The Great
Contemporary
Issues Series
Set I Vol. 5

BLACK AFRICA

The Series

1. DRUGS
   Introduction by J. Anthony Lukas
2. THE MASS MEDIA AND POLITICS
   Introduction by Walter Cronkite
3. CHINA
   O. Edmund Clubb, *Advisory Editor*
4. WOMEN: THEIR CHANGING ROLES
   Elizabeth Janeway, *Advisory Editor*
5. BLACK AFRICA
   Hollis Lynch, *Advisory Editor*
6. VALUES AMERICANS LIVE BY
   Garry Wills, *Advisory Editor*
7. CRIME AND JUSTICE
   Ramsey Clark, *Advisory Editor*
8. THE PRESIDENCY
   George E. Reedy, *Advisory Editor*
9. POPULAR CULTURE
   David Manning White, *Advisory Editor*
10. SCIENCE IN THE TWENTIETH CENTURY
    Walter Sullivan, *Advisory Editor*
11. THE MIDDLE EAST
    John C. Campbell, *Advisory Editor*
12. THE CITIES
    Richard C. Wade, *Advisory Editor*
13. INDEX AND BIBLIOGRAPHY

The Great Contemporary Issues Series
Set I Vol. 5

BLACK AFRICA

The New York Times
ARNO PRESS
NEW YORK / 1978

HOLLIS LYNCH
Advisory Editor

This softbound edition of Great Contemporary Issues is distributed exclusively in the United States by
GROLIER EDUCATIONAL CORPORATION
Sherman Turnpike, Danbury, CT 06816

Library of Congress Cataloging in Publication Data
Main entry under title:

Black Africa.

(The Great contemporary issues)
"A Hudson Group book."
Selections from the New York times, 1870 to the present.
Bibliography: p.
Includes index.
1. Africa, Sub-Saharan—History—Sources.
I. Lynch, Hollis Ralph. II. New York times.
III. Series.
DT352-5.B55 1977 467 77-18022
ISBN 0-405-11114-2

Manufactured in the United States of America

The editors express special thanks to The Associated Press, United Press International, and Reuters for permission to include in this series of books a number of dispatches originally distributed by those news services.

A HUDSON GROUP BOOK
Produced by Morningside Associates. Edited by Gene Brown.

Contents

Map of Colonial Black Africa vi
Map of Black Africa Today vii
Publisher's Note About the Series viii
Introduction, by Hollis Lynch ix
1. Imperialism 1
2. Independence 75
3. Southern Africa 175
4. Political and Economic Development 319
5. Africa and the Modern World 461
6. Update 503
Suggested Reading 533
Index 534

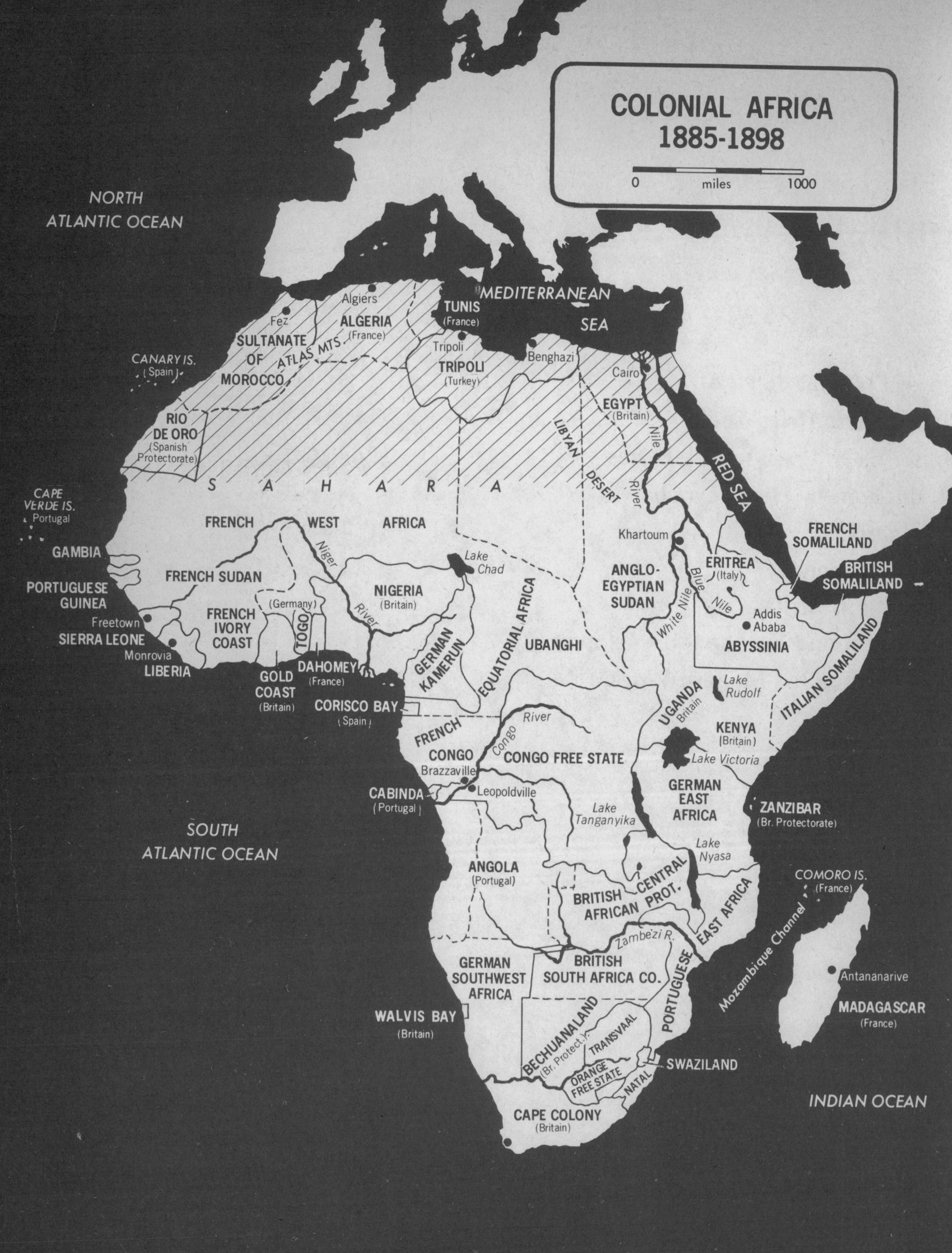
COLONIAL AFRICA
1885-1898
0 miles 1000
NORTH
ATLANTIC OCEAN
MEDITERRANEAN
SEA
Algiers
Fez
ALGERIA
(France)
TUNIS
(France)
SULTANATE
OF
MOROCCO
ATLAS MTS.
Tripoli
TRIPOLI
(Turkey)
Benghazi
Cairo
EGYPT
(Britain)
CANARY IS.
(Spain)
RIO
DE ORO
(Spanish
Protectorate)
LIBYAN
DESERT
Nile
River
RED SEA
S A H A R A
CAPE
VERDE IS.
Portugal
FRENCH WEST AFRICA
GAMBIA
FRENCH SUDAN
Niger
River
Lake
Chad
NIGERIA
(Britain)
Khartoum
ANGLO-
EGYPTIAN
SUDAN
ERITREA
(Italy)
Blue
Nile
White Nile
FRENCH
SOMALILAND
BRITISH
SOMALILAND
PORTUGUESE
GUINEA
Freetown
SIERRA LEONE
Monrovia
LIBERIA
FRENCH
IVORY
COAST
(Germany)
TOGO
GOLD
COAST
(Britain)
DAHOMEY
(France)
GERMAN
KAMERUN
EQUATORIAL AFRICA
UBANGHI
Addis
Ababa
ABYSSINIA
ITALIAN SOMALILAND
Lake
Rudolf
UGANDA
Britain
KENYA
(Britain)
CORISCO BAY
(Spain)
FRENCH
CONGO
Congo
River
CONGO FREE STATE
Brazzaville
Leopoldville
Lake Victoria
CABINDA
(Portugal)
SOUTH
ATLANTIC OCEAN
Lake
Tanganyika
GERMAN
EAST
AFRICA
ZANZIBAR
(Br. Protectorate)
Lake
Nyasa
ANGOLA
(Portugal)
BRITISH
CENTRAL
AFRICAN PROT.
EAST AFRICA
COMORO IS.
(France)
Mozambique Channel
Zambezi R.
GERMAN
SOUTHWEST
AFRICA
BRITISH
SOUTH AFRICA CO.
PORTUGUESE
Antananarive
MADAGASCAR
(France)
WALVIS BAY
(Britain)
BECHUANALAND
(Br. Protect.)
TRANSVAAL
ORANGE
FREE STATE
SWAZILAND
NATAL
INDIAN OCEAN
CAPE COLONY
(Britain)

Maps by Andrew Sabbatini

Publisher's Note About the Series

It would take even an accomplished speed-reader, moving at full throttle, some three and a half solid hours a day to work his way through all the news The New York Times prints. The sad irony, of course, is that even such indefatigable devotion to life's carnival would scarcely assure a decent understanding of what it was really all about. For even the most dutiful reader might easily overlook an occasional long-range trend of importance, or perhaps some of the fragile, elusive relationships between events that sometimes turn out to be more significant than the events themselves.

This is why "The Great Contemporary Issues" was created—to help make sense out of some of the major forces and counterforces at large in today's world. The philosophical conviction behind the series is a simple one: that the past not only can illuminate the present but must. ("Continuity with the past," declared Oliver Wendell Holmes, "is a necessity, not a duty.") Each book in the series, therefore has as its subject some central issue of our time that needs to be viewed in the context of its antecedents if it is to be fully understood. By showing, through a substantial selection of contemporary accounts from The New York Times, the evolution of a subject and its significance, each book in the series offers a perspective that is available in no other way. For while most books on contemporary affairs specialize, for excellent reasons, in predigested facts and neatly drawn conclusions, the books in this series allow the reader to draw his own conclusions on the basis of the facts as they appeared at virtually the moment of their occurrence. This is not to argue that there is no place for events recollected in tranquility; it is simply to say that when fresh, raw truths are allowed to speak for themselves, some quite distinct values often emerge.

For this reason, most of the articles in "The Great Contemporary Issues" are reprinted in their entirety, even in those cases where portions are not central to a given book's theme. Editing has been done only rarely, and in all such cases it is clearly indicated. (Such an excision occasionally occurs, for example, in the case of a Presidential State of the Union Message, where only brief portions are germane to a particular volume, and in the case of some names, where for legal reasons or reasons of taste it is preferable not to republish specific identifications.) Similarly, typographical errors, where they occur, have been allowed to stand as originally printed.

"The Great Contemporary Issues" inevitably encompasses a substantial amount of history. In order to explore their subjects fully, some of the books go back a century or more. Yet their fundamental theme is not the past but the present. In this series the past is of significance insofar as it suggests how we got where we are today. These books, therefore, do not always treat a subject in a purely chronological way. Rather, their material is arranged to point up trends and interrelationships that the editors believe are more illuminating than a chronological listing would be.

"The Great Contemporary Issues" series will ultimately constitute an encyclopedic library of today's major issues. Long before editorial work on the first volume had even begun, some fifty specific titles had already been either scheduled for definite publication or listed as candidates. Since then, events have prompted the inclusion of a number of additional titles, and the editors are, moreover, alert not only for new issues as they emerge but also for issues whose development may call for the publication of sequel volumes. We will, of course, also welcome readers' suggestions for future topics.

INTRODUCTION

Black Africa

This volume is a compilation of selected *New York Times* articles and feature stories on Africa from the 1870's to the present. As a background for an appreciation of the selections, and also to fill some of the gaps not covered by them, I have attempted in this introduction to delineate the major developments in Africa since interaction with America began, as well as sketch the nature of this interaction. Finally, I shall attempt to assess the nature of the *New York Times* coverage of Africa and indicate the merits of this volume.

Since 1619 when the first blacks were brought to Virginia, there has been a sustained interaction between Africa and the territory which later became the United States of America. Americans were not slow to participate in the lucrative slave trade. From the first half of the 17th century, American slavers sailing from New York and increasingly from New England ports obtained slaves illegally in West Africa or else on the east coast of Mozambique and Madagascar.[1] From 1698 when the monopoly on the West African slave trade held by the Royal African Company ended, American slavers greatly extended their operations in this area trading rum from New England distilleries and tobacco from Virginia in a thriving enterprise. Although American participation in the slave trade was outlawed by Congress in 1808, it continued clandestinely right up to the Civil War. Simultaneously, American legitimate trade to West and East Africa expanded, rum, tobacco and cotton goods being exchanged for gold dust, ivory, peanuts and spices. Just before the Civil War, American legitimate trade with Africa was valued at $7,000,000. During the Civil War European commercial establishments, equipped with steamships, largely replaced American traders. However, a desultory American trade with Africa continued which spurted to $150,000,000 during World War I.[2]

According to the latest scholarship, some 427,000 Africans were landed in the United States during the entire period of slavery.[3] If that is accurate, the black population must have grown rapidly because the 1790 federal census put blacks at 757,000, comprising 19.3 per cent of the population, and by 1860 their number had increased to almost four and a half million, comprising 14.1 percent of the population.

During the antebellum period some 10 percent of the black population was technically free but suffered severe discrimination. Some of this westernized quasi-free black population developed an articulate interest in Africa, which, combined with the interest of the humanitarians and slaveholders who wished for altruistic and selfish reasons respectively to settle free blacks in West Africa, led to the formation of the American Colonization Society in 1817 and the founding of Liberia in 1822. Up to the outbreak of the Civil War some 12,000 black Americans settled in Liberia. In 1847 Liberia declared itself independent and won widespread recognition as a black republic, but not until 1862, during the Civil War when the influence of Southern slave-holders was removed, did the United States recognized the new state.

The end of the American Civil War coincided with the demise of the slave trade in West Africa. The following years were marked by increased European activities and rivalries in Africa, which led to the paper partition of Africa at the Berlin Conference of 1884–85, and the establishment of European colonial rule by the turn of the century. The new colonial powers were Britain, France, Germany, Portugal and King Leopold of Belgium, who personally owned the Belgian Congo. The United States, engaged in expansive imperialism on its own continent and as yet conscious of its anticolonial past, was represented at the Berlin Conference, but did not enter the competition for African colonies. In black Africa only a truncated Lib-

[1] Daniel P. Mannix and Malcolm Cowley, *Black Cargoes: A History of the Atlantic Slave Trade* (New York, 1962), pp. 67–68.

[2] Vernon McKay, *Africa in World Politics* (New York: Harper and Row, 1963), p. 248.

[3] Philip D. Curtin, *The Atlantic Slave Trade—A Census* (Madison: University of Wisconsin Press, 1969), p. 88.

eria and the ancient kingdom of Ethiopia survived as independent nations, the one partly through its own diplomacy and with the support of the United States, the other only after it had thwarted the colonial ambitions of Italy and whipped that nation's invading forces at the Battle of Adowa (1896)—one of the glorious events in black military annals.

If the establishment of European colonial rule in Africa was a triumph of European trickery, savagery and superior arms (for instance, Belgian atrocities in the Congo from the late 1880's to the early 20th century) it should also be stated that there was sturdy resistance to European conquest, as exemplified by the prolonged military efforts against the French of Samore Toure, the West African Muslim warrior; and of Gezo, King of Dahomey. There was also early rebellion against alien rule, examples of which are the Hut Tax rebellion of Sierra Leone in 1898 and the Maji Maji rebellion of Tanganyika in 1906.[4]

The situation in southern Africa in the last part of the 19th century deserves special comment. In South Africa itself, the main actors were the Bantus, a vigorous people who comprised the vast majority of the population; other "nonwhites" of substantial numbers were the Cape Coloreds, the products of various admixtures of Bantu, Malay and European. In addition the two white elements—the Boers and the British—were contending for supremacy. The Boers, better known today as Afrikaners, were hardy Calvinistic descendants of mixed Dutch, German and French stock who had settled in and around the Cape in the 17th and 18th centuries and were imbued with a sense of exclusiveness and mission. In 1805, the British became colonial overlords of the Cape Colony which it had captured during the Napoleonic wars. Thus began a long conflict which was further intensified by the discovery in 1870's and 80's of gold and diamonds in the Transvaal, and which was to have its climax in the Boer War of 1899–1902. The man who had done most to exacerbate the conflict was the legendary British imperialist Cecil Rhodes, diamond magnate and former premier of the Cape Colony, whose incredibly grand imperial schemes included the building of a railroad from the Cape to Cairo. This never materialized, but Rhodes succeeded in giving his name to two major territories in Central Africa—Northern Rhodesia (today's Zambia) and Southern Rhodesia—and in introducing the still unsolved settler problem in the latter. Ironically, the war's end brought a policy of appeasement of the Boers at the expense of the Bantus. In 1910 when the Union of South Africa was established, nonwhites were virtually disfranchised and were permitted few civil rights. This state of affairs prompted the birth in 1912 of the African Nationalist Congress whose goal was to unify black Africans to press for full participation in the life of their country.

In the period between the end of the Civil War and World War I American groups with an active interest in Africa were largely limited to black Americans, Protestant and Catholic missionaries and a few commercial establishments. There was little general or governmental concern for Africa. Perhaps the interests of black Americans loomed largest; they sympathized with Africa's plight and some dared hope that the continent would be the source of their own freedom and dignity, for the exercise of political and civil rights on the part of the former slaves had been shortlived. From the end of Reconstruction on, black Americans were steadily disfranchised and jimcrowed. The same racial Darwinist philosophy that had justified European imperialism in Africa was used to deny blacks the status and opportunity of first-class citizenship in the United States.

Although many black Americans were ambivalent about Africa, particularly since it had come largely under white rule, there were those who advocated a "return" to Africa as a solution to their problems; at least Liberia was free, and, as some argued, the chances of ending minority white colonial rule in Africa were greater than of revolutionizing the attitude of white Americans toward blacks. At any rate, hundreds of thousands expressed the desire to emigrate, but only a small number of these had the means to do so.[5] Some 3,000 emigrated to Liberia in the post-Civil War 19th century, and in 1914 some 60 blacks succeeded in reaching the Gold Coast aboard the black-owned ship *Liberia*.[6]

Black Americans showed their interest in other ways: they were aware of and protested against the atrocities in the Congo. But the major impact of American blacks on Africa came from missionaries scattered throughout the continent who were agents either of white denominations or of two black churches—the African Methodist Episcopal Church and the African Methodist Episcopal Zion Church. These black missionaries frequently arranged for African students to study at black colleges in the United States.

[4] Robert I. Rotberg and Ali Mazrui, eds., *Protest and Power in Black Africa* (New York: Oxford University Press, 1970), pp. 3–373.

[5] See Edwin Redkey, *Black Exodus; Black Nationalist and Back-to-Africa Movements, 1890–1920* (New Haven: Yale University Press, 1969).

[6] William E. Bittle and Gilbert Geis, *The Longest Way Home; Chief Alfred C. Sam's Back-to-Africa Movement* (Detroit: Wayne State University Press, 1964).

The First World War and the Interwar Years. World War I, partly fought on African soil, resulted in Germany's loss of her colonies there, and with Britain, France and South Africa assuming trusteeship of Tanganyika, Togoland and the Cameroons, and South West Africa respectively. It also stimulated African pride and nationalism, for black soldiers fought both on their continent and abroad, an experience which lessened their awe of the white man. Their return and subsequent unemployment was a source of some tension and unrest in the postwar colonial society.

The interwar years further accelerated African nationalism. The increase of western education, largely through missionary agencies, in Europe as well as America; a cash economy and increasing urbanization brought into being both an urban middle class and a protetariat, each demanding a greater share in the running of their country. This nationalism was further fed by the activities and propaganda of Marcus Garvey's American mass-based Universal Negro Improvement Association of the 1920's with its strident cry of "Africa for the Africans." The nationalist spirit found its strongest expression in the formation in 1920 of the National Congress of British West Africa. In the 1920's the Congress held four major interterritorial meetings and proclaimed its political goal of a self-governing federation; all it achieved was the introduction on a very modest scale of the elective principle in urban areas between 1923 and 1925. However, this stimulated the creation of political parties, which were not to become national in scope until the 1940's. The Congress collapsed in 1930 with the death of its main inspirer, J.E. Casely Hayford of the Gold Coast. The 1930's in West Africa witnessed more widespread and more effective protest journalism and the growth of trade union organization and youth movements. The two men in the vanguard of these movements were the American-educated Nigerian Nnamdi Azikiwe and the Communist-trained Sierra Leone radical I.T.A. Wallace-Johnson.

In West Africa there was at least some slow advance; other parts knew only stagnation or reversal. In South Africa, the best efforts of the African Nationalist Congress and the Industrial Commercial Workers Union—the two major black organizations—were unable to halt the march of white oppression and exploitation. In Kenya, black Africans suffered a major setback: during the interwar years the Kikuyus were systematically dispossessed of their lands and exploited by the rapidly growing and properous European farmers, planting the seeds of future trouble.

One event had repercussions in all of black Africa and, indeed, the black world—Italy's imperialistic and vengeful conquest of Ethiopia in 1935–36. Everywhere that action called forth expressions of pan-African solidarity and increased the rising tide of black nationalism. But Italy's triumph was short-lived: a combined Ethiopian and British force defeated and expelled the Italians in 1941.

World War II. The war further accelerated African nationalism. Once again, Africans as well as black Americans were asked to fight for democracy abroad while they were denied it at home. African and Afro-American soldiers fought by the thousands in the various theatres of war. At the end of the conflict colonial peoples everywhere were more determined than ever to apply democracy to their own situation; in French Africa, the goal was political and cultural assimilation with France; in English-speaking Africa, complete political independence of England. This determination to free Africa from colonial rule was expressed at the 1945 Pan-African Conference in Manchester, England, which was attended by some of the most dynamic leaders of the black world, including Dr. W. E. B. DuBois of the United States, George Padmore of the West Indies, Kwame Nkrumah of the Gold Coast and Jomo Kenyatta of Kenya. In 1947 Kwame Nkrumah returned to the Gold Coast to implement the new strategy of liberation worked out at the Manchester Conference. Ten years later, the nationalist struggle culminated in the winning of independence by the Gold Coast—the first black African colony to do so. Throughout tropical Africa the nationalist tide had become irresistible: by the early sixties more than 30 African countries had been catapulted into independence.

Black/White Confrontation. However, the settler problem in East, Central and Southern Africa and the Portuguese doctrine of the inalienability of their overseas territories were serious obstacles in the way of political freedom for all black Africans. And up to this time Africans have won only partial victory. In Kenya the way to African political success was paved by five years (1951–55) of Mau Mau guerrilla activities on the part of the Kikuyu against their British exploiters and African accomplices. In the struggle Jomo Kenyatta, the future President of Kenya, was arrested, tried and imprisoned on the grounds that he was a Mau Mau supporter. The Mau Mau movement was certainly the most determined and sustained challenge to a colonial power in Africa. Quelled by superior force at great expense and the loss of thousands of African lives, Mau Mau, nonetheless, ensured that Africans would be paramount in Kenya and set the stage for Kenyan independence in 1963.

In Central Africa, white pressure brought into being in 1953 the Central African Federation, encompassing Northern and South Rhodesia and Nyasaland. It was, frankly, a white attempt to retain supremacy in this area. But determined African opposition brought the federation to an end in 1963 and permitted independence for Northern Rhodesia, renamed Zambia, and Nyasaland, renamed Malawi. In Southern Rhodesia, the territory in the former federation with the greatest ratio of whites to blacks, the whites have clung tenaciously to power. In 1966 Rhodesian whites defied Britain in unilaterally declaring the country independent. Although it has failed to win any formal recognition, Rhodesia has, nonetheless, had moral and practical support from South Africa and Portugal. With the Afrikaners politically dominant since 1948, the South African government has sought to rationalize gross white exploitation of blacks through the doctrine and practice of apartheid. Portugal is the only major European colonial power which has resisted the tide of decolonization. This has led to continuing wars of liberation in Portuguese Guinea, Angola and Mozambique. These struggles are already more than ten years old and no end is in sight. Thus Southern Africa remains a bastion of minority white supremacy and thus potentially explosive.

Post-Independence Problems. The euphoria of independence had hardly worn off when Africans realized that they were still faced with difficult problems. It became apparent that there was a need to forge a sense of nationhood among disparate peoples on whom artificial colonial boundaries had been imposed. Such a sense of nationhood does not seem to have existed, for instance, in the Congo (present-day Zaire); indeed, the Congo was one of the least prepared among African countries for modern nationhood. Here independence was quickly followed by virtual anarchy which in turn led to a four-year military occupation by a United Nations peace-keeping force, and a new painful groping toward unity. In Nigeria, the loyalty of the major ethnic groups—Hausas, Yorubas and Ibos—to nationhood remained fragile enough to cause a 30-month civil war (July 1967–January 1970), immediately precipitated by the Ibo attempt to secede as Biafra. Post-independence Sudan expended most of its energies in a civil war between the Arabized Muslim North and Christian and pagan African South which only recently came to an end. In Burundi, conflict between the ruling minority Tutsi and the majority Hutu erupted into massive massacres largely of the latter.

An even more pressing problem for the emerging nations has been the failure, in the face of enormous expectations in part excited by the relatively lavish life-style of the small middle class, to improve the standard of living of the masses. In this largely elusive quest millions have flocked since independence to urban centers, creating or aggravating the problems of housing, sanitation and unemployment.

Political corruption, the failure to solve basic economic problems, differences in ethnicity, culture, religion and ideology have all been factors creating instability within African countries and often leading to military coups. Today there are some dozen military regimes in black Africa, including such large and populous countries as the Sudan, Nigeria and Zaire.

African leaders have long seen the need for closer cooperation among their countries to solve their common problems, but there have been serious differences of opinion as to the means and structure of bringing this about. Since 1963 the Organization of African Unity has sought with modest success to foster voluntary cooperation—political, economic, cultural and diplomatic—among African nations. But as yet, various attempts at closer political and economic regional groupings have not shown much success.

American Interest in Africa since World War II. American interest in Africa has grown enormously since the beginning of World War II. This new attention can be explained in terms of the strategic importance of Africa during the war, the desire for African friendship during the postwar period of Cold War politics with Russia and China and an interest in the continent as a major source of strategic raw materials. This has been expressed in terms of vastly increased investments; the establishment since the late 1950's of such educational and cultural organizations as the African-American Institute, the African Studies Association, the American Society for African Culture, and Cross Roads Africa; and in the growing involvement of American labor organizations on the continent.

By 1970 U.S. investments in sub-Saharan Africa had grown to a substantial two and a quarter billion dollars, about 40 per cent of which had been invested in the white-dominated territories of southern Africa, particularly South Africa and Angola. As a result the United States has been charged with supporting the minority white ruling elements against the legitimate aspirations of Africans for freedom. Additionally, through NATO as well as bilateral agreements the U.S. government supplies arms to Portugal, and again critics have charged that these arms are used against African freedom fighters in Angola, Mozambique and Guinea.

The influence on black Americans has been of a special kind: an independent black Africa has removed much of the ambivalence which has historically characterized attitudes to that continent, and thus to stimulate a pride in blackness. Since 1957 when black African countries began achieving independence, first with Ghana, hundreds of black Americans, including major leaders, have yearly visited the continent. In addition to this sentimental interest, black Americans are still engaged in the process of seeking to establish a functional, mutual-aid pan-African relationship with Africa. Black American leaders are as concerned as their African counterparts in seeing an end to white minority rule in Southern Africa. They have been critical of U.S. policy in this area, but so far have not formed an effective lobby.

Recently, there has been a relative diminution of U.S. governmental and public interest in Africa. An end to the Cold War, a new rapprochement with China and Russia and preoccupation with Vietnam have contributed to this. But growing U.S. investments in Africa, the steady interest of black Americans and a shrinking world will ensure that Americans will never again become oblivious to Africa.

The New York Times *and Africa.* Until World War II, American interest in Africa was confined to small and well-defined groups: some black American intellectuals, American missionaries and a few businessmen. This lack of a general public or governmental concern with Africa was reflected in the desultory, uncertain and spasmodic American reporting on that continent. *The New York Times* was no exception. But even in this period *The New York Times* reports, while not free of distortions, had the advantage of reflecting, at least partially, the point of view of a country which had no formal colonies in Africa. Reporting since World War II, as the selections below indicate, has been much more regular, but has still been open to the charges of being inadequate and sometimes biased and inaccurate. But perhaps these charges are unavoidable even for the best newspapers given their propensity to reflect the interests and biases of their readers. At any rate, over the last hundred years, of all American newspapers, *The New York Times* has generally been in the vanguard both in terms of the quantity and quality of its reporting on Africa. Thus this volume is bound to serve as a rich source of information on Africa to both interested scholars and laymen.

Hollis R. Lynch

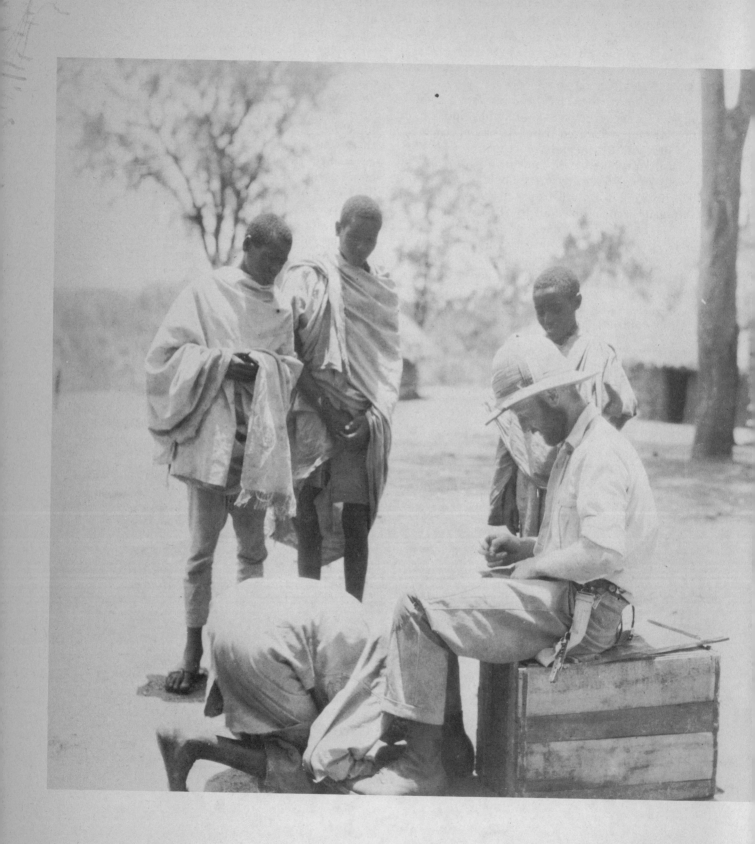

CHAPTER 1
Imperialism

An Ethiopian slave kissing the foot of a white visitor.

Courtesy Compix.

MINOR TOPICS.

The African slave trade is not over yet by a great deal, although its suppression on the West coast of Africa leads many to think so. There is a lively Asiatic demand for negroes, and the African tribes on the East coast find no business so profitable or exciting as chasing and selling each other to the Oriental dealers who come to buy them. It is of course plain that so long as they can do this, they will prefer it to working, and that the effect of the trade—since several are usually killed in battle for each one captured and sent into bondage—must also be steadily to reduce the population of the country. To stop the trade by a naval blockade is said to be impossible, because of the immense length of the coast; and it is suggested, as the sole way of combating the evil, that the Christian Powers should pay the Eastern potentates, who make money by the business, a fixed subsidy to forbid and prevent the importation of blacks into their dominions. There are manifest objections to this plan, but anything is better than to allow the shocking practice to go on unchecked, and practically unrebuked.

August 29, 1872

AFRICA.—The history of that dark continent, so far as known to us, presents an awful retrospect, and one all the more dreadful when we take into account the kindly and affectionate qualities of so many of its primitive people to which Mungo Park, Livingstone, Grant, Schweinfurth, and Cameron have borne witness. It is inexpressibly sad to think of the unnumbered ages through which these poor dark savages have continued, scarcely advancing beyond the elements of art and science and even of language; from within, destroying and devouring one another, willingly offering their throats to the knives of sorcerers, or paving the deep grave-pit of some bloody monarch with the living trembling bodies of a hundred of his young wives: from without, hunted down and destroyed or captured by aid of the weapons of civilization, until every man's hand is turned against his brother, and terror reigns over vast regions. The bounty of Nature has provided for them such abundance that they continue to exist despite all the cruel conditions of that existence. But they are arrested at a position, not so much between heaven and earth, as between earth and hell. There is an old touch, a tertiary or pre-tertiary touch about them, affiliating them with the ancient hippopotamus and the crocodile; but there is also a touch of a sensitiveness and of an affection as keen as any to which the more civilized races have attained. This has exposed them to a torture which the crocodile and hippopotamus do not know; but it has been insufficient to elevate them to a platform of order and happiness. Surely here is a case where the introduction of European civilization would be most justifiable, and might well repay the cost. But if this is to be done at all, it should be done effectually—not as in India, to the great loss of the agents of civilization, and in the fostering of a weak native conceit, in itself incapable of developing or even retaining the benefits which have been conferred upon the country—not as in America, to the extermination of the aborigines. In the interests of England, the African continent might be made really to correct the balance of the Old World, and enable us to keep in front of such expanding nations as Germany and Russia. Then, perhaps, it might be given to England, in the evening of our days, to wander meditatively on the shore of Tanganyika, that mighty Ulleswater of Africa, or of Lake Nyassa, its softer Windermere. It does not seem at all likely at present that England will undertake such a work, but Germany has of late displayed some distinct symptoms of being inclined to do so. But however that may be, it is to Englishmen belongs the glory of having first penetrated into the centre of tropical Africa, and of having achieved there a series of grand individual explorations which has no parallel in the history of the human race.—*Blackwood.*

July 1, 1877

PERIL OF ETHIOPIANISM.

Signs of Unrest Among Natives in British South Africa.

LONDON TIMES—NEW YORK TIMES
Special Cablegram.

JOHANNESBURG, Transvaal Colony, South Africa, May 22.—Persistent rumors of unrest among the native tribes have been rife for some time. "Unrest" is perhaps too strong a word to use at present. The natives have been talking a good deal and feel themselves dissatisfied, but only in a vague manner.

It seems likely that if a check is put upon the activity of the Ethiopian movement the natives will eventually settle down again. Should Ethiopianism, however, produce a leader capable of overcoming the mutual jealousies of the various tribes and uniting them in common action, the native question will then assume an acute form and must be left to the people of South Africa to settle it once for all.

Ethiopianism is an importation from the United States which, under the guise of religious teaching, preaches the doctrine of Africa for the native races. The propaganda has sown and still is sowing seeds of discontent among the native tribes, and serves to perpetuate the unsettled condition of the natives.

May 23, 1904

THE BASIN OF THE CONGO.

The conflicting claims of European powers in the heart of the Dark Continent have attracted but little attention since the beginning of hostilities in Madagascar and Annam. While the French were bombarding the Hova ports and shipping troops to Tonquin STANLEY was pushing his way up the Congo River, and it is now announced that he has reached Brazzaville with 1,000 followers, and has met there M. DE BRAZZA, who is said to have made but little progress. Mr. STANLEY is the agent of the international and neutral organization known as the Comité d'Etudes du Haut Congo, at the head of which is the King of the Belgians. The Association Internationale Africaine, of which King LEOPOLD is the moving spirit, undertook to open a path from Zanzibar, on the east coast, to the great lakes of the interior. A path was opened and a station was established on the eastern shore of Lake Tanganyika. The other organization undertook to explore the course of the great River Congo from its mouth on the west coast to its source, and to make roadways around the cataracts that divide the basin of the Upper Congo from the navigable waters, which extend for 115 miles eastward from the river's mouth.

The roadways were built and a steamer was placed in the waters above the cataracts, at Stanley Pool, beyond which navigation is unimpeded for nearly one thousand miles into the heart of the continent. All this work was done under a neutral flag by an association that represents no nation, and that advocates the opening of the rich valley and basin of this great river to the commerce of all nations. Already the trade of this region is great, the gross exports and imports amounting, it is said, to $10,000,000 a year. The association that undertook to make a path westward from Zanzibar granted out of its funds 20,000f. to a French committee that desired to do part of the work. This committee sent out M. DE BRAZZA as its agent. He discovered another and a better route from the western coa... to the Upper Congo by avoiding the Lower Congo and the cataracts and following the course of the River Ogowe, that empties into the Atlantic north of the mouth of the Congo. The spirit of acquisition and annexation that has taken possession of the French nation took possession of M. DE BRAZZA. He passed from the service of a neutral organization into the service of France, induced a native chief to cede to France the northern shore of Stanley Pool, and raised the French flag upon this territory

In this way the French gained a foothold in the basin of the Congo. The Portuguese suddenly discovered that the King of Congo had been their vassal since 1491, and laid claim to the region above and below the mouth of the river. So that the international scientific and philanthropic associations that have undertaken to open a belt across the continent, and have already accomplished so much, are confronted by the pretensions of two European nations. This could have been foreseen. The great wealth of the basin east of the mountains, covering thirteen degrees of longitude and fourteen degrees of latitude, having been revealed by bold explorers, aroused the predatory instincts of Europe, and the peaceful work of King LEOPOLD and his associates must soon give way to a struggle between colonizers and conquerors.

There will be great changes in Southern and Central Africa in the next fifty years. A large area of rich land is to be explored and opened to civilization. The colonizing nations of Europe may contend among themselves for a division of the spoil. Ancient and forgotten claims, like the claim brought forward by Portugal, will be revived by other powers, and the Dark Continent may be lighted up by the fires of great conflicts.

June 23, 1883

THE CONGO DISPUTE.

No river in the world absorbs at this moment more of the attention of Kings and Cabinets than the one which the intrepidity of STANLEY discovered to be among the mightiest streams of the globe. The Nile itself, whose long supremacy among the watercourses of Africa must henceforth be shared by this modern candidate for international commerce, is not more of an object of current political interest and anxiety.

Portugal, England, France, Germany, and Belgium are doubtless the five European nations most concerned in the rivalry for the possession of the Congo country, although others are watchful and have their claims upon it. Austria, for example, apparently intends, in the breaking up of the territory under colonial domination, to secure a bit of it herself, hard by the German annexations, as if to parallel in Africa her geographical relations to Germany in Europe, and two war vessels are expected soon to leave Trieste for the mouth of the Congo. The Netherlands have a very clear interest in the river from the old Dutch trading settlements on its banks. Even our own country has become involved in the question, through the pronounced recognition of the rights of the African International Association by President ARTHUR.

A remarkable feature in this international controversy is furnished just now in some apparent leanings of England toward supporting the sovereignty claimed by Portugal. This claim, based on the original discovery of the stream when Portuguese explorers were among the most famous and adventurous of all, and on Portuguese settlements along its banks has been repeatedly set aside by England during the last half century in treaties made with the natives, ignoring any European rights of sovereignty. Nevertheless, it has of late seemed advisable, apparently, to the English Government to listen respectfully to the claims of Portugal, as if thereby to avoid a still less desirable political result. Not long ago, when a Portuguese envoy presented to the various Governments a memorandum of the Lisbon Geographical Society containing an abstract of the Portuguese claims to the whole coast from Kabinda to the Lower Congo, Earl GRANVILLE was credited with assenting to the Portuguese scheme for an international conference to discuss these claims. Since then this scheme has been abandoned, Prince BISMARCK being quoted, whether rightly or wrongly, as considering it premature, so long as the share of German subjects in the territory remained ill-defined.

One would say that the proper time for such a conference, if called at all, would be before any more decisive seizures, raising conflicting jurisdiction, should be made. But if the German Chancellor's cynical avowal means that he will first, by possession, get his nine points of the law over a selected portion of the Congo country, and then leave conferences to wrangle as they may, he has certainly succeeded in this policy. At one time we find it asserted that the German Special Commissioner for West Africa has annexed all the coast south of the Cameroons River as far as Baltava; at another, that he has added Little Popo, on the Dahomey coast, to the German colonies; again, that Germany has annexed the entire territory between the Orange River and the twenty-fifth degree of south latitude, hoisting the German flag along the coast to Berseba, and placing herself directly side of England; finally the latest advices are that the commander of a German gunboat has taken formal possession, in the name of Germany, of the entire west coast between the eighteenth and twenty-sixth degrees of latitude, except Walfish Bay, which was formally annexed during the past Summer to British possessions by the Cape Colony authorities. This would apparently give to Germany a coast line of about 550 miles, independently of windings.

France, meanwhile, has not forgotten the Congo in her preoccupation with Madagascar and Tonquin. She has ratified a treaty with MAKKO for the cession of lands in the district which is said to have been ceded to DE BRAZZA, between the Imkila and the Gordon Bennett River, and she is prosecuting further quests. She has lately sent a detachment of troops to Porto Novo, which act was quickly announced as a fresh annexation, although France claims that she has held this place for twenty years.

The King of Belgium stands firmly by the rights of the International African Association, and these rights, if we can credit Mr. STANLEY's rather confident assertion, are unassailable. It is even intimated that Prince BISMARCK would prefer Belgium as a general Congo custodian after German desires are satisfied.

What conflicts are yet to come out of these and other rivalries in the Congo country? No one can foretell the result, but it is certain that elements of international controversy are there.

September 19, 1884

COLONIZATION IN AFRICA.

BERLIN, Oct. 4.—The Government of England has made a proposition that an international commission be formed to decide upon the rights of British traders in the districts of the Cameroons, Batanga, and Angra Pequeña, in Africa, which have been annexed to Germany. The proposal aims to secure protection to British merchants from differential duties.

The *Universal Gazette* says the Government's policy on colonial matters will be fully explained in the Reichstag.

PARIS, Oct. 4.—The *Gaulois* says that Prince Bismarck has made a proposition to the Cabinets of France and England to hold a convention for the purpose of fixing the limits of the territories upon the coast of Africa.

LONDON, Oct. 4.—The activity of the German movements for colonizing the west coast of Africa is exciting grave alarm among English merchants. Several influential Chambers of Commerce have sent strongly worded petitions to Lord Granville, the Foreign Secretary, declaring that the interests of British shippers and traders doing business in Africa are seriously menaced by the German invasion, and praying the Government to take energetic measures to protect this important trade. The petitions take the ground that the Germans, if allowed to establish themselves firmly in the Cameroons district and the other places they seek to occupy, would be certain to levy differential duties, discriminating against British und in favor of German products, and thus crushing fair competition. It is known, however, that Lord Granville is disposed to favor German colonization as a counterpois to that of France. He has recently expressed the belief that the Germans would prove more kindly neighbors than the French, and would do less than the latter to hamper British trade.

It is reported that the Government is preparing a scheme to form a confederation of the South African colonies.

October 5, 1884

TALK OF THE DAY IN PARIS.

The *Temps* publishes a letter from Brussels which states that delegates representing the Governments of England, America, France, Portugal, Spain, Holland, and Belgium will attend an international conference, to be held in Berlin, probably in the latter part of November, at which the West African question will be considered. The letter states that France and Germany have agreed to submit proposals to the conference securing freedom of commerce to all nations in the Congo country and upon the River Niger. The necessity of determining the right of any power to occupy any of the unannexed territory in Africa, it is expected, will result in the creation by the conference of an International Commission of the Congo, similar to the Danubian Commission.

October 9, 1884

SETTLING CONGO QUESTIONS.

THE CONFERENCE ADOPTS THE REPORT OF ITS COMMITTEE.

BERLIN, Nov. 27.—Count von Hatzfeldt, Minister of Foreign Affairs, presided at to-day's session of the Congo conference. The Congo Committee made its report, which was adopted. It contains a provision in favor of the extension of the Congo Basin boundary eastward, duly respecting the rights or Portugal, Zanzibar, and one native King. The powers will offer their good offices on the spot for the settlement of any important questions that may arise. A second committee was appointed, which will to-morrow arrange the details, and a third committee was appointed to conclude the labors of the second committee and compile their report. The resolutions of the committee were then adopted. The question of free trade will be discussed when the frontiers have been settled. The American proposal for an extension of the Zanzibar territory caused surprise in the conference, but it is believed that the replies of the different Governments to their delegates will authorize its acceptance.

King Leopold of Belgium has telegraphed to the Emperor William his thanks for convening the conference. The question of the existence of the African International Association after the death of King Leopold has been the subject of much discussion, owing to the fact that the reversion belongs to France. The association claims that only the territory acquired prior to the agreement can be ceded to France, even if it is a failure. This view is generally approved.

Mr. Kasson, the American delegate, has lately less actively supported the International Association, which organization has been well received by all the powers except Portugal. King Leopold has already spent $2,500,000 in promoting the association, and promises to endow it with sufficient capital to insure an annual income of $200,000.

Henry M. Stanley will depart from here on Sunday to fulfill an engagement to deliver a lecture in Edinburgh. It is stated that he asks of the International Association a salary of $20,000 per annum.

November 28, 1884

The Congo Free State---What Is It?

Account of the Origin of the Government Whose Rule Over Central Africa Is Denounced for Inhumanity.

THE fierce dispute over the conduct of the Congo Free State Government and the demand that a concert of Europe interpose in the alleged interest of humanity makes important the question whether the Congo State is an independent State and, if so, how it became such.

In 1860 Leopold, King of the Belgians, began to turn his attention toward Africa. Two years before Sir Richard Burton, Capts. Speke and Grant had discovered Lake Tanganyika, the sources of the Nile, and Lake Victoria. The great discoveries of Livingstone and Stanley had just startled the world. Leopold saw in the Congo region an outlet for the manufactures of Belgium, which is not only one of the most densely populated of countries, but depends entirely for subsistence on the marketing of its manufactures in foreign lands. In 1876 King Leopold invited expert geographers of international repute to convene at Brussels. Calling themselves the Brussels Geographical Conference, they held their first meeting on Sept. 12, 1876. In 1883 they formed "The International Association for the Exploration and Civilization of Central Africa." It consisted of an International Commission sitting in Brussels, assisted by Dependent National Committees in each of the countries taking part. The executive power of the International Association was vested in an Executive Committee, of which King Leopold was appointed President. The principal countries of Europe, as well as the United States, were represented in the association.

Working in the interests of King Leopold, Henry M. Stanley began to travel through the Congo region, buying land, establishing stations, and making treaties in the King's name with native chiefs. This aroused the distrust of other European nations, which at that period were looking with longing on the few promising places for colonization left unoccupied by the British. The French raised their flag at Brazzaville, on the Congo; the Portuguese set up a claim to the Congo River because a Portuguese navigator had discovered the mouth of it 400 years before; Germany, too, began to look longingly at the Congo region.

Alarmed by these encroachments, King Leopold conceived the idea of a Congo State, with himself as sovereign ruler. But first of all it was necessary to secure the assent of the great powers interested.

Matters were made more complicated for Leopold by the Anglo-Portuguese Convention, made on Feb. 26, 1884, in which England recognized the Portuguese claims to the Congo. But, fortunately for the King of the Belgians, this convention was not only unpopular on the Continent of Europe, but in England itself. A British mission dispatched to the West Coast of Africa to investigate the validity of the treaties made in Leopold's name with the African chiefs in that part of the Congo which Great Britain proposed to recognize as Portuguese territory, reported that the treaties in question were valid and the allegations of the Portuguese baseless. Thereupon the Anglo-Portuguese Convention died a natural death.

Short-lived and unimportant as it had been, this convention showed that there existed a growing necessity for giving the Congo region a definite political status. On April 22, 1884, the United States officially recognized the flag of the International Association as that of a friendly Government, a course adopted soon after by France and Germany. The latter power, on the very day that she gave recognition to the association, invited all the powers interested to a conference on African affairs in Berlin.

Fourteen nations accepted the invitation and formed the Berlin International Conference.

Presided over by Prince Bismarck, it met on Nov. 15, 1884. The practical business at the first sitting was to decide what territories constitute the basin of the Congo and its affluents. Eight experts, selected by the eight powers chiefly interested, reported at the third sitting of the conference as follows:

"The basin of the Congo is delimited by the crests of the contiguous basins, to wit, the basins in particular of the Niari, the Ogowe, the Schari, and the Nile on the north; by Lake Tanganyika on the east; by the crests of the basins of the Zambesi and the Loge on the south. It comprises consequently all the territories drained by the Congo and its affluents, including Lake Tanganyika and its eastern tributaries."

At the tenth and last sitting of the conference, held on Feb. 26, 1885, the representatives of the powers assembled at Berlin formally acknowledged the International Association as a friendly and sovereign State whose flag—a golden five-pointed star on a blue field—they agreed henceforth to recognize.

In the anti-Belgian campaign which has since arisen one of the main contentions of Leopold's enemies is that the Congo Free State was created by this act of the Berlin International Conference. Those arguing on the other side maintain that recognition of a State implies its existence already. The foundation of the Congo Free State, they say, really dates back to the beginning of the organized work of the Comite d'Etudes du Haut-Congo on Nov. 25, 1878. Between that date and the convening of the Berlin Conference stations were established, treaties concluded, administrative and police service organized, and other essentials of an actual Government established.

Another fact, which the pro-Belgians do not fail to point out, is that the British, who are active in the campaign against King Leopold in the Congo, have territories to the north and south of the Congo State, which tends to make any change in the status of the latter advantageous to themselves.

Leopold II., who is also King of the Belgians, is sovereign of the Congo. Formally there is no connection between the Government of Belgium and that of the Congo State, except through the fact that one man is head of both. King Leopold has willed his sovereignty over the Congo to Belgium, to whom it will pass at the King's death.

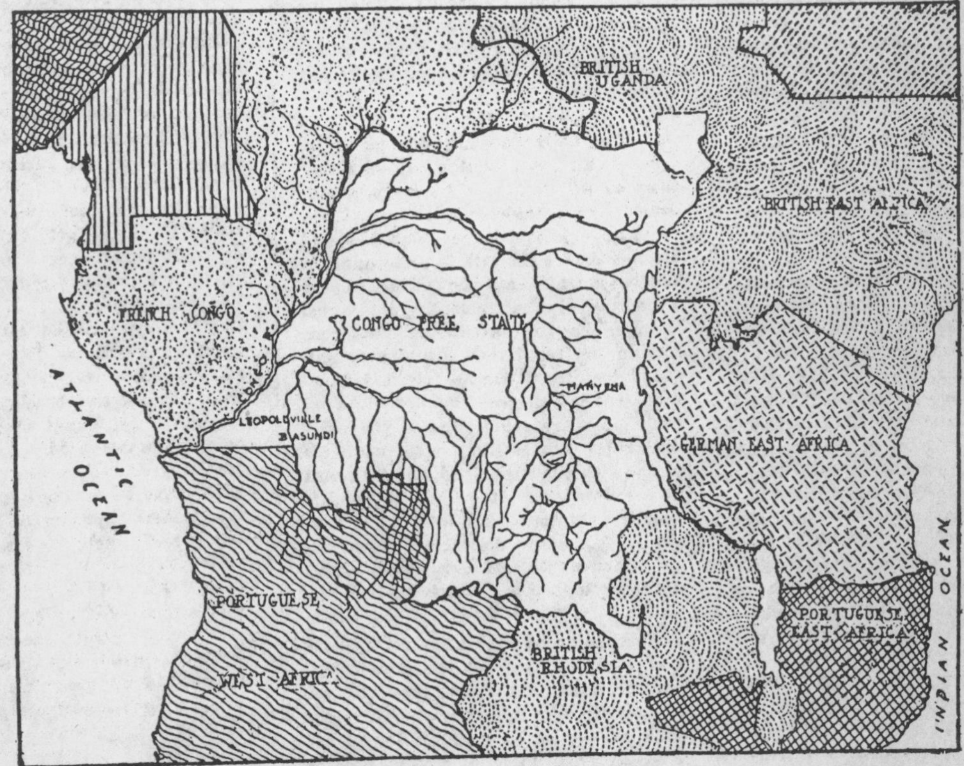

The country lying between the Niger and its great tributary, the Chadda or Benoueh, which European enterprise is now endeavoring to open up, has already figured conspicuously in African history as the seat of the first self-organized negro federation which West Africa has yet seen. In the earlier part of the present century the Yorubas and other local tribes attempted to protect themselves against the terrible slave hunters of Dahomey by establishing a colony eighty miles inland from the port of Lagos, near the mouth of the Niger, and building a large fortified town there, which they named "Abbeokuta," (foundation stone.) Here they formed a federation under a Constitution which, though simple, might be copied with advantage by more civilized nations: "We will all be freemen, all brothers, and all Christians." The new capital repulsed, with the loss of several thousand men, the invading armies of Dahomey, and elected as its first Bishop a Yoruba convert named ADJAI, better known now as "Samuel Crowther." This curious settlement still exists, and may not improbably play an important part in the projected development of the Niger Valley.

December 10, 1884

A NEW NATIVE KING.

King LEOPOLD of Belgium is now King of the Congo. There will be no attempt to unite the two kingdoms, and, as in the case of Sweden and Norway, the only connection between Belgium and the Congo will be the fact that the King of one is also the King of the other.

King LEOPOLD is greatly pleased with his new dominions, which are many times larger than Belgium. Indeed, it is thought that in view of the disturbed state of things in Belgium, due to the quarrel between the Liberal and Clerical parties, the King may resign the Belgian crown and retire to the Congo. Whatever may be the King's intentions, it is well understood that he will soon pay a visit to Africa. His royal robes, consisting of a blue jean shirt and a silk hat artificially roughened so as to present a second-hand appearance, have been prepared, and he frequently wears them in the palace when the Queen is not at home. He has studied under Mr. STANLEY the art of making pombé—or native African beer—and has become very fond of that simple beverage. A gross of old tomato cans was recently bought by the King with the view of converting the bottoms of the cans into decorations for the members of the "Order of the African Tin Knights on Wheels"—an order of knighthood which LEOPOLD proposes to establish in his African dominions. A rumor, not as yet wholly authenticated, also informs us that the King is devoting several hours every day to the banjo and the bones, and is studying the late DANIEL BRYANT'S "Theory and Practice of Colored Conundrums," the Court chaplain assisting him in this study by assuming the character of "Mr. Johnsing," and propounding the conundrums, which the King answers.

This shows that King LEOPOLD has the laudable intention of fitting himself to be a native King. He knows that were he to carry to Africa the manners and customs of a Belgian King his darky subjects would misunderstand him and would be dissatisfied. As he cannot by royal decree turn them into civilized and clothed Belgians, he means to convert himself as far as possible into a native African. The motto already adopted for the great seal of the Congo State is, "We study to please," and it doubtless expresses the wise and amiable intentions of the monarch.

If King LEOPOLD really does go to the Congo with the intention of remaining there he will doubtless be warmly welcomed by his subjects when he first appears among them in his high hat and his blue shirt. His skill in performing on the banjo will please the people, and his knowledge of the ancient and classical conundrums of the African race will gain for him the reputation of a man of profound learning. Has he reflected, however, that as a native King he will be expected to make rain? One of the chief duties of a native King is to supply his people with rain on demand, and the result of a failure to meet such a demand is usually a revolution, followed by a banquet, at which the dethroned monarch is the principal dish. If King LEOPOLD is not ready to face this danger he had better not go to Africa. He knows very well that no European can make rain, whatever a native King may be able to do, and he need not expect that he can compromise with his subjects by establishing a weather bureau. On the whole, King LEOPOLD would be wise to stick to his Belgian capital. The Belgians may perhaps accidentally shoot him in the course of a heated and public theological argument, but they will never think of putting him to death in consequence of a prolonged drought.

April 30, 1885

GIN AND MISSIONARIES.

There has been a great deal of talk in Europe about carrying to the inhabitants of the Congo basin and of the west coast of Africa the blessings of civilization. The nations that were almost ready to fight among themselves for slices of African territory were apparently convinced that the blacks were perishing in degradation and ignorance for the want of the blessings that would accompany trade. Reports from the Congo and from other parts of "the Dark Continent" now show what those blessings are. Trade with the Congo basin has grown rapidly in the last two or three years. The exports and imports amount to many millions of dollars. Two years ago the annual exports from Liverpool alone were said to reach $5,000,000 in value. Almost the entire Congo trade is now controlled by two Liverpool companies, one Paris company, a Hamburg company, and a company formed in Rotterdam. Before these European traders lies a rich country of 1,500,000 square miles containing 60,000,000 blacks. What is the staple article imported for the use and civilization of these blacks and in what way is the work of civilization carried on?

Half of the stuff exported from Europe by these traders is gin and rum of a wretched quality. Gin alone forms 40 per cent. of the companies' stock in trade. This "firewater" is made in Hamburg expressly for the African. Europeans would not drink it. There is greater profit for the trader when he uses gin than he can get by the use of any other European product. With gin go European guns and knives. The natives are fond of the gin, but they hate the white man who makes them drunk with it. Two tribes excepted, the natives of the Congo basin are wild, savage, and cruel. The men are loafers. They lounge about, drink, and fight, while their women are compelled to do the work. European gin and rum have made them so quarrelsome that the traders are forced to maintain an armed police for their own protection. In Zanzibar, on the other side of the continent, "the real achievement of civilization," writes one correspondent, "is neither missions nor emancipation, but the success that has crowned its efforts to introduce drunkenness among the native population." The stuff used by traders in Zanzibar, where the traffic in "firewater" is protected by commercial treaties, is called brandy. Like the Congo gin, it is made in Hamburg, where a dozen bottles of it cost one dollar. This trade in so-called "brandy" is controlled by the Germans and the English.

But the civilizing nations of Europe may say that with the gin and brandy they send missionaries. This is true, but what an missionaries do with the poor creatures who are poisoned and maddened by these rivers of foul spirits? Does not the aborigine see that the missionaries come with the rum and are allied to the traders who pour the rum down his throat? Is it strange that he gets a distorted view of European religion and a prejudice against European civilization? If he becomes converted, is it to be wondered at that he backslides? There is the instructive example of Prince ALLACOGHA, who recently relapsed into a condition of barbarism. He was "well known to the missionaries, and had always been looked upon," we are told, "as a professing Christian." But he became offended and seized nine villagers to be held as hostages. These unfortunate villagers were cooked and eaten by him and his companions.

The industrious, self-sacrificing missionaries have a hard time of it. Some of them have gone out from this country. Doubtless they will do some good, but there are also European missionaries who mix trade with their religion. One of these, named BENTLY, returned to England last Summer and carried on there a little crusade against the Portuguese. He gave a glowing description of "the vast opportunities for trade" and assured the English that everything was "going on very quietly and satisfactorily." Trade was the burden of his remarks, and he did not forget to say that gin and gunpowder held prominent places in the list of imported products.

Why should the missionaries go to the Congo basin? Liverpool, Hamburg, Rotterdam, and Paris are more inviting fields for their work. If they could check at its source the stream of poor gin and rum that sustains European "trade" in Africa, they would do more for the civilization and elevation of the blacks than they can accomplish on those fever-stricken coasts in a century by their teachings.

July 12, 1885

CAPE TOWN, May 13.—Sir Arthur Havelock, the Governor of Natal, has been instructed to proclaim Zululand, excepting that portion constituting the new Boer Republic, a British possession. The new Boer Republic occupies the western part of Zululand and does not reach the coast. Its area is about 1,800 square miles. The capital is Vryheid.

May 14, 1887

ENGLAND'S NEW HOLD ON AFRICA

The British Government has again altered the political map of Africa, and a new colony is about to be placed under the political protection of John Bull. The exact limits of the territory are not fixed, but it extends, roughly speaking, from the territory of the German East Africa Company northward to the Somati country, and westward to the Albert Nyanza. A year ago in the general scramble for the Dark Continent Germany and England made an agreement dividing up the whole country back of the Zanzibar coast. A company called the British East African Company has now been formed to take charge of the British half. The objects as usual are commercial and philanthropic. The Baroness Burdett-Coutts and others are interested. By royal letters patent the new State in a few days will be handed over to the company, which is empowered to levy customs and taxes, to maintain an armed force, and to assert authority. The movement meets with serious opposition from some of the leading journals. They say that enormous powers over an unknown region, to which England has no right whatever, are to be given to a company of which nothing is known. It is also said that the inhabitants of the territory, numbering 12,000,000 about the lakes alone, may have their own views of the advisability of annexation. The Sultan of Zanzibar has consented, however, and the annexation is nearly a consummated fact. The Government reason is that it will be unwise to leave to other nations the entire control of routes and trade between the Zanzibar seaboard and the great equatorial lakes. They also say it will result in crushing the slave trade, as the territory in question is the great hunting ground of slave dealers. It is more than surmised that there is a nigger in the fence somewhere, and that the philanthropic plan is possibly made to cover less noble ends. The region is as large as a great European State, almost wholly unexplored and undeveloped, and the scheme has been kept so quiet up to the final consummation that the English public have not yet recovered from their surprise or made up their mind about it.

May 27, 1888

THE ZANZIBAR TROUBLES

ACCOUNTS OF TERRIBLE NATIVE MASSACRES.

THE SULTAN'S BLOODTHIRSTY POLICY —A FIERCE TRIBAL WAR—SLAVERY, THE CAUSE OF THE REBELLION.

LONDON, Dec. 19.—A dispatch from Zanzibar says that in pursuance of the Sultan's orders four natives who were awaiting trial for murder were horribly and cruelly executed in the streets of the town, their heads cut off, and their bodies left where they had fallen, exposed and unguarded, until the evening of the day of execution. The Sultan has also ordered that 24 prisoners, including one woman, who had been sentenced for life, be put to death in a similar manner during the next week, a few to be executed each day. The British Consul has vainly protested against these atrocities. The Sultan has proclaimed that in the future he will be guided by the Mahommedan law only. He has bestowed the power of capital punishment on the local Governors, and has ordained that their sentences shall not be subject to appeal.

News has been received of an outbreak between the Arusha and Masai tribes. The former tribe had enticed the Masai warriors into a cow-lifting expedition, and during their absence the Arushas raided the Masai settlement, massacred the old men and women and children, and seized the young women for concubines. They also carried off 14,000 head of cattle. The Masai warriors returning from the expedition and finding their homes devastated, lamented for three days and then began a war against the Arushas which will probably last for three years and result in the devastation of the country west of the Kilima-Njaro Mountain.

LONDON, Dec. 20.—The *Times's* correspondent at Zanzibar announces that the German Club there is about to be closed, and declares that serious results will follow. He says that there are continuous riots in Zanzibar, created by unemployed and drunken Germans, and that the matter loudly calls for stern interposition on the part of the German Government.

BERLIN, Dec. 19.—The Director of the German Plantation Company says that no instructions have been sent to Zanzibar to migrate to Borneo, and that there must be some mistake in the report to that effect.

The existence of trouble on the east coast of Africa has been made evident during the past month from the cable dispatches coming in quick succession from Zanzibar and the beleaguered stations on the mainland. These dispatches show that the Zanzibar country is in a state of rebellion, and that the German colony on the mainland would have been wiped out of existence but for the hurried dispatch of vessels-of-war with double crews from Germany to the scene of the disturbance. Furthermore we learn that the Sultan of Zanzibar has nearly lost his throne; that the whole Arab population in Africa is arrayed against the Europeans, and, finally, that 2,000 miles of African coast is being guarded by the warships of England, France, Germany, and Portugal. These are some of the events which the cable has enabled the newspapers of the day to chronicle from time to time, and now that the powers of Europe are taking a hand in the difficulty the interest in the "East African question" increases daily.

The present difficulty on the coast of Africa is a direct outcome of slavery. To properly realize the situation prior to the present rebellion necessitates a study of the slave traffic which has been carried on between the east coast of Africa and the Mohammedan countries during the past 300 years. This traffic England, France, Germany, Portugal, and the Papal power are now exerting their efforts to suppress and crush out of existence the temporal powers by a vigorous blockade of the whole Zanzibar coast.

It is well known that the continent of Africa has been open to colonization ever since the voyage of Vasco de Gama in 1499, and to see to what extent this colonization has been carried on the charts show that the British have possessions at the Cape of Good Hope, Sierra Leone, Natal, and on the Gold Coast, that the French have possessions, aside from Algeria, in Senegal and Gambia, and that on the east coast in Mozambique and on the west in Angola and Benguela the Portuguese are strong in the dependencies which they there possess.

During the last five years Germany has joined the ranks of colonizers in Africa, and the advance of this nation has been so steady and at the same time quiet that were it not for the attention suddenly aroused in all Europe few Germans and fewer foreigners would have realized the amount of work that has already been done in Africa by the German companies. At the present time there are six companies in Germany carrying out the plans of colonization, all having originated from the "Deutsch-Ostafrikanischen Company."

This "East African Company" was organized about five years ago with the German Emperor at its head. Its sole object in colonizing other lands was to effect the spread of German power, irregardless of any pecuniary return to the company. By providing German territory outside of the "Fatherland" homes are established for the surplus population, at the same time retaining to Germany the people who would be merged in other nations were they to emigrate to foreign lands. When this company cast about for territory for a colony in Africa it selected the country forming part of the dominions of the Sultan of Zanzibar. Negotiations resulted in the securing of some 20,000 German square miles, extending six degrees along the coast back of the ten-mile strip belonging to the Sultan of Zanzibar, and thence across the continent to the Congo State. Two seaports were secured—Dares Salam and Paugani—each being the terminus of a great caravan route.

The charter granted the company on its acquirement of this territory gives almost sovereign rights, but where serious criminal cases are to be tried decision is rendered by the Consul-General at Zanzibar. International rights were also obtained for the new German territory and a system of tolls arranged whereby the Sultan of Zanzibar receives 5 per cent. on all products carried through his territory. Although there has been no official support by the German Government until now, it has always been understood that the association of such names as the Emperor, the Prince of Pless, and the Duchess of Saxe-Weimar among the members of the "East African Company" has virtually denoted royal support.

Dr. Peters, who has been the prime mover in all attempts at German colonization, led the first band of colonists from Germany. He was accompanied by five officers of the German Army, furloughed in order that they might join the expedition. Stations were established throughout the territory, and their defense placed in the hands of a corps of 400 native troops. These troops were officered by the Germans. Later on two more bands were sent out from Germany, each consisting of 25 people. These numbers have been augmented from time to time by smaller acquisitions. At the breaking out of the rebellion there were about 100 Germans in the colony.

As remarked before, the colonization so far effected is the work of six companies. Some of these companies have as many as 15,000 members on their rolls, including some of the most prominent names in Germany. The German Colonization Society devotes itself to stirring up public enthusiasm through the medium of the press and public gatherings. There are 8,000 members on its rolls.

The German Wituland Society has for its object exploration and exploitation.

The German East African Plantation Society deals with the development of plantations in the annexed territory and the growing of tobacco.

Notwithstanding the efforts of these combined companies it has been no easy matter to recruit the ranks of the colonists. The domestic characteristics of the German race have made the Fatherland far dearer than the prospective homes in distant lands, and it has only been from the result of enforced eviction due to the increase in population that the Germans find themselves looking for homes elsewhere. As soon as the Germans had established their stations in the acquired territory a vigorous, home-like, well-nigh Bismarckian policy was put in operation. Now, it must be borne in mind that the territory bought by the Germans was inhabited by tribes who were far advanced ahead of the heathen hordes in the interior in the matter of civilization. The result of this new German rule over the natives was evident from the first to one acquainted with the tribes of Zanzibar. Outbreaks were continually occurring, and the little corps of 400 men was severely taxed in its efforts to quell insurrection.

The German power, however, continued to increase until within the last two months, when, like the rush of a whirlwind, the natives rose in one great rebellion as terrible in its object as the sepoy rising in India. The colonists were forced back to the Sultan's dominions and were saved from annihilation only by the arrival of the German men-of-war.

December 20, 1888

Under the repeated punishments inflicted upon them by British troops the natives of West Africa will at length realize that it is dangerous to interfere with the march of trade. The destruction of the chief town of the Wandab tribe, in the interior, northeast of Sierra Leone, is the latest practical lesson taught them. Of late years a great impetus has been given to commerce in this region by the tribes converted to Mohammedanism, who have welcomed Europeans on the coast and have become the intermediaries between them and the negroes of the interior. These latter, however, resent the intrusions and encroachments of the traders and their go-betweens, and have for generations been in the habit of blackmailing and plundering travelers. Occasionally also they have attacked the trading stations. While commerce doubtless does not appear as sacred in African eyes as in European, yet the progress of trade is unquestionably that of civilization, and wherever the sway of white men extends the horrible natives' practices of beheading and of making human sacrifices by the hundreds are checked or abolished. The advance of European civilization also diminishes slavery. Our American merchants are interested in these movements, there being a growing use of American products in West Africa.

April 28, 1889

GERMANS IN AFRICA.

BERLIN, Oct. 22.—A German protectorate has been proclaimed over the east coast of Africa, from Vitu to Kismaya, with the consent of the native chiefs. The rights of foreigners are preserved.

The Zanzibar Mission had a cordial interview with Prince Bismarck to-day and started for London.

ZANZIBAR, Oct. 22.—Lieut. Gravenreuth of Capt. Wissmann's expedition surprised Bushiri's camp and put his forces to flight. Lieut. Gravenreuth's men are continuing the pursuit of the rebels.

October 23, 1889

If the conflict going on between his Majesty of Dahomey and the French Colonial authorities in West Africa ends in the permanent overthrow of the despot who holds the lives of all his subjects at his mercy or his whim, it will be a gain for civilization. The horrible sacrifices of human beings at the political and religious celebrations, called "grand customs," have long been known, and within the last few years instances of this savagery have been recounted. The superstition of the Dahomians, who regard their sovereign as divine, makes it hopeless to expect an end of these and other atrocities save through the application of some exterior force. France, which has steadily pushed its interests in Upper Senegal and on the Upper Niger, might do a good work by annexing Dahomey, but it is not certain that England and Germany would consent. They might even, perhaps, prefer letting the ceremonies of immolation go on to allowing anybody to annex Dahomey but themselves. The number of victims sacrificed on peculiarly grave, impressive occasions, such as the ascending of a new monarch to the throne, may have been sometimes exaggerated in the accounts, but it is known that they mount into the hundreds. If France can reasonably interfere with the performance of one horrible festival of this sort, which is said to be down upon this year's programme for Dahomey, she will do a good act.

March 4, 1890

The British East African Company had only a brief enjoyment of the march it had stolen upon its rivals. Its agent, Mr. JACKSON, in concluding a treaty with MWANGA, the restored King of Uganda, for putting the latter country under British influence, secured a very great advantage. Fortune favored his energy and enterprise. King KAREMA had been overthrown after his brief lease of power and MWANGA reinstated through the help of the Christians, and the English missionaries had established a claim on MWANGA's gratitude during his flight and exile by giving him shelter and succor. But now the news comes that the Arabs have swarmed to the assistance of KAREMA, who has again expelled MWANGA and the missionaries from the capital. While these stirring events were going on in Uganda Mr. JACKSON's expedition had been making its way toward Victoria Nyanza and founding stations as it went along. He reached Uganda just about the right time for profiting by MWANGA's brief return and his friendly disposition toward the British. The British East African Company must now defer its project for opening and maintaining a trade route of its own from Victoria Nyanza to the sea.

May 11, 1890

THE PARTITION OF AFRICA.

If discovery carries with it the right of possession, to England belongs all that vast territory in Eastern and Central Africa about which an agreement has just been reached in Berlin. It was her explorers, not those of Germany, that made this region known to the civilized world. Germany is the merest tyro in the art of exploration and the civilization of primitive lands and peoples. But she it is that has snatched from England almost half of the region brought to light by English travelers and English traders. Her new-born enthusiasm for colonial empire, her daring and almost reckless energy, her shrewd and subtle diplomacy have vanquished the timidity of her more experienced but more cautious rival. While England has permitted her interests in Eastern Africa to look after themselves, Germany has watched with an eager gaze the movements that her colonists have made since they were permitted, less than fifteen years ago, to gain a foothold in the coveted continent of the negro. When BISMARCK first made an agreement with Lord BEACONSFIELD, in 1875, he could hardly have dreamed that here the Fatherland would soon have an empire many times larger than united Germany. But so vigorously has the colonial policy been prosecuted, so freely has German gold been given to encourage trade and commerce in Eastern Africa, so summarily have those obstacles presented by native hostility been swept away by German arms, that had it not been for the alarm sounded by the greatest of her travelers, England's share of the disputed region would, we cannot doubt, have been much less than it is. But had she sooner come to a realizing sense of her rival's greed, we cannot doubt, either, that she could have retained a far larger share than she has of that vast strip of territory stretching from the Juba on the north to the Rovuma on the south, and extending back in the interior to an irregular line from Albert Nyanza to Tanganyika and the southern end of Lake Nyassa.

This strip originally belonged to the Sultan of Zanzibar. Although he had no treaties with the tribes of the interior, his was the sole authority that they recognized. His subjects alone had the right to settle among them and receive protection. As late as 1877 England could have acquired for the sum of £200,000 whatever sovereignty he possessed. In that year Said BARGASH proposed to Sir WILLIAM MACKINNON that England should virtually make his kingdom a part of her empire, but as Sir WILLIAM received no encouragement from the Foreign Office, the offer came to naught. The authority of the Sultan remained undiminished and up to 1884 it was unquestioned. But at the conference in Berlin the next year the powers entered into a general agreement in regard to Africa. Two years later, on the 2d of [illegible], England and Germany made a more specific engagement. Sitting down together, the representatives of these powers divided the royal garments of the Sultan, paying no more attention to his rights and wishes than the savage plunderers of an African kraal. But with more delicacy than the savage ever knows, they designated their shares of the spoils as spheres of influence. The English sphere on the north followed the Tana River to near the intersection of the equator with the thirty-eighth degree of east longitude, and continued to the intersection of the first degree of north latitude with the thirty-seventh degree of east longitude. The southern limit began at the mouth of the River Wanga, pursued a northwesterly course, deflecting to the north of Mount Kilimanjaro, and ended at the intersection of the first degree of south latitude with the eastern shore of Victoria Nyanza. This line was the northern limit of the sphere of German influence. The southern limit was the Rovuma River. The western limit was not fixed, and this omission has been provocative of heated and almost endless discussion in the German and English press. The framers of the agreement of 1887 were also guilty of another grave omission. They neglected to make any disposition of that part of the Sultan's dominions lying between the Juba River, the southwestern limit of Italy's African protectorate, and the northern limit of England's sphere of influence. Germany has been taking advantage of this omission. Much to the annoyance of Englishmen, her traders and explorers have been invading this remnant of the Sultan's domain and laying claim to the choicest parts. The islands of Manda, Patta, and Somali, on the coast, excited their greed and envy, and they sought also to annex the kingdom of the Sultan of Witu. Dr. PETERS sailed up the Tana, penetrated the region on the north of Victoria Nyanza, making treaties with the tribes he encountered, and invaded the kingdom of Uganda. It was the hope of the *National Zeitung* that this "pearl of Central Africa" would fall into Germany's lap, but it is doomed to disappointment.

If the cable summary of the agreement between England and Germany is correct, Uganda remains under British control. The Germans also lose Manda, Patta, and Somali. They surrender Witulaud, but they get in return the worthless island of Heligoland in the German Ocean. They repudiate all the treaties that Dr. PETERS has made, and abandon all the unoccupied territory between the English sphere of influence and the borders of the Italian protectorate. They also permit the establishment of an English protectorate over the Sultanate of Zanzibar, and cede to England the islands of Pemba and Zanzibar. But in return Germany gains a recognized sovereignty to the vast territory that belongs to her neither by the right of discovery nor the right of conquest. She is permitted to extend the undefined western boundary of her sphere of influence to the eastern limit of the Congo State. The Hinterland, about which so much has been written in the English and German press—the section lying between the Congo State and the shadowy line of the German sphere of influence—now becomes hers forever. The western limit of her territory is washed by the waters of Lake Nyassa; it then follows the old Stevenson road made, to quote the words of the London *Times*, "by British capital and surrounded by British missions and trading stations"; it is next washed by the waters of Tanganyika; from the upper end of Tanganyika it crosses to the shore of Victoria Nyanza, traverses the lake, and unites with the southern limit of the English possessions.

It is the surrender of Heligoland and the Hinterland, particularly the former, that has aroused such a storm of opposition in England. But they are sentimental considerations only that give any value to Heligoland. The argument against the surrender of the Hinterland is not without force. The territory on which the caravans of England would pass from her possessions in Central Africa to those in Southern Africa now belongs to Germany. But by the Berlin agreement her goods and subjects are permitted without customs or other obstructions to pass across German territory to and from the Congo State. Similar privileges are granted to German goods and subjects. As to the other features of the treaty—the rectification of the boundary of N'gamiland in Southwestern Africa and of Togoland on the Gulf of Guinea—these are of small consequence compared with those that have been considered and stand stamped with the approval of so competent a judge as Mr. STANLEY and of so able and experienced a politician as Mr. MORLEY. They will in no way affect the fate of the agreement when it comes before Parliament for approval.

June 22, 1890

The partition of Africa between the nations of Europe goes on rapidly in these days. Lord SALISBURY'S announcement in Parliament shows that France and England have already come to an agreement upon the great region between Senegal and Lake Tchad, which it had been proposed to submit to a joint commission for delimitation. By this agreement the province or empire of Sokoto, whi has long been under the influence of the Royal Niger Company, will be conformed to it, and this part of the Soudan, lying between the Niger and Lake Tchad, is recognized as under British influence. Its dominion extends to the southern portion of the west shore of the lake. The region north of Sokoto beginning at the northern part of the west shore of Lake Tchad, and extending westerly and northwesterly, is recognized as under French influence. In this way France gets a connected zone from Lake Tchad along the Upper Niger to Senegambia and the coast. This has of late been one of the most marked scenes of French activity, and a short time ago, in the region between the Upper Senegal and the Niger, treaties with five chiefs greatly extended French influence. From their post at Bomaku the French have gone down the Niger as far as Segu and captured it, and very likely are now much further advanced through Massina on the way to Timbuctoo.

August 16, 1890

The French exploring expedition in the Congo region, of whose return to Brazzaville the cable speaks, is one of three which had been planned to push French interests in that part of Africa. The other two go respectively from the Niger and from Algeria toward Lake Tchad. It daily becomes more evident that France has conducted both her diplomacy and her practical operations on the Dark Continent, of late, with great success. Measured by actual area, she has annexed through the recent international agreements a far greater territory than either Germany or England. It is true that much of this is in Sahara and the Western Soudan; and the former is held at small value, especially by those who are guided by old ideas in regard to the great desert. But with a trans-Saharan railroad to Lake Tchad, which the French are seriously meditating, and which has gained the approval of STANLEY as being both practicable and wise, the value of the French acquisitions will be more manifest. The sphere of influence conceded to the French is further increased in importance by the treaties of , rotection they have lately made with native tribes.

September 10, 1890

GETTING SICK OF AFRICA.

There have been signs for several months that Africa was losing her charm for many of the enthusiasts that had dreamed of her speedy rescue from the dominion of savagery. The difficulty of raising the fund to place a German steamer on Victoria Nyanza was one; the report that the Berlin Government had discovered more sand than soil in the vast territory on the southwest coast, and had all but decided to abandon it as of no value to German colonists, was another; the growing belief in England manifesting itself in frequent articles in the reviews that a great and needless fuss had been made over getting what would soon be regarded as not worth having, was still another. But the most important and significant of these signs is the announcement that the British East Africa Company is about to withdraw from Uganda.

This famous kingdom on the northwest shores of Victoria Nyanza is known as "the Pearl of Equatorial Africa." Some of Mr. STANLEY'S finest rhetoric has been expended in describing its great natural beauty and boundless agricultural and mineral wealth. In a speech at Newcastle, just after the Anglo-German agreement was signed, he declared its inhabitants to be "the finest in all Africa." So fired was his patriotic imagination by the news that it had been lost to Germany, which had set her heart on possessing it, and that it had been included within the sphere of British influence, that he saw Victoria Nyanza in the near future covered with steamers "conveying missionaries" and "carrying supplies" to the country, thus "gradually lifting the people from the slough of barbarism." Aroused by pictures of a land almost literally flowing with milk and honey, British greed could not let such a prize slip through its fingers or the grass grow under its feet before seizure.

But possession and examination have divested this pearl, as they will doubtless divest many other African pearls, of its priceless value. The discoveries of Capt. LUGARD and Mr. F. J. JACKSON, who led expeditions to Uganda in 1889-90, show how absurd Mr. STANLEY'S rhapsodies were. They show, moreover, that the German tears shed over its loss were ill spent, and that the English joy over its acquisition was premature. They make clear also the reason for its abandonment. "A network of rivers has to be crossed, enormous forest-covered gorges are met with, rendering traveling difficult and dangerous," says an article in the London *Times* giving an account of these expeditions; "many donkeys, cattle, and even men, succumbed to the hardships which the magnificence of the scenery did not mitigate." Fancy the years that it would take to reduce such a region to cultivation, even if it presented no other obstacle to European settlement. But the explorers encountered other obstacles, and one of them not only closes Uganda but the whole of equatorial Africa to civilization. That obstacle is the climate. "Of course," says the *Times* article, alluding to this feature of the country, "white colonization is not to be thought of." "What are wanted," it adds, "are cheap and rapid means for getting from the coast and settlers suitable to the climate and physical conditions."

When the Anglo-German agreement was before the House of Lords, the British Premier gave precedence to "the task of developing the vast and untrodden field of Africa, thus making them new outlets for colonization by excessive populations at home and new fields for industry and trade." But if white colonization is not to be thought of in Uganda, in what part of equatorial Africa is it to be thought of? No other part of it is more healthful or more free from that terrific heat, which, according to Prof. DRUMMOND, makes "moving a torture." As to the universal prevalence of the fever that has almost converted Africa into a graveyard for Europeans, there is an abundance of testimony of the highest character. "No prediction," says Prof. DRUMMOND, "can be made beforehand as to what regions are haunted by it and what are safe." "From 0 to 5,000 feet above the sea," says Mr. STANLEY, "there is no immunity from it." Moreover, where are the "suitable" settlers to be found? When the natives and Arabs fall victims to the fever as readily as Europeans, it would be a waste of time to seek them outside of Africa.

Would it not be quite as vain also to provide a "cheap and rapid means for getting from the coast" to the interior? A people sunk in "the slough of barbarism" does not have those varied wants and tastes that create a great and profitable trade and thus justify the establishment of expensive lines of transportation. Such, at least, is the view that English investors are beginning to take. The stream of money that they poured into African enterprise is not so large as it was. Their pious desire to see the people of the Dark Continent converted to Christianity and their country opened up to commerce has found but slight encouragement in the "dividends in philanthropy" that the President of the East Africa Company hoped the stockholders would be satisfied with. Already this company has found the purse of the English capitalist closed against it, and has been forced to call on the Government for assistance, forgetting or ignoring the declaration of the African enthusiasts that they asked for nothing beyond the opportunity to prosecute their glorious work undisturbed by other nations. "All we want," said Mr. STANLEY in his plea for protection against the encroachments of Germany, "is the privilege of putting in the seed." This privilege, as all the world knows, was granted at the cost of a heavy addition to the responsibilities of England. But the further petition that the Government provide the seed shows how public confidence in the future of Africa has decreased. It proves also that English philanthropy and private enterprise are already sick of the charge that they assumed with so much enthusiasm.

December 1, 1891

GERMANY IS WELL PLEASED

REGARDS FAVORABLY ENGLAND'S ACQUISITION IN AFRICA.

BERLIN, May 27.—The Anglo-Belgian agreement as to sphere of influence in Central Africa has roused the Colonial enthusiasts to the usual outcry against English greed. In the Foreign Office, however, a totally different feeling is noticeable. The officials there, while acknowledging that the French have been thoroughly outwitted, contend that they have been cognizant of the Anglo-Belgian negotiations almost from the first, and have found their tendency highly advantageous to Germany.

The agreement between London and Brussels is recognized as another step in England's policy of creating a buffer territory between French and English possessions in Africa, keeping France from access to the Nile, and securing to England unbroken connection between Cape Colony and Egypt.

England tried at first to obtain a German buffer by ceding to Germany territory east of the Shari River. The Franco-German Cameroons Convention foiled this aim, and prevented the utilization of Germany as a go-between, for by it France obtained that which England had abandoned to Germany.

The local newspapers which assert that the German Government probably will support France in refusing to recognize the Anglo-Belgian agreement are entirely misinformed. The Foreign Office intends to hold aloof from the dispute, satisfied that the new situation tends to lessen Germany's Colonial difficulties with France. If France should propose a Colonial conference of the powers interested in Central Africa, as she is expected to do, the Berlin Government, before assenting, would undoubtedly consult with England and agree with her upon a common course of action.

May 28, 1894

THE PARTITION OF AFRICA.

It is already plain that, as the partition of America was the principal European question of the seventeenth and eighteenth centuries, the partition of Africa is to be the chief European question of the twentieth. The process has already begun. It is rather curious that to-day there should be reported three collisions of native Africans with the representatives of different European nations. The siege of Bulawayo, which is a native protest against British rapacity in Matabeleland, is still going on, and the issue is still doubtful. Far to the north, in Abyssinia, a conflict is reported between the natives and the Italians. Finally, "German Southwest Africa" has been the scene of a small conflict in which the Germans appear to have got the worst of it.

Of course, these affairs are mere eddies in the stream of European invasion, and a hundred such affairs would not suffice to obstruct or to deflect that stream. The resistance of the Matabeles to the forcible acquisition of their country seems more absurd to the British, naturally, than it does to the Matabeles, or even to the Boers, who are not remotely threatened by it. It is quite possible that this resistance may give trouble for many years to come. The Matabeles are so numerous that they are reported to have 30,000 men now under arms, though this is very likely an exaggeration. What is more to the purpose is that they are brave and that from some quarter they have been furnished with quite as good weapons as those possessed by the invaders.

German Southwest Africa is not, like German East Africa, a mere "sphere of influence," marked out because it may possibly become a valuable possession at some future time. It is a German possession already, and contained, at the last reports, about 1,200 whites to 200,000 blacks. As the blacks are scattered over a region which allows a square mile and a half to each of them, the odds are not so formidable, even in point of number, as they would at first appear. It is, however, likely that there are more Germans among the Uitlanders in the South African Republic than there are in all German Africa, so called. The little reverse that the Germans seem to have experienced is of an importance rather moral than material, since nothing could in the long run be more expensive than to let the natives believe that as soldiers they are equal to the Europeans. It must be owned that as colonizers the Germans seem to be, like the French, somewhat amateurish as compared with the English, of whom, whatever else may be said of them, it can never be denied that they are "on business." The Italians in Abyssinia, on the other hand, have not at all the air of being on business, but only of having been sent to Abyssinia to divert Italian attention from what is going on in Italy.

April 26, 1896

THE ITALIANS IN AFRICA

RESULTS OF CRISPI'S BRILLIANT POLICY.

DECLARATION OF A PROTECTORATE OVER KING MENELICK'S DOMAINS—EUROPE'S ASTONISHMENT.

From the month of December to the present time Italy has achieved triumph upon triumph in Africa. After the defeat of Ras Alula and of the successor of King John in the battle of Haramat, after the submission of all the tribes, after the occupation of Heren and the surrounding territories, the troops of King Humbert have now entered Adowa, the capital of Abyssinia. They have been welcomed by the natives as liberators, and have taken possession, established and lasting possession, in the name of the Italian Government.

Thus the bold and at the same time prudent policy of Crispi has had a magnificent termination, and one which will be excusably envied by other diplomats and other nations. Without the excessive expenses that invariably attend a campaign, even though of small proportions, in the inhospitable and barbarous regions of "mysterious Africa," without too much spilling of blood, if we except two or three feats of arms, without risks of diplomatic conflicts or possible conflicts with other powers, Italy, from the small possession of Massowah, has gradually pushed and fought her way to a new eastern territory of superior commercial advantages, and has concluded a treaty of alliance with King Menelick (Emperor of Abyssinia) by which he acknowledges the protectorate of Italy and guarantees it a peaceful possession, with free access to his own kingdóm.

The policy of Crispi, so different from that of England in the same regions and under almost the same circumstances, has obtained merited success. This success has cost infinitely less, and has produced incalculably more.

Crispi is not a nephew of Machiavelli for nothing, and his methods, slow but sure, must and will conquer. They are methods applied in the face of the instinctive diffidence of friends and the badly simulated indifference of competitors, in silence, without effrontery, without "*cœur léger*," proceeding straight to their object.

Europe now marvels and perhaps scarcely credits its own eyes. Italy in Adowa! Is it true or is it a dream? It is reality that nothing in the world can alter or destroy, just as nothing in the world has the power to drive the Italian troops from their central position.

We could not thus speak, however, if the programme of Italy in Africa was one of pure conquest, because exploits exclusively military are in too great opposition to the sentiments of progress, of peace, of work, of companionship, that should form the pivot of modern life. But, instead, we may rejoice in and applaud this conquest, because to a certain extent it is a conquest of civilization and Christianity over barbarians and savages, over unbelief, over habits of ferocity, over brutal ignorance of every human law, religious, social, and civil.

The water roads of Africa and the large commercial arteries in the hands of Italy signify that they are also in the hands of the civilized world, which can now introduce without fear the benefits of commerce, of exchange, of relations of any and every sort, and in a short time produce the best profits from the immense natural wealth existing there.

Still this advance of Italy in Abyssinia appears to have met with an obstacle a few days ago, in a protest attributed by the French press to Russia. We say appears, because the dispatch stated that Crispi had made known to the Baron di Uxhult, Ambassador of the Czar to the Quirinal, that while grieved at Russia's opposition Italy would continue to follow her own judgment.

The right of the Ethiopian Emperor to regulate his international relations in the manner which appears to him most opportune is indisputable. After long centuries this is the first time that Ethiopia has come in contact with Europe; after long centuries its Princes are now no more confined to the sea, and with the interior of Africa their relations are no more limited to barbarous tribes.

When Ethiopia came in contact with another power Egypt was for making war, victorious war. Completely inclosed in the continent of which she forms a part, she had no political relations of any kind with others, and this is the first time that she resolutely emerges from the uncivilized regions with the intention of taking her place in the civilized world. Who after this could prohibit the right to direct itself rather to one State than to another?

Geography and history unite in rendering clear and incontestable the diplomatic situation created by the relations which Ethiopia now intends to assume with the rest of the world by means of Italy. Italy by precedence or by the position which she had already occupied on the Red Sea, and by which she conquered the interior, was the only power to which naturally and logically Ethiopia could address herself. Now all that is too evident not to be at once accepted by European Cabinets, and of the question raised by a faction—limited, it must be admitted—of the French press, nothing remains but a new proof of its inability. It is indeed inability, for it is clear that, if the Cabinet of Paris had been so badly advised by its own councils, still the fact itself would not be changed. Italy would still have continued to be the intermediator in the relations of Ethiopia with the rest of the world, and only France would have given proof of an unjustified rancor, by which it would have gained nothing, but would have lost instead Italian sympathy. The Cabinet of Paris equally with others has been better advised, and many wise and thoughtful Frenchmen, understanding the true interests of France, acknowledge themselves to be satisfied and pleased.

In point of fact the plan of Italy in Africa is not circumscribed. Assab, Massowah, Kerim, Asmara, Adowa, are so many points upon which to march forward and extend the prize of possession. The places upon the coast of Suakin to Assab comprise the first of these localities, and will belong in a future more or less distant to Italy.

Nor is this all. The plan of occupation extends also to Berber, to Khartoum, to all the strips of territory on the right and left of the White Nile. Therefore it is inadmissible that Italy acts out only a colonial plan, in which we must also include the countries of the Bogos and the Tigré. Many points are in the possession of England, which, following the traditions of her policy, will leave freedom of action to Italy, in view of being assisted in the formidable and decisive war with the Soudanese; for Italy—ally and protectorate of Menelik (negus of Abyssinia)—is in a condition to facilitate the success in the Soudan without direct interference.

As is known, the natural enemies of Abyssinia are the Soudanese, or Mahdists, who in battle killed King John. The influence, therefore, of Italy, in order to favor the Anglo-Egyptian action, should exercise itself in the sense of inducing Menelik to attack the Mahdists. Upon this influence England relies to take the Soudanese between two fires. With her forces united to those of the Egyptians Menelik could march north and England herself could move to the south.

Little things produce great effects. Thus, from the action of Italy, which invaded Africa to obtain Massowah, only issues the protectorate of King Menelik and the dominion of the entire province. From this also may issue the extermination of Musselmanism and the disappearance of all the States of slavery and barbarism in the Soudan.

"Videbimus infra."

A FRIEND OF AMERICA AND ITALY.

February 2, 1890

ITALY IN AFRICA.

The colonial projects and proceedings of Italy are even less explicable than those of France. At the beginning of our Revolution BURKE pointed out in the House of Commons that colonies were maintained because they were serviceable to the mother country. That description is quite obsolete as applied to the recent colonial enterprises of more than one power. It can no more be pretended that Abyssinia is serviceable or gives any prospect of being serviceable to Italy than a like proposition can be maintained respecting France and Siam or France and Madagascar.

In the case of Italy the colonization is stranger than in that of France, because Italy has so much less money to waste. Everybody knows that Italy is very fast approaching, if she has not reached, the point at which the enormous armament she has undertaken to maintain puts upon her resources a breaking strain. In a very careful article a year or two ago Sir CHARLES DILKE showed how near she was to succumbing, and certainly her condition has not improved since that time. Yet here has the Italian Chamber of Deputies been cheerfully voting a credit of $4,000,000 for the prosecution of operations in Africa for which nobody can reasonably pretend to see a return.

Indeed, there has been no time since Italy assumed her protectorate over King MENELEK, in 1889, when the transaction has promised to show a profit. But though quite useless to Italy, a protectorate in Africa may be very "serviceable" to Italian politicians. It is always possible to create a rumor of war, to make a pretense of winning some cheap glory, and thus to distract attention from troublesome questions at home. This seems to be the chief function of a "colonial policy" for more than one European power.

December 19, 1895

ITALY'S TERRIBLE DEFEAT

Three Thousand Men Killed, Sixty Guns and All Provisions Lost.

BARATIERI'S STRATEGY CONDEMNED

All Available Steamers for Transport of Reinforcements to Abyssinia Are Ordered.

PERSISTENT RUMOR OF MINISTRY'S FALL

Te Deum and Diplomatic Banquet Countermanded by the Pope—Misadventures of Erythrean Colony.

ROME, March 3.—The present campaign against the Abyssinians threatens to become one of the most disastrous in which the Italian arms have ever taken part, and what the final outcome will be it would be hard to predict. It was rumored to-day that the latest defeat of the Italians by the forces of King Menelik had compelled the Ministry to resign, owing to the popular disapproval of the Government's policy, but to-night this report is denied.

Details received here to-day of the defeat on Sunday of the Italian Army show that the Italian losses were very heavy, they being placed by some at 3,000 killed. It is still impossible to ascertain the precise losses, but popular opinion credits the report that the number of killed is not overstated. Thus far the reports make no mention of the number of wounded. Among the dead are Gen. Albertone, Commander of the Left Brigade, and Gen. Dabormida, Commander of the Right Brigade.

The news of this latest disaster has caused the greatest excitement throughout Italy, and the Opposition Party is taking advantage of it to make violent attacks upon the Government's policy in attempting to extend the sphere of Italian influence in Abyssinia.

The scenes in the streets to-day were very exciting, the populace being greatly incensed against the Government. The Pope is greatly disturbed by the news. He has ordered the suspension of the Te Deum and diplomatic banquet which were to be given in celebration of the anniversary of his coronation.

A meeting of the Cabinet was last night immediately upon the re the news of the Italian reverse. isters met at midnight and session until late t the situation. Th of Deputies to- ment regar

March 4, 1896

Emperor and Empress of Abyssinia.

March 7, 1896

MOZAMBIQUE REBELLION ENDED.

Gungunhama and His Son Gudide Captured by the Portuguese.

WASHINGTON, Jan. 6.—Consul General Taveria, in charge of the Portuguese Legation here, this afternoon received the following cable dispatch from his Government, at Lisbon, in regard to the Mozambique (east coast of Africa) rebellion:

"Gungunhama and his son, Gudide, have been imprisoned by the brave Capt. Mousenlio. They have already reached Lorenzo Marques, and will be conveyed at once to Lisbon, on board the Portuguese troopship Africa. The strongest enthusiasm prevails at Lisbon."

The Consul General says this practically marks the end of the rebellion, which has been in progress in Mozambique for over a year.

Gungunhama and his son are African chiefs who have caused the Portuguese colony a great deal of trouble for years past, and the Government has spared no pains or expense to catch them. They had been in hiding since last November, when the chief's army, nearly 10,000 strong, and composed of members of the Massapa and Vatuas tribes, was met by the Portuguese troops, attacked, and repulsed.

The battle was fought Nov. 7, near Lake Coella, in the Province of Mozambique. The rebels and the Portuguese soldiers, the latter numbering 1,500, again fought Nov. 11, and once more the rebels were put to flight.

Chief Gungunhama and his son fled toward the Transvaal, and all trace of them was lost until their capture by the Portuguese authorities.

In both battles mentioned the rebels had a number of killed and injured, and the Portuguese troops had a few casualties.

January 7, 1896

PEACE AGAIN IN ABYSSINIA.

The Treaty Signed with Italy and Its Conditions.

ROME, Nov. 15.—It is officially stated that King Humbert has received a telegram from Menelik, Emperor of Abyssinia, stating that a treaty of peace between Abyssinia and Italy was signed on Oct. 26.

The new convention abrogates the Uccialli Treaty, by the terms of which Italy claimed a protectorate over Abyssinia, and recognizes the complete independence of Ethiopia. Menelik declares free all the Italians taken prisoners by the Abyssinians during the recent campaign, but Italy will have to indemnify him for their support while in captivity.

Major Nerazzi, the special envoy sent to Menelik by Gen. Baldissera, Governor of Erythrea and Commander in Chief of the Italian forces in that colony, signed the treaty on behalf of Italy.

November 16, 1896

ITALY OUT OF AFRICA.

The report that the Italian Government has decided to abandon its ill-fated enterprise of African colonization has been expected for some time. It is the logical conclusion of the treaty with Abyssinia, withdrawing all claim to an Italian protectorate, and is, moreover, made necessary by the fact that the colony thus circumscribed must be a heavy tax upon the Italian Treasury without bringing any commensurate advantage to Italian influence.

The history of the enterprise furnishes an excellent illustration of the methods of modern colonial expansion. An Italian ship owner in 1869 purchased from the Arab chiefs a small tract of land near the Straits of Bab-el-Mandeb for a co[illegible]ing station. The next year he enlarged his property by additional purchase, raised the Italian flag over it, and after some years of private rule formally handed it over to the Italian Government in 1882. Three years later the Egyptian Government announced that it must give up its occupation of Massowah, about 300 miles to the north, and next to Suez the most important port on the Red Sea. This gave an opportunity which the Italians seized eagerly, and, probably with an understanding with England, they occupied the place, for a time conjointly with the Egyptian troops, but soon alone. The next step was to secure the high land back from the coast. Massowah was low and unhealthy and thus unfavorable for the establishment of an Italian colony which it was hoped by the more sanguine would be the beginning of an Italian African empire. This naturally met with opposition from the Abyssinian chiefs, who, however, were generally worsted in battle, until by a treaty with one of them, MENELEK, an Italian protectorate over the whole land was recognized.

The colony, however, proved a failure, as the Italians persistently refused to emigrate, preferring good wages and comfortable living in America to no wages, a bare subsistence, and a most uncomfortable climate in Erythrea. The failure of the colony carried with it failure in securing any financial returns, and the drain upon the Treasury at Rome became constantly more serious. With the consolidation of the power of MENELEK the assertion of Italian authority became more difficult, and it was not long before the disastrous Abyssinian campaign resulted in the defeat of Adowa and made necessary the giving up of the protectorate.

Since then the question before the Italian Government has been whether it is worth while, merely for the name of an African possession, to continue such a draft upon the almost bankrupt Treasury as made home development impossible. It should be remembered that the wisest of the Italian leaders were opposed to the whole scheme from the beginning, and CRISPI, DI RUDINI, and others only gave their assent because they found it impossible to stem the tide of popular enthusiasm. Now that their first judgment has received such emphatic indorsement, it is natural that they should seek in the most practical way possible to retrace the wrong step. For the present, it is stated that they will retain Massowah. That, however, can scarcely be permanent. The city without the highlands is of no advantage and a positive drag. It will in all probability not be long before that, too, will be given up, and the Italian possessions on the Red Sea be reduced to the original purchase of Signor RUBATTINO.

February 2, 1897

THE WEST AFRICA PROBLEM

French and British Claims to One of the Richest Regions in the Continent.

THE ORIGIN OF THE DISPUTE

Scheme of France to Reach Upper Egypt — The Agreement of 18[illegible] Touching the Occupation of Borgu—Work of the Commission Now in Paris.

The West Africa question, about which the cable dispatches have so much to say, with meagre actual information, is likely to assume an aspect of vast and serious importance in European diplomacy before the

ri[illegible] to station a Resident and an escort at N[illegible]

In 1895 M. Ballot, the Governor of Dahomey, acting presumably under orders from Paris, or those of M. Chaudie, the Inspector General of the West African colonies of France, who has supervision of Senegal, the Western Soudan, French Guinea, and Dahomey, led an expedition to Sokoto. He arrived at Gando, and is said to have concluded treaties with the chiefs there. The same year the expedition of Commandant Toutée journeyed northward from Dahomey, across the disputed strip and up the Niger to Tibi-Farka, in French Soudan. He then descended the river and did not meet a single Englishman until he reached Igga, in Lagos, undisputed British territory.

Grounds for British Claims.

According to the British claims their rights to the territory are prior to all expeditions of the French. In 1885 Joseph Thompson is said to have obtained treaties with the chiefs in the disputed strip which place that area completely under British control. Queen Victoria's Commissioners in Paris have about 400 of these documents whose dates are prior to those of the French. The English, however, confine their claims to the Lugard treaties of 1890 and 1894.

Capt. Lugard was sent to Borgu because the French designs upon it were suspected. His instructions were to avoid conflict with Commissioners to determine—the exact course to be taken by the frontier from Say, southward, until it meets the line which divides Dahomey and Lagos, and the northern limits which shall be set to the English sphere of operation along the Gold Coast and in Ashantee.

The Present Aspect.

At present there are two French expeditions in Borgu, and although they graciously evacuate their posts on the approach of the English, by so doing they are gradually working eastward, thus dangerously imperilling England's position in Upper Egypt. There is no mistaking the recent speech of M. Lebon, the French Colonial Minister, when he openly declared the other day that the cardinal feature of French policy in Africa is the extension of French influence from the west coast to the Nile Valley, and thence to Ethiopia, with uninterrupted series of posts and protectorates. And underlying all this is the provoking rumor that the French Colonial party is secretly subsidized by German money.

While the commission in Paris is procrastinating, both parties are secretly moving reinforcements toward Borgu—the French from Senegal toward Say, and the English up the Niger to Rabba and Badjibo on the Sokoto border; and Capt. Lugard, the British officer, formerly in command of Kalahari, South Central Africa, whence he was ordered to report in Downing Street, has been sent on a secret mission to the Niger delta.

November 14, 1897

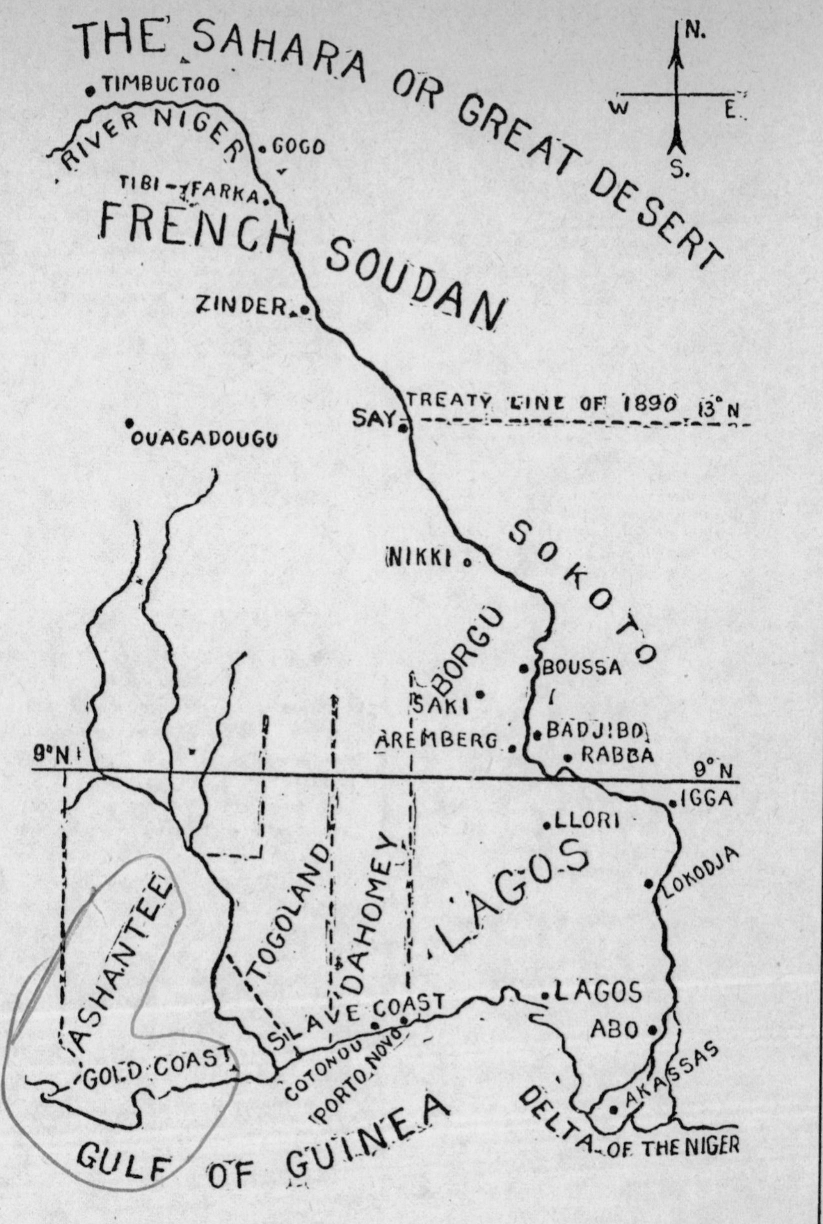

November 14, 1897

THE NIGER CONVENTION.

London Newspapers Reproach Salisbury for Letting France Get the Better of It.

LONDON, June 14.—The Anglo-French convention with reference to the disputed territory in the Niger Valley was signed yesterday.

France agrees to evacuate Kissi, Boria, Ashigere, Kiam, Boussa, Gorba, and Ilo, but she retains Nikki. Furthermore on the left bank of the Niger the French get a triangular piece of territory whose base extends from Say to Ilo. In return they give Great Britain Bornu, including the portion east of the meridian passing through Darua.

On the right bank of the Niger the French get the country from Say to Ilo and also Gurma. Beyond this they get thirty-year leases of bonded areas at Liaba and facilities for transit in bond. This is to secure the benefit of the navigable portion of the river.

In return they give thirty years of reciprocity for the whole west coast colonies, from the Liberian frontier to the Niger. With respect to the Gold Coast, the French evacuate Wa and probably Pumu and Leo. In return, Great Britain gives up Bona and Dawkita, and accepts the Volta as the best natural boundary. The French retain Moss, which they have held for eighteen months.

The editorials in the morning papers express satisfaction that the threatening dispute in the Niger Valley has been arranged.

They confess, however, that M. Hanotaux, the French Foreign Minister, has made an excellent bargain for France, some of them sorrowfully reproaching Lord Salisbury with allowing England to be "over-squeezed."

June 14, 1898

THE CONGO FREE STATE

Belgian Parliament Discussing the Question of Its Annexation.

RICH IN IVORY AND RUBBER

Leopold II. Now Its Absolute Ruler—The Natives Make Good Workingmen if Kindly Treated.

BRUSSELS, March 24.—In view of the probable annexation in 1900 of the Congo Free State to Belgium, (which annexation is under discussion just now in the Parliament at Brussels,) the work published lately by A. J. Wauters is of great present interest. The volume in question, "L'Etat Independent du Congo," is by far the most comprehensive work yet published on the Congo, and the wide reputation Mr. Wauters long since achieved as a savant and political economist is sufficient guarantee of the intrinsic merit of this his latest contribution to science.

As at present constituted, the Congo Free State is an absolute monarchy, Leopold II., a constitutional monarch in Europe, being the sole arbiter of his African subjects' destinies. There is no constitution, in the ordinary sense of the word, which limits the power of Leopold II. as Sovereign of the Congo. The Congo Government, in its present form, is, however, only temporary. In virtue of the convention of July 3, 1890, Belgium has the right to annex the Free State in 1900. Moreover, King Leopold has, as is well known, bequeathed the State to Belgium in the event of his death before the question of annexation is voted upon by the Belgian Parliament. If, contrary to all probability, the Belgian Chambers were to refuse the royal legacy, it would be difficult to say who would be the next Sovereign of the Congo. Until now no legal steps have been taken to regulate the question of succession to the throne of the Free State, but this question can be settled by King Leopold himself. If he bequeaths the Congo to his successor on the Belgian throne, this successor—presumably Prince Albert, the King's nephew, son of the Count of Flanders—must, before accepting the gift, be authorized to do so by Parliament, since the union between the two crowns is entirely personal, and has not the character of a dynastic or hereditary union.

The Free State is therefore, at present, the personal property of King Leopold. The annexation of the Congo to Belgium as a colony would be of the greatest importance both for the future of the Free State and to Belgium, who would thus become a great colonial power, holding much the same position as Holland does to-day.

The present commercial and industrial position of the Congo is very clearly set forth by Mr. Wauters. At the time when the Belgians first made their appearance in the Lower Congo, the only products exported from the district were palm oil, cocoanuts, and ivory. A few years later, owing to the rapid progress made by the Belgians in settling the country, attention was given to the india rubber industry. Ivory and india rubber have, so far, been the principal articales of export. But now that the Matadi-Leopoldville Railway, (which will carry freight at low rates,) is open to traffic, a great number of other products will be exported.

THE CONGO IVORY TRADE.

The figures relating to the ivory trade in the Congo are significant. According to the latest statistics the annual production of ivory in the world is about 700 tons, of which Africa produces 600 tons. It may, therefore be said that, with the exception of a small stock of fossilized ivory derived from India and Liberia, the entire production of ivory is furnished by the Dark Continent. Half a century ago all this African ivory came from Egypt and Zanzibar, but to-day the Congo Free State holds the first rank among ivory-exporting countries. In 1897 no less than 245 tons were exported to Europe, this being half of the total output from Africa. The Antwerp ivory market, which started on July 31, 1888, with a sale of fifteen tons, had already surpassed the Liverpool market in 1890 and the London market in 1895. The Antwerp ivory market is to-day by far the most important in the world. Four great public sales take place there every year, at the begining of February, May, August, and November.

The following statistics show the quantity of ivory sold on the Antwerp market from 1889 to 1897:

In 1889 90,000 pounds were sold, the total value of which was $264,000.

In 1890 152,000 pounds were sold, the total value of which was $339,000.

In 1891 118,000 pounds were sold, the total value of which was $249,600.

In 1892 236,000 pounds were sold, the total value of which was $450,000.

In 1893 446,000 pounds were sold, the total value of which was $718,000.

In 1894 370,000 pounds were sold, the total value of which was $559,800.

In 1895 546,000 pounds were sold, the total value of wh'ch was $885,400.

In 1896 49[illegible],000 pounds were sold, the total value of which was $781,200.

In 1897 560,000 pounds were sold, the total value of which was $976,400.

The average price of ivory on the Antwerp market, at present, is $8.47. The question naturally arises, How is the ivory obtained which the Congo Free State exports in such large quantities? Some imaginative writers are responsible for wonderful legends circulated, from time to time, concerning those "fabulous cemeteries of elephants hidden in the depths of the Congo forests, mysterious spots where ivory tusks have been accumulating for centuries." The truth of the matter is far simpler. Herds of elephants are still extremely numerous in the immense virgin forests of Central Congo. The natives hunt these animals, more on account of their flesh, which the Congolese greatly appreciate, than for their tusks. But these hunts are, on the whole, far from lucrative, and only furnish a small proportion of the tusks exported to Europe; most of these come from former harvests. Thus, during 1897 of the 29,985 tusks sold on the Antwerp market, 8,539 alone came from freshly-killed animals, the remaining 21,446 tusks being what the natives term "dead ivory."

For centuries the aborigines have been gathering and collecting elephant tusks, which they considered as of little intrinsic value in themselves, but useful as articles of exchange. The ivory accumulated in this manner remained hidden for a long time, there being practically no demand for it in the remote districts of the Congo. The Khartoum merchants were the first to discover these hidden reserves of ivory, first in the region of the Upper Nile, in the district of Bahr-el-Ghazal. Later on, the Zanzibar traders pushed on to Katanga, and thence to the very heart of the Congo, with the result that the ivory trade soon became the principal industry of the country.

The Congo ivory, as indeed all African ivory, is far more highly prized and sought after than the Asiatic product. It is harder, of a finer grain, lends itself more easily to workmanship, and has fewer fissures. The tusks of Congolese elephants are, as a rule, very large, and weigh on an average 60 pounds. Some of them are of extraordinary size. At the Brussels Exhibition a pair of tusks were exhibited from the Congo, each of which weighed 156 pounds.

By a decree passed in 1889 elephant hunting is forbidden throughout the whole territory of the Free State without special permission from the Government. The carcasses of all animals killed in violation of this law are confiscated by the State.

GREAT QUANTITIES OF RUBBER.

The great future wealth of the Congo, however, will not be ivory, but india-rubber. There is small probability of even coffee or oleoaginous substances taking a preponderating position over india-rubber as an article of export.

The india-rubber industry in the Free State is a recent one. Some forty years ago the first Europeans who settled in the Lower Congo regions began to develop this industry, but on a very small scale; and it was only in 1889 that the Belgians turned their attention to the great gutta-percha forests of the Upper Congo. Since then the progress made in the rubber trade has been such that at the present moment the Free State holds the first place among the rubber-producing countries of Africa, with an annual output of nearly 2,000 tons. In 1897 the total production of rubber in the world was about 34,000 tons, 22,000 of which came from South America, 10,000 from Africa, and 2,000 from Asia and Australasia.

Stanley had, at the time of his first exploration, already pointed out the great future of the india-rubber trade in the Congo. "On the islands of the river alone," said he, "I estimate that enough rubber can be gathered in a year to pay the expenses of building the railroad!" Cameron is even more emphatic. He says: "The day will come when enough rubber will be gathered in the forests and jungles of the Congo to meet all the requirements of the civilized world."

The most numerous species of rubber plants in the Congo are the Landolphias, which produce a first-class grade of rubber; but there are several other varities of the plant. In the Summer of 1898 Mr. Hennebert discovered great numbers of Kickxia Africana in the districts of Lagos and Accra, where new rubber factories have been established in the past few months. Other varieties of gutta-percha plants have lately been found at Bangaso, Kwango, and Wamba.

Since the development of the rubber trade in the Free State the natives have been in the habit of cutting the entire bark of the gutta-percha plants, instead of making incisions, thus obtaining a great deal of gum in a short space of time. Were this process to continue the plants would soon be exhausted. By decree of the sovereign it has recently been forbidden to gather the rubber otherwise than by incisions.

POPULATION OF THE STATE.

Concerning the population of the Congo Free State, about which so many discussions have taken place of late, it is not an easy matter to get exact figures. But, already in 1888, when means to determine the extent of the population were necessarily very limited, Mr. Elisée Reclus estimated the figure at more than twenty millions. This estimate is certainly too small. Stanley places the number of inhabitants of the State at twenty-nine millions, and the Governor General Wahis, after visiting the regions of the upper river and obtaining information and statistics on the spot from the agents of the Government, thinks that Stanley's estimate must be held as a minimum.

The population is very unequally scattered over the territories of the State. Side by side with districts where it attains an extraordinary density there are regions where the villages are few and far between, and others which are almost entirely deserted. The region of the Falls, from Noki to Kimpese, the banks of the Congo River between the Pool and Bolobo, the Lower Ubangi, and certain districts of the Bomu Basin, have but few inhabitants. While certain regions of the great forest, notably the basin of the Lopori, have a large population, there are others, notably those which the Stanley and Dhanis expeditions explored, between Basoko and the Falls to Lake Albert, which are hardly inhabited. On the other hand, a number of explorers mention certain districts as having populations of extraordinary density.

Following are the most reliable statistics concerning the population of the principal Congo districts. The Belgian, Lieut. de Berghe, after several months of exploration, estimates the population of the Boma district at 15, and that of Mayombe at 20 inhabitants per square kilometer. The district of the Falls, which is but sparsely populated, has an average of only 3 inhabitants per square kilometer. According to the explorer Costermans, the country extending between the Pool and the Kwango is very thickly populated. In the district of Sankuru are to be found the largest villages in the Free State, one of them, Mutombo, has, so Major Parmenter relates, a population of at least 10,000 inhabitants. The natives along the shores of Lake Leopold II. number about 20,000, and those of Lake Tumba, 36,000. From these figures, and from those of other explorers, it may be concluded that Stanley's figure—29,000,000—comes near to the truth. This gives the Free State an average of 12 inhabitants per square kilometer.

NATIVES EASILY CIVILIZED.

The Congolese negroes, with few exceptions, adapt themselves easily to civilization, and make excellent workingmen if they are kindly and justly treated. The history of the Congo Railroad, from Matadi to Leopoldville, is in itself proof sufficient of the adaptability of the Congolese to the habits of civilized life. It took no less than five years to build the first twenty-four miles of the railroad. During these five years the negro laborers employed on the road were treated with extreme harshness, practically like slaves, the whip and rattan being frequently used by the Belgian overseers.

It was only after the unsatisfactory results of the first five years, that the company decided to change their system of coercing the blacks. From that time on the negro laborers were no longer treated like slaves, and kept at work by the whip, but were put exactly on the same level as working men in Belgium, or in any other civilized country, and paid, not by the day, but according to the actual labor performed.

Stimulated in this manner by the prospect of gain in proportion to their efforts, the natives then showed what they were really capable of doing, and in four years the remaining 216 miles of the railroad were covered, as against twenty-four miles for the first five years.

This astonishing contrast can only be explained by the difference in the two methods of treating the laborers, for the difficulties of building the road were the same throughout. Henceforth, owing to the successful experiment of the Matadi-Leopoldville Company, it is certain that any great undertaking requiring native labor can be accomplished in Equatorial Africa. This, in itself, is of the greatest importance for the future development of the Upper Congo. There is now every probability that new means of communication will, before long, be established in the extensive territories of the Upper Congo, which have an area of five times that of France.

BRADFORD COLT DE WOLF.

April 16, 1899

REVOLT IN CONGO STATE.

All the Whites on the Upper Reaches of the River Reported Slain.

BERLIN, Jan. 11.—According to private advices received by the Taglische Rundschau from missionary sources, an uprising of natives has occurred in the Congo Free State.

The trouble originated in the upper reaches of the Congo River, where, it is reported, all the whites have been murdered.

Catholic missionaries and missions are said to have suffered severely.

A dispatch to the same paper from Brussels says that the news of the uprising is not confirmed officially, but unofficial reports affirm in the most positive manner that a revolt has broken out in the Mongalla district.

The Alabua native troops are reported to have mutinied and killed their officers, the American Mission has been stormed, and the posts of the Kasai Company have been destroyed.

January 12, 1905

KING LEOPOLD DENIES CHARGES AGAINST HIM

Is Poorer Instead of Richer Because of the Congo, He Says.

NOT A MONSTER, EITHER

May Have Been Misjudgment and Even Crime in the African Region, but No Countenanced Atrocities.

BRUSSELS, Belgium, Dec. 10.—In an interview given personally to-day to the correspondent of the Publishers' Press, King Leopold of Belgium denied categorically the reports which have been circulated so widely of atrocities practiced in the Congo.

His common sense would have kept him from indulging in cruelties such as those he is accused of practicing, the King declared, even if he was not moved by humanity to do so.

The old King also paid a high tribute to America and Americans, especially to President Roosevelt, whom he described as a "splendid type of the splendid American Nation."

The correspondent was received by King Leopold in his working room in the royal palace at Laaken, outside of Brussels, where the monarch resides. His Majesty was alone in the room, busy at his desk, when the correspondent was announced. He at once arose and shook hands with the visitor, saying:

"I am very glad to see a representative of the American press. I have great admiration for most of the newspapers of America. I know most of them try to be honest and straightforward and usually judge an international question on its merits.

"Your Minister asked me to receive you and I am happy to have the opportunity of meeting you as a citizen of one free country talking to a citizen of another."

Would Like to Visit America.

Asking the correspondent to be seated, the King continued:

"The whole of America is full of wonder to me. I have often wished to visit the United States to see all for myself, but I fear that dream will not be realized. I am an old man now, and no longer have my former strength. There are many great men in America to-day. In the two houses of Congress are many brilliant minds. Occasionally it has been my good fortune to meet American legislators in Belgium, and I highly prize the remembrance of these gentlemen. Any country might be proud of such men.

"President Roosevelt I esteem highly for his great qualities. He is a splendid type of the splendid American Nation."

The conversation turned on the subject of the charges of cruelty and misgovernment in the Congo, and Leopold said:

"It is curious what satisfaction certain people get spending their lives libeling others. I suppose there is nobody in Europe painted as a monster of such blackness as I am. The words used in picturing my perfidy cannot be repeated in polite society. Nero, it is said, was a saint compared to me. I am an ogre, who delights to torture helpless African negroes."

The King mockingly congratulated the correspondent because he had visited him without trembling, and said.

"Let me see if you have a revolver in your pocket to protect yourself. Have you armor under your coat? No. I am surprised. Why do you risk your life in this foolish manner?"

"Then it is not true that atrocious conditions exist in the Congo region?" was asked.

"Of course not. People should credit us with common sense, even if they will not allow that humanity exists outside their own country. It would be absurd for us to mistreat the blacks because no State prospers unless the population is happy and increasing. America knows, perhaps, better than any other country, how true this is.

New Trade of Calumination.

"Many of the people maligning us are doing so from interested motives. It seems a new trade has arisen in the world, that of calumniation. There are those who make their living by forming associations to protest against everything under heaven.

"Recently a certain American missionary made sensational Congo charges and bitterly attacked me. Some one wrote him, protesting against the vehemence of his language and received a letter from him saying he had never been to the Congo. All his charges were based on hearsay. In this manner many reports as to the Congo circulated, while those who speak from first-hand evidence magnify particular incidents into generalities. Charges about Congo cruelty have been so often repeated that I believe their constant reiteration leads those spreading the false reports finally to believe they are true.

"I do not deny that there have been cases of misjudgment on the part of Congo officials. Most likely cruelties, even crimes have been committed. There have been a number of convictions before Congo tribunals for these offenses. I do deny that every effort, as far as possible, has not been made to stop the ill-treatment of natives, not only by white people, but by natives themselves.

"No Government in the world has remedied all the grievances within its own jurisdiction. It is a curious fact that when one country seeks to produce a local millennium it always seizes on territory belonging to some one else for the experiment. The Scripture parable about the beam and the mote is of as much significance to-day as nineteen centuries ago. It would be more philanthropic to strengthen our hands, more for the benefit of civilization, for all white persons to stand united than for some to abuse us, which certainly does not augment the respect it is good for the African natives to have for the white race. It would be of more interest to civilization to show the natives that Christians have good feelings for their neighbors.

"Our God says we must all have Christian fellowship one for another. Certainly this example is not being shown the blacks by those white men who attack the Congo so maliciously."

What Has Been Done in Congo.

Leopold dwelt at some length on what has been accomplished in the Congo, saying:

"We have been fortunate in reducing smallpox in Central Africa by the introduction of vaccine. We have stopped the Congo slave trade and prohibited alcohol from entering the country, but steamers on the rivers have built and are building railways and introduced the telegraph. Now we are sending out motor cars.

"All this is only the beginning of our work. By the concessions we have given, especially concessions to Americans, we have reduced almost to nothing the territory of barbarism. Now we must fight the dreadful disease known as sleeping sickness, which has depopulated not only the Congo but also Uganda. We hope with the help of Almighty God to succeed in stamping out this scourge in Africa. In dealing with a race composed of cannibals for thousands of years, it is necessary to use methods which will best shake their idleness and make them realize the sanctity of work."

"It is asserted you are financially interested in the Congo and make a huge fortune there yearly. Is this so?"

Leopold replied:

"It is absolutely false. I am the ruler of the Congo, but the prosperity of the country no more affects me financially than the prosperity of America increases the means of President Roosevelt. I have not one cent invested in Congo industries, and I have not received any salary as

Congo Executive in the past twenty-two years.

"In no shape or form have I bettered myself financially through my relationship with the Congo. On the contrary, I have spent large sums of my own in developing the country, sums amounting in the aggregate to millions. I am poorer and not richer because of the Congo. The betterment of the country and the improvement of the conditions of the natives are the only objects of my efforts.

"I know there are persons so constituted that they are unable to appreciate such a statement. They believe readily enough, however, false charges that I am rolling in wealth at the expense of dying natives. They see me as a boa constrictor, squeezing the life out of the blacks in order to put gold into my purse.

Wants No More Money.

"Why should I do such a thing? Of what use is money to me? I am not in the prime of life. I have passed threescore years and ten on my earthly journey. I cannot take money out of this world, why should I pile up gold for the sake of wealth? I have sufficient for my wants and do not wish for more. I am not a business man. I am a ruler, anxious only for the welfare of my subjects. It is more to me than money to a miser for me to know my work in the Congo has not been vainly spent. From a wild African forest, inhabited by cannibals, the Congo is developed wonderfully, its revenues increasing from nothing to $10,000,000 annually.

"But what has been accomplished is nothing to what will be. There is fabulous wealth in the country. I am making every effort to see that it is properly developed. I cannot conceive anything that will give a greater return than planting rubber trees there. Rubber sells for $2,000 a ton, and the Congo is the natural rubber region of the world. To care for the future supply of rubber is one of the objects of the new so-called American Company, formed to invest money in Congo realty.

"This is not purely an American corporation; half of the shares are held by Belgian financiers. The new company has two objects—first, to prospect for and work mines, and, second, to plant rubber forests on modern principles. I have no pecuniary interest in the company, but the Congo has, for, as in the case of all concessions given in the Congo, shares have been allotted free to the Government. The interest on these shares meets the expense of the Congo Government, and the dividends it now receives are sufficient to pay the whole interest on the Congo national debt. To see this development of the Congo is my reward."

Leopold rose, extended his hand, and asked the correspondent to extend his compliments to the American Minister, thus indicating that the audience was at an end.

December 11, 1906

SAYS LETTERS WERE STOLEN.

Col. Kowalsky Talks of His Mission from King Leopold.

In answer to the charge of a morning paper of yesterday that he was a paid lobbyist in the service of King Leopold and to the statement of the newspaper that it would publish his letters to the King, Col. Henry I. Kowalsky of 40 Wall Street charged that portions of his correspondence had been stolen.

It was quite true, he said, that he had been commissioned by Leopold to prepare a brief on conditions in the Congo Free State, to be submitted to President Roosevelt, together with a letter from the Federation for Defending Belgian Interests Abroad. The whole affair had been perfectly open. He had seen the President in October, 1904, when he had submitted the brief and his authority for doing so. At that time he had talked freely with newspaper correspondents, making no secret of his mission.

"If the newspaper in question," said Col. Kowalsky yesterday, "prints tomorrow my letters to King Leopold I have no hesitancy in saying that they have been stolen from this office. The letters I wrote were informal in tone. I find upon examining the files that many of them are missing. I filed this correspondence in cabinet files here. Whoever gained possession of them may have entered through the janitor after hours or may have bribed the stenographer. I have found no evidence of a breaking in."

"Did you employ a lobby or a press bureau in connection with your work for Leopold, as charged?" was asked.

"I did not. There was no lobbying in the matter at all. My service consisted in the submission of my brief. The whole agitation against Leopold in the Congo Free State was started by the British, who want the land. They are adopting their familiar expedients. First they get in their missionaries to set up a howl, their troops follow, and then of course their occupation follows. In this case they got the missionaries in, and the howl promptly followed. A memorial was presented to the President by the Congo Reform Association, supported by the British and Foreign Anti-Slavery Society and the Aborigines' Protection Society. I then presented my brief as an answer to that memorial.

"My printed brief carried at its end an appendix in which was, first of all, a letter under date of Oct. 4, 1904, from Leopold to me, in which he informed me that 'I have instructed you to defend in the United States the case of the Congo Free State, which is now being attacked by a group of English merchants and missionaries at present represented in Washington by Mr. Morel.' This letter further stated that 'under the stress of the indignation aroused in Belgium by the English calumnies' an association had been formed consisting of prominent men in the army and in commercial and industrial life. This association wished to point out to the President the untruths contained in the memorial submitted to him by Mr. Morel. I received the appointment of counsel to the Congo Free State. At the request of this association I was to present a letter written in the name of the association, as well as my brief."

Col. Kowalsky denied that he was counsel to Mayor Schmitz of San Francisco, now under graft charges. He also said that the alleged agreement printed by the newspaper as being between him and Leopold was not what it purported to be.

"I don't know what that section of the newspaper story is," he said. "Some of it appears to be a sort of circular. That the rest of it is an agreement between me and Leopold I deny. Those were not the terms."

"Do you know anything about the newspaper's intimation that Secretary Root was indirectly influenced through a concession in the Congo of 2,500,000 acres given to Thomas F. Ryan?" was asked.

"I know nothing about any such concession," was the reply. "No money or favor was given to any one in connection with the matter."

December 11, 1906

MOROCCAN TREATY TERMS DISCLOSED

France Cedes 96,525 Miles to Germany, Who Recognizes Protectorate.

GERMAN DISSATISFACTION

Compensation Inadequate, Says Colonial Secretary, Whose Resignation Follows the Councilor's.

PARIS, Nov. 3.—The contents of the Franco-German accord, officially made public to-day, show that Germany recognizes the right of France to establish a protectorate in Morocco, while both nations engage to obtain the adhesion to this accord of the other signatories to the Algeciras agreement.

France, as compensation for German recognition of her protectorate in Morocco, cedes to Germany about 250,000 square kilometers, or about 96,525 square miles, in Northern French Congo, touching the German Kameruns. The territory ceded is inhabited by about 1,000,000 negroes, and has a commerce valued at $2,400,000 annually. The new German frontier starts at Monda Bay and extends to the Sanga River, thence to Kandeko, thence through the Congo, finally attaining Lake Tchad by way of the Ubanga and Logone Rivers.

France retains the right to run railroad lines across German territory, so as to connect the different parts of French Central Africa. The accord does not affect Togoland, but Germany cedes her "duck's bill," extending from the Charl River to the Logone River. France and Germany agree to submit to The Hague Tribunal all difficulties arising from the operation of the accord.

In reference to Morocco, France agrees to safeguard the economic equality and commercial liberty for which provision is made in existing treaties. The only reference to commercial rights in the ceded territory is the mutual agreement to take over the rights and obligations in connection with the companies holding concessions there.

The whole French press is pleased over the conclusion of the Franco-German accord as terminating a four months' political crisis which looked at times as though it might result in war, and while deploring the loss of so much of the French Congo, hails with satisfaction the creation of a great French empire in the north of Africa, consisting of Tunis, Algeria, and Morocco.

The Temps says: "The historic work commenced by Charles X. is thus crowned by the Third Republic."

November 4, 1911

A SOUTH AFRICAN QUESTION

BOERS AND BRITONS.

THE TWO DUTCH REPUBLICS OF ORANGE AND TRANSVAAL IN CONTROVERSY WITH THE ENGLISH COLONY OF SOUTH AFRICA

Republics are at a discount just now in the Old World. One of them stepped down and out last week from the banks of the Manzanares. and voices are heard prophesying a like fate for the French and Dutch Commonwealths. That of Switzerland looks steady in virtue of its rugged barrenness, and the out of the way ground it stands on. It is not worth anybody's while to overthrow it—as yet.

Those who remember how Napoleon I. obliterated the famous old Dutch Republic of The Hague, which the Vienna Congressmen refused to restore, may for a moment fancy the use of that style is a mistake. But there are really two Dutch Republics in existence—two little curiosities of modern civilization, flourishing in a solitary way among the group of colonies composing the southern apex of the African peninsula, and a few words about themselves and their antecedents may give some idea of the controversy, rather muffled by distance, which now occupies men's minds in that part of the world. Africa itself has been coming a good deal into the light latterly, reminding us of its earlier periods when the Roman *Africa semper aliquid novi offert* was a proverb in good standing. In those days that huge, sequestered peninsula was always offering something new, in the report or presence of its monsters of all sorts, sphinxes, pigmies, moon-mountains, pyramids, lions, crocodiles, and other things terrible or extraordinary; and still, in our own, it furnishes us with new sensations and matters of moment. like the Suez Canal, the wild war of Kassai Jugurtha Theodore, the Madagascar Queen and her five millions of subjects coming over in a body to Christianity, and the great story of David Livingstone, to say nothing of Du Chaillu's gorillas, or the Gondokoro achievements of Baker and Long.

In the pre-Christian times, the further cape of Africa seems to have been doubled by some Red Sea mariners of an Egyptian king or *necho*. But, about four hundred years ago, the Portuguese were certainly the first to pass round it on their way to the Ganges and the Golden Chersonese, led by Diaz and Da Gama, in 1487. They (or tradition before them) named that promontory the Cabo Tormentoso, which meant "Cape of Storms" or "Cape of the Lower-end." The old word *Torment* had the meaning of Hades, (an inferior region and "place of torment,") and it was a term of such ghostly and uncomfortable import to the ears and fancies of all ancient mariners that they were glad to exchange it for the good *Esperansa*. The Portuguese made no colony at the Cape, and at the end of a hundred years the Dutch, in 1598, occupied it as a convenient halfway-house to the Indies, and planted a little colony. At the same time the English took the benefit of Table Bay, north-west from the Cape, and tried to colonize Robben Island, on the eastern side, with some of their convicts. But the men would not stay there, preferring the Hottentot *kraals*. Meantime an English and Dutch Post Office was established at the Cape. It had neither clerks nor a Postmaster, being, in fact, a certain bowider under which all passing ships posted their news for the benefit of the next comers to the place.

The Hollanders held the Cape for 143 years, till 1796, when it was seized by the English, to save it from the French masters of Holland. In 1802 the Dutch got it back for a time, as they once got back New-Amsterdam; but in 1806 it finally became a British colony, with a strong Dutch flavor, which, in spite of the lapse of years, "will hang round it still" in a very perceptible degree. In colonizing the Cape, men turned their faces rather to the eastern side, where the long ridges of the Drakenberg Mountains run up to the north-east, beside the coast level, something after the manner of the South American Cordilleras, lying over against them across the Pacific, and produce those conditions of land and water most favorable for settlement. In 1820 the colony covered an area of 128,000 square miles, (nearly three time as large as New-York State,) with a population of 110,000 persons, half of whom were whites. In moving eastward, the colonists, both English and Dutch Boers, came always into rough contact with the native tribes, the most formidable of which have always been the Kaffirs, a stalwart and powerful race of many tribes haunting the hills and gorges of that region, and only giving way before the superior force of musketry. These pagans, with a religion as simple and scanty as their style of dress, hung on the edges of "civilization," stealing cattle, killing the intruders on all convenient opportunities, and also, as in 1835 and 1839, waging united and savage war against the colony. The names of their chiefs, Hintza, Tola, Kreli, Saudilli, Macomo, &c., received much distinguished notice in the English newspapers, and Lord Glenelg and other men in office were of opinion that these Kaffirs were very badly treated. But the fate of the natives was inevitable, and like our own red men, they were forced to give way before the advance of "the fittest," who drove their cattle and plows still eastward and northward, to the Kishamma, (the Great Fish,) and the Kei Rivers, and so took gradual possession of the great mountain tract subsequently styled British Kaffraria. Other colonists, chiefly Boers, went by water still farther north, to the port of Natal, on the Pacific side, and there, about 1840, founded the Natal colony, over a thousand miles from the Cape. This colony has at present an area of about 17,000 square miles, with a population of 18,000 persons.

In those movements the Dutch had a natural desire to go together, and they were always foremost of those who went as far as possible from the Cape and its English Governorship, which they never liked. In 1840 Governor Napier stopped their onslaughts on the Zulus. They were going too fast for the main body. But they kept doggedly to their purpose of wandering off, and in a short time spread themselves as much as possible over a tract of ground lying beyond the lines of the colony. This is the elevated country now known as the Orange Republic. It is bounded on the north and west by the river Vaal, on the east by the long Drakenberg range of mountains, and is watered by the Orange River, and other streams that rise in the aforesaid range. The Orange River, falling westward into the Atlantic, once bore the native name of *Gariep*, and this was also the name of the Vaal, which has its source in the Drakenbergs still further north, and takes the name of the Orange at the boundary of the two Dutch Republics, where both streams combine. Thus the long superior Gariep has two nomenclatures, needlessly enough. On this ground, about twenty-five years ago, the Dutch farmers, led by a Boer, very happily named Pretorius, made an independent government, a thousand miles from Cape Town. But they were challenged and worried by the Governor, for several good reasons, and then beaten at the battle of Boomplatz. This instead of conciliating only disgusted Pretorius and the bolder spirits, and inspanning their oxen they determined to go still farther off. They crossed their boundary, the Vaal, and went northward, leaving the rest of their Orange brethren to argue the matter with the Englishmen.

The latter were not without arguments and grumblings among themselves in their two provinces of the East and West. The Easterns, among the high grounds of the Drakenbergs, were always agitating for home rule, seeing that their little capital of Grahamstown was six or seven hundred miles away from Cape Town. These difficulties were greatly aggravated by the Kaffirs, who in 1851 broke out with another fierce war, the fifth in the space of thirty-five years. It was a general insurrection of Sandilli, Kreli, and the other chiefs—something in the style of the Indian mutiny of 1857, but on a smaller scale—and the Hottentots themselves, so long the trusted servants of the colony, "went out" under their chief, Uthalder. The country was wasted over an area of thirty thousand square miles, and the war of two years cost the British two millions of money. But the Kaffirs suffered most. A famine in their mountains followed the defeat, and completely broke their spirit for a time. In 1865 their country, with its six hundred miles of coast on the Indian Ocean, was incorporated with the Cape Colony and called British Kaffraria.

Meantime, the two elder provinces, the Western and the Eastern, had been united in 1854 under a Constitution and a Parliament of two chambers—the Legislative Council and the Assembly—the former numbering about fifteen, appointed under control of the Executive, and the forty-eight members of the House chosen by the suffrage of every man, white or black, possessed of £25—a system sufficiently liberal for that motley community.

The Boers in the north were making progress in their own way. The Transvaal Republic was the first organized, (1850,) on a broad area within the great eastern ridge there called the Quathlamba, having the Vaal on the south, and on the north the twenty-second line of latitude and the tropical ground of the River Limpopo. It covered at first a space of 78,000 square miles, and was subsequently enlarged, so that now its area is set down as 117,000 square miles, gathered in from the Zulus and other wild tribes of that region. This territory has a rich, well-watered soil, with a powerful vegetation of all sorts, and a magnificent forestry, in the midst of which is a population of 150,000 persons, 20,000 of whom are Dutch, who, as well as the natives, subsist mainly by cattle culture and hunting. Their Government is a pure Democracy—the rascalliest thing in the world, according to Edmund Burke—and every citizen of the Republic has a right to receive three thousand acres of the Transvaal domain, and then hold them against the incursions of the original owners, if he can. At the same time those Boers are more afraid of the civilized Englishmen than of the wild Zulus.

The Orange Republic. below, the Vaal, was recognized by the English Government in 1854, and has its *Volkrad*, or Parliament, its *landrosts*, (Governors of districts,) and *heemraden*, like its neighbor on the north. Its area is about forty-two thousand square miles, (a little less than that of New-York State,) with near fifty thousand inhabitants, of whom fifteen thousand are whites. But these republicans find themselves very much "in the force and road of casualty." "Civilization" is all about them, keeping them on the sharp and ragged edge of political uncertainty. The fate they have visited on the Kaffirs and other native tribes threatens themselves, and their strokes of good fortune are anything but blessings in the end. In 1869 some of their Orange people were so unlucky as to find diamonds in the district where the Vaal mingles with the Orange River, and in 1870 a Koranna man found the "Star of Africa," a gem at present in the coronet of the Princess of Wales. Then rose the great outcry of the "Diamond Fields," and people crowded in from all points of the compass. The *copays*, or mounds, along those rivers had their swarms of earth-grubbers, and Clip Drift, Priel, Gong Gong, Sevenelli, Du Joit's Pan, and other names of that sort became familar in men's mouths as household words. In 1871 there was over five thousand men picking up a few diamonds here and there, among the *copays* and *karroos* (barrens) of that sunburnt wilderness, and the diggers, chiefly English, found it necessary to make laws for the rough society which then took shape sufficiently to make the Orange Republicans uneasy. Officers were sent to the diamond grounds to demand license-money and acknowledgment, and these the miners refused, not finding any mention of them in their own improvised code. Altercation followed, in the midst of which Waterboer, a native chief, stood up to claim the ground in dispute. A Dutch force advanced to interview the Waterboers; but before a blow was struck, the republicans found, to their dismay, that the tribe was under British protection. Sir Henry Barkley, the Cape Governor, then came up, showed the dull Boers how it was, and soon after took possession of the diamond ground, naming it Griqualand West. President Brand protested, and the Orange Republic is still protesting. for this and several other reasons. The Transvaalers, on their side, find, also, that they are not yet beyond the reach of the Britons. They had a fierce dispute with the Basutos on the subject of a common boundary, and were proceeding to settle the matter in the usual Boerish way, when it came out somehow that the Basuto Chief, Moshesh, was under British protection. The result was, as in the other case, that Basutoland was soon a part of the British territory.

Simultaneously with the diamond outcry came (1870) a gold outcry, from a locality in the Natal colony, which had its own swarm of "prospectors" in a very short time, exploring the hills and river sides as far as the Jatin, a large stream near the northern boundary of Natal. Lindley, an Englishman, went there with his party in 1871, but made nothing of it, except a book, from which we learn something of the snakes, leopards, rhinoceroses, and other dangerous creatures of the region, but nothing about gold. The delusion of gold in this case was kept up in England and elsewhere by the fact that the Ophir of the ancients was believed to be in that land of the Kaffirs, around the Pacific seaport of Sofala; the sound of the word probably misleading the old writers, as in a great many other instances. But all those ravenous incursions have tended to benefit the English colony, by introducing a crowd of settlers, and thus affording an opportunity of intermeddling with the slow and exclusive Boers, who have now seen their boundaries of Transvaal pushed in by the British-Basutos, and about 15,000 Europeans, under British protection, occupying a place on the ground claimed by the Orange Republic.

The foregoing may give an idea of the condition of things in that region of South Africa. It shows the tendency of the English to take Africa as they have taken India. They are moving up from the Agulha, or Point of the Cape, in 35° south latitude, toward the Limpopo, (near 20°,) and those other great waters recently brought to light by Livingstone and the rest; while the march of invasion from the upper end of the great peninsula, as it may still be called, is led by Baker, Gordon, and Long. The settlement of Natal, still an independent colony, will soon find itself an incorporated province, like Kaffraria and the others. A federation of Natal and the two Republics with the Cape Colony has been much discussed latterly, and this seems significant of the end. Those Dutch Republics went off as far as possible, meaning to be isolated among the mountains; but they see themselves overtaken and surrounded by those who will soon be masters of all Southern Africa, and afterward push their colonists still further into the heart of the peninsula, and they must be aware that the federation and then the incorporation are merely questions of time. They have at present many reasons of complaint against the encroachments of the English, and their Presidents, Burgess and Brand, have had a world of discussion with the Cape authorities. Mr. Froude, the historian, has been for some months past in South Africa, commissioned by the Secretary of State, Lord Carnarvon, to learn as much as possible on the subject at the Cape, and also visit Natal and the Republican Presidents, the better to comprehend the entire controvery. If those Dutch Presidents have read any of Mr. Froude's histories they will probably be afraid of him as an envoy. He is not the man to sympathize with the bucolic and easy-going people who want to mind their own quiet business and be let alone. He is for the prompt and peremptory hand of a strong government such as Oliver Cromwell once exercised in Ireland, but did not exercise long enough for the good of that unhappy country, and he will be for bringing out the Boers from their *plaats* into the great highways of English progress, and merging their interests in a federal way wit.. 'hose of the colony.

That colony certainly bids fair to be a prosperous concern in the course of time. From its area of 222,000 square miles, and its population of 680,000, of whom 190,000 are whites, it exports, chiefly to England, wool, hides, coffee, copper, cotton, sugar, wine, rice, ivory, ostrich feathers, and a variety of other products 'o the value of two million of pounds sterling yearly, while its inhabitants import from the United Kingdom, to the value of three millions, in those articles held necessary to the comfort of a colony that imitates in most things the social life of the mother country. It has its army, of about 6,000 men, its Parliament, its two Bishoprics, its two or three colleges, its telegraph line of six hundred miles between Cape Town and Graham's Town, and its one railway running sixty miles from the capital, north and by east, in the direction of the Gariep and the Limpopo, and the great lacustrine region of mountain plateaus uncurtained by Livingstone and the other explorers of the tropics. The soil of the country is fertile in most places, especially on the eastern side, where the Drakenbergs, those mighty cloud-compellers, bring down the rivers that rush along the gorges and irrigate the level pasturages and fields of agriculture. In many of the level districts, chiefly at the Atlantic side, the want of water is much felt, and few showers fall in the course of the year. But a remedy for this will yet be found in a system of artesian wells, such as the French have sunk with such success in the dry soil of Algiers. The climate of South Africa is, on the whole, very salubrious and friendly to European constitutions. The region is interesting in itself, and still more in its natural contact with tropical Africa, a region that, with its vast lake system and lofty mountain plateaus, so favorable to every form of life, animal and vegetable, seems destined at no distant date to swarm with colonists from the more crowded societies of the Old World.

January 17, 1875

THE TRANSVAAL REPUBLIC.

ABSORPTION OF THE TERRITORY OF THE DUTCH BOERS BY GREAT BRITAIN—PROTEST OF PRESIDENT BURGERS.

LONDON, May 7.—A dispatch to Reuter's Telegram Company from Capetown April 17, via Madeira, announces that the Transvaal Republic has been annexed to the British Empire, and the British flag hoisted at Pretoria. Mr. Shepstone informed President Burgers that he could wait no longer, and proclaimed Transvaal British territory on April 12. President Burgers has issued a protest against the annexation, but has at the same time counseled peaceable submission. Messrs. Jorrison and Paul Kruger, two leading inhabitants, will proceed to Europe and the United States to protest against the annexation to powers who have recognized the Republic. A body of British troops have entered Transvaal. Some rioting is thought likely, but armed resistance is improbable. Mr. Shepstone has abolished the war tax. The Cape Colony Ministry agreed, in accordance with Lord Carnarvon's wishes, to incorporate Griqualand-West with Cape Colony.

May 7, 1877

THE ZULU WAR.

Whether or not Providence is on the side of the heaviest battalions, there can be little doubt of the result of a contest between a civilized nation, with great military and naval power and inexhaustible resources, and a primitive and barbarous tribe, however brave and unyielding. When the British High Commissioner in South Africa undertook to bring the Zulu King into subjection to his demands, and was supported therein by the Government of the Empire, there could be no question of his ultimate success, however unjustifiable his course may have been, and whatever incompetency and disastrous blundering might be developed in the course of the undertaking. Sooner or later, the powerful nation was destined to bring the savage tribe into abject submission or demolish it utterly. The justice of the cause had nothing to do with this foregone conclusion. After more than half a year of war, the most discreditable in which England has been engaged within the memory of the living generation, there are indications that CETYWAYO is ready to acknowledge himself beaten, and will soon accept any terms that may be imposed. What to do with the vanquished Zulus, and their territory will be a question with which the British Government will soon have to deal. It is not likely that in this, any more than in the origin of the war, will the requirements of justice be heeded.

Never was there a struggle from which a civilized nation could derive less honor, or which it could remember with less pride. That the Zulus were a warlike and somewhat troublesome people upon the borders of the South African colonies is not disputed, but nations that plant colonies in uncivilized regions, against the will of the original occupants, can hardly expect to find them altogether meek and submissive to whatever restraints may be put in their way. CETYWAYO had his quarrels with rival tribes, and there was a dispute as to the boundary between his dominion and the Transvaal colony. He kept an army on foot, and was somewhat too eager to give it steady employment, which of itself disturbed the minds of timid settlers. His modes of internal administration were by no means in accordance with the time-honored principles of the English Constitution, but it is just possible that his people were not ready for their application. The Zulus were feared and hated by the colonists of Natal and the Transvaal, who were anxious for a war that should either drive them off or subjugate them to the British power, and doubtless not the less so as the war would be conducted by the home Government at its own proper cost, while the colonists would profit by dealings with the Army. But what was to be the pretext for such a war? The boundary dispute was in a fair way to a settlement, and CETYWAYO showed no disposition to make aggressions upon British territory or British rights. A year ago this time a little incident happened. Two native women, fleeing from the consequences of their own crimes, took refuge in a British kraal across the border. The pursuers, a powerful chief and some of his relatives, followed and seized them and dragged them away to punishment. Of this violation of British territory much was made. No apology or promise of indemnity would be accepted, but the occasion was taken, after much negotiation and delay, to offer an ultimatum which no ruler with a sense of pride and importance, however savage, could be expected to accept. The King was required to disband his Army, to change his laws restricting marriage, to restore missionaries who had been expelled for fomenting trouble, and to accept a British Resident in his dominion under conditions that would utterly destroy his independence.

It was the 11th of January last that the time for accepting the ultimatum expired, and no submission came from the savage King. Sir BARTLE FRERE, the High Commissioner, was responsible for the war that followed. It is doubtful if his course would have been sustained had there been closer communication between Natal and London, but events had gone so far before there was a chance for interposition, that it was considered out of the question. Then, the Government must perforce support its agents in South Africa, and carry on the war to the end. The military commander was a holiday soldier, owing his place to aristocratic influence and political favor, and discreditable blunders and humiliating disasters were the result. But in spite of Isandula and Rorke's Drift, and less important fiascos, Sir GARNET WOLSELEY will doubtless gain the prestige of a speedy and victorious conclusion of the war after his assumption of the supreme civil and military command. The Zulus will be beaten and there will be peace without much honor, but what will be the after-result? The history of the Cape colonies is a record of one difficulty after another with the natives and the old Dutch settlers, ending with the extension of the British authority over the domain of the weaker party. The Orange Free State and the Transvaal became a refuge only to fall into the hands of the aggressor at last, and there is but one final solution of the difficulty with the Zulus, according to British precedent. The King must submit his domain to the rule of the conqueror in one form or another, with a certainty of its ultimate annexation to the colonies.

But how long will this process continue with the consent of the English people? There may be advantage in it for the colonists, but the colonists do not do it or pay for it. They have, practically, self-government. They conduct their internal affairs to suit themselves, and even get into trouble with uncivilized neighbors at their pleasure, and then the home Government has to take up their quarrel and make their defense. The Army of the British Empire fights their battles, and the English people pay for it. How far this is worth while for the English people, or how far they may be willing to consent to it, may become a serious question. Since the road to India has been deflected to the north of the African Continent, the Cape colonies have become of comparatively little consequence to England, and it would not be surprising if a policy were to be adopted ere long making self-defense a concomitant of self-government, and leaving them virtually to take care of themselves at their own expense. Otherwise, it is difficult to see where the process of encroachment upon the native tribes is to stop.

July 25, 1879

The British seem destined to ceaseless trouble with the native tribes of Cape Colony, or, to give its official title, the Colony of the Cape of Good Hope, as the almost daily dispatches from Cape Town testify. Just now they are at war with the Basutos, as they have been, from time to time, with the Kafirs and other aboriginals of the country, and they appear likely to be at war indefinitely. The colony forms the southernmost part of the continent of Africa, and has an area proper of nearly 182,000 square miles, divided into an eastern and a western division. There are, besides, large and irregular outlying districts, such as Basutoland, British Kaffraria, Fingoland, Griqualand, and Transvaal, the last, once a Republic, having been annexed three years ago, as other adjacent lands have been since. The Cape region, settled by the Dutch in 1652, passed in 1806 into possession of the British. The former had only intended at first to use the Cape as an intermediate station between Holland and their East Indian colonies, occupying but a small tract of ground on the slopes of Table Mountain, with a portion of the adjoining flats. Finding, however, that they had in their immediate neighborhood scattered tribes of careless, feeble natives, they naturally increased their territory as soon as immigration had largely set in from the mother country. In entering upon the Government of the colony, the British saw themselves confronted with a totally different race from that of the purposeless Hottentot—the Kafirs, mainly of Arab descent, tall, athletic, finely formed, of warlike disposition, with an irresistible passion for stealing from everybody outside of their own tribe. After a succession of wars, which were unavoidable, the Kafirs were driven back, and the British have advanced to the north-east corner of the colony, as far as the mouth of the River Kei. The country is occupied at present by a variety of people. The Portuguese were the first Europeans to land there; then came the Dutch, who are, in all probability, still the most numerous, and then the English, inhabiting the eastern parts almost exclusively. The French are also largely represented, many refugees having gone thither after the revocation of the Edict of Nantes. A number of Germans have settled on the frontiers, near the Kafirs, for purposes of defense. The natives—Hottentots, Bushmen, Kafirs, negroes, and Bechuanas—yet form a majority. A great many Kafirs have been retained in the districts they originally inhabited, and others have repaired thither as servants and shepherds, wool being the principal product of the colony. A large number of the people are of Malay origin, and live in and around Cape Town, the capital, and in towns on the East Coast, and are employed as fishermen, porters, and heavy laborers. The name Africander properly belongs to a few Mozambiquers and Hottentots, as well as to a number of half-castes. The present population of the colony, estimated at about 900,000, is as motley as any that can be conveniently found.

November 10, 1880

THE PARTITION OF AFRICA

LONDON, Dec. 20.—The charter of the South African Company is gazetted to-day. The charter describes the regions of the company's operations as immediately north of Bechuanaland and west of the Portuguese possessions, and north and west of the dominions possessed by the Transvaal Company. This includes, therefore, the vast tract of Central Africa north of the Zambesi River and west of the coast line in Mozambique, to which it is now the policy of England to limit the Portuguese. The company is bound by the conditions of the charter to oppose and discourage the slave trade and the trade in ardent spirits.

December 21, 1889

BOERS READY TO FIGHT

ANOTHER WAR EXPECTED IN SOUTH AFRICA.

THE INVASION OF BRITISH TERRITORY OPENLY THREATENED—PLANS FOR ESTABLISHING THE "REPUBLIC OF THE NORTH."

LONDON, May 7.—Replying to a question in the House of Commons to-day in regard to the reported Boer "trek" being prepared for the invasion of Mashonaland, Manicaland, and other South African territory, for the purpose of establishing the so-called "Republic of the North," the Hon. Edward Stanhope, Secretary of State for War, intimated that troops were being sent to British Bechuanaland in order to oppose the proposed Boer "trek."

Some weeks ago it was announced that a force of 5,000 Boers contemplated "treking" into or invading a portion of the territory now in dispute between Great Britain and Portugal, and which has already resulted in strained relations between those two countries, the seizure of the British South Africa Company's steamer Countess of Carnarvon, the stoppage of the Willoughby British expedition on its way up the Pungwe River, and the subsequent dispatch of three British war vessels to that river with instructions to the senior officer in command of the British ships to act as he judged best in defense of British interests, without waiting to consult with the home Government.

This announced movement of the Boers and intimated counter-movement of British troops in Bechuanaland seem to be the prelude to another "little war" in South Africa. The Boers have never forgotten their successes over the British troops in the Transvaal, where their superior marksmanship enabled them to inflict severe loss upon the less skillful British troops sent against them. When it first became known that the "trek" was projected, 5,000 Boers were calculated to be on the point of forming the army of invasion. There was no attempt to conceal the projected raid, and the apparent indifference of the British Government to the movement caused great indignation at Cape Town and elsewhere, so much so that meetings of South African subjects of Great Britain were called and it was openly said that if no help against the Boers was to be expected from Great Britain, it was time for the Cape colonies to declare themselves independent.

This seems to have somewhat stirred up Lord Salisbury's Government, for the British High Commissioner and Commander in Chief at Cape Town, Sir Henry Brougham Loch, was instructed, some ten days ago, to inform President Kruger of the Transvaal Republic that any movement of the Boers into the disputed territory would be considered as an act of hostility to the Queen of England. To this President Kruger replied briefly that he had "damped the trek," and it was supposed that the affair was ended. A day or two later, however, it became known in Cape Town and elsewhere that the force of Boers which proposed to establish the Republic of the North was composed of 20,000, instead of 5,000, as at first supposed, and it was added that, in spite of President Kruger's anxiety to live up to the obligations entered into between the Transvaal and Great Britain, it would possibly be beyond his power to prevent 20,000 well-armed Boers from carrying out any "treking" plan which they might have formed. The trekers are understood to be upon the point of massing together from the Transvaal, the Free State, and from the Cape Governments.

According to the plan announced, these warlike farmers will assemble on the southern bank of the Limpopo River between the 15th and 31st of this month, and will cross the Limpopo on June 1 and immediately proclaim the Republic of the North. The leaders of the "trek" include men of position from both the Free State and

Cape Colony, and all steps taken are said to have met with the approval of the famous Afrikaner Bund, which was recently in session at Kimberley, the well-known mining town in West Griqualand, South Africa. It will thus be seen that the Boer movement to the north is a South African movement in the direction of northward expansion and is of a serious nature, and it is bound to conflict with the claims of the British chartered company, to say nothing of the claims of the Portuguese South African Company. In fact, one of the objects of the raid is said to be the extinction of the claims of the chartered company and the replacement of the company by a popular South African movement free from all control of the Imperial Government.

The idea prevailed in England that as the Afrikaner Bund supported the Premier of Cape Town, the Hon. Cecil Rhodes, it would also support him in the policy of the chartered company. This, it is said, is not the case. Recent events are said to have convinced the Afrikaner Bund that Mr. Rhodes is not entitled to the Bund's support. He is charged with having dallied entirely too much with the imperial schemes and imperial ideas, and the restablishment of any form of imperial control in South Africa is a proposition which the Bund would not listen to for a moment. Consequently there has arisen a strong spirit of opposition to Mr. Rhodes and to the chartered company, accompanied by the determination to settle the interior of Africa independent of Mr. Rhodes and of the chartered company. This determination was doubtless hastened by the conduct of the company's officers in the Countess of Carnarvon affair, and may have led up to the proposed "trek." The state of public feeling in this matter can be best judged from the utterance of an influential journal published in Cape Town and known as the mouthpiece of the moderate section of the Dutch party. Referring to the seizure of the Countess of Carnarvon, this journal remarked that the news of the seizure was only lacking in one respect to make it entirely acceptable—that it did not include a report that the Captain of the British steamship had been killed by a shot from a Portuguese cannon.

The leaders of the "trek," however, say little or nothing about the chartered company, claiming to base their proceedings upon concessions granted long before the chartered company existed. There is a wide district between the eastern boundary of Matabeland and the western frontier of the Portuguese settlements, and it is in this district which extends northward from the Limpopo to the Zambesi, that the new "Republic of the North" may be established. The new republic will be founded on the constitutional laws of the South African Republic, and is expected to attract men of high character and abitity from all parts of South Africa. It is easy to estimate the strength of the movement from the open manner in which its plans are discussed. Therefore, taking past experiences into consideration, it will require a very strong force of British troops, many more than are now available in South Africa, to make any practical stand against 20,000 well-armed, fighting Boer farmers, who are dead shots and capable of suffering the most severe hardships without complaint.

May 8, 1891

THE "BIG TREK" A FAILURE.

CAPE TOWN, July 2.—A body of armed Boers, composed of about one hundred men and their families, crossed the Limpopo yesterday, thus raiding Mashonaland and taking the first steps toward founding the Republic of the North. These men were the pioneers of the "big trek" which has been so long talked of, and to prevent which President Kruger promised to use his utmost endeavors when he was informed that the British Government would consider any such invasion as an act of hostility against the Queen.

The pioneers of the "big trek" seem, however, to have met with a reception somewhat different from what they expected. They were no sooner in Mashonaland than they were met by police and troops in the employ of the British South African Company, who drove the Boers back and arrested their leaders.

July 3, 1891

WHITE AND BLACK IN SOUTH AFRICA.

Having a race problem of our own, there is always a certain interest to us in observing the peculiarities of the relation between whites and blacks on the native African soil. The relations of Europeans and natives in South Africa are very different from those which exist between white and black Americans. In South Africa the Kafirs and Zulus have not been the slaves of the English. Furthermore, the superior and conquered races speak different languages, a fact which must very much increase the natural difficulties in the way of a correct understanding of one another. That warm friend of the Zulu, Miss COLENSO, has an article in the *Contemporary Review* in which she sets forth the injustice done by the English to the natives. The strength of Miss COLENSO's feelings in this matter is of course well known; and yet the statement that the English in their dealings with a subject race are not controlled by the most generous and unselfish sentiments and the nicest and most scrupulous sense of justice is not upon the face of it so improbable that we may not be prepared to hear what she has to say regarding the misfortunes of Kafirs and Zulus.

The theory by which the Governor of Natal, who happens just now to be also Governor of Zululand, holds the supreme rule over the natives rests upon the idea that he has absorbed the rights of the old native chiefs and that these powers were absolute. The fact is, however, that these powers were not absolute. This fact was established by the testimony of CETEWAYO before the Cape Town Commissioners. CETEWAYO'S testimony was to the effect that there was an unwritten law in Zululand, and that the duty of the supreme chief was to administer in accordance with it. If he does not do this, the supreme chief knows that he is liable to removal by the assegai. The notion of an irresponsible supreme chief was an invention of the white man. It is conceded, however, that there is such a thing as native law, and there seems to be an effort on the part of the Colonial Government and courts to recognize its existence and to accept suggestions from it. We presume that the English local magistrates, in theory at any rate, profess to consider it. But these local magistrates, according to Miss COLENSO, are not a first-rate class of men—not to be compared, for instance, to the same class in India. The salary attached to the office is small, and it is intimated that the career is a refuge for half-educated youths who are not good for much else.

The young magistrate does not know the language. He has often seen a circle of elderly natives seated on the shady side of a kraal, talking long and earnestly and marking off their points in the dust with a little stick. These are Kafirs, discussing the different problems of their judicature. An old Kafir Nestor is no doubt telling his juniors what their fathers would have done in the days of his youth. If the magistrate might consult these authorities—and if he would condescend to do so—he might get valuable suggestions to assist him in the administration of his office. But as a matter of fact, the only authority to whom he has recourse is the "boy" who blacks his boots. The "boy" is human and is open to inducements from the Kafir litigants who come before his master, and the litigants are also human. It is not surprising, therefore, that the decisions should be such as to puzzle Kafir ideas of equity. There are appeals to the courts, but it is said that the courts never decide twice alike.

There have been attempts made to codify the native law, but this law has no binding force. The Governor, acting upon a false theory, considers himself the supreme law. He issues a proclamation, and the Zulus are supposed to be made acquainted with it by word of mouth, and are often flogged for violating edicts of which they never heard. The pass law of Natal is a specimen. A native who wants to pass from Zululand into Natal must get a pass out of one country and a pass into the other at a cost of a shilling for each. Failure to comply with this formality is punishable by a fine of £1 and a flogging. But the main accusation which Miss COLENSO brings against the white rule concerns the case of ZIBEBU. Before the English invaded Zululand in 1879 it had given no trouble at all in thirty-five years. After the invasion the trouble began. The English set up thirteen independent chiefs, who were known in the colony, from their continual fighting, as the "Kilkenny cats." ZIBEBU was one of these. ZIBEBU seems to have been a very bad man and to have been the cause of all the trouble. After CETEWAYO'S death, in 1884, his followers, the Usutu, drove out ZIBEBU'S people, and there was peace for three years. Then in 1887 the Government determined to restore ZIBEBU, which was the more difficult because the Government had already confirmed the Usutu in the possession of these lands. The new crops were about half grown, but ZIBEBU and his people, backed up by the white police, came into the country, drove out the Usutu, numbering many thousands, the magistrates flogging those who had not, in their opinion, been quick enough in getting out. ZIBEBU then did a great deal of killing, and the Usutu again drove him out. For this action the leaders of the Usutu have been banished to St. Helena for high treason. It is said that ZIBEBU will be again forced on the Zulus, a step the bloody consequences of which the English at home can form no idea. But the Zibebu question is but a part of the general subject of the treatment of the blacks, which is in need of radical reform.

March 26, 1892

NEW-YORK, TUESDAY, DEC. 13, 1892.

The latest English papers are filled with the speech of Mr. CECIL RHODES before the shareholders of the British South Africa Company, of which he is President, and with comments on the speech. Certainly the achievements of that gentleman and of his First Lieutenant, Dr. JAMESON, are of the most impressive character as reported by Mr. RHODES. He has, in the name of his company, and, apparently, with the aid of his authority as Premier of Cape Colony, succeeded in acquiring a more or less definitely-acknowledged sovereignty over a territory in Southern Africa larger than the whole of Central Europe, which he reports to be entirely healthful, fertile, and with rich gold-bearing ridges. He has started a railroad toward each coast, and a telegraph line to Uganda, which he proposes to carry northward to Egypt. He has brought in some thousands of colonists, has organized an army, and has beaten the Portuguese into peace. And now he comes home to appeal to the sentiment and imagination of the English people, to make a public opinion that will sustain him. He is getting much admiration and volleys of the most ecstatic praise from the papers. But the Government looks a little askance, and we shall be much surprised if the Ministers do not keep him at arm's length until the popular mind is quiet, and then call him to account, for it is plain that the responsibilities he is incurring would fall on the empire if he failed, or if his company would not or could not give him money enough, or if other Governments interested in Africa should check his career. His enterprise is magnificent, his pluck is unquestioned, and his ability is remarkable. He has many of the qualities of CLIVE, but England might well hesitate to back even a Clive in these days.

December 13, 1892

INVASION OF TRANSVAAL

British South Africa Company's Action Condemned at Home.

JAMESON CUT THE TELEGRAPH WIRES

President Kruger's Call May Entail a Battle at Any Moment—Berlin Journals Protest Violently.

LONDON, Jan. 1.—It is rumored here that advices have been received announcing the arrival of Dr. Jameson with his followers in Johannesburg.

The Right Hon. Joseph Chamberlain Secretary of State for the Colonies, has issued an official statement that he is now in communication with President Kruger of the South African Republic in an effort to avert serious consequences of the unauthorized and altogether unjustifiable act of Dr. Jameson, the administrator of the British South African Company, in leading a force of from 500 to 700 men into the Transvaal to assist the Uitlanders in their contention against the South Afrioan Republic.

Gov. Robinson of the Cape Colony has issued a proclamation publicly repudiating the act of Dr. Jameson, and has caused to be published in the newspapers of Pretoria and Johannesburg an injunction in the name of the Queen to all her Majesty's subjects in the Transvaal not to give aid to Dr. Jameson, but to obey the law and observe order.

Messengers have been sent to overtake Jameson, conveying orders to him and every officer accompanying him that they shall retire from the Transvaal territory, immediately. The situation is very much aggravated by the fact that Dr. Jameson cut the wires behind him, rendering telegraphic communication with him impossible.

Mr. Chamberlain sent a dispatch to the British South Africa Company asking them to repudiate Jameson and his acts. To this the company replied that they were entirely ignorant of Jameson's acts or purposes. Cecil Rhodes, Prime Minister of the Cape Colony, in connection with this reply, stated that Jameson had acted without authority. Rhodes had tried to stop him when he learned that he had gone into the Transvaal, but found that the wires had been cut, and that, consequently, he could not communicate with him.

Dr. Jameson wrote a letter to the commandant at Maricoland, refusing to withdraw from the Transvaal, and avowing that he would proceed upon his original plans, which, in acceptance of the invitation of the principal residents of Rand, were to assist them in their demands for justice.

President Kruger, according to the latest information received here, has called the burghers to arms and a large force of them is proceeding against Johannesburg. They are advancing rapidly and a battle is hourly expected.

The Standard to-morrow, will print a dispatch from its Berlin correspondent, saying that the news of the invasion of the Transvaal has caused in the German capital a storm of indignation that has rarely been witnessed.

Emperor William yesterday summoned by telegraph to the New Palace Baron Marschall von Bieberstein, Secretary of State for Foreign Affairs, to discuss the situation. The correspondent adds that there is excellent reason for believing that German statesmen expect a peaceful and satisfactory settlement of the affair.

The Times to-morrow will print a dispatch from its Berlin correspondent, in which he says: "The crisis in the Transvaal endangers British relations with Germany. The Government hitherto has endeavored to restrain the newspapers over which it has some control, but, judging from what has already been written, one does not like to contemplate what will happen when the restraint is removed."

The newspapers to-morrow will unanimously express approval of the action of Colonial Secretary Chamberlain in ordering the return of the Transvaal expedition. The Liberal newspapers especially laud the statesmanlike wisdom of the Colonial Secretary, while they denounce Dr. Jameson as a lawless freebooter. The Conservative papers recall proofs of Dr. Jameson's ability and discretion, and urge that he be not condemned until the reasons for his action shall have been made known.

The Times gives a qualified approval of Mr. Chamberlain's course, and expresses the strongest sympathy with the foreign residents of the South African republic.

BERLIN, Jan. 1.—Considerable excitement prevails here over the crisis in the Transvaal, and the attitude of Great Britain is denounced upon all sides. The National Zeitung says:

"The South Africa Company, holding the charter of the Queen, has committed a grievous breach of the peace and violation of the law of nations. Germany's interests demand that the independent republic shall be maintained intact, and we expect Germany to interpose with all possible emphasis to assist President Kruger."

The Vossische Zeitung says: "The proceedings of the British South African Company cannot be tolerated, and Germany must immediately take energetic steps to protect the South African Republic."

Advices have been received from Pretoria that 800 more armed men of the British South African Company have crossed the Transvaal frontier. The Government, the dispatches say, is resolved to drive back the intruders by force. A rising has occurred at Johannesburg.

The Cologne Gazette says that Germany has sent an official inquiry to Great Britain as to what steps are to be taken by the British Government in regard to the invasion of the Transvaal by the British South Africa Company.

The paper expresses hope that Dr. Layd, the Secretary of State of the South African Republic, who is now in Berlin and in close communication with the Foreign Office, has already telegraphed to Pretoria that Germany will grant the Boers protection that will not be merely diplomatic.

January 2, 1896

ENGLAND AND GERMANY

Intense Anger Provoked by the Kaiser's Message to Kruger.

By Commercial Cable from Our Own Correspondent.

LONDON, Jan. 4.—Since England was breathlessly following the bloody progress of the British relief expedition up the Nile toward Khartoum, eleven years ago, I have witnessed no such rapt universal popular excitement as has reigned in London in these opening days of the new year. No matter how deeply opinions may differ on the rights and wrongs of the Transvaal business, there is no doubt that everybody, high and low, is profoundly stirred up about it.

It would be an easy enough matter to satirize the English attitude toward this extraordinary and probably momentous catastrophe and to give an air of epigrams to numerous commonplaces about English greed, perfidy, and the rest, in which the whole Continental press is reveling delightedly, but that would be to beg entirely the true character of the episode. What is really to be seen in it is a strange survival of the original processes by which the British Empire was created, suddenly revealed and expounded to people five generations removed from knowledge of them by the magical operations of modern electrical science. If England 140 years ago could have followed Lord Clive with the telegraph wire, British India would never have existed. Englishmen now, even while they curse the inexplicable block in the communications which kept them for forty-eight hours without news from Johannesburg, dimly understand that they are witnessing something to which they are ancestrally related, but which they thought had been dead and buried for a century or so. Their judgment commands that they should disapprove it sternly, but all the inherited impulses of their blood impel them to cheer and wave their hats. It is a genuine conflict between their respectable modern civilization and the old Berserker Island instincts in their veins. If they were left alone there would be no doubt as to the result of this struggle. The nineteenth century would win, and, in their calmer mood, they would see to it, as in 1880, that the Boers had scrupulous justice dealt to them.

But suddenly the German Emperor leaps into the middle of this perplexing situation with drawn sword and infuriates everybody. Yesterday seven-eighths of thinking England was against Cecil Rhodes and his South African dummy company, and was glad to hear that Dr. Jameson and his filibusters had been soundly whipped by the Boers, but last evening, when the terms of the German Emperor's insolent dispatch reached London, this mood began to change as swiftly as the newspapers could spread the news. To-day, while nobody has altered his mind specifically about Dr. Jameson's part in the affair, it is also true that nobody speaks or thinks of Germany's interference without an angry glisten in the eye. Every aspect of that imperial message, upon examination, reveals a fresh ground for wrath. If it were intended to enrage England on as many sides as possible, it is a triumph of ingenuity. Its rejoicing that English blood has been spilled, its reference to friendly powers which would have intervened if President Kruger had asked them, its calm denial of England's suzerain treaty rights, the fact that it was sent after an imperial council at the Foreign Office, in which naval members ostentatiously predominated—all these give to it the character of a deliberate, intentional affront. No living Englishman remembers any such other premeditated slap in the face. What counsels second thoughts may bring it is impossible to say, but England to-night wants to fight Germany more passionately than she has desired anything else since the time of the Georges.

January 5, 1896

CECIL RHODES.

The resignation of CECIL RHODES as Premier of Cape Colony is perhaps the most important result of the collapse of JAMESON'S filibustering expedition. The telegram of congratulation sent by the Emperor of Germany to the victorious Boers is for the moment more conspicuous, and certainly it is adapted to excite more emotion in England. But it is too evidently personal permanently to affect the German or the British policy. In our day even an hereditary ruler with so much personal ascendency as an Emperor of Germany possesses does not shape a policy in the spirit in which he may be moved to compose a telegram.

In the first place, the resignation of CECIL RHODES emphasizes the complete dissociation of the British Government from JAMESON'S attempt and assumes the responsibility of it for the Premier himself. There really has not been any substantial reason for distrusting the good faith of Mr. CHAMBERLAIN and of the Government he represents in their disavowal of any complicity with JAMESON'S attempt. It is only fair to remember that prompt and energetic measures were taken to put a stop to the expedition as soon as it was known in London that it had been undertaken and before the fate of it could have been known or even plausibly guessed. It is this fact which deprives the irregular and impulsive action of Emperor WILLIAM of what would otherwise have been very near a justification of it. If the expedition had succeeded, if the Boers had been surprised and their country successfully invaded, there is, indeed, reason to suppose that the British Government would have profited by its success. But now that it has failed the responsibility for it must be borne by the actual instigators of it. This responsibility CECIL RHODES fully assumed, when the expedition turned out disastrously, by offering his resignation of the place which he had worked so hard to win, and which was of value to him mainly for the foothold it gave him for translating into action what he has avowed was the dream of his life.

It was in 1883, when he was publicly known only as a successful speculator in the diamond fields, that CECIL RHODES is said to have drawn a line across the map of Africa including the mouth of the Congo and the great lakes, and to have exclaimed: "All that shall be English; that is my dream." It was not an ungenerous dream, and at times it has seemed to be in course of realization. But it was not a dream which the aspiring politicians of "Little Britain" found attractive. For the visionary never concealed his intention to make an independent power of the region which he meant to be "English" only in the sense that it was to be controlled by men of English birth or descent. He meant to make of South Africa a new Australia or Canada, a federation for which these two furnished the models, and in which a constituent State that happened to be Dutch should have as much individuality and freedom as, for example, French and Catholic Quebec now enjoys in the Dominion of Canada. He did not conceal his impatience that South Africa should be governed from ten thousand miles away by men who were neither very well informed about its needs and desires nor very much in sympathy with them. To British statesmen an outlying possession is necessarily little more than a pawn in the "imperial" game, even when it is more than a pawn in the game of domestic politics. It is the ignorance and indifference of British statesmen that have brought about the actual independence of the United States and the virtual independence of Canada and Australia, of all the great British possessions, indeed, excepting British India, where an infinitesimal minority of Britons who have not expatriated themselves govern meek millions of natives. That South Africa should be a British dependency is the view of Downing Street; that it should be British and independent has been the dream of CECIL RHODES.

It has seemed that if anybody was capable of realizing this dream, it was he. He has shown himself to be of the stuff of which the "conditores imperii" were made in the largeness of his conceptions, in the fixity of his purpose, and also in the absence of any scruples that might interfere with success. His most formidable opposition was not that of the Colonial Office, although the struggle in which he has been worsted has been described as a "duel" with Mr. CHAMBERLAIN. Up to a certain point the ambitions for a colony of the colonial and of the metropolitan statesman are the same. It is only when the colony has become powerful and homogeneous enough to be worthy of being called a nation that they begin to diverge. And even the threat of divergency has not been very formidable, since for the last half century, at least, the course of British policy has been in the direction of allowing the colonies virtual independence rather than to allow them to become troublesome or expensive. In the primary object of extending the British possessions in South Africa it has seemed that RHODES, with his knowledge, energy, and resource, was the most valuable ally the home Government could possess. The obstacles to this extension were offered by the European powers which had claims or the settlers of European descent who had possessions that blocked the path of RHODES's ambition. Germany was the chief of the powers, and the Boers were the principal settlers. It has been related, however, how RHODES had devoted himself to conciliating the leading men among the Boers, and how he was making progress in that undertaking. It seems that nothing could have been more injudicious for him than to have countenanced a forcible invasion of their country led by his old companion "Dr. JIM." Such an invasion was sure to exasperate both the Boers and Germany and to be very disastrous, if not entirely ruinous, to his project if it failed. His resignation seems to be an acknowledgment at once of complete responsibility and of complete failure. But it would be premature to say that it closes the career of the most important Englishman in South Africa.

January 7, 1896

GOVERNMENT OF CAPE COLONY.

Changes Looking to Home Rule Approved by Mr. Chamberlain.

LONDON, Feb. 24.—The Secretary of State for the Colonies, Joseph Chamberlain, as set forth in a Parliamentary paper just issued, proposes that in future the differences between the British South Africa Company and the natives must be submitted to the Secretary of State, whose decision will be binding. In addition, the Administrative Council of Southern Rhodesia is to be augmented by four elected members to the Council, and sufficient of the Company's nominees to insure the Company a majority. Further, while the responsible expenditure of the Commandant of the forces will be paid by the Crown, he will cease to be a Deputy Commissioner, and the control of the High Commissioner will be based on information from the Imperial Resident Commissioner.

Mr. Chamberlain has also agreed that there shall be separate Administrators for Matabeleland and Mashonaland, and that there shall be only one Executive Council. The Government of Cape Colony has approved Mr. Chamberlain's proposals, regarding them as clearing the way for self-government and the probable eventual federal union of the Cape.

LONDON, Feb. 25.—The morning newspapers and all parties concerned raise a chorus of approval over Mr. Chamberlain's scheme, which begins with the conversion of Rhodesia into a Crown colony. The arrangement is regarded as reassuring for the Transvaal, since the British Government is now responsible for any attack upon the Transvaal. The scheme does not affect Northern Rhodesia, which is left for future consideration.

February 25, 1898

ENGLAND'S PLANS IN AFRICA.

Cecil Rhodes, the Developer at Work on His Scheme to Build a Great Railroad.

LONDON, Jan. 21.—Great Britain seems to shake to its foundations whenever Cecil Rhodes steps foot on the island. Peers, Cabinet Ministers, promoters with Munchausen schemes, Duchesses craving for tips on "Kaffirs" or South African securities, workmen who cherish dreams of emigration, and Bishops solicitous for African souls haunt his hotel and beg for even the briefest interviews, as though he had already realized his aspiration. The popular mind credits him with being the potentate of the African continent. An inconsiderate newspaper has described how Mr. Rhodes ate his meals to the accompaniment of business, dismissed a couple of millionaires while he cracked an egg, sold mines over his beefsteaks, and ate oatmeal while organizing a company or two. It was therefore suggested that the breakfast hour was the surest time to see him, and the result is that while he breakfasts his secretaries repel the invasion of mobs of importunate speculators.

The Cabinet met yesterday, specially, to discuss Mr. Rhodes's scheme for Government guarantees of the Cape to Cairo Railroad and Telegraph. Mr. Rhodes afterward conferred with Mr. Joseph Chamberlain, the Secretary of State for the Colonies, and Sir Michael Hicks-Beach, the Chancellor of the Exchequer. Mr. Rhodes says £10,000,000 will cover the entire cost of the work, and there is little doubt that he will carry his point with the Government and raise all the money he needs in the City. Before the projectors can act in the matter there will be a formality in the shape of a Parliamentary bill, but the Imperialists may be backed to drive over the so-called "Little Englanders," who are preparing an opposition to the scheme, declaring that the Rhodesian Empire is making for a gigantic fiasco, and that Mr. Rhodes wants the Government to lift him out of a hole by throwing good money after bad, into a railroad through a wilderness. They also find a coincidence in Mr. Rhodes's homecoming, and the revival of newspaper outbursts against the Boers' oppression of British subjects in the Transvaal.

By slow steps, so as not to arouse the violent antagonism of the powers, but in pursuance of a definite plan, Great Britain is tightening her grip on North Africa. The Egyptian Convention, so far as the Soudan is concerned, accomplishes all that those who prodded the Marquis of Salisbury to declare a protectorate could have desired. Great Britain no longer governs through the Khédive. She becomes a co-equal ruler and ignores the mixed tribunals. This means that the Governor General is responsible only to Downing Street and Parliament.

The comment of the Liberte of Paris, that "Great Britain does not annex the Soudan as she palms it like a sleight-of-hand professor," is a specimen of the spirit in which France, already incensed at Great Britain, regards this Government's progress toward absolute sovereignty in Egypt.

January 22, 1899

THE REAL ISSUE IN THE TRANSVAAL.

The Duke of DEVONSHIRE, who is the Lord President of the Council in the Cabinet of Lord SALISBURY, made a frank and even naïve statement on Saturday regarding the Transvaal question. He expressed little hope of a pacific outcome, and thus explained the situation:

> The obstacle which seems to stand in the way of a peaceful settlement appears to be the rooted conviction of the Boers that we cherish designs hostile to their independence. That such apprehensions are unfounded has been asserted as strongly as possible—officially in our dispatches and unofficially by members of the Government.
> The unfounded suspicions of President KRUEGER and his Government cannot relieve us of the duty of taking measures for the protection of our fellow-subjects and in the interests of peace and good government.

In plain English this amounts to declaring that the pretensions of the two parties are entirely irreconcilable. The Boers claim independence, which certainly includes the right to determine under their own Constitution and laws what share any class of residents shall have in the Government, and also the right to determine that any class admitted to a share in the Government shall renounce allegiance to any other Government and shall assume all the obligations of citizenship, not excepting service in the army. Great Britain, on the contrary, while insisting, as the Duke of DEVONSHIRE does in terms, that the Government has no "designs hostile to the independence" of the Boers, still regards the English in the Transvaal as "subjects" and "citizens" of her own, for whose "protection" she is responsible.

The Duke says that the negotiations have reached a stage where the Government of Great Britain does not see "any advantage in pressing the proposals they had made in regard to the franchise," and he adds that these "have never been an essential point of difference." It is not hard to understand that there is no advantage in pressing these proposals, for it is really absurd to talk of one nation respecting the independence of a second nation and at the same time demanding from it the suffrage for the "subjects" of the first nation. Either the English in the Transvaal are not the subjects of her Majesty the Queen or they cannot be entitled to a vote in the South African Republic if that republic is independent. And it is plain indeed that the question of the suffrage is not an essential point of difference. The essential difference is as to the nature of the independence which the Boers claim and that which the British Government is ready to concede. They use the same word, but they mean very different things. Practically what the Duke of DEVONSHIRE states to be the purpose of the British Government is that it shall decide for itself what the rights of the English in the Transvaal shall be, and how their interests shall be protected.

It may be admitted that the claim of the British Government will ultimately have to be conceded. The interests of the Outlanders in the Transvaal, the great body of whom are English, are undoubtedly of greater value and importance than those of the Boers. They are, moreover, in harmony with the way the world is going, while the ideas, customs, and purposes of the Boers are opposed to that way and will have to yield. Not only are the Boers out of the current of modern life, but their claims are clearly contrary to the modern notions of justice and right. They are seeking to maintain what in effect and in spirit is a despotic oligarchy, which is at once harsh, stupid, narrow, obstructive, and corrupt. It is the bad rule of a minority that they would perpetuate and extend, and such a rule is bound to perish and ought to perish. Nor can it be denied that if the pretensions of the British Government were granted or enforced the result would be beneficent. The Outlanders would get no more than their rights and the Boers would lose none that they ought in fairness and equity to possess.

But the question still remains whether this end ought now to be sought through war. It has seemed to us and still seems that it ought not so to be sought. The evil and the cost of war are out of proportion to the gain to be got from that settlement of the problem. Practically the gain is only in time. There is no doubt as to the final outcome. With the steady increase of the Outlanders in numbers, in wealth, in enterprise, and in the influence these bring, the Boers are bound to yield. The endurance for the time necessary of the evils and wrongs that undoubtedly exist cannot be so bad as the terrible consequences of war.

October 2, 1899

BOER ULTIMATUM REACHES LONDON

Demands Instant Removal of British Troops from Frontier.

Failure of Great Britain to Reply a Declaration of War.

LONDON, Oct. 10.—The South African Republic has sent an ultimatum to Great Britain, demanding that the points in dispute be referred to arbitration, that all troops on the border be instantly withdrawn, that reinforcements sent to South Africa since June 1 be removed, and that no further troops be landed. An answer is demanded by 5 P. M. on Wednesday, Oct. 11.

The text of the ultimatum, on arriving this morning, was sent with all speed to Lord Salisbury, who came to town this afternoon, and a dispatch box was sent to the Prince of Wales, which is only done in cases of especial urgency.

The ultimatum of the Transvaal Government is the absorbing topic of conversation at the clubs and in political circles to-night, and the late editions of the afternoon papers containing the text of the document met with a good sale in the central parts of London, the newsboys doing a thriving trade on the closing of the theatres. There was no apparent excitement, however, but a general feeling was expressed that the Boers had made a mistake, tending to alienate the sympathy which might have been extended to them had they thrown the onus of declaring war on Great Britain.

The diplomatic circumstances surrounding the presentation of the ultimatum are probably without precedent. Ordinarily a foreign power, when addressing peremptory demands to another, sends them through an Ambassador or Minister accredited to its adversary.

The Transvaal Government, however, has no diplomatic representative recognized by Great Britain. Montague White, the Transvaal Consul General in London, would not be received by either the Foreign Office or the Colonial Office. Consequently President Krüger was reduced to handing the ultimatum to Conyngham Greene at Pretoria, who in turn wired it to Sir Alfred Milner, British High Commissioner in South Africa, by whom it was retransmitted to Joseph Chamberlain, who thus becomes the first Secretary of State for the Colonies who has ever received an ultimatum.

In ordinary circumstances, as Great Britain is the Government making the demand, she would be the dispatcher of the ultimatum, and the fact that the Boers have taken the initiative is regarded as rendering the situation more serious and increasing the hopelessness of averting war.

The only wonder is why, if President Krüger is resolved upon fighting, he has waited so long. The explanation seems to be that his hand has been forced by the fact that the Boers have got out of control, or that, if he awaited the arrival of the British army corps, the chances of military success for him would be of the slimmest possible character.

The expiration of the time limit of the ultimatum to-morrow evening does not leave Great Britain much time to strengthen the present military position, although there are still a few troops at Durban, Natal, available for dispatch to the front, and the Government will doubtless now adopt the suggestion to form the refugees from the Rand into volunteer regiments, and thus, while relieving their distress, utilizing excellent material.

October 11, 1899

INVASION OF NATAL BY BOERS REPORTED

Rumored Advance on Ladysmith by Free State Troops.

A BRITISH GARRISON THERE

Reinforcements Arrived Tuesday, 6,000 Men at Dundee.

British Telegraph Censorship Just Established Prevents Receipt of Definite News from the Scene of War.

DURBAN, Oct. 11.—There are persistent rumors in Pietermaritzburg that a large body of Free State Boers have entered Natal. The rumor, however, lacks confirmation.

LONDON, Oct. 11.—A dispatch from Pietermaritzburg, Natal, says intense excitement prevails there owing to persistent reports that the Orange Free State troops have already crossed the border and are advancing on Ladysmith.

A later dispatch says the invaders entered Natal by the important Pass of Cundy Cleugh, thirty-seven miles southwest of Newcastle.

The military authorities in South Africa have instituted a censorship over all telegrams in order to prevent information regarding British movements from reaching the Boers.

It is not surprising that the Boers should have already crossed the border, as they would be entitled to do so in virtue of the notification contained in the last paragraph of the ultimatum and also of the British acknowledgment, which reached Pretoria so speedily as to justify a belief, amounting almost to certainty, that the war party in Great Britain was eagerly awaiting its chance, and, despite newspaper attempts to veil the real feeling, is in reality delighted that diplomacy has said its last word and that action can now proceed.

There will inevitably be a long period of suspense, together with a great deal of chafing at delay, as all indications go to show that Great Britain is so unprepared as to be compelled to remain on the defensive for some weeks. All the aggressiveness must come from the Boers.

It seems highly probable that the "tongue of Natal" as far as Newcastle will be in the hands of the Boers before many hours. From that point, however, in the event of a further advance, they would probably find British forces at Ladysmith and Dundee capable of repelling their attacks.

At Ladysmith the garrison, which has to guard against an onslaught from the Orange Free State, was reinforced yesterday by the Gordon Highlanders and a strong contingent of the Indian troops, and the authorities are now confident of their ability to protect the place in the event of an attempt to rush the position.

At Dundee there are about 6,000 men. This force ought to be sufficient to stem a Boer advance by way of Zululand, and to maintain the line of communication with the base at Pietermaritzburg, the headquarters of Gen. Sir George Stewart White.

WHERE WAR OPERATIONS ARE IN PROGRESS.

On the Bechuanaland border the situation seems to give the Boers a temporary advantage. There is considerable anxiety in the districts of Vryburg and Mafeking, although it is hoped that the reinforcements recently dispatched there will be sufficient to protect the rich town of Kimberley.

Newcastle and Umvoti in Natal are both Boer centres and it had long been expected by the British Colonial Office that these places would be the objective points of the Transvaal and Orange Free State troops respectively. Along the line, west and east of Charlestown, is Sir George White with some 12,000 troops, while menacing the Transvaal from the southwest is Sir Redvers Buller, with from 30,000 to 35,000 men, whose line of advance is connected with two railroads. It has been reported that no attempt will be made by the British to force entrance into the Transvaal along the line from Newcastle to Volksrust, including Majuba Hill and Laing's Nek—the theatre of operations in 1881—but that the attack will be made south of this line, along the route from Border Siding to Klerksdorp, below Potchefstroom, at which point it is the intention to seize the Pretoria-Klerksdorp Railway. At the same time a descent may be made from Tuli, which is in Rhodesia, on the right bank of the Limpopo. These are the two obvious lines of British attack, but there is another—from the east, with its base at Lorenzo Marques, the chief town of Delagoa, from which a line of railway runs directly to Pretoria, the Transvaal capital, a distance of 370 miles. The distance by rail of Pretoria from the other South African ports, which will form the British bases of supplies is as follows: Durban, 484 miles; East London, 665 miles; Port Elizabeth, 414 miles; and Cape Town, 1,013 miles.

Thus it will be seen that three distinct columns supplied by five lines of railway may move on Pretoria. It is expected that eventually the Boers will be obliged to fall back on their capital, where they will make their last stand. The capital is surrounded by mountain ranges, and access is only to be obtained through the "poorts" or defiles. Each poort is guarded by a fort placed in a commanding position.

It is said that the line of advance from Border Siding to Klerksdorp has been adopted rather than the "Jameson route" to Krügersdorp, because while the latter is hilly and well defended in anticipation of just such an invasion, the former route passes through an entirely flat grass land practically free from such obstacles as rivers and hills.

In the last Transvaal war in 1881, even while the battle of Majuba Hill was being fought, British reinforcements were on the way to South Africa, and a most elaborate campaign was being prepared by the Colonial Office. It all came to nothing, however, when Mr. Gladstone caused an armistice to be declared. Military critics have declared that if "Gladstone had not stopped the war" the Transvaal would have been completely subjugated within three months after the Majuba Hill affair.

The battle of Majuba Hill was not conducted on a very large scale. The engagement was precipitated by the British commander, who desired to whip the Boers and end the war before the arrival of the troops that had been sent to reinforce him. On the night of Feb. 26, 1881, 600 British infantry set out for the summit of Majuba Hill. Four hundred men finally reached the summit, and were disposed in various positions about the rim of the mountain. The first shots were fired at 6 o'clock on the following morning, and the contest raged for several hours. In the final stages the main party of Boers crept up to within forty yards. The fighting ceased at 10 o'clock by the flight of the British, who left on the field, in killed and wounded, 280. The Boer loss was one killed and four wounded. The Boers have asserted that their force consisted of 400 riflemen; British reports place the number at 1,000.

October 12, 1899

BOERS, BRITISH, AND NATIVES.

Nothing is more interesting, in the existing war in the Transvaal, than the attempts of the combatants to throw on each other the onus of employing "natives" in war. We are not aware that it has cut any figure in the official and diplomatic correspondence. And no wonder. Because this controversy, of its own nature, begins where official and diplomatic correspondence ends. It is recognized, however, that the employment of "native" allies by a professedly Christian and civilised combatant is a disreputable operation, even though there has been no international prohibition of it at the conference at The Hague or at any of its predecessors.

It is a queer situation, because part of the case of each combatant is that it commands more of the sympathy of "the natives" than its opponent, and yet it has to disclaim turning this sympathy to practical and armed account. In our own Revolutionary War Lord CHATHAM made it a ground of reproach against the Ministry of the day that it had invoked the aid of the savages against white men. The latest recrudescence of the same spirit is the British explanation of the stampeding of the ammunition and battery mules. The explanation is that the "native" mule drivers were in sympathy with the Boers and that the stampede was really the work of these drivers.

But how does this explanation go with the contention that the natives are hostile to the Boers on account of the cruelty with which the Boers have treated them? Obviously it does not go at all. Neither does it go with the report that the warlike Basutos are rising up to help the British beat the Boers. This report would be "important if true," looking to the situation of Basutoland, between Natal and the Orange Free State. The truth we suppose to lie, as usual, between the two extremes. The natives do in fact loathe both Boers and British. The answer to the question which do they loathe the more probably depends upon the question which they have encountered the earlier and the oftener. It also depends largely upon "the personal equation," upon what kind of Boer or Briton the native has first encountered and from what specimen he has formed his impression of the species. No doubt the "native" loathes the Boer. No doubt he also loathes the Briton. If he has seen more Boers than Britons, or if he has seen more of the Boers than of the Britons, then he loathes the Boers the more warmly, and vice versa. We have nothing to boast about in such a comparison, because it was only the other day that an American officer, and therefore an expert witness, returning from the Philippines, gave it as his opinion that, although the Filipinos used to hate the Spaniards very bitterly, yet, now that they had come to know us, we had entirely displaced the Spaniards as objects of animosity. The ultimate conclusion is that there is really no conclusion to be drawn from these animosities, or these comparative animosities, of savages for comparatively civilized people. Least of all can any conclusion be drawn from the contradictory statements that the savage tribes have suffered cruel wrong from one combatant and that they are also taking his part against the other.

November 7, 1899

WINSTON CHURCHILL'S ESCAPE

British Correspondent Tells How He Got Out of Pretoria and Eluded the Boer Watchers.

LONDON, Dec. 27.—Winston Spencer Churchill has cabled and The Morning Post publishes to-day an account of his escape from captivity with the Boers, after having been taken prisoner in the reconnoissance of an armored train at Estcourt.

The dispatch, which is dated Lorenzo Marques, Dec. 21, says:

"On the afternoon of Dec. 12 the Transvaal's Secretary of War informed me that there was little chance of my release. I therefore resolved to escape, and the same night I left the State School's prison, in Pretoria by climbing the wall when the sentries' backs were turned momentarily. I walked through the streets of the town without disguise, meeting many burghers, but was not challenged in the crowd. I got through the pickets of the town guard and struck the Delagoa Bay Railroad. I walked along it, evading the watchers at the bridges and culverts, and waited for a train beyond the first station. The 11:10 goods train from Pretoria had arrived before I reached the place, and was moving at full speed. I boarded it with great difficulty and hid under coal sacks.

"I jumped from the train before dawn, and was sheltered during the day in a small wood, in company with a huge vulture, who displayed a lively interest in me.

"I walked on at dusk. There were no more trains that night. The danger of meeting the guards of the line continued, but I was obliged to follow it, as I had no compass or map. I had to make wide detours to avoid bridges, stations, and huts, and so my progress was very slow. Chocolate is not a satisfying food. The outlook was gloomy, but I persevered, with God's help. For five days my food supply was very precarious. I was lying up by daylight and walking by night.

"Meanwhile my escape had been discovered, and my description telegraphed everywhere. All trains were searched and every one was on the watch for me. Four times the wrong people were arrested.

"The sixth day I managed to board a train beyond Middleburg, whence there was direct service to Delagoa.

"In the evening I concealed myself in a railway truck under a great pile of sacks. I had a small store of good water. I remained hidden so, chancing discovery. The Boers searched the train at Komatipoort, but did not search deep enough. After sixty hours of misery I came safely here. I am very weak, but am free. I have lost many pounds in weight, but am light in heart. I shall avail myself of every opportunity henceforth to urge earnestly the unflinching and uncompromising prosecution of the war."

December 28, 1899

ROBERTS BELIEVED TO BE IN PRETORIA

JOHANNESBURG CAPTURED

The War Is Now Regarded as Practically Over.

LONDON, May 31.—Yesterday at noon the British were only about two hours' march from Pretoria, and the Boer military forces had abandoned the city. This intelligence comes from the Reuter agent at the Transvaal capital, and from the Earl of Rosslyn in a dispatch to The Daily Mail. The two messages left Pretoria at about the same time. Lord Rosslyn's telegram was as follows:

"Pretoria, Wednesday, May 30.—11:40 A. M.—Pretoria will be occupied in about two hours, without resistance. The President has gone to Waterval Boven. Burgomaster De Souza is authorized to receive the British. He, with an influential committee of citizens, including Chief Justice Gregorowski, has been appointed to preserve life and property during the interregnum.

"Everything is quiet, but crowds are waiting expectantly in Church Square for the arrival of the British.

"Fearing a possible disturbance and bloodshed among the prisoners of war at Waterval, United States Consul Hay and Mr. Leigh Wood insisted upon twenty officers being liberated on parole to go to the men. Their action cannot be too highly praised.

"I was permitted to accompany the officers. Everything was quiet."

At 2 o'clock this morning the War Office had received no news from Lord Roberts which the officials would make public; but it is assumed that the press advices are correct. Most of the London morning papers, through the courtesy of The Daily Mail, print Lord Rosslyn's dispatch and comment upon it, treating the war as ended. Some of the more cautious critics think that guerrilla warfare is likely to be carried on for some time in various parts of the conquered territories.

The Times says this morning: "The war is practically over. By this time the British flag is flying in Pretoria. Mr. Krüger has fled, and is ere this half way to Delagoa Bay."

Confirmation of part of Lord Rosslyn's dispatch comes in another message from Pretoria, as follows:

"At a public meeting called this morning by the Burgomaster of Pretoria a committee was appointed to keep public order.

"The committee consists of Judge Gregorowski, N. C. Marais, Loveday, De Villiers, Zeederberg, and F. Grobler."

Another Pretoria dispatch of yesterday's date says:

"British officers are now at Johannesburg dictating terms of surrender.

"The British advance guard is half way between Johannesburg and Pretoria. It is reported that there is a force also at Hatherly.

"All the forces have been dismissed from the forts around Pretoria.

"President Krüger is now at Waterval Boven."

Waterval Boven, or Waterfall Hoven, is 130 miles due east of Pretoria, on the Delagoa Bay Railway. It should not be confused with Waterval, ten miles north of Pretoria, where the British prisoners are. Waterval Boven is a small place, in a mountainous country. The seat of the Boer Government what there is left of it will probably be Lydenburg, to the north. Dispatches published yesterday said Krüger was preparing to flee to Holland, by way of Lorenzo Marques.

A dispatch from Lorenzo Marques, dated Wednesday, says:

"Commandant Kraus has surrendered Johannesburg to Lord Roberts.

"By to-night's train from Pretoria arrived a few Greeks, who say they were told to leave Pretoria on Tuesday. They affirm that the train in which they left was shelled by the British and that half of the train was cut off, the remainder steaming away. This incident probably occurred at Eleandsfontein Junction.

"Passengers from Pretoria assert that the town is utterly demoralized. There is a mad rush for the coast. Five trainloads of fugitives are expected here to-night."

Although the Boer forces are dissolving, Lord Roberts, apparently, has not yet taken any considerable quantities of artillery, arms, or stores. Large bodies of Boers must still be somewhere in the field.

The British authorities at Bulawayo think the Boers will retire into Southern Rhodesia.

By the release of the British prisoners at Waterval a full brigade will be added to the army of Lord Roberts, as there were 177 officers and 4,182 privates among them.

Events elsewhere in the field of war seem to dwindle in comparison with the Pretoria news. Gen. Buller re-entered the Transvaal at Marlbogopan on Tuesday. The advance was made off the railway. Water is scarce, and all the farms are deserted. Yesterday Gen. Hunter reached Geysdorp with ten ten days' supplies.

Marlbogopan is half way between Vryburg and Mafeking. Geysdorp is from twelve to fifteen miles east. Gen. Hunter meets with no resistance.

Gen. Baden-Powell is invading the country further north, without opposition.

In Northern Natal Utrecht has surrendered to Gen. Hildyard, and Gen. Lyttleton is moving to Vryheid. Three correspondents estimate the number of Boers at Laing's Nek at about 10,000.

Two Australians who escaped from Pretoria on April 28 have arrived at Mafeking, having spent a month on the veldt, with but little food and no blankets. They slept by day and marched at night. They complain bitterly of the treatment they received at Pretoria.

May 31, 1900

THE FREE STATE ANNEXATION.

BLOEMFONTEIN, May 28.—Amid salutes and cheers and the singing of "God Save the Queen" the Military Governor, Major Gen. George T. Pretyman, at noon formally proclaimed the annexation of the Free State under the designation of the Orange River Colony. The ceremony was somewhat imposing, and the scene in the market square inspiring. An immense concourse had gathered, and the town was gay with bunting. The balconies and windows surrounding the square were crowded with women, among them Lady Roberts and the Misses Roberts, the Countess of Airlie, and the Ladies Henry Bentinck and Settrington.

The troops were drawn up under command of Gen. Knox. The Governor, accompanied by Gen. Kelly-Kenny and their staffs and escorted by the Welsh Yeomanry, was greeted with a general salute, after which, amid an impressive silence and in a clear voice, heard in every part of the square, Gen. Pretyman read Lord Roberts's proclamation annexing the Orange Free State, conquered by her Majesty's forces, to the Queen's dominions, and proclaiming that the State shall henceforth be known as the Orange River Colony.

Lusty cheers greeted the concluding words of the proclamation, and these were renewed with increasing volume as Lord Acheson unfurled the royal standard and the bands struck up "God Save the Queen," all present joining in singing the national hymn.

The ceremony concluded with cheers for the Queen, Lord Roberts, and the army, and a salute of twenty-one guns.

May 31, 1900

TERMS OF PEACE WITH THE BOERS

Burghers Required to Swear Allegiance to King Edward.

Dutch Language Retained in Schools and Courts—Permission to Carry Arms—$15,000,000 to Aid in Restoring Homesteads.

LONDON, Jui e 2.—Not in years has the House of Commons been so thronged with a brilliant and enthusiastic audience as when the First Lord of the Treasury and Government leader in the House, A. J. Balfour, announced this afternoon the peace terms concluded with the Boers.

An hour before the House met a large crowd on Whitehall vociferously cheered the notable politicians, particularly the Colonial Secretary, Joseph Chamberlain, who walked unconcernedly from the Colonial Office, with a broad smile on his face.

Long before the customary prayer the galleries of the House were packed. Joseph H. Choate, the United States Ambassador; Henry White, the Secretary of the Embassy; Lord Rothschild, and many members of the Cabinet patiently waited through the answering of questions in the House for the momentous announcement. An unusually large number of peers sat in their gallery, and behind the ladies' grill aristocratic women were closely packed. Noticeable among them was Lary Sarah Wilson, who thus saw the end of the drama in which she played such an active part.

Mr. Chamberlain and Mr. Balfour received great ovations as they walked to their seats, Mr. Chamberlain's reception being by far the more enthusiastic of the two.

The lobbies and waiting rooms were crowded with disappointed seekers for seats, among whom were many Americans.

The period of waiting finally came to an end. Amid breathless silence, broken a few seconds later by applause such as the House of Commons seldom hears, Mr. Balfour stood up and announced the terms on which the war in South Africa had been ended. The reference to the Boers acknowledging King Edward as their sovereign made the hit of the day, being greeted with a salvo of "Hear, hears!" and applause from the galleries, the occupants of which refused to be silenced.

As the liberality of the terms grew plainer, the cheers on the Government side of the House diminished, while the Opposition's satisfaction was proportionately increased.

Through all this the Irish members sat impassive, though earlier in the afternoon they had startled the House by a demonstration, which at first was thought to be in honor of peace, but which, it was soon discovered, was caused by the reappearance in the house of William Redmond, who has just returned from the United States.

Mr. Balfour arose at 2:40 P. M. and announced the terms of peace in South Africa, as follows:

THE TERMS OF PEACE.

"His Excellency Lord Milner, in behalf of the British Government; his Excellency Mr. Steyn, Gen. Bremner, Gen. C. R. De Wet, and Judge Hertzog, acting in behalf of the Orange Free State, and Gen. Schalk-Burger, Gen. Reitz, Gen. Louis Botha, and Gen. De la Rey, acting in behalf of their respective burghers, desiring to terminate the present hostilities, agree to the following terms:

"The burgher forces in the field will forthwith lay down their arms and hand over all their guns, rifles, and ammunition of war in their possession, or under their control, and desist from further resistance, and acknowledge King Edwad VII. as their lawful sovereign.

"The manner and details of this surrender will be arranged between Lord Kitchener and Commandant General Botha, assisted by Gen. De la Rey and Chief Commandant De Wet.

"Second—All burghers outside the limits of the Transvaal and Orange River Colony, and all prisoners of war at present outside South Africa, who are burghers, will, on duly declaring their acceptance of the position of subjects of his Majesty, be brought back to their homes so soon as means of transport can be provided, and means of subsistence assured.

"Third—The burghers so returning will not be deprived of their personal liberty or property.

"Fourth—No proceeding, civil or criminal, will be taken against any burghers surrendering, or so returning, for any acts in connection with the prosecution of the war. The benefits of this clause do not extend to certain acts contrary to the usages of war, which had been notified by the Commander in Chief to the Boer Generals, and which shall be tried by court-martial after the close of hostilities.

"Fifth—The Dutch language will be taught in public schools of the Transvaal and Orange River Colony where the parents desire it, and will be allowed in the courts of law for the better and more effectual administration of justice.

"Sixth—Possession of rifles will be allowed in the Transvaal and Orange River Colony to persons requiring them for their protection, on taking out a license, according to law.

"Seventh—The military administration of the Transvaal and Orange River Colony will, at the earliest possible date, be succeeded by a Civil Government, and, so soon as circumstances permit, representative institutions, leading up to self-government, will be introduced.

"Eighth—The question of granting the franchise to natives will not be decided until after the introduction of self-government.

"Ninth—No special tax will be imposed on landed property in the Transvaal or Orange River Colony to defray the expenses of the war.

"Tenth—So soon as the conditions permit it, a commission, on which the local inhabitants will be represented, will be appointed in each district of the Transvaal and Orange River Colony, under the Presidency of a Magistrate or other official, for the purpose of assisting in the restoration of the people to their homes, and supplying those who, owing to war losses, are unable to provide for themselves, with food and shelter, and the necessary amount of seed, stock, and implements, &c., indispensable to the resumption of their normal occupations. His Majesty's Government will place at the disposal of these commissions the sum of £3,000,000 ($15,000,000) and will allow all the notes issued under the law of 1900 of the South African Republic, and all receipts given up to officers in the field of the late republics, or under their orders, to be presented to a judicial commission, which will be appointed by the Government, and if such notes and receipts are found by this commission to have been duly issued in return for valuable considerations they will be received by the first-named commissions as evidence of war losses suffered by the persons to which they were originally given.

"In addition to the above-named free grant of £3,000,000, His Majesty's Government will be prepared to make advances, on loan, for the same purposes, free of interest for two years, and afterward repayable over a period of years with 3 per cent. interest. No foreigner or rebel will be entitled to benefit under this clause."

After he had concluded reading the peace agreement, Mr. Balfour proceeded:

"There are certain important points not dealt with in the document I have just read, and which was signed on Saturday night. Therefore it may be convenient if I read a dispatch from Lord Kitchener to the Secretary of State for War, dated May 30, as follows:

"'After handing the Boer delegates a copy of the draft of the agreement I read them a statement and gave them a copy of it, as follows:

"'"His Majesty's Government must place on record that the treatment of the Cape and Natal colonists who have been in rebellion, and who now surrender, will, if they return to their colonies, be determined by the Colonial Courts and in accordance with the laws of the colonies, and any British subjects who have joined the enemy will be liable to trial under the law of that part of the British Empire to which they belong.

"'"His Majesty's Government are informed by the Cape Government that their views regarding the terms to be granted to British subjects in Cape Colony, now in the field, or who have surrendered or been captured since April 12, 1901, are as follows:

"'"With regard to the rank and file, they should all, after surrender and giving up their arms, sign a document before the resident magistrate of the district in which they surrender acknowledging themselves guilty of high treason, and the punishment to be accorded them, provided they are not guilty of murder or acts contrary to the usages of civilized warfare, shall be that they are not entitled, for life, to be registered as voters, or vote in any parliamentary or provincial Council or municipal election.

"'"With reference to Justices of the Peace, Field Cornets, and all others who held official positions under the Government of Cape Colony, or who have been occupying a position of authority, or who have held commands in the rebel or burgher forces, they shall be tried for high treason before the ordinary courts of the country, or such special courts as may hereafter be constituted, their punishment to be left to the discretion of such court, with the proviso that in no case shall the penalty of death be inflicted.

"'"The Natal Government are of the opinion that rebels should be dealt with according to the law of that colony."'

"These arrangements," concluded Mr. Balfour, "the Government have approved."

Sir Henry Campbell Bannerman, the Liberal leader, in behalf of the opposition, said unbounded satisfaction would be felt throughout the empire at the conclusion of peace. They were unanimous in admiration of their late enemies, now their friends and fellow-citizens, whose military qualities, tenacity of purpose, and self-sacrificing devotion to liberty and country, had won them the respect of the whole world, and, foremost of all, the respect of their opponents. Every member would offer congratulations to the King and to the country, on the thrice blessed restoration of peace.

Mr. Balfour, having announced that the Government would take an early opportunity of moving a vote of thanks to Lord Kitchener and the forces in South Africa, the members of the House of Commons returned to their ordinary avocations.

The tension was over, and when Mr. Balfour's statement was concluded every one seemed glad of the opportunity for a hearty laugh, caused by the Government leader's humorous quashing of the suggestion that the Commons adjourn in honor of peace. Then the House, in which even members could not find seats, was emptied, and diplomats, Indian Rajahs, in gorgeous robes; Peers and Peeresses, and Commoners and their guests trooped into the lobby, when general congratulations followed.

Various objections to the peace terms were expressed, but they did not appear to be very serious. The Irish viewpoint was that the Government has given up practically everything and that the regulations affecting the Cape rebels will be done away with, in consequence of the King's amnesty proclamation.

Mr. Choate did a lot of handshaking and took part in the general congratulations.

In the purlieus of Westminster large crowds waited long after it was seen that the day's session of the House of Commons was over, hoping for another chance to cheer some of the leaders.

June 3, 1902

NEW NATION BORN TO-MORROW

United South Africa to Come Into Being—Gen. Botha's Cabinet.

CAPE TOWN, May 30.—The first Cabinet of United South Africa is being formed by Gen. Louis Botha, who has himself taken the portfolios of Premier and Minister of Agriculture.

The other members of the Cabinet so far as selected are:

Gen. J. C. Smutz, Minister of the Interior, Mines, and Defense.

J. W. Sauer, Minister of Railways and Harbors.

Gen. J. B. M. Hertzog, Minister of Justice.

F. S. Malan, Minister of Education.

H. C. Hull, Minister of Finance.

United South Africa was formed recently by the Federation of Cape Colony, the Orange River Colony, Natal, and the Transvaal. Viscount Gladstone is the first Governor General. The union will come into operation to-morrow.

Gen. Louis Botha, the new Premier, was the Premier of the Transvaal. Gen. Smutz and Mr. Hull were respectively the Colonial Secretary and Treasurer of the Transvaal. Messrs. Sauer and Malan were respectively Commissioner of Public Works and Secretary of Agriculture in the Cape Colony Cabinet. Gen. Hertzog was Attorney General in the Ministry of the Orange River Colony.

The Union Parliament, the members of which will be elected immediately, will consist of a Senate and a House of Assembly. Cape Town will be the seat of the Legislature and Pretoria the seat of the Executive Government.

May 31, 1910

ASSAILING GERMAN AFRICAN COLONIES

German Southwest Africa Being Attacked from Sea and Land Sides.

TOGOLAND ALREADY LOST

East Africa Wireless Station Destroyed by British—Fighting in Kamerun.

Although, of course, overshadowed by the campaigns in Europe, events are occurring in Africa that, according to the British view, will contribute to the destruction of the German Empire.

The announcement by Gen. Botha at the opening session of the Union of South Africa Parliament on Sept. 9 cabled to New York that a military organization had been completed for offensive purposes in German Southwest Africa conveys but a vague idea of the real position. That colony is now being attacked from the sea and by two expeditionary forces operating on the land side, with, it is said, the certainty that—if this has not already occurred—it will be taken in the course of the next few days, or weeks at most. The recent unsuccessful attempt by a small party of Germans to invade British Bechuanaland and their abandonment of the coast towns of German Southwest Africa indicate the straits in which the local German forces are placed. They have already removed the guns intended for seaward defense from Luderitzbucht to Windhoek, where they have intrenched themselves with an enormous stock of provisions, and it was from that inland town that the sortie which met with disastrous results to the Kaiser's troops was made into Upington, Bechuanaland.

Pre-war maps show that Germany had four colonies in Africa, namely:

1. Togoland, on the Gold Coast.
2. The Colony of Kamerun, in the Gulf of Guinea, with a hinterland extending inland to French Equatorial Africa.
3. German East Africa, which lies immediately south of the equator, and,
4. German Southwest Africa, which is hemmed in on three sides, respectively, by Portuguese West Africa, Bechuanaland, and the Cape Colony, while the only harbor of importance on the coast of the vast areas (322,000 square miles) of that German possession—Walfisch Bay—is owned by the British.

Of these colonies, Togoland has already been taken as the consequence of a combined British and French attack by sea and land. The capture of this territory is of great value, as, apart from the fact that it was the only one of the German colonies that did not encroach on imperial revenues, it was the chief station of a German over-sea wireless system, which will probably soon be converted from the Teutonic Telefunken to that of the better-known Marconi.

The Kamerun colony, where some desultory fighting has taken place, is entirely destitue of harbor accommodation or navigable rivers, and, although possessing a rich soil, the climate is of a deadly character. It is, moreover, surrounded by British, French, and Belgian territory, which would render its seizure and occupation by the Allies a comparatively easy task.

German Southwest Africa is of vastly greater importance from many points of view, and it has always been a sore point with British South Africans that Germany was ever allowed by Great Britain to annex the territory, which, by its geographical situation, should, it is asserted, have formed part of the Cape Colony. It is developing great mineral and agricultural industries, and during 1913 produced diamonds to the value of more than $10,000,000.

The white population of German Southwest Africa is slightly under 15,000, of whom about 2,000 are South African Boers, loyal to the British Empire, and a military force of approximately 3,000 men, including (before the war) quite a number of British colonists who were ex-members of the Cape Mounted Rifles when that famous corps assisted the German authorities to quell a native rising. The natives number some 80,000.

In German East Africa British cruisers have destroyed the powerful wireless station at Dar-es-Salam, thus cutting off Germany's imperial communications and practically taking possession of the only German port of importance on the east coast of Africa, the retention of which would give Great Britain an exclusive control—subject to the Protuguese ports of Beira and Delagoa Bay—over the Eastern and Western trade routes of South Africa. On the other hand, Portugal, England's ancient ally, is at present co-operating with the British forces in East Africa.

South Africa has probably the most effective military organization of all the British oversea dominions. Not only are there the fighting forces of the Government of the union but also the citizen forces, consisting, to a great extent, of veterans of South African wars, and it is due to that combination, available for offensive as well as defensive operations, that the British Government has been able to release the imperial garrison of about 5,000 men for service in Europe.

The cabled announcement of the publication by the London War Office Press Bureau of the correspondence relating to the resignation of Gen. Beyers from the Commandant Generalship of the South African Union Citizen Army, is not regarded as an indication that any considerable number of Boers in South Africa are out of sympathy with their fellow-British subjects in regard to the war, its necessity, or its justice. On the contrary, Gen. Beyers is believed to be the only representative Boer who is not heart and soul with the otherwise general unanimity of spirit prevailing in South Africa. Even Gen. Hertzog, the leader of the small recalcitrant Dutch Party in the Union Parliament, has, with his followers, become an active supporter of the Government, while one of the Transvaal's former most powerful Boer commanders, Gen. Schalk Burger, is an active member of the Union Council of Defense, and—with Gen. Beyers—took part in the preparation of the plans for the invasion of German Southwest Africa.

Looking for the moving causes of the sudden change on the part of Gen. Beyers, who, a few days after the outbreak of war, declared that "Briton and Boer are one, with identical interests and national aspirations," it is recalled that in 1912 Gen. Beyers visited Europe to study military questions for the purpose of preparing a scheme of defense partly intrusted to him by the Union Government. During that visit he was present at a review at Potsdam, subsequently accompanying the Kaiser to the Swiss manoeuvres, and, on his return, proudly distributed the snapshots of himself taken with the Kaiser. About this time Gen. Beyers gave an interview to the publication South Africa, which said:

"The Kaiser, who had a long conversation with Gen. Beyers in English, expressed his admiration of the work done under the Swiss system of national training, upon which, by the way, the South African scheme of defense is largely based. The German Emperor also intimated to Gen. Beyers his gratification that South Africans were now so happily developing their country under responsible Government."

Gen. Smuts, the Union Minister of Defense, said in his reply to Gen. Beyers that it was more than strange that Gen. Beyers should, at this moment, take exception to the execution of operations which he himself largely assisted to plan. It was also not without significance that, having undertaken the formation of a South African Citizen Army composed almost equally of Boers and British, Gen. Beyers should at this time urge that Great Britain had been guilty of acts of barbarity during the last war in South Africa. Gen. Smuts asserts that there is not a particle of truth in the statement.

The invasion and capture of German Southwest Africa is likely to take place notwithstanding Gen. Beyers, and will be followed by a similar move in regard to the other German African colonies.

September 27, 1914

KAMERUN CHIEF EXECUTED.

Accused of Fomenting a Native Revolt Against the Germans.

LONDON, Oct. 22.—A dispatch to the Exchange Telegraph Company from The Hague says that Magna Bell, the native chief of the German Colony of Kamerun, has been executed because he attempted to foment among the natives a rebellion against Germany.

The announcement is credited by the correspondent to Herr Ebermayor, German Governor of Kamerun.

Kamerun, formerly known as the Cameroons, is a German Colony of Western Equatorial Africa on the Bight of Biafra, with a coast line of 200 miles. It was annexed in 1884. Nigeria is on the north and the French Congo on the south and west.

The colony has a population of 3,500,000, of whom about 1,400 are whites. Its area is 191,000 square miles. It is administered by an Imperial Governor, who resides at the capital, Buea, and a Government Council of three.

As in the case of most of the German colonies, Kamerun is not self-supporting. An annual grant of over $500,000 is given to it, and the exports are a good deal less than the imports.

Disaffection in other German possessions in Africa has recently been reported

October 23, 1914

FRENCH VICTORY IN CONGO.

Drive Germans from Most of the Territory Lost in 1911.

BORDEAUX, Tuesdoy, Nov. 10, (via Paris.)—It is officially announced that in the region of the Sanga River, in the Congo, French troops, commanded by Gen. Aymerich, drove the Germans from the larger part of the territory lost in the 1911 convention. The military post of Nzimou was retaken after two days' heavy fighting on Oct. 29.

The Belgian Congo put at the disposition of the French forces the steamer Luxemberg and 150 soldiers. On Oct. 22 a column commanded by Col. Hutin captured Nola and made prisoners of several officers and many sharpshooters. Four quick-firing cannon and munitions were also taken.

The operation, it is stated, assures to the French the possession of the town of Basanga.

November 10, 1914

"AFRICAN WAR A BLOT."

German Society Condemns Attacks on Colonies.

The German Colonial Society has issued a protest to the neutral world concerning what it terms the "inhuman procedure of the English and French in the German colonies." The protest is signed by the Duke of Mecklenburg, President of the society, and states that the actions of the British and French are destroying the civilizing work of Europeans in Africa and that this procedure constitutes "a mockery of the law of nations and definite international agreements." The protest was issued here yesterday by the German Information Service, under the caption "Allies' African War a Blot on History."

The protest contends that no military interests necessitated the extension of the war to the German colonies in Africa, which it says were not protected against European attack. The destruction of German colonizing work in Africa, it is added, "can have no bearing whatever on the final issue of the world war."

"Before the eyes of natives," the protest reads, "white men, with the aid of blacks, now engage in the slaughter of white men. The effect of that unhappy racial encounter can be only fatal to the future colonizing work of every European nation in Africa."

It is charged that the French transported Germans from Togo and the Cameroons to French Dahomey and thence 300 miles further inland, compelling the captives to walk all the way, where the Germans were compelled to do manual work under the supervision of black men. In Southwestern Africa it is charged that the British conveyed German captives to concentration camps in South Africa, previously having confiscated privately owned diamond fields.

"It is a criminal offense," the protest concludes, "against the moral sentiments of our age that from the beginning of the war until now the English have forcibly prohibited any exchange of news between the African colonists and their families at home. Such cold blooded prohibition tears the family tie asunder, deprives the separated parties of every hope and solace and abandons them to endless anxiety and agony about the fate of their beloved ones.

"These facts cannot be disputed. The English and French in their procedure against the German colonies in Africa have trampled on the sanctity of international obligations which they have guaranteed. Not only in our colonies, but all over the world, wherever German economic enterprise was manifested, the English and French have seized private property, destroyed it and expelled the Germans in order to ruin systematically German labor and German methods and substitute their own. Instances of this are the procedure of the French in Morocco, of the English in Hongkong, Ceylon, and other British colonies."

March 20, 1915

MAKING HISTORY IN THE DARK.

Almost unnoticed, while our eyes have been fixed on Europe, a struggle is going on which will take a place in history along with the contest of the French and English for the possession of the North American Continent in the eighteenth century; and the place of General BOTHA among the world's famous men may be beside that of JAMES WOLFE. That which engrosses the attention of contemporaries is not always that which interests the historian most. In the Seven Years' War no one talked, and only statesmen thought, of what was going on in the forests of America; even the statesmen did not know that some day a great nation would think of it, not as the Seven Years' War, but as the French and Indian War, and that the doings of such Generals as BRADDOCK with small commands on little missions in a far-off wilderness would have a place in history. Still less could they imagine that colonial militiamen whose names they did not know, such as Major WASHINGTON of Virginia, would become an object of interest through the future centuries.

But some day great nations that now are colonies will trace through the history of 1914 the now unnoticed battles in Africa, and Europe and America will find interest in them, too. Historians will search through the publications of today for comment on these battles and record their inability to find it with the same amusement as that with which now they hunt for European comment on the American contests that decided the future of another continent. BOTHA's capture of Windhoek the other day may rank as one of the world's gre[illegible] events.

Africa is [illegible] last of the continents to be Europeanized, and her significant modern history began in our own times. Her partition was accomplished in a quarter of a century; it began about 1875. Prior to that time Britain, France, and Portugal alone had any large interests there; but when Germany entered on an expansion policy, South America being barred to her by the Monroe Doctrine, she turned her attention to this last continent. LEOPOLD of Belgium precipitated the struggle by creating the Belgian Congo in 1876 and the Franco-British agreements of 1898 and 1906 marked its end as a peaceful contest. Today, exclusive of Egypt, Great Britain's African possessions amount to 2,101,411 square miles; France's, 3,866,950; Germany's, 910,150; Italy's, including Tripoli, 600,000; Portugal's, 787,500; Belgium's, 900,000; Spain's, 79,800. There are only three separate States left, Liberia, Abyssinia, and Morocco, and the total independent area is only 613,000 square miles.

The development of Africa as a site for future nations and civilizations has been going on rapidly. The war is to decide its future; and that future is being decided with great speed. Germany is being excluded. The war is continental in size. British soldiers are fighting in Nigeria and Cameroon, far up on the west coast, British and German East Africa are locked in a struggle to the death on the east coast, and down in the south BOTHA is making the continent his own to the southern border of Angola, the Portuguese province. This is why Portugal made that declaration, early in the war, that her old alliance with England was still in force. It was commented on with tolerant amusement; what did Portugal expect to do? What Portugal expected to do was to keep the last remains of her old empire; it is perhaps not doing her an injustice to suspect that she decided in her own mind which side was likely to be the winner and declared herself on that side. Windhoek is the capital of German Southwest Africa, which will change its name when the Germans are swept out of the continent and Africa becomes English and French.

In a letter from a soldier about a bloody struggle in which he had taken part in some unknown and desolate region in Nigeria there was a complaint that he and his comrades were dying unseen and unheard; that there was not even glory, for the very names of the battlefields would never get to Europe. Some day, however, when the young nations of Africa are grown to full size, those battlefields will be searched out, and the descendants of the participants will wear their names as proudly as our Colonial Dames wear the names of theirs. When the war is over, unless all signs fail, the German dream of expansion will be ended, and France and Great Britain will face the question whether there is to be another Anglo-Saxon continent.

May 28, 1915

GERMANS' SURRENDER TO BOTHA COMPLETE

Property of Protectorate Government and All War Materials to be Transferred.

PRETORIA, July 10.—The supplementary terms of surrender signed by Dr. Seitz, the Imperial Governor of German Southwest Africa, provide for the transfer to the Union of South Africa of the entire property of the Protectorate Government as well as all war material and all the military forces.

The choice of abode of the German officers on parole is subject to the concurrence of the Union of South Africa Government.

July 11, 1915

GERMAN EAST AFRICA FINALLY CONQUERED

Official Announcement Made in London That Territory Is Cleared of Foe.

KAISER'S LAST COLONY

Is 180,000 Square Miles Larger Than His Empire in Europe—History of the Campaign.

LONDON, Dec. 3.—"East Africa has been completely cleared of the enemy."

This official announcement was made tonight.

The text of the announcement reads:

Telegraphing under date of Dec. 1, General Vandeventer (commander of the military forces in East Africa) has reported that reconnoissances have definitely established that German East Africa is completely cleared of the enemy. Thus the whole of the German overseas possessions have passed into our hands and those of our Belgian allies. Only a small German force now remains in being. This has taken refuge in adjoining Portuguese territory, and measures are being taken to deal with it.

With the surrender or dispersal of the few surviving forces in East Africa the German Empire loses the last, largest, and most valuable of its overseas possessions. Of these possessions, having a total area of 1,027,820 square miles, German East Africa accounts for 384,180 square miles; of their total population of 25,000 whites and 15,000,000 natives, German East Africa accounts for 15,000 whites and 8,000,000 natives.

The last of Germany's foreign dependencies to fall to the Allies is 180,000 square miles larger than the empire in Europe. Its revenues in 1911 were $4,127,500, and it expenditures were $5,942,500; its imports amounted to $15,000,000, and its exports to $9,750,000. Rich mineral mines, the exact nature of which is not yet known, exist in the territory, whose partly developed wealth consists so far of rubber, copra, ivory, coffee, and wax. Its potential wealth is estimated in billions. In 1912, 1,034 vessels, totaling 1,913,743 tons, entered the various ports, whose chief connections before the war were only with Zanzibar and Germany.

Two months before the beginning of the war a railroad more than 700 miles long was completed through the centre of the possession from the Indian Ocean to Lake Tanganyika, where it was destined to tap the limitless resources of the Belgian Congo and Central Africa generally, which it brings weeks nearer to the European markets. This road now will certainly connect with the All-British Cape-to-Cairo Railroad, in course of rapid construction, and which Germany had refused to permit to pass through her colony.

Other Colonies Germany Lost.

How and when Germany lost her other dependencies in this war, together with some data concerning their characteristics, is told as follows:

Togland, captured by a Franco-British force Aug. 26, 1914; area, 33,700 square miles. In 1914 estimated revenue $875,000 and expenditures $1,045,000. In 1913 imports were valued at 10,000,000 marks and exports at 9,100,000 marks.

German Samoa, captured by a New Zealand expedition Aug. 30, 1914; area 1,000 square miles, (Savali and Upolu.) In 1914 estimated revenue $2,975,000 and expenditures $3,450,000. In 1913 imports valued at 5,700,000 marks and exports at 5,300,000 marks.

German New Guinea, consisting of Kaiser Wilhelm's Land, (70,000 square miles;) Bismarck Archipelago, (20,000 square miles,) captured by an Australian expedition Sept. 11, 1914. Imports 5,872,000 marks and exports 5,041,000.

Caroline, Solomon, Marshall Islands, captured by the Japenese Oct. 7, 1914; area 10,500 square miles. Revenue estimated at $525,000 and expenditures at $957,500

Kiao-Chau, surrendered to a Japanese and British force, former taking precedence, Nov. 7, 1914; area 200 square miles. Revenue for 1914 estimated at 8,980,000 marks and expenditures at 18,410,000. In 1912 imports valued at 121,254,000 marks, and exports at 10,040,000.

German Southwest Africa was captured by General Botha with the Union of South Africa troops, July 9, 1915; area, 322,450 square miles. In 1914, estimated revenue, $5,875,000, and expenditure, $10,085,000. In 1913, imports valued at 43,400,000 marks, and exports at 70,300,000 marks.

The Kamerun was completely occupied by a Franco-British force Feb. 18, 1916; area, 300,000 square miles. In 1914, estimated revenue, $2,827,500, and expenditure, $4,315,000. In 1913, imports valued at 34,000,000 marks, and exports at 29,100,000 marks.

No German foreign dependency, not even German Southwest Africa, has revealed such a thorough preparation for the great war as German East Africa. Although the white force consisted of only three regiments, there had been organized, armed, and drilled a native Arab and negro force of 50,000 under white officers. Over 100 Krupp 77 millimeter field pieces had been imported, together with several hundred machine guns and quantities of barbed wire, engineering implements, and munitions of all sorts. Finally, a great wireless station had been erected in the Kilimanjaro, which, via the station at Togoland, on the other side of the continent, could communicate with Berlin.

So elaborate had been the German preparations that the Allies could do little during the first year of the war. With the conquest of German Southwest Africa completed, however, the army of the Union of South Africa was released and preparations were made to reduce the vast territory by investing its most populous and civilized regions.

To Generals Botha and Smuts, assisted by British, Belgian, and Portugese Staff officers, is due the comprehensive plan of offense which has finally been crowned with victory. The army of the Union of South Africa was sent by water from Cape Town to Mombasa, on the British East African coast, the terminus of the railway which runs southeast almost parallel with the frontier, from Port Florence on Victoria Nyanza. These troops, who numbered 25,000 white veterans, were under the command of General Jan Christian Smuts.

In the middle of December, 1916, General Sir Horace Smith-Dorrien, relieved in the previous July by his own request from the command of one of the six British armies under Sir John French in Flanders, was sent out to take supreme command. Ill-health, however, soon compelled him to give up, and the chief command was again offered to General Smuts, who accepted it, with the rank of Temporary Lieutenant General.

General Smuts, born in 1870, was educated at Stellenbosch and Christ's College, Cambridge. By profession he is a lawyer; as one of the Boer leaders against the British in 1890 he revealed great military talent, which was later shown in the manner he helped to put down the Boer rebellion in the Transvaal and in the victorious campaign under General Botha in German Southwest Africa. He was then Minister of Defense in the Union and Colonial Secretary to the Transvaal.

Sir Horace had done little beyond consolidating his forces along the northern frontier and attempting to drive the Germans from the positions hey had actually secured in British territory near the Port Florence-Mombasa Railway, in the vicinity of Moshi.

The plans finally put into execution by General Smuts consisted of three columns operated by himself from the Port Florence-Mombasa Railway, (1,) against Kondoa Irangi, a highway junction 85 miles north of the Central Railway; (2) against Wilhelmstal and the Moshi-Tanga Railway, and (3) against the Nguru Hills section, between Kondoa Irangi and the coast.

The ultimate objective of these columns was to be the Central Railway. Meanwhile, a Belgian column under General Tombeur was to operate southeast from the Belgian Congo and gain possession of the western end of the Central Railway, and later form a junction with a column under General Northey, which would advance from Rhodesia northward, recovering the northern shores of Lake Nyasa and covering the eastern shores of Lake Tanganyika and the territory between them. The Portuguese were to hold the line of the Rovuma River in the southeast. The fleet was to assist the land forces in capturing the coast towns.

These plans have been carried out, integrally, though their execution took far longer than was ever dreamed of and involved heavy losses in men from fever and dysentery. Smuts himself, a few months ago, when the campaign had been virtually won and the Germans split up into guerrilla bands, was stricken down with fever and had to return to the Cape. He is now a member of the War Council in London.

December 4, 1917

ASK FOR GERMAN COLONIES.

Negroes Want Land Captured in Africa Turned Over to Natives.

That the captured German colonies in Africa be turned over to the natives and that educated negroes be placed in leadership there, is one of the requests that the negroes of New York as represented by the Universal Negro Improvement Association and African Communities League, will make to this Government and to the Allies. These requests were contained in a resolution adopted at a meeting of 5,000 negroes in the Palace Casino in 135th Street, near Madison Avenue, yesterday.

The meeting was presided over by Marcus Garvey, head of the League and representatives of the race made speeches. The resolution set forth that it would only be through the granting to the negro his rights and the rights of all weaker peoples at the Peace Conference that future wars would be obviated. It was also asked that negroes be permitted to travel and to reside in any part of the world; that they be permitted the same educational facilities as Europeans; that all segregative and proscriptive ordinances against negroes be repealed and that they be given political, industrial and social equality.

November 11, 1918

SAYS COLONIES FAVOR BRITAIN

Injustice to Give Them to Any Other Power, Long Declares.

LONDON, Dec. 5.—Natives of Germany's colonies want to come under British rule, said Walter Hume Long, Secretary of State for the Colonies, speaking at Westminster tonight.

"Our representatives at the Peace Conference should see that the case for our retention of those colonies is put forward in full strength," he said. "It will be a gross injustice to our great dominions to tell them that these colonies, which, in a large measure, they conquered by their blood and valor, are to pass under the control of anybody but the empire to which they belong."

December 7, 1918

Definite Accord Is Reached on German Colonies; Conquered Regions To Be Detached From Turkey

PARIS, Feb. 1, (Associated Press.)—The accord reached by the council of the great powers concerning the disposal of the German colonies and the occupied regions of Turkey in Asia is much more definite than was generally supposed. In addition to acceptance in principle of the American plan of mandatories, the plan embraces the following main features:

The allied and associated powers are agreed that the German colonies shall not be returned to Germany, owing, primarily, to mismanagement, cruelty, and the use of these colonies as submarine bases.

The conquered regions of Armenia, Syria, Mesopotamia, Palestine, and Arabia are to be detached from the Turkish Empire.

Provision is made whereby the well-being and development of backward colonial regions are regarded as the sacred trust of civilization, over which the League of Nations exercises supervisory care. The administration or tutelage of these regions would be intrusted to the more advanced nations, who would act as mandatories in behalf of the League of Nations.

These mandatories would not be uniform, but vary according to the degree of development of the colonial region and its approach to the stage of self-government. The mandates in Palestine, Syria, and other portions of Turkey, where well-developed civilization exists, would be comparatively light and would probably permit of provisional recognition of the independence of these communities.

On the other hand, colonies like those in Central Africa would require a mandatory with large powers of administration, responsible for the suppression of slave trade, liquor, ammunition and arms traffic, and the prevention of exercise of military authority on the part of the natives except for native police purposes.

Other colonies and localities, such as those in German Southwest Africa and some of the South Pacific islands, have such sparse and scattered populations and are so separated from other communities that the laws of the mandatory country would probably prevail in these regions.

The mandatories would report at stated intervals to the League of Nations concerning the manner in which a colony was being administered.

The foregoing general outline indicates on broad lines the terms whereby, it is stated, the conflicting views were finally reconciled and a common agreement was reached, acceptable to all the great and colonial powers.

February 2, 1919

SMUTS SPEAKS OF MANDATE

Tells South African Parliament of the Plan for Southwest Africa.

CAPE TOWN, Sept. 10, (via Montreal.) —The debate in the Assembly on the bill giving the Union of South Africa the mandate to administer German southwest Africa was opened today by Premier Smuts.

The Premier dwelt on the two great principles of the mandate: First, that there should be no military training of the natives, and, second, that equal opportunities should be given members of the League of Nations for trading in the mandated area.

General Smuts pointed out that safeguards would be introduced on behalf of the natives. He announced that the actual terms of the mandate had not yet been approved by the Supreme Council in Paris, but said it would be necessary for the Government to have provisional interim powers pending the passing of the act by Parliament.

September 15, 1919

FRANCE TO DECLARE AFRICAN MANDATES

New Regime in Cameroons and Togoland Will Be Set Up Without League Approval.

DELAY DUE TO OUR NOTE

Council Had Given Permission to Powers to Go Ahead Within Scope of B Mandates.

Special Cable to THE NEW YORK TIMES.

PARIS, March 24.—The French Government has just taken rather remarkable action with regard to the Cameroons and Togoland, former German colonies in Africa assigned to France under Class B mandates. Because of the recent note from the United States Government to the Council of the League final action by the Council upon Class B mandates was postponed until May or June. However, M. Sarraut, the French Minister for the colonies, has drafted a scheme of administration for the Cameroons and Togoland and it is announced that the plan will be published in the official journal as a decree tomorrow morning, which is the French method of putting laws into effect.

It certainly remains that the Council of the League at the session to which it has invited an American representative may review the administrative plan, but it seems worth while to remark in speculating upon changes that the action of the Council is by unanimity.

In publishing this news the Temps tonight adds a note in which it says that the ministerial decree will "take into account the legitimate pre-occupations of the League of Nations." The reason advanced for the action by the French Government is that the two great countries involved will suffer permanent injury if left longer under wartime régime such as that which has been in force during the past six years.

The two territories will have practically the same constitutional standing. The Cameroons, which is the more important territory, will have what the Temps describes as "full financial and administrative autonomy." That presumably is to say that it will be independent of the Government of French equatorial Africa and its resources will be consecrated to its own development, except in certain cases when there is a question of common interest. The French Commissioner will be liable to be called upon to sit in the General Court of French equatorial Africa to ssure the political and economic liaison between the various districts.

At the French Foreign Ministry tonight it was stated that at the last Council meeting of the League permission was given to each mandatee to go ahead with the formation of administrative régimes within the scope of the terms of the B mandates as already drafted and presented to the Council, though not yet approved. That being so, there is nothing in the least irregular in the French proceedings. With the actual régime in operation it will, however, be somewhat difficult for the League to alter its terms when it does come up for approval, and should the new statute contain a provision for raising black troops or any other such controversal matter it will be certainly more difficult for the League to procure an alteration than if it had not been placed in the presence of what is virtually a fait accompli.

March 25, 1921

BELGIUM IS SEEKING AFRICAN MANDATE

Formally Objects to British Taking Control of German East Africa.

RECONSIDERATION ORDERED

Lloyd George Summons Milner for a New Conference on the Subject.

PARIS, May 9.—After Paul Hymans, head of the Belgian delegation, had discussed the rights of Belgium in German East Africa today, Premier Lloyd George telegraphed Viscount Milner, British Secretary for the Colonies, to come to Paris. On his arrival here questions concerning the East African mandate will be considered again.

The Belgian delegation yesterday issued a note relative to Great Britain being appointed mandatary for German East Africa, saying that it was "unable to believe that this action had been taken by the Council of Four."

"In view of Belgium's important military operations in Africa, her sacrifices to insure the conquest of German East Africa, and the fact that her situation has given her rights on that continent," the note says, "Belgium is unable to admit that German East Africa could be disposed of by agreements in which she has not participated."

The Belgian delegation called at American headquarters yesterday and made energetic representations regarding the mandate for German East Africa. The members also complained strongly of the omission from the peace treaty of a provision indemnifying Belgium for the 7,000,000,000 marks of German money forced into circulation in Belgium during the German occupation, which has depreciated to one-fourth of its face value.

May 10, 1919

Lloyd George Announces Mandates for Colonies

LONDON, March 15. — David Lloyd George, the British Prime Minister, in the House of Commons today announced that the following mandates had been allocated:

German East Africa to Great Britain and Belgium; German Southwest Africa to the Union of South Africa; German possessions in the Pacific Ocean south of the Equator, other than Samoa, to the commonwealth of Australia; Samoa to New Zealand, and the German Islands north of the Equator to Japan.

March 16, 1920

HUGE AFRICA AWAKENS TO A NEW DESTINY

The Prince of Wales Goes to Do Royal Advertising for Britain's Colonial Empire, as Quickening Development of a Continent Holding One-Fifth World's Area Has Great Commercial Significance

By P. W. WILSON.

ONCE again the Prince of Wales, accompanied this time by his brother, the Duke of Gloucester, has set forth as a pilgrim of publicity to promote the interests of the British Empire. Ostensibly, it is his object to shoot big game in Africa. In reality, there are issues involved in his tour of far-reaching significance, which have to be considered, not from the British standpoint alone but as they affect the world.

The greatest of Africa's pioneer statesmen was Cecil Rhodes. His ideal was, frankly, an "Africa all red"—that is, as British as India. It is a dream which, as a result of the war, has been brought at any rate within partial realization. In Egypt, Britain's influence is dominant and from Cairo to the Cape her territory is, in effect, continuous. With the Dominions declaring their autonomy, Africa has become the real Colonial Empire of Britain, and it is to advance the development of this empire that the Prince of Wales, an Ambassador of Commerce, is proceeding on his tour.

An International Concern.

But it would be a great mistake to regard the situation as specifically British. It affects mankind. As a continent, second only in size to Asia, Africa has arrived at an epoch in her destiny. Ancient Athens divided the world into Greek and Barbarian. Africa has been looked upon hitherto as a barbarian region, excluded by the curse of Ham from the amenities of civilization. In the words of Stanley, she was Darkest Africa. But what Africa has now to face is the dawn. Even the twilight is over. It is day.

There are published numerous books on Africa and, for the better understanding of the continent, there have been two elaborate inquiries initiated in the United States. The Phelp Stokes Fund organized a commission under Dr. Thomas Jesse Jones and more recently Harvard has sent out Dr. Raymond Leslie Buell. On the problem of Africa, racial and economic, these investigators have brought to bear a detached vision, the very negation of that buccaneering impulse which is expressed by a frank realist like Trader Horn. Africa has been despised in the past as the continent of slaves. Today she is included, at any rate prospectively, in the household of citizenship.

The Map Now Complete.

To begin with, the map of the continent, broadly speaking, is complete. Explorers like Livingstone have played their part and nothing remains of their task except the details, still to be filled in. As a field for adventure, Africa still remains herself. But to adventure there must now be added investment. The trustees for Africa's future are the administrator, the merchant, the scientist, the doctor, the educator and the missionary. It can hardly be doubted that the days of big game are numbered. As the bear and the wolf have disappeared from America, so is it likely that the lion and the giraffe, the hippopotamus and great snakes will be exterminated, slowly but surely, as man establishes his kingdom along the Congo, the Niger and the Zambesi.

There are those who argue that it would have been well for the native if his continent had been closed to the white man. Even today there is a determined attempt along the eastern seaboard from Cape Town in the south to Mombasa in the north to exclude the Asiatic, at any rate from British territory. It is an exclusion fiercely resented in India, and it is uncertain whether it can be sustained. For an isolated Africa is today unthinkable. The flash of a diamond on Fifth Avenue is a searchlight on the mines at Kimberley. The gold reserve of the world is guarded by nature in her volcanic vaults on the Rand at Johannesburg. Wash the hands and the skin is cleansed by the vegetable oils of Angora. A cup of cocoa owes its fragrance to the plantations of S. Thomé and Principe. It is from

Africa that rubber has been derived and Africa grows cotton, breeds cattle and harvests cereals. Her manufactures may be negligible, but her raw materials, actual and potential, are to be included among the dominant economic factors that contribute to the wealth of mankind. So far from separating Africa from the world as a whole, fate will elaborate the contacts already effected. Coffee grown on the shores of Lake Victoria Nyanza will rival, so it is predicted, the coffee of Brazil. So with a score of other products.

The trade of Africa is rapidly increasing. The exports, mainly oversea, are about $1,250,000,000 a year, while the imports are $1,440,000,000, an excess of imports which indicates new investment in the continent. Of this commerce, inward and outward, three-quarters is attributable to areas in Africa classified as British. The share of the United States is, at the moment, less than a tenth of the whole, but is increasing, as shown by these figures:

United States.	1925.	1926.
Imports from Africa	$89,000,000	$101,000,000
Exports to Africa	92,000,000	96,000,000

The railways in Africa, all told, exceed 33,000 miles and construction is proceeding. More than half of this mileage is within the British sphere of influence. It is to be realized, of course, that a mile of railway in Africa does not represent the same capacity for traffic as a mile of highly developed double or quadruple track in a country like the United States.

Vastness of the Continent.

The magnitude of Africa has yet to be appreciated. This vast and varied region extends from the Mediterranean in the north, a distance of 7,000 miles, to the latitude of Tasmania in the south. Not long ago that distance was traversed for the first time by a party, including a woman, Mrs. Treatt, in automobiles. We may thus assume that Africa, like Arabia, will yield her deserts to the motor car and the airplane. But it was the dream of Cecil Rhodes, the real founder of African democracy, that a railway be constructed from Cairo to the Cape.

It is a dream about to become a reality. To the north that railway extends in the Sudan beyond Khartum. To the south it traverses Rhodesia. The remaining links lie through Tanganyika and Kenya; and the fact that Tanganyika is no longer German East Africa means that, as Rhodes desired, the whole railway will be under British control. With branches radiating like ribs to the Atlantic and Indian coasts, this Cape-to-Cairo Railway is the destined backbone of the continent, and through Palestine it will be linked with the railways of Asia and of Europe herself.

The land on this planet covers an area of 55,000,000 square miles. The area of Africa is no less than 11,500,000 square miles or more than one-fifth of the land area of the world. Africa is three times as big as Europe and half again as big as North America. The continent is nearly four times the size of the United States.

As yet the peoples of Africa, taken as a whole, have not been enumerated in a census, and in considering statistics of population we have to depend on estimates so diverse as to be obviously uncertain in their accuracy. The population of the world is put at 1,800,000,000. If we allow 150,000,000 for Africa—apparently a generous figure—it follows that, with one-fifth of the land on this planet, the continent is sustaining only one-twelfth of the people.

It is true that the Sahara Desert in the north and the much smaller Kalahari Desert in the south suffer from an undervegetation which man has been unable as yet to counteract. But, on the other hand, Africa contains no Arctic zone. She may have to endure heat, but she is immune from ice.

Indeed, we have here in the main a continent of highlands. Almost the whole of South Africa lies at an altitude of more than 2,000 feet above the sea, and these splendid plateaus sweep northward through Abyssinia. Yet we have the curious and significant fact that the very uplands where the white man is making his home have been only sparsely populated by the black man. The equatorial colonies to be visited by the Prince of Wales are, roughly, half the size of India. But whereas the population of India is 330,000,000, this African area supports only about 12,000,000. Here is an obvious under-development, nor is its explanation merely climatic.

We need to examine the human factor. It is true that Africa includes many races. But the body of Africa is black. Of her people at least 100,000,000 are of negro blood. It is the negro who has made Africa what she is or, as some would put it, failed to make Africa what she should be. As it has been said, the African negro has founded no stone city, built no ship, produced no literature and suggested no creed.

The Mediterranean Minority.

The minority in Africa consists mainly of Semites and Hamidians. But it is along the shores of the Mediterranean that they have their home. On the one hand, they occupy provinces like Egypt and Tripoli, which in other days belonged to the Roman Empire—Morocco being geologically a continuation of Spain. On the other hand, they have been cut off hitherto from the real and essential Africa which we are here considering. The route, let us say, from Algiers or Alexandria to Sierra Leone or Durban is not by land but by sea.

It should be added that a distinction is to be drawn between the negro who has and the negro who has not acquired an American background. Education and an infusion of white blood have transformed the negro of the New World into a new race. In Liberia we can see the difference between the African population and the governing class which migrated eastward when that experimental republic was founded.

The native African has his arts, his music and his virtues. But his social and industrial inactivity has had deplorable results. It may be that, in North America, the forests were too recklessly hewn down. In Africa the forests have had it too much their own way. The inevitable undervegetation of deserts like the Sahara and Kalahari is still supplemented by the overvegetation of scarcely penetrable jungles, covering immense areas within the tropics. Hence, in no small measure, the ill reputation of Africa for fever, sleeping sickness and other epidemics which have so gravely reduced and sometimes obliterated her peoples. It is now realized that these scourges are, in large measure, preventable. Just as yellow fever was eliminated from the Caribbean, so should this and other maladies disappear from the Congo, situated along a similar latitude. Exceptional mortality is seldom inevitable. It can be and, in Africa, it is being prevented.

There were other evils in Africa than disease. Organized under chiefs in villages, the natives—often lacking a wider organization—were a prey to inter-tribal war and slave raiding. If there had been no continent except Africa on this planet, these abuses would have prevented an advance along the path of progress. It was this pre-existent and internal traffic in human flesh and blood which, in due course, was extended overseas, not to America alone, but throughout the entire middle east of Asia.

Europe's Work in Africa.

Under these circumstances, the association of Africa with Europe has been by no means the calamity which sometimes we are apt to assume. Doubtless, exploiters of red rubber and cocoa have been and may be ruthless. The treatment of the natives, whether in compounds, as on the Rand and at Kimberley, or in reservations, or as forced laborers on public works and even private plantations has been subject to vigilant exposure. But the broad fact is that, taking Africa as a whole, the blacks, unlike the Maoris in New Zealand and other Polynesians, are increasing in numbers. There is no question of these vigorous races dying out. On the contrary, their sal-

Photograph by Ewing Galloway.

A Model Sanitary Village for Negro Copper Miners in Belgian Congo.

vation from bloodshed and disease has already enhanced their vitality. By suppressing the slave trade, by introducing modern medicine and by instituting the rudiments of what is already an influential education, the white man is producing a very different race of black men.

It is a situation by no means devoid of difficulty. With the blacks increasing in numbers and in mental capacity, the whites remain a small minority. In the United States there are ten whites to one black. In Africa there are fifty blacks to one white. Indeed, even this is an understatement of the case. For where do the 3,000,000 European whites live? One million of them are to be found in the extreme north. A further 1,500,000 are gathered in the extreme south. Of the others, most live near or on the coast. In mid-Africa the European whites are a mere handful of individuals, surrounded by multitudes of natives, and their security depends on the support of Europe behind them. Today the whole of Africa is under foreign sovereignty except Abyssinia with her 10,000,000 people and Liberia with a population of not more than 2,000,000.

If this political structure is still haphazard, it is no wonder. In the main, it is the creation of only forty years. In the early '80s European sovereignty was limited to a fringe of settlements, still clinging to the seaboard—Cape Colony, Lagos and the rest. As a continent, Africa consisted of a vast and largely unknown hinterland.

Today the political map of Africa covers the entire continent. Every foot of the soil is owned by somebody. The two paramount powers are France and Britain, each of them governing about 50,000,000 people and holding about one-third of the continent. Under the French flag we find almost the whole of the northwestern territory, including the Sahara, but also including Morocco, Algeria and Tunis. With Madagascar in her hands France is stronger in Africa than ever she was in America or India.

Britain holds, broadly, the east of the continent, with an isolated Nigeria, Gold Coast and Sierra Leone to the west. It is a vast territory and, what is more important, mainly continuous.

Three other powers exercise an African sovereignty—Belgium on the Congo, Portugal in Mozambique to the east and Angola and Guinea to the west; and, last but not least, Italy. Her possessions are strategic. Somaliland hugs the frontier of Abyssinia and over this ancient kingdom Italy has endeavored to impose a protectorate. At the Battle of Adowa in 1896 the Abyssinians were able to defeat this claim and assert their independence.

On the other hand, Italy was able in 1912 to seize Tripoli, now called Libya, and this province makes her the neighbor of Britain in Egypt and France in Tunis, where many Italians reside. It is admitted that Italy desires to extend her North African sovereignty westward along a coast that directly confronts her own.

Arbitrary Partitions.

If, then, the map of Africa is now highly colored—red for British territory, green for French, and so on—it is, for this reason, deceptive to the mind. Countries like Egypt and Abyssinia embody a historical tradition. But there is no pretense that such a tradition supports the British in Tanganyika or the French on the shores of Lake Chad. These occupations may fairly be described as accidental.

The Continent has been subjected by Europe to a partition, at once arbitrary and artificial. Except in treaties, the frontiers have no existence. By a stroke of the pen the German colonies in Africa were transferred to France, Britain and Belgium. By a similar stroke of the pen they could be returned to Germany. Nor has there been audible one whisper of comment from the peoples whose sovereignty has been thus changed. Africa has acquiesced not only in the rule of Europe but in the rule of a disruptured Europe, whether the rule be good or bad.

This, however, is a situation that cannot long continue. What has now to be faced is the Africa not of diplomatic fiction but of ethnic fact—an Africa neither British nor French nor Belgian nor Portuguese, but African—an Africa in whose well-being, in whose resources, mankind as a whole is intimately concerned. Africa is not really divided. She is and always will be one of the world's great unities, and for Africa the world is responsible.

That growing sense of responsibility has been embodied in a series of historic treaties. The first of them was signed at Berlin in February, 1885. To this treaty the United States is a party and its object was "the development of trade and civilization in Africa, the free navigation of the rivers Congo, Niger, &c., the suppression of the slave trade by sea and land, the occupation of territory on the African coasts," &c. Out of that treaty there arose the Congo Free State, a disgrace under King Leopold of Belgium, but reorganized under King Albert.

In 1890 a second treaty, to which once more the United States was a party, was signed at Brussels, its object being a more rigorous suppression of the slave trade, and in 1919, after the war, the collective responsibility of civilization for Africa was yet again emphasized. The transferred German colonies are held by Great Britain, France and South Africa under the direct mandate of the League of Nations as defined in Article XXII of the Covenant. This clause is the Magna Carta of "peoples not yet able to stand by themselves under the strenuous conditions of the modern world." A characteristic and operative paragraph may be quoted:

Mandate Responsibility.

"Other peoples, especially those of Central Africa, are at such a stage that the mandatory must be responsible for the administration of the territory under conditions which will guarantee freedom of conscience or religion, subject only to the maintenance of public order and morals, the prohibition of abuses such as the slave trade, the arms traffic and the liquor traffic, and the prevention of the establishment of fortifications or military and naval bases, and of military training of the natives for other than police purposes and the defense of territory, and will also secure equal opportunities for the trade and commerce of other members of the League."

The human issues affecting Africa are here clearly stated. First, we have an assertion of an equal right of all countries to develop trade in the occupied regions. Next, it is laid down that such trade must not include arms and liquor, which are calculated to militate against native interests. Thirdly, there is to be no slavery, and, fourthly, religion is to be freely permitted. In the Treaty of St. Germain, signed 1919, it is expressly stipulated that "missionaries shall have the right to enter into, and to travel and reside in, African territory with a view to prosecuting their calling."

The organized conscience of mankind refuses, then, to permit Africa to be treated as a sphere of exploitation where "there ain't no Ten Commandments." It is, however, idle to pretend that as yet the continent is a paradise. The employment of natives industrially in the mines and agriculturally on the plantations creates a new social situation. Even if there be no ill treatment, it may not contribute to well-being, nor need work be slavery in order to be a form of servitude.

A Color Bar Applied.

Under Prime Minister Herzog and against the warnings of General Smuts, South Africa has applied to the blacks a color bar. This means that the negro, however enterprising he may be, is excluded, merely because he is a negro, from skilled positions in industry, which are thus reserved for the whites. In Kenya the struggle is over land, the right of the native to an adequate reservation, and the protection of the native against implied compulsion to leave that reservation in order to work for the white man. It is fair to add that, as her native policy, Great Britain has adopted recently and in a formal manner the development of education, as the path to be pursued. If that policy be steadily persisted in, not by one suzerain power alone but by all, if the education be manual as well as mental and suited to African conditions, and if the native, so educated, is treated with industrial equity, Africa will become—so it is argued—not merely a producer of raw materials for the white man, but a market for the consumption of commodities which the white man has to sell.

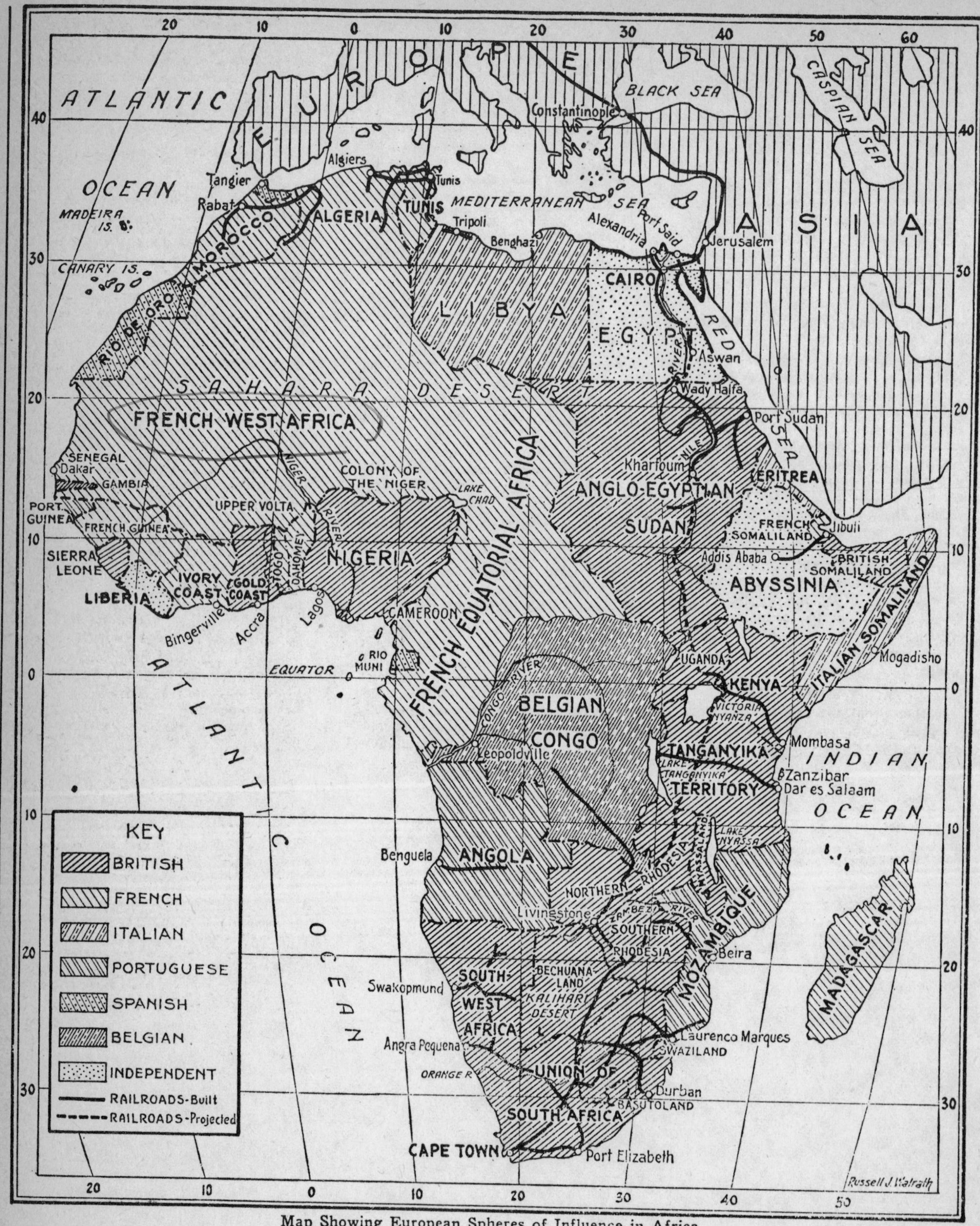

Map Showing European Spheres of Influence in Africa.

Flurry in League on Hottentot Revolt Over Dog Tax; Natives Killed by Bombs

By EDWIN L. JAMES.
Copyright, 1922, by The New York Times Company.
Special Cable to THE NEW YORK TIMES.

GENEVA, Sept. 8.—On the rostrum of the League of Nations Assembly today the first delegate from Haiti came to the defense of his colored brethren in Southwest Africa and tonight around the polyglot dinner tables of Geneva the discussion on whether a country holding a mandate under the League has a right to drop airplane bombs upon the Hottentot inhabitants of mandated territory when they refuse to pay a dog tax, drives into the shade even the talk about "Bob" Cecil's effort to make the naughty world behave.

The Bondels live down on the Fish River in what was a German colony before the world was made safe for democracy. The territory was mandated to the British Empire in general and South Africa in particular.

Just the other day the South African delegation reported that there had been an uprising, and said they would put a report about it in the League library. Almost every one forgot it until Delegate Bellegarde of Haiti, after a speech praising the League and surprising his hearers by unfashionably nice words about the United States, called attention of the Assembly to the "so-called punitive expedition against the Bondels, Hottentots, who are under the protection of the League of Nations."

"Taxes were levied on the dogs which guard the herds of these poor people," he continued, "that is the manner in which civilization first manifests itself among these savages. As the tax was very heavy the Bondels who would have had to sell their flocks to pay, refused to pay it. Then, without there being any act of rebellion, they were attacked with all the weapons of modern war, machine guns, cannon and airplanes.

"These natives, almost disarmed, were massacred and inasmuch as bombs cast from the air cannot chose their victims, women and children were killed in great numbers."

After the Assembly adjourned there was a general rush to the library to see the report. The Bondels were described as a quarrelsome people by nature. It was recounted that some years back the Germans chased out Jake Christian and Abe Morris, native leaders, who in 1919 went back and were permitted to stay. Jake wanted to be chief and the tribe wanted him but the mandate administrator named Tim Beukes and backed him up.

Then in 1921 the dog tax was levied at the rate of one pound sterling on one dog and a graded scale up to ten pounds on five dogs. The official reason given was that the natives used dogs to hunt and would not work. It seems the natives tried to some extent to raise the money to pay the taxes but found so much difficulty that they refused to pay.

In fighting at the end of May and the beginning of June, eighty or a hundred natives, including some women and children, were killed and Jake was put to flight. The report admits that airplane bombs were used.

The official record contains the sad story of a donkey which, after serving as motor power for Jake's lines of communications, was killed and eaten. * * *

Unfortunately for Jake's political prospects, there seems to be little chance of the mandate being taken from Great Britain, but the dog tax has been reduced 50 per cent.

September 9, 1922

FULL RIGHTS DENIED KENYA COLONY INDIANS

British Government Compromise Decision Expected to Cause Dissatisfactiin in India.

LONDON, July 24 (Associated Press).—In a Parliamentary paper issued tonight the Government communicates its decision on the long-disputed question of the status of Indians in Kenya Colony. The colony and protectorate were formerly known as the East Africa Protectorate.

The decision has been awaited with intense interest in India, as it is regarded as affording a test case governing the status of Indian immigrants in all parts of the British Empire. It is a frank compromise and is expected to be received with great dissatisfaction in India.

The Indians had claimed complete equality of treatment in all respects with both Europeans and natives, not only in the franchise question, but in the right of unrestricted freedom of entering or leaving the colony, the right to buy or sell land in any part of the colony on equal terms, the right to enter any branch of the civil service on equal terms, and no segregation.

The Government's memorandum at the outset says that Kenya is African territory and that the interests of the African natives must be paramount, and when these interests and the interests of immigrant races conflict the former shall prevail.

The essential points of the memorandum are:

That responsible self-government for the colony is out of the question; that the Indian demand for equal franchise cannot be granted, but that the Government is prepared to grant the Indians and Arabs representation on the Legislative Council through the communal system of election; that the elected members of the Council shall comprise five Indians, one Arab and eleven Europeans. This leaves the franchise unchanged as regards white settlers.

The policy of segregation as between Europeans and Asiatics in townships must be abandoned, but the existing practice of reserving agricultural land in the highlands for British and Europeans must be maintained. The Government undertakes temporarily to preserve an area in the lowlands to ascertain when demand exists for agricultural land on the part of the Indians.

The Government declares it cannot countenance racial discrimination with respect to British immigrants, and that some further control over immigration in the economic interest of the natives is required. The Governor of Kenya is instructed to investigate this matter.

Finally, the Government suggests that the whole question may be re-examined after a period of years, with a view to improving the position of the Indians.

July 25, 1923

LIGHT SWIFTLY COMING IN THE DARK CONTINENT

Journey Through East Africa Shows Schools Increasing and the Natives Eager for Education—British Praised for Civilizing a Benighted Land

THE author is President of the Slater and the Jeanes Funds, amounting to more than a million dollars each, devoted to the education of colored people in the South. He is also a member of the General Education Board founded by John D. Rockefeller. His recent visit to East Africa reveals educational progress in the Dark Continent that would amaze people of Livingstone's day.

By JAMES H. DILLARD.

WHETHER we are thinking of railroads or of schools, we must soon stop calling Africa the Dark Continent. This was evident when E. Alexander Powell in 1912 published his book entitled the "Last Frontier," and since then more miles of railroad have been built and more schools established. I traveled in East and South Africa more than 4,000 miles by rail, and I visited both mission and Government schools that seemed to be doing as good work as the ordinary schools of similar grade in America. The leading schools have courses in industrial branches and they are all feeling their way toward making their work count for thrift and better living conditions.

In Abyssinia the train from the coast up to Addis Abeba, the capital, does not run at night, so you spend two nights in hotels; but the trip is over a smooth track and is comfortable.

Educational progress is slow, but if the present intelligent ruler, Ras Taffari, can have his way there will be steady improvement. The Ras is a handsome man, in the thirties, and strikes one as interested in progressive movements and as a ruler who has the good of the people at heart. He seemed especially interested in agricultural improvement and was glad to talk of agricultural and educational conditions in Europe and America. He is now visiting in Europe.

In his reception hall there are photographs of President Wilson and President Harding. He spoke of his desire to come to America some day. He has taken great interest in, and has personally contributed to, the hospital which an American missionary, Dr. Lambie, is building in Addis Abeba.

Central Africa Accessible.

The main objective of the education commission of which I was a member was Kenya, Uganda and Tanganyika. When American tourists find out how easy and agreeable is the visit to these regions many will be going. You can take a boat from Marseilles to Mombasa and at Mombasa board a good train running through Kenya up to Nairobi or on to Kisumu, situated on the Gulf of Kavirondo, which is an arm of Victoria Nyanza.

At Kisumu you can almost step from the train to the deck of a delightful little steamer, with about a dozen staterooms and excellent meals, which takes you across the lake, 175 miles, to Entebbe and Kampala, in Uganda. Or you may take another steamer which will take you southward on a trip around the lake. In going up to Nairobi, if the traveler can get a view of Kilimanjaro, with its top of snow, which is just over the border in Tanganyika, that alone would justify the trip.

Such a tour would be an agreeable variation from the much-frequented Nile excursion. Of course, it is longer and would involve a bit more of preparation. The distance from Port Said to Mombasa is a little greater than from New York to Liverpool, and the journey by rail from Mombasa to Kismu covers 587 miles, but there are interesting stopping places both on the sea voyage and on the railroad journey.

A stop at Jibuti, which the French spell Djibouti, would be worth while, even if the visitor should spend his time in the town, contenting himself with short automobile excursions. There is a satisfactory hotel, with spacious rooms, broad verandas, a fine view out to sea and a fair share of refreshing breezes. As in many African towns, there are at least two distinct sections. In Jibuti, around the hotel, you are in a French town, but a five minutes' walk will bring you into a typical native quarter, with its circular huts, scanty clothing and lean camels.

Where Races Mingle.

There are three towns in Mombasa—English, Indian and native. Altogther it is much more of a city than Jibuti. The English Club is charming and the golf course is one of the most picturesque in the world. A drive in the late afternoon around this course, along the shore and then back up the bay to the Indian School will give many striking views and present on the way many contrasts of vegetation, from the huge baobab to a familiar rose; of costumes, from an English sport suit to a native loincloth, and of buildings, from the stately stone of the Standard Bank to the conelike hut of the native. It is hot during the day, and visitors must never venture out without the helmet, but in February I felt the heat there less than during several days in Washington and Richmond this July.

Going up from Mombasa the traveler bent on seeing Kilimanjaro may leave the main line at Voi and take a branch road to Moshi, which is at the foot of the mountain. But the chances are that he will get the view from other points without taking this extra trouble. A stop should certainly be made at Nairobi, the capital of Kenya Colony. Altogether I spent a month there and most agreeably. The altitude is something over 5,000 feet. Out in the sun in the middle of the day it is hot, but I do not recall a night when I did not sleep under a blanket.

There are two good hotels. When I sat the first evening after dinner in the lounge of the New Stanley, sipping coffee and listening to selections from "Faust," I hardly knew where I was; and when, a few days later, I was taken out to the handsome country club the wonder grew. The English population numbers about 3,000 and there are numerous "settlers" in the neighborhood, engaged mainly in the cultivation of coffee and sisal. So far as a stranger may judge, the social life is hospitable and delightful.

There are perhaps as many as 10,000 Indians in Nairobi and 12,000 natives. The Indians are merchants and clerks. The natives are laborers of various kinds. Many are working in the extensive shops of the railroad, and some are aspiring to clerkships. I saw twenty in a night school learning typewriting. These elements in the population are an interesting study, but the visitor will want to see other and far different sights from those in the town. Nor will he have far to go.

A Land of Sudden Contrasts.

There are good roads leading in several directions and American automobiles are to be seen everywhere. A drive of eighty miles northward toward Mount Kenya and the equator, into the heart of the Kikuyu country, will supply all the strange sights that the most curious may wish to see and bring you into regions of wild game and native life such as have been described and pictured in the many books that have been written about Africa. At the present stage of progress Africa is more than anything else the land of sudden and overwhelming contrasts.

Around the foothills of Mount Kenya, in the midst of rudest human life, there are dozens of mission and village schools into which the children are crowding, some walking as far as seven miles, and there are large churches built of grasses, reeds, poles and banana leaves which cannot contain the people in Sundays. In such a building I heard the service of the English Church and a sermon by a native preacher, all in the Swahili language, when the crowd filled every part of the building and left perhaps a third as many outside.

There are stops which may be made between Nairobi and Kisumu, especially in the region of the wonderful Rift Valley. At one station the train reaches an altitude of more than 8,000 feet. Even after the descent to Kisumu you are still 3,700 feet above sea level.

Before taking the steamer there we made trips northward to several mission schools. The largest of these is a mission of the English Church at Maseno, situated directly on the equator. As I stood watching a game of soccer played by the students in bare feet, the teacher of science in the school informed me that the equator ran through the football field. And yet I do not remember suffering from heat.

This is an excellent school. I was particularly struck with the good work of a large class in drawing and with the fine exhibition of drilling officered by native sub-teachers. It was at this school that I had the queer experience of speaking through two interpreters. The audience was composed about half and half of people from two tribes.

Across the lake in Uganda there are as great surprises as in Kenya. I heard that more than two thousand bicycles have recently been sold to natives. The steamer lands first at Entebbe, where the English Governor has his spacious and delightful residence, set in a park of great beauty with charming views over the lake. The next stop is at Kampala, the capital, where the "King" lives and the native Parliament sits. Three of us had the honor of addressing the Parliament, which is composed of about 200 chiefs.

We were introduced by the Prime Minister, who had a dignified and commanding presence. He has held office longer than the lifetime of the present King, and is recognized by every one, English as well as native, as a man of unusual ability. There seems to be entire harmony between the native Government and the English officials, who are the real Government and have learned to use wisely and well the native machinery. Efforts are being made through cooperations of Government, missionary and native influences for improvement in agriculture among the native workers. The main crop is cotton.

Kampala is the centre of both education and religion for Uganda. Here is the beginning of what will be a large Government school, and here are a large school of the English Church Missionary Society and two large schools of the White Fathers and the Mill Hill Mission, both Roman Catholic. In fact, throughout Uganda only two churches have missions, the English Church and the Roman Catholic Church.

The Cathedrals of these two churches, situated on commanding hills, are among the surprises of East Africa. Each of them, handsome structures of yellow brick and built by native labor, can hold from 5,000 to 6,000 worshipers and they are thronged at the Sunday services. Here you may see every grade and variety of the natives. You will see some sitting on the tiled floor in the native garbs, and others sitting in chairs and dressed like Europeans. Two girls sat in front of me with wrist watches and dressed as girls might be in Harlem.

Here the English service was in the Luganda language. The hymns were sung and the responses given with great heartiness. English is being learned in the upper schools, and in some of the higher classes you may speak in English and be understood. I may say here that two months later in passing rapidly through some of the higher native schools in South Africa I found that English was generally understood. It will not be many years before it will be so in the English regions of East Africa.

A fact that strikes the visitor in East Africa is the number of nations or tribes having different languages and customs and looks. There are perhaps more than a dozen distinct tribes and languages around Lake Victoria, and these people are jealous of the preservation of their language. Along the coast Swahili is a sort of lingua franca, a mongrel of native and Arabic dialects, but the people of the interior highlands will have none of it.

The Kavirondos, who live to the northeast of Victoria Nyanza, are particularly fine looking and upstanding, proud of their race and language, yet ready to welcome the religion and education that come from the presence and influence of the English.

The readiness, or it might be better said keenness, for education is another outstanding fact about the native peoples of British East Africa. The mission schools are largely attended, and also the few Government schools that have been established. In Uganda practically all the education is in the hands of the missions, the Government making grants in aid.

Under German rule education in Tanganyika was carried on mainly by German missions. These were closed during the war. Since the war the English and other churches have established missions, and there is talk of allowing the German missionaries to return. In Kenya there is more activity in the way of State education. Throughout the three States there are signs of increasing activity on the part of the Colonial Governments.

Schools Increasing.

It is inevitable that the number of Government schools will increase, and an important problem will be cooperation between the Government and the missions. In Kenya there has been formed an advisory council of education composed of representatives of the Government, the missions and the settlers. In remote sections where no school has been established you will sometimes find that a village school has been started by the native people themselves, led by some of their number who have had the advantage of attending a mission school.

One of the most pressing problems is the improvement of these little "out" schools. Both Kenya and Uganda are forming plans to solve this problem. The Indian question, especially in Kenya, is also vital in the matter of education, as well as economically. Separate schools have to be provided for the Indian population. The Indian is persona non grata to both native and European, yet he is there and he does much of the work, especially as clerk and trader.

There are many problems of education, business, agriculture, religion and race which East Africa has to face, but the visitor will likely leave with the feeling that they will be settled in good time. The English Colonial Office and the Colonial and Provincial Governments are desirous of dealing justly with all the elements of the population. Much depends upon the attitude of the English "settlers," increasing numbers of whom are becoming convinced of the wisdom of helping to provide education and means of betterment for the large native population.

ACCUSES PORTUGAL OF AFRICAN MISRULE

'Worse Than Slavery' Says Report by Americans on Forced Labor in Angola.

PEONS UNPAID AND ILL-FED

Men and Women Leased to Planters Whipped and Even Tortured—League of Nations Appealed To.

There was made public here yesterday a Report on Compulsory Labor in Portuguese Africa by Dr. Edward A. Ross, Professor of Sociology of the University of Wisconsin. The report has been submitted to the Secretary General of the League of Nations with the request that the League of Nations Slavery Commission interest itself in the matter.

The report does not charge that slavery exists in the simple form of ownership of the blacks by whites, but describes a complicated system of peonage under which the Portuguese Colonial Government requisitions labor on a wholesale scale and uses it without pay on Government projects or leases it to planters and other private interests.

In some respects, it is said, the system is worse than slavery, because the peon is not only not paid, but is often not fed. If the labor, for instance, is on highways near his home, the native is often not only compelled to work for nothing, but to feed himself. Women with babies on their backs are requisitioned like other laborers, it is asserted. The period of compulsory labor without pay may run from a few months, it is said, to twelve months a year. Some gangs are treated kindly, others flogged with the djambock, or hippo lash, and tortured.

Native Crafts Declining.

Constant preying on black women by ruthless whites is charged. The arts and crafts, which had reached a fairly high development among the natives, are being destroyed by their systematic exploitation as day laborers for the planters and the Government, it is charged.

Dr. Ross's colleague in the investigation was Dr. R. Melville Cramer, a physician of New York. Their mission had the backing of prominent Americans including George Foster Peabody, Raymond B. Fosdick, E. E. Olcott, Mrs. Carrie Chapman Catt, Dr. John H. Finley, Thomas S. McDonough, Dr. John Grier Hibben, Joseph P. Chamberlain, Newton D. Baker, Glenn Frank, William Jay Schieffelin, Henry N. MacCracken, Ernest W. Riggs, Hamilton Holt, Dr. James Shotwell, A. L. Warnshuis, Dr. James R. Angell, James G. McDonald, Henry Goddard Leach.

Drs. Ross and Cramer visited nineteen villages in widely separated parts of Angola to obtain a comprehensive view of the Portuguese labor system. Through interpreters, they report, they questioned between 6,000 and 7,000 natives, besides local pastors and teachers.

"Slavery ceased," says the report, discussing a typical village, "with the downfall of the Portuguese monarchy in 1910 and the new system began about 1918. In the interval when republican principles were supposed to prevail, the Portuguese landholders constantly complained that the natives were hopelessly lazy, that the planters could not obtain workers for their farms; yet all this time the blacks thronged the mission estate delighted if they could earn 5 cents a day, skilled labor 10 cents. Most Portuguese thought they ought to get labor for nothing or at most 20 cents a month, with perhaps 2 cents worth of food a day. Moreover, on the plantation, labor is ruthlessly driven.

Flogged When Baby Cries.

"If the mother lays a baby under a tree and rises up from her work when it cries, she may get struck for it.

"Much of the brutality from which the natives suffer is inflicted by the native police who are given virtual carte blanche by their Portuguese superiors. A year ago the police came to the mission, collected the men, went to the pounding rocks where the women pound their manioc and had their meal spread ready to dry and took them off to work on the road without even giving them a chance to gather up their meal and carry it to their homes.

"Children had to quit the mission school saying, 'Father has been taken to work on a plantation, mother and the older brothers are working on the roads, so I must stay out of school to hoe the fields, pound the manioc into meal and feed my little brothers and sisters.' Furthermore, the child will have to pound the meal and carry it to mother working on the road with the baby on her back."

Conditions in thirty-two villages are discussed separately, the narrative in nearly every case being one of brutality and oppression, differing only in detail from the others. In his conclusions, Dr. Ross says:

"While the evidence we have amassed may seem to justify a severe condemnation of the system under which native labor is exacted in Portuguese Africa, there is much evidence in our report which shows that we have been as willing to set down favorable statements when we could do so as unfavorable statements."

Dr. Ross's Findings.

Dr. Ross sets forth ten findings as follows:

"1. The labor system—virtually State serfdom—which has grown up in the Portuguese colonies in recent years, often claims so much of the natives' time and strength that they are no longer able to give adequate attention to the production of food in their own gardens and fields.

"2. There is little evidence that any considerable part of the wages turned over in trust to the officials by the employers of natives hired from the Government actually reached the hands of those to whom it belongs. It appears that the typical thing is for the earnings of those commandeered laborers to be embezzled.

"3. The amount of unpaid labor exacted of skilled natives is not infrequently so excessive that the young men see nothing to be gained by their acquiring skill in the missionary schools.

"4. Motor roads have been extended far beyond the needs of the colony and the construction of such roads by conscripted, unpaid, unrationed natives—for the most part women—with only the most primitive implements imposes in some cases an almost crushing burden.

"5. There appears to be widespread labor-stealing; i. e., the planter arbitrarily refused to give credit or pay for certain days or half days of labor which have been rendered him. We heard of no effort made by any official to curb this despicable practice.

"6. The official does not appear to be in a strong position with respect to his fellow nationals, the traders and the planters, and hence rarely ventures to stand up for the rights of the native as against the claims of a white man. The blacks feel that the Portuguese are leagued against them and that there is no recourse against the white man's violence and injustice.

"7. The native policemen, utilized among stranger or enemy tribes, grossly abuse their authority for purposes of lust, spite or extortion.

"8. The Government provides practically nothing in the way of schools, medical care, emergency relief or justice, against the white trader, for the people of the villages, as recompense for the heavy burden of unrequited toil it lays upon them.

"9. The treatment of the natives in Portuguese territory compares so unfavorably with that experienced by the natives of Rhodesia or Belgian Congo that there is a strong tendency to emigrate across the frontier.

"10. In Portuguese East Africa the amount and manner of collection of the hut tax impose severe hardships upon the natives."

July 10, 1925

COLORS CLASH IN SOUTH AFRICAN UNION

Whites, Outnumbered By Blacks, Want to Segregate the Native Race

By WYONA DASHWOOD

COLOR clashes threaten the peace of South Africa. Black natives number five and a half million to a colonist white population of one and a half million. The native vote in the Cape Province alone has so increased that it has been the deciding factor in the election of twelve out of the fifty-one members representing that Province in the Union Parliament.

Within the comparatively short space of fifty years, it is estimated, the native voting strength in the Cape will exceed that of the white man.

Statesmen and politicians in the past have wished to solve this problem of the white colonist and black native, but, not caring to risk their political standing by the experiment, they have kept discreetly aloof.

Now General J. M. B. Hertzog, Prime Minister of the Union and the first of its statesmen in all its stormy history to admit the exigency of a ticklish problem, says that the five and a half millions must be segregated.

General Jan Smuts, who is also campaigning for return to power, and has a party platform of his own, is scathingly critical of the plan.

Encouraged by Smuts, a small band of native agitators are openly threatening the white man, who is "asserting his superiority by an act which would make of the native a thing without the power to vote in his own country."

Summarized, the Hertzog measure involves:

The disenfranchisement of the Cape Province native and the extension of the colored vote to the rest of the Union.

The placing of all natives on reserved areas like that of Swaziland and Basutoland.

The granting to the native of direct Parliamentary representation by means of seven native-elected European members, and the partial election of members to a Native Council, to function as a Native Parliament in collaboration with the Union Parliament.

The idea behind it is to give the native a chance to develop along his own lines and afford him the opportunity to lay a sound national foundation on which to ground the more advanced economic, social and political system of the white man's civilization. Without this intermediate step, it is held, modern European civilization is apt to be to the semi-civilized native of much the same use as a razor in the hands of a monkey.

Reservations already exist for the native, created—as Basutoland, Bechuanaland and Swaziland—to check tribal fighting, or—as Transkei, Tembuland, East Griqualand and Pondoland in the northeastern Cape Province—to clear other land for mining and farming. The discovery of diamonds at Kimberley was a signal for the movement of the natives there to reservations. This so impressed the native consciousness that the chiefs forbade their tribesmen to uncover mineral findings.

In Basutoland some of the natives uncovered coal deposits and began selling to white missionaries, traders and Government officials, but when word of the commerce reached the paramount chief he ordered it stopped and the diggings covered. In Bechuanaland, where there is believed to be considerable gold, even the sinking of wells is prohibited for this reason. Sooner or later the native will grasp the fact that the land he now occupies is his own, dependent upon himself for development, and not to be encroached upon in any way by the white people.

The danger, if more subtle, is even greater than in the violent past. For the main point with the native now seems to be multiplication, and he works reluctantly. Whole acres of cotton have had to be plowed under when the native, having enough money for his taxes and enough corn in his kraal, has refused to come out and pick. Out of a heritage of fear that alternated between the terror of annihilation or slavery by another tribe and of the dreadful charms of the witch doctor, he has evolved a philosophy of living for the present which reduces his reliability to a minimum.

Only Three Wives Taxed

This characteristic has been combated in great part by the Government, which, in return for bringing him its protection, exacts a "huut" or "head" tax from each native over 21, whether single or married. Since polygamy is general, the premium for having a second wife is a double head tax, and for a third wife it is tripled. One wife is not counted as extra. He is not charged beyond the third, either—the Government perhaps believing that such a man has trouble enough on his hands.

Somehow the native must obtain this money for the yearly tax-gatherer, and there is ample employment for him in the towns. The chiefs act as agents for labor bureaus and receive 5 shillings for every youth they enroll. To the white people facing the costly task of developing a new country, the low cost of native labor seemed the solution to their problem.

But from being a convenience, the native has become a necessity. Those who agree with General Hertzog believe he is a drain upon the whites in his present juxtaposition; that the dependence upon him for physical labor of all kinds serves to reduce the sense of the dignity of labor among the young white generation; that native labor, cheap as it is, will prove incalculably expensive since it will undermine the energy of the white; that segregation of the native, with the necessity for making his living from his own territory, will impel young whites to participate in labor.

So South Africa begins to feel the menace of its indolent, ignorant five and a half millions—seven and a half, if you count all the territory south of the Zambesi—upon the wise disposal of whom depends the prosperity of its future.

To the casual visitor, the native appears ubiquitous and, after the marvelous industrial development throughout the Union, the most interesting object there to study

At Durban he pulls the rickshas about the streets, dressed terribly in colored feathers that do not in the least match his amiable grin. In the great gold mines of the Rand 185,000 of them are at work beside 22,000 whites, and you hear his chant. You see him as chef, waiter, porter, coachman, chauffeur, gardener, navvy, miner, plowman. And you see him in the kraal.

Work in the diamond mines at Kimberley has fascination for him. When his contract terminates he is kept five days under guard because of his propensity for stealing, and is allowed to take only soft clothing away with him; even his footwear must be left behind, for he is clever at secreting diamonds in his boot-heels. One native who fell under suspicion had swallowed stones to the value of $3,700, and another a 152-carat diamond. Once the company doctor found gems hidden in a hole made in a native's leg.

The trek back to the kraal is delayed no longer than necessary. And with the first mile out, off come his boots, for it is hot walking, and he has scarcely resumed his life in the shaggy huts before he strips off every stitch of the white man's garb. Presently he shows no trace of ever having tasted the life of the towns.

At Cape Town, the first landing you make, you look everywhere for the "native." You realize at last that these fellows in wide trousers and straw hats are native grandees. You feel that it is too bad to see the clothes of Western civilization on them. They do not compare in interest with the dashing young men who parade the streets of Johannesburg on Sundays in red blankets, tinkling and jingling with metal and ivory ornaments.

Native women can wear white women's clothes less patently, when they choose bright colors and a simple style, and wear no shoes and stockings. But even so, you prefer their own red dresses trimmed with beads and bootlaces.

The Road to Zululand

In Zululand, they don't wear very much of anything, although the women do put on petticoats to go to the white settlements. Among Zulu young women it is the vogue to plaster their hair with red clay, as a way of saying they are married and from the country.

But it is something first to get to Zululand. You pass through mango groves, where the Sykes monkeys sleep through the hot hours or walk in a procession through the steaming air, where sometimes a flamingo flashes to the lakes beyond, and sometimes an antelope streaks from its lair.

Perched on the hills are the little thatched huts of the Zulus, hills sometimes separating a dwelling from its neighbor, always separating the kraals. It is a patriarchial land in these native reserves, where each man receives for tillage such soil as his needs suggest, living in solitary state upon his own little hill, or as a unit of the more clannish life of the many kraals. The Zulu King has been deposed for the peace of the country but there are tribal chiefs under supervision of the Union Government.

For thirty years the Government has tried to introduce individual land tenure in place of the communal system of holding land among the natives, but it is not popular. Natives who do farm work small fields.

As a rule the women are mentally inferior to the men, but now and then you come across a self-assertive old dame, accustomed to rule her husband, his other wives, all relatives within reach, and even the kraal, as oracle or caster of nativities. One such among his wives is the affliction of the first headsman you meet in Zululand. Her costume is scant and maladorous, her manner vindictive. She hurls grim jests and quips at all who pass her way, with frank allusions to the intimate affairs of village maids and matrons.

She mistakes you for the periodical tax-gatherer and growls at you "Gone are the mighty days when, did the rains hold off or sickness come, the diviners saw and told who wrought the evil so that some one suffered greatly. But now the law forbids this. The law! And what does the law, but pry, hampering men and working evil with this tax and that tax, seeking always peace and money, money and peace? And to what end?

"See how the people toil. And what avails it? The cattle kraals are empty, the crops grow scant. But in the days of long ago, when no true Zulu worked, if aught were wanted we needed but cross the border and find it there. Cattle in plenty. Corn ready ground. Women for barter and toil

"What matter that the weak were slain and that for miles the Fingo smeared the face with ashes? What matter, so that we, the victor, lay fully fed! Wow! Those were the days when kings were truly kings, eating whole tribes at will; and men were very bulls, prancing with ill-pent vigor. While now, Inkos, behold the men!"

It is true that these men no longer garner enemies. They are a carefree lot, though, and out of their heritage, proud-looking. One of the retained customs is that of having their wives plant and manage the crop of mealies (corn), sweet potatoes, pumpkins, while the small boys look after the cattle and goats. That leaves them much time for loafing and they do that thoroughly, remaining within doors most of the days, in the huts that their wives have built.

Women greatly outnumber the men among the natives, which takes their importance down several pegs. Since the Government placed a head tax on its native population a man does not take too many wives without due consideration; the high cost of living burdens him. It is true that two of the Basuto chiefs have thirty-five wives apiece and various of the wealthy tribesmen ten to twenty each, but the average native observes moderation.

Cattle Pay for Wives

It is still customary that cattle shall be turned over by the bridegroom to the bride's parents before he can lead her away to his own kraal. Many of the men go to work in towns to earn enough money to buy cattle to pay for a wife—that is to say, six or eight head.

The law provides for lack of domestic harmony. When great trouble comes to the woman through her husband she is not irrevocably bound but may return to her parents and demand that they support her from the cattle paid for her. These include the offspring of those cattle, so careful count must be kept of the calves.

If a woman is left a widow with only female children she inherits her husband's goods. But if her brother-in-law contributes toward the maintenance of the children he is entitled to a portion of the proceeds from the sale of his nieces.

If a man is found guilty of seducing or abducting an unmarried woman the fine is six head of cattle, or as much as if he had taken the trouble to marry her. Long ago Moshesh established the law of thefts and this remains today: a beast shall be repaid by a beast, a second beast for compensation, a third as a fine to be paid to the court.

An induna, or village counselor, passes you on your way, stalking superbly along, ringed, club and shield in hand. His snuffbox flaps from the lobe of one ear, his snuff-spoon from the other. He is stalwart and haughty, wrapped in a worn kaross and true African dignity. Behind him his three lithe wives pad soft-footed in Indian file. There is harmony among the three, for "is there not less work to be done by one when there are three?"

It is true the kraals are not overclean, but each is a place to warm the heart of the Arcadian—lazy laughter, song and labor ranking in the order named. Wants are few and apparently easily satisfied from the untidy little fields around. The possessions of that haughty Philistine of an induna, for instance, are worth perhaps $2.50, excluding live stock.

In the dawn, a short distance out of the village, your horse shies at a prostrate witch doctor overcome by Kaffir beer. In these cultivated sections the Kaffir cornfield stands side by side with the field of mealies. The beer made from the former contains only 2½ per cent. alcohol, but it is sufficient percentage to make the native very drunk.

Spirits and Witch Doctors

Witch doctoring is profitable in a land as drenched as this with the primitive superstitions. The native believes spirits are there, good and bad—especially bad. The woods are full of them. Some even live under the water. A few bring rain. But others—and these have the ascendancy—are occupied in keeping it off, in binding the soil so that hoeing is doubly hard, in tampering with cattle and in carrying evil between man and man.

Tell the raw native that there is dignity and manly satisfaction in labor, and he sees the fallacy at once. Speak about a benign God whose good-will reaches to all men, and his interest wanders. But get started about some new and peculiarly malignant devil, and you have him spellbound, fascinated beyond all thought of time or reason.

The witch doctor juggles with them all. In spite of the prohibition against witchcraft, he does a brisk trade in charms for curing impotency in field or stock, compounds love philters for destroying opposition in young women coveted by aged polygamists, manipulates certain bones which when cast permit interpretation of fantastic dreams and visions that on hot nights beset overfed people sleeping in stuffy huts.

In Southern Rhodesia, high on the summit of a mountain of the Motopos range, is the cave of the Umlimo spirit, malignant, causing death, illness, personal harm and famine. Offerings of tobacco, antelope, horns, pottery, are left at the door of his cave for appeasement. This spirit speaks only through a priest, and his oracles in days past have been the cause of many massacres. In one rebellion that rose out of advices from the Umlimo spirit the Government had to pay $1,800,000 to settlers for losses suffered.

Education, in the circumstances rather experimental, is extended to the native. In places he has his own press, his native teachers of European learning, his own Christian ministers, his own carpenters, masons, bootmakers, tailors, and even graduates in law and medicine. But those who work with him say his qualities are of the immature brain.

Segregation is the first definite policy advanced toward the solution of the South African dilemma. History keeps ominous record of what has happened whenever the native and colonist have been brought together—one or the other inevitably succumbing. In America it was the native; in ancient Africa the colonist. In Asia Europeans have never established themselves except as a small ruling caste. In South Africa it remains to be seen. Party differences are interfering with the suggested solution. But that is history, too.

BRITISH STRIKE SNAG IN AFRICAN EMPIRE

Governors Disagree on Whether United Territories Should Be Black or White.

CAMERON FOR NATIVE RULE

Grigg Champions Caucasian—Both Going Home to Have It Out With Foreign Office.

Wireless to THE NEW YORK TIMES.

LONDON, Dec. 13.—The British scheme to group the mandated Tanganyika territory with the colonies of Uganda and Kenya and to develop the whole vast area into a rich new African empire has struck its first snag. That is a dispute between the Governors of the Tanganyika territory and Kenya colony as to whether East Africa in future is to be a white man's country or a black man's.

Sir Donald Cameron, administering the former German possession under the League of Nation's supervision, holds that East Africa will inevitably be a black man's country. His scheme of government involves building, so far as possible, on the present tribal rules, teaching to the chieftains British ideas of law and order, and incidentally of commerce, and slowly civilizing the natives so that they will be able to run their own country under British guidance.

Sir Edward Grigg, however, Governor of the aristocratic Kenya colony, holds that his portion of Africa anyway is going to be a white man's country. Britons, like Lord Delamere, are staking out great ranches there. The climate is cool and it has a high altitude. The natives are to receive reserves—like those that the builders of the United States accorded to the Indians across the Mississippi—but the white man is to own and rule Kenya in the traditional British fashion.

To Consult Colonial Office.

The proposition to federate Britain's East African holdings, therefore, has encountered two diametrically opposed conceptions of the land's future. That is the reason, it was learned today, why the long awaited report of the Hilton Young commission on federation has not been made public. The disputes waxed so warm between the protagonists of the two ideas that each was fearful the commission would lean too far toward the ideas of the other, so that both Governors are coming home early in January to wrestle the matter out with the Colonial Office.

It is already apparent that the political federation will not proceed as far as its ardent advocates have desired. It may not go beyond a small board to coordinate the development of roads, railways, the postal and telegraph systems and customs.

But political unity in East Africa, Britain realizes, is not a vital matter for the new empire's development, except in a small degree. The main problem is commercial rather than political. The first task is road building and the development of transport for the products of the inhabitants. A small committee has just been appointed here to "study every aspect of mechanical transport likely to further economic development in the overseas empire."

Railroads Held Impossible.

According to one member of the new committee, Brig. Gen. D. S. Hammond, it will be impossible to use railroads to open up the country, as the late James J. Hill did in the American Northwest. The committee is exploring the potentialities of new types of motor trucks capable of carrying tremendous loads over relatively primitive roads. The six-wheeled trucks now doing heavy work in some portions of the empire are believed to be a step in the right direction in design, but Britain is looking for some bigger type, and also one capable of using other fuel than gasoline.

Alcohol has been made and sold as motor fuel in Uganda. But the committee is now studying the potentialities of a "producer of gas" which can be made from charcoal, anthracite or wood, all of which are plentiful throughout the territory. The possible use of the Diesel engine is also under inquiry.

Since vast distances are involved and since loops of the new road which it is planned to build to link outlying areas to the railroads cannot be macadamized, the committee is going to bring road designers having tropical experience and vehicle designers together to have them evolve a road type and vehicle type to match each other instead of tackling the two problems separately.

December 16, 1928

SMUTS URGES NEED TO SAVE AFRICANS

World Would Be Poorer if It Lost Negro Culture, He Tells Oxford Audience.

SEES DANGER OF UPHEAVAL

Former Premier of Union Says the Retention of Tribal Local Rule Is Stabilizer in South.

By CHARLES A. SELDEN.

Wireless to THE NEW YORK TIMES.

OXFORD, England, Nov. 16.—General Jan Christian Smuts, former Premier of South Africa, gave the third and last of his course of Rhodes lectures at Oxford University today on the specific subject of "Native Policy in Africa."

General Smuts said that what is wanted in Africa now is a far-sighted régime whereby what is excellent in the native stock would be preserved.

"If we could evolve and pursue a policy which would promote the cause of civilization of Africa without injustice to the African and without injury to what is typical of and specific in the African," he continued, "we should be rendering a great service to the cause of humanity. For there is much that is good in the African which ought to be preserved and developed.

"The negro and negroid bantu form a distinct human type which the world would be poorer without. Here, in a vast continent with its wide geographical variety and immense climatic differences, this unique human type has been fixing for thousands of years. It is even possible, so some anthropologists hold, that this was the original mother-type of the human race and that Africa holds the cradle of mankind. But, whether this is so or not, at any rate we have vast results of time which we should conserve and develop with the same high respect we feel toward all great natural facts.

"This type has some wonderful characteristics. It has largely remained a child type, with a child psychology and outlook. A childlike human cannot be a bad human, for are we not, in high spiritual matters, bidden to be like unto children? Perhaps, as the direct result of this temperament, the Africans are the only happy humans I have come across.

Need for Different Policies Seen.

"It is clear that a race so unique, so different in its mentality and culture, from those of Europe requires a policy very unlike that which would suit Europeans. Nothing could be worse for Africa than the application of a policy the object and tendency of which would be to destroy the basis of this African type, to de-Africanize the African and turn him either into a beast of the field or into a pseudo European.

"We have tried both alternatives in our dealings with the natives. At first we looked upon the African as essentially inferior or subhuman, as not having a soul and as being only fit to be a slave. As a slave he became an article of commerce and the greatest article of export from this continent for centuries. But the horrors of this trade became such that the modern conscience finally revolted and stamped out African slavery, peacefully in the British Empire, but in the United States with the convulsions of a civil war and a million dead.

"Then we changed to the opposite extreme. The African has now become a man and a brother. Religion and politics combined to shape this new African policy. The principles of the French Revolution, which emancipated Europe, were applied to Africa, so that liberty, equality and fraternity could turn bad Africans into good Europeans. The political system of the natives was ruthlessly destroyed in order to incorporate them as equals into the white system. The African was good as a potential European, but his social and political culture was bad, barbarous, only deserving to be stamped out, root and branch.

Past Policies Called Bad.

"These are the two native policies which have prevailed in the past, and the second has been only less harmful than the first. If Africa is to be redeemed, if Africa is to make her own contribution to the world, if Africa is to take her rightful place among the continents, we shall have to proceed on different lines and evolve a policy which will not force her institutions into an alien European mold, but which will preserve the unity of her own past, conserve what is precious in her past and build her future progress and civilization on specifically African foundations. That should be the new policy, and such a policy would be in line with the traditions of the British Empire.

"It is a significant fact that this new orientation of African policy had its origin in South Africa, as its author was Cecil Rhodes. In his celebrated Glen Grey Mr. Rhodes's African policy embodied two main ideas—white settlement to supply a steel framework and stimulus for an enduring civilization, and indigenous native institutions to express the specifically African character of the natives in their future development in civilization.

"The principal innovation of Mr. Rhodes in his new legislation was, so far as possible, resolved on direct native rule of the natives in their local and tribal affairs. The system of native councils was inaugurated for the smaller areas, from which, again, delegates met to form the larger general council under the chairmanship of the resident magistrate of the area.

"Powers of taxation, administration and recommending legislation to the government were conferred on these councils.

Private Property Instituted.

"His second innovation was to make it possible for the natives in their tribal areas to become possessed of their own separate plots of agricultural land instead of the traditional communal holding and working of the land, which is the universal native system through Africa.

"His provision for individual agricultural holdings has been a great success and has been the principal means of native advance where it has been adopted in the South African Union.

"The new policy is to foster the indigenous native culture or system of cultures and to cease to force the African into alien European molds. As a practical policy of native government it has worked most successfully. Gradually the system of native councils and native self-government through their own tribal chiefs elected to the councils, has been extended from one native area to another in the Cape province until today about two-thirds, or roughly over a million, of the Cape natives fall under this system and manage their own local affairs according to their own ideas, under the supervision of European magistrates.

"The new departure is most far-reaching and has come none too soon. Already the African system is disintegrating everywhere over the whole African continent. Many factors have combined to produce this situation. Missionaries share the blame with the administrators and the fight against native religious ideas has been not less destructive than the deposition of native chiefs and the institution of European organs of government. Unfortunately, the earlier efforts of missionary enterprises were made without any reference or knowledge of the peculiar native psychology or the light anthropology has thrown on the past of human cultures.

Creeds and Sciences One to Natives.

"For the natives religion, law, natural science, social customs and institutions all form one blended whole, which enshrines their view of the world and the forces governing it. Attack this complex system at any single point and the whole is endangered. The introduction of the Christian religion meant not only a breakdown in the belief in primitive spirits, magic and witchcraft and abandonment of the practice of polygamy, it meant a breakdown of the entire, integral native 'seltanschuung,' or outlook on life and the world.

"A knowledge of anthropology would have enabled the missionary to differentiate between what was barbaric and degrading in the native system and what was merely different from the Christian European system without being morally or socially harmful to the natives.

"The events of the great war on the African continent also contributed to this general disintegration. If the bonds of native tribal cohesion and authority are dissolved, African governments will everywhere sit with vast hordes of detribalized natives on their hands, for whom the traditional restraints and discipline of chiefs and elders will have no force or effect. The old social and religious sanctions will have disappeared while no new sanctions, except those of the white man's laws, will have been substituted.

Unprecedented Situation Seen.

"Such a situation would be unprecedented in the history of the world and the results may well be general chaos. The natives of Africa, from time immemorial, have been subject to stern, even ruthless, discipline, and their social system rested on the despotic authority of their chiefs. If this system breaks down and tribal discipline disappears, native society will be resolved into its human atoms with possibilities of universal bolshevism and chaos, which no friend of the natives or orderly civilization on this continent would contemplate with equanimity.

"There remains the big question of how far the parallelism of native and white institutions is to go. Is it to be confined to the local government, or is it to go all the way up to the level of full political or parliamentary government? Should the black and white cooperate in the same parliamentary institutions of the country? If so, should they separate their representatives in the same parliamentary institutions?

"I do not think there can be, or, at bottom, there is among those who have given the subject serious attention, any doubt that in the supreme legislature of a country with a mixed population both colors should ultimately have representation. It is repugnant to our civilized European ideas that the weaker in a community should be unheard or should go without representation either by themselves or through European spokesmen where their interests are concerned. There can be but one sovereign body in a country and that body should represent the weaker or less than the stronger. As to the mode of representation of color in a supreme parliament, there can be legitimate differences of opinion."

Before delivering his last lecture, General Smuts received the honorary degree of Doctor of Civil Law. The students who packed the historic Sheldonian Theatre gave him a rousing welcome.

Referring to General Smuts's visit to the United States next month, Dr. A. B. Poynton, public orator, said he hoped that Halcyon would "calm the seas for this Ulysses of many travels and wide experience who is now about to visit the West."

NATIONS' METHODS IN AFRICA SCRUTINIZED

France Would Assimilate Her Colonies, While Britain Tries Indirect Rule

By DOUGLAS WOODRUFF.

FRANCE has agreed to give to Italy portions of her territory in Africa. The areas are not large; indeed the whole of Italy's African possessions in Libya, Eritrea and Somaliland looks very small on the map beside the vast empires of England and France. But Italy cares intensely about her standing and repute in the African Continent. She is a late-comer who was not reckoned a great power at the time of the final partitioning of Africa in the Eighties and Nineties.

The French concessions to Italy are a gesture arising out of the new fear of Nazi Germany, and as such they are true to the diplomatic tradition of the last century which made African ambitions subsidiary pieces in the game of European rivalries.

The Italians under the leadership of the new Governor of Libya, the illustrious airman Balbo, are determined to make their presence felt, and it is even mooted that Italy too, must begin to consider the technique of tropical administration if her responsibilities in the difficult country bordering Abyssinia, that solitary survivor of the old order, should ever increase.

Two Vast Experiments.

The Italian, like the German, watches today a continent containing among its inhabitants some 80,000,000 of aboriginal Negroes, where two sharply contrasting imperial experiments, the French and the British, are being worked out side by side. Today Great Britain has withdrawn from Egypt, though she is still credited in that country with much more responsibility than she is really carrying because the presence of troops to guard the Suez Canal suggests, naturally enough, that the policy of the King of Egypt, even in home affairs, is under British control. The preoccupation of Great Britain is with peoples further south, and France too is much more concerned with her new tropical colonies than with maintaining the well-established order that is Marshal Lyautey's legacy among the Arabs of Algiers and Morocco.

With not many exceptions the whole of tropical Africa, from the Sahara to the Cape, is now included in either the British or the French empires. The boundaries of their possessions are arbitrary enough, the results of the jealousies and compromises of the European powers at the end of the last century, when the scramble for spheres of influence led to rapid boundary-drawing which has left subsequent administrators with territories of the most incongruous and inconvenient shapes.

Early Days—And Now.

There is a profound divergence of views and methods between French and English rulers. In the early days of effective occupation by European governments this divergence was concealed by the common need to put down slave trading and intertribal wars and to establish the essentials of law and order. But today there is no unknown or darkest Africa. The tasks of law and order, except in a few back pockets like Somaliland, are easily achieved, and the government has no serious natural or human opposition to overcome in making itself obeyed.

Hence the question may now be fairly put to France and Britain: What are you trying to do? What do you envisage as the future of these African peoples for whom you have so often declared yourself to be the trustees?

The French are clear and self-confident in their reply. France would incorporate into itself its subject peoples. The Africans under the French flag are to become Frenchmen, sharing the rights no less than the duties of proud French citizens. There is no color or class barrier, but there are high tests to be fulfilled. Only the Africans who really fit themselves for citizenship can expect to enjoy it.

The assimilé is accorded social in clerical or minor administrative tasks, is the pivot of French policy.

In a recent speech the Governor General of French West Africa stated: "Although we have renounced the out-of-date policy of all-embracing assimilation, we have left a door ajar to permit individual accessions to French citizenship. It is the fitting reward for successful efforts to raise themselves to our level."

"The assimilé is accorded social equality, and for social equality much in the way of administrative vexation and dictatorial centralization, slightly tempered by elective councils, is cheerfully borne.

The Essential Difference.

When Clemenceau toured British India after the World War, he expressed in a single sentence the root difference between French and English approaches to subject peoples. "You do not mix enough with these people," he said to his English friend, "but you pay far too much attention to what they say." The French attitude pays little enough regard to formal requests for more constitutional representation, and an autocracy, itself governed from Paris, rules the French colonies. But the large class of the assimilés, men vehemently French because French by adoption and as a proof of personal qualities, forms a cushion or buffer between the administration and the mass of its subjects.

It follows that the French have little enthusiasm for the idea of indirect rule through native chiefs. This method is an accepted pillar of the British system, cherished alike on grounds of economy and statesmanship. Its essence is to change as little as possible, to maintain the prestige and authority of native rulers, and to lead instead of driving them. It is the treaty principle, by which Indian rajahs and Malayan sultans are guaranteed in their possessions in return for accepting a British resident at their court and handing over their foreign relations and defense and other similar subjects to British direction.

In Africa this system was established in its classic form in Northern Nigeria, where Mohammedan emirs of considerable dignity and capacity were already ruling millions of native Africans when the British arrived. The arrangement with the emirs forbids Christian missionaries to enter their territory. Such an attitude horrifies Frenchmen, even when they are not only anti-clerical but atheistic themselves. It is an illustration of trepidity and lack of belief in European civilization, for which the French reproach the English.

The French Way.

In the French colonies, from Senegal and Dahomey to French Equatorial Africa, there is no desire to preserve native civilization; in the French view, to give large powers to native rulers, to let them enjoy revenues instead of salaries and encourage their people to look to them is to hinder the spread of European ways and beliefs. The most anti-religious French Cabinets have continued to make subventions to French missions abroad, from a realization that French missionaries, men and women of a very high stamp, are inevitably spreaders of the culture and prestige of France.

Senegal, as an old French settlement, sends a Deputy to the Chamber of Deputies in Paris, but it is in that respect unique among the seventeen different units of administration which make up French Africa. To date, the native element in French colonial councils is very much a minority, generally a third, whereas two-thirds of such local councils are elected by those enjoying French citizenship; but it has been indicated already that such citizenship by no means represents pure European blood.

Military service, the training of the black regiments whose presence in occupied Germany proved such a provocative aggravation of the Treaty of Versailles, is another powerful link making France the real country of Senegalese and Dahomey and other Africans. The wireless, organized under a special company, Radio-Coloniale, sends out to French Africa programs very often above the heads of the listening public, but all designed to reiterate the pre-eminence of France in the arts and in knowledge.

British Doubts.

If the Frenchman is free from doubts and misgivings as to policy in Africa, doubts and troubled indecision are all too common in England today. Africa societies abound in London, at Oxford and Cambridge; grants are eagerly earmarked for anthropological research and field work, because the present generation of men responsible for policy has few clear ideas about education and civilization.

The Englishman's dilemma is that his own education is a glorification of political independence, a literary education in the old tradition which has already produced, in colonies like the Gold Coast and Southern Nigeria, natives who would be assimilés if they were in a French colony, but for whom there is neither niche nor welcome in an English one. The native rulers, precariously defending the old customary order against the disturbances of modern invention, hate the smart native lawyer, and the administration dislikes his loquacity and the uncomfortable fact that both his talents and the drawbacks of his position incline his mind toward political life. The young African, like the young Indian, catches from the Englishman on the scene his real beliefs. For all the French boast about assimilation, the English spread the contagion of their own ideals no less effectively if reluctantly.

Aspirations Aped.

It is embarrassing for the English, especially for the English settlers in the Kenya highlands, to find all their own aspirations toward control of their colony and free political institutions for Europeans, mimicked, as it were, both by the Indian element in East Africa and by the educated natives. These political ideals, these visions of sovereign legislative bodies carrying out the will of the people, may have little glamour in Europe today, but they burn very brightly in British colonies.

It is difficult for educationalists to make Africans understand that the curriculum in the best African schools ought not to follow English models. Talk about helping the African to make his own distinctive contribution, about avoiding the errors of the European literary education which only turns out redundant clerks, is met with the greatest suspicion. The African wants the best. He is unwilling to be given anything different from the English model, because he thinks there is a motive for the discrimination.

Yet there is a mass of strong reasoning in favor of such discrimination, based not only on the difference in future conditions between African and European children but still more on the difference of mental habits. As things are today, the African is asked, in field after field—law, medicine, public work—to learn to work English methods without an English mentality.

"Light Touch Needed."

Having little belief in the value of tribal life and custom, the French find it simple to apply civilized standards, but the Englishman, who is keen to preserve what he finds and to make it the structure on which something else will one day arise, must bring a light touch even to the dark sides of the native inheritance. He must do this because he is already faced with the problem of the detribalized native, an unhappy individualist who belongs nowhere and who derives all his inspiration from people much richer than himself. The isolated or town native has every temptation to drift into debt and to succumb to the salesmanship which sees in him a buyer for every kind of European merchandise, and in particular the bicycle and the phonograph.

It is among the major misfortunes of African history that the collapse of world prices in the last five years should have hit the African native so hard. He has been taught to grow crops—cotton in Uganda, cocoa in the Gold Coast, palm oil in Nigeria, maize in East Africa—whose price has been outside his control. The catastrophic falls to less than half or a third have not only spread among natives grave suspicions about the business system into which they have been encouraged to enter, but have left governments with greatly shrunken resources, compelled to retrench and cut salaries and postpone improvements.

An Effect in Britain.

It is a bad introduction to the modern world, this sudden collapse of prices for causes quite inexplicable to native peoples, and it has strengthened the case of the advocates in Great Britain of closer economic relations with the colonies. They say that as natives have been encouraged to take up tropical agriculture, for marketing and not for subsistence, and to become regionally dependent on single crops, what matters to these colonies is regularity and fixity of income, which could be guaranteed within limits by large-scale undertakings to relieve a colony of its crop, year by year, in return for the purchase of goods from Great Britain.

What is reasonably certain is a change of policy in Great Britain toward the African colonies, based on a recognition that it is of little use to talk at length about what the African of the future should be like, and what government policy should be, if the governments responsible live in a state of penury, compelled to be self-sufficient, unlike the French colonies, and yet only able to derive revenue from the indirect taxation of very poor populations. If these populations are denuded of their income by being exposed bare and unprotected to the full wind of world competition, they will undergo violent fluctuations of fortune.

These primitive peoples must take their first steps in agricultural industry behind a wind-break. In proportion as it is found that there is little in the cultural inheritance of the Africans that they are deeply bound to, and that the solicitude from above to go slowly in changing modes of life and beliefs is not met with any similar conservatism from below, does it become vital that the economic foundations of the new Africa of peasant producers shall be firmly laid; because being civilized **is an expensive affair.**

January 13, 1935

ABYSSINIA ENCIRCLED BY COVETOUS POWERS

Proud Black Empire Opens Resistance to Encroachments Upon Her Independence

By JOSEF ISRAELS 2D.

GEOGRAPHICALLY and economically beleaguered by the great powers of Europe, the Ethopian Empire, last stronghold of monarchy in Africa, is now engaged in what will probably be a life-or-death struggle for an independent existence.

Abyssinia, or Ethiopia, as its own people call it, has been fighting an economic battle ever since the conclusion of the World War permitted its territorial neighbors to turn their attention from defense to trade. Now, with the sharp conflict of Ethiopian and Italian interests projected into the news, and with Mussolini rejecting the League of Nations as an arbiter, European attempts at absorption of Africa's last empire enter more definitely into the military stage.

Underlying the Italian ambitions toward Ethiopia are two chief factors: First, the desire of Mussolini's Fascist government to demonstrate to the Italian people its ability to acquire more territory and thus strengthen Italy's Colonial empire; and second, the Italian desire to beat France, Germany and, most particularly, Japan to the control of vast potential sales to Abyssinia's millions, who are now reaching increasingly capacious hands for the necessities and luxuries of Western civilization.

Geographical Handicaps.

Ethiopia's position in Northeast Africa just toward the southern end of the Red Sea has, for centuries, been geographically disadvantageous to a people immensely nationalistic and strongly concerned with keeping their country free and independent under a royal line which is proud to date its ancestry back to the Queen of Sheba and King Solomon.

Through a long series of commercial, military and, in earlier years, religious invasions of what should be its natural coastline, Ethiopia finds itself today without access to the sea save through foreign territory. Therein lies the greatest obstacle in its path of progress and protection as a free State. Italy, Great Britain and France divide among themselves the thousand-odd miles of sea coast to the north and east that, geographically, might well be part of Ethiopia's map. To the west and south, the Anglo-Egyptian Sudan and British East Africa (Tanganyika, Kenya and Uganda) complete the foreign enclosure of Ethiopia.

Comparatively safe and secure in her mountains, Ethiopia has yet had to transport all of her goods and carry all her communication with the outer world through the territories of these ambitious powers. The ambitions of European nations with respect to this region date back in concrete form to the Portuguese religious and commercial missions which the Abyssinians drove from their country in the fifteenth century and to the unsuccessful Italian military campaign against the black empire in 1896. This invasion resulted from an imperialistic interpretation of a commercial treaty. There was a fast and fierce clash, the battle of Adowa, in which a quarter of a million savage black warriors, equipped mainly with spear and shield, slaughtered nearly 40,000 Italians practically in their tracks and in spite of the Italian rifles and artillery.

Indemnity by Italy.

In order to preserve its trade in Northeast Africa, Italy paid the Emperor Menelik heavy indemnity in cash for that ill-starred adventure. But the insult of defeat has rankled in the breasts of Italian militarists these many decades. Fully as strongly has burned the Ethiopian conviction that, having once beaten Europe at her game of war, Abyssinia could do so again.

Let there be no mistake in European or American minds as to the psychology of the Ethiopian. The true Abyssinian, ethnologically a member of the Amharic race (traced anthropologically from a mixture of Hebraic and Arabian lines), considers himself vastly superior to a white man. He brooks no condescension from any one, and is ready to excel any European in fierce protection of his country's pride and race. Under this comparatively small group of pure-blooded ruling class are some 20,000,000 blacks, a conglomerate of many tribes, not far from savagery, and yet sharing their nobility's feeling for a fierce defense of Ethiopian independence.

It must be borne in mind also that Ethiopia is a Christian country—in fact, the first Christian country in the world, since it was St. Mark himself who carried the gospel thence. The Ethiopians have a culture, they have a tradition, and they are too intelligent to be tricked by European diplomacy of their birthright of independence and freedom.

Embarrassing Treaties.

The Emperor Menelik, great-uncle of today's ruler, Haile Selassie, paved the way for European development of Ethiopia, but in doing so he made two treaties that have returned again and again to plague his successors on the throne. The first is a phrase in a commercial treaty, consummated with Great Britain in 1902, in which Menelik bound himself "not to construct or allow to be constructed any work across the Blue Nile, Lake Tsana or the Sobat which would arrest the flow of their waters into the Nile except in agreement with His Britannic Majesty's Government and the Government of the Sudan."

The second of these was the granting to France of a perpetual monopoly in the operation and construction of railway transportation between Addis Ababa and the coast. In return for this, France built the railway which is still Ethiopia's only modern link with world commerce, but the restriction of railway operation to the French is a thorn in the Ethiopian's side, because it has prevented the making of any deal with Italy for a free Ethiopian port on the Red Sea.

When the World War began the Colonial Ministries of the world were already endlessly involved in intrigues concerning the eventual domination of Ethiopia's trade and government. All these plans were hastily dropped in the scramble to defend colonial empires during the conflict, only to be resumed with the coming of peace and the realignment that followed Germany's elimination as a power in Africa.

Mussolini's Plans.

Italy began to look southward with more definite interest in colonial expansion. Mussolini drew a line across the Abyssinian map, a line bisecting Ethiopia, on which he has hoped to build a railroad knitting closer together his separated colonies of Eritrea on the north and Italian Somaliland on the south. More and more Italian troops have been sent to these colonies, and only a few months ago King Victor Emmanuel himself visited them to show the world in general, and Ethiopia in particular, their importance to Italian ambitions.

At the same time France has guarded jealously her railway monopoly and thus effectively blocked Ethiopian negotiations with Italy through which a trans-Abyssinian railroad franchise might be exchanged for an Ethiopian corridor to a free port at Massowa on the Red Sea. Polite but firm threats on the part of the French indicated that they would not consider removal of the French railway terminus from the French port of Djibouti, now the principal port of entry for Ethiopia, or consent to the construction of an Italian railway.

Great Britain joined with Italy in a two-way treaty which angered Haile Selassie and his people. Italy would cooperate in urging Ethiopia to grant British control of a dam on Lake Tsana for year-round control of the waters of the Nile, and Great Britain, in turn, would urge the granting of the Italian railway concession. Neither plan made any headway until the British, in 1930, compromised on granting permission to the Ethiopians to have an American company build the Tsana dam. Depleted national finances have blocked the carrying out of this dam construction, but the agreement is still in existence.

Meanwhile, Italy, checkmated, has until the last few weeks contented herself with strengthening her colonial armies and staging military and naval demonstrations along the Red Sea coast.

Cooperation of Powers.

France and Italy have managed, despite their rivalries, to work in harmony for the exploitation of interests they have already established in Ethiopia. France runs the railways; the Bank of France shares on an even basis the exploitation of gold and platinum mines that have yielded Golconda-like fortunes for the thousands of years they have been worked, and which as yet show no signs of exhaustion. Italy controls Ethiopian communications through cable and wireless contact with the outer world. The Church of Rome has established friendly relations with the Coptic Church of Ethiopia and Egypt, and papal emissaries are received with honor at Addis Ababa.

In the years since the war, Italy, France and England have maintained an unofficial, yet effective, arms embargo against the Ethiopians. Protests to the League of Nations have been unavailing. Officially there has been no blockade, yet actually legal shipments of arms or ammunition have been blocked because they cannot enter Ethiopia without passing through these countries' possessions. But the Arabian, Syrian and Greek gun runners have not been idle. Great quantities of guns and ammunition, much of it obsolete but most of it effective, have penetrated the embargo.

Japan and Germany have recently appeared on the economic horizon, sending their salesmen to unload quantities of the cheap gimcracks which so fascinate semi-civilized populations. At the same time, Russia could not forbear agitation within the African empire. Quietly, and with little notice from the outer world, the Ethiopians in 1929 expelled a Russian "economic mission." The mission had been too active in forming Communist cells within the Ethiopian Army and in employing Red workers to spread the doctrines of Moscow to a people already in ferment because of the rapid westernization of their country. Russia's hand has not openly reappeared in the boiling African pot.

Border Troubles.

Italy of late has trained great numbers of troops along Ethiopian borders and has hastened to establish definite military outposts at points along the Somali and Eritrean frontiers to mark borders long disputed, but about which no one has ever before been seriously concerned. It was the establishment of such an outpost at the town of Ualal, on the Somali border, that precipitated the armed clashes of the last few weeks.

The Emperor Haile Selassie and a few of those around him well understand the military significance of these comparatively small engagements. They know that an Ethiopian Army, equipped only with ancient rifles, small artillery and a few ramshackle airplanes, can accomplish little against a fighting machine such as Mussolini is prepared to throw into his African possessions, though their people are ready to brandish their shields, don their war capes of lionskin and dash boldly into a fray.

Haile Selassie has counted on the League for protection, but Mussolini denies the jurisdiction of the League. There will perhaps be Abyssinian apologies, drawn more painfully than blood, from a race of land-proud people, or there will perhaps be quick Italian annexation of most or all of Ethiopia, with another King falling from the world's small roster of absolute rulers, either to occupy his throne as a tragic puppet or go into eclipse. The next few months will be crucial in Ethiopia's history.

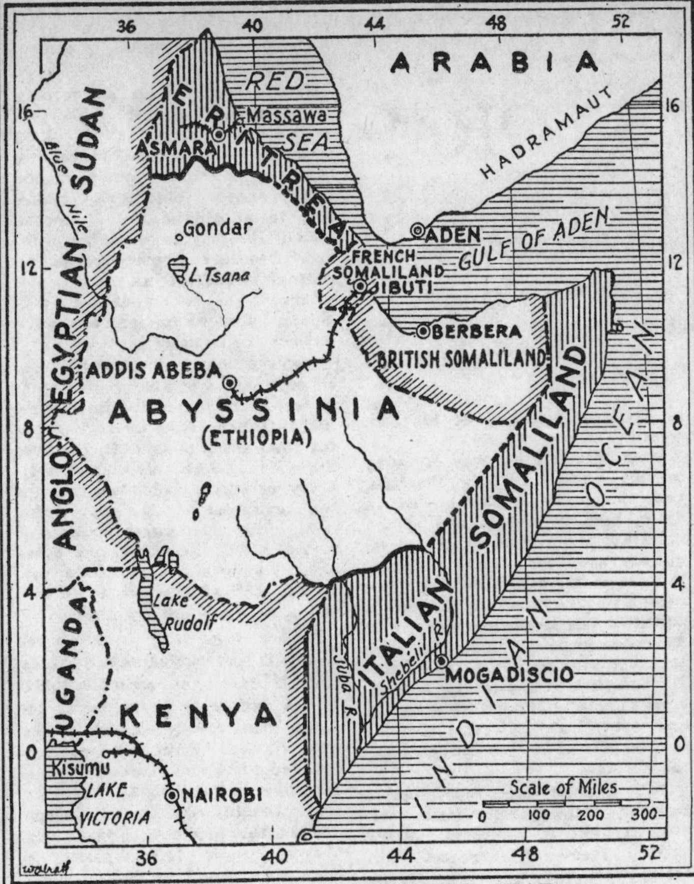

SCENE OF THREATENED WAR.

An engagement between Italians and Abyssinians on the border of Italian Somaliland has caused Italy to threaten reprisals and Abyssinia to appeal to the League of Nations. The place does not appear on available maps, but is probably near British Somaliland. Previously Italians had been attacked at Gondar and Abyssinia offered amends.

December 16, 1934

Haile Sellassie I. Rejects Idea of an Italian Sphere

Asserts Granting of Police Powers Would Lead to Annexation—Reaffirms Nation's Readiness to Defend Itself, if Invaded.

Emperor Haile Sellassie of Ethiopia, in response to an invitation from The New York Times to state his position as regards Italy, cabled as follows:

By **HAILE SELLASSIE I,**
Emperor of Ethiopia.
Special Cable to THE NEW YORK TIMES.

ADDIS ABABA, Ethiopia, July 13.—Under no circumstances will we accept a railway or other zone in or through Ethiopia administered or policed by Italy, because history teaches that the creation of such zones inevitably is followed by annexation.

No such zone exists in the case of the railway from Addis Ababa to Djibouti, and our government has demonstrated its capacity and willingness to accord every protection during more than twenty-five years.

Our repeated efforts to secure a peaceful arbitral settlement have been constantly resisted by Italy, which originally refused arbitration and only accepted with bad grace after three appeals to the League of Nations, and now again manifests repugnance toward an arbitral and peaceful settlement by refusing to hear the presentation of Ethiopia's case and refusing to appoint a fifth arbitrator, declaring this unnecessary.

Our attitude toward Italian territorial and political aspirations in Ethiopia remains unchanged since our illustrious predecessor, King Menelik, declared in 1894 that he would not remain an indifferent spectator if foreign powers attempted the partition of Ethiopia, which had been for more than fourteen centuries an island of Christians in a sea of pagans, and that as the All-Powerful had protected Ethiopia up to that time, he was confident that the same protection would be accorded in the future, and that Ethiopia would not be permitted to be divided among other powers.

Imbued with the same ardent faith, we will continue our efforts to secure a peaceful settlement in conformity with the (Briand-Kellogg) pact and our treaty of 1928 with Italy. And only if these fail and when Italy commences a further invasion of Ethiopian territory will we offer armed resistance in defense of our political independence and territorial integrity, leaving to Italy the odium of repudiating international obligations.

We nourish no illusions of the difficulty of the task confronting us, but we are confident of Divine aid and of the sympathy of the civilized world in resisting the territorial aspirations of a power which, while seeking to disguise these as a mission of civilization, rejects every means of pacific settlement elaborated by modern civilization.

July 14, 1935

ETHIOPIA'S EMPEROR FACES THE STORM

Haile Selassie Stands Alone, Endeavoring to Protect His Ancient Nation Against an Encroaching World

By JOSEF ISRAELS 2d

IN the sprawling, haphazardly built palace, or "Gebbi," at Addis Ababa lives the man who is today the storm centre of the Ethiopian crisis. He is medium-sized, dark, with a black beard and the slight, sensitive features that characterize his proud Amharic race. The baptismal name he bears as Emperor of Ethiopia is Haile Selassie, meaning, in the Geze (classic) tongue, the Power of Trinity; his titles are more imposing, though scarcely more dignified, than the simple royal figure who bears them.

Haile Selassie, born Tafari Makonnen, is Lord King of Kings of Ethiopia, Conquering Lion of the Tribe of Judah, the Elect of God, the Light of the World, Defender of the Faith. He stands alone, an almost prophetic figure, against an encroaching world, perhaps the last representative of the absolute monarchs. His country, the last free territory of Africa, is threatened with attack by Italy; his fate and the fate of his people involve, perhaps, the peace of Europe.

Haile Selassie's position has always been difficult. On the one hand he has been faced with the necessity of maintaining his power and popularity at home in his semi-Oriental kingdom and on the other of dealing in a modern manner with the Western world. He has never lost touch with the one or with the other. He has always remained free of conceit, bombast or autocracy. He, of all people, realizes best the dangers that Ethiopia faces, yet he has never lost heart, and remains today his country's only great bulwark against the Roman tide from the north.

At home his political difficulties have arisen chiefly out of conflicts with the reactionary element which centred in his aunt, the late Empress. Almost every move he has made to introduce education, mechanical devices or other Western symbols of civilization into his country has been opposed and hampered by members of her party. They are still at his heels to harass him in his preparations for the war that may come. He recognizes that Ethiopia may be facing a struggle for her life, whereas these oldsters, knowing nothing of European fighting methods and made confident by the Ethiopian defeat of the Italians at Adowa in the last century, believe their primitive armies invincible.

* * *

THE proudest boast and tradition of the people of Ethiopia is that their kings are the descendants of Solomon and the Queen of Sheba. The legend, as authentic as any dating from biblical times, runs that Makeda, black Queen of Ethiopia, journeyed with her court to Jerusalem and there shared the couch of the gorgeous Solomon. The son she bore and who returned to Ethiopia as Menelik, the first King of Kings and first ruler of a united Ethiopia, is supposed to have been the founder of the royal line which continues to this day.

Although the royal line is far from direct in its course to Haile Selassie, the best historians and scientists will not deny the Semitism of the Amharic, the ruling Ethiopian race.

The Emperor, who recently celebrated his forty-fourth birthday, is some 5 feet 6 inches in height, with features rather strongly Semitic. His hands and feet are small and lightly boned, and his large eyes have that liquidity which is often deceptive to a European, who may mistake softness of eyes for weakness of mind.

He is a keen statesman, a well-informed man. His education was largely gained in a French mission school at Harrar, where he was born. Here he passed his youth and the province he still considers his home. From the missionaries, and later from foreign tutors, he learned to speak and write fluent French and to understand most conversations in English.

In 1924, keenly conscious of the necessity for absorbing the culture of Europe, he went on a state visit to Italy, France, England and Switzerland, taking with him the principal chiefs of his provinces, who might have been expected to create trouble if left at home to their own devices. He was received with great acclaim in the capitals of Europe. He brought back with him not only a new understanding of the ways of the Western World but many human and mechanical aids to the modernization of his own country.

After that trip his way of living became almost entirely Western, and, though he retains his native dress, both in private and at the elaborate ceremonies which so frequently are held at Addis Ababa, the palace has been filled with European furniture and the Emperor's private meals are now served in the European manner. At state dinners to the diplomatic corps or distinguished visitors, the service is from a set of solid gold platters designed and cast in New York from Abyssinian metal sent by the Emperor for the purpose.

Haile Selassie is an indefatigable worker. He generally rises soon after daylight. His bedroom is rather stuffily furnished, crowded with plush and leather, and he makes his headquarters in a small and not impressively decorated study. Here the private work of the State is carried on. Unable to make use of many of the mechanical conveniences enjoyed by other rulers, he must depend mainly upon swift-footed native carriers for communication with the outlying provinces. Even at the very best speed of the messengers it is sometimes two or three weeks, particularly in the rainy season, before word can be brought from one of the northern provinces to Addis Ababa.

There is a telephone at his elbow, but it is connected with only the local exchange, and this has few subscribers beyond the postoffice, the other government offices and the foreign legations. Yet the Emperor's soft and pleasant voice is often heard over the wire by the Ministers of the foreign countries, whom he frequently consults.

* * *

IN his communications with the outer world he is also considerably hampered. The only reliably swift cable from Addis Ababa passes via Eritrea to Rome, and is, obviously, of little use in the present situation. There is also the antique and uncertain telegraph which follows the railroad down to Djibouti, where a French wireless station relays messages to Paris. Recently, under Italian auspices, the first of what was to be a series of short-wave radio stations was set up in Addis Ababa. Others were to be installed in the outlying provinces, but this work has, of course, been suspended.

The Emperor spends his morning receiving the messages of his Governors and chiefs, greeting callers from the legations and transacting business in connection with his large private holdings — mining and farming lands. He lunches usually in private with his wife, and takes the customary rest period during the heat of the day. In the afternoon he is available to outsiders, native or foreign, who have business to transact.

Twice a week the sovereign presides in person at a Supreme Court, to which the major civil and criminal litigation of the country comes for final adjudication. In the evenings he reads in his elaborate library, continually supplied, through the Abyssinian foreign representatives, with the newest books and periodicals of the world, and occasionally entertains at a state or private dinner, after which the diversion is usually motion pictures.

He has never had much leisure, and in these troubled days he finds himself scarcely a moment to spare to the family to whom he is devoted. This family consists of his wife, Waizeru Menin, the Empress; two daughters and three sons. One daughter is married to the Ras Desta Demtu, who visited Europe and the United States in 1934. The Crown Prince, Asfa Wassen, is busy being educated by American and European tutors.

The favorite child of the Emperor seems to be his second son, Makonnen, on whom he has conferred the title, new to Ethiopia, of the Duke of Harrar. This boy is a great favorite, and is rarely away from his father's side, hearing with him all the affairs of state and learning the lessons that the Emperor later hopes will fit him to be an important member of the ruling class, if not the Emperor. Under Ethiopian custom, the Crown Prince need not necessarily succeed to the throne. It is the Emperor's privilege to nominate another member of his family, if he so desires.

Incidentally, Haile Selassie has been married twice. His first wife died childless. He is devoted to his second, and does not avail himself of the Ethiopian aristocrat's privilege of marrying or "protecting" additional wives or concubines. He is pious, but not fanatically so. He attends the Coptic church, but no more than convention requires.

* * *

FOREIGN visitors are generally first received by the Emperor at a formal audience in a small throne room in the substantially built stone part of the rambling and rather unattractive palace. The Emperor asks polite questions and receives conventional answers and the audience is swiftly terminated.

It was the writer's good fortune to be summoned to the palace on other occasions, generally for informal dinners at which the principal guests were members of legation staffs and some of the medical, educational, engineering and other foreign experts brought to the country by the Emperor's desire for Western counsel on modern developments.

At such gatherings the conversation flows steadily, the Emperor drawing information from his visitors and stating his desire to take the lessons of the rest of the world to heart. He believes, he has said, in the slow development of Ethiopia; he knows that he must avoid shocking, with swift changes, a people whose manner of living is practically unchanged from that of their ancestors a thousand years ago.

He believes in bringing the Ethiopian women out of their retirement and gradually projecting them into the forefront of life and affairs, and toward this end he has at his own expense brought European and American teachers to Addis Ababa to conduct a girls' school, which supplements the educational facilities created for the male youth of the country. At government expense youths from the better families have traveled to Europe and America for training.

* * *

THE Emperor has created a printing house to publish Abyssinian literature, both in the Amharic and Geze (religious) languages. His printing house has succeeded in publishing and widely distributing through the nation stories about Ethiopia's modern life and the country's history, as well as an informative geography of the world.

He has also published a newspaper called Berhanana Salam (Light and Peace), containing native poetry, news of Ethiopian events and articles on economics, politics and other matters in which he believes the learned class of his country will be interested.

Considering his difficult position, and the grave necessities he has always labored under to conciliate not only the opposing factions among his own people but the Western World, Haile Selassie remains outstanding as a combination of Emperor and diplomat, truly a protector of his own people.

From the Film "Abyssinia." Courtesy of Wardour Film Company

Lord King of Kings of Ethiopia.

BIG ITALIAN FORCE INVADES ETHIOPIA

ETHIOPIA WILL ARM TODAY

Emperor Tells League 50,000 Foes Have Crossed Border.

ITALIAN AIR BASE READY

Addis Ababa Fears Casualties Among Journalists in Hotels if Radio Is Bombed.

EMPRESS TO AID DEFENSE

250,000 Men Are Marching to the Border in Advance of General Mobilization.

By G. L. STEER.

Special Cable to THE NEW YORK TIMES.

ADDIS ABABA, Ethiopia, Oct. 2.—The Ethiopian frontier has been invaded by Italian forces in the neighborhood of Assab, the Ethiopian Government announced today on the receipt of a telegram from the Jibuti Consul, Lij Anderge Masai.

[General mobilization will be ordered in Ethiopia today, according to The Associated Press. The Emperor decided on this step after protesting to Geneva that 50,000 Italians had crossed the frontier.]

French sources reported that the frontier, which is east of lonely Mount Mussa Ali, was crossed last week when the Italians hurriedly pushed forward from the terminus of one of their six roads leading inland from Assab. The Italians, with the aid of armored cars and trucks and without encountering any opposition, were said to have occupied a good advance base for airplanes in the western foothills more than fifty-six miles from the sea.

French Guard Their Border.

French authorities, on hearing the report, sent a detachment of native troops to the northern frontier of French Somaliland. Between their line and the southern slope of the mountain there is space only for a track for sixty-three miles. The Italians are said to have already run a track for supplies to the new base, where there is a large number of native troops with a few white officers. This base has armored cars and airplanes of the latest colonial type, including some new Savoia-81 planes ordered from Rome early this year.

Between this post and Assab there are reported to be 60,000 troops, but in view of the shortage of water in this country, which was mapped only recently by friends of the late Baron Franchetti, it is improbable that more than 15,000 can be accommodated at the new base. As there is no concentration of Ethiopian troops nearer than the Aussa Sultanate these troops can soon threaten the Diredawa-Harrar railway without danger to themselves.

Fears are felt here for the Hulhul Bridge between Diredawa and French Somaliland, which thus far has been only lightly defended by Lij Worku, former chief of the railway police and now Governor of Aisha, and a few men with automatics, all that can be sustained in this dry, volcanic region.

Frontier Fixed in 1908.

According to the latest Italian military maps, which were issued publicly in Rome last June or July, there is no frontier between Eritrea and Ethiopia anywhere south of a point west of the potash mines at Kululli near the River Endeli. This, however, is not an accurate geographical statement because under Article I of the Eritrean delimitation treaty signed by Ethiopia and Italy on May 16, 1908, the frontier was delimited as running southwest parallel to the coast for sixty kilometers till it reaches French Somaliland.

Demarcation upon the ground did not follow, but, as the next article said, the demarcation was to adapt the frontier "to accidents of the terrain" and there is no article defining the frontier in relation to the tribes, which gave some initial plausibility to the Italian claim at Ualual.

It is almost certain now that Empress Menen will go to Dessye when the fighting starts with an extremely strong contingent of the Imperial Guard. Mules for the journey are being purchased. Dessye is the capital of her old province of Wallo and perhaps the purpose is to show confidence in the Crown Prince, who is in command at Dessye, because he has been subjected to adverse Italian propaganda.

In Chercher the price of camels is mounting to record heights. It is indicated the Chercher forces will operate speedily in the desert north of the railway, supporting the army of Dedjasmatch Mohammed against Italian forces from Assab.

Count Luigi Orazio Vinci-Gigliucci, Italian Minister, had a long conference with the legation staff until late last night, ending with an hour's conversation with the Military Attaché, Colonel Calderini. Three taxicabs left the Italian Legation for the Addis Ababa railroad station this afternoon, carrying archives. Later the legation staff was seen making bonfires in the garden, probably destroying other documents.

The consular staff from Debra-markos has crossed the Blue Nile, despite the flood. Nothing is known in Ethiopian or Italian official circles of what has occurred at Magalo.

The Italian commercial agent at Adowa was officially reported to have locked up his office after burning his papers and to have left secretly at night, probably over the Eritrean frontier. The radio telegrapher who was occupying the Italian agency office at Makalle also closed the office after destroying essential parts of the radio apparatus, but is believed to be still in Makalle. The Italian commercial agent at Gondar is expected shortly at Gallabat, and the Italian Consul at Dessye is due in Addis Ababa Saturday.

Emperor at Church Service.

Emperor Haile Selassie today visited the Church of Miriam the Virgin on Mount Entoto for the monthly Festival of the Virgin. The steep, winding road, climbing 2,000 feet above Addis Ababa to the church, was early thronged with pilgrims bearing gay cotton cloth which they customarily purchase to present to the clergy at these feasts.

The clergy, seated around the church, in which the usual Coptic mass was chanted to the accompaniment of bells and silver rattles, received the cloth as well as gifts of wheat for the sacramental bread and green tapers and candles for burning in the church. In return the clergy gave parcels of gray earth from an ancient well near by which is considered a powerful panacea and cathartic.

The Emperor, who was received with shouts of "Li-li-li-li," remained in the church ninety minutes. Afterward he walked around the octagonal building, shouldering a rifle with a golden stock.

The only untoward incident came when one of the hermits inhabiting the hill, who was clad in a hairy goat skin, had a fit in the church.

The Emperor evidently appreciated the enthusiasm of the reception on the famous mountain, from which could be seen wide, misty views of Addis Ababa, shrouded by eucalyptus trees, and a plain yellow with Maskal daisies. Entoto was Emperor Menelik's original choice for his capital and the foundations

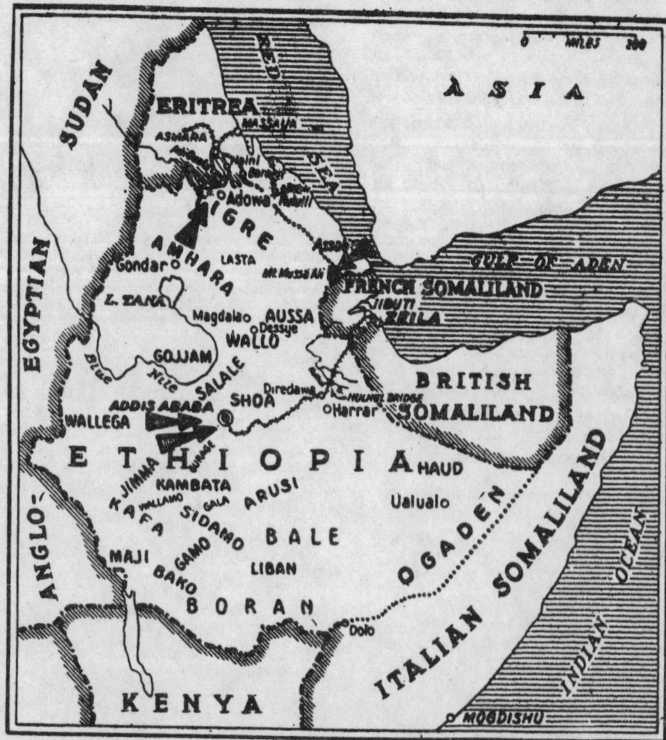

WHERE ITALIAN INVASION IS REPORTED.

The black arrow indicates the point at which the Ethiopian frontier was broken. The border in this area is not sharply defined. The lighter arrows indicate movements of large bodies of Ethiopian troops, 160,000 marching toward Adowa and 80,000 toward Addis Ababa.

of his houses remain, overgrown with grass.

Mr. Purves, a representative of the British Ambulance Service, interviewed a committee of the Ethiopian Red Cross today and encountered the difficulty facing every neutral auxiliary organization here. He was invited to produce a list of the personnel of his proposed service and found the Ethiopian members of the committee objected to all transport officers, contending the organization should rely on transport of the Ethiopian Government.

After an argument it was decided the Foreign Minister should confer with the Minister of War, who has firm control over traveling permits and has already forbidden a Swedish military doctor, who left this morning for Harrar, to take any Europeans except doctors. This indictates the government's tendency to tighten all central control, especially over travel in the provinces.

October 3, 1935

Kenya Group Asks Natives to Aid Ethiopia, Then Fight to 'Emancipate' Africa's Negroes

NAIROBI, Kenya, Oct. 6.—A meeting of Africans convened by the Kikuyu Central Association, a political body not recognized by the government, passed a resolution today declaring that East African natives should "go and fight for their Ethiopian brothers" and appealing to the Negroes of Africa to take the present dispute as the right opportunity for the emancipation of colored peoples "from oppressive imperialist foreign governments."

The resolution, however, congratulates the British Government on its attitude at Geneva and requests that all who wish be permitted to go to Ethiopia to aid in the fight for that country's independence. It also urges an embargo on colonial goods intended for Italy. Kenya is a British colony.

It is most unlikely that Kenya natives generally take more than a passive interst in the conflict, especially the tribes living at a distance from the frontier. Phrases such as "colored workers of the world" and "imperialist governments" suggest that the resolution originated outside of Africa.

October 7, 1935

The League of Nations Stands Firmly On Covenant in Italo-Ethiopian Conflict

ITALY'S adventure in Ethiopia in 1935 cannot be traced to the successful invasion by Lord Napier in 1868, for his engineers found no mineral wealth; nor to the unsigned treaty of Ucciali of 1889 giving Italy a protectorate, for that was repudiated by the Italian defeat at Adowa, in 1896.

In 1923, Ethiopia was admitted to the League of Nations over British opposition, and five years later the Negus complained to the League that Britain, France and Italy had made a secret pact to dispose of his realm—for Britain the region of Lake Tana, for France railway concessions, and for Italy a quasi protectorate. There were repudiations all round with the Negus feverishly urging the United States to raise its consular agency at Addis Ababa to the dignity of a legation.

Late in 1934 and early in 1935 there were clashes on the frontiers with French and Italians; the former were amicably adjusted; the latter (the Ualual affair) went to the League, which decided that neither party was to blame.

This was the situation when Italian conversations at Paris assured Rome of a common Franco-Italian front "on possible eventualities," and similar conversations at London awakened merely British indifference. On April 11-15 the Stresa conference brought about an Italo-Franco-British front—with Germany indicated as the party confronted.

Jan. 3—Ethiopia complains to the League that Italy meditates aggression.

Feb. 12—Italy demands an apology and indemnity for the frontier clash, and on March 5 Ethiopia and Italy agree on a neutral zone, while Italy continues to mobilize and is made war-conscious by the head of the government.

May 7—Il Duce warns the powers to refrain from intervention.

May 20—The Negus appeals personally to the League to enforce the covenant on Italy, and on May 25, the League Council appoints a committee of conciliation, which requires a settlement by Aug. 25.

June 22 and 24—Anthony Eden, British envoy to the League, confers at Paris and Rome; at Paris he sounds France on a Mediterranean naval pact; at Rome, Il Duce reminds him of British possessions in Africa and that the time has come for Italy to have some too. [See Foreign Relations.]

July 25—Italy proposes resumption of arbitration of dispute and the proposal is laid before the Council of the League when it meets on July 31; Britain had already prohibited export of arms to either belligerent. Italy continues to dispatch troops to her possessions bordering on Ethiopia.

Aug. 22—The British Cabinet decides to leave the Italo-Ethiopian question to the League and invokes a collective front against Italy's alleged transgression of the covenant.

Aug. 31—The Ethiopian oil concession to F. W. Rickett is announced and immediately repudiated by the concessionaires, and, for them, by Great Britain and the United States.

Sept. 3—The committee appointed by the League on May 25 decides that neither Italians nor Ethiopians were to blame for the Ualual affair.

Sept. 6—Five-power commission of conciliation is created by the League.

Sept. 11—Sir Samuel Hoare, British Foreign Minister, is supported by France, Russia, and the smaller members of the League, except Austria and Bulgaria, in pledging "collective maintenance of the covenant in its entirety" and demanding that the League act against Italian aggression.

Sept. 18—Italy rejects the Five-Power Committee's suggestion for settlement.

Sept. 23—Italy increases her army to 1,000,000 and mobilizes, as a demonstration, 10,000,000 Fascisti. Great Britain sends her home fleet into the Mediterranean.

Sept. 26—The Council of the League unanimously supports the Five-Power Committee and decides to proceed against Italy under Article XV of the covenant.

Oct. 2—The invasion of Ethiopia by Italy is announced. [See In the Field.]

Oct. 18—France, having won Italian consent to the withdrawal of the super-garrison in Libia Italiana, if Great Britain will order the return of her home fleet, agrees to support Great Britain if she is attacked by Italy.

Oct. 22—Military sanctions against Italy having been debated by the Five-Power Committee, Sir Samuel Hoare assures the House of Commons that they can be avoided. **He supports the formula that financial sanctions will be sufficient.**

Nov. 11—Italy warns the nations of the League that the imposition of sanctions would mean retaliation in kind.

Nov. 18—The League, supported by fifty-one members, applies economic sanctions.

Dec. 7—At the Quai d'Orsay, Paris, Premier Laval and Sir Samuel Hoare, British Foreign Secretary, agree on a plan to dismember Ethiopia to Italy's imparted satisfaction; the plan is submitted to the British Cabinet, and its publication stirs the British public and causes Anthony Eden to replace Sir Samuel at the Foreign Office.

Dec. 11-15—The League shelves the Laval-Hoare agreement, but delays the resort to oil sanctions against Italy.

Dec. 20.—The Mediterranean powers consent to aid Great Britain if she is attacked by Italy, and the prestige of the League is correspondingly strengthened.

IN ETHIOPIA.

Nov. 14-Dec. 20—With Adowa, the site of the Italian defeat in 1896, recovered, the Italian armies from the north, east and south slowly advance with varied success, and Marshal Pietro Badoglio succeeds the aged General Emilio de Bono in command of the armies, while General Grizzoni is withdrawn from the field and made vice-governor of Eritrea.

Dec. 20—With the Laval-Hoare plan shelved by the League and the imposition of the oil sanctions indefinitely postponed, Mussolini decides to proceed to his goal—"Italia farà da sè."

January 1, 1936

ETHIOPIANS SUFFER IN BIGGEST AIR RAID

Jijiga Bombed for Third Day, Supposedly to Bar Imports From British Colony.

Haile Selassie Disappointed by Failure of Powers to Bar Gas —Italians Plan Drive.

By G. L. STEER
Wireless to THE NEW YORK TIMES.

ADDIS ABABA, March 25.—The greatest losses suffered by Ethiopians from Italian air raids were inflicted today on Jijiga and surrounding villages, including El Bhai and others nearer the frontier of British Somaliland when they were heavily bombarded by more than twenty Italian airplanes. This third attack in three days continued for two hours.

The object of these intensive daily bombardments of Jijiga, the largest town between Berbera and Harar and until the end of last year the storehouse of the Ogaden Province army, seems to be to prevent the Ethiopian Government from importing arms from British Somaliland, transport by the railway from French Somaliland having already been refused by the French Government.

According to information from a trustworthy British source the casualties resulting from the first bombardment now amount to about 40 killed and 140 wounded.

Red Cross Reports Gas

Gas bombs apparently have not been used at Jijiga. The Norwegian Red Cross report of the bombardment of Ergalem on Friday charged today that two large mustard gas bombs had been dropped there. One of these exploded, causing thirty-five persons to suffer from the effects of the gas.

Contact was re-established today with Emperor Haile Selassie after a break of five days. It is understood he reported that yesterday, for the first time since both parties agreed to the proposal for new peace negotiations, the Italians failed to drop gas bombs on his men in Northern Ethiopia.

The Emperor asked whether any answer had been received from those powers to which his note protesting against the use of gas had been addressed and was disappointed to hear from his advisers that none had arrived.

This is the first time in history that gas attacks have been made on a black people and they have been employed generally only since Italy has been certain of the postponement of new sanctions because of the long negotiations of the Committee of Thirteen, according to the Emperor's view.

Mustard Near Emperor

A correspondent at the northern front said the Emperor was sitting in his headquarters surrounded by eddying men and mules littering the north plain, which is drenched with mustard gas.

After several experiments the Ethiopian Womens Work Association has evolved a gas mask on the lines of the earliest masks used against German gas in the World War. This consists of a flannel headpiece soaked in a chemical solution and a respiratory tube closed with a gas resistant chemical. It has been tested successfully in a gas chamber.

Harar, which was evacuated yesterday morning after the sound of explosions in Jijiga, fifty miles away, reported the Italians were moving up the Fafan valley and had occupied the Ethiopian camps at Sasa Baneh and Anale.

March 26, 1936

DEFEAT IS IN SIGHT, ETHIOPIANS ADMIT; BLAME POISON GAS

HAILE SELASSIE IN PERIL

Foe May Surround Him if His Troops Fail to Stem Advance.

MUSTARD GAS HITS MANY

Women and Children Among Victims Burned by Chemical Dropped by Enemy Fliers.

By G. L. STEER
Wireless to THE NEW YORK TIMES.

ADDIS ABABA, April 3.—The next few weeks hold fateful possibilities for the whole world. It is clear in that period Ethiopia will either lose the war or by a superhuman heroic effort postpone its end.

It is equally clear that the measures taken by the League of Nations four and one-half months ago have been, from a military standpoint, without the slightest effect and that half-measures taken now would be equally ineffective. There are things this writer knows but cannot write, and from them it can be seen that the League stands on the edge of final failure.

A vast gap now exists on Emperor Haile Selassie's western flank, which it is the duty of Ras Seyoum and Ras Kassa to protect against inroads by an Italian force descending by the Fenaroa-Socota road. If these chiefs fail in their duty, the Emperor himself stands in danger of being surrounded, as it is known he is unwilling to retire any further. The final words of his latest communiqué, "Our troops have advanced," reflect his present mood.

Gas Causes Gaps in Line

Meanwhile gas is reported being used in great quantities in the north. Asphyxiating gases have begun to predominate in the last three days, it is stated. There can be no shadow of doubt that this intensive use of gas caused dangerous gaps in the Ethiopian line which have been apparent since the beginning of March.

A British ambulance unit arrived at Addis Ababa last night from Quoram, following the Netherlands ambulance and all other northern units. Red Cross work has been made impossible for all by Italian aviation, and all units have been forced either to withdraw or to re-equip. The Emperor's army is now completely without medical aid, and the only white man remaining by his side is Konvaloff, a White Russian without a country.

The Ethiopian Government and advisers here were surprised to learn from reports of the recent debate in the British House of Lords that official evidence of the use of gas by the Italians had not yet reached Great Britain.

The Ethiopian Red Cross received statements from a Swedish ambulance unit bombed in the Ganale Denja sector of the south and from Dr. Hooper, a Canadian who headed an Ethiopian ambulance unit at Noghelli, that gas cases among Ras Desta Demtu's troops during December were seen and treated by them.

A Norwegian Red Cross unit established at Erga Alem reported in a letter dated March 19 that gas containers had been dropped there and that one had exploded, injuring twenty-one persons.

Britons Chronicle Cases

British Ambulance Unit No. 1 chronicled the use of gas by the Italians on the northern front regularly from March 1 until the bombing of the unit by Italian aircraft forced it to leave Quoram to re-equip and reorganize here.

Dr. J. W. S. MacFie, at present in Addis Ababa, stated yesterday that he had personally seen and treated between March 1 and 18 several hundred men, women and children suffering from mustard gas burns.

This writer and correspondents of British newspapers have seen and photographed gas cases in the Quoram area.

Emperor Haile Selassie has told people he has been accosted by old friends whom he could not recognize because of burns caused by gas and that he could not sleep at night for misery and because of the screaming and groaning of his fighting men and the country people who had been burned inside and out by mustard gas.

THE NEW YORK TIMES's correspondent on the Northern front, who has just returned to Addis Ababa, expresses astonishment that any one in Europe should doubt the use of poison gas by the Italians.

"My own first experience in a gas bombardment in this campaign," he said, "occurred Sunday, March 1, in the bush between Alomata and Kobbo, about ten miles south of Quoram. Italian planes flying over the area dropped several mustard gas containers whose contents soon impregnated the surrounding atmosphere with a pungent, biting vapor of whose character I, as a chemist with previous experience in war gases, could have no doubt.

"The containers fell amid dense bush, thus producing an effect which was particularly barbarous, as I learned during a visit later the same day to the British ambulance base at Alomata. A large number of sufferers arriving showed burns on their legs and other parts, from which in some cases considerable areas of skin had already been entirely removed.

"These injuries arose from contact with foliage on which the corrosive liquid lay, retaining its potency as long as two or three days. Many of these victims were peasants who received burns while using their customary routes through the bush.

Container Photographed

"The same day a container brought to an ambulance was examined and photographed by the American Military Attaché, Captain John A. Meade, the Russian cinematographer Zeitlin and myself. It was torpedo-shaped and about four feet long. On striking the ground, the nose broke, releasing about forty pounds of liquid.

"During the subsequent three weeks I spent at Quoram and in the neighborhod of Lake Ashangi, I witnessed almost daily bombardment and spraying of mustard gas by Italian planes. Against the latter method there seems to be little protection, unless possibly something in the nature of a diving suit.

"Ethiopian soldiers and peasants, including obviously women and children, not being provided with the slightest protection, receive ghastly burns, sometimes covering their entire heads and shoulders.

"One evening, while riding across Quoram plain shortly after a gas spraying by an Italian plane, I met a British ambulance warrant officer named Atkinson administering first aid to victims. The news that a 'doctor' was present spread rapidly, and within two hours over a hundred received treatment.

"Among the wounded, who throughout my stay streamed in from Makale, Tembien and other areas, were a great proportion of old gas cases, many with wounds so gangrened that doctors expressed despair of their recovery.

"All the facts I have told here have been observed by a company of European witnesses."

April 4, 1936

'ETHIOPIA IS ITALIAN,' SAYS MUSSOLINI AS HIS TROOPS OCCUPY ADDIS ABABA

BADOGLIO REACHES GOAL

Leads 30,000 Men Into Capital as Fifty Planes Swarm in Sky.

RAISES ITALIAN TRICOLOR

Marshal Orders Machine Gun Units to Guard Legations and Troops to Patrol City.

FINDS 'MISERABLE SCENE'

Forces Start Clean-Up and Take Over Services—'New Labor Begins,' Says Chief.

By HERBERT L. MATTHEWS
Wireless to THE NEW YORK TIMES.

ADDIS ABABA, May 5.—Ethiopia's era of independence, which had lasted since biblical times, ended at 4 o'clock this afternoon [10 A. M. in New York] when the Italians occupied Addis Ababa. The newer empire founded by Menelik received its quietus at the same time, and a new epoch in the history of this ancient country begins.

This account is being typewritten in the automobile in which this correspondent came to Addis Ababa from Dessye with Marshal Pietro Badoglio. The marshal with his staff is standing at salute several yards away while the Italian flag is being hoisted over the former Italian Legation, which had to be abandoned when the hostilities commenced.

Act to Restore Order

The first preoccupation of the Italians was to restore order, and this can be said to have been already accomplished, although a shot or two can be heard every now and then.

[Machine-gun troops in armored cars were ordered by the Italian commander to surround and protect the foreign legations last night, The Associated Press reported. Troops afoot patrolled the avenue leading to the legation quarter and Royal Carabinieri were posted all over the city. The force occupying Addis Ababa numbered 30,000 soldiers, who had entered the city in 1,000 trucks, while fifty airplanes flew overhead.]

Marshal Badoglio had made tremendous haste in the past two days in getting here. He traveled for no less than eighteen hours yesterday without a halt and resumed this morning after four hours of sleep.

He entered the native part of the city at exactly 4 P. M., moving through streets lined with saluting natives and past the British Legation, where foreigners have been taking refuge against the burning and pillage to which the city has been prey for four days. The foreign population was evidently in great danger for a while, but so far the only death reported to the Italians was that of Mrs. A. R. Stadin, American missionary.

Before the marshal's entry engineers and other technicians had arrived to take over the city services, as well as the telegraph and wireless.

Marshal Badoglio, speaking to the small group of journalists who had accompanied him from Dessye, said:

"The Negus, following his great victories, has been obliged to flee from his capital. We, following the defeats we received, have arrived here. You have seen in this march from Quoram to Addis Ababa what tenacity and force the Italian soldiers are capable of. You have seen them work in rain, make paths through mountains, drag trucks out of the mud and across fords and all this with enthusiasm and vigor.

"The Duce told me to reach Addis Ababa. I have been able to do so because I have had the high honor to command Italian officers and soldiers.

"You have seen the welcome the populations have given us along the road. They feel themselves freed of the heaviest yoke. Now begins a new labor for us, as arduous as that of the war we won, to give civilization and progress through peace and tranquillity to these people for all."

May 6, 1936

ITALY WELDS A UNIT OF AFRICA COLONIES

Five Regional Governments Set Up Under Central Regime in Addis Ababa.

NATIVES TO ADVISE VICEROY

Six Chiefs to Serve on Board of Consulters—Religious and Ethnical Lines Preserved.

By ARNALDO CORTESI
Wireless to THE NEW YORK TIMES.

ROME, June 1.—The Cabinet, meeting this morning under Premier Benito Mussolini's chairmanship, approved a law, effective immediately without waiting for parliamentary sanction, laying down the main lines of organization of Italy's East African empire.

The empire is to be administered, at least for the present, as a colony. This lays at rest reports that it would be organized on lines similar to the British Dominions in order to give Italy an extra League of Nations vote.

However, although all legislative and executive power is concentrated in the hands of appointees of the home government in Rome, provisions are made for giving white colonists and native populations a voice in the affairs of the empire. This seems to indicate that Ethiopia may, at some later stage of its development, be raised to dominion rank.

African Colonies Combined

All Italian possessions in East Africa are to be organized into a single unit, to be known as Italian East Africa. The capital will be Addis Ababa. For administrative purposes the territory will be divided into five "Governments," all subordinate to the central government in Addis Ababa but nevertheless enjoying a degree of autonomy.

Addis Ababa and the territory immediately surrounding it will not be a part of any of the five Governments but will have a status somewhat similar to that of the District of Columbia in the United States with a special administration of its own with a Governor at its head.

The central government in Addis Ababa will be composed of a Governor-General, who will also be the Viceroy; a Vice Governor-General and a Chief of Staff. Its main function will be to coordinate, by indicating the general policies to be followed, the political and administrative action of the five regional governments. For this purpose it will make use of the superior directorates which will have charge of the various civil and political services.

Two consultative organs will be placed at the central government's disposal. The first is the Council of Government, presided over by the Viceroy or in his absence by the Vice Governor-General and composed of the empire's highest officials. The second is the Board of Consultors, composed of prominent white colonists and six native chieftains. All members of the Board of Consultors will be appointed by the Viceroy.

Regional Governments

The five regional Governments will be:

The Government of Eritrea, with its capital at Asmara, comprising the old colony of Eritrea plus Tigré and Danakil Provinces of Ethiopia as far south as French Somaliland.

The Government of Amhara, with its capital at Gondar, comprising all Amharic populations of the high plateau from the region of Lake Tana as far south as and including Shoa.

The Government of Galla and Sidamo, with its capital at Jimma, comprising all the territories of Southwestern Ethiopia inhabited by the Gallas and Sidamos from the great lakes to the Sudan frontier.

The Government of Harar, with its capital at Harar, comprising all the lands inhabited by the Moslem populations of Harar, Arussi and Bale Provinces.

The Government of Somaliland, with its capital at Mogadiscio, comprising the whole of the old Italian Somaliland, plus Ogaden Province of Ethiopia.

The regional Governments are to be headed by and represented by Governors, each of whom will have at his service a secretary general in charge of civil affairs and a commander of troops in charge of military affairs. Technical officers will be in charge of civil and political services. Each Government will be divided into districts known as Commissariats, which in turn will be divided into smaller districts known as Residencies and Vice Residencies.

The most important inhabited centers, including the capitals of the five regional Governments, will be raised to the rank of municipalities.

Some Regional Autonomy

The five regional Governments will be subordinate to the central government at Addis Ababa for matters of internal policy, empire administration, justice, military defense, colonization and spread of civilization. They may, however, correspond with each other and with the home government in Rome on "everything that concerns their ordinary development and administrative affairs."

Today's communiqué emphasizes that the empire has been organized in such a way as to respect the interests and traditions of native populations. It points out that the empire has been divided into territories homogeneous from ethnical, geographical and historical viewpoints. Each great racial stock in the empire is to have its own territory and government.

The rights of the Moslem population are fully guaranteed and protected. Throughout the empire they are to be allowed to reopen their places of worship, religious institutions and schools. Controversies among Moslems are to be settled by their own cadis in accordance with Islamic law and local customs. The teaching of Arabic will be compulsory in all schools for natives in Moslem territories.

The Ethiopian Coptic Christian Church is also fully guaranteed and protected. Agreements are to be reached with the clergy to provide for the greatest development of religion in the Christian territories of the empire and of the cultural and other ties that unite the Ethiopian church to the Egyptian Coptic Church.

The Viceroy must ask the opinion of the Board of Consultors on all questions affecting the life of the native populations of the empire. As the principal representatives of the native population are to have places reserved for them on this board, they will collaborate directly in the government of the empire.

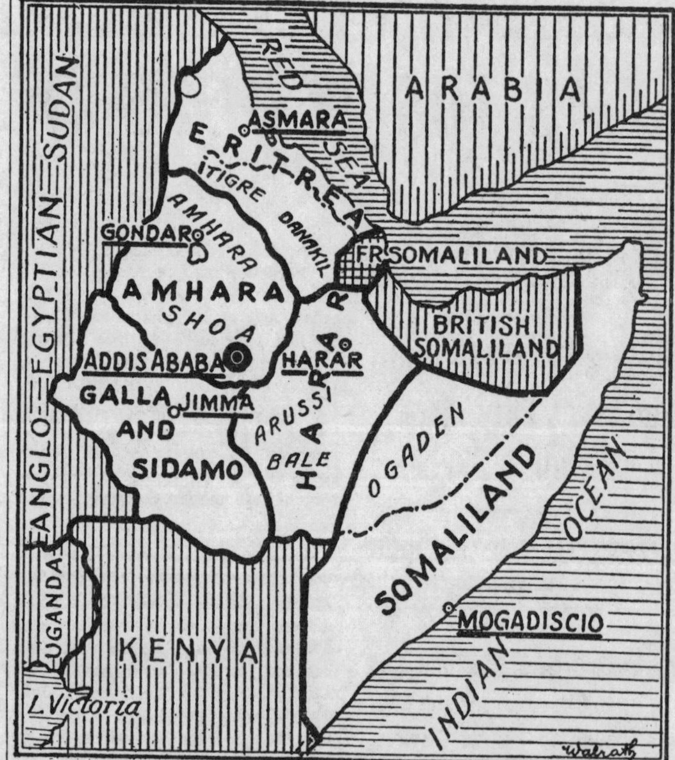

ITALY DIVIDES CONQUERED ETHIOPIA

With Eritrea and Italian Somaliland included and enlarged five governments have been set up. Their boundaries are shown approximately and the capitals are underlined. Addis Ababa, with some surrounding territory, will be kept as a separate entity, the seat of the central authority.

June 2, 1936

CONQUEST OF AFRICA COMPLETED

By the Seizure of the Last Large Independent Region Italy Presents the Other Powers With a New Set of Problems

By P. W. WILSON

Italy's triumph in Ethiopia completes four centuries of a territorial transition that now embraces the whole of the once-Dark Continent of Africa with its 12,000,000 square miles and about 150,000,000 inhabitants. Omitting the single and comparatively unimportant exception of Liberia—a Negro republic on the Atlantic seaboard—the whole of Africa has been brought under the dominion of white men of European origin.

Il Duce won his war despite the League of Nations and despite the British Empire. The security promised by the league has been severely shaken, and questions are asked. Is it probable that the present partition of Africa will be permanent? Three colonial powers—Spain, Portugal and Belgium—are minor countries unable of themselves to defend their colonies against attack by a strong dictatorship. Yet these possessions cover in the aggregate 1,850,000 miles, with 17,500,000 people.

Effects on Britain

The refusal of Italy to submit either to the League supported by the British Empire or to a peaceful settlement of the Ethiopian question with France and Britain outside the League has humiliated Britain and affected her interests in three ways:

(1) Britain's route to India through the Mediterranean, the Suez Canal and the Red Sea has become a line of Italian communications, naval and military.

(2) The Cape-to-Cairo corridor under British control is now flanked by a power strong in Europe as well as in Africa, instead of by an independent Ethiopia, only strong in herself. Ethiopia adjoins the Sudan, Uganda and Kenya Colony.

(3) Italy now controls Lake Tana, out of which flows an important tributary of the Blue Nile, a river essential to the irrigation of the Sudan and Egypt.

Italy has been credited with a desire to build up a consolidated East African empire. By conquering Ethiopia she has united that country with the previously separated colonies of Eritrea and Italian Somaliland. There remains Libya on the Mediterranean, and Libya is separated from the Greater Ethiopia by Egypt and the Sudan, now under the influence of Britain.

Italy has large forces in Libya, and she has been stirring up anti-British feeling in Egypt and Palestine. Is there any reason to suppose that her ambitions extend to a realm which would unite Libya, Egypt, the Sudan and Palestine with Greater Ethiopia—a realm that would include practically the whole of the regions watered by the Nile and its tributaries as well as the whole western shore of the Red Sea and control of the Suez Canal?

This question is answered, after a fashion, by Mussolini himself. He says that Italy is now among the "satisfied" powers and that she is not harboring the more ambitious designs attributed to her. The expense of war is known to have been large and sanctions have severely restricted Italy's trade. Also, there is the prospect of further investment in the development of Ethiopia on which Mussolini indicates a readiness to cooperate with other countries.

Africa Divided by Six

The new map of Africa, surveyed as a whole, is the result of a prolonged colonial expansion, usually peaceful, sometimes accompanied by war. Politically the map is divided among six sovereignties. Two-thirds of the continent is shared about equally by France and Britain. The other third has fallen to Italy, Belgium, Portugal and Spain.

In Africa the average density of population is about twelve to the square mile, compared with more than forty to the square mile in the United States. The population is unevenly distributed. One-fourth

'AFRICA AFTER FOUR CENTURIES OF CONQUEST

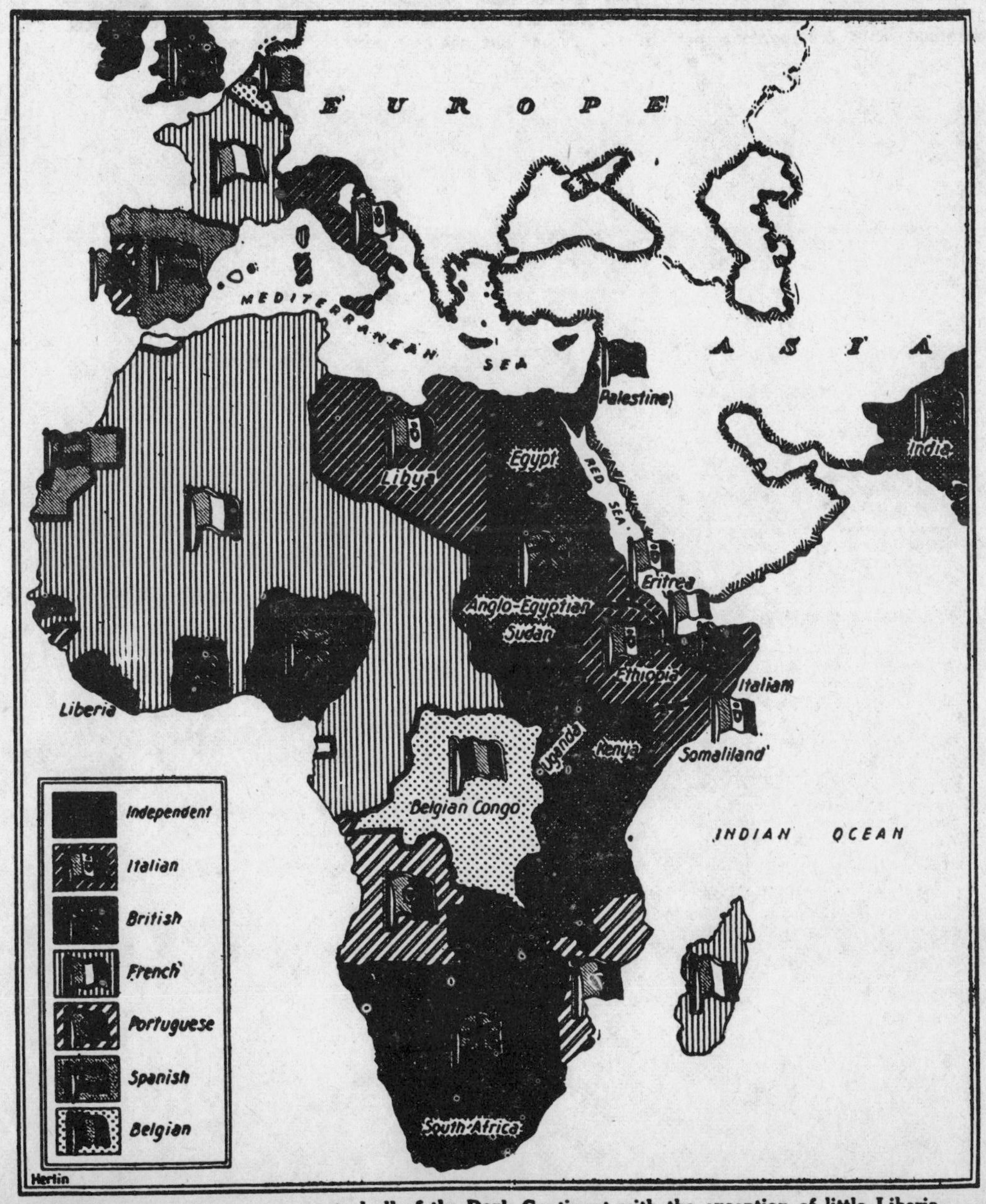

Six European powers now control all of the Dark Continent with the exception of little Liberia.

of the continent, being desert, is almost uninhabited. The Sahara in the north, covering 3,500,000 square miles, is nearly as large as Europe. There is also the Kalahari Desert in the south. Moreover, the equatorial jungle is sparsely populated.

The extent of empire in such a continent matters less than soil, climate and resources. We have the broad fact that British Africa has a population per square mile which exceeds the African average, while the other five powers govern populations which in every case fall below the average. A reasonable conclusion is that the British sphere includes, on the whole, the best of the territory.

France, Britain and Italy

France holds the largest slice of Africa—4,232,732 square miles. Her empire includes the island of Madagascar, in the Indian Ocean, and also the valuable Mediterranean States, Morocco, Algiers and Tunis. But the hinterland of this northern and western seaboard embraces much of the Sahara Desert; hence the number of inhabitants under the French flag is only 38,500,000, or nine per square mile.

Britain (with Egypt) holds 3,925,288 square miles, in which the population is 65,000,000, or over sixteen to the square mile. Most of the British realm lies in the east and south of Africa. It is seen to be almost twice as habitable, on the average, as the French empire. As for Italy, the large increase in her empire is shown thus:

	Sq. Miles.	Population.
Eritrea	45,754	621,766
Somaliland	194,000	1,010,815
Libya	677,000	717,663
Total	916,754	2,350,244
Ethiopia	350,000	10,000,000
New total.....	1,266,754	12,350,244

Without Ethiopia, Italian Africa sustained only 2.5 persons per square mile; with Ethiopia, the population is 10.5 to the square mile.

Belgium owns the immense equatorial basin of the Congo—920,600 square miles, with 9,584,936 inhabitants or about ten to the square mile. This territory includes much jungle, and an important question is what will be its value, and its climate, when the jungle is cleared.

Portugal owns Angola to the west and Mozambique to the east, with one or two smaller colonies, a total area of 796,721. The population is 7,023,860 or nine to the square mile.

Spain's possessions—in Morocco and on the North Atlantic seaboard—cover 140,000 square miles with 900,000 inhabitants, about 6.5 to the square mile.

The evaluation of Africa as a white man's empire is subject to emotional factors, and especially pride of possession. Realism suggests an exceedingly sober estimate. Europe has not been saved from depressions by her empires, whether in Africa or anywhere else. The standard of life, let us say, in Portugal with her colonies compares none too favorably with the standard in Scandinavia where sovereignty is confined to the countries themselves.

As an outlet for European population, Africa so far has been a disappointment. The whites in Africa—say 3,000,000—are only about one in fifty of the people. They are gathered chiefly at the Cape, which is now independent of European control, and along the Mediterranean seaboard.

The present value of Africa as a market for European products is, in terms of Western values, surprisingly small. Take a department store. Only a few of its commodities, the very cheapest and simplest, would have any sale at all in an African village. African trade is as yet but a small percentage of trade in the world as a whole.

GANDHI FOR A PEACE WITHOUT A DEFEAT

Suggests U. S. Halt War Aid Until Britain Pledges Liberties

WARDHA, India, Oct. 12 (AP)—Mohandas K. Gandhi today expressed the hope that Britain and Germany would both become exhausted and come to terms with neither defeated. He suggested that the United States give no more active aid to Britain without getting guarantees.

"She should ask what will happen to India, Asia and African possessions," he said. "She should withdraw any help unless there are guarantees of human liberties. If America is true to her tradition, she should say what Abraham Lincoln would say. America would lose nothing by making stipulations concerning her war help."

With the war drawing closer to India, Mr. Gandhi said that he personally would stick to his policy of non-violence, which he said "is a life policy with me." He added the possibly important proviso, however, that "if the Congress [Indian Nationalist party] assumes power and revises its policies, it has a perfect right to do so."

Congress leaders who are not jailed will meet soon with Mr. Gandhi, but the leader denied that there would be "any important change in policy."

October 13, 1941

M. P. DEFENDS EMPIRE AGAINST U. S. CRITICS

Bars Post-War Tampering—Bahamas Riot Debated

Wireless to THE NEW YORK TIMES.

LONDON, April 15 — Some friends of Britain in the United States still show a complete lack of understanding of what the empire means to Britons, it was declared in the House of Commons today by Sir Leonard Lyle, Conservative. Even in the last fortnight, he said, there had been statements by such Americans.

He expressed the hope that the Prime Minister and the Colonial Secretary would continue "strenuously to uphold the view that there must be no tampering with the British Empire," which he viewed as one of the greatest instruments for good the world had ever seen.

While members of the House seemed thoroughly united behind Mr. Churchill's assertion that Britain had every intention of "holding our own," they had varying points of view on corollary matters relating to the West Indies.

Subjects brought up included the Bahamas labor riots of last June, the possibility of making sugar to the West Indies what coal is to Britain, the salaries of teachers and the need for labor legislation in the islands.

April 16, 1943

Britain to Aid West Africa

Wireless to THE NEW YORK TIMES.

LONDON, May 26—The government's plan for promoting the native manaufactures of West Africa was outlined today at a meeting of the Royal African Society. The British Treasury will make grants totaling £127,000 over the next five years, and an institute for the development of native arts and crafts will be established. In this way it is hoped that the economic independence of native communities will be established in advance of their political independence.

May 27, 1943

Abroad

Africa of Yesterday, Today and Tomorrow

By ANNE O'HARE McCORMICK

By Wireless to THE NEW YORK TIMES.

CAIRO, Dec. 31 (Delayed) — Not until the rough winds of the Mediterranean shake you out of the gripping drama of Europe and the plane skims along the African coast do you remember again the long, long trail that led the Allied armies to the doorstep of Germany. Who thinks now of Tobruk and El Alamein? As the decisive year of 1944 ends, who recalls the days when victory meant winning a desert outpost farther from the outermost gates of Europe than Aachen is from Berlin?

The journey from today's battlefield to that of yesterday is a journey backward.

The storm has passed over the desert and left it much as it was before. There are more hummocks than there were and fewer towns. Skeletons of iron caravans corrode beside the bones that once littered old camel tracks. The face of Europe will never be the same again when the bombs cease falling, but the shifting sands have already obliterated many marks of the African war.

Not all, however. If flight from the fresh ruins of the Italian mainland to the rubbed-out vestiges of Italy's empire is a flight backward it is also a journey forward. For Africa is the main stage of all those reactions visible in a lesser degree wherever liberating armies have passed by.

Africa is a colonial problem. It is the newest, longest link in the war-born aerial network that ties the hemispheres together. It is the last stronghold of protectorates, mandates and condominiums. It is a rude caldron wherein new nationalisms simmer and backward peoples begin asking what's going to happen to them in the war settlements. One disadvantage of piecemeal victory is that it leaves too many issues hanging fire, too much time between question and answer.

Africa's question is written in large letters that can be read as soon as the traveler descends from the murky air of Europe in these wide empty spaces the armies have left behind. What will Allied victory mean for this continent? Will there be a new dispensation or not? Who will inherit what Italy has lost?

The last is the key question. The Naples-Cairo plane stopped at Bengasi, and in a single hour in that ghost town the most pressing problems of Africa came trooping into view.

Bengasi six years ago was a bustling little port parked and embellished with modernistic architecture to form part of the plaster façade of Mussolini's empire. Bengasi today is almost deserted. Farms in the "green belt" surrounding the town are abandoned and revert to the desert. Only a handful remains of the Italian population, one-third whereof was killed in battles that swept back and forth along the coast. The rest was evacuated or fled. The Arab population wanders among ruined houses like shadows of the pre-Italian era when the country belonged mostly to the tribes.

There are besides about a thousand Jews in the town, including former residents and some refugees. These repatriates, said to be the first allowed to return by the British in charge of military administration, raise the question of Allied intentions in regard to Libya. In Italy, despite Mr. Eden's declaration to the contrary, it is still hoped that the pre-Fascist colonies will either be restored to the Italians or placed under international control wherein Italy will have a voice. But on the ground it is assumed that Italian colonists if they return will live under another flag—French or British—or the recent arrival of five hundred Jews gives rise to speculation on the existence of a plan to open coast cities as refuges for Jews or other displaced persons who do not wish to go back to the countries of their origin.

This seems too inadequate a solution of an immense post-war problem to be taken seriously. While other parts of Africa offer possibilities for large-scale colonization, Italian colonies are mostly desert, valuable to Italy for prestige rather than for settlement and economic exploitation, and coveted by other powers only for their strategic importance.

Here again Bengasi illustrates the African story. Today it is only the corpse of a town, the remains of a Fascist dream of trans-Mediterranean glory.

This correspondent saw it last when the airfield was full of planes plying from Addis Ababa, Teheran and points east to Rome, when the port was alive with trig little ships weaving back and forth on Mare Nostrum. It was during the week when Neville Chamberlain visited Rome in a last effort to reconcile Italian and British interests and keep Germany from the Mediterranean. That was the day of Bengasi's brief flourish in the sun. It was the day of Italy's opportunity. The new wreck of Bengasi is flanked by two new airports, one British, one American. It is the hub of a system of airfields and bases built or in process of construction in the Libyan desert.

These airlines and installations, wherein the United States takes so large a part, may influence the future of Africa as much as the ambitions of rival powers or the aspirations of awakening peoples. Africa is already tied in with a larger world than it has ever known. It is not by chance that the post-war problems and post-war atmosphere hit you like a rising wind the moment you strike these shores.

The desert looks as it did before the armies drove across the wastes but actually it stirs with new restlessness. There is no immediate prospect of peace on this continent.

January 3, 1945

CHARTER HOLDS OUT HOPE TO COLONIALS

Requires Responsible Nations to Report to League on Conditions of Peoples

By JOHN H. CRIDER

Special to THE NEW YORK TIMES.

SAN FRANCISCO, June 19—Under the trusteeship section of the charter agreed upon last night all the nations of the world having charge of peoples not wholly independent will for the first time in history undertake to report to a world organizaion on the health and well-being of these peoples.

This aspect of the trusteeship sections, experts pointed out today, seemed by far the most significant advance represented by the new approach to the problems of dependent peoples. It was hailed as a reflection of how far the world has moved in its attitude toward such peoples in the last quarter century.

Moreover, from the point of view of the United States, the first of the two parts of the trusteeship portions of the charter, which applies to all areas governed by nations of which they are not an equal part. It is understood that the United States would be obliged to report to the new league on the health and well-being of the peoples of Puerto Rico, Alaska and Hawaii, for example.

Beyond this, the trusteeship sections assure that all member nations of the world organization may decide on the basis of national interest alone, if they please, what they will do regarding the administration of such areas which may be assigned to them at the forthcoming peace conference.

Choice for United States

This would mean that the United States would have the choice with regard to such strategic islands in the Pacific which may be assigned to it, whether to physically annex them, which would require the United States to administer them under the standards of Section A of the trusteeship document relating to all dependent areas, or whether to put them under the new trusteeship system.

In the latter case their administration would be governed by the terms of agreement entered into between the United States and the proper organ of the new league, plus the general standards laid down in Section B, which relate specifically to trusteeship areas.

Prime Minister Fraser of New Zealand, chairman of the technical committee on trusteeships, expressed the conviction at a press conference today that since the United States was "the main belligerent power in the Pacific it was quite clear that it would have a prior claim," to such of the Pacific islands as it needed for strategic purposes, and that the other powers would have no objection to this.

While there had never been any suggestion that the United States had any aspirations to be a colonial power there was no question, Mr. Fraser said, that while she had no mandates now, she certainly would have some trusteeships in the Pacific—referring to strategic islands—because "the security of the Pacific demands that."

He predicted that the United States would put under trusteeship such islands formerly Japanese-controlled as the Peace Conference might assign to us. Senator Arthur H. Vandenberg asserted that he would stand on the language of Section B, which says "it will be a matter for subsequent agreement" as to which areas will be brought under trusteeship arrangements.

Conflict of Interpretations

Mr. Fraser went even farther, making the general statement that in his opinion the signing of the charter would imply "a solemn pledge" on the part of nations now having mandates to put such mandates under the new trusteeship system. However, others who have worked on the trusteeship document declared there was no obligation, implied or otherwise, for member nations to do this, each being at liberty to make its own decision in the matter.

There was no official statement as to what areas were included under the term "territories whose peoples have not yet attained a full measure of self-government," to which Section A and its subsection "E," relating to the reports which have to be made by the responsible powers, apply.

The subsection says these powers must transmit regularly to the Secretary-General "for information purposes, subject to such limitation as security and constitutional considerations may require, statistical and other information of a technical nature relating to economic, social and educational conditions in the territories for which they are respectively responsible, other than those for which Section B of this chapter applies." (Section B applies to areas brought under trusteeship.)

While there seemed no question that the United States would have to report on these points as to Puerto Rico and the Virgin Islands, American experts said it was still arguable whether it would apply to territories such as Alaska and Hawaii. Some said it would, others said it would not.

New Status for India

But one of the most curious aspects of the new situation is that India, which one would think was not wholly independent, obtains under the charter a status of "sovereign equality" with all other United Nations. The same applies to the Commonwealth of the Philippines, which, while not yet wholly independent, is a member of the United Nations and thus sovereignly equal, under the new charter, with all other United Nations.

Thus, while under Section A of the trusteeship section it would appear that the British would have to account to the organization for the wel-being of the Indian people, under the preamble of the charter India will be recognized as sovereignly equal with the United Kingdom.

While Section B, which defines the new trusteeship system, is regarded as a decided improvement over the League of Nations mandate system, it perhaps loses some of its force because the system is elective rather than compulsory.

Mr. Fraser could argue, on the one hand, that there was an implied obligation upon signers of the Charter to put their old League of Nations mandates under the trusteeship system, while other officials could argue just as emphatically that no such obligation was even remotely implied.

Public Opinion a Factor

But on Prime Minister Fraser's side were all of the high principles stated in the charter, plus the combined force of public opinion in the dependent areas and in the world at large, which would operate as powerful forces to compel nations to use the trusteeship system so far as possible.

Much newer in history, however, is what amounts to a pledge on the part of all nations with dependent peoples in whatever category, that they will look after their welfare and aid them toward the goal of self government, which one official said represented "a first faltering step toward acceptance of the principle that nations are accountable to civilization for the well being of dependent peoples."

It was recalled that the League of Nations mandate system applied only to the areas which the Allied powers put under the system.

June 20, 1945

EAST AND WEST

The collapse of the Japanese Empire, marking the end of a reign of violence and terror, has inevitably released forces throughout Asia and the Pacific which are now manifesting themselves in a revolt against the old imperialisms as well. In Indonesia, in Indo-China, in India itself, in Malaya, Burma and Korea the voices of a growingly conscious Eastern nationalism, demanding of the West the right to independence and self-government, are growing louder. In some cases a stage has been reached in which there is open conflict and new bloodshed.

These stirrings of an awakening continent are still uncertain and confused. There can be little doubt that in some cases they are inspired and aided by the remaining Japanese troops, sowing dragon's teeth before final disarmament. But the voices of new nations being born are already loud enough and widespread enough to bestir the older empires into hurried offers of concessions and reforms. Unless all signs deceive we are approaching the end of the colonial era which began with the discovery of America nearly five hundred years ago and spread European civilization and European power throughout the world.

In a sense, Asia and Oceania are today turning the tables on their European masters. For while Europe has exhausted itself in this war, and large sections of that Continent have become semi-colonial areas ruled by larger Powers or their puppet governments, Asia and Oceania are able to look forward to greater freedom than they have ever known in the past. China, long the prey of all imperialists, and all but swallowed by Japan at the height of its power, is free today with but minor disabilities which it can hope to shake off in time. Korea has already been promised independence "in due course." India, Burma, Indo-China and Indonesia have all been offered increased self-government of varying degrees. Though the results of these offers are still to be seen, the offers themselves are sweeping enough to remove these areas from the classification of colonies. This, together with the decision to place the Italian colonies under the trusteeship of the United Nations, would leave but few spots in the world where that classification could be truthfully applied.

However, the decline of Europe's power is but one cause of this development. Far more important is the growth of freedom and democracy which is in progress throughout the world. The proclamation of the right to life, liberty and independence, with which the Americas first interrupted Europe's colonial expansion, has since been extended to the right of self-determination for all nations, first proclaimed in Wilson's Fourteen Points and again in the Atlantic Charter. Though these principles are being violated in Europe itself, in certain cases, they have found all the greater acclaim in the East, where their translation into independence for the Philippines has set a goal for all other subject peoples.

The questions that must still be settled are whether complete independence is the proper goal and whether it shall be achieved by revolution, as was done in the Americas, or whether there shall be a gradual increase of self-government through an evolution toward dominion status within a commonwealth of nations that preserves long-developed political, economic and military ties, as illustrated by the British Commonwealth of Nations. The former goal and method are the choice of the Asiatic and Oceanic nationalists; the latter are the offer of Britain, France and the Netherlands.

Whatever the solution to this problem is, however, three considerations remain paramount. There must be no rule by collaborators intent on keeping the door open for a Japanese return. There must be no reversion to tyranny, whether by native potentates or by small minorities attempting to bolster up their rule with terror. Last but not least, there must be no impairment of the security of that part of the world for which America and other United Nations have poured out their blood and treasure.

October 21, 1945

BRITISH VOTE BIG SUM TO ADVANCE COLONIES

By Wireless to THE NEW YORK TIMES.

LONDON, Dec. 12—Despite the "unparalleled" strain on Britain's finances, £120,000,000 is being provided for colonial development and welfare under an act that comes into force on April 1, 1946, the amount to be spread over ten years, it was announced today.

The allocations include £10,000,000 for research, £4,500,000 for higher education, £2,500,000 for training schemes for the colonial service and £2,000,000 for geodetic and topographical surveys.

Amounts allocated to specific territories include £23,000,000 to Nigeria, £6,500,000 to Jamaica, £5,250,000 to Tanganyika and £5,000,000 to Malaya.

In a message to the colonial governments, George H. Hall, Secretary for Colonies, declared that "in spite of the manifold difficulties confronting the United Kingdom on all sides the additional effort to provide these funds is being gladly made because of the desire to see colonial welfare and development advanced."

The Colonial Office also issued proposals for streamlining the interterritorial organization in East Africa, including an East African high commission consisting of the Governors of Kenya, Uganda and Tanganyika, a central legislature and an executive, supported in appropriate cases by advisory boards.

December 13, 1945

WELLES DENOUNCES 'IMPERIAL SYSTEM'

WASHINGTON, Feb. 17 (U.P.)—Former Under-Secretary of State Sumner Welles said tonight that the United Nations' General Assembly must face squarely the demand of millions of colonial peoples for freedom and self-government if it were to build a lasting peace.

He said in a broadcast that a new world order based on freedom and justice would not permit the continuance of the "imperial system" and its "exploitation of the weak by the strong."

"It is impossible to conceive of a peaceful world," he said, "were the new world order to be founded * * * upon a recognition of the right of a few nations of western Europe to dominate almost three-quarters of a billion of human beings, many of whom are at this moment struggling for liberty, and many of whom are ready for self-government.

"This is a decisive moment. Unless the United Nations meet this challenge the new international organization will not become the agency which is so desperately needed for the construction of a prosperous, a decent and a free world."

Mr. Welles hailed as "a step in the right direction" the Charter amendment proposed by American delegates that would require Britain, France and other colonial powers to develop, under the UNO's control, self-government and free political institutions within their colonies.

February 18, 1946

BRITAIN OFFERS UNO 3 TRUSTEESHIPS IN AFRICAN AREAS

Bevin Tells Assembly of Plan to Submit Tanganyika, the Cameroons and Togoland

Palestine Proposal Awaits the Inquiry—Security Council Meets, Vishinsky Absent

By JAMES B. RESTON

By Wireless to THE NEW YORK TIMES.

LONDON, Jan. 17—British Foreign Secretary Ernest Bevin told the United Nations General Assembly today that his Government would place the mandated territories of Tanganyika, the Cameroons and Togoland under UNO supervision and establish Trans-Jordan as a sovereign independent state.

In a speech that was altered at the last minute to eliminate references to Iran's troubles with the Soviet Union and Britain's opposition to the Big Five veto power, Mr. Bevin said that his Government's plans for Palestine must await the report of the Anglo-American Commission of Inquiry. It is known, however, that the British Cabinet still favors some form of trusteeship—preferably a joint one with the United States—for that divided and unhappy land.

Other Developments of the Day

The speech of the Foreign Secretary, which emphasized that Britain was determined to give the UNO responsibility, was the highlight of a busy day that also saw these developments:

First, the eleven-nation Security Council, which is authorized under the San Francisco Charter to act for all fifty-one nations in preventing or repelling aggression, met for the first time. Edward R. Stettinius Jr., who has not fully recovered from a recent operation, represented the United States. The chief Russian delegate, Andrei Y. Vishinsky, was not present but is due to arrive tomorrow. Russia was represented by Andrei A. Gromyko. The meeting, held under the chairmanship of N. J. O. Makin, Australian Navy Minister, who was elected its first president, dealt only with routine business and was open to the public.

Second, the Iranian Ambassador to London, Seyed Hassan Taqizadeh, indicated that he had received the approval of his Government for the form in which he proposes to place the Iranian dispute with the Soviet Union before the Security Council. This will be done when the Ambassador feels that the time is favorable to his case and when he feels sure of support from other members of the organization.

Third, Mr. Gromyko, who is the Russian Ambassador to Washington and deputy head of the Soviet delegation, prepared to speak before the General Assembly tomorrow. He is expected to refer to the presence of Soviet troops in northern Iran—now estimated by American official quarters at 75,000—and to tell the Assembly that Russia will withdraw these troops as she has promised by March 2.

The speech of the British Foreign Secretary, which opened the tenth plenary session of the General Assembly this morning, was well received, particularly because it announced the first territories to be promised to the Trusteeship Council and offered independence to Trans-Jordan.

All these territories are held by the British under the mandatory system of the League of Nations, and by agreeing to put them under the supervision of the UNO the British were carrying out the recommendation of the United Nations Preparatory Commission, which adopted a resolution urging all nations holding mandates to negotiate trusteeship terms as soon as possible. The territories involved are the following:

Cameroons—Situated on west coast between French Equatorial Africa, on the east, and Nigeria, on the west, it was captured by the British from the Germans in 1916 and divided between the British and French under a declaration signed in London July 10, 1919. The country is administered under a mandate granted July 20, 1922, and the British area, with a population of 868,637 in 1939, covers 34,000 square miles.

Tanganyika – This territory, formerly a German colony, is situated on the east coast of Africa between the Belgian Congo and the Indian Ocean. The most important of the three trusteeships offered by the British, it was conquered in 1918, divided between the British and the Belgians in 1921 and administered under a mandate approved by the League of Nations. It has a total area of 360,000 square miles and in 1944 had a population of nearly 5,500,000; the revenue that year was £3,553,000, against expenditures of £3,906,255.

Togoland—This was captured by the British from Germany early in World War I. The British part of it lies just off the Gulf of Guinea between Ashanti and Dahomey on the west coast of Africa. It has an area of 13,000 square miles and a population of 391,000. It is administered by the British Governor of the Gold Coast.

The British announcement does not mean that these territories will go under United Nations trusteeship immediately. At present there is no Trusteeship Council, and it is far from certain that there will be a council before the end of the present General Assembly meeting because the terms of trusteeship must first be negotiated.

January 18, 1946

END AFRICAN CONFERENCE

London Announces Preparations for 'Important Developments'

Special to THE NEW YORK TIMES.

LONDON, Nov. 21—A conference of Governors and Governors-designate of Britain's colonies in Africa ended today after sitting in private for two weeks.

A statement issued tonight by the Colonial Office said that there had been discussions on "many important questions of policy" at a time when "important political developments have recently taken place or are impending."

These developments, it said, affect "the composition of legislature councils, the central executive machinery of Governments and the development of local Government bodies" and "far-reaching plans for economic and social development."

These headings cover problems that have already arisen or are expected to arise from the withdrawal of British power from Egypt and Palestine and the consequent insecurity of the Mediterranean and Suez Canal route as an imperial highway.

November 22, 1947

British Parley on Africa Scored

K. Ozuomba Mbadiwe, president of the African Academy of Arts and Research, 55 West Forty-second Street, charged yesterday that the Conference of African Governors, recently held in London, was "a conference for the execution of the further exploitation of African peoples." He criticized Great Britain for "barring native legislators from the meeting."

November 30, 1947

BELGIUM GIVES REPLY ON TRUST TERRITORY

Special to THE NEW YORK TIMES.

LAKE SUCCESS, N. Y., June 18—The Government of the Belgian trust territory of Ruanda-Urundi is not based on the electoral system because the inhabitants do not understand the western concept of democracy, Maurice M. Simon, Governor of the territory, reported today to the United Nations Trusteeship Council.

Acting as Belgium's special representative for Ruanda-Urundi before the Trusteeship Council as it considered the Belgian Government's 400-page book of answers to the Council's written questionnaire on conditions in the territory, Governor Simon made his statement in answer to questions from the members of the Council, particularly from Semyon Tsarapkin, the Soviet Union delegate.

Mr. Tsarapkin asked Governor Simon what the Belgian Government had done to educate the natives of Ruanda-Urundi in the significance of electoral government. The Governor replied that there had been no such educational program because the natives must first understand their responsibility in political affairs.

Ruanda-Urundi is the third administered territory to be examined by the Trusteeship Council. The examination will be continued on Monday.

June 19, 1948

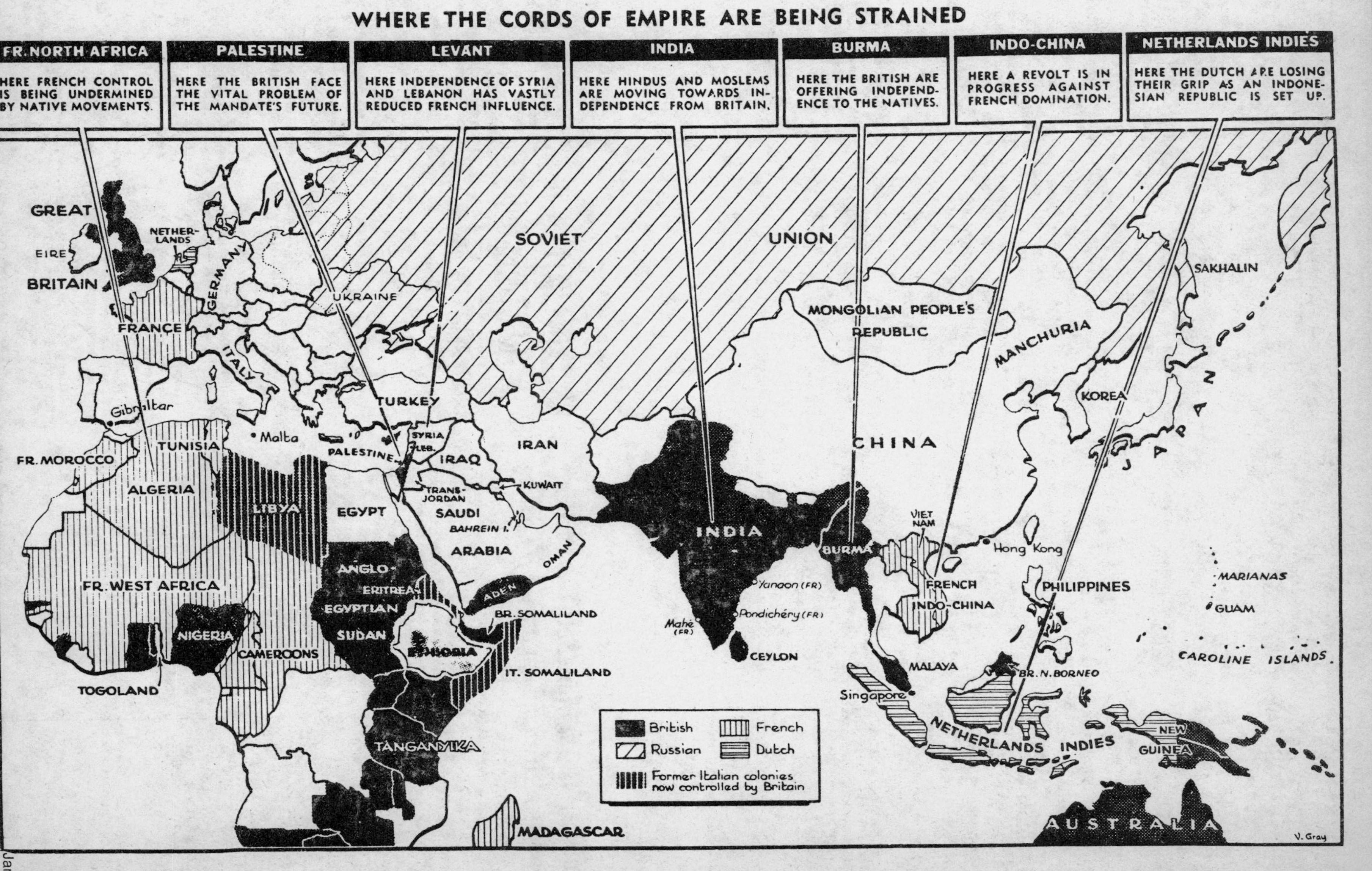

January 5, 1947

TANGANYIKA GETS MILD CRITICISMS

U. N. Trusteeship Council's Report Is Denounced by Both Sides in Debate

By A. M. ROSENTHAL
Special to THE NEW YORK TIMES.

LAKE SUCCESS, N. Y., Aug. 3—Britain's rule of Tanganyika was criticized sparingly today in a United Nations Trusteeship Council report that was denounced roundly by delegates on both sides of the administrative fence.

The forty-two-page report was adopted, 5 to 3, with four abstentions, after morning and afternoon sessions at which most Russian and Mexican amendments—largely harsher comments on Britain's administration—were defeated.

The drafting committee that drew up the report was composed of the United States, Australia, Mexico and the Soviet Union and it turned in a report that was largely an accounting of its failure to agree. Most of the criticism was based on charges that the report gave no clear picture of the Council's feeling, was confused and sometimes inaccurate and contradictory.

Russia's Semyon K. Tsarapkin took his usual unfavorable view of the report because it did not go far enough. Several administering powers also attacked it.

New Zealander Shocked

John Reid, of New Zealand, who joined the Russian and French delegates in voting "No," had this to say:

"My sense of shame at this report is so deep that I cannot vote for it. It is a shocking piece of work. The only impression it will create is that we are thoroughly confused and unable to grapple with our problems."

Sir Alan Burns, British delegate, appealed to Mr. Reid to abstain for fear that the report would be defeated.

"I view with horror going through this process again," said Sir Alan.

Mr. Reid shot back: "It is less a horror than this report."

As in the debates on Belgium's government of Ruanda Urundi and Australia's rule of New Guinea, one of the main issues was the proposal of the administering authority to combine the trust territory in an administrative union with an outright possession.

In 1947, Britain passed an order linking Tanganyika administratively with Kenya and Uganda, and the Council's report asked that it be kept informed of the effect of the reorganization on the chances for advancement of the people of the trust area. Mr. Tsarapkin tried several times to put the Council on record as opposed to the administrative union but all his proposals were defeated.

Almost twenty votes were taken. In most cases the winning side was composed of the United States, Britain, France, Belgium, Australia and New Zealand, the six administering powers. The line-up of votes, however, did not hold in all cases and on many ballots the administering powers were joined by some non-administering nations.

As finally adopted, the report, on the critical side, noted that no electoral system existed and none was contemplated, that the existing tribal structure was an "obstacle" to advancement of natives, that educational facilities were inadequate, that more money should be spent for schools and teacher-training and for mass education.

August 4, 1948

AFRICANS' DISTRUST OF WHITES DEPLORED

Special to THE NEW YORK TIMES.

LONDON, Aug. 3—The distrust and suspicion that the African native has for the European at present is poisoning life on the Gold Coast, it was stated in the report of a British commission of inquiry, issued today.

The commission, which investigated the disturbances in the colony in February and March, exonerated the police who fired on the rioters. Twenty-nine persons were killed and 273 injured during the riots.

Among the underlying reasons for the clashes the report said, was the fact that African soldiers were disappointed at the conditions in their homeland after war service, "either from specious promises made before demobilization, or a general expectancy of a golden age for heroes."

The commission found that other causes of unrest were "a feeling of political frustration among the educated Africans who saw no prospect of ever experiencing political power under existing conditions," and the Government's failure to realize that with the spread of liberal ideas and increasing literacy the star of rule through the chiefs was on the wane.

August 4, 1948

U. N. Mission Urges More Self-Government In Report on British Tanganyika Territory

Special to THE NEW YORK TIMES.

LAKE SUCCESS, Dec. 7—The British administering authorities of the African Territory of Tanganyika have been urged by an on-the-spot United Nations mission to encourage the 6,000,000 African inhabitants in the area to seek increased participation in government affairs.

In a 205-page report on their inspection of Tanganyika, made public here today, the visiting United Nations mission urged also the expansion of educational facilities as a major factor in accelerating the inhabitants' progress toward self-government.

The Tanganyika report, based on a six weeks' study of the African Territory by a four-nation mission, comments favorably on the work undertaken by the British authorities to develop the natural resources of the Territory and promote its commerce and industry through a ten-year development and welfare plan.

In the mission's report, which will be submitted to the Trusteeship Council at its next session, the four visiting officials recommended greater political planning for the Territory and the appointment of more African inhabitants to government boards and committees, such as the labor board. The mission proposes also that agricultural development be broadened, that textile factories be established to use locally produced cotton and that labor conditions for workers and their families be improved.

December 8, 1948

BRITAIN LIMITS U. N. IN TRUST MERGERS

J. M. Martin Tells Committee Decisions on Colonies Are Not Open to Interference

By WELLES HANGEN
Special to THE NEW YORK TIMES.

LAKE SUCCESS, Oct. 25—Britain told a fifty-nine-member committee of the United Nations General Assembly today that she never would permit the world organization to intervene beforehand in projected mergers between British Crown colonies and United Nations trust areas under British administration.

In a long statement before the Trusteeship Committee, J. M. Martin, former Colonial Office Adviser to Winston Churchill, delivered what appeared to be Britain's final word on the controversial question of preserving the separate identity of African and Pacific trust areas, with a population of 15,000,000 persons, in relation to outright colonial possessions.

Mr. Martin expressed adamant opposition to the suggestion that the United Nations should supervise administration of colonial holdings with which trust territories have been merged. His government could "in no circumstances" allow international control of parts of its colonial empire, Mr. Martin insisted.

Fear for System Expressed

The British policy declaration came on the heels of a bitter debate in the Assembly's Trusteeship Committee, in which many delegations expressed fear that the continued existence of the system of international jurisdiction over colonial areas was dangerously jeopardized by so-called administrative unions of such territories with ordinary imperial holdings.

Britain has unified the trust territories of Togoland and the Cameroons in West Africa with the adjoining colonies in the Gold Coast and Nigeria, respectively. In East Africa she has created an interterritorial union between the former German colony of Tanganyika, now under the trusteeship system, and the British colonies of Kenya and Uganda.

France, Australia and Belgium have similarly combined trust areas under their administration with adjoining colonial possessions.

Mr. Martin rejected a joint Cuban-Guatemalan resolution that would have the United Nations condemn, by implication, political combinations between trust areas and colonies that threaten to destroy the special status of territories under international supervision.

The British delegate also opposed any enumeration of "criteria" that should govern administering powers in setting up amalgamations of this sort, urging that the Assembly merely instruct the Trusteeship Council to keep the subject under study.

October 26, 1949

Expedition Finds Africa Suffering Pains of Growing Into Civilization

By MURRAY SCHUMACH

One of the few major expeditions into Africa in recent years produced proof yesterday that civilization had penetrated Africa's last holdouts of the simple life. The natives now want more money for less work and better working conditions.

The story of inflation and the rising cost of expeditions amid lush jungle and arid desert of the "dark continent" was told by Dr. James L. Clark, who led an 8,500-mile expedition for the American Museum of Natural History.

In other respects, though, Dr. Clark found the expedition business holding up pretty well. At least he and his party managed to come up with a few thousand insects for scientific study and 16,000 feet of color film. Dr. Clark also found time to test watches, radios and ballpoint pens for American companies.

The "growing sophistication of the African native," however, surprised him almost as much as the expedition's catch of stalk-eyed flies and giant termites.

"Africa,' Dr. Clark decided, had fallen heir to "pains of growing up to become a civilized country."

"It's got so that when you take on a cook he won't work unless he has an assistant and he won't do anything but cook. You have to pay $40 a month for a gun-bearer or trained skinner, plus food and blankets and tent, of course. And try to get the gun-bearer to skin! Why, the natives have become as independent as can be!"

Dr. Clark said the natives picked up these inflationary customs because a "boom in hunting has brought sportsmen who pay high wages and give lavish tips." Also, he pointed out, inflammatory printed matter was being passed around in some parts of French Equatorial Africa. The literary work, he said, was done by Communists.

August 11, 1948

'Point 4' Census

In British East Africa, first steps toward rehabilitation and development of backward areas have taken the form of a census of the tribes. Since most of them are nomadic, the task had to be done in seven days by 20,000 enumerators. Prime fact learned was that the population of a region of 640,000 square miles was 17 million, almost 4 million more than earlier estimates. Once the region's "Athamaki" or "wise old men" were satisfied of the value of the count, it went well.

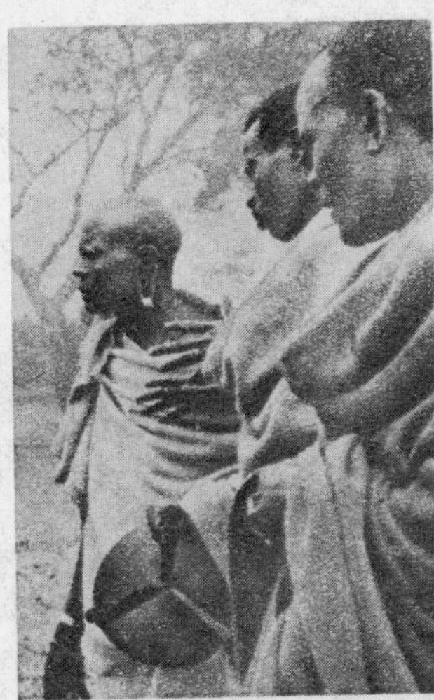

Kenya "wise men" gather to learn about the counting.

The wise man Muiruri obliges the census man, while his "bibi" (wife) ritualistically conceals her features from the camera.

The Chief Supervisor, David Waruhui, right, presents a corps of census takers to patriarchs of the village of Kamariari.

A British District Officer launches a regional drive.

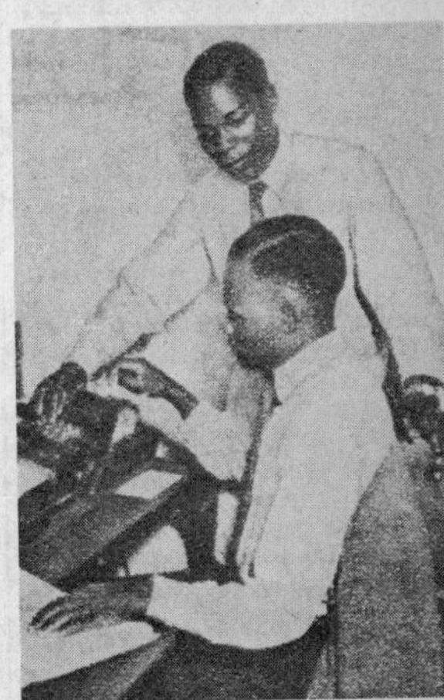

A clerk learns the use of a keypunch recording machine.

August 21, 1949

Belgium Plans Aid to African Territories To Develop Resources for Mutual Benefit

Special to The New York Times.

BRUSSELS, Belgium — Belgium is one of the world's few colonial powers which, in a year of growing nationalism in dependent territories, has escaped any grave or immediate problems of colonial relationships.

In an attempt to forestall trouble in the future, however, the Belgian Government worked in 1949 on plans for developing the Congo and Ruanda-Urundi into prosperous areas which can contribute to and draw from the Belgian economy to mutual advantage.

The Congo, whose uranium is only a minor item on the list of vital resources, is the main beneficiary of these projects. Ruanda-Urundi, which the Belgians took from Germany after World War I as a mandate, is less important and also, to the dismay of the Belgians, less certain in status since recent action was taken by the United Nations on administration of mandated and trust territories.

A plan for the investment of $1,000,000,000 in the Congo over the next ten years has been drawn up. It aims at developing light industry so as to achieve a better balance in the colony's now predominantly agricultural and raw material economy and also internal purchasing power as a safeguard against a sudden drop in world market prices.

The project also is directed toward drawing more and more of the native population into organized, productive enterprise. Of the Belgian Congo's 10,000,000 population, some 90 per cent of the natives still live in the bush, existing in the most meager fashion on primitive agriculture and roaming from one place to another in the attempt to make a bare living.

Financing of the plan is to come from the Government and half from private investors, who, the Government hopes, will be largely Belgian. The Government is interested in aid from President Truman's Point Four program, but on a limited scale which would not represent reorientation of the colony's economic ties.

Experts from the Congo and Ruanda-Urundi have, during the first eight months of 1949, been running at the rate of 11,000,000,000 francs a year. This is a slight increase over 1948. Products of the Congo's mines, mainly copper, make up 51 per cent of the exports. The United States is the Congo's third best customer, after Belgium and the United Kingdom.

A new contract for the sale of uranium ore recently was negotiated with the United States. Its terms have been kept a closely guarded secret, as are the production figures, but it is known that the Belgians had been seeking an increase in price.

January 4, 1950

BRITAIN RESENTED IN AFRICAN CIRCLES

Many Whites and Negroes Feel Colonial Office Talks Well but Acts Autocratically

By G. H. ARCHAMBAULT

Special to The New York Times.

PRETORIA, South Africa, Jan. 5—Few whites in British lands in Africa seem to have a goood word nowadays for the Colonial Office in London or for its twin, the Commonwealth Relations Office. Native opinion is difficult to assess—it all depends on the assessor.

Yet one may gather from a New Year message from Arthur Creech Jones, the Colonial Secretary, that the opinion is not altogether favorable. It began: "I ask you to trust our friendship," and went on to enumerate colonies where local government is being evolved. Therein lies most of the story.

Loudest recriminations come from settlers in Northern and Southern Rhodesia, whose aspirations toward a Central African Federation as the germ of "British Capricorn Africa" have been checked by the insistence in London on "obligations to the African populations" and "the wishes of the Africans."

From personal survey and trustworthy reports, the writer can define these wishes on broad lines: Negro intellectuals (a small minority) demand equality with the whites; the still primitive Negroes (the great majority) are instinctively suspicious of any change and cling tenaciously to what they have.

In reality, British policy has remained fairly constant since William Ewart Gladstone became Colonial Secretary in 1845. As the future apostle of "Gladstonian liberalism," he believed in trusteeship and representative assemblies, a doctrine culminating today on all sides in a sprouting of councils and committees of all sorts—all-white, mixed, or all Negro.

As to trusteeship, the whites urge that if it implies retirement of the guardian when the ward matures, they have no inducement to spend time, effort and money on development. As to councils, the Anglican Bishop of Nyasaland, after having served six years on the Legislative Council, described it recently as having "an ornamental democratic façade," but as remaining "essentially oligarchic" because Government officials held the majority. The Bishop is not alone in protesting that "London talks democratic but acts bureaucratic."

Mr. Jones said also in his message:

"Some among you may still think that advances have to be wrung from Britain by strenuous opposition to the Government and by continued agitations."

There are indications that not only some, but many, still think so, whites as well as Negroes.

In Northern Rhodesia, because of obstacles to federation, agitation has begun for a change of status from a Crown colony to a self-governing colony. For the same reason, Southern Rhodesia, now a self-governing colony, is considering agitating to become a dominion.

In the view of observers on the sidelines, West Africa, particularly the Gold Coast, is well on the way to "home rule" as a result of native agitation, attended at times by bloodshed. In East Africa, on the other hand, pressure from white settlers has stayed a similar trend.

In the protectorates, also, there is uneasiness, not only because the Union of South Africa is demanding their incorporation. Bechuanaland has been disrupted by the marriage of the Chief-Designate of the Bamangwato to a white girl, and a movement is afoot to make tribal rule "more democratic."

In Basutoland, the Paramount Chief (a woman) is petitioning the Crown for intervention because of "lack of liaison" between herself and British officials.

London is damned even in retrospect. When the Voortrekker monument was inaugurated here in December, it was explained on various occasions that the early Boer pioineers went north 115 years ago "in resentment at dictation from the Colonial Office."

January 15, 1950

FRENCH BAN RALLIES OF PARTY IN AFRICA

Special to The New York Times.

PARIS, Feb. 1—The French Cabinet today decided unanimously to forbid gatherings and public meetings of the Communist-affiliated African Democratic party in French West Africa.

The action was taken after Jean Letourneau, Overseas Minister, had reported on Monday's riots in the Ivory Coast village of Dinbokro during which twelve persons were killed and fifty seriously wounded.

M. Letourneau told the Ministers that the riot had occurred when the police charged 2,000 members of the African Democratic party who were attempting to hold the Dinbokro market place by force.

In a communique issued early this morning Paul Bechard, Governor General of French West Africa, reported that order had been restored in Dinbokro and other centers of agitation in the Ivory Coast. A judicial investigation had been ordered in an effort to bring the ring leaders to justice, he said.

Felix Houphouet-Boigny, Deputy from the Ivory Coast and president of the African Democratic party, and Gabriel Darbourssier, Councilor of the French Union and vice president of the party, are both at present in the Ivory Coast.

February 2, 1950

AFRICA IS BUILDING 'PORT OF FUTURE'

A modern port designed to attract overseas trade is now under construction on French West Africa's Ivory Coast and is expected to be partly opened this summer, according to a report by the Economic Cooperation Administration.

Under Marshall Plan aid Abidjan, described as Africa's port of the future, is being developed to bring potential wealth out of the desert and into the world's markets. At present the city is still a surf port where ships anchor off the coast and discharge and load by means of tenders.

In addition to a dredging program, plans for the port include the building of piers and quays and the establishment of modern facilities in the inner harbor.

The work here is not expected to be completed for two or three years. It is only a part, in fact, of a large-scale program under which French West Africa is being developed with ECA funds.

A total of $31,000,000 worth of American goods and machinery has been allocated for the improvement of roads, ports and airfields, the mining of gold and other ore deposits and the cultivation of rice and peanuts.

In the so-called "dead" delta left by the Niger River a 200,000-acre rice project has brought thousands of natives out of the jungle to irrigate and develop the fields. Nearly 40,000 acres are already under cultivation, according to the report. The rice, it continued, will supplement the native diet, which consists mostly of millet and sorghum.

American machinery also has gone into the Senegal region where two projects are under way to expand the peanut industry. More than 3,000 acres have been planted with peanuts, and eventually 80,000 acres are expected to be used for this purpose. Peanuts are an important produce in France where cooking oils and oilcake for cattle are urgently needed.

In 1948 peanuts and peanut oil accounted for 44 per cent of the territory's total value of exports, the report noted.

The French colony's transport and communications system, which has been the chief drawback to industrial and agricultural development, is scheduled to be improved with $1,500,000 worth of American machinery. The ECA announces that it has financed new equipment for the Dakar-Niger railroad and machinery for the expansion of the Bamako airfield.

Development of extensive iron ore deposits in the Conakry region has also been made possible by the use of more than $337,000 worth of Marshall Plan aid.

February 25, 1950

PARIS TO INTEGRATE COLONIES IN NATION

Political Mergers in Republic on Imperial Preference Basis Fixed as Policy

By MICHAEL CLARK
Special to THE NEW YORK TIMES.

PARIS, May 15—The political and economic integration of French colonial territories with the French Republic on the basis of imperial preference was defined as France's colonial policy at a meeting of the Overseas High Commissioners in Paris last week.

The French officials were aware that this doctrine, which was announced today, was not in accord with United States encouragement of nationalism and independence in colonial areas, as exhibited by Secretary of State Dean Acheson's statement on Indo-China in Paris last Monday.

The French press also has given prominence to a statement attributed to Assistant Secretary of State George C. McGhee to the effect that the United States favors the progressive development of African peoples toward political autonomy or independence. The view commonly held in French circles here is that Mr. McGhee's words reflected conclusions reached by the United States diplomatic and consular representatives at their regional conference in Lourenço Marques, Portuguese East Africa, last February.

Commenting on Mr. McGhee's remarks Jean Letourneau, French Overseas Minister, told a press conference today that a gap often existed between the decisions of international conferences and the public statements preceding them. "We must thank the Lord for this," he added.

M. Letourneau, who was flanked by the High Commissioners of French West Africa, French Equatorial Africa, the Cameroons and Madagascar, said that the policy of integrating these territories into the republic, provided for by the present Constitution, had become a basic goal of French colonial policy. He emphasized, however, that this policy did not apply to the associated states of Indo-China.

Political autonomy or independence for African peoples, M. Letourneau said, would lead to a "Balkanization" of the Continent, would hinder economic development and backfire on the same statesmen who made generous but purely verbal pronouncements.

M. Letourneau declared that while no one in France wanted to base the economy of the French Union on what he called an imperial pact, some degree of imperial preference still appeared to be highly desirable. Such a system, he said, would hasten the reduction of trade barriers sought by the European Marshall Plan Council. He added that a concomitant readjustment of customs tariffs was in progress throughout the French Union.

According to M. Letourneau, the primary object of the conference of high commissioners was to coordinate the application of the long-term plan for equipment and modernization of territories coming under the Overseas Ministry, a plan designed to increase productivity and stimulate trade.

The Overseas Minister said that although the great strategic importance of France's African territories had been proved in two world wars, the program for their modernization and equipment had not been influenced by the imperatives of national defense. "You cannot hastily push these areas toward excessive industrialization," he commented.

May 16, 1950

Africans in a Plea to U. N. Charge French Retaliation

Special to THE NEW YORK TIMES.

LAKE SUCCESS, June 15—French administrators in West Africa have been accused of arresting a Cameroon tribal chief for signing a telegram of complaint addressed to the United Nations.

The charge came in two petitions sent to the United Nations Trusteeship Council from the French Cameroons, a territory run by France under agreement with the world organization. Postmarked Duala, the petitions were signed by the Union des Populations de Cameroun.

The petitions, both sent out April 25, 1950, said that Mathias Djoumessi, "traditional chief of the Bamileke people, who rules over a population of more than 10,000," was arrested April 21 and committed to prison.

"On what charge?" continued one of the petitions. "That of having signed a telegram which the people had decided to send to the United Nations in protest against the arrest of our Secretary General, Nyobe Um, and of the Secretary General of the Union des Syndicates Confederes du Cameroun."

June 16, 1950

BRITISH FACE VAST AFRICAN PROBLEM

Seretse Khama Case Points Up Difficulty Of Their Task

By CLIFTON DANIEL
Special to THE NEW YORK TIMES.

LONDON, March 18—Semakula Mulumba, Secretary General of the African League in London, remarked this week that no African problem had ever created so much publicity as the case of Seretse Khama, young Bamangwato chief, who has been prohibited by the British Government from assuming leadership of his tribe because of his marriage to a white girl.

"The consequences throughout the whole colonial empire are serious and particularly in Africa it is likely to bring every aspect of British colonial policy into disrepute," said The Economist, London weekly.

Government's Defense

The Khama case, it was thought in London, would surely be discussed wherever there were politically conscious and literate people and would be used by agitators against British rule in every colonial capital.

The Government defended its specific action in the Khama case as the only one possible. It pointed out that Seretse's marriage had caused upheavals within his own tribe. Seretse's uncle, Tshekedi Khama, regent of the Bamangwatos for twenty years, had left the tribe in protest against the breakdown of traditions by miscegenation. He took his advisers with him, and tribal affairs had since fallen into decay.

Colonial experts said that the Khama case—relating to only one man and his wife and a tribe of 100,000 people in a backward British protectorate—was largely irrelevant to the main issues of British colonial policy: economic development, educational advancement and progress toward self-government. In their opinion the issue of race relationships which arose with Khama's marriage was not the principal one in most African territories.

In the southern part of Africa where the Bamangwatos live in the protectorate of Bechuanaland, there is, of course, a racial problem, one that would be familiar enough to Southerners in the United States. The fundamental long-term question there is who, ultimately, shall rule—the 2,500,000 whites or the 12,000,000 blacks in the Union of South Africa and adjacent territories. For the moment South Africa's answer to the question is strict segregation and control of the Negro population.

Extent of Self-Rule

In areas where the British and not South Africans are in control segregation is practiced, but without legal compulsion. The general policy is that the natives shall participate in government and be guided toward ultimate self-rule within the British Commonwealth.

The extent of self-government at present varies widely with local conditions. The color problem figures in the political situation in varying degrees, usually in proportion to the number of white settlers in each territory and the degree of advancement of the native population. These points are illustrated by the difference between East and West Africa.

While the British arrived in West Africa 300 years ago, they have been in East Africa only fifty years. On their arrival, as has been said by Sir Philip Mitchell, Governor of Kenya, who has been in East Africa off and on for thirty-six years, they found no alphabet, no culture and no wheel.

East African Handicaps

So far as colonial experts in London can recall, there has so far been only one Oxford graduate from all of East Africa while there have been hundreds from the other side of the Continent. In these circumstances, the white people in Kenya hold the candid opinion that it will be many generations before East Africans are capable of ruling themselves.

Meanwhile, the people are governed in one way or another by a minority of white settlers, some of whose families have been in Africa for three generations, and by delegates from Whitehall. East Africa's increasing prosperity has been due mainly to the exploitation of minerals which would not have been possible without European skill. The most prosperous colonies are those of Kenya and Southern Rhodesia, where the proportion of white people is the largest.

On the west coast the racial issue does not arise as much as it might because the only white people are those in government and commerce. Opposition to white supremacy mainly takes the form of a demand for replacement of white officials with educated Negroes. There is considerable political agitation, but the disturbances in West Africa lately have had nothing to do with racial problems as such.

Agitation for self-government is regarded tolerantly by experienced colonial officials; they would be surprised if with the advance of education and spread of political ideas Africans did not demand control of their own affairs.

Because of the absence of a large white population and because of the level of education in West Africa, the British have been able to follow a clear policy of gradual approach of self-government. The Gold Coast is just now acquiring a Constitution that will place a majority of natives in executive and legislative positions.

One of the fundamental principles of British colonial policy is that economic development should keep step with political development and that territories should not become autonomous or independent until they are capable of supporting themselves. More money than ever before is now being spent on colonial development. Some of the colonies are important dollar-earners for the sterling area and the British hope that in due course they will contribute substantially to the Empire's self-sufficiency and Britain's own larder.

In the meantime, the colonies are costing this country more than they contribute and the emphasis is on developing the territories rather than benefiting Britain.

IMMEDIATE FACTORS AFFECTING BRITISH POLICY IN AFRICA

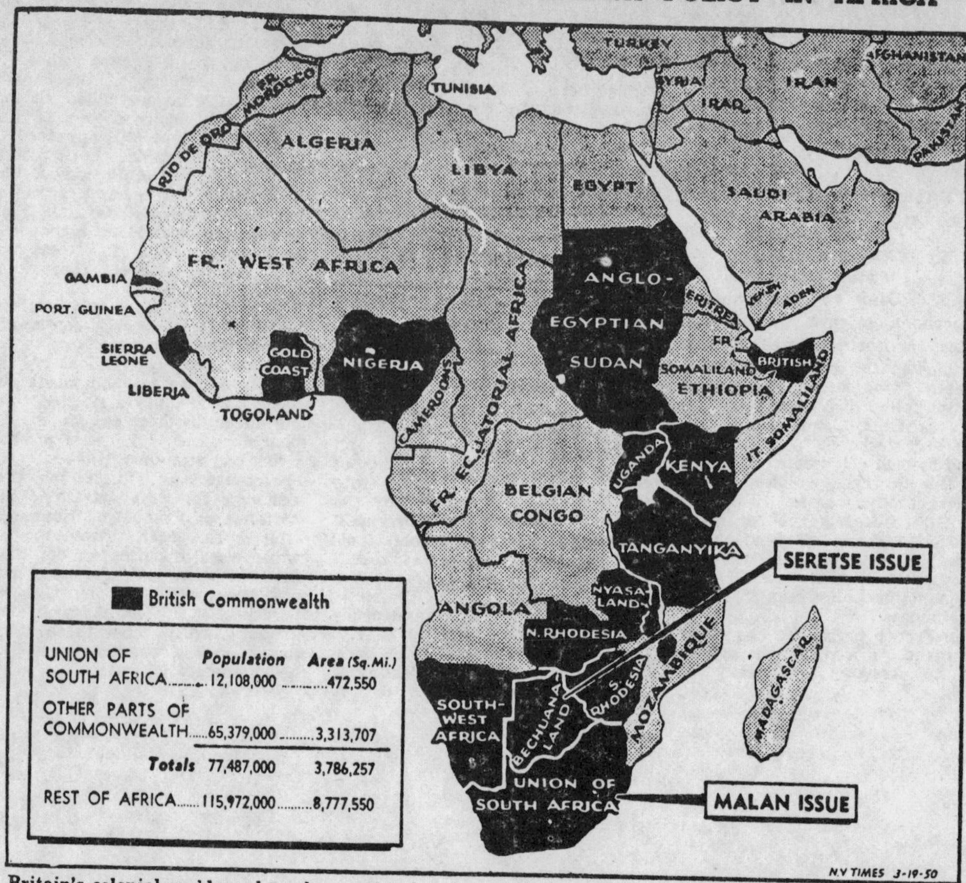

Britain's colonial problems have been pointed up by the case of Seretse Khama. The case is complicated by the fact that the white supremacy issue is so agitated in the Union of South Africa, where Prime Minister Malan's Government follows a policy of strict segregation of the Negro population.

March 19, 1952

BRITISH BAR KHAMA AS CHIEF FOR LIFE

Deny Title to the African Heir Who Wed White Woman—Labor Protest Voted Down

Special to THE NEW YORK TIMES.

LONDON, March 27—The British Government announced today the permanent and final exclusion from chieftainship of the Bamangwato tribe in Bechuanaland Protectorate in Africa of Seretse Khama, Oxford-educated heir to the title who married a white English girl in September, 1948.

At the Labor Opposition's insistence, the House of Commons interrupted its business to debate the decision for three hours. The Liberals joined Labor in denouncing the action as a concession to the racial views of the South African Government but a vote gave the Conservative Government a majority by 308 to 286.

The Government's statement, read by the Marquess of Salisbury, new Secretary for Commonwealth Affairs, in the House of Lords said that Mr. Khama had permanently disqualified himself from the chieftainship and would not be permitted to return to Bechuanaland until "an alternative chief has been securely established." At the same time a post in the colonial administration of Jamaica in the West Indies was offered to the deposed ruler in addition to the pension he now receives from the British Government.

Also barred from the chieftainship was Mr. Khama's uncle, Tshekedi Khama, the former regent of the territory, who strongly opposed the return of Mr. Khama and his wife.

Mr. Khama, now in London continuing his law studies, said he would not abandon his claim to the chieftainship so long as the people of his tribe wanted him back. He said he would be quite willing to go back and work with them as an ordinary citizen. He said he would decline the Jamaican post because there were plenty of Jamaicans who could fill it and he himself could be of greater service to the Bamangwato people.

Mr. Khama charged that the Government was "desperately determined to placate South Africa * * * even if it means alienating thousands and thousands of Africans who sincerely believe in Great Britain." John G. Foster, Parliamentary Undersecretary for Commonwealth Relations, who gave the Government statement in the House of Commons, acknowledged, under questioning, that at the latest "kootla," or meeting, of the Bamangwato tribe Mr. Khama's return had been favored.

Patrick Gordon-Walker, who two years ago as Minister for Commonwealth Relations in the Labor Government had banished Mr. Khama from the Bamangwato reserve for five years, said that today's action constituted a change, not a continuance of the Labor Government's policy.

Anthony Wedgwood Benn, a Laborite, said that since then the situation had changed and the

PARTED FROM TRIBE

Associated Press

Seretse Khama

Bamangwato had rallied to their chief, his wife and child. Behind the whole matter, he charged, was the crisis in the Union of South Africa.

When Liberal party leader Clement Davies asked whether Prime Minister Daniel F. Malan of South Africa had anything to do with the decision, Mr. Foster replied that he had not, directly or indirectly.

LONDON, March 27 (UP)—Mr. Khama charged the government with "apparently trying to placate South Africa." He told reporters nearly all his tribe were "unanimous in wanting me back." He said Britain apparently was trying to placate race-conscious South Africa by offering him a job as far away as possible.

Mr. Khama, 31 years old, and his 29-year-old white wife, Ruth Williams, were banished to London in March, 1950. The decision was subject to review in five years, but today's announcement made the exile permanent.

He was removed as chief in March, 1950, following his marriage. After his exile was announced, Mr. Krama was allowed to visit Bechuanaland briefly while his child was born.

March 28, 1952

Ethiopia Gets $7,000,000 Loans From World Bank to Build Roads

Grants Are the First to an African Nation and First for Non-Self-Liquidating Project —Borrower Also to Put Up Capital

By MICHAEL L. HOFFMAN

Special to THE NEW YORK TIMES.

PARIS, Sept. 13—The International Bank for Reconstruction and Development made two loans totaling $7,000,000 to Ethiopia today.

Although small in amount, both loans break new ground in World Bank financing. They are the first to any African nation and the first to have been negotiated in the borrowing country by a bank mission instead of at headquarters. They are also both loans of a type that the bank is always accused of never being willing to make—that is, loans for general development projects that are not in themselves self-liquidating.

The first loan, for $5,000,000, is for the rehabilitation and maintenance of the highway system. The Ethiopian Government has undertaken to furnish 5,000,000 Ethiopian dollars (about 2,000,000 United States dollars) for the same purpose immediately, 6,000,000 Ethiopian dollars for each of the next three years, and 5,000,000 dollars annually thereafter for the remainder of the twenty-year life of the loan.

The second loan, of $2,000,000, will provide foreign exchange required for projects to be financed by a new Ethiopian Development Bank. This is a type of loan of which the bank's circles expect more to be heard.

The new development bank will be financed entirely by Ethiopian capital, including the local currency counterpart of the $2,000,000 to be furnished by the International Bank. The new bank will develop and finance projects that are too small for the International Bank to undertake individually but are nevertheless vital for the country's development.

Commenting on this new type of financing in a conversation with this correspondent the other day, Eugene R. Black, president of the World Bank, said:

"We have found that there are dozens of small industries that most of these underdeveloped countries need to make the miscellaneous kinds of supplies and equipment to use in carrying out the bigger projects. We cannot finance each $10,000 or $20,000 project individually, so we are going to try mobilizing local capital resources and let them do it with the bank's counsel and guidance."

After the loans were approved by the International Bank's board of governors, the agreement was signed for the bank by Mr. Black and for Ethiopia by Ato Menassie Lemma, Vice Minister of Finance. Both loans are for twenty years and bear 3 per cent interest plus the standard bank commission of 1 per cent. Amortization will begin in 1956.

The governors of the International Monetary Fund elected members of the fund's executive board, the real seat of power in that organization—in a closed meeting today. The only notable thing about the elections is that Czechoslovakia, while remaining a member of the fund, has no director and no vote to be exercised through another director.

World Fund Directors Named

The group of countries in which Czechoslovakia belongs for purposes of representation on the executive board (Yugoslavia, Turkey, Thailand, Ceylon and Czechoslovakia) elected Neda Popovitch of Yugoslavia, as its representative.

Other new directors elected were Leslie Melville, of Australia, representing South Africa and Australia; Raul Ostos of Mexico, representing Panama, Mexico, Guatamala, El Salvador, Colombia, Costa Rica, Ecuador, Cuba and Venezuela.

Re-elected directors are J. W. Beyen of the Netherlands, representing also Norway; Guido Carli of Italy, representing also Austria and Greece; Louis Raminsky of Canada, representing also Iceland; Ernest de Selliers of Belgium, representing also Finland, Denmark and Luxembourg; Octavio Paranagua of Brazil, representing also Peru, Paraguay, Nicaragua, Honduras, Chile, the Dominican Republic; and Zaki Bey Saad of Egypt, also representing Syria, Lebanon, Ethiopia, Iraq, Iran, Pakistan and the Philippines.

The directors of the United States, Britain, France, China and India, the five biggest contributors to the fund, do not change biennially like the others.

September 14, 1950

TRUSTEESHIP COUNCIL IN PLEDGE TO NATIVES

The United Nations Trusteeship Council, in a rare series of unanimous decisions, agreed yesterday to tell the natives of trust territories that the United Nations objective was to give them self-government and to encourage respect for their freedoms without regard to race, creed or color.

The council, meeting at Flushing Meadow, Queens, approved a statement to this effect which will be issued by United Nations missions when they visit trust territories.

United Nations trust territories are being administered by Australia, Belgium, Britain, France, Italy, New Zealand and the United States.

The draft statement introduced yesterday by a committee of the council had no specific proviso against racial discrimination. It merely asked respect for human rights and freedoms. Inclusion of the added proviso was proposed by A. A. Soldatov of the Soviet Union and was adopted without opposition.

A note from the secretariat informed the council that the United Nations had set aside for Africans sixty fellowships in the fields of economic and social development and public administration.

June 7, 1951

MALANISM ABSENT IN BELGIAN CONGO

Natives Found Well Paid and Happy Under Enlightened Colonial Administration

RACE FRICTION HELD PERIL

Mid-Continent Parley Called by U. S. Proposed to Seek Agreement on Policies

By WILLIAM S. WHITE.

Special to THE NEW YORK TIMES.

LEOPOLDVILLE, Belgian Congo, May 11—It is raining in the Congo, rain that falls in measureless melancholy, but this nevertheless is one of the brightest spots in many an African mile.

Leopoldville, seat of this Belgian colony, is alive and happy while so much of Africa south of the Sahara is lethargic and struggling in gloom with insoluble problems of race and politics.

Here, in what is frankly a colonial world, though an enlightened one, there is no trace of the sharpest of all frictions between black and white—the friction of political rights—because here nobody votes, and that goes for whites, and everyone simply looks to Brussels for political guidance.

In this permanent holiday from the highest responsibilities, that of making some political accommodation between whites and Negroes, the Congo's Belgian administrators are making a land of good living for whites and fairly tolerable living for Negroes.

A Reminder of Bayonne

Along the banks of the Congo for three miles and more a fast growing industrial nexus is rising and to go along the dirty river in a speedboat is like passing a little bit of Bayonne, N. J., a little bit of Hoboken and a great deal of St. Louis on the Mississippi. Across the Congo, shimmering in watery heat, stands Brazzaville in French Equatorial Africa—which is belatedly being developed now that France is menaced in Indo-China and having trouble in Tunisia.

The river is aswarm with traffic—modern Diesel-powered barges and old wood-burning steamers—and four miles to the north an old Mississippi stern-wheeler is being used as a training ship for Negro maritime cadets while other Negroes paddle about half naked in hollowed out logs.

Here in the Congo are now meeting, amid French "mercis" and mostly pseudo American "okays," the oldest and newest in this world. Leopoldville itself is an astonishing mixture of continentalism and Americanism.

Natives Earn Fine Pay

So great is the need for labor in the Congo, which has 12,000,000 Negroes and 60,000 whites, that natives earn fine pay by other African standards. In the Leopoldville area—a region where crocodiles may still be seen—10,000 Negroes earn above $120 a month and are paying income taxes in some instances while still praying to heathen gods.

While there is no tally here of political equality or any other kind of equality, every white man employing a Negro must provide absolute guarantees to furnish that Negro housing, food, clothing, and medical attention, including such drugs as penicillin when needed.

The Belgian Congo administrators are a strange lot—unmoved by political talk but generous in an economic sense in dealing with the Negro compared with much of the rest of Africa.

This country, which sells vast quantities of minerals, including uranium, to the United States, is as far away from Prime Minister Daniel F. Malan's South African concept of "white supremacy" as could be imagined.

The leaders here are not "kind" to the native in a sentimental sense, but in a pragmatic sense they are developing magnificent hospitals for his care and in Leopoldville they are building a 72,000-seat stadium for his recreation.

They are well aware of what Malanism is doing to set aflame the entire African Continent with its 200,000,000 Negroes. At the other end of the stick they look with great misgiving, though expressed without resentment, toward what is happening against the white man's interest in Mediterranean Africa.

See Clock Being Turned Back

They think that while Dr. Malan is trying to turn the clock back fifty years or so the British are trying to run it ahead by at least twenty-five.

Accordingly, responsible Belgians here would like to see called a mid-African conference—with the United States taking the initiative—either in the United Nations or North Atlantic Treaty Organization.

They would like this conference to exclude both the Union of South Africa and all Africa north of the Sahara. It therefore would encompass Belgian, British, French and Portuguese Africa. Its purpose would be to try to develop agreed policies with which to resist both Malanism and "premature north African liberalism."

The Belgians think that is the way to save Africa from what happened to China—the extirpation of the middle way by extremes of left and right.

They think that the outside world and particularly the United States has far too little understanding of what an indispensable and inexhaustible storehouse Africa has become for the whole world's industrial civilization.

They think, and they are immensely practical people, that time is running out for the salvation of this vital mid-earth position and that the free world's whole future may be won or lost in Africa within five years.

May 12, 1952

BRITISH U. N. AIDE LAUDS TRUST ROLE

Burns Outlines Progress in 5-Year Review on Cameroons, Tanganyika and Togoland

Special to THE NEW YORK TIMES.

UNITED NATIONS, N. Y., Nov. 19—British administration in Tanganyika and two other colonies in East Africa was defended today by Sir Alan Burns, British representative on the Trusteeship Council. In reporting to the United Nations General Assembly's Trusteeship Committee, he said:

"It is a long road from tribal warfare to the apparatus of parliamentary democracy. We must build a nation. It is to this task that we have set our hands. Our achievement during the five years which I now review is, I think, a good augury for our final success in the not too distant future."

The statement was the first to be delivered by an administering power in the opening of debate on a report from the Trusteeship Council on the 30,000,000 persons living in eleven trust territories operated under the United Nations system in Africa and the Pacific.

Criticism was anticipated by Sir Alan with the observation that the "most extreme" opposition would doubtless come, as usual, from the Soviet bloc,

Sir Alan warned the committee in general that "the best will in the world" applied to the best of all policies could not hasten the development of "those peoples who have, through accidents of history and geography, remained over-long in a backward state."

A year is not long enough to serve as a yardstick for measuring improvement, he said, in explaining why he was reporting on a five-year basis.

The report he submitted on Tanganyika, Cameroons and British Togoland covered economic expansion, education, political evolution and social progress on a broad range.

"The primary need is to insure that the development of food supplies outstrips the growth of population and that the fertility of the soil is enhanced and not diminished by these increased yields," said Sir Alan. "Our habit is to build from the bottom up and our critics are sometimes impatient because they do not see suddenly flowering a fully self-sufficient central administration based on the pure principles of democracy. Such a flower, without roots, would perish."

British control over the trust territories, he added, has been leading the people "surely toward the goal of self-government or independence."

In the Social, Cultural and Humanitarian Committee, Jamil M. Baroody of Saudi Arabia denounced THE NEW YORK TIMES for its editorial, "The Bogy of Colonialism," published Nov. 10, which, he maintained, was "propaganda being made in the West against the right of self-determination."

A key sentence in the editorial was:

"In reality, national sovereignty of itself solves no problems, and usually creates new ones temporarily which are worse than the old."

The editorial, in Mr. Baroody's opinion, was evidence of a clash between two fundamental freedoms: that of information and that of self-determination. THE NEW YORK TIMES' editiorial was typical of "reams" of newspaper copy published in this country in opposition to the trend for independence abroad, he said.

"I feel constrained to tell those who are writing such editorials that they are not helping the cause of freedom and peace in the world," Mr. Baroody added.

November 20, 1952

Industrialization Causing 'Growing Pains' In Africa

Africa's economic "growing pains," including the hurried adjustment of "virtually neolithic tribesmen" to industrial society, were described yesterday by two Columbia University professors who returned Saturday from a fourteen-week journey through the central and southern parts of the continent.

They are Kingsley Davis, professor of Sociology, and William A. Hance, Associate Professor of Economic Geography, who made the 17,000-mile trip, costing $20,000, under the sponsorship of the Carnegie Corporation of New York to stimulate interest in areas that are "still too little known and understood in America."

African industry has developed tremendously since the war, they said, because of favorable trade relations and increased European investment, principally along the Ivory and Gold Coasts, in the Belgian Congo and in Southern Rhodesia.

"Hostility toward whites is not characteristic of these regions," Professor Davis declared, adding that the natives generally regarded industrialization by whites as necessary to their economic betterment. Further development, he said, would require improvements in public health conditions, in schools for vocational education and transportation facilities.

"Africa is in for a tremendous increase in population in industrialized areas," he said, adding that while a high mortality rate generally occurred where primitive groups were "rushed" into an industrial society, "some parts of Africa are over this hump." This situation, he continued, "confronts administrators with the problem of balancing funds between capital investment and public health."

The two professors with Sanford Mosk, Professor of Economics at Stanford University, and Eric Larrabee of Harper's magazine, comprised the third group sent to Africa by the Carnegie Corporation since 1951.

December 18, 1952

TROPIC AFRICA PUT IN ECONOMIC CLAMP

Special to THE NEW YORK TIMES.

UNITED NATIONS, N. Y., April 11—Tropical Africa has reached a critical stage in its economic development, United Nations experts reported today in a new regional study of the countries south of the Sahara.

Future economic progress, they concluded, will depend in large measure on improved agricultural techniques and the extension of transport facilities to bring remoter regions within range of markets.

In their report, the experts commented that the native population of 140,000,000 was in the process of moving away from complete dependence on the land for food and toward cash-earning labors. However, only a small part of the population has reached the point where a cash income supplies the "essential" means of livelihood.

The experts observed that the arrival of settlers in East and Central Africa had resulted in considerable land transfer and caused the native peoples to seek employment outside their subsistence environment. Elsewhere, non-native settlers have undertaken transport or mineral and power development programs that have created demand for native labor.

The report, prepared for the Economic and Social Council, excluded from its economic survey of the region the Union of South Africa, which is almost entirely outside the tropics.

It said that in tropical Africa a number of new operations were under way to develop natural resources. All the Governments have stepped up geological surveys, the experts found. Mineral projects are under way to develop iron ore deposits in Liberia, lead in Tanganyika, copper in Uganda and bauxite in the Gold Coast. It is hoped that health programs will put additional grazing and farm lands under cultivation in many parts of the region. It is expected water-conservation projects will also increase the cultivable land and permit more intensive farming methods.

The experts warned that such programs would intensify problems of soil deterioration and declining productivity and that the need for new agricultural techniques would become urgent.

April 12, 1953

Uganda Bans Tarzan Film

KAMPALA, Uganda, May 1 (Reuters)—An old Tarzan film showing Johnny Wiesmuller in battle against African natives was banned in this British colony today because of the racial tension throughout Africa. A member of the Uganda Board of Censors said: "Some scenes which might have been all right years ago are not suitable for showing before an African audience now."

May 2, 1953

POLICY CLASH SEEN IN WESTERN AFRICA

Britain's Encouragement of Self-Government Is Opposed to French Integration

By MICHAEL CLARK
Special to THE NEW YORK TIMES.

DAKAR, French West Africa, Nov. 6—The divergent colonial policies of Britain and France in West Africa are expected to make international cooperation increasingly difficult south of the Sahara.

The British territories, especially Nigeria and the Gold Coast, are progressing rapidly toward self-government. Meanwhile French West Africa is being closely integrated with metropolitan France on the basis of a common citizenship and of interlocking political institutions.

Can two systems so radically different exist harmoniously side by side? The French authorities here are afraid the answer is "no," and they are bracing for trouble ahead.

Relations between the French and British territories in West Africa since the end of World War II have been excellent on the whole, both on the diplomatic level and on the administrative level locally. Technical liaison and cooperation have been particularly close and effective.

It is, however, greatly to be feared that home rule and "Africanization" in Nigeria and the Gold Coast will upset the present arrangements. Liberia has hitherto been the only independent country in West Africa. It took Britain and France more than twenty years to work out their relations with Liberia on a more or less satisfactory basis.

Artificial Political Frontiers

The territorial borders inside West Africa are wholly artificial. They are the result, not of any natural geographic or ethnic division, but of the varying fortunes of colonial expansion in the past. There is, therefore, always a danger of agitation along borders that frequently cut right through various African tribes.

Already Kwame Nkruma, Prime Minister of the Gold Coast, is demanding the annexation of Togoland, a contiguous British trust territory, formerly a part of German Togo. The French, who administer the other part of the former German colony, take a poor view of Mr. Nkruma's expansionist ambitions. The Togo trust territories, they say, already have caused enough trouble because of the complaints of the local Ewe nation about being cut in two by the boundary between the British and French sides.

The French are committed to their policy of integration and assimilation. The British are equally committed to their policy of local emancipation. Both policies appear to have consent of the populations involved. Which of the two will ultimately prove more attractive to the African? At this point few observers would dare venture a guess.

However, the economic centers of gravity lie mostly in British territory, and these are likely to set in motion currents of migration away from French territory.

Repercussion from the Sudan

The French also anticipate difficulties in the vast Sudanic region between the Sahara to the north and the tropical forests to the south. The new factor here is the forthcoming independence of the Anglo-Egyptian Sudan. The French in Equatorial Africa have more than 600 miles of common frontier with the Anglo-Egyptian Sudan, and their relations with that country will probably have to be worked out all over again.

Meanwhile the flow of men and goods along the Khartum-Kano axis is bound to continue through French territory. Khartum, the capital of the Anglo-Egyptian Sudan, will be the seat of an independent government beginning in 1956. Kano is the principal center in northern Nigeria, and Nigeria, too, is to be self-governing by 1956. Both Khartum and Kano are focal points of African Islam, the expansion of which is causing increasing anxiety among the French.

Autonomy and Islam—these are the forces that are expected to complicate matters between the French and their neighbors in West Africa.

To the extent to which the maintenance of peace and order in West Africa remains the ultimate responsibility of London and Paris, the objectives of the two countries will remain the same and their entente will undoubtedly endure.

But as the British territories become more and more a law to themselves, the danger of friction with the French territories must increase. Moreover, problems that formerly could be solved by arrangements on the spot will in the future probably have to be handled in a political context on the diplomatic level. In other words, practical solutions are likely to be infinitely harder to arrive at than before.

November 14, 1953

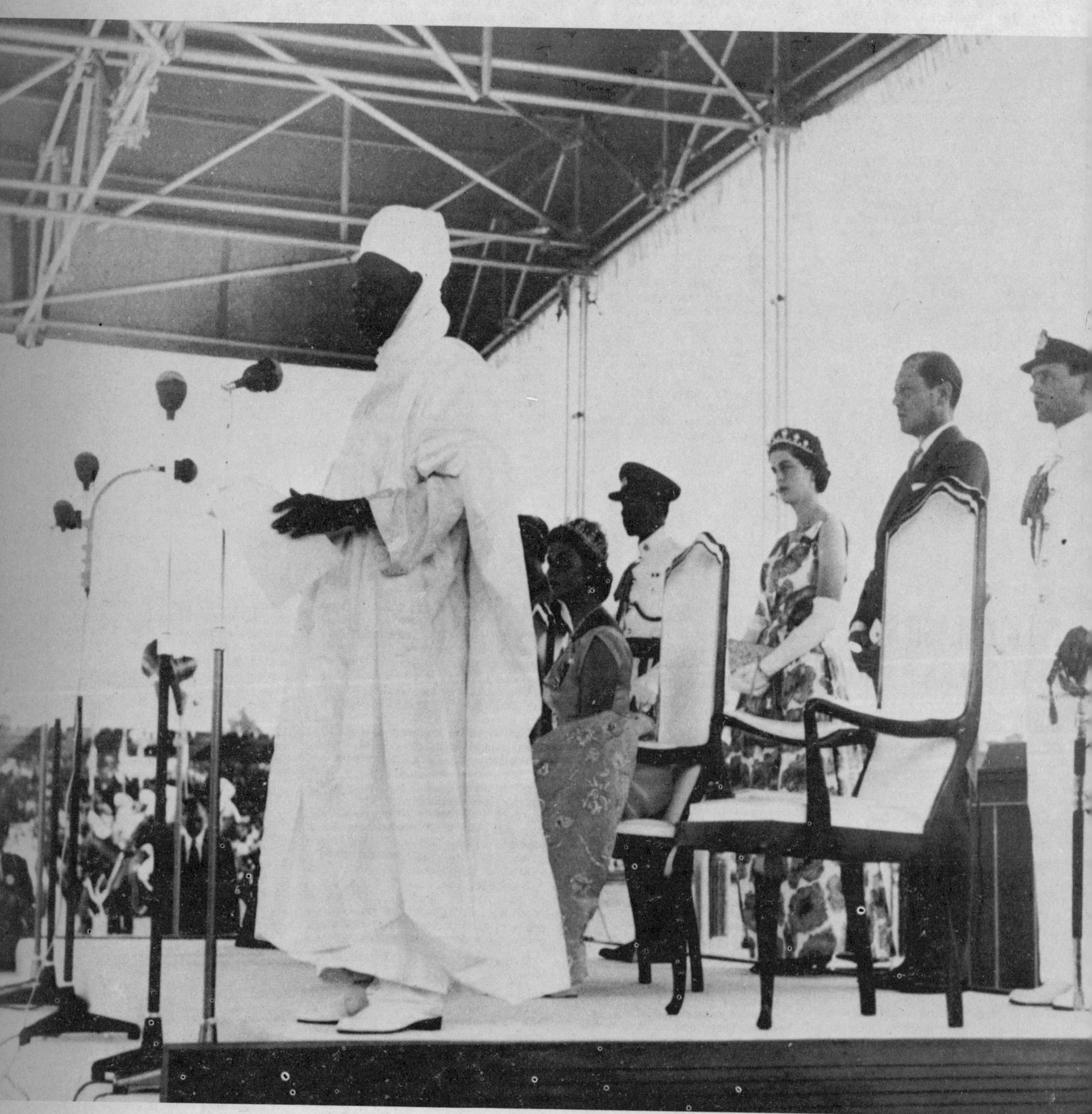

CHAPTER 2

Independence

'ndependent Nigeria's first premier broclaims his nation's freedom.

Courtesy Compix.

Colonialism: The Good, the Bad, the Lessons

The easy explanation of Africa's current troubles is that they are the fruit of colonialism. But was that system the unmitigated evil it is often held to be?

By GEORGE H. T. KIMBLE

ALTHOUGH Africa was never as dark as our ignorance of it, some of the news coming out of it these days is far from bright. And not only from the still-colonial territories either. Dispatches from the Congo tell of grave social disorder and political instability, and of leaders who are seemingly unwilling or unable to do anything about either. In Algeria, formation of a government to lead the newly independent nation has been delayed by power struggles while economic conditions have deteriorated and violence, though sporadic, continues. From Ghana and elsewhere come other intimations that the accolade of independence is no magic wand. It confers dignity—but not prosperity, peace or even, alas, order.

The quick and easy diagnosis of the continent's continuing trouble is that it is the fruit of colonialism: that colonialism was poor soil for the growth of independence—worse, that it was poor seed, and poor seed is incapable of producing good fruit. As developed by the people concerned, it is a plausible diagnosis, and one that is supported by many doctors of the African body politic, both in and out of the United Nations. But how accurate is it? Was colonialism the unmitigated evil it is so often represented to be? Was trouble its only bequest? Let us take a look at the colonial record, which by now is clear for all to see.

AS practiced in its heyday by every European power, colonialism was a conceit wrapped in a concern that was frequently less religious than sanctimonious and less charitable than mercenary. It proceeded on the premise that it was dealing with, as Kipling wrote, "lesser breeds without the Law," or, as a Southern Rhodesian administrator put it in 1925, that "we are in this country because * * * we are better men." It employed methods that were bossy, when not dictatorial, or worse. It was everlastingly telling people what was good for them, and what was bad. And all too often it failed to practice the good it looked for in others or to eschew the bad it abhorred in them.

Granted, there have been vast differences in the records of the various colonial powers. Not all of them have made the same mistakes. Thus, the French did not mistakenly classify people by the color of their skins and build separate and unequal schools, churches, park benches and washrooms for those not of their color.

On the other hand, the British did not presume to think that their wards wanted to speak English and to live like Englishmen, or that the chief end of man was to glorify the British Constitution and enjoy it forever. Of course, they did not stand in the path of those who wished to adopt British ways. Indeed, they eagerly helped them to attain this end, but the matter was not one on which they insisted. They assumed, almost from the start, that sooner or later most educated people want to be themselves and manage or mismanage their affairs in their own way.

AND neither the French nor the British made the mistake of supposing that it was possible—in the words of a Governor General of the former Belgian Congo—"to live together with the African, while remaining ourselves," or, as the Portuguese did, that nobody should be allowed to remain himself but, rather, that every African should be exhorted (if need be, by methods more punitive than persuasive) to live in an orderly, regimented society purged of the old tribal excesses and hostilities.

Then, not all of them have made equally serious mistakes. Thus, the French, for

all their sense of mission, interfered surprisingly little with African customary law and its enforcement. Further, they took the view that some of the higher values of African culture were not incompatible with those looked for in a community of civilized men. Wherever the organization of a group was found to be reasonably efficient, they sought to protect and strengthen it. As a result, they had fewer lawbreakers on their books, and fewer enemies, than the Spanish and Portuguese.

AGAIN, not all of them were equally slow to learn from their mistakes. For example, as deeply attached as the British are to precedent and tradition, they have not hesitated to ignore both when the occasion served and, instead, either to take their cue from their critics or to sit down in front of a piece of blank paper and wait for a new idea to strike them.

Some of these ideas, such as indirect rule (whereby indigenous systems of government were called into the service of the colonizing authority) may not always have been any more to the liking of their critics. However, none can doubt that the willingness of the British to try almost anything once, has won them more friends than were won by the Belgians who, it is to be feared, did little trying and did it too late.

Where all the colonial powers failed, it seems to me is in the following respects:

First, they failed to forecast the rising of the "winds of change." In a recent book, Margery Perham, one of Britain's most highly respected students of colonialism, confessed that she was "taken by surprise" by these winds, and that as late as 1939 the feeling about West Africa in the "official world," that is, the British Colonial Office, was pretty much that "we can be sure that we have unlimited time in which to work." As things turned out, the British had less than twenty years in which to work.

MANY French people, we may assume, were taken even more by surprise, since down to the mid-Nineteen Fifties the common official view seems to have been that France would stretch from the Rhine to the Congo. As for the Belgians, as recently as 1958 they were still affirming their intention to stay in the Congo

—because "the Congo needs us even more than we need the Congo."

Yet, for those with eyes to see them, there had long been signs of the coming change. From World War I onward there had been international conventions devoted to the subject of "African liberation." From the Nineteen Twenties there had been African student organizations (notably in the United Kingdom) that served as seedbeds for the germination of nationalist ideas and programs.

From the Nineteen Thirties there had been political congresses, parties and undercover organizations that worked to the same end in several British and French territories. From about the same time there had been African newspapers which sought to form—and sometimes to inflame—public opinion. And for a generation or more there had been Africans who journeyed to Moscow and other unpatriotic places.

As the colonial powers now see, they failed to understand African nationalism—both the source of its strength and passion, and the reasons for its surging discontent with servitude in any guise.

In the second place, they failed to provide the African with sufficient "protection" when the winds did rise. None of the newly independent countries had enough skilled African administrators to run their own show; not infrequently, independence meant an increased, rather than decreased, reliance on outsiders. (As one wit put it, "It takes a lot of Europeans to Africanize a place.")

None of the countries had enough African technicians to keep their public utilities working smoothly, or enough African professional men to ensure that the health of their people would be protected and their economic and legal interests adequately served. Somalia had no indigenous doctors when it became independent; Nigeria less than one dentist for every million people; Tanganyika only two engineers; the Congo one engineer, and no doctors, dentists, lawyers or public accountants.

And no country had an electorate that knew what independence was all about or what the keeping of it would cost in self-discipline, or cold cash.

THIRD, the colonial powers failed either to understand the nature of the African's environment or to live up to their understanding of it. They underestimated the difficulty of getting the environment to "go to work" for the African, and so of establishing economies that were at once strong enough to take the strain of independence and durable enough to keep those who worked them independent.

All too frequently they regarded the African's land as a bank to be robbed for their profit rather than as a trust to be husbanded for his. Only belatedly did they come to perceive the delicacy of Africa's physical and biological balance: the hunger of its soils, the variability of its rainfall, the scourge of its heat and humidity, and its hostility to sustained effort and large-scale enterprise.

Today, roughly half the lands of Africa are in poorer shape than they were fifty years ago. In at least one-third of the continent wind and water are removing topsoil faster than it is being replaced, and ground water levels are receding because of the consequently increased evaporation and run-off. In at least one-half of the forest country timber is being cut for fuel, lumber, wood ash and a dozen other purposes faster than it is growing.

THE agricultural picture is scarcely brighter. In many areas the rest period given to land that has been cropped—as most of it periodically is—to the point of exhaustion, is now shorter than it used to be. While this is partly because of growing population pressure on the cultivated land, it is also because in many, areas the farmers are now restrained from following their traditional "bush fallowing" system of soil conservation, under which sections of land are allowed to return to "bush" for a number of years. The Government feels that this method removes too much acreage from cultivation.

Needless to say, there are ways of stabilizing the soil and of increasing its yield of water, wood and crops; but up to now these have been more often talked about than tried. When tried, they have more than once been on the wrong scale or in the wrong place.

Perhaps the colonizers' greatest failure of all was their failure to understand the African—his hopes and fears, his capacities, needs and sensibilities. True, they did much better by him in the Nineteen Fifties than in the days of H. M. Stanley and Joseph Conrad. But they (and, for that matter, we) have lost little of the old-time zeal to make over (if not to take over) his economy—to convert him to Western ways of running farms and ruining the soil, of making money and creating unemployment, and of arousing desires that cannot be satisfied.

NEITHER have they (or we) lost much of the old-time zeal to teach him Western ways of organizing academies and armies, of behaving toward God and neighbor, of marrying and raising a family, of dressing, drinking and dying. (Already in some territories the automobile kills more people than the anopheles mosquito.)

All this has quietly undermined, when it has not destroyed, the African's self-respect, his sense of being valued for what he is and not merely for what he can do. It has also forced him to do virtually all of the taking and none of the giving. If we are to believe Laurens van der Post, the writer-explorer, who has lived closer to the African than most, it is this denial of the African's creativeness that has embittered his spirit, inflamed his passion and been responsible for much of the continuing "darkness" of his continent.

This is not to say that the colonial powers are called upon to renounce their record, let alone to stand trial for it. As George F. Kennan observed in his Reith Lectures in England in 1957: "The establishment of the colonial relationship did not represent a moral action on somebody's part; it represented a natural and inevitable response to certain demands and stimuli of the age. It was simply a stage of history." To judge the colonial powers in the light of the standards of a later age is unfair.

Furthermore, some of the things to come out of the "colonial relationship" are cause more for praise than for shame. To begin with, independence came out of it. The fact that there are independent states in Africa today is very largely the result of the European "presence." Without this, it is hard to see how the people living there could have bridged the gap between tribaldom and nationhood, between anarchy and order in so short a time.

For all its faults, colonial government was a hundred times better than the unregulated dealings of men like Conrad's Kurtz, who were armed with power to destroy and corrupt and had no scruples about using it. It provided security of person and property in lands that had known little of either, and so, enlarged the borders of the world in which a man could wander and work, live and die. It also provided experience in the running of business, industry and civil services for people who had hitherto shown few signs of developing these for themselves.

Then, too, it provided education (little enough, to be sure) that enabled men to know of Jefferson and Burke, the Magna Carta, the Bill of Rights and the no less revolutionary doctrines of the New Testament. In other words, it provided the grain of opportunity on which the pearl of independence could be cultured.

IT did more than this. It provided much of the sustenance for the growing pearl. For it was the colonial powers who were largely responsible for the opening of the region to the lumberman, miner, planter and other men of means without whom its wealth would have continued to lie fallow.

Before colonial times, almost the only tropical African "goods" to command an overseas market were slaves, ivory and gold. There was a little trade in hardwoods such as ebony, and in kola nuts, spices and incense, but none at all in cocoa, coffee, rubber, peanuts, sisal and a dozen other commodities that are now indis-

---

Lost Empires

Throughout most of Africa, the flags of empire are down. During the past ten years the French flag has been lowered in eighteen territories and the British in seven. The Belgian flag no longer flies in the Congo or Ruanda-Urundi, nor does the Italian in Somalia. Five years ago there were less than fifty million people in the whole of the continent who managed their own affairs; today there are less than forty million out of some 261 million who don't—and five years from now the number of those who don't is likely to be nearer four million than forty.—G. H. T. K.

---

pensable revenue-earners in as many countries.

The colonial powers were also responsible for a great deal of development that was not, and could not have been, financed from export revenues. The French Investment Funds for Economic and Social Development, the Belgian Funds for Native Welfare, the British Colonial Development and Welfare Grants and the Portuguese Colonial Development Fund — to name only four sources of such development money — provided the means, and often the ways, by which people could learn to overcome the handicaps imposed on them by a difficult environment and by centuries of isolation and apathy. In precolonial times there were no high schools or colleges in tropical Africa, nor any hospitals, clinics, dispensaries or other health services, and no roads or railways.

A number of uncovenanted gains also have come out of the colonial relationship. Among these is the mutual esteem—affection is not too strong a word—which has frequently developed between the colonial administrator and those he administered. Many Africans have been frank to admit that, if they have to be shoved around by somebody of another tribe, they would just as soon he was of a European "tribe."

Among them, too, is the interest taken in the African and his world by philanthropic and social agencies; and the realization by those who have gone to the African as tutors that they, also, have much to learn.

Which brings me to what the colonial relationship has done for the colonizers. It has shown them that, in many respects, they were not so good as they thought they were; that they didn't always know what was best for others; and that, not infrequently, their best—including, as it did, parliamentary democracy, paper work and plumbing—held little appeal for others.

It has shown them that the African was, in many respects, better than they thought he was; that his own ways of raising crops and family, of dealing with offenders and having fun were frequently as sensible as their own, and much less costly.

Again, it has shown them—the British and French, at any rate, and perhaps even the Belgians—that the only kind of power worth wielding is the one that decreases rather than grows with exercise. And it has encouraged them to believe that dying empires can be transformed into living commonwealths.

At the moment, it is true, this transformation is little more than a possibility in most parts of Africa; in some it is scarcely even that, for Ghana, Guinea and the Congo show no sign of wanting to be transformed into anything that can be taken for a family likeness to those who sired them. Yet none of the new states is unaware of the impossibility of being a standout in a world where the trend is increasingly toward "togetherness." After all, none of them has enough revenues, skills, experience or manpower to "go it alone."

What, then, will happen to the new states? Will they form durable regional federations among themselves, complete with common markets, common laws, armies and so on? Will they seek to establish a United States of Africa? Will they try to turn themselves into a "third world" that is independent of both East and West?

One thing we can be sure of. The new states have no intention of changing one colonial relationship for another—whether the relationship be with fellow Africans or foreigners. They have had colonialism—and the subservience, the second-class citizenship, the economic and social disabilities, the rule by outsiders that goes with it.

Henceforth they intend to go their own way, just as we in this country have gone our own way. By the look of things, their way may not be greatly to our taste, for as yet it shows little sign of coinciding with ours in such matters as order and efficiency, to say nothing of how to deal with communism. Nor does it show any sign of being comfortable to live with.

Not that there is much any of us can do about it—except one thing. When asked (and we shall be, increasingly, as we set our own house in order) we can play the almost forgotten role of servant; clearing up a mess here, giving a helping hand there, and demonstrating that we are at least as well-fitted for the role as the Russians, the Chinese and all the other people who will be playing it, too.

BRITAIN KEEPS CURB IN GOLD COAST PLAN

LONDON, Oct. 26 (AP)—Britain turned down today demands for full self-government for the 4,000,000 people of West Africa's Gold Coast. She thereby risked what many colonial administrators fear is a threatened link-up between European Communist agitators and Nationalist leaders in West Africa.

Nigeria, the Gold Coast's neighbor on the east, also is demanding full independence outside the British Commonwealth. A Government commission studying the Nigeria question is to make a report about the first of the year.

Arthur Creech Jones, Colonial Secretary, in rejecting the Gold Coast's demands for full self-government, agreed to give somewhat more freedom to the colony.

He approved a plan to set up a twelve-man Cabinet and for the indirect election of a Legislature. But he turned down a proposal to make the Cabinet responsible to the Legislature, the key point of the West Africans' demands. Instead, the Cabinet will be answerable to the Governor, who is picked by the Colonial Secretary.

The proposals were formulated by an all-Negro thirty-eight man commission chosen by the Gold Coast Government. The group was named after extensive unrest, which in February, 1948, erupted into riots at Accra, the capital.

October 27, 1949

Gold Coast Railmen Strike

ACCRA, Gold Coast, Jan. 7—(Reuters)—Railroad engineers and firemen defied the Government today by starting a general strike called by the local Trades Union Congress. The Government, which had declared the strike illegal, warned the railmen they would be liable to penalties. The general strike was proclaimed last month to compel the British Government to grant dominion status to the Gold Coast and to demand the reinstatement of sixty-one Government workers dismissed in November.

January 8, 1950

Gold Coast Ends Emergency

ACCRA, Gold Coast, March 18 (Reuters)—Gold Coast Gov. Sir Charles Arden-Clarke Oday ended the state of emergency, proclaimed over two months ago after riots and widespread strikes instigated by nationalist extremists. The leader of the movement, Dr. Kwame Nkruma, and four of his supporters are serving one-year jail sentences.

March 19, 1950

Gold Coast Nationalists Win

ACCRA, Gold Coast, April 1 (Reuters)—Dr. Kwame Nkruma's Convention Peoples' party, which is strongly nationalist, swept the polls in local elections here today, winning all six municipal wards for the first time. Only about one fifth of the electorate voted.

April 2, 1950

GOLD COAST IN 1ST VOTE

People's Party Wins 34 Out of 38 Elective Seats

ACCRA, Gold Coast, Feb. 8 (Reuters)—The Convention People's party, which stands for immediate self-government, swept the polls at yesterday's first Parliamentary election in this British African colony. It will demand the immediate release from jail of its leader, Kwame Nkrumah.

Mr. Nkrumah himself, a one-time divinity student in the United States and a London University graduate, won a Parliamentary seat by an overwhelming vote. He is serving a jail term for having organized a general strike last year and is not due for release until November.

Kamlo Gbedemah, who leads the party in his absence, said he would seek an immediaate interview with Gov. Sir Charles Arden Clarke to have him freed.

The party won thirty-four seats, out of thirty-eight elective seats in the eighty-four man Parliament, plus one more held by an independent supporter. Three seats were gained by the only other successful party, the United Gold Coast Convention. —

February 10, 1951

GOLD COAST LEADER WIELDS BIG POWER

Nkrumah Called West Africa's 'Gandhi'—Attitude Toward West Closely Watched

ACCRA, GOLD COAST, West Africa, May 30 (Reuters)—Kwame Nkrumah, officially styled "Leader of Government business in the Gold Coast Assembly," but actually undisputed leader of the whole territory, is puzzling all political observers who are attempting to forecast his future attitude toward cooperation, not only with Britain but with all the Western world.

Mr. Nkrumah occupies a position in West Africa such as Gandhi had in India. In the Gold Coast he is regarded as a saint and special hymns have been written in praise of him, which are sung at political gatherings.

In the other West African territories, too, Mr. Nkrumah is gaining in power. In Nigeria, the largest native state in Africa, he is regarded as even more important politically than the noted Nigerian leader, Dr. Nnamdi Azikwe (Zik).

Could Lead All Africans

"Nkrumah could become the leader of all the African peoples," a European political leader at the Gold Coast Assembly said.

Mr. Nkrumah won the recent election on a program of "full self-government now" and his party has a vast majority in the House. He controls every office save those of finance, defense and justice. The governor, however, has the power of veto, which, so far, he has never exercised.

Mr. Nkrumah has taken no steps to carry out the policy of "self-government now", and is being assailed by some of his more revolutionary supporters on this account. In an interview, he said:

"We shall give the Constitution a chance. Both sides are determined to cooperate and if the Constitution fails it will fail by its own weight.

"But in the present circumstances the most important questions which face us are what is happening here and what is happening in the Union of South Africa. We cannot close our eyes to what is going on there.

Favors Congress of Peoples

"For the good of West Africa as a whole we favor the idea of a West African Congress of peoples.

"We have one great fear at present and that is that if the Conservatives come to power in Britain at the next election they would obstruct the political development of the colonies.

"This fear is producing a situation that could be dangerous. There is pressure from some quarters that we should force the issue of self-government at once in case the Conservatives do come to power. It is felt that even they could not put back the clock once self-government was a fact.

"We are determined to make this experiment a success. The Gold Coast wants all the help it can get from Britain, particularly in the matter of ships to take our produce away.

"We are pressing ahead with our development plan and we are tackling first essentials first. But to do this we need help and equipment, and the next Empire Conference should consider all the available resources and their allocation in order to make it easier for countries like ourselves to get rapidly onto their own feet."

June 3, 1951

'CULTURAL BRIDGE' TO AFRICA SOUGHT

Gold Coast Official Here Asks for Aid to 'See Imperialism Wiped Off Continent'

Kwame Nkrumah, Leader for Government Business of the West African Gold Coast, called upon Negro American educators, technicians, scientists and medical men yesterday to set up a cultural bridge between his countrymen and persons of African descent here.

He spoke at a reception for himself and Kojo Botsio, Minister of Education and Social Welfare, at International House, 500 Riverside Drive. The meeting of 400 persons was arranged by the New York alumni of Lincoln University, Pa., from which Mr. Nkrumah was graduated and which gave him an honorary degree of Doctor of Law last week.

Mayor Impellitteri greeted the ministers of the British dependency that received partial self-government last February. He tendered "a warm hand of friendship" to the visitors—who left yesterday by plane for London—and called their stay here a step "toward cultural goodwill and understanding."

Advocating a new "back-to-Africa movement" in a cultural sense, Mr. Nkrumah asked for technical aid to help "see imperialism wiped off the continent of Africa." He declared that "democracy is a fine word, but it doesn't work so well on an empty stomach."

Standards of Living

Mr. Nkrumah said that British colonialism had not advanced Gold Coast standards of living very much. He declared that, although the area had heavy rainfalls, there was a water shortage, roads were bad, tremendous natural resources were untapped and, because there was no free education, the 4,000,000 inhabitants had only 10 per cent literacy.

In addition to plans for economic expansion and a Tennessee Valley Authority type of hydroelectric program, Mr. Nkrumah said, free primary schools soon will be established in his country. He welcomed aid from non-Negro Americans, because "we are not fighting against race or color but against an economic system that exploits our people."

Mr. Nkrumah said that the aims of his Convention People's party were being embraced by natives of other African countries. He expects that his people eventually will win full dominion status in the British Commonwealth.

"A new day is dawning in Africa," Mr. Nkrumah said. "A gigantic movement is now under way in all West Africa. The old Africa is gone forever and I hope it never comes back again."

As one step in the nationalist revival in his country, Mr. Nkrumah declared, his party intends to change the name of the Gold Coast, "because it brings back to mind the old slave days." He is proposing the name Ghana, its name in the eleventh century, "when we had emperors, large cities and a high level of culture."

June 10, 1951

Native Gold Coast Leader First Premier of Colony

The New York Times

Kwame Nkrumah

By Reuters

ACCRA, Gold Coast, March 5—Kwame Nkrumah, African politician who left prison in February, 1951, to lead the Gold Coast's first elected government, today became the country's first Prime Minister.

Announcing the appointment to a packed audience in the Assembly Hall, Sir Charles Arden Clarke, British Governor of the Gold Coast Colony, said Queen Elizabeth II approved the change.

The Prime Minister will rank in precedence in the Cabinet immediately after the Governor.

Kwame Nkrumah is leader of the Convention People's party, which was returned to power in the 1951 elections on a program of "self-government now." At that time he was serving a two-year jail sentence for trying to incite a general strike in 1950 and for a seditious newspaper article. He was released by the Governor.

Once a student at the London School of Economics, Kwame Nkrumah is a graduate of Lincoln University in Pennsylvania.

March 6, 1952

GOLD COAST RICH IN OTHER PRODUCTS

African Country Also Exports Diamonds, Minerals, Rubber—World's Chief Cocoa Source

All that glitters is not gold along Africa's Gold Coast.

True, the British-governed West African country stands in sixth place among the world's gold-producing regions. Its annual production exceeds half a million ounces. The ore at Obuasi, 100 miles inland from Takoradi, the Gold Coast's only deep-water port, assays high—an ounce of gold to the ton.

However, in 1919, panners of river gold, discovered diamonds. A newly found diamond field midway between Takoradi and Obuasi, described as "phenomenal," is expected to increase Gold Coast diamond export volume. Gem stones have been rare in the past, the National Geographic Society says, but small, industrial diamond production in some years has exceeded 1,000,000 carats.

Then there is the Gold Coast's greatest glitter of all—cacao pods ripening to a canary-yellow brilliance under a tropical sun. Like diamonds, they are a comparatively recent Gold Coast harvest. Imported from tropical America seventy years ago, the cacao tree took to the new soil and humid climate.

World's Chief Cocoa Source

The beans, yielding cocoa and chocolate, are the Gold Coast's leading export, normally worth twice its output of gold. The colony is well entrenched as the world's chief chocolate and cocoa source.

Aluminum ore and manganese are newly important mineral exports. Mahogany and other hardwoods are cut for world trade. Kola nuts, palm kernels, copra and rubber follow cocoa on the agricultural list. Rubber was the Gold Coast's money crop early in the century before East Indian rubber forged ahead.

Centuries ago Portuguese and other seafarers from the north established a few small trading forts, bartered European goods for native gold—and the Gold Coast on the Gulf of Guinea shore was named. Today, belying the second half of its name, the state slices north 440 miles into the West African bulge—a distance one-third greater than its shoreline.

The Gold Coast approximates Minnesota in both size and shape. Fronting the gulf is the Gold Coast Colony proper, where live half the area's 4,000,000 inhabitants. Inland and northward lie Ashanti and the larger, heavily forested Northern Territories. Part of Togoland to the east is administered from Accra, the Gold Coast capital, under United Nations trusteeship to Great Britain.

Negroes in Vast Majority

Native Negroes outnumber non-Africans more than 600 to 1. The majority adhere to their tribal lands, live in mud-hut villages, sleep on grass mats and eat little meat. On the coast, and in the Ashanti country they work on cocoa plantations. On higher land of the north they raise cattle and sheep. The educated few include doctors, lawyers, teachers. A small number ardently advocate complete and immediate self-rule.

The 900-mile Volta River system drains the entire country. About 2,800 miles of roads are passable for motor cars. About 365 miles of railroad lines and branches run northward from Takoradi and Sekondi to Kumasi, the Ashanti capital, then southeastward to Accra.

World War II brought boom times to Accra as a station on major air routes to eastern fronts. Even without good harbor facilities, its population tripled in the Nineteen Forties to a present total of about 135,000. Kumasi, ranking second, counts half as many, while the current estimate for Takoradi-Sekondi is 44,000.

August 19, 1951

New World of Africa's Gold Coast Arises From Ashes of Colonialism

Although Land Is Still British, Black Men Are Masters in Their Own House

By WILLIAM S. WHITE

Special to THE NEW YORK TIMES.

ACCRA, Gold Coast, May 15—The black man's brave new world is slowly rising here on the backs of those who once were his white masters and now do his bidding—the British Civil Service men.

Britain, once ruler of the Gold Coast, is in headlong flight not simply from a long past imperialism; here is being worked out a suicide of colonialism as well. Nowhere else in the world has there been such an experiment as is in progress here.

The natives, after rioting bloodily in 1948 and again in 1950, have had a growing measure of self government since 1950 under a native Prime Minister, Kwame Nkrumah (pronounced "Krooma").

Now they are after absolute independence and their declared design is to throw out the British altogether except insofar as British experts in the science of government may care to remain as paid assistants to a Cabinet of Africans.

Today in the Gold Coast Cabinet, three of the eleven Ministers are still British. With an ironic detachment they are cooperating—on the word of Mr. Nkrumah himself—in the process of making themselves expendable. For the short run they are indispensable, as the Prime Minister himself concedes, until the Africans learn enough about government to take on the whole show.

In their hearts the British hope they can stay on for perhaps twenty years more. Mr. Nkrumah's plans for them, however, are different. He would like to get rid of them tomorrow and his highly nationalistic followers consistently press him toward such a course.

Foreign Capital Is Needed

But he is restrained for the moment by several practical considerations—of which the greatest is a need for foreign capital to develop this country's big project, a Tennessee Valley Authority type of project on the Volta River. This job will cost $150,000,000 and the money must come either from the United States or Britain, and probably from the United States. Accessible to the Volta is $5,000,000,000 worth of aluminum ore.

Mr. Nkrumah, a small neat man who was educated at Lincoln University in Pennsylvania and at the University of Pennsylvania, therefore is walking softly for the moment. But he does not hide the fact that his forbearance toward the British is temporary and tactical only.

On the British side life is hard. In the Nkrumah Government, which is controlled in a ratio of eight to three by the natives, it is the British who do the work; but the future lies wholly with Mr. Nkrumah and his people. The British do not permit themselves to forget that.

The British are enormously correct toward the black Prime Minister and the other Africans; among themselves they deal in shirt sleeves but they never enter the office of an African Cabinet Minister without putting on ties and coats and long pants to replace the shorts that otherwise are worn.

They still have a very large measure of practical influence and in some areas of Government practical control, but they walk a very slippery tight rope.

The British Governor, Sir Charles Arden-Clarke, still has the power to veto acts of the Gold Coast Parliament, but he has never done so and he probably never will. What he does do is to work with tact and patience—with what the Gold Coast Information Officer, Maj. James Lillie-Costello, calls "a gentility of explanation"—to persuade the Africans never to insist on doing anything that would force the use of the veto.

The whole experiment therefore is a fantastic one. The essential picture is that self government is being given to the Africans long before they are ready for it and it is being given to them simply because the British decided after the troubles of 1950 that it was either a white retreat or civil war. They reckoned that they could not shoot, either morally or practically.

In the curious ad lib sort of policy followed by the British Colonial Office it was therefore decided not simply to give concessions to the African but actually to fling concessions at him.

The policy here is the very opposite of British policy elsewhere but there are long reasons for it and the immense, seeming contradiction of it does not worry the Briton.

Asked why self government is being put hurriedly into practice here and wholly withheld elsewhere, the Briton murmurs an old Biblical quotation: "In my Father's house are many mansions * * *."

Nothing whatever is said officially here about Prime Minister Daniel F. Malan and South Africa. It is nevertheless perfectly plain tha the British here are raising the most dramatic—and even slightly melodramatic—contrast to "Malanism" of which they can conceive.

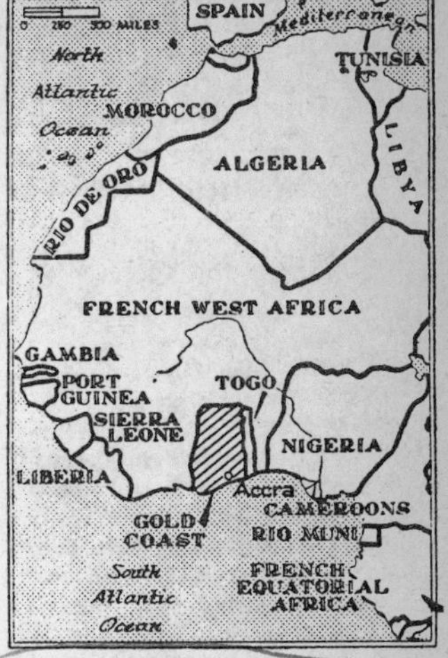

The New York Times May 16, 1952

'British control of Gold Coast (diagonal shading) is giving way to Negro self-government.'

They know that in a real sense they are on the way out in the Gold Coast; but they know also that the Gold Coast has ties to Britain—including the English language—that no Nkrumah can ever wholly break.

When the time comes for the last British withdrawal it is the British hope that what is left behind will not be another embittered India but a country that might willingly take its place in the British Commonwealth.

With moving forebearance and with moving gallantry, the British are working toward their own extinction in the Gold Coast—but also toward their own re-emergence in another form.

May 16, 1952

British Give More Self-Rule to Gold Coast; Natives to Get Ministries Whites Now Hold

Special to The New York Times.

LONDON, April 28—The Gold Coast is to take another big step toward self-rule. The British Government has accepted proposals from Prime Minister Kwame Nkrumah and his Government under which the last three British Cabinet Ministers will be replaced by natives.

This announcement was made in Parliament by Henry L. Hopkinson, Minister of State for Colonial Affairs. The developments were outlined in an exchange of letters between Colonial Secretary Oliver Lyttelton and the Gold Coast's Governor, Sir Charles Arden-Clarke, that was published as a White Paper today.

The new constitutional proposals for the former colony in West Africa will be laid before Britain's Privy Council shortly, Mr. Hopkinson declared. They include extension of the direct ballot to areas that now vote by tribal groups and a definite reduction in the initiative the Governor normally will exercise. Like the British sovereign, he will carry out his day-to-day prerogatives with the advice of a group of ministers, but he will retain emergency powers, including certain direct controls over the police and civil service, in case of need.

These provisions reflect concern that has been increasingly felt by the Nkrumah Government at losing the services of the trained Europeans who have run the colony for so many years.

Only by keeping the public service in British hands for the time being would it be possible to recruit Europeans or hold those who are there.

Eventually the judiciary and the civil service will be supervised by commissions to be specially set up.

The Gold Coast has proposed to insert a constitutional guarantee that any business enterprise that is nationalized will be given fair compensation, Mr. Hopkinson revealed. This clearly was made necessary by the past radicalism of Dr. Nkrumah and his Convention People's party.

April 29, 1954

PREMIER APPEARS GOLD COAST VICTOR

Survey of Electorate Shows Widespread Ignorance Among the Voters

Special to The New York Times.

ACCRA, Gold Coast, June 11—Next Tuesday's general election in the Gold Coast is expected to establish Prime Minister Kwame Nkrumah as "master in his own house."

The expression has been used by Mr. Nkrumah himself, and there is no doubt that fanatics of the Convention People's party look upon self-government and Mr. Nkrumah as identical. This is particularly true of Mr. Nkrumah's early "beer cellar" companions, for whom prison was sometimes the price of their devotion.

The constitutional advance in the Gold Coast has virtually destroyed the indigenous social structure of the country. Mr. Nkrumah, a man of humble birth, has done more than anybody else to crush the power and prestige of the traditional chiefs. His own rise to power would have been impossible if he had acted otherwise. But it seems odd that an "Africa firster" like Mr. Nkrumah should base his entire strategy on alien forms.

In practice these forms have been totalitarian rather than democratic. In the Gold Coast representative institutions have no roots at all.

A pre-election survey completed last Wednesday showed that in Accra, where the literacy rate is particularly high, only one intending voter in four knew the names of the candidates or the parties they represented. The symbols of the Opposition parties were known to one in two of the intending voters.

However, four out of five intending voters knew the symbol of the Convention People's party—a red cockerel—and three out of five knew the name of the candidate of the party. This is not surprising, because Mr. Nkrumah's political organization is the only one in the country that could be called efficient.

The survey was conducted by a group of forty African students under the direction of Walter B. Birmingham, senior lecturer in economics at the University College of the Gold Coast, and Dr. Gustav Jahoda, lecturer in the University College Department of Sociology. Both Mr. Birmingham and Dr. Jahoda are Europeans.

Using the "random sample" method worked out by the British Institute of Public Opinion, Mr. Birmingham, Dr. Jahoda and their assistants canvassed the three Accra constituencies (82,000 registered voters). The results showed that, in the event of good weather, the Convention People's party should get 82 per cent of the votes. The investigators concluded that rain would tend to favor the Opposition parties.

June 12, 1954

GOLD COAST CHIEF HAS EASY TRIUMPH

Nkrumah Has Big Edge in New Assembly—Will Be Asked Today to Form Regime

Special to The New York Times.

ACCRA, Gold Coast, June 16—Prime Minister Kwame Nkrumah of the Gold Coast, whose party won a substantial victory at the polls yesterday, will call on the Governor, Sir Charles Noble Arden-Clarke, at Christiansborg Castle here tomorrow.

When the nationalist leader meets the Governor within the massive walls of the castle, a relic of the slave trade period, he will be asked to form a new Government, the first to assume power in a fully self-governing African colony.

Dr. Nkrumah and his lieutenants have made it clear they regard home rule as a mere prelude to complete independence and dominion status within the British Commonwealth.

The Convention Peoples party, of which Dr. Nkrumah is life chairman, took an early lead in yesterday's general election.

Rural returns were far from complete at a late hour today. However, the Convention Peoples party already had won an absolute majority in the new Legislative Assembly, with fifty-four seats to the opposition's twenty-five.

As was expected, the Convention Peoples party made a poor showing in the northern region, where the influence of the traditional chiefs remains strong. But the party's most significant defeat occurred in British Togoland, a trust territory administered as part of the Gold Coast.

Candidates in the Transvolta region who had campaigned strenuously in behalf of permanent integration of Togoland and the Gold Coast were opposed by the Togoland Congress, backed by the Ewe tribe, which is striving to promote unification of French and British Togoland.

June 17, 1954

BRITISH TOGOLAND AWAITS U.N. ACTION

London's Aim of Integrating Area With Gold Coast Blow to Ewe Nationalists

By MICHAEL CLARK

Special to The New York Times.

ACCRA, Gold Coast, June 21—Political leaders here were astounded to learn today that the British Government had decided to relinquish its responsibilities as administering authority in the British Togoland trust territory as soon as the Gold Coast attained full independence within the Commonwealth a year or two hence.

An announcement to this effect was issued here after Oliver Lyttelton, British Colonial Secretary, had put his Government's views on the future of British Togoland before the House of Commons in London. These views were also contained in a memorandum sent to the Secretary General of the United Nations by the permanent British representative.

In effect, the British decision means that the future of British Togoland is to be settled on the basis of integration with the Gold Coast, rather than on reunion with the French Togoland trust territory. It is a stunning blow to the Ewe nationalist movement, which has been striving to resurrect the German Togoland of pre-World War I days.

Northern British Togoland long has been integrated with the northern territories of the Gold Coast and appears to be happy with the arrangement, which insures unity of the powerful Dagomba tribe.

Last year southern British Togoland became part of the newly formed Transvolta Togoland region of the Gold Coast. The idea was to link Ewe members living in the Gold Coast with those in southern British Togoland.

But the Ewe problem cannot be so easily solved. Many members also live in southern French Togoland. Agitation for unification of British and French Togoland under Ewe leadership has continued unabated the last year.

Last week's general election in the Gold Coast disappointed those who had hoped that results in the Transvolta Togoland region, and particularly in the six southern Togoland constituencies, would reflect a clear desire for permanent integration with the Gold Coast. This did not materialize.

Prime Minister Kwame Nkrumah's Convention People's party, which was returned to power with a substantial majority, had campaigned in southern British Togoland on the strength of its promise to achieve "unification through integration."

An attempt to win Ewe votes by depicting French Togoland as the Gold Coast's unredeemed land was not altogether successful. Convention candidates won in only three southern British Togoland constituencies. It was clear the party had failed to penetrate the heart of Eweland.

London's position is that British Togoland cannot be administered as a small isolated unit, and that union with the Gold Coast is a proper solution. But it will be for the United Nations to decide whether the territory should continue to be a trust territory.

The British announcement suggests that the United Nations should arrange to ascertain the wishes of the territory's inhabitants. If a plebiscite is held in British Togoland and if this precedent is eventually followed in French Togoland, the Togoland problem may resolve itself in the end on the basis of irrevocable separation.

June 24, 1954

COCOA PRICE ISSUE SPLITS GOLD COAST

Native Regime's First Major Crisis Has Coastal Province Aligned Against Interior

Special to The New York Times.

KUMASI, The Gold Coast, Dec. 10—A controversy over cocoa prices has brought the Gold Coast its first major internal crisis under African government.

The situation has caused considerable tension in this, the country's second largest city. A new political party has emerged here, its aim being a federal form of government in the Gold Coast. It has accused the Government of using the proceeds of cocoa sales to swell its party coffers.

In recent weeks, at least one political assassination has occurred, numerous bloody clashes have given the city a mood of riot at times and a curfew has had to be imposed.

This amounts to the first big crack in the political unity that gave impetus to the Gold Coast's successful drive for independence from British rule. It also is a challenge to the popularity of Prime Minister Kwame Nkrumah.

Two Regions in Dispute

The dispute lies between two of the country's three regions, the Coast Province (the former Gold Coast colony) and Ashanti, the central province. The two regions roughly represent the poles of political thought in the Gold Coast. The third region, the Northern Territories, while not economically involved, is sitting this one out, although giving an occasional hand to the Ashanti side.

Ashanti is cocoa country, and cocoa is the hinge of the Gold Coast's economy. World cocoa prices soared after World War II, incidentally cutting the size of the 5-cent chocolate bar in the United States and bringing record prosperity to most levels of Gold Coast life.

Dr. Nkrumah's Government has been conservative in its sharing of the cocoa proceeds—the grower receiving less than half the world price of about $780 a ton. Dr. Nkrumah has argued that any increase in the price to the producer would be inflationary.

But the Ashanti leaders have maintained that talk of inflation has been merely a shield to hide both improper use of cocoa proceeds and partisan appointments to the cocoa administration boards.

The whole problem goes well beyond cocoa, however. The price issue actually has served only as a lever to pry loose resentments and suspicions that are traditional between the "coasters," the detribalized Africans whose agile intellectualism led the movement for self-government, and the Africans of the center and north, most of whom are still amenable to tribal influence and tradition.

Specially, the rising crisis between Kumasi and Accra, seat of the Gold Coast Government, is a test of strength between Prime Minister Nkrumah and the Asantehene, spiritual leader and hereditary chief of the Ashanti. They are the two most powerful men in the country.

The Asantehene is the embodiment of the power of the chiefs, a system of rule Dr. Nkrumah's Convention People's party is determined to replace with popularly elected district councils. In Ashanti, where tradition is steadfast, the Asantehene is regarded as virtually a sacred person.

The Ashanti, historically an aggressive and turbulent people who have always resented their lack of direct access to the sea and dependence upon the "coasters" for the export of their crops, have not taken kindly to the Government's attitude toward the chieftaincies.

The views of the new Federalist party, which calls itself the National Liberation Movement, were expressed by a spokesman as follows:

"We in Ashanti believe that the unity of the Gold Coast should not abuse the economic, historical and cultural background of the component units. When people glibly decry tribalism, do they seriously consider that tribalism could be more injurious to this country than party loyalty when either of them is adhered to blindly?"

December 30, 1954

GOLD COAST SEEKS LEAD IN INDUSTRY

Ambitious Project Foresees Country's Becoming Chief West African Center

Special to The New York Times.

ACCRA, Gold Coast, May 1—The Gold Coast Government, eager to establish the country as the leading industrial center of West Africa, has embarked upon an ambitious development program. It includes some of the biggest harbor installation, agricultural research and power projects on the Continent.

The program, if fulfilled, would give the country within ten years the three most modern ports on Africa's west coast, a great power and river development project, the world's leading cocoa research institute and a highly efficient system of interior communications.

At the moment this self-governing African state, once one of Britain's richest colonial possessions, is trying to balance an economy that is largely and, according to local economists, dangerously dependent upon the cocoa market boom.

Faced by the prospect of full political independence within eighteen months, the all-Negro Government of Prime Minister Kwame Nkrumah is intent upon providing assurance that the Gold Coast, when on its own, will be economically stable and will offer reasonable investment opportunities to the international market.

While overseas observers here have felt that some of the plans are overly ambitious, especially in view of the leisurely pace common to African labor, which often drains financial resources through time lag, they also have been anxious to see general encouragement of the development program. The British Colonial Office, through its $360,000,000 Colonial Development and Welfare project, has channeled large sums into the Gold Coast.

Equipped with rich natural resources, a strategic coastline, an ancient international trading tradition and an aggressively commercial-minded people, the Gold Coast is thus making a strong bid to match its acknowledged political leadership in West Africa with a similar lead in industry and commerce.

The major plans in its development program involve overseas interests, either the British Colonial Office or free enterprise, or both. The biggest one of these is the $432,000,000 Volta River plan whereby the waters of that stream, which runs almost diagonally across the country, would be harnessed and used principally for the production of aluminum from the country's bauxite resources at an ultimate rate of 210,000 tons a year.

The capital outlay is to be shared between the British and Gold Coast Governments and Aluminium Limited of Canada and Aluminium Company of England. A preparatory commission of British, Canadian and Gold Coast officials has been studying all aspects of the plan and will submit a report this year. If accepted by all parties, construction may get under way by 1957. The plan, which will provide the West with a valuable new reserve of aluminum, will take about seven years to complete.

Linked directly to the Volta project are several major undertakings that are now under way. The principal of these is construction of a new deep-water harbor at Tema, near the mouth of the Volta.

Port to Be Finished by 1958

The Tema port will be finished by 1958. A thirty-six-mile railway linking Tema with Achimota, near Accra, was opened last year. Work also has started on a main trunk road that, when completed, will give a first-class route from Tema to Bawku, in the northeast corner of the country.

Roads and railways throughout the country are being improved and extended. The ports at Takoradi and Accra are being improved. Prime Minister Nkrumah, in a recent review delivered to the Legislative Assembly, said development expenditure is now four times as much as it was in 1950-51. The entire cocoa industry is being reconstructed, he said. Emphasis is on research, eradication of disease, cultivation of improved strains and protection of the watershed.

During the past four years, he added, electricity has been increased 60 per cent. Telephone capacity has been increased threefold; hundreds of miles of new roads and railroads have been built; and cash crops such as coffee and the oil palm are being encouraged.

May 15, 1955

GOLD COAST VOTES ON INDEPENDENCE

Issue Is One of Centralism Versus Federalism Within British Commonwealth

By THOMAS F. BRADY
Special to The New York Times.

ACCRA, Gold Coast, July 17—Citizens of the Gold Coast went to the polls today to tell Britain what kind of independence they want within the Commonwealth. Their choice is between centralized government and a federal system.

The problem will be difficult for Britain to solve if the voters have not spoken clearly—that is, if there is not a "reasonable majority" for one system or the other.

By the time the polls closed tonight it was apparent that the issue was a burning one only in Ashanti territory, the stronghold of the federalists, who are grouped under the label of the National Liberation Movement.

In the Central Gold Coast where the Ashanti tribesmen live the voting was heavy; in the coastal "colony" section it was moderate to light and in the sparsely populated backward northern territories it was even lighter.

From first reports reaching the capital it was doubtful that the ratio of votes cast to the voters registered would reach the figure of 58 per cent attained in the 1954 election.

The voters, about 85 per cent of whom are illiterate, had a choice between the red rooster of the Convention People's party, which stands for centralized government, and the green cocoa palm of the National Liberation Movement, which champions federalism.

Results were slow. By 11 P.M. thirteen Convention candidates and one opposition candidate had been posted as winners. Five of thirteen won uncontested seats.

Rooster Found a Favorite

Here in the capital the rooster was a visible favorite. Nevertheless the Convention People's party headed by Prime Minister Kwame Nkrumah is expected to lose some of the seventy seats (out of a total of 104) it held in the Legislative Assembly just dissolved. It won this parliamentary majority by a popular majority of only 52 per cent in 1954.

It is generally expected that the party will retain control of the Government, but whether the British Parliament will view its prospective victory as a "reasonable" mandate for a centralized state is not clear.

The Opposition coalition, headed by the National Liberation Movement and led by Kofi Abrefa Busia, combines the tribal conservatives with elements of the intelligentsia and the economically important cocoa farming bloc. Mr. Nkrumah's support, on the other hand, comes from the urban masses.

The campaign was marred by violence and killings in the Ashanti country. At least a dozen persons died and several times that number were wounded.

The use of coercive juju (black magic) in the campaign was forbidden by Gold Coast law

Innocuous juju was permitted however. The Prime Minister, himself, went Sunday with several thousand supporters to the Accra Lagoon and poured a palm wine libation to the water gods in an appeal for victory for the Convention People's party.

The economic issue behind the constitutional question of federalism or centralism lies in the cocoa farms of the Ashanti region which produce the Gold Coast's big money crop and give the country the most viable conomy in British West Africa.

Farming is entirely in the hands of small African farmers whose crops are bought by the Accra Government marketing board at a fixed price well below the fluctuating world price.

The difference is used for development throughout the Gold Coast.

Advocates of the federal system would give each region financial autonomy and thus would keep the cocoa money in the Ashanti region where it is produced. The rest of the country would be left in a state of relative impoverishment by such a change.

The Opposition has charged corruption and mismanagement by the cocoa marketing board and a recent investigation and earlier scandals have lent some weight to the charges.

July 18, 1956

GOLD COAST DUE FOR SHIFT TODAY

Nkrumah Expected to Name New Regime to Receive Freedom From Britain

By THOMAS F. BRADY
Special to The New York Times.

ACCRA, Gold Coast, July 22—Dr. Kwame Nkrumah, United States-educated Prime Minister of the Gold Coast, is expected to form a Government tomorrow that will see his country become independent of Britain.

The experiment in establishing a Negro nation in the British Commonwealth is the object of antagonistic but attentive observation from those sections of Africa ruled by a white minority, Chief among them is the Union of South Africa.

Other colonial powers, especially France and Belgium with their vast neighboring African dependencies, also are watching with anxiety lest Britain's way of dealing with the Gold Coast upset their own patterns of rule.

No less attentive are sympathetic independent nations of the Asian-African bloc. But most concerned of all, like any parents who must turn their offspring out into the world, are the British, whose credit and justification as imperial leaders of underdeveloped peoples will rise or fall with the success or failure of the Gold Coast. Britain has been the mentor of the area for about a century.

Some Britons Dubious

There are misgivings among the British, in London possibly more than in Accra. But the British observers feel strongly that to hestitate now would be more dangerous than to pursue the charted course toward independence that should culminate early in 1957.

Dr. Nkrumah's Convention People's party won seventy-one seats out of 104 in the Gold Coast election last week. The election was held to determine whether his constitutional plan for a unified, independent Gold Coast had the support of a "reasonable majority" of the people, as required by Britain.

The Convention People's party received nearly 58 per cent of the total popular vote, but it gained only about 45 per cent in the central and northern sections of the Gold Coast. The tribal peoples of these areas would prefer a federal type of government to centralization, so that the heavily populated and somewhat more advanced southern coastal region could not dominate them after independence.

One reason for British misgiving is the possibility that the great Ashanti federation of the central Gold Coast may develop into a war-like dissident minority in the new nation.

Nevertheless, observers here feel that there remains no alternative to full cooperation with Dr. Nkrumah. The Prime Minister and his associates have worked with Governor Sir Charles Arden-Clarke and other British officials since 1950 under a system of internal autonomy. One official commented: "It's a damn good thing they won. Otherwise we would have to train a whole new team."

Another reason for British misgiving is the allegation of corruption aimed at the Government in an investigation of state marketing of cocoa. This is the Gold Coast's major money crop and a very lucrative one, on which the economic viability of the new nation will depend.

Grave suspicions were aroused by the recent investigation. The findings have not yet been published, but the Opposition parties threw mud effectively enough to make some of it stick to the targets.

If British traditions of honest government should disappear when the Gold Coast becomes independent, British prestige as well as the ideal of colonial self-determination would suffer a severe blow.

London opinion was shocked on the eve of the election by Dr. Nkrumah's government's dismissal of Kodwo Mercer, Gold Coast Commissioner in London, without explanation. Mr. Mercer, an African, had been called home to testify in the cocoa marketing investigation and had severely criticized the Government in his testimony.

July 23, 1956

ACCRA BODY LINKS REGIME TO ABUSES

Cocoa Inquiry Report Says It Connived at Corruption in Purchasing Company

Special to The New York Times.

ACCRA, Gold Coast, Aug. 31—An official inquiry report said today that the Government had connived at and condoned irregularities in the Gold Coast Cocoa Purchasing Company.

The concern was established in 1952 as a subsidiary of the Cocoa Marketing Board, which controls and fixes prices paid to Gold Coast Cocoa producers and buys, sells and exports cocoa.

The report of the commission of inquiry said it was satisfied that bribery, corruption and extortion existed among some of the company's officials and that A. K. Djin, the company's first managing director, had abused his office and defrauded the company in a number of ways. Mr. Djin resigned his position before the inquiry began.

The Government, headed by Prime Minister Kwame Nkrumah, appointed an inquiry committee into the operations of the company following allegations of irregularities and corruption made against the company by the Opposition. Its chairman was O. Jibowu, a judge of the Federal Supreme Court of Nigeria, sister colony of the Gold Coast in British West Africa.

The committee met for the first time last May. Its status was later changed to that of a commission with wider powers.

The commission report stated that allegations that the company was controlled by the Government party, the Convention People's party, were justified. The commissioners said they were satisfied that the company gave loans only to members of the pro-government United Ghana Farmers Council.

The commission recommended that the section of the company responsible for granting loans to indebted farmers be wound up. It proposed the formation of a new board, nominated by the Government and the Opposition and with the chairman named by the Governor, to trade with all farmers, irrespective of their political affiliations.

In a paper accompanying the report the Government said the commission had departed from accepted procedure. In particular, it said, the commission did not hear counsel at the end of the inquiry with the result that a number of grave imputations had been made that were not supported by the record of the evidence.

Nevertheless, the Government said, it believed the commission had been helpful in revealing irregularities and shortcomings of the company previously unknown to the Government.

However, the Government said it could not accept the commission's recommendation about the constitution of a proposed board to take over the produce section of the Cocoa Marketing Board. It said its constitution was unlikely to produce a congenial board and would lead to appointments being made on political grounds rather than upon merit.

The Government said it had decided that the Cocoa Purchasing Company should cease to be responsible for making loans to cocoa farmers and that an agricultural credit board should be established to take over responsibility for loans to all types of farmers as long-term measures.

September 1, 1956

TOGOLAND CHANGE APPROVED BY U. N.

Assembly Votes to Conclude Trusteeship Under Britain, Backs Gold Coast Merger

By KATHLEEN McLAUGHLIN
Special to The New York Times.

UNITED NATIONS, N.Y., Dec. 13—The General Assembly approved today termination of trusteeship for British Togoland and merger of the territory with the Gold Coast in an independent state. The vote was 63 to 0, with 9 abstentions, mainly by Latin-American delegations.

The Assembly decision came on the tenth anniversary of the signing of the trusteeship agreement for the area between the British Government and the United Nations. The people of British Togoland are the first to win termination of their status as a dependent population under United Nations auspices.

By its action the Assembly signified its concurrence with the British view that the economic, social and political advancement of the Togolese had reached a point at which the people were capable of administering their own affairs.

Today's vote also constituted an endorsement of the results of the plebiscite held in the territory last May—the first such polling to be conducted under United Nations supervision. At that time 58 per cent of the voters signified their desire to be released from trusteeship status and to affiliate with the Gold Coast, which is scheduled to achieve sovereignty within the British Commonwealth next March 6 under the name of Ghana.

Representatives of the United States and other delegations expressed the hope that the dissident Togolese groups that had protested against the prospective merger with the Gold Coast would reconcile themselves to the new situation.

Frank C. Nash, the United States spokesman, recalled that the views of minority witnesses heard by the Trusteeship Committee had revealed conflicting opinions as to the courses they would have preferred to see adopted.

"We would strongly urge these groups to accept the principle that political maturity seeks to achieve political change by peaceful means, and to operate on the democratic premise that minorities should yield to majorities as long as there is a complete freedom for the minorities to seek to become a majority," he said.

The Assembly will deal later with the problem of the French half of Togoland, in which a similar 'popular consultation" was held last October under French auspices.

December 14, 1956

Negro Nation of Ghana Is Born in Africa

Gold Coast Becomes Ninth Member of Commonwealth

By THOMAS F. BRADY
Special to The New York Times.

ACCRA, Ghana, Wednesday, March 6—A new Negro nation was born at midnight.

As the British flag was lowered from the staff of the Legislative Assembly here and the new red, green and gold flag bearing a star rose in its place, the British colony known as the Gold Coast ceased to exist and the sovereign state of Ghana became the ninth member of the Commonwealth.

Prime Minister Kwame Nkrumah had told the final session of the colony's Legislative Assembly a few minutes earlier that the "chains of imperialism and colonialism which have hitherto bound us to Britain" were left behind as Ghana redeemed "her lost freedom."

Ghana is the name of the ancient West African empire that flourished about a thousand years ago. After it disintegrated, it remained a legend of Negro power and magnificence.

Attending the celebrations of the rebirth of Ghana are representatives of more than fifty nations, including the Soviet Union and Communist China. Vice President Richard M. Nixon heads the United States delegation. He is accompanied by his wife.

Thousands of Ghanians marched in the streets of Accra this morning singing, thumping drums and shooting firecrackers. At least 30,000 of them came from the polo grounds where the Prime Minister had told them in English and in the Fanti language that they were free people—no longer "slaves"—and that they must throw out their chests when they walk.

Mr. Nkrumah addressed them after his long and serious speech in Parliament House. He was still inside when the flag of Ghana rose on the mast and the crowds in the streets began to cheer and yell.

The independence of modern Ghana, which includes the former British Togoland, has been achieved without any significant violence since 1948. Then, riots in Accra grew out of shooting by the police of two Africans among a crowd of demonstrators.

Shootings and subsequent disorders cost twenty-nine lives and marked the beginning of constitutional reform and self-government in the then British colony.

The Duchess of Kent, who represents the British Crown at the current celebrations, dedicated a triumphal arch built at the point on the road where the demonstrators had been shot.

As a consequence of the riots Mr. Nkrumah was imprisoned without trial under the emergency powers of the Governor. After his release he organized the Convention People's party, which has held a large majority of the seats in the Assembly.

He preached a campaign of peaceful "positive action." Arrested and tried on charges of fomenting an illegal strike, he was sentenced to three years' imprisonment.

Further constitutional reform led to new election, and the result was so decided a victory for the Convention People's party that the Governor pardoned Mr. Nkrumah and released him from prison after he had served only nine months. He became Leader of Government Business, a post that has since

African Nation Gains Independence

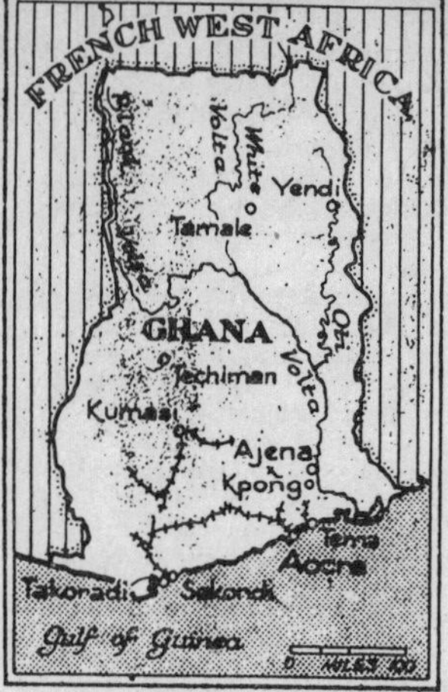

The New York Times March 6, 1957

The former British colony of the Gold Coast has become Ghana (cross-hatching), a member of the Commonwealth.

evolved into that of Prime Minister.

Mr. Nkrumah said in his speech that he intended to take over the portfolios of defense and external affairs himself. These departments have been under British control, and their transfer to African hands is one of the major changes that independence brings.

In a foreign policy statement, the new Prime Minister said:

"The Government of Ghana feels that at this stage the country should not be committed in any aspect of its foreign policy and that it should not be aligned with any particular group of powers or political bloc."

Monday Mr. Nkrumah told Mr. Nixon that Ghana "could never be neutral" in the "cold war."

Mr. Nkrumah told the final session of the Assembly that the Government would seek to help "all African peoples in their pursuit of freedom and social progress." He also emphasized that foreign investment would be encouraged.

In an economic summary, he said that the "material basis for the independence of Ghana exists."

"We can stand on our own feet," he continued.

He said the per capita income here averaged a little more than $140 a year for a population of slightly more than 4,000,000 in an area of nearly 91,700 square miles.

The figure is regarded as high for an African nation whose non-African population is fewer than 10,000, most of them civil servants and traders.

The per capita income is two and a half times that of Nigeria and more than three times that of Tanganyika. The Prime Minister said it exceeded the per capita incomes of India, Pakistan and Ceylon.

He warned, however, that much of the wealth was based on the nation's position as producer of about half the world supply of cocoa. Mr. Nkrumah emphasized the need to diversify the economy.

March 6, 1957

Independence Leader

Kwame Nkrumah

THE first citizen of Ghana, a cocoa-rich land on the under side of the hump of West Africa that became independent today, went to college in Pennsylvania and was voted the "most interesting" man in his class.

Kwame Nkrumah was the first Negro to become Prime Minister of a British colony. As popular leader of one of the first European colonies in Africa to gain full independence, he is of interest and concern to statesmen around the world. The success or failure of Britain's "experiment" with the Gold Coast colony and Mr. Nkrumah's plans for the new state are bound to affect for decades the history of Africa.

Man in the News

Mr. Nkrumah, a goldsmith's son, was born in primitive bush country forty-seven years ago. Now he heads the first Black dominion in the Commonwealth.

Called by Many Names

The man called often the African Nehru; and sometimes the Eagle and the Lion of Africa—and sometimes affectionately and proudly Show Boy by those who look on him as a prize personage for all to admire—is legally known by a name that means Saturday's Thirteenth Child.

Kwame Nkrumah, born in the mud-hut village of Nkroful in 1909, is pronounced as if it were spelled Qua-meh En-kroo-mah—sometimes run together as Quam' En-kroo-mah.

After he completed schooling at a Roman Catholic mission and the colony's Achimota College, Kwame Nkrumah was given funds by a diamond prospecting uncle for a trip to the United States. He enrolled at Lincoln University, Oxford, Pa., in 1935, receiving his B. A. four years later and later becoming a Bachelor of Sacred Theology. He was a philosophy instructor at Lincoln for a while, and earned an M. A. in anthropology at the University of Pennsylvania.

The young scholar was an active leader of the African Students Association of America and Canada, and early in his student career began attacking British colonialism. In 1945 he attended the London School of Economics, following the pattern of other colonial leaders who have decided to learn from the British how to replace them.

Mr. Nkrumah returned to his homeland in 1947 and soon after that the determinative phase of his career really began. Following a fatal riot in February, 1948, a British Parliamentary Commission that had been rushed to Accra blamed the colonial regime for denying the Negroes a voice in the Government. The upshot was a new Constitution and popular elections.

Spurred by the less patient wing of native leaders, Mr. Krumah denounced the new charter and demanded "positive action"—defined as "strikes based on perfect nonviolence." But the policy did not work. Mr. Nkrumah was jailed.

Arresting officers found in his pocket an unsigned membership card in the British

British Information Services.
Personifies the new Africa

Communist party. He explained later that he had used it to gain admission to meetings so that he could "learn their techniques."

A Hero to the People

Being in prison made Mr. Nkrumah a hero and martyr when the election was held. His Convention People's party got 80 per cent of the votes—cast after elaborate sound-truck education of the illiterate natives in the technique of voting—and Mr. Nkrumah's first big fight was won.

Sir Charles Arden-Clarke, Colonial Governor, freed him and appointed him Leader of Government Business, with powers approximating those of a Prime Minister. Later he assumed the title and position of Prime Minister. The Gold Coast's prison director resigned, protesting against being put in a position to take orders from a former inmate.

Mr. Nkrumah and his aides occasionally sported a "P. G." ("Prison Graduate") as a badge of honor, but he insisted he was a friend of Britain, aiming for dominion status for the Gold Coast. Ghana will be a member of the Commonwealth. He has tended to use the word "imperialism"—once his favorite whipping boy—much less frequently. Now he describes his job as keeping "things level and steady."

He is the personification of the contrasts in the emerging Africa. With Western education and Western tastes, he likes to pride around in a big, black Cadillac. Yet he consults a juju, or medicine man.

Mr. Nkrumah has a comb of frizzy hair, big soulful eyes and a manner that has been described as Messianic. The Prime Minister, who is unmarried, has declared, "Every woman in the Gold Coast is my bride."

March 6, 1957

BRITAIN ACTS IN NIGERIA

New Constitution Enlarges the African Colony's Home Rule

Special to The New York Times.

LONDON, July 1—A new constitution for the colony and protectorate of Nigeria in West Africa was announced by the British Government tonight. The Constitution, providing for a Central Legislature and Executive Council and three regional Legislatures and Executive Councils was promulgated by an order signed by King George VI on Friday.

The three regions of Nigeria will now have greater autonomy within a united country, and native Nigerians will receive a larger share of governmental authority. Twelve of the eighteen members of the Central Council of Ministers will be Nigerians.

July 2, 1951

32 Die in Moslem-Nationalist Riots Over Self-Rule in British Nigeria

By Reuters.

LAGOS, Nigeria, May 18—The death toll in political rioting at Kano, Northern Nigeria, rose to thirty-two tonight.

More than 200 persons have been injured in the Nigerian factional political violence that broke out during the week-end and continued today.

During the week-end five persons were reported killed. In the fighting today twenty-seven more were slain.

The situation in Kano was reported earlier today to be "getting out of hand." The Government already has declared a state of emergency throughout Northern Nigeria and rushed police and troop reinforcements to the scene.

The riots so far have been confined to Kano, the third largest city, with a population of 107,000.

The British Colony and Protectorate of Nigeria spreads over 373,000 square miles of West Africa and has a population of 24,000,000.

The riots began when supporters of the North Peoples Congress, representing 11,000,000 Moslems, demonstrated against a meeting of the rival Action Group. Moslems who fear domination by Nigeria's non-Moslem majority want self-rule only "when practicable."

The Action Group and affiliated organizations, representing both Christians and pagans, demand self-government by 1956. The group represents the Eastern and Western provinces south of Moslem territory.

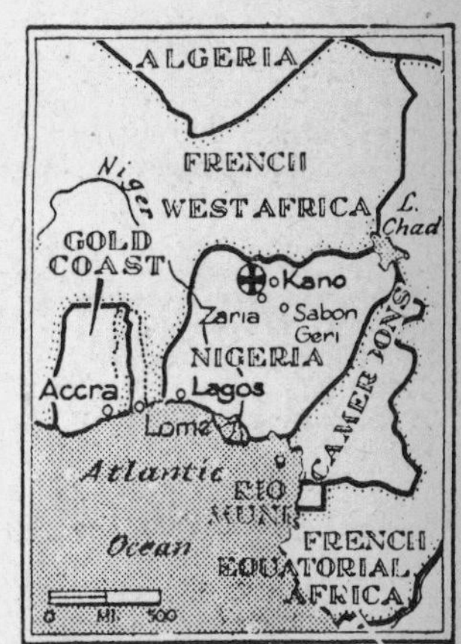

The New York Times May 19, 1953
Site of the rioting (cross)

Under the present constitution, the northern, eastern and western regions each have their own elected assemblies. Each sends four ministers to the Central Government in Lagos, the capital, and delegates to the Central House of Assembly.

The Moslem north has asked Britain to permit it to secede and form a separate colony, it was learned yesterday.

When the self-government demand came before the Central House of Assembly last March northern members opposed it. Members of the Eastern and Western Provinces promptly walked out. Tension through Nigeria has been mounting since.

May 19, 1953

NIGERIAN BODY DROPS BAR TO FEDERATION

Special to THE NEW YORK TIMES.

LONDON, Aug. 7—A long step toward agreement was taken unexpectedly today at the conference of delegates from the British West African colony of Nigeria who have been meeting here since last week to draft a new Constitution for their country.

Delegates representing the Northern Peoples Congress agreed in principle to a form of federal government which they had previously been thought to oppose.

There was great excitement at the conference when the northerners' decision was announced, for the question of the form of government had been one of the principal obstacles to agreement.

Earlier this year it became apparent that the Constitution of Nigeria, which has 20,000,000 inhabitants and is the most populous of Britain's African dependencies, was not working well.

Instead of full unification of the country and early independence within the British Commonwealth the northerners wanted only a very loose confederation in which there would be a central agency but no central legislature. Their decision to accept a federal government was a major concession.

August 8, 1953

NIGERIA TALKS SET ROLE OF CAMEROONS

Special to THE NEW YORK TIMES.

LAGOS, Nigeria, Jan. 21—The Nigerian constitutional conference agreed today that the Southern Cameroons trust territory should become a separate unit within the contemplated federation of Nigeria.

Oliver Lyttelton, British Colonial Secretary, who is presiding over the conference, presented a series of proposals that he had formulated last night in consultation with the delegates from the British Cameroons, a trust territory under the United Nations.

The conference endorsed these proposals, the most important of which were:

¶That the Northern Cameroons would remain a part of the northern region of Nigeria.

¶That the Southern Cameroons would cease to be part of the eastern region of Nigeria but would be included in the contemplated federation as a "quasi federal territory."

¶That the Federal Government would accept contingent liability to assist the Southern Cameroons financially in the event of deficits.

Mr. Lyttelton's proposals went far to meet the demands of Dr. E. M. I. Endeley, whose Kamerun National Congress swept the polls at last month's general elections in the Southern Cameroons.

The Southern Cameroons will have its own Legislative Assembly and Executive Council, but a British commissioner of the Cameroons, his deputy, a financial officer and a legal officer will sit in the council and in the assembly. Assent of the Governor General of Nigeria to legislation will be necessary.

The Southern Cameroons will be represented in the Federal Legislature by six members and there will be one minister from the Southern Cameroons in the Federal Council of Ministers.

January 22, 1954

SELF-RULE DELAY URGED IN NIGERIA

Northern Leaders Say They Have Not Enough Trained Native Administrators

By THOMAS F. BRADY

Special to The New York Times.

KANO, Nigeria, Aug. 26—This part of Africa is remarkable among colonial regions: its leaders admit they are afraid of achieving self-government and independence too soon.

The Sardauna of Sokoto, Prime Minister of Northern Nigeria, said yesterday in Kaduna, the northern capital 270 miles south of here, that his Government expected to have full autonomy in 1959. But he spoke without enthusiasm and emphasized reasons for waiting.

Basically, his thesis was that there were not enough trained northern Nigerians to man an autonomous administration and that British administrators were preferable to administrators from the more evolved southern regions of the Nigerian federation.

The Emir of Kano, ruler of the largest of the northern provinces, said here today he thought 1959 was too soon for self-government.

Both men represent the traditional Fulani ruling class of Northern Nigeria.

The Sardauna, Ahmadu, who is the nephew of the Sultan of Sokoto, is his probable successor. The Sultan, besides ruling the province of Sokoto, is the traditional leader of the faithful in Moslem Nigeria, and as such he has primacy over the other rulers of the northern region.

Sardauna is a title given to the Sultan's chief military executive. But the present Sardauna has gone into politics and is a leader of the Northern People's Congress, which controls virtually all the seats in the Northern House of Assembly.

A Polished Orator

An equally powerful leader of the congress, Abubaker Tafawa Balewa, Minister of Works in the Nigerian Federal Government, is of humbler origin. A Hausa, that is, a member of the largest, but not the ruling, ethnic group of the North, he is the son of a butcher.

He is viewed in this conservative region as something of a radical because he would not regret a drastic curtailment of the power of the traditional rulers.

Despite his undistinguished birth, Mallam (Mr.) Abubakar is one of the most polished orators in English that Nigeria has produced.

Mallam Abubakar has done a good deal to move the North toward self-government, and he commented recently that the northern chiefs had become surprisingly complacent about the prospect. They appeared to be unaware, he said, that democracy and party politics would inevitably end their ascendancy.

But the Sardauna and the Emir of Kano alike expressed the opinion that the "loyalty and affection" of the people toward their traditional rulers would survive independence and British withdrawal.

Still the chiefs of the North owe their continued authority and prestige to the British system of "indirect rule," and it seems most unlikely that their powers could increase with independence.

For the first time in Northern Nigeria, there will be direct popular election of legislators in the urban districts in the coming winter. The rural districts will continue to choose their representatives through graduated electoral colleges.

But the traditional chiefs will no longer be authorized to "inject" by direct nomination 10 per cent of the electors into the last stage of the electoral process. The traditional rulers will still sit in the Northern House of Chiefs, an upper chamber equal with the elected assembly in the bicameral system established in this region.

Once the election is completed, the Northerners will sit down with their fellow Nigerians from the South in a constitutional conference. This is scheduled to give the Southerners (of the Eastern and Western regions) full regional self-government, and carry the North one step further toward the 1959 goal of full self-government and the federation one step further toward independence in the Commonwealth.

September 9, 1956

BRITISH ADVANCE NIGERIA FREEDOM

Agree to Broaden Self-Rule Though Not Meeting Demand for Independence in '59

By LEONARD INGALLS
Special to The New York Times.

LONDON, June 26 — Britain agreed today to broaden self-government in Nigeria. The step would be taken in preparation for the possible independence of the West African dependency in 1960.

The British agreement was the result of a conference on constitutional improvements for Nigeria that began May 23. It was a disappointment to the Nigerian representatives who had come here with the support of their people to seek independence within the British Commonwealth in 1959.

Nigerians had been encouraged by the achievement of independence by their neighbor Ghana, formerly the Gold Coast, in March and by the agreements on approaching independence for the Federation of Malaya and for Singapore, British dependencies in Southeast Asia.

Early in the conference Britain indicated her reluctance to accept a fixed date for Nigerian independence. This caused the Nigerian representatives to postpone their ambitions for a year.

1960 Resolution Planned

Alan Lennox-Boyd, Colonial Secretary, noted that the Nigerians now proposed to adopt a resolution in their federal Parliament early in 1960 calling for independence within the Commonwealth that year.

He said Britain would consider the resolution sympathetically but could not "at this stage give any undertaking that the date would be the same as asked for in the resolution."

Mr. Lennox-Boyd added, however, that Britain would do her utmost "to meet the resolution in a reasonable and practicable manner."

Britain agreed at the conference to steps in the next three years to give Nigeria greater experience in self-government. Foremost among these would be a strengthened federal Government of the three Nigerian regions, Eastern Nigeria, Western Nigeria and Northern Nigeria, under a newly created post of Federal Prime Minister and an enlarged Federal Parliament.

Senate to Be Created

It was agreed that the Federal House of Representatives would be increased from its present membership of 194 to 320 members in 1959 and that a second legislative house, to be known as the Senate, be created.

On the question of the inclusion of the Cameroons, a United Nations trusteeship territory, in an ultimately independent Nigeria, the Colonial Secretary said this would have to depend on a vote by the people of the north and south sectors of the Cameroons. Under the United Nations trusteeship, the Cameroons has been administered by Britain as an integral part of Nigeria.

However, Mr. Lennox-Boyd said there could be no question of the Cameroons remaining part of an independent Nigeria against its wishes.

June 27, 1957

NIGERIA FEDERATION GETS FIRST PREMIER

Special to The New York Times.

LAGOS, Nigeria, Aug. 30—Governor General Sir James Robertson asked Alhaji Abubakar Tafawa Balewa today to become the first Prime Minister of the Federation of Nigeria. Mr. Balewa is the leader of the Northern People's Congress party.

The necessary constitutional changes had previously been made, leaving only external affairs and defense in the hands of the Governor General.

The Prime Minister's list of Cabinet members had been accepted. It includes, as he had wished, two members of the Action Group, majority party of the Western Region, and, until now, the official opposition in the Federal House of Representatives.

The Prime Minister will take on the additional duties of Finance Minister. The new Cabinet will be sworn in Sunday before the ceremonial opening of the Federal House of Representatives here Monday.

The National Council of Nigeria and Cameroons, Dr. Azikiwe's Eastern Region party, is not entirely happy about the appointment of the Action Group ministers. Although holding six seats in the new Cabinet, the National Council fears that inclusion of the Action group will threaten the smooth cooperation that has hitherto existed with the Northern People's Congress party in all federal matters.

August 31, 1957

TRIBE, NOT PARTY, COUNTS IN NIGERIA

Old Clan Loyalties Hamper Unity Amid Desires to Gain Independence

By RICHARD P. HUNT
Special to The New York Times.

IBADAN, Nigeria, Nov. 10—The old loyalties to tribe and clan still outweigh party political slogans here in the Western Region of Nigeria.

A Cabinet minister in the regional government, the leader of the Opposition and a young intellectual agreed on that a few days ago. But they would differ in the great debate going on in Nigeria: What should be done about it?

"Nigeria is an artificial creation, and the process of coalescing the people into one national bloc has been a failure so far," the young intellectual said, talking quietly in the humid heat of a late afternoon. "Many people feel there is no such thing as Nigeria."

Chief Anthony Enahoro, Minister of Home Affairs in the cabinet of regional Premier Obafeme Awolowo, pondered the same problem later in his cool office as he sat behind a big desk.

Regime Dimly Sensed

"The man in the village knows that somewhere in Lagos [the Federal capital of Nigeria] there is another government, but he does not know quite what it does," said the Minister, a brawny, handsome young man in a crisp white shirt.

"He is loyal to his village and his tribe, but beyond that his loyalty is not very strong," Mr. Enahoro continued.

In a crowded quarter among the twisting streets of the city, Adegoke Adelabu, leader of the Opposition, his face striped like a tiger's with tribal scars, walked back and forth across the room in his mud-walled house.

"When the British withdraw," he said, "if any regional government decides to secede from the Federation, how can the Federal government keep the regions together? There will be a war!"

These are the moods a visitor finds in Ibadan, Nigeria's largest city and capital of its Western Region. The region, which became autonomous in local matters last Aug. 8, is one of four in the Federation. The Federation is under British rule, but hopes for independence in 1960.

Lively Confusion

Ibadan, the home of 460,000 people, is a city of rusty tin roofs and lively confusion. It is a truly African metropolis. The crowded bazaars provide a shifting panorama of women in gay prints, with bundles on their heads and babies on their backs; men in flowing robes and little round hats; and grave schoolboys in khaki shirts and shorts.

On the outskirts of Ibadan the marks of the twentieth century are beginning to appear. There lie the new divided highway, the 500-bed teaching hospital on the university campus and the new ten-story Cooperative Bank Building.

Chief Enahoro puts his trust in these things. His party, the Action Group, believes the country should be divided into as many regions as can be made viable, within a decentralized federation.

To Mr. Adelabu, the answer is a strong central government, dominated by a Socialist mass movement. "What kind of unity is it when all the vital powers of government rest with the regions?" he asked.

The young intellectual had no ready answers. But an older man said he felt Nigeria's problems could not be solved as long as the British remain here to referee the disputes.

Nigerians, he said, must suffer and learn for themselves. A bit sadly, he added: "I am not looking forward to independence, but I still desire it as soon as possible."

November 15, 1957

NORTHERN NIGERIA RECEIVES SELF-RULE

LAGOS, Nigeria, March 15 (Reuters)—The last of Nigeria's three regions achieved internal self-government today in the final step before Britain's largest colony becomes completely independent in October, 1960.

Northern Nigeria established its own government to join the eastern and western regions as autonomous units of this 373,000-square-mile country of 30,000,000 people.

The Northern Nigerian Premier, Alhaji Ahmadu, the Sardauna (paramount leader) of Sokoto, was handed the Presidency of the Executive Council by the British Governor, Sir Gawain Bell. The ceremony took place at Kaduna.

The transfer of power came on the fifty-sixth anniversary of Britain's conquest of the former Sokoto empire, from which the new Premier derives.

March 16, 1959

CAMEROONS AREA TO STAY AS TRUST

Northern Section Plebiscite Favors Retaining British Under U. N. Mandate

Special to The New York Times.

YOLA, Northern Nigeria, Nov. 9—The Northern Cameroons has voted in favor of a continuation of British trusteeship, according to conclusive results received here today.

Of 108,992 votes, 67,879 were in favor of a continuation of the United Nations trusteeship and 41,113 in favor of the territory's becoming part of Northern Nigeria when it attains independence next year.

Fewer than 4.000 votes are outstanding.

The voting throughout the territory was heavy for a predominantly illiterate population exercising the secret ballot for the first time.

The territory is 175,000 square miles, mainly of poor scrubland. It was part of the former German Cameroons colony that came under British rule after World War I under a League of Nations mandate. Since 1946 the British have administered the area under a United Nations trusteeship.

Moslem Tribes Advanced

The British administer the territory as an integral part of the northern region of Nigeria. Nigeria is to become independent next Oct. 1.

The territory's population is made up of a majority of animist. or spirit worshiping, tribal groups and a minority of Moslem tribes which are more advanced and better organized politically.

The administration of the territory by the British as part of Northern Nigeria meant, in effect, an extension to the territory of the power and dominion of the emirs and sultans of Northern Nigeria.

The Moslem minority controls the territory's local government institutions and local administrative jobs. This touched off anti-Moslem resentment among the animist tribes.

The plebiscite was organized by the British Government as administering authority. It appointed Sir John Dring, retired Indian civil servant, as organizer. To insure the impartiality of the plebiscite and the validity of its results, the voting was supervised by twenty United Nations officials headed by Djalal Abdoh, an Iranian diplomat.

The result of the vote will require separation of the territory's local government institution and administrative machinery from those of Northern Nigeria as soon as possible.

The territory will have to decide eventually whether it wishes to remain independent or form a union with one of three neighboring states—the French Cameroons, the southern section of the British Cameroons, or the Federation of Nigeria.

November 10, 1959

African in Nigerian Post

IBADAN, Nigeria, July 8 (Reuters)—The first African to be appointed Governor of a British colonial territory, Sir Adesoji Aderemi, 71-year-old Paramount Ruler of Ife, was sworn in this morning as Governor of Western Nigeria. Sir Adesoji, former president of Western Nigeria's House of Chiefs and Minister Without Portfolio in the old Central Government of Nigeria, succeeds Sir John Rankine.

July 9, 1960

NIGERIA UNION FAVORED

Northern Cameroons Voters Back Merger With Neighbor

Special to The New York Times.

LAOS, Nigeria, Feb. 15—Provisional totals of voting in the Northern Cameroons plebiscite last Saturday show that those who favored joining Nigeria won by 47,611 votes. After the final count today figures stood at 145,265 for union with Nigeria and 97,654 for union with the Cameroon Republic.

More than 83 per cent of those eligible cast votes.

The final results in six constituencies in the Southern Cameroons are not in yet, but indications are that those who favor joining the Cameroon Republic have won overwhelmingly.

February 16, 1961

Nigerians Achieve Their Independence

By PAUL HOFMANN

Special to The New York Times.

LAGOS, Nigeria, Saturday, Oct. 1—Nigeria became an independent nation within the British Commonwealth today.

Until her independence last midnight, Nigeria was Britain's largest colony, with a population of 35,000,000.

Among the dignitaries here for the independence celebration was Governor Rockefeller, President Eisenhower's personal representative.

In a prepared statement, the Governor stressed that the United States was not seeking allies in Africa but free and independent friends. He advocated ever closer and stronger ties between the United States and independent Nigeria.

Mr. Rockefeller later attended a midnight outdoor flag-raising ceremony that marked the rise of Nigeria as Africa's most populous sovereign state.

Before Nigeria's colors—green and white—were given a salute by massed military honor guards, prayers for the future of the new nation were offered by an Anglican Bishop, a Roman Catholic Archbishop and Moslem Chief Imam of Lagos.

Princess Alexandra of Kent, who represented her cousin, Queen Elizabeth II, and the other foreign guests were cheered by the Nigerians.

Following a fireworks display, thousands remained in the brightly illuminated streets of the capital to await the dawn of independence day.

After having emphasized the interdependence of the world's nations, Mr. Rockefeller made it clear that the United States Government and the American people did not "expect the newly independent nations like Nigeria to stand besides the United States as a kind of active and committed ally in all struggles and conflicts that today are dividing the world."

Alluding to the Nigerian Government's professed policy of "nonalignment" in the "cold war," Governor Rockefeller urged the Nigerians to "be yourselves, to take and hold your own free place in the world of nations."

Nigeria, the Governor added, should "guard this place against all threats from without or perils from within."

Mr. Rockefeller, sporting a Nixon-Lodge campaign button for the Republican candidates in the United States, was accompanied by his wife, Mary; Tom Chauncey, an Arizona business man serving as special United States Ambassador to the Nigerian independence ceremonies, and James K. Penfield, Deputy Assistant Secretary of State for African Affairs.

Representative Charles C. Diggs Jr., Democrat of Michigan, who is here for the independence celebrations, said he would comment on his return home next week on the failure to include some prominent Negro in the official United States mission. The Representative is a member of the House Foreign Affairs Committee.

The United States delegation arrived here yesterday in a Boeing 707 jet plane.

Governor Rockefeller and his party were welcomed at Ikeja Airport by J. Modupe Johnson, Nigeria's Minister of Labor and Welfare. Also present was Joseph Palmer, 52-year-old career diplomat who has been appointed as the first United States Ambassador to Nigeria.

Delegates from about sixty governments attended the independence celebration.

The Soviet Union was represented by S. M. Arushanyan, deputy chairman of the the Presidium of the Supreme Soviet, and Yakov A. Malik, a Deputy Foreign Minister. They arrived here earlier this week.

To handle Nigeria's role as a sovereign state, Prime Minister Sir Abubakar Tafawa Balewa expanded and shuffled his nine-month-old federal Government last night. He announced that he would serve as his own Foreign Minister and Minister of Commonwealth Relations.

Muhammadu Ribadu, formerly Minister of Lagos Affairs, was named Minister of Defense. Among other Cabinet appointments, Jaja Wachuku Upto, speaker of the Federal House of Representatives, was named Minister of Economic Development.

October 1, 1960

Nigeria: Contrast to the Congo

The latest state to achieve independence in 'Africa's year,' it has had a course of practical training in self-government.

By ARCH PARSONS

LAGOS, Nigeria.

THE birth of another African nation, coming toward the end of a year that has seen so many other states on this continent gain their independence, and arriving in the midst of the Congo explosion, might seem by now to be anticlimactic. But Nigeria's achievement of independence yesterday is nevertheless one of the most significant events of "Africa's year."

Nigeria, a former British territory shaped roughly like a shovel and situated where the underside of Africa's western bulge begins to turn south, is not a big country in terms of land mass. It is less than half the size of the Congo, about a third larger than Texas and about a third smaller than Alaska. But its thirty-five million inhabitants, increasing at an estimated rate of one million every eighteen months, will make it the most populous independent nation on the African continent. It contains more than twice the population of the Congo and six times as many people as near-by Ghana. It will be, in fact, the twelfth most populous nation in the world.

Is it "ready" for independence? One must begin by warning that nothing angers a politically sophisticated African more these days than a discussion of that question. On the one hand, he may argue that he was "ready" as soon as he felt that it was necessary (he is inclined to recall that, two centuries ago, the United States did not waste much time on this point). On the other hand, he is likely to say, "Ready or not, here I come."

THE fact is, however, that Nigeria has been in training for independence since the end of World War II. It has been a practical course of preparation, developed through a combination of African nationalist fervor and a more enlightened colonial policy than Britain has shown in some other of its African territories. At times there has been no small amount of conflict between these two forces, but on the whole the two combined to create what could grow to be the most viable, influential nation in Africa. The potential is here.

What may be the country's greatest asset is its ability to run the day-to-day machinery of government and to maintain public order with some degree of impartiality.

Thousands of Nigerians have gone to the United Kingdom (and now in increasing numbers to the United States) for training and education. Nigeria has its full-fledged scholars. The university college at Ibadan is a first-class institution.

There are thousands of Nigerians, at all levels up to that of Permanent Secretary, in the Federal and regional civil services. To be sure they are still undertrained and still in insufficient numbers, but crash programs are rapidly filling the gap.

The Nigerian Army is a small but disciplined military force in which a quarter of the commissioned officers are African, some trained at Sandhurst, Britain's West Point. The United Nations requested that, immediately after independence, a Nigerian battalion be sent to join the U. N. force in the Congo. It will be under the command of a Nigerian lieutenant colonel.

NIGERIA'S arrival—less dramatic but also less likely to become erratic, may, in the long run have more meaning for Africa. For, precisely because of Nigeria's population and potential, it is no exaggeration to say that Africa's role in world affairs, particularly its ability to gain and hold the confidence of other nations, depends to a considerable extent on this country's ability to succeed where the Congo thus far has failed.

All this is in sharpest contrast to the condition the Belgians left behind in the Congo—where there were just sixteen or seventeen Congolese college graduates in a population of fourteen million and where the Force Publique had no African above the rank of sergeant. Few events could be more dramatic—and more tragic for Africa—than the Congo's arrival on the world scene, spinning and banging and crashing its way into international politics.

The Congo situation, regardless of where the blame for it lies, gives grounds at present for little beyond despair; Nigeria offers hope. Put simply, no one here expects the Congo to happen again.

A look at Lagos, the seaport capital of this new nation, confirms this. The city was in a turmoil as independence day neared, but there was none of the atmosphere of impending disaster that hung over Leopoldville on the eve of Congolese independence.

Near by is Ikoyi, a suburb of handsome houses that was once mainly the residential preserve of the "expatriate"—the term Nigerians use to describe the British and all white people in general. Affluent Nigerians live here now, too. As independence approached, no one left.

THERE was no sign of an expatriate locking his door and running out of Nigeria with a bundle of personal belongings under one arm and his dog under the other. Neither had anyone heard from a Nigerian who believed that "freedom" meant he might take over the house of the "white master," come Independence Day.

Nigerian servants do still call the man of the house—expatriate or Nigerian—"master." But if anybody had the idea of bringing off a domestic coup, there would be a good chance that he would find that "master" merely was a tenant and that the African landlord expected anywhere from $3,000 to $9,000 in annual rent, three to five years in advance, cash on the barrelhead, please.

Belgians deserted Leopoldville out of fear; Lagos simply has a housing shortage. There is no "white settler" problem here. Most of the land is owned by the Nigerian "community"—a family or village or tribe—and contrary to what the British may have done elsewhere in Africa, in Nigeria they have maintained that tradition.

Lagos, however, is hardly representative of all Nigeria. First of all, it is a city with modern department stores, office buildings, slums of unbelievable squalor and traffic chaos that rivals New York City's garment district at noon. Most of Nigeria is "bush," as the expression goes here. In the States, we would probably say "boondocks."

MORE important, perhaps, Nigeria, like the United States, is a federation of tremendously diverse areas and peoples. Lagos, like Washington, D. C., is geographically set apart from the rest of the country. It no more explains Nigeria than Washington explains the fifty United States.

NIGERIAN VISTA

It has been found that within the borders of this country, 249 distinct languages are spoken. Basically, Nigeria consists of three regions: Northern, Eastern and Western. "West and East Nigeria are as different as is Ireland from Germany," a Nigerian politician said a few years ago. "The North is as different from either as China."

In one sentence, and with only slight exaggeration, he was explaining that the basis of the division into three regions is more tribal than geographical. The result has been a political system that is still somewhat fragile. The issue of whether Nigeria can maintain itself as an independent nation turns to a great extent, as we have seen in such newly independent African states as the Congo and the dismembered Mali Federation, on the willingness of tribes to live together.

Northern Nigeria is basically Moslem. The faith of the Eastern and Western Regions is Christian, when it is not pagan.

The Northern Region is the least developed of Nigeria's three main areas. Its predominant tribe is an intermingling of the Hausa and the stately Fulani, who conquered the North in the nineteenth century and never forget their links with the medieval kingdoms of ancient Sudan and with Mecca. They are traders; few tourists leave Nigeria without at least one stiff bargaining session with the "Hausa man."

THE dominant tribe of the Eastern Region is the Ibo, who have been called both the "Jews of Africa" and "Nigeria's Irish." They are individualistic, quick to learn and industrious.

The Western Region, best developed of the three, is the land of the Yoruba, the most "Westernized" of Nigeria's tribes. The West is the home of the first television station in Africa, Nigeria's first "skyscraper" (ten stories), political leaders who campaign in helicopters, soap operas complete with commercials ("Has upset stomach and constipation got you down?") and one of the finest universities on the African continent.

THE idea of creating a single political unit out of this diverse trio of tribes was originally a British concept. For centuries, this was the scene of intertribal warfare touched off by the demand abroad for slaves; victorious tribes sold their captured victims to European slave traders. James Coleman, an American political scientist who has studied Nigeria closely, has called the "pacification" of the country part of "the greatest contribution the British have made to Nigerian unity."

The name "Nigeria" was born in a London newspaper only in 1897, and it was not until 1914 that the entire territory was merged into the Colony and Protectorate of Nigeria.

The result is that Nigeria today faces two alternatives. Should anyone decide to leave the three-member *ménage*, Nigeria would become merely another victim of "Black Balkanization," lying around in bits and pieces; another example of a growing African phenomenon that can only lead to violent rivalries and continental strife. As one household, Nigeria will be a major African power. Its political leaders appear to realize the alternatives and thus far have opted for the latter, despite their regional backgrounds.

The Prime Minister of the Federation of Nigeria is a northerner, Alhaji Sir Abubakar Tafawa Balewa, a dignified, astute politician whose Northern Peoples Congress is the largest party in the national legislature. The most imposing political figure in the North, however, is Alhaji Sir Ahmadu Bello, the towering, Oxford-accented Prime Minister of the Northern Region and the only major politician in Nigeria thus far to have shunned a role in the Federal Government in favor of continuing his regional position.

Dr. Nnamdi Azikiwe is the leading Easterner and perhaps the Nigerian best known abroad; he is variously called "Zik" (pronounced "Zeke"), the "Father of Nigerian Nationalism" and "Mr. Nigeria." Articulate, magnetic and American-educated, he is to take over the post of Governor General, generally regarded as "above politics." There is speculation, however, that he sees Nigeria, like Ghana, becoming a republic and himself, like Kwame Nkrumah, becoming Nigeria's first President. No one expects him to remain above politics for very long.

PRECISELY because Nigeria consists of a Federal Government with a delicate political alignment, Chief Obafemi Awolowo, studious, intellectual representative of the financially more prosperous Western Region and a pioneer nationalist, can continue to look beyond his present post as opposition leader.

Assuming these men can carry Nigeria over the first hurdle of independence, what of its future? What kind of role is it likely to play in world politics?

Nigeria has indicated its intention of applying for membership in the British Commonwealth. At the same time, Prime Minister Tafawa Balewa made it plain in a recent statement on foreign policy that "we shall nevertheless have a free hand to select those policies which we consider to be most advantageous for Nigeria. • • • We consider it wrong for the Federal Government to associate itself as a matter of routine with any of the powerful blocs."

ESSENTIALLY, Nigeria is oriented to the Western world—but this should not be looked upon with complacency. The West must make up its mind that while Nigeria needs plenty of economic aid and probably will seek it first from our side of the world, it is determined to play a "neutralist" role in cold-war politics.

If this role causes the West to be hesitant in offering aid for Nigeria's development, it is being made clear by political leaders here that Nigeria will show no such hesitancy in turning to other possible sources.

In regard to its fellow nations on the African continent, Nigeria is expected to be strongly "pan-African" but extremely cautious in approaching any plan for converting this feeling into formal and binding ties. In his statement the Prime Minister made it plain that Nigeria is not about to rush headlong into anything like the Ghana-Guinea union and expressed the view that any start toward a "United States of Africa" should be made by "emphasizing and building upon the cultural and economic links which already exist."

At another time, he was more candid; he told reporters that Ghana is interested in an African federation only if that country is "boss of the show."

Nigeria's domestic future at this point carries too many unknowns to be predictable. The country's new constitution is untried. The balance of power between the Federal and the regional governments is unknown. If the country's basically regional political parties attempt to expand into national groups, as is expected, what this may do to tribal relationships cannot now be determined.

The heritage of British parliamentary government — or any other form of democratic government—is no guarantee that democracy will automatically meet the needs and peculiarities of a new African nation. Nigeria's greatest chance for democracy may lie, paradoxically, in the very condition that could pull the country apart: the delicate balance of its tribal-regional-political system of federalism. In present circumstances, there is little possibility of one-man rule here for some time to come. No would-be ruler has that power nor could he obtain it unless he is satisfied to rule a fragmented section of the country.

IN an address in New York in July, the Northern Region's Prime Minister Bello summed up the situation this way: "Our country presents a picture of political stability. There is no absence of politics, and at times controversy runs high, as it does in any free country, but the basic factor in our political life is stability. We have not rushed unprepared into independence, but we have advanced step by step over the years.

"Our taking over the reins of government from our British tutors has been gradual and without rancor on either side. There need be no feeling that the emergence of Nigeria * * * presages a time of turmoil or disturbance."

October 2, 1960

CALMNESS RULES IN SIERRA LEONE

Colony Prepares for Stable Independence—Plans to Stay in Commonwealth

By HOMER BIGART

Special to The New York Times.

FREETOWN, Sierra Leone, March 17—Under the cautious leadership of Sir Milton Margai, Sierra Leone gives evidence of emerging next year as the most stable of the new African nations.

There seems to be no danger that Sierra Leone will follow her neighbor Guinea into providing a vacuum that the Communists might fill.

All political groups, including the Opposition, agree that Sierra Leone should remain within the British Commonwealth after independence is attained in April, 1961.

Sierra Leone is on the coast of the hump of West Africa between Guinea to the north and east and Liberia to the south.

Compared with most of West Africa, Sierra Leone is a haven of temperate, civilized thought. The frontiers are tranquil. Despite minor friction between the aristocratic "Creoles"—descendants of freed slaves that were the founding settlers of the colony—and the "natives" of the protectorate, there is internal harmony.

Guinea Stirs Concern

Sir Milton, the Premier, feels no urge to throw his Opposition into jail. He confesses some anxiety over events in the neighborhood of Guinea, where agents from the Communist bloc are settling. He is perturbed over the visits to Conakry by his embittered brother Albert. But he has put no hindrance on his brother's activities.

Recent Guinean visitors to Freetown have complained of police surveillance. They say their hosts are questioned about their reasons for being here, where they go and whom they see. Albert Margai said that his mail from Guinea had been mysteriously delayed.

"President Touré [Sékou Touré of Guinea] sent me an invitation late last Summer to attend a convention of his party," Albert said in an interview. "It took that letter a month to get here. I finally received it on the very morning that the convention was to open."

"I went to Conakry to explain why I hadn't answered the invitation," he said.

He denied Sir Milton's implication that he had sought President Touré's aid in building up the People's National Party, which he founded last year to oppose his brother's Sierra Leone Peoples' Party.

There is considerable unemployment in Freetown. The country faces a heavy budget deficit. Yet, according to the Governor, Sir Maurice Doorman, solvency could be assured if some way could be found to eliminate illegal digging and smuggling of diamonds.

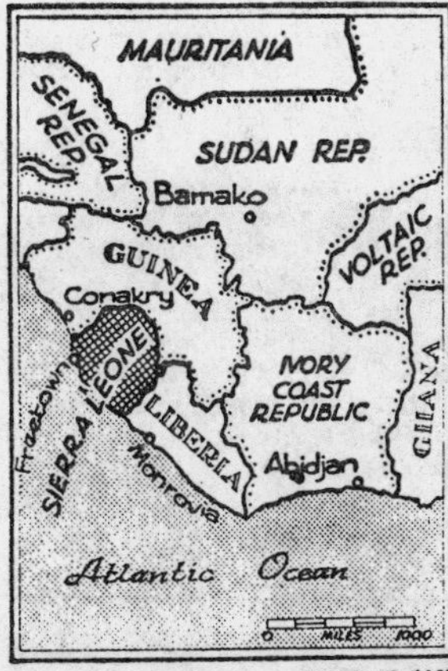

The New York Times March 27, 1960

A STABLE TERRITORY: Sierra Leone (shaded area) is scheduled to obtain its independence in one year.

Diamonds of gem quality were discovered in 1930. They were so near the surface that they could be found with a pick, a shovel and a sieve.

In 1933 the Government gave the Sierra Leone Selection Trust all rights to diamond mining in Sierra Leone until 2033. But bootleg mining was so easy that it was impossible to safeguard the company's rights.

Illicit mining and smuggling reached a peak in 1955. In that year the Government persuaded the Selection Trust to release its monoply rights over all but 450 square miles in return for compensation of more than £1,500,000 ($4,200,000).

The released land was then opened to Africans. More than 6,000 licenses were issued to diamond miners in the first year. By October, 1956, more than 75,000 persons were digging.

In a move against smuggling, Sir Milton expelled 20,000 Liberians and Guineans who were digging diamonds illegally. He also reduced taxes.

The results were encouraging. Legal dealings in diamonds in the last four months of 1959 were double the rate of the same period in 1958, and sales for the year set a new record of almost £6,000,000 ($16,800,000). But even so, the majority of diamonds continued to slip out of the country illegally.

Besides diamonds, Sierra Leone has important mineral wealth, particularly iron ore and chrome ore.

Sierra Leone is primarily an agricultural country. Most of the 2,200,000 inhabitants grow their own food. Export crops include palm kernels, coffee, cocoa and kola nuts.

March 27, 1960

STATEHOOD BEGUN BY SIERRA LEONE

Midnight Ceremony Marks Colony's Independence

FREETOWN, Sierra Leone, April 27 (Reuters) — Sierra Leone celebrated its independence today after nearly 175 years as a British colony.

Independence came to the West African territory of 2,000,000 persons in a dramatic midnight ceremony. About 15,000 persons jammed the Freetown sports stadium and stood together to sing the hymn "Lead, Kindly Light," followed by the new Sierra Leone national anthem.

At midnight, lights were extinguished. Ten seconds later they flashed on, focused on the new green, white and blue flag that had replaced the Union Jack on the staff in front of the royal pavilion. Cheers roared through the city as fireworks festooned the starry sky.

The celebrations were not attended by thirty-one members of the opposition All People's Congress party. They have been jailed by the Government on charges of having planned to disrupt the independence celebrations. The Prime Minister, Sir Milton Margai, has promised to free them as soon as the independence festivities are over.

At a state banquet before the independence ceremony last night, Sir Milton said his regime had no intention of suppressing "responsible criticism" and always would welcome comments made in a "democratic" manner. He also said the Government intended to encourage foreign investment.

Today, at the opening of the Sierra Leone Parliament, the Duke of Kent, representing Britain, read a message from Queen Elizabeth II, his cousin. He also handed Sir Milton the formal documents making Sierra Leone a sovereign state.

The Government plans to join the British Commonwealth and seek a seat in the United Nations. It also will negotiate a defense treaty with Britain.

Sierra Leone, about the size of Ireland, was ceded to Britain in 1787 by African chiefs as a haven for destitute freed slaves living in England. At the time, settlers did not know they were walking on one of the world's richest diamond areas.

April 28, 1961

GAMBIA A NATION, TINIEST IN AFRICA

Dancing and Singing Mark the End of British Rule

By LLOYD GARRISON
Special to The New York Times

BATHURST, Gambia, Thursday, Feb. 18—The Union Jack fluttered down over Gambia at midnight this morning, bringing an end to the last outpost of British colonial rule in West Africa and giving Africa its smallest and poorest independent state.

Thousands of Gambians pressed around the old cricket grounds in Bathurst's McCarthy Square for the ceremony. They drummed and danced and sang. A barefoot sixth grade school boy exclaimed over and over: "It's just like New Year's Day."

But Prime Minister David K. Jawara captured the mood of most adult citizens when he cautioned that freedom would not bring miracles.

In a brief speech he thanked the British for the "atmosphere of harmony, friendliness and cooperation that prevailed in the transition to independence." Then he warned his people: "We must realize, however, that we are entering into independence with many grave problems."

The most urgent, he said, was to achieve a sound economy in a one-crop land—peanuts—that will depend for years on a subsidy from London of more than a million dollars a year.

The Ritual of Independence

The evening's ceremonies reflected the now-standard procedure for a British colony's shift to independent status. A few minutes before midnight British Royal Marines marched in solemn half-step, taking the salute of the Queen's representatives here, the young Duke and Duchess of Kent.

Then the crowd stood at attention as the band struck up "God Save the Queen." The flag descended and the lights dimmed. There was a hush during the darkness of the next moments, then a joyful cry as the blue, green and red flag ran up the pole to the blare of Gambia's national anthem.

Fireworks lit up the bay. The drums pounded on and on. All of Bathurst's 28,000 people seemed ready to dance until dawn.

Gambia, which is entirely surrounded by Senegalese territory except for her coastline on the Atlantic, twists 300 miles along the banks of the Gambia River, but is only 30 miles wide. The country has no railroad, no airline, no army.

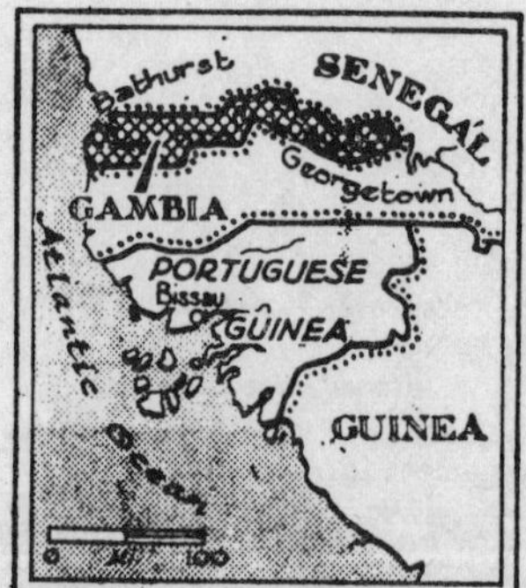

The New York Times Feb. 18, 1965

WINS INDEPENDENCE: Gambia (in cross-hatching) is newest African nation.

Gambians are highly sensitive about their country's small size, but as one member of Parliament said the other day: "If independence seems to make little sense, it is Britain's fault, not ours."

Many Britons would agree with Sir Thomas Southorn, a former Governor General, who described the colony as "a geographic and economic absurdity."

Gambia was squeezed out of the heart of French-speaking Senegal during Europe's headlong scramble for colonies four centuries ago. Even the British realized their mistake. As late as 1876 they were still trying to strike a deal with France to let Gambia be absorbed into Senegal in exchange for a slice of French-ruled Gabon.

The cost of staging the independence ceremonies stands as a grim reminder of present economic reality here. Britain and Gambia have split the expense of fireworks and receptions, providing hotel rooms for foreign guests and stringing up miles of flags and colored lights.

The cost comes to $95,000. This is modest compared to what other African countries have spent. But it is still almost as much as Gambia earns each year in income tax.

Gambia is the 36th land in Africa to win independence. With Prime Minister Jawara at the helm her foreign policy is likely to follow the moderation of Nigeria and Sierra Leone, two of her West African English-speaking neighbors.

G. Mennen Williams, Assistant Secretary of State for African Affairs, arrived for the ceremonies and brought Washington's Independence Day contribution of $125,000—so far Gambia's largest gift. It will be spent on agricultural machinery and a mobile dock crane.

February 18, 1965

TANGANYIKA ASKS BETTER SCHOOLS

Trust Area's British Rulers Agree on Aim—Economy of Area Is Deteriorating

By ALBION ROSS

Special to The New York Times.

DAR ES. SALAAM, Tanganyika, June 8—When a United Nations investigating commission visits this trust territory, the Negro natives' representatives will call attention to the fact that their opportunities for education are limited.

The issue came up recently in the Legislative Council. Britain is the trustee power here, and under the trusteeship system the primary task of the governing power is to prepare the population for eventual control of their affairs. The British Government has accepted this principle. Colonial Secretary Oliver Lyttelton told Parliament last month that it was the golden thread of colonial administration accepted by all political parties.

Julius Nyerere, president of African Society, the only active Negro political organization in Tanganyika, said in the Legislative Council recently that at the present rate it would be 1986 or 1990 before all African children could go to primary schools. The present plan calls for providing such schools for 34 per cent of Negro children by 1956.

Technical Training Stressed

The importance of technical schooling rather than "academic" education was emphasized. Mr. Nyerene, himself a teacher, suggested that this was impossible without at least a minimum of grammar school education.

Mr. Nyerere is a moderate recently appointed to the Legislative Council by Governor General Sir Edward Twining. Extremism is not a problem here and racial relations are the best in this part of Africa. The Government is consistently trying to build up a multi-racial society and is firm on the primacy of the Africans' interests. Only an extremely small part of the population is European or Asian.

Mr. Nyerere proposed that as a part of the education of Africans for self-government, the town of Dar es Salaam elect one or more African representatives to the Legislative Council instead of their being appointed by the Governor. He also proposed that European and Indian reprentatives here be elected instead of appointed.

Nowhere in British East Africa are Negroes elected to Legislative Councils. The white authorities here and in Kenya and Uganda are loath to see election of Negro members.

East Africa's increasing economic stagnation and falling income have put the brakes on the development of Tanganyika, the biggest and most backward of the area's territories.

Drop in Exports Noted

Tanganyika's exports, on which it is largely dependent for anything above bare subsistence, fell by more than a fourth last year. High cotton and coffee prices are being watched anxiously. The loss was due largely to a fall in the price of sisal fiber, Tanganyika's principal product.

Tanganyika's falling exports and shriveling economy are an aspect of the general recession in East Africa, which, in terms of percentages, is exceptionally severe compared to most parts of the world.

A bill has been introduced providing for Tanganyika to take over the Tanganyika Agricultural Corporation, the wreck of the spectacular groundnuts plan on which the British Treasury lost the equivalent of $100,000,000. The failure was a demonstration of the essential poverty of the soil in the vast bushlands and of the rapid deterioration that sets in when they are exposed to the tropic sun.

The remark of one Legislative Council member that the peanuts plan had "put Tanganyika on the map" received a rather mixed reception—including the British version of what would be known in the land of the Giants and the Dodgers as the Bronx cheer.

June 13, 1954

TANGANYIKA GETS NEW LEGISLATURE

Revamped Council Stresses Racial Parity but British Retain Majority of One

Special to The New York Times.

DAR ES SALAAM, Tanganyika, April 19—Gov. Sir Edward Twining today opened this British-mandate territory's new Legislative Council in which those of British, African and Asian origin have parity representation.

The reorganized Legislative Council represents the biggest constitutional advancement in the history of Tanganyika and follows hard on the controversy that shook the area after a visit of a United Nations Trusteeship Council mission.

That mission's report, issued last January, suggested the establishment of a timetable for self-government in a period not less than twenty years.

Tanganyika has been regarded as a model trusteeship territory and an example of unusual racial harmony.

Although the report was severely criticized here by members of all races as inaccurate and misleading, it also found its champions, especially among the more nationalistic of African organizations.

The recommendation that caused the most unhappiness among Europeans and Asians, who share equally the burden of the administrative and commercial life of the territory, was the mission's belief that an African majority should be seated on the "unofficial" side of the Legislative Council within three years.

All Members Nominated

There are no elections in Tanganyika. All members are nominated and those not actually sitting with the Government on the Administration benches are termed "unofficials."

Tanganyika Africans generally are still backward and primitive. Even the most advanced among them have not reached the standards common to energetic tribes, such as Kenya's Kikuyu. A common topic among Europeans and Asians here in recent weeks has been the problem faced by the Government in finding suitable African applicants to fill the African seat quota in the Legislative Council.

To facilitate its search the Government decreed that Swahili, the native language common to most of the East African tribes as the form of communication over tribal dialect, could be used as the medium in the new house.

This allowed the selection of senior chiefs from the hinterland districts who speak no English.

Generally, despite rumblings from the Europeans and scattered complaints from the Africans, the new Constitution has been acclaimed by all races as an example to the rest of Africa.

Although the colored races have no Cabinet representation, the reconstituted Legislative Council seats more non-whites than any chamber in Africa outside of the West African territories.

The new house represents the first major change in the Constitution since Britain assumed responsibility for the former German colony in 1919.

Total Membership Is 61

The new house has a membership of sixty-one, thirty-one of whom are "officials," the Government thus having an official majority of one. All Cabinet and Government seats are held by the British. The thirty unofficial seats are divided equally among the races, ten to each.

An unusual feature of the council is the nomination of three women, one from each race. This is regarded as a step without precedent in Africa.

The selection of "unofficial" members was made in consultation with the principal political associations of the various racial groups, a method that was generally regarded as unsatisfactory.

The Tanganyika European Council, the largest of the white groups, is virtually confined to Dar es Salaam. The Tanganyika African National Union is composed almost entirely of urbanized Africans of grade school education.

The Asian Association is by no means representative of all the Asian groups, which are inclined to organize on a religious basis, either Moslem or Hindu.

Tanganyika is an arid and agriculturally poor state, with a population of 8,000,000 Africans, 60,000 Asians and 18,000 Europeans, a large proportion of the last group being government servants and administrators.

April 20, 1955

BRITISH SET VOTE FOR TANGANYIKA

Announce First Elections in '58 for Minority Groups on Multi-Racial Basis

By RICHARD P. HUNT
Special to The New York Times.

DAR ES SALAAM, Tanganyika, March 28—Britain is preparing a tethered constitutional experiment in the uneasy political atmosphere of Tanganyika.

The Government here has just announced proposals to hold the country's first election in 1958. Minority members of the Legislative Council will be chosen in three or four of the nine constituencies.

Talk of a boycott was heard at once from the rapidly growing Negro nationalist movement. A group of whites also is beginning to ask whether the Government is going far enough.

The official view is that Tanganyika must tread carefully because the great majority of its inhabitants have no experience, little education and meager economic resources on which to found a modern self-governing state.

The accidents of history have made Tanganyika something of a stepchild in the British family of nations. Pacified by Germany at the turn of the century, it was ceded to Britain after World War I and is now administered as a United Nations trust territory.

Within its 362,688 square miles live 25,000 persons generally of European descent, 94,000 Asians and Arabs and 8,205,000 Africans. The last named range from primitive tribes in remote bush country to business-minded coffee farmers on the slopes of snow-capped Mount Kilimanjaro.

Few Schools for Negroes

There are primary schools for less than half of the Negro children, and only twenty-five secondary schools for them. There are few Negro university graduates and fewer civil servants. Communications are poor and the uncertain natural resources are undeveloped.

Britain is required by her mandate to bring this backward country, second in size and population only to Nigeria among her dependencies, to independence. Her solution is suggested by the electoral proposals.

These call for voting on a common roll, which means that all voters, regardless of race, choose among the same candidates. But each voter will be required to vote for one European, one Asian and one African.

The two chosen will jointly represent each constituency. Under the present method ten members of each race are appointed to the unofficial minority, which holds thirty of the sixty-one seats.

A voter must be 25 years old and have one of three qualifications: at least eight years of education or an income of at least £150 ($420) a year or service as a council member, local adviser, chief, headman or clan leader.

A Multiracial Regime

The implicit policy is to create a multiracial government dominated eventually by an African electoral majority. The theory here is that progress will be timed by the education of that majority.

About a year ago the multiracial United Tanganyika party was formed with Government blessing to pursue similar objectives. It now has 4,000 to 5,000 members of all races.

Lately a group within the party has begun to feel that Africans are not accepting the idea of multi-racial government and that their party lacks appeal because it does not have a program for swift advance.

Therefore, this group wants to adopt a timetable for self-government, giving the African more council seats at once. Some are prepared to walk out and from a party more critical of the Government.

Clearly, a multi-racial government is opposed by the Tanganyika African National Union, a party of about 150,000 members demanding self-government within twelve years.

As an all-Negro party it cannot put up a full slate of candidates in any constituency. Therefore, its likeliest course is to boycott the elections in an attempt to discredit them.

The New York Times March 30, 1957

VOTING IS SCHEDULED: Plans have been issued for an election in Tanganyika (shown in black) next year.

March 30, 1957

TANGANYIKA EYES WAY TO STATEHOOD

But Delicate Relationship Between Tribalism and Nationalism Is Hurdle

Special to The New York Times.

MOSHI, Tanganyika, Feb. 27—The relationship between African nationalism and traditional tribalism is delicate in Tanganyika.

Paradoxically, the relations between the outstanding nationalist leader and the paramount chief of the best-known and most prosperous tribe are excellent.

The nationalist is Julius Nyerere. He heads the Tanganyika African National Union. It has just completed a sweep of two-stage elections that have generally been taken as the surest indication that this United Nations trust territory under British administration is headed for African statehood.

In the elections, each voter had to choose one candidate from each of three groups, African, Asian and European. In every case the Asian and European endorsed by the African union was elected.

Independence Sought

The paramount chief is Thomas Lenana Mlanga Mareale of the coffee-growing Wachagga of the slopes of Kilimanjaro. He is the 43-year-old Cambridge-educated elected leader of 350,000 people, who refer to him as the Mangi Mkuu, or top man.

In June, 1957, both Mr. Nyerere and Mr. Mareale appeared before the Trusteeship Council of the United Nations. Each praised the other, and since then each in his own way has been a firm advocate of eventual independence, to be achieved by moderation and nonviolence.

Both Mr. Mareale and Mr. Nyerere, in talks at Dar es Salaam, capital of Tanganyika, a few days ago, closely examined the latest outbreaks of violence in Nyasaland, which borders Tanganyika to the south, and sought to assess the effect on the situation here.

But what really took Mr. Marealle to the capital was a series of confidential discussions growing out of his difficulties with other chiefs as a result of his close harmony with Mr. Nyerere.

In May, 1957, Mr. Mareallc suggested an organization of all tribal chiefs for periodic discussions of common problems. He was chosen as executive chairman of the group, in which all tribes of the eight provinces are represented.

Last Fall Mr. Mareale formally suggested that the chiefs' group invite Mr. Nyerere to speak at a December meeting.

Mr. Nyerere was not invited and Mr. Mareale resigned his chairmanship of and membership in the group. This development worried the territorial government, and eventually Mr. Mareale agreed to base his withdrawal on the pressure of other activities, with no public reference to the central issue.

February 28, 1959

TANGANYIKA SETS MODEL FOR AFRICA

British-Held Trust Region to Install a Multiracial Government July 1

By MILTON BRACKER

Special to The New York Times.

DAR ES SALAAM, Tanganyika, June 20—Multiracial government will reach a new stage in Africa July 1.

On that day twelve new ministers will be sworn in in Tanganyika. Three of them will be Africans. But even more significant, two others will come from a multiracial-elected bloc that is led by an African of the bloc's own choice.

The bloc is made up of ten persons of European descent, ten Asians and ten Africans so that numerically the Africans are outnumbered 2 to 1.

In fact, this United Nations trust territory administered by Britain is so far advanced along the lines of multiracial government that it poses delicate questions for the British Colonial Office.

Reaction Expected

For to the degree that London smiles on the progress here, or agrees to further increases in the number of elected ministers, there is expected to be uneasy reaction in areas like Uganda, Kenya and the Federation of Rhodesia and Nyasaland.

Tanganyika, formerly German East Africa, has 20,000 "Europeans," 80,000 Asians and 20,000 Arabs. But it has about 9,000,000 Africans, of whom 2,-500,000 are Moslems.

Until now it has had nine ministers—all "official," or non-elected, and all white.

But a two-part election was held in September, 1958, and last February. Under the so-called parity Constitution, each of ten constituencies was to elect ten members of each main ethnic grouping to the Legislative Council.

The result was that in twenty-eight instances the winners, white, African or Asian, had the support of the Tanganyika African National Union headed by Julius Nyerere.

Moreover, the two other candidates, both whites who ran unopposed in an effort by the unsuccessful multiracial United Tanganyika party, promptly joined the Tanganyika Elected Members Organization.

Not only did this group choose Mr. Nyerere as chairman, but it has in every instance so far followed his leadership unanimously. In fact Temo, as the organization is known, has worked so smoothly that it has occasionally been referred to as "Teamo."

In mid-March Gov. R. G. Turnbull announced that the number of elected ministers would be increased from none out of nine to five out of twelve as of July 1. On the legislative side, the "official," or non-elected members, still outnumber the elected ones by thirty-four to thirty.

However, as a responsible British official put it "Nyerere is the key to everything in Tanganyika."

The 37-year-old former school teacher declined to accept one of the five Ministries himself. He feels that, as the unquestioned leader of the elected bloc regardless of race, he is in a stronger position than ever to press for a greater share of Ministries in the future.

The situation here is thus a far cry from that in Kenya and much farther from that in Central Africa. Two key factors make it possible:

First, the personality, skill and absolute dedication of Mr. Nyerere to nonviolence and anti-discrimination against Africans and non-Africans alike.

Second, the fact that of the 20,000 whites 17,000 work here but are not settlers. And the 3,000 settlers include men, women and children; there are only 1,000 householders among them.

June 21, 1959

Tanganyika in 4-Day Celebration As Nation Gains Independence

Flame Lighted on Mountain to Symbolize Aspirations —British Rule Ends

By LEONARD INGALLS

Special to The New York Times.

DAR ES SALAAM, Tanganyika, Saturday, Dec. 9—Tanganyika became an independent sovereign state today.

An instant after midnight the green, gold and black Tanganyika flag was raised in a ceremony here that brought to an end the territory's years as a German colony and then a British-administered United Nations trust territory.

Tanganyika, the twenty-eighth African country to gain independence, will remain a member of the British Commonwealth.

A simultaneous flag-raising was held on Mount Kilimanjaro, which rises 19,340 feet in northern Tanganyika. A young second lieutenant of the new Tanganyika Army, Alexander Nyirenda, raised the flag and lit a symbolic torch atop the mountain in a snowstorm.

Flame Represents 'Hope'

The Kilimanjaro ceremony was in keeping with a wish voiced in 1959 by the Prime Minister of Tanganyika, Julius K. Nyerere. He said at that time: "We the people of Tanganyika would like to light a candle and put it on top of Mount Kilimanjaro to shine beyond our borders, giving hope where there was despair, love where there was hate and dignity where before there was only humiliation."

More than 70,000 people crowded the new National Stadium in Dar Es Salaam for the transfer of authority from Britain to the Tanganyika Government. They witnessed a military tattoo and a fireworks display and greeted the moment of independence with a mighty roar.

The people of Tanganyika began a four-day public holiday yesterday to mark the achievement of their freedom.

The first of many events on a crowded program of celebrations proved to be a moving one. It was the unveiling of a monument to the country's independence by Prime Minister Nyerere. It stands at a site in the center of Dar Es Salaam where Africans held many of their largest political meetings during the years they were campaigning for independence.

Associated Press

Julius K. Nyerere

About 3,000 Africans gathered for the unveiling ceremony in the old meeting place, known among them as Mnazi Mmoja, which in Swahili means The Place of the Lone Cocoanut Tree. With Prime Minister Nyerere were members of his Cabinet and visiting African political leaders, including Jomo Kenyatta of neighboring Kenya.

"The real monument is yet to be built," Mr. Nyerere said. "It is going to be a nation, a nation that we can with pride bequeath to the posterity of our country, and the torch at the top of this modest monument is merely to show us that we have not yet achieved this objective."

Later yesterday Mr. Nyerere went to the airport with Sir Richard Turnbull, who was serving his last day as British Governor of Tanganyika, to greet Prince Philip, Duke of Edenburgh. The Duke is representing his wife, Queen Elizabeth II, at the independence celebrations. He was given a military welcome by Tanganyika troops.

December 9, 1964

UGANDA SELF-RULE AIDED BY BRITAIN

Constitutional Expert to Help Tribe—Governor Defends Banishing of King

Special to The New York Times.

LONDON, Feb. 23—The British Governor of Uganda today defended the dismissal of the native ruler of one of its provinces while plans were being announced for a new step toward self-government for that colony.

Sir Andrew Cohen, home from the colony to consult the Colonial Office, said he recommended the discharge of the Kabaka (king) of Buganda last November when that young native ruler became "absolutely rigid" in his demands for separation and independence for what is now a province in the Uganda Protectorate.

Sir Andrew acknowledged that a majority of the members of the Baganda tribe certainly wanted the Kabaka to return to his throne from his present exile in London, but that he would not be permitted to do so.

Uganda must not be split up, he said, nor should it be federalized, as has become the avowed objective of the more moderate Baganda who have abandoned the notion of separatism since the Kabaka's deposition.

Sir Oliver Lyttelton, the Colonial Secretary, announced in the House of Commons today that a constitutional expert would be sent to Uganda to give the Baganda tribe his help in working out a new relationship to the central Uganda Government.

The announcements were taken as first move in an attempt to get the Great Lukiko, the native governing council, to elect a new Kabaka. Replacement of the ruler is being held up until a Uganda court hears a suit against the Governor's appointment of delegates to the Council. A victory for the Governor will establish the legality of what has been done and it is thought the tribesmen will resign themselves to the deposition of their ruler.

Sir Andrew and Sir Oliver Lyttelton today re-emphasized the determination of the British Government to protect the Uganda natives from white and Asian infiltration. No industrial color bar will ever be tolerated, Sir Andrew promised. The Colonial Government maintains strong controls on any immigration and land alienation.

February 24, 1954

EIGHT UGANDA CHIEFS REMOVED BY BRITAIN

KAMPALA, Uganda, June 3 (Reuters)—Britain today ousted eight tribal chiefs in Buganda province in her drive to subdue a growing wave of anti-British feeling in the East African protectorate of Uganda.

The ousters came three days after Colonial Governor Sir Andrew Cohen declared a state of emergency, called up special police and alerted British troops.

Buganda African leaders became incensed last November when the British Government banished the province's 29-year-old Kabaka (king) on the ground he was not cooperative. A month ago the Uganda National Congress organized a trade boycott to protest native resentment over the king's removal and exile to London.

[In London, Congress President Ignatius Musazi charged that the ouster of the eight tribesmen was "yet another political blunder" by General Cohen, and hinted that the Buganda people might have to use violence to win their case.]

The British Resident Commissioner in Buganda, J. P. Birch, said some of the ousted chiefs had taken active roles in the trade boycott, and that one had urged his tribesmen not to buy or sell goods. He criticized longstanding "unsatisfactory work and attitudes" of the tribal leaders.

Governor Cohen proclaimed the state of emergency after charging that African leaders had intimidated those who defied the Uganda National Congress boycott order. A group of Africans is reported to have cut off the hand of a man because he bought bread.

June 4, 1954

PRESS IN UGANDA COURTS TROUBLE

African-Language Papers Prosecuted for Sedition by the Colonial Regime

By LEONARD INGALLS
Special to The New York Times.

KAMPALA, Uganda, July 6—Strong political feeling in Uganda has resulted in a wave of prosecutions for sedition this year against the African-language newspapers in Kampala.

The British Protectorate Government has brought the prosecutions for inflammatory advocacy of Uganda's burning desire for self-government.

A recent report of political speeches in the newspaper Gambuze, which freely translated means "The Answer," cost editor a fine of $140. His story quoted speakers as having said:

"All of us should strike for self-government Foreigners pack up and go home. The people of Uganda should unite to clamor for self-government and if we are to die then we shall die until we are exterminated."

The superintendent of the Criminal Investigation Division of British colonial police testified in case that the quotation amounted to an exhortation to fight to the death.

The two publishers and two editors of Emambya-Esage (The Dawn) are awaiting trial on a sedition charges for having printed an article titled "How Can Peace Come to the Country while Britain Uses Robbery!"

The government charged that this incited dissatisfaction and discontent among Africans and promoted feelings of ill-will and hostility among them.

The owners of The Uganda Post paid a $280 fine for having printed a letter containing the following:

"There are many reasons why the people of this country wish to govern themselves. Racial discrimination, being made to work like slaves and being cheated in a cunning manner, failure to realize that the African was created in the same way as the Europeans (whites), are some of the many reasons, so when we hear that other countries are fighting for self-government we should not sit back and watch."

The Uganda Post and The Uganda Express, now defunct, were suspended by government order from June, 1954, to January, 1955, at the height of the crisis over the exile to London of Kabaka, the King of Buganda, Uganda's largest province, after he refused to cooperate with British officials here. The Post's editor is in prison for accusing a tribal chief of witchcraft.

July 1, 1956

NATIONALIST TIDE SLACK IN UGANDA

No Leader Has Yet Emerged Who Can Command a Large Following

By MILTON BRACKER
Special to The New York Times.

KAMPALA, Uganda, Jan. 29—The Belgian Congo is a neighbor to Uganda, but the continuing turmoil in the Congo has not had any detectable impact on African nationalism here.

The same applies to the first apparent signs of unrest in Portuguese East Africa, Mozambique, which have been reflected in local newspapers this week.

Although big news travels just as fast to Uganda as elsewhere, its significance is rarely apparent even to those Africans who read the English language or vernacular papers. Moreover, the braking effect of the Kingdom of Buganda on its subjects, the Baganda, within this protectorate is such as to slow modern nationalist progress and temper nationalist feelings anyway.

In addition, no leader of the nationalist cause has emerged who can command a big following. The main nationalist party is badly splintered, and in Africa as elsewhere the strong personality is often more important than the detailed program.

Thus the name of Kwame Nkrumah means something here. There has been plenty of time for the role and achievements of Ghana's leader to sink in. Five members of the Uganda Nationalist Congress, the oldest and strongest of the parties demanding independence, attended a meeting in Accra in December, and Dr. Barnabas Kununka, secretary general of the party, returned proud of the fact that the Ugandans had had not one but three audiences with Prime Minister Nkrumah.

The Uganda Nationalist Congress was founded in 1953 by Ignatius Musazi, a former theological student. But recently, in a complicated split, Mr. Musazi dismissed the Central Committee, and it reacted by dismissing him. The best bet for eventual leadership of a united party is Abou Bakar Mayanja, at present finishing a law course at Cambridge.

Briton Aided Student

Mr. Mayanja was ousted from Makerere College here for having stirred up a student strike. Sir Andrew Cohen, former Governor of Uganda and now a member of the British mission to the United Nations, was instrumental in getting Mr. Mayanja a scholarship to Cambridge.

Meanwhile, some concern has been raised here over the existence in Cairo of a branch of the Uganda Nationalist Congress. Its leader is John Kale, who recently visited the United States and appeared at the United Nations. A former teacher said Mr. Kale had an expressed craving to "organize the masses." In the course of the party squabble, Mr. Musazi actually charged opponents, including Mr. Kale, with getting money from "Cairo and beyond," that is, Moscow.

U. S. Neglect Charged

Dr. Kununka ridicules this. He says Uganda Moslem students have always gone to Cairo to study and, like expatriates many places, tended to give vent to collective patriotic feelings.

The attitude of young educated members of the Nationalist Congress to the United States is interesting.

Samuel Nsubuga, 18-year-old pre-medical student, speaking slowly and gravely, asserted that the United States was not doing its duty as the leading power, and not using its influence "to see countries in bondage liberated."

He said such duty was best done within the United Nations. When it was recalled the United States had supported Guinea's bid for membership in the United Nations, Mr. Nsubuga acknowledged promptly:

"Yes, and I thank you for that."

Governor Sir Frederick Crawford, who returned today from talks in London, said merely that nationalism in East Africa had been among the subjects discussed there.

January 30, 1959

NATIONALIST RUSH HALTED IN UGANDA

Province of Buganda Balks at Unifying Government for Independent State

By LEONARD INGALLS
Special to The New York Times.

KAMPALA, Uganda, Dec. 9—In the race of East African countries toward independence Uganda has dropped behind Tanganyika and Kenya, her neighbors.

Four years ago Uganda, a protectorate, was considered the most likely of the three to become independent first. But now Tanganyika is on the threshhold of forming her own government to replace the United Nations trusteeship administration dominated by Britain. Kenya, a British colony, is expected to move rapidly in the next year toward control of her own affairs.

The efforts of the British administration to prepare Uganda for independence have struck a formidable obstacle.

The obstacle is the kingdom of Buganda, headed by the 35-year-old Kabaka, or King, Mutesa II. Buganda is one of four provinces that make up Uganda. Its opposition to a unified government for the whole country led to the exile in 1953 of the Kabaka.

When he returned from London in 1955 and agreed that Buganda would participate in the Uganda Government it was hoped that a smooth road lay ahead toward independence.

However, loyal subjects of the Kabaka have gradually revived their opposition to a unified government. They advocate a federation with strong local governments in Buganda and the three other provinces. Their Kabaka is a constitutional monarch and the political power rests with a representative assembly called the Lukiko. The Lukiko is extremely jealous of its power.

Buganda has refused to send representatives to the Uganda Legislative Council and the Lukiko has opposed the formation of strong national political parties. Thus far no outstanding political leader has emerged in Uganda with the stature of Julius Nyerere in Tanganyika or Tom Mboyo in Kenya.

The people of Buganda fear that their Kabaka would be eclipsed by a Uganda Prime Minister. They regard the other tribes of Uganda as inferior.

Another reason why no strong national spirit has developed in Uganda is the absence of a common language. Swahili is the Lingua Franca in Tanganyika and Kenya. In Uganda there are five languages and fourteen principal tribes.

In the last four years at least a dozen political parties have been started in Uganda but none has succeeded on a country-wide scale. The latest was the Uganda National Movement, which was formed by elements of six other parties. Its strength was confined to Buganda. It was banned after it organized a boycott which was more economic in aim than political.

The boycott was directed at Asian shops and at products produced by white-owned companies. It has kept Buganda in turmoil since March.

In summing up the Uganda situation one high government official said, "We are skating on the thin ice of civil disturbances all the time."

Meanwhile efforts of the protectorate government to build up an African civil service have encountered difficulty. The best educated Africans have been going into the Kabaka's Buganda provincial government or into tribal governments in the other provinces.

December 10, 1959

Uganda Celebrates Independence From Britain

Head of New African State Pledges to Back Kenya's Campaign for Self-Rule

BY ROBERT CONLEY

Special to The New York Times

KAMPALA, Uganda, Tuesday, Oct. 9—Uganda attained independence at midnight last night after 68 years under British rule.

Uganda and her 6,845,000 people thus became the 16th member of the British Commonwealth.

The African country is scheduled to become the 110th member of the United Nations.

Delegations from seventy countries and the Vatican were invited for the independence ceremonies, which began a three-day public holiday. Schools are closed and most Government departments and business concerns gave their employes a bonus or a salary advance for the celebration.

"Uhuru," or freedom, came to Uganda just a century after the first white man appeared here. He was John Hanning Speke, the explorer who discovered the headwaters of the Nile at what is now Murchison Falls.

Flags and bunting covered buildings downtown. There was a last-minute rush in the shops for "uhuru" shirts, dresses and ties in the new national colors. of black, yellow and red. Outside a thatched-roof house in a banana grove near Entebbe, a man put out a sign. "My country," it said.

With independence the old colonial view toward Africa also passes. It was expressed by Henry Stanley, the explorer and journalist, in 1875 with this appeal to Britain:

"But oh that some pious practical missionary would come here! What a field and a harvest ripe for the sickle of civilization."

Prime Minister Milton Obote said Uganda would throw her full weight behind neighboring Kenya's demands for independence if Kenya's two main political parties formed a coalition.

Mr. Obote spoke at a mass rally attended by political leaders of the East African territories of Kenya Uganda and Tanganyika as well as Uganda.

Strong anti-British feeling at the rally struck a discordant note a few hours before Uganda achieved independence.

Kenya must become independent at once, Mr. Obote told the crowd of several thousand Africans in calling for a coalition of the Kenya African National Union and African Democratic Union parties.

Tom Mboya, Kenya's young African nationalist and her Minister of Labor, taunted the Ugandans.

"How can you hold up your heads and talk about your own Uganda freedom when British imperialists continue to oppress us in Kenya?" he asked. "How can you claim to be proud and free when your brothers remain under imperialist rule?"

Uganda takes over control of her affairs with a background rare in emerging Africa: a multiple party system and no white-settler problem. There are 11,800 whites here, but they have rarely been able to purchase land.

"I am not color-minded," Mr. Obote has said. "I do not care about color."

He has offered citizenship to the 77,400 Indians and Pakistanis who are the merchants and shopkeepers of Uganda if they learn English or a vernacular Ugandan language.

Uganda's emergence into nationhood leaves Kenya and the Federation of Rhodesia and Nyasaland as Britain's most pressing colonial problems in Africa.

October 9, 1962

Kenya to Fight Terrorists

NAIROBI, Kenya, Sept 6 (UP)—The Legislative Council will be summoned to pass emergency laws strengthening the Government's hand in fighting a secret society terrorizing thousands of natives and threatening to drive all whites from Kenya, authorities announced today. The council was expected to meet in about two weeks. The society calls itself Mau-Mau.

September 7, 1952

Roads to Nairobi Closed At Night to Bar Terrorists

By Reuters.

NAIROBI, Kenya, Sept. 17—Main roads in and out of Nairobi will be closed to all traffic between 7 P. M. and 5:30 A. M. starting Sept. 23, the police announced today.

Anyone wishing to use the roads during the day hours will have to apply for a special pass.

This is another move to combat activities of the Mau Mau, a fanatical African anti-European terror society in Kenya colony.

Yesterday the Government extended the existing curfew to include the Kiriku mission area where the Mau Mau tried to murder European priests last week.

The Police Commissioner said today that his new order was necessary to "combat crime."

September 18, 1952

British Put Troops in Kenya To Halt a Reign of Killings

Cruiser Is Also Dispatched to Colony in Africa—State of Emergency Ordered

By The Associated Press.

NAIROBI, Kenya, Oct. 20—The British sent a battalion of troops and a cruiser to Kenya and declared a state of emergency tonight in this East African colony in an effort to control the fanatic, secret, anti-white society known as Mau Mau.

The Mau Maus, who took a blood oath to drive the British out of Kenya, have murdered at least forty-three persons, set buildings and crops on fire and slaughtered cattle in the last few weeks. The organization is said to number 200,000 of the Kikuyu tribe.

The announcement of a state of emergency—equivalent to martial law—followed by a few hours the arrival in Kenya of a battalion of the British Lancashire Fusiliers flown in from the Middle East, Uganda and Tanganyika.

An airlift of twelve planes with about 800 men made night landings at the Nairobi Airport. Use of the airport after nightfall is considered an emergency operation.

The New York Times Oct 21 1952

AFRICAN EMERGENCY: British troops were flown to Kenya, where violence gripped Nairobi (1). A cruiser was on the way to Mombasa (2).

The action was taken under the military code name Operation Sterling. The men came equipped with rifles, light machine guns and Sten guns.

[The Colonial Office announced in London Monday that the Cruiser Kenya would go to Mombasa, 400 miles from Nairobi, to support troops in the Kenya capital.]

It was the first major show of force Britain had made in East Africa in years. Britain fears Kenya could become another area of guerrilla warfare like Malaya. So far as can be learned, however, the Mau Mau has no Communist leadership or backing.

Two thousand European volunteers joined policemen and British soldiers in patroling Nairobi after a new wave of Mau Mau atrocities. Kenya's exclusive Nyeri Polo Club, where Queen Elizabeth II watched the Duke of Edinburgh play earlier this year, was burned to the ground by Mau Mau raiders last night.

It was in this African colony that Queen Elizabeth learned of the death of her father, King George VI. She returned home from here to become Queen.

The anti-European arsonists set ablaze 300 acres of grazing land belonging to White farmers near the polo club. Police officials said they had raided a Mau Mau oath-taking ceremony in a field near a Kikuya police station, arrested forty-one African men and women and seized symbols associated with the secret society.

Police Witness Found Slain

Thirty Kikuyu also were arrested in connection with the discovery in Laikipia, North Kenya, of the body of an African police witness. His hands had been cut off and his clothing buried. The man disappeared in mid-September. Three of those seized have been charged with murder, the remainder with taking part in a Mau Mau ceremony prior to the killing.

Kenya has clamped down a curfew nightly and passed emergency laws to deal with the Mau Mau but the organization's activities have reached menacing proportions in the last three months. It grew out of the outlawed Nationalist Society, Kikuyu central association. Mau Mau had thrived in the rural areas and has now moved into towns and cities.

Oliver Lyttleton, British Colonial Secretary, told the House of Commons in London last week that the Mau Mau members had taken oaths to kill European farmers—or die themselves. Many natives have been murdered for not agreeing to join the society, Kenyan authorities have declared.

The society's first objective is, through terror campaigns, to drive out the 3,000 Whites who monopolize almost all the fertile land in the cool "white highlands." Then all Whites must be thrown out of Kenya, its leaders insist.

October 21, 1952

BRITON TO SURVEY TERROR IN KENYA

Colonial Secretary to Visit Scene—Troops Arrive in Nairobi—Arrests Rise

Special to The New York Times.

LONDON, Oct. 21 — Britain's Colonial Secretary, Oliver Lyttelton, will leave for Kenya next week for a personal survey of events there and to discuss with the Kenya Government plans for the future development of the colony.

This was announced today in statements made to both houses of Parliament on the progress of the police operation against the Mau Mau, the secret organization whose campaign of terror to drive the British out of Kenya has been responsible for nearly forty murders and many more beatings and attempted killings among natives and Europeans alike. The subject was discussed by the Cabinet earlier in the day.

Report Made to Peers

The Earl of Munster, Parliamentary Under Secretary of the Colonial Office, told the House of Lords that the state of emergency had been proclaimed in Kenya with the British Government's full approval and had been timed to coincide with the arrival in Nairobi, the Kenya capital, of the first battalion of the Lancashire Fusiliers from the Middle East. More troops, he said, are being moved into Kenya from Uganda and Tanganyika. So far all troops are merely being used as a reserve, he explained, and all action against the terrorists is being taken by the police.

The Earl said that since the middle of September the Mau Mau had become so bold it carried out its attacks in broad daylight frequently with the use of hired assassins. Firearms and gelignite, gelatin dynamite, were stolen he said and the leaders of Mau Mau began to establish their own courts in an attempt to usurp the functions of the legal government and to destroy all authority with the people except its own.

Mr. Lyttelton made a similar statement to the House of Commons at the end of which he read a message he had just received from the Governor of Kenya. This reported the arrest up to this morning of eighty-nine persons. A dispatch from Nairobi said ninety-eight had been arrested by nightfall.

The Colonial Secretary also foreshadowed the appointment of a royal commission to investigate the troubled area and to study long term problems of social and economic development there.

In reply to questions about the arrest of Jomo Kenyata, leader of the Kenya African Union, Mr. Lyttleton said he had been arrested not as president of the union but as an "individual concerned with Mau Mau terrorism." The Kenya African Union, he added, is not being proscribed.

Kenyata, who first came to Britain twenty-three years ago to seek land reform for his tribe, last returned to his country in 1946 to become president of the Kenya African Union, which has sought through democratic methods to gain various benefits for its people. He left behind him in England his English-born white wife and their son, now 9.

October 22, 1952

DISORDERS IN KENYA EXPECTED TO GO ON

Special to The New York Times.

LONDON, Nov. 7—Colonial Secretary Oliver Lyttelton cautioned today in the House of Commons that Kenya might have to undergo several more months of unrest because of the activities of the Mau Mau secret society. He described the group as "the unholy union of dark and ancient superstition with the apparatus of modern gangsterism."

Mr. Lyttelton, who was reporting to the House on his return from Britain's troubled East African colony, said that the Mau Mau did not thrive on economic discontent, but on "perverted nationalism and a sort of nostalgia for barbarism."

The Secretary emphasized that Britain would restore "freedom from fear" for the Europeans and natives in Kenya, who for nine months have been terrorized by the Mau Mau. How soon this will be achieved depends on the cooperation of the law-abiding Africans who, until recent weeks, have been too frightened to testify against the underground organization, he explained.

Mr. Lyttelton said he would expedite the creation of a royal commission to study economic problems in Kenya, but cautioned that the commission might need a year to make its report.

November 8, 1952

The Mau Mau Strikes

RAID ON MAU MAU

Colonial police make a raid on a Kikuyu village where the Mau Mau is believed to have a powerful following.

Suspects are rounded up by the police, which angers the innocent and may drive some into the Mau Mau.

LONDON.

OVER the equatorial landscape of Kenya, the British Crown Colony in East Africa, lies the frightening shadow of Mau Mau, a secret tribal society whose campaign of murder has forced the imposition of emergency law. The British Government and the Colonial Government of Kenya, trying to crush the movement, are not sure what they are fighting, not even what the name means. It is known that the members of Mau Mau swear to a ritualistic vendetta against all whites and Christians, and that the society is responsible for scores of killings, especially among blacks who have given information to the authorities. But who its leaders are or what their ultimate objectives may be remain mysteries.

The outbreak of terrorism is in the territory of the Kikuyu tribe, which numbers about 1,000,000 out of the 5,500,000 black peoples of Kenya. The first aim of the Mau Mau, with its voodoo apparatus of disemboweled animals for warnings and long machete-like knives for their killings, seems to be to drive the 36,000 whites out of Kenya. But whether the movement is a spontaneous native uprising or was instigated from outside, the authorities do not know. However, the organization does seem to bear some resemblance to the cells of a Communist organization. Jomo Kenyatta, who is held for trial as the suspected leader of Mau Mau, received part of his education at the London School of Economics, married a white English woman and thereafter visited Moscow.

An underlying cause of the movement is probably native resentment because white settlers have much of Kenya's good farmlands. Now, because the authorities have resorted to such measures as rounding up the whole populations of villages to restore order, there is a fear that the innocent who suffer will become sympathetic with the Mau Mau movement and it will grow.

Here are scenes from the bitter struggle.

—RAYMOND DANIELL.

A Kikuyu tribesman swears he is not a Mau Mau.

December 7, 1952

Soviet-Trained Mau Mau Terrorist Is Sentenced to 7 Years' Hard Labor

KAPENGURIA, Kenya, April 8—Jomo (Burning Spear) Kenyatta, Moscow-educated tribal leader, was found guilty today of organizing the dreaded Mau Mau secret society, which aims to throw the white man out of Kenya.

After fifty-eight days of trial in a barricaded former school house here, British Magistrate R. S. Thacker sentenced Kenyatta to seven years in prison on charges of inspiring and assisting the brutal savagery of the Mau Mau terrorists who have arisen among the Kikuyu tribesmen.

He was also found guilty of being a member of the secret band and sentenced to three years on this count. The sentences, involving hard labor, are to run concurrently.

The court also found that five others had worked with Kenyatta in instigating or assisting the Mau Mau uprisings in which whole families have been brutally butchered in a wave of murder and arson. Each of the five drew seven-year sentences.

[According to Reuters the five were: Fred Kubai, executive member of the Kenya African Union and a leader of the Kenya Transport Workers' Union; Richard Achieng Oneko, former editor of an African newspaper and African councilor on the Nairobi City Council; Bildad M. Gaggia, secretary of the Nairobi branch of the Kenya African Union; Kunga Karumba, member of the African Union's executive council; Paul Ngei, an African Union representative among the Wakamba tribe.]

The sentences are subject to confirmation by the Kenya Supreme Court. All the defendants had protested their innocence.

A defense lawyer, D. N. Pritt, the London barrister who defended Gerhart Eisler against extradition proceedings when the German Communist jumped bail in the United States and arrived in Britain, immediately announced he would appeal the magistrate's decision.

A member of the million-strong Kikuyu tribe from which Mau Mau springs, Kenyatta, about 50 years old, has lived a number of years in Britain where he has a white wife and son.

In England he was a close friend of Paul Robeson, the American Negro singer. In 1932 he went to Moscow, where he remained two years studying at Moscow University. He lived in a place furnished by the Communist International.

April 9, 1953

KENYA ZONE CLOSED TO CHECK MAU MAU

British Seal Off the Colony's Central Area as Anti-White Terrorist Drive Spreads

By ALBION ROSS
Special to THE NEW YORK TIMES.

NAIROBI, Kenya, May 29—Central Kenya, including all three Kikuyu tribal reserves, and the Meru and Embu districts to the east were ordered sealed off today from the rest of the country, except for through travel on certain main roads and railroads. No one may enter the area or leave it without special permission of the district commissioners.

At the same time, three areas on the west side of the Great Rift Valley were declared "special areas," in which anyone moving about will be shot on sight. Previously, the only "special area" had been the Aberdare Mountains, rallying ground of the Mau Mau, a secret society of Kikuyu tribesmen sworn to curb white control.

The Mau Mau fighting is taking on increasingly the character of all-out guerrilla warfare. Virtually all forested mountain areas are now being used by the Mau Mau guerrilla forces as hide-outs and centers of forest and bush warfare similar to the type of fighting found in Malaya.

The extension of the "special areas" meant that the Mau Mau had spread across the Rift Valley from its original territory in and near the Kikuyu reserves to the mountains bordering the western Kenya highlands. It was announced officially that the Mau Mau were in fact operating in this mountain area known as the Mau Mountains.

The fact that the Meru and Embu districts east and southeast of Mount Kenya were included in the areas sealed off was also an indication that the Mau Mau movement has spread east as well as west. The districts are not Kikuyu districts, but are inhabited by related tribes. The orders indicated that the greater part of the Kenya highlands is now infested by the Mau Mau.

The guerrillas have also started to destroy bridges in the Kanyanyeni and Tuso regions. Patrols moving up have also discovered road blocks. It was reported previously that explosives had been found in at least one raid.

Three Kikuyu guard posts have been attacked by the Mau Mau in the last forty-eight hours. In the attack on the post at Ngunjiri village, two Kikuyu home guards were killed, one shop was burned and another sacked. The attacking Mau Mau were dressed as native police.

The Kiruri guard post was burned down in a successful Mau Mau attack on Wednesday night. Two Kikuyu home guards were killed. The attack on the Ichichi guard post was beaten off.

The Mau Mau forces are carrying off their dead into the bush and patrols have found evidence that they kill their seriously wounded. Bodies are constantly being found.

Regular Cattle Raids

The guerrillas are now apparently making regular cattle raids, driving off the cattle to their hideouts. In the latest cattle raid 400 head of cattle were rounded up and driven off. The reserves are filled with cattle as the keeping of cattle is deeply rooted in tribal custom and connected with the purchase of brides.

By stealing and killing cattle the Mau Mau can supply themselves readily with food. On the other hand nothing probably is so calculated to embitter the rest of the Kikuyu against them as the slaughter of their beloved cattle.

There appears to have been a quiet period during which the Mau Mau were apparently reorganizing or resting. Now their campaign of terror in the reserves has apparently been resumed. Smaller groups are evidently moving about fairly freely and attacking at will while larger units attack guard posts.

The reports are rather discouraging as it had been hoped that the Mau Mau were being driven back into the forests and that wholesale terror in reserves was being stamped out.

The destruction of bridges, the building of road blocks, the cattle raids, widespread terror raids of small units, larger attacks on guard posts, and the spreading guerrilla warfare would indicate that the Mau Mau were still strong.

The Government hesitated a long time before declaring so large a section of the country as a forbidden zone. Now it has acknowledged in effect that the zone is a battle area in which there is no place for noncombatants. On the edges of the forests a scorched-earth policy has been adopted in the fields to deprive the Mau Mau of food.

May 30, 1953

TROUBLED KENYA—A PROBLEM FOR BRITAIN

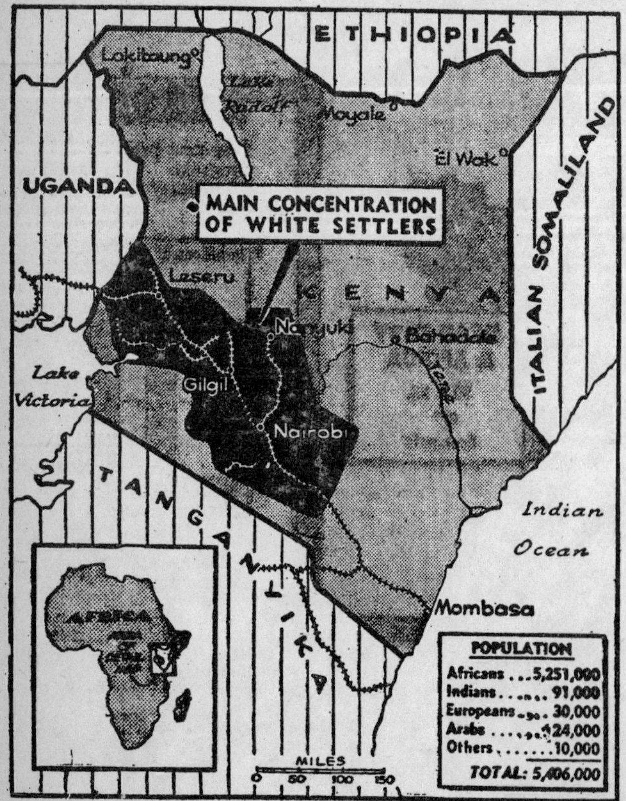

May 10, 1953

NAIROBI REQUIRING SERVANT QUARTERS

City Council Ruling on Homes for Whites Reflects View One 'Simply Must' Have Help

By ALBION ROSS
Special to THE NEW YORK TIMES.

NAIROBI, Kenya, June 3—The Nairobi City Council has forbidden the construction of houses for white occupants without servants' quarters. The decision has aroused considerable interest here because it is the sort of thing that holds up to society a mirror in which it can see itself.

The construction of houses for white occupants without servants' quarters has been forbidden, it is explained, not because the City Council has adopted the attitude that whites must have servants but because its records prove that there is no such thing as a white family in Kenya without Negro help.

Accordingly, when a license was sought to build sixteen low-priced houses for white clerks and the like, the city authorities noted that no quarters had been provided for Negro servants. The builder was proceeding on the theoretical basis that such families would not have servants, but the city fathers told him to stick to the facts of life in this little city. Nairobi is a "you simply must have servants" community.

Asked why one must have servants in Nairobi, the immediate past president and present public relations representative of the Kenya Women's League explained that social life—luncheons, sundowners, dinners and whatnot—normally is intense and on a large scale. She added also that a good many women sought employment because the cost of living is high here. The cost of living, it was conceded, consists to a considerable extent of the expensive social whirl and the liquor bill.

A woman member of the City Council suggested that as long as women could earn enough by working to afford servants, there would be "very few women in Nairobi prepared to go back to the sink."

The issue of no white without servants, or, at least, without servants' quarters, is indicative of the psychology of the Kenya white settler and even of the more or less temporary resident who has found a job.

The white settler is a person with a "don't fence me in" complex. His great fear is to find himself once more hemmed in and living the rationed, restricted life of Britain.

June 4, 1953

MAU MAU GROWING DESPITE REVERSES

Terrorist Movement in Kenya Spreads Even as It Loses 100 Killed in Week

Special to THE NEW YORK TIMES.

NAIROBI, Kenya, June 5—Government forces killed 100 Mau Mau terrorists and captured fifty-four during the last seven days, it was announced today. In addition, the killing of six terrorists was listed in tonight's report.

Despite this apparent success of the measures against the Mau Mau, agents of the movement have been able to gain new adherents.

The Mau Mau organization still exists and its mobilizing heads are calling in reserves and setting up areas of action that have been, during the first months of the struggle, free of terrorism. Agents of the Mau Mau now are giving the oath throughout the Meru Reserve east of Mount Kenya, in the Embu district southeast of Mount Kenya and have created a state of emergency on the west side of the Rift Valley.

Resurging of Outbreaks

This spreading movement has created a new problem in crushing of the Mau Mau. It had seemed up to two weeks ago that the Mau Mau was being driven back into the Aberdares Mountains and immediately adjacent areas and bottled up. Success of its agents in spreading the movement to other regions at this point in the campaign is puzzling.

Natives of the Meru and Embu districts are tribes related to the Kikuyu but are defined as Kikuyus or as separate groups depending on the system of classification. They have been permitted to plant coffee, which is a big money earner in Kenya, and have been encouraged and aided by the Government. It had been thought that they were doing reasonably well and were fairly well satisfied with the degree of economic progress that had been made.

That it is possible to recruit new bands in the Nairobi slums, induce them to try to get up into the cold, wet Aberdares to share hunger and the dangers of the groups already there, also is a rather remarkable evidence of the strength which the Mau Mau organization still has.

Basically, these developments appear to be evidence that the desperate, real proletariat of the Kikuyu tribe, who have no shamba (patch of land), no hope of getting one, who live from hand to mouth and are seldom employed, are still ready for anything. Native African spokesmen have been largely silenced under stress of the emergency. Any suggestion that the Mau Mau movement is, in effect, a brutal native African form of an agrarian revolution in which the landless have been driven to savage fury is cried down by the white settlers here.

Settlers Furious at Critics

Representatives of the British Colonial Service who have, in fact, a strong conviction that the Mau Mau movement is at base an agrarian revolutionary movement also have closed their mouths in view of the red-faced fury of the white settlers who insist that anyone who mentions such a thing is a Communist and virtually seditious.

The statement in London of a member of the Royal Commission on Land that there must be equality of races here has been bitterly resented by the white settlers. Among the Colonial Service people who have been dealing with the natives professionally the fact nevertheless is considered significant that now, when Mau Mau followers are being tracked down and are dying in the forests of the Aberdares and are known to be half starving, that new areas should be turning to the Mau Mau, that young natives still are ready to leave their towns and villages to join them.

Despite the bestial savagery of the Mau Mau, there is evident at this stage an element of a desperate spirit of heroism which chooses to die rather than to live on the terms offered.

There is an increasing tendency among those here who are not white settlers but who by profession are more immediately concerned with the future of British Africa to feel that it is time for the British Government to take a long look at Kenya and decide whether continued existence of 3,000 white-owned plantations in the Kenya highlands are worth the price. It is no secret that all plans for an East African federation and the like have been stalemated by detestation of the Kenya white settlers in Tanganyika and Uganda.

The report of the week's success against the Mau Mau followed clashes all up and down the Central Kikuyu Reserve as the Mau Mau organization tried to bring in reinforcements to its main forces in the Aberdare Mountains and raided desperately for food in the reserves. As for today's record, in addition to the six terrorists killed, the Mau Mau killed two Kikuyu Home Guards.

June 6, 1953

KENYA SUPPRESSES CHIEF NATIVE BODY

African Union, Two of Whose Leaders Were Jailed, Is Said to Be Terrorist Front

By ALBION ROSS

Special to THE NEW YORK TIMES.

NAIROBI, Kenya, June 8—The Kenya Africa Union, outside of the West African parties and South Africa's National Congress probably the most famous African political organization, was proscribed as an unlawful society by the Kenya Executive Council today. Its assets were seized by an African Courts officer and membership in it was made a criminal offense.

Jomo Kenyatta, African author, anthropologist and political leader who was found guilty by a court here of having managed the Mau Mau movement and who now is in prison, had been president of the Union. He never resigned as presdent, nor was he expelled, and his picture continued to hang in the Kenya African Union headquarters.

His successor as acting president, Faniel Odede, a member of the Legislative Council, was detained early in March on the ground he had sought to spread agitation in his native province of North Kavirondo, near Lake Victoria.

Action has been taken because the Government has satisfied itself that there is ample evidence to show that the Kenya African Union has often been used as cover by the Mau Mau terrorist organization and that both before and after the emergency there has been a connection between many members of the Kenya African Union and Mau Mau terrorists. Not only have a number of K. A. U. officials been deeply implicated in the organization of Mau Mau but in many cases local organizations of the two societies have been identical. It is significant that in 1948 the K. A. U. adopted the technique of ritual oath-taking to bind its members to secrecy."

Basically the Kenya African Union, and its predecessor, were agarian reform organizations which ended up as proponents of what amounts to an agarian revolution.

The issue in Kenya is the 3,000 white-owned plantations and ranches occupying 12,000 miles of the Kenya highlands reserved for European occupation. Both the Kikuyu Central Association and latterly the Kenya African Union demanded that the lands be given to the natives of Kenya. The bloody Mau Mau revolt was a direct outgrowth of this demand and was almost certainly directly linked to the agitation of the Kenya African Union.

June 9, 1953

Life Goes On Under the Mau Mau's Shadow

But the surface calm of Kenya's white colony is penetrated by the perils and anxieties of racial unrest.

By SANTHA RAMA RAU

PEOPLE in Nairobi, the capital of Kenya, are fond of describing their city as a frontier town. Although it is the largest and most important town in that curious association of protectorates, colonies and trust territories known as British East Africa, still it is a very young city. Everywhere one can see signs of its youth—the newness of its buildings in the center of town, some of the Government departments housed in temporary barracks, roads that suddenly stop in the middle of nothing, the ease with which one can get out of the city into the game reserve where giraffe canter casually among the thorn trees. But perhaps the most striking of its pioneer characteristics, certainly to the stranger in the city, is a sense of danger everywhere. Sometimes this amounts almost to an air of panic, at other times simply to an increased caution. The reason for this, of course, has been the sudden and brutal murders of the secret society of terrorists known as Mau Mau.

Only fifty years ago on the site of Nairobi there was nothing much besides a water hole where the Africans of the nomadic Masai tribe led their cattle from time to time. In those days the first railway was being built into the interior of East Africa, a project that seemed even to many Englishmen so far-fetched that a British periodical labeled it the Lunatic Line. But since then, the Lunatic Line which attracted from India the thousands of laborers who built the railroad, has carried into the heart of Kenya the equipment, supplies, machinery and food necessary to the growing town of Nairobi. It also carried British colonialism inland. With the first few thousand Europeans who bought farms on the plateau surrounding Nairobi and on the slopes of the snow-capped mountain that straddles the equator, Mount Kenya, and with the Indians who decided to settle in East Africa rather than return home, came the beginnings of the intricate racial, economic and political problems which half a century later were to grow into the explosive conditions which bred Mau Mau.

THE White Settlers, as they came to be known to distinguish them from the white Colonial Office officials (who didn't settle), and the brown Indians (who did) were led by the famous expatriate Lord Delamere with his dream of Kenya's great future as "White Man's Country." They saw the possibility of leading, in Kenya, the kind of life that was rapidly becoming impossible for most people in Europe. One of the Englishmen who came to Kenya fairly early in the history of the settlement told me that "this seemed to be about the only place I could afford to keep polo ponies."

AS news spread of the enormous possibilities of the land, of the wonderful climate, the magnificent countryside, the cheap and easy living, more immigrants arrived. They hadn't quite the style of the first pioneers, and even today one occasionally hears the rather supercilious comment that Kenya has become a "place in the sun for shady people." Whatever their social status may have been, in Kenya they were White Settlers, the only people permitted to own land in the White Highlands around Nairobi.

This alone would have been enough to cause trouble because the White Highlands contain some of the best land in Kenya. Other problems have been added more recently. The Kikuyu tribe who originally owned the land have so increased in number that they now need room to expand beyond the tribal reserves which the British assigned to them. Some of the Kikuyu spokesmen claim that the land was never sold to the White Settlers—only

IN THE FIELDS—Scion of a wealthy English family, Lord Waterpark owns 750,000 Kenya acres. In work clothes and armed, he looks over his domain of crops and cattle.

leased—and added the further grievance that Africans are not allowed to grow the more profitable crops like pyrethrum or coffee, and that they have inadequate political representation.

The White Settlers, in turn, claim that the land was bought in the first place, and that their modern farming methods have materially increased the output of the White Highlands, and consequently the wealth of Kenya. Politically they say, the African is "not ready" for self-government, or even for greater participation in government than his present very small role. This stalemate has led to relations between the races tense enough to result in appalling atrocities from those Kikuyu who joined Mau Mau, and equally fierce reprisals from the Europeans.

INEVITABLY the resulting tension penetrates most aspects of living in Nairobi. On the surface, the measured activities of a colonial capital continue undisturbed. There are the teas and garden parties at Government House, socially prominent ladies organize field days and bazaars for the Girl Guides, amateur concerts are given for the relief of flood victims in England.

Inside the famous New Stanley Hotel, the European jeunesse dorée (known in Kenya as the Pink Gin Set), meet for lunch in the grillroom. In the dark, paneled New Stanley bar will be the farmers in riding clothes who have just come in from up-country, or Boers with beards drinking beer, or the sunburned young men from the isolated places where they study locust control.

OUTSIDE the hotel, standing in the brilliant crystal sunlight of Kenya, on one of the city's busiest street corners, there may be a group of Masai tribesmen barefoot, carrying their spears, dressed only in a dusty blanket slung over one shoulder and with their bodies and hair rubbed with red ochre. Possibly they are in town to shop or perhaps to sightsee. A group of Indian school children may wheel by on bicycles on their way home for lunch. Veiled Muslim women of Arab descent may be peering at the things displayed in the shop windows—cloth from India, canned goods from England, dresses from South Africa.

These three main population groups—the European, the Asian and the African—live in the same city with a high degree of mutual exclusiveness or, as a friend of mine described it, as a racial pousse café, each element necessary to the whole, each retaining its separate identity, and, in the opinion at least of most Europeans and some Indians, a disastrous and unpalatable failure when the various elements mix.

Immediately beneath this seemingly calm surface lie the anger, bewilderment and consciousness of danger that all the racial groups seem to share. The first time I realized how seriously Nairobi took the threat of terrorism was after a dinner at the house of some friends in one of the residential suburbs of the city where the gardens are fairly large and there is virtually no traffic on the streets at night. The guests were leaving, saying their final goodnights on the verandah. Somebody asked if he could give us a ride back to the hotel. I said we were going by taxi. He said, with a certain polite concern, "You're armed, of course?"

I thought for a second he was joking, but clearly he wasn't because from the pockets of well-cut English dinner jackets and trousers revolvers were produced, from the jeweled evening bags of a couple of the women, from among the lace handkerchiefs and lipsticks smaller guns appeared and were most generously offered to us as protection during the taxi trip. Our host told us, "In the old days one never walked unarmed or alone in Nairobi at night because of the lions on the streets, now one doesn't because you can't take chances with Mau Mau." Somehow the serious voice made it sound like an ordinary remark to make in the huge starry quiet of the African night, among the departing guests, against the neat provinciality of a garden suburb.

AT HOME—White Settlers in Kenya cling to a formal social life in the colonial tradition. Dressed for dinner on their estate, Lord and Lady Waterpark await their guests.

AFTER a while in Kenya you begin to expect the signs of tension, and every day you notice fresh evidences of this sense of danger. Many of the sons of your friends will have enlisted in the homeguards or the Kenya Police Reserve, and will spend week-ends or a regular tour of duty helping to protect the farms in the troubled area. Almost daily the newspapers warn you not to leave your child with African servants, however reliable you may think they are. The East African Women's Association, as a public service, helps to check the credentials of ayahs, and gives its approval only to those that are beyond question loyal, or those that come from a remote group of French-African islands in the Indian Ocean called the Seychelles, and who are, consequently free of Mau Mau influence. If you have a baby-sitter in the evening, she will certainly refuse to go home by bus; she will probably refuse to go home in a taxi unless you accompany her to her door.

ONE of the most impressive reminders of trouble in Kenya is the crowded transit camp for Kikuyu, the only one of East Africa's 220 tribes involved in Mau Mau terrorism, which is situated in an open, unused space, almost opposite one of the city's chief hotels, and slap in front of the imposing new building of the Kenya National Theatre. If you sit on the terrace of the Norfolk Hotel, or on the balcony outside the bar of the theatre, you can see the barbed wire enclosure to which the Kikuyu rounded up in the night-time raids or in the course of the day are brought. Some time about the middle of the morning you could see them being herded on to trucks, standing tightly packed together and guarded by the young European men of the special police. By then a crowd of Africans would have gathered and there would be many exchanges of shouts between them and the Africans jammed against the board railing of the truck. Mostly they were arrested for not having their identity card which carries the proof of their employment in the city. Without it they are not allowed to live in Nairobi.

As the trucks drove slowly out of the camp one day when I was watching, the Africans began to sing. I asked one of the waiters in the hotel, a Kikuyu, what the words of the song were. He said, "They sing, 'We don't care, we don't care.' Like that they are singing."

"Why do they sing that? Is it a proper song?".

"They sing like that because they are angry people."

WHILE incidents like these keep you constantly reminded of the perilous tensions in Kenya, in Nairobi, itself, there is really no particular reason for the elaborate, almost melodramatic, precautions because there has been no Mau Mau activity in the city. Up country, however, in the isolated farm houses and even on the big, well-protected estates the danger is both more real and more grimly prepared for. Local papers, word of mouth, magazines, special pamphlets all suggest precautions of the most drastic kind. Never, they warn the White Settler and his family, move an inch without your gun—even from your bedroom to the bathroom, or when you step into the hall to answer the telephone, or when you walk across to the liquor cabinet to make yourself a drink. Your gun should always be within reach of your hand, "always loaded and cocked with the safety catch off," one list of instructions read, "not buttoned up in a holster, not on the mantelpiece, not in your handbag or under a cushion; but always, always, always within inches of your hand on your lap, on the arm of your chair, on the edge of the bath, on the table beside you. The criteria should be: can you shoot within one second?"

IN Kitale, one of the more remote outposts of White Settler country, feeling ran high because just outside the town Jomo Kenyatta was on trial for being the leader and organizer of Mau Mau. There on a Friday, which is market day, the European farmers come in from their maize, or pyrethrum, or coffee plantations which are set in the foothills of Mount Elgon, surrounded by some of the loveliest scenery in the world. After their work in town is done they gather in the bar of the Kitale Hotel for a few drinks before they return to the uneasy prospect of nighttime on their farms. Beside each glass is a gun. On the bar, among the bowls of potato chips and peanuts are more guns.

Mothers who can afford it or who have obliging friends in Nairobi or on the coast send their children away to safety. A friend of mine who used to make the long tedious bus trip into the city every week-end to see her 1-year-old daughter, had tried at first to keep the child on the farm. "But it simply became too exhausting. If I went out to the garden for a few minutes for some flowers, I had to pick her up and take her along too. We used to put her to sleep in the living room and then carry her crib into the dining room with us when we went in for dinner. She didn't even get any fresh air because it was much easier to watch her indoors than out, and at night all the bedroom windows are kept tightly closed." In the end even the bus trip seemed a more convenient arrangement, not because she hadn't a car, but because she felt she couldn't risk a breakdown even during the day.

IN the extraordinary and dramatic chasm of the Great Rift Valley which cuts through the middle of the White Highlands, one of the most eminent of the White Settlers still maintains the full ritual of a formal dinner, but with certain unusual trimmings. As the guests are seated, each man present is assigned a door or window to cover. Each sits with his side to the table and eats and converses as best he can with half his attention fixed on possible movement outside the house. As the servant enters with the soup he is covered. While he serves and until he leaves the room the gun is kept trained on him and the door locked behind him because in many of the Mau Mau attacks the terrorists have entered through the kitchen, intimidated the servants and used the house-boys as shields to get to the front of the house and attack the settler and his family.

The papers, however, tell the settlers to be even more careful than that, to change their meal hours every day, never to fall into a routine that a possible enemy can learn to count on, to cook and serve their own evening meal, to clear all shrubbery and trees for at least thirty yards around the homestead. It is easy to understand why the settlers and their wives who come to Nairobi these days have lost their interest in the conventional attractions of the big city. They don't bother much with movies and theatres and night clubs. Most of all they want a couple of nights of uninterrupted sleep.

This whole situation with its tense atmosphere, its guarded living, atrocities and reprisals holds far more extensive dangers than simply frayed nerves. As the Kikuyu are rounded up and sent back to their tribal reserves, and as thousands more return voluntarily, the labor shortage on the farms becomes extremely severe. The huge ranches, the farms covering thousands of acres cannot survive without African workers, of whom the Kikuyu are the best and most numerous. There is the added danger that the political tension will spread to other parts of East Africa. The longer the situation is drawn out, and the longer conditions in Kenya remain unsettled and hazardous, the more likely general discontent becomes.

WORST of all, perhaps, is the fact that distrust between the races in Kenya, and by contagion in most of East Africa, is growing. Race relations in East Africa were never ideal (although the more diehard of the White Settlers speak nostalgically of the Good Old Days when there was no trouble from the Africans, when they were "Nature's gentlemen" uninterested in political or economic advancement). The only way some sort of community could function, apparently, was by complete segregation of the various racial groups.

The British, for the most part, then lived their own, self-contained lives in their homes in the special suburbs reserved only for them, pursued their amusements and their sports entirely in white company, and met the Indians and the Africans only in the course of business and on the streets. The Asians, similarly, lived in their special residential areas the other side of "Grogan's Swamp"—a rather slummy, neglected strip of the city owned by one of the most conservative of the early White Settlers and leased extremely profitably to Indians and Africans. The Indians still have their own clubs, restaurants, schools and hospitals, but not from choice. Only very recently has there been some breakdown of this social barrier which they feel very keenly.

FOR the Africans, so far, there has been no breakdown. Many Europeans have a rather tiresome phrase for this. They call it a "Culture Bar, not a color bar" and insist it is justified. But whatever they call it, to the visitor there who wants, for instance, to talk to African leaders, members of the Legislative Council, or just to friends, this segregation is a great embarrassment. Africans are not allowed in hotels, restaurants, or even in the shops. There is one restaurant that allows a multi-racial clientele. It is called the Blue Room, though many Africans call it the Blue Moon because of its rarity. Even there you cannot offer an African anything stronger than beer.

Their own social life has been considerably hampered by the banning of all public meetings of Africans in the White Highlands. This has cut out, as was intended, all the political meetings, but it has also suppressed the huge and popular *ngomas*—communal dances which were the chief African amusement of a Saturday night. Besides this, Africans are not allowed on the streets after dark. If for any reason they must be out at night, they have to get a pass signed by a European proving that they are on legitimate business.

THESE ever-present social insults seemed to me to be very deeply wounding to the Africans. In many ways they seemed to cause more bitterness than political injustices or economic grievances. The effect on the educated Africans is both corrosive and dangerous.

Mau Mau, itself, may easily be a relatively short-lived affair—already the terrorism is being brought under control—but the social and racial tensions will certainly remain.

If Nairobi is ever to get out of the stage of being a frontier town, and up country, if the White Settlers look forward to a time when they can ride across their estates unarmed, if visitors and Kenyans want to travel through their fabulously beautiful country to hunt or holiday or admire, somehow a working multi-racial society will have to be evolved. It is a tricky thing to build at the best of times, and requires, I imagine, great sophistication and understanding and endless concessions on every side. But when it is achieved, even though Kenya will probably never again match Lord Delamere's original vision, it may well turn out to be one of the world's pleasantest places for people of all nationalities to live.

July 19, 1953

AFRICAN WILL SIT ON KENYA COUNCIL

Lyttelton Plan Also Opens Way for Asians and Arab—Mau Mau Drive Reorganized

NAIROBI, Kenya, March 10 (Reuters)—Britain gave the Africans, Asians and Arabs ministerial posts in Kenya today as a first step toward multi-racial government in this troubled colony.

Recognizing a sharp change in public opinion since the fight against the terrorist anti-white Mau Mau cult began seventeen months ago, Colonial Secretary Oliver Lyttelton greatly modified the colonial system that dates to the beginning of British rule nearly sixty years ago.

He announced a new Council of Ministers—"the principal instrument of government in the colony"—to include two Asians and an African. All will be members of the present Executive Council, which also is to include an Arab Under Secretary.

At the same time, the visiting Minister set up a War Council of four members, including Gov. Sir Evelyn Baring, to pursue with "the utmost vigor" the war against Mau Mau terrorism. The Governor retains supreme authority.

This will be the first time that an African has held a portfolio in any British East or Central African territory. Because native leaders are resentful at not being given greater representation, he may have to be nominated by the Governor instea of being chosen by his own people.

Kenya's 5,500,000 Africans will be represented by one official in the sixteen-man Council of Ministers. Two Ministers will speak for 154,000 Asians, mainly Indians and Chinese. The remaining thirteen Ministers will be drawn from the 42,000 whites.

The present twelve-man Executive Council will be broadened to include the Council of Ministers, plus an Arab and two additional Africans. Two of the three Africans and the Arab, who represents 24,000 Arabs in the colony's coastal region, will be given posts as under secretaries to gain administrative experience.

Meanwhile, Capt. Gerald Selby Lewis Griffiths, a British officer charged with cruelty to Africans, declared at his court-martial today that he thought it "quite proper" for a Mau Mau prisoner to be led by a wire run through a hole in his ear.

Captain Griffiths, who has pleaded innocent to charges of causing "grievous bodily harm" to Africans, told the court that leading a native by the ear "would not cause pain."

March 11, 1954

MULTI-RACE PARTY FORMED IN KENYA

White-Sponsored New Group Maps Election Campaign on Non-Discrimination Basis

NAIROBI, Kenya, July 9 (Reuters)—A new white political party whose program is the uniting of all races by backing a multi-racial government was launched in Kenya today.

The party, with the declared object of inviting other races to join its ranks in the future, will be known as the United Country party.

Formed by a group of white men who are determined to fight the next election in the colony on a platform of multi-racialism, the new party is the first attempt to establish a political body in Kenya on a non-racial basis.

Supporters see the party as a solution to the present crisis in Kenya in which militant anti-white natives are grouped together in the Mau Mau cult fighting the white populace, often led by militant anti-Negro groups.

Nearly 500 whites are understood to have promised to back the new party, including a number of big business interests.

Observers here see the new party as a determined attempt to prevent the continuing deterioration in relations between the three main races—white, African, and Asian—and also a "declaration of war" by the more liberal white elements on the extremists.

A manifesto issued by the organizers of the new party declared that there were three political choices before the people of Kenya—domination by one race, political division of the country into communal areas, or the formation of a government broadly based on cooperation among the main races.

The Kenya security forces have killed 2,500 Mau Mau terrorists and captured and wounded 3,000 others this year, Maj. Gen G. D. Heyman, British Chief of Staff in East Africa, said at a conference here today.

General Heyman said that in the same period, 200 of the security forces had been killed, and 509 loyal civilians murdered.

July 10, 1954

BRITISH PROPOSE AFRICAN REFORMS

Royal Commission Urges End of Racial Bias on Land—Maps Economic Moves

By LEONARD INGALLS
Special to The New York Times.

NAIROBI, Kenya, June 9—Major land reforms and a pattern for future economic development of East Africa were recommended today by a British Royal Commission.

In a report expected to stir up a storm of controversy the Commission advised permitting Negroes to use more land in the fertile highlands of Kenya, hitherto reserved mostly for white men.

The Commission was created on Jan. 1, 1953, by Queen Elizabeth II to study the population, land and economic problems of Kenya, Tanganyika and Uganda, the three British Colonial territories of East Africa. Its report was published simultaneously today here and in London.

Tribal and racial barriers must be removed, the Commission declared, to bring white man, African and Asian into a modern economy operating for the benefit of all.

The Commission held that the East African colonies were badly in need of improved railways and roads, wider use of irrigation, the newest agricultural techniques, greater attention to public health problems and vastly extended educational opportunities for the Africans.

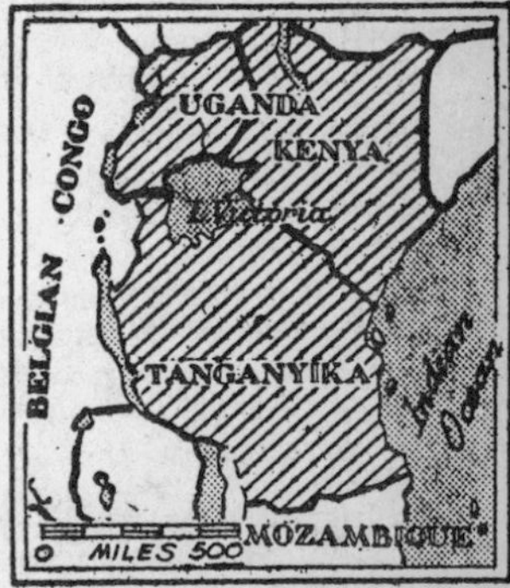

The New York Times June 10, 1955

A British proposal called for economic development of Kenya, Tanganyika and Uganda (diagonal shading).

East Africa cannot progress as it should, the Commission said, without the loyalty, advancement and active help of its 18,000,000 native population. It was in outlining ways that this goal might be attained that the Commission made possibly its most controversial point. It concerned the use and ownership of land, one of the hottest issues in sub-Sahara Africa today.

Race Bias on Land Use Scored

The commission condemned the restriction of land-use and ownership on a racial basis, as has been done in the so-called White Highlands, Kenya's most desirable farming land. It advocated leasing available land free from color bars to anyone who could make the best use of it.

The commission warned that progress in obtaining a more direct contribution to a modern society by the natives would be slow.

In recommending that the natives be encouraged to settle and work in cities or rural areas rather than following their present widespread migratory practices, the commission said:

"In this connection it is important that a new sense of security and stability appropriate to his participation in a modern economy should replace in the African mind the former sense of these values which was associated with his tribal order of society and which cannot be reconciled with the material progress which is now devised."

Incomes that would enable the natives to support themselves and their families are essential, the commission observed.

Other important points made by the eight-member commission, headed by Sir Hugh Dow, in its 482-page report were:

¶Low productivity of ordinary African labor is due not merely to a lack of technical skill but also to malnutrition, poor physique, disease, inadequate supervision and lack of interest in ordinary economic incentives.

¶Tribal and racial barriers in East Africa have prevented the migration of skill, enterprise and capital and large-scale exploration or development of new natural resources, have retarded the growth of communications and of towns and have restricted markets.

¶East Africa must cast off customs or vested interests that continue to lead to the waste of resources through ill-used land or useless cattle, through conspicuous consumption based on privilege or status, through ill-trained labor or through outworn restrictions on employment based on race, through agricultural production protected by monopolistic devices or state regulation and through restrictions on the use of land for agricultural or urban purposes.

¶A new land law should be introduced to recognize individual rather than tribal ownership and to permit land to be bought, sold or leased between Africans and others under Government supervision.

¶Credit should be made available to Africans, but restrictions must be placed on the natives' right to mortgage land and on the recovery of debt through the sale of land.

June 10, 1955

AFRICAN LEADER LOOMS IN KENYA

Tom Mboya, 25, Secretary of Labor Federation, Achieved Fame by Ending Strike

By LEONARD INGALLS

Special to The New York Times.

MOMBASA, Kenya, Oct. 24—They are still talking in Mombasa about a young Negro labor leader who settled a strike that crippled the port here for a week last March.

He is 25-year-old Tom Mboya, general secretary of the Kenya Federation of Labor.

Until June Negro political organizations were under a two-year ban in Kenya as a result of the Mau Mau uprising. A program for renewed recognition of African political parties has been approved by the colonial Government headed by British Governor Sir Evelyn Baring.

The Mombasa strike tied up the port, which serves all British East Africa, for a week. There was violence and the situation was growing worse. Troops fighting the Mau Mau in the vicinity of Nairobi were flown to Mombasa.

Mr. Mboya also hurried here. After a series of meetings with the 4,000 striking African stevedores and representatives of the employers he persuaded the men to return to work. Subsequent bargaining by Mr. Mboya led to a 30 per cent wage increase for the strikers and other benefits.

As a result of this, his experience as a union official and his standing with the politically conscious Kenya Negroes, Mr. Mboya is regarded as a man who easily may become the political leader of the Africans in a land where since the imprisonment of Jomo Kenyatta, alleged top Mau Mau chief, no important African leader has appeared.

Mr. Mboya, who is unmarried, is a member of the Luo tribe. He comes from Nyanza in Western Kenya. He was born on Rusinga Island in Lake Victoria and ws educated at Roman Catholic mission schools and at a secondary school in Nairobi.

After having begun his career as a sanitary inspector in Nairobi he left the job in 1953 to become secretary of the Kenya Government Workers' Union. He also was treasurer of the Kenya African Union, the Negro political organization that was proscribed in 1953.

At present Mr. Mboya is studying international relations for a year at Oxford University.

In Kenya Mr. Mboya is a member of the Government's Labor Advisory Board, Wages Advisory Board and Rural Wages Committee.

Mr. Mboya has cordial relations with extremist white settlers whose influence in Kenya is waning as the realization dawns on many white persons that multiracial Government must succeed if Kenya is to progress.

The extremists have tried to pin the Mau Mau label on Mr. Mboya, but he is not a Kikuyu and has successfully fought efforts to discredit him.

In his labor union work Mr. Mboya recently has had the assistance of James Bury, a Canadian, who represents the World Confederation of Free Trade Unions in East and Central Africa. Mr. Bury was a former member of the Vancouver Legislative Assembly and of the Executive Council of the Canadian Congress of Labor.

October 25, 1955

Mau Mau Campaign Is Ended by Britain

Special to The New York Times.

LONDON, Nov. 13—British military operations against the Mau Mau terrorists in Kenya ended today, Colonial Secretary Alan Lennox-Boyd announced in the House of Commons.

The announcement was accompanied by a review of progress toward self-government in Nigeria, Malaya, Cyprus and other colonies.

Mr. Lennox-Boyd emphasized that the new state of Ghana, Gold Coast of West Africa, would become independent within the Commonwealth just when Britain was being charged with "nineteenth-century colonialism" abroad.

Since 1952 Kenya has been disturbed by the Mau Mau, a secret society of Kikuyu tribesmen pledged to the extermination of Europeans and the end of British rule.

This morning, Mr. Lennox-Boyd said, Sir Evelyn Baring, Governor and Commander in Chief, had announced the withdrawal of military forces from active operations and assumption by the police and the civil administration of full responsibility for law and order.

The number of terrorists has been reduced from 8,000 to a few hundred, the Minister reported. Although there are still more than 30,000 Africans detained and 10,000 imprisoned the process of restoring them to peaceful tasks is accelerating.

The end of the military emergency, Mr. Lennox-Boyd said, has allowed the Government of Kenya to strengthen its racial base. Under constitutional changes announced today the Governor can now appoint an additional African minister and an additional European minister. He can also invite the leader of of the Arab community to participate fully in the work of the Council of Ministers and appoint two additional African representatives to the Legislative Council.

November 14, 1956

KENYA'S EUROPEANS ADAMANT ON RIGHTS

Special to The New York Times.

NAIROBI, Kenya, Feb. 20—European elected members of the Legislative Council said today they were determined to prevent the "achievements of the pioneers in Kenya" from being "undermined by irresponsible people to the detriment of all races and creeds."

Over the signature of Sir Alfred Vincent, chairman of the group, the statement declared that Kenya was home to Europeans and Asians as well as to Africans.

It concluded with the assertion that "no abdication by Her Majesty's Government from its responsibilities in Kenya can be contemplated" if the people here were to avoid the unhappy consequences so apparent elsewhere.

There were originally fourteen elected Europeans in the Legislative Council of seventy-seven, which resumed its session Wednesday. But one was expelled by the group on the eve of the meeting. He is E. L. Howard Williams, who represents the most extreme of the white settler viewpoints.

The European members who joined in the statement said they rejected any suggestion that Africans had any preferential land rights in Kenya to any land outside the so-called native land units.

This meant that the Europeans stood firm against the increasing African insistence that Kenya is basically an African country and that even those who have settled and cultivated the rich **"White Highlands" for fifty years are merely immigrants.**

February 21, 1959

KENYA RESTRICTS MBOYA'S ACTIVITY

African Leader Forbidden to Make Political Talks Outside the Capital

By LEONARD INGALLS
Special to The New York Times.

NAIROBI, Kenya, July 15—The political activities of Tom Mboya, Kenya nationalist leader, are being restricted in a number of ways.

At a time when the political awareness of Africans is growing rapidly throughout the continent, the organization headed by Mr. Mboya, the People's Convention party, has been confined to Nairobi by government regulation. Nor is Mr. Mboya, who is eager to organize a Kenya-wide African political party, permitted to make political speeches outside Nairobi.

Even as an officer of the African Labor Federation he had to get official permission to hold union meetings in Nairobi, Mombasa and Nakuru. Discussion of political matters at union gatherings is banned.

Office Crowded Daily

Mr. Mboya has tried to organize party district or neighborhood committees within Nairobi, but this, too, has been forbidden. Nevertheless, the public meetings he is permitted to hold here are heavily attended by Africans.

His office is crowded daily by Africans whom he and his staff help with a variety of personal and civic problems. But Mr. Mboya has yet to gain a country-wide political position or organization comparable to that of his friend, Julius Nyerere, African political leader in neighboring Tanganyika.

Mr. Mboya was detained for several hours by authorities at Nairobi Airport on his return recently from a trip to the United States. On suspicion of possessing banned literature and seditious documents, he was searched, but no such papers were found. Africans who had gathered to greet him were dispersed.

The whites here, who control the multiracial Government, contend that Mr. Mboya's speeches are provocative and that to give him a free hand politically would lead to revolution. They scoff at his appeal for "undiluted democracy" with an African majority in the Government and say 98 per cent of the Africans do not know what he means.

Newspaper Ignores Meeting

Nairobi's principal English-language daily newspaper, The East African Standard, did not report Mr. Mboya's latest public speech, delivered at a meeting of more than 3,000 Africans.

Mr. Mboya spoke in Swahili, the lingua franca of East Africa, and distributed an English translation of his remarks. He reported on a meeting with Michael Blundell, leader of the New Kenya Group, which is a multiracial organization seeking a compromise agreement among all races on the future Government of Kenya.

Mr. Mboya said he found "no common ground" with Mr. Blundell. He went on to say that "Kenya's European [white] community needs to face a complete revolution in their thinking."

Mr. Mboya also said that Kenya could not be treated in isolation from developments in West Africa and that the fact must be accepted that Kenya was "primarily an African country." He charged that the New Kenya Group's advocacy of "a parliamentary system" was ambiguous and vague.

July 17, 1959

KENYA PARTY FORMED

New African Group Headed by Mboya, Nationalist

NAIROBI, Kenya, Aug. 24 (Reuters) — A new political party—the Kenya Independence Movement—has been formed, with Tom Mboya, general secretary of the Kenya Federation of Labor, as its leader, it was announced today.

The new party proposes to operate throughout the British colony, although African political parties are forbidden to do so under emergency regulations here.

Mr. Mboya, who is president of the Nairobi People's Convention party, led a group of six African-elected members of the Legislative Council that split during the week-end from the eight other African members, who supported the recently formed Kenya National party.

The National party is a moderate group. Mr. Mboya and his supporters have made stronger demands for greater African participation in Kenya's government.

August 25, 1959

KENYA WILL END EMERGENCY RULE

Anti-Mau Mau Curbs Will Be Eased Early in '60—More Political Freedom Seen

By LEONARD INGALLS
Special to The New York Times.

NAIROBI, Kenya, Nov. 10—Gov. Sir Patrick Renison announced today that the seven-year state of emergency in Kenya would end early in 1960.

The emergency was imposed Oct. 20, 1952, because of the uprising by Mau Mau terrorists, who sought to overthrow the British Colonial Government by violence.

Calling for "a new approach to the future," Sir Patrick indicated that there would be opportunity for greater African political activity in Kenya. He spoke at the opening of a new session of the Kenya Legislative Council.

The Governor also announced an "act of grace" under which 1,079 persons imprisoned, detained or restricted as a result of the emergency would be given a chance to regain their freedom.

This is being done, he said, "to emphasize the reorientation of our plans and policies toward the constructive future and the closing of the tragic chapter of the last seven years."

New Laws Planned

However, in keeping with his responsibility to preserve law and order, Sir Patrick said that certain provisions of the emergency regulations would be enacted into the permanent law of Kenya. These would give the Governor power at his discretion to impose censorship, prohibit or restrict public meetings and control the movement of individuals or detain them.

In effect, the proposed laws would give the Governor broad power to combat any movement similar to the Mau Mau that might develop in the future.

Sir Patrick said that in deciding whether to abandon controls on political organizations and public meetings, he would be guided "not by race or politics but solely by my judgment of the needs of law and order."

He added significantly: "I hope that experience will show me that I do not need these controls. I intend in the coming weeks to give sufficient rope to judge for myself how much, if at all, they must be used."

In this connection, the Kenya African nationalist leader Tom Mboya has been given permission to hold meetings outside Nairobi. His political activity had formerly been restricted to this city.

Sir Patrick appealed to the Legislative Council, which includes Africans, whites, Asians and Arabs, to "stop scurrying in small, frightened, selfish parties to all points of the compass."

He also announced that the delegates to the Kenya constitutional conference scheduled to begin Jan. 18 in London would include all elected members of the Legislative Council as well as the Governor, his legal adviser and one or two appointed members of the Council.

In announcing that persons imprisoned, detained or restricted as a result of the Mau Mau uprising would get a new chance for freedom, Sir Patrick emphasized that the clemency did not apply to Jomo Kenyatta, who was convicted in 1954 of having organized the Mau Mau movement.

November 11, 1959

KENYA ADVANCES NEW LAND POLICY

Details Published for Plan to Open All-White Area to African Farmers

By LEONARD INGALLS
Special to The New York Times.

NAIROBI, Kenya, June 15—Kenya's land problem moved a step nearer solution today.

The Government published details of its plan to open to African farmers an area of more than 12,000 square miles of arable land that is now restricted to whites. The area, known as the "White Highlands," includes some of most fertile land in this British colony.

African nationalist leaders have long contended that too much of it was lying fallow while Africans were going land-hungry.

The Government's proposals are designed to provide a basis for settling the land controversy that has threatened to become a major obstacle in Kenya's progress toward self-government and independence.

Advisory Board Proposed

In a White Paper submitted to the Legislative Council, the Government declared again that its objective was "the progressive disappearance of racial and tribal land barriers. "It proposed that a start be made with the White Highlands, which lie near the Equator, northwest of Nairobi, at altitudes ranging from 5,000 to 10,000 feet.

Under the plan a multi-racial Central Land Advisory Board would be established to advise the Governor on land policy. The board would be composed of six Africans, six Asians and six whites, with the Minister of Lands as chairman and the Commissioner of Lands as deputy chairman.

One of the board's chief responsibilities would be to advise the Governor in cases where a ruling is sought from him on land transactions involving persons of different races.

Racial Bars a Target

The board also would advise on the removal of racial bars on all of Kenya's land. These include restrictions that prohibit Africans from residing in certain parts of Nairobi, the capital of Kenya.

The Government proposals also would provide freehold title to land regardless of race.

Kenya, which is about the size of Texas, has an economy that is based almost exclusively on agriculture. Nearly half of the country is arid. The efficient farming of virtually every inch of available arable land has become a national goal for Kenya's growing population.

The present population is estimated at more than 6,000,000 Africans, nearly 200,000 Asians and 65,000 whites.

Self-Rule Misunderstood

Despite the progress in Kenya's land re-allotment plans, two other developments are causing concern in the colony's transition to self-government and independence.

One is a misunderstanding among Africans of the meaning of self-rule, which they know as "uhuru." This is the Swahili word for freedom.

The other cause for concern is friction between members of the Kikuyu tribe who were loyal to the Government during the Mau Mau uprising and former Mau Mau members who were released from detention after the seven-year state of emergency in Kenya ended earlier this year.

The misunderstandings about self-rule was reported by Government representatives in Kenya's Central and Rift Valley Provinces, two of the most heavily populated of the colony's six provinces. Many Africans in these rural areas are uneducated and primitive.

"They know that uhuru means they will be running things all right, but they also think that when that time comes they can quit work and sit around," an official said. "Their attitude results from exaggerated promises being made by African politicians, and one of our big jobs is going to be to put them right."

Ill-feeling between former Mau Mau members and Africans who remained loyal to the Government has led to the imposition of curfews and the restriction of movement of Africans in the Nyeri district of Central Province, about 100 miles north of Nairobi.

June 16, 1960

KENYA VOTING WON BY MBOYA'S PARTY

Special to The New York Times.

NAIROBI, Kenya, Feb. 28—As the counting of votes in Kenya's common-roll election for fifty-three Legislative Council seats ended tonight, the Kenya African National Union emerged as the dominant party in the Parliament. It held sixteen seats, against nine won by the Kenya African Democratic Union and four by independents.

Results of the voting for ten European, eight Asian and two Arab reserved seats were announced earlier today. Only four results from isolated North Nyanza, Tana and Lamu and Northern Province West constituencies were awaited.

The elections have proved an overwhelming victory for the Kenya African National Union, which so far has polled 404,800 votes against 100,700 by the Kenya African Democratic Union.

Aided by a mass African vote, Michael Blundell's moderate New Kenya party has won four of the ten European reserved seats, with three going to Sir Ferdinand Cavendish-Bentinck's Kenya Coalition and three to independents.

Election officials said today that throughout Kenya the voting had proceeded quietly. However, the police used tear-gas bombs in Nairobi early today to disperse crowds rejoicing at the victory of Tom Mboya, Kenya African National Union leader, over four rival candidates.

April 6 has been set as the tentative date for the first sitting of the new Kenya legislature, which will be the first to have an African majority.

March 1, 1961

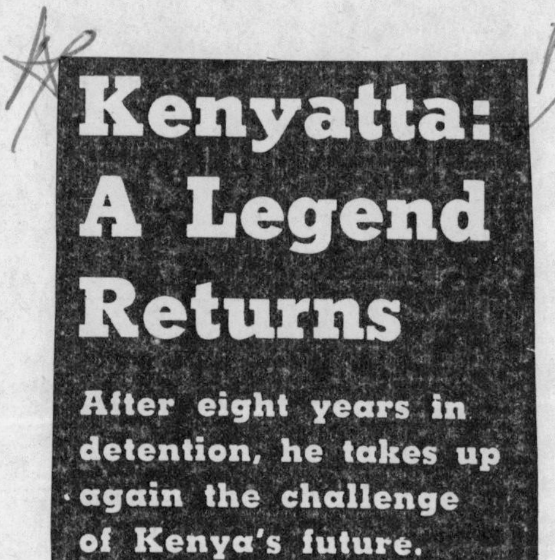

Kenyatta:
A Legend
Returns
After eight years in detention, he takes up again the challenge of Kenya's future.

By RICHARD COX

NAIROBI, Kenya.

THE crowd that waited for Jomo Kenyatta on the drizzling early morning of his release after eight years of imprisonment and restriction sang in Kikuyu: "People were locked up while fighting for *Uhuru* but now it is inevitable. *Uhuru* is coming, Kenyatta is in the country with us, he is the leader of Africans." And inside the compound of his new house the women of his family sang in the same chanting kind of melody: "This lovely country of ours, Kenya, has room for everybody with *Uhuru*."

If the simple emotions of these songs reflect not merely the feeling of Kenyatta's own tribe, the Kikuyu, but of other tribes, too, then the hope of his fulfilling his obvious role in Kenya's future is bright.

RICHARD COX is a British freelance journalist who has traveled extensively in Africa.

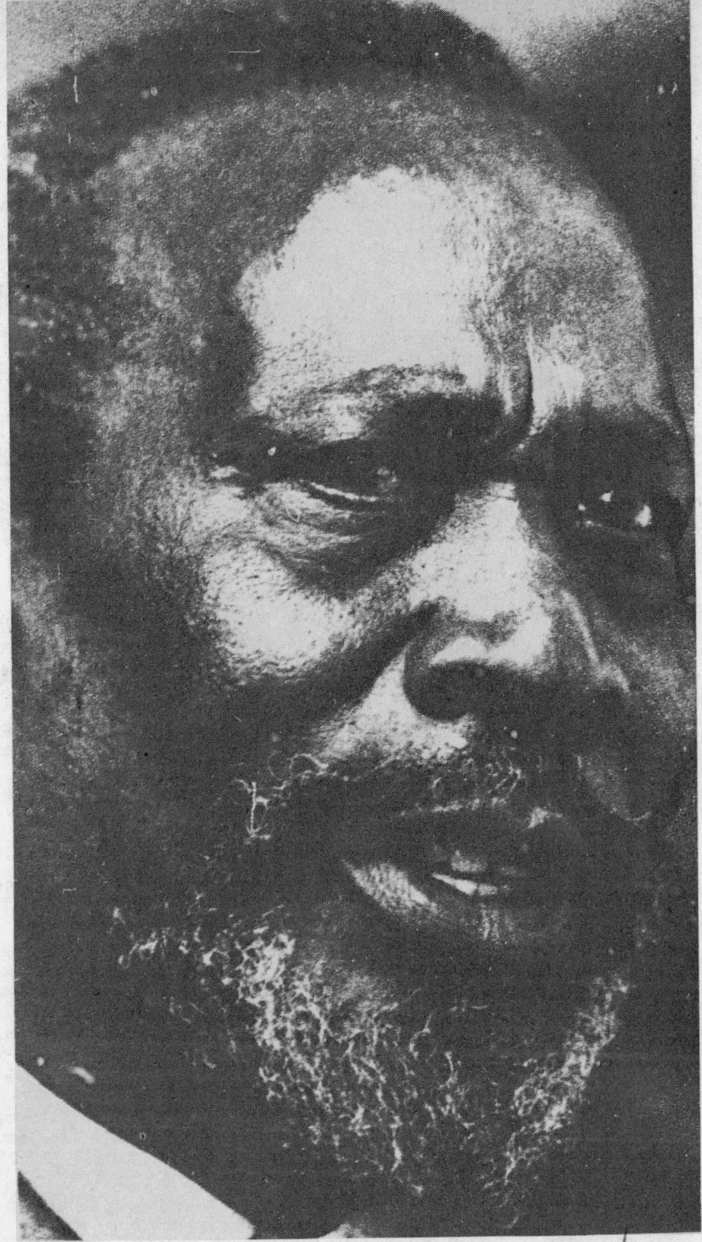

Jomo Kenyatta, septuagenarian apostle of Kenya's freedom.

Today Kenyatta is far and away the biggest factor in Kenya politics, as indeed he was in 1952, before he was arrested and convicted for managing the Mau Mau terrorist organization. The difference is that during his absence he has become a legend, too, for which the explanation is simple. Three years ago he was a forgotten man, drinking himself to death in prison, never expecting release. When "the wind of change" began to blow through Africa the younger African leaders, notably Tom Mboya, took up the issue of Kenyatta's freedom as a stick with which to beat the British Government. By the time of the elections of March this year, when Africans first acquired a majority of seats in the Legislative Council, the electorate had become so aware of Kenyatta's imprisonment, and he had been made so much a hero of the African cause, that the only electioneering slogan Mboya and the others needed was *"Uhuru na Kenyatta"* ("freedom and Kenyatta").

MEANWHILE Kenyatta himself, with remarkable self-discipline, had given up smoking and drinking, and was preparing for his return. Now that he is free, all the races in Kenya—Africans, Asians, Europeans and Arabs—are waiting to see if the godlike figure he has become can survive the descent to earth and if he will really be the national statesman that Kenya so badly needs.

Kenya's 6,450,000 population is made up of more than 6,000,000 Africans, 170,000 Asians, 66,000 Europeans and 37,000 Arabs. The first white settlers came at the turn of the century and created a modern economy by developing the land. In the main, they settled on unoccupied land; other land they bought. The tribe most affected is the Kikuyu, whose 1,500,000 members now believe—as the result of being continually told so by their leaders, not least Kenyatta himself—that the land was stolen from them. This presents the strong implication (at least to some of those concerned) that under *Uhuru* all present holdings by Europeans might be declared null and void. So the security of land title is a major issue not merely for Europeans, but also for the economy, which depends largely on European agriculture.

If Kenya is to make a successful transition to independence, it must have a constitutional framework under which all races can live together. But the African leaders are frighteningly divided. Apart from personal bickering, the main division is between the two parties, the Kenya African National Union (KANU) and the Kenya African Democratic Union (KADU). KANU is backed by the Kikuyu and the Luo tribe (numbering 750,000). KADU is a coalition of the smaller tribes, including the Masai, Kipsigis, Kalenjin and others, many traditional enemies of the Kikuyu and all fearful of Kikuyu domination after independence.

At the moment the Government is made up of KADU representatives, KANU having refused to cooperate with the British Government until Kenyatta was released. Now the two parties are negotiating over the future constitution with the Governor, Sir Patrick Renison. A major need for Kenya is that they should continue to cooperate and not allow politics to develop further along tribal lines. If anyone can bring about such unity, it is Kenyatta.

HE is also widely regarded as the probable president of an East African Federation, if this comes into being after Kenya, Tanganyika and Uganda are all independent. They already have a customs union, the makings of a common market, similar British administrative systems and so on. Together, as a bloc of 22,000,000 people, they would exert far more influence politically and economically than they could singly. Tanganyika's Prime Minister, Julius Nyerere, has been advocating federation for about a year. Kenyatta is the only East African leader with the prestige to lead it. Thus he is bound to become a major figure on the African continent and much depends on him and how closely he is still tied to his Kikuyu origins.

Kenyatta's character is complex and difficult to analyze even though the reasons for his immense appeal are clear. His very appearance is somewhat awe-inspiring. He is of only average height, but broad, and the set of his great, bearded head on his shoulders bespeaks power. His voice is normally calm, deep and convincing—except when he is annoyed, and then it is harsh and tough. When talking of "my people," he is fatherly and benevolent.

In private conversation he appeals by being both understanding and charming. Indeed he is a past master at telling people what they want to hear. Perhaps as a result of an intensive study of comparative religion during the past two years, he was able to send no less than seven different sects away satisfied from his house; furthermore, four local political leaders have returned from talks with him at various times and announced themselves chosen to be his political heir. He is also unquestionably vain and enjoyed the constant stream of pilgrims who came to his last place of restriction, Maralal, like mortals to the oracle.

BUT whether he is being devious or direct, humorous or bitter (all of which he can be within the space of a single interview), what strikes the observer most is the force of personality that he can project, especially through his eyes. These are very dark, pupil and iris sometimes seeming one, and yet there is a pale blue green depth flickering in them. They can be dull, saying nothing; they may blink innocently from behind reading glasses, or they may be compelling, hypnotic and sinister.

Kenyatta's intense magnetism has often been compared to hypnosis and the reverence in which the Kikuyu hold him includes a definite element of fear. He knows well how to hold, almost to transfix, a crowd and was the first African leader to develop the art of the mass meeting. His popularity with the Kikuyu also owes a lot to his lifelong occupation with their grievances and aspirations.

HE estimates his age to be 71 or 72. At the age of 10 he was saved from death by Church of Scotland missionaries who had him operated on for a severe spinal disease. In 1920 he first identified himself with the Kikuyu *mystique* of the land by interpreting for Chief Kioi in a big land dispute heard at the Nairobi Supreme Court. He wrote in 1938 that, to the Kikuyu, land is "the most important factor in the social, political and religious life of the tribe. * * * Communion with the ancestral spirits is perpetuated through contact with the soil in which the ancestors of the tribe lie buried."

Because the Kikuyu tribal lands were more affected by colonization than any other tribes', and because the Kikuyu have a penchant for intrigue, they took the lead in Kenya politics. By 1928 Kenyatta was general secretary of the Kikuyu Central Association, a party which aimed to get back the "stolen lands" and was strongly anti-European.

In 1929 Kenyatta went to London to promote the Kikuyu case, visited Moscow, returned briefly to Kenya and then, in 1930, left again for what was to be a sixteen-year absence. At this point he had emerged as one of the most prominent Kikuyu nationalists.

In 1932 he went to Moscow again and is alleged to have attended the Lenin School there (a school at which innumerable agitators, including Mao Tse-tung, studied), though he denies this. He joined the Communist party and, back in London, studied anthropology at London University. While continuing to put the Kikuyu case fervently, even virulently, he consistently avoided returning home. But he was not forgotten and received money from Kenya.

In 1938 he published the book from which the foregoing remarks on land are taken. "Facing Mt. Kenya" was a sociological study of the Kikuyu, to which Kenyetta added some of his own views on politics. In it, he wrote: "The people were put under the ruthless domination of European imperialism through the insidious trickery of hypocritical treaties."

Of missionaries, he said: "They set out to uproot the African body and soul from his old customs and beliefs and put him in a class by himself with all his tribal traditions shattered and his institutions trampled upon." Missionaries had particularly offended him by their attempts to end female circumcision, a custom basic to Kikuyu tradition.

The book's dedication was to "Moigoi and Wamboi [Kikuyu clans] and all the dispossessed youth of Africa: for perpetuation of communion with ancestral spirits through the fight for African freedom and in the firm faith that the dead, the living and the unborn will unite to rebuild the destroyed shrines."

THE distoration and cynical exploitation of tribalism for political ends in these passages speak for themselves, even though Kenyatta believed fervently in the value of tribal ritual and expounded the idea that magic is "one way of transmitting thoughts telepathically from one mind to another."

During the war Kenyatta worked as a farm laborer in Britain and married an English girl, whom he subsequently deserted. He is a polygamist, as are many other African leaders and, though European-educated, he by no means thinks in a purely European way.

After the war, he and Kwame Nkrumah of Ghana, then the British Gold Coast, founded the original Pan-African movement in Manchester. Today he feels that their ideas are "working out splendidly." Then in 1946 he was persuaded to come home and lead Kenya to independence. The K. C. A. had been proscribed for subversion and replaced by the Kenya Africa Union, of which he soon became president. It was now that he began addressing rallies of 30,000 or 40,000 people.

BEGINNING with a characteristic, long-drawn-out "Eeeee!", which drew not only attention but wild applause, he would express himself with compelling clarity: "I want you to know the purpose of KAU [pronounced cow]. It is the biggest purpose the African in Kenya and it is their mouth-piece which asks for freedom." Easily and quickly he became the undisputed leader of African nationalism, though KAU remained predominantly Kikuyu.

However, at the same time, former members of the K. C. A. were working underground organizing the Mau Mau terrorist movement, a purely Kikuyu affair whose rituals and methods revolted the sensibilities of other Kenyan tribes. The Mau Mau aimed to take back the land by violence. A State of Emergency was declared in October, 1952, and Kenyatta was arrested and later convicted of managing the Mau Mau.

Today opinion is still divided as to whether he was guilty or not. He firmly maintains his innocence and claimed at his trial that the case was arranged "in order to strangle KAU, the only African political organization that fights for the rights of the African people."

The evidence was flimsy but administrators point out that many of the witnesses the Crown wanted to call were murdered before they could testify. Yet other people assert that the Mau Mau elected Kenyatta their leader whether he liked it or not and would have murdered him had he denounced them. Certainly he was the only African who could have stopped its spreading, had he denounced it unequivocally, but this he never did.

The issue is most relevant now because the inheritor organization, called the Kenya Land Freedom Army, estimated to number anything up to 2,000 terrorists, had to be outlawed on Aug. 9. One K. L. F. A. official, recently arrested, told the police bluntly "If Kenyatta gets in our way, we shall cut him down like anyone else."

Kenyatta has so far avoided denouncing the K. L. F. A., protesting that nobody has given him any specific information about it, and he cannot denounce what he does not know. But he cannot lead Kenya into anything but disaster if he does not set his authority against insurrectionist movements within his own tribe.

NAMES

Jomo Kenyatta has had several names in his seventy or so years. He was born Kamau, son of Ngenge, a herdsman. Orphaned early, he was raised in part by his grandfather, who called him Jomo, meaning "Burning Spear," and in part by Scottish missionaries who baptized him as Johnstone Kamau. When he became a leading political figure in the Nineteen Forties, he took as his last name Kenyatta, a Kikuyu word for the traditional ornamental beaded belt that Kenya men wear and which he made a sort of trademark.

The Kikuyu always have been, and probably always will be ridden with secret societies. The problem facing Kenyatta is tricky but, with African unity at stake, he will have to back up statements like "there is no room for tribalism" with actions if he is to convince Kenya that he is no longer a tribalist himself.

In the short time since his release, he has been almost evasively careful not to commit himself in any detail on current issues, always stressing his lack of up-to-date knowledge and the need to get back in the swim of affairs, though he has given some indications of his thinking.

WHILE it is hard to see why eight years in the wilderness should have lessened his hatred of the Europeans, he has acknowledged the place of the European farmers and technicians in Kenya. "They will be treated as Kenyans so long as they behave themselves as such and don't want so many privileges." He has said they can keep land they are working but "all land that is not developed must be handed over to landless Africans." He has constantly reiterated the need for unity between the various tribes and races.

ROUND-UP — Kikuyu men, accused of membership in the Mau Mau during the violence of 1952, await their fates in a Kenya detention compound.

On the whole these opinions are viewed hopefully in Kenya, though his remarks are often capable of misinterpretation. What exactly does "so long as they behave themselves" mean?

On the question of East-West relations, he is emphatically neutralist and denies that he is a Communist. He says: "East and West are competing in Africa for their own good, not for the good of Africans and their rivalry is very, very dangerous to Africa."

HE also says he will not be dictated to by either East or West. Whether his pre-war friendships will, after independence, lend a pro-Eastern bias to his neutrality, it is impossible to say. But it is gratifying that in a private interview he implied criticism of the international gadding-about of some of Kenya's leaders with the words: "It is only fair that we put our own house in order before going about other peoples' business."

Kenya's house does indeed need putting in order and there is no doubt of Kenyatta's sincerity in wanting to travel all around the country to improve his knowledge of it and to preach his political philosophy, which, he says, is "Love thy neighbor as thyself."

He has already had discussions with the Governor and, although he is not yet a member of the Legislative Council himself, he is likely to exert considerable influence on the KANU-KADU constitutional negotiations scheduled to start with the Governor soon. But, again, of this he will only comment that he will help choose the best sort of constitution for Kenya.

THERE are two possible explanations for his extreme reluctance to make his thoughts known. One is that he is far better at being the prophet than the detailed thinker and, while retaining enormous influence over the crowds, will come to grief when pitting his brains against men like Mboya around the conference table. One young African politician even goes so far as to suggest in private that a single interview on American television would reveal Kenyatta's inadequacies and kill his international reputation stone dead.

What, however, is more likely is that Kenyatta, a shrewd and very experienced politician, knows what he wants but is making certain he puts no foot wrong during his re-entry to the political scene. His niche in the African arena is assured by his fame. Precisely what he will do with his power may not be revealed for many months. Perhaps not until the shadow of British authority is finally removed from Kenya and he has only his fellow Africans to contend with.

Britain Bows to Kenya Somalis, Agrees to Regional Autonomy

By ROBERT CONLEY
Special to The New York Times.

NAIROBI, Kenya, March 8— Britain bowed to Somalia today in her dispute with Kenya. She agreed to let the Somalis in Kenya's Northern Frontier Province, estimated at 200,000, form their own region.

London's decision was disclosed here by Duncan Sandys, Colonial Secretary, as he announced that elections for Kenya's first African government would be held May 18 to 26.

The decision to give the Somalis greater autonomy was expected to ease tension with the Somali Republic, which had been mounting for a week and had British troops on the alert.

Constitution Agreed To

It came at the end of the day in which Mr. Sandys and this British colony's Council of Ministers or Cabinet reached agreement on a constitution for transferring further political control in Kenya to the Africans.

The constitution will give Kenya's 8,300,000 Africans internal self-government under their own Prime Minister as the first stage on the road to full independence.

Independence is expected about the middle of 1964.

At the same time, Mr. Sandys announced that the Sultan of Zanzibar had agreed to allow Kenya's prospective African government to continue to administer Coast Province as British Kenya has since 1895 under a $28,000-a-year lease from the Sultan.

Thus after a three-week visit to East Africa, Mr. Sandys was able to announce decisions on three main stumbling blocks to Kenya's independence—the Somalis on the frontier, a constitution and coast Province.

Only ten miles wide along Kenya's Indian Ocean coast, the Coast Province is nonetheless a key to Kenya's economic future because it contains Mombasa, the largest port in East Africa and Kenya's door to world commerce.

Mr. Sandys reflected British concern over the growing crisis on Somalia's demand that Somalis on Kenya's northern frontier be allowed to secede and rejoin their "homeland."

He said Britain hoped that Somalia would accept the decision to give Kenya's Somalis a greater say in their own affairs as a sign of London's "genuine and sincere goodwill."

Specifically, Britain decided to establish a seventh region within Kenya to pull together the Somali-settled areas of the Northern Frontier Province, a parched land of camel corps, mud huts and 120-degree heat that suggests a scene from "Beau Geste."

The new region will cover the eastern sector of the district in a strip about 150 miles wide along the Somali border, from the Ethiopian border in the north to the Tana River in the South. Wajir is expected to be the regional capital.

As will the six other regions in Kenya, the Northern Frontier Somalis will have their own regional assembly.

Some political figures expressed concern that creation of a Somali region carried danger of a "British Katanga." They feared that the Somalis with their own assembly might secede and present Kenya's future African government with a showdown similar to the one caused in the Congo by Katanga's breakway.

Voting for internal self-government under the new Kenya constitution will take eight days because three elections will be held to take over further political control from the colony's 66,000 whites.

One election will be held to fill the seats in the seven regional assemblies. The two other elections are for the 170 seats in Kenya's new National Assembly, an expanded parliament based on the lines of the United States Congress.

One election will fill 41 seats in the upper chamber or Senate. The other will fill 117 seats in the lower chamber or House of Representatives. The House, sitting as an electoral college, will elect 12 special members to represent such interests as labor, women, business and industry.

March 9, 1963

Integration Grows In Kenya's Schools

By ROBERT CONLEY
Special to The New York Times.

NAIROBI, Kenya, Jan. 13 — An educational revolution will take place here this week in an atmosphere of tranquility remarkable in white-settler Africa.

Without fuss or fanfare, Kenya's white primary schools will open their doors to Negro and Asian pupils for the first time.

About 365 Negro and 50 Asian children have applied for admission to this British Colony's previously all-white primary school for the term beginning tomorrow. It will take about two weeks, educational authorities say, before the number actually admitted will be known.

The new desegregation policy has been accepted by all but one of the county's 28 white, or "European," primary schools. The lone holdout is in Molo, a conservative farming community in the heart of Kenya's white highlands.

In each case, the Government left the decision to the local primary school commitee.

This week's action will end more than a half century of white exclusiveness in Kenya's classrooms. It follows desegregation of the colony's seven white high schools with the beginning of the 1962 term last January.

Educational authorities say the primary school's decision to desegregate without direct Government intervention is a result of an "extraordinary revolution" in the attitude of Kenya's 66,000 whites toward her estimated 8,300,000 Negroes and 178,000 Asians, mainly Indians, Pakistanis and Goans.

Five years ago it would have been unthinkable in settlers' eyes for a Negro or Asian to sit next to a white child in Kenya's school system.

"We can't lower the standards, you know old boy," was the usual reaction.

In Northern and Southern Rhodesia, two British colonial areas in Africa with an even larger concentration of whites, racially mixed classed are still possible.

Yet the change in Kenya is passing relatively unnoticed. There are no newspaper headlines or radio bulletins about it, only action-quiet, firm and no less effective for its lack of thunder.

Nor is anything said about the end of years of embarrassment to "colored," or mixed-blood, families.

Until recently their children's educational future was determined by eyesight. If a child's hair was deemed too buzzy or his skin too dark, he was assigned to a Negro school. If the hair appeared straight to a white school admission officer and the skin light, the child might be assigned to a white school.

White enrollment has dropped sharply in some schools, mainly because many families have left Kenya as she approaches independence, presumably next year or early 1965.

Five years ago Kenya had 604,900 Negro pupils in 3,879 primary schools, 636 intermediate schools. She now has more than 50 per cent more Negro pupils.

January 14, 1963

Clanging Oil Drums Punctuate Vote Rallies in Kenya

By ROBERT CONLEY
Special to The New York Times

NAIROBI, Kenya, May 22— Jomo Kenyatta extended his arms, threw back his head and sent the Swahili words "uhuru, uhuru!" ("freedom, freedom!") booming over the crowd.

Twenty thousand Africans at an election rally shouted and cheered, banging oil drums with stones and hurling the words back at the leader of the Kenya African National Union.

Kiyuku women, their heads shaved, jumped up and down, the bells around their waists jingling. They chanted over and over, "We will not sleep, we will not sleep, we will not sleep until Kenyatta wins!"

There is little chance that anyone will sleep much until the results of Kenya's election

East African Standard

Jomo Kenyatta, leader of the Kenya African National Union, at rally during the campaign

are known next week. Out of the voting will come an African government with an African prime minister who will lead this British colony, with a population of about 7,300,000, into independence within a year.

Fur Hat and Elder's Cape

Upcountry the same joyous din greeted Mr. Kenyatta's opponent, Ronald Ngala, president of the Kenya African Democratic Union, the colony's other principal nationalist party.

A Kalenjin tribesman in a fur hat and an elder's cape made from black and white monkey skins leapt on the platform beside Mr. Ngala to rouse the crowd. "Freedom and Ngala!" he shouted with flicks of his fly whisk.

Again and again he called out, and the crowd responded. The rhythm was carried over the clearing by the feet of Nandi tribal dancers, bright, bouncy women from the Rifs Valley with coils of beads piled high on their necks.

A Bit of Nonsense

On occasion a noisemaker is some flattened bottle caps nailed loosely to a stick. A woman with loops of colored beads in her ears wears a pair of smoked welder's spectacles. A bit of "maridadi," or nonsense, they make her friends laugh, so she is nappy.

Election campaigns in Africa are a fusion of politics and tribal heritage, of music and dancing, part festival and part revival meeting, alive with evangelical fervor and stomping feet, all reflecting the spirit of an emerging people.

The rallies and campaigns are part of a continuing search for identity—an attempt to link the present with the past—on a continent where history seldom goes back more than a century and all the rest is silence.

That is one reason for the silver-topped tribal cane Mr. Kenyatta carries, and for the fly whisks and monkey skins.

Mr. Ngala wears a beaded cap and a printed robe of the Luo tribe, but underneath is a business suit from London. Mr. Kenyatta's first name used to be Johnstone. It was not African enough, so he is Jomo Kenyatta now, a big, bearded, bear of a man, whose name means "burning spear."

Most political speakers put their points across in parables and folk images.

"If someone is blind and he falls in the mud," one tells a crowd, "he can still see that the slavery of the Africans is finished."

The thought stirs the crowd, and the ululations of thousands of women fill the clearing and spread in the gathering dusk toward the hills where their tribal forebears lie buried.

May 24, 1963

KENYATTA NAMED PRIME MINISTER

Party Now Holds 64 Seats of 112 in Kenya House

By ROBERT CONLEY
Special to The New York Times

NAIROBI, Kenya, May 28—Jomo Kenyatta was named today to be the first Prime Minister of Kenya.

Mr. Kenyatta, the 73-year-old leader of the Kenya African National Union is expected to take office Saturday. He was named Prime Minister after his party's victory in the national elections.

A three-day national holiday was declared for next weekend to celebrate the achievement of internal self-government by this British colony's 8,300,000 Africans.

As Prime Minister, Mr. Kenyatta will lead the colony to full independence under an African Government within a year.

Mr. Kenyatta will be sworn in by Gov. Malcolm MacDonald on Saturday on behalf of Queen Elizabeth.

At the end of the second day's counting of the election results, Mr. Kenyatta's National Union held 64 of the 112 seats in the House of Representatives, against 32 for Ronald G. Ngala's Kenya African Democratic Union. Fifty-seven seats are required for a majority.

Paul G. Ngei's African Peoples party held eight seats. Independents took eight others.

Independent Support Likely

The National Union is likely to hold at least 66 seats. At least four independents are expected to align themselves with Mr. Kenyatta.

In the Senate, Mr. Ngala's Democratic Union won 16 seats and Mr. Kenyatta's party won 18 of a total of 38. Two independents and one African People's party candidate won seats. One seat is still undecided.

Mr. Kenyatta's supporters took control of two regional assemblies and Mr. Ngala's supporters two. Two of the races for the assemblies remain undecided.

The National Union Government will control all of Kenya's domestic matters with the exception of the police. The Governor will retain control of internal security, defense and foreign affairs until Kenya achieves full independence.

At a news conference, Mr. Kenyatta reaffirmed his National Union's intention to form a Government "committed to a path of democratic African Socialism."

His government will do away with the "terrible poverty of so many of our people," he said.

"We do not expect to do all this from foreign charity," he said. "We are not going to compromise our independence by begging for assistance."

May 29, 1963

Kenya to End Jury Trials As 'Discriminatory Practice'

NAIROBI, Kenya, July 30 (Reuters)—Trial by jury is to be discontinued in Kenya, Justice Minister Tom Mboya told the House of Representatives today.

Mr. Mboya termed trial by jury "a discriminatory practice" because in Kenya it had been applicable only to residents of European extraction.

He said that to have an effective trial by jury it was necessary to have reasonable jurymen who would understand what was going on. While it is easy to find such jurymen among Europeans Mr. Mboya added, the Government is not certain they can be found in every part of the country.

"We are dealing with a legal system that in many cases is completely foreign to the people of our country," he said.

July 31, 1963

Do White Men Have A Future in Africa?

Yes, says a leader of Kenya—provided they do their part to build the nations emerging.

By T. J. MBOYA

IS there a place for the white man in Africa? I believe the answer to this question must be a definite yes. The European has a place in Africa, just as the Negro has a right to live in America. But, in both situations, agonizing readjustments are needed. In the United States, the Negro is battling for political, economic and social equality with his fellow countrymen. In many parts of Africa, on the other hand, Europeans are fighting to retain their privileged status. Some of them are not prepared to be treated on a basis of equality with other citizens.

While the answer is definite enough, it is necessary to look behind the question and discover why it is so often asked. After all, no one asks whether the Negro has a right to remain in America, whether the Arab has a right to stay in Zanzibar or, for that matter, whether the Normans have a right to remain in Britain.

The question stems primarily from the guilty conscience of white men in Africa. I know that many will deny this. These people—and not all of them are reactionary Colonel Blimps—will point to the achievements of Europeans in Africa. They will instance the selfless service of missionaries, the introduction of Western systems of law and administration, the economic benefits brought from Europe by businessmen, farmers and entrepreneurs.

WE do not deny this, but it does not wipe out all that Africa and its people have suffered at the hands of colonialism and white domination. Imperialism took many forms, according to the circumstances it found in various parts of our continent. During the struggle for independence, we were sometimes told that there was a big difference between East Africans and West Africans. This was said in order to justify the withholding of freedom in East Africa when Ghana already had hers. We knew that this was not true. The West Africans happened to be luckier than we because they had so many more mosquitoes. Because of its freedom from them, Kenya became a "white man's country." Other areas of Africa which Europeans considered suitable for their own use suffered the same fate. Eastern, Central and Southern Africa, together with some of the Northern fringes, notably Algeria, became areas of settlement. It is mainly with regard to such territories that the question whether the white man has a place in Africa is asked.

Straightforward colonialism does not leave the same scars as white settlerism. I think that in West Africa today a European with some special skill—academic, technical or what you will—is generally as acceptable as, say, an American in France or a Frenchman in Italy. In such parts of Africa, Europeans have been mere birds of passage—administrators, doctors, missionaries, engineers, managers. But in places such as Kenya it was a different matter. The Europeans who came to my country put down roots. By virtue of their economic contribution and their attachment to the country, they demanded and received from a sympathetic metropolitan government many of the privileges and powers they wanted.

ONE of the most bitter controversies which has raged between the indigenous people and the settlers in Kenya and elsewhere is that concerning land. I do not intend to enter into this now, but what cannot be denied is that, at the end of it all, thousands upon thousands of Africans whose forefathers have been in the country for generations are today without land and without jobs. At the same time, large tracts of the country are owned by Europeans with high standards of living—none of whom have been there for more than two, or perhaps three, generations.

Naturally this creates a deep sense of grievance among the Africans and a corresponding sense of guilt and uncertainty among the Europeans. In Kenya, the Government is doing what it can to relieve the tension. Some of the more glaring examples of land alienation, and some of the grabs which took place most recently, are being put right. In these areas, land is being bought—note that, *bought*—from settlers on a willing-buyer, willing-seller basis at a fair price. It is then redistributed to the original owners and their descendants—who *pay* for it by installments.

Larger and more general schemes are also in operation to take the pressure out of the explosive situation created by land hunger. I must stress that there is no question of expropriation. We are *not* driving out Europeans. They are receiving fair prices, and legal sanctions are not used to force them to sell against their will. Nor does the buying up of a farm mean that the European owner has to quit the country. In fact, some of them are reinvesting their money in Kenya by buying farms in areas which are not in dispute.

IN the election manifesto upon which our party, the Kenya African National Union, won its great victory this year, we had this to say: "The problem of the unemployed landless will be vigorously tackled, and resettlement in the Scheduled Areas (i. e. European areas) has a part to play in meeting their desperate needs. At the same time, we are aware that this process cannot continue indefinitely.

"We cannot afford to fragment economic farms which are making a vital contribution

> **to our national prosperity into units producing little more than subsistence. . . . The KANU Government will not tolerate the holding of large underdeveloped tracts of land by anyone. At the same time, those who have farms, estates and ranches making a full contribution to the economy need have no fear of expropriation."**

Since the elections, the Prime Minister, Jomo Kenyatta, has gone even further. He has given an undertaking that it is not the Government's intention to limit landholding to citizens. Foreigners will also have the right to remain and farm without becoming Kenyans.

WHILE land became one of the most burning issues between the races in Kenya and other colonies with European settlers, it was not the only problem. Everywhere the settlers went, they introduced a form of racial discrimination. While in Kenya the excesses and inanities of apartheid on the South African pattern were never reached, the bitterness remaining from the type of racialism employed cannot be ignored.

Many United States citizens will know the sort of thing we had to put up with: the separate queues and counters, the exclusion from hotels, restaurants and clubs in our own country. Hospitals, schools, housing and social services were provided on a descending scale of adequacy—Europeans, Asians, Africans. An individual African's ability to pay opened no doors for him. To the racialist settlers, he was a Black, just a "boy," hardly human. As a sanitary inspector for Nairobi City Council, I was on the receiving end of a great deal of racial discrimination myself. I was sometimes thrown out of premises I was sent to investigate by Europeans who demanded a white inspector.

THEN, of course, there was economic discrimination. The African inspectors received only a fifth of the pay received by European inspectors. While the best education was available for all Europeans — indeed, it was compulsory—only the luckiest of Africans reached a stage at which they

could train for a professional qualification. The discriminatory wage scales operated not only in local government, but also in the civil service and industry—for those who were lucky enough to rise above menial levels.

Sometimes during our struggle for freedom, I wondered whether we would be able to wipe out the memory of this treatment. We in the nationalist movement believe in democracy and the brotherhood of man. We had no intention of replacing one kind of racialism with another when we came to power. Yet would we be able to convince the mass of the people who had suffered insult and suppression for so long that the white man was their brother?

Now I am more hopeful. In our election manifesto we declared: "The KANU Government will welcome those non-Africans who choose to join with us in the noble task of building a Kenya nation. Their training, their skills and their knowledge will be of the greatest value to us. We are confident that those who show confidence in us will appreciate the need to pass on to the nation what they can teach the people. They will be fully accepted by us, not only through legal forms, but in our hearts.

"Far from accepting the inevitability of tribal and racial antagonisms, we believe these differences are a challenge and an opportunity for creating a nation united in its purpose, yet rich in the diversity of its peoples."

HUNDREDS of thousands of copies of this message went out in English and Swahili to the people of Kenya. It was received and accepted by the electorate who gave us the mandate we sought for our policies. Today, our people — all our people, black, white and brown—are making rapid adjustments in human relations. We are moving beyond the stage of mere "cocktail integration," which started in the fifties when a few tame Africans were selected to attend formal gatherings to give an impression of liberalism to the occasion. While I would not suggest that everything is solved, large strides forward have been made.

In place of the unnatural atmosphere of those earlier days (was it only half a decade ago?), genuine, deep and unselfconscious friendships exist across the racial barriers. And I am not thinking only of people in political life, although it is here that the developments are most striking. The contrast with the past is seen here most vividly because it was in the political sphere that the clash between African nationalism and white supremacy was most clearly exposed.

THE attitude of British colonialism to the indigenous people in countries such as Kenya was at best negative and protective. It was the intention from the start to make our land "a white man's country" and only as an afterthought were the needs of the natives to be considered. In the nineteen-twenties, a struggle for power took place between the European and Asian settlers. The Africans were not considered, except as pawns, although each side claimed to have the interests of the Africans at heart.

As a result of this struggle, the colonial government decided to retain power, instead of handing it over as it had in South Africa and as it did, in part, in Southern Rhodesia. The 1923 Devonshire Declaration, another result of the European-Indian clash, said that the interest of the indigenous people of Kenya should be paramount. But they did not become so until nationalism grew strong enough to challenge the combined forces of colonialism and settlerism.

In the face of the nationalist challenge after the Second World War, the colonialists adopted new tactics. East and Central Africa, it was declared, were "multiracial" states. This was supposed to mean that each race would have some rights but that they would be kept in separate departments. From the European department would come the leadership, since they were the upholders of civilization.

When we rejected multiracialism, it was dressed up a little and returned to us as "partnership." But to most of us it looked like the same old "multiracialism" with a slightly more liberal tinge. A few Africans, the sort with an inferiority complex, who accepted the idea of holding a permanently junior status, agreed to the new notion, but the nationalists rejected it. It was Lord Malvern, the first Prime Minister of the Rhodesian Federation, who let the cat out of the bag when he told the British House of Lords that it was the "partnership of horse and rider." There was no need to ask who was the horse and who the rider.

WHEN we had rejected both multiracialism and partnership, further advances were made. (I might add that the swiftest advances came only after the Africans had been driven to violence. This was true both in East Africa and Central Africa as well as in Algeria.) A number of liberals then came forward claiming to represent a halfway house between white supremacy and African nationalism. People such as Sir Michael Blundell in Kenya and Sir John Moffat in Northern Rhodesia held the stage for a while. They helped to foster the acceptance of change among the European communities, but their positions could obviously not provide the final answer to our countries' needs.

WHAT we really want—and what we are now getting—are people who will adapt themselves to the new Kenya and to the new Africa as individuals. As I have said, the most spectacular advances have been seen in the political arena. Some of our most trusted and respected colleagues in the Government and in the party are non-Africans.

Nor am I just thinking of those at the top. In my election campaign this year, there were many Europeans doing the run-of-the-mill work of addressing envelopes, distributing leaflets, driving cars and so forth. When it was all over, we had a celebration party. As I looked around the room and saw the happy, jostling crowd of people of all races, I knew that here was the spirit of the new, nonracial Kenya the Government aims to build.

It will not be easy. There may be troublemakers on both sides. Anyone stirring up racial animosities will be dealt with, whoever he may be. Those Europeans who remain as foreigners must show respect for the people. There is certainly no room for any who harbor the old ideas of racial superiority. Some, realizing this, have already left, seeking temporary refuge in South Africa. A change of domicile will do them no good. Only a change of heart and attitude will suffice, for we know that the whole of Africa will soon be free.

THE leaders of the new countries are doing all they can to foster a change of heart among the African people and will not tolerate *agents provocateurs* who disrupt their work. The Europeans for their part must also make an effort. Instead of bleating, "Am I acceptable? Do I have a place in Africa?" they should *make* themselves acceptable and they should *secure* a place for themselves by their own actions.

They can engender faith by taking out the citizenship we are offering without any racial strings. They can continue wholeheartedly to serve with their skills, their experience, their capital and their managerial ability. They must understand the feelings of the Africans about their past treatment and, by their own present conduct, they must demonstrate their rejection of the past. They must not look to the Africans to make all the concessions. They must make some themselves.

It should be obvious from what I have said that there is a future for the white man in Kenya and Africa. What is this future? This question, too, is already answered. The white man's future in Kenya must be identical to that of every other citizen of Kenya. As we grapple with the task of nation-building — building new villages, cooperatives, farms and roads — so must they be prepared to dirty their hands and sweat with us in this task.

As I have already shown, the white man has the advantage over his fellow African citizens. He has skills, experience, managerial training, education and even capital. He should make these available to his country and be ready to help the country move forward. This can be done without resentment on the part of the African if it does not become a question of "big brother" helping the poorer ones.

TO emphasize this position of equality and complete acceptance of the white man, we in Kenya have decided against dual citizenship. Those white men who become Kenya citizens will first have to renounce their other nationality. This is a step made necessary by the history of our country. It will convince the African that the European who takes on Kenya citizenship is not a mere opportunist but a determined "nationalist," ready to give up everything for his country. It will remove the problem of divided loyalty. It will insure total commitment — without emergency exits. I believe that we shall be able to demonstrate to the world that all the inhabitants of our country can live and work happily together under the leadership of Jomo Kenyatta.

When our hopes and ambitions are fulfilled, we shall demonstrate to the world that people of different races *can* exist within one state without oppression of one group by another. We shall show those unhappy states in Southern Africa that the white man can maintain a place for himself in Africa not by force, but on a basis of individual equality

Joyful Kenya Gets Independence From Britain

London Frees Final Colonial Holding in East Africa— Seat in U.N. Assured

By ROBERT CONLEY
Special to The New York Times

NAIROBI, Kenya, Thursday, Dec. 12—Kenya emerged today as Africa's newest independent state.

Jubilation swept through the new country.

With Britain's Union Jack replaced by the black, red and green flag of the new state, political power in Britain's last East African colonial holding slipped from the grasp of its 55,759 whites and was taken up by its 8,365,942 Africans.

Young and impatient Africa thus pushed the remaining areas of white control all the way down to the Zambesi River, which is farther from here than London is from the Alps.

Ten years ago, white men controlled nearly all of Africa, from Cairo to Capetown and from Dakar to Dar es Salaam. The only free states were Ethiopia, a monarchy as old as the Bible, and Liberia, which was founded by former American Negro slaves.

Now the aspirations of African nationalism have pressed the whites back toward the southern end of the continent, where the first white settlers stepped ashore three centuries ago.

Whites have lost all of East Africa. They have also lost Nyasaland and Northern Rhodesia in Central Africa. Nyasaland is to receive independence from Britain next July. Northern Rhodesia, with an African majority already in limited control, is expected to follow soon afterward.

That leaves white authority below the Zambesi confined to a diminishing bit of ground made up of Southern Rhodesia and South Africa and the Portuguese territories of Angola and Mozambique, on the continent's opposite coasts.

There are about 3.6 million whites in those areas roughly as many people as live in Chicago. They intend to make their final stand there against a continent with 250 million people, one-fifth of the world's land mass and an area bigger than the United States, India and China.

Kenya, a land about the size of Texas, is the 35th independent state to emerge in Africa. In a matter of days she will also become the 18th member of the British Commonwealth and the 113th member of the United Nations. Zanzibar, free of Britain since Tuesday, will be the 112th.

Kenya's emergence is particularly significant as a clue to faced with a settled white population.

It is increasingly accepted here that Prime Minister Jomo Kenyatta is determined to submerge the racial bitternesses of the past and to assure whites of a place in "nation building." This is something none of the whites ever offered him.

Mr. Kenyatta has extended the same assurances to the country's other settlers — her 176,600 Asians of Indian, Pakistani and Goan descent, who are the shopkeepers, carpenters and mechanics of Kenya, and her 34,000 Arabs, whose forebears sailed to Kenya's Indian Ocean coast before Jesus was born.

"We are all human beings," the Prime Minister says. "We all make mistakes. But we can all forgive. That is what we need to learn in Kenya. Where I have harmed you, I ask forgiveness. We must put the past behind us."

The only settlers who will not be wanted are those who consider themselves "bwanas," or masters, who look down at Africans as "boys" the term that whites used until a short time ago in addressing an African of any age.

"Anyone who still wants to be called 'bwana' should pack up and go," Mr. Kenyatta says, "but others, who are prepared to live under our flag, are invited to remain."

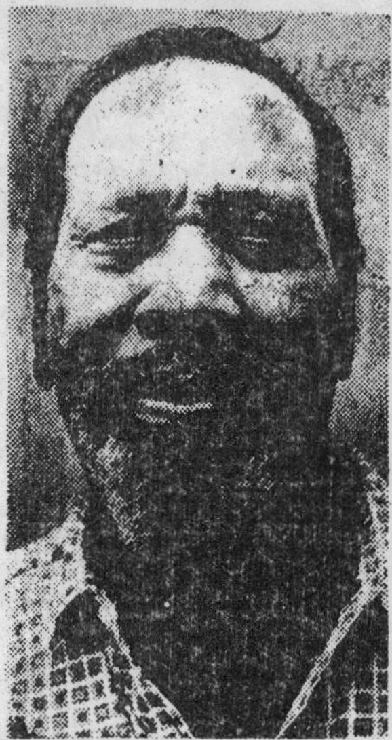

Keystone
Prime Minister Jomo Kenyatta, who has assumed an image of a tribal elder.

Associated Press
Tom Mboya, 33 years old, is the Minister of Justice and Constitutional Affairs.

Change Is Pervasive

Change is evident everywhere, from mud-hut villages on the slopes of Mount Kenya to old Arab towns on the coast, where carved front doors still bear great brass spikes to keep elephants from butting their way in.

In Nairobi, a bronze statue of the first Lord Delamere, who opened the highlands to white farming half a century ago, is gone from the main square in front of the New Stanley Hotel. An Independence Fountain rose in the statue's place.

The main street is no longer Delamere Avenue but Kenyatta Avenue. Photographs of Mr. Kenyatta gaze at passers-by from every shop window. Henceforth Oct. 20 will be Kenyatta Day, one of the country's 10 national holidays.

There is every indication that Kenya will evolve into a one-party state in the pattern of nearly every other black country on the continent.

In the House of Representatives the Prime Minister's Kenya African National Union has increased its majority among the 124 seats to near 4 to 1. This is partly because of recent defections from the Opposition Kenya African Democratic Union, led by Ronald G. Ngala.

Thus Mr. Kenyatta is gaining additional support to create a strong central government and a unitary state while Mr. Ngala has lost almost all chance of creating the dispersed series of regional administrations he advocated.

Zanzibar Regains Independence After 73 Years Under Britain

Island Off the African Coast Will Continue as a Member of the Commonwealth

By Reuters

ZANZIBAR, Tuesday, Dec. 10—With a volley of rifle fire by soldiers, sailors and policemen, and the distant boom of guns over the harbor, this island off the east coast of Africa regained its independence today after 73 years as a British protectorate.

Crowds estimated unofficially at more than 70,000 broke out in claps and cheers of "Uhuru!"—"Freedom!"

Thousands crowded the arena, where the ceremonies were held, or stood outside.

Speeches by Prince Philip, the Duke of Edinburgh; the Sultan of Zanzibar, Seyyid Jamshid bin Abdulla; and the Prime Minister, Mohammed Shamte Hamadi, were all read twice—in English and in Swahili.

A parade of Gordon Highlanders and a pipe band, sailors from the British aircraft carrier Ark Royal and units of the Zanzibar mobile police stood at attention while the national anthems of Zanzibar and Britain were played.

The new national flag, a yellow clove on a green circle against a red background, was hoisted along with the Sultan's flag.

Kenya, another British East African territory, will become independent Thursday. Kenya received internal self-government last June.

The Duke, representing his wife, Queen Elizabeth II, was among representatives of some 70 countries who arrived to help celebrate the independence of Zanzibar and its tiny twin island of Pemba.

About 500 Africans, Indians and Arabs, along with a few Europeans, crowded the airport for the Duke's arrival. Small groups waved the national flag along the five-mile journey into the city.

Among the others here for the celebration were Philip H. Hoff, Governor of Vermont and leader of the American delegation; the British Commonwealth Secretary, Duncan Sandys; Mrs. Indira Gandhi, daughter of the Indian Prime Minister, Jawaharlal Nehru. and the Aga Khan, spiritual leader of several thousand Moslems here.

Britain established the Protectorate of Zanzibar—including the islands of Zanzibar and Pemba—on June 14, 1890, during the period when the European nations were securing control of much of Africa.

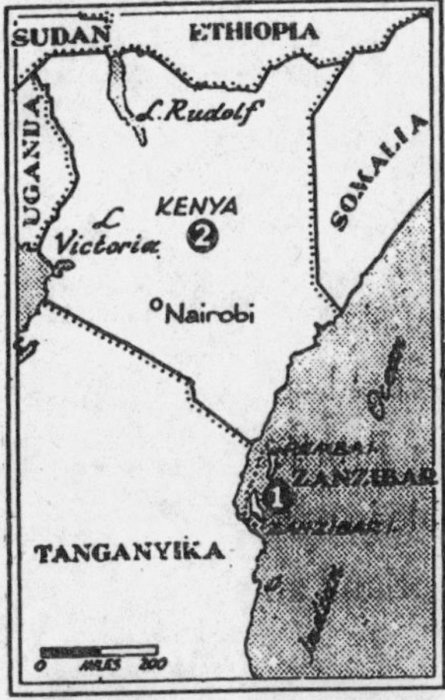

The New York Times Dec. 10, 1963

Zanzibar (1), the newest sovereign African state. On Thursday Kenya (2) will receive her independence.

Last-Pix

A SCENE IN ZANZIBAR, off the east coast of Africa, which became independent at midnight, but remains in British Commonwealth. Here, men stem cloves for export.

December 10, 1963

Somaliland Marks Independence After 73 Years of British Rule

HARGEISA, Somaliland, Sunday, June 26 (Reuters)—Crowds danced in the streets here, bonfires blazed from the hills and fireworks burst in the sky as last midnight spelled the end of Britain's rule in Somaliland.

The country became independent after seventy-three years as a British protectorate.

Political parties gave receptions to guests from all communities. The rejoicing was to continue tomorrow, a public holiday.

Newly independent Somaliland plans to unite with neighboring Somalia Friday when Italy gives up her United Nations trusteeship there.

The five-day hiatus between independence and merger was seen as a period of potential danger. There was fear of possible clashes with Ethiopian tribes along Somaliland's ill-defined borders. [Emperor Haile Selassie of Ethiopia said Friday he hoped for peaceful border adjustments with free Somalia soon.]

Thousands of Somalis turned out to say farewell to the British Governor, Sir Douglas Hall, and his wife. They flew to Aden.

A delegation arrived from Mogadishu, the Somalia capital, led by the President of the Somalia Legislative Assembly, Adan Abdullah. He said the people of Somalia were eagerly awaiting independence.

June 26, 1960

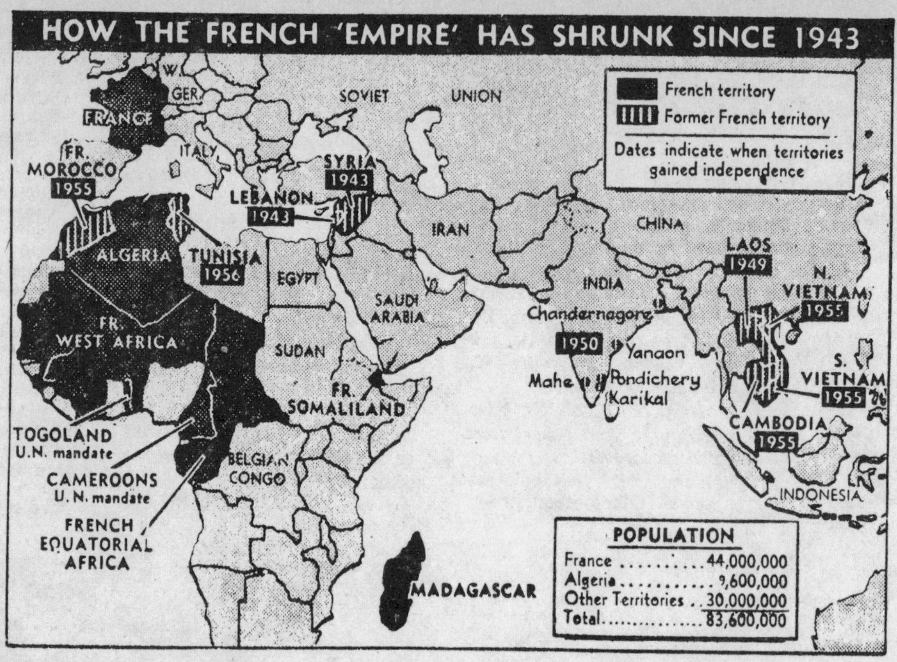

May 18, 1958

FRENCH IN AFRICA ASSIMILATE NEGRO

Movements for Independence in Gold Coast and Nigeria Have No Repercussions

By MICHAEL CLARK

Special to THE NEW YORK TIMES.

DAKAR, French West Africa, Aug. 12—The French authorities here are betting on their policy of assimilation to secure their vast West African territories against the convulsions that have made things so awkward for the British in Nigeria and the Gold Coast.

So far that policy has paid dividends. The political peace of French West Africa is cited as evidence that the idea of integration with France is "catching hold" and producing a climate of confidence in which Frenchmen, both white and Negro, can get on with the vital tasks of social and economic betterment.

The drive for home rule in the Gold Coast has had no noticeable repercussions here, although the educated few are obviously keeping an eye on constitutional developments in neighboring countries. Only a handful of Leftists and intellectuals appear to find special virtue in the nationalist medicine dispensed by the Gold Coast Premier, Kwame Nkrumah.

Except in rare instances, the political aspirations of local natives remain rather vague. What the African here wants is a place in the sun. The impact of the Gold Coast will, it is thought, be felt in the future only if that country makes a marked success of its independence. Liberia has been independent for 106 years without causing a flicker of enthusiasm on this side of the border.

Integration Process Continues

Meanwhile the process of integration with France continues to develop.

The old distinction between citizen and subject disappeared in 1946 when, under the new French Constitution, all the inhabitants of French Africa automatically became French citizens without loss of personal status. A pagan or Moslem African may now keep several wives and still vote and even become a deputy in the French National Assembly.

The accession of the African to French citizenship put an abrupt end to such practices as requisitioned labor and a separate system of native justice. Political parties and trade unions appeared as soon as the right of association was proclaimed.

French West Africa is an unwieldy entity eight times the size of France. Its heterogeneous population of 17,000,000 includes Moors and Tuaregs in the Sahara to the north, Peuls of mixed blood and a wide variety of Negro peoples, the most important being the Mandingos, the Mossi and the Wolofs.

The eight territories — Senegal, Guinea, Ivory Coast, Upper Volta, Dahomey, French Sudan, Mauritania and Niger—form a federation and have their own elected assemblies. A Grand Council emanating from the territorial assemblies meets twice a year at Dakar and votes the federal budget. Together the territories send twenty deputies and twenty senators to the French Parliament in Paris.

The electorate has expanded greatly in recent years. Heads of families and mothers with two or more children are now eligible to vote. Universal suffrage is just around the corner.

Although the territorial assemblies and the Grand Council are not legislative bodies, their deliberations carry considerable weight. The administration has shown an increasing tendency to seek the advice of the assemblies, and the assemblies frequently insist on being heard even when not consulted.

In Paris the African deputies have become a force to be reckoned with. The fate of a Cabinet may depend on their collective vote.

Léopold Sédar Senghor, deputy from the Senegal and leader of the group of overseas independents in Paris, wants to revise the French Constitution so as to make France and the French Union a federal entity with equal status for the overseas territories. These, he says, should not become associated states or overseas departments but partners in a vast federal system. This view won the support of some thirty overseas representatives gathered at Bobo-Dioulasso in Upper Volta last February.

The French Union Intergroup headed by Fily Dabo Sissoko, Socialist deputy from the French Sudan, and supported by Lamine Gueye, Mayor of Dakar, advocates the maintenance of the present system. The African Democratic Rally led by Félix Houphouet-Boigny, deputy from the Ivory Coast, broke with the Communist party in 1950 and now cooperates with former Premier René Pleven's Social and Democratic Union.

For the moment Communist influence here is slight. It is felt principally in the ranks of the African trade unions affiliated with the Communist-dominated General Confederation of Labor in France.

August 23, 1953

FRANCE EXPANDS MINING IN AFRICA

Engaged in a Supreme Effort to Lift Vast Territory Out of Indigence

By MICHAEL CLARK

Special to THE NEW YORK TIMES.

DAKAR, French West Africa, Nov. 24—France is engaged in a supreme effort to lift her West African territories out of their immemorial indigence.

The task is one of staggering proportions. These territories, once thought to conceal untold reserves of wealth, have all too often been prodigal only of discouragement and lost illusions.

French West Africa is a vast, sprawling federation eight times the size of France but with a native population of only 17,124,000.

Its eight component territories lie between the desert wastes of the sub-Sahara to the north and the lush coast of the Gulf of Guinea to the south. Cocoa and coffee have made the Ivory Coast rich. An artificial prosperity prevails in the larger cities. Elsewhere dismal poverty has kept the people at a subsistence level. In volume of foreign trade, the whole federation lags behind its little neighbor, the Gold Coast.

Stagnation here is the heritage

of centuries. The climate is debilitating. Ancestral methods of agriculture have depleted the soil. Internal communications are difficult and costly. Improvement is an uphill battle every step of the way, but for France victory is an inescapable imperative. Her position as an African power depends on it.

Development Plan Changed

In 1947, the Fourth Republic, conscious of its stake in Africa, launched a ten-year economic and social development plan for its overseas territories. By then, West Africa, weakened by the improvident policies of the Third Republic and by the strain of World War II, was gasping for breath.

Railways, roads, ports, airfields, schools, hospitals and facilities of all kinds had to be restored and improved. Production had fallen off, and the circulation of produce within the country was impeded for lack of transport. These major deficiencies were remedied. Production slowly crept back toward pre-war levels. But solvency was, and is still, nowhere in sight.

The official view here is that French West Africa will continue to need the protection of currency control and preferential markets in France for a long time. Any move in the direction of free convertibility at this point would, it is felt, imperil the fragile progress so far made.

Last June the books were closed on the first development plan although only six years, instead of ten, had elapsed since its inception. Available funds were beginning to run low, and a thorough review of the whole situation was in order. A new plan, this one to run for four years, was drawn up and is now being put into effect. Its emphasis is on production and on works directly related to production.

The authors of the new plan never lost sight of the fact that, although mining shows great promise in some areas, notably in French Guinea, agriculture remains the mainstay of the country's slender economy. In 1951 agriculture accounted for 66 per cent of a total national income estimated at 323,000,000,000 francs ($922,857,000). It was evident that agriculture would have to be given a strong stimulant.

Seven-eighths of the population lives on the soil, but the lot of the peasant is by no means everywhere the same. The coastal areas, far more prosperous than the hinterland, produce about 90 per cent of the country's exports.

Some areas depend for their livelihood on a single crop. This makes them particularly vulnerable in times of price fluctuation. The peanuts and peanut derivatives make up 93 per cent of the exports of Senegal.

The most significant development of 1953 was the opening of iron ore and bauxite mines in the region of Conakry.

Extraction of iron ore on the Kaloum Peninsula began in February, 1953. By the middle of the year 175,000 tons of ore had been exported. The production goal is 3,000,090 tons a year.

The bauxite mines on the Los islands off Conakry were put into operation in November, 1952. By the end of that year, 109,750 tons of ore had been mined and 59,120 tons exported. In the first three months of 1953, 43,857 tons was mined and 30,589 tons exported. The production goal is 450,000 tons a year.

Phosphate production in the Senegal was 64,550 tons in 1952 and 31,088 tons in the first three months of 1953. The production goal is 500,000 tons a year, but the present slump in world prices may impede expansion.

The mining prospects are held to be extremely hopeful in Mauritania, the poorest of the eight territories.

Deposit of Copper Found

An exceptionally rich deposit of iron ore, estimated at 100,000,000 tons, is being prospected near Fort Gouraud by a company in which Canadian and British as well as French interests are represented. Tentative plans call for the construction of a railway 345 miles long and of loading facilities on the Atlantic near Port Etienne. Th eoperation would, it is thought, be worthwhile on the basis of an annual production of 4,000,000 tons. A public investment of 22,000,000,000 ($62,857,000) is contemplated.

A copper deposit at Akjoujt has attracted particular attention because France has virtually no copper of her own at present. The deposit, containing an estimated 500,000 tons of metal, is being explored by a company combining public and private capital in equal parts. The idea is to develop the mine in connection with a processing plant capable of producing 60,000 tons of copper concentrate or 20,000 tons of blister a year. The anticipated public investment is 15,000,000,000 francs ($42,857,000).

Despite the progress of recent years, French West Africa remains very poor in electric power. Consumption in 1952 reached 60,000,000 kilowatt-hours, or only about four kilowatt-hours per capita, compared with 100 kilowatt-hours per capita in the Belgian Congo. And yet the mountainous district of Fouta Djallon in French Guinea contains one of the richest water reserves in Africa—enough to produce 12,000,000,000 kilowatt-hours a year.

The most ambitious single development project now in hand involves a scheme to harness the Konkouré River in French Guinea for electric power and the production of aluminum at the rate of 100,000 tons of metal a year. The project is expected to cost 109,000,000,000 francs ($311,428,000), of which 39,000,000,000 francs ($111,428,000) is to be provided under the new four-year plan.

Financing of Development

The over-all development plan is financed largely through the Investment Fund for the Economic and Social Development of the Overseas Territories (F. I. D. E. S.). This agency receives grants from the French Government and loans from a state credit bank known as the Caisse Centrale de la France d'Outre-Mer. Grants are supposed to represent 50 per cent of the total provided for economic development and 66 per cent of the total provided for social development, but the territories will probably not be in any position to repay the loans for many years to come.

Some projects of interest to the French Union as a whole are financed entirely by grants channeled through a special section of F. I. D. E. S. Other sources of financing include local appropriations on the federal or territorial level and loans from the Caisse Centrale to agencies of local government or to private concerns engaged in activities that dovetail with the development program.

The following comparative table shows the total volume of expenditure absorbed by the first development plan and estimated for the new one. Sums are converted into dollar equivalents.

	First Plan (1947-53)	Second Plan (1953-57)
Productive works—	$125,200,000 (24%)	$156,900,000 (36%)
Non-productive works—	269,600,000 (53%)	137,685,000 (36%)
Social development—	111,914,000 (23%)	119,677,000 (28%)
Totals—	$506,7144,000	$434,262,000

Agriculture development is expected to result in an increase of 12 per cent in national income by the end of 1957, while mining is expected to provide an increment of almost 4 per cent. Thus, if production goals are met, the national income should reach about 375,000,000,000 francs ($1,070,000,000) in 1957. It is hoped that this will provide an increase of 8,000,000,000 francs ($22,800,000) in state revenue, or enough to carry the added burden of expanded social services and a heavier public debt.

January 5, 1954

AIR OPENS MARKET TO FRENCH AFRICA

Development of Cargo Lines Permits Chad Territory to Export Beef Cattle

By MICHAEL CLARK
Special to The New York Times.

FORT LAMY, French Equatorial Africa, April 24—The development of air cargo links with the outside world promises to give the remote Chad Territory it first real economic stimulus.

Occupying what is probably the geographic center of the African continent, the Chad has from time immemorial suffered the consequences of fantastic distances and impossible communications. Until recently little in the way of progress could be expected from its primitive economy based on the ancestral methods of a nomadic and pastoral people, part Negro and part Arab.

But now, with five airlines already in the picture, it begins to look as though the Chad might be able to break out of its economic isolation at last and to get its produce to market for the first time on reasonable terms.

The French authorities here are, in any case, determined to give the territory its maximum opportunity. The Foreign Operations Administration of the United States is reported to be interested in several projects here.

As cattle constitutes the principal wealth of the Chad, Fort Lamy, the territorial capital, may one day soon emerge as a meat-packing center of first importance, as a sort of Chicago of central Africa.

A modern slaughterhouse and refrigerating plant is now under construction here. Four airlines, three French and one Belgian, already are carrying meat to areas near the coast where trypanosomiasis, a fatal illness to animals carried by the tsetse fly, and climatic conditions make cattle raising difficult.

Cotton, which flourishes in the southern part of the territory, is the second major resource of the Chad. Most of the cotton produced is laboriously evacuated by road and river transport, but one company has started taking cotton out in a flying boat operating between Léré on Lake Mayo Kebbi and Douala on the French Cameroons coast.

The possibilities of air transport as a means of opening up the Chad were first recognized, not by private enterprise, but by a Government veterinarian Pierre Receveur, territorial director of animal husbandry.

In 1947 M. Receveur and his associates brought their point home by flying three tons of fresh lamb south across the tropi-

The New York Times May 9, 1954

AFRICAN BEEF SOURCE: Air lines are beginning to make cattle supplies of Chad Territory (diagonal shading) available to other areas.

cal jungle to Brazzaville, 1,130 miles away, as a Christmas present to the Governor General of French Equatorial Africa.

The following year, with the help of a Government-sponsored native provident society, they shipped forty tons of beef to Brazzaville by air. Private enterprise, having caught on by this time, took out an additional twenty tons that year.

Since then M. Receveur has let the private companies carry the ball. In 1952 and 1953 the air-lines took away all the meat that the existing installations could handle—2,100 tons a year.

M. Receveur's new slaughter-house at Fort Lamy, scheduled to reach full production early in 1955, will be equipped to pack 6,000 tons of meat a year. The capacity of the installations at Abéché and Fort Archambault also is being increased.

Meanwhile M. Receveur and his associates are doing their utmost to protect the cattle of the territory, estimated at more than 4,000,000 head, against disease and to improve its quality.

A central laboratory at Fort Lamy for the preparation of serums already is functioning, although much of the equipment is still awaited. In arid areas the construction of watering points is being pushed.

Two research stations have been set up, one at Abéché and one at Fianga, in the cotton belt.

In the north the aim is to increase the weight of the hump-back Zebu cattle raised there and to bring the animals to maturity in four years instead of six.

In the south, where peasant farming has created the demand for an all-purpose animal, an attempt is being made to improve the N'dama or African Shorthorn and to increase its resistance to trypanosomiasis.

May 9, 1954

Togoland Deputies Back Amended French Plan

ACCRA, Gold Coast, Aug. 14 (Reuters)—The Territorial Assembly of French Togoland adopted today, subject to twenty admendments, the French Government's draft plan for making French Togoland autonomous.

The plan was prepared in Paris and published last week in Lome, chief city of French Togoland. It is to give the territory home rule, while retaining defense and foreign affairs in French hands.

Under the French plan, a Togoland legislative assembly, elected by universal suffrage, will choose a premier, who in turn will select a cabinet of eight ministers with the approval of the French Governor or commissioner.

August 15, 1954

MOLLET UPHELD ON RULE IN AFRICA

French Assembly Defeats Bid for Full Autonomy—

By HENRY GINIGER
Special to The New York Times.

PARIS, Feb. 2—The Government defeated attempts in the National Assembly today to provide France's African territories with full-fledged local governments. However, some concessions were made to African demands for greater self-rule.

On the Assembly floor the discussion on how far to go in loosening France's highly centralized control over her overseas territories came toward the end of a week-long debate. The discussion was on a series of governmental decrees affecting the administration and political organization of these territories.

These decrees, authorized by an Act of Parliament last year, were designed to give the native populations a greater voice over their own affairs. They also were designed to meet demands for autonomy before they take on an aggressively open nationalistic character that could end in rebellion.

The areas at issue were the eight territories composing French West Africa, the four composing French Equatorial Africa, and the island of Madagascar. The decrees organize governmental councils and assemblies in each of them and confer powers of decision on purely local matters.

The Government stipulated that each council should be presided over by a French commissioner appointed by the Cabinet. The commissioner would appoint three-eighths of the councils' members and the territorial assembly would elect the remainder. In no case would be councils be responsible before the assembly, as the Government in Paris is before the National Assembly.

The African deputies in the French Assembly saw an opening through which their territories could gain greater power without openly breaking with France, at least not immediately.

With support from the Communists and members of the Roman Catholic Popular Republican Movement, they moved that each governmental council be chosen entirely the assembly. The council, in turn, would name a premier who would preside over it. It would be responsible before the Assembly, which could vote it out of office.

Regime Opposes the Move

The move was unacceptable to the Socialist-directed Government and to a majority of the National Assembly, which feared that the Africans were going too far and too fast. The nationalist rebellion in Algeria has encouraged a more liberal policy in other French territories to prevent similar outbreaks. But sweeping concessions in "black Africa," it was felt, also would encourage the rebels in Algeria to hold out for more than the Government is now prepared to give.

It was contended that setting up full governmental systems would violate the Constitution, which provides for an "indivisible" republic.

Days and nights of bitter argument produced a compromise, to which some Africans were not entirely reconciled, whereby each governmental council would be presided over by the commissioner. However, it would in each case be elected entirely by the territorial assembly. It could choose to resign if it felt that it no longer had the confidence of the assembly. This text was approved by 322 to 199.

Attempts by the Africans to extend territorial powers to customs, radio, postal and educational services were defeated, the Government preferring to keep these powers in its own hands.

Gaston Deferre, Minister of Overseas Territories, described the formation of governmental councils as a profound reform. He said an "immense step has been taken between what existed yesterday and what will be built tomorrow."

February 3, 1957

France Sends Troops to Crush Red-Led Uprising in Cameroons

Acts to Prevent New 'Algeria' in African Territory Where Rebels Burned 60 Villages

By The United Press.

PARIS, Jan. 5—France shipped troop reinforcements to the Cameroons today to crush a Communist-led uprising before it could develop into a struggle like that in Algeria.

Jacques Chaban-Delmas, Defense Minister, assigned to the West African equatorial territory two companies of infantry at the request of the Cameroon Premier, André-Marie M'Bida, officials disclosed.

The reinforcements will help the 1,500 troops already in the French Cameroons fight against forces of the Union des Populations du Cameroun, a Communist-led movement.

About 800 members of the extremist group, armed with hatchets, shotguns and sabers, are reported to have taken refuge in the Bamiléké and Sanaga-Maritime regions, terrorizing the populace of surrounding areas.

The rebels have murdered dozens of villagers and burned down sixty villages in their campaign to win independence for the African territory, which is a French trusteeship under United Nations auspices. The French Cameroons has a population of 3,100,000 in an area of 166,000 square miles.

The leader of the rebel movement is 40-year-old Ruben Um Nyobe, a former court employe educated in French mission schools who later became a Communist. Most of his armed followers are not concerned with politics. They regard him as a prophet with magic powers and swear death to anyone who betrays him.

Mr. Um Nyobe, a member of the 155,000-strong Bassa tribe, says he is a Christian, although his followers offer sacrifices to him during night feasts in the deep jungles. There the French soldiers do not penetrate and the U. P. C.'s flag flies—a black crab against a red background.

The revolutionary movement

was formed in 1948. It was disbanded in 1955 after its first armed disturbances. Nationalistic insurgents lost much influence after France gave her African possessions a large measure of home rule in 1956.

In elections for the new Cameroons Assembly a year ago, three candidates were elected by the Bassa tribesmen, while Mr. Um Nyobe's movement was badly beaten. Later the three Bassa Assemblymen were slain by the rebels.

Most of the seventy Assembly members back the French-sponsored regime, which does not preclure total independence in the near future.

But the Union des Populations du Cameroun has decided to step up its activity to "regain the lost ground by terror," officials said.

The New York Times Jan. 6, 1958
Disturbed area is shaded

Mr. Um Nyobe's movement was the only group from French Equatorial Africa to have delegates at the recent Left-wing Asian-African Solidarity Conference in Cairo.

January 6, 1958

UNION WITH FRANCE IS GOAL OF AFRICANS

Special to The New York Times.

PARIS, Feb. 18 — Leaders from France's Central African territories proclaimed today as their ultimate goal independence within a French federation.

A communiqué, following a three-day conference here, reaffirmed the necessity of a French-African community and rejected "separatist tendencies" that would seek immediate independence.

However, the communiqué indicated that the right of independence should be accorded to the territories, notably French Equatorial and West Africa.

The African leaders reiterated their demands for a reform of the French Constitution leading toward the formation of federal republics uniting France and her four territories in Equatorial Africa and eight territories in West Africa on a basis of "free cooperation and absolute equality."

February 19, 1958

DE GAULLE LANDS IN FRENCH GUINEA

Continues Tour After Ivory Coast Leader Supports French Community Plan

By THOMAS F. BRADY
Special to The New York Times.

CONAKRY, French Guinea, Aug. 25—Thousands of Guineans gave Premier Charles de Gaulle a warm welcome here today. But Sekou Touré, their political chief, changed the tone of the greeting two hours later with a tough, aggressive nationalist speech.

M. Touré, like Felix Houphouet-Boigny of the French Ivory Coast, a Minister in the Paris Cabinet, belongs to the African Democratic Rally. This party has declared in principle for the federal community General de Gaulle is seeking to establish with Metropolitan France and her African colonies as members.

But the contrast between the political tone in Abidjan, the Ivory Coast's capital, and Conakry, 600 miles to the northwest, was marked.

General de Gaulle left Abidjan on his 12,000-mile African tour shortly before noon to fly here. This morning he and M. Houphouet-Boigny exchanged cordial speeches before 40,000 dancing, applauding Ivory Coasters in the Abidjan stadium.

Ivory Coast Loyalties Pledged

M. Houphouet-Boigny pledged the Ivory Coast's allegiance to the proposed new federal community and General de Gaulle replied that the "community has become a fact here in Abidjan."

The capital of the Ivory Coast gave General de Gaulle a wild African welcome on his arrival last night from Brazzaville, French Equatorial Africa.

Tonight at a territorial assembly here, M. Touré, a tough nationalist politician who has had Marxist training, stood beside General de Gaulle and spoke harshly of "French colonial injustice."

He said 2,500,000 Guineans would vote in favor of a new French Constitution only if it guaranteed to African members the right to independence, equal status with France in the federal community, complete internal autonomy and the grouping of African territories into a big unit.

General de Gaulle, who had already offered the first three guarantees in speeches in Brazzaville and Abidjan, was clearly angered by M. Touré's intransigeant tone. He replied that he would not be here if

OVERSEAS FRENCH TO CHOOSE STATUS

Charter Offers Continuance as Territories, Federation Role or Integration

Special to The New York Times.

PARIS, July 19—France will offer three choices of future status to her overseas territories under the new constitution—continuance as territories, integration with France or membership in a federation.

This was announced today as a ministerial committee put the finishing touches on the draft Constitution for the Fifth Republic that will be considered by the full Cabinet next week.

At the end of the month the draft will be submitted to a consultative committee of legislators and jurists for advisory opinions.

Finally, after what promises to be a sharp electoral campaign, with the Communists leading the opposition, it will be submitted to the voters at a referendum, probably Sept. 28, instead of Oct. 5 as previously believed.

To the provisions setting up a strong executive Presidency cut to the measure of Gen. Charles de Gaulle, the current Premier, and to the modifications of the legislative system, the committee today added a section defining the relationship of France with her overseas territories.

21 Overseas Territories

There are twenty-one of these, most of them in the two big African dependencies of French West Africa and French Equatorial Africa, but also including Madagascar and other island possessions. All are now regulated by a framework law giving them a measure of home rule under French-appointed governors.

Even before the committee's decisions were announced a group of African leaders entered a demand that the options to be presented to the territories include that of full independence. The Government has not commented upon it but the constitutional draft made it clear that full independence is excluded for the present.

Following the meeting, presided over by Premier de Gaulle, Felix Houphouet-Boigny, Minister of State, himself an African leader, and Bernard Cornut-Gentille, Minister for Overseas France, outlined the terms of the triple choice to be presented to the territories.

The decisions did not apply directly to Algeria, but Premier de Gaulle in a recent speech clearly indicated that Algeria, too, would have the option of federal relationship with Metropolitan France instead of its present status as an integral part of it.

After having participated in the Constitutional referendum, the peoples of the territories, through local assemblies, will be called upon to choose:

¶Continued territorial status within the French Republic. Under this choice they would continue to exercise some local autonomy, be governed by local laws and would send representatives to the French Parliament.

¶Transformation into French Departments—that is, full integration with France, participating to the full in French law, social legislation and governed from Paris through prefects just as are the Departments of France.

¶"Association" in the framework of a federal system as "federated territories." Under this solution the territories would be their own masters in all but certain "common affairs"—notably, defense, diplomacy, money, higher education, justice and common economic policy. Definition of the degree of common action in these domains would be a subject for negotiation.

July 20, 1958

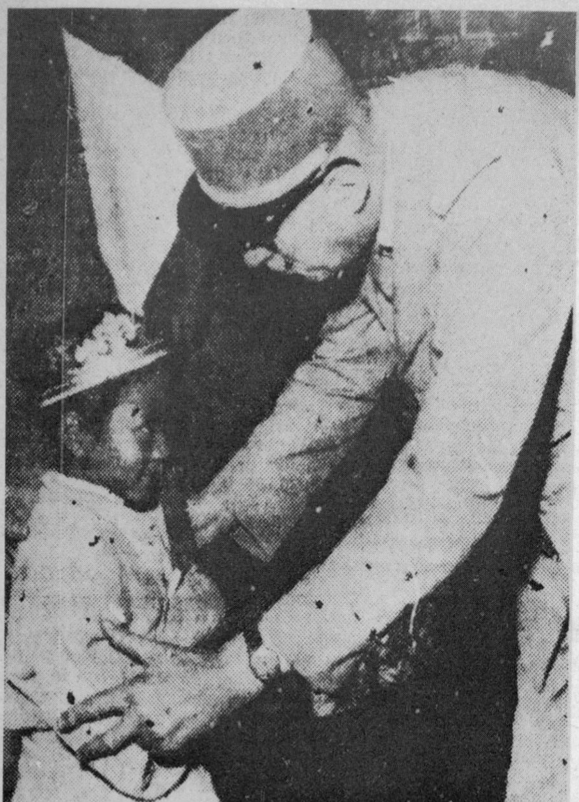

Associated Press

YOUTHFUL GREETER: This little girl was part of the reception for Gen. Charles de Gaulle at airport near Tananarive, capital of Madagascar. The French Premier, who was in French Guinea yesterday, is on tour of French African territories seeking support for new Constitution.

France had "any thing to blush for in her work in Guinea."

He repeated coldly his promise that a negative vote in a Sept. 28 referendum on the draft constitution would automatically give a territory independence. He said that if Guinea wanted to go its own way, France would make no objection.

The proclamation of this principle earlier in Bruzzaville was cheered by Europeans in the grandstand as enthusiastically as by the delighted Africans.

It was the first time Premier de Gaulle had used the word independence, although he had previously talked of "secession" and the "separate destiny" of the territory from that of France.

Bernard Cornut-Gentille, Minister for Overseas France who is accompanying Premier de Gaulle on the swing around African territories, disclosed at a news conference that the principle and magic word, independence, had been written into Article 72 of the proposed constitution before General de Gaulle left Paris.

In reply to a question, M. Cornuta Gentille said the new principle did not apply to rebellion-torn Algeria because "Algeria is metropolitan France" and not technically an overseas dependency.

General de Gaulle alluded to his enunciation of the principle of a French Union in Brazzauille in 1944 by saying historic destiny brought him to this city at significant moments. Actually, he had chosen the moment and the place deliberately.

The Premier, who wants Africans to vote yes in the Sept. 28 referendum on the draft Constitution, stressed the advantages for the under-developed territories in remaining in the French community headed by a Federal government that would control diplomacy, defense, money and economic affairs.

But he said that if a territory wanted to go its own way it could do so immediately by rejecting the draft constitution or later by demanding independence.

He reserved two basic rights for France: the right to withdraw from the community and the right to force any other member of the community to get out.

The new principle applies to Madagascar, French Equatorial Africa and French West Africa with a combined population of 28,000,000.

August 26, 1958

OVERSEAS AREAS FAVOR FRENCH TIE

Only Guinea in West Africa Votes for Independence —Turnout Is Large

Special to The New York Times.

PARIS, Monday, Sept. 29—Incomplete returns from France's overseas territories showed overwhelming acceptance of a Federal community with France.

Only one territory, that of Guinea in West Africa, appeared thus far to have chosen complete independence.

Voters in the territories were asked to accept or reject the Constitution just as those of France and of Algeria. But the meaning of their decision was different. Acceptance will mean joining a newly proposed community as fully autonomous states. Rejecting it will mean secession from the French Union and independence, with further French aid becoming problematical.

Despite the rainy season and vast distances, Negro voters turned out in large numbers to accept a federation with France in Mauretania, Dahomey, Senegal and Upper Volta in West Africa; in Chad, Middle Congo, Ubangi-Shari and Gabon in Equatorial Africa; in the islands of Madagascar, the Comores and Reunion off the east coast of Africa and in New Caledonia in the Pacific.

The islands of St. Pierre and Miquelon, off Newfoundland, voted by 2,325 to 46 to accept the Constitution. The city of Dakar, capital of Senegal, which had given Premier Charles de Gaulle a somewhat hostile reception during his visit there

The New York Tim Sept. 29, 1958

The new French Constitution appeared to have lost in Guinea (shown by cross-hatching) in West Africa.

last month, gave him a ten-to-one majority. French Somaliland also was favoring the Constitution.

Complete returns from Madagascar showed 973,000 for the Constitution and 259,000 against.

In Guinea, Sekou Toure, head of the local government, who had announced his opposition to federation, showed his hold over the electorate with results as impressive as those registered in the opposite way elsewhere. The first figures for Conakry, the capital, showed more than 97 per cent opposed to federation.

The territories that accept a community may leave it to become independent states when they wish.

The Niger in West Africa, which some had feared might follow Guinea's lead, appeared headed toward federation with France on the basis of first returns. Voting was running at more than 3 to 1 in favor of the Constitution and against the local Government head, Djibo Bakary, who had taken the same stand for independence as Sekou Toure.

September 29, 1958

PARIS CUTS TIES TO FRENCH GUINEA AFTER 'NO' VOTE

By HENRY GINIGER

Special to The New York Times

PARIS, Sept. 29—France lost no time today in pushing the West African territory of Guinea out of the French community as a result of its rejection of the Constitution yesterday.

Guinea was the only member of the community to turn down the Constitution.

Even before the final returns were in, a note was handed to Sekou Touré, head of the Guinea Government, informing him that Guinea was separated from other territories of French West Africa and could no longer expect administrative or financial aid.

Premier Charles de Gaulle thus made good his warning that territories that chose to secede from France would do so "at their own risk and peril."

Others Back Premier

Except for Guinea, Premier

de Gaulle had France and its possessions in his hands as a result of the surprising 4-to-1 vote of confidence in his Constitution yesterday. But there was no clear indication what he planned to do with his virtually unlimited power.

The speedy and peremptory manner in which Premier de Gaulle acted on Guinea was seen here as a possible warning to the seventeen other territories that voted to accept a federal community with France but might be tempted later to follow Guinea's example.

A new independent state is thus born in Africa under the leadership of a tempestuous and outspoken young nationalist who yesterday demonstrated his powerful hold over the electorate. Guinea, on the west coast of Africa, has 95,000 square miles, a population of more than 2,000,000, a port at Conakry, the capital, and a mountainous and forested interior.

Bauxite a Key Resource

A start at industrialization has begun through exploitation of bauxite deposits for the manufacture of aluminum through French and some United States capital. Otherwise the country is agricultural, with bananas a major export.

In contrast to a general rise on the Paris stock exchange as a result of General de Gaulle's triumph yesterday, stock in the Pechiney aluminum concern with interests in Guinea, went down somewhat.

Premier Touré announced his opposition to the new Constitution and its provision for a federal community well before the referendum and the French Government therefore knew what to expect. Jean Risterucci, a high official of the Ministry of Overseas Territories, arrived in Conakry yesterday morning.

With about half of 1,692 polling places still to report, the latest count was 636,281 against the Constitution and 18,012 for.

The firm French note was handed over this morning. It said the Constitution would not be promulgated in Guinea. Guinea would have no valid representation within the new community. Furthermore, "Guinea can no longer normally receive the aid either of the administration of the French state or of funds for equipment." The note declared the responsibilities assumed by the French state would have to be "profoundly revised."

Premier Touré was informed that France did not wish to disturb the administrative or financial functioning of the territory and that consequently French civil servants would be removed gradually.

It was indicated in Paris that the possibility of negotiation of accords with Guinea was still open so that the severance of ties was not yet complete.

In the seven other territories of West Africa, as well as in the four territories of Equatorial Africa, in Madagascar, Somaliland, the Comores, Polynesia, New Caledonia and St. Pierre and Miquelon, the new Constitution rang up decisive majorities.

99.99% in Ivory Coast

In West Africa, for example, 98.03 per cent of Ivory Coast voters went to the polls and turned in a majority for the Constitution of 1,553,704 to 197, a percentage of 99.99. The Ivory Coast is led by Felix Houphouet-Boigny, a Minister of State in the French Government and a champion of cooperation with France. He and M. Touré are members of the same party, the African Democratic Rally.

In Equatorial Africa, the Chad registered a majority of 98 per cent. Probably the smallest majority was registered in Polynesia, which includes Tahiti, where 65 per cent of the voters were in favor of the Constitution, according to incomplete returns.

The new French community will be organized within six months. Each territory will gain its full autonomy. Matters common to members of the community, such as defense, diplomacy and currency, will be handled by special institutions in which the French voice will be preponderant.

The head of the executive is the President of the French Republic, assisted by a Government made up of the French and territorial premiers and French ministers dealing with matters of community interest. A Senate and a court of arbitration are also provided.

According to Article 76 of the Constitution, the territories may choose to keep their present status of limited autonomy, become overseas departments or join the community. Once in the community, they may leave it and become independent.

The four overseas departments, which were not given these choices, also turned in heavy votes for the Constitution yesterday. They are Reunion, off the east coast of Africa; Guadeloupe and Martinique in the West Indies, and Guiana in South America.

September 30, 1958

FRANCE TO LOOSEN GRIP ON TOGOLAND

Paris Indicates Internal Autonomy Will Be Given Under Pledge to U.N.

By HENRY GINIGER

Special to The New York Times

PARIS, Oct. 2—France announced today that she had recognized Togoland's desire for independence.

Bernard Cornut-Gentille, Minister for Overseas France, indicated Togoland would receive full internal autonomy as a step toward independence. He said the change in the country's status would be made in conformity with a promise made to the General Assembly of the United Nations in November, 1957.

Under that pledge France would control only Togoland's foreign affairs, defense and currency. All other matters presumably would be left in local hands.

The announcement today followed a visit here last week by Sylvanius Olympio, Togoland's Premier, who conferred with Premier Charles de Gaulle.

M. Cornut-Gentille said the procedure for lifting the trusteeship exercised by France under the United Nations would be pursued during the present session of the General Assembly. He said France's objective was abrogation of the trusteeship in 1960.

Guinea Recognition Expected

Meanwhile, it was indicated in Paris that France would recognize the Government of the new Republic of Guinea probably next week. Recognition would make explicit what was implicit in the somewhat harsh note sent to Premier Sekou Touré Monday after Guinea's rejection of the new French Constitution.

The note had told Guinea that she was now separated from the rest of French West Africa and could no longer expect financial or administrative aid from France.

However, the de Gaulle Government was understood to be under some pressure from French business circles with interests in Guinea not to cut ties in such a way as to compromise their position.

The New York Times Oct. 3, 1958

STATUS IS CHANGING: Guinea has become independent and France will give Togoland internal autonomy. Both areas are shown by cross-hatching.

The Ministry for Overseas France said that final settlement of Guinea's new situation would await the formulation of conventions between the two countries.

There is a feeling in Government circles here that France cannot give the same treatment to Guinea that she would give to the seventeen other territories that accepted the Constitution and, consequently, a Federal Community with France.

It is thought probable that Guinea would like to remain in the franc zone. The problem, as financial and banking circles here see it, is to conciliate Guinea's independent status with the need for monetary solidarity among all members of the franc zone.

Territories in the Community will continue to have all their deficits covered automatically, in return for which France will have full control over their commercial policies

Despite Guinea's severance from the seven other territories of West French Africa, an expression of solidarity with Guinea was voiced today by Sourou Migan Apithy, head of the Government of Dahomey, which voted Sunday overwhelmingly in favor of the new Constitution.

M. Apithy sent a note to M. Toure assuring him of Dahomey's friendship. The note said that Guinea and Dahomey had merely taken different roads toward the same goal, that of African unity.

October 3, 1958

REPUBLIC IS SET FOR MADAGASCAR

Big Island Declares Itself Autonomous State Within French Community

By HENRY GINIGER
Special to The New York Times.

PARIS, Oct. 14—Madagascar declared itself today an autonomous republic within the French Community.

The large island off Africa's southeastern coast thus became the first of seventeen French territories that approved France's new Constitution Sept. 28 to choose its new status. The eighteenth territory, Guinea, in West Africa, rejected the Constitution, thus becoming automatically independent.

The sixteen territories that, like Madagascar, voted for the new French Community, at least for a while, are expected to follow Madagascar's example and choose the status of an autonomous state federated with France.

The Constitution approved overwhelmingly in France, Algeria and the rest of the French Union offers overseas territories the choice of remaining semi-autonomous territories, of becoming simple overseas departments virtually identical with the departments of continental France or of gaining their full autonomy in federation with France. They have been given four months to make this choice.

Provincial Bodies Decide

The six provincial assemblies of Madagascar met in Tananarive, the capital, and made their expected choice today.

A considerable body of local opinion favors independence and this is the path Madagascar may take some day when it feels ready to carry its own financial and administrative burdens. The Constitution gives any member of the Community the opportunity of leaving it when it wishes.

Under the Community questions of foreign relations, defense and currency will be handled by Community institutions in which the French voice will be predominant.

Off the southeast coast of Africa, Madagascar is the largest of the French territories. Its 227,602 square miles makes it slightly larger than France. The island has about 4,000,000 people.

The choice of status in West and Equatorial Africa is being accompanied by a harsh political battle between two rival parties, the moderate African Democratic Rally and the more extreme Party of African Regrouping.

The latter tends to regard autonomy as a mere step to independence and favors eventual replacement of federation with France by a loose association.

Leaders of the Party of African Regrouping met in Paris today and decided to push for "primary federation"—meaning federations of all the territories of French West Africa and of all those in Equatorial Africa, which in turn would federate with France.

The chiefs of the Party of African Regrouping, which controls Dahomey, Senegal and Niger, all in West Africa, called upon France to recognize Guinea's desire to remain part of the French family even though independent.

The party warned France against attempts to dissolve the Government of Niger because it favored a no vote in the referendum. Félix Houphouet-Boigny of the Ivory Coast, who as Minister of State in the French Government wields great influence in Paris and others in that government favor such a dissolution on the ground that the Nigerian Premier, Djibo Bakary, has been disavowed by the local electorate.

But the party of African Regrouping is contesting the validity of the referendum in Niger, charging irregularity in the manner in which it was held.

The New York Times Oct. 15, 1958

NEW STATUS CHOSEN: Madagascar (1) has become a republic in the French Community. Guinea (2) already is independent. The validity of the vote in Niger (3) on the French Constitution has been questioned.

October 15, 1958

CAMEROONS GETS FREEDOM PLEDGE

Paris Backs Independence for African Trust Territory After Interim Self-Rule

By THOMAS F. BRADY
Special to The New York Times.

PARIS, Oct. 19—France has recognized the right of her United Nations trust territory of the Cameroons to choose independence.

This move is the latest step in a general liberalization of French colonial policy in Africa, which has already given independence to Guinea and the promise of independence in 1960 to Togoland.

Ahmadou Ahidjo, Premier of the already quasi-autonomous Cameroons Government, told the Legislative Assembly of the territory yesterday in Yaoundé, the capital, that he had concluded an agreement with the French Overseas Ministry for a transitional statute of full internal autonomy for the territory.

"If you desire it, and if the country confirms our decision," he continued, "the Cameroons will be independent Jan. 1, 1960."

The Premier disclosed that he had received a letter from Bernard Cornut-Gentille, French Overseas Minister, declaring that France would support a resolution before the United Nations for termination of the trusteeship.

This termination must precede independence, M. Ahidjo said, adding: "It is logical the United Nations should prescribe a referendum" to learn the views of the people of the Cameroons. Such a procedure, he indicated, might require two years to complete. The territory's population is about 3,000,000.

M. Ahidjo said also that his Government expected to explore means of reunifying the French trusteeship area with the smaller Cameroons territory under British administration.

Like Togoland, the Cameroons was a German colony until the end of World War I. After the Treaty of Versailles, both territories were split into British and French mandates under League of Nations authority. The mandates were converted into trusteeships by the United Nations after World War II.

British Togoland was absorbed into independent Ghana in 1957 after a referendum that terminated the trusteeship. The British Cameroons, with a population of about 1,100,000, has been attached to Nigeria for administrative purposes and participates in Nigerian self-government. Nigeria is expected to become an independent member of the British Commonwealth in 1960, as Ghana, the former Gold Coast colony, did in 1957.

The transitional statute of autonomy for the French Cameroons will give the territorial government full legislative and administrative powers, including most of those hitherto exercised by the French high commissioner, M. Ahidjo said.

M. Ahidjo added, however, that the new statute was accompanied by conventions defining relations between the French and Cameroons Governments in matters of money, defense, external commerce and transfer of judicial powers. France may thus be expected to retain final authority in these domains during the transition period, as well as in the field of diplomacy.

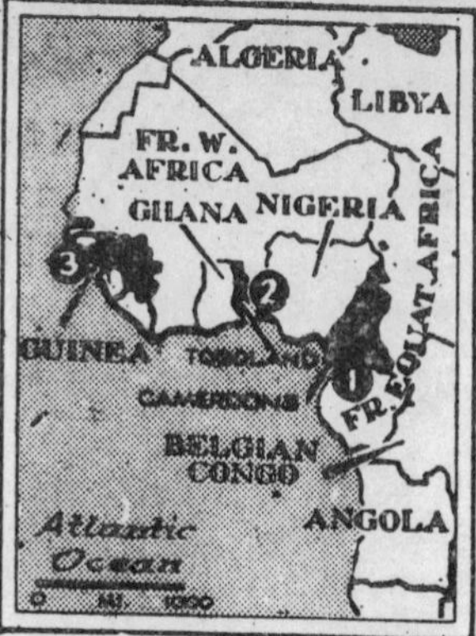

The New York Times Oct. 20, 1958

INDEPENDENCE OFFER: France has told the Cameroons (1) that it may have independence. Togoland (2) has received a pledge of independence, and Guinea (3) already has its freedom.

October 20, 1958

Senegal to Become Autonomous And Enter French Community

3d of African Territories to Take Step—Plans Ties to Proposed Federation

Special to The New York Times.

PARIS, Nov. 25—Senegal, in French West Africa, decided today to enter the French Overseas Community as an autonomous republic.

It was the third territory to take the step among seventeen that approved the French Constitution last September. The others were Madagascar and the French Sudan. The remaining territories are expected to follow suit.

Autonomy was approved by the Territorial Assembly at Saint-Louis. Senegal also plans to adhere to the prospective federation of former colonies in West Africa.

Under a resolution that it adopted, the Territorial Assembly became a Constituent Assembly charged with drawing up a Constitution for the new state along republican lines. It also will study and adopt a federal constitution in agreement with the other former territories and will establish organic laws.

The New York Times Nov. 26, 1958

Senegal (shaded) will be republic in French Community.

Dia Outlines Plans

Mamadou Dia, head of the Senegalese Government, outlined plans for the new state in a radio address. He asserted that tasks ahead would be accomplished in close association and friendship with France.

Senegal, situated on the Atlantic coast, was explored first by Portuguese navigators, then by the French, English and Dutch. The first French settlement was founded about 1626.

Senegal is 80,600 square miles in area and has a population of more than 2,000,000. Saint-Louis is the captial, but Dakar is the principal city. The biggest crop is peanuts.

November 26, 1958

4 AFRICAN AREAS ALTER FRENCH TIE

Chad, Gabon, Mauritania, Middle Congo Join Overseas Community as Republics

By W. GRANGER BLAIR

Special to The New York Times.

PARIS, Nov. 28—Four more former territories elected today to join the New French Overseas Community as autonomous republics.

Three of the new states are Gabon, Chad and the Middle Congo in French Equatorial Africa. The other is Mauritania in French West Africa.

Their entrance into the French Overseas Community, established by the Constitution for the Fifth French Republic, brings the total of territories to have taken such action so far to seven.

Autonomy within the community had been decided upon previously by Madagascar, French Sudan and Senegal.

As republics, two of the former territories have changed their names somewhat. The Middle Congo is to be known as the Republic of Congo and Mauritania as the Islamic Republic of Mauritania.

The decision to join the community was taken in each territory by the Territorial Assembly. It is expected that the assemblies of the remaining ten territories that approved the new Constitution last September will take similar action soon.

The rush of the French African territories to associate themselves with the new Overseas Community is not unexpected. But some observers note a quickening of pace since the announced intention of Guinea, the only French territory to vote for independence in the constitutional referendum, to unite with Ghana, a member of the British Commonwealth.

In Togoland, a French trusteeship that is to receive its independence in 1960, Premier Sylvanus Olympio expressed hope today that the "Ghana-Guinea union" would extend itself to other West African states. He also said he hoped that Togoland, which borders on Ghana, would be able to join an "eventual federation" of that nature.

A declaration like M. Olympio's and the message sent today to the President of Senegal by Sekou Touré, President of Guinea, are hardly likely to please the French since they run counter to French interests in Africa.

M. Touré congratulated President Mamadou Dia of neighboring Senegal on the birth of the Senegalese republic "to which Guinea is attached by geographic, historic, economic and cultural ties."

"We ardently hope for the development of your future institutions toward the rapid attainment of African unity and independence," M. Touré said, in a manner not calculated to improve his already troubled relations with France.

The New York Times Nov. 29, 1958

AFRICANS AFFILIATE: The seven former French territories shown by cross-hatching have chosen to remain in the French Overseas community as autonomous republics. Five (diagonal shading) have not yet decided. Only one, Guinea, shown in black, has voted for independence.

Chad Largest of Group

The biggest of the French territories that acted today is Chad, with an area of 496,000 square miles and a population of about 2,250,000. Much of its territory is semi-arid steppes, with livestock and cotton as important products. It came under French control late in the nineteenth century.

Gabon and Middle Congo, both of which touch on the Atlantic Ocean, came under French control late in the last century.

Gabon, with its major product, wood from its dense tropical forests, has a population of about 420,000 and an area of 103,000 square miles. Middle Congo, a producer of wood, minerals, rubber, tobacco and bananas, has a population of 700,000 and an area of 132,000 square miles.

Mauritania, a vast desert in the western Sahara, became French at the turn of the century. Its population is about 565,000 and its area 415,900 square miles. France and Morocco have quarreled over the northern boundaries of the territory.

November 29, 1958

8th African Area Joins French Union

Special to The New York Times.

PARIS, Dec. 1—The number of former territories to join the new French Overseas Community rose to eight today with the accession of Ubangi-Shari in French Equatorial Africa.

The Territorial Assembly at Bangui, capital of the territory, voted unanimously to turn the region into an internally autonomous republic linked to France under the new Constitution.

The Assembly gave it the name of Central African Republic. The French name chosen is "Centrafricain," a manufactured word.

Other former territories that already have joined the overseas community are Madagascar, French Sudan, Senegal, Gabon, Mauritania, Middle Congo and Chad. Nine other territories are expected to take action soon.

December 2, 1958

NEW REPUBLIC FORMED

Upper Volta Decides Status in the French Community

Special to The New York Times.

PARIS, Dec. 11—The French West African territory of Upper Volta became a republic within the new French overseas community today.

However, two other territories, the Comoro Islands and French Somaliland, decided not to change their status. Thus their relationship with Paris will be far closer administratively than is the case with the new internally autonomous republics.

The Upper Volta was the eleventh former territory of seventeen that approved the new French Constitution to set itself up as a republic. Four remaining territories have yet to decide what their future form of government within the community will be.

December 12, 1958

U. N. VOTES TO FREE FRENCH CAMEROONS

Special to The New York Times.

UNITED NATIONS, N. Y., March 13—The General Assembly voted tonight to grant independence to the French Cameroons next Jan. 1 without further elections.

The eighty-two-nation body also voted to hold plebiscites in the northern and southern sections of the British Cameroons as a step toward ending the trusteeship system there.

The Assembly thus upheld the decisions of its Trusteeship Committee, which in thirty-six sessions ending this afternoon debated the future of the two West African territories.

The vote on the French Cameroons was 56 to 0, with twenty-three abstentions. Three nations were absent. On the British Cameroons the vote was 56 to 0 with twetny-four abstentions and two nations absent.

The votes were taken after speakers for the Soviet bloc and some African states had objected again to the Trusteeship Committee's draft resolutions.

The Assembly also, by 58 votes out of 65 cast in a secret ballot, named Djalal Abdoh of Iran to supervise the United Nations plebiscites in the British Cameroons. The northern section of the British area must decide whether it wishes to unite with independent Nigeria as a member of the Commonwealth. The southern section may decide to become independent, to join the French Cameroons or to retain the trusteeship system.

March 14, 1959

2 NEW REPUBLICS SET

Dahomey and Ivory Coast Join African Community

Special to The New York Times.

PARIS, Dec. 4—Dahomey and the Ivory Coast, both in French West Africa, became today the ninth and tenth former territories today to join the new French Overseas Community as republics.

The action was taken by territorial assemblies in Porto-Novo, capital of Dahomey, and Abidjan, capital of the Ivory Coast.

The new republics will be internally autonomous although closely linked to France under the new Constitution. Other territories that have joined the community as repubilcs are Madagascar, the French Sudan, Gabon, Mauritania, Middle Congo, Chad and Ubangi-Shari.

December 5, 1958

WEST AFRICANS JOIN IN LINK TO FRANCE

PARIS, Jan. 17 (AP)—Four territories of France in West Africa today took a step toward more control of their own affairs but still decided to remain within President Charles de Gaulle's now French Community.

Dahomey, Upper Volta, Senegal and French Sudan voted to form a federation and named it "Mali" after the ancient Negro empire that stretched from the coast of Guinea to the deserts of the Sudan six centuries ago.

They made their decision in a Constituent Assembly at Dakar, capital of French West Africa. They had already joined in an economic federation. Now the four autonomous republics within the French Community will rule all their internal affairs from Dakar, with France still in control of defense, foreign affairs and finance.

Three other territories in French West Africa—which has 15,000,000 inhabitants—did not send delegates to the Dakar meeting. They were Niger, the Ivory Coast and Mauritania.

Guinea, the other territory in French West Africa, voted for complete independence from France in last September's constitutional referendum.

January 18, 1959

SUDDEN FREEDOM TROUBLES AFRICA

Tribal Strife Marks New Nations That Still Lack a Sense of Nationhood

By THOMAS F. BRADY

Special to The New York Times.

BRAZZAVILLE, Congo Republic, March 10—Nationalism has hardly begun to replace tribalism in Equatorial Africa yet self-government is here.

In French West Africa nationalism had reached the stage of mounting agitation when Gen. Charles de Gaulle established his community of autonomous states at the end of last year.

But here, in more backward Equatorial Africa, the problem is to create enough national cohesion to make internal autonomy work.

To have kept the Equatorial Africans at a lower level of emancipation than the West Africans would have been dangerous for French authority. But the fact that they obtained self-government before they demanded it has now created a danger for the Africans themselves.

The uneasy peace that lies over this former capital of French Equatorial Africa, after the killings of last month, is regarded by most observers as an indication of the continuing need for French "arbitration" in politics here.

Of the four territories of French Equatorial Africa, now autonomous republics, only the comparatively rich and developed Gabon appears to be wholly stable.

Its government is pro-French, but the term has only a relative significance here, because there are no anti-French leaders or parties of any significance in Equatorial Africa. Every important political group campaigned last fall for a yes vote in the referendum and thus for continued association with France.

The instabilities are internal. Chad, biggest and most populous of the former territories, is divided between Arabized Moslems in the north and Christians and animists in the south.

Barthelemy Boganda, Premier of the Central African Republic (formerly Ubangi-Shari), a veteran reformer and once a subversive in French eyes, appears to be securely in the saddle in his territory. His Opposition, led by young Socialist intellectuals educated in France, accuses him of having turned bourgeois.

His Movement for the Social Evolution of Black Africa party has passed election laws that virtually assure a one-party legislature. Even now he has a top-heavy majority.

The risk is that the frustrated young élite of the small Opposition will turn violently subversive, some observers suggest.

Here in the Congo Republic tribal politics have set the north and south against each other. Last month Jacques Opangault's African Socialists—or, to give them a tribal name, M'Bochis—and Premier Fulbert

Youlou's Democratic Unionists, or Balalis, spent three days killing each other.

When the French Army moved into Poto Pote—at M. Youlou's written request—to separate the antagonists, not a shot had to be fired. At least 103 persons had been killed, but not a single European had been touched. Since then Africans have tended to criticize the French administration for not acting sooner and more vigorously.

Premier Youlou has promised to hold elections, which may or may not confirm the tenuous majority he holds in the legislature. He has proposed to hold a referendum, in the north before the elections, to permit his opponent's stronghold to secede and join Boganda. M. Opangault is in jail awaiting trial on charges of fomenting violence.

March 21, 1959

2 AFRICAN STATES SEEKING FREEDOM

Malagasy Republic Obtains Paris' Approval—Dahomey Makes Similar Request

Special to The New York Times.

PARIS, Dec. 20—Two more autonomous states of the French Community are following the African Republics of Senegal and Sudan toward independence.

Philibert Tsiranana, President of the Malagasy Republic (Madagascar), said here today that France had agreed to independence for his country. He reported that Dahomey also had asked President Charles de Gaulle for full sovereignty.

The President of the Malagasy Republic, in a statement at the airport on his way home to Madagascar, said he had obtained French approval during a week of talks here with members of the Government and President de Gaulle.

In making his statement, M. Tsiranana emphasized Madagascar did not want "to break with the community." This point of view is shared not only by Paris but also by other member states. What is expected to develop, therefore, is a French version of the British Commonwealth.

M. Tsiranana said he probably would return to Paris in January to begin negotiations with France that eventually would lead to the transfer to individual states of those powers now largely held by France in the direction of community affairs.

A week ago, when President de Gaulle and African leaders attended a meeting of the Executive Council of the French Community at Saint-Louis in Senegal, he promised independence to the Federation of Mali, made up of Senegal and Sudan.

Negotiations on the transfer of powers with the Mali states are scheduled to open here in January.

One of the principal pressures on France by her African partners has grown out of the desire of the young republics to have their own diplomatic representation at the United Nations and in states outside the community.

Thus it is that four out of eleven new African republics, established slightly more than a year ago with the approval of the Constitution of the Fifth Republic, are well on the road to full control over their own affairs.

Originally this was not General de Gaulle's conception of how the community would evolve. But now it is clear that he believes the best way to maintain solid links with former French territories is to accede to their aspirations rather than risk an explosion such as broke out in Algeria five years ago.

December 21, 1959

FEDERATION OF MALI GAINS INDEPENDENCE

DAKAR, Senegal, Monday, June 20 (AP)—A skyrocket arched high over the Federal Assembly Building and exploded in a burst of fire at midnight last night to signal the independence of the Mali Federation, the latest of the African territories to become a sovereign nation.

Although Mali is casting off the last vestiges of official control by France, she will remain within the French Community and retain close economic ties with Paris.

The Mali Federation unites Senegal and Sudan in a country two and one-half times the size of France but with a population of only six million. Sudan is more than five times as big as Senegal.

Dakar, the capital of Senegal, will also be the capital of the new Federation. Premier Modibo Keita of Sudan will be President of the Federation and Premier Mamadou Dia of Senegal will be Vice President.

June 20, 1960

4 AFRICAN STATES ATTAIN FREEDOM

France Gives Independence to Ivory Coast, Niger, Dahomey and Volta

By W. GRANGER BLAIR
Special to The New York Times.

PARIS, July 11—Four West African autonomous republics in the French Community today received a pledge of full independence from the French Government.

Accords giving complete sovereignty to the Ivory Coast, Niger, Dahomey and Voltaic Republics were signed this evening by leaders of the four African republics and Premier Michel Debré at the Hôtel Matignon, the Premier's official residence.

It is expected that the formal proclamations of independence by the four states, which are grouped into what is known as the Council of the Entente, will take place the first week in August, after the ratification of the accords by the French and African Parliaments.

At the close of the signing ceremony, Hammani Diori, Premier of Niger and president of the Council of the Entente, said:

"Today is a solemn day for a France faithful to its ideal of liberty, equality and fraternity. It is equally a great day for the four states of the Council of the Entente, which offer their gratitude to France."

M. Diori asserted that it was his belief that today's step in the evolution of the French Community was leading to "the constitution of a great ensemble, based on the liberty and equality of the peoples of Africa and of France."

Premier Debré also spoke in warm words of cordiality between France and members of the Community. But he warned the African states of dangers from within and without to their democratic development.

There are private ambitions loose on the African continent and in this perspective cooperation between France and the African states. [in the Community] takes on a significance unlike anything that has occurred over the past centuries." M. DeBré said.

Sovereign Members Growing

With today's action and the virtually certain approval of the independence agreements by the Parliaments, the number of autonomous republics in the Community to achieve full sovereignty soon will increase to seven.

Already independent are the Malagasy Republic (Madagascar), of the Eastern coast of Africa, and the Mali Federation, made up of Senegal and Sudan in West Africa. Soon to follow the Council of the Entente into independence are the Chad, Congo, Gabon and Central African Republicans, whose leaders are now in Paris negotiating with the French Government.

Next year, when the West African republic of Mauritania becomes independent in accordance with the pledge given by President De Gaule, all twelve African republics in the Community will be sovereign and equal to France.

The negotiations between the leaders of the Council of the Entente and French officials began last week. The fourt states in the Council had demanded and received their independence first. Once their candidacy has been presented to the United Nations under French sponsorship, the Council members are expected to negotiate cooperative accords in such fields as defensce, economic development and finance.

July 12, 1960

3 More Nations Gain Freedom Through Pacts Signed by France

Congo, Central African and Chad Republics Are Given Sovereignty in Paris

By W. GRANGER BLAIR
Special to The New York Times.

PARIS, July 12—The rush to freedom in the French Community continued today as three more autonomous African republics signed independencet accords with the French Government.

The formal designation of the Congo, Chad and Central African Republics as independent states brought to seven the number of African members of the Community to be granted full sovereignty in the last twenty-four hours.

The republics that received their independence today are grouped into what is known as the Union of Central African Republics. Yesterday independence was pledged to thet Council of the Entente, which is composed of the Ivory Coast, Niger, Dahomey and Voltaic Republics in West Africa.

Besides signing independence accords with Premier Michel Debré of France, the leaders of the Congo, Chad and Central African Republics also initialed cooperation agreements with France.

Ratification Is Required

When the independence accords have been ratified by the French Parliament and the legislative Assemblies of the Union Republics, the three new states will proclaim their independence.

The republics making up the Council of the Entente are expected to proclaim their independence the first week in August. It seems likely that the Union republics will follow suit soon after.

France has agreed to support the seven republics in their candidacy for membership in the United Nations as she has done in the case of the already independent Malagasy Republic (Madagascar) and Mali Federation, made up of Senegal and Sudan.

A note of satisfaction over the way France has shepherded her former African territories toward complete sovereignty was sounded this evening in Premier Debré's remarks at the close of the formal ceremonies at the Hotel Matignon, the Premier's official residence.

"Very soon you will be at the United Nations," the Premier said. "And you can demonstrate more than other African states, without any doubt, how far you have come to a high degree of political maturity when you take your place at that immense table where all the nations of the world are represented."

Premier Calls For Unity

As he did yesterday before the leaders of the Council of the Entente, M. Debré warned the leaders of the Union of Central African Republics of difficulties and dangers that lie ahead for the young African states.

The New York Times July 13, 1960

Independence is set for the Chad Republic (1), the Central African Republic (2) and the Congo Republic.

He asserted that the African states were directly threatened by an "external ambition" that views the continent "without any desire to concern itself with the fate of Africans."

Africa is also threatened, he said, by internal subversion, which "far from aiding the progress of men and states, pushes the one to ruin and the other to slavery."

"In this effort to resist both external threats and subversive dangers, union is necessary," M. Debré asserted.

Premier David Dacko of the Central African Republic replied that in gratitude for what France had done for her former African possessions "we will remain faithful to her and we will always remain faithful to the Community."

"Our independence is now complete and we will know how to meet our obligations," President Fulbert Youlou of the Congo Republic said.

Premier François Tombalbaye of the Chad Republic said that France had spent fifteen years teaching her African possessions a sense of public affairs.

"The results are fruitful," M. Tombalbaye said. "It [the Chad Republic] will know how to remain faithful to its friendships."

Out of the Community grouping France and twelve African republics, ten of the African members are now either fully independent or have concluded independence accords.

The Central African Republic of Gabon, now negotiating sovereignty and cooperation agreements here, probably will receive its independence in a few days. The Republic of Mauritania in West Africa is expected to become independent next year.

July 13, 1960

Gabon Is Granted Sovereignty; Remains in French Community

Debre Hails the 11th African Republic Made Free Under Paris Accords in 1960

By W. GRANGER BLAIR
Special to The New York Times.

PARIS, July 15—The Republic of Gabon became today the eighth autonomous African state in the French Community to be granted full sovereignty by the French Government this week.

Accords giving independence to Gabon were signed this afternoon by Premiers Michel Debré of France and Leon M'ba of Gabon. At the same time, the two leaders initialed agreements for cooperation during a brief ceremony at the Hotel Matignon, the French Premier's official residence.

Premier M'ba warmly expressed his gratitude to France, President de Gaulle and the Government of M. Debré. Then he turned to the French Premier and declared solemnly:

"You can count on Gabon's remaining with France for better or worse."

M. Debré asserted that in "the immense African continent, which is undergoing such change," Gabon can place herself at the forefront of the new African states.

Eleven Are Independent

With the accession of Gabon to full sovereignty, eleven of the twelve African republics that form the Community with France have become independent or have completed accords to that end in the last ten days.

The one remaining Community member, which has yet to open independence negotiations in Paris, is the Republic of Mauritania, in West Africa. It is expected to attain complete sovereignty early next year.

Last Monday, the French Government granted independence to the Council of the Entente, made up of the Ivory Coast, Niger, Dahomey and Voltaic Republics in West Africa. The next day independence accords were signed with the Union of Central African Republics, composed of the Chad, Congo and Central African Republics.

Although Gabon is geographically and economically linked to the Union of Central African Republics, Gabonese leaders preferred to negotiate independence and cooperation agreements separately. Gabon, like the Union and Entente republics, will be offered by France for admission to the United Nations next fall.

The Malagasy Republic (Madagascar), off the eastern coast of Africa, and the Mali Federation, made up of the West African republics of Senegal and Sudan, were granted independence in March.

July 16, 1960

De Gaulle Promises Mauritania Freedom Nov. 28

Advances Independence for West African Republic in Talk With Its Premier

By W. GRANGER BLAIR
Special to The New York Times.

PARIS, July 28—President de Gaulle has pledged that the autonomous Republic of Mauritania, in French West Africa on the Atlantic, shall have its independence next Nov. 28.

The President's promise of full sovereignty for the last of the twelve African republics in the French Community to seek it came at the end of an unobtrusive two-day visit to Paris by the Mauritanian Premier, Moktar Ould Daddah.

While the spotlight was on the just completed state visit of Premier Ahmadou Ahidjo of the Republic of Cameroon, the Mauritanian Premier was quietly discussing independence for his country with President de Gaulle and other Government officials.

The decision to grant sovereignty to Mauritania in November represented an advance in the original time schedule. M. Ould Daddah some time ago requested and received French approval of independence for early next year.

The Mauritanian Premier is expected to return to Paris in the fall to open negotiations for independence. Cooperation accords in the defense, economic aid and cultural fields will be drawn up at the same time.

Four months ago the twelve African republics in the French Community were autonomous states tightly linked to and dominated by Paris. Since that date full sovereignty has been granted or promised to all twelve.

With the decision to give full sovereignty to Mauritania this year instead of next, the amazingly swift evolution of the Community will have been completed in eight months.

Although the African republics remain heavily dependent on France for technical and financial assistance, the Community is in the process of being transformed into a juridically equal partnership of states similar to the British Commonwealth.

Most of the African leaders who have come to Paris seeking independence have credited the orderly and democratic transformation to the foresight of General de Gaulle, who, as far back as 1944, promised the colonies that France would lead them to self-management of their affairs.

July 29, 1960

PARIS RECOGNIZES SENEGAL REPUBLIC

Step, Marking End of Mali, Raises Questions for French Community and U. N.

By W. GRANGER BLAIR

Special to The New York Times.

PARIS, Sept. 11—France officially recognized the West African Republic of Senegal today as an independent state.

The action served formally to end the Federation of Mali, which, until Aug. 20, had united Senegal with the neighboring Republic of Sudan.

A communiqué from the office of Premier Michel Debré "took note of the independence of Senegal." It further stated that France would recommend the admission of Senegal to the United Nations.

Since the secession of Senegal, Premier Modibo Keita of Sudan had insisted that Mali was a still going concern. Mr. Keita was also Premier of Mali. Furthermore, the United Nations has two candidacies to deal with, one from Mali and the one from Senegal.

Problem of the Community

More important, from France's standpoint, is what the consequences of the day's act may be on the solidarity of the French Community, the not clearly defined union of states that once made up France's colonial empire.

Both Senegal and Sudan are members of the Community as the result of accords signed with France last April. Since conflicts of interest split the Mali union, French officials have expressed fear that Sudan might break with the Community and drift into the orbit of the Lefist-oriented Republic of Guinea. Guinea was the only former French colony in Africa to break with Paris two years ago when the Community was formed. Since then, Premier Sékou Touré of Guinea has developed close relations with the Soviet Union and Communist China.

The communiqué from Premier Debre's office said France's efforts to mediate the Senegal-Sudan quarrel had failed. It expressed a willingness on the part of France to do all possible to bring about a "free regrouping" of the two African states.

The decision to recognize Senegal's independence was a logical outgrowth of President de Gaulle's remarks at last Monday's news conference when he stated that Senegal had the same right to leave the Mali Federation as it had to form a part of Mali in the first place.

As to the United Nations, when the Mali union was proclaimed as an independent entity last June, France sponsored the entrance of the Federation of Mali, not each republic separately, into the world organization. That sponsorship would now presumably be canceled.

September 12, 1960

AFRICA CHANGES, RED-TAPE DOESN'T

Immigration Controls Rigid, Air Traveler Discovers—New V. I. P.'s Created

By PAUL HOFMANN

Special to The New York Times.

PORT GENTIL, Gabon Republic, Oct. 8.—A journey across equatorial Africa exposes the traveler to some of the "winds of change" that are sweeping this continent. And the "winds" blow plenty of official questionnaires his way.

From the center of Lagos progress to Ikeja Airport is cumbersome because the road is thronged with bicycles and mammywagons—rickety trucks jammed with Africans in gaudy dresses seated on wooden boards. The two conveyances are rapidly opening up the back country, cutting tribal bonds and creating a new mobile city-oriented West African society.

The bunting and decorations of Nigeria's independence celebration last Oct. 1 are going to shreds and the capital's festering slums are again bared in their ugliness.

A Madison Avenue Touch

Huge billboards advertise soft drinks and department stores picturing satisfied clients as athletic young Africans with self-assured smiles. On the edge of a teeming suburban shantytown a new drive-in bank that might stand in New England caters to a couple of Nigerians in identical German Mercedes.

At the airport a group of turbaned Moslems gaze toward the east and bow deeply in their prayers. The bartender expertly trades dollars and francs against Nigerian pounds and a souvenir vendor peddles stuffed baby crocodiles.

The aircraft is a battered DC-4 that once a week flies down the Gulf of Guinea. The plane is devoid of hatracks and other amenities and a section of seats has been removed to make space for livestock in an enclosure.

During the bumpy flight through thick banks of humid vapor a French-speaking African points at a peak suddenly visble in a hole in the clouds—Mount Cameroon, a 13,370-foot volcano.

Also on board are two African mothers in bright tribal costumes with a swarm of children, a missionary and a couple of American school mistresses who write feverishly in notebooks embossed "My Trip."

An Africa-wise travel companion jokes: "In Douala be careful not to be fired at in the airport bus and at the hotel be sure to shake your bedclothes before you go to sleep. You know, snakes."

Curfew Is Imposed

Douala, in the state of Cameroon, is a town with a 10 P. M.-to-dawn curfew. Bush terorism preceded and followed independence last Jan. 1. Immigration control is rigorous even for transit passengers. The weary African traveler cannot help thinking that Stanley at least did not have to fill in so many forms.

A group of five assertive young Africans in blue serge suits that are obviously too hot for the tropical evening cut into the line of debarking passengers without explanation and are cleared at once. They are an official delegation, one of the many traveling this continent these days.

The Douala hotel is air-conditioned, snakefree and expensive. In the fifth floor dining room a party of European residents, the men in white dinner jackets, finish off Chateau-Briand steaks washed down with French wine. The Europeans are eager to get home before 10 P. M.

The pre-dawn hour finds the hotel wide awake, with travelers scrambling to catch another plane under another tropical downpour. Customs, health and police controls are as stringent as the night before. Again a blue-suited African in his early twenties is accorded V.I.P. treatment. He is the Minister of Public Works of one of the new African Republics.

The airliner from Paris is disgorging large European families returning to Africa after vacations, a few taciturn Belgians and more African delegates.

New passengers going aboard at Douala are informed by the hostess that they will cross the equator at 9:57 A.M. At 9:57 one stares wistfully into the Atlantic Ocean below and thinks of gay shipboard parties that used to be held when one sailed over the equator.

Port Gentil looks ungentle under a thunderstorm at the edge of a tropical rain forest. Three earnest Americans fill in more questionnaires and wait for the small plane that will fly them over gorilla and hippopotamus country to Lambaréné, where they hope to see Dr. Albert Schweitzer.

The other passengers re-embark for Brazzaville and discuss how to get into Leopoldville across the Congo without a visa. The few Belgians aboard remain silent.

October 9, 1960

Ruanda Tribal War Intensified As Africans Struggle for Power

300 Killed in 2 Months—Bahutu Press Political Advantage as September Vote Nears in U.N.-Guided Area

By DAVID HALBERSTAM

Special to The New York Times.

ASTRIDA, Ruanda-Urundi, Sept. 2—Fierce conflict has caused about 300 deaths in the last two months in this overpopulated and impoverished country, where independence is eagerly awaited.

The conflict is not between Africans and whites but between Africans—between the intelligent, aristocratic Watusi and the numerically superior but long suppressed Bahutu.

It is the dry season here and the Africans are nervous and tense in this United Nations trusteeship that has been under Belgian mandate since World War I.

On Sept. 25 the people will vote in a legislative election by casting pieces of colored paper. The election was ordered by the General Assembly of the United Nations April 21. The Assembly called also for a United Nations commission to oversee the elections and for a referendum in Ruanda to decide whether to retain the Mwami (King.)

It is this democratic election that has provoked a bloody struggle in Ruanda.

There are two powerful forces at work here. There is first, as in the rest of Africa, a growing unrest and desire for independence—the desire to take the country away from the white man, to run it better, to make everyone richer.

But in Ruanda an even more powerful force exists: The determination of the peasant Bahutu tribe to rise up against its Watusi oppressors.

The desire is to reverse the feudal past when the Watusi owned all the cattle and the land, and the Bahutu, serf to the Watusi, bowed to him, tilled his land, and could not break bread with him.

Social Revolution

This is also a social and economic revolution. The Bahutu, shorter, and darker than the Watusi, compose 85 per cent of the population. The Watusi, the Africans of King Solomon's mines, ruled here traditionally by self-proclaimed divine right and with the consent and aid first of German and later of Belgian colonial administrators. the Watusi composes about 14 per cent of the population.

The bush attacks go on constantly, day after day and night after night. The Bahutu want mostly to overwhelm the Watusi. The Watusi want to throw the country into such chaos that the United Nations will reject the election results—expected to give the Bahutu a sure victory.

The tribal war is a strange one. A night foray by two or three Watusi, traditionally the superior warriors, is answered the next day by a retaliatory attack by a larger Bahutu force. Huts are burned, men are beaten and killed and cattle are killed and stolen.

Only the Belgian paratroopers keep this from turning into a war of tribal extinction. The Belgians come out of the sky in helicopters, land on the hills where there are telltale burning huts and disarm the warriors of their spears, bows and arrows and stones.

These days are considered mild compared with what may happen in the days following the election. For the Bahutu nationalist party, the Parmehutu, seems sure to win, and there will be fewer Belgians here.

In November, 1959, there were bloody bush skirmishes between the two tribes that caused about 1,000 deaths and the political exile of many Watusi leaders, including the Mwami (King), who is still in exile.

This year the Bahutu staged a coup d'état and set up their own Ruanda government. This coup was accepted by the Belgians and rejected by the United Nations observers—a move that heightened friction between the United Nations and the Belgians.

There are about 50,000 Watusi refugees here—some in neighboring Bukava and some in neighboring Uganda. Many are expected to return to vote.

The open Belgian support of the little Bahutu against the taller Watusi, has caused criticism from United Nations quarters. The Belgians are touchy on this point.

"Always in the past they say to us, you always support the tall one against the little ones and so now we support the little ones and they are still mad at us," a Belgian administrator said.

The switching of sides has brought a paradox. On one hand the Pan-Africans and the Communists favor the monarchist Watusi. On the other hand, the Belgian colonialists are supporting the peasant Bahutu.

If the Belgians are somewhat sensitive about their role here, it is because Ruanda, like the adjoining territory of Urundi, is no great prize. The Belgian Government has for years been putting in more money than it has taken out. This year it will go about $20,000,000 into the red.

This is a small mountain country. It is overpopulated and it has too many cattle, which have great value as possessions and currency, but little value for milk and beef. There are about 2,500,000 people and about 500,000 head of cattle. There is a coffee crop, but this year it has been cut in half because of the unrest.

It is a land of poor people. Periodically the police go into the native market to try to collect taxes. Then there is a great stampede of men, women, children, dogs and goats. A few unfortunates are hauled off to jail. One of the reasons the tax money is needed is for a proposed expansion of the jail.

Urundi, to the south—which has virtually the same ethnic composition but less tribal conflict—is comparatively calm in the face of the coming elections.

Independence Next Year

Independence for Ruanda-Urundi, expected sometime in 1962, is almost certain to see the formation of two separate countries, linked at best by a common currency. There is no move for unity and the Bahutu-led nationalists of the north have no desire to form a government with the moderate, monarchist Watusi of the south.

The Watusi domination in Urundi has never been arrogant or complete. In Ruanda it was strict and overpowering.

The Watusi arrived in Ruanda about 400 years ago from the east and announced to the resident Bahutu that they were descended directly from heaven. They decreed it better and nobler to be tall and light than to be short and dark.

The Watusi held power through the manipulation of the cattle — ugly, long-horned animals valued as the chief currency of the nation. The Mwami owned all the cattle, which meant that the Watusi owned all the cattle. The only way a Bahutu could have any cattle was to become a servant of a Watusi.

September 3, 1961

RUANDA AUSTERE ON FREEDOM'S EVE

Officials and People Aware of Nation's Poverty

By DAVID HALBERSTAM

Special to The New York Times.

KIGALI, Ruanda - Urundi, June 28—In this tiny capital city high in the mountains, the impoverished people of Ruanda await Sunday and independence with an austerity program already in progress.

Ruanda, as she will be known after independence, when she will be separate from what will become Burundi, is an unbelievably poor country, and the Government and people know it. There is already what one diplomat calls "a mystique of austerity" here.

The outgoing Belgian regime gave the Rwanda Government here a sizable grant to spend on its independence celebrations, but the Government decided to use only a small part for the celebration—essentially a cold-plate buffet on Sunday— and put the rest aside for such things as new schools.

The ministers here drive small cars and dress in patched clothes—purposely, according to observers, who say they can afford to dress much better—in order to impress the people with the economic difficulties ahead.

The ministers draw salaries equivalent to about $100 a month, approximately a fifth of comparable salaries in neighboring Urundi and a tenth of those in the Congo.

The wife of Gregoire Kayibanda, the President and Premier, still works in the fields like other peasant women.

'More Work Than Ever'

Mr. Kayibanda, a quiet, cautious, strong man, told his people today how they should welcome independence Sunday.

"Our population is like a young couple getting married," he said. "We are adult now and we have been taught by the Belgians. On Sunday we should drink and celebrate and then the next day, like any young married couple, we should go to work, for there is more work than ever to do."

There has been so much uncertainty about the time of independence that the Ruanda Government had to print its program without giving the date. Only yesterday it sent messages to foreign countries asking dignitaries to attend the ceremonies.

Anything but the simplest ceremonies would seem out of place in this beautiful village of about 2,000 people 5,000 feet up. One of the smallest villages, it was selected as the capital because it was the traditional home of the Mwami, or King, of Ruanda, who was ousted when the present Government started its political and social revolution in 1957.

Until recently there were about 700 Europeans here, but political and economic uncertainty caused all but about 120 to depart. Their vacated premises will, in some cases, be put to new uses.

The butcher shop will become the United States Embassy, the grocery the Belgian Embassy and the chemist's shop the national bank.

The countryside is calm as independence approaches. There has been considerable fear of tribal violence from the ruling Bahutus and their former masters, the taller and more sophisticated Watusi. But most of the Watusi extremists are in exile and the Belgian troops are prepared to contain any attacks.

The Government, according to most predictions, is likely to be relatively moderate, pro-Belgian and pro-Western. Mr. Kayibanda, who is considered an astute and careful politician, has recently traveled up and down the countryside attempting to strengthen himself with the people, keep the local politicians under his command and replace the legend of the Mwami with his own legend.

The people he has been visiting are simple, cautious, reserved and extremely proud, used to working hard and long on the land. In the Kyniarwanda language, the word for strong is derived from the word for strong of leg.

June 29, 1962

Rwanda and Burundi Become Independent African Countries

By DAVID HALBERSTAM
Special to The New York Times.

USUMBURA, Burundi, Sunday, July 1 — At the stroke of midnight last night independence came to Rwanda and Burundi, two of the smallest, poorest and least-known territories on the African Continent.

Both countries are overpopulated and lack trained personnel. Together they have formed a land known as Ruanda-Urundi in Central Africa. Originally part of German East Africa, it has been administered by Belgium since 1916, for the last sixteen years as a United Nations trust territory.

Because the two countries are so poor, most Belgian and United Nations officials who have come here to discuss their independence have suggested that they form one country under a federal form of government.

Apparently the only people against the idea are the leaders of Rwanda and Burundi. These are the African names by which the independent states will be known.

The fact is that Rwanda does not like Burundi much and Burundi does not like Rwanda much. Each is deeply suspicious of the others aims and ambitions. Even though Belgium and the United Nations have convinced them to enter economic agreements on customs, telecommunications and foreign exchange, many sources here are extremely skeptical that the joint operation will work out.

Both countries—Rwanda with 2,500,000 people and Burundi with 2,000,000—have essentially

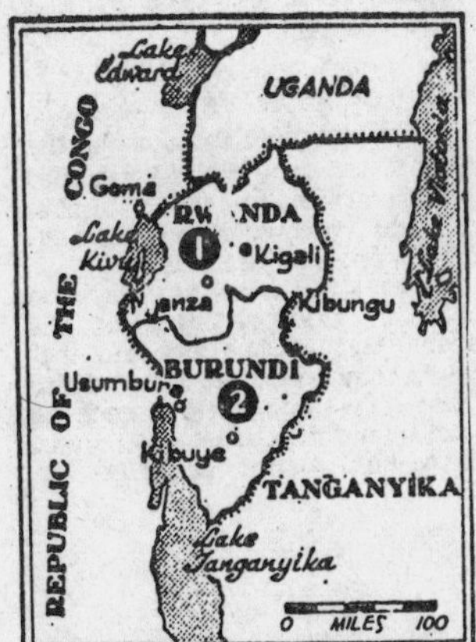

The New York Times July 1, 1962
Rwanda (1) and Burundi (2) became independent today.

the same ethnic composition, one of the most colorful in all Africa. 10 to 15 per cent of them are Watusi, a tall, thin, aristocratic people of Hamitic background; about 1 per cent are Batwa, or Pygmies, famed hunters and court jesters, and the rest Bahutu, mountain peasants of the Bantu type, shorter and less sophisticated than the Watusi.

On the other hand, the governments and ruling classes are strikingly different, and this accounts for unusual suspicion.

Rwanda is a republic headed by a President and Premier, where a recent social and political revolution by the Bahutu brought on widespread and violent tribal fighting—it is estimated that 5,000 Africans died—and ended with the Bahutu in the ascendancy over their former masters and nearly 150,000 Watusi in political exile.

The Kingdom of Burundi is a constitutional monarchy headed by the Mwami (King) Mwambutsa IV, an immensely popular sovereign who has so far not committed himself on the role his will play in the new Government.

Unlike Rwanda, the Watusi in Burundi did not rule so autocratically over the Bahutu, and there was less segregation and more intermarriage. The result is that there has been no social revolution, and the predominantly Watusi party and Government enjoy considerable Bahutu support.

On the eve of independence, and despite the execution today of the paid European assassin of Prince Rwagasore I, the Mwamisson, both countries are strikingly calm. In fact, some observers see the execution as an an attempt to head off angry mobs.

Violence Was Feared

Observers have feared violence in both countries: another tribal outbreak in Rwanda, and in Burundi, where the Government is essentially anti-Belgian, anti-European rioting of the kind that marked independence in the Congo two years ago.

In tiny Kigali, in Rwanda, workmen have spent the last two days making arches of triumph—wooden poles laced with pine boughs. Here workmen have painted the curbs and red, white and green flags have been made.

In addition, the Burundi radio has repeatedly broadcast messages in the African dialect and in French telling the African population that while there is to be fun and celebrating, no one is to molest Europeans because Europeans are friends.

Nevertheless, the Belgians, still sensitive about the Congo tragedy, are taking no chances. There has been a major exodus of Europeans, mostly Belgians, in the last couple of months. About three-fourths of the European population of about 8,000 in both countries have departed.

Belgian troops, unwanted in Burundi, will probably stay on indefinitely in Rwanda, where they will be a major safeguard against terrorist attacks by Watusi exiles.

July 1, 1962

BELGIANS FEEL U. N. HARMS CONGO AIMS

Withdraw From Commission Because They Say Own Plan Is Best for Africans

By ALBION ROSS

Special to THE NEW YORK TIMES.

LEOPOLDVILLE, The Belgian Congo, Aug. 20—Belgium's refusal to participate in the work of the United Nation's Committee on Information from Non-Self-Governing Territories is believed to be traceable to its program of gradual political and economic development of the Congo, the course of which she believes should not be changed.

The basic first principle of this program is that the 12,000,000 native Africans must become responsible citizens, capable of judging their own interests and producing more or less on a European level before self government or, eventually, autonomy or independence can be considered.

The negative side of this principle of determination is not to permit a native African political class and a native African political movement to emerge until the mass is educated to understand.

A second principle is that Belgium in the Congo is obligated to provide every opportunity for the native African to acquire skills and enter every branch of activity, and to improve his agriculture. This is known as the principle of the open door.

A third principle is that Belgium is obligated to provide increasing educational facilities, with emphasis first on primary education of the masses.

A fourth is that Belgium must create a native middle class, which will emerge into a status of economic and social equality with the white settler.

A fifth principle is that the white settler should not be permitted to play any major role in politics and should not be given the franchise until the native masses are sufficiently advanced also to use the franchise intelligently; accordingly, the ultimate authority must remain in Brussels, and the native African Crown and its Ministers as the final, decisive authority above both the white-skinned man and the black-skinned man in the Congo.

The Congo now has educational facilities for about 1,000,000 of the estimated 2,500,000 native African children of school age. It is steadily opening new schools. The number of middle schools is increasing. A program now is under way to increase the number of professional and trade schools.

The Congo Administration has rejected the French principle of education entirely in the French language and is using fourteen native languages in three primary grades and graduating children slowly into French. The explanation is that a completely French education would alienate the advanced African from the mass.

A high official of the Education Department has stated officially that the present policy of limited admittance of Africans to white schools will be gradually eased until separate education of races is done away with.

In industry and commerce, the practice is to replace white workers with Negroes and push the whites up to supervisory positions. Accordingly, too many colonists are not wanted, which is a sore point with the colonist group.

Governor General Leo Petillon, in his official annual discourse this year, was quite specific about the administration here. He held that United Nations intervention was a menace.

"We know these tendencies," he said. "They are inspired by ideologies which are generous at first glance but are utopian. They are built on impatience. They are calculated to incite us to do things, no matter how, in impatient haste. They are calculated to lead us to ignore the lessons of long experience, dearly acquired, for reasons of political opportunism."

August 21, 1953

NATIVES PROSPER IN BELGIAN CONGO

New Economic Middle Class Plays Increasing Role in Affairs of Colony

By LEONARD INGALLS

Special to The New York Times.

LEOPOLDVILLE, Belgian Congo, May 12—The emergence of a middle economic class among the Negroes in Leopoldville is regarded as one of the important recent phenomena in Africa.

An economic middle class among Negroes is virtually unknown elsewhere in Africa south of the Congo River. Belgians cite the development here as an example of their policy of encouraging native participation in all phases of community life.

Political rights for both whites and Negroes still are barred in the Belgian Congo. However, legislation is pending in Brussels to grant everyone the right to vote in municipal elections.

This plan is considered here to be the first step toward the eventual achievement of self-government for this colony.

The existence of an economic middle class of Negroes in Leopoldville became known last year. The distribution of income tax questionnaires disclosed the development.

It was found that there were 7,000 independent native business men here. They support 30,000 persons—one-tenth of the total native population of 300,000 in this capital of the Belgian Congo.

At least 100 of them reported earnings of more than $14,000 yearly and several hundred placed themselves in the $6,000 to $14,000 income group.

The largest native enterprises are furniture factories and retail stores, transportation and trucking concerns and various repair shops.

Of Leopoldville's 300,000 Africans only about 100 have qualified for complete freedom of the city. They have met educational qualifications, abandoned tribal ties and received character affidavits from white friends.

Several thousand natives have most of the privileges of the white part of the city but, because they have not surrendered their tribal connections such as land ownership, they must dwell in the native area. A curfew law closes the white's part of the city to natives after 10 P. M. and the native city to whites at the same hour.

Within the next five years Leopoldville's African population is expected to reach 500,000, with a proportionate increase in the size of the Negro middle class.

Much emphasis is given here to the development of natives as responsible and useful citizens.

There are several native business men's associations that have established their prestige and now work closely with white colonists' organizations to present the African point of view.

At present the Government is working on the elimination of legal obstacles to the ownership of land by natives. The inability to own land has prevented Negro business men from obtaining credit.

May 13, 1955

TRIBAL VOTE HIGH IN BELGIAN CONGO

Special to The New York Times.

LEOPOLDVILLE, Belgian Congo, Dec. 9—Tribal ties dominated African voting yesterday in Leopoldville, the first in the history of the Belgian Congo.

A tribal group known as Abako, which includes about half the Congolese population of the city, captured about 130 of the 170 seats for Negroes on their eight township councils.

Jean Tordeur, who has been appointed Mayor of the city, siad this tendency had been expected. It is considered possible that the Belgian Government may redress the tribal balance by its appointments to the City Council.

The voting, first for the Belgians here, as well as the Africans, passed without incident. There were no organized party tickets either for whites or Africans.

The only real surprise was the unexpected turnout of 40,-083 of the 46,957 Africans eligible to vote. Of 4,001 whites eligibles, 3,097 voted. Suffrage was open to all adult male Belgian subjects with residence qualifications.

December 10, 1957

15 DIE IN RIOTING IN BELGIAN CONGO

Mobs Loot and Burn Shops —Troops Patrol Capital

By Reuters.

LEOPOLDVILLE, Belgian Congo, Jan. 5—African troops commanded by Belgian officers patrolled the African quarter of this city tonight after rioting that cost fifteen Negroes their lives and injured about 100.

A curfew, ordered this evening after twenty-four hours of sporadic looting and rioting, was enforced by armored cars and jeeps carrying soldiers armed with machine guns.

About twenty Europeans were among those treated in hospitals for injuries.

Three Africans died today when soldiers opened fire to check rioters in Leopoldville's main market place.

The trouble started Sunday evening after an African political meeting had been called off. The police said that at one time rioters were marching through the streets several thousand strong. Stores were looted.

A state of alert was declared today and soldiers were called in from Thysville, eighty miles away. Public meetings of more than five persons were banned and the Congo River ferry service between Leopoldville and Brazzaville, capital of French Equatorial Africa, was halted.

Many of the rioters are believed to have come from the 50,000 Congolese unemployed.

Earlier today angry crowds of Africans clashed with troops stationed across Boulevard Baudouin, which links the African with the European quarter. The Africans shouted anti-European slogans, the police said.

In some places, the police said, machine-gun fire was used to disperse the demonstrators.

Demonstrators piled up stones and signposts to form barricades in the Matete suburb on the road leading to the airport. European cars were stoned, the police said.

Also in Matete, the crowd burned books and maps in a new mission school, according to police reports.

Tonight the usually bustling Congo capital appeared deserted except for soldiers behind barbed-wire roadblocks.

Arthur Pinzi, African burgomaster of a suburb, attributed the disorders to "overhasty" action by the police.

M. Pinzi said he had been invited to address a meeting about a trip he had made to Belgium, but refused because he was not ready. This meeting had been organized by the Abako, the Association des Ressortissants du Bas Congo, an African nationalist group.

After his refusal, the meeting was canceled but the crowd refused to leave, M. Pinzi said. The police intervened and trouble broke out. Some police officers were injured, a police car was set on fire and shots were fired in the air.

January 6, 1959

BELGIUM PLEDGES CONGO SELF-RULE

Decree Stresses Universal Suffrage and Equality

By HARRY GILROY
Special to The New York Times.

BRUSSELS, Belgium, Jan. 13—The Belgian Government announced today measures aimed at organizing in the Congo "a democracy capable of exercising sovereignty and making decisions about its independence."

The declaration was prepared by Maurice van Hemelrijck, Minister of the Congo. He read it to the Senate and Premier Gaston Eyskens read it to the House of Representatives.

The Government made plain that during the evolution to self-rule in the Congo it intended to maintain order and to control administration in the interests of efficiency.

Emphasis was placed on the intention that "every vestige of racial discrimination will disappear in practice and from all written documents."

King Baudouin supported the declaration in a radio address today. He said:

"It is our firm resolve to lead the Congolese populations, without petty recriminations but also without undue haste, to independence in peace and prosperity."

A schedule of political developments projected for the next fourteen months contained the Belgian Government's basic offer to the Congolese people.

By the end of this year councils to deal with local problems in municipalities and in rural areas would be elected by universal suffrage.

Councils composed largely of members chosen by universal suffrage would be formed this year to govern the 135 territories into which the Congo is divided.

These elected councilors would select members for councils for the six provinces. These councils would be constituted by March 1, 1960. They would advise the provincial governors, who represent the Governor General of the Congo.

Later the elected local councilors would select the majority of the members of a general council. This body would replace the present Government Council, which advises the Governor General.

The new general council would be "a prelude to a House of Representatives," according to the plan.

A new legislative council would be formed as a fore-runner of a Senate. Each of the six provincial councils would designate two members to the legislative council.

While these political and administrative developments were going on, executive authorities at all levels would be assisted by committees from the local councils involved.

New consultative bodies would be set up immediately in the offices of the Governor General and of the provincial governors.

Unity Is Emphasized

The Belgian Government said the Congo had become unified by seventy-five years of collaboration between white and Negro populations. Now, it said, it is time to decentralize administration so the government can be brought closer to the people.

Attention was directed to a Belgian law, in force since Jan. 1, giving the Congolese the right of access to all levels of administration.

A promise was given that labor legislation would be improved and that meantime the basis of calculation for minimum pay would be revised.

The Government declaration said that "in the interests of the Belgian Congo and Belgium it is desirable that at the end of the evolution the two nations maintain bonds of association about which they can freely decide at that time."

The basic aim of the Belgian Government, according to the declaration, is the "well-being of the Congolese populations."

Their well-being, it added, is dependent on the development of the economy and this requires "a climate of order, confidence and work." The government said it would "do everything possible to prevent disturbance of this order."

A state of confidence is also necessary, the statement said, to assure the cooperation of technicians and "the help of Belgian and foreign capital, of which the Congo continues to be in need."

The statement said that development of education in all forms was "one of the essential elements of the emancipation of the Congo." It promised that in this respect no effort would be spared.

The New York Times Jan. 14, 1959
Belgium has announced steps to lead the Congo (shaded) to democracy.

The declaration said: "The Congolese people will prove its wisdom and maturity by undertaking with us the building of new structures and by conscientiously assuming the grave responsibilities of the future."

Belgium, it was said, "makes a solemn undertaking vis-a-vis the Congolese population," thereby reinforcing the "spirit of fraternity and collaboration" so that the two peoples can associate in freedom and help one another.

January 14, 1959

CONGO SETTLERS WARY OF CHANGE

Europeans Warn Belgium Against Undermining Their Position by 'Weak' Policy

By MILTON BRACKER
Special to The New York Times.

LEOPOLDVILLE, Belgian Congo, Feb. 4—Maurice van Hemelrijck, Belgian Minister for the Congo, has run into the first trouble of his tour of the territory. It arose not from Africans but from white settlers.

The Minister was visiting the eastern Congo city of Bukavu on Lake Kivu. Over the weekend the shops displayed flags at half-staff and on Monday they stayed closed.

Moreover, in show windows and on vehicules there was displayed a celebrated utterance by King Leopold II, made shortly before he was impelled to turn over the Congo, which he had ruled from 1885 to 1908, to the Belgian Government.

The King's remark can be translated idiomatically as "So long as they don't mess up this Congo for me." The settlers of Bukavu were in effect saying to the present Belgian Government, as represented by the traveling Minister, "All right, reform if you must, but don't mess up our situation in the Congo."

The flags at half-staff and the closed shops also represented a warning by the Europeans against any Government policy that might be regarded as displaying weakness in the face of rising African nationalism.

New Parties Organized

At the same time as M. van Hemelrijck was making his visit, a new party called the Congolese Rally was formed at Bukavu. It described itself as being in absolute opposition to the policy of "weakness and demagogy" that ended in the tragic riots at Leopoldville last month.

Another new party was formed at Stanleyville, calling itself the Congolese National Union. Like the Congolese Rally, it wants an "independent" Congo with continued ties to Belgium.

Before leaving Bukavu, M. van Hemelrijck declared that there was no question of Europeans' being forced to leave the Congo. He also said there was no question of Belgium's abdicating her authority until she was assured that chaos would not result.

He continued his trip to Stanleyville, where he was warmly received, and the air of tension surrounding his tour abated.

Both Government and diplomatic sources regard the new political groups as of doubtful long-range significance. Parties have been mushrooming here ever since the riots.

There appears to be no doubt, however, that the white settlers are determined to show resistance to what they fear may be a new Congo policy tending to lessen their economic and social position in relation to the African majority.

Europeans a Small Minority

The situation is somewhat parallel to that in Algeria, except that the European settlers here represent a much smaller proportion of the total population. There are about 13,000,000 people in the Congo; no more than 110,000 are white. Leopoldville has more than 350,000 inhabitants, of whom 17,000 are whites. There are only about 5,000 Europeans in the Bukavu area.

In this humid capital today, the authorities continued a round-up of Africans unable to show cards identifying them as regular residents. Those who do not belong here are being held in a transient camp pending their return to their home areas by truck, train and river boat.

The Government has attributed the recent troubles partly to the floating population, including unemployed adults, delinquency-prone adolescents and vagrants. The number of unemployed in Leopoldville is put at 22,000. The number has increased lately because of several factors, including a drop in prices for copper and farm products.

February 5, 1959

ELECTION NERVES UPSETTING CONGO

Fearful Legend and Threats of Boycott Stir Tension as First Vote Nears

By JOHN B. OAKES
Special to The New York Times.

LEOPOLDVILLE, Belgian Congo, Sept. 18—The coming December general elections are threatened with a boycott by two of the leading nationalist parties here.

If they carry out their threat, they could seriously undermine the first major effort of the Belgian Government to provide, through the ballot box, a guided outlet for the pressures rapidly pushing this colony toward political freedom.

But at the moment it is neither a political party nor an electoral candidate that is causing the most agitation among the nervous inhabitants of this simmering city on the banks of the Congo. It is, rather, "the white man with the light."

His name is Mundele Na Nwinda, and—according to the legend here—he prowls the streets at night with a lantern looking for little African children—to chop them up and sell them as mincemeat. He is everywhere and he is nowhere; yet he is powerful enough to cause bitter outbursts of hate and fear.

Can Label Misunderstood

The legend is said to have started during World War II when the picture of a happy young African decorated cans of American corned beef. It was misinterpreted by some Congolese as indicating the contents of the tin.

Why this gruesome fable has sprung up again no one can say; but it has resulted in several violent incidents in the last few weeks. Cars have been burned and stoned when rumors spread that an agent of Mundele Na Nwinda was about.

A few days ago a white clergyman was reported to have been almost mobbed for offering candy to children in a public square. The belief arose that he was poisoning them.

One result of the legend is that attendance at the United States Information Service's library here has fallen off markedly.

The tension seems likely to increase as the elections approach. The voting will be for members of 136 territorial councils. About two-thirds of the members will be selected by universal male suffrage, the remaining third to be appointed by the Belgian Government.

These territorial councils will, in turn, elect 60 per cent of the members of provincial councils. The provincial councils will select the members of a National Assembly. All this is to be accomplished by next spring.

Belgium Changes Policy

The creation of this structure of elected bodies represents a revolutionary change in the Belgian method of governing its huge and wealthy territory. Until recently all the emphasis had been on a kind of conomic and social paternalism with virtually no political freedom.

Suddenly — and the bloody Leopoldville riots of last January emphasized the need for speed—the Belgian Government recognized the pressures and moved to create political institutions reflecting, at least partly, the Africans' newly discovered political self-consciousness.

"Of course we're going too fast for ideal arrangements," mused a top Belgian official here, as he watched the broad Congo flow past his door. "But we're not working in a laboratory."

Fast as it is, the pace toward independence is not fast enough or complete enough for the more articulate African nationalists.

"This place up to a year ago was like a boat smoothly floating along the surface of a placid river," said one foreign observer. "Now all of a sudden it's come to the rapids, almost without warning; and in all the rocks and spray and whirlpools, you can't see where it's going."

With no political base from which to start, many African political parties have sprung up overnight. Few have clear programs or outstanding leaders. As in all the rest of Africa, tribalism is strong with no single coherent voice speaking for all or even most of the Africans.

Secession Threatened

In this southern part of the country, spokesmen of the dominant Bakongo tribe talk about creating their own state, if not independent then at least autonomous in a loose federal structure. This is much looser than the arrangement the Belgians and many of the Congolese of other tribes have in mind.

A Bakongo leader expressed his people's view:

"We aren't going to take part in the election, because it isn't complete, it isn't direct, and we have no confidence it will lead to a National Assembly. If we vote in assembly, we'd be voting for a trick expressly designed to deceive us."

The Africans of both the Abako party and the National Congolese Movement—the two principal nationalist groups—want nothing to do with the pyramidal structure the Belgians are belatedly trying to build up.

They demand instead the immediate creation of a provisional government for the express purpose of holding general elections to determine the future form of the state.

They are not worried about the fact that virtually the entire economy of the Congo, the entire civil service, the entire machinery of government is in European hands and that a sudden turnover in power would disrupt the community.

"We're ready for independence now," says Joseph Kasabuvu, nationalist leader who has served his time in jail.

Whether the Congo will develop into a unitary or a federal state is a burning question here. Yet the fact that it is heading for ultimate self-government in some form is recognized by the Belgians themselves.

The best-informed among the Belgians say that the recent shift in Ministers of the Congo, from the liberal Maurice van Hemelrijck to August de Schryver, will make no difference in the rate of progress to self-government.

A huge new gubernatorial palace is now being built by the Belgians in the best part of Leopoldville. Some unkind critics point to it and say with bitter irony: "They're building that for Kasabuvu."

October 11, 1959

TROOPS PUT DOWN CONGOLESE RIOTS

Belgians Report 20 Killed at Stanleyville—Leader of Africans Arrested

STANLEYVILLE, Belgian Congo, Nov. 1 (Reuters)—The security police restored calm today and arrested Patrice Lumumba, an African nationalist leader, after a hunt that touched off two days of rioting.

A Government statement today said twenty persons died in clashes Friday and yesterday when war-painted Africans fought with stones and spears against Belgian-led territorial troops and policemen using guns and tear gas bombs. Well-informed sources insisted the figure was actually between seventy and seventy-five, with more than 200 persons injured.

The area was reported "absolutely calm" today. But strongly reinforced policeman and military patrols were busy in the city and surrounding districts, dispersing groups of Africans and preventing pillaging.

The riots flared up Friday when the police first tried to arrest Mr. Lumumba, who was at a closed-door meeting of leaders of his Congolese National Movement in the African suburb of Mangoba.

He had failed to answer a summons to appear before the police to explain statements he made Thursday night at the wind-up of a convention in Stanleyville of his movement.

Mr. Lumumba had called for a nation-wide campaign of civil disobedience aimed at forcing Belgium to grant the territory immediate independence. He had ordered the Congolese not to cooperate with the Belgian administration and announced his movement would not take part in elections scheduled for December.

Observers said feelings among the 2,000 to 3,000 Africans who stood outside the convention hall had been whipped to a high pitch by Congolese national movement speakers.

The attempted arrest Friday of Mr. Lumumba, who escaped in a haze of tear gas and a welter of fighting bodies, "put the match to the powder keg," the observers said.

Africans fought with troops and policemen, attacked European cars, stoned many city buildngs and wrecked others.

On Saturday, the police fired on strong bands of Africans roaming the banks of the Congo River and broke up groups who were looting deserted buildings.

Official reports said many buildings had been burned and sacked, including social and education centers and other official buildings. Social workers living or working in African quarters have taken refuge in their homes or have asked for shelter in military camps.

Shortly before the announcement of Mr. Lumumba's arrest, political opponents in his own party called on him to come out of hiding and attend their three-day congress, which opened in Elizabethville today. Cyrille Adoula, elected president of the congress executive, said in a speech that the single aim of the group was immediate independence, but by "nonviolence."

November 2, 1959

CONGO MILITANTS CLAIMING VICTORY

By HOMER BIGART
Special to The New York Times.

LEOPOLDVILLE, Belgian Congo, Dec. 21—Militant Congolese nationalists today claimed a sweeping victory in the local elections yesterday.

Elated by the defeat of the moderate Party of National Progress in the major cities, the militant leaders were hopeful that a convention of radical parties hastily summoned to hammer out a united front program would assume new importance.

They want to confront King Bauduoin with minimum demands for swift independence when the Belgian monarch reaches Leopoldville Dec. 28 near the conclusion of his tour of the Congo, a Belgian colony.

Tribal rivalries and acute regionalism are major obstacles to the orderly development of an independent Congo. The convention starting Christmas Eve will try to prove that the Congolese are capable of unified political action.

The convention will be held in Kisantu, eighty miles south of Leopoldville, under the auspices of the Association of Bakongo People, known as Abako, the dominant political party of Leopoldville Province. Five other groups have been invited, including two rival factions of the National Congolese Movement, the only radical party with a following in all provinces.

Landu Nzeza, vice president of Abako, said the parties might agree to boycott the new roundtable conference with the Belgians scheduled for mid-January unless Brussels gave "an absolute formal guarantee of general elections with universal suffrage at the shortest possible date."

He also warned that Congolese party leaders must be invited to the roundtable meeting whether or not they participated in yesterday's elections. The Abako president, Joseph Kasavubu, had ordered his followers, mostly Bakongo tribesmen, to abstain from voting. Abako contends the election is invalid.

Only about 31 per cent of the eligible voters in the African communes of Leopoldville, the capital voted yesterday. Mr. Nzeza claimed this was a result of the boycott, calling it a "tremendous victory for Abako."

Even with the Abako boycott, the moderate Party of National Progress won only one of the city's thirteen communes. It had entered candidates in three communes.

Outside Leopoldville Province the Congolese Nationalist Movement claimed big victories. In Stanleyville the movement received 80 per cent of the vote.

Agence-France-Presse

ROYAL SURPRISE: King Baudoin arrived without advance notice Thursday in Stanleyville, Belgian Congo. There were demonstrations for him and for independence. A native ex-soldier is shown kissing his hand at airport.

December 22, 1959

5 CONGO PARTIES ASK LIBERTY NOW

Nationalist Leaders Open Congress to Form United Front Against Brussels

Special to The New York Times.

LEOPOLDVILLE, Belgian Congo, Dec. 25—Five nationalist parties called last night for "complete, immediate and unconditional independence" for the Belgian Congo.

The demand was voiced in Kisantu, seventy miles south of this capital, where the nationalists opened a congress to formulate Congolese claims and present a united front for the coming negotiations with Brussels.

The opening session was held in a modest African beer hall decorated with slogans for local stout. There were about 200 delegates from the Congo's fast-blossoming political parties.

In the chair was Joseph Kasavubu, president of the Association of the Lower Congo, the Abako. The strength of Abako has been confirmed by massive absentions in the recent municipal elections, which it boycotted

The vice chairman was Albert Kalondji, leader of one wing of the Congolese National Movement, which swept to victory in the municipal elections in the cities of Kasai Province. Also represented were the African Solidarity party, the Socialist People's party and Abazi, the party of an ethnical group of 1,000,000 in the Kwilu district.

The absence of the Lumumba wing of the Congolese National Movement, whose leader, Patrice Lumumba, is in jail, and of other invited nationalist parties showed that the goal of forming a united nationalist front was not yet attainable, because of the deep rifts between leaders and parties.

But the present coalition has a wide enough representation to lend weight to the independence claims it will probably present to King Baudouin, whose "study tour" through the Congo will bring him to Leopoldville Monday.

Shouts of "Long Live the King of Congo" greeted Mr. Kasavubu when he arrived yesterday in Kisantu. Disregarding heavy rains, a mass of Africans poured through the streets and surrounded his car, shouting "ruau" (their version of "roi," the French for king).

Belgian troops patrolling the town in jeeps kept at a discreet distance.

The opening session got under way with a speech by Mr. Kasavubu. The Abako leader laid down the line for the congress by an unequivocal call for independence.

He praised the "kind, courageous and Christian but misinformed Belgian people" and said the Congolese wanted to negotiate with Belgium as free and equals but also as friends.

He asked the Congolese to remain calm and disciplined in "these historical days" and avoid trouble and bloodshed.

The only party leader who did not echo Mr. Kasavubu's words was Alphonse Nguvulu, leader of the Socialist People's party, a small group of intellectuals. Mr. Nguvulu applied a Marxist analysis to the colonial situation. He said Africans were exploited economically as workers, politically as victims of colonial oppression and racially as blacks.

During the congress, which will end Sunday, Mr. Kasavubu is expected to urge Abako militants to be patient. They are demanding independence Jan. 1.

December 26, 1959

TRIBE WAR PERILS LIBERTY FOR CONGO

Barbaric Fighting Dismays Africans Who Seek Early Withdrawal by Belgians

By HOMER BIGART
Special to The New York Times.

MUTOTO STATION, Belgian Congo, Dec. 26—A barbaric civil war in the heart of the Belgian Congo may wreck Congolese plans for speedy independence.

The savagery of the fighting has upset even some militant nationalists, who are beginning to dread what might happen if the restraining influence of Belgian authority were suddenly lifted.

Equally macabre has been the discovery by Belgian authorities of the mass poisoning of scores of members of the Bushongo tribe, which has been neutral in the fighting.

The Belgians say investigations revealed that 226 tribesmen were poisoned during a recent series of tschipapa, or occult ceremonial trials in which whole villages participate. Drinking bouts are held in which the contents of some cups are poisoned. Those who receive them are presumed to have been guilty of some offense.

Old Customs Revived

The Belgians have outlawed tschipapa. But the agitation for independence apparently has encouraged the Bushongo to revert to old customs. Cynics believe that the tschipapa are rigged by witch doctors who slip poison into the cups of tribesmen of whom the chief wants to be rid.

The war, cruder and more horrible than the tschipapa, involves two closely related tribes, the Lulua and the Baluba.

They are wrestling for control of Kasai Province, which is fertile, well populated and the world's biggest producer of industrial diamonds. Here the aggressive Lulua are trying to cast out the more docile and more advanced Baluba.

King Baudouin of the Belgians, who is touring the Congo, arrived this morning in Luluabourg, the provincial capital. He received a dignified, restrained welcome from a city gravely threatened by violence.

Congolese troops with fixed bayonets lined the three-mile route from the airport to the city. The atmosphere was strained and abnormal.

Among the official welcomers was old King Lukangu of the Baluka tribe, who recently was questioned by the Belgian authorities in connection with the outbreak of ritual murders among the Bushongo. King Lukangu has been cleared of complicity and the Belgians say he has given help to the police.

The war between the Lulua and the Baluba is being fought with primitive spears, bush knives and arrows dipped in deadly poison. The Lulua are spurred on by naked women who brandish long wooden pot-stirrers, which they clack together overhead while chanting "Benyi baye kuabo." This means, in their Tshiluba dialect, "Strangers go home."

By "strangers," they mean the Baluba, whom they regard as ungrateful poor relations. The Lulua came to this region first. The Baluba arrived later.

Contact with the white man gave the Baluba an immense advantage over the Lulua, who remained in the forest. The Baluba acquired Western education, learned trades and got jobs in the provincial government.

Job Rivalry Causes Friction

Competition for jobs caused the first tribal friction. The Lulua, awakening from the torpor of a primitive culture, suddenly realized that the Baluba commanded all the strategic posts. Even the trucks that carried the Lulua's corn, peas, peanuts and cassava to Luluabourg were owned by the Baluba.

When the fever for independence spread to the Kasai a year ago, the Baluba, having evolved faster than the Lulua, enlisted in the Congolese National Movement. The Lulua, thoroughly alarmed at the prospect of being governed by their former slaves—the Baluba now outnumber the Lulua in many districts, including Luluabourg—held a council of war last August.

The Lulua King, Kalamba, gave an ultimatum to the Baluba: Withdraw eastward beyong the Lubilash River by the end of summer or be massacred. The Lubilash is a tributary of the Kasai River.

The Baluba ignored the ultimatum. In October, the Lulua warriors daubed their faces with white clay and soot and while the women clacked their spoons and marched up and down the village streets shouting, the men set out to burn, plunder and kill.

Mutoto Station, an American mission post of the Southern Presbyterian Church thirty-five miles northeast of Luluabourg, was in the midst of the fighting.

In the first outbreak, the Lulua succeeded in frightening the Baluba, who fled several villages without offering resistance. But as the element of surprise wore off, the Baluba sometimes elected to stay and fight. Occasionally they repelled

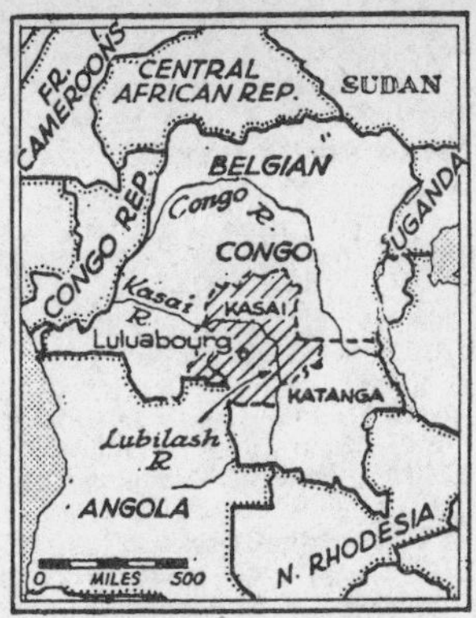

The New York Times Dec. 27, 1959

AREA OF TRIBAL WAR: The Lulua and Baluba tribes are fighting for control of Kasai Province (shaded) in Belgian Congo.

the Lulua, but usually they got the worst of it.

One can only guess at the casualties. The Belgians counted forty-six known dead in the province in October. After a November lull, there were renewed outbreaks, stimulated in part by political agitation attending the Dec. 10 election in Luluabourg, which the Baluba won.

Perhaps eighty persons have been killed. Terror grips a huge area, and the Luluabourg railway terminal is jammed every evening with Baluba refugees heading southeast for Katanga Province.

Two weeks ago the Mutoto mission was swamped with hysterical Baluba who streamed in with their goats and chickens, begging for protection. The missionaries were embarrassed because the Government policy discourages mass evacuation. But for the Baluba to remain in their villages would have meant wholesale slaughter.

The missionaries had only a few shotguns which they use to discourage snakes. Lights were kept burning all night for security and the next morning the Presbyterians got two trucks and carried the refugees to safe country east of Lake Munkamba.

Many Bodies Mutilated

The Baluba terror was understandable. The fighting had become nasty. Many of the dead were found beheaded and with their feet and hands severed.

Two days ago this correspondent visited a Lulua village chief, then crossed a four-mile-wide no man's land of abandoned Baluba country to hear a Baluba chief's version of the difficulties.

Chief Tshibata of the Lulua is a man of medium height, lean, with a thin, taut face and coldly arrogant eyes. He drinks much palm wine, but he seemed sober. Sitting outside his mud-and-reed hut, with the village elders standing about dressed in shabby Western clothing, he spoke with passionate bitterness of the Baluba.

"The Baluba must go," he said. "When they came to us originally, we took care of them, considered them our relatives. We even gave them dowry money to get married. When the state said no more slavery, we set them free. They mixed with the white men and got all the jobs. Our children couldn't find work.

"After all this, they no longer respected us. They called us wild people or little fish. They were very offensive.

"So one day we said: 'Enough, you must leave this land forever.' "

The visitor asked whether the chief wanted Congolese independence.

"Independence," he shouted with aversion. "That's one of the basic reasons for this fight. It is the Baluba who want independence. We want the white man to stay.

"We told the Baluba: If you want to chase the whites out, go back to your own country and chase them out. We want the whites to stay here and teach us."

The chief was not finished. "My final word," he announced, "the Baluba must go back across the Lulibash. Either they leave or we will have to kill them off."

Over in Baluba territory, Chief Tshikungu said the Lulua were jealous. Besides, he added, the Lulua were not the first settlers of the Kasai—"the pygmies were here first."

A mild-mannered man with a fat, bewildered face, the chief let his head men do most of the talking. A babble of confused counsel ensued.

"We came here because the white people needed us," one man cried. "The whites told us to settle here. It's up to them to say whether we go or stay."

"Now we are waiting instructions from Albert Kalonji," another shouted. M. Kalondji is a leader of the Congolese National Movement and a Baluba.

"We want independence," a youth insisted. "This doesn't mean the whites have to leave. We want to govern ourselves, but we want the whites to stay and protect us and give us work."

A warrior appeared and pranced about, ragged as a scarecrow. He brandished a knife and scowled ferociously. But the chief was not comforted.

"We want to live in peace but they keep attacking us," he said. "What shall we do?"

December 27, 1959

DOUBTS ARE AIRED BY CONGO CHIEFS

Tribal Heads Fear Power of Rising Party Leaders After Independence

By HARRY GILROY
Special to The New York Times.

BRUSSELS, Belgium, Feb. 5—Tribal chiefs of the Belgian Congo indicated today that they were dubious about a complete break with Belgium June 30 when the colony is to receive independence.

They also expressed misgivings about some political leaders who are coming to the fore.

A news conference was held by nineteen of the chiefs and their right-hand men attending the Belgian-Congolese round-table conference that is planning for the Congo's independence. The chiefs said that 80 per cent of the Congo people still lived under the rule of tribal chiefs.

They attacked a statement by Patrice Lumumba, president of one wing of the Congolese National Movement, that he was forming a syndicate of parties, including tribal chiefs.

Chiefs Get Support

A representative of the National Progress party, Ignace Kanga, supported the chiefs in warning against placing too much emphasis on new combinations formed by M. Lumumba and other leaders.

The Progress party is a Congo-wide group formed from twenty-seven smaller parties. It won the largest vote in the December elections and is classed in Brussels as a "moderate" party.

The chiefs gave the impression that they were a formidable force. Their general theme was that independence should be approached under peaceful conditions. Several expressed fear there would be trouble after independence.

Some chiefs denounced "political adventurers" who claimed to lead large parties. Several said they feared dictatorship might result when Belgium freed the Congo.

Chief Lwaka Bwanga from Kasai province, which is now under martial law because of tribal conflict, said he felt an election would not establish a firm enough control in that region to achieve peace.

Chiefs Strong in Rural Areas

The chiefs complained that the press tended to emphasize the views of the political parties, which are centered in the cities, but to ignore the views of tribal leaders, who have been conducting rural affairs for many years in concert with Belgian colonial officials.

Chief Luhina Mwenda-Munongo of Katanga province said that of 1,600,000 votes cast in the December elections, 1,300,000 came from rural areas, mostly ruled by the chiefs.

He said the chiefs were not opposed to independence or to economic development or social change. However, they feel they should play a major role in bringing their people up to the level of broad democratic institutions, he said.

He said that Belgium should probably have provided greater aid to the chiefs in their desire to see their people advance, but now he asked for continued cultural, scientific, administrative and economic assistance from Belgium.

He suggested that the person of King Baudouin might provide a basis for a personal union of Belgium and the Congo.

February 6, 1960

EUROPEANS QUIT CONGO PROVINCE

Flight Laid to Anxiety Over Independence—Mine Aide Holds Many Will Return

By HOM ; BIGART
Special to The New York Times.

ELISABETHVILLE, Belgian Congo, May 3 — A male nurse and a bankrupt trader are seeking to become the first African political boss of Katanga, the richest province of the Belgiar Congo, when the Congolese attain independence June 30.

Both are regarded as tolerant of Europeans and anxious to avoid racial tensions. This makes the nervous flight of Europeans from Katanga seem unreasonable. But as one Belgian put it: "Nobody knows what will happen."

The exodus has been exaggerated by newspapers in South Africa and Rhodesia, which have portrayed it as a stampede.

However, every outbound plane is fully booked. Normally about 3,000 of the 12,000 Europeans of Elisabethville go home to Belgium each summer, according to the local chamber of commerce, but generally vacation travel does not start until late June.

An official of the Union Minière du Haut Katanga, a huge copper mining company, explained the premature flow.

"This year many Europeans have advanced their annual leave in order to miss the Congolese elections late this month and the four-day independence feast starting June 30," he said. "They are afraid some drunken Congolese will make trouble. But very few are leaving for good. If the independence celebration passes quietly, and I'm sure it will, they will come pouring back."

He conceded that the Union Minière, which pays more than one-third of all the Congo's taxes, was having trouble signing young engineers in Brussels to three-year contracts here.

To bolster confidence in the future, the Union Minière has announced it will spend 1,000,000,000 francs ($20,800,000) a year for next twelve years on plant expansion. And the chamber of commerce, seeking to reassure whites, points out that racial animosity remains remarkably low despite the heady atmosphere of approaching freedom.

This seems true. A visitor from South Africa is amazed by the casual, friendly contacts between the races here. The only segregation is economic. If they have the price, Congolese can eat, drink and sleep at Elisabethville's leading hotel.

A few months ago, none of the Europeans had heard of the male nurse and the bankrupt trader now striving for political power. The nurse, Jason Senowe, heads a coalition of three tribal parties.

The former trader, Moise Tshombe, is president of the Conakat party, which represents other tribes.

The two are running neck and neck, according to European observers. Both are considered moderate. Both say they need the white man and want him to stay.

May 4, 1960

CONGO TRIBES WAR IN LEOPOLDVILLE

5 Slain in Street Fights With Spears and Machetes

By HOMER BIGART
Special to The New York Times.

LEOPOLDVILLE, Belgian Congo, May 13—This city's African quarter was put under a state of military occupation today following communal fighting. Five tribesmen were slain by machetes and spears.

Lulua and Baluba warriors, brandishing three-foot bush knives and primitive spears, gave the city four hours of chilling terror in the morning as they hunted each other out in streets and backyards of the African quarter. At 11 A. M. a conference of civil and military leaders decided to call on the army to assist the police in restoring order.

Anarchy Is Feared

Today's clash signaled the extension to Léopoldville of the bitter Lulua-Baluba tribal war that broke out in Kasai Province six months ago. It came only a day after Governor General Henri Cornelis warned that continued tribal fighting would produce a dictatorship after the Congo achieves independence June 30.

What frightens the 20,000 whites remaining in Léopoldville is not so much the specter of dictatorship as of anarchy. They believe that this is already threatened by another tribal war, between the Bakongo and Bayaka tribes. The latter are the dominant ethnic groups in Léopoldville Province.

Most whites and many Congolese would prefer even martial law to the present state of uneasiness. Earlier this week provincial Governor Jan-Baptist Bomans was relieved of his post after having resisted pressure for military rule.

The tiny Congolese Army of 25,000 Africans led by 1,000 Belgian officers could not maintain effective martial law throughout this vast colony, which is eighty times bigger than Belgium. It could only hope to maintain order in the key cities of Léopoldville, Elisabethville, Stanleyville, Coquilhatville, Bukavu and Luluabourg.

The Association of the Lower Congo, the Abako party of the Bakongo tribe, has been agitating for removal of the Belgian general commanding the army and his replacement by a general to be selected by the United Nations.

Today's fighting was the sharpest in Léopoldville since the riots of January, 1959, when the police fired on Abako mobs killing more than 100.

The state of military occupation proclaimed today is a degree less severe than a state of siege. It means that the army is alerted, with troops standing by police stations to assist in smashing riots.

A night curfew was put on the outlying commune of Matete, where trouble started at 5 A. M. A Lulua worker was set upon by Baluba and killed with machetes.

Later a Pepsi-Cola truck driven by a Baluba was halted by a revengeful Lulua mob in Kinshasa, two miles from the center of the city. The driver was slain by a spear.

Then Baluba warriors went on a rampage, driving Lulua from Kinshasa streets and setting fire to two Lulua houses.

Councilman's House Sacked

Their main target was the house of Sylvan Kabongo, a Lulua member of the Municipal Council. Finding him away—a notice on the door said in four languages "I receive nobody at midday"—the Baluba stormed into the house through broken windows, slashing legs off tables and arms off chairs and setting fire to bedding.

Waving their knives they approached two frightened overseas newsmen warning them against taking pictures.

A Baluba youth brandishing a knife, his face contorted with wrath, said his brother had been slain by Lulua and cried out that M. Kabongo was "the man who gave the orders to kill."

Some neutral Bakongo standing by were eager to blame the Belgians. "They wanted this to happen," they said. "They want trouble. The police sit in their cars and do nothing."

Police jeep patrols were observed, but the situation was out of hand. In near-by Bandalungwa a Lulua was stabbed to death. Toward noon a carload of Baluba was halted in Kinshasa by Lulua, who killed the driver and a passenger and wounded two others.

Late today the police set up road blocks searching all traffic and arresting passengers with machetes. They wore tear-gas goggles on their steel helmets and carried metal shields against spears and arrows.

White Elements Accused

Albert Kalonji, Congolese nationalist leader, said here yesterday that tribal fighting was fomented by white elements in the Congo and could be controlled easily after independence.

He said that Belgium was acting in good faith but that some of the officials and some of the settlers in the Congo "have prepared this far in advance."

M. Kalonji, who is a Baluba, said the Lulua tribes had been encouraged because they had not been punished for past violence. He said they had also been told that if they did not drive out the Balubas before independence it would be too late.

"Some Belgians are trying to create panic by all means," he said. "They are predicting the worst catastrophes."

Despite that, M. Kalonji said, few Belgians are preparing to leave the country and a large part of the civil servants are expected to stay on after independence.

M. Kalonji has been here on the invitation of the State Department since Saturday. He will leave for Brussels today.

May 14, 1960

LUMUMBA RISING AS A CONGO RULER

Defies Belgians as He Builds Power in Interior Region

By HOMER BIGART

Special to The New York Times.

STANLEYVILLE, Belgian Congo, May 17—Belgian authority is collapsing in part of the Congo.

Patrice Emergy Lumumba, Congolese nationalist leader, is taking over as virtual dictator of this city and much of the Stanleyville and Eastern Provinces.

Not even the arrival of Belgian troop reinforcements is likely to halt the rapid erosion of the colonial administration's authority. Forty-five days before Congolese independence the Belgian administration already seems subservient to the nationalists.

Ban on Meetings Defied

M. Lumumba saw reports of troops arrivals at the Kamina military base in Katanga Province as an "attempt to intimidate the voters and influence the election in favor of Belgian selected candidates." He said he had sent a telegram to King Baudouin of the Belgians demanding the recall of the troops. He did not seem unduly worried, however.

Yesterday, in a moment of painful humiliation for the Belgian settlers, M. Lumumba defied a ban on public meetings. He did it in the heart of the city that jailed him last October for inciting riots.

The incident marked the beginning of a triumphal tour by M. Lumumba of the region north of Stanleyville. There, in villages deep in the equatorial forest, he demanded and received assurances from Belgian officials that watchers from his party, the National Congolese Movement, would be allowed at polling places during the current election. The election will select political leaders to guide the Congo to independence June 30.

Emerging from a confectionery where he had provisioned for an eighty-mile drive to Banalia on the Aruwimi River, M. Lumumba was cheered by a few hundred Congolese. As he spoke, from a cream-colored American convertible, Congolese troops arrived.

Troops Called Provocation

"This is a provocation," M. Lumumba cried through a loudspeaker as a young Belgian officer dismounted and approached.

"These people came here only to see me," he said. "They are not attacking Europeans. They are perfectly peaceful."

The crowd shouted, "Uhuru," the Swahili word for freedom.

"I must disperse them," the officer countered. Stanleyville has been under a state of military occupation since rioting occurred May 6. All gatherings of five or more persons are prohibited.

The officer turned and ordered his men to dismount. As they climbed from the truck M. Lumumba, carrying his megaphone, advanced to meet them. Ignoring the officer, he told the Congolese soldiers:

"Aren't you satisfied with the trouble you provoked last October? [M. Lumumba's arrest sparked rioting in which several were killed.] Wasn't that enough for you? You get back in your truck and don't provoke anything."

The soldiers grinned and obeyed.

Soldiers Wave to Truck

En route to Banalia M. Lumumba passed the same troops on the outskirts of the city. "Uhuru," bellowed his loudspeaker truck. The soldiers grinned and waved.

At Bangamisa M. Lumumba paused at the headquarters of the Belgian territorial administration. Congolese gendarmes stood at attention and a bugler played. But M. Lumumba's followers, now swollen to more than a thousand, swept them aside.

"How many political prisoners are here?" he demanded of a Belgian official who served him beer.

"None," replied the Belgian. "But we have some prisoners who attacked a European and burned his truck because he had run over a drunk." M. Lumumba was assured that the European had not done it deliberately. He then said:

"We have decided that prison conditions must be improved. No longer may European prisoners be favored over the Congolese. They must receive equal treatment; otherwise independence is meaningless. You must improve prison conditions for the Congolese at once."

"Right," said the Belgian. "But where is the money coming from. People are not paying taxes. We had to close three roads because there was no money for repairs."

It took spunk on the part of the Belgian to say this. A howling mob of Congolese surrounded the house. The Belgian's wife, his small son and a police dog kept glancing nervously out of window.

"I am not blaming you personally," M. Lumumba said. "I know its not your fault."

They walked together from the porch into the heart of the crowd. A youth aimed a kick at the Belgian but M. Lumumba grabbed him and twisted his ear.

For three days Bangamisa voters had boycotted the polls been appointed by the Belgian administration. The fact that all of them favored M. Lumumba in a town where his party was unopposed made no difference. M. Lumumba told the crowd that the Belgians had agreed to permit party officials to witness the balloting and that voting would resume at once.

M. Lumumba then drove on toward Banalia, passing through villages where the population lined the road to cheer him and to pile his car with gifts.

A crowd in front of a Protestant mission carried the only Belgian flag seen all day. M. Lumumba told the children, "Study hard and I will send you to Britain and America for higher training. Then you can come back and save the Congo."

At Banalia, a steaming settlement on the crocodile-infested river, M. Lumumba proceeded to the district administration headquarters for a talk with the Belgians.

A dozen gendarmes in front of the building were powerless against the thousands of Congolese who came streaming after their leader. M. Lumumba obtained a two-hour stay of the curfew so he could address a night rally.

In the darkness he told the crowd that the Belgians were permitting "great abuses" in the election and he promised that those responsible would be punished.

He refrained from the violent attacks on the Belgians that have characterized his previous speeches, possibly because British and American newsmen were present.

Interviewed later, M. Lumumba denied reports he had received funds from Belgian Communists.

He concedes his party cannot achieve a majority in the national parliament but he hopes to come to power through a coalition with other groups that prefer a strong central government to tribalism.

May 18, 1960

'Messiah' in the Congo

Patrice Emergy Lumumba

PATRICE EMERGY LUMUMBA, Congolese nationalist who is emerging as virtual dictator of two of the Belgian Congo's six provinces, has been hailed as the messiah of Congolese freedom.

As president of the National Congolese Movement, which is expected to sweep Stanleyville in the voting for a national government and provincial assembly, he has maintained strong pressure on the Belgians.

Man in the News

Less than four months ago, upon his release from Jadotville Prison in the Congo, M. Lumumba joined a round-table conference in Brussels at the invitation of the Belgian Congo Minister, August de Schryver. He had been sentenced to six months' imprisonment on the charge that he made an inflammatory speech in Stanleyville that started a riot in which twenty persons died.

His defense was that his remarks were in favor of freedom but not of violence.

M. Lumumba thanked the Belgian people for his release, requested a general amnesty of "other political prisoners" and ended by saying:

"All of us together, in a union of hearts and sentiments, are working to build a powerful and proud Congolese state in the center of black Africa."

He has long espoused a unified Congo state. At Brussels he urged that a central government be established with a President elected on a nation-wide basis.

This is the only way to prevent tribal warfare and inefficient administration, he asserted. He opposed a federation of Congo states as too weak to deal with the problems that would face a new Government.

He thus took a stand contrary to that of Joseph Kasavubu, president of the Association of the Lower Congo. M. Kasavubu advocated a federation of states, which presumably would give his party predominance in the region of the present colonial province of Leopoldville.

Belgians in the Congo fear and distrust M. Lumumba, a former postal clerk who was

Feared and distrusted by Belgians in the Congo.

once convicted of embezzlement. They accuse him of fomenting racial hatred in the Stanleyville region, where Europeans have been insulted, spat upon and stoned by Congolese.

The Belgians call him an opportunist who has accepted money from Belgian Communists and they fear he either will control a coalition in the new Parliament or will become a terrorist leader. He has asserted that only he can maintain order.

M. Lumumba was born 34 years ago in Kasai Province in the southern part of the Congo Basin.

He is a slender man, more than six feet tall. He recently was described as looking like a dark, bespectacled Davy Crockett under his chieftain's headdress—a feathered sheepskin cap.

He is married to a girl of his neighborhood in the jungle. They have four children, a girl and three boys. The two older children are studying in a Belgian school in Leopoldville.

M. Lumumba, who thinks of himself as a father, while at the same time trying to be a revolutionist, would like to have his children study in Europe. "The atmosphere in Africa is not good," he said.

He was educated in the Belgian schools of the Congo. He completed high school and later studied law and literature through correspondence courses.

He started work at 19 in the post office at Stanleyville. His ability was recognized, but eleven years later he was charged with fraudulent conversion of $2,500. He was imprisoned for more than a year.

On his release he assured the Congolese that he had been compelled to use the money he embezzled only to keep up his activities in the nationalist circles of the Congo.

May 18, 1960

'Magic' of Freedom Enchants Congolese

By HOMER BIGART

Special to The New York Times.

LEOPOLDVILLE, Belgian Congo, June 4—"Does it come wrapped in paper and do we go to the bank and get it?" Lulua tribesmen asked an American missionary in Kasai Province.

They were asking about independence, a kind of magic box that will be given to them June 30. As the hour of freedom from Belgian rule nears, "In-de-pen-dence" is being chanted by Congolese all over this immense land, even by pygmies in the great equatorial forest.

Independence is an abstraction not easily grasped by the Congolese and they are seeking concrete interpretations. All seem to agree that it means an easier life.

To the forest pygmy independence means a little more salt, a little more beer. To meat-starved tribes living near the national parks, it is freedom to invade the game preserves and slaughter the magnificent herds of antelope and buffalo and the hippopotamus, elephant, wart-hog and lion.

Among the proud Bakuba, the most artistic of all Congolese tribes, independence means a revival of illicit practices such as ordeal by poison, the traditional way to eliminate the witches and sorcerers that have proliferated among them under Belgiam rule.

Detribalized Congolese living in cities put a strictly materialistic interpretation on independence. To the clerk in a government office, independence means a major rise in personal status—perhaps he will even become a Cabinet minister or a diplomat.

Other popular fantasies concern an immediate redistribution of wealth. City sharpers are selling "independence tickets" that entitle the holder to take over the homes, automobiles and other property of departing Belgians. Some innocent Congolese have purchased mysterious boxes marked "Do not open until June 30" that contain nothing but rocks and dirt.

A number of mystical doctrines, some of which had been banned by the Belgians, have been revived. Among these is Kibanguism, a xenophobic dogma founded about forty years ago in the Lower Congo by Simon Kibangu, who died in an Elisabethville prison in 1951.

The Belgians tried to suppress Kibanguism because they considered it anti-white. Its members believed in the coming of a black messiah and preached civil disobedience. Outlawed as subversive during World War II, Kibanguism has just been permitted by Belgian authorities to emerge from underground.

Meanwhile, the flight of Belgian colonists on the eve of independence has reduced the white population from around 100,000 to about 80,000. Since March the Belgians have been leaving by plane and ship at a rate of nearly 4,000 a month.

Belgian colonial officials have decried the panicky flight. They say there has been no serious molestation of Europeans by the Congolese despite some fanning up of anti-white sentiment, especially in the Stanleyville area by the nationalist leader Patrice Ernergy Lumumba.

American missionaries have encountered some slight hostility at Bibanga in Kasai Province. Congolese politicians demanded that the mission pay rental for grazing land to the still unborn Congo Republic instead of paying it to the Belgian administration.

They also demanded that the missionaries pay for all gravel taken out of the ground and all wood used in the construction of the mission's school, hospital, church and leper colony since the station was set up forty-three years ago.

Southern Presbyterian missionaries who run the station are trying to reach an agreement with the political leaders, but fear the station will have to close if the harassment continues.

Generally there has been no overt hostility. The fears of the departing Belgians seem to be based on the possibility that the independence fete will produce excesses.

Belgian officials hope independence day will pass without incident. They think the decision of King Baudouin to attend the celebration and proclaim Congolese independence will have a calming effect on the Belgians remaining here.

June 5, 1960

LUMUMBA VICTOR ON CONGO REGIME

Named to Form Government After Rival Bloc's Defeat in Parliament Vote

By HARRY GILROY

Special to The New York Times.

LEOPOLDVILLE, Belgian Congo, June 21—Patrice Lumumba won his first test of strength in the Congolese Parliament today. As a result, he replaced Joseph Kasavubu as the man designated to form a Government of the Congo, which will become independent of Belgian June 30.

Walter Ganshof van der Meersch, Belgian Resident Minister, said that he had withdrawn the mission to form a Government from M. Kasavubu after he discussed the Parliamentary vote with him. The Belgian authority said that he then had called in M. Lumumba, who had sent the Minister an offer to take over the mission.

M. Lumumba told newsmen that he would hold further talks with other leaders and present a list of cabinet ministers to M. Ganshof van der Meersch tomorrow night or Thursday morning.

Eearlier, the Lumumba bloc scored a significant victory by electing one of its members as President of the House of Representatives. He is Joseph Kasongo, who was originally elected to Parliament on the ticket of M. Lumumba's wing of the Congolese National Movement.

Confidence Vote Seen Assured

M. Lumumba mustered 74 votes for M. Kasongo, while the Kasavubu bloc produced 58 for Jean Bolikango, former Assistant Commissioner of Information in the Belgian Colonial Service at Leopoldville. One vote was cast for another candidate and four members of the 137-member House were absent.

The immediate implication was that M. Lumumba could obtain a majority vote in the House that would be required for a vote of confidence if he were given the opportunity of presenting a Cabinet.

M. Lumumba said at a news conference, after he had been named to form a Government that he felt that the attitude of the Belgian Government had changed and that he hoped for sincere friendship and economic cooperation with Belgium.

June 22, 1960

Lumumba Assails Colonialism as Congo Is Freed

Associated Press Radiophoto

King Baudouin speaking in Leopoldville. At lower right is Joseph Kasavubu, President.

By HARRY GILROY

Special to The New York Times.

LEOPOLDVILLE, Republic of Congo, June 30—An attack on colonialism by the Premier of the new Republic of Congo marred the ceremonies today in which King Baudouin of the Belgians proclaimed the territory's independence. [Early Friday the republic of Somalia was proclaimed.] The Congo independence ceremony before the two chambers of Parliament was attended by leading Belgian officials and diplomats from all over the world. It began in an atmosphere of friendship but was abruptly transformed by the militant speech of Premier Patrice Lumumba, who recited the sufferings of the African people at the hands of the whites.

Two hours later at a state dinner however, Mr. Lumumba toasted King Baudouin and praised Belgium for the magnificent work she had done in building the Congo. He said the Congolese people were grateful that Belgium had given them freedom without delay and he said the two countries would remain friendly.

The ceremonies were held in the beautifully draped circular hall of the National Palace that was to have been the residence of the Belgian Governor General.

Kasavubu Expresses Goodwill

Joseph Kasavubu, the new nation's Chief of State, expressed goodwill toward Belgium and won hearty applause from the members of Parliament. Apparently as a result of behind-the-scenes discussion, Mr. Kasavubu dropped the last section of his prepared address, which was to have ended with the declaration: "I proclaim in the name of the nation the birth of the Republic of the Congo!"

Instead, Mr. Lumumba moved from his place alongside Premier Gaston Eyskens of Belgium and went to the lectern to speak. He wore the maroon sash of the Order of the Crown, Belgium's highest decoration, which he received last night.

He said that June 30, 1960 would be known for the "glorious history of our struggle for liberty" He asserted that no Congolese would ever forget the struggle in which "we have not spared our strength, our privations, our sufferings or our blood.

Cites 'Wounds' of Colonialism

It was a struggle that was indespensable, he said, for putting an end to the "humiliating slavery which had been imposed on us by force." He commented that colonialism had left wounds too keen and too painful to be wiped from memory.

Premier Lumumba reminded the members of the new Parliament of "the ironies, the insults, the blows that we had to submit to morning, noon and night because we were Negroes."

He declared Congo must be made the "rallying point of all Africa" and that the nation must put an end to the oppression of free thought and give to all citizens the fundamental liberties guaranteed in the United Nations Declaration of the Rights of Man.

He said Belgium had finally understood the meaning of history and had not tried to oppose Congo's independence. He noted that Belgium was ready to provide help and friendship and that a treaty had been signed that would be profitable to both countries.

King Baudouin was cheered as he drove to the ceremony. In the first speech of the day he gave a careful statement of Belgium's claim to have delivered the Congolese from the Arab slave trade and to have created the fabric of civilization on which their parliament now rests.

The territory was acquired in 1885 by King Leopold II, Baudouin's great-grand uncle, as a personal empire. Belgium took it over as a colony in 1908.

King Baudouin foresaw as the principal dangers threatening the Congolese the inexperience of the people, tribal struggles and "the attraction that you exercise for certain areas of foreign powers desiring to profit from weakness."

He urged the Congo Parliament to continue the services established by the Belgians and to turn to Belgium for help whenever it was needed. He concluded: "My country and I recognize with joy and emotion that the Congo has acceded on June 30, 1960, in full accord and friendships with Belgium, to independence and international sovereignty."

Premier Lumumba's speech produced comments of surprise and disappointment among Belgian and other Western representatives. The Soviet diplomats present seemed to be enjoying the occasion.

Robert Murphy, former Under Secretary of State and head of the United State delegation to the independence ceremonies, presented credentials to Mr. Kasavubu and gave him a bust of Abraham Lincoln sent by President Eisenhower.

Mr. Murphy said the United States was prepared to finance the training of 300 Congolese in United States schools or institutions of other countries.

Clare H. Timberlake, who has been counselor of the United States Embassy in Bonn and who accompanied Mr. Murphy, is scheduled to become the United States Ambassador.

July 1, 1960

KATANGA PREMIER IN CONGO SECEDES; ASKS BELGIAN AID

Economic Tie Is Proposed—Lumumba Seeks Help of U. N. in Uprisings

By Reuters.

LEOPOLDVILLE, the Congo, July 11—The Congo's richest province declared itself an independent state tonight.

Premier Moise Tshombe of Katanga Province asserted in a radio broadcast that the copper-rich province was declaring its "total independence" from the Congo.

He added, however, that Katanga would retain an economic bond with Belgium.

The Katanga Premier made his announcement in Elisabethville after having declared a state of emergency as the rebellion of Congolese troops continued.

Earlier he had asked in vain for the aid of troops or policemen from Northern Rhodesia, a member of the British-ruled Federation of Rhodesia and Nyasaland.

'Astonishment' Expressed

Premier Patrice Lumumba of the Congo, which became independent of Belgium June 30, took off for Elisabethville before Mr. Tshombe's declaration. Mr. Lumumba earlier expressed "astonishment" at the call for troops from neighboring Northern Rhodesia.

Mr. Tshombe declared Belgian troops in his provincial capital would remain there. He said he had asked for more of them to be sent into Elisabethville.

Mr. Tshombe said he wanted Premier Lumumba to keep out of the province and had sent instructions to his Cabinet ministers to tell Mr. Lumumba so upon his arrival at the Elisabethville airport.

As Congolese Army mutineers battled Belgian troops today in two centers, Mr. Lumumba appealed for United Nations military specialists to help reorganize the rebellious armed forces. He made the request through Dr. Ralph J. Bunche, United Nations Under Secretary, who has been here since the Independence Day celebrations.

[At the United Nations, Secretary General Dag Hammarskjold plans to ask nine African members to send officers to the Congo to restore discipline to the mutinous army.]

Bunche Issues Statement

Dr. Bunche issued a statement here tonight saying he assured Mr. Lumumba and Chief of State Joseph Kasavubu yesterday that the United Nations would give the new republic "as much assistance as possible."

This assistance, he said, would be given within "the framework of the Charter of the United Nations and of the principles according to which the organization functions."

"On a purely personal level, I would like to say that I was profoundly impressed in the course of this interview by the ardent desire of all those who took part in it to surmount the present difficulties in the country," Dr. Bunche added.

Dr. Bunche said he had submitted a detailed report on his discussion here to Secretary General Hammarskjold at the United Nations.

Mr. Lumumba has been rushing from one trouble center to another in an effort to restore order. He hurried to Matadi over the week-end and flew this afternoon to Luluabourg on his way to Elisabethville.

Before taking off, he declared his Government's determination to "have law and order respected and to defend the territorial integrity of our country."

Radio reports received here described a continuing battle between Belgians and Congolese in the uranium center of Shinkolobwe, 100 miles northwest of Elisabethville.

The battle began when the Europeans rejected a demand to hand over their weapons. Rebel gunfire drove off a planeload of troops trying to land reinforcements in Shinkolobwe.

Missionaries Surrounded

Sixty American missionaries and their families at Kapanga in northern Katanga Province found themselves surrounded by Congolese rebels. They radioed a message from their mission station that so far they had not been molested.

Congo Area Declared Independent

The New York Times July 12, 1960

As violence continued throughout the Congo, Katanga Province (shaded area), which is adjacent to Northern Rhodesia, announced that it was seceding from republic.

July 12, 1960

U. N. Force Due in Congo; Disorders Continue There

Bunche Expects Troops by Tomorrow—U. S. Missionaries Abused

By HENRY TANNER
Special to The New York Times.

LEOPOLDVILLE, the Congo, July 14—Dr. Ralph J. Bunche announced this afternoon that United Nations troops were expected to reach Leopoldville by Saturday.

The United Nations Under Secretary said the first United Nations forces to arrive would be drawn from the African states of Ghana, Guinea, the Mali Federation, Morocco and Tunisia. By early next week at least four battalions will be here, he added.

[A European slapped Premier Patrice Lumumba at the Leopoldville airport, The Associated Press reported.]

Maj. Gen. Carl Carlsson von Horn of Sweden, now head of the United Nations truce supervision organization in Jerusalem, will head the operation here, Dr. Bunche added. He has been conferring for the last six days with Congolese and Belgian officials trying to ease growing tension and to keep the two-week-old state from drifting into chaos.

Mutinous Congolese soldiers have forced the ouster of their Belgian officers and have harassed Belgian civilians in various parts of the Congo. Their interference with fleeing refugees culminated yesterday in a clash with Belgian troops at the Leopoldville airport.

Belgian paratroopers occupied key positions in the European part of Leopoldville this morning, against bitter objections by the Congo Government.

The Belgians now control the

city's airport and two main highways leading to the city and they have patrols at main intersections in the downtown area.

Dr. Bunche came to the Congo to represent the United Nations at independence ceremonies June 30 and to study the possibilities of technical assistance by the world organization.

In his first statement since the outbreak of unrest a week ago, he said that the "sole purpose of the United Nations in this operation is to assist the Government of the Congo Republic in the restoration of conditions of calm and good relations."

He said that the resolution adopted last night by the United Nations Security Counsel "envisages the withdrawal of Belgian troops from the territory of the Congo Republic" but that the timing of the withdrawal was up to the Beligians.

He added it was his understanding that the Congolese had not objected to the presence of Belgian forces but to their going into action without a Congolese request.

Missionaries Molested

A graphic report about the Congolese reaction to the intervention of Belgian forces was given by American missionary sources this afternoon.

Until yesterday the missionaries had not reported any difficulties with the African population. This morning, however, the Congolese, in apparent anger over the Belgian action, turned against missionaries in several places, missionary sources said. They said several missions will now leave the Congo.

At Sona Imponga, 150 miles west of Leopoldville, seven missionaries and eleven children were molested this morning. Arrangements are being made for a plane to fly from Brazzaville, in the French Community Congo Republic, to evacuate them.

In African quarters of Leopoldville the Congolese turned against their own ministers to vent their anger over the Belgian intervention.

"They called us traitors," a minister said after returning from that section of city. "They hooted and jeered us and told us we sold out to the Belgians."

Albert Delvau, Congolese Resident Minister in Brussels and a member of the Cabinet, was reported to have been stoned when he tried to reason with an excited crowd in a Congolese section of Leopoldville.

Congo Leaders Return

Premier Patrice Lumumba and Chief of State Joseph Kasavubu returned to Leopoldville this afternoon. They had been touring the interior since last Sunday in an effort to establish the authority of the central government. Despite their efforts the situation remained confused in the rich Katanga province, which announced its secession four days ago.

The two Congo leaders were involved in an angry scene at the airport with Lieut. Gen. Charles P. Cumont, Belgiums army chief of staff, and Col. Roger Gheysen, commander of the Belgian paratroopers in Leopoldville.

A Belgian honor guard met the Congolese leaders. When General Cumont told Premier Lumumba that Belgian forces were in the Congo only to protect the whites, Mr. Lumumba gestured agrily and retorted, "we don't need your presence." He then stalked away.

Belgian reinforcements continued to arrive this morning and moved into Leopoldville in large convoys. Some Belgian soldiers said they had come from Germany.

Congolese officials said their Government had protested to the Belgian Ambassador, Baron Jean van den Bosch, last night and had requested the withdrawal of Belgian forces by 5 o'clock this morning. They said the Ambassador had told them he would transmit their request to Brussels but could not act on it himself. They said at noon today Brussels had not yet acknowledged receipt of the request.

Belgian troops appeared in the center of Leopoldville just before nightfall yesterday. They drove through in convoys. For a while it looked as if they would fraternize with Congolese army patrols. The Congolese soldiers were taken aboard Belgian command cars for what appeared to be joint patrols.

Cooperation broke down, however, after less than an hour when the Belgian soldiers sought to disarm the Congolese patrols that continued to cruise without Belgian supervision. Fighting broke out at that time and continued sporadically during the night.

American Fired On

An American newspaper man was fired on by a Belgian paratrooper, who then explained his mistake by saying, "You looked like a Congolese in the dark."

This morning Congolese ministers complained that they had been "tricked" by a Belgian "ruse." They said that in order to avoid bloodshed they had agreed to joint patrols and had ordered their soldiers not to use their weapons. They charged that Belgians then infiltrated into the center of the city and disarmed dozens of Congolese soldiers, wounding or killing others. They said that "about ten Congolese soldiers" had been killed in the night's fighting.

At dawn two or three Belgian planes, rockets showing plainly beneath the wings, made several passes over the city.

A Congolese Army ambulance drove slowly through streets near the European section and picked up the bodies of three Congolese soldiers killed during the night.

Congolese watching the scene broke into sobs. Congolese youth in the area motioned European cars to stop, then stoned them and robbed the passengers. They set fire to two cars. At least one civilian was severely wounded by rocks.

The United States Embassy consulted Congolese and Belgian officials today on plans for relieving a serious food shortage in Leopoldville. The shortage results from a strike of Congolese workers.

There was hope that a plan might be worked out by tomorrow for large quantities of food to be flown in by United States Air Force planes.

This reporter and three other American newsmen, driven into the Congolese quarter in a Congolese army jeep with an armed Congolese escort, were rushed by a frenzied crowd brandishing rocks. The escort, a sergeant, shouted that these were not Belgians but Americans.

Almost unbelievably the word "American" turned the mob into a laughing cheering crowd that pressed forward to hug the Americans and shake their hands.

July 15, 1960

KHRUSHCHEV TELLS THE WEST TO KEEP HANDS OFF CONGO

Replies to New Republic's Appeal for Intervention by Soviet if Needed

By SEYMOUR TOPPING
Special to The New York Times.

MOSCOW, July 15—Premier Khrushchev acceded quickly today to an appeal by the Government of the Congo for Soviet intervention if the West does not end its "aggression" against the new African republic.

The Premier declared that the Soviet Government's demand to the West was "hands off the Republic of Congo."

The Kremlin made public a message from the Chief of State of the Congo, Joseph Kasavubu, and Premier Patrice Lumumba. The message accused Belgium and "certain Western countries" of threatening the republic's neutrality and independence. The telegram added:

"At present the Congolese state territory is occupied by Belgian troops and the lives of the Republic's President and Prime Minister are in danger."

U. N. Action Is Ignored

The telegram, dated yesterday, did not take cognizance of the United Nations Security Council decision on the previous day to send an emergency force to the Congo to replace Belgian troops.

In his reply Mr. Khrushchev termed the Council's decision "a useful thing." But the Soviet Premier also gave this assurance to the Congolese leaders:

"If states which are directly carrying out imperialist aggression against the Congo and those who are pushing them on continue their criminal actions, the U. S. S. R. will not shrink from resolute measures to curb the aggression."

[In Washington the State Department denounced Mr. Khrushchev's statements as "intemperate, misleading and irresponsible."]

The Congolese appeal to Mr. Khrushchev dismayed Western diplomats here, who saw it as a propaganda coup that would enhance the Soviet leader's efforts to pose as the guardian angel of the African peoples. It was believed here that unless the Congo can be pacified quickly the situation could provide an opening wedge for Soviet penetration into the heart of Africa.

According to the text of the telegram published by Tass, the Soviet press agency, the Congo's leaders asked Mr. Khrushchev "to watch hourly over the development of the situation" in the Congo. It continued:

"We may have to ask for the Soviet Union's intervention should the Western camp not stop its aggression against the sovereignty of the Republic of the Congo."

Mr. Khrushchev hastened to publish the ninety-word telegram together with his reply of 800 words.

He employed the reply as a

platform for calling on the peoples of Africa, Latin America and Asia to align themselves with the Communist states against the Western powers, headed by the United States.

"Your struggle is the struggle of hundreds of millions of people of Africa, Asia and Latin America, Indochina, Algeria, Suez, Guatemala, Lebanon and Jordan, Guinea, Cuba." Mr. Khrushchev told the Congolese leaders. "It is an established fact," he added, "that the old Congo was not only a Belgian colony. The bayonet was Belgian but the bosses were the United States, Belgian, British and West German big monopolies."

The Khrushchev telegram followed the line laid down in yesterday's Soviet statement, in which the Kremlin sought to shift responsibility for the police action in the Congo from Belgium to all the Atlantic powers. It charged the West with seeking to restore the Congo to colonialism.

The Soviet Union has made the Congo and Cuba pivotal positions in its contest with the West for the sympathy of the uncommitted peoples. The tempo of the Soviet push into what had been preserves of Western influence seems to have quickened after the Bucharest Communist party congress last month, which was attended by Mr. Khrushchev and leaders of Communist China and the East European Communist states.

July 16, 1960

ECONOMIC CRISIS STIRS CONGO FEAR

Threat of Violence Revives as Hunger Spreads and Unemployment Grows

By HENRY TANNER

Special to The New York Times.

LEOPOLDVILLE, the Congo, July 25—The Congo is facing a new threat. Unless quick solutions are found, the new republic's economy may grind to a halt.

Unemployment has more than tripled in Leopoldville in three weeks. Even Congolese workers who still have jobs say their wages buy barely enough food for their children, with nothing left over for adults.

Observers fear unemployment and hunger will lead to looting and riots. They predict that if hungry Congolese start descending on the European section of the city looking for food, the result may be much more serious than the mutiny of the Congo Army two weeks ago.

Meanwhile, the United Nations reported its forces here had reached 7,300 following the arrival of additional troops from Tunisia and Ethiopia. A spokesman said the total would be 9,000 by Wednesday.

Agitation is reported rising in Leopoldville's African quarters as economic stagnation continues.

For the first time in the Congo crisis, looting is being reported in Leopoldville's well-to-do European areas, where many houses were abandoned during the height of the crisis.

United Nations specialists say the Congo is in "desperate financial straits." Many doubt that the Congo treasury will have enough banknotes to pay state employes next Monday.

One reason given by experts for the money shortage is that few banknotes were printed by the Belgians as independence approached. Another reason is that many notes apparently vanished in the confusion of the past.

The Congo's Finance Minister, Pascal Nkayi, flew to Stanleyville last week in a United Nations plane to get money that had piled up there.

United Nations officials are cials about the banknote shortage.

United Nations experts say the food shortage is particularly severe in urban centers. This is a result of the breakdown of the distribution system. For the last three weeks trains have not run. River and road traffic has been halted. The port of Matadi at the mouth of the Congo River has been idle.

The river below Matadi is badly silted because dredging operations were discontinued when trouble broke out.

Lieut. Gen. Raymond A. Wheeler United States Army, retired, who cleared the Suez Canal after Egypt's conflict with Britain, France and Israel in 1956, arrived yesterday to take charge of opening the river below Matadi.

U. S. Flour Just in Time

The first United States flour shipments arrived just in time to prevent disaster in Leopoldville. The city's flour stocks ran out last Wednesday. The United Nations was able to start putting American flour on sale the same day. Officials reported that 300,000 pounds were sold in the first two days. The United States has sent 350 tons of flour so far.

Food shipments have arrived or are on the way from West Germany, Denmark, Britain, Sweden and India, the United Nations reported.

The proceeds from United Nations food sales are being placed in a trust fund jointly administered by the Congo Government and the United Nations. The fund will be used for relief work.

No one is willing to predict what will happen if the state is unable to meet its payroll next Monday. About 12,000 Congolese are reported to be dependent on state salaries and 90,000 more are working for the state as contract laborers.

The halting of exports and imports, which normally account for a large share of state income, has further depleted the treasury. Taxes are not being collected.

Moreover, the mass exodus of Belgian merchants and industrialists has contributed heavily to unemployment. Experts estimate that 70,000 workers in Leopoldvile are without jobs. This is a fifth of the city's African population. The figure is up from 20,000 three weeks ago.

Prices Rising Sharply

Sharp price increases are compounding the effects of unemployment. A pound of meat that cost a dollar three weeks ago now costs $1.50. The average pay for skilled Congolese workers is about $50 a month. Unskilled workers earn $18 to $20 a month.

A Congolese trade union leader attacked the Government this morning, charging that all the "advantages" won by workers since independence had been wiped out by inflation. The workers received an "independence bonus" and, in some cases, a pay increase of 30 per cent.

United Nations technicians are working with nearly all ministries. They are training policemen and soldiers and have taken the country's telecommunications in hand.

In such areas as finance, government administration and health services, the United Nations technicians are making surveys of the Congo's need.

An Israeli medical team in on hand, made up of a general health adviser, two surgeons, two internists, an orthopedist, a pharmacist and nurses. A Ghanaian team is expected in the next few days.

Present estimates are that 400 to 500 physicians will be needed to replace the Belgians who have left.

At one Leopoldville hospital, which has 1,800 beds, there is one doctor left, a United Nations spokesman said.

July 26, 1960

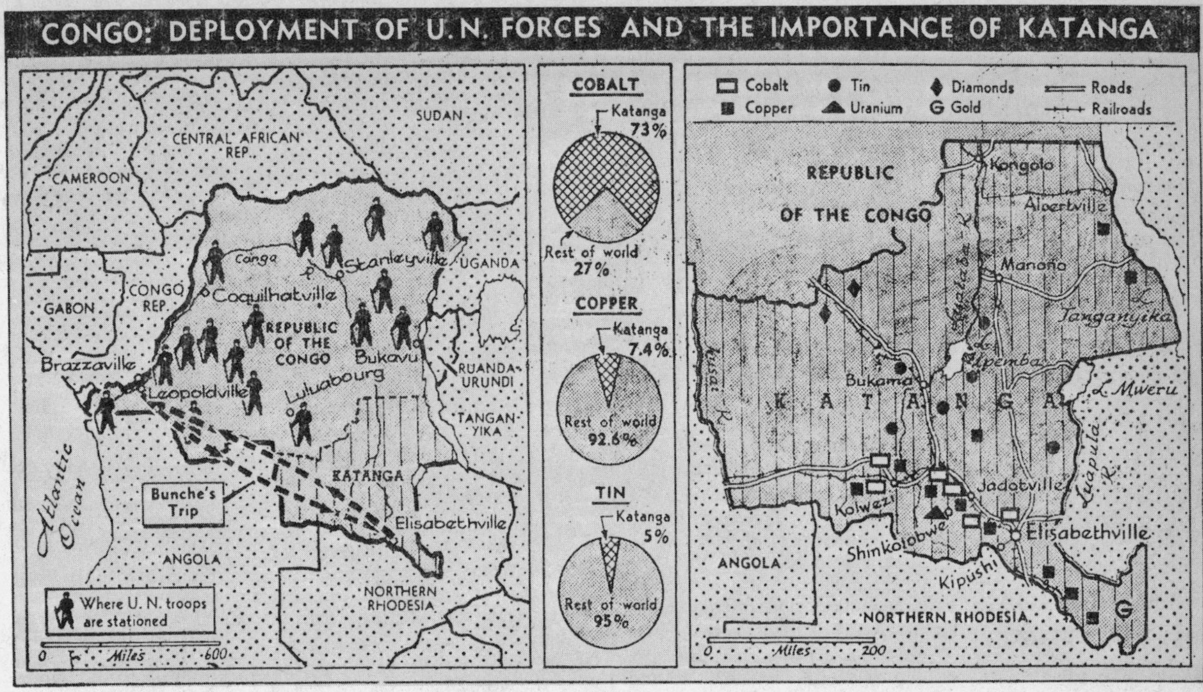

CONGO: DEPLOYMENT OF U.N. FORCES AND THE IMPORTANCE OF KATANGA

Katanga, with only 10 per cent of the Congo population, produces more than half the country's wealth.

August 7, 1960

U.N. TROOPS ENTER KATANGA IN FACE OF NEW DEFIANCE

Hammarskjold Averts Move to Block the Landing of 7 Planes With Him

CROWD JEERS SWEDES

Tshombe Greets Secretary Warmly—Two Men Hold Preliminary Discussion

By HENRY TANNER

Special to The New York Times.

ELISABETHVILLE, the Congo, Aug. 12—Katanga Province accepted United Nations troops today with a last gesture of defiance. Secretary General Dag Hammarskjold refused to change his plans, however.

On instructions from the Katanga Government the airport control tower told the pilot of Mr. Hammarskjold's plane to land but withheld clearance for seven troop-carrying planes that followed.

Five trucks, a bus, a fire engine and a big excavator had been posted along the runway at the last moment. Their operators were to have been ordered to move into the path of the troop carriers once the lead plane had landed. About 200 Katanga troops also were on hand.

Airport officials said Mr. Hammarskjold's pilot had radioed back that unless all eight planes were permitted to land the Secretary General would fly back to Leopoldville.

Tshombe Clears Way

Katanga's President, Moise Tshombe, who was waiting on the landing field apron with his ministers and two Belgian diplomats, then instructed the control tower to give clearance to all the planes.

Mr. Tshombe said that there had been a misunderstanding and that the control tower had been acting on instructions given several days ago.

The acceptance of United Nations troops was a reversal of the stand Katanga had taken earlier. The province, which has declared its independence from the Congo, has insisted that United Nations forces were not needed because its own forces, assisted by Belgian troops, were able to keep order.

Katanga authorities refused to let United Nations civilian specialists leave a plane that landed at Elisabethville last Saturday. This led to an urgent session of the Security Council, which adopted a resolution calling for the immediate withdrawal of Belgian troops from Katanga.

The resolution also assured the province that the United Nations forces replacing the Belgians would not be a party to the province's dispute with the central Government of Premier Patrice Lumumba.

After the clearance order was given Mr. Hammarskjold's plane landed. The Secretary General was greeted by Mr. Tshombe, smiling and obviously unawed. The Katanga leader carried a tourist booklet entitled "Elisabethville Invites You."

Mr. Tshombe led Mr. Hammarskjold past a Congolese honor guard and paused in front of the red, white and green flag of independent Katanga. The Secretary General, his face set, acknowledged the flag briefly after a moment's hesitation, then moved on.

Crowd Cheers Tshombe

Katanga officials reported today that the Secretary General had agreed to Mr. Tshombe's demand that control over the movement across provincial borders of persons and goods would remain in the hands of the Katanga government.

Mr. Tshombe's main purpose in meeting with Mr. Hammarskjold is to get a firm United Nations pledge against interference in local affairs and thus to prevent Premier Lumumba from using United Nations intervention to bring Katanga under his control.

The arrival of Mr. Hammarskjold and the Swedish troops accompanying him was observed by several hundred Belgians and a few Congolese.

The crowd shouted, "Long live Tshombe!" and Long live independent Katanga!" There were no cheers for Mr. Hammarskjold or the United Nations.

On the fringe of the crowd, however, was a small group of Congolese carrying a banner reading "Down with independent Katanga, Long live united Congo." The banner identified the group as members of the Cartel group of opposition parties in Katanga.

A Belgian army officer wearing a military police armband tore the banner down just as Mr. Hammarskjold passed.

One man in the Cartel group was arrested by a Belgian officer and handed over to Congolese soldiers.

As the Swedish soldiers

marched across the field they were mildly jeered. There were some shouts of "Down with Hammarskjold!" and "Down with the United Nations!"

Mr. Hammarskjold waited for the Swedes at Mr. Tshombe's car. He had been overheard to say to the Katanga President that he did not want to leave the airport before the troops had arrived.

After the Swedish commander had reported to him, Mr. Hammarskjold turned smilingly to Mr. Tshombe and said: "Now that I have made my little gesture of greeting my troops, we can go."

Brig. I. J. Rikhye of India, who is in charge of the United Nations troops in Katanga, said 240 men had arrived today. Half will stay at the airport and half will move into the city, he said.

Mr. Hammarskjold met for nearly two hours this afternoon with Mr. Tshombe and his aides. The two parties exchanged documents that will serve as a basis for further discussion tomorrow. The Secretary General dined with Mr. Tshombe at the President's residence tonight.

Mr. Hammarskjold is staying in a villa put at his disposal by Union Minière du Haut Katanga, the large mining concern that has its headquarters here.

August 13, 1960

CONGO TROOPS FLY TO KASAI TO STOP SECESSION EFFORT

Lumumba Acts to Crush Bid to Create a New State in Area of Tribal Conflict

By HENRY TANNER
Special to The New York Times.

LEOPOLDVILLE, the Congo, Aug. 24 — Premier Patrice Lumumba sent Congo Army units today to Luluabourg, capital of Kasai Province, in his first serious effort to check a secessionist movement there.

The movement follows nearly two months of bitter fighting by two hostile tribes, the Lulua and the Baluba. It is led by Albert Kalonji, a Baluba chief and political opponent of Premier Lumumba.

Mr. Kalonji has declared the independence of a part of Kasai Province that he calls Mining State and has turned to President Moise Tshombe of the secessionist Katanga Province for support.

Three Companies Sent

Three companies of Congo Army troops — 200 men — left Ndjili Airport at Leopoldville this morning in five planes. This was the first major troop movement by the Congo Army since independence June 30. It was the mutiny of the army early in July that led to United Nations intervention in the Congo.

The Congo Government requisitioned the planes from Air Congo, a subsidiary of the Belgian airline Sabena. The United Nations had refused to make its planes available for the troop movement. Some of the planes bore United Nations markings because they had been chartered earlier by the world organization.

While the official reason given for sending the troops to Luluabourg was to end the tribal fighting that is reported to have cost several hundred lives, officials made it clear that the real reason was to strike at Mr. Kalonji.

New State a Baluba Area

Mr. Kalonji claims the territory to the east, south and west of Luluabourg. His is an all-Baluba state. There have been reports of large-scale population movements, with the Balubas moving south and the Lulua crowding into the Luluabourg area.

Mr. Kalonji formerly was allied with Mr. Lumumba in the Congolese National Movement. Differences before independence caused them to split and each thereafter headed separate factions of the party.

Meanwhile, the United Nations sent Col. Henry Byrne of Ireland to Albertville, in Katanga, to investigate reports that Mali soldiers had mutinied and had killed two Congolese.

Heavy fighting was reported in the Albertville area yesterday but reports conflicted about whether the Mali forces had mutinied. Belgian sources said the Mali soldiers had fought with Balubakat tribesmen who oppose the Tshombe regime.

Another ranking United Nations officer, Gen. Iyassu Mengasha of Ethiopia, went to Stanleyville, in the northern Congo, to investigate reports of incidents between Congolese soldiers and United Nations personnel. He was accompanied by Gen. Victor Lundula, commander of the Congo Army.

In another development, Leopoldville prepared for the arrival tomorrow of representatives of independent African states convening for a five-day conference.

The conference was first proposed by Premier Lumumba and King Mohamed V during Mr. Lumumba's visit to Rabat, Morocco, three weeks ago. At that time it was described as an "African summit conference."

The project later was reduced to a "preparatory" session intended to explore the possibility of holding a summit meeting here later this fall.

Tunisia is sending Habib Bourguiba Jr., Ambassador to France; Mongi Slim, delegate to the United Nations, and Sadok Mokkadem, Foreign Minister.

The United Arab Republic will be represented by Hussein Zulficar Sabry, Deputy Foreign Minister. M'Hammed Yazid, Minister of Information in the Provisional Government of Algeria, is expected to arrive tonight.

Congo officials said the conference would not deal with the Congo but principally with the problems of African unity.

Congo Government sources made no secret of the fact that for Premier Lumumba the conference was above all an opportunity to seek recognition as an African leader.

Leopoldville, meanwhile, remained sealed off from Brazzaville, the neighboring capital of the French community's Congo Republic across the Congo River.

Congolese soldiers refused permission to cross the river even to persons producing safe-conduct passes issued by Premier Lumumba.

Many airline passengers with tickets on planes leaving from Brazzaville were stranded. However, Sabena airliners operated normally from the Leopoldville airport, which is occupied by the United Nations.

August 25, 1960

AFRICAN NATIONS ASKING LUMUMBA TO SUPPORT U. N.

By THOMAS F. BRADY
Special to The New York Times.

LEOPOLDVILLE, the Congo, Aug. 30—The pan-African conference meeting here decided today to urge Premier Patrice Lumumba to maintain "close cooperation with the United Nations." This became known as it was announced that the last Belgian combat troops had left the secessionist province of Katanga.

Most of the thirteen states represented at the conference, which was convoked by Premier Lumumba, have called on him to exercise prudence. One North African delegate said the conference theme had become "calm down Lumumba."

The conference decision will be made formal in a final declaration to be published tomorrow.

Troops Leave on Schedule

A United Nations spokesman said he had been informed that the Belgian troops in Katanga—the last in the Congo—had left on schedule last night at the end of an eight-day limit announced by Dag Hammarskjold, United Nations Secretary General.

The departure of the Belgians constitutes the achievement of one of the major goals of the United Nations intervention in the Congo. However, Premier Lumumba is expected to take exception to the fact that certain noncombat technical military personnel have remained at the former Belgian base at Kamina in Katanga.

Mr. Lumumba has said also that once the Belgian troops had gone he would press for the withdrawal of United Nations troops.

A three-man United Nations committee, headed by Brig. I. J. Rikhye of India, left for

Kamina to study problems facing nearly 15,000 Congolese supported by the base who will now be without employment.

Dr. Ralph J. Bunche, who has been Mr. Hammarskjold's personal representative here, crossed the Congo River this afternoon to board a plane in Brazzaville for his return to New York.

Before leaving, he and his temporary replacement, Andrew W. Cordier, executive assistant to Mr. Hammarskjold, called on Chief of State Joseph Kasavubu. United Nations quarters reported that Mr. Kasavubu had apologized for Saturday's incidents at Stanleyville, in which eight American airmen and two Canadians were beaten by Congolese.

The Stanleyville incidents were discounted tonight by Serge Michel, French Leftist who is Mr. Lumumba's press spokesman.

Returning with Mr. Lumumba from a three-day visit to Stanleyville, M. Michel said:

"It was simply an altercation that lasted three or four minutes between the American aviators and the Congolese, astonished at having seen the American plane circle repeatedly above the Stanleyville airport. None of the aviators was seriously wounded, as anyone knows who has visited them at the Leopoldville hospital where they are being cared for."

The Americans said they circled the airport because its beacon was functioning poorly and they wanted to be sure where they were. The maneuver was said to have provoked rumors among the Congolese, who were excited by Mr. Lumumba's repeated exhortations against "Belgian spies," that the plane was dropping Belgian parachutists.

Visitors reported the injured Americans and Canadians were recovering their sense of humor. When asked if they would like to make an automobile tour of Leopoldville, one replied: "No thanks. What this country needs is tourists who are more resistant than we are."

African Parley Ends Work

The pan-African conference here concluded its major work after five days of deliberations. Its final declaration is said to include the following major points:

¶Support of Congo unity and territorial integrity and backing of the Central Congo Government, without specific mention of Katanga.

¶Agreement that African aid must be "in harmony with the United Nations." The conference apparently did not raise the question openly of direct military aid to the Congo.

¶An exhortation to the Congo and to the United Nations for cooperation. This appears to imply the continued United Nations presence in the Congo.

¶A call for an "African summit meeting" at a place and time not fixed. The declaration indicates, however, that the conference should be held in time to formulate a consensus of African views for this year's session of the United Nations General Assembly, which opens Sept. 20.

The conference also made clear that Africans support the United Nations and Mr. Hammarskjold despite Mr. Lumumba's bitter criticisms. Mr. Hammarskjold was reported to have addressed notes to some of the African powers represented asking them to urge prudence.

The conference sent a letter to Dr. Bunche, one delegation chief said, expressing gratitude for his work here and asking him to convey the thanks of the conference to Mr. Hammarskjold for the efforts of the United Nations. This action appears almost to constitute a censure of Mr. Lumumba.

The delegates said that they intended to meet privately with Mr. Lumumba to express their disapproval of Saturday's beatings of United States airmen and Canadian technicians. Although Mr. Lumumba called the conference, he absented himself from it for his visit to Stanleyville.

A United Nations military source disclosed today that reports from Bakwanga in Kasai Province indicated that several persons had been killed in fighting between the Congo Army and Baluba tribesmen who support the secessionist move of Albert Kalonji in that region.

Premier Lumumba's troops entered Bakwanga Saturday, as Tunisians in the United Nations garrison there remained aloof from the "internal issue." Nevertheless, a United Nations plane evacuated five wounded Congolese soldiers to Leopoldville yesterday on "humanitarian grounds," military sources said.

Reports to the United Nations said "many dead bodies" were lying in front of the headquarters of the eighty-man Tunisian garrison in Bakwanga. A United Nations spokesman, who did not confirm these reports, said the Belgian population of Bakwanga, which is not numerous, was living in a club of the diamond mining company there, guarded by Tunisian soldiers.

The spokesman said that the diamond mine was reported to have been closed because of the arrest of one of its executives.

August 31, 1960

Soviet Planes Sent To Help Lumumba In Katanga Dispute

By THOMAS F. BRADY
Special to The New York Times.

LEOPOLDVILLE, the Congo, Sept. 2—The Soviet Union appears to be providing Premier Patrice Lumumba with air and surface transport for a possible invasion of secessionist Katanga Province.

Mr. Lumumba has repeatedly stressed his determination to subdue Katanga, where Moise Tshombe, Provincial President, has proclaimed independence.

Soviet pilots have flown fifteen twin-engine Ilyushin 14 planes to Stanleyville in the northern Congo in the last few days, according to reports from reliable observers there. Observers also reported that "Republic of Congo" was being painted on the planes.

Reports from Stanleyville indicate that each plane brought with it a "crew" of at least eight, or a minimum of 120 persons, including mechanics, relief crews, ground crews and interpreters. The reports said the planes carried "large quantities of spare parts."

A spokesman for Mr. Lumumba confirmed the arrival of ten Ilyushins in Stanleyville and said the Soviet Union had agreed to put them at the disposal of the Congolese Government for an indefinite time.

The fleet of propeller-driven Ilyushins, classed as civilian passenger planes, can carry a total of more than 500 persons exclusive of their crews.

In addition, the Soviet Union has sent to Mr. Lumumba 100 trucks capable of transporting a total of 2,000 troops. With the trucks, which landed at Matadi, the Atlantic port of the Congo, came technicians to maintain them.

Observers are wondering where the Ilyushins could land in Katanga.

The airports there are held by the United Nations forces. The most important airport is the former Belgian base at Kamina, which the United Nations took over this week. The last Belgian troops left there yesterday.

In his latest statement to the United Nations Security Council, Secretary General Dag Hammarskjold said:

"No military or civilian personnel will be admitted to these bases or will be permitted to remain there, except those serving the goals of the United Nations in administering the bases or giving assistance to the Republic of Congo."

U. N. Assumed Responsibility

Mr. Hammarskjold also said that the United Nations had assumed "the entire responsibility for management of the bases." The Congolese Army has no paratroopers and there is every reason to believe from Mr. Hammarskjold's statement that the United Nations would not permit the Ilyushins to land at Kamina or other bases held by the United Nations forces in Katanga.

The arrival of the Ilyushins underlines the reasons for the disputes between the United Nations and Mr. Lumumba over control of Congolese airports, and throws new light on Mr. Hammarskjold's public decisions. It also seems to explain why Soviet representatives in New York and the Congolese Government have objected to United Nations control of the bases.

In a speech Tuesday, Mr. Lumumba said with reference to Kamina that "there can be no question of bases in the Congo controlled by foreigners —not even by the United Nations."

African Stand Noted

In addition, the arrival of the Ilyushins gives new meaning to the emphasis of delegates to the Pan-African Conference here earlier this week on the need for the United Nations to stay in the Congo as long as "the threat of outside interference continues."

Soviet influence here is growing in many directions. Including medical teams, maintenance men for trucks, personnel brought in by the Ilyushins this week, the crew of Mr. Lumumba's private Ilyushin—a gift of several weeks ago—and members of the Soviet embassy, the number of Soviet citizens now in the Congo is known to exceed 250. None of these is under United Nations administration.

September 3, 1960

CONGOLESE ARMY ASSUMES POWER; BACKS KASAVUBU

CHIEF DENIES COUP

Lumumba Is Reported Fleeing to Home in Stanleyville

By **HENRY TANNER**

Special to The New York Times.

LEOPOLDVILLE, the Congo, Sept. 14—The army took over the Congo tonight.

In a broadcast to the nation Col. Joseph Mobuto, Chief of Staff of the Congo Army, announced that the army command would take over the reins of government until Jan. 1, 1961.

"This is not a coup d'état," Colonel Mobuto declared. He said the army was taking over because the country had been plunged into chaos as a result of the conflict between President Joseph Kasavubu and Patrice Lumumba.

Mr. Kasavubu had named Joseph Ileo to replace Mr. Lumumba as Premier. The struggle between the two factions had grown more bitter from day to day and it had become increasingly unclear which side held the reins of power.

[Mr. Ileo declared in Leopoldville that the Congo Army was swinging its support to President Kasavubu, according to The Associated Press. It reported that he had credited Mr. Kasavubu with having promoted Colonel Mobuto to Commander in Chief of the army. Mr. Ileo also was reported to have said that most senior army officers had pledged their loyalty to Mr. Kasavubu.]

Mobuto Unclear on Premier

The army move left the Leopoldville picture unclear. Colonel Mobuto said both the President and Premier would retain their positions.

But it was not clear whether he meant Mr. Lumumba or Mr. Ileo would be Premier. Colonel Mobuto is known to be a stanch follower of Mr. Kasavubu.

Mr. Lumumba tonight was reported to have fled to Stanleyville, the capital of Oriental Province, by plane. The report could not be verified. Stanleyville is Mr. Lumumba's home town.

The army's seizure of power came after it had become known that President Kasavubu was working quietly behind the scenes to bring the army firmly to his side in his conflict with Mr. Lumumba.

Mr. Kasavubu called top-ranking officers to his residence for the second consecutive day.

Earlier, his office said Gen. Victor Lundula had been dismissed as Commander of the Congo Army. [Colonel Mobutu was named by Mr. Ileo to replace General Lundula as new Commander of the Congo Army, according to Reuters.]

General Lundula, Mr. Kasavubu's supporters charged, was responsible for releasing Mr. Lumumba from Camp Leopold II the city's military garrison after his arrest Monday.

Mr. Kasavubu also ordered the suspension of both houses of Parliament for a month.

September 15, 1960

Journalist-Strongman

Joseph Desire Mobutu

VISITORS to the 1958 World's Fair in Brussels may have seen a tall, slim, bespectacled young Congolese who was in the Belgian Congo section as a representative of the Congolese press. If they did, they were seeing a possible "strongman" of the Republic of the Congo, Col. Joseph Désiré Mobutu, who, as Chief of Staff of the Congo Army, has taken over temporary control of the country. In 1958, Colonel Mobutu was a civilian, the chief news editor of a Leopoldville newspaper, Actualités Africaines. He had turned to newspaper work in 1956 after leaving the army organized by the Belgians and called the Public Force. He had served as a clerk in the quartermaster corps.

Man in the News

While still in the army, Colonel Mobutu did some newspaper writing. When he was discharged in 1956 after seven years' service, he began work for the L'Avenir. He soon left for Actualités Africaines, where he was an assistant editor. He became chief news editor in 1957.

He was active in politics, as were most Congolese newspaper men, and rose quickly to prominence in the Congolese National Movement, whose leaders were Patrice Lumumba and Joseph Ileo, now the rival Premiers, and Albert Kalonji, leader of the secessionist state of South Kasai.

A Lumumba Lieutenant

When the party split in 1959, because of Mr. Lumumba's dictatorial actions, Mr. Mobutu remained as one of Mr. Lumumba's chief lieutenants.

Mr. Lumumba repaid this loyalty by sending him to Brussels for the round table conference early this year where the framework for independence was hammered out. He was in charge of the Brussels headquarters of the delegation.

On independence, Mr. Mobutu, who is 29 years old, became a Secretary of State without portfolio in the Lumumba Cabinet. He left that post to return to the Congo Army as a colonel and Chief of Staff to Gen. Victor Lundula, who has been ousted as commander.

London Daily Express

A moderate voice in military and political circles.

Neither had officer rank in the Public Force, which was staffed entirely by Belgians.

Colonel Mobutu was born at Lisala, the Congo, Oct. 14, 1930. After finishing a secondary school education at Coquilhatville, capital of Equator Province, he was sent to Brussels by the Belgians for study at the Institute of Social Studies.

On his return to the Congo, in 1949, he enlisted in the Public Force. He was discharged in 1956.

Since assuming his rank and duties as Chief of Staff in July, Colonel Mobutu has been a moderate voice in military and political circles.

Soon after his appointment, in several of the incidents between the Congolese soldiers and United Nations forces, he interceded to restore order.

Disregarding his recent actions, Colonel Mobutu's political history seems to indicate he is a "Lumumba man." But he has consistently pursued a course of cooperation with United Nations forces in the Congo and had talked moderately while his former mentor was breathing defiance of everyone except Moscow.

September 16, 1960

MOBUTU APPOINTS HIGH COMMISSION TO GOVERN CONGO

Youthful 'College' Approved by Kasavubu—Lumumba Calls It Ridiculous

By HENRY TANNER

Special to The New York Times.

LEOPOLDVILLE, the Congo, Sept. 20—A caretaker government of students and young university graduates was named today to take over the administration of the Congo.

A fifteen-member "College of High Commissioners" was installed by order of Col. Joseph D. Mobutu. The Commissioners were chosen by President Joseph Kasavubu.

Colonel Mobutu, who took over the Congo in the name of the army on Sept. 14, read a communiqué over the national radio station. He said the new body would "conduct the general policy" of the country, impose "respect for legality" and "assume representation of the republic abroad." No other body is entitled to carry out these functions, he said.

Political Appointees Ousted

Key members of the caretaker government introduced themselves to newsmen at an impromptu news conference called on the steps of the administrative building. Soldiers sent by Colonel Mobutu blocked all entrances to the building this morning and evicted political appointees from their offices. Only civil servants remained on the job.

The new appointees, some of whom returned from European universities recently at Colonel Mobutu's request, looked like a group of graduate students posing for a picture during a reunion. One said he was 26 years old.

A spokesman for the group explained that they had put themselves at the disposal of the nation for a limited transition period to assure a continuity of administration and to give the politicians a chance to iron out their difficulties. They described themselves as strictly nonpolitical.

Vice President Named

Political confusion has reigned supreme in the Congo since Mr. Kasavubu dismissed Patrice Lumumba as Premier and named Joseph Ileo to replace him. Mr. Lumumba insists he still is the head of the Leopoldville regime.

The president of the new body and High Commissioner for Foreign Affairs is Justin Bomboko. Mr. Bomboko, who is 32 years old, had been named Foreign Minister by Mr. Lumumba. He is now one of the major allies of Mr. Kasavubu.

The vice president of the new body and High Commissioner for Financial Affairs is Albert Ndele. Until now he was principal adviser to Finance Minister Pascal Nkayi, a member of Mr. Kasavubu's Abako party. The official name of the party is the Association of the Lower Congo.

The new group includes High Commissioners for Defense, Information, Education, Justice, Public Health, Public Works, and Economy and Planning. Some of the Commissioners have one or two deputies.

In spite of the careful display of nonpartisanship by the new commission it was clear tonight the appointment of the commission was a severe blow to Mr. Lumumba.

Colonel Mobutu warned newsmen that any reporter who "published contradictory communiqués by rival parties" would automatically be expelled.

Mr. Ndele, asked for an explanation of the colonel's statement, said it meant only that nobody outside the new commission had a right to issue communiqués in the name of the Congo government.

Mr. Lumumba, however, continued to do just that. He called reporters to his official residence today, where he remained with a dwindling group of faithful aides. He charged that this "student government" was both ridiculous and illegal.

He also distributed mimeographed copies of an "agreement of conciliation," which he said both he and President Kasavubu had signed.

Kasavubu Issues Denial

Tonight Mr. Kasavubu issued a statement that, in effect, accused Mr. Lumumba of having forged the document he showed to newsmen. "Lumumba was dismissed and remains dismissed," Mr. Kasavubu declared.

Mr. Lumumba, meanwhile, renewed his attack on Secretary General Dag Hammarskjold. Mr. Lumumba said the United Nations had refused to fly him to New York because the Secretary General "was afraid of a confrontation."

Mr. Lumumba was understood to have advised the United States Embassy last night that he intended to leave for the General Assembly session in New York today and that he would make a formal application for a visa this morning.

No formal application has been made, however, and visa has been issued.

Officers at the Ndjili airport said today that Congolese military police at the airport would arrest the "deposed Premier" if he tried to leave the country.

Mr. Ileo remained silent about today's developments. Mr. Ndele implied, however, that the College of High Commissioners had had Mr. Ileo's approval.

September 21, 1960

KASAVUBU WINS SEAT IN U.N.

LUMUMBA LOSES

French-Linked Lands in Africa Back U. S. Against Red Bloc

By THOMAS J. HAMILTON

Special to The New York Times.

UNITED NATIONS, N. Y., Nov. 22—The General Assembly, after a long and bitter debate, seated today a delegation headed by President Joseph Kasavubu as the representative of the Congo.

The Assembly accepted a recommendation by its Credentials Committee by a vote of 53 to 24 with 19 absentions.

The vote was a victory for the United States and other Western powers. The victory was made possible by the support given by most of the African members of the French Community.

The Soviet bloc, Ghana, Guinea, India and other African and Asian suporters of Patrice Lumumba, whom Mr. Kasavubu deposed as Premier last September, were in the minority.

New Barrier to Lumumba

The Assembly's action today is expected to make it more difficult for Mr. Lumumba to regain power. His supporters have contended that he is still the legal Premier and that the Congolese Parliament should be promptly called back into session to confirm him in power.

At the time the Congo was admitted to the United Nations the Assembly did not seat either a Kasavubu or a Lumumba delegation pending action by its credentials committee.

Today's decision, one of the major actions taken at this Assembly, gives at least implied recognition not only to Mr. Kasavubu as chief of state —this was not contested even by his enemies—but to Justin Bomboko, Congolese Foreign Minister, and other commissioners now serving under Col. Joseph D. Mobutu, Chief of Staff of the Congolese Army.

November 23, 1960

LUMUMBA SEIZED IN CONGO; MOBUTU ORDERS HIM TRIED; U.N. URGES FAIR TREATMENT

EX-CHIEF JEERED

Troops Display Bound Captive to Crowds in Leopoldville

By PAUL HOFMANN

Special to The New York Times.

LEOPOLDVILLE, the Congo, Dec. 2—Patrice Lumumba, his hands tied behind his back, returned here tonight as a prisoner of Col. Joseph D. Mobutu, head of the army regime.

Mr. Lumumba, the deposed Premier, had been a fugitive since Sunday. He was reported to have been arrested by Colonel Mobutu's forces in Port Francqui in Northwest Kasai yesterday.

He arrived at Ndjili Airport near Leopoldville shortly before 5 P. M. today in a DC-3 Belgian aircraft that had left here this morning with six Congolese military policemen aboard.

The former Premier was taken from the airport by truck. Congolese rushed into the streets, booing and cursing Mr. Lumumba as the soldiers displayed their prisoner in triumph.

Mobutu Looks to Trial

Colonel Mobutu said it was "up to the judiciary" to decide Mr. Lumumba's fate. He indicated that the deposed Premier would be brought to trial. A warrant signed by President Joseph Kasavubu early in October charged Mr. Lumumba with having misused his powers as Government chief by persecuting political opponents and having them subjected to atrocities.

[Colonel Mobutu said Mr. Lumumba would be tried for having incited the army to rebellion and other crimes, The Associated Press reported.]

Mr. Lumumba and other prisoners boarded the plane in Port Francqui, where they were held by Congolese gendarmerie. The United Nations said it had ordered its Ghanaian forces in the area to "refrain from any interference whatsoever."

A strong army force secured Ndjili Airport this afternoon. After landing, the aircraft taxied to the far end of the runway and Mr. Lumumba, surrounded by Congolese soldiers, was led to an open truck.

Mr. Lumumba was wearing faded blue trousers and an open-necked white shirt with sleeves tucked up. He was bareheaded. The truck was followed by other military vehicles. The second vehicle was filled with soldiers.

Mr. Lumumba kept his head bowed and did not look at the soldiers, who laughed and jeered. In the truck he sat on the floor, his head between his knees. His face appeared dust-stained, but he bore no signs of mistreatment.

Four other bound prisoners, including a woman, were led from the aircraft. Their identity was not disclosed.

The motorcade reached the outskirts of the capital in fifteen minutes and skirted the African city.

Taken to Headquarters

Mr. Lumumba was taken to Colonel Mobutu's headquarters at Binza on the western outskirts of Leopoldville. Congolese army detachments encircled the suburban area where Colonel Mobutu lives and works, barring excited crowds of Africans who were shouting death threats against Mr. Lumumba.

It was assumed the former Premier would spend at least the night as the personal prisoner of the army chief of staff.

While announcing Mr. Lumumba's arrest, Colonel Mobutu said earlier that the gendarmes of Port Francqui had warned him by telephone that they would shoot the former Premier unless he was flown out today.

According to Colonel Mobutu, the deposed Premier was captured while he was on his way by a circuitous route to Stanleyville, capital of Oriental Province. Stanleyville is controlled by Mr. Lumumba's followers.

U. N. Charges Brutality

Later, the United Nations issued a report charging that brutality had been suffered by many of the more than 1,000 "Europeans" in Stanleyville. The victims, it was said, included United Nations personnel who had been rounded up by Lumumba supporters this week. The term European in Africa covers foreigners in general.

According to some reports, some Americans suffered beatings in Stanleyville.

United Nations officials, recalling that their troops had protected Mr. Lumumba while he was in his residence in Leopoldville, said they were in no way responsible for his movements thereafter.

Colonel Mobutu said Mr. Lumumba would not be tried until Alphonse Songolo was freed. Mr. Songolo, a member of Parliament, was arrested in Stanleyville in October after having turned against Mr. Lumumba.

An International Red Cross inspection team reported that he had lost an eye and suffered other injuries as a result of beatings while a prisoner.

Colonel Mobutu said three Lumumba followers had been arrested in Port Francqui. They were Anicet Kashamura, pro-Communist Minister of Information; Joachim Masena, former Minister of Labor, and Georges Grenfell, former Minister of State.

Joseph Okito, vice president of the Senate and a Lumumba supporter, was also arrested in the area, Colonel Mobutu dis-

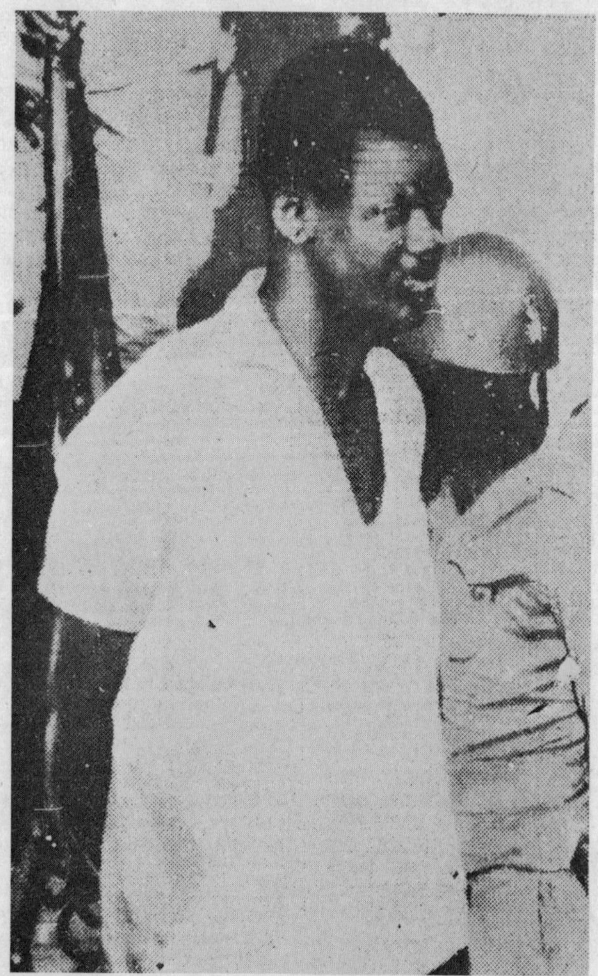

Associated Press Radiophoto

CAPTURED AND RETURNED: Patrice Lumumba, deposed Premier of the Congo, leaves plane at Leopoldville airport under Congolese Army guard. His hands are tied.

closed. He confirmed that Maurice Mpolo, a pro-Communist aide of Mr. Lumumba, had been detained in another part of the country and was being brought to Leopoldville by army escort.

Europeans Rounded Up

The United Nations report on Stanleyville was released after the return of a Ghanaian liaison officer who had been sent there to make an inquiry.

The report said the turbulence broke out when provincial authorities proceeded to check the credentials of all Europeans with a view to expelling all who lacked a newly issued identity document.

Early Sunday, the report said, all Europeans in Stanleyville were brought at gunpoint to the military camp.

"Many were ill-treated, slapped and kicked by the soldiery during this process," it said. "The gendarmerie entered the Catholic church and forcibly removed priests and nuns awaiting the celebration of mass. A woman member of the United Nations staff was threatened with a loaded machine gun while explaining her identity."

Persons of all ages and both sexes, the report said, were kept waiting in the sun for up to seven hours and many were again ill-treated, slapped and kicked.

More than seventy, including four women and a child, were kept in a small unventilated room without food and water, it was said.

According to the report. Stanleyville authorities agreed to relinquish the prisoners to the United Nations on condition that they would leave the country.

The United Nations said it had rejected responsibility "for enforcing a police measure like deportation" and suggested that the Europeans be flown to Usumbura, capital of Ruanda-Urundi, the Belgian trust territory east of here.

December 3, 1960

Pro-Red Lumumba Aide Claims Authority to Rule

Gizenga Tells Zorin Legal Government Has Moved Seat to Stanleyville

By PAUL HOFMANN
Special to The New York Times.

LEOPOLDVILLE, the Congo, Dec. 13—Antoine Gizenga, the Communist sympathizer who was Vice Premier under Patrice Lumumba, proclaimed in Stanleyville today that he represented the Congo's lawful government.

In a message to Valerian A. Zorin, chief Soviet delegate to the United Nations and this month's President of the Security Council, Mr. Gizenga formally served notice that the seat of "lawful government" had been moved from Leopoldville to Stanleyville, the capital of Oriental, or Eastern, Province.

Stanleyville is the pro-Lumumba stronghold where whites were threatened with death last week unless Mr. Lumumba, the deposed Premier, was freed from prison in Thysville. Mr. Lumumba is being held by the Leopoldville regime.

In Leopoldville, meanwhile, President Joseph Kasavubu was reported in favor of reviving Joseph Ileo's claim to the Premiership. Col. Joseph D. Mobutu, head of the army regime, was said to be opposed to the plan.

The United Nations command in Leopoldville was worried by Mr. Gizenga's move. High United Nations officials talked of a "potential civil war situation." They voiced fear that the Soviet Union, Ghana, the United Arab Republic and other countries favoring Mr. Lumumba might recognize Mr. Gizenga's "government" and send diplomatic missions to Stanleyville.

But the possibility that Col. Joseph D. Mobutu, Army Chief of Staff and head of the military regime, might start military action to bring Oriental Province under his control was discounted in United Nations quarters.

Gizenga Troops Tallied

Mr. Gizenga and his Left-Wing regime in Stanleyville said they had 3,000 loyal troops in Stanleyville and 3,000 more in the rest of the province.

Colonel Mobutu, United Nations quarters said, has neither the forces nor the transport system to venture on a military expedition into Oriental Province.

Mr. Gizenga took part in the recent conferences in Stanleyville during which the United Nations mission attempted to obtain assurances that the province's 2,000 Europeans would not be harmed.

United Nations and Western diplomatic officials here appeared to feel tonight that the outcome of the Stanleyville talks so far had been disappointing and that the plight of Europeans and other foreigners in Oriental Province remained serious.

Western observers in Leopoldville tonight voiced the suspicion that Soviet or other Communist agents were in Stanleyville in Mr. Gizenga's entourage. Mr. Gizenga is a graduate of the Prague Institute for African Studies, a training center for Communist agitators.

If diplomatic missions were to be established in Stanleyville, the next step might be the arrival of "technicians" and other "volunteers" to assist Mr. Gizenga, it was thought here.

As Mr. Gizenga acted in Stanleyville, signs of strain showed in the Leopoldville alliance of Lumumba opponents over the issue of who is to be Premier.

Colonel Mobutu is apparently opposed to Mr. Ileo, who was named by President Kasavubu to succeed Mr. Lumumba early in September. A Cabinet list was drawn up, but the Ileo Government never functioned.

Shortly after Mr. Ileo had been appointed, Colonel Mobutu assumed power in the name of the army. He said then he had acted temporarily, until Dec. 31, to end the political confusion caused by Mr. Lumumba's refusal to bow to his dismissal.

The New York Times
Antoine Gizenga

Colonel Mobutu named a governing commission of young intellectuals to rule the Congo under the army. Mr. Kasavubu approved the naming of the commission.

Mr. Kasavubu is now said to want Mr. Ileo to reshuffle his Cabinet and call a conference of Congolese politicians.

But as Dec. 31 approaches, Colonel Mobutu and his closest associates say that deadline for his regime to relinquish power no longer exists. They say the military governing commission will continue in office after Dec. 31.

December 14, 1960

Congo Army Rule Ended; Ileo Named New Premier

By PAUL HOFMANN
Special to The New York Times.

LEOPOLDVILLE, the Congo, Feb. 9—President Joseph Kasavubu proclaimed the end of the Congo's five-month-old military regime today and named a Provisional Government composed of members of the suspended Parliament.

Joseph Ileo, president of the suspended Senate and a close associate of Mr. Kasavubu, was named Premier.

President Kasavubu promised that Parliament would be reconvened "as soon as possible." The new Government was regarded here as a move to strengthen Mr. Kasavubu's Administration before the United Nations Security Council acts on the situation in the Congo.

The Cabinet took office at once, replacing an army-appointed governing commission of young intellectuals that was named after the army assumed power Sept. 14.

Bomboko Retains Post

Justin Bomboko, who was chairman of the governing commission, remains in charge of foreign affairs under the new Government.

Jean Bolikango, an influential representative of Equator Province, was appointed Vice Premier and Information Minister. Cyrille Adoula, a labor leader, was named Minister of the Interior.

The new Public Works Minister, Alphonse Ilunga, and two or three other Cabinet members, have in the past shown sympathy for Patrice Lumumba, the imprisoned former Premier. Most of the new ministers, however, have opposed Mr. Lumumba.

In a proclamation announcing the new Government, President Kasavubu said he dismissed the Lumumba Cabinet last September because it had "betrayed the country and its people."

The President said the Congolese National Army had restored public order. He added: "Maintenance of order in the country and defense of its territory represent the exclusive prerogative of a sovereign state."

This was understood as a new warning to the United Nations not to attempt to disarm the Congolese Army.

Maj. Gen. Joseph D. Mobutu, named commander in chief of the army last month, was absent from Leopoldville today. He is reported to be in Equator Province, where detachments of his troops are being shipped up the Congo River, presumably in a move against the pro-Lumumba forces in Eastern Province.

General Mobutu told members of the United Nations Conciliation Commission last week that he considered his political role ended and that he would henceforth devote himself exclusively to military tasks.

Mr. Kasavubu said he appreciated the work that had been done by the youthful members of the governing commission. Three members of the commission left for Belgium yesterday to resume their college studies.

The President noted that he had acted within his powers under the Provisional Constitution in naming a new Government before Parliament was convened. He said the Chamber and Senate could not be reopened immediately because many members were being prevented from reaching the capital.

Five ministerial posts in the new Cabinet were kept open for representatives of regions now separated from Leopoldville.

Mr. Kasavubu said the round-table talks on constitutional reform and the political crisis would continue. The parley is in its preliminary stage under the chairmanship of Mr. Ileo.

New Cabinet Members

Following is the list of members of the new Provisional Government:

Premier—Joseph Ileo.
Vice Premier and Information Minister—Jean Bolikango.
Interior—Cyrille Adoula.
Foreign Affairs and Foreign Trade—Justin Bomboko.
Finance—Pascal Nkay.
Instruction and National Education—Cleophas Bizala.
Labor—Felicien Kimvay.
Economic Affairs and Middle Classes—Jean-Pierre Dericoyard.
Planning and Coordination—Alois Kabangi.
Public Works—Alphonse Ilunga.
Agriculture—François Mopipi.
Civil Service—Paul Bolya.
Minister Resident in Belgium—Albert Delvaux.
Social Affairs—Jacques Massa.
Minister of State in Charge of Semi-Government Workers—Charles Kisolokela.

The Ministries of Defense, Justice, Communications, Public Health and Mines and Electricity will remain vacant until the posts can be filled with representatives from what Mr. Kasavubu called the "separated regions." These are the secessionist provinces of Katanga and South Kasai and the areas dominated by Lumumba supporters.

February 10, 1961

LUMUMBA MURDERED IN KATANGA; HIS BACKERS PREDICT A CIVIL WAR; U. N. CHIEF CALLS FOR FULL INQUIRY

SITE KEPT SECRET

By PAUL HOFMANN
Special to The New York Times.

LEOPOLDVILLE, the Congo, Feb. 13—Patrice Lumumba, deposed Premier of the Congo, was killed yesterday by tribesmen, the Katanga radio announced today.

The broadcast said Mr. Lumumba, who was 35 years old, and two associates were murdered by inhabitants of a village they had passed while in flight. The three men had been in the custody of Katanga authorities acting on behalf of the Leopoldville Government, which Mr. Lumumba opposed, until they escaped Thursday night.

[A spokesman for the Katanga Provincial Government refused to identify the village where Mr. Lumumba was killed and where he was buried. He said that vengeance might be taken against the tribal inhabitants.]

The village where the three men were killed was said to be in the area of Katanga known to be violently opposed to the policies of the late Premier.

Slain Associates Identified

The two other victims with Mr. Lumumba were identified as Maurice Mpolo, Minister of Youth in the Lumumba Government, and Joseph Okito, vice president of the suspended Congolese Senate.

Congolese followers and foreign supporters of Mr. Lumumba's policies predicted that civil war would result from his death. Fears arose that new anti-white violence might break out in Eastern Province and other areas dominated by pro-Lumumba forces.

The United Nations disclosed

today it had warned President Moise Tshombe of Katanga that the responsibility would rest with him if United Nations troops clashed with his forces, which are fighting rebels in Katanga.

Force by U. N. Hinted

The warning was interpreted as reflecting new orders to United Nations detachments in Katanga to use force if necessary to stop the operations of Mr. Tshombe's troops.

A United Nations note to Mr. Tshombe was said to have requested that he halt his offensive against Baluba tribesmen in the northern part of his province who oppose his regime.

The announcement that Mr. Lumumba was dead was received with outward calm in Leopoldville, the capital of the Congo.

The news was first broadcast by the radio station in Brazzaville, in the former French Congo across the Congo River.

A United Nations spokesman voiced "shock and horror" over the news. He said, "The slaying of political personalities is bound to have repercussions. The question of the responsibility now arises."

The Katanga radio announced last Friday that Mr. Lumumba and his two imprisoned associates had escaped the previous night.

However, for several days before that announcement persistent rumors spread here that the three men had died in prison.

United Nations troops throughout the Congo were alerted for possible incidents, but the United Nations command said tonight it had received no reports of any major disturbances.

No comment on Mr. Lumumba's death was available from the Congo Government or from President Joseph Kasavubu.

The United Nations instructed Brigadier Iyassu Mengasha of Ethiopia, chief of staff of the international force in the Congo, to stay on for the time being in Elizabethville.

Brigadier Iyassu and two United Nations investigators flew there yesterday for an inquiry into Mr. Lumumba's disappearance. President Tshombe refused to receive them, however, on the ground that the Lumumba case was an "internal Katanga matter."

A spokesman here said the United Nations had taken emergency measures to make more of its troops available in northern Katanga. At the beginning of Mr. Tshombe's offensive last week-end only a few Moroccan and Swedish platoons were in the area. The spokesman declined to disclose the details of the United Nations military movements.

The spokesman denied today that the latest United Nations protest to Mr. Tshombe had contained the term "genocide" to denounce the Katanga regime's action against the rebellious Balubas. Last night the spokesman had said that United Nations headquarters here felt that the offensive was marked by "elements of genocide."

The charge, implying indiscriminate extermination of an ethnic group, was said to have been based on a report given by a member of the Katanga forces to a Swedish United Nations officer. He was said to have reported that orders had been given to burn Baluba villages.

There was no confirmation that villages had actually been burned. United Nations sources estimated that approximately 2,000 Katanga soldiers, led by European officers, were employed in the military operations.

February 14, 1961

CONGO CHIEFS MAP KASAVUBU REGIME WITH WIDE POWER

Draft Constitution Indicates a Strong Central Control on Federal Pattern

By HENRY TANNER
Special to The New York Times.

LEOPOLDVILLE, the Congo, May 12 — Congolese leaders made public today a project for a "United States of the Congo" with a strong central Government.

A draft project for a new Constitution was read to a plenary session of the conference at Coquilhatville, capital of Equator Province, after three weeks' work in commission. The conference will vote on it in a few days. Its adoption without major change is expected.

At that time it will be decided whether the new state will be called a federation or a confederation. The draft project uses both terms.

In a federation, sovereignty would be vested in a central government with wide powers in military, economic, financial and diplomatic affairs. In a looser confederation, sovereignty would lie with individual member states, which would delegate some of their prerogatives to a weak central executive.

Kasavubu to Be Head

The principal point of the project is that the chief of state would have strong powers. There is no doubt that Joseph Kasavubu, the present President, will hold that position.

The draft project thus completes the defeat of President Moise Tshombe of secessionist Katanga Province, who managed to get acceptance for his concept of a loose "confederation of independent states" at the conference of Tananarive in the Malagasy Republic in March.

The leaders of the Central Government developed second thoughts about Mr. Tshombe's project after they returned from Tananarive. They went to Coquilhatville determined to defeat him.

Mr. Tshombe was arrested after he walked out of the conference. He has been held in a villa at Coquilhatville and there have been unconfirmed reports that his transfer to Leopoldville may be imminent.

Premier to Share Power

The draft states "the executive power belongs to the President of the confederation." The President's decisions would have to be countersigned by the Premier of the Central Government or by the minister directly involved.

There would be a Federal Congress, presumably identical with the Assembly and Senate that came into existence with independence nine and a half months ago. The draft stipulates that the Congress would be elected by popular vote, but it is not clear when the election would be held.

In addition, there would be a Council of States, consisting of the heads of individual member states, mostly tribal chiefs.

The new federation or confederation would consist of an undetermined number of states, including Albert Kalonji's "Kingdom of South Kasai" and the "Federal city of Leopoldville," the capital.

The draft thus leaves to the future the difficult problem of drawing boundaries of member states. A majority of the Congolese leaders are understood to be in agreement that the six provinces established by the Belgians should be increased to twelve or thirteen, carved out along tribal lines.

Central Powers Defined

The Central Government would have exclusive control of foreign affairs, defense, internal security, currency, Federal finance, customs, communications, the Federal judiciary and legislation on citizenship.

Federal legislation would be promulgated by the Congress, but could be vetoed under certain circumstances by the Council of States. The President might proclaim a state of emergency if the federation was faced with an external threat.

The Government leaders are understood to be planning the convocation of a commission of constitutional lawyers from several countries to give the Constitution its precise final terms. After that the Constitution is expected to be submitted either to Parliament or to the nation in a popular referendum.

Prior to carrying out this plan, however, the Central Government has to establish control over secessionist Katanga Province and to convince Antoine Gizenga, head of the Lumumbist regime in Stanleyville, to give up his own brand of secession.

May 13, 1961

The Tshombe Riddle

Everything is at odds and ends in the Congo and nobody seems to know what's what and who's who. A prime example is the case of Moise Tshombe. Shortly after the Congo won its independence a year ago, Mr. Tshombe took the mineral-rich province of Katanga out of the Congo and proclaimed it a separate state and himself its President.

Last April, after Mr. Tshombe walked out of a "unity" conference sponsored by the Central Government of President Joseph Kasavubu, the Kasavubu regime arrested him. Since then President Kasavubu has been trying to set the stage for a new and peaceful era in the Congo. He has called for a tightly knit federation of Congolese states including Katanga, under a strong central government. He has recalled Parliament, which was suspended during the factional strife last September. He has sought a compromise settlement with his chief rival, Antoine Gizenga, the Soviet-backed leader in Stanleyville.

Until two weeks ago, his efforts had appeared to be successful. Mr. Gizenga agreed to attend the new session of Parliament, which was originally scheduled to convene today, under U. N. protection.

Then, week before last, the commander-in-chief of the Congolese army, Gen. Joseph D. Mobutu, released Mr. Tshombe. Last weekend in Leopoldville, before he returned to Katanga, Mr. Tshombe signed an agreement with the Central Government which was reported to have ended Katanga's secession.

But last Monday Mr. Tshombe went back to Elizabethville, his capital, castigated the Central Government as "corrupt and weak," and said he would keep Katanga independent "at all cost."

As a result, there is uncertainty about what lies ahead in the Congo. Mr. Tshombe insists on new negotiations among the various Congolese leaders before Parliament meets. The feeling now is that Parliament is unlikely to convene before the end of summer.

As for the role of the United Nations, it has sought all along to bring peace to the Congo without taking sides in internal disputes. It has been operating under serious handicaps. For one thing, its neutrality policy has been strongly attacked by the Soviet bloc and some African nations. Secondly, its operations in the Congo—including the maintenance of 18,000 troops and a group of civilian technicians — are costly and many U. N. members have been unwilling to pay their share. Nonetheless, the U. N. has succeded—so far, at least—in averting an all-out civil war in the Congo. Despite Mr. Tshombe's statements last week, U. N. officials still hope the Congo will be reunited under a federal constitution.

July 2, 1961

ADOULA ELECTED PREMIER IN CONGO

Landslide Vote Is a Victory for Kasavubu and U. N.

By HENRY TANNER
Special to The New York Times.

LEOPOLDVILLE, the Congo, Aug. 2—A landslide vote in Parliament swept Cyrille Adoula, a staunch follower of President Joseph Kasavubu, into office today as the new Premier of the Congo.

The Chamber of Deputies or lower house, voting first, gave Mr. Adoula and his Cabinet of National Unity a near-unanimous vote of confidence. There was only one abstention. The Senate then indorsed him by acclamation.

The verdict was a smashing victory for President Kasavubu who designated the new Premier yesterday. It was regarded as a bitter defeat for Antoine Gizenga, head of the Soviet-backed regime in Stanleyville who had sought the Premiership.

The outcome was also interpreted as a victory for the United Nations and for Dr. Sture C. Linner, the Swedish head of its mission here. Dr. Linner and his aides played a key role in bringing about the Parliament session under the protection of United Nations troops.

Gizenga Is Silent

Mr. Gizenga was listed as First Vice Premier in the Cabinet list that Mr. Adoula presented to Parliament. It was not known whether Mr. Gizenga would accept that post or whether he would repudiate the verdict of Parliament.

The Stanleyville leader never showed up at the Parliament session despite pledges that he intended to come. He has raised various arguments with procedures here from Stanleyville and thus laid the ground for a possible repudiation of today's vote.

Christoper Gbenye, Mr. Gizenga's top aide, was named Interior Minister. Mr. Gbenye was present at the session and presumably is willing to take his post.

The key positions in the new Government — with the exception of those reserved for Mr. Gizenga and Mr. Gbenye — went to men who are strong supporters of President Kasavubu or at least have been willing to work with him.

Mr. Adoula will keep his old post of Defense Minister in addition to the Premiership. Justin Bomboko will remain as Minister of Foreign Affairs and Joseph Ileo, the outgoing Premier, will take over the Ministry of Information.

Tshombe Foe Named

Jason Sendwe, a tribal leader from northern Katanga and a bitter rival of the provincial President of Katanga, Moise Tshombe, was named Second Vice Premier. Jean Bolikango, outgoing Minister of Information, is the Third Vice Premier.

The Cabinet is believed to include a total of twenty-seven ministers and about fifteen secretaries of state.

The Parliament's verdict appeared to indicate a further decline of Mr. Tshombe's political power. The decision by Parliament showed that Mr. Kasavubu did not need Mr. Tshombe's vote and that Mr. Tshombe did not have the balance of power in the Congo.

Mr. Tshombe boycotted the Parliament session and forbade his twelve Senators and Deputies to attend.

Later in the evening Mr. Adoula told newsmen he would "bring Katanga into line as soon as possible." The new Premier is known to believe in a strong central government.

Mr. Adoula also said he was going "to try bringing peace and order to the Congo and to reunify the army."

The vote took Congolese and foreign observers by surprise. Most had expected Mr. Adoula to scrape by on a narrow margin. But many had refused to rule out a victory by Mr. Gizenga.

August 3, 1961

GIZENGA TO JOIN ADOULA'S REGIME

Stanleyville Leader Accepts Post as a Vice Premier in New Congo Government

By DAVID HALBERSTAM
Special to The New York Times.

STANLEYVILLE, the Congo, Aug. 18—Antoine Gizenga publicly recognized today the Government of Premier Cyrille Adoula as the only legal Congolese Government.

Mr. Gizenga, leader of what had been a dissident Soviet-backed regime here, made a rare public appearance to announce that he would accept the post of first Vice Premier in the Adoula Government.

Mr. Gizenga spoke with Premier Adoula at his side. Standing arm-in-arm, they embraced and smiled.

Nevertheless, there were disturbing undertones. Mr. Gizenga, leader of the pro-Lumumba forces, gave no indication when he might go to Leopoldville. He told a crowd of 30,000:

"The Government will have to follow the Lumumba line and if ever the Government departs from this line of truth, I am ready to fight again."

Mr. Gizenga was referring to Patrice Lumumba, the slain former Premier. By the Lumumba line, Mr. Gizenga said he meant the Congo for the Congolese.

During Mr. Gizenga's speech, when he mentioned the possibility of going to Leopoldville, some of the people in the crowd shouted: "Don't go! Don't go!"

The warnings stemmed from suspicion here of the head of the Congolese Army in Leopoldville, Maj Gen. Joseph D. Mobutu. In Stanleyville, capital of Eastern Province, General Mobutu is pictured as a traitor who is ready to destroy all pro-Lumumba forces.

The shouts apparently disturbed Premier Adoula. Moments later, in his own speech, he said:

"There is only one thing that pains me and that is when you said that Gizenga should not go with me. You are probably frightened because the country is divided.

"In Leopoldville people said the same thing, they told me the same thing—they said I should not come here because it was too dangerous and I would be killed. But I did not listen to them and I came."

Then the Premier said that Mr. Gizenga would be his "right hand."

"Do you want me to work without my right hand?" He asked. He added:

"We have achieved what Lumumba wanted—one Congo, one Congo, one Congo."

The speech and a parade ended a three-day visit here by Mr. Adoula. After the parade Mr. Gizenga accompanied Mr. Adoula to the airport and the Adoula party returned to Leopoldville.

It is expected that the Soviet bloc and the African nations that had recognized the Gizenga regime will now move their diplomatic missions to Leopoldville. Many of these missions had been expelled from Leopoldville by President Joseph Kasavubu.

Gen. Victor Lundula, head of the Stanleyville army, made no pledge of loyalty to the Congolese National Army. But he appeared friendly throughout Mr. Adoula's visit. United Nations officials felt his loyalty was assured.

Even the Communist-bloc newsmen who attended the parade seemed somewhat surprised that Mr. Gizenga showed up. It was his first public appearance in five months.

Mr. Gizenga is a small, delicate-looking man. He wears glasses and has the look of a schoolteacher. Some African diplomats refer to him as "the headmaster."

As a speaker Mr. Gizenga is not so forceful or emotional as many other African leaders. But he spoke for a long time today under a broiling equatorial sun.

Mr. Gizenga's decision to recognize the Adoula Government publicly was made last night. It was then that he summoned to his home all the diplomatic missions accredited here to inform them that he recognized Mr. Adoula as Premier and that they would move their missions to Leopoldville.

August 19, 1961

U.N. ARMY TAKES KATANGA; DEFEATS TSHOMBE FORCES IN FIGHT ENDING SECESSION

BATTLE IS FIERCE

32 Dead, Many Hurt in Street Fighting —Tshombe Hiding

By DAVID HALBERSTAM
Special to The New York Times.

ELISABETHVILLE, the Congo, Sept. 13 — United Nations forces seized control of this city today in fierce fighting with troops of Katanga Province.

The United Nations announced that Katanga was now under the authority of the Congolese Central Government at Leopoldville, after fourteen months of secession.

At least thirty Katangese and two United Nations soldiers were killed in the fighting. Many more were wounded, among them a score of United Nations troops.

The sharp resistance met by the United Nations forces and the open bitterness of the Belgian community and many Africans here left some doubt whether the violence had ended.

Action Begins Early

Moise Tshombe, President of the province, who led it into secession soon after the Congo won its independence from Belgium last year, was in hiding, reportedly in Elisabethville. A friend quoted him as saying: "The United Nations lied to me all along."

Also missing was Godefroid Munungo, Mr. Tshombe's Minister of Interior and a leading opponent of the United Nations' effort to unify the country. Mr. Munungo's home was one of the first targets of the United Nations take-over, which began at 4 A. M. But apparently he and other Katangese had been forewarned, for he was gone. One report said he had fled to near-by Northern Rhodesia.

Other Ministers Arrested

Two other Katanga ministers were arrested. It is believed that the United Nations forces have orders for the arrest of several ministers and probably for the arrest of Mr. Tshombe himself, but spokesmen here said the United Nations still regarded him as provincial President, under the authority of the Central Government.

Efforts were apparently being made through intermediaries to persuade Mr. Tshombe to surrender. Meanwhile, the Congo Government at Leopoldville dispatched an aide here to direct provincial affairs.

Although his name was not announced here, he was believed to be Egide Davidson-Bocheley, a former police official of the Left-wing regime at Stanleyville, the capital of Eastern Province.

The United Nations representative here, Dr. Conor Cruise O'Brien, said the take-over had been requested by the Leopoldville Government of President Joseph Kasavubu and Premier Cyrille Adoula.

Before dawn, the United Nations command sent one company of Indian Gurkhas to seize the post office in the center of the city, which houses communications; another company of Gurkhas to the radio station, and two platoons of Swedish troops to Mr. Munungo's home.

To their surprise, the United Nations troops found Katangese soldiers dug in at all three points. What had been expected to be a swift and bloodless take-over developed into wild hand-to-hand fighting. While the three key points had been taken by 8 A. M., sporadic clashes occurred through the day and after nightfall.

The United Nations troops at first addressed the Katangese over portable loudspeakers. In French and Swahili, they told the defenders that they were surrounded, and that the United Nations was not seeking to disarm them but only to take over the key points.

The Katangese replied with machine-gun fire.

About thirty paratroops held the post office, with two machine guns mounted on the roof. The Gurkhas, accompanied by armored cars, dashed into an alley and entered the building, then fought their way from room to room, hurling grenades and firing submachine guns.

As the fight was still raging, a reporter telephoned the post office. A Katangese replied: "We are all dying."

Two hours after the shooting began, it suddenly ended. Katangese prisoners filed out, their hands in the air, amid the shouts of Gurkhas and onlookers. Minutes later a Katangese armored car reached the scene and the shooting resumed.

Twenty Prisoners Taken

When it was over, the United Nations had twenty prisoners. The post office was strewn with shattered furniture, equipment, weapons and bodies. More weapons and bodies and wrecked jeeps littered the street outside.

As the shooting ended, the square in front filled up with Europeans, shouting curses and obscenities at the Ghurka troops. The whites, many of them former Belgian officers in the Katangese army, waved their fists and cried: "Give us arms!" until they were driven off by the United Nations soldiers.

A car filled with Katanga policemen slowly turned a corner en route to the post office. From the United Nations hospital near-by, a machinegun chattered. An Indian officer rushed to stop it, but he was too late. Two of the policemen had been killed instantly, two more were dying and a fifth was walking dazedly away, wounded in the arm.

Some Europeans followed the wounded man shouting at him: "Why don't you fight? Why do you leave your men? Fight, coward!"

A Red Cross ambulance arrived to pick up wounded. Some jittery United Nations soldiers fired at its tires. A machinegun bullet creased the leg of Ray Wilson, a British correspondent for the National Broadcasting Company.

September 14, 1961

HAMMARSKJOLD DIES IN AFRICAN AIR CRASH

12 OTHERS KILLED

Lone Survivor Reports Explosions on Flight to Tshombe Talks

By DAVID HALBERSTAM

Special to The New York Times.

NDOLA, Northern Rhodesia, Sept. 18—Secretary General Dag Hammarskjold of the United Nations was killed today with twelve other persons in the crash of a plane carrying him to a meeting with President Moise Tshombe of Katanga Province. The meeting had been called in an effort to end the fighting in Katanga.

The bodies of the Secretary General and his staff were found about four miles from the Ndola airport in Northern Rhodesia. The plane had been scheduled to land at the airport last night.

[The Associated Press said that mistaken identity and tight security led it to report erroneously Sunday night that Mr. Hammarskjold's plane had reached Ndola.]

The site of the crash is close to the border of the Congolese province of Katanga. The Congo is an area that has demanded much of Mr. Hammarskjold's time and patience in the last fifteen months.

Crash Stuns U. N. Aides

The news of the crash stunned this area. Earlier today United Nations officials at Elisabethville seemed dazed as they kept hearing reports that Mr. Hammarskjold had not arrived in Ndola.

[The Associated Press reported that the lone survivor, Harold M. Julian, a United Nations security guard, said that a series of explosions had preceded the crash. He also said that the plane had turned away from a landing, apparently on Mr. Hammarskjold's orders.]

At near-by Kitwe, in Northern Rhodesia, President Tshombe was holding a news conference and was saying that he hoped to meet in a few minutes with the Secretary General and end the war when a newsman said:

"President Tshombe, Mr. Hammarskjold is dead. His body lies not far away in the wreckage of his airplane."

Mr. Tshombe's face reflected shock and horror seemed to show in his eyes.

Tshombe Expresses Regret

"I regret it very much if what you say is true," he said. "He was a man who enjoyed the respect of many African nations and I had hoped to reach a settlement with him that would leave Katanga free."

Earlier in his news conference Mr. Tshombe had attacked United Nations policy in the Congo.

Mr. Hammarskjold's plane was a United Nations DC-6B. It left Leopoldville yesterday. Much concerning the crash remains inexplicable.

The Secretary General's plane apparently crashed after it had circled the Ndola airport twice and had been waved in. No one here could offer any explanation for the crash.

It was believed that the plane might have taken a circuitous route to avoid the Katanga area, which is patrolled by one Katanga jet fighter. This might account for the plane's late arrival here and it might account for some fatigue on the part of the pilot.

There apparently was only one survivor, a man who was found severely burned and in a delirious state near the plane. He was taken to a hospital.

Those who have been trying to end the Katanga fighting believe that Mr. Hammarskjold's death was a terrible blow to hopes for a truce.

Mr. Tshombe has refused to meet with United Nations officials in Elisabethville, the Katanga capital, since the United Nations took over there last Wednesday in an attempt to restore the province to the control of the central Government in Leopoldville.

It is now feared that the Katanga fighting will become worse.

At the scene of the crash in the tree-covered African plain there was a long scar of broken trees and torn up dirt where the plane had rammed through. A giant anthill stood at the end of the path. All that remained of the main fuselage was a gray circle of ashes.

The only recognizable part of the plane was an engine cowling that had been thrown sixty yards behind the wreck.

Only Mr. Hammarskjold's body was practically unburned and immediately recognizable. Rescue workers said they had found a total of twelve bodies and that one appeared to be the body of a woman. The one survivor had lain in agony for fifteen hours.

The decision of the 56-year-old Secretary General to fly here to meet Mr. Tshombe was a last-minute one, prompted by the Katanga fighting.

Before the fighting, United Nations officials worked hard to persuade President Tshombe to come to Leopoldville to meet the Secretary General. Mr. Tshombe refused.

He said he had not been invited by Mr. Hammarskjold to meet him in Leopoldville, but had rather been invited to a meeting of officials of the central Government that Mr. Hammarskjold would attend. The next day the fighting started in Katanga.

British Urged Meeting

The planned meeting of Mr. Tshombe and Mr. Hammarskjold appeared to have been prompted by British diplomatic officials in Elisabethville and in and in London. It was a well-kept secret until the moment that both parties were virtually on their way here.

It also appeared that Ndola had been a site suggested by President Tshombe. Rhodesian officials are considerably more sympathetic to his cause than to that of the United Nations.

Mr. Hammarskjold's plane was originally scheduled to land here at 10:30 last night. At 12:10 A. M. the plane was in contact with the control tower and was talked down to 6,000 feet. That was the last contact with the plane.

After the normal interval, overdue procedure was put into operation. Yet even this morning when Mr. Hammarskjold had not arrived there was no general state of alarm.

Spotter planes searched hundreds of miles. The police were alerted and they searched the countryside checking country roads for any sign of the plane. Airports for hundreds of miles around were queried as to whether the Secretary General had landed.

Then the first charred wreckage was spotted by a Royal Rhodesian jet plane. Col. Don Gaylor, United States Air Attaché at Pretoria, flew his plane slowly in on the course taken by the Hammarskjold plane when it was last in touch with the Ndola tower. His course brought him right over the wreck.

September 19, 1961

KATANGA'S RICHES BOLSTER TSHOMBE

Mining Industries Have Paid Levies to His Regime

By HENRY TANNER
Special to The New York Times.

LEOPOLDVILLE, the Congo, Dec. 10—The amazing resilience of Moise Tshombe, President of Katanga Province, in standing up thus far to all military and political pressures brought against him has many sources.

The most obvious is the wealth of the secessionist province, which has increased since the Congo became independent of Belgium in June of 1960. Katanga, a source of turmoil in the Congo, is again the scene of fighting between Katangese and United Nations troops.

Katanga, which produces copper, tin, cobalt, manganese, zinc and uranium, was the source of two-thirds of the Congo's exports before the Congo became independent.

Since independence and the province's secession from the central Government, the huge ore industries have been paying their taxes, export duties and other levies to the provincial Government. This has made Mr. Tshombe's regime one of the richest in any region of comparable size in the world.

Union Minière Aids Tshombe

A large part of Katanga's new wealth has emanated from the Union Minière du Haut-Katanga, the Belgian-controlled mining concern that is the largest in the province. Neutral observers and United Nations officials are convinced that the Union Minière has put its entire organization — workshops and an elaborate communications and transport system — at Mr. Tshombe's disposal in his fight against the United Nations.

Mr. Tshombe has used Katanga's wealth to buy planes, to provide his troops with modern military equipment and to pay large salaries to as many foreign advisers and military mercenaries as were willing to enlist.

The United Nations is now acting, under a mandate voted by the Security Council Nov. 24, to expel all mercenaries and foreign advisers from Katanga. It also acted militarily in Katanga last September, under a Security Council resolution authorizing the use of force, if necessary, to prevent civil war in the Congo. That action led to eight days of fighting that was ended by a cease-fire Sept. 21.

At the outbreak of the new fighting last Tuesday, which followed a denunciation of the latest Security Council action by Katanga, Mr. Tshombe was believed to have about twelve modern planes including transports. Twenty-two European fliers were reported to have been enlisted to fly them.

Arms Seized in September

In September, United Nations troops at Albertville, in northern Katanga, captured nearly 100 tons of arms and ammunition from the Katangese garrison there. According to United Nations sources, the arms included most of the modern weapons used by forces of the North Atlantic Treaty Organization, including Belgian submachine guns, bazookas and triple-barrel rocket projectors.

While Mr. Tshombe's forces gained strength, the Congolese National Army was disrupted after independence when mutinous soldiers expelled all but a handful of their Belgian officers. Discipline broke down and the Congolese National Army has been almost unmanageable ever since.

The Katangese army suffered no such disruption. After independence Mr. Tshombe dismissed and deported all soldiers who were not members of his own tribe, the Lunda. With the help of Belgian officers he then built a relatively efficient force.

Other institutions in Katanga also had the benefit of an orderly transition that was denied to the rest of the Congo.

Belgian officers and officials stayed on in the police and all branches of the civil administration. Belgian advisers continued to play an influential role in ministerial offices and many Belgian and other European business men continued their operations.

In other parts of the Congo Belgians fled. They stayed away for several months before they started to drift back in sharply reduced numbers.

The cooperation between Mr. Tshombe's government and Europeans in Katanga and the orderly transition from a colonial regime to independence is rated as Mr. Tshombe's major achievement.

December 11, 1961

GIZENGA RETURNS TO LEOPOLDVILLE

U. N. Guards Ousted Official —His Former Troops Are Said to Slay 5 More

By DAVID HALBERSTAM
Special to The New York Times.

LEOPOLDVILLE, the Congo, Jan. 20—Antoine Gizenga, deposed Vice Premier of the Congo, returned here today from Stanleyville on a United Nations plane. He went immediately to guarded quarters provided by the world organization.

Mr. Gizenga's arrival went almost unnoticed by the Congolese public. It was ignored by the central Government, which sent no representative to the airport to greet the plane.

From the moment the transport landed, Mr. Gizenga and his party were protected by Danish military policemen and a platoon of Nigerian infantrymen from the United Nations forces in the Congo.

[Rebel Congolese troops formerly loyal to the Gizenga political faction in Stanleyville were reported to have killed five Europeans in new attacks, sources in Ruanda-Urundi told The Associated Press.]

Mr. Gizenga had asked the United Nations to bring him here from his headquarters in Stanleyville, the scene of recent fighting between troops presumably loyal to Mr. Gizenga and those of the central Congolese Government.

The United Nations, apparently fearful of the tense situation in Stanleyville, where Mr. Gizenga's status had been almost that of a prisoner, agreed to the change. The organization said today, however, that Mr. Gizenga was being brought to Leopoldville at the request of the central Government.

It was revealed here that rebel Congolese troops once loyal to Mr. Gizenga, but now outlaw, had fired on a United Nations jet and had attacked another village in North Katanga.

United Nations jets, on a reconnaissance flight in the Kongolo-Sola area, found the village of Kilubi in flames. It is just south of Sola. The pilots reported that several smaller settlements between Sola and Kilubi were in flames.

On the road between Kilubi and Kongolo, one jet came upon a column of troops. They opened fire on the jet.

The pilot did not return the fire. A United Nations spokesman said he did not know whether the pilots had orders not to fire on the rebel troops.

The pilots saw no troop activity of any kind at Sola, which was presumed to have been attacked by the outlaw troops. The reconnaissance flights were started yesterday after the United Nations was told by the Red Cross representative in Elisabethville that rebel troops were mounting an attack on the large Roman Catholic mission at Sola.

Two Soldiers Sighted

The pilots arrived, sighted two Congolese soldiers and two military vehicles at the mission but saw no sign of the priests or nuns assigned there.

Catholic church sources in Leopoldville say they did not believe there were any priests or nuns left at the Sola mission by the time the Congolese troops arrived. The sources noted that the massacre in the Kongola of nineteen priests and Catholic workers had been reported more than two weeks earlier, giving the officials at Sola time to flee.

The renegade troops reported at Kongola were originally from Stanleyville and went into Katanga Province as part of an invasion force. They are believed to be responsible for the slaying of thirteen Italian airmen in Kindu in November. Their commander, Col. Alphonse Pakassa, a close personal friend of Mr. Gizenga, was arrested two days ago in Stanleyville by Gen. Victor Lundula.

The United Nations has pledged all possible assistance, including military aid, to the central Government in stopping and apprehending the rebel troops. But the United Nations spokesman said there were no new developments on possible retaliatory action against the rebels.

At the airport to greet Mr. Gizenga, the political heir of the late Premier, Patrice Lumumba, were about thirty members of his divided political party, who cheered and pushed forward to shake his hand.

Mr. Gizenga was met at the airport by Ahmed Abdoun, a Sudanese member of the staff of Dr. Sture C. Linner, the United Nations chief of the Congo operation.

Mr. Gizenga was driven to his guarded quarters in a United Nations car, protected by an escort.

Mr. Gizenga, who has been in defiance of the Central Government since early October, was censured by the Congolese Parliament this week and then deposed as Vice Premier. Premier Cyrille Adoula said earlier this week that legal proceedings were being started against Mr. Gizenga.

January 21, 1962

TRIBES REASSERT POWER IN CONGO

Aim Is to Revise Provinces to Follow Ethnic Lines

By DAVID HALBERSTAM

Special to The New York Times.

LEOPOLDVILLE, the Congo, Aug. 5 — Tribal political power is reasserting itself strongly in the Congo. It is manifest in the powerful desire of the Congolese to form new provinces along basically tribal lines.

When the Congo won independence from Belgium on June 30, 1960, there were only six major provinces in this huge country. With the sanction of Parliament, seven new provinces have been approved. A total of nineteen provinces is foreseen shortly.

Observers view the trend as essentially federalist and traditionalist and thus anti-nationalist and against the mainstream of pan-African political development. It marks, in effect, these observers believe, the failure of the late Patrice Lumumba and his nationalist movement to make any deep inroads into the traditional tribal alignment in the Congo.

There are, the observers note, about forty ethnic groups in the Congo, of which about twenty are major groups. The new provinces are generally being developed along major ethnic lines.

The new province of South Kasai, for example, is essentially a Baluba tribal area, Cuvette Province a Mongo area and Kasai Central Province a Lulua area.

In addition, to meet requirements of size, some of the new provinces will encompass a major tribe and one or two smaller friendly tribes.

The new provinces are expected to be formalized in September or October after President Joseph Kasavubu has approved final petitions. In several disputed areas referendums will be held.

Observers here regard the following as the basic course of events:

The immense Congo, with its ethnic groupings and suspicion between tribes, had always been tribally oriented before independence. Yet, in the immediate pre-independence elections, Patric Lumumba, campaigning as a nationalist, made considerable headway against tribalism. Elected Premier, he became the leading political figure in the Congo.

According to the observers, Mr. Lumumba, as a detribalized figure urging national unity, represented the major pan-African force in the Congo. For this reason and others he was strongly backed by Ghana, Guinea and other countries with a pan-African outlook.

In the chaos that followed independence — the rioting, the secession of Katanga Province, the ouster and slaying of Mr. Lumumba — no government, including the present regime of Premer Cyrille Adoula, managed to extend its authority into the interior.

Period Called Crucial

Yet the post-independence period was a crucial time, according to observers, for it was then that the power of the tribal chiefs had to be broken and an illiterate people made aware that they are a nation, not a collection of tribes.

Instead, the observers say, what occurred in the interior was a breakdown of authority. In the vacuum created by the end of Belgian colonial rule, the tribal chiefs, traditionally strong, reasserted their power. To most Congolese deep in the interior the chiefs are the most important symbol of authority.

For more than a year the Congolese Parliament has been debating the criteria for the new provinces. In April the Interior Ministry worked out the basic requirements: a province must have at least 700,000 inhabitants and be economically strong enough to support its own budget.

Belgians here contend that the new provinces will closely resemble the former Belgian colonial districts. They also say the formation of the new provinces may ease some of the acute tribal tension that occurred when two traditionally hostile tribes were lumped in one province.

August 6, 1962

Mystery—and Tragedy —of Tshombe

Disdained by his fellow African leaders as a 'white-man lover,' he yet inspires in his people a fierce loyalty. Here a reporter probes what he is—and might have been.

By DAVID HALBERSTAM

ELISABETHVILLE, the Congo.

ONCE upon a time, when it was already getting too late, the white man said to the Africans: You are free. The Africans were a bit surprised by the decision but they celebrated anyway, and one of the first things they set about doing was meeting other Africans. The British Africans met the French Africans, and in time both met the Belgian Africans. At first they met in twos and threes and then in small groups and finally they began to have conferences. At the conferences they had good times and sat around and talked about Portuguese Africans and white people. They all joined the United Nations and they began to use it as a social club. But there was one African who claimed he was free but, try as he might, he never was asked to the parties and never was invited into the club. In fact, whenever the members got together, they spent more and more time deciding what to do with him. This African was a very lonely African. His name was Moise Kapenda Tshombe.

Though it is officially winter now in this lovely land of the Congo, the sun is bright but there is hardly any time to go to the swimming pool and watch the Belgian girls in their bikinis. The old Elisabethville uncertainty is back—the old game of cat and mouse between the United Nations and the Katangan-ese (and sometimes it is hard to tell who is the cat and who is the mouse).

Here in Elisabethville there are the same demonstrations by the Katanganese against the Americans and the Indians; the same protests by the *Femmes Katangaises* to Mrs. Kennedy and Mrs. Khrushchev, and by the Katanganese Boy Scouts to other Boy Scouts; and Moise Tshombe is, as always, spending more time talking about his good intentions than revealing them. In New York, once again, the Security Council is about to decide whether there should be a new mandate on the Congo and Acting Secretary General U Thant is bringing new pressures to bear — trying to divert Union Minière tax revenues from Katanga and closing Elisabethville airport to all but U. N. planes. But in Elisabethville itself there is little new to report—oh yes, the people who were tired of the Congo problem a year ago, oh my, are they tired of it now.

THERE is a peculiar rhythm to Katanganese and Congolese negotiations. Relations are usually very bad but every third or fourth month there is a flicker of agreement. Leopoldville likes Elisabethville, Elisabethville likes Leopoldville and the United Nations beams proudly in the background. Two weeks ago, after an intensive month of cat and mouse, there was the beginning of agreement over a Federal constitution proposed by Premier Adoula of the Leopoldville Government and there were the usual sighs of relief. The U. N. promised to send constitutional experts. But in the Congo it remains traditionally easier to disagree on a constitution than to agree on one and optimism in Leopoldville remained cautious—as befits people after a twenty-five-month losing streak.

The man Leopoldville is wary about, even in dealings over a Federal constitution, is the very charming, very ingratiating President of Katanga Province, Moise Tshombe. If he is not the most popular African of his time, he is at least the most controversial; if not the most profound, then certainly one of the most clever and resilient. The son of an African millionaire, he is disdained by his fellow African leaders as a white-man lover. Yet he inspires in the black people of his region a loyalty as fierce as the debate he inspires in the rest of the world.

Curiously, his greatest detractors—the radical pan-Africans. who detest him beyond belief as a Quisling—and his greatest admirers, whose strange assembly includes segregationist Americans, have one thing in common: they both see Tshombe as a white African. For Africans, it is a case of the white man's money corrupting one of their number. For them, the trouble in the Congo has nothing to do with mutinous troops or irresponsible leadership or pan-African influence. It is due simply to the white man's neo-colonialism.

FOR his supporters, the case is equally plain. Tshombe is safe against communism and opposed to nationalization.

The true situation is not, sadly, that simple. For one thing, no matter what Tshombe may have been before, he is no one's puppet today. (For many observers, he now has as much leverage over the Union Minière in Katanga as this Belgian mining company has over him. Tshombe makes his own basic political decisions and although each may eye the other a bit suspiciously, each benefits the other immensely. The Belgians obviously find a business man like Tshombe easier to deal with than a nationalist like the late Patrice Lumumba.) The white man's political influence in Katanga is decreasing all the time. Indeed, Tshombe now appears to be a very *black* African — emotional (he will lose his temper at a messenger who brings him bad news), mercurial, stubborn, aware of the tribal roots of his people and sometimes, according to one observer, behaving more like a great tribal chief than a new nationalist leader.

AT a time when the new African nations are assuming more and more power and voice in the United Nations, it is perhaps only fitting that it should be a very obstinate African who is testing it to the limit. And it is also fitting perhaps that in a time of something like diplomatic sentimentalism toward Africans, Tshombe should be cashing in on it. Robert Gardiner, a United Nations' official in the Congo—and a Ghanaian himself—once complained bitterly over this sentimentality. "If it had been a Frenchman or an Englishman who was indirectly responsible for the death of Hammarskjold," he said, "can you imagine the uproar? But with him no one says anything."

There is, of course, a mainstream of African leadership (national unity is good, de-emphasis of tribal power is good, liquidation of opposition parties is understandable — these are some of the general rules) and Tshombe is clearly outside it. But the feeling is gaining on this continent now that it is dangerous to regard some African leaders as good and others as bad. Instead, it is felt, there is a tendency of all African leaders to adjust to their circumstances and rarely to rise above them. If circumstances make it convenient to shut off freedom of debate and freedom of the press, for instance, then it will be shut off.

It is entirely possible that some of the honored African nationalists of today would, in Tshombe's circumstances, have acted as he acted. And, conversely, Tshombe, under different conditions, might easily have become a great unitarist.

But there is no getting away from the fact that a secession, dubious under any conditions, becomes even less admirable when it happens to involve one of the richest little areas in the world. Nor is there anything admirable in signing agreements and then repudiating them or in offering money to the unemployed in Leopoldville—who Tshombe claims are the victims of Adoula's administration. In the Congo tragedy, Tshombe must take much of the blame.

Yet if Tshombe is a guilty man, it is part of the never-ending pathos of this Congo story that he is also a sad and tragic figure.

For here is the man who desperately wants the West to back him, and yet who is such an embarrassment to it. One is torn by the thought of what Tshombe might have been, the immense potential of this man. Had he been Prime Minister of a unified Congo, he would probably have been the most popular African ever to visit the United States.

One listens to his speeches proclaiming himself a pan-African, demanding economic unity of all African nations and warning that unless the United States gets its Katanga policy right it will inevitably face a solid bloc of anti-American African nations, and all this, too, is a bit sad somehow —like a little Negro boy in a classroom always raising his hand and being ignored.

Start with the Tshombe charm, which is considerable and not unimportant in the history of Katanga. He is a fine story-teller, acting out every event (his enemies, it seems, are always trying to cut off his head or, at the very least, placing knives at his throat, and so his fingers are always going to his neck). His marvelously expressive face changes back and forth between extreme joy and a sad downcast look—a "black Fernandel," as one reporter said. His unhappy expression was used in a famous Katanganese poster after his arrest at Coquilhatville. The message read: "He suffers for you. Be worthy of him."

He is immediately disarming. And Tshombe is aware of his appeal. Recently, a high United Nations official was trying to entice him into joining the Leopoldville Government, saying he might become a powerful force there because of his political ability. "People can't resist you," he declared. "I know," Tshombe answered.

He is a consummate politician and his power in South Katanga — the only area he cares about — grows stronger all the time, abetted by the sense of nationalism which two military conflicts with the U. N. has produced. Probably more than any other Congolese politicians, he has visited the interior regularly since independence and each time he makes a trip, he stops his car almost every time he sees two Africans and gets out to shake hands and chat.

AT an Indian military party, he told the Indians with considerable feeling that it was an Indian trader in North Katanga who taught him the meaning of independence. On Israeli Independence Day, he dons a yamilke and with his entire Cabinet goes to the local syngogue to tell the congregation that what Israel wanted is what Katanga wants—that no nation has more to teach Katanga than Israel.

For all his declarations of anti-communism, he was not above holding his delegation back from the Lovanium Conference and thereby risking a radical Leftist take-over of the central Government. Similarly, in Leopoldville today, his parliamentarians work regularly with the radical Left in an attempt to unseat the moderates. (According to some observers, the idea is that if the Government should fall to the Leftists, his secession would look far better to Western eyes.)

But for all his vanity, he has, as the United Nations has learned, a sharp and quick mind, and it is hard to get the better of him. The most recent to learn this was U Thant who, angered at Tshombe's inevitable stalling, recently referred to him and his Government as "a bunch of clowns." "Why, that was not only an insult but something of a surprise," commented Tshombe, referring to the fact that the day before Thant's representative in the Congo had offered Tshombe the job of Congo Vice President. "Me, the clown!"

He is deeply stubborn, and while there has at times been a United Nations theory that there were two Tshombes—a good one and a bad one—and it was simply a matter of getting enough time with the good one, it is now generally conceded that from the U. N. point of view there is only the bad Tshombe, that he has as little intention as possible of joining with Leo and that only the threat of military and economic force will bend him.

For an African nationalist, Tshombe is a strange mixture. He is, first and foremost, a conservative, deeply impressed with the power and use of money. His response when asked about the difficulties of living under colonialism is not to tell of the human and social problems but of the economic hardship of running a black man's store in a white man's world.

"If there is one African in the Congo who has suffered under colonialism, it is I," he declares. "Kasavubu and Adoula—they were only clerks. But every day I had to fight it out to make a living. The Belgians put many obstacles in my way. The Tshombes have come out of this so well because we are so courageous. The Tshombes don't run off. They will fight."

He is also something of an aristocrat. Tshombe was born to a great tribe and he is still acutely aware of the power of the chiefs. At a time when other African leaders are engaged in breaking it down, Tshombe works actively with it. "In Katanga today, chiefs are just as strong as they were before independence," says a European observer.

This explains in part why Tshombe is not a member of the pan-African Club but there are other and far better reasons: his secession, which is a cardinal violation of the rules (African leaders have a deep fear of splinter movements in their own countries); his comment when Lumumba died on Katangese soil ("The fuss over this evil man will soon die down. The people have no memories here. It is finished"); his constant opposition to the United Nations and thus pan-African will in the Congo; his frequent discussions with Sir Roy Welensky; the belief that he imports arms through Angola and the Rhodesias; his use of white mercenary troops, including Belgians and South Africans. All this is enough to make him odd man out.

HE was born forty-two years ago in the village of Musumba. His father, Joseph Kapenda Tshombe, was the most successful Congolese business man of his time. Tshombe senior spent the early years of this century traveling throughout the Congo with the Belgians helping to pacify many of the troubled regions, according to his son. "He was a very good diplomat. The chiefs trusted him and he kept the Belgians from using force," Moise says.

From this, Tshombe's father went into business—an unusual thing for a Congolese to do in 1914. The elder Tshombe knew Europeans liked potatoes and so he bought them up from African farmers and made trips on foot to sell them. Business boomed and by 1925 he was walking nearly 600 miles to Elisabethville — but now with fifty bearers porting meat, vegetables and other staples. There he used some of the cash to buy textiles to carry back to the village to sell to Africans. It was the beginning not only of a big retail store but also of a seven-thousand-acre farm and a transportation service.

AS far back as 1940, Tshombe senior employed a white accountant at $600 a month to take care of his business. Estimates are that the family fortune, before trouble struck, reached nearly $400,000. Tshombe claims his father was the first Congolese millionaire (in Belgian francs); the first Congolese to go to Europe on his own money; the first to have credit at the bank; the first to have his own car (a 1928 Chevrolet) and the first to be allowed to travel second-class with his family on the local railroad (there are three classes and the third was traditionally reserved for Africans).

Tshombe himself was educated by American Methodist missionaries. In a land where the Catholic Church was virtually an arm of the colonial administration, American Protestants and even the minority of Africans who followed them were considered, according to Tshombe, as "foreigners and captes." In 1935, he was doing well in school and wanted to become a minister himself. He had been encouraged by the Methodists to study in America and his father had the money. But the Belgians, he says, refused him permission to go.

It is a point that rankles deeply. He believes that if he had somehow been able to go to school in America, he might have been the African to whom everyone turned at the time of independence—an African with many contacts on the continent and in the West.

HIS bitterness is particularly sharp now because it is the same America, which he always saw as helping to fulfill his own ambitions and whose missionaries were his closest friends, that is now thwarting his chances of recognition and financing the United Nations—his opponents. His feeling toward America is similar to that curious blend of love and hate which other African leaders feel toward their former colonial masters.

Eventually, the Tshombe family went bankrupt. Trying to find out what happened today is extremely difficult for no two people tell the same story. Tshombe claims that the Belgians feared his father and encouraged him in deals that were bound to fail. His enemies say that his father was solvent but that Moise and his brothers frittered the money away.

Several years later, Moise himself went bankrupt. At this point, Belgian creditors seem to have shown considerable leniency. The farm and retail store business were returned and the Tshombes were soon solvent again.

IT was from business and trading that Tshombe, already president of the African Chamber of Commerce in Elisabethville, where the Tshombes had opened a second store, went inevitably into politics. With his own and his wife's tribal standing, he was a formidable man among the Katanga Lundas. In 1956, he became head of the Confederation of the Mutual Associations of the Lunda Empire and with the leaders of several other tribal associations, formed what was in essence a tribal coalition party. His Confederation of Associations of Katanga, or CONAKAT, is to this day one of the best-organized and best-disciplined political parties in the Congo.

Tshombe, with Katanga's Interior Minister Godefroid Munongo, was co-founder and became its first president. With typical modesty he noted recently: "They asked me to become president but I refused because I was a business man. Munongo wanted to be president but he was not very brave. He was a civil servant in the Belgian administration and the Belgians said either you can work for us or you can make politics. So he made his choice. I went back to Sandoa and in my absence they elected me president. I wanted to stay in Sandoa—I was becoming a rich man. But they said you must help us and so I made the sacrifice."

The idea of Katangan independence was an early one in CONAKAT. It was, according to observers, both a black and a white idea—or a white idea that the blacks quickly and eagerly adopted.

For Europeans in Elisabethville, the desire to get out from under Leopoldville was old and nagging. They saw Leopoldville as a city whose skyscrapers were built from their work and taxes while their own city was never able even to have its hospital completed.

And there was another marked difference. The Belgians in hot, muggy Leopoldville were rarely settlers. They came and went every few years and were thus regarded somewhat disdainfully by the Elisabethville Belgians who, under one of the most delightful climates in the world, had become deeply rooted. Leopoldville, they declared, was "the milk cow." "We deal in copper, you deal in paper," they said. In independence, the Europeans saw the perfect time to sever the link; in the

Africans, they found willing partners.

The Katanganese sensed not only the financial benefits of separatism but the political excitement of it too—having their own country, foreign ministry, flags, parades and postage stamps. Moreover, the Belgians had ingrained in them a certain hostility toward Leo ("They speak different languages there and they are very far away, you know").

By the time independence arrived, Tshombe—already rebuffed at the round-table conference by the unitarists—had already made up his mind for secession. According to friends, he planned to declare it only two days before independence and was only prevented from doing so by the Belgian Vice Governor who threatened to arrest him. Since independence, the secession has continued—to the bewilderment of virtually everyone. More than two years have passed and while there is a feeling that time is Tshombe's greatest enemy and that it is closing in, it is a rash man who would predict the outcome now.

THE secession remains one of the most divisive international issues of the day—a deeply emotional issue and as draining a problem for the West as it is a crushing tragedy for the Congolese.

In the United States, it has become a simple matter of anti-communism. Critics of American policy see Tshombe as the hero of Central Africa, as a buffer between spreading black Africa and the remaining white Africa. For them, Leopoldville is a den of radical and unpredictable Africans and Tshombe is the one sound African. And Tshombe himself contributes to this idea. Everyone else in Africa, and the Congo in particular, is inevitably described as a Communist or a Communist dupe.

The State Department has a more sophisticated brand of anti-communism: it believes that if the Katanga secession continues the sound and moderate Leo Government will inevitably fall into more radical hands, and that even apart from what happens in Leo, the Katanga secession is a great open sore for the West—an issue on which the East can continue to flog the anti-colonial line in Africa without ever making a positive contribution itself.

MANY of the same people who now see Katanga as a historically separate entity are also the people who are loudest proclaimers of Tshombe as the greatest of all Africans. The tragedy of this is that if Tshombe is such an outstanding man, why didn't these same people see his qualities earlier, send him out of the country, build his prestige and make him what he himself wanted to be—the African all the others turned to when independence came?

This is the tragedy of Tshombe and another small part of the whole Congo tragedy—the endless waste of men and effort.

At the very best, all that Tshombe can do now is to continue his *de facto* secession and stand as a source of embarrassment to the West. For the West, he might have been a great man, but now in the West there is very grave doubt whether he is even a good man.

August 12, 1962

U.N. DRIVES ON IN KATANGA, VOWING END OF SECESSION; TSHOMBE OUT OF COUNTRY

RESISTANCE EBBS

Key Towns Captured—Leader of Province Remains Defiant

By J. ANTHONY LUKAS
Special to The New York Times.

LEOPOLDVILLE, The Congo, Dec. 30 — The United Nations command set up its offensive in Katanga today and vowed it would continue until the province's cessation was ended.

(President Moise Tshombe of Katanga arrived in Salisbury, Southern Rhodesia, Sunday, the Associated Press reported. He denied that he had fled Katanga. He charged that the United Nations was trying to force a solution on his cessessationists province.)

As United Nations forces continued to advance virtually unresisted, Robert K. A. Gardiner, the organization's chief officer in the Congo, declared, "We are not going to make the mistake this time of stopping short."

To Press for Decision

"This is going to be as decisive as we can make it," he said at a news conference at United Nations headquarters here.

This was the first firm statement of United Nations policy in the third round of fighting with Katangese forces. It indicated that the United Nations would not stop short of total victory, as it did in September and December of last year.

Reports from commanders in the field indicated that the United Nations forces were well on the way to that victory.

Late in the afternoon, the United Nations announced that a Ghanaian battalion had captured Kamina, 270 miles northeast of Elizabethville. **The Ghanaians were stationed at the big United Nations air base in Kamina. The base has been in United Nations hands for months, but the city had been under control of a gendermarie.**

Little resistance was encountered during the attack. The Ghanaians also captured two key railway bridges and a highway at the town of Kiowa, near Kamina.

Earlier in the day, an Irish battalion captured Kipushi, which straddles the Northern Rhodesian border 25 miles southwest of Elisabethville.

The Irish troops met no resistance from the gendarmerie, which fled into the bush, discarding weapons, equipment and armored cars. Not a shot was fired during the Irish advance for the time the force left Simba Hill, on the outskirts of Elisabethville.

President Tshombe and his ministers had been reported planning a last-ditch stand there.

United Nations troops were reported moving up the road from Elisabethville toward Jadotville and Kolwezi, both centers of the operations of Union du Miniere Haut-Katanga, the huge Belgian-controlled mining company in Katanga.

Officials here believed the attacks on Jadotville and Kolwezi would indicate whether the Katangese intended to put up any further resistance.

These centers would be the logical place for a final stand if one was to take place. But so far the gendarmerie has given no indication that it will respond to President Tshombe's appeal for resistance to the death.

Katanga Plains Destroyed

The Katangese capacity to hold out at either Kolwezi or Jadotville has been limited by United Nations air strikes during the last few days, which have apparently knocked out most of the Katangese air strength.

The United Nations reported that these attacks had knocked out all installations at the Kolwezi airport, including underground shelters, hangars, the control tower and the administration building.

Swedish Saab aircraft destroyed a light Harvard trainer on the ground at Kolwezi today. An earlier attack was said to have destroyed three other planes there, although one apparently was repaired and escaped.

Four or five more Harvards and two Vampire jets were destroyed at Hgule, another airfield near Kolwezi.

No planes were sighted on six other airfields inspected by United Nations aircraft. Four of the fields were blocked by gasoline drums.

The United Nations appealed tonight for all Katangese aircraft to be handed over. It said all such aircraft should be flown to the airfield of Manono between 6 A.M. and noon Tuesday. During this time pilots will be guaranteed free passage, it said.

The United Nations cleared the last resistance in the Elisabethville area. The Fourth Rajputana Rifles, Indian regiment, captured the last of 20 Katangese road blocks in the area, at Navundu.

It also seized a radio transmitter at Kilobolobe, on the eastern outskirts of the city. The Elisabethville radio station has been in United Nations hands since Friday.

African Group Approves

Meanwhile, the Pan African Freedom Movement for East, Central and South Africa adopted a resolution strongly backing the United Nations action in Katanga.

The organization which has been meeting here for three days, sent messages to President Kennedy, Prime Minister Macmillan and Secretary General U Thant.

The message to Mr. Kennedy praised the United States for its "enlightened Congo policy." It said the organization opposed pressure for a cease-fire before Katanga's gendarmerie was integrated and Katanga reunited with the Congo.

The message to Mr. Macmillan said the organization was "distressed" by reported British pressures to obtain such a cease-fire and "British manuevers in support of the secessionists."

Among the signers were Kenneth Kaunda, Northern Rhodesian nationalist leader; Milton Obote, Prime Minister of Uganda; Jomo Kenyatta, leader of the Kenya African Nationalist Union, and Rashidi Kawawa, Prime Minister of Tanganyika.

December 31, 1962

KATANGA'S BREAKUP COMPLETED BY CONGO

Special to The New York Times

LEOPOLDVILLE, the Congo, July 9—Moise Tshombe lost his position as President of South Katanga Province today.

Mr. Tshombe, whose secession ist regime defied the Congolese Government and the United Nations for two and a half years, was stripped of power by two bills signed into law.

The Congo's President, Joseph Kasavubu, signed the bills, which set up the provinces of East Katanga and Lualaba. The complete the dissolution of Katanga, begun last year with the establishment of North Katanga Province.

Mr. Tshombe may seek the presidency of either of the new provinces.

He is in Paris, where he went last month, ostensibly to seek treatment for eye and kidney diseases. Most observers believe that he fled to avoid arrest.

July 10, 1963

Insurgents Terrorize Kwilu Province in Congo

Special to The New York Times

LEOPOLDVILLE, the Congo, Jan. 16—Insurgent bands, armed by a former Congolese ambassador are causing panic in Kwilu Province, 250 miles east of here. It is feaerd that they are getting encouragement and help from abroad.

A curfew is enforced in Kikwit, capital of the province. Policemen and troops do not dare venture into rebellious territories inhabited by the Bapende and Babunda tribes. Rebels have virtual control over a third of the province.

The wives and children of four American missionaries have been evacuated from their post, 22 miles south of Kikwit.

Some diplomatic observers here view the situation as serious. They believe an attempt at yet another secession from the Congo may be in prospect.

Other observers take a less somber view. They note that the rebellion is limited to only two tribes. Troop reinforcements, which arrived in Kikwit yesterday by road from Leopoldville, may be able to contain it, they say.

Pierre Mulele, who was Ambassador to Cairo of the deposed secessionist Government headed by Antoine Gizenga, is leading the rebellion. He is secretary general of the left-leaning party of Mr. Gizenga, who has been imprisoned for the last two years.

Mr. Mulele returned to the Congo clandestinely last summer after a year and a half in exile in Cairo and Communist China. He joined his followers in Kwilu, where he had been elected a national Deputy in the 1960 elections before the Congo became independent.

Soon after his return, isolated acts of terrorism began in Mr. Mulele's region. Some administrative buildings and schools were burned and small bridges and ferries were damaged. A reward for Mr. Mulele, dead or alive, was posted by the provincial government.

Guerrilla training camps of "Mulele partisans" were discovered in the forests. Among articles said to have been found in the camps were two Russian fur hats, Soviet-made cameras, a portable combat radio, copies of a dissertation on guerrilla warfare by Mao Tse-tung, the Chinese Communist leader, and beer bottles filled with gasoline that could be used as bombs.

Mr. Mulele is known to have made several trips recently to Brazzaville, capital of the former French Congo, where he met with a group of insurgent Congolese politicians who are reported to receive support from Communist countries.

This group calls itself the National Committee of Liberation and vows to "free" the Congo from "foreign oppression." It consists of about 50 Congolese politicians, headed by Christophe Gbenye, a former Deputy Premier.

Last November the entire staff of the Soviet Embassy was expelled from Leopoldville following the arrest of two Soviet diplomats on their return from Brazzaville. Among documents found in their possession was a memorandum from Mr. Gbenye warning the Russians that Mr. Mulele was receiving Chinese Communist support.

Another note, addressed to a Soviet diplomat from a Gizenga Deputy in Brazzaville, said, **"Please don't give the money to Pierre, we will pass it on to him." Pierre is understood to mean Pierre Mulele.**

Informed sources believe that the Congolese exiles in Brazzaville have arms and they expect that these arms will soon show up in Kwilu. For the time being, however, the Mulele partisans use only bows and arrows, machetes and gasoline-filled bottles.

Within the last week, the guerrilla bands stepped up their activities. They ransacked a Portuguese-owned plantation at Lutshima, about 60 miles from the provincial capital. They destroyed 10 trucks and cars—all the vehicles in the region—burned the administrative buildings and fled with food and money.

Kwilu Province is a rich agricultural area. Palm oil plantations provide the main source of revenue. Until recently it was considered as one of the best administered provinces of the 21 created since the middle of 1962.

January 17, 1964

TSHOMBE CABINET IS SWORN IN CONGO

7 of the 18 Ministries Taken Over by the Premier and Another Katangese

By J. ANTHONY LUKAS
Special to The New York Times

LEOPOLDVILLE, the Congo, July 10—Moise Tshombe, President of Katanga Province when it was in secession, was sworn in today as the Congo's fourth Premier.

Godefroid Munongo, who served as Mr. Tshombe's interior minister during the Katangese secession, was named to head the Congolese Interior Ministry. He was also appointed Minister of Civil Service, an important patronage-dispensing post.

Between them, Mr. Tshombe and Mr. Munongo control seven of the 18 portfolios in the Cabinet.

In addition to the Premiership, Mr. Tshombe took four other ministries: Foreign Affairs, Planning, Foreign Trade and Information.

Radio Broadcasts Decree

Eight of the ten new ministers took the oath of office with Mr. Tshombe in a simple ceremony at President Joseph Kasavubu's residence on a hilltop overlooking the Congo River.

The ceremony took place 13 hours after Mr. Kasavubu issued a decree naming Mr. Tshombe head of a six-to-nine-month "transition" Government. The decree, broadcast by the national radio at 9 P.M. last night, ended 10 days of feverish political negotiations following Premier Cyrille Adoula's resignation June 30.

The Cabinet bore only superficial resemblance to the "national reconciliation Government" for which Mr. Tshombe has been calling since he returned from exile in Europe two weeks ago.

Settlement Is Sought

All the country's factions were represented in the Cabinet. However, none of their ministers appeared to be of sufficient stature or ability to stand up to Mr. Tshombe and Mr. Munongo.

The only two other men in the Cabinet with a national reputation were Albert Kalonji, the former "Mulopwe" [god emperor] of the secessionist state of South Kasai, who was named Minister of Agriculture, and André Lubaya, a member of the Communist-backed National Liberation Committee, who was named Minister of Health.

Desire for a political settlement with the Committee, which is backing revolts in Kivu, Kwilu and North Katanga Provinces, was a main motive for formation of the Tshombe Government.

However, observers doubted that Mr. Lubaya could speak for most of the Committee's other leaders, who are in the former French Congo and in Burundi. Christophe Gbenye, the Committee's president, has denounced Mr. Lubaya as a traitor for dealing with Mr. Tshombe.

There was no minister of defense listed in the Cabinet. However, informed sources said this post would be retained by President Kasavubu. He will run the ministry through a special commission headed by Gen. Victor Lundula, a former army commander, who has been serving as the President's military adviser. Maj. Gen. Joseph D. Mobutu, the army commander, is expected to remain in his post.

Prisoners to Be Freed

In its first session, the Tshombe Cabinet took three decisions apparently aimed at appeasing the National Liberation Committee and other leftwing movements.

First, it ordered the liberation of all political prisoners. Although he was not mentioned by name, this almost certainly will include Antoine Gizenga, the leftist leader, who has been imprisoned on the island of Bulembemba in the mouth of the Congo River for two and a half years.

Mr. Gizenga's liberation has long been demanded by the followers of the late Patrice Lumumba, the Congo's first Premier, who was murdered in 1961. Mr. Gizenga is widely considered Mr. Lumumba's political heir.

Opposition spokesmen have charged that there are about 600 political prisoners in addition to Mr. Gizenga, but there is no reliable information to confirm this.

Curfew Lifted in Capital

The new Government also ordered the lifting of the unpopular midnight to 5 a.m. curfew in Leopoldville. The curfew was imposed several months ago after a series of bombings attributed to the National Liberation Committee.

The Government's other action was to abolish the post of Resident Minister in Stanleyville, thereby lifting the virtual state of emergency in that northern city which is a stronghold of Lumumbist sentiment.

Following the afternoon meeting, Mr. Tshombe and the Cabinet made a triumphant tour of the city. Large crowds lined the streets to cheer their new Premier.

The 44-year-old Mr. Tshombe stood in the back of an open limousine acknowledging the ovation by clenching both hands over his head.

Earlier, following the swearing-in ceremony, Mr. Tshombe received another tumultuous welcome when he drove to the Premier's official residence, which Mr. Adoula had vacated only yesterday.

Several hundred persons massed along the fence bordering the garden crying "Vive Tshombe" and "Down With Adoula." Mr. Tshombe, dressed in his formal blue morning coat, gray-striped trousers and black tie, did a little jig of joy on the lawn and led the crowd like a cheerleader.

Secession Ended in 1963

Mr. Tshombe was enjoying to the full one of the classic comebacks of recent political history.

Eighteen months ago, in January, 1963, the Katangese secession was ended in the third round of fighting with United Nations troops.

Mr. Tshombe stayed on in Katanga until June, 1963. Then, after the Central Government cut away two-thirds of his province and threatened him with arrest for treason, he went into exile in Paris and later in Spain.

The Cabinet formed by Mr. Tshombe was the smallest in the Congo's history. It was well below the 18-minister limit prescribed in the new Constitution. Mr. Adoula's outgoing cabinet had 27 ministers and 6 secretaries of state.

Members of the Cabinet are:

Premier, Foreign Affairs, Planning, Foreign Trade and Information—Moise Tshombe.
Interior and Civil Service—Godefroid Munongo.
Finance—Dominique Ndingw.
Justice—Leon Mambuleo.
National Economy—Jean Ebosiri.
Agriculture—Albert Kalonji.
Public Works, Transport, Communications—Jules-Leon Kidicho.
National Education—Frederic Baloji.
Public Health—Andre Lubaya.
Youth and Sports—Joseph Ndamu.
Mines and Energy—Dolphe Kishwe.

July 11, 1964

MERCENARY UNIT IS READY TO FIGHT REBELS IN CONGO

Mixed Foreign Force Called Prepared to Act in Days, Despite Regime's Denial

By J. ANTHONY LUKAS
Special to The New York Times

LEOPOLDVILLE, the Congo, Aug. 24—A foreign mercenary force will begin military operations against rebels in the eastern Congo within a few days, authoritative sources said today.

Although a Government spokesman denied reports that mercenaries were being hired, the sources said such a force had been assembled at the Kamina military base in Katanga and would be pressed into use almost immediately.

According to the sources, about 80 mercenaries are training at Kamina, a huge former Belgian base 260 miles northwest of Elisabethville.

Most of the mercenaries at Kamina are South Africans or Rhodesians, many of whom fought for Premier Moise Tshombe when he was president of secessionist Katanga Province.

30 Arrive in Leopoldville

Another group of about 30 mercenaries, including men from most European countries, arrived in Leopoldville today. They are expected to go to Kamina within the next few days.

The Government denial was issued by Emmanuel Sinda, Premier Tshombe's official spokesman, following reports from Johannesburg, South Africa, that mercenaries were being recruited there for the Congolese Army.

Mr. Sinda said: "We have no intention of recruiting mercenaries to fight against the rebels. We will fight the rebels with our own soldiers. We have enough."

Newspapermen have talked with a number of mercenaries who have been here for a month. Some are now in Kamina.

Group Stays in Hotel

One group of about a dozen South Africans and Rhodesians has been staying at the Hotel Memling here since shortly after

Mr. Tshombe became Premier on July 9.

Among these is J. C. Puren, a South African who formerly fought for Mr. Tshombe in Katanga. Mr. Puren is reported to be the chief recruiter for the mercenary force.

Another member of the group is Michael Hoare, a former British Army officer, who has recently been seen wearing the uniform of a Congolese major. Mr. Hoare is reported to be heading the operation at Kamina.

A number of other South Africans and Rhodesians who have been here for a few weeks are flying Harvard trainers against rebel forces in the Kasai region.

Observers here have known for weeks that Mr. Puren and Mr. Hoare were negotiating with Premier Tshombe to provide a substantial number of mercenaries. They were said to have more than 200 men available in South Africa.

Both the Belgian and the United States Governments participated in planning for the force.

They are reported to have agreed at talks in Brussels last month that some sort of mercenary force would have to be organized to supplement the Congolese Army, which has virtually collapsed in the face of the rebel assault.

However, the United States also brought heavy pressure on Mr. Tshombe's Government to appeal to African Governments for troops.

The rebels, who are believed to be motivated by tribal dissatisfaction, are supported by leftist Congolese exiles in the former French Congo and by Chinese Communists from Peking's embassy in neighboring Burundi.

Diplomatic Cover

The United States hoped that a Congolese appeal to other African countries would at least provide a diplomatic cover for the mercenary operation and and that at best, if troops were provided, it would limit the number of mercenaries needed.

After talks here last week with G. Mennen Williams, Assistant Secretary of State for African Affairs, Mr. Tshombe appealed for troops from Ethiopia, Liberia, Nigeria, Senegal and Malagasy.

None has yet replied officially. The news that the mercenary force is being organized makes it unlikely that black Africans will intervene. They bitterly oppose the South African regime and its policy of apartheid, or complete racial segregation.

The use of South African mercenaries would merely confirm most Africans' view of Mr. Tshombe as a pawn of the white man. This reputation arises from his leadership of the two-and-a-half year secession of Katanga, during which he was supported chiefly by Belgian financial interests and used many European mercenaries in resisting Congolese governmental forces.

The precise role that the mercenaries will play here is still not clear. Reports from Johannesburg yesterday indicated that they would be organized in a single "Foreign Legion" brigade to be called the Congolese Army's Command No. 5.

Six Special 'Columns'

However, authoritative sources denied this. They said current plans called for organization of six special "columns," to be composed of mercenaries and Congolese soldiers.

Each column is to be headed by a Congolese officer and will have about 300 Congolese soldiers and 50 mercenaries.

The 50 mercenaries will be used as a spearhead at the head of the column to break through rebel positions.

It will be headed by a white officer but he will report, at least nominally, to the Congolese column commander.

The sources concede that in practice the spearhead will probably often act independently, but in theory it will always be under Congolese command.

The Congolese soldiers in the columns will be the best soldiers to be found. This means they will be drawn largely from the former Katangese gendarmes who have recently been reintegrated into the army.

The mercenaries will also occasionally be used in larger groups for what the sources call "special operations." One such operation might involve a lightning move to take an important rebel position. There were indications that the first use of the mercenaries in the east will be for such an operation.

The sources said the mercenaries would be members of the Congolese Army and would wear Congolese uniforms. Their salaries are said to range from about $400 a month for privates to about $1,100 for the top officers.

The salaries will be paid in either dollars or pounds sterling and will be deposited in foreign bank accounts.

Foreign Financial Help

The sources said the money would come from the Congo's own foreign-exchange reserves. However, observers believe the United States and Belgium have indicated they will help meet the cost of the operation.

The mercenaries will be armed with Belgian automatic weapons, standard in the Congolese Army.

They will use jeeps and trucks and other heavy equipment provided to the Congo by the United States under the military aid program.

Each column is expected to have air support, provided by planes of the Congolese Air Force flown by pilots on contract to the Congolese Government.

The sources said that the six columns would be organized at Kamina and that the first should be ready within two weeks. Other columns are expected to be made ready at intervals of about two weeks.

It is believed the columns will strike first against rebel positions in North Katanga and then move north toward Fizi, Uvira, Bukavu and Kindu. Finally, it is said, they will attack the chief rebel stronghold of Stanleyville.

August 25, 1964

BELGIANS DROPPED AT STANLEYVILLE TO SAVE HOSTAGES

Special to The New York Times

WASHINGTON, Tuesday, Nov. 24—The State Department announced early today that a battalion of Belgian paratroopers had been landed at Stanleyville to rescue more than 1,000 foreigners being held as hostages by the rebel Congolese government.

The 600 paratroopers, carried by United States military transport planes, apparently met little or no resistance and quickly captured and secured the Stanleyville airport.

Within an hour after it had announced the operation the State Department said that 117 of the hostages had been freed and were gathered at the airport on the outskirts of the city.

The State Department said it had received unconfirmed reports that many of the foreign hostages had been attacked by the rebels as they tried to make their way to the rescue force at the airport. These reports indicated that many of the foreigners had been wounded and that some of them had been evacuated to Leopoldville.

There were other unconfirmed reports that some of the foreigners had been killed.

Flown to Ascension

The first paratroopers were dropped shortly after dawn in Stanleyville (about 11 P.M. Monday New York time). After the airport was secured the rest of the paratroopers were landed.

As a precautionary move, the Belgian battalion had been flown to Ascension Island in the South Atlantic last Wednesday. They were moved on Sunday to a base at Kamina in the Congo, about three hours by air from Stanleyville.

The State Department emphasized that the decision to move the paratroopers into the rebel-held capital had been undertaken with great reluctance and concern, and only after it became apparent that the lives of the hostages were imperiled.

A total of 1,288 Europeans and Americans and 325 Indians

and Pakistanis had been held as hostages by the rebels. Among them are 59 Americans, including Dr. Paul E. Carlson, a missionary doctor condemned to death on charges of spying.

Action Held Last Resort

A State Department statement emphasized that the purpose of the action was "humanitarian" and designed "to save the lives of innocent men, women and children, both Congolese and citizens of at least 18 foreign countries."

The decision to send in a rescue force, the statement said, was taken "when every other avenue to secure the safety of these innocent people was closed by rebel intransigence."

The decision was made jointly by the United States and Belgian Governments and with the full knowledge and agreement of the Congo Government. The State Department made public a letter from Premier Moise Tshombe approving the rescue mission.

Secretary of State Dean Rusk was in the State Department operations center in the early morning hours following radio reports of the operation. The department was in periodic contact with President Johnson at his ranch in Johnson City, Texas.

The State Department said that when the rescue mission was accomplished, the force would be "withdrawn promptly."

The mission is "designed to avoid bloodshed—not to engage the rebel forces in combat," the department said. It added that the paratroopers were under orders to use force "only in their own defense or in the defense of the foreign and Congolese civilians."

From the first radio report it was not clear whether the paratroopers had encountered any resistance by the rebel forces.

American officials were uncertain of the whereabouts of the hostages.

In the last few days diplomatic discussions had been held in Nairobi, Kenya, with rebel representatives in an attempt to work out arrangements for release of the American hostages.

However, the department said, "it quickly became clear that the rebel representative was not concerned with the safety of the hostages or other humanitarian considerations but rather sought to use the lives of these civilians for political purposes."

November 24, 1964

TSHOMBE OUSTED AS CONGO PREMIER

He Violates Constitution by Staying, Kasavubu Says

Special to The New York Times

LEOPOLDVILLE, the Congo, Oct. 13 — President Joseph Kasavubu dismissed the 15-month-old Government of Premier Moise Tshombe today, touching off diplomatic anxiety for the Congo's stability.

One hour after dismissing Premier Tshombe, President Kasavubu named Evariste Kimba, once Mr. Tshombe's Foreign Minister in secessionist Katanga Province, to replace him.

President Kasavubu told a joint session of Parliament that he had dismissed the Government because it had not fulfilled the constitutional requirement that it resign on its own initiative.

The President has long said that the mission of the Tshombe "transitional government" would end with the opening of the new Parliament.

Addressing the opening session of Parliament, President Kasavubu said, "It is an evident fact that the present composition of the Government neither conforms to the constitutional norms nor to the electoral results nor to the imperatives that condition the political equilibrium of the country."

Under the present Congolese Constitution, the President holds the power to dismiss the Premier. President Kasavubu and Mr. Tshombe have been embroiled in a long dispute that, politicians and diplomats agree, concerns the forthcoming presidential election.

President Kasavubu, a candidate for a second term, was reported to be fearful of a Tshombe challenge because of the showing Mr. Tshombe's party made in last spring's general elections.

Aided by former Cabinet ministers, the President rallied small regional parties and renegades from the Tshombe party into an anti-Tshombe bloc. With this strength, President Kasavubu swept aside Mr. Tshombe's contention that he need not resign until a new President was elected.

Western and African diplomats had been pressing both sides to reach a compromise that would not further impair the country's stability. Until early this morning it appeared some formula had been reached.

Mercenaries a Big Question

The main fear arising from Mr. Tshombe's downfall is that the 600 white mercenaries bolstering the Congolese Army in the northeast will now abandon the Congo.

The primary allegiance of the

tion of the Government neither conforms to the constitutional

mercenaries, brought in by Mr. Tshombe and his advisers last summer, is unclear. Diplomats believe that many — especially the English-speaking South Africans and Rhodesians under Lieut. Col. Mike Hoare — may want to leave.

Military sources say that if this happens, the almost dead Congo rebellion could revive.

The Kasavubu alliance, called the Congolese Democratic Front, includes all of the men who ruled the Congo for four disorderly years.

Mr. Kimba, leader of the North Katanga Balubakat party, commands little allegiance. He is now canvassing support among other small regional parties to gain enough support to hold a majority in Parliament.

It was said to be likely that the 39-year-old Mr. Kimba, who is generally respected, would eventually have to turn to some members of the Tshombe party to get the necessary votes. The Tshombe party is the Congolese National Convention, called Conaco.

Such maneuvering for a coalition government makes Western diplomats here apprehensive. They noted that there was a similar government under Cyrille Adoula when the most recent rebellion began.

Meanwhile, one of Mr. Tshombe's aides said that Mr. Tshombe would remain in Leopoldville as a Member of Parliament. He said he could not say whether Mr. Tshombe would try to run for President from the Opposition benches.

October 14, 1965

Kasavubu Regime Ousted By Army Coup in Congo

By Reuters

LEOPOLDVILLE, the Congo, Thursday, Nov. 25—President Joseph Kasavubu was deposed early today in a bloodless military coup by Maj. Gen. Joseph D. Mobutu, the Congolese Army commander. General Mobutu installed an Army Government under his own direction.

Announcement of the coup was made in a dawn proclamation over the Leopoldville radio.

The proclamation of the new government named Col. Leonard Mulamba, 34 years old, as Premier in place of Evariste Kimba, who was named by President Kasavubu only 10 days ago to try to form a new government.

Maj. Gen. Louis Bobozo, head of the army command in the Katanga provinces, was named to replace General Mobutu as head of the army while General Mobutu assumed the role of President.

Leopoldville Is Calm

The proclamation said a meeting of high ranking army officers yesterday decided to remove the Kasavubu Government because of its "absolute failure" in the political field.

Leopoldville remained calm throughout the change of leadership and there were no extra military patrols evident in the city. But a handful of paracommando troops were stationed at the radio station and all transmissions were controlled.

Mr. Kasavubu, 53 years old, spent the night at his presidential palace in suburban Leopoldville.

He was due to leave the residence during the morning, a source close to the deposed President said.

This is the second coup by the 35-year old General Mobuto. In 1960, he deposed President Kasavubu and headed a college of Commissioners for nine months before handing back control to the parliament.

Today's coup follows a tense conflict between President Kasavubu and former Premier Moise Tshombe, the Katanga leader, who was removed from office as Premier by Mr. Kasavubu on Oct. 13.

But, led by Mr. Tshombe's Conaco party alliance, the Parliament refused on Nov. 14 to approve a Government led by Mr. Kimba, a North Katanga politician.

Figures in Leopoldville Shake-Up

Joseph Kasavubu

Camera Press-Pix

Maj. Gen. Joseph D. Mobutu

November 25, 1965

How C.I.A. Put 'Instant Air Force' Into Congo

Intervention or Spying All in a Day's Work

Special to The New York Times

WASHINGTON, April 25—At the Ituri River, eight miles south of Nia Nia in the northeast Congo, a government column of 600 Congolese troops and 100 white mercenaries had been ambushed by a rebel force and was under heavy fire. Suddenly, three B-26's skimmed in over the rain forest and bombed and strafed a path through the rebel ranks for the forces supported by the United States.

At the controls of the American-made planes were anti-Castro Cubans, veterans of the Bay of Pigs invasion of Cuba in 1961, three years before. They had been recruited by a purportedly private company in Florida. Servicing their planes were European mechanics solicited through advertisements in London newspapers. Guiding them into action were American "diplomats" and other officials in apparently civilian positions.

The sponsor, paymaster and director of all of them, however, was the Central Intelligence Agency, with headquarters in Langley, Va. Its rapid and effective provision of an "instant air force" in the Congo was the climax of the agency's deep involvement there.

The C.I.A.'s operation in the Congo was at all times responsible to and welcomed by the policy-makers of the United States.

It was these policy-makers who chose to make the agency the instrument of political and military intervention in another nation's affairs, for in five years of strenuous diplomatic effort it was only in Langley that the White House, the State Department and the Pentagon found the peculiar combination of talents necessary to block the creation of a pro-Communist regime, recruit the leaders for a pro-American government and supply the advice and support to enable that government to survive.

In Dark and Light

From wiretapping to influencing elections, from bridge-blowing to armed invasions, in the dark and in the light, the Central Intelligence Agency has become a vital instrument of American policy and a major component of American government.

It not only gathers information but also rebuts an adversary's information. It not only organizes its own far-flung operations but also resists an adversary's operation.

Against the Soviet Union alone, it performs not only certain of the services performed in Moscow by the K.G.B., the Committee for State Security, but also many of the political, intelligence and military services performed by pro-Soviet Communist parties around the world.

When the Communist and Western worlds began to wrestle for control of the vast, undeveloped Congo in 1960 after it had gained independence from Belgium, a modest little C.I.A. office in Leopoldville mushroomed overnight into a virtual embassy and miniature war department.

This was not to compete with the real United States Embassy and military attachés but to apply the secret, or at least discreet, capacities of the C.I.A. to a seething contest among many conflicting forces.

Starting almost from scratch, because the Belgians had forbidden Americans even to meet with Congolese officials, the C.I.A. dispersed its agents to learn Congolese politics from the bush on up, to recruit likely leaders and to finance their bids for power.

Capable of quickly gathering information from all sources, of buying informants and disbursing funds without the bureaucratic restraints imposed on other government agencies, the C.I.A. soon found Joseph Mobutu, Victor Nendaka and Albert Ndele. Their eventual emergence as President of the country, Minister of Transportation and head of the national bank, respectively, proved a tribute to the Americans' judgment and tactics.

So pervasive was the C.I.A. influence that the agency was widely accused of the assassination of Moscow's man, Premier Patrice Lumumba. Correspondents who were in the Congo are convinced the C.I.A. had nothing to do with the murder, though it did play a major role in establishing Cyrille Adoula as Mr. Lumumba's successor for a time.

Money and shiny American automobiles, furnished through the logistic wizardry of Langley, are said to have been the deciding factors in the vote that brought Mr. Adoula to power. Russian, Czechslovak, Egyptian and Ghanaian agents were simply outbid where they could not be outmaneuvered.

In one test after Mr. Adoula had been elected, rival agents of East and West almost stumbled over each other rushing in and out of parliamentary delegates' homes. On the day of the roll-call, American and Czech representatives sat one seat apart in the gallery with lists of members, winking at each other in triumph whenever a man pledged to the one turned out to have been picked off by the other. Ultimately Mr. Adoula won by four votes.

More Than Money

By the Congo period, however, the men at Langley say they had learned that their earlier instincts to try to solve nasty political problems with money alone had been overtaken by the recognition of the need for far more sophisticated and enduring forms of influence.

"Purchased?" one American commented. "You can't even rent these guys for the afternoon."

And so the C.I.A. kept growing in size and scope.

By the time Moise Tshombe had returned to power in the Congo — through American acquiescence, if not design — it became apparent that hastily supplied arms and planes, as well as dollars and cars, would be needed to protect the American-sponsored government in Leopoldville.

This, apparently, was a job for the Defense Department, but to avoid a too obvious American involvement, and in the interests of speed and efficiency, the Government again turned to the C.I.A.

The agency had the tools. It knew the Cubans in Miami and their abilities as pilots. It had the front organizations through which they could be recruited, paid and serviced.

It could engage 20 British mechanics without legal complications and furnish the tactical expertise from its own ranks or from Americans under contract.

Moreover, some C.I.A. agents eventually felt compelled to fly some combat missions themselves in support of South African and Rhodesian mercenaries. The State Department denied this at first — then insisted the Americans be kept out of combat.

But it was pleased by the overall success of the operation, in which no planes were lost and all civilian targets were avoided.

Meanwhile, in Other Areas . . .

In the years of the Congo effort, the C.I.A. was also smuggling Tibetans in and out of Communist China, drawing secrets from Col. Oleg Penkovsky of Soviet military intelligence, spying on Soviet missile build-ups and withdrawals in Cuba, masterminding scores of lesser operations, analyzing the world's press and radio broadcasts, predicting the longevity of the world's major political leaders, keeping track of the world's arms traffic and of many arms manufacturing enterprises and supplying a staggering flow of information, rumor, gossip and analysis to the President and all major departments of government.

For all this, the C.I.A employs about 15,000 persons and spends about a half billion dollars a year.

Its headquarters, the brain and nerve center, the information repository of this sprawling intelligence and operations system, is a modern, eight-story building of precast concrete and inset windows — a somewhat superior example of the faceless Federal style — set in 140 acres of lawn and woodland overlooking the south bank of the Potomac eight miles from downtown Washington.

In this sylvan setting, somewhat resembling an English deer park, about 8,000 C.I.A. employes — the top managers, the planners and the analysts —live, if not a cloistered life, at least a kind of academic one with the materials they are studying or the plans they may be hatching.

Formerly, the C.I.A. was scattered through many buildings in downtown Washington, which increased the problems and expense of security.

In the early nineteen-fifties, a $30-million appropriation for a new, unitary headquarters was inserted without identification in the budget of another agency—and promptly knocked out by a Congressional committee so befuddled by C.I.A. secrecy that it did not know what the item was for.

When Allen W. Dulles, then director of the C.I.A., came back in 1956 with more candor, he asked for $50,-million, and Congress gave him $46-million. He justified the bite that he proposed to take out of a 750-acre Government reservation on the Potomac by saying the site with "its isolation, topography and heavy forestation" would provide the agency with the required security.

While the whitish-gray building is undoubtedly as secure as fences, guards, safes and elaborate electronic devices can make it, the location is hardly a secret. A large sign on the George Washington Parkway pointing to "Central Intelligence Agency" has been removed, but thousands of people know you can still get to the same building by turning off on the same road, now marked by the sign "BPR"—"Bureau of Public Roads."

There, beyond the affable guard at the gate, is the large, rectangular structure with four wings, the ground-level windows barred, which stands as the visible symbol of what is supposed to be an invisible operation.

For organizational purposes, C.I.A. headquarters is divided into four divisions, each under a deputy director — plans, intelligence, science and technology, and support.

What the Divisions Do

The Division of Science and Technology is responsible for keeping current on developing techniques in science and weapons, including nuclear weapons, and for analyzing photos taken by U-2 reconnaissance planes and by space satellites.

The Division of Support is responsible for procuring equipment and for logistics, communications and security, including the C.I.A. codes.

The Division of Plans and the Division of Intelligence perform the basic functions of the agency. They represent the alpha and omega, the hand and brain, the dagger and the lamp, the melodrama and the monograph of the intelligence profession. Their presence under one roof has caused much of the controversy that has swirled about the C.I.A. since the Bay of Pigs.

It is the responsibility of the Intelligence Division to assemble, analyze and evaluate information from all sources, and to produce daily and periodical intelligence reports on any country, person or situation for the President and the National Security Council, the President's top advisory group on defense and foreign policy.

All information — military, political, economic, scientific, industrial — is grist for this division's mill. Perhaps no more than one-fifth — by volume and not necessarily importance — comes from agents overseas under varying depths of cover.

Most information is culled from foreign newspapers, scientific journals, industry publications, the reports of other Government departments and intelligence services and foreign broadcasts monitored by C.I.A. stations around the world.

All Sorts of Experts

The Intelligence Division is organized by geographical sections that are served by resident specialists from almost every profession and discipline — linguists, chemists, physicists, biologists, geographers, engineers, psychiatrists and even agronomists, geologists and foresters.

Some of the achievements of these experts are prodigious, if reports filtering through the secrecy screen are even half accurate. For instance:

¶From ordinarily available information, reliable actuarial and life-expectancy studies have been prepared on major foreign leaders.

¶In the case of one leader, from not-so-ordinarily available information, physicians gleaned important health data: They made a urinalysis from a specimen stolen from a hospital in Vienna where the great man was being treated.

¶C.I.A. shipping experts, through sheer expertise, spotted the first shipment of Soviet arms to Cuba before the vessels had cleared the Black Sea.

¶Some anthropologists at C.I.A. headquarters devote their time to helpful studies of such minor — but strategically crucial — societies as those of the hill tribes of Laos and Vietnam.

¶One woman has spent her professional lifetime in the agency doing nothing but collecting, studying, collating, analyzing and reporting on everything that can be learned about President Sukarno of Indonesia — "and I mean everything," one official reported.

Heavy With Ph.D.'s

It is the agency's boast that it could staff any college from its analysts, 50 per cent of whom have advanced degrees and 30 per cent of whom have doctorates.

Sixty per cent of the Intelligence Division personnel have served 10 years. Twenty-five per cent have been with the C.I.A. since 1947, when the agency was established. The heaviest recruiting occurred during the Korean War — primarily, but by no means exclusively, among Ivy League graduates.

The Division of Plans is a cover title for what is actually the division of secret operations, or "dirty tricks." It is charged with all those stratagems and wiles — some as old as those of Rahab and some as new as satellites — associated with the black and despised arts of espionage and subversion.

The operations of the C.I.A. go far beyond the hiring and training of spies who seek out informers and defectors.

It was the Plans Division that set up clandestine "black" radio stations in the Middle East to counter the propaganda and the open incitements to revolution and murder by President Gamal Abdel Nasser's Radio Cairo.

It was the Plans Division that masterminded the ouster of the Arbenz government in Guatemala in 1954, the overthrow of Premier Mohammed Mossadegh in Iran in 1953 (two notable successes) and the Bay of Pigs invasion in 1961 (a resounding failure).

Among the triumphs of the Plans Division are the development of the U-2 high-altitude plane, which, between 1956 and May, 1960, when Francis Gary Powers was shot down by a Soviet rocket, photographed much of the Soviet Union; the digging of a tunnel into East Berlin from which C.I.A. agents tapped telephone cables leading to Soviet military headquarters in the Eastern Zone and the acquisition of a copy of Premier Khrushchev's secret speech to the 20th party congress in 1956 denouncing Stalin's excesses and brutalities.

Liberals in the C.I.A.

The C.I.A. analysts of the Intelligence Division, in the opinion of many experts, are aware of the embedded antagonisms and frustrations of peoples just emerging into nationhood. Thus they are likely to be more tolerant than the activists in the Plans Division of the flamboyant nationalism and socialist orientation of the leaders in former colonies and more flexible than many of the State Department's cautious and legalistic diplomats.

In discussing the Portuguese territories of Angola or Mozambique, for example, the analysts are said to take the attitude that change is inevitable, that the United States has to deal with a pluralistic world. The State Department, on the other hand, tends to be diverted by Portuguese sensitivities and the North Atlantic Treaty Organization base in the Azores, also a Portuguese territory.

Regarding the C.I.A. analysts, one State Department officer said that "there are more liberal intellectuals per square inch at C.I.A. than anywhere else in the government."

The operators and agents of the Plans Division, on the other hand, are described as more conservative in their economic outlook and more single-minded in their anti-Communism. This is particularly true of those engaged in deep-cover operations, many of whom are ex-military people or men formerly in the Office of Strategic Services or the Federal Bureau of Investigation.

It has been said, however, that many of the agents who are essentially information gatherers and who work under transparent cover are as sophisticated as the analysts back home, and like them are sympathetic to the "anti-Communist left" in underdeveloped countries.

The C.I.A. agents abroad fall into two groups — both under the Plans Division.

First, there are those engaged in the really dirty business — the spies and counterspies, the saboteurs, the leaders of paramilitary operations, the suborners of revolution. Such agents operate under deepest cover, and their activities become known only when they are unfortunate enough to be caught and "surfaced" for political or propaganda purposes.

While such operatives may be known to "the chief of station" — the top C.I.A. officer in any country they are rarely known to the American Ambassador, although he may sometimes be aware of their mission. In fact, these deep agents are not known to the C.I.A.'s Intelligence Division in Washington, and their reports are not identified to it by name.

Correspondents of The New York Times say they have never, with certainty, been able to identify one of these agents, although they have on occasion run across some unaccountable American of whom they have had their suspicions. Often unknown to each other, the deep agents masquerade as businessmen, tourists, scholars, students, missionaries or charity workers.

Second, there are those agents, by far the larger number, who operate under the looser cover of the official diplomatic mission. In the mission register they are listed as political or economic officers, Treasury representatives, consular officers or employes of the Agency for International Development (the United States foreign aid agency) or United States Information Agency. The C.I.A. chief of station may be listed as a special assistant to the Ambassador or as the top political officer.

A Thin Cover

This official cover is so thin as to be meaningless except to avoid embarrassment for the host government. These agents usually are readily identifiable.

The chief of station is recognized as the man with a car as big as the Ambassador's and a house that is sometimes — as in Lagos, Nigeria — better.

In practically all the allied countries the C.I.A. agents identify themselves to host governments, and actually work in close cooperation with Cabinet officials, local intelligence and the police.

In some embassies the C.I.A. agents outnumber the regular political and economic officers. In a few they have made up as much as 75 per cent of the diplomatic mission.

The chief of station often has more money than the Ambassador. Sometimes he has been in the country longer and is better informed than the Ambassador.

For all these reasons the host government, especially in underdeveloped areas of the world, may prefer to deal with the chief of station rather than the Ambassador, believing him to have readier access to top policy-making officials in Washington.

Well Kept Secret

Obviously the number of agents abroad is a closely held secret, kept from even such close Presidential advisers in the past as the historian, Arthur M. Schlesinger Jr. In his book "A Thousand Days," Mr. Schlesinger states that those "under official cover overseas" number almost as many as State Department employes. This would be roughly 6,600. The actual number, however, is believed to be considerably less, probably around 2,200.

The secrecy of identification can lead to some amusing situations. Once when Allen Dulles, then C.I.A. director, visited New Delhi, every known "spook" (C.I.A. man) was lined up in an anteroom of the embassy to greet him. At that moment a newspaper correspondent who had been interviewing Mr. Dulles walked out of the inner office. A look of bewilderment crossed the faces of the C.I.A. men, plainly asking, "Is this one we didn't know about?"

Mr. Schlesinger has written that "in some areas the C.I.A. had outstripped the State Department in the quality of its personnel."

Almost without exception, correspondents of The New York Times reported that the men at the top overseas were men of "high competence and discipline," "extremely knowing," "imaginative," "sharp and scholarly" and "generally somewhat better than those in State in work and dedication."

But they also found that below the top many C.I.A. people were "a little thin" and did not compare so favorably with Foreign Service officers on the same level.

The C.I.A. screens and rescreens applicants, because it is quite aware of the attraction that secrecy holds for the psychopath, the misfit and the immature person.

The greatest danger obviously lies in the area of special operations. Although it is generally agreed that the agents — overt and covert — have been for the most part men of competence and character, the C.I.A. has also permitted some of limited intelligence and of emotional instability to get through its screen and has even assigned them to sensitive tasks, with disastrous results.

One example was the assignment of a man known as "Frank Bender" as contact with Cuban exile leaders during the preliminaries of the Bay of Pigs operation. A German refugee with only a smattering of Spanish and no understanding of Latin America or Latin character, Bender antagonized the more liberal of the leaders by his bullying and his obvious partiality for the Cuban right.

Offices in This Country

The C.I.A. maintains field offices in 30 American cities. These offices are overt but discreet. Their telephone numbers are listed under "Central Intelligence Agency" or "United States Government," but no address is given. Anyone wanting the address must know the name of the office director, whose telephone number and address are listed.

At one time these field offices sought out scholars, businessmen, students and even ordinary tourists whom they knew to be planning a trip behind the Iron Curtain and asked them to record their observations and report to the C.I.A. on their return.

Very little of this assertedly is done any more, probably because of some embarrassing arrests and imprisonment of tourists and students. While the C.I.A. deals frankly with businessmen, it reputedly does not compromise their traveling representatives.

Most of the work of domestic field agents involves contacts with industry and universities. For example, an agent, on instructions from headquarters, will seek evaluation of captured equipment, analysis of the color of factory smoke as a clue to production, an estimate of production capacity from the size of a factory, or critiques of articles in technical and scientific journals.

The Human Inadequacy

In greater secrecy, the C.I.A. subsidizes, in whole or in part, a wide range of enterprises — "private" foundations, book and magazine publishers, schools of international studies in universities, law offices, "businesses" of various kinds and foreign broadcasting stations. Some of these perform real and valuable work for the C.I.A. Others are not much more than "mail drops."

Yet all these human activities, all the value received and the dangers surmounted, all the organization and secrecy, all the trouble averted and all the setbacks encountered, still do not describe the work of the C.I.A. For the most gifted of analysts, the most crafty of agents — like all human beings — have their limitations.

At the time when the Americans were successfully keeping the Congo out of the Communist orbit, it still took the same men several months to slip an African agent into Stanleyville in the Congo to check on the lives and fate of some arrested Americans.

Men are fallible and limited, and the demands on the C.I.A. are almost infinite; that is why, today, some of the most valuable spies are not human and some of the most omnipotent agents hum through the heavens, and above.

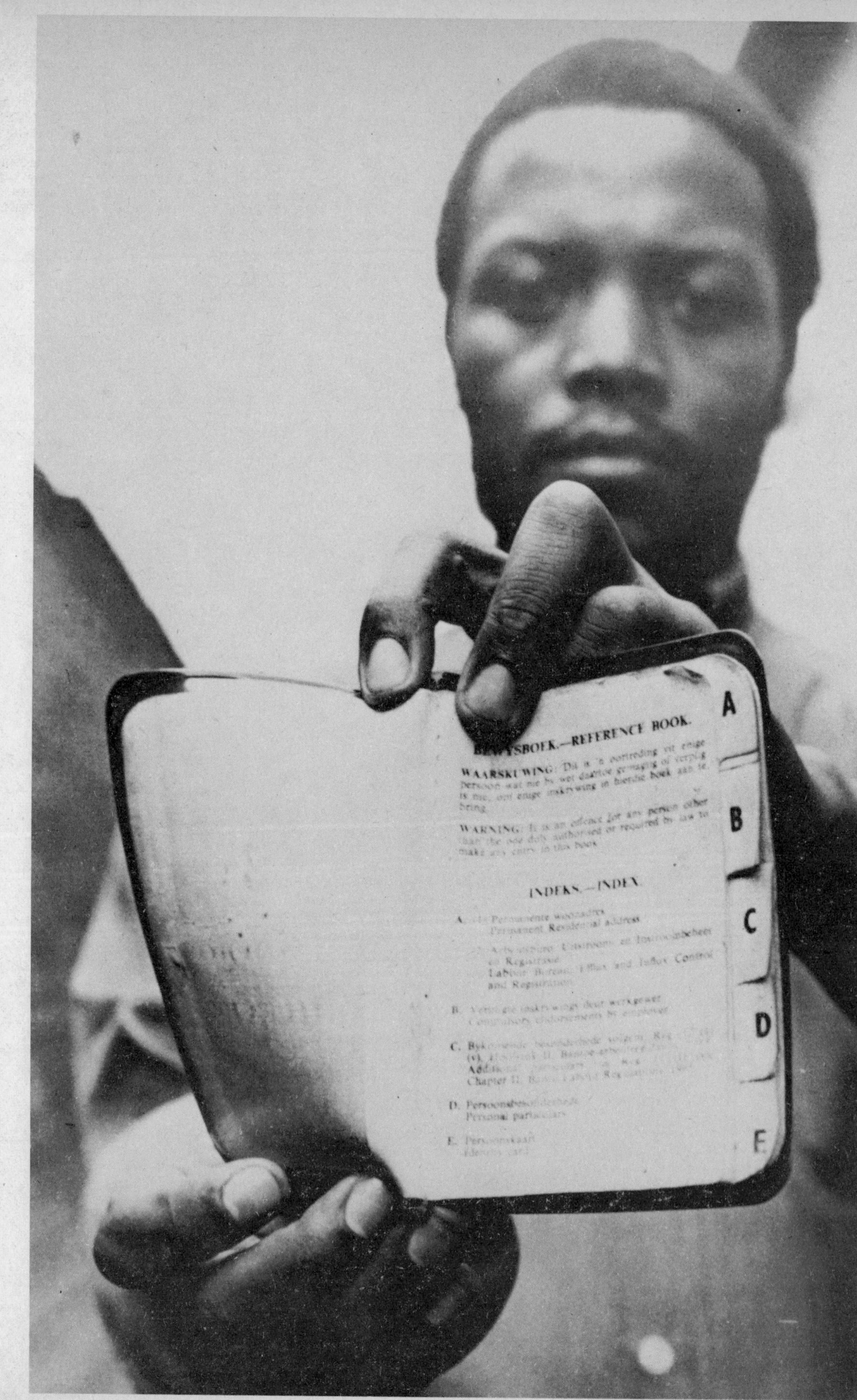
A
REFERENCE BOOK.
WAARSKUWING:
B
WARNING:
INDEKS.—INDEX.
C
Permanent Residential address
Labour Bureau: Efflux and Influx Control
and Registration
D
Personal particulars
E

CHAPTER 3

Southern Africa

The most important possession for any South African over 16 years of age is his pass-book. Without it on his person, he can be arrested and charged for failing to produce it on demand.

Courtesy Compix.

Smuts Resigns, Leaves Public Life; Nationalist Asked to Form Cabinet

By G. H. ARCHAMBAULT
Special to THE NEW YORK TIMES.

PRETORIA, South Africa, May 28—Prime Minister Jan Christiaan Smuts handed the resignation of his Cabinet to Governor General Brand von Zyl this morning. Then, escorted by a single secret service man, the defeated Prime Minister passed through the pillared corridors of the Union Buildings to return to his farm at Irene, away from the stress of politics.

The 78-year-old Field Marshal was obviously disappointed over his own and his party's defeats at the polls but he remarked philosophically:

"These things do happen. There it is—there it is."

He has declined to become leader of the Opposition in Parliament and insists on disappearing from the public scene, for the time being at least.

Immediately after having accepted the Cabinet's resignation, the Governor General invited Nationalist leader Dr. Daniel F. Malan to form a new government. This is scarcely an enviable task.

With all election returns in, the Nationalist party and its ally, the Afrikaner, have a majority of only eight votes over Field Marshal Smuts' United party and its allied Labor party. As the governing groups will have to elect a speaker of the House of Assembly from their membership, this majority will be reduced to seven.

Moreover, three white members representing the non-white populations may be expected to vote against the Nationalists on most major issues.

Even with a bare majority of four, however, Dr. Malan can scarcely hesitate to attempt to form a government, since his lieutenants and also the party's rank and file are thirsty for power after having been in the minority since 1939.

It may be presumed therefore that the new Government will not concern itself immediately with major problems but will call a session of Parliament merely to vote appropriations to carry on the nation's routine affairs. Former Prime Minister Smuts, imagining that the time was favorable for an appeal to the nation, deliberately postponed the presentation of his budget and called for the national elections.

In these conditions, it seems possible that new elections may have to be called before many months have passed to obtain a more decisive victory for one side or the other.

It is becoming clearer that one reason for Field Marshal Smuts' downfall is that, while he was immersed in world problems, he was losing touch with conditions in his own country. Black bread, the shortage of meat, the housing crisis, the ever-rising cost of living and innumerable restrictions and controls perpetuated from the war days influenced the electorate in a great measure.

In addition, Field Marshal Smuts, always loath to delegate authority, became submerged in innumerable details and his immediate aides tended to present reports calculated to please the "old master" rather than reflect actual conditions.

There was discontent also in industrial and commercial circles over the restrictions on imports from the South African Union enacted by the British Colonies in Africa itself, which, under directions from London, included this country among those with hard currencies.

SUCCEEDS JAN SMUTS

Dr. Daniel Francois Malan
Associated Press

May 29, 1948

SEGREGATION PROTESTED

South Africans Demonstrate Against Jim Crow Law

Special to THE NEW YORK TIMES.

CAPETOWN, South Africa, Sept. 5—Although it developed that the demonstrators had no thought of violence, a strong force of railroad policemen was on hand at the central station here today following an open-air protest meeting against the Nationalist Government's extension of Jim Crow regulations to suburban trains in the Cape peninsula.

There were sufficient indications, however, that the "Cape Colored"—the half-castes chiefly affected by the new measures—were considering taking a leaf from the late Mohandas K. Gandhi's book and were ready to practice the form of civil disobedience that Mr. Gandhi initiated in this country nearly forty years ago.

At a meeting today 250 young persons pledged themselves to defy the new regulations by riding in railroad cars marked "European only." The meeting was sponsored by extreme Left elements.

September 6, 1948

SOUTH AFRICA FIRM OVER SEGREGATION

Aide in U. N. Strongly Opposes Human Rights Code—Denies Race Dignity Is Involved

By GEORGE BARRETT
Special to THE NEW YORK TIMES.

PARIS, OCT. 1—South Africa came out strongly today in the United Nations against the Draft Declaration of Human Rights and subjected to special attack the provisions in the declaration barring racial segregation.

In the General Assembly's Social, Humanitarian and Cultural Committee Eric H. Louw, South Africa's chief delegate, contended that the declaration was in error in holding that human dignity would be impaired if some persons were told that they could not reside in particular areas of a country.

While not making any specific references to India's renewed complaint before the Assembly charging South Africa with mistreating and segregating some 300,000 Indian residents in the country, Mr. Louw argued that it was not at all self-evident that human dignity was damaged because particular areas of land were set apart for the reception of certain population groups "in the interests of the state or of racial harmony."

"We in South Africa could not possibly accept such a proposition as it would destroy the whole basis of our multi-racial structure," Mr. Louw said. "This certainly would not be in the interests of our less-advanced native population for whom large tracts of territory have been set aside for their exclusive use and development and in which no European is permitted to acquire or occupy land."

Mr. Louw contended that the whole scope of the declaration was much too broad and suggested that it would be better to promote respect throughout the world for a limited category of human rights and fundamental freedoms. He advocated support only for the generally recognized fundamental rights, such as freedom of religion and speech, liberty of the person, the inviolability of the person and property and free access to courts of impartial justice.

Mr. Louw asserted that it was not the United Nations' function to codify a whole philosophy of life and cautioned against accepting a human-rights code that attempted too much. Approving a declaration that might be honored in the breach rather than observance would be destroying it in advance, he said.

South Africa was the only country of the thirteen heard in committee today to present vigorous opposition to the draft declaration. Other delegations presented minor objections, but the feeling of most speakers during the preliminary debate was that the declaration was an important step toward eventual acceptance of a convention on human rights.

October 2, 1948

NEGROES DEFIANT IN SOUTH AFRICA

Council Hits White Supremacy As It Learns of Abolition—Malan Majority Imperiled

By G. H. ARCHAMBAULT
Special to THE NEW YORK TIMES.

PRETORIA, South Africa, Jan. 5—Political relations between whites and Negroes in South Africa were broken off today. The consequences cannot be foreseen. Whether they are immediate or remote probably depends more on world events than on domestic developments.

Negro speakers today dwelt on such points as President Truman's civil rights policy, progressive ideas in British lands in Africa compared with the "retrograde South African Union" and implications in the Indian Ocean of "fast-developing Asian freedom."

The occasion of the rupture was a meeting here of the Negroes' Representative Council called by the new Nationalist Government "so that requirements of law might be carried out" but in reality to hear its own death sentence since the present administration is pledged to end such representation under its segregation plan.

Council Set Up in 1936

The Council was created in 1936 by the late Gen. J. B. M. Hertzog, then Prime Minister, as an embryo parliament to be consulted on legislation affecting Negroes. It came as compensation for abolition of the Negro franchise in the Cape colony.

In practice by general admission the Council degenerated into a mere debating society ignored by successive administrations and taken seriously only by itself. Two years ago the councilors rebelled —Field Marshal Jan Christiaan Smuts was then Prime Minister—and adjourned indefinitely in protest against a "breach of faith toward the African people."

The Council reconvened today to learn that the Government not only intended to abolish it but would not restore the Negro franchise. Faced by impending dissolution, the Council set out to deny white supremacy and at the same time to defy it in the following resolution:

"This Council deprecates what in its opinion amounts to dereliction of duty on the part of the Minister of Native Affairs, namely his failure to place before it the new Government's policy of racial segregation."

Reign of Harmony Expected

The irony of the situation lies in the fact that twelve years ago General Hertzog sought to solve the racial problem by creating the Representative Council — purely advisory — representing 8,000,000 Negroes, compared with 2,500,000 whites represented by the Legislature in Capetown. The two were expected to work in harmony.

One reason now advanced for the suppression is that the "Council has turned its mind to politics." The Council retorts that by statute its advice was to be sought on questions of racial policy that it claims cannot but be political.

Today's decision may react in other ways, since Nicholaas C. Havenga, Minister of Finance and leader of the Afrikaaner party, says that he is pledged to follow the Hertzog tradition. He holds the life of Prime Minister Daniel F. Malan's administration in his hands, since the governmental coalition is at the mercy of the Afrikaaner party's seven votes.

Negroes Accept the Split

Negro speakers today agreed that this was the parting of the ways. They were for the most part professors and editors with a complete mastery of the English language and observing all the proprieties of debate. Their general theme was that racial segregation could not be unilateral. They decided to continue to boycott meetings "until the Government through a Minister of the Crown lays before the Council * * * full details of its native policy."

Obviously the Government cannot accept dictation at the hands of the Council. On the other hand, there are increasing signs that the Africans are becoming restive.

January 6, 1949

DURBAN RIOT TOLL 100 DEAD, 1,000 HURT

Indians Suffer Most in Clash With Natives—Smuts Warns Regime on Repressive Laws

By G. H. ARCHAMBAULT
Special to THE NEW YORK TIMES.

CAPETOWN, South Africa, Jan. 15—One hundred dead, 1,000 injured and untold damage to property were estimated tonight as the outcome of the three-day communal clashes between natives and Indians in Durban and its suburbs. The majority of the casualties and all the damage were sustained by the Indians. The outstanding feature of the rioting was that the white population was nowhere involved.

Earlier estimates had been much magnified and the present figures may still be reduced. The authorities believed tonight that they had the situation in hand.

The outbreak of communal strife was both unexpected and unprecedented. It reached its peak in the early hours this morning but began to subside when troops were brought to the scene under a proclamation from the Governor General and when police reinforcements arrived by air.

Both the Minister of Justice and the Minister of Defense are on the spot to take all necessary measures. Refugee camps have been opened to care for thousands of fleeing Indians. Two emergency hospitals have been set up.

At the height of the trouble Indian stores were looted indiscriminately and Indian homes were set on fire. Charred bodies were still being removed tonight from the smoking ruins.

The disturbing aspect of the riots is how and why they happened. Ostensibly, it all began with a rumor, later proved false, that a vendor in the Indian market had beaten and killed a small Negro boy. Thereupon the natives sought vengeance and violence bred more violence. Obviously, there must have been deeper causes, traceable partly to the general feeling of unrest among both whites and non-whites.

Natives in Durban and Natal Province are mostly Zulus, a warrior race that a few generations back humbled British arms in a series of resounding defeats. They remain a proud people whose chief recreation is to revive war dances in which the men appear with traditional oxhide shields and heavy clubs. And, as in the old days, their "bush telegraph" carries news swiftly from hill to hill.

The Zulus do not like the Indians and the antipathy is mutual. In the case of the Zulus it is fostered by the example of the whites of Natal who fear the encroachment of the "coolies," and seek not only their complete segregation but their repatriation.

It is common knowledge that many Indian traders and employers exploit their native customers and servants who, in turn, harbor resentment.

It is said also that the Indians themselves have been "playing with fire." Ironically enough, the executive committee of the South African Indian Congress party was scheduled to meet in Durban this week-end "to review the political situation." One of the most recent acts of its president was to send confraternal greetings to native organizations in which he spoke of South Africa's "becoming another Malaya, Indonesia or Viet Nam."

Several Indian Congress party leaders are avowed members of the Communist party.

The problem for the Government is to ascertain if the Durban riots were spontaneous or concerted. Moreover, it must be prepared to face accusations before the United Nations that the Indians in this country, 99 per cent of whom are South African nationals, remain unprotected

January 16, 1949

NEGRO DAY OF PRAYER HELD IN SOUTH AFRICA

Special to THE NEW YORK TIMES.

PRETORIA, South Africa, Aug. 21—Negroes in South Africa today observed a national day of prayer "in this period of humiliation and dispossession," in the hope of achieving unity.

The observance was organized by the interdenominational African Ministers Association and supported by the African National Congress.

Hitherto, repeated attempts to achieve political unity have failed chiefly because of rivalry among leaders of the Negro community. Spiritual unity may prove as difficult to achieve because of the diversity of sects. There are several hundred on the Witwaters Rand alone.

Advocates of unity are hopeful, nevertheless, because they believe that the present Nationalist Government's policy of segregation is calculated to advance their cause by accentuating the feeling of frustration and humiliation among the Negro population.

Government departments are working on large-scale segregation plans, but their execution is likely to be retarded indefinitely by the present period of financial and economic stress. In the meantime, segregation is being applied methodically in public places such as railroad stations and post offices. There also is stricter control of films and publications to ban everything related to racial problems, as in the cases of the film, "Home of the Brave", the British magazine Picture Post and Life magazine.

The commission inquiring into native education was told last week by Prof. C. J. Uys of Bloemfontein University College that "development of a native (Negro) national consciousness is one of the most dangerous trends to be seen in South Africa at present." Therefore, he declared, the white policy should be "divide and rule."

August 22, 1949

URBAN MOVE HELD AFRICA RIOT CAUSE

Much Expected of Creation of Special Mobile Unit Under Police Head's Direction

By G. H. ARCHAMBAULT

Special to THE NEW YORK TIMES.

CAPETOWN, South Africa, Feb. 18—Although riots in Negro townships on the fringes of Johannesburg have occurred generally at weekends, authorities report today that there is little likelihood of any immediate trouble in view of measures taken under personal direction of the Police Commissioner. Much is expected from the creation of a special mobile force, which this morning began patrolling the townships and their approaches. Nevertheless police action can only be repressive, and the real problem is to remove the causes of the trouble.

Moreover, there is urgency. The newspaper Cape Argus recalls that in the Johannesburg area, riots have occurred at least once a month for the last six months. Since Negroes there outnumber the whites in a ratio approaching three to two, the city council's manager of native affairs has described the situation as "explosive." Mrs. Margaret Ballinger, one of the three whites representing the Negroes in the House of Assembly, said this week: "The riots are not an episode but a symptom; not the end but only the beginning."

Most South Africans believe that urbanization of the Negroes is at the root of the matter. It began years ago when an agricultural people began to turn to industry, and it has developed at the same pace as industry, with its constant demand for cheap labor. Thus several million Negroes have become sort of "displaced persons," living in overcrowded locations on the fringes of cities and losing toucch with tribal laws and traditions. In the main they are law-abiding, but inevitably some of the younger generation have taken to running wild.

Gradually the attitude of the Negroes toward the whites has been changing. A magistrate at Port Elizabeth remarked this week: "These days one is apt to encounter impudence from the natives."

The present Nationalist Government's remedy is racial segregation, with Negroes developing their own mode of life in their own reserves. This implies restoring tribal conditions to the same extent. That would be a long process. Meanwhile, the Government is striving to stem the influx to the urban areas by turning back all who do not hold "passes" as proof that they have work. That is the reason for the systematic police raids.

In telegrams to Prime Minister Daniel F. Malan yesterday and today, Negro leaders held that these raids were the determining factor of the riots. The Anglican Archbishop of Capetown declared: "The law-abiding element among the Africans is large, but it is not prepared to help the police against law-breakers."

In Parliament this week there was a tendency to discuss the riots on party lines, but with an agreement that the situation called for rapid action and that white civilization must be maintained. Few suggestions were made. The Natal Mercury, an opposition organ published in Durban, has one:

"What is wanted is the setting up of a national convention charged with the task of drawing up a new charter of race relationships in South Africa, a charter which will steer a middle course between the reactionaries on one hand and the so-called Liberals on the other.

February 19, 1950

South Africa Reds Dissolve Just Ahead of Suppression

CAPETOWN, South Africa, June 20—Anticipating final approval tonight in the House of Assembly of the Government's bill to suppress communism, Sam Kahn, lone Communist member of Parliament, read an official statement from the central committee of the South African Communist party that it had decided "to dissolve the party today."

Soon afterward the bill was approved on third reading by 64 votes to 49.

The implications of Mr. Kahn's announcement are being examined in political circles, but if it means that the Communists have decided to go underground the bill adopted tonight is wide enough to track them down. Its rapid passage through the Senate is assured.

Both the governmental Nationalist party and the United party, the main opposition group, agreed, during debates, on the principle of fighting communism but differed on method. In the end the Government won its point that Communist organizations and individuals might be "proclaimed" without prior trial.

Several amendments moderated some of the most drastic clauses of the original draft, such as granting the possibility for any person to prove in court that he had joined, a suspected organization without knowledge of its unlawful character.

In its broad lines the measure gives the Government power to declare any organization unlawful if it is satisfied that its aim is to propagate the principles of communism or to promote the spread of communism. Such organizations will thereupon be "liquidated" under the wide powers given to the Minister of Justice.

During the debates on the bill, the Government conceded the reservation that the Minister could exercise these powers only after receiving a report from a committee of three members, including a Government law adviser and a senior magistrate. Nevertheless, the Opposition still considers that the Minister's powers are too great.

The South African Communist party, small in number so far as whites are concerned, has had a special appeal in that it knows no color bar and accepts members of all races.

June 21, 1950

South African Race Act Out

CAPETOWN, South Africa, July 7 (Reuters)—The South African Government promulgated today the Groups Areas Act of 1950—designated to separate white and colored people into different living areas—in a Government gazette extraordinary. The act provides "for the establishment of group areas, for the control of Acquisition of immovable property and the occupation of land and premise."

July 8, 1950

SOUTH AFRICA SPLIT INTO THREE GROUPS

Apartheid, Which Segregates Blacks, Also Acts to Divide the White Population

By WILLIAM S. WHITE

Special to THE NEW YORK TIMES.

CAPETOWN, South Africa, April 15—South Africa's system of apartheid does not merely divide the 2,600,000 whites from the 8,500,000 blacks of this country. In a nonlegal sense, there is also sharpening apartheid among whites themselves—English-speaking whites on one side and Afrikaans, or colloquial Dutch-speaking people on the other.

The literal meaning of the word, which is pronounced apart-tate, is "apartness," and apartness is profoundly the real thing in all South African life.

Where it operates to contain the blacks it has the support of all but a handful of the members of the white community, whether in the currently dominant Nationalist party of Dr. Daniel F. Malan or in the minority United party. In this field the United party is "liberal" in the sense that it wants to maintain the present vast barriers between the races, but to erect no more barriers, and even to consider, though in a somewhat vague way, some sort of possible future concessions to the natives.

The Nationalists, on the other hand, want to raise still more and higher barriers.

Apartheid was put forward in the old days of United party control of this country, and is by no means an invention of Dr. Malan. The difference really is one of methods and approach. The United party believes that added pressure for utter political isolation of the blacks, especially against a world movement that for better or worse is in the other direction, will one day create so confined an explosive force as to detonate and blow away all this white-run civilization.

Called Beyond Solution

The Nationalist party believes any breach in a policy of continued pressure would drive the thin end of a wedge into the whole apartheid structure.

The white man here feels that the race problem is beyond ultimate solution, and so discussions of it are to him rather like discussions of how to get nations to quit making war on each other.

It is apartheid in the white community that is South Africa's present most somber manifestation. Here there is a dualism within a dualism—two sides where white meets black and then two sides again among the minority whites.

This land has two capitals—Pretoria for administrative departments and Capetown for Parliament, not to mention a third quasi-capital for the judiciary, which is at Bloemfontein. Apart from native dialects, it has two languages, English and Afrikaans. All public places divide blacks and whites physically; they also in the deepest sense of common understanding divide English-speaking persons and Nationalist Afrikaners.

There are two sets of public schools, English-speaking and Afrikaans-speaking, and sometimes this dualism even extends to hospitals.

The young son of an American friend here of this correspondent recently was run down in a street accident and rushed off bleeding from his head to the nearest hospital. It was an Afrikaans-speaking hospital, and he was English-speaking. He was not admitted, although possibly mainly for some mysterious bureaucratic reason in this profoundly bureaucratic country.

In any event, in the two sets of schools, supported by what amounts to double taxation, forces are at work driving the whites farther and farther apart.

While this is not a matter subject to exact proof, one is convinced on all the evidence that in the Afrikaans-speaking schools a tireless, extremely nationalistic indoctrination is going on so effectively that the next generation of Afrikaners is likely to be far more nationalistic than the present one.

In the English-speaking schools also there is a type of indoctrination, less planned and conscious, and it is basically indoctrination in the English way of life, which in certain fundamental matters is as far from the Afrikaner way of life as if these two sets of peoples lived in different worlds.

There is, to an outsider, a fundamental incompatability between these two white groups, of which the English-oriented group is steadily declining in long term political power whatever may happen over the short run. In all this scene, nothing seems so basic as this impression.

It is in this atmosphere that South Africa's countless clubs flourish—athletic clubs and mellow but dusty clubs among the English-speaking that are more British than those in Britain.

It is in this atmosphere that such militant groups as the Torch Commando, led by Group Capt. A. G. (Sailor) Malan, wartime Royal Air Force ace, and the Skiet (target shooting) Commando operate. They are quite lawful—the Torch Commando demonstrates against the Nationalist Government and the Skiet Commando is for that Government—but to an onlooker there is something a little frightening in the possible future implications of all this commando business working outside the framework of ordinary political parties.

Lack Voting Right

As for the natives, some of whose organizations plainly have been captured at the top by Communists, all this is more or less irrelevant to him.

They have in substance no voting rights, although their 8,500,000 are "represented" by three white members of a white Parliament of 159 members.

They have no right to buy land outside the overcrowded reserves set aside for them. They must live in restricted areas, and their movements are subject to complicated passes that they must carry about with them.

The native can be removed from urban areas if he is out of work. His home may be raided by the police at any time without warrants. He must pay a head tax, and to pay it he must have a job.

Apart from all this—and this analysis of native restrictions was made for this correspondent by a disinterested outside authority—the black has further troubles.

The Malan Government has gone farther and provided that a native living within a "black spot" area of a city may be removed to an area chosen for him by local authorities, even if he lives on land belonging to him.

To him, the most pervasive sign in all life is "slegs vir blankes" (Europeans only).

There are no posted signs reading "only for English-speaking" or "only for Afrikaans-speaking."

Among the whites, they are not posted on walls, but to a very considerable extent they are posted in the hearts of men.

April 16, 1952

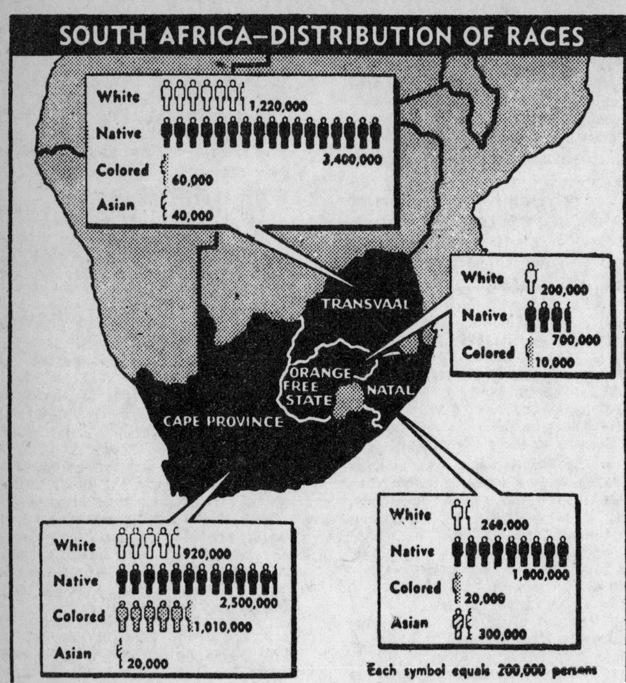

HOW TOTAL POPULATION IS DIVIDED

WHITE 2,600,000

NATIVE 8,400,000

COLORED 1,100,000

ASIAN 360,000

Each symbol equals 200,000 persons

November 23, 1952

South Africa Club to Train White Women in Shooting

JOHANNESBURG, South Africa, Feb. 19—A pistol club to train white women as marksmen has been formed at Pretoria under the auspices of the Skiet Commando (Shooting Commando), a defense force unit composed mostly of Boer farmers.

Die Transvaler, Johannesburg newspaper of the Nationalist Government, said today that interest in revolver shooting had been aroused by reports from Kenya of Mau Mau violence.

A club to teach self-defense has been in existence at Bloemfontein since last November. Its first member was Mrs. J. J. Fouche, wife of Nationalist administrator (Governor) of Orange Free State Province.

February 20, 1953

TOP TRIBUNAL VOIDS PARLIAMENT COURT CREATED BY MALAN

Appeal Body in South Africa Is Unanimous in Declaring Anti-Colored Move Illegal

ENTRENCHED RIGHTS STAND

Ruling Says Chamber, by Use of Judicial Name, Cannot Act Contrary to Constitution

Special to THE NEW YORK TIMES.

JOHANNESBURG, South Africa Nov. 13—The Appeal Court, South Africa's highest tribunal, ruled unanimously today that the High Court of Parliament set up by the Malan Government was illegal.

The High Court of Parliament, consisting of Parliament's entire membership, had been created by the Nationalist regime to override the lower courts that had upset the Voters Act which took 48.000 voters of mixed blood off the common election rolls and put them on a separate list. The Appeal Court acted after an appeal by the Government against the lower court's decision.

In delivering the verdict of the five judges of the Appeal Court, Chief Justice A. van de Sandt Centlivres said:

"Parliament cannot, by giving itself the name of a court of law, come to any decision which will have the effect of destroying the entrenched provisions of the Constitution."

Constitutional Safeguard

The entrenched provisions safeguard the voting rights of the non-whites and, under the Constitution, can be altered only by a two-thirds majority of both houses of Parliament.

The verdict confronts Prime Minister Daniel F. Malan with a grave choice—whether to abide by the Constitution or defy the law and create what the Opposition leader, J. G. N. Strauss, said would be anarchy. Mr. Malan has said that the Government cannot afford to lose, and he may show his hand when he addresses a meeting tomorrow night.

The anti-Government Torch Commando, a former servicemen's organization, stated:

"We await with the gravest concern the vital decision by Mr. Malan. Prominent members of the Government have indicated that in the long run they will not be balked by the decisions of the courts."

Mr. Strauss, calling on Mr. Malan to honor the Constitution, commented:

"If the numerical inferiority of the white man causes many to fear for the future, that fear won't be removed by injustice to the colored (half-caste) people. The answer lies in a larger white population."

Not a Court of Law

Chief Justice Centlivres said:

"The so-called High Court of Parliament is not a court of law but simply Parliament functioning under another name."

In a separate opinion Associate Justice C. P. van den Heever said:

"No legislative organ can perform an act of levitation and lift itself above its own powers by the bootstrap methods."

Dismissing the Nationalist standpoint that the imperial abdication of Britain in South Africa had weakened the checks in the Constitution, the judge said:

"That contention assumes that as soon as a policeman is round a corner there is no law."

He said that altering the colored franchise without the requisite two-thirds majority at a joint sitting of the two houses of Parliament had "no greater validity than if the City Council of Bloemfontein had presumed to do so."

The Nationalist propaganda suggests that Mr. Malan will seek a "mandate" in the spring elections to sidetrack the colored vote on a bare majority if returned to power. He could do this by passing a bill through Parliament with a simple majority giving him power to pack the Senate with Government-nominated members to assure the required two-thirds majority of both houses meeting together.

Alternatively, he could treat an election victory, however small, as a "mandate" to scrap the Constitution.

Cabinet Reported Split

Mr. Malan's Cabinet was reported to be split on its next move, some urging defiance of the courts and the holding of elections, with the colored voters off the register. This would virtually assure Mr. Malan's re-election. Other ministers, notably Finance Minister N. C. Havenga, were reported to be insisting on putting the issue to the people at the elections.

Dr. A. B. Xuma, leader of the moderate Negro group, said today that non-white defiance of the race discrimination laws could be called off—on conditions, which he did not specify.

"As a person not involved in the defiance movement," he said, "I say that the Government will miss the full meaning of the situation if they hold the leaders of the defiance movement responsible for the riots. If the Government goes on as at present we shall soon all be in defiance."

He said it was misleading to draw a comparison between the Mau Mau terrorists in Kenya and the defiance movement in South Africa.

"It has not been suggested that Europeans should be driven out of South Africa," he said.

November 14, 1952

South Africa Court Backs Natives On Equal Facilities With Whites

By ALBION ROSS

Special to THE NEW YORK TIMES.

JOHANNESBURG, South Africa, March 23—The Supreme Court of Appeals of the Union of South Africa handed down a constitutional decision today invalidating racial segregation unless equal facilities were offered to both whites and other races in the union. In principle, the doctrine espoused by the court would necessitate something like an economic revolution in South Africa and immense expense to the state, municipalities and other public bodies, if the principle of racial segregation were to be upheld.

The case itself was small but came at the end of a series of similar decisions less clear cut. It started in a railway station at Capetown, where an African native, George Lusu, sat in a waiting room reserved for whites. A policeman arrested him when he refused to leave. The Magistrates' Court and the Cape Province Court of Appeals upheld Mr. Lusu's contention that when facilities provided for African natives are not equal to those provided for whites, a native has a legal right to use the whites' facilities.

The issue is of tremendous significance because in transportation, housing and utilities and in every aspect of South African life the state, municipalities and other public bodies provide far more facilities for whites than for Negroes. This is notably true in the expensive field of education. The tension that arose while the decision of the Supreme Court of Appeals was awaited has been considerable.

In handing down the decision, Chief Justice A. van de Sandt Centlivres declared that the Act of 1916 giving the railways racial segregation powers did not intend that members of different races were to be treated with a substantial degree of partiality and inequality.

Attorneys for the Government had not disputed that facilities for Negroes at the station were, as is universal, far inferior to those provided for whites. The Government based its case on the contention that the railways had the right, under the law, to provide facilities for Negroes inferior to those provided for whites.

The Government could hardly take any other stand, since the whole South African economic and social system and standard of living of the white South African is based on inferior wages and inferior facilities of all sorts provided for the Negro majority of the population.

The decision brought into the foreground of the election campaign now under way the issue of the Nationalist party's determination to empower Parliament to overrule the constitutional functions of the Supreme Court of Appeals and, in effect, do away with the constitutional form of government in South Africa and replace it with the complete sovereignty of Parliament.

Minister of Justice Charles R. Swart, referring a couple of weeks ago to the Supreme Court of Appeals' decision last year denying the Government the right to take away the vote from the mulatto population of Cape Province, which is rooted in the constitution of 1910, stated:

"Is it right that I who appoint these judges should go to them to ask whether they approve of a law which I present in Parliament."

On the same day, Paul Sauer, Minister of Transport, said:

"It is undemocratic that six old men at Bloemfontein [seat of the Supreme Court of Appeals] should have all the say. Who is boss? Bloemfontein or you?"

Last night the Minister of Lands, Johannes G. Strydom, a powerful leader of the Nationalist party in the Transvaal who may be slated to succeed Prime Minister Daniel F. Malan, said that after the elections the Government would pass a law "re-establishing the supremacy and sovereignty of Parliament" and that the courts would have no testing rights.

It was the Government effort to do this last year through the Supreme Court of Parliament Act, which subsequently was declared unconstitutional, that brought on last year's constitutional crisis. In the dispute, the Torch Commando organization of veterans warned of open rebellion if the Government went outside the law, and threats to secede from the Union were made in the Province of Natal.

The opinion of political experts in the press here is that the new decision upholding the rights of Negroes to equal facilities will aid the Nationalist party in the election. Their argument briefly is that decisions upholding the rights of Negroes are not popular with the white electorate here and that there will be more sympathy for the Nationalist Government's efforts to put the courts in their place.

March 24, 1953

MALAN WINS POWER OVER SOUTH AFRICA FOR 5 YEARS MORE

Nationalists' Election Victory Adds to Parliament Majority Pushing White Supremacy

By ALBION ROSS

Special to THE NEW YORK TIMES.

PRETORIA, South Africa, Friday, April 17—Prime Minister Daniel F. Malan's Nationalist party has been returned to power as a result of Wednesday's election with its majority increased from thirteen votes in the previous Parliament to twenty-nine in the new Parliament of 159 seats. The opposition United and Labor parties have been completely routed.

There is a distant chance that one of the three country constituencies still outstanding may reduce the Nationalists' majority, but there is little likelihood of it. Three seats of white representatives of Cape Province were not involved in the election and polling for another was deferred by the death of a candidate.

The estimated total vote was 626,000 for the Nationalists and 758,000 for the United and Labor parties combined. These figures include the customary adjustment made for unopposed seats, of which eighteen went to the United party and two to the Nationalists.

Vote Nearly Balanced

Final returns from the small outstanding constituencies were not expected to change the relative standing of the parties materially. Therefore, disregarding the adjustment for unopposed seats, the United and Labor parties combined polled only slightly more votes than the Nationalists.

In the last election, in 1948, the Nationalists received 462,000 votes and the United and Labor parties 617,000, with the figures adjusted for unopposed seats.

The election victory puts the Nationalists into power for five more years. They are pledged to segregate the races in South Africa and to guarantee uncompromising white supremacy. There are just over 2,500,000 whites in South Africa and roughly 10,000,000 African natives and mulattos and some Indians.

The party also has promised, without defining by what means, to strip the Supreme Court of Appeals of the power to pass on the constitutionality of laws passed by Parliament, meaning rule for the next five years by Nationalist party caucus. It likewise has promised to take the franchise away from about 1,000,000 Cape Province mulattos. They have had the vote for more than a century with various property restrictions.

The Nationalist Government also has promised to change the laws to guarantee the principle of inequality it desires in providing public facilities for whites and non-whites. The Government likewise has prepared over a period of years elaborate legislation to prevent native Africans from participating in collective bargaining and to prohibit membership of whites and non-whites in the same union organizations.

The so-called Transvaal language ordinance, which prevents Afrikaans and English-speaking children from going to the same schools, also is expected to be extended now to other provinces. The Nationalists, primarily Afrikaner, resent expansion of the English language as a threat to Afrikanerdom.

The size of the total vote and of the majorities built up by the United party for seats it was known to hold safely was considered indicative of the dangerous development of white public opinion. United party voters were responding partly to their party's slogan, "Vote so that you may vote again."

There was a general feeling that Mr. Malan's election was decisive, not for five years, but indefinitely. The Nationalist party's determination to remove mulattos from the Cape Province franchise roll, the creation of six constituencies in South-West Africa, where the voters are so few that each one in effect has several votes, plus the determined attack on the courts' control over legislation, have strengthened belief that the Nationalist regime is determined to remain in power for good.

The situation is summed up in the commonly heard statement that the real purpose of the Nationalist party is to reverse the result of the Boer War, fought at the beginning of this century, and set up an Afrikaner-dominated state and society.

The party is officially pledged to the idea of secession from the British Commonwealth, or at least from allegiance to the British Crown, and setting up of a republic. Mr. Malan has promised that this will not be done without a referendum, but the way obviously is open for such a referendum and fanatical Nationalists, such as Johannes G. Strydom, leader of the powerful Transvaal section of the party, are expected to press for a quick decision on a republic.

Mr. Malan is 79 years old and, although always an extremely active campaigner, he made only three speeches during this campaign. Who will be his successor is one of the most discussed questions in South Africa. There is a general fear among moderate Nationalists that Mr. Strydom, who stands for extreme authoritarian government and no compromise on anything, may be his successor.

The reaction of the investing public was shown in the early hours on the Stock Exchange in Johannesburg, when prices of South Africa's gold and uranium mining stocks tumbled sharply from hurried sales. Later, professional operators checked the fall and the market waited for the reaction of the London market to the news of the Nationalists' election victory.

The National African Congress, the principal political organization of Negroes, and the small South African Indian National Congress had, in a rather backhanded way, come out in favor of the United party because it left the door open for consultation with non-European "moreate" leaders, a course that Mr. Malan refuses to envisage. Their partisans had shown iron discipline recently in refraining from any demonstrations that would only have served to further the Nationalist party's "black peril" propaganda.

The native elements now see no further hope in compromise or in the usual forms of cooperation. The evidence indicates, however, that they do not know what to do. They are not in a position to challenge the Nationalists, who are armed with the so-called "whipping-post law," passed in the last Parliament, and the public security law.

The future of the United party also is in question. There are important elements in Natal, profoundly British, that talk occasionally in terms of secession from the South African Union. The old wholly English-speaking Natal Dominion party has disappeared, but a movement in Natal against the United party after its failure is not out of the question.

Steps already have been taken also for the formation of a Liberal party and, with the recent death of John Christie, an old-line compromising labor man who headed the Labor party, the young men of the party may choose to give up their alliance with the United party and take a bolder course.

Some political experts prophesy that before the five-year term of this Parliament is over the United party will collapse, with part of its following passing into the ranks of the Nationalists, who will have a good deal to offer men wandering in the political wilderness.

It is no secret that many United party members of Parliament regard J. G. N. Strauss as a weak leader. It also is known that rapidly developing and predominantly British Rhodesia is exercising a strong attraction for some English-speaking families that are averse to living in an Afrikaner-dominated state.

April 17, 1953

Whites Launch Two New Parties In South Africa to Fight Malanism

One Group Asks Full Rights for Negroes. While Other Urges Better Conditions

Special to THE NEW YORK TIMES.

JOHANNESBURG, South Africa, May 10—For the first time since the Union of South Africa was formed forty-three years ago a crack has developed in the solid front that the ruling whites, now totaling 2,600,000, have invariably presented toward the non-white majority, now numbering 10,000,000. Hitherto the whites, though bitterly divided into Afrikaner nationalism versus the British element supported by the moderate Afrikaners, have united in applying race segregation, in blocking any extension of political rights to non-whites and even in reducing the voting rights of non-whites, as in 1936, when the Negroes were struck off the white register in Cape Province.

This week-end the Liberal party was set up by Alan Paton, author of "Cry the Beloved Country," and other whites. They advocate full citizenship rights for all civilized people irrespective of race, color or creed. At the same time the national executive of the war veterans' Torch Commando, which met here to decide the future of the organization, declared unequivocally that the "non-European must be advanced economically, culturally and politically."

The Liberal party elected Mrs. Margaret Ballinger, the leader of seven white Parliament members who represent Negroes, as president, and Mr. Paton as one of the vice presidents.

New Party's Principles

The Liberal party took its stand on the following principles:

¶The essential dignity of every human being irrespective of race, color or creed and maintenance of his fundamental rights.

¶The right of every human being to develop to the fullest extent of which he is capable consistent with the rights of others.

¶Maintenance of the rule of law.

¶No person should be debarred from participation in government or other democratic processes of the country by reason only of race, color or creed and political rights based on a common franchise roll should be extended to all suitably qualified persons.

¶The party will employ only democratic and constitutional means to implement its principles and will oppose all forms of totalitarianism. The membership is open to all persons irrespective of race.

Prime Minister Daniel F. Malan's Nationalist party is jubilant at the formation of the white Liberal party, which the Nationalists believe will drive more whites into their extreme right-wing camp.

The tendency toward the South African Union's disintegration gained further momentum today with the formation of the Federal Union party, drawing support mainly from the British elements in Natal Province. The Federal party reflects the gulf between the British section and the Afrikaner Nationalists who won the April elections and talk of converting the Union into an Afrikaner republic.

The Federal Union party is sponsored by L. Kane Berman, Maj. Gen. A. R. Selby, Brigadier J. T. Durrant and other Torch Commando leaders who will continue as Torchmen and it responds broadly to the recent call by Senator C. Heaton Nicholls, veteran British leader in Natal, for conversion of the Union into a federated state that would leave Natal free to maintain its British traditions should Prime Minister Malan's Nationalist party turn the Union into an Afrikaner republic. Senator Nicholls will be the Natal leader of the Federal party.

May 11, 1953

NEGROES FLOCKING INTO SOUTH AFRICA

Six Years of Apartheid Fail to Halt Many Thousands Seeking Better Life

Special to THE NEW YORK TIMES.

CAPETOWN, South Africa, Feb. 21—After six years of apartheid, the regime of Prime Minister Daniel Malan is having little success in warding off thousands of Negroes seeking to enter South Africa every month.

According to available statistics, South Africa offers the highest wages and the most education, health care and welfare aid available to Negoes south of the Equator. Figures released by the Ministry of Native Affairs show that there are 255,000 illegal Negro immigrants in the country whose presence is known to the police.

How many whom the police have not caught up with is not reported. Heavy patrols on the frontiers and adjacent roads have been strengthened. Negroes caught entering illegally are subject to a fine, imprisonment at forced labor and, unofficially, rough treatment.

Cover Long Distances

This is known from the experiences of those who have been punished for illegal entry and have returned home after expulsion. But still they come. They have not the means to use ordinary forms of transportation, and as illegal travelers they dare not use them.

They walk hundreds and sometimes a thousand miles on foot, dodging the police, falling sick and occasionally dying on the road. But still they seek their mecca—Dr. Malan's ultra-race-conscious South Africa.

The known illegal immigrants, chiefly those whom the police have caught, are forced to accept work on farms so that they may be kept out of the cities. The Ministry says this policy has been adopted because it has been proved useless to return the Negroes back across the frontier. They just came back again, having learned in the meantime how to avoid patrols.

Besides the illegal immigrants, 245,000 Negroes are admitted legally. Of these, 195,000 work in the coal and gold mines, in commerce and on the land. They do 67 per cent of the semi-skilled work and 16 per cent of the skilled work in industry; own stores, run businesses and the like, in addition to furnishing the entire unskilled working force in the country.

Figures on wages, medical care, education and welfare indicate the extent to which the South African, in relative terms, has been pushing the Negro toward actual participation in white Western civilization while talking apartheid and adopting ineffective apartheid laws.

The figures bear out the charge made through three weeks of parliamentary debate that the Malan Government, while proclaiming a policy of barring the Negro from the white men's heritage, actually has aided and abetted Negro advancement and improvement of standards.

February 22, 1954

MALAN WILL MOVE HUGE NEGRO AREA

Law to Enforce Segregation and Reduce Slums in Vast Johannesburg Trade Zone

Special to THE NEW YORK TIMES.

CAPETOWN, South Africa, March 1—Hendrik Verwoerd, Minister of Native Affairs in the Malan Government, introduced a bill today that would empower his ministry to settle elsewhere the largest body of city dwelling industrialized Negroes in Africa.

The legislation, already approved by a majority caucus, will therefore become a law. It provides for the "removal of natives from any area in the magisterial district of Johannesburg or any adjoining magisterial district and their settlement elsewhere.

The legal reference to magisterial districts means Witwatersrand, the wealthiest industrial, financial and commercial center in Africa and the world's principal source of gold.

A large proportion of the Negro population live in Johannesburg and Witwatersrand Negro slums and in so-called "slums in the sky," boxlike constructions on the roofs of buildings in white sections of the city.

Others Also Face Ouster

The power to remove and resettle Negroes of the Witwatersrand is being asked at the same time a process is being completed empowering the Ministry of Native Affairs to drive Negro squatters and tenants of various sorts off white-owned farms without the obligation to provide other homes for them.

The principal purpose of the new law is to enforce apartheid, or separation of races, on the industrial Witwatersrand, with its constantly swelling Negro labor force. However, it also is intended, the Minister of Native Affairs has stated, to enable his ministry to break up the great Negro slums and to provide air, light and an opportunity for decent living for the Negro masses.

The slum problem had reached a hopeless dead end. The wealthy municipality of Johannesburg has been building a very limited number of houses annually to rent to Negroes in locations. At the same time Johannesburg scheduled millions of dollars to be spent on new civic centers in white districts and expended great sums every year in improving the splendid white suburbs that stretch for miles.

Slum clearance plans have been drawn up, but recently the municipality even refused a request of the Ministry of Native Affairs to provide water standpipes and cesspools on municipal land for natives living in shack towns with no source of clean water and no sanitation whatever.

Needed Labor Lacking

Millions of pounds provided by the government to build accommodations for Negroes have been turned back, apparently because the labor needed in white sections of the city was not available to work on housing for Negroes.

An official report on conditions in the old Johannesburg Negro slum showed 25 per cent of the Negro families had only one room and shared that one room with another Negro family. An additional 50 per cent of Negro families lived in one room.

The Government of Prime Minister Daniel F. Malan has presented a plan for an extensive Negro city with an eventual population of hundreds of thousands, with large, airy lots, broad streets, sanitation facilities and other amenities. It has also presented a program for creating model Negro settlements throughout the Witwatersrand area.

March 3, 1954

AFRICAN DEFENSE PERPLEXES MALAN

Continental Parley at Dakar Poses Issue of Native Army in Face of Racial Policy

By ALBION ROSS

Special to THE NEW YORK TIMES.

CAPETOWN, South Africa, March 13—South Africa's color bar has placed the Government in a quandary in regard to the defense of Africa, now being discussed at the Dakar defense conference.

The delegation that South Africa has sent to Dakar has a watch-and-wait brief.

Prime Minister Daniel F. Malan's Government is anything but ready to plunge into any definite commitments and there is reason to believe there is some hesitation here about the conference although South Africa could not avoid participation.

The issue, as the South African Government sees it, was presented in Dr. Malan's address on foreign policy last Aug. 11 in Parliament here. The address was a formal statement of South African policy with regard to all foreign issues and the Government and the delegation at Dakar are bound by it. Dr. Malan said:

"We should prevent Africa from becoming militarized. Africa should not follow the road taken by other parts of the world by becoming militarized. It should not be dragged into wars in other parts of the world. If it were done, Africa would be a danger to itself and a danger to the European in Africa and danger to South Africa."

Malan States the Case

On this statement of foreign policy the Prime Minister received broad nonpartisan support to an extent that he has seldom experienced. The conviction is virtually universal here that to arm the native African and involve him in wars between the great powers can result only in a pan-African revolution.

Strong publicity has been given here recently to reports from Kenya that the Mau Mau rebellion there was the work of men who learned about guerrilla warfar eand a nationalist movement against colonialism during World War II.

Dr. Malan stated clearly enough what he feared and what is feared here. He said:

"After the end of the World War, in which France had large numbers of natives of Madagascar in Europe to participate in the struggle, a rebellion broke out in Madagascar. Who took part in that rebellion? Who led it? The natives who had taken part in the war in Europe. Therefore, our interest and their interest is: Do not allow the natives of Africa to become militarized. One does not hand a rifle to a child."

In the same address Dr. Malan had proposed an "African charter to guard Africa against Communist penetration and Asian penetration, with special reference to India, regarded here now as South Africa's sworn enemy. He said that the principle of not "militarizing Africa" should be included in the charter.

Defense Minister François C. Erasmus, in previous statements here, indicated that South Africa's participation in any defense of Africa would be with only limited manpower.

Vaguely, the suggestion has been made that South Africa could provide a small air force and a small armored force. Her chief contribution would have to consist of war material and general supplies.

With Negro nationalism and Communist propaganda as far advanced as they are here now, the South African Government would be faced with a serious job of policing inside the country and she has only 2,600,000 white, including women and children.

There are international reasons why policing has become an important function. An official Government publication entitled "South Africa, 1954," released here yesterday, states that South Africa is the world's largest source of uranium. After reviewing the great expansion of mining in all fields, the publication says:

"These developments mean that South Africa has now become the biggest source of the world's two most precious metals, gold and uranium."

The South African stand presents a serious, and possibly, a decisive problem, to the other powers dealing with the question of the defense of Africa. Events in Asia since World War II and events in Africa in the last few years present the possibility that arms given to the native races of Africa would conceivably be turned against the colonial powers in Africa.

In any case, in any negotiations concerning the defense of Africa, South Africa's opinion is bound to bear weight.

This is the only actual manufacturing area, with well-developed industry and a many-sided economy within the African Continent.

The defense of Africa is likely to take place under one of two sets of contingencies. Either Europe will be using every resource for its own defense, it is believed, or Europe will have been entirely or largely overrun or a large part of its industrial potential destroyed.

The United States is likely to be deeply involved, supplying any number of fronts. Accordingly, South Africa, with her constantly developing industrial potential, has a large say in matters concerning any future defense of Africa.

Will she ever agree to arm her large native African forces, with the possibility that the arms will eventually be used against the white man in Africa? That is the question.

March 14, 1954

PRETORIA ORDERS TRIBAL CONFINES

South Africa to Put Negroes With Their Own Groups in Segregated Towns

Special to The New York Times.

PRETORIA, South Africa, Aug. 8—Dr. Hendrick Verwoerd, Minister of Native Affairs, has issued orders that new residential cities and settlements for Negroes are to be subdivided according to tribal allegiance.

The big meadowlands area on Witwatersrand outside Johannesburg, to which Negroes living in western Johannesburg slums are to start moving at the end of this month, is being subdivided in this fashion. The new Negro town of Vlakfontein, near Pretoria, is being subdivided in the same fashion. Negro children are educated on the basis of ten major tribal language groups and the schools are to be situated to fit the tribal subdivision pattern.

The measure is an extension of the Ministry of Native Affairs program for building up a system of Negro society and self-government based under the new formula on old tribal loyalties. In the part of South Africa that is given over to Negro reserves this pattern has been to a considerable extent preserved and is being reintroduced where it was breaking down.

The basic doctrine of the ministry, as explained here, is that the 9,000,000 Negroes of South Africa have an essential way of life and a society of their own and should not be regarded simply as a black mass but as tribal national groups.

The contention of the ministry is that Negro self-government in reserves and Negro towns throughout South Africa can be created only on a oasis of reform and modernization of existing African institutions, social class levels, common religious, occupational, and cultural activities.

Politically, the program appears to be part of a long-term policy of divide and rule.

Meanwhile, the South African National Police this week-end instructed the public in certain areas to report immediately to the police any sign of fire in mailboxes, post offices, houses, or on farms. The purpose of the instruction is to facilitate a quick check on possible arson.

August 9, 1954

Strydom, an Extreme Nationalist, Is Named Premier of South Africa

Havenga, Nominated by Malan as Successor, Quits Race and Political Life

Special to The New York Times.

JOHANNESBURG, South Africa, Nov. 30—Johannes Gerhardus Strydom succeeded Dr. Daniel F. Malan today as Prime Minister of the Union of South Africa. The new leader, 61 years old, is an extreme nationalist and an advocate of an eventual republic.

He was elected leader of the Nationalist party after Nicholaas C. Havenga, Dr. Malan's nominee, withdrew, saying he would refuse office in a Strydom Government and would retire from politics.

The election of Mr. Strydom (pronounced stray-dom) by the Nationalist caucus ended a seven-week struggle between the advance and rear guard of nationalism. It was a pointed rebuff to Dr. Malan, who had done everything possible to install Mr. Havenga as his successor.

Both Dr. Malan and Mr. Havenga, in cautiously worded utterances, gave the impression that they doubted Mr. Strydom's ability to maintain Afrikaner unity—the foundation of nationalism's power.

Die Transvaler, Mr. Strydom's own newspaper, said that the spirit and direction of the Strydom Government would be the same as that of the Malan regime. It is unnecessary to greet the new Prime Minister with shuddering and fearful curiosity, the newspaper remarked, because no revolution will take place; the ship of state will be steered in the same direction as before.

"The new Prime Minister will not be an incarnation of Satan," the paper added.

Tribute to Malan Printed

Mr. Havenga's newspaper, Die Vaderland, in a tribute to Dr. Malan, warned:

"He who stands at the helm and glances over the whole scene observes dangers of which the masses are not always aware. A leader who takes fickle mass feeling as his guiding light will not be able to lead the people to the heights. History has taught that the masses who shout hosanna today can just as readily be moved to erect gallows tomorrow."

J. G. N. Strauss, leader of the United party Opposition, said the Nationalists "have elected as leader and Prime Minister an uncompromising extremist and apostle of a republic completely and finally divorced from the British Commonwealth, in preference to a man [Mr. Havenga] who could have done much good for our country as Prime Minister."

"I appeal [to Mr. Strydom] to allay the fears an anxiety of many South Africans by publicly declaring that he will respect our Constitution and leave the independence and prestige of our courts intact and undamaged," Mr. Strauss added.

Associated Press

Johannes G. Strydom

Stand on Voters Cited

The Opposition leader was referring to a constitutional crisis caused by Dr. Malan's attempts to segregate voters of mixed blood on a register of their own. Several Malan laws doing this were declared unconstitutional by the courts. The issue is still unresolved.

Judging by his past statements, Mr. Strydom will not hesitate to act to change the colored franchise. He once said in Parliament:

"Coloreds who are on the common roll with Europeans today must be separated and given separate representation, and Negro representatives in this house [the Assembly] must be eliminated. The Indians must be regarded as outsiders who cannot enjoy political rights in South Africa."

December 1, 1954

130 Negro Families Forced Out Of Johannesburg Under Guard

By LEONARD INGALLS
Special to The New York Times.

JOHANNESBURG, South Africa, Feb. 9—The forced removal of natives from their homes in Johannesburg began today.

The transfer of the first 130 Negro families from their slum dwellings to a new Government housing development beyond the city limits was carried out under close surveillance of 2,000 heavily armed policemen.

Although disturbances had been feared, there were no incidents and no arrests.

The resettlement of the natives to areas outside Johannesburg represents the application of the National Government's policy of apartheid, or separation of white and native communities.

The law under which the resettlement is taking place was introduced in Parliament last year by Dr. Hendrik F. Verwoerd, Minister of Native Affairs.

The first group of native families had been scheduled to be relocated Saturday, but the operation was advanced three days in a surprise move to thwart demonstrations.

This step followed a ban yesterday on public gatherings in the Johannesburg area for the next twenty days because of apprehension over the possibility that violence might result.

Notices were served last night on 150 families in the native community of Sophiatown to be ready at 6 o'clock this morning to leave their homes and move to the new Government community at Meadowlands, eleven miles from the center of Johannesburg and four miles more distant than Sophiatown.

At 4 A. M. detachments of white and native police assembled in the pre-dawn darkness at Sophiatown and Meadowlands and on the route between them to enforce the removal plan. White officers were armed with pistols, rifles, submachine and machine guns. Native policemen carried steel-pointed spears, known as assagais, and clubs.

The actual moving, in three-ton Army trucks, was supervised by motorcycle military police.

Although 150 families had been scheduled to be moved, twenty took refuge in the Anglican mission and refused to go. No action was taken against them for the present since they had vacated their slum dwellings and taken their furniture and possessions to the churchyard. Later many of them went to live with relatives in crowded Sophiatown homes not yet affected by the removal plan.

It is planned to move about 150 native families a week from Johannesburg until 57,000 have been shifted outside the municipal boundaries.

Opponents of resettlement of the Sophiatown residents have complained that many of those affected have lived there for nearly fifty years and are being forced out against their will. These critics declare that some are being deprived of property they rightfully own; that there are worse slums that should be cleared, and that Meadowlands is too far from the city for persons employed here to commute easily every day.

As soon as the native families and their possessions were taken from Sophiatown dwellings this morning, fumigating squads moved in with cyanide gas equipment to destroy pests and vermin. They were followed by demolition crews who quickly tore off the roofs and made the structures otherwise uninhabitable.

The first cavalcade of trucks, piled high with native belongings, rolled away to Meadowlands in pelting rain. Mothers and babies rode in the cabs. Fathers and older children crawled in among the furniture and other possessions in the rear of the trucks.

Most of those interviewed said they were glad to be going to new homes. They had been paying up to $6 a month for hovels. Rents at Meadowlands will range from $3 to $13 a month.

The Meadowlands dwellings are small one-story brick cottages of three or four rooms. The roofs are of corrugated asbestos sheeting. The floor area varies from about 300 to 750 square feet. The larger ones are for families of up to eight persons.

Each house has a cold-water tap and a flush toilet. In many cases these facilities are in a small yard building. A six-room school building has been built and stores and improved transportation facilities have been promised.

February 10, 1955

The Grim Drama at Johannesburg

Forced resettlement of Negroes there, says Alan Paton, is yet another example of the end justifying the means—and 'this end is white supremacy.'

By ALAN PATON

JOHANNESBURG.

THE attention of the world has been focused on the removal, now begun, of 58,000 Africans from the western areas of Johannesburg to new housing made available farther west at Meadowlands. What are the facts of this situation?

Johannesburg is the most important city in Africa south of the Sahara and, with its immediate environs, has a population approaching 1,000,000, rather more than half of whom are native Africans. In all southern Africa, Johannesburg has been the scene of the greatest cityward migrations.

Of these half-million Africans in Johannesburg, very few are mine laborers. In any event, mine laborers are not the subject of this report, for they come to the city temporarily and, after their contract is completed, they return to the Reserves, which are country areas set apart for Negroes. While they are in the city they live in mine compounds. They are not therefore property owners, tenants or sub-tenants.

The majority of the adult Negro workers are employed in white-owned factories, shops and homes. All South Africa is passing through an industrial revolution, and white-owned factories are clamoring for African labor.

Johannesburg, like many other cities, just keeps on growing. When I was a boy, we usually reckoned that any city population was half white people and half non-white people. One can no longer do this. In many cities there are two non-white persons to each white person.

IN America the average Negro income is approximately 50 per cent of the average white income, and this figure is steadily rising. But America is an old industrial society and South Africa is a new one. The average income of the native African is a great deal less than 50 per cent of the average white income. However, thanks to increased industrialization, this low figure is slowly rising.

Nevertheless, the lowness of the income should make it clear that most urban Africans work in lowly positions as domestic servants, messengers and low-paid clerks and as factory hands.

Now there has been a traditional, long-established way of dealing with African workers in the white man's towns and cities. Such workers, if they were domestics, lived in the servants' quarters of the white home, or they lived in a part of the town or city set aside for them and called a location. This location and all its land and houses belonged to the municipality. No African could buy his land or his house. The theory behind this arrangement was that the real home of the African was in the Reserve, and that he was only a temporary sojourner in the white man's city.

This theory grows less and less tenable. But in various parts of the country there were exceptions to this traditional location system. Three of these exceptions were in Johannesburg; their names are Sophiatown, Martindale and Newclare. They are, in fact, the western areas that are now being evacuated. How did they come into being?

In 1905 Sophiatown was established as a township. Certain stands, or as Americans would say, lots, could not be sold to non-white people, but most could. It was a freehold township; if you bought a stand there, it was yours and presumably no one could take it from you except, one supposes, in the interests of some public service or benefit. If you built a house on your lot, the same applied.

SOPHIATOWN became predominately non-white, and in 1921 even the remaining restrictions were removed. Nevertheless, many of the properties were owned by Europeans and Indians.

Also in 1905, Martindale was established with no restrictions in respect of occupancy, and in 1912 Newclare was established with restrictions against white occupancy.

The Western Areas were accepted as non-white areas. They were near a municipal sewage farm and no one wanted particularly to live near there. In fact, in 1918, the City Council established the western native township as a controlled location in the same area.

But Johannesburg went on growing as before and subsequently the land to the east and west of Sophiatown was offered for white purchase. Westdene and Newlands were two of these new white suburbs. By 1939 there was a growing demand on the part of white owners and tenants to evacuate the Western Areas and to move their non-white inhabitants farther to the west. In 1944 the City Council was prepared to approve such a scheme.

It should be noted that the present Nationalist Government was not in power at that time. This is an important feature of the total situation—the great majority of white South Africans favor residential segregation.

THE Nationalist Government came into power in 1948. It came into power very largely because it promised to solve the racial problems of multiracial South Africa. It promised to do this through apartheid. Apartheid means the separation of the races—residentially, socially, politically. Total apartheid includes even territorial separation on the grand scale.

One of the cardinal principles of apartheid is that the African has his home in the Reserve and that if he wishes to work in the white man's towns and cities he must not expect to receive any benefits other than those of a temporary dweller. He must certainly not expect to own land in the white man's territory. If he does so, this is due to the mistakes of previous governments.

For some years the City Council made no provision for more African housing, though the population continued to increase. The existing African areas were full to overflowing. Owners and tenants took in lodgers to increase their meager incomes. Slum conditions developed, but these were largely due to the failure of the City Council.

At last the extent of the congestion was exposed when the lodgers, finding the conditions more and more intolerable, overflowed into the famous shantytowns and built for themselves dwellings of any pieces of wood, sacking and galvanized iron that they could lay their hands on. They lived in great discomfort, but struggled valiantly to avoid squalor. An investigation revealed that the vast majority were employed people and that their presence was essential to the well-being and prosperity of Johannesburg as a whole. One might have thought that they had

ALAN PATON is a South African author who writes often of the racial tensions that exist in his native country. He wrote "Cry, the Beloved Country," and "Too Late the Phalarope."

a prior claim on any new housing. But no.

It is the intention of the Government to evacuate the 58,000 Africans in the Western Areas to the new location of Meadowlands, farther away from the city. These 58,000 people live on 1.885 stands situated on some 440 acres of ground. It is estimated (variously) that only from 350 to 600 of these stands are actually owned by Africans; the others are owned by Europeans and Indians, although Europeans could not occupy them,

There was gross overcrowding in these areas and whole families, sometimes large families, lived in one room; also, slum conditions were common and much of the property was fit only for demolition.

Against this, it must be stated that the property on one quarter of the stands was in good condition. This was very often the property owned by Africans. Their savings had gone into it and they were proud of it and took good care of it.

The material conditions of many of these families will improve by transfer to Meadowlands. Each family will have one house. The new area is twice the extent of the old. Those families whose material conditions were abject—and there were many—will benefit materially; and many of them are not in general concerned with the loss of property rights which will be sustained by others. Press photographs show that many of these families left with joy the hovels in which they had been living.

IT should be known that Meadowlands is six miles farther from Johannesburg than the Western Areas and that the present transport facilities are overburdened. It should also be known that Sophiatown was, in a way that no other native location has ever succeeded in being, a community—it had schools, churches, cinemas, shops.

No shopkeeper who is moved to Meadowlands knows whether his business will ever be the same again. No elderly woman dependent on some domestic service for her living knows whether she will be able to face the new and more arduous undertaking of getting to her work. And clerics such as the Rev. Trevor Huddleston, the Anglican priest who has opposed the removal, could be kept out altogether.

NEVERTHELESS, the first removals, which many feared would cause violence and disorder, have gone off quietly. These removals were carried out, not by the City Council, but by the Government, which had created a Resettlement Board to effect removals when a City Council proved difficult.

It is estimated, however, that twenty to forty of the first fifty families were not in their homes or lodgings when the Resettlement authorities came to remove them. They had been helped to move during the night and had found other lodgings in the already congested lodging rooms of Sophiatown. The authorities have stated that some of those families have since asked to be forgiven and removed.

A large number of police stood by during the removal. On the night before the second removals, some "volunteers" of the African National Congress were arrested while helping other families to leave their homes before the arrival of the removal vans.

These new houses at Meadowlands are for Negroes removed from areas of Johannesburg.

Father Trevor Huddleston, leader of the opposition to resettlement.

The removals themselves, like the first, went off quietly.

Lastly, it should be noted that, while the right to own land outside the Reserves has been taken away, Africans will be entitled to buy the new houses on leasehold for a period of thirty years and also to build houses in the new areas.

WHY, then, has the removal attracted such worldwide attention? Why has it caused such opposition? Why have the African National Congress, the Liberal party and churchmen, like the Bishop of Johannesburg and Father Huddleston, opposed the removals so vigorously?

The Minister of Native Affairs, Dr. D. H. F. Verwoerd, who is responsible for the removals, has the answer to the questions: These people are agitators, opposed to the Government and anxious to foment any dissatisfaction.

The Minister stated that he had abundant information that a great number of Africans welcomed the move, and he promised them protection from any who tried to intimidate them.

But what is the basis for these objections? The objections have been clearly stated by Dr. Xuma, an African doctor living in Sophiatown.

Dr. Xuma by no means bases his case wholly on the taking away of freehold rights. He bases it rather on the removal of human rights without consultation or consent. He bases it on the denial of rights which should belong to all human beings and should be sacred to any government.

He points to other slum areas which could have been cleaned and maintains that the Western Areas were cleared first in order to destroy the freehold rights. He regards the whole scheme as an offense against justice and morality, and concludes that it can only create hatred between white and black.

Dr. Xuma's case is unanswerable. It shows that apartheid, whatever flowery things may be said about it, is something that is done by people with power to people without power.

Many Africans are docile and acquiescent, and it is a myth propagated by the Government that they represent true African opinion. But many are not, and it is another myth that these are agitators and unrepresentative.

The removal of the Western Areas is a test step for the Government. It will be the first of many. The Minister of Native Affairs will probably attempt in the near future to remove Alexandra Township on the northern edge of Johannesburg, another freehold township with 75,000 inhabitants.

But he seeks still greater powers under proposed new legislation. This removal of "black spots" and the taking away of freehold rights is only part of the apartheid program. The greater part lies ahead.

THIS will be to check further industrial development in white territory and to prevent the further migration of African labor to the industrial areas. The attempt will be made to shift new industrial development to the impoverished Reserves and to make them capable of sustaining a greater African population. Eventually, it is hoped to attract African labor away from the cities back to the Reserves and to replace this by white immigration.

The great dream of total separation will then be approaching realization and white civilization will be saved. Then in the Reserves all the human rights which could not be granted to Africans in white territory will be granted to them, and the black nation and the white nation will be able to live in harmony side by side.

CAN this fantastic ideal be realized? How far can one go toward it?

It must be the realization of the equally fantastic difficulties that causes the Minister sometimes in the House to rest his head on his hands and withdraw temporarily from active pursuit of his messianic ideal. His energy and drive no one doubts. But consider his difficulties.

White immigration has always been a problem to the Nationalist Government. South Africa is not like America. Its white population speaks two languages, English and Afrikaans, and the two groups are uneasy neighbors. There is no guarantee that white immigration from Europe would strengthen the Afrikaner group - descended from the original Dutch settlers. It might strengthen the English group and weaken the Afrikaner power.

Can industry be safely diverted from its present centers without imperiling the growing affluence of the country? We are witnessing a struggle between economic forces and apartheid ideology.

But English South Africans are not so sure as they were that economic forces must win. They have learned that apartheid ideology is fiercely powerful, deriving much of its strength from the Afrikaner will to survive.

Prominent Nationalist leaders have told their followers time and time again that one cannot achieve a great victory without great sacrifice. One threat has always hung over the head of white South Africa and that is that the African could paralyze the country by withdrawing his labor. But if greater and greater separation could be achieved, would not the danger of such a threat be correspondingly lessened? Would not the African paralyze himself? It is a great race against time and world opinion.

The Government is trying to create a new world before it is too late. In this world there will be justice for all under the rule of the Afrikaner Nationalist. It is the Afrikaner Nationalist who knows what is just for all. And so great is his power that opposition is at the moment at its lowest ebb. The parallel with pre-war Germany is frighteningly close.

Can the great feat be brought off? Can complete separation under white domination be achieved? To anyone who knows only South Africa and the strength of its Government it seems to be possible.

There is also evidence that some non-whites are beginning to accept the doctrines of the present Government. The Government thinks that this is free choice. It is not. It is a yielding to power.

AS for white South Africa, it has accepted the evacuations with unconcern. It has become used to deciding the fortunes of non-white people without consulting them. It is prepared to overlook dispossession when it is accompanied by material improvements. It is prepared to believe that domination is good if it wears a paternal smile, so long as it is not challenged.

It is day by day, year by year, beginning to accept more and more that the end justifies the means. This end is white supremacy; but it is often called racial peace, and conscience is thereby stilled.

Let us make no mistake about it. The Johannesburg evacuations, whatever ills they remedy, whatever benefits they confer, however quietly they may be carried out and however attractive the goal of harmony they aim at, are fundamentally unjust. They may remove occasions of conflict, but they leave the causes untouched; they even multiply them. They are a blot on the name of our unhappy country.

Strijdom's Grip Strengthened By South African Parliament

It Adjourns After Adding to Power of Nationalist Regime—Long Tenure for Government Is Foreseen

By LEONARD INGALLS
Special to The New York Times.

JOHANNESBURG, South Africa, June 23—The South African Parliament adjourned today, ending one of its most significant sessions of recent years.

Actions taken by the Parliament at Capetown since its 1955 meeting began Jan. 21 are believed by observers here to have made it possible for the National party of Prime Minister Johannes G. Strijdom to remain in power for many years.

Two items in particular are cited in support of this view. One is the packing of the Supreme Court by increasing its membership from five to eleven. The second is an increase in the size of the Senate from forty-eight to eighty-nine members, which will have the effect of insuring a two-thirds majority for the Nationalists.

The session also was marked by legislation extending the Nationalists' apartheid policies for separating races, and further limitations on the liberties of all South Africans.

The parliamentary session has been called one of the "unhappiest" in the nation's history and has been condemned as leading toward "a republic" and a one-party system.

[The Union of South Africa, in spite of a steady weakening of its Broederbond with Britain, is still a member of the British Commonwealth of Nations. Creation of a republic would have the effect of eradicating the last vestiges of British influence in the Union.]

Role of Secret Society

The reference to the Broederbond by critics of the Government applies to a highly secret society of Afrikkaner Nationalists which is said to be the real ruling group of South Africa. The organization's membership is reputed to include Government ministers and leaders of the Nationalist party, as well as some of the nation's top business and financial interests.

Most of the criticism of the Strijdom Administration comes, of course, from members of the major opposition, the United party, which will lose parliamentary representation as a result of changes in the composition of the Senate.

In addition to denunciations of the Administration legislation the opposition also has charged in recent week that its members' mail has been opened while in the hands of the post office, and that their telephones are being tapped. The only comment from Government sources was a statement by Minister of Justice Charles R. Swart that under certain circumstances the police had the right to do the things complained of.

Nationalists Grip Tightened

While strengthening their grip on the Government, the Nationalists took no direct step toward establishing the long-promisedd republic. One aspect of the increase in the size of the Senate is that it would make possible the creation of a republic by a majority of both Houses of Parliament sitting together. The Nationalists will have a majority of sixty-five in the new Senate instead of twelve.

Other major legislation enacted by Parliament included:

¶Further segregation of the races into what are known as "group areas."

¶Increased control and limitation by the central Government of education for the nation's 10,000,000 Negroes.

¶Extension of the powers of police to enter homes and to attend private meetings without warrants.

¶Restriction on the issuance of passports and provision of stiff penalties for persons leaving South Africa without official permision.

¶The grant of wide powers to the Minister of Economics for the control of monopolies in business.

The over-all significance of the major legislation enacted is that it grants the Nationalist Administration virtually unlimited opportunity to do exactly as it wishes in determining the political, social and economic structure of South Africa.

Warnings by the opposition that the Nationalists are creating a police state and threatening the nation's prosperity with racial segregation measures that affect the availability of native labor have not deterred the Nationalists in pushing through their program.

June 24, 1955

KIMBERLEY BEGINS TO CLASSIFY RACES

Some Who Had Considered Themselves Coloreds Are Placed in Negro Bracket

Special to The New York Times.

KIMBERLEY, South Africa, Aug. 20—The life of scores of South Africans of mixed and Negroid blood is being drastically reshaped by the compilations of a population register.

In one-half hour yesterday six Kimberley men, who regarded themselves as colored—mulatto—were reclassified as Negroes, thrusting them back to the bottom of the social ladder up which they had attempted to climb. Many others are similarly affected in informal courts being held by Government officials at main centers.

The director of the census, J. I. Raats, told the press today that so far 7,000 persons of doubtful racial origin had been classified into one or other of the main racial categories. Of this number, 260 had given notice of appeal.

Compilers of the register have dealt with most of the difficult cases in Pretoria and are now working in Johannesburg, Kimberley and other towns. The classification is being done by specially selected officials picked for their impartiality, integrity and humanity.

The population register is required by law to classify people into three main groups of whites, Negroes and Coloreds.

Mr. Raats personally classified 700 persons after separate interviews. If a white man is classified as a Colored it may mean a personal tragedy for himself and his family. Similarly, a Colored who is reclassified as a Negro goes to the bottom of the social scale.

The population register, which is the cornerstone of the Government's policy of segregating the races, will eventually make it impossible for borderline cases to "escape" into a higher racial category. Each person will receive an identity card containing his classifiction and photo.

Of total white, Colored and Asian population of 3,753,000, 1,542,000 have been photographed. The Government expects to photograph the rest by the end of the year. Of the 8,500,000 Negroes, 1,700,000 have been photographed and given identity cards.

August 21, 1955

POLICY TEST NEAR FOR SOUTH AFRICA

Segregation Stand Found to Soften in Bid to Be Leader in Area South of Sahara

By LEONARD INGALLS
Special to The New York Times.

CAPETOWN, South Africa, Jan. 31—South Africa's desire to act as leader of the nations south of the Sahara has produced subtle changes in the country's policy in the past year, according to observers here.

Whether South Africa realizes this aim is expected to be tested this year at a conference on African defense for which the nation has been pressing.

Diplomatic representatives and other persons who have been watching developments closely believe that the first important move in the Government's drive was a statement early last year by Prime Minister Johannes G. Strijdom. This said that South Africa sought friendship and co-operation with non-European, or Negro, states of Africa.

For the Prime Minister of South Africa to have recognized and accepted a need for dealing with Negro states was considered quite a step, compared with the narrower attitudes of his predecessor, Dr. Daniel F. Malan.

At the time Mr. Strijdom said there would be no departure from the Nationalist party's plan of separate communities and development for Negroes in South Africa. But he added that South Africa would be ready to live in peace with fully matured Negro states elsewhere on the continent.

This of course has raised the question of what adjustments and accommodations would be made with respect to South Africa's color bar should a delegation from a Negro state visit the country on official business. The Department of External Affairs recently undertook to seek an acceptable and inoffensive solution to the problem.

Meanwhile, a second step believed aimed toward helping enhance South Africa's international standing has been taken by Mr. Strijdom, who has been Prime Minister a year and two months. This is an apparent acceptance in a speech in Parliament of the principle of economic intergration for Negroes in South African society.

Here Mr. Strijdom is on difficult ground because of political dangers involving the overwhelming fear most of South Africa's 3,000,000 whites have of being swamped by the country's 10,000,000 Negroes. Nevertheless, good propaganda value was seen in the indication by the Prime Minister that the Nationalists were yielding in their former strict segregation policies.

One of the Government's major aims at the present session of Parliament is to remove persons of mixed blood from the election rolls permitting them to vote for white candidates. But there is considerable informal talk in this legislative capital of South Africa about the international propaganda advantages of extending the franchise more widely among the nation's Negroes.

There is little doubt in the minds of persons familiar with the situation that one of the big questions to be asked by the African defense conference will be whether South Africa is prepared to use Negroes in the armed forces. Negro troops are common in defense forces on the continent outside South Africa.

February 5, 1956

South Africans Urge 7 Areas for Negroes

By LEONARD INGALLS
Special to The New York Times.

JOHANNESBURG, South Africa, March 27—A blueprint for enforcing on an unparalleled scale the racial separation theories of South Africa's governing party was submitted today to Parliament in Capetown.

A Government commission called for establishment of seven areas in which the nation's 9,000,000 Negroes would be segregated to live and work, leaving the rest of the country to the whites. Some Negroes, however, would continue to be used as migrant labor in white areas.

The commission said the greatly broadened application of apartheid (racial segregation) would require the expenditure of $290,000,000 in the first ten years of the program for economic development of the seven areas. These areas are now largely agricultural. The chief aim of the plan would be to prevent at all costs integration of Negroes with South Africa's 3,000,000 white persons and 1,100,000 persons of mixed blood, known as Coloreds.

Complete segregation as a national policy in South Africa as compared to the United States policy of gradual integration is influenced chiefly by the fact that the whites here are outnumbered 3 to 1 by Negroes.

The commission, which has worked for five years on the plan, warned that the whites must be prepared to work harder and bear most of the initial cost of the program if they wanted to preserve their supremacy in South Africa.

The recommendations and results of the commission's studies were contained in seventeen volumes totaling 3,755 pages plus a 277-page summary. The report is expected to lead to the introduction of legislation, based on its recommendations, by the Government of Prime Minister Johannes G. Strijdom.

The commission also advocated incorporation into the Union of the three British protectorates of Bechuanaland, Basutoland and Swaziland. They would be used as the nucleus for the seven Negro areas.

The South African Government has long campaigned for annexation of the protectorates, but thus far transfer has been resisted by the British Government.

In arguing for acceptance of its plan the commission asserted that the alternative would be that 17,000,000 Negroes and 6,000,000 whites would be living in a common society, integrated politically, economically and socially, by the year 2000. The result, the commission contended, would be friction and possible domination of the whites by the Negroes.

The report said that the commission was "convinced that there is no midway between the two poles of ultimate total integration and ultimate separate development of the two groups."

Consolidation of the 260 areas where Negroes now live into seven also would mean elimination of 154 so-called black spots or centers of Negro settlement in predominantly white areas, the commission said.

All Negroes living in the Western part of Cape Province would be removed and the area would be restricted to the nation's 1,100,000 colored persons.

Some whites would be forced to move out of the proposed Negro areas, but Negroes would continue for the foreseeable future under jurisdiction of whites, the commission said. It added that eventually increasing degrees of self-government, up to the provincial level, might be granted to the Negroes, but the National Government would remain under white control.

Great emphasis was given by the commission to economic development of the seven Negro areas to make them self-sufficient. Reduction of the present number of African farmers from 4,000,000 to 2,000,000 was envisioned. Seven million persons would make their livelihood within the Negro areas in thirty years and 2,000,000 would continue to work as temporary immigrants in white sections.

The commission proposed that about half of the $290,000,000 required for industrialization of the Negro areas be sought from private sources, including Negro savings and income. It urged that the other half, for social and economic improvements, come from public funds.

Mining, manufacturing and various businesses in 100 cities and towns in the segregated areas would be owned and operated by Negroes, the commission said.

March 28, 1956

SOUTH AFRICANS BAR BIG NEGRO AID

Strijdom Regime Turns Down Area Development Plans—Vote Laws in Court Test

By LEONARD INGALLS

Special to The New York Times.

JOHANNESBURG, South Africa, April 24—The Administration rejected today the major recommendations by a Government commission for large expenditures to develop seven areas inhabited by 9,000,000 Negroes.

However, the Government said in a White Paper presented to Parliament in Capetown that it welcomed the unequivocal rejection by the commission of the integration of whites and Negroes.

The report of the commission on the sociological-economic development of the Bantu (Negro) areas compiled after five years of study was submitted last month to Parliament. It is known here as the Tomlinson report after Prof. F. R. Tomlinson, commission chairman.

The Government embraced all of the commission's favorable comments on the apartheid program, which is the fundamental policy of Prime Minister Johannes G. Strijdom's Administration.

Among those rejected was a ten-year plan for the expenditure of $290,000,000 for the industrial and social development of Negro areas. Individual land tenure in place of the present tribal ownership and the introduction of modern mining in Negro areas also were rejected.

The White Paper gave the impression that the commission's report would be used to support apartheid legislation. However, the Government would not court any possibility of unpopularity by creating a large financial burden. There was, however, a suggestion that some small amounts might be required from the white community to insure that the Negro areas were developed in "the right manner."

It was indicated that any funds for improvement of the largely agricultural Negro areas must come from the Negroes themselves. Small industries, particularly those providing services, will be encouraged, the Government said, but there will be no large manufacturing or other enterprises that would compete with white industries for many years.

More than $1,000,000, it was said, is available in Negro trust funds held by the Government and can be used immediately for afforestation, irrigation and soil conservation. This indicates that the Administration foresees that the Negro areas will continue to be devoted chiefly to agriculture.

A recommendation that industries be set up by whites in the Negro areas was rejected, although assistance was promised to businesses that set up plants adjacent to Negro areas to obtain labor.

Another aspect of the Government's race issues came to the fore. The removal by the Government of persons of mixed blood from South Africa's common voters' roll was challenged in the Supreme Court.

The action was brought in Capetown on behalf of the Opposition United party by two men of mixed Negro and white parentage. Such persons are known in South Africa as Coloreds. Their suit attacked the constitutionality of two acts of Parliament.

A final decision in the cases is not expected before August. Should the high court rule against the Nationalist party Government, it would be a major upset for Prime Minister Strijdom and his followers and could result in the dissolution of the Government. A favorable decision, however, would leave the Nationalists more firmly entrenched than ever.

One of the acts of Parliament in question increased the size of the South African Senate to give the Nationalists an undisputed two-thirds majority in Parliament. This made possible the passage of a second law that removed 40,000 Coloreds from the common rolls.

April 25, 1956

South Africa Court Upholds Separation Of Half-Caste Vote

Special to The New York Times.

JOHANNESBURG, South Africa, Nov. 9—South Africa's Constitutional Court of Appeal upheld today a Government-sponsored act fought by the opposition as "Senate-packing."

The vote of the court, in which all justices participated, was 10 to 1.

By the court's decision, South Africa moved into a new political era. A total of 38,000 Coloreds (half-castes) in Cape Province were placed on a separate voting roll by the enlarged Senate. For the first time in 100 years they will vote as an electoral group segregated from whites in the 1958 general election.

The Coloreds have been given four whites to represent them in the lower house of the Assembly and one Government nominee in the Senate. The voter with both white and Negro antecedents have lost their right to elect two Colored representatives to the Cape Province Council. Now they may elect only two whites.

Voting rights of Colored people on a common roll with whites were guaranteed in the South Africa Act of 1910 and could be removed only by a two-third majority of Parliament with both the Assembly and Senate sitting together.

Removal of Colored voters from South Africa's common roll has been a major goal of Prime Minister Johannes G. Strijdom, an advocate of racial segregation as a basic South African policy.

Today's court decision ends a five-year constitutional struggle during which the Nationalist Government tried one measure after another to get the Cape Coloreds off the common voters' roll. The only non-whites now left on it are about 1,000 Coloreds in Natal. Their names will remain but no more will be added. When they die, the common roll will be all white.

November 10, 1956

South Africa Seizes 140 in Race Dispute

Special to The New York Times.

JOHANNESBURG, South Africa, Dec. 5— Detectives of the political branch of the South African police arrested 140 persons today in various parts of the union on charges of treason.

Those arrested, under the Suppression of Communism Act, included whites—men and women—Negroes and Asians. Among them was L. B. Warden, a white member of Parliament who represents Negroes in Cape Province.

[The Nationalist Government of Premier Johannes G. Strijdom enforces a policy of strict segregation of the races. The Suppression of Communism Act nominally provided for the outlawing of communism, but it has been called a formidable engine for the stifling of opposition to the Government's policies.]

Attorneys, surveyors, architects and trade union officials were among those taken into custody.

The Rev. Douglas Chadwick Thompson, superintendent minister of the Methodist Church circuit, was ordered out of bed at 4 A. M. and taken to a police station, where he was being held pending trial with others arrested.

Many others appeared in local courts today, and all were similarly charged and remanded to Johannesburg for trial. Military planes brought persons arrested at other places to Johannesburg, where they were held in custody for hearing Dec. 19.

Mrs. Helen Joseph of Johannesburg, secretary of the South African Women's Federation, appeared in court this afternoon with several white, Negro and Asian men, also charged with treason. A few months ago she led a march of Negro women to Prime Minister Strijdom's office in Pretoria to protest against Negro women's having to carry "passes."

The arrests are the result of raids last year on hundreds of organizations and private homes in a search for evidence of treason and offenses under the Suppression of Communism Act. Among the homes raided then was that of the Rev. Trevor Huddleston, an Anglican priest and an enemy of the Government's racial policies.

In today's raids detectives carried warrants authorizing them to search for documents covering about forty-eight organizations.

In addition to raids where arrests were made, the police raided many other homes in their search for evidence.

When a group of nineteen Negroes was driven up to the court, they shouted "Long Live Africa!" and sang the anthem of African National Congress, a Negro political organization.

December 6, 1956

NEW CURBS NEAR IN SOUTH AFRICA

Measures Empower Cabinet Aide to Bar Negroes From Areas Used by Whites

By RICHARD P. HUNT
Special to The New York Times.

CAPETOWN, South Africa, May 25—In a few days the South African Government will be armed with a series of new laws to prevent Negroes from "causing a nuisance" in white areas.

These measures have been adopted by both houses of Parliament in an omnibus native laws amendment bill. They await only the signature of the Acting Governor General and formal promulgation.

They empower the Minister of Native Affairs to bar Negroes from churches, clubs, hospitals, schools, places of public entertainment or public meetings outside their own residential areas if he thinks their presence undesirable.

The definition of "a nuisance" is left to the opinion of the Minister, and that is not subject to review by the courts. In most cases, he cannot be required to say how his opinion was formed.

The sitting Minister, Dr. Hendrik F. Verwoerd, holds that these powers are needed to insure that the relations between black and white here be those of guardian and ward, and consistent with the policy of rigid racial segregation.

Antiracist Group Protests

To the antiracist South African Institute of Race Relations, these laws seem to give the Minister "powers of dictatorship over the lives of citizens."

It was the so-called church clause of the omnibus bill that stirred sharp criticism here and abroad on the ground that it would empower the Minister to interfere with religious freedom. Dr. Verwoerd denied any intention of doing so.

However, the main Dutch Reformed Church in South Africa gave at best only equivocal support to the clause, and this lukewarm attitude caused rumblings of dissent deep within the governing Nationalist party. In the end, Dr. Verwoerd agreed to some tempering safeguards.

The law will require him to grant a hearing before banning Negroes from a white congregation, to consider the availability of other facilities for Negro worship and to act only with the consent of local government officials.

Nevertheless, the Right Rev. Ambrose Reeves, Anglican Bishop of Johannesburg, declared: "This clause gives the Minister the power to determine who shall or who shall not worship in any particular church."

'Duty to Disobey' Cited

He said it was the Church's duty to disobey.

There is some doubt that churchmen will have the opportunity to do so in the near future. Political pressures indicate that the Minister may move slowly, and that the wording of the law could make it difficult to find a test case.

The direct penalties for disobedience of the church measure fall on the Negro members of a congregation rather than on the clergymen. This may limit the ability of the churches to find effective protests.

But the same rule does not apply to secular gatherings where sponsor and visitor alike are liable to punishment. Whites who test the law can share the risks fully.

In these fields, the Minister's powers will be unhampered and he will not be subject to the moderating pressure of the Dutch Reformed Church, which is an important influence in his party.

For these reasons, it is expected here that the more vigorous attack will be made upon nonchurch meetings and associations.

May 26, 1957

Verwoerd Is Named South Africa's Head

JOHANNESBURG, South Africa, Sept. 2 — Dr. Hendrik Frensch Verwoerd, Minister of Native Affairs, was elected Prime Minister of South Africa today. He succeeds Johannes G. Strijdom, who died Aug. 24.

Dr. Verwoerd, 56 years old, also became the new leader of the Nationalist party. The election was by secret ballot at a party caucus held in Capetown.

There were three candidates: Dr. Verwoerd, Charles R. Swart, Minister of Justice and acting Prime Minister, and Dr. Theophilus E. Donges, Minister of the Interior.

Dr. Verwoerd is the leader of the Nationalists in the Transvaal, the home of national extremism, and his election means that the Government will pursue relentlessly its policy of apartheid, or racial segregation, and drive for the establishment of a republic.

Dr. Verwoerd was born in the Netherlands and came to South Africa at the age of 2.

He is a former Professor of Applied Psychology at Stellenbosch University and former editor of the Nationalist Transvaal newspaper Die Transvaler.

A controversial figure, he entered politics in 1936 when, with five other professors, he protested against the immigration to South Africa of Jewish refugees from Nazi Germany.

As a newspaper editor he disapproved of South Africa's war effort. He was appointed Senator after the Nationalist victory of 1948 when he failed to win the Parliamentary seat of Alberton, near Johannesburg.

He ended the system of allowing natives to acquire property rights in urban native townships and is regarded as the chief architect of the Nationalist party's policy of apartheid.

September 3, 1958

South African Racist

Hendrik Frensch Verwoerd

THE Union of South Africa's new Prime Minister is one of his country's most unyielding advocates of white supremacy. In a nation where whites are outnumbered 4 to 1 by non-whites Hendrik Frensch Verwoerd (pronounced fair-VOOT) has based his political career on extremism. He has been the driving force for the last ten years behind South Africa's racial segregation program, which is called apartheid.

Man in the News

When the Nationalist party attained power in 1948, Dr. Verwoerd became Minister of Native Affairs in the Cabinet. In the opinion of many observers he has used his vast ministerial powers over Negroes and persons of mixed color to promote himself as a strong candidate for the post he won yesterday.

The picture that has emerged over the years has been one of a dominant public official who would stand for no nonsense about which race was boss in South Africa. He has introduced in

the South African Parliament some of the nation's most repressive race laws.

At the same time Dr. Verwoerd has served as one of the chief political and social theorists of the Nationalist party. The party derives its support from 1,600,000 South Africans of Dutch ancestry who call themselves Afrikaners.

Dr. Verwoerd is a psychologist by training and an expert on social services. During his tenure as Minister of Native Affairs many schools, hospitals and housing developments for Negroes have been built. But they have been insufficient to make more than a small dent in slums, illness and ignorance among Africans.

Increased Barriers

At the same time the programs administered by Dr. Verwoerd have tended to increase the barriers between whites and non-whites. The new Prime Minister often has declared that the ultimate aim of his country must be complete territorial segregation.

Last year he had the Native Laws amended to give himself control of nearly all social contact between the races in schools, hospitals, clubs and churches, even in white areas. Critics of the measures charged that Dr. Verwoerd was a dictator.

His racist attitudes became apparent early in his career. After studying at the Universities of Hamburg, Leipzig and Berlin in Germany during the Nineteen Twenties, Dr. Verwoerd returned to South Africa to become Professor of Applied Psychology at the University of Stellenbosch, cultural center of Afrikaner nationalism.

In 1936 Dr. Verwoerd joined with five other Stellenbosch professors to object publicly to plans for South Africa to provide a haven for a shipload of Jewish refugees from Nazi Germany.

The following year he entered political journalism to become the editor of Die Transvaler, a daily newspaper that the Nationalist party had established in Johannesburg. His editorials caused another newspaper, The Johannesburg Star, to accuse him of being a supporter of the Nazis in Germany. He sued the paper for libel and lost.

The Star charged that "his spiritual home is nearer to Bechtesgaden" than to South Africa. The court held, in dismissing the suit, that Dr. Verwoerd had consciously aided the war aims of Adolf Hitler.

Dr. Verwoerd was born in the Netherlands in 1901 and was taken to Africa by his parents when he was 2 years old. The family lived for a few years in Southern Rhodesia and then went to South Africa.

The new South African Prime Minister, a large man just over six feet tall, has a shock of silver gray hair and icy blue eyes.

He boasts that not one of his seven children has ever been bathed or put to bed by a Negro servant.

Like most stolid Afrikaner Nationalists, Dr. Verwoerd frequently argues that there is spiritual justification for keeping the races apart. He is a member of the Dutch Reformed Church and uses Old Testament references to support his argument.

He also is a courageous man. When his life was threatened during a bitter internal fight in the Nationalist party during World War II, he ignored the threat and went to a public meeting where he had been warned he would be killed if he appeared.

Opponents of the Nationalist Government in South Africa have often publicly expressed the fear that Dr. Verwoerd would one day become Prime Minister. They regard him as the Nationalist party's most dangerous extremist.

September 3, 1958

New Interest in Africa

JOHANNESBURG, South Africa, Feb. 10 (AP)—David Rockefeller, vice chairman of the Chase Manhattan Bank of New York, said today he expected an increasing number of American concerns to invest in Africa, particularly in South Africa.

Mr. Rockefeller told a news conference that 128 concerns were operating in the Union of South Africa and he expected the number to increase. The United States, he said, was becoming increasingly dependent on foreign sources for raw materials.

Mr. Rockefeller said the opening of the bank branch here was an indication of the "confidence we feel in the economic potential of South Africa."

February 11, 1959

ARRESTS ABOUND IN SOUTH AFRICA

On Average, Every Urban Negro Is Jailed Once a Year on a Trivial Count

Special to The New York Times.

JOHANNESBURG, South Africa, Feb. 16—Every male Negro in every city of South Africa can expect to be arrested once a year on the average.

Every year more than 1,250,000 Negroes are arrested for infringement of the pass laws, which require them to carry identity documents, and of labor regulations, curfews and restrictions on residence.

The Negro walks in constant danger of arrest for some technical offence. Thousands who have never so much as stolen a loaf of bread have records of "previous convictions" that would make a hardened criminal in any other country shudder.

But all their previous convictions are for things that in the broad sense are not offenses at all. These include forgetting to carry identity documents, being out after curfew, failing to register unemployment or moving from one area to another without the authority of a native affairs officer.

The recent arrest of an elderly Negro who had been a trustworthy worker for twenty-five years at one concern serves to illustrate the problem. He lived in a cottage in the non-white Johannesburg suburb of Sophiatown.

One warm summer evening, while cooking his supper on a kerosene stove, he stepped outside in his shirtsleeves to knock out his pipe on the curb. A pick-up van stopped and a young policeman demanded to see the old man's pass.

Laws Grow Tighter

The old man argued in vain that the document was in his jacket, hanging inside the door. He was bundled into the van and taken to the nearest police station. The policeman refused even to allow him to enter his cottage to turn off the stove.

Next day he was fined £1 for "being without a pass." If he had been a younger man and had not been able to pay his fine (in fact his employer paid it), he would have been given the choice of serving ten days in jail or two weeks on a potato farm and no one would have known what had happened to him.

In fifty years of progress in South Africa, time has stood still on such things as pass laws and curfew regulations. In fact, new prohibitory laws have been added. They are cluttering up the courts to such an extent that even the Government that has added to these laws is now seeking some method of keeping out the million or so Negroes that find themselves there for trivial reasons every year.

In Pretoria, policemen on beat have been instructed to use more discretion when applying the laws controlling the movements of Negroes. Warnings instead of arrests and checking of bona fides are suggested.

Last year yet another Criminal Law Amendment Act gave the courts the right to impose the death penalty for armed robbery. Last week three Africans were executed under this law.

March 1, 1959

APARTHEID DRIVE RECEIVES IMPETUS

South Africa Lists Places Suitable for Industries Near Bantu Reserves

By MILTON BRACKER
Special to The New York Times.

JOHANNESBURG, South Africa, April 14—The Government took another step today toward the ultimate separation of races, which is the goal of the apartheid policy.

It issued a detailed report listing fifty-seven towns considered to be suitable for white industrial centers near the borders of the "Bantustans," or African reserves.

The report, available so far only in Afrikaans, also maps about the same number of Bantu towns the Government hopes to build near existing European settlements.

In general, the arrangement is to assure that African labor can work in white enterprises but will live in the sectors reserved for Negroes.

Data on Sites Presented

The newly envisaged border areas are described as places "where industrial development and investment can take place through white initiative in white areas but where Bantu families will be able to work while still living within the reserves."

The report was prepared by the Natural Resources Development Board and other Government departments. It gave particulars on climate, population, water supply, power, communications and other factors of interest to potential industries.

Cheap African labor for white industry is a basic fact in the Union's economic development and prosperity. But the hint of many new industrial complexes near native areas is significant in view of an imminent debate in the Assembly at Capetown.

Bill Based on Report

After the current budget is debated, the Legislature will take up the "Bill to Promote Self-Government among the Bantu."

The measure had a first reading in the Assembly March 24. It was the ultimate legislative projection of a program suggested three years ago in the controversial report of the Tomlinson Commission (named for the chairman, Prof. Frederik Rothmann Tomlinson of the University of Pretoria).

As introduced three weeks ago, the bill divides the Bantu population into eight national units—North Sotho, South Sotho, Swazi, Tsonga, Tswana, Venda, Zhosa and Zulu.

These units will advance rapidly toward internal self-government, according to the Nationalist regime. Their interests will be communicated to the union Government by five appointed white commissioners general, who, in effect, will link the Minister of Bantu Administration and Development to the inhabitants of the "Bantustans."

But at the same time the nonwhites will lose their present representation in the union Assembly.

The most cogent protest is likely to be that the bill would seal the fate of the Bantus as a kind of captive second-class population restricted to their own areas and related to the country as a whole only by the familiar ties of manual labor.

The Government insists, however, that opportunities will steadily improve within the areas. Eventually the Bantustans will amount to about 41,000,000 acres.

At present more than one-third of the total Bantu population of 9,000,000 lives in reserves amounting to about 13 per cent of the union's territory. The white population is about 3,000,000.

April 15, 1959

CRITIC IS CURBED IN SOUTH AFRICA

National Congress' Leader Is Barred From Meetings —Travel Prohibited

Special to The New York Times.

JOHANNESBURG, South Africa, May 27—Albert Luthuli, president general of the African National Congress, has been banned by Justice Minister Charles R. Swart from attending any meetings or gatherings anywhere in South Africa for five years.

The action was taken under the Suppression of Communism Act. Under the Riotous Assemblies Act, Mr. Swart also banned Mr. Luthili from leaving his home district in Lower Tugela, Natal Province. The ban on attending meetings is effective immediately and the ban on leaving the district takes effect in seven days.

[The Suppression of Communism Act, passed in 1950, gives the Minister of Justice power to ban organizations or individuals deemed to be propagating the principles of communism. It has been used on occasion to curb labor leaders—both white and nonwhite—and other leaders of defiance campaigns against segregation laws. Under the broad terms of the act, any person may be named as a Communist who seeks a change by unlawful acts or omissions or by threat of such acts or omissions.]

Mr. Luthuli was scheduled to be the main speaker at a mass meeting of the African National Congress in Johannesburg Saturday, which is Union Day.

A crowd of 30,000 is expected to attend this rally of the African nationalist political organization, at which it was thought details would be announced of a proposed economic boycott of companies controlled by members of the governing Nationalist party.

It has been expected also that a fresh campaign would be launched against the laws requiring all Africans to carry identification passes at all times.

May 28, 1959

Foe of White Rule

Albert Luthuli

Man in the News

WHEN South Africa barred Albert Luthuli yesterday from meetings throughout the country it chose a worthy foe. His inflexible ambition is to free the African people from white rule.

This 61-year-old former teacher dominates every gathering at which he speaks, whether his audience consists of semi-illiterate Africans in the reserves or white liberals with university affiliations. Last month he told an audience in Capetown:

"We, the nonwhites, have come to hate white rule, but not the whites themselves. The whites are grinding us down with repressive measures but they will never destroy us spiritually. The nonwhites today are fighting against slavery."

Stockily built, gray-haired and always dressed in black or dark gray, Mr. Luthuli has something of an old-world courtesy about him. He smiles readily and his frank eyes show a twinkle behind the glasses he often wears.

Many white persons mistakenly interpret his good manners as the traditional respect an African pays to a white man. Mr. Luthuli, who grew up on the Groutville Mission Station in Natal founded by American missionaries, developed an early respect for the white men who dedicated their lives to the Africans. Yet he has the same polite manner for any member of his own race.

Father Was Interpreter

His father was an interpreter for the Mission Society and the Luthuli family were important members of the mission community. Young Albert developed deep religious convictions which he still holds today.

He attended the mission school and completed his education at Adams College in Natal. After two years of teaching at a country school, he accepted a post on the college staff.

In 1935 Mr. Luthuli gave up his teaching career to become chief of the Amakholwa tribe of Zulus. This tribe chooses its leader democratically and submits its choice to the Government for approval.

He was soon seen to be more than a figurehead leader. He urged his people to save their soil and conserve their water resources. Under his leadership agricul-

Cloete Breytenbach

"South Africa is large enough to accommodate all people if they have large enough hearts."
(Mr. Luthuli in a garland given him at a rally)

tural production increased, and he helped to organize farmers' associations that represented important steps forward for the Africans.

Soon afterward he became a member of the African National Congress, chiefly through his association with Dr. John Dube, first president of this African nationalist organization.

He continued also to maintain his interest in the Congregationalist Church. In 1948 he visited the United States on a lecture tour to speak on the work of the Christian Mission in Africa.

It was on his return from this trip that he began to devote much of his energy to the work of the African National Congress. After his election as president of the organization's Natal branch he was in the forefront of all the Congress' campaigns against segregation laws.

Separate Facilities Opposed

He helped organize the passive resistance campaign of 1952-53 against separate facilities for whites and non-whites in post offices, railway stations and other public places.

The Nationalist Government came to regard him as an agitator and deposed him from his chieftainship. Two months later, in December, 1952, he was elected president general of the African National Congress.

Mr. Luthuli has never been anti-white. Cooperation with the whites has always been his basic policy, even though he has lost some support among followers by his refusal to accept a program of "Africa for the Africans."

In 1953 the Government imposed on Mr. Luthuli a twelve-month ban on travel and attendance at meetings. Then, late in 1956, he was one of 156 persons arrested on allegations of treason.

On and off for twelve months Mr. Luthuli sat among the suspects at a preliminary inquiry. When it was over he and sixty others were freed.

Mr. Luthuli is married and is the father of two sons and three daughters. He is widely regarded as a typical embodiment of moderate African nationalism. He hates domination of one race by another.

"South Africa is a multiracial country and it is not our intention to elbow anyone out," he says. "South Africa is large enough to accommodate all people if they have large enough hearts."

May 29, 1959

AFRICAN WOMEN RENEW ATTACKS

Protesting Regime's Curbs, They Block Highways and Assault Natal Workers

DURBAN, South Africa, Aug. 18 (Reuters) — African women set up roadblocks and attacked workers in the fields today as a wave of anti-Government violence continued through its fifth day.

About 200 Africans were arrested at scattered points in the southern tip of Natal Province. Two Africans have been killed by the police since the disturbances started last Friday.

A group of more than 100 women attacked workers in the can fields in the Umtwalumi area, demanding that they quit their jobs and strike for wages of £1 ($2.80) a day. The men drove the women away, but all work in the fields stopped.

In court later, 118 women were ordered to pay fines of £10 ($28) or go to prison for two months at hard labor for trespassing on private property. No fines were paid. The women will be brought to jail in Durban.

A hundred women were arrested between Isipofu and Hibberdine for piling stones two feet high on a road. Later, seventy-five of the women were sentenced to three months in jail.

At Highflats, also in the southern tip of this east coast province, eighty women were arrested after they had commandeered a bus and demanded to be taken to the native commissioner.

Seven Africans were arrested near Pietermaritzburg when they stopped a bus and threatened to stone it if the driver continued his journey.

The main causes of the unrest are increased taxes and laws restricting the entry of Africans into cities and towns. The Africans say the measures are aimed at forcing them to work on farms instead of in the cities, where they can earn more money.

August 19, 1959

The New York Times Aug. 19, 1959

DISORDERS CONTINUE: Violence has swept Natal Province (shaded) in South Africa for last few days.

August 19, 1959

AFRICANS PLAN PROTEST

Negro Leader Asks Flouting of South African Pass Laws

JOHANNESBURG, South Africa, March 18 (AP)—The Pan-Africanist Congress issued a call today for a nation-wide campaign of nonviolence against South Africa's pass laws for Negroes.

Starting Monday, Negro men who heed the call will invite arrest by going to police stations and declaring they are not carrying the passes required by law.

Robert Mangaliso Sobukwe, president of the Congress, said at a news conference that the campaign was meant to crowd the jails and courts and cripple industry.

Mr. Sobukwe said he would appear at a police station at 8 A. M. Monday.

March 19, 1960

South Africa Business Men Plan Drive to Win World's Goodwill

By LEONARD INGALLS
Special to The New York Times.

JOHANNESBURG, South Africa, Jan. 6—A new campaign to "sell" South Africa to the world is being organized by some of the country's leading industrialists, financiers and business men.

They are concerned over foreign reactions to the Government's policies, particularly those dealing with matters of race. Boycotts of South African goods have been threatened abroad and it has been difficult to obtain investment capital from overseas.

The South Africans are prepared to spend at least $1,500,000 yearly to counteract the unfavorable impression of South Africa, particularly in Britain and the United States. Their contribution would bring the annual total spent on publicizing South Africa to $3,000,000 since the Government is now providing $1,500,000 annually for its State Information Office, which has branches in Europe and North America.

Twenty-five industrialists, financiers and business leaders have formed the South African Foundation to conduct the sales campaign.

Among them are Harry F. Oppenheimer, chairman of the Anglo American Corporation; Dr. Hendrik J. Van Eck, chairman of the Industrial Development Corporation; Anton Rupert, chairman of the Rembrandt Tobacco Company; Charles W. Engelhard, chairman of Engelhard Industries of Newark, N. J., whose company has large investments in South Africa; Dr. Michiel de Kock, chairman of the South African Reserve Bank, and Dr. John E. Holloway, former South African Ambassador to the United States and Britain.

The membership of the foundation is significant because it includes top representatives of both the English-speaking and Afrikaans-speaking elements in South Africa. Nationalistic differences have hindered cooperation between these two groups in the past.

The foundation has emphasized that it is nonpolitical, but the difference between politics and economics in South Africa is almost invisible. Many shades of political opinion are represented in the foundation, from extreme Right-wing Nationalists to supporters of the new Progressive party, which is slightly left-of-center in South African politics. Some observers believe the foundation could become a formidable pressure group in South African affairs.

The immediate task it has set itself is to analyze the reasons why South Africa is unpopular and to present facts about economics, social and industrial accomplishments here. The foundation expects to enlist the aid of experts in many fields, including public relations in Britain and the United States, to tell its story.

Branches of the foundation are expected to be set up in London and New York. Mr. Engelhard has agreed to be chairman of the group's American committee.

In discussing the foundation's task, one Johannesburg newspaper, The Star, declared that it was impossible to explain abroad such circumstances in South Africa as the use by the police of firearms where tear gas would suffice, banishment and banning orders against individuals, the arbitrary refusal of passports, the reservation of jobs for whites that might otherwise be filled by Africans and the Government's policy of opposition to television.

January 7, 1960

50 Killed in South Africa As Police Fire on Rioters

Special to The New York Times.

JOHANNESBURG, South Africa, March 21—The police opened fire today on thousands of Africans besieging a police station at Sharpeville, thirty miles south of Johannesburg. Officials reported twenty-five Africans had been killed and fifty wounded. Unofficial reports indicated about fifty had been killed.

The Africans were demonstrating against South Africa's laws requiring Africans to carry passes at all times. The police arrest any African found without his pass.

The demonstration followed a call by the Pan-Africanist Congress for all Africans to leave their passes at home and to go to police stations to surrender to the police for not carrying them.

At Sharpeville a crowd of Africans gathered at the police station and began stoning the police and armored cars that had been brought to the station.

The police, behind a wire fence, fired into the crowd.

Casualties were taken to a native hospital in near-by Vereeniging. The hospital soon was filled and the wounded were treated on the surrounding lawns. Every available doctor was called to the hospital.

A senior police official said: "I don't know how many we've shot." He is reported to have added: "If they do these things they must learn the hard way."

Earlier, South African Air Force planes flew over the trouble spot in a show of force. But the Africans ignored all orders to disperse.

As tension rose, the police charged with clubs and used tear gas against the demonstrators. One African was reported shot dead in this clash and several policemen injured. The police forced through reinforcements from Witwatersrand in armored cars.

Another trouble spot was Vanderbijl Park, five miles west of Vereeniging. Reports have been received also of clashes in Langa, Capetown, between African demonstrators and the police. There was no reports of violence elsewhere in South Africa.

Mangalise Robert Sobukwe, president of the Pan-Africanist Congress, and some of his officers were arrested this evening. Mr. Sobukwe, a lecturer on African studies at Witwatersrand University, had led one group of "no pass" demonstrators to a Johannesburg police station.

March 22, 1960

SOUTH AFRICA SET TO OUTLAW FOES

By LEONARD INGALLS
Special to The New York Times.

JOHANNESBURG, South Africa, March 25—Political organizations of Africans are to be outlawed in this country.

Plans for this drastic step were announced today by the Government. Legislation giving Governor General Charles R. Swart, former Minister of Justice, power to impose the ban is to be introduced Monday in Parliament, now sitting in Capetown. The bill is to be enacted with the utmost speed.

This was the latest development in a momentous week that has seen South Africa stiffening in her determination to stifle political expression by Africans while elsewhere in the continent Africans are gaining greater political rights.

Meanwhile, preparations were made to cope with further outbreaks of violence over the week-end. All leaves for the more than 20,000 and members of the south African police force were canceled.

The nearly 7,000 members of the defense force and thousands of members of the white civilian force remained on a stand-by alert. This was ordered Monday after fatal clashes between African political demonstrators and the police near Johannesburg and Capetown. A bill to amend the Riotous Assemblies Act and "make watertight" the ban imposed yesterday on public meetings also is to be submitted Monday.

Indoor and outdoor gatherings of more than twelve persons were made illegal until June 30 in twenty-four major cities and towns.

Africans in Sharpeville, the dwelling area near Vereeniging south of Johannesburg where the worst violence occurred Monday, remained away from work again today, crippling local industries.

Several Groups Affected

The new legislation will give the Governor General power to ban the African National Congress, the Pan-Africanist Congress and other organizations that were not identified. It is understood that these include the Indian National Congress and the Congress of Democrats, an organization of whites sympathetic to African and Asian causes.

The Pan-Africanist Congress was established last April 6 by young Africans who were dissatisfied with the African National Congress. The Pan-Afgricanists organized the demonstrations earlier this week against laws restricting the movements of Africans. The protests led to the death from police bullets of seventy-two Africans and the wounding of 184.

A deputation from the Afri

can National Congress conferred today in Capetown with the three white members of Parliament elected to represent the Africans. The congress representatives made two requests, which they said would ease the present situation.

They asked that there be some relief from the stringent pass laws. They suggested that channels be created between the Africans and Government authorities and between the Africans and industry for negotiation about wages. Although a number of African trade unions exist in South Africa they are not officially recognized.

About 2,000 Africans defied the ban on meetings today when they assembled in Capetown outside a police station to demonstrate against the laws requiring them to carry passes.

An African leader addressed them through a police loudspeaker, however, and they dispersed peacefully. No arrests were reported.

In a sharp reaction to the week's events The Rand Daily Mail, a Johannesburg morning newspaper, called today in a front-page editorial for the resignation of Prime Minister Hendrik F. Verwoerd.

March 26, 1970

CAPETOWN DROPS IDENTITY PASSES IN WAKE OF RIOTS

Suspension of Hated Curbs Indicates Major Change in Strict Racial Policies

MEETING BAN IS WIDENED

By LEONARD INGALLS
Special to The New York Times.

JOHANNESBURG, South Africa, March 26—Prime Minister Hendrik F. Verwoerd's Government suspended today a requirement of many years' standing that Africans must carry identity passes.

The suspension went into force less than a week after rioting against the passes that resulted in the killing of seventy-two Africans and the wounding of 184.

The action came in the form of an announcement by the police that Africans would not be arrested for failure to carry the passes, heretofore required for moving about in South Africa. Policemen were told not to arrest Africans for trivial offenses.

Major Grievances Noted

The two steps were an effort to recognize and eliminate some of the Africans' principal grievances. It appeared that a major change of policy might be in the making to give the Africans at least some formal voice in the affairs of a country where strict racial segregation is maintained.

[In Washington, South Africa protested to the United States against the scheduled United Nations Security Council meeting on the rioting. The session was postponed from Tuesday to Wednesday at the South Africans' request.]

Meanwhile, the situation continued to be potentially explosive. This was indicated by the action of François C. Erasmus, Minister of Justice, who banned public meetings until June 30 in forty-nine more magisterial districts in South Africa. Meetings in twenty-four major cities and towns were banned Thursday. The Government announced plans yesterday to outlaw political organizations of Africans.

Suspension Called Temporary

Mr. Erasmus insisted in a statement in Capetown that the suspension of pass requirements was temporary. However, observers, including many South Africans, believed it would be impossible to reimpose the hated requirements without generating a violent reaction.

The instructions to policemen said that, instead of making arrests for trivial offenses, they should warn the Africans involved or issue summonses.

Such offenses include violations of laws barring Africans from drinking strong alcoholic liquor and requiring them to observe curfews.

The announcement was a big victory for the Pan-Africanist Congress, organized about a year ago as a political organization, and for the older African National Congress. Both have been campaigning for abolition of the pass laws and the Pan-Africanists led the demonstrations this week.

Since then South Africa has been in a state of extreme racial tension. Many Africans, who comprise the bulk of the labor force have stayed away from work in anger at police violence as well as to demonstrate the strength of their complaints. On the Johannesburg Stock Exchange share values have plummeted with losses at week's end about $300,000,000.

Reason for the Move

In announcing that there would be no arrests for pass violations Maj. Gen. C. I. Rademeyer, Commissioner of Police, implied that the move was necessary because some Africans were being intimidated by others into not carrying the papers. He referred to the passes as reference books, the official euphemism by which thye have been described in the last few years.

"In view of the fact that the Bantus [Africans], as a result of intimidation, are so gripped by fear to carry reference books or other documents and are even afraid to carry any money, I have decided to relieve this tremendous tension and to prevent innocent and law-abiding Bantus from landing in trouble." he said. "I have instructed that no Bantu, male or female, is to be asked for his or her reference book or any other documents. No Bantu will be taken into custody because he is not in possession of his reference book.

"Bantus must not be arrested and detained for all sorts of petty offenses. They must be warned or summoned to appear."

One important effect of the order is that it will end the notorious farm-labor system. This provided that Africans found guilty, at the rate of hundreds weekly, of violations of the pass laws or other minor offenses were given the alternative of paying cash fines or serving several months working on private farms designated by the Minister of Justice. Most could not pay the fines.

Farmers Built Jails

In many parts of South Africa farmers built jails at their own expense from which they could draw Africans convicted of pass offenses.

The pass system was adopted many years ago to control movements of Africans and to confine them to various areas unless permission was granted for them to go elsewhere. For example, passes have been used to limit the number of Africans moving from rural to urban areas to seek work.

Passes at present in use contain about fifty pages in which are recorded such information as employment, arrests and tax payments, as well as vital statistics and the photograph and home address of the holder. Each month the employer of an African must sign his pass or the African can be arrested and, in many cases, sent to an African reserve.

In recent years failure to have valid passes in their possession has meant for many Africans harsh treatment by the police, summary hearings in the courts, loss of employment and great humiliation. The extension of the pass laws to women in the last two years has aroused the African community.

Business Pressure Reported

There is considerable speculation here that in making their conciliatory gesture today Prime Minister Verwoerd and his Administration have been under great pressure from leading industrialists and financiers.

On Thursday Dr. Verwoerd hurriedly left Capetown, where he had been attending a session of the South African Parliament. He flew to Pretoria, administrative capital, where, it is believed, he heard views on the present crisis from representatives of the South African Reserve Bank, the South African Iron and Steel Industrial Corporation and other industrialists and African affairs experts.

In Capetown, meanwhile, milk, bread, fuel and newspaper deliveries were critically curtailed when Africans stayed away from their jobs. The loading and unloading of twenty ships in the harbor was affected.

The influential Capetown newspaper Die Burger, which supports the Nationalist Government, said today that "we must discover what grievances are so far as we do not know already and see what we can do to reduce friction to a minimum."

Verwoerd Calls for Calm

In a speech tonight, Dr. Verwoerd appealed for calm. Speaking at a Nationalist party rally in Meyerton, near Johannesburg, he said:

"I want it to be quite clear there is no cause for uneasiness.

"I want you to know we shall protect the rights of all in this country, white as well as black."

More than 4,000 people gathered to hear the Prime Minister, who was cheered and applauded.

"Do not be alarmed, law and order will be maintained in this country," Dr. Verwoerd said.

He asserted that political demonstrations by Africans were caused "by small groups who exploit them."

"We must solve our problems on the basis of goodwill," he added.

"Not only the rights of the black man of Africa have to be protected, there is also a white man in Africa."

March 27, 1960

SOUTH AFRICA PUT IN STATE OF ALERT; OPPONENTS JAILED

PARLIAMENT IS GUARDED

30,000 Negroes in March on Capital—Premier Warns Force Will Meet Force

By LEONARD INGALLS

Special to The New York Times.

JOHANNESBURG, South Africa, March 30—A state of emergency was declared today in much of South Africa.

The declaration followed by a few hours the arrest and jailing before daybreak of 234 white, African and Asian opponents of the National party Government led by Prime Minister Hendrik F. Verwoerd.

These dramatic steps came amid mounting unrest and new mass demonstrations against the Government by Africans protesting strict policies of racial segregation.

Troops Ring Parliament

Steel-helmeted policemen and soldiers armed with rifles and submachine guns ringed the Parliament buildings today as 30,000 Africans marched on Capetown. Armored cars blocked approaches to the building and an air force helicopter carrying police observers droned overhead.

Eighteen regiments of the civilian force were mobilized to supplement the police, the army and the air force, which have been on the alert since last week's outbreak of African violence.

Dr. Verwoerd declared in a Parliament speech that the situation was "completely under control." He added that because of the "arson and violence" in the last few days "the Government had to take strong action."

"If the natives [Africans] go over to greater violence, their actions will be met with greater force in order to hold them back," he warned.

Interference Charged

The Prime Minister also asserted that the United Nations Security Council's discussion of the South African situation was "interference in South Africa's domestic affairs" and contravention of the United Nations Charter.

"It is my duty to point out that interference in South Africa's domestic affairs by such an important body as the Security Council could have the effect of even greater encouragement of agitating and rioting in South Africa," he said.

"It could lead to a situation where vigorous action may be required, causing further bloodshed," he added.

The racial differences that have plagued South Africa throughout its history have finally plunged the nation into a terrible convulsion. Engaged are 10,000,000 Africans, more than 1,000,000 persons of mixed blood known as coloreds, nearly 500,000 Asians and about 3,000,000 whites.

The Government of the white supremacist National party was still in control, but there were South Africans as well as foreign observers who wondered how long it could survive.

If force of arms could contain the situation, there was no doubt that the Verwoerd Government would continue. But the pressures upon it to soften the harsh apartheid policy that makes nonwhites third-rate citizens appeared to be building significantly. This was particularly so because of the economic effect of the present crisis, which was causing a loss of confidence among investors.

New Stoppage Expected

Thousands of Africans are expected to stay away from work again tomorrow in protest against laws requiring them to carry passes. The demonstration has been scheduled by the African National Congress and the Pan-Africanist Congress, the major African political organizations, most of whose leaders are in jail.

A similar work stoppage Monday crippled Johannesburg, Capetown and other areas and led to violence.

The demonstrators who marched on Parliament went several miles from Langa, an African dwelling area several miles away. They were demanding the release of leaders arrested after last week's violence. It was at Langa that the police shot some of the African rioters killed last week.

After massing at the Caledon Square police station, a few blocks from Parliament, the throng dispersed peacefully.

At Worcester, sixty miles from Capetown, the police used tear gas to break up a procession of demonstrators. At Stellenbosch, thirty miles from Capetown, police baton charges were made against demonstrators, forcing them back into their dwelling area. Government buildings in the area were set alight.

The New York Times March 31, 1960

CRISIS DEEPENS: Africans demonstrated in the Capetown area (1). Riot dead were buried at Sharpeville (2).

Reports of Panic Selling

There were reports of panic selling on the Johannesburg Stock Exchange after the emergency was declared. Stock prices dropped as much as $2 a share.

The chairman of the South African Wool Board, Dr. J. H. Moolman, called for an appeal by business and industrial leaders to the Government for a change of policy because of the possibility of "repercussions on our markets and exports."

The state of emergency was proclaimed in eighty of the country's 300 magisterial districts. The areas affected are those in which public meetings were banned last week by François C. Erasmus, Minister of Justice.

They include principal cities and towns and most heavily populated areas. The major cities involved are Johannesburg, Capetown, Durban, Port Elizabeth, East London, Pietermaritzburg, Kimberley, Bloemfontein and Pretoria.

The proclamation was made under the Public Safety Act, which also empowers the Government to detain individuals without charges for an indefinite period. The state of emergency may be continued for twelve months.

Virtually dictatorial powers are conferred on the Government, including censorship and direction of labor.

Chief Luthuli Arrested

Persons roused from their beds and arrested included Chief Albert Luthuli, president of the African National Congress, and Peter Brown, national chairman of the Liberal party.

Others included top officials of labor unions and of various African National Congress subsidiary organizations and of the Indian National Congress, the Congress of Democrats, an organization of whites that supports African and Asian causes, and the South African Federation of Women.

Also among those seized were the Rev. Mark Nye, head of the Pretoria Anglican mission, and Miss Hannah Stanton, warden of the Tumelong Anglican mission near Pretoria.

Robert Mangaliso Sobukwe and eleven other leaders of the Pan-Africanist Congress have been under arrest since last week.

The police refused to give reasons why any individuals had been arrested. Many documents were taken from the homes of those detained and from the offices of organizations involved.

The state of emergency was retroactive to yesterday but the arrests were made before it was proclaimed.

At Sharpeville, 1,000 Africans attended a mass funeral for thirty-four Africans killed by police bullets during last week's violence. They were carried to their graves in plain wooden coffins. The police would not permit white persons to attend the funeral.

The current crisis started ten days ago with violence at the Sharpeville and Langa townships. In two days seventy-two Africans were killed and 184 injured.

They were demonstrating for relief of grievances and particularly against laws restricting their movements and requiring them to carry the passes, which the Government calls reference books. These contain records of employment and tax payments as well as the person's photograph and the record of the area in which he is permitted to live and work under the segregation laws.

The Africans were compelled to produce the passes on demand by any policeman and faced arrest, fines and prison if they were not in order. As a result of last week's rising and the discontent, the Government temporarily suspended arrests for failure to carry passes. This suspension was still in effect.

March 31, 1960

PASSES RESTORED BY SOUTH AFRICA; EASING IS HINTED

Identity Documents Required for Africans but Study of System Is Planned

BUSINESS MEN AROUSED

Commercial Leaders Press for Softer Policy—Day of Prayer Scheduled

By LEONARD INGALLS
Special to The New York Times.

JOHANNESBURG, South Africa, April 6—South Africa announced today it was reintroducing the enforcement of laws requiring Africans to carry identity passes. It was this requirement that touched off the current racial violence in the country.

Arrests for failure to produce passes and for other minor offenses were suspended by the Government March 26 in what was interpreted as the recognition of the Africans' grievances over severe restrictions on their liberty.

The Minister of Justice, François C. Erasmus, warned that the police henceforth would be empowered to demand passes or temporary identification papers, which would be issued in the place of passes. Many Africans burned their passes in protest against the pass laws.

Arrests for pass violations were suspended as violence spread through the country after more than 300 Africans had been killed or injured in police shootings March 21.

Need for Passes Stressed

Mr. Erasmus emphasized the importance of the passes as proof of the right of Africans to be in urban areas.

In a tacit admission that enforcement of the pass laws had been humiliating to the Africans, Mr. Erasmus told Parliament that the Government would explore ways of making the system more palatable.

He suggested that the police might be instructed to check the passes "in such a way as to lay more stress upon the advantages" that the passes hold for the Africans.

But any amelioration, he added, will have to be achieved "without sacrificing the necessary control measures."

The passes are the keystone of the apartheid system for the separation of the races. The African must have his pass signed each month by his employer. Otherwise, he forfeits his right to live in an urban location and is herded back to an African reservation.

Business Men Seek Talk

Meanwhile, South Africa's business and industrial leaders appealed urgently for a meeting with Prime Minister Hendrik F. Verwoerd because of the severe economic effects of the racial crisis.

It became known today that they plan to place before the Prime Minister a demand for a radical change of policy. The men who run South Africa's economy are said to be frustrated and angered over the enormous cost of the emergency.

Economists say there is no way to calculate the exact losses caused by the internal disruptions and the loss of confidence by foreign investors. It is estimated that the loss in production in the last three weeks as a result of the refusal of Africans to work has cost industry more than $60,000,000.

Until the uprising two weeks ago the police were so severe in enforcing pass laws that a housewife who wandered a few hundred yards from her hut to get water could be arrested if she left her passbook at home.

Mr. Erasmus warned employers that the law required them to see that the passes of their African workers were in order. Employers should immediately arrange that Africans without passes obtain temporary documents, he said.

"The police will also render assistance to the Bantu [Africans] to obtain the necessary temporary documents," he said. "For this purpose, as well as to reintroduce control measures, the police will henceforth again be able to demand reference books or temporary documents."

Day of Prayer Set

Leaders of Protestant, Catholic and Jewish faiths called today for the observance Sunday of a national day of prayer and penitence.

South Africa was quiet today as it observed a national holiday commemorating the first Dutch settlement in South Africa 308 years ago.

It is understood that the business delegation seeking to meet with the Prime Minister will include representatives of the Federated Chamber of Industries, the Chamber of Mines, the Association of Chambers of Commerce and the Board of Trade and Industries.

The proposals they plan to put to Dr. Verwoerd will include the following points:

¶Immediate consultation between the Government and acknowledged leaders of the Africans must be held.

¶Present identity passes must be replaced with identity cards and restrictions on the Africans' liberty modified.

¶Controls over the influx of Africans into cities and towns must be confined only to areas where an accommodation problem exists. The African labor force otherwise is to be given complete mobility.

¶Continuous discussions with responsible Africans must be held to find out what the Africans are thinking.

The business men are expected to press for the immediate release of Chief Albert Lithuli, president of the African National Congress, who is considered to be a moderate man of high integrity. He is believed to be the best man to build a firm bridge between the Africans and white authority.

Chief Luthuli at present is one of more than 300 African, Asian and white critics of the Government in jail under emergency regulations.

The business men plan to suggest that a strong campaign against the hooligan element among the Africans must be undertaken but only after the Government's racial policy has been modified and the goodwill of responsible Africans won.

An indication of the rigid attitude held by the Afrikaners, descendants of the Dutch settlers who are the main supporters of the Verwoerd Government, was given today by the newspaper Die Burger in Capetown.

The paper warned that any flexibility by the Government would give African nationalists the impression that black supremacy over South Africa was possible. It said any concession would sharpen the appetites of African nationalists and hasten the day of white capitulation.

The appeal for a national day of prayer on Palm Sunday was made by leaders of the Dutch Reformed, Roman Catholic, Methodist, Presbyterian, Baptist and Congregationalist churches, the Salvation Army and the United Hebrew Congregation of Johannesburg.

Their statement noted that the Dutch Reformed Church, which has the largest number of members among the whites of South Africa, had "already called their people to humiliation and prayer."

Most of the thousands of Africans who had stayed away from their jobs in the crisis have returned to their jobs.

At Vereeniging, thirty-six miles south of Johannesburg, several hundred Africans have been refused their jobs. Their employers are replacing them with Africans brought in from the near-by Orange Free State and from tribal reserves. The Sharpeville settlement where the March 21 shootings occurred is outside Vereeniging.

April 7, 1960

African Statements In Sharpeville Case To Be Given to U.N.

By WAYNE PHILLIPS

Copies of sworn statements by Africans wounded in a police attack at Sharpeville in the Union of South Africa have reached New York and are to be presented to the United Nations this week.

The attack, on March 21, touched off the wave of violence that has swept the Union of South Africa. Seventy-two Africans were killed and about 250 wounded when the police opened fire at the original demonstration against the passbooks Africans are required to carry.

The Africans who made the eighteen statements received here said the police had opened fire without any provocation from the crowd, which had gathered under the impression that an announcement would be made regarding the passbooks.

All said they had been shot from behind while fleeing.

The copies of the statements were shown to reporters yesterday by Allard Lowenstein, an attorney representing African groups. He said they would be circulated to United Nations delegations this week. Mr. Lowenstein said he had received the copies by "a round-about route" from the Anglican Bishop of Johannesburg, Ambrose Reeves.

The statements were taken by two white attorneys for Africans arrested after the shootings. The attorneys, John Lang and Ernest Wenzel, have since been arrested. Bishop Reeves has fled to Swaziland to avoid arrest.

Mr. Lowenstein displayed a handwritten note on the Bishop's printed letterhead that had accompanied the copies of the statements. It was dated March 29 and read in part:

"Since last Wednesday lawyers who have been instructed by the arrested to represent them have been taking statements from them. A selection of the documents is enclosed. I convey them to you in the hope that you will be able to bring this to the attention of the American people and that they will be useful to you at the U. N."

Statement by an African

Following is one of the more detailed statements:

"My full name is Adam Sakoane. I am married with four children and I live at 5618 Sharpeville.

"I work at Garcia, where I earn £2 15s 9d a week.

"I went to the police station at Sharpeville at about 12 o'clock. I went to hear about the passes. I do not like carrying a pass. The pass is too troublesome because we get arrested if we don't carry our passes and cannot seek work where we wish.

"While I was at the police station I saw Saracen tanks, airplanes and police with machine guns. I was standing next to the wire. Amongst us were lots of little children and women. These children had come to see the Saracens.

"The people were standing against the fence in an orderly fashion and were not pushing against it. I saw police coming from all over the Reef. The first troop came from Vereeniging, the next from Boksburg and the third from Springs. I know that they came from these areas because I observed the car numbers of the vehicles. All these police went into the yard of the police station. The last three trucks to arrive had Johannesburg number plates and there were also two cars.

"As soon as these police arrived all the police formed into a line along the fence. At that stage one of the persons who had arrived in a car—a man in plain clothes, well built with blond hair balding in front, and a red face—arrested one of our leaders. Our leader said to him in English several times, 'we have come here to talk not to fight.' They arrested him and pushed him inside. After this the police lined up. They loaded their rifles. The troops in the Saracens also loaded the guns in the Saracens. We took it very easily as we were not there to fight. Some of the police had revolvers.

"The police, without any warning, suddenly raised their weapons and started to fire. No order had been given to us to disperse nor had there been any talk. No provocation of any sort was offered to the police.

"It has been alleged that stones were thrown but if stones were thrown, I certainly did not see them. As soon as the police raised their weapons, I turned to run and was shot in the buttocks. I fell, then managed to get up and run. The police went on firing for a long time. Certain children were shot during the firing.

"We did not leave the scene because we were expecting a statement to us at 2 o'clock about ...

April 10, 1960

SOUTH AFRICAN PREMIER WOUNDED BY WHITE ASSASSIN AT EXPOSITION

2 SHOTS IN HEAD

Verwoerd Is Gaining After Operation—Attacker Beaten

By LEONARD INGALLS

Special to The New York Times.

JOHANNESBURG, South Africa, April 9—Prime Minister Hendrik F. Verwoerd, champion of white supremacy in South Africa, was shot and wounded by a white man today in an attempted assassination.

The Prime Minister was struck by two shots as he sat in a box at the Union Exposition here. He fell back, blood streaming from head wounds and from his nostrils.

The shooting threw South Africa back into turmoil just as the racial tension that has gripped the country in the last few weeks appeared to be ebbing significantly.

Motive of Attack Unclear

Whether the attack on Dr. Verwoerd had direct political motivation was not known. However, emotions have been running high as a result of his National party Government's racial segregation policies.

Spectators and policemen threw themselves on the assassin and knocked him to the ground. He was severely beaten and cried out "God help me!" before being taken away by the police. He was described as a middle-aged cattle breeder of English extraction, who had never been involved in politics.

Further drastic emergency measures, including possible imposition of martial law and a curfew throughout South Africa, were expected here. The nation is already under a state of emergency imposed March 30.

[A declaration of martial law by Governor General Charles R. Swart was forecast by the Johannesburg Nationalist newspaper Die Vaderlund, which also predicted a dusk-to-dawn curfew, The Associated Press reported. The news service said the assassin had been identified as David Pratt.]

Verwoerd 'Resting Well'

Dr. Verwoerd, 58 years old, was rushed to the Johannesburg General Hospital, where an immediate emergency operation was ordered. His wounds, inflicted by a .22-caliber pistol, were reported to be serious but not lethal. He was said to be "resting well."

"One bullet entered the right ear and the other the right cheek," an official announcement said. Both the lower jaw and right upper jaw were found to have been fractured.

The gunman had approached the Prime Minister and said softly "Dr. Verwoerd." Prime Minister Verwoerd turned toward him smiling, and the man fired at point-blank range. The assailant was said to be a senior member of the agricultural society that helped organize the exposition and wore an official's badge that enabled him to slip through the security forces.

During the period that the Prime Minister will be incapacitated, the Deputy Prime Minister, Dr. Theophilus E. Donges, Minister of Finance, will head the Government.

In a special radio broadcast tonight, Paul Sauer, Minister of Lands, appealed on behalf of the Government for calm. The "callous attempt on the life of the Prime Minister," he said, "must inevitably inflame feelings."

He reported that Dr. Verwoerd's condition was "reassuring" and added: "We must thank providence his life has been spared."

A hospital bulletin described Dr. Verwoerd's condition as "satisfactory." He was said to be conscious.

For the first time since the present crisis began nearly three weeks ago, policemen armed with rifles patrolled the streets in the vicinity of the main post office in Johannesburg tonight.

The shooting took place in full view of more than 20,000 persons who had gathered in the grandstand of the Johannesburg Show Grounds for the official opening of the Union Exposition by the Prime Minister. The exposition celebrates the fiftieth anniversary of the formation of the Union of South Africa. It had been open to the public since Monday, but was closed after the attack on the Prime Minister.

Only a few minutes before he was shot, Dr. Verwoerd had made a thirty-minute speech. In a reference to world criticisms of South Africa, he said:

"We desire the utmost in good relations because no country in the world today can exist alone. And no country can achieve greater heights by treading on the corpse of another nation.

"We shall be nobody's corpse. We shall not be killed. We shall fight for our existence and we shall survive."

Audience Enthusiastic

There were cr[illegible] Hear" cheers fr[illegible]

April 10, 1960

STRIKE CALL FAILS IN SOUTH AFRICA; TENSION SUBSIDES

165 Seized in Port Elizabeth —U. N. Chief to Meet With Government Leaders

By LEONARD INGALLS
Special to The New York Times.

JOHANNESBURG, South Africa, April 19—African workers flocked back to their jobs today after a four-day Easter holiday, ending a threat of a week-long strike.

For the present the racial strife that has gripped the country for a month appeared to have subsided. The work-stoppage threat was a gesture of defiance by African political organizations that have been driven underground.

[Dag Hammarskjold, United Nations Secretary General, announced that he would meet with South African leaders next month in London for conversations on their racial policies. He said he would visit South Africa, probably in July or August.]

Large police forces supported by armored cars and troops were on hand at main centers this morning and tonight but no disturbances developed.

Strike Call Ignored

At dawn long, orderly lines of Africans began to form at railway stations and bus stops. It soon became apparent that the call for South Africa's large African labor force to stay at home had been ignored. The call had been issued by an emergency committee of the African National Congress and had been supported by the Pan-Africanist Congress. Both organizations have been banned for a period of a year.

At Port Elizabeth, an important Indian Ocean port and manufacturing center, the police and troops seized 165 Africans. They first protected Africans in the area who wanted to go to work and then moved in to arrest what they described as "undesirable elements."

At East London, another Indian Ocean port, 400 Africans who had been arrested yesterday were sentenced to fines of $2.80 or eight days in jail each for being in an African township without permission. They were found guilty of having violated laws requiring Africans to carry identity passes to move about.

School Boycott Fails

From all over South Africa came reports of a normal turnout of African labor. In such vital industrial areas as Johannesburg, Durban, Capetown and Port Elizabeth full staffs of African employes were on hand this morning.

A threat that African children would be kept out of school today also went unfulfilled and school attendance was normal.

There are several reasons why the demonstrations called for today did not occur. One is that more than 400 African leaders and white and Asian supporters of African causes have been jailed under emergency laws.

Another is that stiff penalties for withholding labor and for encouraging others to do so have been established.

In addition, many Africans could not afford to stay away from their jobs for a week. There was also the threat by the Government that Africans engaging in work stoppages faced the loss of their jobs and banishment to reserves in remote areas.

A former officer of the African National Congress explained the failure of the strike call by saying:

"It was badly timed. After a holiday and the free and easy spending that goes with it nobody was prepared to lose pay. There is one simple honest reason why the campaign failed—the people were broke."

Many businesses and industries were reported to be increasing African wages or to be contemplating doing so to help restore economic stability. Low wages have been one of the major complaints of the Africans.

13 Africans Sentenced

In Durban today thirteen Africans were sentenced to two years in prison for participating in a protest march April 1. They were among several thousand Africans from the Cato Manor slum area who marched to the center of Durban. Three were shot and killed and others wounded by the police who broke up the demonstration. One year of the sentences imposed today was suspended.

Another African was sentenced to two years but eighteen months of his sentence were suspended.

The convicted Africans were accused of having participated in an unlawful gathering constituting a danger to public safety. It was charged that their action had been a clear indication that they had intended to overthrow law and order in Durban.

In Capetown, Francois C. Erasmus, Minister of Justice, said in Parliament that thirty-four churches, schools and other public buildings had been destroyed or damaged by fire since the racial disturbances started March 21. He estimated the total damage at $170,000.

Mr. Erasmus said fifteen married couples had been detained under the emergency regulations and 422 Africans had been arrested for violation of pass laws since the order suspending such arrests was withdrawn.

He disclosed that among those arrested was Mrs. Zainunnissa Gool, a member of the Capetown city council and a strong opponent of all forms of racial segregation.

It became known today that Josua François Naudé, Minister of the Interior, had discussed the Government's plan to increase white immigration to South Africa with Gregory Esgate, chief representative here of the Inter-Governmental Committee for European Migration.

Mr. Esgate said he had told Mr. Naudé that there was a considerable pool of skilled workers to draw from in Europe. He noted that Greece, Italy, Spain and the Netherlands were countries from which South Africa might expect to attract immigrants.

Paul O. Sauer, Minister of Lands, who has been acting as Government spokesman during the recuperation of Prime Minister Hendrik F. Verwoerd, said today that the whites in South Africa must try to dispel the idea among the Africans that they were being suppressed. Dr. Verwoerd was shot April 9 by David Pratt, a white cattle farmer.

Mr. Sauer called for "a new approach" to the situation and an effort to convince the Africans that the Government's policies were the right ones for dealing with South Africa's problems.

April 20, 1960

The Bantu Listens to a Louder Drum

The South African Negro hears the call to freedom being sounded in countries to the north, and is responding with a degree of determination that frightens ruling whites.

By ANTHONY SAMPSON

JOHANNESBURG.

IN the middle of Johannesburg stands a large, ornate department store known as the "O. K. Bazaars." Recently, between its tall Corinthian columns, elaborate decorations have been erected to celebrate the fiftieth anniversary of the Union of South Africa on May 31. Four enormous bronzed white men hold hands across the facade of the store, representing the four colonies that came together in 1910—Transvaal, Natal, the Orange Free State and the Cape Colony. Beneath the bold white statues a crowd of Negro shoppers—who make up a large proportion of the custom of the O. K. Bazaars—mill in and out of the store.

The contrast might be taken as a symbol of the present state of South Africa. For, ironically enough, it is just at the moment when South Africa is celebrating its all-white jubilee that the South African Government has become abruptly aware of the power of the black three-quarters of the population.

Among the 9,000,000 black people, it is the 3,000,000 who live in the cities who have been the crucial factor in the crisis of the past month. But it is precisely those 3,000,000 that successive Governments have been most determined to ignore.

NO Government since 1910 has been prepared to face fully the fact of this disorganized population of Africans streaming into the towns to work in the great new urban centers of Johannesburg, Capetown or Durban. For their very presence in the white men's streets or shops constitutes a contradiction of the theory of *apartheid*. While the white South African leaders have been building up their elaborate theories of racial segregation, they have found the Africans becoming steadily more Westernized, urbanized and detribalized on their very doorsteps.

No Government has come to terms with this, and the Afrikaner Nationalist Government, which has been in power since 1948, has positively turned away from it. It is the very basis of the policy of Dr. Hendrik Verwoerd, the present Prime Minister, that Africans have no place in European cities, and that they are merely temporary visitors from what he calls the "Bantu homelands"—the bleak tribal reserves that constitute 13 per cent of the area of South Africa.

Dr. Verwoerd's chief theorist on African matters, Dr. Eiselen, describes the 3,000,000 urban Africans as an "unattached mass of Bantu individuals." Whenever any Cabinet Minister refers in general to the black population, it is clear that he means not the city dwellers, but the 3,000,000 tribal people who live in the reserves, or the remaining 3,000,000 who work, very close to the breadline, on the South African farms.

But during the past month, to ignore this "unattached mass" of town people has become impossible. For it is precisely these people, who the Government has liked to think did not really exist, who have—as it were—hit it in the stomach. It is they who have walked to the police stations to defy the pass laws; it is they who have emerged in a column, 30,000 strong, to march into Capetown; it is they who have reminded the white people of their dependence upon them by staying away from work for a time.

THE urban Africans have, in fact, become suddenly aware of their power. The awareness is apparent in any conversation between Africans — inside their beer halls, in the bus queues from the cities or in their "shebeens," the illegal drinking places which are the hub of the more sophisticated black world. "Now we know," said one young African clerk in a shebeen outside Johannesburg the other day, "that the white fellows are really *scared* of us."

A messenger boy was sitting next to him, gazing at a map of Africa in an American magazine that indicated the newly independent states. "Why should all these guys up there be free," he said in the American drawl much favored in the shebeens, "while we're still in chains, man?"

The odd thing about the question is not that it should be asked, but that it should be asked so late. For the chains of the black people in South Africa are not entirely made by whites. The practice of white supremacy could never have succeeded so well if it had not been for the passive consent of the Africans.

COMPARED to the more volatile, tribal people of Ghana or Kenya, the black South Africans are long-suffering and much less confident. The reason is obvious: They have been uprooted and confused by the harsh impact of the twentieth-century cities.

South Africa is much the richest and most industrialized country on the continent. While Ghanaians or Kenyans have acquired a steady confidence, still half-rooted in their tribal heritage, the cream of black South Africans have found themselves pitchforked into chaotic cities, subjected suddenly to Hollywood, juke boxes, comics and alcohol, not sure whether they were meant to be white, black, tribal or urban.

Only in the past few years have they begun to emerge from this turmoil, to look around and decide that they have a claim to the country.

At the time of union fifty years ago, their grandfathers had few such thoughts. When a group of African lawyers in 1912 founded an organization called the African National Congress—the same organization that two weeks ago was finally banned by Dr. Verwoerd — they were concerned more with defending their rights than with enlarging them.

"The white people of this country," said the first President of the Congress, Dr. Pixley Seme, "have formed what is known as the Union of South Africa — a union in which we have no voice in the making of the laws and no part in the administration. We have called you, therefore, to this conference so that we can together devise ways and means of forming our national union for the purpose of creating national unity and defending our rights and privileges."

"Nationalism" in those days meant not a militant African front but the sinking of tribal differences in a new nation. The sedate, top-hatted African politicians of 1912, many of whom came from hereditary chiefly families, would have been as horrified as any white

ANTHONY SAMPSON is a London newspaper man (The Observer) who once edited a paper for Africans in Johannesburg and has periodically revisited South Africa.

leader by the thought of "one man, one vote."

OVER the past fifty years the Africans have hardened their political thoughts. They have watched the Governments not opening the doors to racial integration as they had expected, but gradually closing them; taking away, act by act, their remaining rights.

The Africans had a limited-roll franchise, freehold property rights in the cities and a liberal educational system, including two mixed universities, that was rooted in the extensive missionary tradition of the nineteenth century. All this is now abolished or being abolished. The mission schools were taken over by the Government to produce a limited form of "Bantu education" and the University College at Fort Hare is being transformed into a tribal college. As a result, the many African leaders who had compared themselves to American Negroes, and had hopefully followed the precepts of Booker T. Washington found by the end of the Second World War that South Africa's racial policies were proceeding in the opposite direction from America's.

Two of the most ardent disciples of Booker Washington in the Thirties, Chief Albert Luthuli and Prof. Zachariah Matthews, found themselves in 1956 arrested for high treason, and in 1960 detained indefinitely under the emergency regulations.

BUT the more decisive change over the fifty years has been not so much the disillusion with white rule as the growth of the new urban African society. The Africans' education came not only from schools, but from the streets, cinemas and newspapers. Pressed together in crowded townships—there are 300,000 Africans in the southwestern suburbs of Johannesburg alone—they have created out of the slums a throbbing and powerful society of their own—a kind of African Harlem, but with an underlying confidence and calm that few Negroes can have in Manhattan.

In the noisy, smoky townships of Orlando, Meadowlands, Moroka or Pimville, clustered around Johannesburg; or Cato Manor outside Durban; or Langa or Nyanga outside Capetown, a new sort of Africa is being beaten out of the chaos.

TO most white observers these seem merely to be distressing "black spots" to which their servants or messengers regrettably have to retreat in the evening. But to the Africans the townships are the great new black metropolis which lures strangers from as far away as Nyasaland or Portuguese East Africa.

The 700,000 Africans in the segregated satellite townships of Johannesburg make this the biggest black city on the continent. This varied and complex society has its own jazz, its own fashions, musicals, journalists and poets—each representing in a different way a new mixed culture between the two worlds of the tribe and the city.

Within the past fifty years, the towns have ceased to be exciting novelties for blanketed tribesmen; most of the Africans now in the cities were born in the cities. When they hear themselves described as "temporary residents from the Bantu homelands" they are as uncomprehending as a Harlem-born Negro would be if told he belonged in Mississippi.

Meanwhile, among the African élite, the self-made generation of pioneers—men like Dr. Seme, Dr. Xumaor, Dr. Moroka, all former presidents of the African Congress—who were too preoccupied with proving themselves to risk losing their jobs for the sake of politics, have given way to a younger generation who were brought up with more confident and daring ideas. One of these is Robert Sobukwe, the fiery young university lecturer who two years ago broke away from the more cautious African National Congress of Chief Luthuli to form his own Pan-Africanist Congress which precipitated the current crisis.

Behind all the long history of African submissiveness has lain one fundamental fear—the fear of shooting. "Whatever happens we have got the Maxim gun, and they have not," wrote Hilaire Belloc of the whites in Africa in 1893. Since the last Zulu tribes were defeated in the Eighteen Eighties the Africans have not forgotten this simple precept.

AT intervals over the past fifty years, the black leaders have tried to defy the most hated law of the country, which compels all urban Africans to carry passes, controlling their movements, their jobs and their daily lives. Each time, in 1919, 1930 and 1946, they have tried to burn their passes, to wreck the system on which their oppression was based. In 1919, when the Africans still looked to Britain for help, they even surrendered their passes while singing "God Save the King."

But each time the burning of passes has been met with shooting, mass arrests and new acts to impose further controls. "Whenever we attack the passes, they shoot," has become a proverb of the African National Congress.

The African memory is long, and the gunfire of 1930, when Africans made a bonfire of passes in Durban, or of 1946, when gold miners on strike were forced back to their mines with shooting, or of 1953, when riots in Port Elizabeth and East London were met with fierce reprisals, still echoes in their minds. The nightmare of a shooting showdown has pressed the Congress leaders to adopt a cautious, nonviolent policy, gradually consolidating their people.

Since 1953, however, the shape of Africa outside the Union has been rapidly changing. For a time it seemed that South Africa was successfully sealed off from the rest of the continent, and that the "wind of change" from the North had been deflected at the Limpopo River. Black South Africans very rarely met their northern counterparts and, when they did, found little in common with them.

BUT the cries for freedom from Ghana, from Kenya and from Nyasaland were beginning to penetrate into the Union. When, in 1957, the Johannesburg Africans staged a two-month-long bus boycott, they shouted "Ghana!" as a rallying cry. After Ghana's independence in 1957 office boys kept pictures of Dr. Nkrumah in their cubbyholes. The urban Africans became aware that not only the rest of Africa, but the rest of the world, was swinging over to their side.

This has been the dominant thought behind the policies of Robert Sobukwe, who has pledged to lead the Africans to freedom by 1963, to accept no help from whites or Indians, and to follow the militant pattern of Nkrumah of Ghana, Mboya of Kenya or Banda of Nyasaland. Sobukwe, with his bold promises, succeeded in giving younger Africans the impression that he had acquired the authentic fire of Africa—the elixir which had transformed the map of the continent, and could transform South Africa, too. As the first major campaign of his movement, Sobukwe, with typical daring, chose to attack the most dangerous enemy of all—the pass laws.

Thus it was that, on the morning of March 21, the campaign began. It resulted, as the older Congress leaders had warned, in massive shooting, with sixty-seven killed at the model township of Sharpeville, south of Johannesburg. But, as Sobukwe had no doubt realized, shooting in 1960 has much wider repercussions than in 1930, 1946 or 1953.

In the subsequent weeks, as the campaign spread to protests and stay-at-home strikes all over the Union, the black South Africans realized as never before that the whole world was on their side, and that the white Government was totally isolated. In spite of the state of emergency which was declared ten days after the Sharpeville incident, and the 200,000 white people under arms, Africans saw clearly for the first time that white supremacy was no longer an immutable law, but a desperate stand against a hostile world.

THE Africans remain a long way from their own liberation. However much their own attitudes have changed since 1910, they retain a strong sense of dependence on the white man, and a reluctance to tear themselves away from the system of domination.

Their reluctance became clear in the reaction to Sobukwe's anti-pass campaign, and the campaign of the rival African National Congress, which told its followers to burn their passes soon afterward. Despite the fact that the police had temporarily stopped arresting people without passes, few Africans could be persuaded to part with the little books that controlled their lives. The machinery of white control, softened by white paternalism, had become so much a part of their thinking that they did not dare defy it.

All through the townships the political organizers argued with the people, trying to persuade them to burn or abandon their passes. But to the simple, law-abiding Africans their passes were part of their very existence. "Who will know who I am?" "Who will identify me if I'm killed?" 'How can people live without passes?" The bewildered replies showed how accustomed the Africans had grown to their chains.

Sobukwe's Pan-Africanists shouted *"Izwe lethu!"*—"Our land!" But the clerks, laborers or truck drivers who had worked their whole lives for white men found it difficult to believe that South Africa was in fact their land.

YET the idea is dawning, and after each round of reprisals it becomes stronger. "We pack it away, we pack it away!" said an African teacher after a recent location raid. "We may not do anything at the time, but we pack everything the white man has ever done to us into a hard lump in the back of our minds—and then suddenly, man, it will take fire!"

However long the Africans in South Africa must wait before they share their liberty with the northern countries, they are facing their country's jubilee with a new sense of confidence since the Sharpeville shootings. They have detected a note of panic in the white men's reactions—more strongly since the attempt on the life of Dr. Verwoerd. And always in the back of their minds is the hope that the white front will divide and collapse with demoralization.

"Those white fellows," an African was saying in a shebeen just after the attempted assassination, "are driving themselves *crazy* with fear." And a quiet musician sitting next to him said, "And we haven't even begun to put the pressure on.

April 24, 1960

SECRET TIES RULE IN SOUTH AFRICA

Broederbond Unites Leaders in Elite Group Dedicated to White Hegemony

By LEONARD INGALLS

Special to The New York Times.

JOHANNESBURG, South Africa, May 3—One of the strongest influences in South African national life is a secret organization called the Africaner Broederbond.

The Broederbond, as it is commonly known, exists to promote the dominance of Afrikaners, the descendants of the Dutch settlers of South Africa, over South Africans of English ancestry and over the country's enormous African majority.

Its nature is such that the Broederbond has been denounced by a former Prime Minister as "fascist" and by other responsible citizens as "vicious and unpatriotic." Some observers of the world scene have compared it to Nazi organizations established in German during the Nineteen-thirties by Hitler.

In South Africa the Broederbond has strong links to the Nationalist party Government headed by Prime Minister Hendrik F. Verwoerd, who as a newspaper editor during World War II displayed pro-Nazi sympathies. Many members of the South African Cabinet, including Dr. Verwoerd, are members of the Broederbond. A majority of the Nationalist party representatives in Parliament also are said to be members of the Broederbond.

State Within a State

Indeed, so strong is its influence in the Government that some of its critics have described the Broederbond as "a state within the state." Others have said that since the Nationalist party came to power in 1948 under the late Prime Minister Daniel F. Malan, the real government of the country has been the Broederbond.

Dr. Malan was one of the founders of the Broederbond and its present head is said to be Dr. Verwoerd. The Minister of Finance in the Verwoerd administration, Dr. Theophilus E. Donges, is a vice president of the Broederbond.

The organization, whose name means "Afrikaner band of brothers," was established in 1918. Membership is confined to white Protestants whose home language is Afrikaans, the derivative of Dutch, Flemish, French, German, English and Hottentot that is one of the two official languages of South Africa. The other is English.

The Broederbond had its origins in the Boer War, which ended in 1902 with the defeat of the Afrikaners by the British. Since that time the Afrikaners have been determined to create an Afrikaner nation in South Africa. The Nationalist party is their political instrument and the Broederbond is the élite corps of Afrikanerdom.

From its inception the Broederbond has had two main aims. One is the establishment of a Christian national republic governed by Afrikaners and the other is the maintenance of white supremacy.

A referendum on the question of making South Africa a republic is expected to be held later this year. Whether white supremacy can be maintained as a long-range policy remains to be seen.

5,000 Members of Order

Of the 1,700,000 Afrikaners in South Africa's white population of 3,100,000, it is estimated that about 5,000 are members of the Broederbond. Most of the members are drawn from occupational groups that are in a position to exert influence in the community. These include teachers, clergymen, politicians, university professors, professional men and civil servants.

The Broederbond operates on the cell system. There is an estimated total of 500 cells throughout South Africa. Each cell has at least five members who are a cross section of the community in which they function. Not more than one in a cell is drawn from the various influential occupational groups.

A group known as the Twelve Apostles (of Afrikanerdom) is the national governing body. There also are regional administrations. The Broederbond has a written constitution. Its meetings and activities are secret, but official investigations and defections by a few members have provided considerable information about the organization.

It was as a result of one such investigation that the late Prime Minister Jan Christiaan Smuts said: "It is clear that the Broederbond is a dangerous, cunning, political, fascist organization."

Field Marshal Smuts ordered that all civil servants who were members of the Broederbond must either resign from the organization or give up their Government jobs. One of those who decided to leave the Government service rather than the Broederbond was the present South African Ambassador to the United States, Wentzel C. du Plessis. He had been a career employe of the Department of External Affairs.

The Broederbond controls the Federation of Afrikaans Cultural Societies and through it gives directions on cultural matters to 150 cultural organizations throughout the country. It also operates through the Reddingsdaadbond, an Afrikaner welfare and lending society, which has large investments in fourteen nation-wide companies, including banks and insurance companies.

One of South Africa's largest banks, Volkskas or "the people's bank", was founded in 1934 by the Broederbond.

In addition to its efforts in the cultural and commercial life of South Africa, the Broederbond has made the public service one of its main targets. A result has been that the top jobs in all Government departments are held by persons acceptable to the Broederbond and appointments to all important posts in the civil service must be approved by the Broederbond.

May 8, 1960

REPUBLIC IS VOTED FOR SOUTH AFRICA; VERWOERD VICTOR

Record All-White Poll Backs Move to End Allegiance to the British Crown

By LEONARD INGALLS
Special to The New York Times.

JOHANNESBURG, South Africa, Oct. 6—Prime Minister Hendrik F. Verwoerd and the ruling Nationalist party won public approval by a comfortable margin tonight for making South Africa a republic.

Final returns in yesterday's all-white referendum gave the proponents of a republic a majority of more than 72,000 votes.

Slightly more than 90 per cent of the 1,800,700 persons qualified to vote in the referendum cast their ballots. This was a record poll for a South African election.

Prime Minister Verwoerd, the controversial leader of South Africa's white supremacists, made no comment tonight on the outcome of the poll, but he scheduled a radio address to the country tomorrow night.

Queen to Be Supplanted

The result of the referendum means that South Africa will cease to be a constitutional monarchy owing allegiance to the British crown and that Britain's Queen Elizabeth II will be replaced by a President as chief of state.

Dr. Verwoerd has indicated that legislation to accomplish this will be enacted by the South African Parliament at its next session, which is scheduled to open Jan. 20 in Cape Town.

Early today opponents of a republic had rolled up a majority of 155,000 against a republic. But as returns continued to flow in from polling places throughout South Africa and South-West Africa, which South Africa administers under a mandate from the League of Nations, it became apparent that a Nationalist victory was in the making.

Poll Points Up Division

Throughout the day the anti-republic majority dwindled. A majority for a republic then began to mount. Early returns were from the cities and towns, where a great majority of anti-Government voters live. Nationalist rural strongholds were heard from later on.

The result showed the great cleavage that exists between the urban business man and the rural farmer: that is, between the white South Africans of British ancestry—most of whom oppose the Verwoerd Administration — and the Afrikaners, who are descendants of early Dutch settlers and are fervid supporters of Dr. Verwoerd.

The poll was confined to the country's 3,000,000 whites, 55 per cent of whom are Afrikaners and 45 per cent of British blood. The country's nonwhite majority of more than 11,000,000 was excluded.

Also at issue in the referendum is South Africa's membership in the British Commonwealth. As a new republic, the country would have to be accepted for continued membership by the other members.

Many South Africans fear that such countries as Ghana, Nigeria, Malaya and India, which strongly oppose the Verwoerd Government's white supremacy policies, would seize South Africa's conversion to a republic as an opportunity to oust South Africa from the Commonwealth.

Dr. Verwoerd has said that he would attend the next meeting of Commonwealth Prime Ministers to discuss the situation.

Meanwhile, it is believed that an actual change to a republic would be delayed until after the Prime Ministers' conference.

Commenting on the outcome of the referendum, Die Transvaler, Johannesburg's Afrikaans newspaper of which Dr. Verwoerd once was editor, said:

"Those who voted against the republic must also be converted to the republican ideal because their contribution to the further building and development of the country are also necessary."

Dr. Jan Steytler, leader of the anti-Government Progressive party, said: "The danger of South Africa is that the rest of the world may regard a majority yes vote as an indication that all whites approve of racial discrimination."

October 7, 1960

South Africa Becomes Republic; Tie With Commonwealth Ended

Swart Is Inaugurated as First President —Country Quiet and Few Africans Show Interest in Day's Ceremonies

By LEONARD INGALLS

Special to The New York Times.

PRETORIA, South Africa, May 31—South Africa became a republic today.

At the same time, South Africa formally severed its affiliation with the British Commonwealth.

The day was marked by the inauguration of Charles R. Swart, former Governor General and Minister of Justice, as the republic's first President. The ceremonies here in the administrative capital were dampened by heavy rain.

Mr. Swart, in his inaugural address delivered from the steps of the Palace of Justice, repeated a warning often given by South Africa's top officials. He asserted that South Africans had "the right to decide for ourselves on matters of domestic policy according to the expressed will of our own electorate without interference from outside."

Today was a holiday throughout the country and all sections were reported to be calm. The threatened general strike by African workers and other nonwhites, which failed to develop Monday, gave no signs of coming to life today. A scattering of Africans, including eight tribal chiefs, attended the Republic Day ceremonies.

Few of the country's vast African majority took part in the day's events or paid attention to what was happening.

Prime Minister Hendrik F. Verwoerd, who appeared at the side of Mr. Swart throughout the observances, said in introducing the new President at the inauguration that this was a "momentous day" in South Africa.

Extraordinary precautions were taken to insure that the ceremonies were held without incident. More than 12,000 armed troops lined the two-and-one-half-mile route from the President's residence to the Groote Kerk (Great Church), a Dutch Reformed house of worship where Mr. Swart took the oath of office. In recent days the police have checked carefully all buildings along the route and in Church Square to ascertain who would be in them and what their movements would be today.

Mr. Swart, 67 years old, wore a black swallowtail coat, striped pants and a tall silk hat for the occasion. When he completed the oath, a purple and gold sash bearing the seal of the new republic was draped over his shoulder and across his chest.

The new President said that the advent of the republic should not be viewed as a victory of one section of South Africa over another.

As for the break with the Commonwealth, he said South Africa took leave of Queen Elizabeth II of Britain, to whom South Africa as a constitutional monarchy owed allegiance, "with friendship, cordial relations and high regard, coupled with sincere good wishes for Her Majesty's own personal welfare, that of her family and also of the countries and peoples over which she rules."

June 1, 1961

LUTHULI, IN OSLO, SCORES APARTHEID

Peace Prize Winner Terms South Africa a 'Relic'

Special to The New York Times.

OSLO, Norway, Dec. 11—Albert John Luthuli characterized South Africa today as "a museum piece in our time, a hangover from the dark past of mankind, a relic of an age which everywhere else is dead or dying."

"Here the cult of race superiority and of white supremacy is worshiped like a god," he said in his Nobel Peace Prize Lecture in Oslo.

Mr. Luthuli received the 1960 peace prize in a ceremony here yesterday. Dag Hammarskjold, the late Secretary General of the United Nations, was awarded the 1961 prize at the same ceremony.

Mr. Luthuli, 62 years old, a former Zulu chief, said it was a great honor to him "to be plucked from banishment in a rural backwater, to be lifted out of the narrow confinement of South Africa's internal politics" to be awarded the Peace Prize.

Mr. Luthuli suggested that Africa could serve as a mediator between East and West. In this connecion he said:

"In a strife-torn world, tottering on the brink of complete destruction by man-made nuclear weapons, a free and independent Africa is in the making, in answer to the injunction and challenge of history:

"'Arise and shine for thy light is come.'"

He said that as a Christian and a patriot he could not "remain neutral in a situation where the laws of the land virtually criticized God for having created men of color" and when systematic attempts were made to "debase the God-factor in man."

Mr. Luthuli said the award was a democratic declaration of solidarity with those who fight to widen the area of liberty in South Africa. He added that the award was also a welcome recognition of the role played by the African people to establish peacefully a society where merit, not race, would fix the position of the individual in the life of the nation.

Mr. Luthuli said that Africa today "is a continent in revolution against oppression." "There can be no peace until the forces of oppression are overthrown," he declared.

He called it a paradox that the Peace Prize should be given to a man from a country where "the brotherhood of man is an illegal doctrine, outlawed, banned, censured, proscribed and prohibited."

"How great is the paradox and how much greater the honor that an award in support of peace and the brotherhood of man should come to one who is a citizen of a country where the brotherhood of man is an illegal doctrine," he said.

The African said that the policy of apartheid, or racial separation, survived in South Africa because those who sponsored it profited from it since it provided "moral whitewash" for conditions.

Mr. Luthuli said that the true patriots of South Africa would be satisfied with nothing less than the fullest democratic rights in politics, in economic matters, in culture and in the social sphere.

"We do not demand these things for people of African descent alone," he said. "We demand them for all South Africans, white and black. On these principles we are uncompromising."

December 12, 1961

On Native Grounds

LET MY PEOPLE GO. By Albert Luthuli. Illustrated. 256 pp. New York: McGraw-Hill Book Company. $5.50.

By EDWARD CALLAN

AFRICA'S first Nobel Prize winner, Albert Luthuli, believes that South Africa's traditional white supremacy policies are unlikely to be reversed at the polls; for most whites support, or consent to, these policies—and only whites have the vote. This white majority is the Pharaoh addressed in this biography, "Let My People Go," which conveys with unmistakable clarity, the African view on the injustice and folly of apartheid.

Luthuli knows that supremacists will not change their policies willingly, but he hopes they may change them peacefully. That is why he can encourage passive resistance and boycott, while insisting on nonviolence "What we want," he says, "is to bring the white man to his senses, not to slaughter him."

Luthuli is well qualified to speak for Africans. As former Chief of Umvoti, he knows the plight of migrant worker and peasant farmer; once a senior member of the teacher training department of Adams College, he knows that Africans want education based on Western values, not the return to tribalism offered by the present Government's Bantu Education Act; and he has a matchless record of success in elective office. But above all, he feels compelled as a Christian to speak out against any debasement of "human dignity—a God-given force."

This book is no drab recital of African woes. The early chapters reveal Luthuli's deep affection for his family, his pride in his Zulu heritage, and his deep-felt religious convictions. The breath of race prejudice hardly enters into this hopeful early period when the world seemed to be opening up for Africans: "There seemed point in my youth in striving after the values of the Western world." Pervading the whole, is Luthuli's keen eye for comic detail — an African trait that never deserts him even in the later somber moments of arrest and banishment.

The greater part of this book deals with the successive stages of the "program for action" of the African National Congress while Luthuli was President-General. The tempo of action and counter-action mounts with tragic inevitability. Deposition from chieftainship follows political action. The harsh Public Safety Act of 1953, which imposed penalties on anyone taking part in opposition to the government program follows the Defiance Campaign of nonviolent resistance by the African National Congress. The Treason Trial in which Luthuli and 155 others of all races were charged under the Suppression of Communism Act, follows the Freedom Charter—a bill of rights adopted by the multi-racial Congress of the People in 1955.

In the account of these events Luthuli does not evade unpalatable truths. That is his great strength. He unhesitatingly reveals his reasons for accepting the support of Communists, and also for encouraging external boycott of South Africa.

He devotes two chapters to the Treason Trial which, begun in 1956, was still in progress when he wrote his postscript on the Sharpville shootings in 1960, when the local police killed and wounded many Africans. Ironically, the long Treason Trial sessions enabled Luthuli and other opponents of apartheid, previously isolated by restrictive banns, to meet regularly and form common policies. Outside the court sessions, he met a cross-section of *his* South Africa—people of all races dedicated to justice and human dignity: "The color-bar dropped away like the fictitious and beastly thing it is, within the borders of the unexpected world which the Treason Trial had created."

UNFORTUNATELY, no one has thought to add a note on the verdict of March, 1961; for the court's findings cleared the African National Congress of the stigma of communism, and vindicated its claims to a policy of nonviolence. It adds substance, also, to Luthuli's outcry against the arbitrary powers by which Ministers ban African leaders, and, indeed, govern many aspects of African life by fiat not subject to control by the courts.

Luthuli's book reaches its climax in an indignant chapter on the Promotion of Bantu Self-Government Act, entitled "A Huge Deceit." In view of the recent South African announcement of self-government for the Transkei, this chapter should arouse special interest.

Luthuli's criticism of white rule in South Africa is valid in broad outline, but controvertible on points of detail. For example, he minimizes the difference between the Nationalist and United parties, and he ignores the likelihood that segregationists chose the Nationalist apartheid platform in 1948 because they feared the United Party would implement the Fagan Commission's report on the impossibility of complete segregation in South Africa and the need for radically transforming laws affecting Africans. But he rightly concludes that to win elections the United Party must pander to segregationist voters.

His understandable partisanship has one great value: it enables him to illuminate a neglected perspective on South African history. In conventional histories, seen from above, the Boer-Briton conflict dominates and "the Native problem" is incidental. Seen from below, Boer and Briton fuse into white supremacist and their squabbles are inconsequential.

Luthuli is not anti-white; he is anti-white-supremacist. And while the supremacists dream of an Eden where all races are fenced off physically and spiritually, he hopes for a New Jerusalem where all may mingle in the market-place and worship in unsegregated temples.

May 13, 1962

South Africa Giving Tribe Limited Rule

By LEONARD INGALLS

Special to The New York Times.

CAPETOWN, South Africa, Jan. 23—Prime Minister Hendrik F. Verwoerd announced today that one of South Africa's largest non-white areas would be granted internal self-government early next year.

Under a proposed constitution for the affected area, the Transkei, members of the Xhosa tribe there would elect a representative assembly and have a ministerial form of administration.

The Transkei consists of 16,000 square miles south of Durban between the Indian Ocean and the Drakensberg Mountains. Its population is about 1,500,000. About 40 per cent of its people usually work in the mines of South Africa.

Prime Minister Verwoerd portrayed the Transkei proposal as a major step in his Government's program of separate development of the races in South Africa. He said it was being taken at the request of the leaders of the Xhosa people.

The Government will take similar steps for other tribes as soon as they feel capable or desirous of making the same request, the Prime Minister added.

There are 264 areas in South Africa reserved for residence by Africans. The Government contemplates consolidating them into seven so-called Bantustans, a name that derives from the word Bantu, the official name for Africans in the republic.

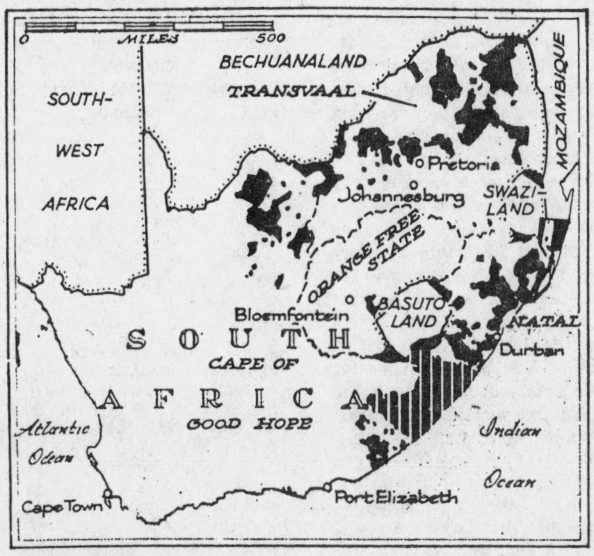

The New York Times Jan. 24, 1962

AUTONOMY OFFER: South Africa will grant internal self-rule to the Transkei (vertical white stripes) and plans a similar status for other African areas (black).

Opponents of the program contend that it is merely a device to continue white domination of Africans and to deny them equal rights.

Called Propaganda Stunt

Sir de Villiers Graaff, leader of the Opposition in Parliament, said during debate today that the Government's separate development program, or "national reconstruction," as it also has been called, was "a political propaganda stunt that must either be proved or be abandoned."

Replying to Sir de Villiers, Prime Minister Verwoerd intimated that the new Transkei constitution would be the first step toward independence for the area. But he added that the Xhosa tribe did not feel ready for independence yet.

The proposed all-African Transkei Parliament, he continued, presumably would have jurisdiction within the area over such matters as agriculture, health and welfare services, lands, roads, education and local authorities.

Foreign affairs, defense and the administration of justice would remain the responsibility of the National Government.

Whites would have no political rights in the Transkei. The Xhosa tribe would decide on voting qualifications for its members.

January 24, 1962

WHITES ARE ADVISED ON BANTU SERVANTS

Special to The New York Times.

JOHANNESBURG, South Africa, Feb. 5—An effort is being made in Johánnesburg to improve relations between whites and their African servants. The Non-European Affairs Department of the city government has issued a booklet of suggestions entitled "Your Bantu Servant and You" on how whites should conduct themselves in dealing with their domestic help.

Referring to Africans as Bantu, the official word for them in South Africa, the booklet says one of the most prevalent fallacies among white South Africans is: "I know the Bantu and how to treat him."

Women are advised to be "exceptionally careful" in the treatment of male servants.

"In tribal life," women are told, "a woman is always regarded as a minor and remains under the tutelage of the man. She must always act with due respect and modesty toward and in front of males."

A basic rule suggested for women in dealing with male servants is: "Do not expect him to make your bed, wash or iron your underclothing or those of girls, nor to wash stained linen. It outrages his sense of what is proper."

February 11, 1962

Drive for White Settlers Is Begun by South Africa

By ROBERT CONLEY

Special to The New York Times.

JOHANNESBURG, South Africa, June 4—The South African Government is starting a major drive to bring in settlers from Europe. The move is one of the most carefully planned and selective immigration projects in modern times.

The purpose is to increase South Africa's white minority of 3,067,000 to the point where the whites about equal in number the country's 12,773,000 Africans, Asians and mixed-blood "coloreds."

Prime Minister Hendrik F. Verwoerd's Afrikaner Nationalist Government hopes to induce 40,000 to 50,000 whites a year from Europe to settle in South Africa.

The goal is to have a white population of 10,000,000 in South Africa by the year 2000.

Recruiting specialists are preparing to go to Britain and the Continent in search of potential settlers.

Cash Grants Offered

Any European who accepts the offer, it is understood, will receive an outright grant equivalent to $84 to ease the costs of setting out for a new country and a new career. He also will be given an interest-free loan of as much as another $84, repayable over two years.

Free rail travel will be provided from the port of entry in South Africa and the Government will make a payment for accommodations until the settler gets a job.

These and other details were disclosed today in a letter to South African business and industrial concerns requesting information on their needs for additional employes.

The letter was signed by Glyn Morris, general manager of the 1820 Memorial Settlers Association, who is going overseas on the recruiting mission at the request of the Immigration Department. He is reported to have scheduled lectures in thirty communities in Britain on the benefits of moving to South Africa.

Appealing to business and industrial concerns for cooperation, he said the association would assist the Government as vigorously as possible to achieve the immigration target. The association was founded in 1920 to perpetuate the memory of the original British settlers of 1820 by introducing "selected" immigrants to South Africa.

His letter is being distributed to an estimated total of 10,000 concerns in South Africa.

Behind the move is a detailed timetable drawn up by Dr. Verwoerd's Government with the stated objective of achieving the "approximate equalization" of white and nonwhite populations by the turn of the century, particularly in industrial areas.

To get the settlers the Government will bring them here, find them jobs and housing and assist them toward what has been termed "full adaptation in the white community and its customs."

The Government is prepared to spend a minimum of $4,200,000 a year on the program. It may even charter ships to carry immigrants if the response is sufficient.

South African immigration and recruiting offices have been set up in Britain, Italy, Greece, Germany, Portugal, Switzerland, the Netherlands and Austria.

June 5, 1962

U.N. FOR BOYCOTT OF SOUTH AFRICA

67-16 Assembly Vote Urges Economic Sanctions

By ALEXANDER BURNHAM

Special to The New York Times

UNITED NATIONS, N. Y., Nov. 6 — The General Assembly called upon members of the United Nations today to impose economic sanctions on South Africa in a worldwide effort to force that country to abandon its policy of racial segregation.

In a show of its growing strength in the world organization, the Asian-African bloc succeeded in defeating Western attempts to water down the strongest condemnation ever voted against a member in the Assembly.

The 34-nation resolution was adopted, 67 to 16, with 23 abstentions. This was an increase of seven favorable votes over its preliminary approval last Thursday in the Special Political Committee.

The resolution also calls upon member nations to break off diplomatic relations with the Government of Prime Minister Hendrik F. Verwoerd and urges the Security Council to consider the expulsion of South Africa from the United Nations if it continues its racial policies.

The vote, which was greeted by loud and sustained applause, was taken after Eric H. Louw, South Africa's Minister of External Affairs, delivered a speech in which he challenged the right of South Africa's critics to condemn his country. He said:

"An unsavory aspect of the anti-South Africa campaign is that a number of delegations and particularly the sponsors of the resolution before this Assembly, knowing of unsatisfactory conditions in their own countries—the insufficiency of schools, of medical care, of social services and of decent housing, to say nothing of discriminatory practices — are quite prepared to condemn South Africa.

"In view of unsatisfactory conditions prevailing in their own countries, they do not have the moral right to judge South Africa."

Mr. Louw repeated his Government's contention that the Assembly was interfering in South Africa's internal affairs. He said that the white population of South Africa had built up and developed in more than three centuries "unquestionably the most advanced and highly industrialized state on the whole of the African continent."

South Africa's opponents, Mr. Louw said, were "asking the permanent white population to abdicate."

Mr. Louw also spoke of what he said was a similarity between South Africa's white population and the descendants of the original immigrants to

United Press International

ADDRESSES U.N.: Eric H. Louw of South Africa.

the United States and Canada. He mentioned the Roosevelts, the Eisenhowers and the du Ponts.

This comparison was rejected by Francis T. P. Plimpton of the United States, who repeated the United States opposition to South Africa's policy of the separation of the races, which is called apartheid.

Mr. Louw repeated arguments advanced by Britain and other countries that any attempt to expel South Africa would be "the beginning of the end of the United Nations."

Trinidad and Tobago tried to introduce an amendment to the resolution before the vote. The amendment would have softened the measures to be taken against South Africa. After three hours of opposition speeches by African delegates, Ellis Clarke, the representative of Trinidad and Tobago, withdrew the amendment.

After a luncheon recess, Alfredo Vasquez of Colombia sought, with United States and Swedish support, to get separate votes on the parts of the resolution that called for "drastic action." This was defeated in a vote.

The United States and Britain were joined by Australia, Belgium, Canada, France, Greece, Ireland, Japan, Luxembourg, the Netherlands, New Zealand, Portugal, Spain and Turkey, as well as South Africa, in voting against the resolution.

Throughout the debate in the Assembly and in the Special Political Committee, the United States and its supporters maintained that they were as much in opposition to apartheid in South Africa as were the Asian-African countries. They questioned the wisdom and legality of sanctions, however, and cited the dangers of expelling a member whose ideas differed with the majority.

The resolution also asks United Nations members to close their ports to South African ships, prevent their ships from entering South African ports, boycott all South African goods and refrain from exporting goods, including arms and ammunition, to South Africa and to refuse landing and passage facilities to all South African aircraft.

November 7, 1962

APARTHEID'S FOES IGNORE TRADE BAN

A Boycott of South Africa Shunned by Its Backers

By KATHLEEN TELTSCH
Special to The New York Times.

UNITED NATIONS, N. Y., March 24—The militant foes of South African race segregation appeared to be ignoring their own call for an economic boycott of South Africa.

The boycott was urged in the General Assembly resolution approved last November that recommended that states shun economic dealings with South Africa to force the Government to abandon its apartheid policies.

Almost six months later, most of the Asian, African and Soviet states that had campaigned for the resolution have been found to be continuing trade with South Africa. Commercial traffic with these states was described by South African sources as "normal and very prosperous, from South Africa's view."

The failure of the boycott has been more or less acknowledged by the states involved and they now are casting around for some other means of putting pressure on South Africa.

Soviet Ships Skip Boycott

Recently, 11 states considered the matter at a private meeting, but apparently they reached no decision on more drastic measures, such as an appeal for Security Council action. Any new move has been promised support in advance from the Soviet Union, which has informed Secretary General U Thant by letter that it is ready to back "any steps" for putting an end to apartheid.

South Africa has said that it was the Soviet Union, ironically, that first violated the assembly resolution calling for economic isolation of South Africa. A short time after the text was adopted, a Russian ship put in at Capetown, made purchases and continued on its way.

The resolution explicitly asked governments to pass laws prohibiting their ships from calling at South African ports. Other provisions called for a break in diplomatic relations, an economic boycott and closing ports and airfields to South African vessels and aircraft. The resolution was the latest, and toughest, of more than a dozen passed by the Assembly over the years in attempts to get apartheid laws changed.

In recent weeks, Polish ships have been making regular calls at South African ports for cargoes of asbestos and chemicals. There have also been indications that trade with other Eastern European states is on the increase.

U. S. and Britain Blamed

The Assembly resolution was opposed by the United States and Britain, which are South Africa's main trading partners. Anti-apartheid campaigners have been quick to blame the two Western powers for the boycott failure, but very little is being said about the continuing traffic with smaller Asian and African states.

In debate, the Western powers and others had expressed doubts that a boycott was either a legal or an effective measure for fighting apartheid. The United States had also held that it opposed apartheid and felt this policy would change, but that reform would have to come from internal pressures and not outside threats or punitive action of dubious legality. This view was rejected by the majority of the Asian and African nations, who cheered the adoption of their resolution by a vote of 67 to 16.

Since November, there has been no significant change in the pattern of trade between South Africa and the Asian-African supporters of the boycott.

Ceylon has continued to sell tea to South Africa and Malaya has continued to export rubber. Even Ghana, one of the most vigorous critics of the South African Government, has continued to supply cocoa. Some of this trade is channeled now through a third party, rather than directly.

South Africa, in turn, is not experiencing much difficulty in finding buyers for her manufactured goods, hides and leather, or the foodstuffs she traditionally sells to the Asian and African states. She has also started shipments of maize to a new customer—Communist China.

March 26, 1963

South Africa's Regime Drops Word 'Apartheid'

JOHANNESBURG, South Africa, July 27 (AP)—The word "apartheid" is dead as far as South Africa's officialdom is concerned. The white Government now prefers the words "separate development" to describe its policy of separation of whites and nonwhites.

The state-chartered radio also uses that term instead of apartheid.

Apartheid is an Afrikaans word that is translated as "separateness."

The Sunday Express of Johannesburg recently declared that apartheid had become a "non-South African" word as far as Government institutions were concerned.

July 28, 1963

U.S. Investments in South Africa Show Big Rise

American Capital There Is Up 15 to 25% Since 1961

Increase Is Noted Despite Government Controls

By JOSEPH LELYVELD

If 28 United Nations resolutions are any sign, South Africa's racist apartheid policies have made her an outcast among nations. But the American investor's reaction to the first 27 makes it a fair guess that he will not be put off by number 28, passed in the Security Council early this month.

American direct and portfolio investment in South Africa is now estimated at more than $600,000,000. Only the British have more money there. Between them, the United States and Britain take 46.9 per cent of South Africa's exports, a figure that shows why their support would be crucial for any program of economic sanctions.

The American investor is proceeding on the assumption that such support will not be forthcoming. He almost seems more confident in the country's future than his South African counterpart.

Until recently, domestic investment was sluggish. Observers say that the South African businessman still has not overcome the trauma of the Sharpesville shootings in the spring of 1960, which led to a vast flight of foreign capital out of the country. To end this flight, the South African Government tightened its import and exchange controls.

A year later, when South Africa withdrew from the Commonwealth of Nations, doubts about its financial future were heightened. Harry Oppenheimer, the chairman of the mighty Anglo-American Corporation of South Africa, Ltd., predicted grave financial consequences. He also described the withdrawal as "a moral disaster."

The American businessman, in the face of these controls and the 28 resolutions, seems to be investing as heavily in South Africa today as he did before the Sharpesville shootings, when the police fired into a protesting crowd, killing 67 and wounding 186.

The Commerce Department estimated last May that American investment in South Africa had risen 15 to 25 per cent since 1961.

The last Security Council resolution "deprecated" the racial segregation code enforced by the white minority, which is outnumbered four to one. Adlai E. Stevenson, the United States representative, deplored apartheid as "a bitter toxic." The white South African now calls it "separate development" instead of " apartheid."

The American investor calls it "politics" and hastens to point out that his decisions are "business decisions."

For instance, a spokesman for General Motors said the company "has not given that racial situation any thought whatsoever, either in its short-term or its long-term planning."

With an eye to future expansion, the spokesman noted, G.M. recently purchased 395 acres in Port Elizabeth where it has its major installation in South Africa.

The First National City Bank plans to open a branch in Durban, its third in South Africa, in November. This, a spokesman for the bank remarked, was tangible evidence of what kind of economic future it foresees for the country. The Chase Manhattan Bank also has South African branches.

The Newmont Mining Company recently became a major participant in a $104,000,000 copper-mining project in the Northern Transvaal. American Metals Climax, Inc., has also invested in the new company, which is called the Palabora Mining Company, Ltd.

"I'd rather invest in South Africa than any other country in the world, except Canada," a Newmont official declared.

Other recent American investors in South Africa are Caltex, Goodyear, American Cyanamid, Firestone, Champion Spark Plug and Kaiser Aluminum.

A Commerce Department official said the department was "neither encouraging nor discouraging" American investment in South Africa. "American business," he remarked, "is doing pretty much as it pleases."

A State Department spokesman put it this way: "We respect the right of Americans to invest where they want to invest."

Such statements do not sit well with the representatives of the newly independent African and Asian nations that have favored economic sanctions. "The more apartheid there is," one of them remarked, "the more prosperous South Africa becomes for foreign businessmen. Their huge profits are built on inequitable labor laws."

Actually the labor laws are a sore point with some South African businessmen, for they give the Government the power to restrict jobs on a racial basis. The result has been an increasingly severe shortage of skilled workers who, almost invariably, are white.

Scale Is Higher

The pay scale of the white laborer is generally four to five times that of the black South African.

The businessmen note that almost all the economic indicators for South Africa are shining brightly. Gold and foreign exchange reserves, which plunged after the Sharpesville shootings, are now at a record high owing to the exchange controls. Last week the ratio of gold reserves to public liabilities was 88.8 per cent.

The country's gold production, the largest in the world, pays for eight months of its imports. Eighty per cent of its manufacturing needs are met at home and in the last fiscal year its gross national product — total output of goods and services — was up 7½ per cent.

A South African banker here described the economic situation in his country as "a reluctant boom."

What holds it back? "You know as well as I do," the banker replied.

August 18, 1963

Durban, Liberal Foes' Citadel, Cheers Verwoerd

British Element Warming to South African Policy

By ROBERT CONLEY
Special to The New York Times

JOHANNESBURG, South Africa, Sept. 2—Prime Minister Hendrik F. Verwoerd is gaining unexpected personal acceptance among British South Africans, long his most vocal domestic critics.

In the last week thousands of British residents have cheered Dr. Verwoerd, and even sung him some choruses of "For He's A Jolly Good Fellow."

This happened at Durban, the resort city on South Africa's Indian Ocean coast, which is usually considered the most anti-Government community in the country.

Nearly 5,000 persons filled the City Hall and overflowed into the public gardens outside to hear the Prime Minister warn that South Africa's whites had to stand together against growing international protests over the country's racial policies or perish.

The crowd was said to be the largest at a political meeting in Durban since the end of World War II.

Whites Pressed Together

A significant body of opinion here holds that the current African campaign to isolate South Africa on the world stage is beginning to blur old political divisions and force the country's whites together for the first time in this century.

Dr. Verwoerd has long had the support of the country's Afrikaner community for his policy of apartheid or complete separation of South Africa's 3,100,000 whites and her 13,000,000 Africans, Asians and mixed-blood "coloreds." Afrikaners, representing just under 60 per cent of the white population, are descendants of the original Dutch and Huguenot settlers.

The recent conference of African heads of state in Addis Ababa that declared what amounted to war against South Africa's racial policy now appears to have given Dr. Verwoerd a gateway into the British community.

At a fund-raising dinner for his Afrikaner Nationalist party, some members of the most prominent families of British descent in Durban paid the equivalent of $7 to $21 a seat to hear the Prime Minister.

"South Africa has been entrusted to us not to lose, but to hand on from generation to generation," he told nearly 500 guests.

Dr. Verwoerd was applauded by spectators on the sidewalk as he entered the building where the dinner was held Inside he spent three-quarters of an hour shaking hands and greeting guests, most of whom were of the British community.

War's Divisions Remain

Only a short time ago the Prime Minister would have been heckled instead of hailed if he had made a public appearance in Durban. This time his City Hall speech was punctuated with cries of "Hear, Hear!" from his audience.

Leaders of Dr. Verwoerd's party hope that his Durban reception marked the beginning of a political "breakthrough" into the British community by the Afrikaners.

The Boer War of 1899-1902, fought over the issue of Afrikaner secession from political union with the British, split the country's whites into two mutually suspicious factions that have persisted to this day.

The Afrikaners are a rural and conservative people. The British element, generally urban and liberal, now accounts for 38 per cent of South Africa's white population. They are leaders of the country's business, industry and commerce.

The opposition United Party, traditionally the party of the British element, contends that the Prime Minister achieved only a personal victory, carrying little, if any evidence of an underlying political realignment.

Throughout his stay in Durban, Dr. Verwoerd continually stressed what he called the need for the country's whites to submerge their internal differences and form a united front against an increasingly antagonistic world.

September 3, 1963

South Africa Shows Early Gain In Recruiting of White Settlers

By ROBERT CONLEY
Special to The New York Times

JOHANNESBURG, South Africa, Sept. 11--South Africa appears to be succeeding far beyond any expectations in attracting white settlers from Britain, Europe and the rest of Africa.

In the first six months of this year, the Government's intensified immigration efforts have given South Africa a net gain of 11,972 white settlers.

This figure is higher than that for the 12 months in 1962 and nearly 10 times that for 1961.

South Africa's carefully planned and selective immigration program was designed with the immediate goal of bringing in skilled workers and professional men, which are in increasingly short supply in South Africa. Its wider purpose is to help increase South Africa's white minority of 3.1 million so it will nearly equal the country's population of 13 million Africans, Asians and mixed-blood Coloreds.

A white population of 10 million by the end of the century is to be sought.

From January to the end of June, 15,143 white people immigrated to South Africa and 3,171 left the country. The departure total was the lowest since World War II. Last year 11,971 more persons settled than left. In 1961, the net gain was only 1,415.

Nearly half of the new arrivals come by plane and by ship from Britain, Ireland, the Netherlands, West Germany, Italy, Greece and Portugal. Others have come by car, truck and bus from Kenya, the Rhodesias and Nyasaland.

Europeans appear to overlook political factors in coming here. The principal attractions for them are the temperate climate, job opportunities and the Government's financial inducements.

To encourage whites from the Rhodesias, the Government grants special customs concessions. They do not have to pay duty on cars, furniture or other personal belongings.

The immigration increase is a first result of the campaign, which was begun last year. Recruiters work out of nine offices—in London, Glasgow, Cologne, Hamburg, Athens, Rome, Lisbon, Belgium and the Netherlands.

Prime Minister Hendrik F. Verwoerd's Government expects to attract 30,000 new white settlers a year before long.

Tactical Balance Sought

Even if 100,000 whites settled in South Africa every year for the rest of the century and none left, there would be little chance of actually having one white for every nonwhite in the country.

What Dr. Verwoerd is seeking, however, is a tactical balance, not an actual one. The key is his plan to transform the country into a checkerboard of white areas and black areas. Ultimately 75 percent of the black Africans will be shifted to black areas or "bantustans" where they will be granted limited local powers.

The rest of South Africa will be for "whites only." It is in that white part that Dr. Verwoerd hopes to make whites the majority.

Discussing the possibility of new security laws, Justice Minister Balthazar Johannes Vorster said at a political meeting during the day that the Government would undertake whatever action it felt necessary against opponents of South Africa's policy of strict segregation of the races "regardless of critism, no matter from what source."

At the same time, the Minister of Transport, Barend Jacobus Schoeman, announced an impending Government move to seal further the main political escape route to Tanganyika.

South Africa would act next week, he said, to close the country's air space to political fugitives escaping by plane from the three neighboring British protectorates of Swaziland, Basutoland and Bechuanaland.

The two ministers spoke at a regional congress of Mr. Verwoerd's Afrikaner Nationalist party at Bloemfontein.

Mr. Vorster told the party leaders that 27,250 white women in South Africa were being instructed by the police in the use of pistols.

An undisclosed number of girls over the age of 16 received similar training at a special camp last April, the Justice Minister said.

September 12, 1963

'Self-Rule' Near for First Bantu Province

South Africa Keeps Whites in Control of Richer Areas

By ROBERT CONLEY
Special to The New York Times

UMTATA, South Africa, Nov. 17 — Here in the rolling hills, where time is counted in the mud-hut villages by when a chief was born or when the floods came, South Africa is setting up the first of her projected Bantustans, or all-black enclaves.

Eight of them are due to be brought into being in a legislated revolution that seeks to rearrange South Africa into a patchwork of white and black areas by the year 2000.

Whites in South Africa now are outnumbered nearly four to one by Bantus, members of various Negroid tribes whose legends indicate a North African origin. The word bantu means "people."

By putting most of the Bantus in enclaves the government hopes to reach the point where Bantus and whites will be about equal in numbers within the white industrialized areas.

A Partitioned Country

Those white areas then will constitute South Africa as far as the Government is concerned.

"It will be a partitioned country, but there won't be any more talk at the United Nations about South Africa's having a 'white minority government,'" one official said. "In our part there will be one of us for every black man."

Bantustans are the ultimate form of segregation—a separate state for a separate race. The Bantus in these "tribal areas" will be allowed to enter white areas as laborers and servants, but their status will be about that of a migrant.

On the 13.7 per cent of the country's land that the Bantustans will occupy, the 11.3 million Bantus are to have a limited political voice. Some form of sovereignty at an unspecified future date is promised.

Within projected homelands, South Africa says, the Bantus can develop along theor own "natural lines" within their tribal heritage and "aspire to the highest levels in all fields of human endeavor."

Each Bantu will be told by the Government where he can live and where he can work. Tens of thousands of Bantu families will be "repatriated" to Bantustans from South Africa's cities.

Eventually half the country's Bantu population will be settled in the enclaves. The other half at work in white areas will be subject to being shipped to Bantustans at any time.

Barred from Rich Areas

The great riches of the country—farms in Transvaal, the financial wealth of Johannesburg, the gold fields of Orange Free State, the industrial areas of Durban and Port Elizabeth —will be restricted to whites only.

Only those Bantus whom the Government deems essential to South Africa's economy will be allowed in white areas. In the words of one Government official, they will be "squatters and nothing more."

South Africa thus has conceived the Bantustan program as a final refinement of her policy of apartheid, or "apartness," which decrees that the country's 3.2 million whites must be separated racially and physically from its 13.8 Bantus, Asians and "coloreds"—those of mixed ancestry.

Bantustans take that policy one step further by stipulating that separation must also be geographic.

The first Bantustan will be Transkei, a tribal reserve about the size of Denmark. Its name means "place beyond the great river."

The largest of South Africa's tribal reserves, Transkei is on the southeastern coast between the Indian Ocean and the inland British protectorate of Basutoland.

On Thursday, the Government will hold an election that will give Transkei's 1.5 million Bantu residents limited internal self-government Dec. 11 with a territorial parliament.

The territory will be a Bantu political and economic dependency partly administered by the Bantus under white "guardianship."

South Africa has contributed the equivalent of $26.6 million for a five-year development plan for Transkei, where tribesmen wearing red blankets roam the hills ond the witch doctors prescribe crocodile meat to ward off evil.

As Transkei's Bantu leaders master what the Government terms "intricacies of modern democratic government," South Africa will grant further autonomy. The territory's status will be comparable to that of a province.

Will Have Own Flag

Initially, Transkei will have its own flag and national anthem, although it will be an integral part of South Africa.

The New York Times (by Robert Conley)

Transkeian women taking home bundles of grass for use in thatching roofs in village

It will be governed by a Bantu chief minister and a cabinet of five. They will answer to a legislative assembly of 103 Bantus. South Africa will have veto powers over all legislation.

The chief minister will be able to sit in forums of the Government in the "bunga" or council building, now being remodeled to house the new assembly, but not in the tearoom across the street, which is for "whites only."

So is all of Umtata, the territorial capital. If the chief minister wants to stay overnight, he will have to go outside the town limits. Umtata's hotels will not take him in.

Whites control all of Transkei's known mineral deposits, all of its industries, its 26 towns and its only potential harbor on the Indian Ocean, Port St. Johns.

South Africa says Transkei's Bantus will displace the territory's 17,369 whites in time, provided they have "capacity for it."

The new Bantu government will take charge progressively of the Departments of Finance, Justice, Interior, Education, Welfare and Labor, and Land, Agriculture and Forestry.

South Africa will retain control of police, prisons, defense, foreign affairs, internal security and the sale of arms and ammunition. She also will control railroads, harbors, national roads, mails, communications, immigration, currency and customs.

Every bill passed by the Territorial Legislative Assembly must be sent to South Africa's State President for his approval. The assembly cannot change Transkei's Constitution, nor can it vote the chief minister and his government out of office unless South Africa agrees.

South Africa intends to put the entire territorial administration in Bantu hands. Already tribesmen fill about 1,900 of the 2,476 civil service posts, a proportion higher than that in Tanganyika when that country attained independence from Britain.

Additional Bantus will be trained to displace th remaining whites "as progressively and as speedily as circumstances permit," South Africa says.

What concerns outsiders is the economic potential of the territory, where cattle are the common currency and mark of a tribesman's wealth. A quarter of the land is not arable. The rest can barely supply the present population, let alone absorb added thousands of Bantus "repatriated" from South Africa's white areas.

Agricultural officials say that Transkei has reached a point where half of the Bantu population, or about 750,000 people, have to be removed from the land now to improve crop outputs, which is now inadequate to feed the territory. Transkei has to import nearly 30 per cent of its corn, the basic food.

The territory's main export remains cheap labor. Its industries as yet are little more than elaborate hand crafts.

November 19, 1963

SEGREGATED CITY GROWS TO 500,000

South Africa Officials Point to Township's Advantages

JOHANNESBURG, South Africa, May 10 (AP)—Thousands of black families live in the model township of Soweto and the South African Government is eager to show that they have found a new life.

Soweto, a multimillion dollar project, is part of white South Africa's rebuttal to those who charge that the Government's policy of apartheid, or separate racial development, means that all black South Africans must live in mud huts.

Soweto (South Western Township), is the fourth largest city in South Africa and the biggest urban concentration of black people in the country. Nearly half a million people live in Soweto, seven miles from Johannesburg. The Government views the community as a keystone in its drive for total segregation of the races.

Whites Must Get Permits

Soweto has 24 sprawling suburbs, covering an area of 26 square miles. No whites are allowed to enter without a special permit and no white may own land or carry on any form of business there.

A Government official said: "Frankly, the African living in this area would be exploited by white and colored [mixed blood] businessmen if they were allowed to operate. High-pressure salesmanship by outsiders would leave little chance for the African businessmen to compete. Residents would be pressused into buying goods they do not require and can ill afford."

In the last decade, 58,000 houses have been built and more than $65.8 million has been spent in developing the showplace community.

Almost 7,000 houses costing $560 each have been purchased, with payments extended over 20 years. The other houses are rented for $2.80 to $11.20 monthly.

More than 2,000 dwellings, comparable to many seen in the upper-class white residential districts of Johannesburg, have been privately built. Some have servants' quarters and garages. The prices range from $5,600 to $28,000.

Three stadiums to seat 30,000 people, 70 sports fields, 58 basketball courts, swimming pools, cycle tracks, tennis courts and tracks are provided.

There are 114 schools for the 70,000 children.

On the boundary of the model township is the slum of Pimville, home of 32,000 black Africans.

One-room shacks house as many as 10 persons; a communal tap serves hundreds of people. The streets are muddy and undrained.

"Here you have the whole picture," the Government guide said, "—and heaven side by side. These slum areas exist and we admit it, but gradually they are being erased. It will take time, money and patience but the effort is being made."

May 11, 1964

South African Court Sentences 8 to Life

By ROBERT CONLEY
Special to The New York Times

PRETORIA, South Africa, June 12 — Eight persons were sentenced to life imprisonment today on the ground that they had plotted a "violent revolution" against South Africa's racial policies.

Nelson R. Mandela, Walter M. E. Sisulu and the other defendants convicted under the anti-sabotage laws stood drawn and pensive before the Supreme Court here as sentence was pronounced. It ended one of South Africa's longest political trials.

Mandela, the so-called "Black Pimpernel" of the South African freedom movement, and the bearded Sisulu are two of the country's most prominent African nationalist leaders.

"Sentence in the case of all of the accused will be one of life imprisonment," the presiding Justice, Quartas de Wet, said from the bench. The trial was conducted without a jury.

It was the severest sentence handed down against African nationalist leaders of the stature of Mandela and Sisulu in Africa.

Mandela, a 45-year-old lawyer and tribal prince, was deputy president of the African National Congress party, South Africa's oldest black political movement until it was banned for opposition to the country's policy of apartheid, or racial separation. Sisulu, 52, was the party secretary general.

The eight were found guilty yesterday of having carried out a campaign of sabotage against the white Government of South Africa's Prime Minister Dr. Hendrik F. Verwoerd.

In addition to Mandela and Sisulu, those sentenced to life imprisonment were:

Dennis T. Goldberg, 33, a Capetown civil engineer; Govan A. Mbeki, 53, a Port Elizabeth journalist, teacher and member of the Congress party's national executive; Ahmed H. Kathrada, 34, former secretary general of the Transvaal Indian Congress party; Elias Motsoaledi, 39, and Andrew Mlangeni, 38, both Congress party members, and Raymond Mahlaba, a party organizer.

June 13, 1964

The Two Worlds Of Jimmy Nkosi

By J. ANTHONY LUKAS

JOHANNESBURG.

WHEN Johannesburg's Africans sing of the city, they call her their "daylight wife":

You are our daylight wife
When the sun shines you beckon us
But at night you frown and we must leave you
To your bright lights and dark ways.

More than 190,000 Africans in South Africa's largest city pass their lives in this schizophrenic state. During the sunlight hours they work in the white world of skyscraper offices, department stores, factories and warehouses. When evening comes, they retreat again into the all-black world of the "Bantu townships," cut off from the city proper by antiseptic buffer strips of grass. ("Bantu" is a word commonly used by South African whites to refer to any black African.)

Lumbering, green buses of the public transport company bounce and jangle their way from the city to most of the townships in less than an hour. Electric trains make the trip in half an hour. White police units, riding in armored cars, can get to most townships in 15 minutes.

But to Jimmy Nkosi, who makes the trip five days a week 50 weeks a year, township and city seem "on different sides of the moon."

Jimmy Nkosi is not a typical African worker. A small, sharp-faced man, with a closely-trimmed mustache, he looks very much at home behind the desk of the Johannesburg advertising agency where he works as a research assistant. He earns 100 rand ($140) a month—about half what a white in a comparable position would make, but substantially more than an African factory worker or miner. The job brings him a dash of prestige and a nodding acquaintance with a few whites who may do him a favor now and then. In short, he is a member of the small African middle class which has begun to develop here within the past two decades.

Yet the two worlds of Jimmy Nkosi are not very different from those of any African who works in the city and lives in the townships. The advantages which he enjoys only heighten the frustration of his divided life. "Every once in a while I get a taste of how the white man must feel," he says, "and then the gate slams down and I remember where and what I am."

HE is never allowed to forget. He can wear his green Tyrolean hat, his well-cut black and white checked suit, his gray rep tie and his pointed shoes, but in the jacket pocket he must always carry his bulky "reference book" which Africans here call their "passport to nowhere." The book will identify him to any policeman or official as Dangenzela James Nkosi—No. 1034514, a "Bantu" of the Swazi tribe.

His father, like thousands of other young Swazis from the British protectorate of Swaziland, was recruited to work in the South African mines—in his case, on the huge Witbank coal mine north of Johannesburg. Jimmy's mother, a Xhosa from the Cape Province, was not permitted to live with her husband. So she set up house in a shanty township across the railroad tracks from Benoni, an industrial town 18 miles east of Johannesburg.

Two years after Jimmy was born there, in 1924, his father died in the mines, probably of silicosis. "He came from the family of the Swazi chieftancy," Jimmy says, "so the family took him back there to be buried. I've only been back to Swaziland once—on business, a few years ago. When I told people who my father was they all nodded and knew him. It was a nice feeling. But I don't think of myself as a Swazi any more. I'm almost completely detribalized."

After his father's death, Jimmy's mother went to work as a nanny for a white family in Johannesburg. With her earnings she brought up Jimmy and the two illegitimate children she later had. But it was the profits from his aunt's shebeen—an illegal African drinking shop—which helped put Jimmy through St. Alban's Anglican Mission School in Benoni, an Anglican boarding school in Pietersburg and then the Diocesan Teachers Training College.

In 1946, armed with a certificate equivalent to an American high school diploma, he went back to St. Alban's as a teacher. He stayed 13 years and might have been there still had it not been for the passage of the Bantu Education Act in 1953. This act, one of the first major pieces of apartheid legislation, placed all African education (including mission schools) in the hands of the Government. It was opposed by many Africans as an effort to "prepare pupils for a subordinate role in the country's life." Nkosi, then a teacher with considerable seniority, was as much concerned by the power the act put in the hands of politicians who, he says, "knew nothing about education."

In 1958 he resigned and decided to seek work in the white world of Johannesburg. At least theoretically, he faced two obstacles—South Africa's "influx control" and the "job reservation" laws.

The "influx control" regulations, designed to limit the number of Africans coming to the city, also provide that Africans must work in the district in which they live. Because Nkosi lived in a Benoni township rather than a Johannesburg township, he was theoretically barred from working in Johannesburg. In practice, this did not hamper him any more than it has thousands of others. With housing short in Johannesburg's townships and skilled labor in great demand, officials are prepared to wink at such violations.

"Job reservation" is likewise honored in the breach these days. Although many skilled jobs in industry and commerce are reserved by law for whites, there are simply not enough whites to fill them. The Government grants exemptions to employers who must hire Africans to keep their businesses going. Moreover, one kind of job for which Nkosi qualified has never been covered by job reservation. Large companies, increasingly aware of the African market, were looking for bright young Africans to help promote their products in the townships. Advertising companies were looking for Africans who could tell them why and what an African buys.

Nkosi began by selling cigarettes. Later he sold insurance and then radios. Finally, last June, he joined Grant Advertising Ltd., a South African subsidiary of an American company. He says the term "'research assistant' means I tell them what will make an African buy toothpaste or orange pop."

He works on the eleventh floor of the Parity Centre, a modern, glass-and-steel office building in the heart of Johannesburg's downtown business district. He shares a room with Beatrice Qubeka, another African research worker, but adjoining rooms are filled by whites.

"It works out pretty well. I've got a job to do and I do it. The whites have their jobs and they do them. When they need me to help solve a problem, they ask me very politely and I respond very politely. There's no scope for a clash. I've never had any trouble there."

Nor does he have any friends there. "We never get on that level. We're completely ignorant of each other's way of life. We don't see each other outside the office and we don't talk about things other than business. If one of their wives died, I would never be invited to the funeral. I probably would never be told."

"One account executive once asked me to call him by his first name, but I knew the others wouldn't approve. So I always just mumble his name when I see him. One secretary once said the same thing. But that's dangerous. If the police suspect that there's anything between a black man and a white woman except the master-servant relationship, you're really in trouble. They can get you on the immorality act. It's best to be careful."

ONCE outside the office, Nkosi must be even more careful. Although there are toilets for whites on each floor, Africans can use only those marked "Non-European Men" (or "Non-European Women") on the ground floor. There is also an elevator in the rear of the building set aside for Africans, but Nkosi and Miss Qubeka usually can use those in the front hall. "There used to be an old Afrikaner porter who would shout, 'Your elevator is back there!' but now that he's not here nobody seems to care."

Lunch poses a more difficult problem. There are no restaurants for Africans anywhere near the building. "The nearest one is about five blocks away, but the food there is horrible. Beatrice and I usually just buy a bread roll and some Vienna sausage at the carry-out counter of a white cafe and then eat it in the office."

Sometimes Nkosi does a little shopping at noon. All stores serve Africans, but some less rapidly than others. "Some salesmen just ignore you as long as there's a white customer around. Others let you stand even if there's nobody there, just to show you who's boss. Every once in a while you find a customer, usually an Afrikaner, who shouts, *'Staan weg, jong!'* ("Out of the way, you!") and elbows in front of you, but that doesn't happen very often these days.

"When you have troubles these days, it's almost always with Afrikaners. An English-speaking man will probably just ignore you. He'll look right through you as if you weren't there. But Afrikaners—particularly the policemen, postal clerks and ticket sellers in the railways—seem to resent us more and feel they have to say something."

When his work takes him elsewhere in the white city, Nkosi must ride either a ramshackle, "second class" (African) taxi or an African bus. If he goes out with company officials, they cannot ride together in a taxi. Usually they take a private car, but this can cause misunderstandings. "Once we were out with the managing director of a client firm. When we got where we were going, he told me to go park the car. When I hesitated, he asked my boss, 'Isn't that your boy?' It was very embarrassing."

Nkosi rarely stays in the white city after the working day is over at 5 P.M. Theaters, concert halls, movie houses and night clubs do not admit Africans. "Occasionally, a visiting stage show will have a one-night stand for black audiences. I always go if I can. I saw 'My Fair Lady' and 'Oliver!' But most shows we can never see. This makes me very sad. I love the theater."

Staying on too late in the city can also be dangerous. There is an 11 P.M. curfew for Africans in Johannesburg and a 10 P.M. curfew in Benoni. "I've been arrested four or five times for curfew violations. Once I slept in a lavatory in the city because I was afraid to go out. I could have tried to get to the train station, but I might have been arrested on the way. There are really only two safe places after curfew—the train station and a police cell."

So most nights he catches the 5:13 train from Johannesburg. The 40-minute ride home—and the one back again in the morning—are "the worst parts of the day," Nkosi says. "There are about seven cars for whites, but only one for Africans. Sometimes we get only part of the parcel van. At rush hours, up to 150 Africans try to cram into the car. We're packed in like cattle. You can hardly breathe."

IT'S a mile and a half walk from Dunswart station to house 689, Wattville Township, where Nkosi has lived for the past 14 years. Wattville, a monotonous series of gray concrete-block houses with corrugated tin roofs, was built in 1948 adjacent to the old Benoni "location" where Nkosi was born. House 689 is on a heavily rutted, red dirt road which dead-ends in a heap of orange peels and tin cans at the railroad track. A scraggly hedge and a fig tree in the front yard ("We planted them ourselves to help brighten the place up") partly shield the house from the clouds of dust which rise when a car bounces past.

Nkosi lives here with his wife, Priscilla, and their three children: 16-year-old Selbourne, 13-year-old Rosalind and 10-year-old Winston Hofmeyr (named after two of Nkosi's heroes: Winston Churchill and Jan Hofmeyr, the late spokesman for South African "liberals"). Most of his neighbors have factory jobs or work in the mines.

The house, for which Nkosi pays six rand ($8.40) a month, has five tiny rooms—two bedrooms, dining room, kitchen and a living room just big enough for two leatherette chairs, a small leatherette couch and a radio which is always on. Unlike many township houses, it has electricity—two naked electric bulbs which are passed through holes in the walls to light whatever room is in use—but there is no water-borne sewage (which most townships have). The outhouse in the backyard must be emptied with buckets.

Nkosi has been pressing for sewage facilities, better roads and better refuse collection as a member of the Benoni Advisory Board, a committee of seven Africans elected by residents of Wattville and Benoni Townships to represent them before the Benoni Town Council and other white officials.

The advisory boards have long been controversial institutions. Some Africans contend that those who serve on them are "stooges" because they work within the framework of apartheid and because they are paid for their services. (Nkosi gets 15 rand a month, compared to 100 rand for a white town councilman). Others argue that the boards, imperfect as they are, are the only means which township-dwellers have of making their grievances known.

Nkosi, who has served on the Benoni board since 1959, agrees with much of what the board's critics have to say. "I've been so disgusted that I've felt like resigning many times. We have absolutely no power and we know it. Any time we protest anything really important, the Town Council or the Bantu Affairs Commissioner merely shrug and say, 'That's government policy.' It all seems completely futile.

"I go on because I think somebody has to keep making a noise about these things. There are so many people in the township who are completely helpless, who have no other way of making their grievances known. In a real democracy they would have their Members of Parliament to speak for them. We don't have Members of Parliament, so we need to scream in the only forum we have available."

Nkosi believes that his noisy complaints have so annoyed some Benoni white officials that they would now like to get him off the board. He tells of a case in 1962, when he and two friends tried to dissuade an African constable who was arresting a man for urinating in the street, a common practice here. "We were arrested ourselves for obstructing a constable in the discharge of his duties. Normally, we would never have been prosecuted for something like that. However, we were taken to court. Why? I told the judge I believed white officials were retaliating for my criticism of them. Once you are convicted of any offense, you lose your seat on the board. We were acquitted."

Although Nkosi has been active in township politics, such as they are, he has kept carefully aloof from national politics.

"There simply is no party which represents my point of view. Among the white parties, the Nationalists and the United party are, of course, out. I reject apartheid. The Progressive party is out, too, as far as I'm concerned, because I could never accept a qualified franchise. I'm closer to the Liberal party, which accepts one-man-one-vote, but I'm afraid that the whites in the party would always insist on some form of white trusteeship. I could never accept that."

The two major African parties—the African National Congress and the Pan African Congress—are now banned, but Nkosi did not belong to either.

"There has never been an African political party in South Africa which really knew what it wanted and how to go out and get it. So far, most African politicians have been either unrealistic political theorists or just personally ambitious men who spent most of their time squabbling with each other."

However, his aloofness from national politics has not spared him the attention of the Special Branch, South Africa's secret police. Last July, during nationwide raids on "subversive elements," two Special Branch agents knocked on his door at 4:30 A.M. and said they were looking for "subversive literature." They found a copy of a pamphlet called "Benoni People Won't Fall Into Apartheid Trap," which attacked a government plan to move residents from Benoni location to a new township miles away. "They wanted to know how the pamphlet came into my possession, and I told them it was drawn up by the residents' association, of which I am a member but not an officer. A few days later they called me to their headquarters for more information about the pamphlet, which I gave.

"Once before, the Special Branch came and asked me whether I had organized a delegation to see a minister. I said I hadn't. The branch used to attend meetings in the townships, at which I was one of the most effective and informed speakers. I think this aroused their suspicion of me But I could assure them that I have never been connected with any subversive activity."

NKOSI has not only eschewed all political affiliations but has also severed his religious ties. He has dropped out of the Anglican church, in which he was brought up and educated and in which he later taught. "I haven't been to church for four or five years now," he says. "I guess the main reason is the church's insincerity on race matters. Officially, it says all Anglicans may worship together. In practice, it's next to impossible for a black to worship with whites here. Oh, there are a few white congregations in Johannesburg where black domestic servants may sit at the back of the church, but that doesn't impress me very much. The Anglican Bishops here make big declarations against government policy, but in practice they are always ready to appease the white section of their congregations and to condone the South African way of life.

"I still believe deeply in the teachings of Jesus Christ, but I find that many so-called Christians in South Africa don't follow those teachings."

Unlike some other Africans who have left the Christian churches, Nkosi does not have an essentially tribal religion to fall back on. "I gave up ancestor worship a long time ago. Most of my friends still slaughter a goat or a calf on any important occasion — like a funeral, a wedding or a birth— as a sacrifice to their ancestors. If I had a death in the family, I'd probably have to slaughter a calf, too, because my people still believe in their traditions and I wouldn't antagonize them. But I haven't slaughtered a beast for any of my children's births.

"My mother doesn't approve. She still thinks I should call in the witch doctor when the children are ill. When I refuse, she just shakes her head sadly. She says the witch doctor always used to cure me when I was a child. I can't remember. In that case I should have marks on my wrists from his knife or razor blade. But you can see I don't."

The only scars which Nkosi bears are from the knives of the *tsotsis*, the young gangsters who terrorize the townships at night. (There are also the "Russians," gangsters of Basuto origin who come into the township from the nearby mines over the weekend.) Nkosi has been assaulted five times in recent years — with fists, stones, bricks and knives. Once, about 10 years ago, he spent six weeks in the hospital with a stab wound which penetrated his left lung. "They didn't even take my money that time; just threw pepper in my eyes, cut me and left me bleeding on the road. That's their idea of fun."

He and his friends stay off the townships' streets as much as possible after 8 P.M., or travel in groups of three or four.

Monday and Friday nights they usually assemble at The Bus Stop, a shebeen operated by a Wattville widow in her parlor. Shebeens are illegal drinking shops which developed here during the years in which Africans were forbidden to drink "white man's liquor." This prohibition has since ended, but the unlicensed shebeens —two years later—still outdraw the cold and impersonal Government-run beer halls and lounges. There are dozens of shebeens in Wattville and Benoni Townships, with names like The Glass House, The Four and Four and Auntie Jane's. But Nkosi and his friends have adopted The Bus Stop as their spot.

"I may go to the Government bar once a month for appearances, or to one of the other shebeens to see somebody, but I feel at home only at The Bus Stop. I always know I'll find some friends, some pretty girls and good music."

MUSIC plays an important part in his life. An accomplished piano player and singer, he was once a member of a Benoni swing band called The African Rhythmers. He also wrote songs, several of which have been recorded. His favorite, is "Wonke Amaxesha" ("All Times"):

All times of my life
All days of my life
I sit alone inviting sympathy
Thinking of you, my Nodoli.

Nkosi rarely plays the piano these days and he has given up songwriting altogether. But he is still an avid jazz and swing fan. He frequently goes to concerts in the townships by such African bands as The Hollywood Swingsters, The Jazz Messengers, The No Name Swing Band and The Jazz Dazzlers.

He is also a soccer fan. On weekends he like to watch The Flying Stars or The Tent Town Hawks in action on one of Wattville's scraggly fields. He is an official of the All-African Benoni Football Association, which recently had a sharp dispute with the Benoni Town Council over interracial sport. "Playing with whites is illegal, of course. We wanted to play with Indians and Coloreds, like many African teams do elsewhere in the country. However, the Benoni Town Council said no. They even pulled out the goal posts until we agreed to play only with Africans.

"That sort of thing really infuriates you because it's so silly. The frustrations are bad enough in the city during the day, but when you come home to the township and find them on the soccer field, too, well, it's enough to make you give up.

"From time to time I've thought idly about just pulling up my own stakes and leaving South Africa. I dream of being somewhere where I don't have all these frustrations and all this insecurity.

"But I don't think I'll ever do it. I love this country. I love it truly from the bottom of my heart. I'd like to see it looking better."

VERWOERD IS SLAIN BY AN ASSASSIN IN THE SOUTH AFRICAN PARLIAMENT; KILLER, WHITE, IS SUBDUED BY M.P.'S

Doctors Are Unable to Save Prime Minister, Stabbed 4 Times

Special to The New York Times

CAPETOWN, Sept. 6 -Dr. Hendrik F. Verwoerd, Prime Minister of South Africa and architect of apartheid, was stabbed to death on the front bench in the South African Parliament today.

The assassin was identified as Dimitri Stifianos, a white South African of Greek and Portuguese origin, about 45 years old.

Stifianos was a temporary parliamentary messenger. His co-workers said he had complained that Dr. Verwoerd, who advocated strict separation of the races, was doing too much for nonwhites and not enough for "poor whites."

[In Washington President Johnson deplored the assassination as "a stroke of violence that shakes the sensibilities of men who believe in law and order."]

Dr. Verwoerd, who would have been 65 years old on Friday, was dead when he reached a hospital within 10 minutes of being stabbed. Five doctors, four of them Members of Parliament, administered mouth-to-mouth resuscitation and intracardiac heart stimulants on the floor of Parliament.

Minister First on Spot

Cabinet Ministers and M.P.s rushed the powerfully built assassin, who appeared to have gone berserk, as he lashed out wildly with his knife.

The first to reach Stifianos was Frank Waring, Minister of Sport and Tourism, a former Rugby football star. The flashing knife ripped Mr. Waring's trousers and grazed the hand of another Government M.P. Finally Stifianos was knocked to the floor and carried from the chamber.

The Prime Minister's wife, Elizabeth, who was in the building, did not witness the stabbeing. She dashed to the floor of the chamber and kissed her husband before he was carried away on a stretcher.

In the tiny office from which he had worked for three weeks as a messenger, Stifianos, according to the other messengers, used to complain about Dr. Verwoerd's Government.

According to the others, he said he was a wanderer who had been born in Mozambique and had held various jobs. He told them he had been a court interpreter in Durban. He had been sent to Parliament by the state employment service in Capetown.

Inquiries built up a picture of a man who was a regular Bible reader yet a member of a small Buddhist group in Capetown, a penniless drifter who was frequently thrown out of his lodgings.

The other messengers noticed this morning that he was restive. He had arrived at 9:30 A.M. Shortly after 2 o'clock, he left the messengers' room for the floor of Parliament.

Pushing aside members, Stifianos thrust his way into the paneled chamber as the bells were ringing to summon M.P.'s for the start of one of the major debates of the session.

Spectators in the crowded public galleries, among them many children, saw him stride rapidly to the Prime Minister's green leather front bench to the right of the Speaker's carved, canopied dais. He pulled a gleaming dagger from under his navy blue messenger's coat and fell forward on Dr. Verwoerd.

The Prime Minister was stabbed four times—near the heart, in or near both lungs and in the carotid artery in the neck. Barely able to raise his arms in self-defense, he slumped forward.

After the first shocked silence there was pandemonium. Ministers, M.P.'s and spectators wept. At least two M.P.'s fainted in the lobby and others shouted with emotion.

An angry cluster of M.P.'s followed Stifianos as he was handed over to the police.

Shock, Then Chaos

After 15 minutes Parliament assembled to hear the Speaker, his voice choked with emotion but his tone level, say the traditional opening prayer. Again many Members wept.

This was the second attempt on Dr. Verwoerd's life. In April, 1960, David Beresford Pratt, a white farmer and businessman, who was subsequently found mentally unfit to stand trial, fired two small-caliber bullets into the Prime Minister's head as he was opening an agricultural show in Johannesburg.

Dr. Verwoerd recovered completely. Pratt hanged himself in a mental institution.

Cabinet Holds Meeting

Parliament adjourned until tomorrow, when a motion of condolence will be adopted. It will then adjourn until after the funeral, for which a date has not yet been announced.

Soon after the assassination the Cabinet met briefly and subsequently the two most senior Ministers, Dr. T. E. Donges, Minister of Finance and senior man in the Cabinet, and Barend J. Schoeman, Minister of Transport and Leader of the House, met briefly.

Dr. Donges, as the senior Cabinet member, took over as Acting Prime Minister. He had been expected to retire at the end of the current parliamentary session but may now reconsider his plans if, as is possible, he emerges as the choice for caretaker Prime Minister.

Dr. Donges, who issued a statement appealing for calm, said that the motives for the attack were still not known and that the police were making a thorough investigation. The message added:

"In these—for South Africa —strange times, I want to appeal to everyone to keep calm. The Cabinet will continue with its ordinary work and the police will leave no stone unturned to get behind the reasons for this dreadful act. This is not a time for rumors or speculation, and still less for people to lose their heads.

"South Africa loses a dedicated, a skilled and dynamic leader who for eight years had stood at the helm and planned and experienced the most spectacular development in every sphere."

At the Peak of His Power

The Prime Minister died at the peak of his power. Earlier this year the National party had continued in office with the biggest majority in the history of South Africa's Parliament. Despite tendencies toward inflation, the economy is booming. Only two months ago, Dr. Verwoerd had won a major victory at the International Court of Justice at The Hague on the issue of the administration of South-West Africa.

Dr. Verwoerd had been expected to make a major policy statement on the future pattern of relations with independent African states and on a still ill-defined concept of an African common market.

Just four days ago he made history by meeting a black Premier, Chief Leabua Jonathan of the enclave of Basutoland, in Pretoria, the administrative capital.

The National party's parliamentary caucus will choose the Prime Minister's successor, but probably not for a few weeks. There is no obvious successor, but the likely claimants are Dr. Donges, Mr. Schoeman and Balthazar J. Vorster, Minister of Justice.

—The nation appeared stunned, but there was little sympathy among black Africans, who hated Dr. Verwoerd.

"Thank God it wasn't one of our people who did it," a black African woman remarked.

Mrs. Helen Suzman, the only opponent of the Government in Parliament and a member of the Progressive party, was present when Prime Minister Verwoerd was assassinated.

"One of the most ghastly shocks I've experienced!" she said.

September 7, 1966

Rigid South African

Balthazar Johannes Vorster

Special t. The New York Times

JOHANNESBURG, South Africa, Sept. 13—South Africa has had four Prime Ministers since the Nationalist party came to power in 1948 on a wave of Afrikaner nationalism and racial fear. Each has seemed more extreme than his predecessor.

Man in the News

In naming Balthazar Johannes Vorster (pronounced FORCE-ter) successor to the murdered Hendrik F. Verwoerd, the Nationalists have gone about as far as they can go. Beyond doubt, he is the hardest man in the party.

In 1948 even the Nationalists thought Mr. Vorster too much the extremist for admission to their ranks. They had not forgiven him for bolting the party at the start of World War II to join the militant Ossewa Brandwag (Ox-Wagon Guard), which was dedicated to sabotaging South African participation in the Allied effort.

Mr. Vorster was fired by the belief that Afrikaner nationalists and the Nazis had a common cause. Asked at the time to say what he stood for, he replied: "You can call it the antidemocratic system of dictatorship if you wish. In Italy it is called Fascism, in Germany National Socialism and in South Africa Christian Socialism."

'General' and Prisoner

He became a "general" of the movement and in 1942 was arrested and interned for two years as Prisoner 2229/2 in Bungalow 48—numbers he has never forgotten—at a detention camp at Koffiefontein, in the Orange Free State.

"I was 26 at the time and decided to go on a hunger strike," he later recalled. "I threatened to continue with it if I was not charged with some offense or released."

Political prisoners detained without trial have made similar appeals to Mr. Vorster since he became Minister of Justice, Police and Prisons in 1961. They have never moved him. Nothing, apparently, has, except a stern sense of mission to preserve the power of the white man in South Africa.

"It is no time to be sensitive about principles," he told Parliament last year in what has become an annual appeal for additions to his arsenal of arbitrary powers.

Sweeping Authority

Those have included the power to ban organizations, to bar individuals from all political activities, to make it a crime to publish anything such individuals have said or written, to keep them under house arrest for up to 24 hours a day, to deprive them of the right of habeas corpus, to hold them in solitary confinement for periods of 90 days to get information, to do the same to possible state witnesses for 180 days and to detain political prisoners indefinitely.

Mr. Vorster has used those powers ruthlessly — first against black nationalists, then against Communists and finally against liberals who persisted in speaking out.

Camera Press-Pix

"No time to be sensitive about principles."

The policeman of apartheid—strict separation of the races—wears power comfortably. He is a large man, barrel-chested and broad-shouldered. His gestures are sharp and emphatic. Because of high blood pressure, his face is usually flushed.

Far more than Dr. Verwoerd, he is a rousing orator, alternately beguiling and caustic, sometimes evangelistic. In an impassioned peroration, he will spread his arms wide and vibrate his fingers like a conductor summoning a last great effort from his chorus.

Cooler in Parliament

His parliamentary style is more restrained, approaching informality. When speaking from the second row of ministerial benches, where he sat as a junior minister until today, he was apt to put his foot on his seat and lean on his knee. The quickest in debate on the Nationalist side of the house, he is sometimes even witty in an icy way.

Balthazar Vorster was born Dec. 13, 1915, on a farm in Jamestown, in Cape Province, the 13th of 14 children.

(It was being said today that 13 is his lucky number, representing not only his birthday and place in his family but also the number of years he has been in Parliament, his ranking by seniority in the Cabinet, his golf handicap and, now, the day on which he was elected Prime Minister.)

He won notice as a Nationalist student leader at Stellenbosch University, where Dr. Verwoerd, then a psychology professor, was one of his tutors. Before the war he practiced law in Port Elizabeth. Afterward he moved north to the Transvaal, settling in Brakpan.

In 1941 he married a university sweetheart, Martini (called "Tini") Malan, daughter of the chairman of the powerful Nationale Pers Publishing Company. They have two sons and a daughter.

Mr. Vorster's policy speeches have invariably been belligerent expressions of white nationalist themes. It was characteristic that he made no reference at all to South Africa's large nonwhite majority in his first remarks as Prime Minister.

Mr. Vorster is closely identified with those in South Africa who believe there is scant difference between Communism and Western liberalism and that white South Africa's only security is to build an impregnable bastion.

He once said he had learned three important truths in life: "never to underestimate an opponent, never to overestimate one's own abilities and never to hesitate to abandon philosophical tenets if the situation requires."

September 14, 1966

South African, Badly Hurt, Awaits Proper Ambulance

DURBAN, South Africa Aug. 1 (Reuters) — A white man critically injured in an auto accident lay on the road for an hour and a half last night because the ambulance that arrived on the scene was for nonwhites only and left without him.

An ambulance for whites reached the scene of the accident, near Mtunzini, 80 miles north of here, after an hour and a half and took the man to a hospital 15 miles away.

A hospital official said the African driver of the first ambulance had been obeying instructions when he left the victim to call for the proper ambulance.

August 2, 1967

SOUTH AFRICA SIGNS MALAWI TRADE PACT

Special to The New York Times

CAPETOWN, March 13—South Africa signed a trade pact with Malawi here today, its first formal agreement with an independent black African state since the Nationalist Government came to power 19 years ago.

The Government said the pact was a breakthrough for Prime Minister Balthazar J. Vorster's policy of establishing links with black states, which have isolated South Africa since 1948 because of the Nationalist Government's apartheid policy.

Malawi's President, Dr. H. Kamazu Banda, has avoided taking part in the Organization of African Unity's boycott campaign against South Africa.

March 14, 1967

In South Africa, Hints of Change

By TERTIUS MYBURGH
Special to The New York Times

DURBAN, South Africa, Sept. 5 — Three years ago tomorrow, Dr. Hendrik F. Verwoerd, Prime Minister of South Africa and architect of the policy of racial separation known as apartheid, was murdered in Parliament by a mentally deranged drifter.

John Vorster, then the Minister of Justice, who had a reputation for toughness in smashing so-called subversive groups through harsh legislation of his own design, became Prime Minister a week later.

Today he presides over a governing Nationalist party that is grievously troubled by internal divisions. He runs a country of 19 million that still practices apartheid, but the policy is undermined daily by the extraordinary growth of the economy. There is internal peace, but it is achieved at immense cost in individual liberty to the vast nonwhite majority and to those in the radical opposition.

Most significant of all, three years after Dr. Verwoerd, the rigidity has gone from the somewhat bewildered Nationalist Government and distinct signs of change are discernible.

First, the Nationalist party is no longer the monolithic political instrument it was under Dr. Verwoerd. Two feuding groups have developed, and only this week Mr. Vorster conceded again at a Nationalist party convention in Port Elizabeth that in the 1971 provincial elections it would have to fight on two fronts — against the opposition United and Progressive parties on the one hand and against extreme racist right-wing Nationalists on the other.

Of the two feuding groups that have developed in the Nationalist party, the majority, the so-called verligtes, or enlightened ones, is grouped around Mr. Vorster, whose reputation as chief jailer is being displaced by a benign if ineffectual image.

The as-yet leaderless verkramptes, or narrow-minded ones, are skirting an open challenge to his authority but are sniping at his policies and attempting to infiltrate key party posts.

The internal dispute has obscure tribal roots but is essentially over whether the Afrikaners, who make up about 60 per cent of the white population of almost four million, should adhere to their dogmatic isolationism and racialism of old or whether their policies should be adapted pragmatically in an attempt to bring them more in line with the demands of the contemporary world.

More specifically, the dispute arises from verkrampte mistrust of Mr. Vorster's policies of seeking friendship with black African states and of recruiting English-speaking whites to a party hitherto almost exclusively for those of Teutonic stock.

As the annual spring series of party conventions gets under way, Mr. Vorster is being accused of weak leadership because, to preserve unity, he attacks the rebels but refuses to flush them into the open and force a showdown. Meanwhile, they are building up a following among white farmers and poor white urban workers who have a vested interest in white domination.

At the same time the implementation of the Verwoerd policy of "big apartheid" — to entice millions of black Africans out of "white" urban areas to rural reserves, which will gain independence and will be the only places where the blacks will have the franchise — is coming to a halt.

The Government has drawn lines on a map demarcating ethnic ministates-to-be and a legislative structure has been erected. But neither artificial lures such as massive state aid, industries on the reserves' borders and promises of the vote, nor laws empowering the state to force the blacks from cities have been able to halt the flow to reviving urban areas. And to the relief of white industrialists, the Government usually looks the other way while they slip blacks into jobs that are technically reserved for the whites.

Costs but No Advantages

Consequently, blacks living in white areas experience all the hurt of apartheid and none of its alleged advantages. In the cities they face segregation in every sphere — even different post-office counters. Harsh restrictions, on such a scale that they are troubling the Dutch Reformed Church, remove all rights of permanency and cause the wholesale break-up of family life, with the unemployed consigned to rural reserves.

Despite all this there are no signs of black unrest in urban areas. Intent on earning more money and working at more skilled jobs, the blacks show scant interest in politics. In any case, black nationalist movements such as the African National Congress and the Pan-American Congress have been proscribed, with their leaders either jailed or forced into exile. A widespread informer network insures that any revival is averted.

The booming economy is based on phenomenal industrial expansion and on South Africa's ability to sell newly mined gold to foreign central banks as well as on the free market -- despite United States opposition. If agriculture, which suffered from a drought, is excluded, gross national product increased by 7 per cent in the last fiscal year. Consumer spending has risen by 7.3 per cent a year for the last decade and stands at more than $9-billion annually.

Prime Minister Vorster's most promising innovation has been in the field of foreign policy. The diplomatic thrust northward to establish links with black states is receiving the highest priority. Close ties have been established with neighboring Lesotho, Swaziland and Botswana and a second black diplomat, from Malawi, arrived in Pretoria this week to become part of a newly nonracial social round in the capital.

Zambia is a special diplomatic target, and a dialogue with President Kenneth D. Kaunda continues covertly despite public animosity. Tentative contacts have been made with Gabon and Madagascar. Kenya and Uganda and, reliable reports have it, even hostile Tanzania trade secretly with South Africa.

In spite of boycotts by the United States and most of the Western world except France, South Africa has built up a defense force to withstand all but a major assault. The defense budget runs to $500-million annually and this week the Minister of Defense Piet Botha, said that South Africa was getting all the arms she wanted. He said she made what she could not buy, including jet trainers.

He has launched a campaign to convince the West of his country's value as a custodian of the east-west sea route since the Suez Canal is closed and Britain is withdrawing from the Indian Ocean.

Power and Resilience

South Africa remains the home of harsh race theories, but when her power and resilience are noted and the new internal pressures examined, fresh possibilities of change are detectable. However, white South Africans who oppose apartheid have little influence and less power. Outspoken people like Helen Suzman, the liberal leader, and Alan Paton are supported by an insignificant number of whites.

The economic sanctions that are often sought at the United Nations might depress the economy slight but would scarcely cause a dent in the Nationalists' hold on the reins of power. A recession could lead to increasing black unemployment and possibly unrest, but the Government has sufficient power to control it.

Peaceful change can come in two ways. As the economy thrusts ahead white politicians who have promised white voters both prosperity and apartheid will find it more difficult to juggle the economy and the race laws in the hope of keeping both. And as blacks gain more economic power, either as producers or as consumers, they must inevitably gain more acceptance.

Perhaps most hopeful of all is the ferment in Afrikaner thinking and the emergence of a powerful and enlightened element willing to face up to contradictions in their thinking as they become more culturally and politically secure and face the demands of an industrialized state and of emergent black Africa.

It is a fragile thing so far, but change is in the air in South Africa. It remains to be seen whether Mr. Vorster either can or wants to override the reactionaries and to force the pace out of the twilight.

September 6, 1969

Zulus Can't See 'Zulu' in South Africa

Special to The New York Times

JOHANNESBURG, South Africa, Nov. 16—Five hundred Zulus waving property-room assagais — or spears — helped make a movie called "Zulu" on location in South Africa a few years ago It dealt with the battle of Rorkesdrift where about 80 British soldiers held out against an overwhelming force of Zulu impis, or battle divisions, on Jan. 22-23, 1879.

But not one of the 500 extras nor any of South Africa's 15 million blacks has seen the movie although it has made the circuit of local theaters twice.

South Africa's Publications Control Board, an autonomous body, decided that the movie was not fit for black African consumption. Presumably the censors felt it might give the now docile Zulus the idea of taking up their assagais again.

In South Africa apartheid policies are as strict on movie-going as they are on living areas, jobs and the use of public transport.

Movies Are Limited

Movies banned to nonwhites have included "The Incident," "Sweet Charity," "The Detective," "Prudence and the Pill," "The Boston Strangler,""Rosemary's Baby," "West Side Story," "Africa Addio" "The Mercenaries," "Valley of the Dolls," and "Che!"

Black Africans, but not coloreds or Indians, have been forbidden to see "Tom Jones," "The Dirty Dozen," "Darling," "The Magnificent Seven," "From Russia with Love," "Spartacus," "A Farewell to Arms," and "One Hundred Rifles," which starred a Negro actor, Jim Brown.

A black African recently complained in a letter to a nonwhite weekly newspaper that black Africans are allowed to see only "second rate secret-service films and rather low-type Westerns."

Recent titles at Johannesburg theaters for black Africans included "Booted Baby," "Busted Boss," "Glory Guys," "Track of Thunder," "Long Ride from Hell," "Stage Struck," "Kiss the Girls and Make Them Die," and "Tarzan and the Huntress."

Film makers here estimate that only 7 per cent of the black African population has ever seen a movie. This is due in part to a shortage of theaters. Soweto, a sprawling African township outside Johannesburg with a population of 600,000, has just opened its second movie theater. Curfews, township crime and inadequate transport limit movie-going.

There are a few multiracial movie theaters in the larger towns and cities.

Demand Increasing

"Not for Bantu. No children 4-12" is the notice frequently displayed outside box offices.

As black Africans become more urbanized and better educated and as their importance as consumers grows, the demand for better movies increases.

Mrs. D. Mabiletsa, director of a welfare center in Alexandra Township — a shanty town outside Johannesburg—says: "Cinema-going is an aspect of our new township culture. Standards and aspirations are rising. More and more Africans have radios and they are asking: 'If you can hear why not also see?"

Johannesburg's Urban Bantu Council recently attacked the Publications Control Board's restrictions. "The judgment of a particular group is being imposed on the freedom of choice of the whole African community," it said.

Censorship has become harsher as the attitudes of international film-makers have changed. The freer use of sex, the appearance of Negroes in dignified and leading roles and the growing emphasis on civil rights make movies increasingly unacceptable to the South African censors.

One certificate issued by the censors said: "No Bantu. No persons 4-12. Excisions: eliminate shot of white man kissing colored girl. Eliminate whole of bed scene."

Local Movies Planned

It is estimated that eight times as many films are banned to Africans as to whites.

South Africa's small movie industry is planning to cash in on this movie starvation. Encouraged by a recent Government decision to increase subsidies for films in Afrikaans — the language of most of South Africa's whites — two groups have announced plans to make films specifically for African consumption.

Thirty-year-old Andre Pieterse, who built up a massive chain of drive-in movies, has set up a new organization called Film Trust. "South Africa has a responsibility toward its Bantu people," he says. "My plan is to develop a Bantu film industry with an estimated annual turnover of 25 million rand (about $35-million)."

"The choice of imported films is becoming increasingly difficult since liberal and permissive thinking seems to predominate in most overseas films," he says. "I intend to make South Africa the Hollywood of Africa. It is we, the people of South Africa, who understand the Bantu. We are better able to produce films to their liking than Hollywood, Moscow or Peking."

Mr. Pieterse is starting with a James Bond-type series of films. Another local moviemaker, Anthony Handley, has already begun filming "Knockout," the first of a projected series of movies. The theme is boxing instead of espionage.

November 17, 1969

SCHOOL GAP FOUND IN SOUTH AFRICA

JOHANNESBURG, South Africa, Feb. 28 (AP) — A black African woman earning $192 a year as a domestic servant pays $90 a year to keep her four children in school.

When schools opened last fall, thousands of black African pupils were turned away because there was no place for them.

An examination of the black school system in South Africa indicates a wide gap between official doctrine—"separate but equal" societies for the races under apartheid—and the reality of education for the black majority.

Black African schools are overcrowded, especially in urban areas where blacks go to work for the white man. Teachers are often badly qualified and teaching facilities rudimentary. The situation is improving but not nearly quickly enough, critics of the Government's education policy believe.

Blacks Pay Fees

The average black African earns the equivalent of $44.80 a month, and many cannot afford the schooling provided by the Bantu Education Department.

Unlike other racial groups, black Africans pay for their children's text books, writing and handicraft materials, secondary school examination fees and sometimes registration and sports fees. Whites, Asians and coloreds, better able to afford the additional fees, pay few of them unless they send their children to private schools.

With too many pupils for too few schools, those who cannot afford the rising costs are consigned to illiteracy.

A recent survey in a township in coastal Port Elizabeth showed that black Africans pay a third to a half of their wages on educating their children.

Books alone cost about $10 for junior school pupils and $30 to $50 for high school pupils. One school principal said he insists his pupils buy books on the first day of term.

"I must do it because parents take too long to buy books for their children. Those who have no books create a problem at school."

Vacancies in Homelands

Under the Government's "separate development" plan, black

Africans are being encouraged to move from the cities to segregated tribal "homelands," where they are eventually to be granted limited autonomy. School building for blacks is therefore not being encouraged in white urban areas.

Officials say there are enough vacancies in homelands such as the Transkei for pupils unable to enroll in the cities. But black families often cannot afford travel costs.

The Government had more than 9,500 schools for the country's 13 million blacks in 1968, and school spokesmen said they were educating 78 per cent of the school-age population.

Yet the dropout rate is so high that only 30 per cent of the children are educated past the fourth school year. Although the number of high school graduates increased by 10 per cent last year, the figure was still only 1,593 of a total school-age population of about 2.5 million. Only 65 qualified for entrance to one of the Government's segregated tribal university colleges.

Critics say the system is "bottom heavy" and concentrates mainly on eliminating outright illiteracy. They feel that adequate secondary education is needed if black community leaders are to be trained for the homelands.

Full Curriculum Scarce

Of the 9,500 schools for blacks in 1968, only 89 provided a full high school curriculum. There were seven technical secondary schools, 30 vocational-training schools and 34 teachers' colleges.

Of 31,705 black African teachers outside the Transkei homeland in 1968, 87 per cent had not been graduated from high school.

An education commission backed jointly by the South African Council of Churches and the Christian Institute recently found that school children of all races are being taught that apartheid is the only acceptable policy for South Africa. There are about 3.5 million whites, compared with the 13 million blacks.

The commission, under the chairmanship of Raymond Tunmer, a senior education lecturer at Johannesburg's Witwatersrand University, criticized Government education for attempting to insure the continuation of racial division and the retardation of "processes of change within these groups."

The commission also criticized the authorities for "making the least privileged group pay to a large extent for their own education."

March 1, 1970

Nationalists' Margin Cut in South Africa

By TERTIUS MYBURGH
Special to The New York Times

DURBAN, South Africa, April 23 — The Nationalist party of Premier John Vorster has been returned to power with a reduced but still overwhelming majority in Parliament.

For the first time in 22 years of rule it has lost a significant amount of support to the opposition United party. The voting yesterday reflected a shift in a mildly leftward direction among many white voters.
ers.

The Nationalists realized Mr. Vorster's aim of completely crushing far right-wing splinter group, the Reconstituted Nationalist party, formed last year by a former Cabinet Minister, Dr. Albert Hertzog. But Mr. Vorster failed in his attempt to bring English-speaking whites into the Nationalist fold.

The Hertzog group, which called for an end to diplomatic contacts with black African states and an even more harsh brand of white supremacy at home, failed to win a single seat. In the old Parliament it had four members, who were elected as Nationalists but bolted to form the new party. The Reconstituted Nationalists' 79 candidates managed to poll only a total of 50,000 votes.

Vet Loss of Two Seats

The liberal Progressive party's sole representative in Parliament, Mrs. Helen Suzman, was re-elected with a greatly increased majority. The votes for the 18 other Progressive candidates showed a substantial increase, mostly at the expense of the United Party.

With only a few predictable results from outlying areas to come, it is clear that in the new parliamental Nationalist party, which advocates territorial apartheid, or separation of races, through creation of separate independent states called Bantustans, will have 117 seats. It had 119 in the old Parliament.

The united party, which resists fragmentation of the country and advocates representation for Africans in Parliament by whites, will have 48, a gain of nine.

In domestic political terms, the election appears to be a severe personal setback for Mr. Vorster. By calling elections a year earlier than required, he had hoped not only a crush the Hertzog group but also to expand the base of the Nationalist into a united white front, including the English-speaking whites.

He all but destroyed the Hertzog movement and he demonstrated that the Nationalist party was able to hold the loyalty of most Afrikaners, the descendants of Dutch settlers.

But the English-speaking whites rejected him and turned out with unfamiliar vigor to vote for their traditional parties. Mr. Vorster had hoped that the English would react to the rightists by supporting him in an attempt to keep the extremists out. But the government majorities were reduced in virtually every contest.

Options for Vorster

This loss of support was viewed as a reaction to a regime that is considered by some to be administratively flabby and inefficient, increasingly careless about bread-and-butter interests of the electorate and less and less concerned about softening or even concealing injustices to nonwhites under the apartheid policy. The cautious United party can hardly be called liberal, and by standards of the outside world the election result may seem to indicate little change. But viewed in the context of South Africa's static political tradition, it does at least reflect what the Rand Daily Mail of Johannesburg called in an editorial today "a trend towards moderation."

The question now is whether er Mr. Vorster, conscious of the slight swing leftward as reflected in the failure of the Hertzog group and gains by the opposition, will press ahead more vigorously with his "outward" diplomatic policies, which appear to be supported by whites of all parties, or whether he will press ahead with apartheid in an attempt to buttress his position within the Nationalist party.

It also remains to be seen whether the United party, with the more liberal Progressives threatening it from the left, will adopt more liberal policies.

While any shifts across the political spectrum will of course be an all-white affair, the primary issue remains what it has always been — what to do about the nonwhites.

As usual, they appeared passively unconcerned in public about the events of the last two days.

The turnout among South Africa's 2.2 million eligible white voters was put at nearly 90 per cent. None of the country's 14.8 million nonwhites — 12.4 million Africans, 547,000 Asians and 1.8 million coloreds (mixed races)—was permitted to vote.

April 24, 1970

Blacks in South Africa Developing a New Awareness

By MARVINE HOWE
Special to The New York Times

JOHANNESBURG, South Africa, July 7—The policy of racial separation, designed to preserve white privileges, is stirring among blacks a new consciousness of their identity that represents a challenge to the Nationalist Government's plan for separate but harmonious racial development.

In almost every domain an atmosphere of resistance is developing as the Government intensifies the application of race laws. Deep resentments are becoming increasingly evident at every point of racial friction.

Also contributing to the establishment of a new black identity is the policy of Bantustans, or black homelands.

International condemnations and boycotts, while cutting off contacts, have helped to dignify South Africa's blacks. Economic progress, which has brought them some satisfaction, has also made them more aware of their rights as citizens.

At the same time the white bridgebuilders, and they are numerous in liberal political circles and church groups and among artists and students, are finding it increasingly difficult to make contact with the blacks.

As for the Government, it has accelerated its vast resettlement program, displacing thousands of black, Indian and mixed-blood families to make room for whites. The numbers involved are not disclosed, but the Government said last year that there were 3.8 million "superfluous" blacks in urban areas who would be resettled.

Plans have just been announced for the removal of 100,000 blacks from the vital Natal watershed under pressure from eight white farm associations.

White liberal groups such as Black Sash and the Opposition press have protested all along against the mass uprooting of people. Now the blacks themselves are beginning to show some resistance.

A branch of the Sotho tribe was suddenly informed earlier this year that its 20,000 acres had been expropriated and concessions given to a mining company. The equivalent of $168,000 was put in trust to pay for resettlement. The tribal chiefs, who hold a deed dating to 1888, have decided to take the case to court.

Platinum for a Pittance

Another tribe sold the rights to a platinum deposits to a British company for a pittance. The chief's son disapproved of the deal and went to management consultants, who are demanding a 20 per cent share in the company and 40 per cent management for the tribe and a guarantee that tribesmen will be promoted to skilled jobs. The company has agreed to rescind the contract and start over.

Many individuals resist removal. The Bantu Affairs Courts are always full of blacks who have not complied with laws controlling movement and have been picked up without the necessary residence or travel documents. It is estimated that nearly two million people, nearly all blacks, were prosecuted as criminals last year for infringements of the pass laws, which restrict freedom of movement, place of residence and choice of occupation. Every black over age 18 must carry a document proving his eligibility to live and work in a particular area.

There are countless cases of blacks who have been ordered out of white areas but simply refused to go.

On 72 hours' notice, Christina, a married woman of 45 living with her husband and child in the vast black township of Johannesburg known as Soweto, was told to go to her "homeland," where she knows no one. "I'll just roam around here until they arrest me and send me away, but I'll come back," she said with a shrug.

4 Children, $5 a Month

A widow from the Transkei Bantustan worked as a farm laborer for $5 a month to support four children. To educate her children she came to Johannesburg and got a job as a servant but she has no legal right to be here. "I know I can be arrested at any time and sent to Transkei, but there's nothing else to do," she said.

An orphan boy from the Ciskei Bantustan who is enrolled in a Soweto high school has been ordered out. His uncle, a legal resident of Soweto, wanted to take him in but that was prohibited. The boy is seeking help from the Black Sash Advice Office, a group of white volunteers who help blacks cope with the pass laws.

There is increasing awareness among blacks that they have some rights and they are beginning to stand up for them.

Blacks will protest more often if they feel they have been shortchanged by shopkeepers.

A student insulted by a white man is not afraid to talk back. If a black and a white fight for the same parking space, the black will not automatically give in to "master," as he used to.

The underlying racial tension is quick to surface. In any serious accident such as a train collision the black victims react with racial hatred. Recent riots at sports events were racial. Blacks and coloreds, as those of mixed blood are known here, systematically cheer any visiting team against the local white team, and the whites resent it.

Black Groups Smashed

On a broader front, the Nationalists have successfully smashed all militant political organizations under what are known as the Suppression of Communism and Terrorism Acts. Virtually all active political leaders have been imprisoned, forced into exile or restricted. However, the blacks are solidifying their ranks or building nonpolitical organizations.

The African Teachers Association is working to improve conditions and consolidate its organization. Up to now it has soft-pedaled the struggle for rights.

The Urban Bantu Council of Johannesburg, a rubber-stamp civic body, is demanding more powers and greater autonomy to deal with black affairs. The Association for Education and Cultural Advancement, formed in 1968, aims to get every black child into school and more blacks into the universities. With education free and compulsory for whites only, the 1969 university enrollment was 68,500 whites in a population of 3.5 million and under 4,000 blacks out of 13 million.

There was an outcry in 1959 when the Government barred nonwhites from English universities, but now the blacks, Indians and coloreds are making the best of their separate colleges and demanding higher standards.

A white clergyman observed that "the Government has done more to create African nationalism by segregating universities than the African National Congress," the forbidden black freedom movement.

Afro Wigs Are In

The new feeling of black dignity occurs among students in particular—to some extent as part of a worldwide accent on negritude but also as a specific reaction to apartheid. Students have begun to call themselves black instead of nonwhite or non-European. Even anti-apartheid Indians now claim to be black.

Advertisements in newspapers are beginning to hail the virtues of blackness. Afro wigs are coming in and whitening creams going out.

The blacks held their first debutante ball in Soweto last month, and it was a glittering affair. The 20 impeccably-gowned girls curtsied in the royal style. "We aren't aping whites but reasserting our identity," one of the organizers said.

The expanding economy is one of the main sources of the black breakthrough. Drastic labor shortages are breaking down restrictive job laws and forcing blacks' wages up. The Government has had to make grudging concessions, bringing blacks into formerly white jobs in such areas as the railroads, the building industry and engineering.

"Economic confidence is making blacks want to be full citizens," the Most Rev. Denis E. Hurley, Roman Catholic Archbishop of Durban, said. He expressed regret that the church had not taken the lead in solving social and racial problems.

Doctors Win More Money

Black doctors have won salary increases through protest. Nurses held a congress in Durban last week to ask for better pay and working conditions.

Even the Bantustan policy is beginning to backfire. Blacks who had fought the plan believe now that a federation of Bantustans could be a springboard to integration.

Gatsha Buthelezi, the new Chief Executive of Zululand, has made it clear that he intends to use the Bantustan policy to get more land and better educations and jobs for his people. He has won support from other Bantustan chiefs who formerly were considered stooges for the whites.

The New York Times (by Marvine Howe)

Women of Kwa Mashu, a Zulu section outside Durban, South Africa, sitting near their huts waiting for job offers

Foreign attitudes have also helped crystalize the new black awareness and have brought some concessions from the Government of Prime Minister John Vorster. The United Nations' condemnations of apartheid since 1946 have strengthened the blacks' belief in integration as a final solution.

It is said that international criticism forced the Government to develop the Bantustan policy in an effort to demonstrate the positive side of apartheid. It was apparent that the rush in 1967 to build schools, hospitals and roads in Namibia, formerly South-West Africa, came in response to world pressures.

Sports boycotts had forced the Government to agree to send a mixed team to the Olympics. Then exclusion from the Olympics raised strong pressure in this sports-minded country for mixed trials.

The Government's attempts to win friends, particularly among nearby black states, has had no effect on internal policy but, again, has elevated blacks here in their own eyes.

'New Expectations' Inevitable

"It is impossible for our people not to get new expectations when they see a black man like Banda, who once worked in a Joburg mine, now fraternizing with the Prime Minister," a black teacher said, referring to the President of Malawi.

The emerging black consciousness is most strongly felt by the white liberals who have struggled to maintain contact in the face of Government restrictions. The Rev. Beyers Naude, director of the Christian Institute, says that over the last two years there has been a large-scale withdrawal of blacks from areas of dialogue.

"It is difficult to meet with businessmen, churchmen, students," he said. "They feel they are wasting their time. They say it is clear the whites have rejected them and so they must work out their own salvation."

Black youth groups are beginning to reject the church as the white man's establishment, according to Mr. Naude. Many are joining independent African churches.

Even the leaders of Black Sash believe that interracial communications are breaking down.

"Blacks and whites are afraid to get together now because of intimidation by the Special Branch," a Black Sash spokesman said, adding that the political police followed many of the people who attended a prayer meeting in Johannesburg Cathedral last March for 22 persons being detained on charges of terrorism.

As the racial gap widens, as apartheid spawns black states and black nationalists and fosters a black counterreaction, it seems that the result of apartheid will be opposing black and white nationalisms—for the whites are determined to hold their domain.

South Africa's 600,000 Indians Having a Bitter Time

By MARVINE HOWE
Special to The New York Times

PHOENIX, South Africa, July 1—The multiracial Mahatma Gandhi Memorial Center here stands as a challege to the increasingly segregated society around it.

Its inauguration the other day, in a rare display of racial cooperation, focused attention on the plight of the Indians, the smallest of the four main South African racial groups and one of those hard hit by the Government's policy of racial separation.

Some 5,000 South African Indians, blacks, persons of mixed blood and whites participated in the ceremony in this community 15 miles from Durban, the capital of Natal Province.

The site for the museum, library and medical clinic was chosen because it is where Gandhi, who had come to South Africa as a young lawyer in 1893 and who began his long struggle for social equality here, founded his first peace settlement in 1912.

The Organizer Was Absent

Honoring Gandhi and the pursuit of his ideals were some of the leading critics of the Nationalist Government's racial policies. Alan Paton, the widely revered author and chairman of the Phoenix Trust, paid special homage to the organizer of the memorial, Mewa Ram Gobin, "who unfortunately cannot be with us today because of the laws of the land."

Mr. Gobin, who is married to Gandhi's granddaughter, was "banned" in 1965 for student activities, and as a banned person he cannot attend gatherings.

Chief Gatsha Buthelezi, new Chief Executive of the Zulus and an outspoken critic of racial discrimination, led the opening prayer.

Fatima Meer, an Indian sociologist and the author of a new biography of Gandhi, expressed the desire that Phoenix "may never be the nucleus of segregated housing like the settlements that are cropping up around us."

Harry Oppenheimer, South Africa's wealthiest industrialist and a leader of the Progressive party, paid tribute to Gandhi and the Indian community, declaring, "Certainly South Africa has not much to be proud of about the way in which, over the years, she has treated her Indian citizens."

Legislatively, the 600,000 Indians are part of the vast nonwhite population—including 13 million blacks and two million coloreds (persons of mixed blood)—which is being pushed to the edges of the cities to make room for the 3.5 million whites.

The Daily News of Durban, a liberal paper, praised the Indians and said that Natal could not do without them. "But instead of receiving thanks," the article continued, "the Indian community is discriminated against at every turn."

According to The Daily News, no section of the population has suffered more than the Indians from the application of the so-called Group Areas Act, which restricts residence by racial group and has resulted in the mass displacement of nonwhites from their homes and businesses, generally with little compensation.

Despite the multiple restrictions, many Indians have acquired wealth, good educations and wide horizons. All the more so do they resent the racial bars that deprive them of security and freedom of movement.

Early Restrictive Laws

Indians have no assurance of land tenure or job security. Many are homeless and many more can be displaced at any time. Those with money may buy their homes but cannot buy the land.

Most of South African Indians are descendants of indentured laborers brought to Natal around 1860 to work on sugar plantations. When a wave of Indians merchants followed, the white settlers, fearing competition, urged restrictive laws. By 1913 most Indian immigration was forbidden and there followed a series of acts controlling Indian property and trading rights.

About a decade ago the mass exodus of Durban's Indian population of nearly 300,000 began. By the beginning of 1969 some 35,000 families had been displaced. Most of the Indian residences there have been eliminated and now the shops are being removed.

There is concern in the Indian community that Grey Street, the last prosperous business and residential area for Indians in Durban, with 15,000 inhabitants, will be the next target.

Springfield Flats, a shantytown on the outskirts of Durban begun as temporary housing for evicted Indian families has 5,000 inhabitants and is still growing.

New Indian Settlements

The largest new Indian settlement is Chatsworth, 12 miles from Durban and described as "a dormitory for urban labor." A mass of concrete and brick boxes spread across the hills,

The New York Times (by Marvine Howe)

Chatsworth, a new settlement for Indians, is 12 miles from Durban, and houses people displaced from homes in the city. South Africa has given Indians full citizenship, but restricts them in many ways. The population of Chatsworth is now 165,000. It is to grow.

with inadequate shopping facilities, poor communications and no means of recreation, it houses 165,000 people and is to grow to 250,000.

Indians were given full citizenship in 1960, but many still feel alien, resenting job restrictions, unequal pay and separate schooling. They must obtain permits to move from one province to another and are confined to nonwhite hotels, restaurants, transportation and public toilets. They are also subject to the Immorality Act, which makes sexual association between white and nonwhite a crime, with the offender liable to five years in prison.

The blacks are subject to the same restrictions and even more, but they have been granted homelands that, theoretically, will become independent states one day.

Activists Were Restricted

Initially the Indian minority tried to incur the whites' favor by keeping quiet and keeping to themselves. When the Group Areas Act threw all the nonwhites together, the Indian Congress and the African National Congress began to cooperate on specific issues, holding joint protests. Later the African National Congress was forcibly dissolved and most activists of the Indian Congress were restricted.

The Government then appointed a South African Indian Council to speak for the Indian minority, but it has not succeeded in easing any anti-Indian measures or preventing new ones.

Recently there seems to have been a revival of efforts, of which the Phoenix gathering was evidence, to promote interracial relations despite the consolidation of the separate-development policy. Durban Indian leaders are planning another multiracial meeting to honor Chief Buthelezi, who has challenge the Government to demonstrate its good faith in leading the tribal homelands to self-rule.

July 14, 1970

Tories Move Toward Sale Of Arms to South Africa

Despite Criticism, Home Tells Commons the Route Past Cape Must Be Guarded —Black Leaders Voice Displeasure

By JOHN M. LEE
Special to The New York Times

LONDON, July 20 — In the face of fierce criticism at home and abroad, the Conservative party Government declared today that it would consider the sale of arms to South Africa for maritime defense.

The decision, which the Conservatives had repeatedly hinted they would make, dramatically reverses the policy followed by the Labor party until its defeat June 18.

The announcement drew immediate protests from critics of South Africa's policy of white supremacy, and the Labor party introduced a motion this afternoon criticizing the decision. The motion is to be debated on Wednesday.

Sir Alec Douglas-Home, the Foreign Secretary, announced the new decision to a taut House of Commons. His brief and broadly worded statement was unspecific on when the final decision would be made.

In response to persistent questioning, he said: "No action in regard to the sale of arms will be taken without a statement to this house." Since the Commons starts a summer recess on Friday that will last until October, any action is presumably some months away.

In his statement, Sir Alec said the decision was based on what he saw as Britain's strategic interest in assuring the safety of the sea route around South Africa against Communist threat. He said any arms sales would be in limited categories and would be prohibited for use in reinforcing racial separation or for internal repression.

Critics, however, see Britain's decision as a contribution to the diplomatic acceptability of the South African Government, and they see no advantage to Britain in such a decision. The strategic argument is dismissed as overstated.

Black countries of the Commonwealth have been particularly vocal in opposition, and Tanzania has threatened to withdraw from the Commonwealth. The Zambian President, Kenneth Kaunda, threatened to take action of an unspecified nature.

Opponents in Britain were out overnight painting "no arms for South Africa" signs near a side entrance to the Foreign Office and next to the front door of the Conservative party office.

Sir Alec told the House that Britain was acting to carry out terms of the Simonstown Agreement. This British-South African naval agreement in 1955 handed over the British naval base at Simonstown, South Africa, to the South African Government, along with responsibility for policing the sea route around the Cape of Good Hope.

Britain also agreed at that time to commercial sales of the sea and air weaponry for South Africa to play this role. In 1964, the newly elected Labor Government halted the sales and placed an embargo on them in line with United Nations resolutions.

Text of His Statement

Following is part of Sir Alec's statement:

"The government has an overriding duty to take account of present and future strategic needs of the United Kingdom and, in that context, particular concern for the free passage of ships in all circumstances on the vital sea route around South Aifrca. It was to that end that the Simonstown Agreement was negotiated.

"It is our intention to give effect to the purpose of that agreement, and we believe that as a consequence we should be ready to consider within that context applications for the export to South Africa of certain limited categories of arms, so long as they are for maritime defense directly related to the security of the sea routes.

"The Government has made abundantly clear its fundamental disagreement with the racial policies of the South African Government. In no circumstances would there be sales to South Africa of arms for the enforcement of the policy of apartheid or internal repression.

"It is on this basis that the Government has naturally been concerned to consult with Commonwealth governments and to discuss these matters with them."

Although a full debate is scheduled for Wednesday, Sir Alec was peppered with questions from former Prime Minister Harold Wilson, former Foreign Secretary Michael Stewart and former Defense Minister Denis Healey.

The Foreign Secretary hinted that Britain might feel compelled to oppose any United Nations resolution imposing a mandatory embargo on arms sales to South Africa. Mr. Healey said Britain's decision would aid the spread of Communist influence in black Africa.

One Labor backbencher shouted: "In view of the idiocy of this decision, is there no way the House can have the Foreign Minister and the Prime Minister safely put away?"

Although details of any arms that might be involved have been kept vague, it is assumed here that the South African list of requests will include frigates and aircraft for antisubmarine patrols and air-sea rescue work.

July 21, 1970

South Africa States Policy Toward Her Chinese

Special to The New York Times

CAPETOWN, July 22—The official racial policy on the 8,000-member Chinese community of South Africa was explained in Parliament here today. The Chinese form a separate racial group with a "separate identity" and may use facilities of the white group "provided the white group does not object."

The statement, by Blaar Coetzee, Minister of Community Development, reiterated the existing position of the Chinese. But it did make clear to the whites that the Chinese were legally entitled to share certain white facilities.

Mr. Coetzee said the Chinese community was so small that it was not practical to provide "separate amenities" for it.

Not 'Honorary Whites'

The big difference between the Japanese, who are classified as "honorary whites," and the Chinese in South Africa is that the Chinese are citizens. There are no Japanese who are citizens. The only Japanese residents are business and professional men on temporary permits.

But several incidents in the last few weeks in which the racial identity of Chinese people had been questioned and raised at Government level led many Chinese to hope that they could be classified, like the Japanese, as "honorary whites" and given absolute access to "white" facilities.

As it is, they are legally a separate racial group, a subgroup of the "colored" classification, and cannot, for example, hold certain property or occupy premises not in their specific "group area."

They are also subject to the Immorality Act, which prohibits cohabitation between persons of different racial groups.

On the other hand, provided the whites in their area do not object, they can attend movie theaters, restaurants, swimming pools, beaches, private schools, hotels and can travel on public transport usually reserved for "whites only."

The most recent incident that highlighted the Chinese position was of Chinese children who were in danger of being removed from a "white" day nursery because they were regarded as "nonwhite."

A Government decision was eventually made that the Chinese children could stay.

July 23, 1970

Embittered Coloreds of Capetown Must Make Way for Whites

By MARVINE HOWE

Special to The New York Times

CAPETOWN—They are beginning to bulldoze brash, bustling District 6, which has been the heartland of the Cape Coloreds for many generations and is to become a white suburb.

The Talk of Capetown

Some of the atmosphere has already faded from central Hanover Street, which seems as if there is a death sentence hanging over it. About 25,000 families classified as colored—the South African term for persons of mixed black and white ancestry — have been disqualified for residence in Capetown under the Group Areas Act, and 10,000 of them must still be resettled, according to an offical statement.

The large-scale uprooting has deeply embittered the coloreds, who were long treated as a favored minority that might one day be integrated with the whites.

The coloreds, largely a result of South African white concubinage with slaves who came from Madagascar and Malaya some 300 years ago, settled mainly in the Cape provinces. While many worked as laborers on vineyards and farms, others were highly skilled artisans.

The colored population, which mixed freely with the whites, acted as a kind of buffer between the main racial groups. Capetown itself, with 600,000 coloreds, 400,000 whites and 100,000 blacks, was far more relaxed and open in its racial relations than other cities.

All this has changed as the Government has strictly enforced its policy of the social compartmentalization of the 3.8 million whites, 14.9 million blacks, 2 million coloreds and 614,000 Asians.

"There are two giants in South Africa," a colored social worker said, "the rich white power that says 'keep South Africa white' and the numerically strong black force calling for 'Africa for the Africans.' We colored are like a dwarf caught in the middle, belonging to both but rejected by both."

•

An informed survey of Capetown's colored élite shows that most of them would have supported the whites in a white-black conflict a few years back but that now the majority would tend to favor the blacks.

"There are a lot of coloreds who would still go in and break up a black strike, but the people that matter would support the blacks," a colored union man said.

On the one hand, the coloreds have made considerable economic progress in recent years, breaking down barriers to certain jobs and getting higher pay. But on the other their political rights have been progressively chipped away, and last year they were deprived of all representation in Parliament and the provincial Assemblies.

Their situation began to deteriorate after the 1948 electoral victory of the Nationalist party, the voice of the Afrikaners, who are mostly of Dutch stock and who feared that the coloreds would support the predominantly English United party in an effort to regain control of the Government.

In 1951 coloreds were put on a separate voting roll, which was abolished in 1968. Last year the Colored Representative Council was established as an advisory body, but it is generally considered useless.

•

Socially too there has been considerable deterioration for the coloreds. Resettlement has taken them out of an established urban environment close to their places of work and moved them miles away to new surroundings in the Cape Flats, which are without amenities.

The removals have not gone without protest. When District 6 was declared a zone of "urban rehabilitation," the coloreds set up a protest commitee and offered to rebuild their houses, but to no avail.

Last year 888 colored families in Capetown simply refused to move under the Group Areas Act and had to be evicted by the Department of Community Development. According to a report to Parliament, there were 3,954 resettlements in Capetown in 1969, of which 3,859 were colored families, 68 Indian and 27 white.

The Progressive Member of Parliament, Mrs. Helen Suzman, recently attacked the resettlement program and called on the Ministry of

Community Development to halt further removals of colored people at least until those living in transit camps had been rehoused.

Mrs. Suzman, who had just visited the Bellville transit camp in the Cape Flats, called it "a disgrace to South Africa." She said 2,000 to 3,000 people were living in tin shacks with communal toilets and without ventilation or running water. She found 19 living in a shack, 17 feet square.

The Cape Flats, where most coloreds are being resettled, is a low-lying, sandy, waterlogged area extending for miles southeast of Capetown's flowering white suburbs. Such new houses as exist are badly insulated, with cement floors and no ceilings or interior doors.

Much worse are the vast shantytowns like Elsie's River, where some 75,000 people live in tin shacks, often without drainage, electricity or proper toilet facilities.

An Anglican priest, the Rev. John da Costa of St. Marks Church in District 6, has asserted that the new townships lack churches, movie houses, community centers and cost residents much more in transit fares and rentals.

In the Capetown area, it is estimated, there is a backlog of 35,000 families needing rehousing because they are inadequately housed or disqualified under the Group Areas Act. The Government has not been able to keep pace with slum clearance, the population explosion and group-area requiremtns; there is a construction slowdown because of labor shortages.

•

Prime Minister John Vorster recently committed what was widely considered to be a gaffe when he went to Graaff Reinet in Cape Province to preside over the opening of a group of restored slave cottages that are to be declared national monuments and will be open to tourists. The colored occupants had been moved to the new colored township.

"They want to keep alive happy, memories of slave days," said a colored businessman, who suggested that it would be better to restore District 6 so that its inhabitants could go on living there.

•

Notwithstanding the official efforts to build up completely separate societies, there are daily reports in the press that the system does not work. The exclusion of coloreds from white society has in fact been much more difficult to achieve than the separation of Africans because there has been so much of what is called "intertwining."

Many coloreds cross the racial lines, but it is an agonizing experience. The "play-whites," as they are called, live in terror of their black relatives and generally see them only at night.

•

A new influx of Southern European immigrants has emphasized the inferior position of the coloreds in their own country. "Many Portuguese are darker than I am, but they are treated like whites even if they can't speak either Afrikaans or English," a skilled worker said.

His economic opportunities are improving, however, for coloreds are appearing where they never dared tread before. With increased industrialization and the shortage of skilled white labor, they are increasingly taking over jobs usually held by whites in textiles, plastics, motor assembly—every kind of job except top administration.

Prospects for coloreds are bright in commerce, too. Some stores are hiring colored salesmen and banks recently got permission to hire colored tellers on condition that they not give orders to whites. Colored women, who used to be confined to teaching and nursing, are getting secretarial work.

More coloreds are also going into the building trades and earning good salaries. Some are even wearing the white helmets of foremen, which would have been unheard of a year or so ago.

Nonetheless, the whites are rising faster than nonwhites, and the gap between colored and white wages is increasing, according to the Institute of Race Relations. Furthermore, there is still widespread poverty among unskilled coloreds, and the majority of coloreds are said to be below the poverty line still.

•

Though many colored professional people have been emigrating in recent years and though there is a good deal of despondency among the better educated, there is a widespread belief that internal and external pressures will crack the racial barriers one day.

South Africa Breaches Black Nations' United Front

By MARVINE HOWE
Special to The New York Times

CAPETOWN — South Africa, at the expense of bending a few of her laws on racial separation, is quietly trying to persuade black African countries that cooperation is more effective than confrontation.

This nation's "African policy" has not won any major converts but has succeeded in making a small breach in the united black front against white supremacy in southern Africa.

The South African Government's breakthrough came with the establishment of diplomatic relations with Malawi on Sept. 10, 1967. Now it is expected that Madagascar, Mauritius and possibly a few other countries will follow suit, putting immediate economic advantage before opposition to white minority rule.

Officials Reluctant to Talk

There is great reluctance in Government circles here to talk about South Africa's new African friends, apparently out of fear that publicity will lead to pressure from other African states, which could spoil this courtship.

Nevertheless the Government proudly told Parliament recently that South Africa had diplomatic relations with 65 countries—46 of these listed publicly and 19 unlisted, with which South Africa has "diplomatic contacts without accreditation."

Evidence of South Africa's great discretion in dealing with the black African states is seen in the annual trade figures —they are published for Africa as a whole without the usual country-by-country breakdown, which might be embarrassing for some black states.

Despite the repeated call of the Organization of African Unity for a trade boycott against South Africa, the nation's exports to Africa last year amounted to about $357.5-million.

This figure included exports to white-ruled Rhodesia and Portuguese Africa, but there were said to be a number of black trading partners as well.

Any question of establishing new diplomatic ties with black nations is officially said to be "premature." Nevertheless, the Government confirms that two houses have been purchased recently next to the Malawi Embassy here and refuses to disclose who will live there.

According to parliamentary speculation, the new villas could be for Madagascar, Mauritius, Lesotho or Swaziland, with which South Africa is developing increasingly close ties.

Several delegations have come here from Madagascar to improve trade and tourist relations in recent months. Last year an official South African mission went to Madagascar and returned with plans to help develop the tourist industry at Nosé bay.

A recent trade mission from Mauritius, led by a Cabinet minister, is said to have resulted in "solid progress" for cooperation between the two countries.

South Africa's relations with Malawi are improving. Members of a parliamentary delegation to Malawi were made honorary members of the Malawi Congress party and described President H. Kamuzu Banda as "the Solomon of Africa."

Ghana is also looked on by South Africa as a potential friend since Prime Minister Kofi A. Busia made a public declaration not long ago in line with Dr. Banda's approach to South Africa.

There have also been approaches to Gabon and the Ivory Coast for improved relations, according to parliamentary sources here.

South Africa politicians said that one effect of the nation's new African policy was the abstention of eight countries of the Organization of African Unity in the recent condemnation of Britain, France and West Germany for supplying arms to South Africa.

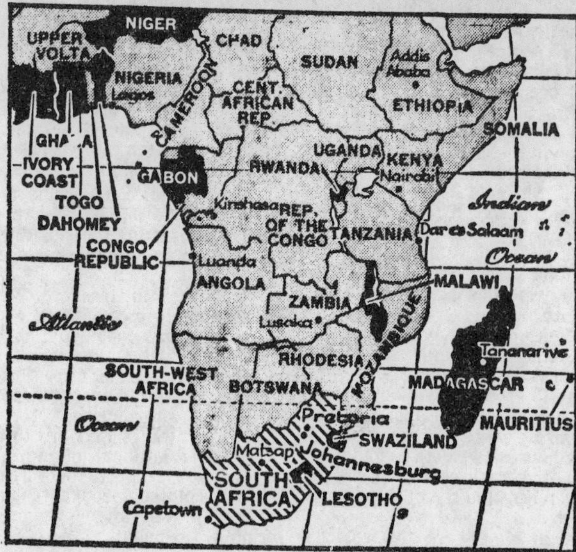

The New York Times Oct. 13, 1970

Countries shown in black are among those considered to be receptive to South Africa's campaign for cooperation.

Some Receptive Nations

These countries, considered a favorable field for the South African diplomatic offensive, are Malawi, Rwanda, Lesotho and five former French territories: the Ivory Coast, Niger, Dahomey, Madagascar and Gabon.

Despite black African attempts to isolate South Africa, South African Airways has succeeded in establishing links with Madagascar, Mauritius and Botswana, in addition to Malawi.

"Kenya's game reserves will be the big loser if Nairobi decides to close its airport to traffic continuing to South Africa," a Government source said, commenting on a resolution by nonaligned nations last month in Lusaka, Zambia, to close ports and airports to South African traffic.

On the other hand, South African leaders view Botswana with pessimism. The landlocked state is part of the South African Customs Union. But Botswana's President, Sir Seretse Khama, has shown—at the United Nations and more recently at the Lusaka conference—increasing determination to follow Zambia out of the South African sphere of influence.

Up to now, South Africa's courtship of black nations has had no effect on the life of blacks inside the country. Foreign black dignitaries in transit from Zambia, Swaziland, Botswana and Madagascar are treated as honorary whites and admitted to the best hotels in Johannesburg and Pretoria.

White liberal critics of the regime feel that both the South African Government and its new black friends stand to lose from what appears to be "short-term political opportunism."

On the one hand, the black countries that cooperate with South Africa lose the respect of their African brothers and tend to become political outcasts.

The South African Government, according to opposition circles, in receiving black dignitaries as whites is undermining its own concept of racial difference, which is the basis of the society of separate development.

Under Apartheid It Is Black Women Who Suffer Most

By MARVINE HOWE
Special to The New York Times

CAPETOWN — Every day they line up in the privately run welfare center—black women, young brides, mothers of large families, widows and the aged, all with the same problem: They have been ordered to leave their homes and families.

It is black women who suffer most under the mass of legislation and regulations that underlie the Government's policy of apartheid, or separate racial development.

One aim is to reduce the number of blacks living in white urban areas. Since black labor is necessary to white industry, African men are allowed to remain in white areas conditionally, preferably as contract labor without family or as "bachelors" in hostels.

Black women and children are officially considered "superfluous appendages," and more and more are being forced to go the black "homelands"—poor, undeveloped areas set aside by the Government.

Here in western Cape Province the restrictions on women are the most severe because the authorities have declared that they do not want a permanent black population. Job priorities have been given to the Cape coloreds, or mulattoes, and businesses have been ordered to reduce black employment by 5 per cent yearly.

Labor shortages are such that industry and farmers are being forced to seek African laborers to replace coloreds, who are being admitted to semiskilled jobs usually held by whites. But there is greater official pressure to get black women and children out.

There are two black townships in the Capetown municipality, with a total population of 81,000 in 1968, of whom 25,000 were women. The trend toward a population of men has been accentuated in the last two years.

The Athlone Advice Office reported hearing 1,800 cases last year, concerning family groups and individuals seeking a way to resist official pressure for resettlement.

The office, in a colored area on the outskirts of white Capetown, is run jointly by the Institute of Race Relations and Black Sash. The institute is engaged mainly in research to publicize the facts of separate development; Black Sash is a white women's volunteer group that has led protests against major racist legislation and action by the Government for 15 years.

Black Sash has embarked on a national campaign to protest against discriminatory legislation affecting black women.

"Great wrongs are being perpetrated upon African women," it declared in a recent appeal to other women's organizations. The main abuses listed are:

¶Women are prevented from living with their husbands who work in white urban areas.

¶Wives of contract laborers can see their husbands only once a year for a couple of weeks at the end of a contract. They live in unnatural communities, where there are only other women, children and old people.

¶Working women in urban areas must send their children to rural relatives; the children then lose all right to reside in urban areas.

Under the widely criticized Urban Areas Act, no black woman may remain in an urban area for more than 72 hours unless she can prove that she has lived there continuously since birth, or for a continuous period of 15 years, or for 10 years working for one employer.

Mrs. Helen Suzman, the only Progressive party Member of Parliament, has led the protest there against the forced removals. After a recent visit to African townships, she deplored the rate at which black women were being expelled from Capetown and said that 29,000 men were living in hostels there under "the most degrading conditions."

The main job of the Athlone Advice Office, which is largely manned by volunteers, is to explain the complicated rulings that regulate the black South African's life and to try to help him cope as well as possible. Black Sash also runs Advice Offices in Durban and Johannesburg.

"There's less and less we can do in the face of revised regulations and tightening up the management of African townships," according to the Capetown office's annual report. Greater pressure, it said, has been put on families that are well established in the townships, with children in local schools, obliging them to tear up their roots and resettle in rural areas.

Divorce the Only Answer

Most of the cases concern couples that cannot reside together. There was the young, happily married couple with one child that had been ordered to separate. The only solution to the problem is divorce, according to the Advice Office. Once divorced, the woman can remain with an aunt as the unmarried daughter of a Capetown resident and can see her "bachelor" husband from time to time.

John and Nombongi, who have four children and a house in the township of Guguletu (which means "Our Pride"), have been told they must leave the Capetown area. John came here in 1947 but worked in the nearby town of Bellville for a few months in 1955, which undermined his claim to continuous residence. He was disabled and discharged from his job in 1962, and has been selling dry goods with a hawker's license since.

Now he has been told that his permission to remain in the area ended a month before he would have qualified as a legal resident. He and his family have been directed to go to a homeland, where there is no work for healthy men, let alone the disabled. The Advice Office has decided to take the case to court.

While the tragic parade of broken families passes through the Advice Offices, separate development has not achieved its aims.

The 1970 census, recently made public, demonstrates the Government's failure to establish racially separate societies. Of a black population of about 15 million, there are some eight million registered in white areas, or twice as many as the white population. When the Government began separate development in 1951, there were five million blacks in white areas.

October 20, 1970

Group in South Africa Advises U.S. Business About Apartheid

By PAUL HOFMANN
Special to The New York Times

JOHANNESBURG, South Africa, June 27—A South African civil rights organization has formulated recommendations for United States business concerns that consider investing here, advising them how to alleviate apartheid "from within."

J. Fred Van Wyk, director of the organization, the South African Institute of Race Relations, said in an interview that "a lot can be done" within the laws on racial separation to give African workers a better deal and more human dignity, and reach across the color line.

The recommendations of the institute, prepared, according to its officers, at the request of some United States businessmen, call for wage scales for nonwhite workers far above the legal minimum, opportunities for them to learn skills, other benefits not contemplated by South African legislation, and "meaningful dialogue" and social contact with Africans.

The Race Relations Institute, a respected private organization with a staff of 50 throughout South Africa, is funded by South African businessmen, the Ford Foundation and its own members.

The 40-year-old institute has 4,500 members, including some in the United States and other foreign countries, and is affiliated with a number of universities and churches.

The institute, an interracial organization, states that it is seeking and publishing the facts on race relations "whether by so doing it is popular or unpopular with any government or party or group."

The Government, though aware of the institute's anti-apartheid stand, has not so far interfered with its activity and on occasion even uses its reports.

The institute's officers noted that not a few United States and other foreign executives adapt very quickly to the South African wage structure with its glaring differences in the treatment of white and nonwhite workers, and seem quite at ease with the maze of apartheid laws.

Apart from the everyday indignities and discrimination that apartheid entails. the disparities in the treatment of whites and nonwhites can best be gauged by the wage differentials.

Earnings Much Lower

In the construction trade, for instance, the monthly average earnings of white workers are $450, of Africans $70. The apartheid argument is that whites are much more skilled, but in practice all too often the blacks do the same or nearly the same work as whites.

Some employers, including church bodies, voluntary pay their African workers more than the legal minimum, provide opportunities for on-the-job training, and give them channels— such as productivity committees—to air grievances.

Civil rights advocates stress that efforts to counter apartheid "from within" are all the more important since the present legislation gives the Government overwhelming powers to deal harshly with clandestine or otherwise illegal opposition.

One liberal said: "There's been sullen lethargy among our Africans ever since the Government removed and silenced one after another of their militants in the early nineteen-sixties. That's why involvement of American firms could be important."

Involvement is Sought

Dudley Horner, who is responsible for a study by the institute covering American investment in South Africa, suggested that American executives here should become seriously involved in the community from which their profits are made and should resist the temptation to be drawn into conformist white South African society.

The institute's officers are perplexed and divided, however, as to whether increased Ameri-corporate involvement here is advisable at all.

"Do new American investments weaken or reinforce apartheid?" Mr. Van Wyk asked during the interview.

"I wouldn't know," he replied. "I would give any new investor from the United States five years time; let him show that he doesn't just mean tokenism."

A researcher at the institute who did not want to be identified said, however, that no more than tokenism — promotion for only a few Africans — would result from the arrival of new American companies on the South African business scene.

"They'll use what they do for Africans in their advertising," the researcher, a white man, said. "If American business involvement in the antiapartheid fight becomes a meaningful movement, the Government will step in with new legislation."

According to the institute study, about 300 United States concerns have at present substantial direct capital investments in South Africa. They are known to employ "tens of thousands" of Africans,

The study places United States investment in South Africa at the beginning of 1970 at $750-million, 14 per cent of all foreign capital here.

United States investors are attracted by South Africa because wages for African workers are very low, manpower, mostly unskilled, is plentiful, strikes are rare, the local economy and market are expanding, and returns are high.

One United States concern that sells its products here, the Polaroid Corporation, announced early this year that while it abhorred apartheid it had decided to "try to influence the system from within."

On the recommendation of a racially mixed investigation group of its employes in the United States, Polaroid has started an experimental one-year program here. The plan provides for improved wages for African workers in companies here that do business with Polaroid, advanced training for them, and grants for 500 scholarships for nonwhite students.

June 28, 1971

South Africa Greets Black Leader on State Visit

Special to The New York Times

PRETORIA, South Africa, Aug. 16—A black African leader, President H. Kamuzu Banda of Malawi, arrived in South Africa today for the first visit o a head o stage to this country in almost a quarter of a century.

The fact that a black is making the first state visit since Britain's King George VI went to South Africa in 1947 is being viewed here as significant in the development of a black-white dialogue in Africa.

A white guard of honor presented arms and was inspected by Dr. Banda as the South African and Malawian flags flew side by side at Waterkloof Air Base in Pretoria.

Dr. Banda arrived in an Air Malawi jet, with an entourage of 10 Malawian Government officials and their wives. He stepped smilingly from the aircraft, carrying a wildebeeste-tail flywhisk, and shook hands heartily with President J. J. Fouché of South Africa.

As the guns boomed and the army band played the Malawian and South Africa National anthems, a squadron of Mirage jets of the South African Air Force screamed past. A crowd of more than a thousand, mainly black city workers, held up traffic outside the plush President Hotel, in the center of Johannesburg, and roared a welcome as President Banda arrived. He will stay at the President Hotel for the week except for one night in Capetown tomorrow.

To Visit Gold Mine

Prime Minister John Vorster gave a private dinner in President Banda's honor at the hotel. Later this week Dr. Banda is to visit a South African gold mine in the Western Witwatersrand region in the Transvaal, near the mine where he once worked as a young clerk-interpreter almost 50 years ago.

He walked from his native Nyasaland to get a job in the gold mines of the Transvaal and put the money he earned into studies. He returned to Nyasaland hoping to become a doctor. He was helped by American missionaries, was sent to school in the United States and received a medical degree at Meharry College in Nashville, Tenn. He returned from practicing in Edinburgh, Scotland, to lead his people to independence. This year he was made Life President of Malawi.

South Africa is involved in technical and financial aid to Malawi and the two countries signed a trade agreement some years ago.

An opponent of apartheid, Dr. Banda has declared consistently that he believes contact with South Africa and not isolation of the white-ruled republic is a realistic approach that could help to change the South African racial separation system.

Although politically the South African Government is not prepared to bend to any pressures for change, Prime Minister Vorster's policy of contact with black Africa echoes some of the realism demonstrated by Dr. Banda. Recently Malawi became the first black country to exchange ambassadors with South Africa.

Apartheid remains unchanged but, to many South Africans, the new approach with Malawi and the historic visit of Dr. Banda has already altered the picture in South Africa.

August 17, 1971

Freedom for The Dean

The crowds at Johannesburg's Jan Smuts airport last Friday sang hymns and recited prayers in a mixture of happiness and regret. They were happy that the stocky, white-haired clergyman around whom they surged had just been acquitted on appeal of subversion charges and thus no longer faced the five-year prison term to which he had earlier been sentenced. But they regretted that he had decided to leave South Africa for his native England.

The center of their affection was the Very Rev. Gonville A. ffrench-Beytagh, the 60-year-old former Anglican Dean of Johannesburg and a leading opponent of South Africa's apartheid policy of racial separation. He had been convicted last November on charges that he had incited members of the Black Sash, an antiapartheid women's organization, to violence and that he had distributed $70,000 to banned organizations in the country on behalf of the London Defense and Aid Fund, an organization prohibited under the Suppression of Communism Act.

But last week a three-man appeal court reversed the conviction and the Dean was freed. A few hours later he departed for London. During his trial, his term at Johannesburg cathedral had expired and he did not seek renewal. Instead he has been offered a post at Norwich Cathedral in England.

As well-wishers, black and white, hugged him, Dean ffrench-Beytagh told them: "I have no plans to return. I don't think I am wanted here now."

April 16, 1972

A Baton Charge Stirs a National Storm

PRETORIA — The confrontation had been a long time coming.

On the one side there was the Government of Prime Minister John Vorster, a regime that is almost obsessional about the allegedly radical, multiracial views of many white students at English-language universities in South Africa. Mr. Vorster is supported by most of the country's whites, who are almost as obsessional as he about such manifestations of student "permissiveness" as long hair and pot — which they believe threaten the foundations of their Calvinist society.

On the other side stood the National Union of South African Students. This organization represents students at all English-language universities; for many years it has been a Government target. Mr. Vorster accuses it of being a "tool of Communists." Many of its leaders have had their passports removed or been forced into exile. It is at present under investigation by a Parliamentary committee.

Ten days ago the confrontation between the Government and the white students finally took place — with anger and violence. By the end of last week, the entire country had been embroiled in vehement debate over the right of dissent.

The trouble began quietly enough on Friday, June 2, when about 200 University of Capetown students staged a poster demonstration on the steps of Capetown's Anglican Saint George's Cathedral. They were protesting against inequalities between black and white education and against the expulsion of a student leader from an all-black university in Transvaal.

There was a brief altercation between a demonstration leader and a police officer over the use of a bullhorn, and 50 policemen waded in with rubber truncheons. Some students were pursued inside the cathedral and beaten as hundreds of spectators (including several opposition M.P.'s from the nearby Parliament) looked on.

The next day dramatic pictures of the students being clubbed appeared on front pages throughout the country —South Africa has no television—and the national storm was unleashed. The original issue of black education was largely forgotten as students at other universities and public figures of many shades of opinion charged the Government with police brutality.

Under attack by the Opposition in Parliament, Prime Minister Vorster retorted: "If the police had not acted in this way, I personally would have been disappointed in them." The Minister of Police, Lourens Muller, said the students were being manipulated by agitators.

By now students at all English-language universities — Capetown, Witwatersrand in Johannesburg, Natal in Durban and Rhodes in Grahamstown — were aroused; massive protest meetings and marches were organized. These universities have a total of about 30,000 students. White liberal spokesmen joined in the nationwide furor.

The Government responded on Monday by imposing a five-week ban on open-air political meetings in all university towns and cities. Citizens' protest meetings were thereupon staged in town halls, and students organized teach-ins on campus.

In Johannesburg, Durban and Capetown a few defied the ban and were fined small sums. But after the violence of what has become known as "Black Friday at the Cathedral," police action against defiant students was almost studied in its moderation, suggesting ministerial orders to avoid further excesses. About 10,000 students and spectators who gathered again at the cathedral last Monday were dispersed with tear gas, but no truncheons were in evidence.

One speaker at the citizens' protest in Capetown City Hall was Dr. Marius Barnard, brother of the heart transplant surgeon, Christiaan Barnard. Marius, who works in his brother's cardiac unit in a state hospital, said he was defying a written threat of dismissal by taking part in a political rally. Christiaan said he would also resign if his brother were fired. So far no action has been taken against either.

Blacks and other nonwhite groups were largely spectators in what was a week of almost entirely white protest activity, although black students of tribal colleges did boycott lectures and stage solidarity teach-ins. The violence of the cathedral baton charge had served to crystallize and dramatize the confrontation among the whites. And white opinion divided along traditional lines.

The conservative majority supported "kragdadigheid" (power) in dealing with the students; the liberal minority saw the week's events as confirmation of the regime's authoritarianism and its intolerance of dissent. Students at Afrikaans universities pledged support for the Government—but, surprisingly and significantly, 1,000 signatures protesting against police violence were collected at the Afrikaans Stellenbosch University.

Violence flared again on Friday night at the University of Witwatersrand in Johannesburg, when students turned fire extinguishers on plainclothes police who broke up a gathering of about 200 demonstrators. Seventy people, including two newspaper reporters, were arrested for violating the Riotous Assemblies Act.

Yesterday, I. A. Maisels, one of South Africa's leading attorneys, addressed the students on campus and persuaded them to stop the demonstrations "for the time being and to assess our position and to determine public support."

—TERTIUS MYBURGH

June 11, 1972

U. N. TRUSTEE BODY HITS SOUTH AFRICA

Adopts for Third Successive Year a Motion of Censure for Policy on Mandate

Special to THE NEW YORK TIMES.

PARIS, Nov. 19—For the third year in a row the Trusteeship Committee of the United Nations General Assembly passed a resolution today censuring the Union of South Africa for failing to place the territory of South-West Africa under the United Nations trusteeship system.

By a vote of 36 to 1 the committee adopted, over the strenuous objection of Eric H. Louw, South African delegate, a Danish, Norwegian, Uruguayan text, by which the "General Assembly maintains its recommendations of Dec. 14, 1946, and Nov. 1, 1947, that South-West Africa be placed under the trusteeship system and notes with regret that these recommendations have not been carried out."

South Africa's delegation has maintained in the Assembly that the matter is within the domestic jurisdiction of the Union and has threatened that the Union would have to "reconsider" its membership in the United Nations if the world organization "persisted in interfering in the conduct of South Africa's domestic affairs."

The joint resolution, as adopted, also calls on the South African Government to continue to report annually to the Trusteeship Council on the administration of the one-time German colony "until agreement is reached with the United Nations regarding the future of South-West Africa."

The resolution notes the assurance given by South Africa that it is her intention to continue to administer the territory in the spirit of the mandate.

The Union is administering South West Africa under a League of Nations mandate granted in 1922 and is the only holder of a League mandate not to have given its territory full independence or placed it under a United Nations trusteeship.

South Africa's new Nationalist government announced several months ago that it intended to grant representation in the South African Parliament to South-West Africa. Many delegates had charged during committee debate that the Union was "annexing" the vast territory, which is extremely rich in natural resources.

Mr. Louw insisted that South Africa merely was "integrating" the mandate for administrative reasons and at the wish of the inhabitants.

November 20, 1948

WORLD COURT BARS SOUTH AFRICA STEP

Decides That Country May Not Modify Status of Territory Without U. N. Consent

THE HAGUE, the Netherlands, July 11 (Reuters)—The International Court of Justice, highest legal authority in the world, today ruled that South Africa could not modify the international status of the mandated territory of South-West Africa without United Nations consent.

But South Africa is not legally obliged to place the territory under United Nations trusteeship, the Court decided.

The United Nations had asked the Court for an "advisory opinion," but the Court held that, in disputes on the interpretation or application of the provisions of the League of Nations mandate, South Africa was under an obligation to accept the "compulsory jurisdiction" of the Court.

The South African Government, which plans to hold elections in South-West Africa for representation in the Union of South Africa's Parliament, had contended that the mandate gave it the right to administer the territory as an integral part of the territory. It denied that its proposals for a "closer association" meant incorporation.

Area Still Under Mandate

The International Court's advisory opinion on the status of South-West Africa and the Union Government's obligations—the climax of a five-year "dispute" between South Africa and other members of the United Nations—was announced today as follows:

1. South-West Africa is still under the international (League of Nations) mandate assumed by South Africa after the First World War.
2. The provisions of Chapter XII of the United Nations Charter provide a means by which South-West Africa may be brought under the trusteeship system.
3. South Africa is not competent alone to modify the international status of the territory. This can be done only with United Nations consent.
4. South Africa has an obligation to submit reports and transmit petitions from the 300,000 inhabitants to the United Nations.
5. South Africa is not legally obliged to place the territory under the trusteeship system.

The Court was unanimous in its opinion on the first three points but divided on the others. The fourth was carried by 12 votes to 2 and the fifth by 8 votes to 6.

Reports Discontinued

South Africa, which has governed South-West Africa as a mandated territory since 1920, last year discontinued sending reports to the United Nations on her administration of the territory.

South Africa has repeatedly held that the United Nations Charter laid down only voluntary conditions for handing over dependent territories to the United Nations. South-West Africa was the only league mandate not placed under the trusteeship system when it began.

The president of the court, Jules Basdevant, summing up the reasons for the court's decisions, said the original mandate given to the Union Government did not involve any cession of territory or transfer of sovereignty to South Africa.

July 12, 1950

APARTHEID FOES IN AFRICA LOSE SUIT IN WORLD COURT OVER SOUTH-WEST AFRICA

AN 8-TO-7 VERDICT

South Africa Is Victor on a Technicality in U.N. Mandate Case

Special to The New York Times

THE HAGUE, July 18 — A legal attack by black African nations against South Africa's system of racial separation, apartheid, failed today in the International Court of Justice.

The Court, the principal judicial organ of the United Nations, dismissed a complaint by Ethiopia and Liberia against the imposition of apartheid in the mandated territory of South-West Africa. It did so without reaching the merits of the complaint against racism.

The ruling was on a technical ground—that Ethiopia and Liberia did not have sufficient legal interest in their claim. The terms of the decision appeared to block any further suit on the issue in the World Court under its existing statute.

The 14 judges who sat on the long-argued case divided 7 to 7 on the procedural issue. The President, Sir Percy Spender of Australia, was then given an additional, or "casting," vote under the rules. He cast it against the complainants, making the vote 8 to 7 for dismissal.

Case Pending Six Years

The result was a bitter, frustrating one for the black African countries and for many others who had seen hope of cracking South African power in the lawsuit.

The case had been carried on for nearly six years—since Nov. 4, 1960. The World Court had handed down several interim rulings, and held almost 300 hours of hearings. The costs to the parties ran to millions of dollars.

Liberia and Ethiopia were acting on behalf of most other African states in their action. The two nations had asked the World Court to rule that the United Nations had supervisory authority over South Africa's administration of South-West Africa and that through her aparthcid regime South Africa had failed to promote the well-being of the more than 400,000 inhabitants of the territory.

U.N. Role Rejected

South Africa controls the adjacent South-West Africa, a former German colony, under a 1920 mandate of the League of Nations, and has steadfastly refused to recognize United Nations trusteeship over South-West Africa.

Court sources said it was the first time that the President had broken a tie with his vote since before World War II, when the tribunal was known as the Permanent Court of International Justice, formed under the League of Nations Covenant.

The burden of the Court's judgment today was that the League, in awarding the mandate, had made no provision for individual members to challenge its execution.

Referring to arguments put forward by the complainants invoking humanitarian reasons, the judgment said it was "necessary not to confuse the moral ideal with the legal rules." The duty of the Court, the judgment declared, "is to apply the law as it finds it, not to make it."

The judgment observed that if individual members of the League of Nations had had the right to challenge the execution of a mandate, as asserted by the complainants, "the position of a mandatory country caught between the different expressions of view of some 40 or 50 states would have been untenable."

Justice Philip C. Jessup of the United Stated voted with the minority, which upheld the right of Liberia and Ethiopia to bring the action.

Those who sided with Sir Percy in the decision were Justices Bohdan Winiarski of Poland, Jean Spiropoulos of Greece, Sir Gerald Fitzmaurice of Britain, André Gros of France, Gaetano Morelli of Italy and Jacques Theodore Van Wyk of South Africa.

Mr. Winiarski, who is 82 years old, has been described as a white Pole. He was legal adviser to the Polish delegation

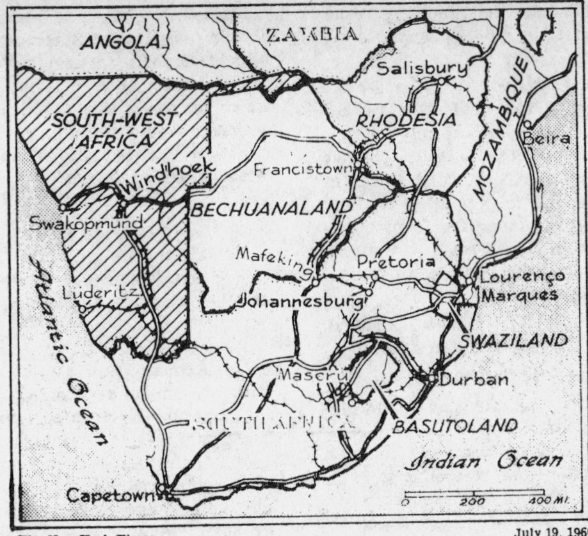

SIX-YEAR CASE ENDS: The World Court refused to consider a plea that South-West Africa (shaded area) was being mismanaged by Government of South Africa.

at the Versailles Peace Conference.

The Seven Dissenters

The dissenters, in addition to Mr. Jessup, were the Court's Vice President, V. K. Wellington Koo of Nationalist China, and Justices Vladimir M. Koretsky of the Soviet Union, Luis Padilla Nervo of Mexico, Kotaro Tanaka of Japan, Isaac Forster of Snegal and Sir Louis Mbanefo of Nigeria.

Justices Van Wyjk and Mbanefo were ad hoc judges designated by the opposing parties in the case and sitting for this case only.

The Court's full complement is 15 judges, who serve nine-year terms. During the case one judge, Abdel Hamid Badawi of the United Arab Republic, died. His replacement, Fouad Ammoun of Lebanon, was appointed too late to take part in the vote.

One of the judges, Muhammad Zafrulla Khan of Pakistan, disqualified himself for undisclosed reasons. Another, José Luis Bustamante y Rivero of Peru, did not participate in the vote because he has been ill for some time.

Renewal of Suit Unlikely

Legal experts in The Hague said tonight that after today's ruling probably no other government would attempt to bring the case back before the World Court. Efforts to change South Africa's policies in South-West Africa would have to be channeled through the United Nations, it was suggested.

The longest of the seven dissents was writen by the American member, Justice Jessup. He described the case as "a procedure of utter futility." Mr. Jussup recalled that the Court held in 1962 that the plaintiff nations could bring action, and sharply disagreed with the majority opinion now that they lacked the legal interest to obtain a judgment on the case's merits.

Mr. Jessup, a former Columbia University professor, said the court had not reversed an advisory opinion, made public in 1950, that the United Nations had supervisory authority in South-West Africa and that South Africa was obliged to report to the world organization.

300 Hours of Hearings

The action by Liberia and Ethiopia entailed nearly 300 hours of oral proceedings, and thousands of pages of written pleadings since formal proceedings started on Dec. 21, 1962. South Africa produced 14 witnesses to dispute the complaints.

The defendant's case was based on the contention that the League of Nations mandate to administer the former German colony had lapsed with the League's dissolution and that the League's supervisory powers had not been inherited by the United Nations.

After Liberia and Ethiopia filed their complaint with the World Court in 1960, South Africa contended that no state had any right to invoke the Court's jurisdiction in a dispute over a mandate. The Court rejected this view, ruling on Dec. 21, 1962, in an 8-to-7 decision that it had jurisdiction in the case.

The Court also dismissed a South African objection that the dispute could be settled by negotiation, although no formal talks had taken place until then. The Court decided that there was no reasonable probability that negotiations would lead to a settlement.

The chief strategist for the complainants was Ernest A. Gross, a New York lawyer and former delegate to the United Nations. He voiced surprise at the ruling.

Speaking to reporters in the courtroom, he said, "I am afraid of the historical consequences of this decision."

Mr. Gross remarked that pressures by African governments to do away with apartheid had been "pent up behind the barrier of this litigation." He suggested that a campaign against South Africa of unparalleled intensity might be unleashed in the United Nations General Assembly this autumn.

Mr. Gross, attired in striped trousers and a black jacket, said the decision pointed up the need to amend the Court's statute to allow the United Nations to seek binding sentences from the tribunal. The statute, an integral part of the United Nations Charter, permits the organization to apply for advisory opinions.

Asked what his next step would be, Mr. Gross said, "Just go to bed, I guess." After a moment he added, "Confer with my colleagues and get the word back to the U.N." Mr. Gross served as deputy United States representative in the United Nations from 1949 to 1953.

The man on whom congratulations were heaped was David P. de Villiers, a Capetown lawyer who came to court in a shin-length black gown and a gleaming white collar. Mr. de Villiers and Mr. Gross shook hands before the court session opened, but did not do so after it ended.

At 3 P.M. an attendant in a tailcoat ordered the throng in the courtroom to rise and the black-robed judges filed in.

The President immediately began reading the judgment. He finished at 5:01 P.M. As he proceeded through a maze of intricate sentences and arguments, the several hundred diplomats and tourists, some standing three deep in the gallery, fidgeted and tilted their heads. Many in the courtroom gazed at the six huge crystal chandeliers overhead.

The courtroom emptied quickly as the session closed. But experts and diplomats clustered in corridors and halls of the Peace Palace, where the Court sits, to discuss the judgment. The palace is a rambling brick and stone building financed by the Carnegie Foundation. It is surrounded by a small, well-kept park.

July 19, 1966

LEAGUE MANDATE IN AFRICA ENDED BY 114 TO 2 IN U.N.

South Africa's Control Over Neighboring Area Is Voided —She Vows to Resist

By RAYMOND DANIELL
Special to The New York Times

UNITED NATIONS, N. Y., Oct. 27—The General Assembly adopted a resolution tonight to terminate South Africa's mandate from the League of Nations to administer the neighboring territory of South-West Africa. The vote was 114 to 2, with 3 abstentions.

The resolution declared that "South-West Africa comes under the direct responsibility of the United Nations." It then went on to create a committee of 14 member states to "recommend practical ways by which South-West Africa should be administered to lead its people to ultimate independence." The committee is to report next April.

The United States, after an attempt to modify the resolution that attracted only 18 supporters, voted with the Soviet Union and Nationalist China in favor of the main resolution. The two other permanent members of the Security Council, Britain and France, abstained, along with Malawi.

South Africa and Portugal voted against the resolution.

Security Council Must Act

The assembly has made its judgment, but it is the Security Council that will be responsible for enforcing it. For that reason, the sponsors of today's resolution had hoped to gain the support of all five permanent members.

It was to that end that the United States sought to amend the resolution in the hope that the big powers could then support it.

South Africa, which contests the right of the United Nations to rescind the mandate unilaterally, has promised to resist with all resources at her disposal any attempt to carry out the terms of the resolution.

James M. Nabrit Jr., in explaining the United States vote, said his country was supporting the resolution, but had "undertaken no commitment on what action it would consider appropriate if the Security Council were called on to act."

U. S. to Weigh Move

He said the United States action in the Council would depend on the situation prevailing at the time.

The resolution was sponsored by 54 African and Asian states with an amendment supported by 21 Latin-American countries. The amendments proposed by the Latin-Americans were adopted by 90 to 2 with 27 abstentions, and by 85 to 2 with 32 abstentions.

South Africa aroused a tumult of shouting, jeers and laughter when she, with Portugal, voted against all the amendments. The South African representative rose in his seat and shook his hands over his head in a boxer's salute.

When the main resolution was disposed of, the assembly defeated a resolution introduced by Jamil M. Baroody of Saudi Arabia calling on it to declare South Africa a "racist colonial power." The vote was 17 in favor, 22 against and 58 abstentions.

The assembly's action tonight was regarded by nearly all delegation—those who favored it and those opposed—as the most important and far reaching likely to be taken at this session.

The mandate to govern South-West Africa was granted to King George V of Britain by the League of Nations after the First World War. The territory had been a German colony. Britain then turned over the mandate to South Africa, then a part of the British Commonwealth.

Under the mandate, South Africa was charged with improving the condition of the territory's people and guiding them to self-determination. This was to be "a sacred trust."

In the 21 years since South Africa became a member of the United Nations her administration of the territory has been the subject of criticism in more than 75 resolutions.

Six years ago, Ethiopia and Liberia, as members of the League of Nations, took their complaint to the International Court of Justice at The Hague.

Last July, the court declined to rule on the merits of the charges before it, holding that Ethiopia and Liberia had no direct interest. The African states then turned to political action in the United Nations.

October 28, 1966

South-West Africa Being Split Into Reserves for Different Races

By PAUL HOFMANN
Special to The New York Times

PRETORIA, South Africa, June 22 — The South African Government is carving up South-West Africa into a mosaic of a dozen or so reserves for whites, persons of mixed blood and various black tribes.

This transformation of the huge, secluded, thinly populated and potentially rich territory noted for its diamonds and copper as well as other minerals is in keeping with the ideology of apartheid, or racial segregation, developed by South Africa's ruling National party.

Confronted with the charge that the Pretoria administration is about to "Balkanize" South-West Africa, officials in Windhoek, the territorial capital, say that decentralization is the only way of administering a territory twice the size of California where many ethnic groups in widely different stages of development are living in pockets of settlements separated by deserts and inhospitable mountains.

The officials deny that South Africa is running the territory —which was redesignated Namibia by the United Nations in 1968 — as a virtual fifth province.

The officials insist that South-West Africa is a separate entity but are at a loss to define its precise status.

Tour by Foreign Newsmen

In a conversation with a group of foreign newsmen who visited the disputed territory earlier this month, South African spokesmen noted only that South-West Africa had its own postage stamps.

A diplomat who is scheduled to assume an important overseas ambassadorship soon compared the relationship between South Africa and South-West Africa with that of Denmark and Greenland, which is part of the Danish kingdom.

The International Court of Justice in the Hague, in an advisory opinion requested by the United Nations Security Council, ruled yesterday, 13 to 2, that South Africa's presence in Namibia, formerly a League of Nations mandate, was illegal and that South Africa should withdraw.

In a broadcast afterward, Prime Minister John Vorster termed the ruling nonbinding and declared that South Africa would go on administering South-West Africa with a view to "self determination for all population groups."

Long-Closed Areas Visited

Officials in Windhoek said that the Pretoria Government might revive an earlier proposal to hold a plebiscite to let the white and nonwhite inhabitants of the territory decide "once and for all" whether they wished to continue living under the present administration or would rather become wards of the United Nations.

The foreign newsmen, who were permitted to visit some areas in South-West Africa that had long been closed to outsiders, were told by officals that the vast majority of the territory's nearly 750,000 inhabitants were in favor of South African rule.

An American among the eleven visiting reporters gained the impression that its strongest element, the Ovambo people, was supporting South Africa's policies.

"The Ovambos know what's good for them," said F. David Tothill, chief of the South-west African division of the South African Foreign Affairs Department, who organized the press tour.

The New York Times June 23, 1971

The land of the seven Ovambo tribes, a bush and savannah area larger than the Netherlands situated just south of the border with Angola, a Portuguese possession, has been designated by South Africa as one of several proposed "Bantustans," or black tribal homelands.

Clearly aiming at making it into a showcase, South Africa has over the last few years appropriated sizable funds—officials speak of $42-million in capital expenditures since 1966—to give the favored Ovambo groups water, roads, schools, hospitals and the beginnings o small industries.

Only 500 whites, mostly officials and missionaries, are said to live among the 350,000 Ovambos. White traders are forbidden to open shops in the area.

At the new ranch-type administration building at Ondangwa, where South African officials are called "Advisers," there are separate lavatories for whites and nonwhites. Yet, despite official apartheid, race relations in Ovamboland seem much more relaxed than in South Africa itself.

The visiting newsmen had little opportunity to meet with Ovambos other than those in the dominant tribal groups.

At a party where white officials, tribal leaders and foreign reporters mingled, a young black clergyman began to tell the foreigners how he had unsuccessfully tried to set up an opposition party last year. Other black men at the party quickly closed in on the clergyman and nudged him away.

The South African Government's Commissioner General for South-West Africa, Jan de Wet, asserted that 85 per cent of all black people in the territory "are with us."

Mr. de Wet conceded, however, that only 30 per cent of the Herero tribe "accept our policy," acknowledging that another 30 per cent were opposed to it and the remainder were indifferent.

The number of Hereros, a black tribal people living in the east of the territory and around Windhoek, is given as 43,000. The South African administration has set aside a vast area in the northeast of the territory as Hereroland.

21,000 Nomadic Bushmen

Another reserve north of this area has been designated as Bushmanland. The number of nomadic bushmen, until recently despised and hunted by other tribes, is estimated at 21,000 in the territory.

The visiting newsmen did not have a chance to talk to a Herero or any spokesman for the other black groups in South West Africa.

Neither were they able to visit the area of a community known as the Rehoboth Basters. The Afrikaans word "basters" means bastard, and the group consists of descendants of white Afrikaners and black women of the Nama tribe.

The community has its own seven-man advisory council. Many of its 16,000 members are well-to-do farmers or breeders of cattle and karakul lambs.

The 90,000 whites who live in South-West Africa have a legislative assembly and are represented by six elected members, all of them members of the National party, in South Africa's 170-seat House of Assembly. The whites, most of them of Afrikaner and German stock, seem to go along with South African policies.

June 23, 1971

South West Africa:

'Legacy of Bitterness'

JOHANNESBURG — The summer rains have been good in Ovamboland and the millet is high. Strong hands are needed to reap and store the grain. That may be one reason why thousands of Ovambo tribesmen in the South Arican protectorate of South West Africa — of which Ovamboland is part — seem unwilling to end a six-week strike against white industries in the protectorate, even though the strike has already won them better conditions.

But there are other reasons and the resistance led last week to a vicious clash between 100 Ovambos and South African police who patrol the region. The Ovambos, armed with pangas (big knives) and bows and arrows, had slain the wife of a headman who sided with the whites, burned his home, tried to close a school and to burgle a bank. Four were killed by the police sent to subdue them.

The continuing friction has stirred fears in some quarters that a major confrontation may be building up. But South African Prime Minister John Vorster asserted last week that there is no crisis.

The clash last week was the latest of a series between the tribesmen and the police in the wild bush country on the South West Africa-Angola border which, by official count, has led to the deaths of 10 natives — eight killed by police and two murdered by their own people.

Minister of Police Lourens Muller said the Ovambos were inspired by the South West Africa People's Organization whose exiles abroad claim responsibility for terrorist activities aimed at the freeing of South West Africa — also known as Namibia — from South African control.

But the labor situation remains basic to the problem, particularly the system that separates the migrant worker from his family. Although the new terms of employment allow the worker for the first time to negotiate for better pay and working conditions with individual employers, the employers are not compelled to accommodate workers' families and most do not have the necessary accommodation anyway.

Some observers saw implications in the affair beyond the borders of South West Africa. In Cape Town, in South Africa's Parliament, Mrs. Helen Suzman of the opposition Progressive party, said the incidents posed a grave warning for South Africa itself, where "a terrible legacy of bitterness and frustration was building up over a . . . labor system identical to that which caused the Ovambo strike."

The warning appeared to be already taken, however. After the Ovamboland debate, the Government surprised even some of its own supporters by announcing that in future some black migrant contract workers in South Africa would be allowed "under certain conditions" to have their families from the homelands living with them in white urban areas.

—PETER HAWTHORNE

February 6, 1972

Malan Tells South Africans He Will Make British Protectorate Rule Election Issue

CAPETOWN, South Africa, May 13 (AP)—Prime Minister Daniel F. Malan touched off another vehement dispute in this racially tense country today by demanding control of three British protectorates.

Dr. Malan shook his fist and banged his desk during a major policy statement to the Senate in which he accused the United Nations of interference in South African affairs and charged successive British Governments with creating dangerous currents among Africa's Negroes through liberal electoral policies.

Since the Nationalists came to power in 1948 they have been pressing Britain unofficially to turn over to the Union of South Africa the rule over the protectorates of Basutoland, Swaziland and Bechuanaland.

Today Dr. Malan announced that in the 1953 general elections he hoped to ask the people to back a formal petition by Parliament to the British Privy Council calling for incorporation of the three territories into the Union.

"The Union no longer is a subordinate country," he asserted. "No free sovereign state would allow a position where territories within its borders are controlled by another country."

The three protectorates, totaling 292,420 square miles with a population of 1,042,000, all adjoin or are surrounded by the South African Union.

The Nationalists contend that Britain promised to turn them over to this country when the Union was formed forty-two years ago. The stand of successive Labor and Conservative governments in London, however, is that repeated promises have been made to the people of the protectorates not to change their status without consulting them.

The New York Times May 14, 1952

Shading indicates the three British protectorates claimed by the South African Premier.

The populations, overwhelmingly Negro, now feel that they have a certain amount of protection under British rule and they are against joining South Africa because of the Malan Government's program of tightening strict white supremacy laws.

South Africa has refused to put her old League of Nations mandate over South-West Africa under a United Nations trusteeship. She also has resented Indian attempts to take to the United Nations complaints on treatment of the Indian minority here.

May 14, 1952

Gains by 3 British Protectorates Causing Concern in South Africa

By LEONARD INGALLS

Special to The New York Times.

JOHANNESBURG, South Africa, Feb. 2—Political developments in three British protectorates are being closely watched by neighboring South Africa.

The territories are Basutoland, Bechuanaland and Swaziland. Basutoland is an enclave in South Africa and the two others have long common boundaries with it. All have strong economic ties to South Africa, which became a republic last year.

Were it not for South Africa's denial of political rights and social equality to Africans, the protectorates might be incorporated in the republic. Such a step was once contemplated, but the protectorates, whose populations are overwhelmingly African, are moving toward self-government and possible independence.

African political parties, which are banned in South Africa, exist in all three territories. Leaders of the Basutoland, Bechuanaland and Swaziland parties met recently to form a united front. Among their demands were early independence, complete elimination of remaining racial discrimination and the submission of any agreements between Britain and South Africa on the protectorates to the peoples concerned.

The greatest fear among the protectorate Africans is that one day their areas will fall under South African rule.

Meanwhile, Africans are being given experience in modern government in Basutoland and Bechuanaland, where they serve in the Legislative Councils.

Studies are under way for the establishment of a similar council in Swaziland.

In Basutoland there are 800,000 Africans and 2,000 whites; in Bechuanaland 350,000 and 3,000 and in Swaziland 250,000 and 8,000.

The British have been trying to develop the territories politically along nonracial lines that would protect both African and white interests. This has been difficult.

The situation is complicated by a clash between tribal chiefs who want to retain their traditional authority and younger, educated Africans who prefer political advancement along Western, democratic lines. Their cry is "one man, one vote," and they would confine paramount chiefs to the role of constitutional monarchs.

Despite their dislike of South Africa, it offers many Basutos, Bechuanas and Swazis their only source of employment. About 150,000 Basutos, nearly half the territory's able-bodied men, are always at work in South Africa, mostly in the mines. In addition there usually are 20,000 Bechuanas and 10,000 Swazis.

Neither mountainous Basutoland nor semi-arid Bechuanaland has much of an economy, but Swaziland is developing rapidly because of mineral resources. About 44 per cent of the land in Swaziland is owned by whites, mostly South Africans.

Heavy Investments Made

British and South African investors are spending $25,000,000 to build a rail link to the Indian Ocean port of Lourenço Marques, in Portuguese Mozambique, so that Swaziland's iron ore can be shipped to Japan under a ten-year, $112,000,000 contract.

South African business men have set up a development corporation to spend $1,500,000 to establish paint, clothing, candy, cigarette, furniture, brick and meat-packing factories in Basutoland.

South Africans are worried lest political and social advance for the protectorate Africans become too rapid and contribute to greater discontent among Africans in the republic. There is talk of ending the freedom of movement between the protectorates and South Africa and of building fences along the borders. The development of a Communist element in Basutoland has caused concern.

The British hope that the protectorates will become models of economic, social and political advance in southern Africa, with Britain continuing for some years as the protecting power.

February 4, 1962

The Changing Face of Southern Africa

Special to The New York Times

GABERONES, Botswana, Friday, Sept. 30—Two southern African territories of Britain — Bechuanaland, which became independent today, and Basutoland, which will become independent on Tuesday are no longer backwaters. They are feeling the winds of change.

Bechuanaland was proclaimed a British protectorate in 1885. Basutoland was administered as a colony by the British from 1884.

For years they have been undisturbed, unambitious, unproductive—economically they are both pitifully poor and independence for them for a long time will have to be bolstered by the same contributions from the outside that have held them together in the past.

But, in their own way, they constitute significant units in a changing Africa.

Both are among the most fascinating countries of the world. Geographically they are fairly remote from the tourist path and their facilities for tourism are few, but their characteristics are most distinct.

Desert and Blue Mountains

When one thinks of Bechuanaland, or Botswana, as the country is to be known, one thinks of desert and Bushmen. Most of the 220,000 square miles of Botswana is desert—its core is the Kalahari itself—and the shrivelled little nut-brown Bushmen of the desert are a constant source of study for anthropologists and adventurers alike.

And Basutoland, or Lesotho, as it will be named, calls up visions of blue mountains, the towering Maluti range that takes up almost three-quarters of Basutoland's entire area and of the blanketed tribesmen who come down from the mountains on their sturdy Basuto ponies.

But the hard facts of economic and political concern are now the dominant realities of both countries.

Above them all looms the big shadow of the Republic of South Africa, whose proximity may become the strongest or the weakest card that will be held by the newly independent territories in negotiations on their future.

The South Africans have realized that Sir Seretse Khama, Bechuanaland's Prime Minister, who now becomes President of Botswana, could turn into one of their most powerful allies in their relations with the rest of black Africa.

The anti-Communist Sir Seretse, is well liked and respected by most of the half a million people of Botswana.

He is similarly trusted by the territory's 3,500 whites for his unswerving policy of non-racialism. The fact that Sir Seretse married an Englishwoman over the objections of his tribe is a factor in this trust.

Sir Seretse is expected to be one of the most stable of African leaders. This stability in a nation on her borders is what South Africa desires and the republic is prepared to go a long way to help it along.

Like Basutoland's Prime Minister, Chief Leabua Jonathan — who met with the late South African Prime Minister, Hendrick F. Verwoerd, on equal terms in Pretoria only a few days before Mr. Verwoerd was assassinated — Sir Seretse is now a black diplomatic contact that South Africa wants to cultivate.

This is the strongest card held by the two black territories. Their weakest is their utter dependence on South Africa for economic necessities.

Out of a population of about a million no fewer than 180,000 Basutos are earning their livelihood outside the territory and most are employed in the Southh African mining industry. This is the cream of the country's young working force. The income in cash and kind from these workers — about $2.8-million a year is virtually responsible for keeping Basutoland alive.

Similarly in Botswana—where the sparse population is ranged predominantly along the Rhodesian Railways line that runs from South Africa's mines. The total of these workers comes to about 60,000 a year, according to a Government source.

A five-year drought, which has brought famine to more than 120,000 in Botswana, has set the country back. Many more Bechuanas have left their arid lands to seek work in South Africa, which has increased the quota to accommodate them.

More than 100,000 people are now being fed by a massive famine-relief operation under United Nations auspices. Under the program Botswand is to get total assistance of about $12.6-million, which is believed to constitute the largest single aid plan ever formulated for an African country.

Britain's own post-independence aid will amount to about $36.4-million over the next three years.

The British Government is also paying the equivalent of almost $7 for each Basuto man, woman and child to enable Basutoland to meet its budget for last year. Britain will have to maintain this sort of subsidy for some years before the future Lesotho can do without it. It is **a legacy of poverty and non-production in Basutoland.**

Politically, the leaders of the new states are well established in personal status and following.

The political opposition in both Botswana and Basutoland is left-wing and strongly Pan-Africanist.

Among the opposition there is frustration and bitterness in arguments against the territories' policies of neighborliness with South Africa.

A Basutoland opposition leader, Ntsu Mokhele, expressed this recently in Masuro, the territory's capital, in a question he asked and then answered himself:

"What happens if we aren't good boys and we go against South Africa? We pay for it—and with South African currency, too."

But the economic and political facts remain.

All in all, the new states of Botswana and Lesotho will have little to give and much to receive before they can achieve any sort of independence in more than just name.

People Show Spirit

But the people have spirit and pride. Bechuanas are at present earning food for themselves and their families by working on community development projects throughout the territory.

This food-for-communal-work plan is expected to take the Bechuanas through the present food crisis and at the same time is to foster a spirit of self-help and self-reliance.

In Basutoland, where factory production is virtually nil, the people look to the mountains for their economic hope.

Basutoland has a chance of striking an economic bargain with South Africa for hydro-electric power and irrigation through the "Oxbow Lake" water plan, centered on a catchment area high in the Maluti mountains of northeast Basutoland where the streams that form the Orange River begin.

Common Market Possible

If the dream of the late Dr. Verwoerd is continued, the two new states will become part of a southern African common market promoted by South Africa.

In this plan Dr. Verwoerd envisaged a sort of confederacy of states — black and white — each independent but having mutually beneficial economic connections. Rich and powerful South Africa would be the focal point of this confederacy, of course.

In this way, Botswana and Lesotho are seen here as a possible bridge over which South Africa can slowly move further afield into the potentially great southern African market.

But the bridge may have a two-way traffic — and Africa hostile to South Africa may be waiting to use it for attacks in the future.

September 30, 1966

Swaziland, Last British Area in Africa,

MBABANE, Swaziland, Friday, Sept. 6 (AP)—Soccer and fireworks, and bonfires atop the twin mountain peaks towering over this tiny kingdom, marked the independence at midnight of the last British territory in Africa.

Swaziland, which is 1,000 square miles smaller than New Jersey, has had the special status of a protected state and internal self-government since April 25, 1967.

The fertile and mineral-rich country, with a population of about 400,000, is a constitutional monarchy under King Sobhuza II, known to his fellow Swazis as Ngwenyama or Lion. The 69-year-old King has been on the throne since 1921. He personifies his country: one foot in the past and the other hopefully in the future.

The King of the Swazis, once one of Africa's great warrior tribes, is equally at home in formal Western clothes or "Mahia," the colorful national costume. He is reputed to have about 170 wives and platoons of children. Statistics are sketchy, but the records do show that the King took his 50th bride around 1933.

King Plans to Move

The royal headquarters is a mud and thatch compound. King Sobhuza plans to move into a relatively modern palace costing $48,000 and keep Swaziland moving forward after "inkhululeko" or independence.

In natural resources and development potential, Swaziland was always the leader among Britain's three landlocked sister territories in southern Africa. It has the only set of traffic lights among the three.

Bechuanaland became Botswana in September, 1966, and four days later Basutoland became Lesotho. Swaziland plans to keep the name it has.

The New York Times

King Sobhuza II of Swaziland is equally at home in the colorful national costume, or in formal Western garb.

More than 50 official visitors are participating in banquets, receptions, concerts and a garden party in honor of independence.

President Johnson is represented in Mbabane by Clifford L. Alexander Jr., chairman of the Federal Equal Employment Opportunity Commission. The United States Consul here, C. C. Pappas, delivered to King Sobhuza today a message from Mr. Johnson offering American congratulations on Swaziland's independence and adding:

"Swaziland has made the difficult passage to statehood with a courage and foresight which will long be an example of peaceful progress."

The Country's Resources

MBABANE, Sept. 5 (Reuters) — Swaziland has rich mineral deposits, including iron ore and asbestos, the Havelock mine being one of the world's five main asbestos producers.

The country's fertile soil nourishes sugar, rice and citrus crops and dense timber plantations.

Annual exports have gone up from 12 million rand ($16.9-million) to 40 million rand ($56.4-million) in the last seven years, but British aid in the form of grants still is needed to balance the budget.

Bordered on the north, west, and south by the Transvaal province of the South African Republic, Swaziland is a 6,705-square-mile enclave, with Zululand and Portuguese Mozambique to the east of its territory.

Its 400,000 mainly pastoral people are akin to the Zulu and other tribes of this region of Southeast Africa.

September 6, 1968

Botswana Offers a Promising Contrast in Africa

By CHARLES MOHR
Special to The New York Times

GABORONE, Botswana, May 28 — Botswana — independent less than four years—offers a pleasant and hopeful contrast to many of the most common trends on the African continent and is fast becoming an encouraging success story.

While the Congo announces she will join a growing number of African states in proclaiming one-party rule; while Kenyan legislators continued to make hostile speeches about white and Asian residents and about tribal nepotism; while crime rates rise among starving Ibos in Nigeria, and while a strong man clings to illegally seized power in Lesotho, the President of Botswana, Sir Seretse Khama, expresses an abiding belief in democracy and is also committed to the principle of a nonracial state.

The discovery of rich deposits of diamonds, nickel and copper promise to bring vital new revenue and free Botswana, the former Bechuanaland protectorate, from British budgetary aid by 1972.

The Government is pragmatic, essentially nonideological and offers the people neither shimmering promises nor scapegoats. Corruption is minimal.

Camera Press-Pix
Sir Seretse Khama of Botswana—independent nearly four years—and his wife, Ruth

'We Have Confidence'

"We probably give this country more aid per capita than any other in the world," one British official remarked. "But we have confidence in their ability not to waste aid."

Problems of tribalism are much less acute than in much of Africa. So are drift from rural areas to urban shantytowns and unemployment among the educated young.

That Botswana seems to be moving toward dignified nationhood and viability is cause for some surprise. As one Briton remarked: "In 1948 the idea that Bechuanaland could be independent was inconceivable." But in 1948 the Nationalist party came to power in neighboring South Africa on the doctrine of apartheid, and any course other than independence for the British protectorate became inconceivable.

Decades of neglect by the British left Botswana with major problems. (Alone among the world's colonies and nations it did not even have its own capital, being administered from South Africa). There were few resources and little revenue and there were only about 30 graduates of secondary schools in the entire country.

Rain Is the Motto

The land is harsh. Six hundred thousand people, mostly cattle-herders, are spread thinly over an area of 220,000 square miles, somewhat smaller than the size of Texas. So sparse and uncertain are the rains that the national motto is "Pula," which means "Let There Be Rain."

Cattle must be driven sometimes hundreds of miles to market in great treks that last as much as four months. Five years of drought from 1960 to 1965 killed a quarter of a million animals, or about 20 per cent of the national herd. Another drought is burning the country this year.

The Kalahari desert covers a huge part of Botswana. Much of the desert is covered with grass and scrub and game roams, but the vegetation grows thinly on a layer of sand 300 to 500 feet deep and there is little ground water.

In the northwest is the Okovanggo Swamp of 8,000 square miles—almost the size of Massachusetts—full of pure, clear water. But it will be difficult to exploit this resource.

Perhaps the most serious problem of all is Botswana's political isolation. The country is almost completely surrounded by the white-supremacist countries of South Africa and Rhodesia. The Rhodesia rail road runs for several hundred miles through Botswana. Botswana uses South African currency and is part of the South African customs union.

Botswana has tried to avoid either provoking or succumbing to South Africa. Diplomacy is conducted, quite successfully, by telephone.

But Botswana has accepted neither South African officials and advisers nor direct aid from the South African Government, believing that to do so would be unhealthy. She accepts and cares for refugees fleeing the countries surrounding her, but carefully prevents the mounting of guerrilla activity from her soil.

Sir Seretse, whose wife is white, has publicly spoken of "our detestation of apartheid" but he has convinced other black states that his great geographic exposure demands that he use less inflammatory rhetoric than they. A Tanzanian official said sympathetically that Botswana's main contribution to the freedom movement in southern Africa should be to survive.

'Must Have Confidence'

"South Africa should realize that Botswana must have the confidence and well wishes of the rest of Africa or it will be fair game for the penetration and infiltration of insurgents," one Western observer remarked. Another said: "If the South Africans are smart they will realize that Seretse is the kind of man who is their best guarantee against trouble."

The President said in a recent interview with the South African radio: "We are confident that we can co-exist with South Africa without sacrificing our national interest or our fundamental principles."

Confident, however, may be too strong a word. In many ways Botswana is an affront to South African racial myths and for the neurotic a source of potential danger.

There is a hopeful sense of racial harmony in Botswana and the young white expatriates working here show an unusual degree of devotion to the country.

One factor that can help prevent South African domination is Botswana's newly found mineral wealth. Almost half the nation's small budget is now subsidized by Britain, but this is obviously not a permanent solution.

Self-Sufficiency Possible

The new mineral developments, however, should quickly achieve what was once considered almost impossible — self-sufficiency.

Bamangwato Concessions, Ltd., an exploration company that is a subsidiary of American Metals Climax, has found nickel and copper at Selebi-Pikwe in east-central Botswana. De Beers, Ltd., is ready to exploit diamonds near Orapa south of the huge Makarikari salt pan. There is speculation it will prove to be one of the richest diamond mines in the world.

Tax and royalties are expected to bring the Botswana Government more than $8-million a year. The nickel and copper mines may bring $8-million to

$13-million a year, or more than present British aid.

But even these blessings are accompanied by problems, and Botswana cannot sit back and collect the money like an oil-rich shiekdom. Totally lacking a structure to support such developments, the country must embark on a program to build roads, pipe water to the mines, create power stations and townships for companies that would otherwise be reluctant to undertake production.

The total program may soak up $150-million, which the World Bank is expected to finance. But Botswana's little bureaucracy has had to cope with the still not resolved problems of getting industrial guarantees for the World Bank loan, marketing agreements to back up the guarantees and other complex negotiations.

It has been helped in this by young British expatriate officials, some of whom are so committed to Botswana that they have become citizens.

Botswana is showing that it is not a comic-opera country—but it sometimes seems like one because it is so small, so poor and so new.

The little capital of Gaborone (formerly spelled Gaberones through an English corruption of a chieftan's name) was begun only shortly before independence. There is no barber shop, no dentist, no place to rent a car and no grass on the central mall, which is surrounded by modern buildings. Next month there will be a movie theater.

It rather resembles a company town in an American mining community, with only five styles of house and 20,000 people.

Still, it has character. The status symbol is not a limousine, but a pick-up truck because many officials like to spend their weekends on their small cattle ranches. The people are quiet, reserved, genial and free. Perhaps this is partly because Botswana, almost unique in Africa, has no preventive detention act.

The parliamentary opposition has only seven seats of 34, but Sir Seretse has expressed a wish that they were stronger.

"I sincerely believe," he said the other day, "that democracy is essential for stability. You can use as much manpower to suppress people as is needed for development itself and where you rule by coercion it's almost inevitable that you will be overthrown by force."

At a national reception one evening almost everyone significant in town seemed to be on hand. As the President entered he shouted the cry for rain "Pula!"

"Pula," the crowd responded, laughing.

Then the national anthem was struck up and it seemed that more whites than blacks knew the words in the local language. When the song stopped, a guest was asked what the anthem said.

"It means," he said, "this land of ours is a gift from God."

BRITISH COOL TO BID FOR AFRICAN UNION

Say Proposal for Dominion in Central Area Must Have Backing of Natives

By CLIFTON DANIEL

Special to THE NEW YORK TIMES.

LONDON, Feb. 18—Reluctant to sanction any possible extension of the policy of white supremacy, British official quarters showed marked coolness and reserve today toward the proposed creation of a new British Dominion in Central Africa. Such a dominion is envisaged by the conference of representatives from Southern Rhodesia, Northern Rhodesia and Nyasaland now being held at Livingstone, Northern Rhodesia.

There exists one great obstacle to the British Government's approval of political federation of the three territories. That is the established British policy that in the protectorates of Nyasaland and Northern Rhodesia the interests of the native Negro population must be paramount. Because of that policy the British Government feels that any act or federation should first be approved by the natives. However, the natives are known to oppose union with Southern Rhodesia, self-governing British colony, because it has a policy of white supremacy similar to that of the Union of South Africa.

Several pertinent facts about the Livingstone conference which was called by Sir Godfrey Huggins, Prime Minister of Southern Rhodesia, were pointed out by the official spokesman here today.

First, the conference is an unofficial one. It is composed of Southern Rhodesian political leaders and unofficial members of the legislative Assemblies in two protectorates. No members of the Northern Rhodesia and the Nyasaland Governments are attending.

Second, the resolutions of the conference are in no way binding upon the London Government, but may be submitted here only for discussion.

Third, the members of the conference are all white Europeans. Out of a total population of 5,500,000 or more in the three territories there only about 130,000 whites and they alone are represented by the conference.

Although the British Government recognizes the desirability of federating the three territories for purpose of operating non-political technical services, it cannot sanction political federation, it was said authoritatively here today, unless the most careful safeguards are provided for the protection of native interests.

February 19, 1949

CENTRAL AFRICANS SPURN BRITISH BID

London Is Unable to Convince Delegates on Federation Plan, but Opens Parley

Special to THE NEW YORK TIMES.

LONDON, April 23—British explanations to African Negroes have not succeeded in overcoming snags in the plan for a central African federation embracing Nyasaland, Northern Rhodesia and Southern Rhodesia.

Official deputations from the first two of those territories declared today that their peoples were unanimously against the plan because they suspected it would mean subordination to the white settlers who already rule Southern Rhodesia. The deputations were explaining their persistent refusal to participate in a conference to discuss the project, which opened here this afternoon without them.

Two Negroes appointed by the Southern Rhodesian Government were the only members of their race to attend the parley. One of them, a newspaper editor, said on his arrival here Monday that a majority of the Africans in the two other territories opposed a federation "because they believe that the less liberal outlook and stricter laws regarding Africans prevailing at present in Southern Rhodesia would then apply to them."

Seeks to Prepare Opinion

The purpose of the conference is to prepare African opinion for ratification of a federation at another parley scheduled here July 8. The attitude of the official African deputations is that European settlers are seeking to railroad a plan that would perpetuate inequalities and close the door to eventual self-government by the African majority.

The educated Negro administrators, who form the official deputations, said that an unofficial delegation that had arrived in Britain to appeal to the public against a federation was fully qualified to speak for the Africans of both territories.

Early Debate Sought

In the House of Commons, A. F. Lennox-Boyd, Minister of State for Colonial Affairs, reassured Labor questioners that the official deputations would be permitted to remain two or three days more to present their case to interested Members of Parliament. The deputations already have expressed their views to Colonial Secretary Oliver Lyttelton, this having been the purpose for which they were invited to London.

James Griffiths, Colonial Secretary in the recent Labor Government, pressed for early debate on the federation plan, and Prime Minister Churchill said that the Government would do its best to arrange one on "these large issues."

April 24, 1952

BRITISH ISSUE PLAN ON CENTRAL AFRICA

Federation of the Rhodesias and Nyasaland Would Have 35-Member Assembly

Special to THE NEW YORK TIMES.

LONDON, June 18—The Government published today a White Paper embodying plans for a Central African Federation, decided upon at an April conference in London with representatives of the white settlers in Northern and Southern Rhodesia and Nyasaland.

The Marquess of Salisbury, Secretary of State for Commonwealth Relations, announced in the House of Lords that a conference to give final form to the draft of a Constitution for the proposed Federation of Rhodesia and Nyasaland would be held in Africa late this year.

The plan, based on proposals put forward by the Labor Government last year, has been opposed steadily by official and unofficial spokesmen of the Negroes who form a large majority of the population in all three territories. They have expressed a fear that

FEDERATION AT ISSUE

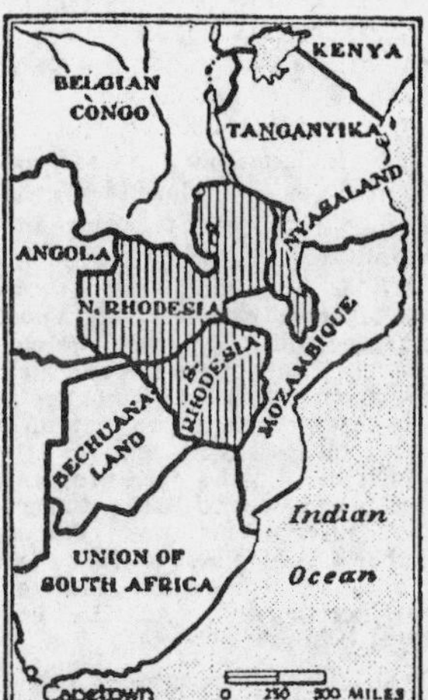

rule by local white settlers would close the door to eventual self-government by the Negroes, already achieved in the Gold Coast colony.

The Negro delegates invited to participate in the April conference declined to attend, with the exception of two from Southern Rhodesia, where the white settlers already enjoy virtual dominion status.

In the preamble of the draft the proposal offered as reassurance to both white and native inhabitants a declaration that "the said territories are the rightul home of all lawful inhabitants thereof, whatever their origin. It offered no explicit formula for determining whose rights would come first.

Under Special Protection

The preamble said that Northern Rhodesia and Nyasaland would remain "under the special protection of Her Majesty." Both protectorates came under the British Crown by agreement with native chiefs in Queen Victoria's reign.

Southern Rhodesia, as a colony occupied and claimed for the Crown without the explicit consent of the local tribes, would continue to enjoy the self-government exercised at present by the white settlers under the safeguards for African interests for which London remains responsible.

The proposed federal assembly would have thirty-five members, roughly proportional to the white population of the three territories —seventeen from Southern Rhodesia, eleven from Northern Rhodesia and seven from Nyasaland. At least six of the thirty-five would be Negroes—two from each territory.

To safeguard the Negroes' rights there would also be an African Affairs Board with seven members—one white and one Negro appointed by the governor of each territory and a chairman appointed by the governor of the federation. All the governors would be appointed, as at present, by the British Government in London.

June 19, 1952

AFRICANS ASK QUEEN'S AID

Opponents of Central Federation Appeal to Her and People

LONDON, Jan. 2 (Reuters)—Five African leaders arrived today to appeal to Queen Elizabeth II—"because she is our protector"—against Britain's plans to unite three central African possessions in a new political federation.

The leaders represent all the chiefs of Nyasaland, which would be united with Northern and Southern Rhodesia under the federation plan involving 6,400,000 Africans, 200,000 Europeans and 14,000 Indians.

In a statement the African chiefs said that "we have come to tell the Queen herself and the British people that we do not want federation."

The federation plan is now being discussed in London at a Government conference boycotted by Africans. They fear the white settlers will dominate them in the proposed federation and that it would mean the end of the African peoples' hopes of self-government.

January 3, 1953

NATIVES PROGRESS, RHODESIAN HOLDS

Welensky, Union Leader, Says Negro Can Become Political Equal of the White

By ALBION ROSS

Special to THE NEW YORK TIMES.

LUSAKA, Northern Rhodesia, Aug. 12—Sir Roy Welensky, with Prime Minister Sir John Huggins of Southern Rhodesia the principal architect of the new Central African Federation, stated in an interview here today that the great issue of the relations of others with the Negro population in this part of the world provided an opportunity for progress.

A dominant political figure in Northern Rhodesia and now one of the most widely known personalities in southern Africa, Sir Roy rose from a locomotive engineer to railway union chief and official leader of the Northern Rhodesian members of the Legislative Council and is the strongest candidate eventually to succeed the 70-year old Sir John as Prime Minister of the new federation.

"I insist on holding out to the African the chance that he can become the political equal of the white," Sir Roy said. "Then it is up to him to see if he can. I do not believe that you can legislate equality. If the white man has any brains he should try to create a middle class among the Africans. I am above all anxious to see that I do what I can to bring that about."

"It is a difficult task to deal with people who are frightened, whether white or black," he continued. "Both races are uncertain about our future. I cannot see as far ahead as some people profess to. I must deal in terms of trial and error. But we must produce a formula in Central Africa to show that different races can live together side by side. Neither those who hold that the black man is an ape, nor those who hold he is an angel help much."

Confident on Copper Price

Sir Roy said he was confident the now falling or threatened price of copper, which is the country's mainstay, would stabilize around the economic price of the producers in the United States, whose costs, he said, are well above the cost of production in Northern Rhodesia and leave Rhodesian industry plenty of room for development. There is a basic long-term shortage of copper that is not a matter of the temporary condition of the markets, he declared.

He said the most important thing for Rhodesian development was the improvement of transportation to deliver coal to the mines and for the export of base metals. This improvement is tied to the development of power resources as electric power saves coal transport. Coal is being produced at a distance of about 600 miles from the mines.

He said the Kafue power project, one of the major power projects in the world, could be completed in five years and then be available just at a time when railway capacity would be completely overloaded. He stated that the engineering studies and all blueprints were ready, but that the snag was the matter of getting around the investment of $87,000,000.

Settling of Nomads

Northern Rhodesia is engaged in an effort to turn an area inhabited by 43,000 largely nomad whites and about 2,000,000 nomad Negroes into a settled state.

About 7,000 or 8,000 whites are arriving annually, but the country is crying out for skilled labor. Two-thirds of the white population is concentrated in the copper-mining area. This white population includes about 6,000 mine employes and their families, with others serving the mining community, on the railroad and in civil service.

For nearly all these people home is somewhere else, either Britain or South Africa. They are Northern Rhodesians in name only. The number of whites for whom this is the permanent home is probably not more than 4,000 or 5,000. This includes the farmers, whose best cash crop is tobacco, but tobacco of such a poor quality that it is hardly competitive on the world market.

About 40,000 native Africans work in the mines. They are unionized and are doing definitely better than the African miners farther south. However, the great majority of the native population lives in native reserves with their grass huts and poor soils in which the Africans carry on the most primitive kind of farming.

August 13, 1953

BRITAIN IMPOSES RHODESIAN RULING

Dictates Charter Change to End White-Negro Rift—Africans Criticize Concessions

Special to THE NEW YORK TIMES.

LONDON, Sept. 22—Faced with irreconcilable differences between the African and European delegates called here to reform the Constitution of Northern Rhodesia, the Colonial Office ended the discussions and dictated a series of Government amendments to the Constitution today.

The changes, to become effective before the next election in the Northern Rhodesian protectorate, made minor concessions to the Africans' demands for a greater voice in the territorial government but left their delegates dissatisfied.

Territorial legislative representatives of the nearly 2,000,000 Africans of Northern Rhodesia will be increased from two to four by the amendments. The representatives will be chosen, as they have been in the past, by a kind of electoral college representing tribal provincial councils.

Representatives of the 37,000 Europeans in Rhodesia, elected by regular suffrage, will be increased from ten to twelve, and the Legislature will continue to include twelve Europeans nominated by the British Government, among them two named specifically to look after African interests. The announcement today said that "when the time comes" the Colonial Secretary would consider "whether it would be desirable" to nominate a Negro as one of the Government's African advocates.

The Colonial Office said that a change from racial representation to a widened franchise was the long-term objective of the British Government. The African delegates to the constitutional conference had asked for the franchise for their people on the same basis as that of British colonials, but the Colonial Office said "this is a difficult problem, which will require very careful consideration."

Oliver Lyttelton, the Colonial Secretary, expects to visit the Central African Federation, of which Northern Rhodesia is a part, next year, and he will look into the question then, the announcement added.

D. L. Yamba, spokesman for the African delegation to London, said he and his colleagues would ask the Governor of Northern Rhodesia to summon the African Representative Council (the body that chooses the African legislators) to consider the points made by Mr. Lyttelton.

"Meanwhile," he added, "we cannot in the name of our people accept the decisions of the Colonial Secretary." He said the amendments did not go "even halfway" to meet African views.

September 23, 1953

Central Africa Federation Is Formally Established

SALISBURY, Southern Rhodesia, Friday, Oct 23 (Reuters) —The Central African Federation came into being today when the new Constitution took full effect.

At the same time the Government issued electoral regulations for Nyasaland that are expected to keep the vote from all but a few Africans. The principal regulation provides that all voters must be members of a political organization or association approved by Governor Sir Geoffrey Colby.

The first Federal election—and the first orthodox political election ever held in Nyasaland —is expected Dec. 15 throughout Nyasaland, Northern and Southern Rhodesia. It will be for the Central Federal Assembly.

The Federation of Nyasaland and the Rhodesias forms a single territory of about 500,000 square miles and a predominantly African population of about 6,287,000.

Queen Elizabeth II sent her "heartfelt good wishes" to the peoples of the federation in a message published here today.

October 23, 1953

BRITISH RHODESIA HAS WHITE SPLIT

Settlers Dispute London's Plan to Give Negroes More Votes —Quarrel Among Selves

Special to THE NEW YORK TIMES.

JOHANNESBURG, South Africa. Nov. 14—Britain has been placed in an invidious position by the quarrel between her and Northern Rhodesia's 50,000 white settlers over franchise rights of the 2,000,000 Africans in that British-protected territory.

Rather than agree to extension of the Negro franchise, Sir Roy Welensky, leader of the whites, and nine other elected members of the Legislative Council have resigned and are refusing to cooperate with the Northern Rhodesian Government.

The Governor has full powers to carry on a Government until a solution is found, possibly when Oliver Lyttleton, British Colonial Secretary, visits the territory early next year. The Governor can act in financial matters by certification and in others through the Executive Council, which is Northern Rhodesia's Cabinet and which has eleven members.

Sir Roy and his followers will continue to sit in the Legislature until the elections in February.

"There are prospects of a first-class row," Sir Roy said recently. "It can lead to only one thing: Europeans will unite for a much greater say in the State Government. Lyttleton's proposals (for changing the Constitution) are quite unacceptable. They mean a 20 per cent increase in the number of white elected members against an increase of 100 per cent in the number of African members to start off with.

"We have been worried and are still worried about his statement that he is considering requests for widening of the native franchise. We say that the African cannot have his cake and eat it too. If the British Government is going to extend direct representation to natives, the natives cannot also expect to enjoy the privileges of the common voters roll."

The crisis follows the recent visit of Sir Roy and other Nothern Rhodesian leaders to Britain where they asked the British Government to increase the number of unofficial elected members and give them more say in running the country. The Colonial Secretary subsequently announced that the number of white elected members of the Legislature would be increased from ten to twelve and African members from two to four.

Whites Split on Future

Observers here see the dispute as a move in the elections due Dec. 15 in British Central Africa —Northern and Southern Rhodesia and Nyasaland—in which the Federal party of Sir Godfrey Huggins and Sir Roy is hard pressed by J. R. Dendy Young's Confederate party.

The Confederate party advocates racial segregation on the South African model and is reported to have won gorund since the three territories were formally joined on the basis of "partnership" between white and Negro. Negroes will sit in the Federal Parliament and some of the Negro candidates have actually been endorsed by the Federal party.

Garfield Todd, the Prime Minister of Southern Rhodesia, has announced that if returned to power in Southern Rhodesia's state elections in January he will order an inquiry into the franchise in that self-governing colony. Mr. Todd said he was determined that the Government of Southern Rhodesia would remain in hands of civilized and responsible people.

November 15, 1953

TINY NYASALAND HAS BIG PROBLEMS

Chief One Is That of Race, Though Negroes Will Have More Voice in Regime

By LEONARD INGALLS
Special to The New York Times.

BLANTYRE, Nyasaland, Sept. 19—Smaller and less well known than most parts of Africa, Nyasaland has the full set of problems that beset the continent. The chief ones are political and racial.

A British protectorate, Nyasaland occupies a long strip of land about 100 miles wide on the west shore of Lake Nyasa between Northern Rhodesia and Tanganyika. It is the home of 2,500,000 Negroes, 5,000 Europeans and 8,000 Asians and persons of mixed blood.

Like all areas that do not have political independence, Nyasaland wants it and has just taken an important step toward self-government.

With the approval of the British Colonial Office a constitutional change has been made to grant a vote to all non-Africans and to give Africans increased representation in the Nyasaland Legislative Council. The latter will consist of twelve official Government members, five African members, an increase of two, and six non-African members.

Negro legislators who hitherto had been appointed by the Governor will be elected by the African provincial councils whose members are elected with the approval of the district commissioners.

Some Negro Resentment

While the new arrangement, which will become effective with the elections early next year, increases the Negro voice in Government there is some resentment among the Negroes that they have not been given representation equal to the elected non-Africans. The Asians, who make up most of Nyasaland's trading group, are fearful that they will not be able to muster sufficient votes to elect a representative. They have an appointed one in the present Legislative Council.

The Nyasalanders also worry about their position as little brother in the Central African Federation. They fear being swamped by the economically and politically more powerful Northern and Southern Rhodesia. Whether their fears are justified remains to be seen, for the federation is still in its infancy.

Possibly Nyasaland's toughest problem, as it is everywhere south of the Sahara, is the one of race. There are signs, however, of a willingness in all racial groups to attack it intelligently. One of these is the formation of the Interracial Association of Nyasaland, headed by Philip Howard, a Blantyre business man.

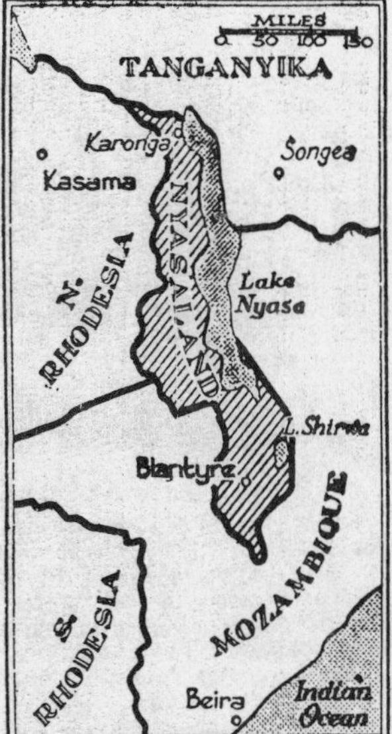

The New York Times Sept. 23, 1955

Color Bar Is Strong

There is a strong, though unofficial, color bar in Nyasaland. In its sixteen months of existence the Interracial Association, which has 200 white, Negro and Asian members has been chipping away at that.

The question of racial discrimination in hotels, restaurants and airport terminals has been taken up with the Government, but thus far appeals for official action have brought the reply that it is a matter of public opinion. The association is also working to eliminate separate salary scales for Africans.

Although association members gather only twice weekly, Blantyre's health officer, a South African, has banned the use of the building donated to the group because it does not have certain sanitary facilities. Mr. Howard cites this incident as typical of the obstacles placed in the association's way.

Negro Rule of Africa Seen

A group of Nyasaland Negroes gathered yesterday afternoon at the home of Wellington Chirwa in near-by Limbe for a discussion and interview. Mr. Chirwa is one of two African members from Nyasaland of the Central African Federation Parliament.

Those present included a politician, a teacher, a civil servant, business men, a student and a housewife. All are members of African National Congress, the Negro political organization which claims the support of the majority of Africans throughout Africa.

Mr. Chirwa and the rest of the group predicted that political control of Africa south of the Sahara would be won by Africans in spite of any efforts by Europeans to prevent it.

September 25, 1955

AFRICAN NEGROES SPUR NATIONALISM

Movement Is Seen Growing in Northern Rhodesia as Labor Unrest Mounts

By LEONARD INGALLS
Special to The New York Times.

NDOLA, Northern Rhodesia, July 13—Negro nationalism is a rapidly growing force in Northern Rhodesia.

In recent weeks it has been showing its strength in two ways. One has been a series of boycotts against shops operated by whites and Asians in copper mining towns. The other has been a series of strikes by Negro copper miners.

African nationalism, as it is called here, is centered in the African National Congress, a Negro political party that is organized to represent the 2,000,000 Negroes in this British territory. The area, with Southern Rhodesia and Nyasaland, forms the Central African Federation.

There are similar organizations in most of the other countries in Africa south of the Sahara that also call themselves the African National Congress. They have a common creed, "Africa for the Africans."

Leadership Held Identical

The leadership of the African Mineworkers Union, which speaks for 37,000 Negro miners, and that of the African National Congress in Northern Rhodesia, which has 60,000 dues-paying members, is said to be identical. Most officers of the union are loyal congress members.

Although the African National Congress is not officially recognized by the Northern Rhodesian Government, its effective use of strikes and boycotts has forced the Government to deal with it on a practical basis.

The boycotts against traders, for overcharging Negroes and compelling them to be served through small windows instead of at counters inside the stores side by side with whites, are forcing changes. A recent court decision upheld use of the boycott.

The recent wave of strikes at the copper mines resulted from dissatisfaction with the advancement programs for Negro miners. Officials of the African Mineworkers Union say the program is "a farce."

They say that in reality it is a "cheap labor" program. And they point to the fact that Negroes promoted to jobs formerly held by whites are being paid one-third for identical work. In this complaint they are supported by representatives of the white miners' union.

Opposed to Federation

The African National Congress also is opposed to the young Central African Federation and denounces its basic principle of racial partnership as "nonsense."

Some responsible persons here suggest that both the African National Congress and the African Mineworkers Union are subject to Communist influence. As evidence, they point to the fact that literature from behind the Iron Curtain is received in the mail by both white and Negro labor unions.

The rise of Negro nationalism is causing great concern among 60,000 whites in Northern Rhodesia. They assert that the Negroes, most of whom have had little or no education and less than fifty years of contact with Western civilization, are trying to move forward politically and economically too rapidly.

There also is, as there is all over Africa south of the Sahara, a determination to maintain white supremacy for many years to come.

July 15, 1956

VOICE OF AFRICA: THE YOUNGER MEN

By RICHARD P. HUNT
Special to The New York Times.

SALISBURY, Southern Rhodesia, July 7—It was the younger men who did the talking when the conversation turned late at night to Negro nationalism.

The three older Africans, sitting back, listened passively and nodded. One yawned and closed his eyes. But the two men in their thirties lighted cigarettes and began to gesture, hunching forward in their chairs.

They were the Negroes who are breathing vigor into the revival in Southern Rhodesia of the political movement known as the African National Congress. They belong to a young men's organization that is to merge soon with the nearly defunct branches of the old congress.

By the light of a kerosene lamp in a new ranch-style house at Highfields, a segregated suburb seven miles from town, the younger men gave a foreign visitor their version of what Africans want and how they propose to get it.

All five were prosperous as Africans go. They wore jackets, shirts and ties. Outside the house, gay flowers bloomed in a little garden beside the unlighted street. A figured rug, print curtains and comfortable chairs decorated the parlor. An automobile stood near the garage.

A Question on Suffrage

Yet sharp words poured in sonorous, short bursts from the smaller, more voluble younger man. The Whites, he said, hold the wealth and power in SouthernRhodesia and they are determined to keep control out of African hands.

Why can his father not vote, he asked, when the old man is wise in the ways of politics even though he cannot read or write? The son expressed the belief that the Europeans would never grant universal suffrage.

"We must take strong measures," he said, but did not elaborate.

The urbane, taller man spoke more calmly and smiled often. Africans in Southern Rhodesia are not anti-white, he said, nor would they deny anyone equal opportunity.

He thought white politicians could be convinced to further African interests, perhaps by political pressures. Beyond that, he hinted, there is always the possibility of passive resistance and boycotts.

Then the tall one laughed and the short one giggled as they told how an official, fearing trouble, had pleaded with them to call off what had been planned as a peaceful demonstration. They had complied.

The older men did not laugh.

It was a conversation similar to talk heard in Nairobi, Kenya; Dar-es-Salaam, Tanganyika, or Johannesburg and Capetown, South Africa. Sometimes the words were more violent, sometimes milder. Usually it was the younger men who did the talking.

July 15, 1957

SOUTH RHODESIA GETS NEW CHIEF

Premier Ousted by His Own Party Over Racial Policy—Aide in U. S. Gets Post

By RICHARD P. HUNT
Special to The New York Times.

SALISBURY, Southern Rhodesia, Feb. 8—R. S. Garfield Todd, Prime Minister of Southern Rhodesia, was deposed by his own party tonight after a quarrel over his leadership and racial policy.

Sir Edgar Whitehead, Minister for Rhodesia and Nyasaland Affairs at the British Embassy in Washington, was elected to replace Mr. Todd as leader of the Southern Rhodesia branch of the United Federal party and hence as Prime Minister. Mr. Todd will continue to head a caretaker government until Sir Edgar arrives from Washington.

Mr. Todd, a 49-year-old former missionary from New Zealand, is identified in the minds of Africans here with a program of rapid advancement for Negroes. African leaders predicted that his fall from power would bring about a turn toward radicalism in the relatively mild African nationalist movement in Southern Rhodesia.

The situation also raised the possibility that independence for the Federation of Rhodesia and Nyasaland might be delayed if doubts were stirred in Britain about the sincerity of the national pledge to a policy of "racial partnership."

Todd Is Silent on Plans

Mr. Todd was silent about his plans for his own political future. However, there is an evident possibility that he may bolt the party and enter open conflict with Sir Roy Welensky, Prime Minister of the Federation and national leader of the United Federal organization.

Mr. Whitehead, 52, is not a member of the Southern Rhodesia Parliament. However, he can legally serve as Prime Minister for three months before he is required to hold a seat. It is expected that a vacancy will be made so that he can be elected.

Sir Edgar served as Finance Minister of Southern Rhodesia for seven years. He retired in 1953 because of an eye ailment, but recently has indicated that he would return to active politics.

He was elected at the close of a tense, eleven-hour party Congress of 300 delegates packed into a Presbyterian Church hall here. Mr. Todd spoke for an hour and three quarters in an effort to save his job, but was unable to swing the delegates.

The Federation of Rhodesia and Nyasaland is made up of Southern Rhodesia, a self-governing British colony, and Northern Rhodesia and Nyasaland, which are colonies administered by the British Colonial Office. Together the three territories hope to gain independent dominion status in 1960.

Mr. Todd is the only white politician in the country who has been able to capture the trust and loyalty of a large following of Africans. Partly as a result, it is believed, Southern Rhodesia is the only territory of the three that has managed to avoid bitter racial flare-ups.

The African movements of Northern Rhodesia and Nyasaland stubbornly oppose the idea of an independent Federation, which they feel would be a sell-out to the whites.

During the four years he has been Prime Minister, Mr. Todd's Government has pressed higher standards in African wages, housing and education. He has promised Southern Rhodesia's 2,000,000 Negroes economic equality with the 200,000 whites in twenty years.

On Jan. 11 all four Cabinet ministers and the one junior minister suddenly resigned. Mr. Todd said they had told him it would be impossible to win the next general election, scheduled for late this year, because of criticism levelled at him.

A spokesman for the ministers said they feared that the opposition Dominion party, which stands for white supremacy without specifically saying so, would have an excellent chance of winning the election if Mr. Todd remained in power.

The dispute has been simmering for some months. It was brought to a boil when Mr. Todd suddenly increased basic minimum wages for Africans by amounts up to 30 per cent. There was also a clash over funds sought for African schools.

Outwardly Sir Roy Wlensky remained neutral in the dispute. The Federal Prime Minister sat patiently through the debate today but never said a word. It was evident, however, that he could have intervened some time ago to save Mr. Todd if he had chosen to.

February 9, 1958

TENSIONS BESET NORTH RHODESIA

Strikes and Boycotts Seen if Africans Do Not Obtain Constitutional Reforms

By RICHARD P. HUNT
Special to The New York Times.

LUSAKA, Northern Rhodesia, Feb. 14—Clouds of political tension are rolling over the warm, flat plains of Northern Rhodesia.

Government officials, white politicians and leaders of the African Nationalist Movement agree that this British colony is likely to experience political agitation and unrest within the next two years.

The feeling is general that a campaign of strikes, boycotts and demonstrations by Africans can be avoided only if the Africans receive substantial concessions in current constitutional talks.

Equality Is Demanded

On the territorial level, Northern Rhodesia's African National Congress organization is asking equal Negro representation on the Legislative Council and universal adult suffrage. Dominant white parties are opposed to both.

The Congress also bitterly opposes the inclusion of Northern Rhodesia in the Federation of Rhodesia and Nyasaland, which links this colony with Southern Rhodesia and Nyasaland. The Congress feels that the independence the federation will seek in 1960 would consign Africans to permanent white rule.

"It is clear we are getting to a time when extreme elements are going to be out of control if we get nothing by a policy on nonviolence," said Kenneth Kaunda, Secretary General of the Congress.

"Unless we can make ourselves heard within the next ten months we will have lost our battle," he added, "and we will know what we are in for." He meant white domination.

The official policy of this colony and the federation is that white domination is not intended. The proposal is to bring about racial partnership between the 70,000 whites and 2,000,000 Africans in Northern Rhodesia and do the same in the federation.

Education a Problem

The problem has been to convince the Africans that partnership means anything other than a partnership like that of horse and rider. The Government's difficulty is that the great mass of Africans still live in primitive conditions and have little education. For example, there are only about twenty Africans in this country with university degrees.

Nevertheless, a great many Africans are emerging into urban life and industrial jobs, especially in the six great copper mines along the Congo border. This class forms the Congress, which now claims 200,000 members in 496 branches.

Last year was one of widespread unrest. In the first nine months there were ninety-five clashes between the police and Congress members. The authorities arrested 545 Africans and fined or jailed 435.

A newspaper here charged the Congress was organizing an army in remote areas, teaching hooliganism and hatred of white men. However, the Government said it had not found evidence to support this.

Nevertheless in the wake of a series of boycotts, petty strikes, stonings and the derailment of a train, stringent new security measures were enacted. These enabled the Government to prohibit any activity it thought tended to create an emergency, to ban public meetings and to disband societies deemed undesirable—all without recourse to the courts.

February 15, 1958

RACISTS ADVANCE IN RHODESIA VOTE

Though Beaten by Federal Party, Dominionites Add to Strength in House

Special to The New York Times.

SALISBURY, Southern Rhodesia, Nov. 14 — Two segregationist trends seem to have been overlooked amid the acclamation here for Sir Roy Welensky's landslide election victory on a platform of white settler paternalism.

Through the general adulation emerges the fact that the Dominion party, which favors white supremacy, although defeated at the polls by Sir Roy's United Federal party, has advanced its cause in British Central Africa.

In the old Federal Parliament of thirty-five members the Dominionites held only one-tenth of the power in the party line-up. In the new assembly, expanded to fifty-nine members, they have climbed to one-sixth. And the latest figures show that the Dominion party's vote represents 35 per cent of the electorate.

In addition, it became known today that thousands of ballots for the election of the four Africans to the special seats in Southern Rhodesia had been deliberately invalidated, left blank or defaced by white voters asked to state their choice of an African candidate. A total of 6,314 such ballots, representing 10 per cent of the total general electorate throughout Southern Rhodesia, were rejected by election officers.

These methods of rejection were most prevalent in Dominion party strongholds in the colony. Before the election, the right wing of the Dominion party, including virulently racist Afrikaner settlers, made it clear they would not vote for an African "in any circumstances." Only one of the Dominion party's four Negro candidates in the colony was elected.

November 16, 1958

MOB IN NYASALAND FIRED ON BY ARMY

Soldiers Used for First Time to Quell Nationalist Riots —One Death Reported

Dispatch of The Times, London.

BLANTYRE, Nyasaland, Feb. 24—Troops fired today on mobs in the market area of Lilongwe, capital of Nyasaland's Central Province.

This was the first time troops had been used to quell the disturbances in this British protectorate. Two volleys were reported to have been fired.

There were two casualties. It was not known whether the injuries were fatal. [One African was killed, according to reports received by Reuters.]

Policemen fired tear-gas shells from riot guns several times to disperse the roaming mobs, but finally African troops and the Rhodesian Air Force had to be called in. Air force planes dropped tear-gas bombs on the rioters.

Late tonight the crowds were dispersed, but the situation remained uneasy. Patrol cars kept on the move in the town.

[The head of the Nyasaland branch of the African National Congress, Dr. Hastings Banda, has been campaigning for the withdrawal of Nyasaland from the Federation of Rhodesia and Nyasaland, a member of the British Commonwealth. He wants to have the protectorate linked, instead, with Kenya, a British colony, and Tanganyika, a United Nations trust territory administered by Britain.]

The situation at Balaka, about fifty miles north of Blantyre, deteriorated again today. An African policeman was slightly wounded by stabbing.

Security forces patroled some areas after sixty Africans mobbed and stoned the Balaka railroad station yesterday. The Riot Act was read, but the crowd refused to disperse and nightsticks were wielded in clearing the area. Four persons were arrested, including one woman.

The Northern Province reported quiet in every district tonight. A political meeting was held at Mzuzu without incident.

The Nyasaland Government announced today that the disposition of Security forces brought in from Northern and Southern Rhodesia to deal with the African nationalist disturbances, was complete and 'the situation has been contained."

Troops are guarding schools, hostels, power stations and airfields.

In Blantyre, the proctectorate's chief commercial center, two policemen were injured in helping to disperse an unruly crowd last night.

Unconfirmed reports of heavy casualties in the Karonga district of northern Nyasaland, which is now closed to correspondents, are still trickling in. Yesterday it was officially announced that the police were starting operations in Karonga to bring to justice persons who had done extensive damage there recently.

The Secretary for African Affairs, John Ingham, said today in Zomba, the protectorate's capital, that the situation was not an emergency.

He said the Nyasaland African Congress' aim of immediate self-government by the Negroes and withdrawal from the federation with the Rhodesias had been pursued until recently by constitutional means.

But lately, he said, Congress leaders are "deliberately encouraging the holding of unlawful meetings and demonstrations."

February 25, 1959

RHODESIA ENACTS EMERGENCY RULE

Leader of Southern Region Aims to Halt Unrest—250 to 500 Africans Seized

Dispatch of The Times, London.

SALISBURY, Southern Rhodesia, Feb. 26—The Prime Minister of Southern Rhodesia, Sir Edgar Whitehead, announced today a state of emergency in the territory and the detention of leaders of the African National Congress under emergency regulations.

The Southern Rhodesian African National Congress, the Nyasaland African National Congress, the Zambia National Congress and Northern Rhodesian African National Congress have been banned as illegal organizations in Southern Rhodesia.

Sir Edgar, whose broadcast came as a surprise, said the Government had advised the Governor to proclaim a state of emergency in view of the general security situation in the Federation of the Rhodesias and Nyasaland and the "grave situation" that had occurred in Nyasaland as a result, the statement said, of the policy of violence pursued by the Nyasaland African Congress among the Negro population.

Action Held Necessary

The fact that this policy is supported by the African National Congress in Southern Rhodesia, he said, has given rise to reasonable fear that a similar grave situation might occur in the territory unless immediate steps are taken to deal with the emergency.

The Government information office in Salisbury said that the acting president of the Southern Rhodesian African National Congress, James Robert Chikerema, and its general secretary, George Nyandoro, had been detained. Later, at a press conference, the Prime Minister revealed that between 250 and 500 persons had been detained.

In his broadcast Sir Edgar said the Government had followed closely the development of extremism in the African

Unrest Is High in the Central African Federation

Troops of the King's African Rifles stage a show of strength in Blantyre, Nyasaland, united with Northern and Southern Rhodesia in Britain's Central African Federation. In Southern Rhodesia, African National Congress was banned and its leaders arrested.

National Congresses in the last few months but that its powers under existing legislation were inadequate to curb this trend.

Sir Edgar said that extreme nationalism, either European or colored, would be fatal to the concept of a multi-racial society. He warned that if the European National Congress members "grew tiresome" he would have no hesitation in putting them behind bars.

The Prime Minister said the Federal Government had given unstinted approval of the emergency proclamation. The action taken against subversive groups in no way involved a change of policy, he said, and the Government was determined to continue its stated policy of giving greater opportunities to colored people in all spheres.

This afternoon in Parliament the leader of the Opposition, S. Aitken-Cade, said the Opposition fully supported the Government's action. Parliament agreed unanimously to an unopposed motion by Sir Edgar that will enable the emergency regulations to remain in force for a month.

Meanwhile, the two-day-old strike of the Kariba dam workers is breaking up. Today about 600 workers went back to work. However, it appears likely that most of the thirteen hundred Nyasa Africans striking at dam will be paid off.

February 27, 1959

NEW OUTBREAKS STIR NYASALAND

One African Dies as Troops Fire at Mob—435 Held in Southern Rhodesia

BLANTYRE, Nyasaland, Feb. 27 (AP)—Security forces used rifles and tear gas to break up an African demonstration near here today. One African was killed and two were wounded in this latest burst of native nationalism in southern Africa.

In Southern Rhodesia, the British rounded up scores of African nationalists and took them to barbed-wire encampments. All was reported quiet in Northern Rhodesia, which with Nyasaland and Southern Rhodesia make up the British Commonwealth's Central African Federation.

British authorities said the latest trouble in Nyasaland began when 200 Africans gathered outside the courthouse at Chigaru, thirty miles south of here.

The crowd demanded the release of two African National Congress officials on trial inside. Those in the crowd brandished stones and iron bars.

Security forces ordered the crowd to disperse. When the demonstrators refused, the soldiers used tear gas, then fired four rounds of rifle shots.

Three Africans have now been killed in skirmishes with security forces. Two were shot fatally in rioting at Lilongwe earlier this week.

Today's shooting was on the main road between Blantyre and Lilongwe.

Minor incidents between rebellious Africans and white policemen and troops were reported from other parts of Nyasaland.

Dr. Hastings K. Banda, president of the Nyasaland African National Congress, said the tense and dangerous situation here would "solve itself, if the Government does not get panicky."

435 Arrested in Dragnet

SALISBURY, Southern Rhodesia, Feb. 27 (Reuters)—A police dragnet has netted 435 African nationalists in Southern Rhodesia since Thursday's declaration of a state of emergency in this self-governing territory, it was officially reported tonight.

Britons Review Policy

By KENNETT LOVE

Special to The New York Times.

LONDON, Feb. 27—Britons concerned with African colonial problems have been spurred into an urgent and searching review of policy by the broad scale of Nationalist rioting in Africa.

The British territory most seriously affected is the protectorate of Nyasaland, where Africans are emphasizing with demonstrations and violence their demand for withdrawal from Central African Federation of Nyasaland and the Rhodesias.

They fear subjugation by the white-settler minority in Southern Rhodesia.

Southern Rhodesia, which has been self-governing since 1923, can act without fear of such British political repercussions as would follow high-handedness by the protectorate Governments of Northern Rhodesia and Nyasaland.

Italy, France and Belgium have also been affected by outbreaks spanning Africa.

United Movement Indicated

The international scope has led to suggestions in parliamentary circles that European colonial powers consult one another on the problem. But most informed politicians and officials feel that such a move, no matter what its motives, would be interpreted by Africans as hostile.

Africans would recall the partition of Africa by Europeans at the conference of Berlin in 1884, some officials said.

Most authorities here believe that African nationalist movements, once kept separate by colonial boundaries and bad communications, have now linked up. This new cohesion south of the Sahara became effective at the All-Africa People's Conference in Accra, Ghana, in December, in the opinion of many observers.

February 28, 1959

GANDHI'S TACTICS PUSHED IN AFRICA

New Movement in Northern Rhodesia Plans Campaign of Civil Disobedience

Special to The New York Times.

LUSAKA, Northern Rhodesia, Feb. 23—A young movement preaching nonviolence has established itself among Africans in Northern Rhodesia.

The movement, called the Zambia African National Congress, plans passive resistance to British colonial rule, following the example of Gandhi.

Zambia has called for a boycott of the territorial elections scheduled for March 20. Its leaders also talk in general terms of a future Northern Rhodesian government "for Africans and by Africans."

Zambia's creed, as expounded in interviews with its leaders here this week, includes a socialistic planned economy on cooperative lines. But the leaders say they are aware of the danger of driving Western capital away.

No blueprint for socialism has been drafted. "We do not want to build castles in the air," they said. The leaders expect, however, that there would be some redistribution of land—with adequate compensation.

Copper Profits Eyed

They also advocate a diversion of copper earnings, now this territory's greatest source of income, to develop rural industry. Mineral rights, owned since 1890 by the British South Africa Company, would be nationalized.

Zambia was formed last October after a split in the ten-year-old African National Congress. The Congress is supporting the March election and running candidates.

The new movement claims more than 75,000 of the 100,000 former Congress supporters. Its main strength is in the urban centers and the large Northern Province. It also has strength in Barotseland.

Zambia's plans for attaining power are vague. The turns its civil disobedience may take are not yet charted. But they will be based on experience in Ghana, according to Kenneth Kaunda, a 37-year-old former Presbyterian minister, who is president of the organization.

"Perhaps we might first seek to withdraw our labor from European employers," he said.

Bars Use of Weapons

A shrug and a smile were his response to the question whether passive resistance would succeed.

"But," he said, "the weapons of violence are in the hands of the imperialists; we will not use them."

Zambia proposes that the tribal chiefs, now organized in a system of native authorities under British direction, form a national council similar to the British House of Lords. The chiefs would have little legislative responsibility, but they would be the conservators of tribal heritage.

Zambia is opposed to the present Federation of Rhodesia and Nyasaland, formed in 1953 from the territories of Northern Rhodesia and Nyasaland and the self-governing colony of Southern Rhodesia. It expects its big test to come in 1960, when the status of the Federation is discussed in Britain.

The Zambia leaders put their stock in majority rule. One of the causes of the split with the Congress was a purported lack of internal democracy.

Mr. Kaunda is confident that the same principle will provide adequate safeguards for minority groups when an African majority governs.

"When a minority is in power they make bad laws to safeguard themselves," he said. "A majority does not need to make bad laws."

The Zambia leaders point to India and Ghana. In both countries, Mr. Kaunda said, the British still have good relations with the nationals.

February 27, 1959

A Symbol of Freedom

Dr. Hastings Kamazu Banda

Man in the News

THE moment of truth for Dr. Hastings Kamazu Banda came when he stepped off a plane in Nyasaland last July. He faced a curious throng of Africans to whom he had become, in absentia, a passionate symbol of freedom. Until that moment he had been a legend in Nyasaland, a British protectorate of 2,500,000 persons. Although he had not set foot in his native land in forty-one years, the grim, gnome-like little doctor had since 1951 been in the forefront of the Nyasa nationalists' fight. They were battling a British plan to submerge Nyasaland in federation with Northern and Southern Rhodesia, where the white minority was stronger.

A roar rose from thousands of Africans as Dr. Banda alighted.

"Kwaca! Kwaca! Kwaca!" they cried.

Kwaca is the African nationalist slogan. It means dawn, or the beginning of freedom. Dr. Banda, the head of the Nyasaland African National Congress, was hailed as a messiah.

Spoke Only English

Stocky, nearly bald and unimpressive in appearance, Dr. Banda, 54 years old, enhanced his mystique with the Africans by speaking only English instead of his native Chinyanja. He wore Savile Row suits, black homburgs and an occasional fawn raincoat. Generally he required an interpreter.

Proudly calling himself "the extremist of extremists," he said repeatedly that he had no use for African moderates.

"We are not going to be bullied by Rhodesian white settlers," he would roar. "To hell with federation!" And the crowd would roar back "Ufulu! Ufulu! Ufulu! (freedom)."

At rallies, crowds scrambled to kiss his hand. "Art thou the second coming of Christ?" he was asked.

The adulation was heady and Dr. Banda, gesturing wildly, would urge his followers to invite imprisonment and even death in the cause of freedom.

'Mean to Be Masters'

White settlers found him an intolerable demagogue. Sir Roy Welensky, Prime Minister of the Central African Federation of the Rhodesias and Nyasaland, began grumbling about "subversive activities." But Dr. Banda would not be silenced.

"In Nyasaland," he said, "we mean to be masters, and if that is treason make the most of it."

He seemed fascinated by the development of the Cyprus crisis and its recent solution of pledged independence for Cypriotes. He hoped Nyasaland would follow the Cyprus path. Some whites found it significant that the recent riots began a few days after the Cyprus settlement.

But during the disturbances Dr. Banda remained quiet and inactive. A dispatch to The New York Times said he seemed "genuinely disturbed at the recent course of events."

Dr. Banda was born in a Nyasa village of poor, uneducated parents who belonged to the Chewa tribe. He ran away at 13 "to acquire an education, because today one does not fight with spears, one fights with knowledge."

His parents thought he had been eaten by lions. But months later the boy turned up in Johannesburg, South Africa, where he got a job in a gold mine.

Lived in U. S. 12 Years

He put together enough money for sea passage to the United States, where he lived

Associated Press

"Extremist of extremists"

for twelve years. He studied medicine at the University of Chicago and later at the University of Edinburgh in Scotland. Then he set up a practice in the London suburbs, where he claimed a prosperous practice of 4,000 patients, mostly white.

Meanwhile, he maintained close relations with tribal leaders in Nyasaland and became the chief spokesman in Britain for extremists in the Nyasaland African National Congress who opposed federation with the Rhodesias. When the federation was established in August, 1953, Dr. Banda left London and moved to the Gold Coast. There, in the Ashanti country, he became a friend of Kwame Nkrumah and watched admiringly when Dr. Nkrumah became Premier of the new Republic of Ghana.

Early last year, when the Nyasaland Congress split on failure to move toward secession, groups appealed to Dr. Banda to go home and become a "Nkrumah" to his own people.

February 28, 1959

RHODESIANS MAP HARSH RACE LAW

Bill Would Outlaw African Groups and Bolster Police

Special to The New York Times.

SALISBURY, Southern Rhodesia, March 11—To combat the campaign for African nationalism, the Southern Rhodesian Government introduced a bill today to give severe repressive powers to the police and civil servants.

The program's harshness shocked even members of the Opposition Dominion party, a champion of white supremacy. While agreeing that stern measures are necessary, they are outraged at the means chosen.

The scattered handful of Southern Rhodesian white liberals, already deeply shocked by the recent proclamation of a state of emergency and the arrest of Guy Clutton-Brock, are talking about a "police state." Mr. Clutton-Brock, the founder of an interracial agricultural project, is one of the few Europeans belonging to the African National Congress.

The bill, introduced by the Minister of Justice, Reginald Knight, seeks to declare the following organizations unlawful in this self-governing British colony:

The African National Congresses of Northern and Southern Rhodesia, Nyasaland and the Union of South Africa, the Zambia African National Congress of Northern Rhodesia, the World Federation of Trade Unions, the World Peace Council, the World Federation of Democratic Youth, the Women's International Democratic Federation and the International Union of Students.

Under the bill the Governor would have the power to add other organizations to the list by proclamation and such action would not be open to question in any court of law.

Other provisions include the following:

¶Any commissioned police officer may call on any person believed to be an officer of an unlawful organization to furnish lists of members and officers.

¶Any member of the police may without warrant, enter any place in which he has reason to believe a meeting of an unlawful organization is taking place, a member of such an organization resides or pertinent documents may be found, and to arrest all persons found and to seize arms, books and papers.

¶Any person who belongs to unlawful organizations indicates he is a member, contributes to or takes part in their activities, allows unlawful meetings in his house or refuses information to the police shall be liable to a fine of £1,000 ($2,800) or imprisonment for five years, or both.

¶Any person alleged to be a member of an unlawful organizaton will be presumed to be so until the contrary is proved; any person attending a meeting shall be presumed to be a member until the contrary is proved.

¶Special jurisdiction will be given to magistrates to impose penalties in summary trials.

¶No legal proceeding may be taken against the governor or any member of the Executive Council, civil servant or policeman, or against any person acting under their direction or with their approval.

March 12, 1959

North Rhodesia Outlaws Group; Nationalist 'Terrorism' Charged

Zambia Congress Is Accused of Using Gang Tactics in Boycott on Election

By MILTON BRACKER

Special to The New York Times.

BLANTYRE, Nyasaland, March 12—The Governor of Northern Rhodesia outlawed the Zambia African National Congress today. The group has been urging Africans to boycott the territorial election a week from tomorrow.

The Governor, Sir Arthur Benson, in a broadcast announcing his action, charged the congress with having terrorized natives by threats of violence and witchcraft. He compared the intimidation to techniques used by gangsters in the United States.

Sir Arthur also announced that the leaders of the Zambia group, including Kenneth Kaunda, its president, had been detained. But he said they would be sent back to their own tribal areas rather than jailed.

The Zambia National African Congress and other nationalist groups opposed to white supremacy would be outlawed by a bill introduced yesterday in Southern Rhodesia.

Northern Rhodesia, like Nyasaland, is a protectorate. With the self-governing colony of Southern Rhodesia they constitute the Central African Federation.

Election Adds to Tension

A state of emergency was declared in Southern Rhodesia Feb. 26 and in Nyasaland March 3. No state of emergency has been declared in Northern Rhodesia, but the situation has become more strained as the election nears.

The vote will choose members of the Legislative Council under the new Constitution, which the Government says will increase nonwhite representation.

The Zambia congress has opposed the vote because, like the Nyasaland African Congress, it contests the whole idea of federation. Northern Rhodesia borders on Nyasaland for more than 300 miles. The congress' main goals transcend geographical frontiers, which in the border areas have little meaning to the people.

Sir Arthur did not take action against the Northern Rho-

British Information Service

Sir Arthur Benson

desian African Congress, which is headed by Harry Nkumbula. Mr. Nkumbula's group has claimed 3,000 members, and he has declared that "nothing could prevent Northern Rhodesia from becoming a self-governing African state."

Sir Arthur noted that Mr. Nkumbula had attended a congress of African nationalists in Accra, Ghana, in December, but that the Northern Rhodesian "disagreed with certain things and left before it ended."

According to the Governor, the Zambia African National Congress was an outgrowth of the post-Accra split between Mr. Nkumbula of the Northern Rhodesian African National Congress on one side and Mr. Kaunda and Dr. Hastings K. Banda, deported leader of the African National Congress in Nyasaland, on the other. The issue, according to the Governor, was the question of violence as a means to attain ends.

Sir Arthur emphasized that the situation in Northern Rhodesia did not justify declaring a state of emergency.

His reference to Accra marked the second time in two days that Ghana has been brought into the situation in the federation. Tuesday at Kitwe Sir Roy Welensky, the federation's Prime Minister, blamed Ghana for the developments here. Yesterday Ghanaian sources in London retorted firmly.

Ghana, formerly the Gold Coast, has won her freedom from Britain and is a leading state in the drive for independence in Africa.

The Earl of Perth, British Minister of State for Colonies, arrived here today to "try to find out what is happening."

The Minister said he would go to Salisbury because he "very much" wanted to see Sir Roy and Sir Arthur. Asked if he would see the congress leaders, he replied, "If the opportunity occurred, of course I would."

Sir Robert Armitage, Governor of Nyasaland, said that communications with the Northern Province were still disrupted but that he thought leaflets being dropped were having "excellent effect."

Terror Tactics Charged

In banning the Zambia group in Northern Rhodesia, the Governor said the congress had sought openly to spread "uncertainty and fear" and to discourage registered voters from going to the polls. But "far worse," he said, is the "reign of terror" instituted by congress members in native villages.

He said the villagers had been threatened with death and mutilation and that witchcraft had been employed to bring the ignorant around to the congress point of view. All this, he said, is done "in private and at night" and is thus "desperately difficult to deal with in law."

"This is on all fours with what happened to millions of law-abiding Americans when the comparatively few Chicago racketeers established their protection rackets," Sir Arthur said.

These racketeers corrupted the local government and ruled by the gun and the knuckle-duster and went on "to establish the organization of killers known as Murder, Inc.," the Governor said.

The Zambia congress, he concluded, is subversive and seditious and the issue is not one of race relations but of Africans attacking Africans.

In various parts of Nyasaland today there were incidents involving the use of tear gas, confiscation of spears and axes and the wounding of one African by gunfire. Sabotage of communications continued in all three provinces. Arrests in Nysaland now total 408.

March 13, 1959

LIBERALS DOUBT RHODESIAN GAINS

Critics of Welensky Regime Describe New Race Policy as 'Panic Partnership'

Special to The New York Times.

SALISBURY, Southern Rhodesia, April 14—The racial policy now being followed by the Government of the Federation of Rhodesia and Nyasaland is described as "panic partnership" by those who are skeptical of the ruling United Federal party's sudden conversion to liberalism.

The newspapers here, which generally support the United Federal policies, have praised the party's recent legislative and administrative acts as great advances toward the concept of racial partnership upon which the Federation was founded.

However, among whites and Africans who base their hopes for the future on the building of a genuine multi-racial democracy, the reaction has been one of considerable reserve.

Would these steps have been taken, they ask, if the racial cauldron had not boiled over in Nyasaland in recent months. Would anything have been done if the governing party's ambition to obtain dominion status for the Federation in 1960 had not received a serious jolt by reason of the British Colonial Office's concern at the trend of events in Central Africa, they say.

Two recent actions by the Federal Government lend credence to Prime Minister Sir Roy Welensky's assertion that he is faithfully implementing the policy of partnership.

One is the appointment of an African to high office in the Federation Government. Jasper Z. Savanhu has been made Secretary to the Ministry of Home Affairs with special responsibility for the Office of Race Affairs.

Post Offices to Be Revised

Sir Roy has also announced the decision to abolish post office "apartheid." No more post offices are to be built with separate entrances for whites and nonwhites, he said, and existing barriers and partitions will be removed wherever practiceable.

More impressive measures to raise the status of the African have been taken by the Southern Rhodesian Government. They include:

¶Legislation that makes it possible for leading African to stay in hotels formerly exclusively for Europeans.

¶Adoption of the Industrial Conciliation Bill, which for the first time provides for racial integration in labor negotiating machinery.

¶Opening of the civil service to non-Europeans, with all attendant rights, including promotion, security and pensions.

In addition, notice has been given that bills to put apprenticeship and workmen's compensation on a non-racial basis are to be introduced.

This record has led the United Federal party's supporters to say that Sir Edgar Whitehead's Southern Rhodesian Government has done more in the last ten months toward positive implementation of partnership than any Government before it accomplished in a full term.

On the other hand, the Government has used strong measures in its effort to stamp out dissidence.

No basic change of heart toward the aspirations of the non-European is discernible among the vast majority of the white electors. Persons of liberal view feel that the mass detentions under the emergency regulations and the proscription of African political groups have probably done no more than drive dissension underground.

Meanwhile, white home owners are preparing protests to the Government against the assignment to Mr. Savanhu of a house in one of the exclusively European suburbs here.

Mr. Savanhu will probably be given a house near the multi-racial University of Rhodesia and Nyasaland. Africans are barred by law from living in "white areas," except as servants.

April 15, 1959

Rhodesia Adopts Security Bill

Special to The New York Times

SALISBURY, Southern Rhodesia, April 28—The Preventive Detention Bill and other controversial security measures received final approval in the Southern Rhodesian Parliament today. The new legislation gives thhe Government wide powers to detain, for periods up to five years, persons belonging or suspected of belonging to "unlawful" organizations.

April 29, 1959

Africans Resent Term 'Boy'

By MILTON BRACKER

Special to The New York Times.

LUSAKA, Northern Rhodesia, May 27—When the constitutional status of the Federation of Rhodesia and Nyasaland is reviewed in London next year, the word "boy" will be on the agenda.

The use of the word in reference to African males regardless of age will be included in a list of challenges against the Government's concept of "racial partnership" to be submitted by the African National Congress of Northern Rhodesia.

Ironically, one of the Federation's own officials newly assigned to London to help prepare for the discussion there has just been referred to as a "boy" in an incident on the Southern Rhodesia side of the Zambezi River at Victoria Falls.

He is Lawrence Vambe, a 42-year-old African journalist, recently appointed Federal information officer in Rhodesia House, London. Mr. Vambe will leave for this post next week.

"Boy" is the traditional form of reference to African males, and not just servants, all over East Central and South Africa.

It is used in either direct or indirect address, frequently by white children addressing or referring to men.

Harry Nkumbula, president of the African National Congress in Northern Rhodesia, confirmed yesterday that the offensive usage would be one of its major targets when the group prepared its case for the London meeting.

Neither the date nor details of the conference have been announced. But in view of developments throughout the Federation since late February, when nationalist agitation was intensified, it is generally accepted that African nationalists will have a direct or indirect voice.

Both the banned Congress movement in Nyasaland and the legal Congress movement here have already announced that they favor withdrawal of their states from the five-and-a-half-year-old Federation.

Nyasaland and Northern Rhodesia are British protectorates. The third unit in the Federation is the self-governing colony of Southern Rhodesia, where the Congress movement also is proscribed.

May 28, 1959

FREE NYASALAND CALLED RED PAWN

Welensky Says Protectorate Could Not Survive as Independent State

By LEONARD INGALLS
Special to The New York Times.

SALISBURY, Southern Rhodesia, Aug. 15—Sir Roy Welensky fears that Nyasaland might come under Communist influence if it becomes independent outside the Federation of Rhodesia and Nyasaland.

The Prime Minister of the federation emphasized his opposition to any break-up of the federation, which is composed of Northern and Southern Rhodesia and Nyasaland. He questioned whether African sentiment in Nyasaland for a withdrawal from the federation and complete independence was as strong as has been represented.

Sir Roy gave his views on the future of the federation in an interview and a public speech this week.

Picturing Nyasaland "a backwater of a state" with limited economic potential, the Prime Minister said is could not survive as an independent country without outside help. He predicted that there would be offers of aid "direct from Moscow."

National Debt Cited

"I do not contemplate with equanimity anything like that happening on my doorstep; let's be blunt about it" he said.

The right to secede from the federation was rejected when the Constitution was drawn six years ago, he went on. Any move to dissolve the federation would be complicated by the national debt of £225,000,000 ($630,000,000) against the assets of all three territories, he said.

Sir Roy contended that the Africans in Nyasaland could not "produce a government of caliber" because the territory has fewer than "twenty-five graduates of any university" and only a few hundred secondary school teachers as its educated class.

Blueprint Suggested

When the federation's Constitution is reviewed next year, the Prime Minister said, he hopes to see the discussion produce a blueprint for self-government for Nyasaland within the federation. "It must include a timetable," he asserted. Nyasaland now has the status of a British protectorate within the federation.

Speaking publicly to a group of school boys, Sir Roy said:

"We are going to get nowhere in this country if we, you and I, and particularly you of the younger generation, do not accept what is absolutely basic to the whole progress of the federation, namely that a man should be allowed to have what he can earn and should not be penalized merely because he happens to be born with a dark skin.

"I say frankly to you that you stand to lose nothing by accepting the emerged African as a normal human being."

Emphasizing the importance of contributions by whites of skill and capital to the development of the federation, the Prime Minister said, "I believe that you are asking the impossible to suggest to him that he [the whites] should surrender what he has created."

Social Mixing Discussed

Turning to the question of the place in the community of Africans who meet the white standards of education and conduct, Sir Roy asserted:

"It does not mean that you've got to mix socially with the African if you do not want to. You do not have to mix with any particular European if you do not want to. Nor does it mean that you have got to lower your standards of culture.

"But it does mean when an African or a colored person reaches that level one must accept him. That does not mean that your sister has got to marry him or that you have got to accept him in your home. But one must accept him as a full citizen of this country, with the rights and privileges as well as the obligations which that implies."

August 16, 1959

AFRICANS EVOLVE NEW MIDDLE CLASS

Sons of Rural Tribesmen Run Businesses in Rhodesia —Some Achieve Wealth

By LEONARD INGALLS
Special to The New York Times.

SALISBURY, Southern Rhodesia, Aug. 17—Six miles from the center of Salisbury, capital of the Federation of Rhodesia and Nyasaland, a new shopping center recently has risen. The proprietors of the dozen modern shops are Africans and their customers are Africans.

These shopkeepers are representative of the growing African middle class, which numbers several thousand in Southern Rhodesia and is expanding rapidly all over the continent. These African entrepreneurs, who constitute an increasingly important part of the economy, were relatively unknown before 1945.

In the last fifteen years the sons and grandsons of primitive tribesmen have left the subsistence life of the bush. They have gained education and have begun the journey up the economic ladder. Some have achieved moderate wealth and there are a few in the Salisbury area whose net worth exceeds $100,000.

Shopkeeper Owns 3 Houses

Typical of the African business men in the New Highfields shopping center outside Salisbury is Aidan Mwamuka, whose grandfather lived in a thatched hut with fellow members of the Manyika tribe. At the age of 49, Mr. Mwamuka owns three shops in Old and New Highfields, where 3,500 African families live. He also has a 300-acre farm and three houses, one for his family and two to rent.

"My father came to work in Salisbury in very early days as a house boy," Mr. Mwamuka said. "He attended a night school and got his first idea of what education was all about."

With the help of missionaries, Mr. Mwamuka's father became a teacher. He insisted that his children go to school. He also arranged for his wife to attend the mission school to learn to read and write.

"Some of his friends regarded him as a fool for sending us to school," Mr. Mwamuka said.

Teacher's Salary Low

Mr. Mwamuka, too, became a teacher. But, he said, "Salaries for teachers were so low that I felt in order to educate my own children I should improve my financial position."

In 1946, he and his wife, who was a nurse, took their $1,120 savings and bought a bus to provide a service for Africans between Salisbury and Domboshawa, eighteen miles to the north, where a government school and African reserve were situated.

By 1949 they had $1,680 to invest in a small shop in Highfields. "It proved a very great success," Mr. Mwamuka said. "It was so good that I gave up teaching completely."

The small general store led to a butcher shop next door and then to the 300-acre maize and vegetable farm. The modern one-story general store and cafe in the New Highfields shopping center was opened last May 1. Mr. Mwamnka estimates the value of his shops, farm and houses at more than $30,000.

Mr. Mwamuka modestly discussed his hopes for his children. "One of our sons is attending boarding school," he said. "If he does well, we hope he'll take up medicine and we hope the other boy will take up law. We are trying to guide them to make up their own minds."

August 28, 1959

Macmillan Denies Independence Of Rhodesia Federation Is Near

By HOMER BIGART
Special to The New York Times.

LAGOS, Nigeria, Jan. 13—Prime Minister Macmillan has thwarted Sir Roy Welensky's dream of early independence for the Federation of Rhodesia and Nyasaland.

Five days before his scheduled arrival in Salisbury, Southern Rhodesia, the Federation's capital, Mr. Macmillan said at a news conference here tonight that Africans in the Federation would remain under British protection until they possessed the political machinery to express their will.

This means that the African majorities of Nyasaland and Northern Rhodesia will not be forced into the Federation against their wishes. It means also that the Federation will not be admitted to the British Commonwealth unless the Africans first approve the Federation.

Vote Extension Likely

It is assumed that the commission headed by Viscount Monckton, now reviewing the constitution of Nyasaland and Northern Rhodesia, will recommend the enfranchisement of the African masses now denied the vote.

Mr. Macmillan had indicated that he would not discuss affairs in south and central Africa until he reached those areas. But this was a hot, fatiguing day and under the persistent questioning of Nigerian reporters the Prime Minister became slightly annoyed.

Asked whether Britain was not trying to "appease" the Federation's Prime Minister, Mr. Welensky, Mr. Macmillan snapped that this was definitely untrue.

"Nyasaland is a backward country, a very poor country," he said. "Now we hope to do what we have done in Tanganyika and give the people self-government. But until that time the people will remain under British protection."

Mr. Macmillan said he hoped the emergency in Nyasaland would soon be ended and that Dr. Hastings K. Banda and other nationalists would be released from preventive custody.

Mr. Macmillan also addressed a colorful joint meeting of the Nigerian Parliament.

African Union Rejected

The Nigerian Prime Minister, Sir Abubakar Tafawa Balewa, held a press conference in which he firmly rejected the proposal of Prime Minister Kwame Nkrumah of Ghana for a United States of Africa.

Sir Abubakar said Nigeria had no intention of surrendering her sovereignty to an African union.

Nigeria has waited 100 years for freedom and does not propose to throw it away right after she obtains independence from Britain Oct. 1, he said.

Growing rivalry between Ghana and Nigeria for the leadership of the free nations emerging in West Africa was evident in the tone of icy contempt with which Sir Abubakar said to foreign newsmen:

I don't know why you attach so much importance to what Dr. Nkrumah says."

Sir Abubakar, a Moslem from Northern Nigeria, answered questions in precise English. He said that Mr. Nkrumah had once invited him to Ghana to discuss federation but that he did not go. He said he felt that the whole question of federation was "very premature."

Of course this does not rule out attempts by newly independent African states to get together and solve common problems, he said.

South Africa Criticized

Sir Abubakar said he thought that the presence of the Union of South Africa in the Commonwealth tended to "discredit" the Commonwealth.

He said South Africa should be dropped from the Commonwealth club "if she does not mend her ways."

He was dubious, however, whether a boycott of South African goods would force the country to scrap her apartheid policy of separating the races. It might make South Africa so bitter that racial hatreds would become even more entrenched, he warned.

He declined to say whether Nigeria would recognize the French-backed Government of Premier Ahmadou Ahidjo in Cameroon, Nigeria's eastern neighbor. Mr. Nkrumah said in Accra last week Ghana would withhold recognition.

Sir Abubakar said Nigerians would demand a rapid rise in living standards after independence. Hence, the Government would need much economic aid from abroad. The biggest project under consideration, he said, is a hydroelectric dam on the Niger River above Jebba. The dam would make the Niger navigable all way to the frontier, he said.

January 14, 1960

SIX MORE KILLED IN RHODESIA RIOTS

120 Wounded, 320 Africans Arrested—Workers Still Stay Away From Jobs

By LEONARD INGALLS
Special to The New York Times.

BULAWAYO, Southern Rhodesia, July 26—Six Africans were killed here today, five by police fire and one by a beating by other Africans in rioting.

The deaths brought to nine the number killed in the violence that started Sunday.

Four of those killed by the police were shot when the security forces opened fire to break up mobs. One of the dead was a looter surprised in the act by policemen.

More than 120 were wounded by the police in a military operation against the rioters during the day. Three hundred and twenty Africans were arrested.

Correspondents asked several Africans the reason for the rioting. Most replied, "I don't know." But one said: "We wanted a meeting on Sunday, but we could not have it. People got angry."

One crowd of 7,000 assembled and demanded an audience with Government officials. They said they wanted the release of the National Democratic party officers who were arrested last week in Salisbury. Two smaller mobs that tried to march to white areas of the city were turned back by the police.

The shooting of Africans by the police broke a record of sixty-four years in Southern Rhodesia. The last time an African was shot by a policeman in this British colony was in 1896.

For the second successive day most of this city's African labor force of 65,000 stayed away from work. Most factories were closed and there were no home deliveries of milk and bread.

Intimidation Charged

Many Africans said they wanted to return to their jobs but had been prevented by intimidators. They responded amicably when questioned by correspondents who entered African townships with police and troops.

Sir Edgar Whitehead, Prime Minister of Southern Rhodesia, told the House of Assembly in Salisbury today that the National Democratic party, which is composed of Africans and a few whites, had organized hooligans "and recent events had shown for what purpose." He charged that whites were advising the African demonstrators.

The police, accompanied by troops with fixed bayonets, worked methodically to restore order in Bulawayo's eight African townships after two days of rioting, looting and arson. In the Old African Township, less than one mile from the city center, one company of troops in battle dress marched through the streets this morning to jeers from African onlookers.

This afternoon hundreds of policemen and a battalion of troops made a house-to-house search of townships for stolen goods. Africans stood quietly by.

The scene in Old African Township was one of destruction and disorder.

A beer hall was destroyed by fire as were those in seven other townships. At least a dozen shops were set ablaze and completely destroyed.

Streets were littered with large boulders and refuse cans that had been overturned to form roadblocks. Broken glass was everywhere. At least two private motor cars had been overturned and burned. A clinic was badly damaged.

While the police and troops worked their way through the streets, planes of the Royal Rhodesian Air Force circled overhead to watch for new mobs. They dropped tear-gas bombs to break up gangs of Africans.

A line six miles long of white and African troops armed with rifles and machine guns stood guard between the white and African parts of the city.

In a letter delivered in Salisbury today to Sir Edgar, Michael Mawema, president of the party, who is free on bail, said Africans "had genuine grievances but have no means to express them."

"Police and soldiers now engaged in ugly battle with the people will only help increase grievances and therefore worsen the situation," he said.

July 27, 1960

Report on Rhodesias Cites Right to Secede

By WALTER H. WAGGONER
Special to The New York Times.

LONDON, Oct. 11 — The Monckton Commission recommended today greater African representation in a revamped Federation of the Rhodesias and Nyasaland and the right of eventual secession for the members of the association.

The twenty-five member commission, with two dissenters, found African distrust and dislike for the white-dominated central African federation too intense and widespread to allow the federal link of the three states to continue in its present form.

But the commission warned that "to break it up at this crucial moment in the history of Africa would be an admission that there is no hope of survival for any multi-racial society on the African continent, and that differences of color and race are irreconcilable."

Stating that granting the right of secession to a territory, such as Nyasaland, might provide a 'safety valve" lessening the likelihood of secession, the commission nevertheless said that "while the federation cannot continue unless it commands general acceptance, a dissolution would lead to hardship, poverty and distress."

Viscount Monckton of Brenchley, chairman of the commission, earned a reputation over many years as a Cabinet Minister and a consultant to the Government on special problems as a man who could see both sides of an argument. The Report of the Advisory Commission on the Review of the Constitution of Rhodesia and Nyasaland, as the 175-page document is formally called, appears to support that reputation.

However, in recommending a middle-of-the-road solution to the Federation's problem of constitutional advancement, it also failed to satisfy the two extremes.

Even before its publication, what was known of the report had already antagonized and frightened some of the white members of the Federation. Today Sir Roy Welensky, Prime Minister of the Federation, denounced it.

The document, which represents four months of interviewing, discussion and field work in the Federation, and nearly as much time in preparation, was ordered by the Government last year in preparation for the constitutional review of the Federal Constitution then planned for late this year.

The commission agreed that if the Federal association of the three states was to continue in any form, the proportion of Africans in the Federal Assembly must be promptly increased.

"We recommend,' the commission said, "a major operation to reduce the functions exercised by the central authority, to change the composition of the Assembly, to widen the franchise, to improve the machinery of cooperation within the constituent states and to introduce safeguards against racial discrimination and for the protection of minorities.

"Our broa aim has been to return to erritorial control those functions of government which directly affect the day-to-day life of the people, while retaining at the center sufficient authority to direct and regulate the economy, and to manage external affairs and defense."

Report Is Attacked

Special to The New York Times.

SALISBURY, Southern Rhodesia, Oct. 11—Sir Roy Welensky rejected tonight the recommendations by the Monckton Commission that right of secession be given to member territories.

At a news conference and later on a nation-wide broadcast the Prime Minister accused the advisory commission of bad faith in including the subject of secession in its report.

Report Scored Here

Joshua Nkomo, director of external and international affairs of the National Democratic party of Southern Rhodesia, said yesterday that the Monckton Commission report was "not acceptable."

Speaking at a news conference at the headquarters of the American Committee on Africa, 801 Second Avenue, Mr. Nkomo said, "Bringing in a few Africans won't solve the question. There must be voting rights for all. They cannot keep the power in the hands of a white minority."

The New York Times Oct. 12, 1960

PLAN FOR AFRICAN REGION: A British report urges changes in structure of the areas in the Federation of the Rhodesias and Nyasaland (shown by diagonal shading).

ENCLAVE OF PEACE IN AFRICAN STRIFE

North Rhodesia Copper Belt Offers Natives a Chance to Learn and Save

By DREW MIDDLETON
Special to The New York Times.

MUFULIRA, Northern Rhodesia, March 2—The Copper Belt is a tiny enclave of peace in an expanse of troubled Africa. There are many, Africans as well as Europeans, who see it as a source of ideas that could lead to stability on the continent.

Here, Europe has offered and Africa has accepted opportunities for economic and educational advancement, social responsibility and public welfare.

The fundamental economic fact of European riches and African poverty underlies much of the continent's political strife. In the Copper Belt, capitalism, acting in enlightened self-interest, has begun to redress the balance and provide an answer to communism.

The African middle class is painfully and slowly emerging in African townships that surround mines. Its members are less than a generation away from "the bush." But already they are showing strong distaste for any extremism in politics that might disturb their economic progress.

Housing Is Comfortable

In the late afternoon sun, miners return from their work. Children run out to meet them and beg rides on the handlebars of their bicycles. Despite weariness, the miners carry themselves with assurance. They are their own masters.

The houses of two, three and four rooms built by mining companies are comfortable. Often there is garden in the rear and there is stnitation and electric light.

The Copper Belt is less than a third of a century old. It owes its existence to two groups of companies—the Rhodesian Selection Trust and the Anglo-American Group. In the late Nineteen Twenties the first working parties of Europeans arrived to fell trees, drain swamps and begin mining operations.

Aside from a few wandering tribes, the area was uninhabited. Today the Copper Belt employs 7,000 Europeans and 37,000 Africans. Including families, the population living on mine properties is at least 140,000.

The total population of the Belt is about 350,000. Of that

October 12, 1960

number 300,000 are Africans. Almost all depend, directly or indirectly, on the mines.

Labor Is Imported

The mining companies imported African labor, most of it from the Bemba tribe living to the north and northeast. But other tribes—the Tonga, the Lovali-Lozi, the Ngonde and the Maravi—have all contributed to building the Copper Belt.

African advancement has been stressed in three mines of the Rhodesian Selection Trust: the Roan Antelope, the Mufulira and the Chibuluma. The management began with workers who had to be taught how to use wheelbarrows. Today a growing number of Africans own stock in the companies.

The average pay today for all Africans—including bonuses and free or subsidized services provided by the company—is £29 ($81) a month. This is on the basis of twenty eight-hour shifts a month.

Some Africans, however, take home as much as £45 ($125) a month.

Equally important to the African miner is the opportunity for advancement opened to him by the companies since 1955.

Company Education

Under a company education plan instruction is provided in English, elementary arithmetic and geography. Each day at three mines about 2,500 workers, often accompanied by their wives, crowd tidy white schoolhouses. They come to learn after eight solid hours of work.

As the African has advanced in status and wages, management has done its best to teach him to save. All Africans earning more than £16 ($48) are entitled to be members of a share-purchase plan. For every two shares purchased by an employe, the company contributes one share. About 5 per cent of Africans eligible participate in the plan at Roan Antelope. The percentage is slightly lower at Mufulira and Chibuluma.

About 60 per cent of the African workers at three mines belong to voluntary savings plans.

Many mine workers carry cards of both major political parties—the United National Independence party and the African National Congress.

Although their economic status provides a certain defense against extremism, African miners here display a reverence for conformity.

An educated and successful African discussing this pattern said that his people "inevitably" would regard any political leader as "the strongest" and expect him to deal vigorously with anyone who opposed his policies. It is not, he conceded, a good omen for future African democracy.

March 5, 1961

HUNGER FOR LAND RISES IN RHODESIA

African Majority Restricted to 42 Per Cent of Space

By LEONARD INGALLS

Special to The New York Times

SALISBURY, Southern Rhodesia, June 30—In this British colony, land is as troublesome a problem as political rights for Africans.

Attention for the moment is centered on the proposed constitution, which would admit Africans to Southern Rhodesia's Legislative Assembly for the first time. But growing pressure from Africans for land reforms has already made the subject highly controversial. The question is receiving increasing attention from the Government of Prime Minister Sir Edgar Whitehead.

The problem is that 48 per cent of the land is reserved for the colony's 220,000 whites and 42 per cent is set aside for the 3,000,000 Africans. The rest is forest, game reserves, parks and unassigned land.

This arrangement was made under the provisions of the Land Apportionment Act of 1930. The act, by establishing who could use what land, became the basis for the color bars that exist today.

Africans Forced to Move

One consequence of the act was that between 1936 and 1959 113,000 Africans were compelled to move from white areas at an estimated cost of $84,000,000.

Africans want the act repealed completely and the land thrown open to all. Many whites regard such a step as unthinkable. This is one reason they are determined to keep control of the Government.

The Whitehead Government has introduced some amendments to the Land Apportionment Act in an effort to assuage African feelings. These changes would transfer 2,000,000 acres of white-owned land already occupied by African squatters to African use. Five million more acres in rural areas now reserved for whites would be thrown open to people of any race.

Africans only recently received the right to buy land in the urban areas set aside for them. Multi-racial industrial areas and multi-racial clubs are to be permitted in designated places, and African business men are to be permitted to trade in some areas hitherto restricted to whites.

Problem Not Tackled

But the major problem of land hunger among rural Africans has yet to be tackled. The situation is complicated by the doubling of the colony's African population in the last twenty years.

Last year a special committee of the all-white Legislative Assembly, which had studied the land problem for two years, said that ultimately 90 per cent of the land in the country should be available to all races. They advocated repeal of the Land Apportionment Act by stages, but this approach is likely to be far too slow to satisfy the Africans.

The Government contends that one of the most serious aspects of the problem is how to insure that the best use is made of the land and how to raise the standard of living above a subsistence level.

Meanwhile, bitter discontent is being caused by the fact that 111,000 African families entitled to land holdings are not able to get them because there is not enough African land to go around, while large acreages of land in white areas are unused.

July 3, 1961

VOTE IN RHODESIA FAVORS CHARTER

New Constitution Would Let Africans Sit in Assembly

By LEONARD INGALLS

Special to The New York Times.

SALISBURY, Southern Rhodesia, Thursday, July 27 — A new Constitution for this British colony providing for direct African representation in the Legislative Assembly was approved by a vote of more than two to one in a referendum yesterday.

The predominantly white electorate gave overwhelming support to proposals upon which the liberalized charter will be based.

The new Constitution will come into effect next year after necessary legislation is adopted in Britain and Southern Rhodesia.

Sir Roy Welensky, Prime Minister of the Federation of Rhodesia and Nyasaland, hailed the result of the balloting as "a great victory for common sense."

He said "this will lead to a considerable easing of tension, and I think the African voters in particular have shown great common sense."

When counting of the votes ended early today, results from thirty-eight of the fifty electoral districts had been reported. The constitutional proposals won approval with 32,928 votes cast in favor and 15,665 against. Votes in the remaining twelve districts are to be counted later.

Polling in the referendum progressed quietly through the day. But at Bulawayo, the colony's second largest city, the police used tear gas to disperse a crowd of 300 Africans who gathered in the morning to greet Joshua Nkomo, president of the National Democratic party.

Africans ignored a call from Mr. Nkomo to stay at home in protest against the new Constitution, which will continue white control of the Government despite the seats in the Assembly for Africans.

Employers reported that nearly all their African workers were at their jobs. The Government had outlawed any strike action by the Africans.

Large contingents of policemen and troops were still on duty in African townships in Salisbury, Bulawayo and other centers. In the last three days more than 200 Africans were arrested for intimidation and assault.

Of Southern Rhodesia's population of 250,000 whites and 3,000,000 Africans, about 80,000 whites and 4,000 Africans were eligible to vote in the referendum.

The proposed Constitution was agreed on by representatives of all races in Southern Rhodesia and was negotiated with Britain at a conference last February. The Africans later repudiated the agreement.

The agreement provided that Africans would be admitted to the Legislative Assembly for the first time and would have fifteen of the sixty-five seats. More Africans would be permitted to vote and a bill of rights would be included in the Constitution.

Britain agreed to the elimination of certain clauses from the present Constitution, under which she reserved the right to cancel legislation adopted by the Assembly.

Africans have complained that fifteen seats in the Assembly are too few for them since they are the majority race in the territory.

July 27, 1961

Protests Sweep North Rhodesia As Kaunda Spurs Disobedience

Special to The New York Times.

SALISBURY, Southern Rhodesia, Aug. 18—Kenneth Kaunda, Northern Rhodesia nationalist leader, launched his "master plan" of civil disobedience today by ceremonially burning his identity card.

Africans in the north responded with a full-scale general strike.

The majority of the African laborers in the remote and largely undeveloped bush territory obeyed the call by their local leaders to stay away from work.

Mr. Kaunda is opposing the new British-supported Constitution for the Northern Rhodesia protectorate as failing to meet African demands for full political rights.

At the same time, reports were reaching Lusaka that a wave of terrorism, arson and sabotage in adjoining Northern Province was spreading rapidly, particularly in the Fort Rosebery and Lake Bangweulu areas. Police patrols have been investigating widespread damage by fire to Government buildings and other property.

At Chinsali, on the Great North Road in Northern Province, yesterday the death toll rose to eleven for the period since trouble started early this month. The police shot to death two African members of a village that had ambushed them near Chinsali. The band opened fire on the police and hurled spears. It was the first such group to use firearms in skirmishes with security forces.

Trouble started today in Fort Rosebery when a crowd of about 200 Africans attacked the Provincial Administration offices. A small police party dispersed the crowd, said to consist largely of women and children, with tear gas.

A crowd of Africans then formed at Mansa Bridge, just outside Fort Rosebery and stoned passing vehicles. Another crowd surrounded the Provincial Commissioner's house in town but was dispersed before causing damage.

The New York Times Aug. 19, 1961

Two Africans were killed at Chinsali (1) and a mob clashed with police at Fort Rosebery (2). In Lusaka (3) a protest campaign opened.

A group of distirct agents had to be escorted into town from an airport outside town because of the danger from armed Africans roaming the outskirts.

They ran into a roadblock set up by about 200 men who hurled stones at the police officer in charge when he demanded that they disperse. The police then fired one warning shot and scattered the band with tear gas.

Two Africans were wounded later at another roadblock.

A Government spokesman said that one large armed band was reported roaming the Government location at Fort Rosebery and that a police contingent had been attacked.

In other parts of the north defiant Africans were continuing to burn identity and marriage certificates and poll-tax receipts. The ashes were being dumped outside local provincial administrative offices.

Security forces sent to Nsombo, on the northern shore of Lake Bangweulu, yesterday to arrest an African as a murder suspect, found the post office had been burned. Rioters also had burned the Government rest house, boat store and schoolteacher's house at Nsombo.

August 19, 1961

RHODESIAN WEEPS IN U.N. TESTIMONY

Kaunda Overcome Telling of People's Suffering

By LAWRENCE O'KANE

Special to The New York Times.

UNITED NATIONS, N. Y., April 17—An African nationalist leader from Northern Rhodesia wept today as he told a United Nations committee of what he called the suffering of his people.

The leader, Kenneth Kaunda, president of Northern Rhodesia's United National Independence Party, accused a "timid British Government" of slowly and "knowingly" giving over control of his people to a "minority of white supremacists with full knowledge of the dire consequences."

Mr. Kaunda, wearing a purple and black toga, addressed the General Assembly's special committee on decolonization. His weeping caused him to stop his testimony until tomorrow.

At the request of the chairman, Chandra S. Jha of India, other petitioners made their statements while Mr. Kaunda regained his composure.

Mr. Kaunda said that a "decadent colonialism that has lost confidence in its strength" had allowed itself to be "bullied and pushed and, finally, compromised" out of its obligations.

This occurred, he said, as a result of pressure from a white minority that intends to maintain its privileges "by the use of force and arms."

He charged that the 70,000 whites in his country had strengthened their power by "harassing, killing, imprisoning, and deporting" those of the 3,000,000 Africans in the territory who had spoken out for freedom and national independence.

Mr. Kaunda said Africans had suffered a variety of oppressions: their movements were limited, their political groups disbanded, whole communities were punished when European property was damaged, emergency governmental powers permitted imprisonment without trial, African opinion was stifled and job opportunities were limited.

Mr. Kaunda was one of four members of his movement who told the seventeen-nation committee today that Africans in their country rejected membership in the federation.

The others were Lieut. Col. Sir Stewart Gore-Browne, an 79-year-old white settler and political leader who has lived more than 40 years in Northern Rhodesia and who now espouses African nationalism; T. L. Gesai, an Indian business man from Ndola, Northern Rhodesia, and A. N. L. Wina, who represents the party in the United States.

Earlier Adlai E. Stevenson, chief United States delegate at the United Nations, announced he was sending Sir Roy Welensky, Prime Minister of the Federation of Rhodesia and Nyasaland, a copy of a recent speech in Lake Forest, Ill. The Prime Minister denounced Mr. Stevenson yesterday for a "bitter and unreasoned attack" on Europeans in the federation.

Mr. Stevenson said that the purpose of the speech had been to explain difficulties in African countries with large white populations. He said that when Sir Roy read the speech "I believe he will find it not 'bitter and unreasoned,' as he charged, but tempered and factual about a situation we are trying to resolve and not aggravate."

April 18, 1962

A Disciple of Gandhi

Kenneth Kaunda

EARLY in his political career, Kenneth Kaunda, African political leader of Northern Rhodesia, read writings of Gandhi that he said "went straight to my heart." Since then he has advocated and practiced nonviolence.

Man in the News

Nonetheless, white settlers in the Federation of Rhodesia and Nyasaland led by Sir Roy Welensky, Prime Minister of the federation, have called Mr. Kaunda responsible for violence in Northern Rhodesia. They have denounced him as an extremist and a hypocrite. Legal and other obstacles placed in Mr. Kaunda's path by the federation government have prevented him from organizing his United National Independence party tightly enough to get his followers to accept his nonviolent philosophy completely.

The New York Times
Passionate orator

In the last six months, however, his record for keeping hot-headed supporters under control has been good.

With this record, Mr. Kaunda appeared yesterday before the United Nations committee on decolonialization to argue for independence under African control of Northern Rhodesia.

A former teacher, farmer and shopkeeper, Mr. Kaunda has for the last ten years devoted himself exclusively to politics.

Son of a Missionary

Mr. Kaunda, who is a Christian, is the son of a Presbyterian missionary who came to Northern Rhodesia from Nyasaland. He was born in Luapula Province in Northern Rhodesia thirty-eight years ago.

His decision to become a politician resulted in part from the treatment he received from whites while teaching in Southern Rhodesia and while working as a welfare officer on the Northern Rhodesia copper belt. He says he decided to fight "for respect."

He came into political prominence in 1958 when he led a split away from the American National Congress to form the Zambia Congress party. In a year the party was banned and Mr. Kaunda was banished to a remote part of Northern Rhodesia to spend "the most terrible months of my life."

Mr. Kaunda suffered dysentery, malaria, respiratory ailments and general bad health in exile. After a few months he was transferred to a jail and tried and convicted of conspiracy and holding unlawful meetings.

When the United National Independence party was founded in 1960 on the remains of the Zambia Congress party, Mr. Kaunda resumed the role of president and the status of foremost African nationalist leader in Northern Rhodesia.

He is a passionate orator. He is gentle, self-effacing and extremely courteous. In private he speaks so softly that listeners must often strain. He neither drinks nor smokes and subsists chiefly on vegetables, fruit, milk and water. He lives in a home in Lusaka, which has no electricity or plumbing, with his wife and six sons.

His demeanor and principles reflect both Gandhi and his other hero, Lincoln. He accepts whites in Africa, he says, not because of what they know and can contribute to the continent but "because they are human beings."

April 18, 1962

BRITISH DEFEATED IN U.N. ON RHODESIA

Assembly, 73-1, Backs Call for Wider African Vote—Longest Session Ends

By SAM POPE BREWER
Special to The New York Times.

UNITED NATIONS, N. Y. June 28—The General Assembly, overriding British legal objections, voted today to call on London to hold a constitutional conference to give adequate political representation to the African inhabitants of Southern Rhodesia.

Seventy-three nations voted in favor of the resolution. South Africa voted in the negative and there were twenty-seven abstentions. Portugal was present but not voting and Iceland was not represented.

The action concluded the longest session in the General Assembly's history, running to 155 days in three sections. The last began June 7.

The President of the Assembly, Mongi Slim of Tunisia, formally closed the session at 5:39 P. M. He remarked that it had dealt with ninety-seven items in a period of twenty-four weeks exclusive of two recesses. The next session, the seventeenth, will begin Sept. 18.

Chief Delegate Absent

Mr. Slim said the session was closing in an atmosphere of "hope and confidence regained."

On the Rhodesia issue, the United States was among those abstaining. Britain had announced in advance that she would boycott any voting connected with the question because she did not consider that the General Assembly was entitled even to discuss it.

Her delegation was present, but the chief delegate, Sir Patrick Dean, stayed away. British sources said the delegation did not wish to stage a walkout. They said they had taken part in the debate in an effort to make the Assembly understand their legal position, which was that the issue was an internal affair of a member state.

Southern Rhodesia, a British colony, is a member of the Federation of Rhodesia and Nyasaland.

Portugal also was present in the Assembly but did not participate in the vote, Iceland was not represented.

The resolution passed by the Assembly was sponsored by thirty-eight African and Asian delegations.

It rejected the British claim that Southern Rhodesia was self-governing in all internal affairs. It asked, therefore, that as "administering authority" Britain call "urgently" a constitutional conference to replace the Constitution of Dec. 6, 1961, with another that would "insure the rights of the majority of the people."

Immediate Steps Asked

It also called on Britain rather than the Southern Rhodesian Government "to take immediate steps to restore all the rights of the non-European population and to remove all restraints and restrictions in law and in practice on the exercise of the freedom of political activity, including all laws, ordinances and regulations which directly or indirectly sanction any policy or practice based on racial discrimination."

An amnesty and "immediate release of all political prisoners" also were requested.

Britain's position has been that since 1923 Southern Rhodesia has been completely independent of London in all internal affairs.

Anti-colonialist forces here have maintained that the "self-governing" status of Southern Rhodesia is a fiction and that Britain could force a new constitutional conference. Their argument is that government in Southern Rhodesia is exercised by a minority of 250,000 Europeans in a total population of about 3,250,000.

The new constitution, due to come into effect after legislative elections next March or April, would allow the Africans a maximum of fifteen of sixty-five seats in the Legislature. There are also provisions to allow the Africans to win some increased representation as time goes on.

Asian-African Bloc Strong

Today's vote reflected the power of the African and Asian delegations, backed by the Soviet bloc.

Delegates said the vote could not coerce Britain into acting its force being purely moral. Most sources here, including the British, feel that continued repression of the African population is building up an explosive situation. However, no solution has been assured.

The second resumed part of the sixteenth session has been concerned solely with two colonial issues, the other being the independence of the Belgian-ruled African trust territory of Ruanda-Urundi. The Assembly confirmed yesterday that Ruanda-Urundi should become free Sunday as the Republic of Rwanda and the Kingdom of Burundi.

June 29, 1962

Nyasaland Seeks to Quit Rhodesian Federation

Land Reshaped With Goal of Independence in 1963

By ROBERT CONLEY
Special to The New York Times.

LIMBE, Nyasaland, July 24 — Nyasaland's Africans are breaking their country away from its federation with Northern and Southern Rhodesia with a determination that amounts to secession in all but the name.

They are planning Nyasaland's economy, conducting their own foreign policy and reshaping the political structure of this British protectorate into what will become, possibly within a year, the independent African state of Malawi.

These developments are occurring less than a year after Dr. Hastings Kamuzu Banda's Malawi Congress party gained a majority in the protectorate's Legislative Council.

They are happening with the consent of the British Government and against the policy of Sir Roy Welensky, Prime Minister of the Federation of Rhodesia and Nyasaland, who maintains that there can be no secession without his approval.

Direct Conferences Held

To carry out his break, Dr. Banda has perfected a technique of negotiated revolution. He has ignored Sir Roy and has conferred directly with the British Government, the United Nations in Geneva and the Portuguese.

He has won public acknowledgment from London on the crucial point that Nyasaland's 2,900,000 Africans have a right to secede from what they regard as Sir Roy's white-dominated federation.

It is now accepted that the only remaining questions are economic. A special team appointed by R. A. Butler, Britain's Minister for Central African Affairs, is here studying the financial consequences of secession.

In Lisbon, Dr. Banda is understood to have won assurances from Portuguese normally allied with Sir Roy that there would be no interference with Nyasaland goods shipped by rail through Mozambique, a Portuguese territory, after secession.

Conference Due in Fall

A constitutional conference on Nyasaland is set for November in London. Dr. Banda says it will be the "final one" before independence in 1963.

Preparations for the day are visible everywhere from the green tea plantations at the foot of Mount Mlanje across the misty lunar valleys around Zomba to the shores of Lake Nyasa in the north, where the scimitar sails of Arab dhows recall the slave trading that pillaged the country a century ago.

A $53,900,000 development program for the next three years has just been introduced in the Legislative Council.

The program would set up Nyasaland's own commercial broadcasting service, although broadcasting is a federal responsibility controlled exclusively by the Federal Broadcasting Corporation.

New Schools Planned

It would establish a daily newspaper to be edited by an "independent person," establish a university college, build classrooms for 1,800 more secondary-school students and start a technical institute.

Britain has promised the equivalent of $8,400,000 in loans and grants for the first year of the development program. She has also just committed herself to provide up to $4,200,000 to help cover a deficit in the current annual budget of $25,760,000 and to review Nyasaland's financial position "from year to year."

The United States has pledged $1,036,000 toward the technical institute. John D. Msonthi, Minister of Trade and Industry, is in West Germany in search of more funds.

Yet Sir Roy's plan to build a $7,000,000 hydroelectric project at Nkula Falls was rejected because it would mean accepting federal money.

Politically, Africans are reshaping the country with sweeping new legislation. They are reducing the powers of district commissioners and tribal chiefs, the two strongest local authorities under the colonial administration, and putting control in hands of local committees made up of persons familiar with their areas' customs and traditions.

They are separating courts today from any connection with law-enforcement agencies, placing responsibility for protecting the land on panels of farmers and overhauling the old "thangata" system of farm tenancy, which is said to have reduced families living on privately owned estates to the status of feudal serfs.

Over everything is an atmosphere of change that extends even to matters like Dr. Banda's name.

The Hastings and its British air has been dropped in favor of his middle name and a title. He now calls himself Ngwazi (the Vindicator) Dr. H. Kamuzu Banda.

The country will be renamed Malawi. The word means "flames," and was used to describe the land by the tribes first encountered by the Portuguese 300 years ago.

Letters still come from the Federal Government. But they are seldom read; they are just torn up.

July 25, 1962

Rhodesian Party, Rejected In Vote Upset, Will Disband

Special to The New York Times.

SALISBURY, South Rhodesia, Dec. 16—As South Rhodesians began to recover today from their biggest political shock in 40 years, the multi-racial Central Africa Party announced it would disband.

The party was rejected in Friday's general elections, which swept the right-wing Rhodesian party into power and ousted Prime Minister Sir Edgar Whitehead's United Federal party.

Ralph Pamer, the Central African leader, received only eight votes, and the party's total vote was only 500.

December 17, 1962

Britain Accepts Nyasaland Split; Welensky Says He Will Fight It

London Agrees in Principle to Area's Secession From Central Africa Federation

By DREW MIDDLETON
Special to The New York Times.

LONDON, Dec. 19 — Britain accepted in principle today the secession of Nyasaland from the Central African Federation.

R. A. Butler s announcement to the House of Commons about Nyasaland, whose secession is expected sometime next year, foreshadowed the early break-up of the nine-year old federation, qualified sources said.

They doubted whether Southern Rhodesia, now ruled by the European right-wing Rhodesian Front, would remain in partnership with Northern Rhodesia, whose government will soon be dominated by Africans.

The Federation, with its 8,500,000 people, 312,000 of them Europeans, will have passed into limbo by the end of next year, qualified sources predicted.

[In Salisbury, capital of Southern Rhodesia, Sir Roy Welensky, Prime Minister of the Federation, refused to accept the British decision on Nyasaland. He said Britain had "ratted" on the Federation and had been guilty of "an act of treachery"].

Mr. Butler, the minister responsible for Central African affairs and Deputy Prime Minister, told Commons he would visit Central Africa soon to confer with the Federal Government of Sir Roy and the territorial governments.

The minister contended bravely that Nyasaland's withdrawal did not mean that the present constitutional relationship between Northern and Southern Rhodesia would be broken up.

This evoked charges of sophistry from Conservatives in both the Commons and the House of Lords. They held that the relationship would be broken all right, but for a different reason. This, they said, is the anti-African attitude of the Rhodesian Front and its leader, Winston Field.

African politicans in Northern Rhodesia, it was said, already have started a movement towards secession. Kenneth Kaunda's United National Independent party and Harry Nkumbula's African National Congress party have formed a coalition in Northern Rhodesia to back the policy of secession.

Northern Rhodesia is the economic key to the Federation. Its copper mining industry produces about $350,000,000 worth of copper a year.

The Government was hotly attacked by Tories in the House of Lords and Commons for granting the principle of secession to Nyasaland without the consent of the two other members of the Federation.

This was the one thing the Conservative government of 1953 had pledged itself not to do, the Marquess of Salisbury told the House of Lords. Evidently, he added mournfully, the Government has found it less embarrassing to break its word to its own "kith and kin" than to delay the ambitions of Dr. Hastings Banda, Prime Minister of Nyasaland.

"It must be clear to everyone that the Government's policy in Central Africa has failed and failed disastrously with all the shifts and shuffles, the chopping and changing we have seen," Lord Salisbury said.

His attack was echoed by other Conservative peers, who charged the Government had "let down" Sir Roy.

Defending himself against similar charges in the House of Commons, Mr. Butler said the Government had the "inalienable" right to take action in such matters. It had tried to gain agreement with Sir Roy, he said, but had failed.

Britain's purpose, Mr. Butler emphasized, is "constructive." It is to secure Central Africa "conditions in which a stable and expanding economy can be maintained and people of all races can live in harmony."

The Labor party, which has long advocated Nyasaland's secession, welcomed the Government's decision.

December 20, 1962

BRITAIN ASSURES RHODESIA BREAK

Says Any Federation Region Has the Right to Secede

By LAWRENCE FELLOWS
Special to The New York Times.

LONDON, March 29 — The Federation of Rhodesia and Nyasaland was in effect dissolved today.

The British Government declared that any of the territories of the nine-year-old Federation had the right to secede.

The protectorate of Nyasaland won the assurance last December that it could withdraw from the white-dominated Federation.

This assurance was extended today in the copper-rich protectorate of Northern Rhodesia, where the Africa nationalists have demanded the right of secession since they assumed power, and to the self-governing colony of Southern Rhodesia, where the European minority is still in authority.

Sir Roy Welensky, the Prime Minister of the Federation, saw the last prop pulled from beneath the crumbling Federation edifice. He angrily accused the British Government of an "act of betrayal" and canceled a luncheon engagement with Prime Minister Macmillan.

North Ready to Secede

Kenneth Kaunda and Harry Nkumbula, the coalition leaders in Northern Rhodesia, said tonight that their country would secede.

"We can now proceed on the road to independence and freedom as a sovereign state," they proclaimed.

"Winston Field, Prime Minister of Southern Rhodesia, said the colony was now entitled to independence from Britain.

He insisted that Southern Rhodesia would attempt no formal conference to dismantle the Federation until its own independence had been assured.

"Southern Rhodesia will have been seceded from," Mr. Field said. "The Federation is at an end and we consider this means we are entitled to the independence we would have had by 1955 had federation not come about."

R. A. Butler, the British Minister responsible for Central African affairs, declared at a news conference tonight that Britain had done no more than acknowledge "that we cannot keep in an association against its will anybody who does not want to be so kept."

"The very fact of accepting that de facto position is, in the Government's view, the only way in which to obtain a talk or conference or discussion on the broad lines of a relationship," Mr. Butler said.

Constructive Help Asked

The British Government has hoped that some of the economic ties in the Federation can be saved, particularly in transportation and power. Mr. Butler appealed for the "constructive help" of the Government concern.

Sir Roy said at a news conference that he had come to London in a "constructive spirit." only to learn that the Northern Rhodesian leaders had walked out of their separate meeting with Mr. Butler, demanding secession and threatening civil disobedience if their demands were not met.

The British Government had "buckled under" to each threat of violence, Sir Roy said.

He declared he could also "act irresponsibly and resort to unconstitutional measures," but would not.

The only other course open to him, Sir Roy said, is to refuse to cooperate in the dissolution of the Federation unless the "vital interests" of the Federation members are taken care of.

The first of these, he said, is that Southern Rhodesia should be granted its independence.

The second, he added, is that the new Constitution of Northern Rhodesia should contain guarantees for the protection of the minority European community there, and of the various regional interests of African communities.

"When I have had assurances on these matters, my Government will work to bring about a new order," Sir Roy said.

The next step toward the formal dissolution of the federation will depend on events in the next few days. As one British official put it, "The dust will have to settle."

A conference in Africa is still hopeful by summer, but much will depend on the reception the Northern Rhodesian leaders get when they return home.

March 30, 1963

BRITAIN REBUFFS SOUTH RHODESIA

Blocks Early Independence for White-Ruled Colony

By SYDNEY GRUSON
Special to The New York Times

LONDON, April 11 — The British Government disclosed today that it had rejected the demand of the all-white Government of Southern Rhodesia for early independence.

R. A. Butler, Minister for Central African Affairs, told Prime Minister Sir Winston Field that no final decision could be taken until after a conference on the future relationship between the three territories of the crumbling Federation of Rhodesia and Nyasaland.

In a series of letters published as a white paper Prime Minister Field said Southern Rhodesia would not attend a conference unless it received written guarantees from Britain on the independence issue.

He had then suggested that Southern Rhodesia be granted independence at the same time as either Northern Rhodesia or Nyasaland was permitted to secede from the federation. Both have African Governments and their secession is expected to take place this fall.

Prime Minister Field wrote that while the impression held that Britain could interfere in Southern Rhodesia's internal affairs, there was a danger of serious disorders "being encouraged from outside in order to compel such intervention."

This was apparently an allusion to reports that Southern Rhodesian black African leaders in exile might order a campaign of violence against the Southern Rhodesian Government.

In the most careful language, necessitated by the sharp division over Southern Rhodesia in the Conservative party, Mr. Butler told Prime Minister Field Britain recognized the colony's desire to reach independence as soon as possible.

But, the minister stressed, the secession of another member of the Federation would not in itself end Southern Rhodesia's membership. This could be achieved only after a conference to discuss "matters which always have to be settled before self-governing territories were granted independence."

Mr. Butler came under sharp attack in the House of Commons from both the Labor Opposition and the right wing of the Conservative party, which has supported immediate independence for Southern Rhodesia

From the Conservative back benches, Patrick Wall told Mr. Butler that there would be no conference on possible association of the two Rhodesias "unless you make up your mind to say either 'yes' or 'no' to Mr. Field."

Mr. Butler refused the request of Harold Wilson, Labor leader, for a "clear assurance" that Southern Rhodesia would not be granted independence until it got a Constitution "which enables the mass of the people of Southern Rhodesia to govern themselves."

John Strachey, Labor's spokesman on colonial affairs, criticized the Government for failing to make clear its intentions toward the Rhodesias.

Nyasaland, where there are about 8,000 Europeans and 3,000,000 black Africans, is headed by Dr. H. Kamuzu Banda. Northern Rhodesia, ruled by a coalition led by Kenneth Kaunda and Harry Nkumbula, has about 75,000 Europeans and 2,500,000 black Africans.

April 12, 1963

WHITE EXTREMIST WINS IN RHODESIA

Smith Forces Field to Quit—Seeks End of British Tie

By ROBERT CONLEY
Special to The New York Times

SALISBURY, Southern Rhodesia, April 13—A conservative extremist gained control of the Government today. There were increasing indications that Southern Rhodesia was heading for a collision with Britain over the question of independence.

Ian D. Smith, former Minister of the Treasury, was named Prime Minister of this self-governing British colony in Central Africa. He took over after a right-wing revolt within the ruling Rhodesian Front party had forced Winston J. Field to resign after 16 months in office.

Meanwhile, the Zimbabwe African National Union, one of the two principal black nationalist movements in Southern Rhodesia, called on the country's Africans to prepare for an "inevitable head - on collision" with the whites.

"The most reactionary element has won the day and the way is cleared for a unilateral declaration of independence," the nationalist party said.

In his first public statement, Mr. Smith denied that the change had anything to do with the efforts of Southern Rhodesia's white minority to gain full independence while it still retained political control over the country's black majority.

But it was said on the highest authority that the party's extremists had forced Mr. Field to step down because he had refused to set a time limit for negotiating constitutionally and legally with Britain for independnce.

The extremists were understood with equal authority to be prepared to seize that independence on their own, once a date was agreed upon.

Mr. Smith, a 45-year-old cattle rancher and wartime fighter pilot, indicated that he would step up pressure for Southern Rhodesia's right as a colony that had governed itself for 40 years to break away from Britain.

"We are desirous to try to have a negotiated independence and we will continue to strive for that," he said at a news conference. "But we can visualize circumstances that might drive us to do something else."

The news of Mr. Field's replacement by Mr. Smith seemed to have brought a sense of shock, fear and despondency to African nationalists and white liberals.

Garfield Todd, who was deposed as Prime Minister in 1957 for being too liberal, called the revolt against Mr. Field an act of "political assassination" and added: "The price this country is being asked to pay to maintain white government is higher than we can afford."

Mr. Field presented his resignation to the Governor, Sir Humphrey Gibbs, with a statement that confirmed his enforced retirement after one of the shortest terms in office in Rhodesian history.

"Serious disagreements have arisen between my party in the House and myself in relation to policy," his statement said, "and I have been requested to retire in order to make way for someone else."

An hour later the Governor called on Mr. Smith to form a new government.

Mr. Smith said he expected to announce his 10-man Cabinet tomorrow. But his ability to hold onto the Rhodesian Front party's narrow five-seat majority was questioned tonight by the Opposition.

The extremists within the Rhodesian Front were known to have felt that Mr. Field, a cautious conservative, lacked "strength" in leading Southern Rhodesias' 223,000 whites in their effort to keep down the political emergence of the country's 3.7 million Africans.

April 14, 1964

Rhodesian Extremist

Ian Douglas Smith

Special to The New York Times

SALISBURY, Southern Rhodesia, April 13—Cecil John Rhodes marched north from South Africa in 1890 with an ox-wagon train of settlers to seize this land in his name for "Christian civilization and commerce." He offered "equal rights for all civilized men," which meant whites only. This policy later evolved into one of supposed racial cooperation between whites and blacks, known as "partnership." Its advocates called it the partnership of "a rider and his horse—and no one had any doubt about who was supposed to be the horse.

Man in the News

The latest white rider is Ian Douglas Smith, who was named Prime Minister of Southern Rhodesia today. He is the country's fourth Prime Minister in the last seven years and by far the most racial minded.

At 45 Mr. Smith is convinced he has the ability to lead Southern Rhodesia's 223,000 whites in their effort to hold firm against the awakening aspirations of the country's 3.7 million Africans. He recently alarmed businessmen and industrialists with a statement on the possibility that the whites might seize independence from Britain to block the political threat of a black majority. He said the British reaction, particularly in financial quarters, would not last more than a weekend.

"For that reason I think a Friday afternoon would be a good time," he added. "By Monday morning all the excitement would be over."

He now says his suggestion of an open rebellion against British control should not be taken literally.

Mr. Smith, a rather humorless and almost abrupt man, expresses amazement at Britain's refusal to grant independence to Southern Rhodesia, which has been a self-governing colony for 40 years, until the whites agree to bring about the political and social equality of the blacks.

"It makes us wonder whether it really does pay to continue along the lines we have been following, to adhere to the ideals and principles on which this Commonwealth has been built up, and whether it would not be just as easy to think of our own convenience," he says.

A cattle rancher, Mr. Smith is tall, raw-boned and blunt. As the first Rhodesian-born Prime Minister, he feels less attachment to Britain than his predecessors did. "He will be a hard rider with plenty of spurs," one of his friends commented.

Associated Press

His youthful appearance seems inconsistent with his record as a fighter pilot in the Rhodesian Squadron of the Royal Air Force in World War II. He was shot down twice while flying Spitfires in the North African and Italian campaigns.

The second time, after bailing out over Italy, he joined Italian partisans and fought for five months behind the German lines. He worked his way north, crossed the Alps on foot in disguise and reached Germany to meet onrushing Allied forces and rejoin the R.A.F.

Mr. Smith was born April 8, 1919, at Selukwe, a small farming and mining town. He broke off his studies at Rhodes University in South Africa in 1941 to join the R.A.F. and returned home in 1946.

He received his bachelor of commerce degree, took up farming and went into politics in 1948, serving in the Legislative Assembly for five years. When the now disbanded Federation of Southern and Northern Rhodesia and Nyasaland was formed in 1953, he moved into its Parliament as a member of the governing United Federal party.

He was chief whip for the Prime Minister, Sir Roy Welensky, until 1961, when he broke with the party and rejected a new Constitution that proposed to give Africans seats in Parliament for the first time. With six other insurgents he helped establish the Rhodesian Front party, a coalition of extreme anti-black conservatives.

When his party swept to victory in 1962, Mr. Smith became Minister of the Treasury and second to Winston J. Field, the man he replaced today. He is married and the father of three children.

April 14, 1964

RHODESIAN POLICE OPEN FIRE ON MOB

265 Rioters Are Reported Held in Wake of Detention of Nkomo and 3 Aides

By ROBERT CONLEY

Special to The New York Times

SALISBURY, Southern Rhodesia, April 18 — The police opened fire on rioting Africans today for the first time as violence and turmoil spread in Southern Rhodesia.

One man was seriously wounded when policemen, dodging a barrage of stones, used shotguns to scatter a crowd of 200 Africans.

At least 265 Africans were reported to have been arrested in the last 48 hours. They were seized in a widening series of stonings, demonstrations and riots that followed the detention on Thursday of Joshua Nkomo and three other nationalists in this self-governing British colony in Central Africa.

All of the country's nearly 5,630 policemen were said to be on full alert.

Mr. Nkomo was ordered sent to a remote area of the colony by the Government of Prime Minister Ian D. Smith. Mr. Smith was named last Monday to replace Winston J. Field, who was considered too moderate by the right wing of the ruling Rhodesian Front party.

Mr. Nkomo's People's Caretaker Council has asked Britain to send troops to protect the African majority in the colony.

The shooting today took place at Bulawayo, in the southern part of the country. It came a few hours after an African had been shot and wounded outside Salisbury, the capital, in what was alleged to be an attempt to escape arrest.

In Salisbury a band of Africans set upon white women shoppers in a downtown store, punching, slapping and beating them in a fury. About 20 African youths entered the store, the OK Bazaar, and mingled with shoppers. At a prearranged signal—a whistle—each youth attacked the white nearest him.

One woman was knocked down a flight of stairs. Another was hit with a glass tray. A man who tried to stop the fleeing band was slashed on the arm.

At Bulawayo a police patrol surprised a mob stoning a beerhall in Imminyela, an African township just outside the city. The patrol opened fire with a riot gun when the crowd turned on it. A man was found later in a house, bleeding badly from gun-pellet wounds.

Houses and Cars Stoned

Roving gangs of shouting Africans stoned houses, community centers and cars throughout the night in and around Bulawayo and Salisbury.

At Bulawayo they set up crude road blocks with rubbish cans and debris to hamper police riot trucks. They also put boulders on tracks in an unsuccessful attempt to derail a train.

Around Bulawayo alone they stoned one store, eight houses, five buses, three beerhalls, three cars, a train and two police patrols.

Two African police reservists were stabbed by members of surging crowds in Highfield township, outside Salisbury. In one incident at least 290 panes of glass were smashed at the Mhiza school. Gangs stuffed kerosene soaked rags under the doors of political opponents' homes and set them afire.

Police with three-foot-long riot clubs patrolled the streets of the capital tonight. In Highfield they carried away several truckloads of suspects.

The biggest mass arrest took place yesterday, when policemen seized 120 women in a protest parade here over the banishment of Mr. Nkomo and two men and a woman to a security camp for a year to preserve "law and order."

The arrested women, many with babies strapped on their backs, were held for trial April 28. Their bail, the equivalent of $84, represents nearly six weeks' wages for their husbands.

April 19, 1964

Lisbon, Pretoria Said to Warn South Rhodesia

Would Not Support It in Any Uprising Against Britain

By ROBERT CONLEY
Special to The New York Times

SALISBURY, Southern Rhodesia, July 11—South Africa and Portugal were reported today on the highest authority to have informed Southern Rhodesia that they could not assist the British colony in any way if it unilaterally declared its independence.

Both countries, whose territories are adjacent to Southern Rhodesia, were understood on equal authority to have gone so far as to state that they would be unable to grant diplomatic recognition if the territory rebelled.

This turn of events was viewed among responsible quarters here as the severest setback to date for Southern Rhodesia's restive Prime Minister, Ian D. Smith, in his determination to preserve the white minority's rule in this self-governing territory in Central Africa.

It meant that Mr. Smith had been denied the backing of his last probable sources of outside support if he chose to act unilaterally to hold back the political emergence of Southern Rhodesia's 3.9 million black Africans.

British Stand Called Basis

It also appeared to insure the prospect, as one informant put it, of the "awful isolation" that Southern Rhodesia's whites would face should they stage what they term a "Boston Tea Party" against the British crown.

South Africa and Portugal were said to have decided on a hands-off policy on Southern Rhodesia for two principal reasons.

First, Britain has let it be known through diplomatic channels that she would regard outside recognition of an insurgent Southern Rhodesian government as an unfriendly act. Second, South Africa and Portugal were understood to be aware of the potential effect on public opinion abroad of open association with "racist rebellion."

South Africa is already confronted with increasing international criticism in her attempts to justify her policy of apartheid, or racial separation. Portugal is under comparable assault from the Asian-African bloc for her policies in her territories of Mozambique, Angola and Portuguese Guinea.

Verwoerd's Views Reported

South Africa's Prime Minister, Dr. Hendrik F. Verwoerd, was understood to have informed Prime Minister Smith that his Government could not interfere in another country's internal affairs because it does not permit outside interference in its own. Mr. Smith indicated part of this in a broadcast this week.

Dr. Verwoerd was understood also to be reluctant to antagonize Britain, South Africa's principal trading partner and her main defender against Asian-African attempts to apply economic sanctions to force the abandonment of apartheid.

Southern Rhodesia, which has a strong military force, is the only territory of the former Federation of Rhodesia and Nyasaland whose political course has not been defined. Malawi, formerly Nyasaland, became independent Monday. Northern Rhodesia will become independent under the name Zambia in October.

Black Africans have demanded that the Southern Rhodesian Constitution be supplanted by one adhering to the "one man, one vote" principle instead of the weighted franchise now underlying white rule. Britain is prepared to grant independence but has been unable to obtain agreement on the basis for it.

The white minority has periodically threatened to seize independence if its demands are not granted, though Mr. Smith indicated Thursday that it would rely on negotiation with London.

African nationalists have said they would set up a government in exile, most likely in neighboring Northern Rhodesia, should a white insurrection occur.

July 12, 1964

RACIAL PROBLEMS HAMPER RHODESIA

Minister Lists Losses of Millions Over Insults

Special to The New York Times

LUSAKA, Northern Rhodesia, May 31—Racial problems continue in Northern Rhodesia despite the efforts of the Prime Minister, Dr. Kenneth D. Kaunda, to create a nonracial state. Both Europeans and Africans are constantly reminded of racial stresses and strains.

Northern Rhodesia has been troubled by strikes caused by alleged racial insults. African workers have walked off their jobs because, they charged, their European superiors referred to them as "kaffirs" and "baboons."

According to recently published government statistics more than 68,500 man-days were lost durning February, March and April because of such strikes. One dispute at Livingstone involving African railway workers cost 10,728 man-days in a four-day stoppage. In Kitwe 200 construction workers walked off the job because of an alleged racial insult.

Arthur N. L. Wine, Minister of Finance, estimated that strikes in 1964 might cut Government revenues by $5.6 million. That much money would pay for the projected University of Zambia.

In Northern Rhodesia economics and race are interwoven. Europeans earn nearly 10 times the wages of Africans in most sectors of the economy. Europeans have most of the top-level skilled positions. All domestic servants are Africans—who earned in 1963 an average of $260.

In the fields of agriculture, forestry and fishing the 39,900 Africans earned an average of $185. The 720 non-Africans, mostly Europeans, in the same fields averaged earnings of $3,700 in 1963. In the better paid mining and quarreying sector of the economy the 41,400 Africans in 1963 earned on the average $834; Europeans in the same industries earned an average of $7,175.

Coupled with the economic disparity is chronic widespread unemployment among Africans. Although there are 3,460,000 Africans in the territory, only 223,000 are employed. In 1954, when there were only 2,660,000 Africans, there were 241,000 employed. Today's figure is a drop of 18,000 in ten years. Of the 74,000 Europeans in Northern Rhodesia 32,000 are employed.

The large number of South Africans in Northern Rhodesia determines the complexion of social life in the territory. Although since the institution of an African government in January many of the barriers, social and economic, have fallen, many facets of racial discrimination continue to exist.

Sometimes Europeans are caught in the African reaction to discrimination.

A multiracially-cast Brecht play, "The Caucasian Chalk Circle," was withdrawn in Lusaka, the capital city, on May 19, a week before its scheduled opening in the Northern Rhodesian Drama Festival. The controversy involved a cabinet minister and a South African European playwright, who has a play, "Blood Knot," on Broadway. Athol Fugard, who came to Northern Rhodesia to direct the Brecht play, left the territory after the Minister of Lands and Works, Solomon Kalulu, threatened to help Mr. Fugard out of the country.

In April an African doctor was arrested when he protested against being refused accommodation as a Livingstone hotel. Dr. Kabeleka Konoso, who received pediatric training at a New York hospital, learned from an African employe of the hotel that rooms were available, and his protests to the hotel manager led to his arrest.

Minister Warns Hotel

The hotel owner explained his refusal by saying that he did not recognize Dr. Konoso. The Minister of Justice, Mainza C. Chona, warned the hotel owner that the law against racial discrimination must be upheld.

Private mine clubs in the wealthy Copper Belt have also been rebuked for their past refusal and present reluctance to accept African members. A few Africans have become mine club members after strong government pressure.

Officials have warned that unless the mining companies integrate the clubs there will be legislation. The governing party charges that the admission of a few Africans to membership has only served to "hoodwink" Africans into believing that racial discrimination had ended. The mining clubs have swimming pools, cinemas, restaurants, barber shops and other amenities for their members. European miners become club members as soon as they are employed.

June 7, 1964

Nyasaland Becomes Malawi, 37th Free African Country

New Name Helps Mark Shift of Control From Whites to Black Majority

By ROBERT CONLEY
Special to The New York Times

BLANTYRE, Malawi, Monday, July 6—Nyasaland became the independent African state of Malawi early today in a din of jubilation.

Africans stomped, shouted and danced at the ending of 73 years of British colonial rule in this Central African land.

"Ufulu! Ufulu!" (Freedom! Freedom!), they cried.

At least 40,000 people had crowded into Central Stadium here for the independence ceremonies. Twelve bonfires blazed into the night sky from the ancient hills where tribal leaders lie buried.

The change came at 12:01 A.M. (6:01 P.M. Sunday, Eastern daylight time).

The acquisition of sovereignty made Malawi the 37th country in restless, emerging Africa to achieve independence. Nearly all its 3.9 million inhabitants are blacks; there are only 8,000 whites.

To emphasize the change from the colonial past, the country's name was altered from Nyasaland, which meant land of "broad waters," to Malawi, land of "flaming waters. The name is taken from a tribal word that described how rays of sun glinted off Lake Nyasa.

A hush fell on the stadium as the moment of independence approached. Official guests from more than 60 countries and the Vatican stood for the final playing of the British anthem, "God Save the Queen."

Prince Philip, Duke of Edinburgh, represented Queen Elizabeth II of Britain.

In the darkness, to the muffled roll of military drums, the Union Jack was lowered for the last time. Seconds later, to a cacophony of screams, exploding fireworks and rattle of bean-filled gourds, the new red, green and black colors of Malawi were unfurled from the ceremonial flagpole.

Celebrators Cheer Banda

The crowd screamed its acclaim for Dr. H. Kamuzu Banda the American-educated physician who will be Malawi's first Prime Minister.

At that moment, miles away to the south, an African climber unfurled a second flag on the 9,843-foot summit of Mount Mlanje, the country's highest peak.

Today was considered a particular triumph for Dr. Banda, now in his sixties. It coincided with the date of his return here six years ago to lead the country's black majority. He had been abroad for four decades.

It also followed his earlier success in breaking Nyasland away from the former Federation of Rhodesia and Nyasland because he felt the federation had been dominated by white-controlled Southern Rhodesia. The federation, which was organized in 1953, collapsed last year as a result.

July 6, 1964

MALAWI KEEPING LINKS TO WHITES

Relies on 3 Regimes Other Africans Try to Shun

By ROBERT CONLEY
Special to The New York Times

BLANTYRE, Malawi, July 8—Malawi, which won independence from Britain this week, became the first black African country in years to invite the Southern Rhodesian and Portuguese Governments to an independence celebration. The rest of Africa might talk of boycotting what it terms the "unholy alliance" of Rhodesians, South Africans and Portuguese but Malawi cannot.

At a state luncheon guests drank Portuguese wine. A $44,-800 Independence Arch was designed by a South African and topped by an aluminum cockerel made in Southern Rhodesia.

The Duke of Edinburgh was met with a 21-gun salute when he flew in as a personal representative of Queen Elizabeth II. The two cannons used had to be borrowed from the Southern Rhodesian Army.

The economic future of Malawi, formerly Nyasaland, which has an estimated population of four million in an area about the size of Pennsylvania, depends upon white areas.

Half of her imports, from tractors to tribal prints, originate in or pass through Southern Rhodesia. The Portuguese control her sole gateway to the sea. White areas are the principal employers of her men — more Malawis have jobs on the farms of Southern Rhodesia and the gold mines of South Africa now than at home.

Poor, Densely Populated

"Our troubles begin with independence," Malawi's Prime Minister, Dr. H. Kamuzu Banda, says of the difficulties ahead of one of the poorest and most densely populated lands in Africa.

She starts on her own with $9.9 million budget deficit covered by Britain, a $1.1 million grant from Southern Rhodesia in return for assuring her continued cooperation as a market, and a hobbling economy in which the average citizen has no more than $17.50 a year to spend.

She also starts out with 239 miles of paved road, 113 backcountry buses and an airline consisting of two prewar American Douglas DC-3's.

Misty, mountainous Malawi contains in miniature all the handicaps of emerging Africa: ignorance, poverty and disease. A total of 64 Africans graduated from her high schools last year and nine in 1960.

"We are not poor," Dr. Banda says, "we are only neglected."

To rectify that, Malawi has a $124.9 million development plan for the next five years, which is more or less a noseprint of her aspirations pressed against the bakery shop window of her tomorrows.

With the plan she hopes to increase her export crops of tea, tobacco, peanuts, cotton and tung oil, which account for half her gross national product; pave and extend her roads to get produce to market; encourage private investment, and expand high schools and advanced courses to create skilled manpower.

Already she was doubled the number of grammar school graduates in three years from 6,092 to 12,843. She doubled in one year the number entering her trade and vocational school

Malawi is also preparing to start a development corporation with an initial capital of $28 million as a "catalyst" for private investment and a $11.2 million sugar project. She is at work on a $6.8 million hydroelectric project.

The United States, Britain, and West Germany are helping in other fields. The United States is building a $1.2 million technical college and an agricultural institute.

July 9, 1964

Northern Rhodesia Reborn as Zambia; Britain Ends Rule

By ROBERT CONLEY
Special to The New York Times

LUSAKA, Zambia, Saturday, Oct. 24—Africa's 36th independent country was born here today. The former portectorate of Northern Rhodesia became the Republic of Zambia, ending 73 years of British rule.

A wave of jubilation swept the country, which takes its name from the Zambezi River, Zambia's border with Southern Rhodesia for hundreds of miles.

Cries of "kwacha!" (freedom) rang again and again through Independence Stadium here as at least 38,000 persons gathered to watch the ceremonies.

The change took place at 12:01 A.M. (6:01 P.M., Friday, New York time).

Kenneth D. Kaunda, head of the United National Independence party, is scheduled to be sworn in tomorrow as Zambia's first President. He will lead 3.6 million people in a country roughly the size of Texas.

In the stadium, Ngoni dancers in lionskins swept back and forth across the field amid a cacophony of tribal drums, war horns and bean-filled gourds.

Moments before 12:01, a hush fell over the stadium in anticipation of the striking of the Union Jack. The lights went out and in the darkness, to the beat of muffled drums, the British flag was lowered for the last time.

At that moment, the last vestige of political power passed, in effect, from the hands of the country's 74,000 whites to her African majority.

Unlike many other emergent states in Africa, Zambia begins independence with a strong potential for economic growth. Her main strength lies in copper, of which she has one-fifth of the West's reserves.

Zambia already stands third behind the United States and Chile as a producer of copper. Her exports last year amounted to the equivalent of $329 million.

Zambia's emergence means that black nationalism has pressed the areas of white control in Africa all the way down the continent to the Zambezi. The only sizable areas left under white control are Southern Rhodesia, South Africa and the Portuguese territories of Mozambique and Angola.

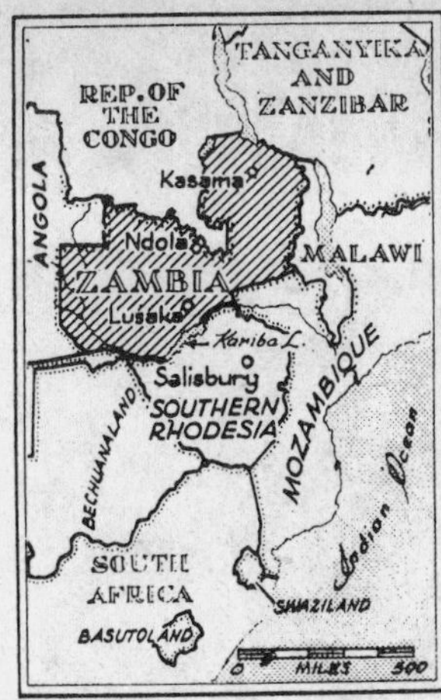

The New York Times Oct. 24, 1964
Diagonal shading defines the new state of Zambia.

October 24, 1964

White Supremacist Wins in Rhodesia

By LAWRENCE FELLOWS
Special to The New York Times

SALISBURY, Rhodesia, May 7—Prime Minister Ian D. Smith swept to victory tonight in Rhodesia's general election, winning all the 50 Parliamentary seats his party was contesting.

He won an overwhelming display of support, from the minority entitled to vote, for his persistent effort to win independence for this landlocked British colony deep in the African continent.

Condemnation of Mr. Smith's Government in the United Nations Security Council this week and an unsuccessful attempt by African states to get Britain to prevent the election, have made little impression in Rhodesia. The mood here is a tough one.

It is widely feared that the election might set the stage for a unilateral declaration of independence.

Mr. Smith's right-wing Rhodesian Front, with a fat cushion over the 44 Parliamentary seats it needed for a two-thirds majority, is now free to push through a program of constitutional reform and tighten the political grip of Rhodesia's white minority. The opposition Rhodesia party was all but shattered. Its leader, David Butler, was beaten in his Highlands North constituency by a margin of more than 2 to 1.

The only two Rhodesia party candidates who were sure of getting into Parliament tonight were black Africans. They had been purposely unopposed by Mr. Smith's party, for they were running on the B roll, which is mainly of Africans.

The Rhodesian Front shied away from this roll in the hopes of bringing about a clearer separation of blacks and whites in the colony, which has been self-governing for about 40 years.

This hope has clearly been realized. In the remaining 13 B-roll seats, the Rhodesia party was swamped and appeared tonight to have lost out to an array of independents, all of them black, but with a wide range of loyalties and aims.

Voters on the B roll must have an annual income equivalent to $739 or own immovable property worth $1,386.

For the first time since Rhodesia obtained self-government, the Opposition, if one can be pulled together when Parliament reassembles, will be entirely black.

Rhodesia's whites, by their show of trust in the tough leadership of Mr. Smith, have revealed their anger at Britain for withholding independence and their disdain for Prime Minister Harold Wilson's warning of the consequences Rhodesia would face if an attempt were made to cut the strings to the mother country.

This morning, the Indian diplomatic mission was withdrawn from Salisbury in a protest against what India called Rhodesia's determination to declare her independence without the consent of the colony's African majority.

In Salisbury City, Salisbury's Asian quarter, persons of Indian origin stayed away from the polls, and the Rhodesia party candidate, who believed he had a chance, was trounced by a margin of 3 to 1.

Voting throughout the country was heavy and orderly. Electoral registers were so out of date that there was no way of telling what proportion of the white electorate cast ballots.

The election belonged to the colony's 217,000 whites. Not many of Rhodesia's 4 million blacks are enfranchised, and if many of the enfranchised ones used their votes, they must have done so by mail.

May 8, 1965

AN HONEST RHODESIAN

TRUST Mr SMITH

TRUST him . . . to <u>negotiate</u> for an honourable Independence

TRUST him . . . to act responsibly in <u>your</u> interests

TRUST him . . . to <u>ensure the safety</u> of us all

TRUST him . . . he has the <u>welfare</u> of the Country at heart

TRUST him . . . he leads a <u>united</u> resolute Party

TRUST HIM ABOVE ALL

. . . HE WILL NEVER 'HAND OVER' RHODESIA

Remember the 'FIRST CHOICE' and unite on May 7

RHODESIAN FRONT

UNITE FOR INDEPENDENCE

Prime Minister of white-run Rhodesia, Ian Smith would divide black Africa from white southern Africa along the banks of the Zambesi River, Rhodesia's northern frontier. Above, a poster widely circulated in his successful election campaign last May.

Would You Give All to Blacks? Rhodesian Asks

By LAWRENCE FELLOWS
Special to The New York Times

SALISBURY, Rhodesia, Oct. 21—At a dinner party here a few nights ago a Rhodesian tobacco farmer summed up in a single crude question his reasons for wanting to see his country independent of Britain:

"Would you give it all to the Kaffirs, man?"

There must be thousands of white people like him who reduce the long-drawn issue of Rhodesia's independence to such simple and precise terms as whether the whites should hand over control to the blacks, especially now that so much emotion has been generated in the country.

Britain has refused to grant independence to Rhodesia unless steps are taken to guarantee the rights of the country's four million blacks. In the interests of white dominance, the Rhodesian Government of Prime Minister Ian D. Smith has threatened to declare independence unilaterally if necessary.

South African Roots

Of the nearly 220,000 whites in Rhodesia, well over a third have roots in the recent or distant past in South Africa and not all of them have shed the prevailing South African views on racial harmony and justice.

A good many of the people who migrated from Britain to Rhodesia in recent years to be plumbers, policemen, nurses, workers and the like grow quickly accustomed to pleasant weather and a standard of living they could never have hoped to experience before.

Their stakes are small but they take easily to this white aristocracy in Africa and they feel, probably rightly, that their jobs would be among the first to be sacrificed to the blacks if everyone in this colony could operate on completely equal terms.

However, there are other white people here who want independence and for whom the arguments were never quite so simple.

Among them are dedicated men, economists. They contend that only with independence and the kind of stability in government that they say the blacks in Rhodesia are not advanced enough to insure can the country expect sufficient capital and skilled manpower to arrive to sustain economic growth.

The Rhodesians are getting virtually no development loans or grants from Britain. As long as Rhodesia remains a colony, on the verge of some agonizing constitutional change, it is not likely to raise any development money on the international market.

White Rhodesians assert that with independence on their own terms, they could get money and proceed with ambitious projects like the dam-building they have started in the dry but potentially rich southeastern part of the country.

The tobacco farmers are the spearhead of the independence movement, but there are groups of them who have spent a good deal of time and money to help the black men around them by plowing their land, showing them how to fertilize and how to cure and market their tobacco.

2,000 Blacks Grow Burley

The sort of flue curing that is needed for Virginia tobacco is expensive, but burley tobacco can be cured in relatively inexpensive sheds. With encouragement from their white neighbors, nearly 2,000 black farmers are growing burley tobacco this year. There were only 500 of them last year and 40 the year before.

Some of the white man's help stems from good neighborliness and some from enlightened self-interest in the knowledge that only by raising the mass of Africans from subsistence-level farming can the whole economy thrive.

One of the white farmers helping on the edge of the Chiweshe Reserve was asked the other day if he thought the black people of Rhodesia were ready for the vote.

"Man, you just don't know your Africans," he said. "It's because of people like you that we need our independence now. You can't push these people."

This is a basic contention, stemming from the pressures the white Rhodesians feel from Britain, from the black African countries to the north, from the United Nations.

The white Rhodesians had their attempt at partnership in government when they belonged to a federation of which Zambia, then Northern Rhodesia, and Malawi, then Nyasaland, were a part. It failed, they say, through no fault of their own, and now Zambia and Malawi, neither with a long record of self-government, are independent. This pains the white Rhodesians deeply.

They are also embittered by the fact that the African nationalists have persistently refused to take advantage of the small part in government that has been offered them and have resorted to violence and intimidation to keep from the polls many of the black people who could qualify.

With independence on their own terms, the white Rhodesians would have the power to roll back the Constitution to their own liking, to make it more and more difficult for the black majority ever to come to power. There are doubtless people in Mr. Smith's Government who would like to see this happen. But Mr. Smith has offered the British a treaty to guarantee that it would not.

With independence the Rhodesians would also be free to pursue their own foreign policy without interference from Britain. They already have their own diplomatic representatives in South Africa and Portugal and there was little the British could do to stop them.

However, with the interests of South Africa, Portugal's African territories and Rhodesia so aligned, the Rhodesians would doubtless find it in their interest to pursue these relations further, perhaps with a common defense arrangement.

October 22, 1965

RHODESIA TO JOIN BRITAIN IN STUDY ON INDEPENDENCE

3-Man Team Is to Canvass Colony on a Possible Pact Retaining Constitution

WILSON ON WAY HOME

He Seeks Cabinet's Backing —Asserts 'Door Is Open' to Accord With Smith

By LAWRENCE FELLOWS
Special to The New York Times

SALISBURY, Rhodesia, Oct. 30—Britain and Rhodesia have tentatively agreed to set up a royal commission to determine whether Rhodesia's people want independence under their present Constitution.

"It gives us time," Prime Minister Wilson of Britain said at a news conference this morning.

"The door is open for agreement," he added. "There is no reason why we can't go forward. There is no excuse for a unilateral declaration of independence."

[At a political meeting in Rusape, Rhodesia, Prime Minister Ian D. Smith said that if the royal commission failed, "this will be the end of the road," Reuters reported.]

Week of Talks Ended

After announcing the decision to form the commission, Mr. Wilson left for London, ending a week of urgent talks with Rhodesians, including Prime Minister Smith, aimed at averting a Rhodesian seizure of independence.

He planned to return to London and seek Cabinet approval after brief conferences in Zambia and Ghana. The two Commonwealth nations share Britain's opposition to an independent Rhodesia so long as the colony's black majority is denied an opportunity to achieve governmental power.

The plan for a royal commission on Rhodesia represented a concession by Britain. Originally Mr. Wilson insisted that before the internally self-governing colony could receive British consent for independence, the entire Rhodesian population must have an opportunity to express its wishes on the 1961 Constitution.

Rhodesian Heads Panel

It is this constitution that provides the basis for rule by Rhodesia's 220,000 whites. The colony's four million blacks are not considered likely to endorse it in any vote.

As an alternative to such a vote, Mr. Wilson has proposed that changes in the 1961 Constitution be weighed by a royal commission appointed by London.

Under the compromise, however, it was agreed that Rhodesia's Chief Justice, Sir Hugh Beadle, would be the commission chairman, and that Britain and Rhodesia would each appoint one other member.

Even before Mr. Wilson boarded his plane, opposition to the plan was welling up in the expected places—among black nationalists and in the more extreme end of Mr. Smith's party, the Rhodesian Front.

The British Prime Minister had taken the occasion of his news conference to state his attitudes toward truculent elements in the colony, and to dispel what he called their dangerous delusions.

He told Rhodesia's black nationalists that they would wait in vain for British military intervention in the colony, for there would be none.

He also told them that there would be no majority rule in Rhodesia for a while because they had a lot to learn before they would be ready to assume power.

Since his arrival Monday night, the Prime Minister had held working meetings with 126 Rhodesians of all races and opinions.

He heard people in industry and commerce voice fear that they would be ruined if Britain imposed economic sanctions to punish Rhodesia for seizing independence.

He heard independent and opposition politicians argue against independence without a promise, at least, that the voting rolls would be widened and the colony's blacks put on the road to political responsibility.

He heard the government's demand that independence be granted with the colony's whites still in power, so that the chaos associated with independence elsewhere in Africa could be averted here.

Mr. Wilson said he would put the plan to his Cabinet and would leave his Commonwealth Relations Secretary, Arthur Bottomley, and the British Attorney General, Sir Elwyn Jones, to see whether a program of work for the royal commission could be agreed upon in the next few days.

Mr. Smith did not see Mr. Wilson off at the airport, but he drove to the city of Rusape to assure party officials that this was not just another time-wasting device.

From the detention camps of the colony's rival black nationalist leaders Joshua Nkomo and the Rev. Ndabaningi Sithole came denunciations of the plan.

"We shall never accept any form of constitutional settlement whereby majority rule is preceded by independence," Mr. Nkomo said. "We regard the proposal as an act of evading responsibility on the part of the British Government."

Mr. Sithole declared: "We must have majority rule first. The problem has gone beyond the proportions of a royal commission."

Mr. Wilson dealt at his news conference with the feats and expectations of the nationalists, and with the problem he had faced in even getting them to sit together at their final meeting.

"The British Government," he said, "do not believe that in the present and tragic and divided condition of Rhodesia that majority rule can or should come today, or tomorrow. A period of time is needed time to remove the fears and suspicions between race and race, time to show that the Constitution of Rhodesia, with whatever amendments may later be made, can be worked, and is going to be worked, and that the rule of law, equally with the maintenance of essential human rights, will be paramount."

Equally obstructive and misguided, the Prime Minister said, are the whites who think they can run away with their independence and survive, whatever the feelings of their countrymen and the rest of the world.

To them, he said: "When nearly two centuries ago, the American states declared their independence from a British Government which to say the least was remote, oppressive and unimaginative, they insisted that their actions be inspired by 'a proper respect for the opinions of mankind.' If Rhodesia acts illegally, do not underrate the consequences of what might be thrown at you, which Britain—even if we had the will—would not have the power to prevent."

October 31, 1965

Wilson Denounces Smith; Commonwealth Tie Is Cut

By ANTHONY LEWIS
Special to The New York Times

LONDON, Nov. 11—The British Government, denouncing Rhodesia's unilateral declaration of independence as rebellion and treason, today took the first counter-measures.

Rhodesia was expelled from the sterling area. Her preferential tariff treatment as a Commonwealth land was suspended. Controls were imposed on all trade and exchanges of currency. Purchases of tobacco and sugar, the main Rhodesian crops, were banned.

Prime Minister Wilson announced these moves to a House of Commons that had about it a sense of occasion, of history.

Mr. Wilson spoke quietly, almost sadly, but his words were not soft as he traced the last few desperate days of negotiations.

Act Called Treasonable

"The British Government condemn the purported declaration of independence by the former Government of Rhodesia as an illegal act and one which is ineffective in law," Mr. Wilson declared. "Action taken to give effect to it will be treasonable."

At 6 o'clock this morning, he disclosed, he talked with Rhodesia's Prime Minister, Ian D. Smith, on the telephone to try again to head off the "illegal act."

"I ended the conversation," Mr. Wilson said, "with a heavy heart, feeling that reason had fled the scene and that emotions, unreasoning racialist emotions at that, had taken command regardless of the consequences for Rhodesia, for Africa and for the world."

The Prime Minister called the white Rhodesians' decision a "tragedy" for them and, referring to the African majority, for "millions more who are denied the inalienable human right of self-expression and self-determination." There are 4,000,000 Africans in Rhodesia and 220,000 whites.

Mr. Wilson rejected, as he often has, the use of British arms to bring about political change in Rhodesia. But he reserved, as always, the right to send troops if necessary "to maintain law and order."

Tonight, on television, Mr. Wilson told the nation that Britain had a trust for all the people of Rhodesia.

"Whatever the cost," he said, "we shall honor that trust."

The television talk was an essential political effort to rally the British people behind stern measures. Because the rulers in Rhodesia are white and many of British extraction, there has been much sympathy for them here.

Recent indications are that public opinion is swinging against the Rhodesian Government. This trend probably will be encouraged by natural resentment of the break from allegiance to the Crown.

Only in the House of Lords today was there expression of a pro-Rhodesian view. Lord Coleraine, a Conservative, attacked Mr. Wilson's speech as "spiteful and vengeful."

'Police State' Denounced

The Prime Minister also emphasized on television what he termed "police state" aspects of the Rhodesian regime—"suppression of news, the sickeningly familiar attitudes of totalitarian rule."

Leaders of the two other parties joined in deploring the Rhodesian action. They also referred to it as the "former Government," thus accepting the official position here that Britain retains sovereignty and that Mr. Smith and his men have been legally removed.

But the Commons session was not without some political bristling. This came when some backbench Tories indicated displeasure at the Government's decision to take the issue to the United Nations.

Mr. Wilson dealt with those cries, and answering snarls from the Labor benches, with this remark: "Why? Because if we don't, somebody else will."

He made every effort to maintain nonpartisan unity, handling Conservative questions with; for him, unusual politeness. He also indicated that he had deferred action on emergency legislation until Monday so the Tories could study it.

Legislation to Be Rushed

The principal purpose of the legislation will be to authorize the British Government to suspend or amend the Rhodesian Constitution — legal steps that might be desirable if the revolt fails and a new Rhodesian political set-up has to be temporized.

The legislation will be published tomorrow, and there will be an immediate further debate in the Commons on the whole crisis. After still another debate Monday, the Government hopes to reach a vote, rushing the bill past all its parliamentary stages that night.

The economic measures announced today are not regarded as "tough." They are the minimum expected in the light of the government's many warnings about the consequences of Salisbury's declaration.

Official sources said the hope was that a change of government could be brought about in Rhodesia with a minimum of economic pain to the people.

Thus the measures include a ban on sale of British arms to Rhodesia. But no step has been taken or is immediately planned to try to cut off supplies of oil, which is essential to civilians as well as the military.

If no sign of a change of heart appears soon in Rhodesia, Britain will unquestionably impose a new and more damaging wave of economic sanctions. She will doubtless be under United Nations pressure to act harder and faster against the rebels.

The Foreign Secretary, Michael Stewart, flew to New York to present Britain's views. He will seek world support for the economic measures so far taken, but will try to restrain African-Asian demands for harsher moves now.

In the long run, one official source said, Britain is prepared to take any economic action to crush the rebellion.

An Appeal to Rhodesians

Mr. Wilson's hope of restoring "constitutional" government in the shorter run rests on two factors—the loyalties of government employes in Salisbury and the state of mind of Mr Smith.

In his Commons speech, Mr Wilson made a direct appeal to Rhodesian civil servants and even soldiers. This was explained officially as designed to let Rhodesian Government employes go on doing routine work, but to arouse their consciences against doing or aiding anything that would have been illegal last week.

For example, the Smith Government might take harsh new measures against free speech. The Wilson moral doctrine is that civil servants and policemen and judges should refuse to apply such orders.

One person who might follow that course of conscience is the Chief Justice of Rhodesia, Sir Hugh Beadle, who returned today from talks here. His past attitudes indicate that he would not hesitate to stand against the rebellious Government.

As for Mr. Smith, Mr. Wilson's theory is that he personally did not want to make the break but was forced to do so by far-right elements in his party, the Rhodesian Front—and that he might, at some point, break from them.

In the telephone conversation this morning, Mr. Wilson told the Commons, Mr. Smith was "a confused and unhappy man." Mr. Wilson added that Mr. Smith had been "under intolerable pressures from some of his colleagues and from the unreasoning extremists of the Rhodesian Front."

Though Mr. Wilson did not disclose this to the House, it is understood that on the telephone he said he did not understand why Mr. Smith let himself be pushed around by "thugs."

In his television talk, Mr. Wilson called the declaration "an avoidable, unnecessary tragedy." He said that in the telephone talk "agreement was in our grasp, but they [the Rhodesian extremist] would not have it."

A tentative agreement on a royal commission broke down when the two governments could not agree on the terms of reference.

The Prime Minister disclosed a new offer to Mr. Smith. This was that his Government would promise to "commend to Parliament" any unanimous commission report if the Rhodesian Government would promise to let the commission draft a new Constitution if it found the old one unacceptable.

Mr. Smith had no objection to this idea, Mr. Wilson told the House. Everything seemed agreed. Then Mr. Smith said their positions were "irreconcilable."

"When I heard this," Mr. Wilson said, "I told him that if anybody could now say that this position was irreconcilable and justifies illegal action, I think they wanted their heads examined or they must have a death wish.

"The differences between us," he continued, "have not been differences of legal drafting.... They have represented a deep difference of philosophy, a gulf that we now know could never be bridged because it was a gulf . . . between different worlds and different centuries."

The Other— And First— Rhodesians

By LAWRENCE FELLOWS

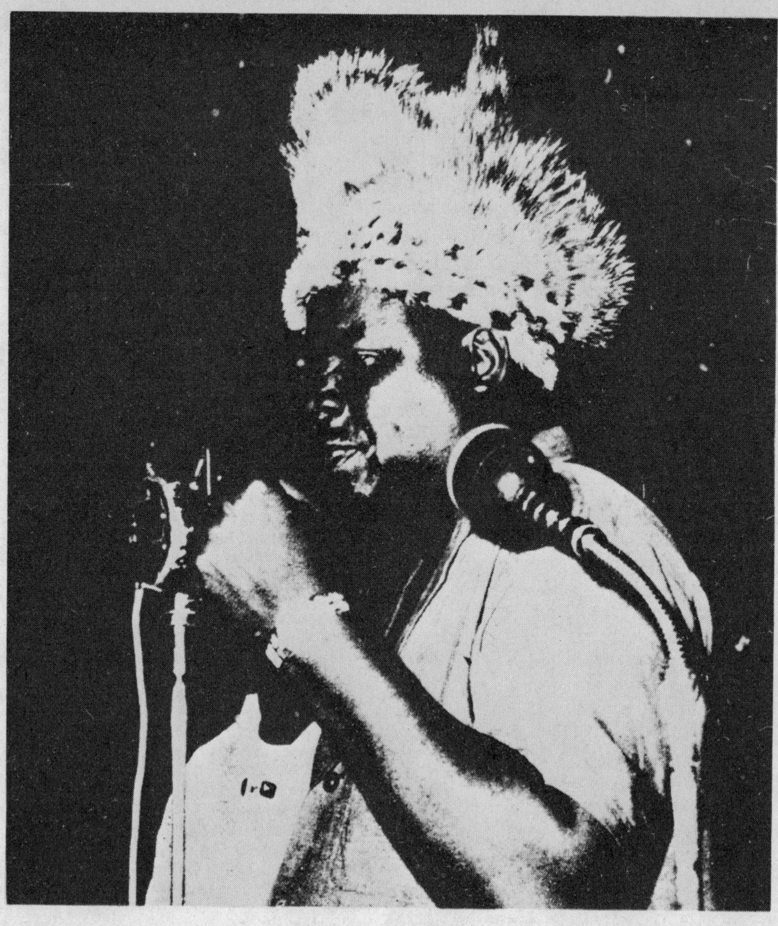

SALISBURY, Rhodesia.

WHEN Lobengula, the last of the great Matabele King, was being pursued northward by Rhodesia's white settlers in 1894 he was a dying man. His nation was being defeated; his kingdom was toppling; he was burning with fever. At the Shangani River he called his chiefs together and told them how he was to be buried: Three oxen should be killed, and his body sewn up in the hides and hidden away in a cave. His remains should not be found by the *Ama-kwa*, the kneeless ones, as the white intruders were called because of their long trousers. It was believed that if the *Ama-kwa* found the remains of Lobengula they would take possession of the spirit of the Matabele people. And the remains of Lobengula were never found.

Neither, it would appear, have the white people of Rhodesia taken possession of the spirit of the Matabele, nor of the Mashona, the Am'kalanga, the Ba'rozwi, or of any of the other tribal groups of Rhodesia. In the 75 years the white people have been here they have put an end to the murderous pattern of tribal warfare. They have checked disease, and brought at least the beginnings of education where none existed before. They have cleared the bush, built dams and irrigated fields, set up industries and made themselves prosperous. Throughout, they have used black labor and the blacks have had a small share in the prosperity. But there are abundant signs that their spirit has not been captured.

"PUZA," a black man shouted in a street in Salisbury a few days before Rhodesia seized its independence. He was arrested and sentenced to three months at hard labor.

It was a simple slogan of defiance, an anagram of the initials ZAPU, standing for the Zimbabwe African Peoples Union, one of several black nationalist parties the Government has banned for acts of intimidation and violence. First the cry of "ZAPU" was banned, then "PUZA." Then the party's leader, Joshua Mqabuko Nyongolo Nkomo, was banished—to Gonakudzingwa, a remote district in the desolate Rhodesian bush, on the border with Portuguese Mozambique.

Banished to Gonakudzingwa with him at the time independence was declared were 241 of his supporters, including most of the party's hierarchy. Another 33 nationalists were in a restriction camp at Wha Wha, 24 others were in a camp at Sikombela. Still another 30 were in preventive detention in the jail at Gwelo, and an unknown number of nationalists were serving sentences at hard labor in prisons—where it is not always easy to determine which crimes of violence are rooted in the politics of black nationalism. Since independence the figures have gone up somewhat as police rounded up a number of nationalists and their sympathizers, some for operating chains of command from the camps to the outside world, some for channeling money from friends abroad to keep the nationalist movements going.

The biggest group of penned-up nationalists still is at Gonakudzingwa. The restrictees there have complete freedom of movement within an area of some 400 square miles but the freedom does not count for much. Except for the town of Malvérnia, on the other side of the border, the area is given over pretty much to a few primitive families, and lions and elephants. The region is malarial, rainfall is low and uncertain, the roads nearly impassable and the heat overpowering. The mail train from Bulawayo runs twice a week in each direction and takes 11 hours.

"ZEEEE, *tikolai inah, tikolai inah*" is what they shout now at Gonakudzingwa, or at least that is what they were shouting before it was declared an emergency area last May, and visitors from the outside were banned. "Zeeee" is an abbreviation for ZAPU and the successor cry to PUZA. *"Tikolai inah"* means "our country," and it is used for everything from greeting strangers to the shout of understanding and approval given, passage by passage, to Nkomo's regular Saturday lectures on current affairs.

The visitors were banned because there were so many. They came in cars, on bicycles and on foot, from all parts of Rhodesia. The railway had to lay on two extra passenger cars for the visitors on Easter weekend.

Some came to see the man who was fighting not just for a measure of political responsibility for Rhodesia's four million blacks, but for immediate majority rule, on a one-man, one-vote basis. Some wanted to be in the good books of Nkomo in case he did take over in Rhodesia, for many had been told of his great magic. Nearly all the tribesmen in the area had heard how Nkomo could hold up his lion-skin hat and then take his hand away and leave the hat hanging in midair. Nearly all had heard about his secret agreement with the British Government to make him King of Rhodesia after independence.

Some were plainly afraid that their homes or kraals would be set afire if they did not visit Nkomo, or that Nkomo would refuse to bring rain to the area. Things got so bad that some tribesmen refused to dip their cattle as the white man had instructed them to do. Even the white man's famine relief supplies were refused.

Tribesmen accepted Zulu-type knobkerries from the nationalists, hardwood fighting sticks like those the Zulu warriors once used; the more primitive Rhodesians believed that Nkomo had given these knobkerries magical powers, to make them especially useful in breaking legs or smashing skulls in battle. They had been told that Nkomo was stronger than the white police, and the proof was in the fact that while the police would arrest anyone wearing a lion-skin hat in the tribal areas they would not dare touch anyone wearing one in Gonakudzingwa. The police finally caught on, and banned lion-skin hats in the restriction camp, too. Now Nkomo and his followers have taken to wearing distinctive tall straw hats which they weave themselves.

THE restricted ZAPU nationalists seem to make the best of their circumstances. There is no self-pity; they regard their lot as part of the inevitable pattern of colonial development and destruction.

Like the other detention camps, Gonakudzingwa has become an education center. Electricity comes from a generator given them by a white benefactor. They have a 16-millimeter projector, a screen, films and books, notebooks and pencils, all supplied by the United States Information Service in Salisbury before it shut down in the diplomatic exodus that began after the proclamation of independence. They conduct their own school, from the fourth grade up, with classes each weekday morning from 8 until 12, and special courses in politics and administration. When it was still allowed, lecturers came sometimes from the University College in Salisbury. Some of the restrictees are working for university degrees by correspondence; the Government pays for their courses.

Education has first priority and Nkomo, for all his back-slapping, corpulent joviality, keeps the restrictees hard at it. He knows how strong are the arguments of the white people of Rhodesia that their black compatriots are not yet advanced enough to hold the reins of power. And he gained his own education the hard way, training first as a carpenter, then driving a bakery truck in Bulawayo to earn enough to finish secondary school in Johannesburg. His education won him a job with the Rhodesian railways in Bulawayo, doing welfare work for the black employes.

He was the first black man to hold that job, and in it he learned to resent the difference between his pay and that of white men doing the same sort of work. He studied by correspondence and got a bachelor's degree in social science from the University of South Africa. A black man with a degree was rare in Rhodesia in those days. Nkomo proudly wore his cap and gown at just about every meeting he attended-- and the railway workers showed their respect by making him secretary of their union.

But Nkomo did not prove a very dynamic trade unionist; he was far too genial and even-tempered. Yet the job led to his political debut. He was known to the Rhodesian Government from having had to put forward his union's views, and the Rhodesian Government turned to him when it needed the black man's point of view represented at the talks that began in London in 1952 on the ill-fated Rhodesian Federation.

The federation, which comprised Rhodesia and the two British territories to the north which have since become independent under black governments as Zambia and Malawi, hobbled along for 10 years before it finally collapsed. Zambia and Malawi feared domination by Salisbury and won from Britain their right to secede. Without the vast copper wealth of Zambia, Rhodesia's dream of riding atop a rich, powerful federation came apart. Her hopes of working her white minority Government very gradually into partnership with the blacks to the north and in her own population vanished. Her trust in Britain to reward her with independence, as the other territories had got theirs, was lost. Nkomo's opposition to federation was not vital, but it helped to undermine the idea and contributed to the bitterness and truculence that led the white Rhodesians to seize their independence.

THAT first trip to London did not do much for the federation, but it broadened Nkomo's own outlook. He was impressed by the sight of white men digging ditches, sweeping streets, doing all sorts of menial work. It had simply not occurred to him in Rhodesia that things could be this way. He was even more impressed by the symbols of British tradition, and on his return he tried to start an organization to erect statues to the great men of the Matabele nation. He began to criticize the teaching of English history to the black children of Rhodesia as a deliberate device to rob them of their heritage and pride. On his trips abroad he took to carrying recordings of tribal music and to showing tribal dances. Even in Gonakudzingwa he makes a point of setting aside Friday nights for tribal dancing and singing.

But the rest of the week is devoted to business. When classes are out, there is bush to be cleared and thatched, mud-covered huts to be built to supplement the corrugated-iron ones which the Government furnishes and which become unbearable in the hot Rhodesian sun. There is a camp journal to be published. There is food to be scrounged to round out the portions of mealie meal, meat and vegetables the Government furnishes. It is normal fare for most Africans, but not for men like Nkomo who grew accustomed in their political careers to *tornedos chasseur* and lobster thermidor.

There are also the ZAPU "Cabinet" meetings at which affairs of state—and doubtless of sedition—are discussed. None of Nkomo's colleagues have commitments elsewhere to hamper their meetings, as was the case when they were all free. If they ever form a Government of Zimbabwe, as they plan one day to rename Rhodesia, they may look back to Gonakudzingwa as the place where they had the time and opportunity to learn how to put a government together.

NKOMO's lieutenants, from all reports, continue to hammer at him to be tougher. But easy-going Joshua, with his plodding ways and his dislike of trouble, is their leader, whether they like it or not. He is only 48 now, but eight years ago, when the young militants of the African National Congress needed a national figure, there was no one else available. With his good command of English and his easy understanding of the ways of the white man's thought, he had to be the choice.

He has been almost deposed a few times — when he failed to boycott the first elections in federation days, and again when he was slow to renounce his participation in the conference that had led to Rhodesia's 1961 Constitution. Its two sets of educational, income and property qualifications, dividing the electorate into so-called A and B rolls, in effect give 15 of the 65 seats in Parliament to black voters and keep the rest firmly in the hands of Rhodesia's 220,000 whites.

In 1959, when the African National Congress, the leading black nationalist movement, was banned in Rhodesia, Nkomo was out of the country. With most Congress officers put into restriction, he was the only one who was in a position to reorganize the nationalist movement into the Democratic party. The party has since gone through a succession of bannings and changes of names. Even ZAPU when it was banned was renamed the People's Caretaker

Council. That was banned, too, in August of last year, but the name ZAPU seems to have stuck.

THE biggest organizational wrench that Nkomo's party has suffered came in August, 1963, when the Rev. Ndabaningi Sithole, fed up with Nkomo's reluctance to condone violent action, led a group of intellectuals away from ZAPU and formed ZANU, the Zimbabwe African National Union. The break was followed swiftly by new waves of terror as the two organizations fought to destroy each other. Homes and kraals were burned, livestock was poisoned, crops were burned, gasoline bombs were tossed through open windows. Hand grenades made in the Soviet Union were picked up here and there by the police.

As each organization sought to impress its superior strength on the black population, boycotts were started against dairies, bakeries, bus companies and stores that were owned by people who supported the wrong party — or neither. A most effective school boycott was effected last year by forms of intimidation that were sometimes subtle, sometimes not. In the beginning, families were told that their children's legs might shrivel, or that their children might never grow fat, if they went to school. In the end, it was enough for a voice to be heard crying out from behind a tree or a building in the darkness: "No school tomorrow."

The 45-year-old Rev. Mr. Sithole served 11 months in prison for handing around a pamphlet instructing black men to have their axes and bows and arrows ready for the day Rhodesia's white Government declared itself independent. Now he is languishing in the sandy woodland at Sikombela. His followers in restriction, for their own safety, have been moved out of other camps and put into Sikombela with him. Life there is rather like life in Gonakudzingwa—on a smaller scale.

Now Sikombela is also closed to outsiders, but a few days before independence, Sithole was living in a rather pleasant thatched, mud-plastered hut which he calls "Confrontation House," furnished with two comfortable beds, crude wooden benches, curtains on the open widows, a record player and a bookshelf sagging with a set of the Encyclopaedia Britannica, Toynbee's "Study of History," a couple of Agatha Christie paperbacks and books on sociology. The plump, scowling divine has a degree from Newton Theological School at Andover, Mass., near Boston. Now he is taking a course in sociology, by correspondence, from the University of South Africa.

His followers have meetings of their "Central Committee" and, because of the inevitable brawling that goes on in a restriction camp, of their "Disciplinary Committee" (the sentences handed out usually keep people at such undesirable tasks as cleaning the crude toilets). They have no electricity, and therefore no movies, for none of their friends seem to be able to afford a generator. But the United States Information Service did send them literature about America, which they were not particularly anxious to get, and notebooks and pencils for which they were grateful. On Sundays, Sithole conducts services in one of the bigger thatched huts. The corrugated-iron ones supplied by the Government are hot and empty.

THE claims of strength all these nationalists put forward are difficult to assess for they have chosen to boycott elections and to ignore the parliamentary system of which they so strongly disapprove. They regard it as futile to struggle constitutionally under Rhodesia's split franchise. On the B roll of voters, the one with the easier qualifications and the only one within reach of Rhodesia's black population, only 1,443 cast ballots in the last election. The leader of the black Opposition in Parliament, Joshua Gondo, won his seat with a total of 124 votes. Yet these black men in Parliament claim to be as fervently nationalistic as any black men in the country.

In the first few days after independence these black parliamentarians were undecided as to what they should do. They were never satisfied to have easy access to only 15 seats in Parliament, but they were willing to make at least some use of them, and to work by constitutional means to improve their lot. Their parliamentary immunity gave them a safe platform from which to attack the Government, and they attacked it vigorously.

There is no reason to think that Prime Minister Ian Smith did not want it that way, for in the general election last May his party, the Rhodesian Front, contested only those members of the opposition Rhodesia party who were white and on the A roll. By this act he demolished the Rhodesia party as a refuge for white moderates and turned it into a black man's party. Five of the 15 men elected on the B roll are independents, the 10 others, black members of the Rhodesia party, have reorganized themselves into the United People's party. Soon, according to the Prime Minister's announced plans, they will be joined in Parliament by representatives of the tribal chiefs. Doubtless, Smith hopes that he can build up the chiefs, by increasing their powers in their own tribal reserves, into a force to shatter the claims of Nkomo and Sithole that they could represent the mass of the black people of Rhodesia.

Sithole, especially in trying to build up his following among the primitive tribes in the bush, has to struggle against everyone's knowledge that he comes from the Shangon, a tribe with a reputation for being small and ineffective, the most easily terrorized and overpowered in the old days by the fearsome Matabele, the first to take up the dirty menial work of the white settlers. And, while he may have the more intelligent of the nationalists around him, he is a poor public speaker, without any of the gift of spellbinding oratory that wins Nkomo bigger crowds.

The ZANU camp pretends not to be worried by such things. They have the tougher approach. They do not encourage their followers who drift out to Zambia, Tanzania or Ghana to take up the offers of guerrilla training given them by the Russians or Chinese, but they take them up anyway. Many of them are caught by the Rhodesian police the moment they step back across the border, for the police here are alert to the danger, and the ranks of the nationalists of both camps are riddled with informers. But some get through and the ZANU leaders do not worry yet about the ideological complications. The important thing to Sithole's lieutenants now is only that the guerrilla training will come in handy when the inevitable test of strength between blacks and whites does come. Besides, they say, Nkomo is not the pure Matabele he claims to be; his father was a Kalango, a member of one of the tribes that was captured and absorbed by the great Matabeles.

IN the simplest possible terms, the question in Rhodesia remains one of brute power. There are 17 blacks for each white in Rhodesia, and they waste no loyalty on their white masters. At one end of the range of feeling there is a kind of day-to-day devotion, an allegiance based on an old acceptance of white paternalism, of holding a job, of fearing the police, of old habits of "borrowing" a bit of money from the boss when you need it and knowing that no one expects it ever to be paid back. At the other end of the range is a deep, abiding, seething hatred. But the whites command an efficient army and air force, a police force that can turn out 30,000 white reservists, and a continuous training program that has turned every young white Rhodesian into a potential soldier.

Such a force could stamp out the initial stages of any black rebellion. It could deal with almost anything the rest of black Africa might reasonably be expected to send against it in the next few years. With South Africa at its back, it would be formidable indeed.

For a long time the black nationalists of Rhodesia courted Britain's power, but when Prime Minister Harold Wilson was in Salisbury during his unsuccessful effort to head off Rhodesia's proclamation of independence he said very plainly that British military intervention in Rhodesia was out of the question. "This is not the right answer," he said, "and I beg those who, because they think in these terms, have closed their minds to cooperative attempts to settle these matters by discussion here and now—I beg them to come to terms with this reality."

For the nationalists there would seem to be nothing to do but wait—and perhaps hope that the confrontation will be hurried along by events. But time, according to a nationalist seeing a visitor out of his restriction camp just before it was closed to outsiders, is a relatively inexpensive commodity in Africa. He recalled an old proverb of the Matabele people: *"Ukozi olu bambayo ngoluzulayo"* — "The eagle which hovers is the one which seizes."

BRITAIN IMPOSES EMBARGO ON OIL FOR RHODESIANS

Order Issued After Wilson's Talks With Johnson—U.S. Backs Airlift to Zambia

By DANA ADAMS SCHMIDT
Special to The New York Times

LONDON, Dec. 17—Britain tonight imposed an oil embargo on Rhodesia.

The order, effective immediately, was issued following Prime Minister Wilson's consultations with President Johnson in Washington and in the expectation that the United States and numerous other countries would follow suit.

British nationals are prohibited from shipping oil to Rhodesia or carrying oil for Rhodesian use by an Order in Council signed by Queen Elizabeth II tonight. It must be approved by Parliament within 28 days.

Orders went out from London to divert a Norwegian oil tanker, the 20,000-ton Staberg on charter to the Shell Oil Company. The vessel is now approaching the Mozambique port of Beira with oil for Rhodesia.

R.A.F. Airlift Ordered

The British Government also ordered the Royal Air Force to begin an oil airlift to neighboring Zambia, which normally receives her oil through Rhodesia. The same planes may also carry copper ore from Zambia.

[In Washington, the United States threw its official support behind the embargo and asked American companies to observe the boycott. The United States also offered to back an airlift to Zambia for oil and other supplies. In Berne, the Swiss Cabinet ordered the freezing of Rhodesia's reserves in Swiss banks.]

Diplomats said these measures had been taken jointly by the British and United States Governments to head off pressure in the United Nations for invoking Chapter VII of the Charter, which deals with United Nations procedures for military and non-military action in cases of threats to peace.

Determination Cited

Under the terms of Chapter VII, much that Britain and other countries are already doing to bring down the white Government of Rhodesia would have to be done by international authority.

Both Britain and the United States feel that the concession of national sovereignty implied in Chapter VII would be a dangerous precedent.

The announcement from 10 Downing Street said:

"Her Majesty's Government are determined to bring to an end the illegal regime in Rhodesia and have already taken a series of economic and financial measures to this end.

"After careful examination they have now decided to take two further measures which relate to petroleum products.

"First, Her Majesty's Government, exercising the power conferred upon it by Parliament which is the sovereign legislation for Rhodesia, are prohibiting the import of oil and oil products into that territory.

"Secondly, British nationals are being prohibited from supplying or carrying oil and oil products for Rhodesian use."

Under British law, anyone who now helps supply oil to Rhodesia could be imprisoned for six months or fined not more than £500 ($1,400) or both.

Rhodesia consumes about 280,000 tons of oil a year supplied mainly from Iran and from the Persian Gulf sheikdom of Abu Dhabi. Although it was believed to have only about six weeks' reserves on hand when the debate on its demand for independence reached a critical point in October, oil company officials now believe it has accumulated six months' supply.

Oil for Rhodesia flows 180 miles by pipeline from Beira to a new refinery at Umtali near the Rhodesian border with Portuguese Mozambique. The refinery is owned mainly by Shell and British Petroleum. Other shareholders are the United States companies, Mobil, Caltex and Aminoil, the French Total, and the Kuwait National Petroleum Company.

Whether this measure, coming on top of other economic sanctions, could bring down the regime of Prime Minister Ian D. Smith is now the big question. Highly placed authorities in London are by no means certain. Some believe that Rhodesian white nationalist fervor will cool when economic pressures are felt seriously early next year. Then, British authorities say, the large proportion of former South Africans in Rhodesia might think about going home. Others predict Rhodesia will "bring the house down" rather than yield to British pressure. Such an effort could include the cutting off of Zambia's power from the Kariba Dam and destruction of the dam if Britain attempts to seize it.

Neighbors Could Help

Theoretically, Portuguese Mozambique and South Africa could keep Rhodesia afloat economically with loans and emergency oil shipments. But British and American diplomats believe neither Portugal nor South Africa wants to pay the price of economic conflict. In any case, Mozambique has a small oil reserve and the possibility of shipping overland from South Africa on the line to Beitbridge in Rhodesia is slight.

The Royal Air Force command in Aden is organizing an airlift of oil to Zambia, possibly flying Britannia transports from Dar Es Salaam and then returning with copper. Help from the United States Air Force is expected.

The principal motivation behind this expensive operation is the importance of Zambian copper to the economies of the West.

The Labor Government's new measure will further strain bipartisan support in Britain for the regime's Rhodesian policy. More than 100 Conservative Members of Parliament introduced a motion in the House of Commons this week deploring the statement by Prime Minister Wilson last week in which he in effect demanded "unconditional surrender" by Prime Minister Smith before negotiations could be reopened.

Edward Heath, leader of the Conservative opposition, refrained tonight from any endorsement of the oil embargo. In a statement, he called it a "grave development" about which he had asked the Prime Minister to provide detailed information at the "earliest opportunity."

December 18, 1965

BLASTS IN ZAMBIA AROUSE RHODESIA

Saboteurs Cut a Power Line to Copper Region—Smith Sees a Red Plot

By LAWRENCE FELLOWS
Special to The New York Times

SALISBURY, Rhodesia, Nov. 26—Rhodesia's relations with Zambia took a sharp turn for the worse today as railway cars piled up on both sides of the border and explosions in the early morning cut power supplies to Zambia's rich copper belt.

The Zambian President, Kenneth Kaunda, continued to press the British to send troops to protect vital installations in his country in the event the dispute with the white-governed state to the south gets out of control.

Prime Minister Ian D. Smith reiterated that Rhodesia had no fight to pick with Zambia and suggested that President Kaunda had fallen victim to the Chinese Communists and other anti-Rhodesian elements he had allowed into his country.

Zambia Victimized, He Says

Mr. Smith recalled that Desmond Lardner-Burke, Rhodesian Minister of Law and Order, said in Parliament yesterday that President Kaunda, by harboring saboteurs in his country, was running an incalculable risk.

"My first reaction is that is precisely what has happened," Mr. Smith said. "People are attempting to step up trouble and to dislocate the economy of Zambia, hoping that they can pin the blame on Rhodesia."

Attempts were made to blow down two power lines. A charge placed against a tower at Luanshiya failed to bring it down. Another, south of Kitwe, cut a 330-kilovolt transmission line from the Kariba power station to the copper belt.

Local Generators Used

While engineers worked to repair the damage, about three-quarters of the power for Zambia's vital copper mines was being supplied by local generators and through lines from the Congo. Still, copper production was affected.

The rail tie-up also worsened as about 400 white railwaymen went into the second day of their strike in the Zambia border town of Livingstone.

The New York Times Nov. 27, 1965

Rail traffic piled up at the Rhodesia-Zambia border (1). An explosion cut electricity from Kariba (2).

They were protesting against the roughing up of white women and children by a gang of Zambian Youth Service members on Tuesday.

Some mail trains were running across the border, but nothing else. Coal from Wankie in the south and copper from the north were piling up by the trainload at Thomson Junction and Livingstone.

Since Rhodesia seized her independence from Britain Nov. 11, it has been feared by Rhodesians and Zambians alike that the services they share—railways, power from the Kariba Dam, and Central African Airways—would be broken over the hardening ridge between white-governed southern Africa and black-governed countries to the north.

At least one C.A.A. plane was turned back from Dar es Salaam because the authorities there would not guarantee safe conduct for the Rhodesians aboard.

The trouble on the railway is rooted in the objections of the white railwaymen, most of them Rhodesians, to being transferred to jobs in the north.

Now the cost of inducement pay is approaching $1.5 million a year. In a year the cost is expected to go up to more than $2.5 million.

In her effort to get around the economic sanctions that Britain applied in the hope of bringing down Mr. Smith's Government, Rhodesia made a gain with a $1.4 million Portuguese order from the Rhodesian Iron and Steel Corporation.

The dispute with Britain is over the speed with which political control should pass into the hands of Rhodesia's black majority.

On another front, in the slow war of attrition against Sir Humphrey Gibbs, the British Governor, who refuses to step down, the typewriters were carried out of his official mansion in Salisbury by a group of white-coated workers. The phone service has long been cut, cars driven away and servants and sentries withdrawn.

Rhodesia—Land Against a Continent

By LAWRENCE FELLOWS
Special to The New York Times

NAIROBI, Dec. 18—Among the Bantu in East Africa there is a saying which holds that the fluttering bird wastes its feathers. The saying was a popular one in the beer halls around here this week, as one African state after another found a way round their resolution that all should break off diplomatic relations with Britain this past Wednesday if she had not by then crushed the rebellious white minority Government of Rhodesia.

The fact that so many of the African leaders seemed to fall all over themselves this week trying to get down off that political limb was probably no more important in a real sense than the fact that they had put themselves out there in the first place, fluttering wildly, their feathers of anger and frustration filling the troubled African air.

There is hardly a politician north of the Zambesi who does not roil at the mention of Rhodesia, for it wounds his pride deeply to think of that small band of whites, outnumbered by the blacks in their own country by more than 17 to 1, turning back by their own efforts the wind of change that swept dark-skinned men into power over most of the rest of the continent.

War Declared

Some African leaders—President Nasser of the United Arab Republic, President Nkrumah of Ghana, President Sekou Touré of Guinea—have declared themselves at war with Rhodesia. But for now, being at war with Rhodesia cannot be much more than a state of mind.

The prospect of any of their neighbors to the north launching a military operation against them does not keep the Rhodesians awake at night. Their own army could probably cope with any African invasion not heavily supported by some major outside power.

Because the African states are aware of this, too, they have been inclined—although with less and less patience—to leave it to the British to find a way to unseat Rhodesia's Government, reassert British authority and hurry the country's four million blacks toward political responsibility.

Until now the British have kept their warfare against Rhodesia on an economic plane, gradually tightening sanctions, hoping to create enough hardship and dissaffection to undermine the Government of Prime Minister Ian Smith.

Britain still has wide support for her efforts against Rhodesia, but even relatively moderate men in Africa, including the Nigerian Prime Minister, Sir Abubakar Tafawa Balewa, President Kenneth Kauanda of Zambia and President Jomo Kenyatta of Kenya, have been insisting that eventually force would have to be used. And eventually this belligerent mood in Africa is bound to limit the room the British have left themselves for political maneuver.

Of the seven African states that did break off relations with Britain this week, Guinea is in the forefront of the radical group of African states, with little to fear for Rhodesia and little to lose in a rupture with Britain.

Tanzania risked a cutback in the development aid she gets from Britain, and might have eroded the confidence of the Britons giving expert advice in that country. But President Nyerere is strongly committed to deposing the remaining white governments in Africa by any means, however drastic.

The other five that broke off relations were Ghana, Mali, Congo Republic (Brazzaville), Mauritania, and the United Arab Republic. That left 29 African states holding back. One of them, Nigeria, began organizing support for a Commonwealth Prime Ministers' conference in Lagos, Jan. 10, to set a new course against Rhodesia.

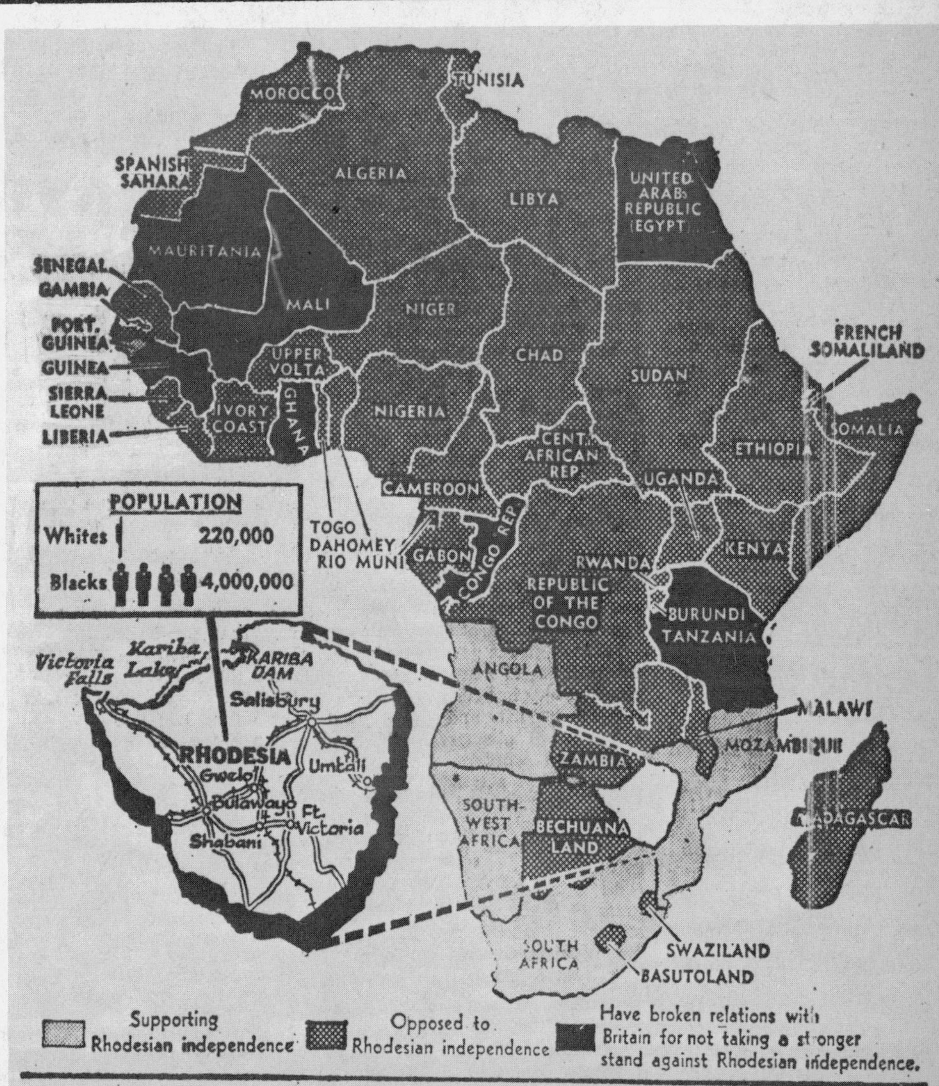

THE ECONOMIC SQUEEZE

More than half of Rhodesia's exports, chart below, go to Britain and the Commonwealth nations. Britain has already taken steps to curtail trade and the Commonwealth nations are likely to follow, putting strong economic pressure on Rhodesia. Last week an oil embargo was announced by Britain and the U.S. agreed to help.

Steps in Rhodesian Crisis

Following are the key events in the crisis over Rhodesia's unilateral decision to declare itself independent:

Nov. 11, 1965—Prime Minister Ian D. Smith declares independence for Rhodesia after 42 years as a British territory.
Dec. 4—Organization of African Unity asks members to break diplomatic relations with Britain unless Smith regime is unseated.
Feb. 3, 1966—Salisbury Parliament approves independence constitution.
April 9—United Nations Security Council authorizes Britain to use force to prevent oil supplies from reaching Rhodesia.
May 9—First exploratory talks on negotiated settlement held in London by British and Rhodesian representatives.
June 2—Talks resumed in Salisbury. Zambia stops importing from Rhodesia.
July—Salisbury's university closed after detention of students and lecturers.
Aug. 28—Terrorist attacks begin in Salisbury.
Sept. 15—Commonwealth Prime Ministers Conference in London gives Britain final chance to settle issue.
Oct. 13—Britain's final proposals are sent to Prime Minister Smith.
Nov. 10—United Nations General Assembly asks Britain to end rebellion by any means.
Nov. 20—South Africa warns of effect of mandatory sanctions on British-South African trade.
Nov. 24—Top Commonwealth officials rush to Salisbury for "last talks."
Dec. 2-4—Prime Ministers Wilson and Smith hold two-day conference on British cruiser off Gibraltar leading to "working document" to which both sides must say yes or no. Britain promptly says yes.
Dec. 5—Rhodesia says no. Britain asks United Nations Security Council to meet on controversy.

December 6, 1966

U.N. COUNCIL VOTES MANDATORY CURBS ON RHODESIA, 11-0

Compulsory Sanctions Are the First by Organization —Oil Embargo Included

Africans Voice Bitterness on Failure to Condemn South Africans and Portuguese

By DREW MIDDLETON
Special to The New York Times

UNITED NATIONS, N.Y., Dec. 16—The Security Council imposed mandatory economic sanctions tonight for the first time.

By a vote of 11 to 0, with 4 abstentions, the Council approved a resolution, basically British but including eight African amendments, banning the purchase of 12 key Rhodesian exports and the supply of oil and oil products to Rhodesia by United Nations members.

The council's action was the second by an international body. The first was the League of Nations' imposition of mandatory sanctions against Italy after she had invaded Ethiopia.

Sanctions were imposed on Nov. 18, 1935, and ended on July 15, 1936, when it had become clear that some members of the League were not observing them and that they had had little effect on the advance of the Italian armies.

Majority Rule an Issue

Britain asked the Council to impose selective economic sanctions after the collapse of negotiations with Rhodesia's white rebel regime, which declared independence in November, 1965. Rhodesia has four million blacks and 250,000 whites. Britain insists that eventual majority rule must be assured.

The resolution voted today lacks the teeth that the African bloc tried to insert. A draft amendment asking Britain to prevent by all means, including force, the transport of oil to Rhodesia was narrowly defeated. So was an amendment deploring the assistance given Rhodesia's rebel regime by South Africa and Portugal.

Led by Chief S. O. Adebo of Nigeria, the African members of the Security Council immediately registered their bitter disappointment over the outcome of the voting, which was preceded by a debate that opened Dec. 8.

Chief Adebo expressed the Africans' strong suspicion that the rejection of another African amendment, demanding the withdrawal of all British offers to the rebels, indicated Britain's desire to reopen negotiations with Prime Minister Ian D. Smith's government in Salisbury.

The absence of a provision to prevent oil and other supplies from reaching Rhodesia through South Africa and Portuguese Mozambique was bitterly attacked by the Africans. Chief Adebo emphasized that this omission robbed the council's resolution of much of its possible effectiveness.

If the resolution does not prove effective in breaking the economic power of the Smith regime, independent Africa will raise the issue anew in the council, the chief promised.

Critical of British

Nor were the Africans much mollified by an amendment presented by Britain earlier today to its original draft resolution. This was a paragraph calling for a ban on the supply of aircraft and motor vehicles and equipment and materials for their manufacture, assembly and maintenance.

Lord Caradon, Britain's representative, tried to convince the Council that this measure would hurt the transportation system of Rhodesia, whose stocks "will shortly run out" and would end any possibility of replenishment from outside sources. But as one African pointed out, British cars and trucks are still being assembled in neighboring South Africa.

The Africans also had attempted to include in the resolution a provision barring the purchase of Rhodesian coal and "all manufactured goods." This amendment, too, was narrowly defeated after Lord Caradon had predicted serious economic damage to neighboring Zambia if it were passed.

The Briton's observations provoked Apollo K. Kironde of Uganda to deplore Lord Caradon's "insufferable priggishness" in attempting to speak for Zambia as though the country were still under British tutelage. Simon M. Kapwepwe, Zambia's Foreign Minister, Mr. Kironde said, has specifically approved the measure.

Lord Caradon did not mention the point in his statement, but Rhodesian smelting coal provides the fuel for the Zambian copper industry, which is controlled largely by United States and British companies.

The Soviet Union voted for the African amendments and supported their viewpoint in the debate. The Soviet delegate, Nikolai T. Fedorenko, lost no time in capitalizing on his country's position as independent Africa's champion.

Britain's rejection of the amendments, he said, had "unmasked" the British as guilty of "the tragedy of the people of Zimbabwe." This is the Africans' name for Rhodesia.

The British, he charged after the voting, want to protect the racist regime in Salisbury.

The Soviet Union abstained in the final vote, along with Mali, Bulgaria and France, Mr. Fedorenko explained, because the completed resolution did not include the five key African amendments.

The fifth of these deplored Britain's refusal to use force against Rhodesia. The four others sought to prevent oil from reaching Rhodesia, to condemn South Africa and Portugal, the withdrawal of British offers to the rebels and an embargo on purchases of coal and all manufactured goods.

The key provisions of the amended resolution, the British contend, will affect Rhodesia's earnings abroad and consequently its balance of payments.

Bans Military Gear

They ask for United Nations members to prevent the purchase of asbestos, iron ore, tobacco, copper, meat and meat products and hides, skins and leather.

To this was added the first amendment on oil offered by the Africans. This called upon all members to prevent "participation in their territories or territories under their administration or in land or air transport facilities or by their nationals or vessels of their registration in the supply of oil or oil products" to Rhodesia.

The approved resolution also calls for a ban on the sale of military equipment of all types to Rhodesia.

The United States Administration, it was learned, will "fully and faithfully" carry out all the sanctions imposed including that dealing with oil. The sanctions, in the American view, are fully justified under the charter and may help convince the Salisbury regime that it has no future.

December 17, 1966

LIFE IN RHODESIA IS LITTLE CHANGED

U.N. Curbs Have Brought Few Signs of Discomfort

By LAWRENCE FELLOWS
Special to The New York Times

SALISBURY, Rhodesia — Thirty-one months after the Rhodesians proclaimed their independence from Britain, the politicians here and in London still talk longingly, sometimes despairingly, about settling their differences, but both sides appear to be losing their ability to influence events.

Britain, which began by insisting that it was her responsibility alone to deal with the rebellion, and that the duty of the rest of the world was to support her, has had to spread the responsibility.

Mandatory sanctions were imposed against Rhodesia by the United Nations Security Council. When the last, sweeping resolution went through the Council on May 29, Britain was left with the "primary responsibility" for getting Rhodesia's whole population, not just the white men in power, to the point of self-determination and independence.

Africans Object

But when Yakov A. Malik, the Soviet delegate, tried to amend the resolution by proposing that Britain compensate Zambia for the losses she had incurred because of her landlocked position behind Rhodesia, it was the Africans in the United Nations, and not Britain, who talked him out of it.

Britain has forsworn the use of force in settling her argument with Rhodesia. But force is being used. Black Rhodesians are being trained as guerrillas in Algeria, North Korea, the Soviet Union, China and Cuba. They get further tactical instruction in camps in Tanzania. In Zambia they are drawn up into fighting units at camps in the outskirts of Lusaka.

Last August a group of Rhodesian and South African guerrillas crossed the Zambezi, and tested the thin lines of Rhodesian troops sorely. Finally, South Africa sent aircraft and ground forces to the battle scene.

The South Africans have helped stave off another large incursion since then, and they are still there, patrolling a stretch of the border from Victoria Falls to the western end of Lake Kariba.

Britain has formally demanded that the South Africans leave, but the troops are still there, and their presence is the frankest admission yet of South Africa's commitment to Rhodesia.

Purpose Is Defeated

There are no illusions in the minds of the Rhodesians in political office about their independent power: If they come to terms with Britain it will have to be on terms South Africa can accept.

Rhodesia has weathered the sanctions well. She has certainly defeated the purpose of them, which was to discourage the white people from supporting Prime Minister Ian D. Smith, and to bring about the quick collapse of his regime.

Exports dropped last year, but imports were cut back. New industries have sprung up by the hundreds. The tobacco farmers, hardest hit by the loss of their easy market in Britain, have had to diversify. The small manufacturers have had to concentrate on what they could produce for the local market.

Rhodesia has had to become more and more self-sufficient. New copper and nickel mines have been opened. Manufacturing and construction have boomed. Agricultural production has risen steadily.

The sourest note is employment, which has receded for the Africans employed on the tobacco farms.

Little Sign of Discomfort

Yet there is little sign today that any substantial part of Mr. Smith's support has fallen away. Salisbury is as quiet, dull and normal-looking as it ever was before independence.

The streets are still choked with automobile traffic. The shops are still full, but the selection leaves something to be desired. All the men's shirts seem to be Rhodesian-made, and there seem to be no more than three or four patterns. But there are none of the discomforts of the sort that would make Rhodesians rue the day they voted for Mr. Smith.

Censorship has been lifted, so a little criticism of the regime has crept into the newspapers' letters to the editor. But most of the critics want to break really clear of Britain; they do not want to capitulate.

The politicians seem to feel little need to reassure the people. The biggest topics of conversation are the frost that has damaged the hibiscus and the tomatoes, and the visit to Salisbury of Gladys Morgan, a Welsh comedienne.

"We don't know what the world is grizzling about," Mr. Smith said when he saw her off the other day. "You can see more happy black faces here than anywhere else in Africa."

That the Rhodesian whites are outnumbered by nearly nineteen to one—4,330,000 to 232,000 — does not seem to worry them.

June 30, 1968

CURB ON RHODESIA IS HURTING OTHERS

By RICHARD J. H. JOHNSTON
Special to The New York Times

UNITED NATIONS, N. Y. Sept. 5—The imposition of economic sanctions against Rhodesia, decreed by the Security Council last May, is working severe hardships on at least three black-ruled African states, according to reports forwarded to the Council by Secretary General Thant.

Botswana, Malawi and the Congo have told Mr. Thant that their economies and possibly their political structures faced increasing dangers as a result of the restrictions placed against Rhodesia, a former British colony that unilaterally declared its independence in November, 1965.

The white minority regime of Rhodesia, under Prime Minister Ian D. Smith, has been repeatedly condemned by the United Nations for its refusal to prepare for eventual black African rule.

While the three black African nations—Botswana, Malawi and the former Belgian Congo —were in full support of the action, they said the sanctions were severely damaging their economies or were threatening to do so.

Consequences 'Disastrous'

"The economic consequences to Botswana of the total applications of the sanctions would be immediate and disastrous," the Botswana report said.

It declared that rail operations, the cattle industry and other operations in Botswana, if cut off from Rhodesia, would come to a halt and Botswana's economic life would "virtually come to a standstill."

The Congo's report, similarly, though less urgently asked the Council to take into account the hardships sanctions were imposing on that country while the United Nations was "trying to find appropriate means of putting a quick end to the Rhodesian rebellion."

The report of Malawi noted that 20 per cent of Malawi's imports came from Rhodesia and that the time lag in search of new supply routes would be damaging to her.

"While Malawi continues to accept sanctions as a preferable alternative to the use of force in solving the Rhodesian dispute, the country cannot be expected to participate in such sanctions to an extent where its own economy will be destroyed," it said.

September 6, 1968

Rhodesia Seeks White Immigrants

SALISBURY, Rhodesia, Dec. 7 (AP)—Large advertisements in Rhodesia announce: "Know anyone living outside Rhodesia? Encourage them to settle here and win one of these great prizes!"

The first prize is a six-day family visit to a lakeside resort ,a game park and the Victoria Falls. All are within Rhodesia, so no foreign currency will be needed. The second prize is a refrigerator, and the third is a radio-phonograph.

The advertisement states the reason for the immigration drive:

"Rhodesia urgently needs skilled immigrants to stimulate the economy and employment and to bring capital and know-how into the country."

It is widely accepted that if the whites are to continue to rule Rhodesia they must build up their numbers dramatically. Rhodesia declared her independence from Britain in 1965 in a dispute over political equality for black Africans.

African Rate Higher

The last official estimate, in June 1968, showed 237,000 whites and 4,410,000 black Africans. The Africans are increasing at a greater rate. Ten years ago there were 3,190,000 and 203,000 whites.

Britain is the main target of the immigration drive. Rhodesia faces severe competition. South Africa, Australia and New Zealand also are seeking English-speaking immigrants and are offering them a perhaps more trouble-free future.

Nevertheless, immigration is increasing. In 1964, when the breakup of the Federation of Rhodesia and Nyasaland caused an exodus of disillusioned whites there was a net loss of 6400. In 1965, as confidence returned, there was a net gain of 4,463, among them many of those who fled the previous year.

Doubts over the declaration of independence in late 1965 led to decline of 983 in 1966. A net gain of 4,142 was reported in 1967, and this trend was continued in 1968 with a net gain of 5,304 in the first eight months.

All these figures refer to whites. Entry into Rhodesia by black Africans from other countries is difficult.

Pieter van der Byl, the Minister of Information, Immigration and Tourism, has announced a new assisted passage plan for families of immigrants already in Rhodesia. Another inducement to immigrants is income-tax concessions.

With a large unskilled African labor force readily available, Rhodesia places emphasis on skilled immigrants. The newspaper advertisement lists 36 professions and trades, from doctors and engineers to welders and bricklayers "which need filling fast."

The last line of the advertisement says: "Help the immigration drive—your future depends on it."

December 15, 1968

SMITH VICTORIOUS IN RHODESIA VOTE

Wins Approval for Republic and Revising Constitution

By LAWRENCE FELLOWS
Special to The New York Times

SALISBURY, Rhodesia, June 20 — Prime Minister Ian D. Smith has won a solid mandate from Rhodesia's tiny white-dominated electorate to give Rhodesia a new Constitution that would clearly separate black voters from white in the country.

With official returns in from 40 constituencies of 65 in the country, it was clear that the voters favored in a referendum a constitution that would institute an apartheid-like way of life by a margin of 3 to 1.

"I would like to say this is a very happy occasion," Mr. Smith said at his party headquarters just after midnight. "It looks as though we have at least 72 per cent in favor of the constitution—that is wonderful."

Voters appear to have approved by an even wider margin a proposal to proclaim Rhodesia a republic and to cut the formal ties with the British monarch that have remained since the Government unilaterally proclaimed its independence from Britain on Nov. 11, 1965.

The two rolls of voters that exist in Rhodesia now have educational, income and property requirements. The requirements of one are higher than the other and it is a predominantly white roll. The other roll is predominantly black.

Few Blacks Can Vote

Taking both existing rolls together, there were 81,583 white people eligible to vote in this referendum, and 6,634 blacks. There are 228,000 whites in the country and 4,818,000 blacks.

The way is now clear for the Rhodesian Government to introduce its proposed constitution when Parliament reconvenes next Wednesday. However, Parliament will have to deal with the budget and other pressing business before debate on the constitution can begin. Elections are due before next May, and it could be a year before the new constitution goes into effect.

Under the proposed new Constitution, there will still be two voters rolls—one for black people and the other for all the rest.

The blacks can hope, under the new constitutional proposals, eventually to elect 50 members to a House of Assembly, as will the others elect 50 members. But the blacks will start by electing only 16 members. The number will rise as does the share of income tax paid by the blacks. For the last three years the blacks have paid about one-half of 1 per cent, and there is little hope that they will soon be paying more.

But in Highfield, the sprawling African township on the edge of Salisbury, there were some faint signs that the normally apathetic black people were stirred at least to vote, knowing that it signified nothing more than a low-key protest.

Posters Are Torn Down

Government officials had worried earlier in the day that the campaigning in the Highfield would lead to trouble, and ripped down some of the political posters that had been pasted up.

Later, however, when all seemed quiet, the officials relented. The posters went up outside the voting booths, and some partisan blacks started out for the center of Salisbury with the posters pinned to their backs.

These men represented too few voters to have had a chance of hurting Mr. Smith in this referendum.

Of far more possible consequence to the Prime Minister was the opposition to the constitution raised by the people on the far right of his own Rhodesian Front, and even further to the right, a new party called the Conservative Association.

They attacked the constitutional proposals on the grounds that they did not go far enough. The Conservative Association and the Candor League, a band of ultraconservatives, warned that the "liberals" and the blacks might eventually have the strength to form a coalition, and take over the House of Assembly and the Government.

June 21, 1969

WHITE RHODESIA OFFICIALLY TAKES REPUBLIC STATUS

The Proclamation Severing Last Ties With Britain Dissolves Parliament

By Reuters.

SALISBURY, Rhodesia, Monday, March 2—Rhodesia's white minority Government formally severed its last tie with the British Crown last midnight, dissolving Parliament and declaring a racially segregated republic.

The proclamation was signed in Government House yesterday by Clifford W. Dupont, the officer administering the Government. Mr. Dupont, a former London lawyer, became interim President at midnight and is expected to become the first President.

The proclamation of the republic comes 80 years after this southern African country was first tied to Britain by royal charter and 47 years after Rhodesia became a colony.

Smith to See Press

White Rhodesians, most of whom long have accepted the country as a republic in effect, are taking the final break without fanfare. No organized celebrations were prepared and radio and television stations did not extend programing until midnight.

The first official reaction to the country's new status is to come later today from Prime Minister Ian D. Smith, who is to hold a news conference. Mr. Smith declared independence without British consent on Nov. 11, 1965.

Mr. Smith who was a fighter pilot with the Royal Air Force in World War II, faces several problems as the republic's first Prime Minister.

The most immediate is general elections April 10 and then questions of economic sanctions, African nationalist guerrilla activities and international recognition.

Despite bitter opposition from white moderates and extremists of the Center and Republican Alliance parties, Mr. Smith is expected to lead his party, the Rhodesian Front, to victory in the elections.

The new Constitution, with racial separation provisions designed to insure continued white minority rule, was overwhelmingly approved by the white electorate in a referendum last year. The country has 4.5 million blacks and 240,000 whites.

Under the new Constitution, the House of Assembly initially will comprise 66 members, of whom 50 will be whites, Asians or of mixed race and 16 will be blacks. When blacks pay more than 24 per cent of the country's personal income taxes, they will be allotted more seats, up to parity with Europeans.

Black Africans — almost all of whom are farmers living on subsistence incomes — now pay only six-tenths of 1 per cent of the total income tax.

Of immediate importance to Mr. Smith is the question of continued foreign representation here and official recognition of the new republic.

Several countries, including the United States, have consulates here, but none have indicated they will officially recognize the new Government. Neighboring South Africa has already said relations between the two countries will continue as before.

Whether the United States Consulate in Salisbury will remain in operation also remains in doubt.

The return to Salisbury last September of the United States Consul General, Paul O'Neill, after a home leave was interpreted by many Rhodesians as evidence that the United States would not sever relations. But authoritative United States sources were reported to have said at the time that no decision had been reached and none was likely to be reached until an over-all review of African policy had been completed.

Secretary of State William P. Rogers, during his 15-nation African trip last month, said the United States deplored governments based on racial discrimination and "identified" with the desire of black Africans for self-determination.

Along with the question of recognition is the problem of international economic sanctions imposed by Britain after the declaration of independence. The sanctions are supported by the United Nations. Although they failed to make Rhodesia submit, there could be a move now to intensify them.

March 2, 1970

Dispute Nears End As Rhodesia Signs Pact With Britain

By ANTHONY LEWIS
Special to The New York Times

SALISBURY, Rhodesia, Nov. 24 — The six-year struggle between Britain and her rebellious territory of Rhodesia neared an end today as a constitutional settlement was agreed upon.

Sir Alec Douglas-Home, the Foreign Secretary, signed the agreement for Britain. Prime Minister Ian D. Smith, who declared Rhodesia independent in 1965, signed for her white minority Government.

A number of steps must still be taken before Britain lifts economic sanctions against Rhodesia. They could take months.

The terms of the agreement will be announced in the Parliaments of the two countries tomorrow.

Some Guarantees Due

Broadly, the terms will confirm the present power of the 250,000 whites in Rhodesia but offer the 5 million Africans some guarantees against discrimination and the hope of eventual political control.

Even before the terms were known, an immediate excitement — even euphoria—swept through Salisbury. Blacks and whites crowded around The Rhodesia Herald building to buy copies of an extra carrying a one-word banner: "Yes."

Another Herald headline said Rhodesia's six years of unilateral independence — not recognized by any other country — were over.

Actually, they were not. First, there will have to be a canvass of black and white opinion to see whether the terms are acceptable to the "Rhodesian people as a whole." Britain is committed to that as the last of her five principles for a Rhodesian settlement.

This test of opinion will be undertaken early next year. It will probably be carried out by a small group, perhaps including members from countries in the Commonwealth.

British Must Approve

Second, the British Parliament will have to approve the terms. The Conservative Government will ask it to do so—after the test of Rhodesian opinion—by presenting a bill to grant Rhodesia legal independence.

The Rhodesian Parliament will also have to make some changes in the constitution and laws to conform with the settlement. For one, it will undoubtedly have to amend the constitutional provision that now bars Africans from having more than half the seats in Parliament.

Britain's Labor party is almost certain to criticize the terms as inadequate. The United Nations will also be critical, because the agreement will leave power in the hands of the white minority. But the odds are still that Britain will conclude the settlement early next year.

Formal Signing Ceremony

Sir Alec spent 10 hard days here negotiating with Mr. Smith and talking with other Rhodesians. In the middle of the negotiations it appeared that Mr. Smith was backing away from the minimum concessions required, as he had in 1966 and 1968 in talks with the Labor Prime Minister, Harold Wilson.

The breakthrough apparently came Monday and yesterday. Today the two sides met for a formal signing ceremony.

At 11:15 A.M. Sir Alec and Mr. Smith came out of the Prime Minister's office smiling broadly and waving appropriately. It was the first really sunny day since the British arrived.

After Sir Alec drove off, reporters questioned Mr. Smith.

Would Rhodesians be happy? he was asked.

"Yes," he replied.

Would black Rhodesians be happy?

"We have the happiest Africans in the world," Mr. Smith said.

The British delegation took off at once for the 16-hour flight home. Sir Alec will make a statement in the House of Commons tomorrow afternoon, probably after reporting to the Cabinet. He will be questioned, and next week there will be a debate.

Mr. Smith will announce the terms at the same hour tomorrow in his Parliament. But there will be no questions, and Parliament will adjourn until after the test of the settlement's acceptability next year.

Smith Maintains Control

Thus Mr. Smith is keeping careful control of his own political situation. But the immediate reaction to the news of the settlement indicated that he would have broad support in his own white electorate.

An African reporter who toured townships said that among Africans there was a feeling of excitement, but that it was mixed with concern at the possibility that the terms could amount to "a sellout."

The British, while keeping silent on the terms, said firmly that they were not a sellout. The Foreign Office spokesman, John Leahy, said:

"They are fully in accordance with the five principles, and I believe that when you have a chance to see them you will agree."

The first four principles call for unimpeded progress toward majority rule, guarantees against regressive amendments to the constitution, immediate improvement in the Africans' political status and progress toward ending racial discrimination.

Sir Alec also signed today an agreement for massive British economic aid. This aid, also to be described tomorrow, will probably be used primarily for African education.

November 25, 1971

The Moral Cost of Chrome

The Nixon Administration has now taken an action that puts the United States in violation of the United Nations Charter and gives moral support, at a critical moment, to Rhodesia's white minority Government. Officials will doubtless say that the Treasury was bound by a provision in the Military Procurement Act of 1971 to lift restrictions on imports of Rhodesian chrome—in spite of the mandatory sanctions invoked against Rhodesia—with American backing—by the U.N. Security Council.

However, there was a thoroughly legal way out if Mr. Nixon had been interested in defending the United Nations as well as the integrity of this country's commitment to that organization. He could have removed chrome from the list of strategic materials on the sound ground that the United States now has a stockpile adequate to meet both military and civilian needs for the next two to three years.

It would be a grave matter at any time for the United States—which has given unlimited support to "the rule of law" and to adherence to international law—to breach unilaterally a Security Council decision, especially one for which it voted. Secretary General Kurt Waldheim must now have a clearer idea of what Mr. Nixon meant, in a White House talk Monday, when he promised "full support" for the United Nations.

Bad as is the undercutting of this newly given commitment to the U.N., it is doubly tragic to give a major boost to the white racists who rule Rhodesia at a time when that country's black majority is dramatizing daily its hostility to Prime Minister Ian Smith's regime. This action will further damage respect for United States integrity—and not just in black Africa.

January 26, 1972

Black 'No!' in Rhodesia

Many Against Anything Smith Is For Despite Benefits in New Proposals

By CHARLES MOHR
Special to The New York Times

SALISBURY, Rhodesia, Jan. 23—Superficially, it was a time of paradox in Rhodesia.

News Analysis

The white Government of Prime Minister Ian D. Smith, which for years has dedicated itself to preventing majority, or black, rule was urging Rhodesians to accept new constitutional proposals. The proposals would cautiously increase black political rights, and, if honestly implemented, would eventually lead to majority rule. Black leaders, many of them only recently released from long detentions, were urging rejection of the proposals, and for the last six days in all corners of this central African country blacks have been shouting "No!"

The catalyst for these events was the arrival here of the British Commission on Rhodesian Opinion.

Britain and her former self-governing colony finally reached agreement last November on terms to end their long dispute on constitutional reform, a dispute that caused Rhodesia's declaration of independence in 1965 and the subsequent imposition of economic sanctions.

Voting Ruled Out

The British were publicly committed to the principle that the terms must be acceptable to Rhodesia's 250,000 white settlers and more than five million blacks. To test acceptability the British, typically, sent a committee.

There were reasons for this. Mr. Smith would not have agreed to a referendum since it smacks of the principle of "one man, one vote," which he abhors. It would also be difficult to let all the blacks vote on proposals that would restrict the number of blacks who would have the franchise in the future.

In any case, many on both sides regarded the work of the opinion commission a mere formality, almost certain to result in a finding of approval for the proposals.

The events of the last few days have thrown this and other assumptions into some doubt and Rhodesia into turmoil.

The commission's chairman is a 70-year-old British judge, Lord Pearce. There are three deputy chairmen, including Lord Harlech, the former British Ambassador to Washington. There are 18 commissioners, the large majority of them former officers in the British colonial service with careers in former British colonies.

At the start Lord Pearce conceded that the commission was not sure how best to operate and would experiment with several methods. One of the early experiments was to issue, from its headquarters in a Salisbury office building called Stability House, a printed questionnaire to assist blacks in giving written opinions.

Thousands of blacks showed up, clogging halls, stairs and sidewalks and — presumably — putting "no" on the forms.

White Rhodesians were furious because the method seemed to be a form of ballot and they charged that blacks were being instructed by leaders in how to fill the papers out.

Forms Are Stopped

The commission, which could hardly get in and out of its own doors, stopped issuing the forms.

Last Monday seven teams of two commissioners each fanned out to begin scheduled and advertised meetings all over the country, including some in the tribal trust lands, or reserves, which cover about 50 per cent of rural Rhodesia.

The results were surprising to many observers. In almost all of the meetings blacks gave choruses of "no" when asked if they favored the new terms.

Urban blacks had been generally expected to oppose the proposals, but more than 80 per cent of blacks live on the tribal trust lands under the authority of 200 chiefs on the Government's payroll. It had been thought that chiefs, tribal councils and the population there would generally give their approval, possibly under the influence of white district officers. Indeed, this was an argument widely used in advance by critics to discredit the validity of the Pearce Commission.

In fact, tribal blacks were as adamant as urban blacks. So far only one chief, with 19,000 followers, has expressed approval.

Some observers said that at many meetings there were "cheerleaders"—black leaders who created an atmosphere in which it was difficult for anyone to voice their approval.

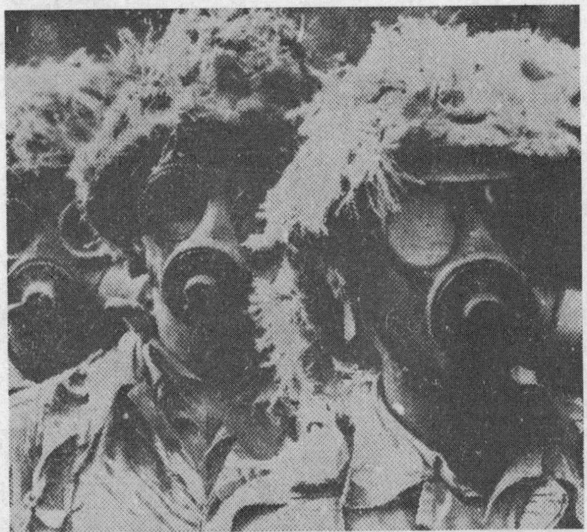

Associated Press

GAS MASKS gave Rhodesian soldiers unearthly appearance as they quelled disturbances in Gwelo recently.

Dissatisfied with the atmosphere of the meetings, many commissioners began to try to urge the blacks to meet them singly or in small groups. In virtually every case the people refused. But no one has yet offered any credible proof that there exist a significant number of blacks who want to approve the proposals but who are intimidated.

In a few days the commissioners, who plan to spend about two months in Rhodesia, will meet in Salisbury to exchange experiences and discuss ways to improve their sampling efforts. It seems possible that they will try to find some substitute for the public meetings.

If they continue to rely primarily on the public meetings and the response does not change it will be almost impossible for the commission to tell the world plausibly that its findings are that Rhodesians accept the terms.

But what can the commission do if blacks continue to boycott private meetings?

Meetings an Embarrassment

Britain and the Smith Government want the agreement to go through. This is why the Pearce Commission meetings have been more of an embarrassment than rioting that erupted last week in five Rhodesian towns and in which 13 blacks were killed by police gunfire.

The British Government wants the agreement partly because it would like to wash its hands of a problem in which it has legal responsibility but no power. Mr. Smith would never have made even the limited political concessions in the agreement unless he felt the need for international recognition and the end of sanctions, which have seriously drained foreign-exchange reserves, hurt farmers and annoyed the business community.

That Mr. Smith wants the agreement is not lost on blacks. It is one of the main reasons that they are opposing it. Some blacks argue that acceptance would make Mr. Smith's declaration of independence legitimate. But many simply seem to feel that they should be against anything Mr. Smith is for.

The complex agreement does promise a degree of political advancement for blacks through a formula that would gradually increase black voters and members of Parliament—if the number who can meet educational, income and property qualifications increases.

Even so, it would take a long time to reach majority rule. Members of the Pearce Commission have had to tell crowds that they simply cannot predict how long.

Although Mr. Smith and the British have warned that there will be no renegotiation if the agreement is rejected, some black leaders say they believe, that renegotiation on better terms would follow a commission finding of rejection. It is difficult to know whether they believe this or whether they feel that a continuation of the present harsh racial situation would do more to promote a real revolution among Rhodesian blacks, who have been, on the whole, docile.

But there is one final factor that struck many observers in the last few days as probably the soundest explanation of all of what is happening.

For the first time, the blacks have been, in effect, given a veto power. There is an almost irresistible temptation to use it, even if it kills a plan that would improve their lot somewhat.

January 24, 1972

British-Rhodesian Agreement Collapses

By ALVIN SHUSTER
Special to The New York Times

LONDON, May 23—The effort to end the six-year dispute between Britain and her breakaway colony of Rhodesia collapsed today.

The British commission assigned to test Rhodesian opinion on a proposed settlement officially reported that the terms were rejected by the people "as a whole." Most of the objections came from Rhodesia's black majority, many members of which felt that the suggested settlement would legalize their inferior status once their country's independence from Britain became official under the plan.

The British team that made the inquiry in Rhodesia about the settlement plan was headed by Lord Pearce, a retired High Court Judge.

The resounding rejection of the settlement plan by black Rhodesians had been generally expected since the commission returned to London. But the formal collapse of the latest effort was left until today with the release of the commission's report and the British Government's reaction.

Sir Alec Douglas-Home, Britain's Foreign Secretary, announced that London would continue its diplomatic and economic boycott of the rebellious white government of Prime Minister Ian D. Smith in Salisbury. He said that sanctions would continue and that "the status quo will remain."

The collapse of the settlement formula, reached last November, represented the latest in a series of failures. Successive British Governments since the fifties have been trying to find a compromise between the ideal of multi-racialism and long-established white power in Rhodesia. The blacks in Rhodesia outnumber the ruling whites by 5,000,000 to 250,000.

Mr. Smith unilaterally declared Rhodesia independent in November, 1965. He did so after Britain refused to grant independence without guarantees that blacks would get a measure of political power in Rhodesia. This led the United Nations in 1966 to impose a series of sanctions, including a trade embargo, now largely ineffective.

In announcing the findings of the Peace Commission, Sir Alec held out the hope that the Smith minority Government and Rhodesia's black majority could reach some agreement among themselves. But he acknowledged that chances of such a compromise were slim.

In reply to questions, Sir Alec left the impression that if a compromise agreement could be reached among Rhodesians, Britain would drop her long-held insistence on sampling opinion, at least in the manner of the commission.

In its 50,000-word report, the commission partly agreed with charges by the Smith Government that some Rhodesian blacks had intimidated others to persuade them to say "no" to the proposed settlement. It said there had been a "certain amount" of intimidation by black nationalists, sometimes acting under the banner of the African National Council, formed last December to urge rejection of the settlement.

"It was our considered view that, had there been no intimidation, there would still have been a substantial majority against the proposals," the commission concluded.

In contrast, the commission reported, most whites in Rhodesia supported the settlement. It said that the whites seemed largely interested on economic grounds—"the end of sanctions and the return of foreign investment."

Many whites also told the commission that they supported the settlement because they felt that it would be tragic to waste this, "possibly the last," opportunity to bring the races together. The commission found that many whites held the view that rule by the black majority was inevitable, but that, if possible, it should come gradually and peacefully.

May 24, 1972

RACE BIAS IN AFRICA SAID TO FLOUT LAW

SPRINGFIELD, Ohio, June 20 (AP)—Dr. José Nunes de Oliveira, former Governor General of Mozambique, said today there was racial discrimination in two Portuguese African territories even though the Portuguese Constitution called for the equality of citizens before the law and especially scorned racial distinction.

He spoke at the North American Assembly on African Affairs, meeting at Wittenberg College here. The assembly is studying the relation of changing social, racial and political conditions in that part of Africa below the Sahara Desert.

Dr. Oliveira is Inspector General of Overseas Administration for Portugal. He said the Constitution drew a line in regard to Portuguese Angola and Mozambique between "citizens and natives, that is to say, civilized and noncivilized."

Robert K. A. Gardiner, head of the Department of Extramural Studies at University College, Ibadan, Nigeria, criticized the non-English-speaking colonial nations for not cooperating with each other. He said the present assembly was the first in which representatives from French, Belgian and Portuguese colonies had gotten together on the same platform.

Gabriel van Laethem, First Secretary of the French Embassy in Washington, said African leaders felt that Russia wanted small African nations that could form alliances on religious or racial bases, all antagonistic to the West.

June 21, 1952

Lisbon to Use U.S. Aid in Colonies; All Africa Will Share in Benefits

Angola and Mozambique Will Be Developed—Migration of Whites Is Planned

By CAMILLE M. CIANFARRA
Special to THE NEW YORK TIMES.

LISBON, Portugal, July 6—Development of Portugal's vast resources of strategic raw materials and basic foodstuffs in her African territories of Angola and Mozambique is one of the objectives in which the United States is deeply interested today.

After United States surveys made in both those areas, the Portuguese Government has received Mutual Security loans for several million dollars. They are to be used to build meat-packing plants and hydroelectric power stations, to start irrigation projects for land reclamation, to improve cattle breeding, to intensify the production of minerals needed for defense, and, above all, to increase the efficiency of the strategically important railway stretching across the whole of Equatorial Africa, from the Atlantic port of Lobita in southwestern Angola, through the Belgian Congo, Northern and Southern Rhodesia, to Beira in Mozambique.

Potentialities of Colonies

United States aid to Portugal is based on an increasing awareness that Angola and Mozambique in wartime not only could help to alleviate the food shortage of Western Europe but also could become a vital artery beyond the range of Soviet bombers for the movement overland of strategic supplies, if the Western powers lost control of the Suez Canal.

Lobita is today the main Atlantic outlet for the shipping of highly strategic raw materials from the Belgian Congo, and copra, timber, diamonds, sugar, cattle and pigs from southwestern Angola. Beira, the gateway to Central Africa from the east coast, is the relaying point for a steady flow of mineral ores, chrome and copper.

The Portuguese Empire is the third largest in the world, after the British and the French. Most of it is underdeveloped and its mineral resources have barely been tapped, partly because Portugal, which has a population of 8,500,000 people with limited resources, does not have the financial means necessary for large-scale development.

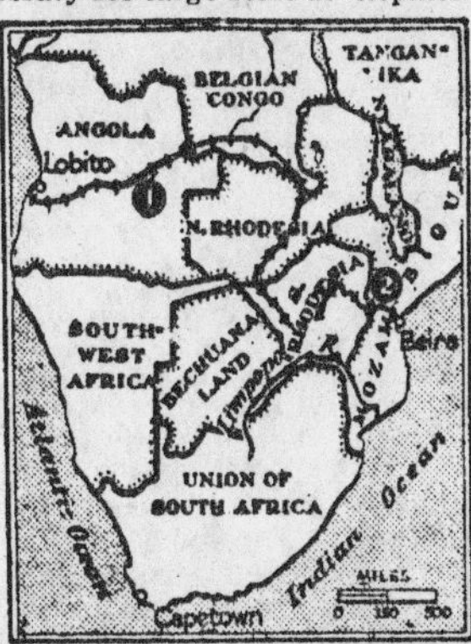

The New York Times July 12, 1952

United States funds are helping Portugal develop Angola (1) and Mozambique (2).

Another reason is the extreme cautiousness displayed by government officials toward all questions affecting the economic structure of both the metropolitan and overseas territories. At present the primitive conditions and extremely low educational level of the native Negro population, estimated at 4,000,000 in Angola and 5,000,000 in Mozambique, is said to be the main reason why nationalism, which is besetting other colonial powers, has not affected the Portuguese territories in Central Africa.

Although Portugal has an excess population of about 3,500,000, no more than 250,000 whites are now living in her two African colonies, most of them along the coasts. A Mutual Security Agency survey completed last April noted that in Angola there was a plateau "including an area larger than continental Portugal and ideally suited by climate and rainfall for European colonization" when properly developed. In Mozambique there are equally satisfactory opportunities for emigration, and the Portuguese Government is now considering a project to settle eventually 9,500 families, or 47,500 persons, in the Limpopo Valley. Each family would receive forty-five acres of land—forty for pasture and five for cultivation.

The Government-owned bank of Angola, which controls the economic life of the colony, has not encouraged large developmental loans to expand agricultural and industrial production. However, there are indications now that this policy is gradually being changed. The Ministry of Overseas Territories has recommended that the present banking laws applying to non-metropolitan areas be revised to allow the entry of new banks that would have their head offices in the colonies. Under this proposal each bank would be obliged to deposit 50 per cent of its subscribed capital with the so-called Province's Bank (Government-owned bank of issue in the colony) before beginning operations—which means that the Portuguese Government would still control all economic activities undertaken by private capital.

Salazar Has Cautious Policy

The same cautious policy is carried out in metropolitan Portugal, where Premier Antonio Oliveira Salazar, who has been ruling the country for more than twenty years, believes that gradual improvement is preferable to rapid expansion that might jeopardize economic stability.

One finds in Portugal an atmosphere of calm and tranquility not to be seen in the rest of Western Europe. There is a virtual absence of communism and the threat of Soviet aggression is not felt as keenly in Portugal as in nations that are more exposed to it because of their geographical position.

The equipment Portugal has been receiving under the supervision of the United States Military Assistance Advisory Group is gradually turning the Portuguese Army estimated at 60,000 men into a small but efficient force.

July 12, 1952

PORTUGUESE AVOID AFRICAN RACE CURB

Mozambique Shows No Visible Sign of Segregation—Tribal Structure Not Disrupted

By C. L. SULZBERGER
Special to THE NEW YORK TIMES.

LOURENCO MARQUES, Mozambique, Jan. 26—There are no visible signs of racial segregation here in Portuguese East Africa, a situation unlike that prevailing in the neighboring Union of South Africa, where apartheid is the rule, and in Southern Rhodesia, where a similar theory applies, if not so blatantly.

Here in this cozy town, with modern houses, and office buildings bordering the best harbor on the continent's eastern shore (its potential capacity is estimated to equal New York's), one sees neither signs reading "Europeans only" nor benches and post office entrances reserved for whites or Negroes.

For Portugal has managed to avoid both the appearance and the formal actuality of discrimination. In theory, at least, any inhabitant of this huge overseas province, regardless of color, is eligible for full Portuguese citizenship and a claim to equal treatment with anyone else who is recognized as a citizen by Lisbon.

The Portuguese, who, after all, have been in Africa since the days of the great explorers in the fifteenth and sixteenth centuries, have managed so far to avoid some of the burning racial problems that are developing elsewhere on the continent.

Tribal Society Untouched

There has been no tendency to break up the native tribal society too rapidly, with the result that there is no problem of a detribalized floating population as there is in Kenya or South Africa. For the vast majority of natives the tribe, with its religion, family bonds, customs and particular form of psychological security, remains the governing social institution. Governor General Gabriel Teixera, a naval captain, is convinced that the native should not be advanced more rapidly spiritually and educationally than materially. He wants to build slowly and avoid upsetting the traditional social structure.

To become "assimilated," or recognized as "civilizado," a native must meet certain requirements. He must go through secondary or commercial school, speak Portuguese fluently and satisfy a native affairs board that he lives in European fashion. Persons of mixed blood, who are called "colored" in the Union of South Africa, have to show only that they live as Europeans, regardless of their education. Portuguese Goans (from India) and persons from Macao (on the South China coast near Hong Kong) are full citizens here.

Few Are in a Hurry

Most natives do not appear in any hurry to seek citizenship. While that status has certain privileges, including a passport and eligibility for better pay, it means foregoing tribal customs and rights. The latest population statistics show only 1,000 assimilated natives out of a total of 5,742,903.

Native education is in the hands of the Roman Catholic Church, which generally gives rudimentary instruction. The majority of natives are not encouraged to advance beyond this. Police justice is swift and tough, but the natives say they prefer to be beaten and released after minor crimes than to be imprisoned. Serious criminals are deported with their families to St. Thomas Island, off the west coast of Africa.

Wage scales for the natives are discouragingly low—far lower than in South Africa. Unskilled labor gets 10 to 25 cents daily. As a result 100,000 natives apply to work in the South African mines each year and twice that number slip over the border illegally.

January 27, 1953

NEGRO MASS HELD IN AFRICAN COLONY

Mozambique Rite Highlights Portugal's Assimilation Aim as Against Malan Racism

By ALBION ROSS
Special to The New York Times.

LOURENCO MARQUES, Mozambique, April 17—The celebration of Easter mass here for Negro soldiers was a symbol of the policy of racial assimilation of the Roman Catholic Church.

The church here is made responsible by the state for the education of this Portuguese colony's Negro men. According to the official policy they are to be raised to a standard where, eventually, they become full Portuguese citizens, equal to all other Portuguese.

Catholicism is the established state religion and it is through the church that the Government is undertaking to draw the Negro natives of its two big African colonies, Mozambique and Angola, into the Portuguese nation and to create a common Negro and white nation.

At the moment the policy is in sharp contrast to that being implemented in the Union of South Africa across the frontier by Prime Minister Daniel F. Malan.

The Government of South Africa has just cut by one half the subsidy to the Christian mission schools. The missions, lacking generally the means to carry on, are being told to turn over their buildings to the new Education Department, established under the Ministry of Native Affairs.

Under the new Government system of education in South Africa Negroes are taught to live apart from whites.

The support to the mission schools is being reduced and probably will be eliminated entirely within a few years because the missions have failed to teach the present South African Government's doctrine of racialism and are charged with giving the natives the idea that racial differences are not important.

Teodosio Cardinal de Gouveia, Archbishop of Mozambique, preaching to the colored soldiers of the garrison, emphasized that Portugal was their country. He said:

"May this and future communions produce in your souls the courage to fulfill your duties to God and to Portugal."

The Cardinal preached on the martyrdom of the Negro Christians at the court of the King of Buganda sixty years ago. He said:

"A little time ago we took part in Uganda in the Catholic Action Congress. On the last day there was a pilgrimage to the tomb of the martyrs. In the little church at the top of a hill a native African Bishop celebrated the mass and another native Bishop prayed, assisted by all the delegates to the Congress, come from all parts of the world to render homage to the twenty-two martyrs who, sixty years ago, were martyred for their faith."

The Cardinal continued:

"They died singing hymns to God and praising our Master serenely in the sincere and calm certitude of their Christian faith. They are today the blessed martyrs of Uganda whom the church praises and exalts in all the world."

Not a Religion for Cowards

The Cardinal told his Negro congregation that though Christianity was a religion of peace it was not a religion for cowards, but one that demanded courage of them in the war against evil, against the enemies of God and against the enemies of their country.

The arming of native Africans is one of the policies against which the Union of South Africa protests. The Cardinal urged his congregation of Negro soldiers to remember the heroic stand made by Portuguese soldiers on April 9 as a source of pride for them. The Portuguese army celebrates the day in memory of the battle in Flanders during World War I.

The mass was celebrated for the Negro soldiers of the garrison but the commander of the Portuguese forces in East Africa and his staff officers took part with them.

April 18, 1954

MOZAMBIQUE BARS BIAS IN LAND USE

Portuguese Colony in Africa Orders Egalitarian Policy in Development Project

By ALBION ROSS
Special to The New York Times.

LOURENCO MARQUES, Mozambique, April 18—Commandant Gabriel Teixeira, Governor of this Portuguese East African colony, has pushed through a race-relations policy that, for South and East Africa, is revolutionary.

White reserves and white colonization will not be permitted under a reversal of policy recently announced. Mozambique will have Negro reserves—90 per cent of the land now is in tribal reserve areas—and white men must settle along with the Negroes or stay away.

The issue arose in connection with the Portuguese Government's Limpopo Valley colonization plan, now starting. Portugal is overpopulated and Mozambique, which has many areas of rich soil and plenty of water, is underdeveloped, with a generally low standard of living.

The colony has a white population of about 50,000, compared with about 5,600,000 Negroes. Probably less than a quarter of the arable areas actually is used.

The Limpopo colonization plan is based on irrigation. A large dam is being built on the Limpopo River and a new railway from the port of Lourenço Marques to the heart of the Rhodesias will open up the valley. The land is marginal and is not being used by the natives, so it presumably was open for exclusive white colonization.

This was the original idea, and irrigation works were put under construction with the intention of creating a white colony in the center of southern Mozambique.

Such white reserves exist all over southern and eastern Africa. The best and largest part of the Union of South Africa is one, and Negroes may not acquire land there. Much of Southern Rhodesia is another, and the 12,000 square miles of white reserve in the Kenya highlands have been made world-famous by the Mau Mau effort to wipe them out.

The Mau Mau affair resulted in some new thoughts here, and the conclusion reached was that the original Limpopo plan, by creating a new white colony, was a guarantee of trouble for future generations. Accordingly, the decision was reached that there were going to be white settlers but that there also was going to be Negro ones, who would have to work the land under supervision and engage in the careful type of agriculture that will not destroy it.

The Portuguese policy of assimilation presumes that eventually all Negroes in the Portuguese "overseas provinces" in Africa will become full citizens, differing from others only in skin color.

Mozambique is geographically part of an area vaguely referred to as white man's Africa. It is in this area that the system of white reserves has arisen in accord with the racial prejudices frequently characteristic of the North European peoples. The Portuguese here apparently were on the verge of stumbling into the same pattern but evidenly have caught themselves in time.

April 19, 1954

INTELLECTUAL FOG DIMS MOZAMBIQUE

Portuguese Colony's Apathy Offers Sharp Contrast With South Africa's Vitality

By ALBION ROSS
Special to The New York Times.

LOURENCO MARQUES, Mozambique, April 19—The racial intolerance and stormy intellectual freedom of South Africa contrast with the racial tolerance and intellectual paralysis of neighboring Portuguese East Africa.

South Africa, in the six years since Dr. Daniel F. Malan's Nationalist Government came into power, has been the scene of an intellectual renaissance in a reaction to the Government's extremist doctrines of race purity. Possibly nowhere else is the art of editorial-page dialectics more highly developed.

Articles by the thousands and books by the hundreds dealing with all aspects of South African life from every viewpoint, but primarily the anti-Government viewpoint, have poured from presses at home and in Britain. They are everywhere available in South Africa.

No corner has been left unexplored in hot Parliament debates. At parties, hotel lobbies and bars, the battle of wits on exchanging opinion goes on incessantly.

Newspapers Join in Attack

Newspapers with the largest circulations in Africa south of the Sahara and with every modern facility for newsgathering attack the Government's stand incessantly. The Church, university professors and men of all ranks offer their opinions freely.

The African National Congress and South African Indian Congress meet and protest Government laws and policies. A Communist organization publishes a weekly newspaper filled with party propaganda and distributes it regularly in Negro or segregated areas.

Student organizations proclaim the Government's position to be wrong. University boards in Government-supported institutions reject the policy of academic segregation.

Some of the books that emerged from these stormy years of intellectual conflict have been international bes-sellers, and several personalities have become known in the Western world. In the meantime, the rapid development of South Africa's industry and commerce has brought a steady increase in the number of Negroes in skilled and semi-skilled occupations.

In neighboring Mozambique no one proclaims that the white man must maintain his supremacy. There are no "Europeans only" signs. Mozambique is Portuguese and ideas of race prejudice and superiority are anathema.

Dearth of Public Activity

The Government undoubtedly would not permit the publication of articles arguing for white supremacy or calculated to encourage race prejudice. However, hardly anything else concerning the affairs of Mozambique is published.

The naming of an official to a new post is hailed as a glorious event. Everyone in authority is dubbed "illustrious." Books dealing with controversial subjects do not exist in this colony. Decisions on public policy are made by the Governor General either on order from or after consultation with Lisbon. There is little debate.

Three hundred thousand Mozambique Negroes are reported to stream over the frontier every year to seek jobs in South Africa. One-third enter legally as mine workers. The rest take their chances at cashing in on the more numerous opportunities there.

Opportunities for Negroes to do anything but remain in the bush are much rarer here. Where there is employment, wages are much lower than what can be had in South Africa.

Political wrangling, Communist talk, organized crime or union organization would not be tolerated by the police. Almost all the Negroes are still under native status and tribal control. Only 4,000 are officially "civilized" and have theoretical equality with other Portuguese.

South Africa, in the long run, with its racialism and intolerance, seems likely to make a greater contribution to the future of the African and the African Negro.

April 20, 1954

PORTUGAL ACCEPTS AFRICAN EQUALITY

Mozambique Governor Sees No Reason to Bar Advance of Natives to Citizenship

By ALBION ROSS
Special to The New York Times.

LOURENCO MARQUES, Mozambique, April 21—Gabriel Teixeira, Governor General of Portuguese Mozambique, sees nothing wrong with a future united Portugal in Europe and Africa in which Negroes would be a majority. He does not believe there is any such thing as Negro nationalism.

The Governor General of Mozambique, the most ancient of the European colonial possessions south of the Equator, explained in an interview the Portuguese attitude on the problem of Africa, which is contrary to the Gold Coast Negro self-government experiment and to South African racial superiority ideas.

He indicated that there were four basic ideas in the modern Portuguese colonial philosophy that guided the country's policy in Mozambique and Angola.

One is that the whole idea of racial superiority was nonsense.

Another is that to try and rush the development of primitive men such as the native Africans, would be to destroy them.

A third is that Christianity is the salvation of the Negro, and for that matter, of everyone else.

Finally, there is the conviction that the Negroes in Africa in time could become full-fledged Portuguese.

Commandant Teixeira, who has been Governor General for more than seven years, said:

"We do not believe in superior and inferior races. The black man in Africa is simply where the white man began thousands of years ago. You cannot rush that sort of thing.

"You must have a balance between a moral advance and a material advance. Too sudden contact of advanced material civilization with primitive peoples destroys primitive people. On the other hand, if the material advance falls behind the moral advance, you have hatred and disorder. The problem is to keep a balance between the moral advance and material advance. The end result which we seek is Brazil."

Senhor Teixeira explained that he mentioned Brazil because of the principle of racial equality and mixture of races that prevail in that country.

The Governor General said the first thing was to get rid of evil superstitions and such practices in the native life, but not to destroy the essential pattern.

He explained that the principle was the settlement of white colonists among Africans, but never to the exclusion of the Africans.

"In South Africa, the natives were crowded into reserves that had nothing to do with the spirits of their ancestors, who according to their beliefs live in the tribal area," Senhor Teixeira said. "Either that, or the natives were crowded into industrial cities. Their society was broken. We do not want to break their society. We want a slow assimilation to the Portuguese life."

He explained that the native administration and Christian missions shared the responsibility of bringing about this slow assimilation.

"A native vote is absurd," the Governor General asserted. "These people's grandfathers were sometimes cannibals. How do they vote? What do they vote for?"

Mozambique has 4,000 Negroes who vote, are full citizens and so-called "civilizados," or "assimilados." The Governor General said that if a hotel or restaurant tried to exclude one of these "civilizados," or Negro Portuguese, the law would intervene.

April 22, 1954

Mozambique Bishop Campaigns Against Segregation of Negroes

Catholic Leader Fights to Prevent Use of Natives' Land as White Reserves From Which They Are Barred

By ALBION ROSS
Special to The New York Times.

BEIRA, Mozambique, May 10—The fight against racial segregation and the creation of white reserves shutting out the African Negro from parts of his native land are being led here by a Roman Catholic bishop.

Bishop Seabastiao de Resend, the outstanding intellectual force in Mozambique, has exercised a decisive influence on the Government. His pastoral letters, each of which constitutes a small book, are published regularly by the Government printer. He warns in his most recent pastoral letter that there is danger in alienating all the best land for white occupation.

Challenging the doctrine of a white man's Africa, represented by the huge white reserves in neighboring South Africa and in the Rhodesias, the Bishop states:

"The soil of Africa was the property of the natives long before it was that of the Europeans [whites]. We must create zones of fixed property rights, continuous territories and intermittent blocks of land where the natives will find possibilities to exercise economic initiative. They must have facilities for progress and development beside Europeans in the fraternal community with them, and free from all racial separation."

The Bishop argued that in place of reserves, which represented the antiquated social ideas of other nations, there must be zones and blocks of native property in all districts near the populated cities and towns.

"In the midst of them," he said, "attention must be given that the soil is good and that there are advantages for the development of commerce and industry. In this fashion the natives will come to recognize that we are opening for them all doors through which they can enter."

The failure to solve these problems is creating agitation and revolts in East Africa "to no one's advantage and to the disadvantage of all concerned," he added.

Mozambique is in danger of creating in the long run problems similar to those of Kenya.

The intention has been to develop some of the most desirable regions in Mozambique as white reserves, in imitation of neighboring South Africa and Southern Rhodesia.

Altogether there are 3,300,000 hectares (a hectare equals 2.47 acres) in such areas reserved on the map for European settlement. There are about ten such reserves. Statistically, these areas are not large in comparison with the total tof 77,000,000 hectares in Mozambique, of which 18,000,000 are native reserves.

However, much of Mozambique is completely or largely useless land, and Europeans have a tendency to occupy the best lands in areas not reserved for either European or native settlement. The rights of natives already on the land in European reserves of Mozambique are maintained here, which was not true in neighboring white-supremacy countries.

May 11, 1954

MOZAMBIQUE MEN FORCED TO LABOR

Negro in Portuguese Colony Must Work for Employer Six Months a Year

By ALBION ROSS
Special to The New York Times.

BEIRA, Portuguese Mozambique, May 8—Negro manpower is still the most sought-after commodity in this Zambezi country, where Dr. Livingstone started his anti-slavery campaign in the last century.

Forced labor still exists. The Negro in Portuguese Mozambique is compelled by law to work for an employer six months a year unless he can obtain a certificate showing that he has put in the necessary quota of work on his land.

Heavy pressure is put on the district administrators who decide whether a Negro is to be shipped away to work. Plantations, both large and small, demand their labor supply as do other employers. Negroes found guilty of crimes are even shipped away to work on the hated sugar plantations of the island of Sao Tome, in the Gulf of Guinea, on the African west coast, which suffers from a chronic shortage of labor. Separated from family, Negroes shipped to Sao Tome believe they will never return.

The Government defends the law which, compels Negroes to work six months a year instead of sitting and watching their wives till their tribal lands. This law is called an essential element in the civilizing process, giving responsibilities.

In the slave-trading days, when Arab slave traders roamed this area, the sought-after-Negro manpower was known as "black ivory." To what extent the existing system of forced labor is part of the civilizing process and to what extent a modified form of the trade in "black ivory" is an issue here.

Sebastiao Soares de Resende, Bishop of Beira, whose pastoral letters regularly call attention to evils that tend to be at least partly unnoticed under the system of complete censorship, has emphasized the evils of separating native families.

There is also foreign competition for the sought-after manpower. Legal and illegal recruiters gather together gangs of labor to work in South Africa and in the Rhodesias. By what means the labor is obtained does not seem to matter much.

One idea that has been put across by the labor recruiters is that work in the mines is what proves that a man is a man, as tribal warfare did in the old days. Women prefer a man who has been to the mines and shown that he is strong and courageous. These tropical natives, however, often come back broken in health, unfitted for life on the colder highlands.

Local administrations are also increasingly worried by the circumstances that the Negro comes back from the mining and industrial centers with ideas about race hatred, expulsion of the white or vague Communist leanings.

June 9, 1954

Mozambique Natives Gain Voice By Means of Legislative Council

Portugal Acts to Promote Negro Progress by Offering Inducements to Assimilation —Area Lacks Official Color Bar

By LEONARD INGALLS
Special to The New York Times.

LOURENCO MARQUES, Mozambique, March 1—Representative government has gained a small foothold in Mozambique.

A newly organized Legislative Council held its first meeting late last year. However, the Council's powers are slight, and the Governor General, representing Portugal, the mother country, still is the supreme authority.

Mozambique, formerly known as Portuguese East Africa, is a possession of Portugal on the southeast African coast, adjoining South Africa. It is a province of Portugal, although it is administered more like a colony. Three representatives from Mozambique sit in the Parliament in Lisbon.

Portugal often has been criticized for the stern way in which she has governed her African possessions, particularly Mozambique and Angola, which lies directly west across the continent of Africa.

Mozambique's Legislative Council and a similar body in Angola are giving the ordinary citizen a voice in his country's affairs, although not a very loud one. Portuguese officials explain that one reason such things as representative government must come slowly here is the comparatively uncivilized state of most of the native population.

There are twenty-four members in the Mozambique Legislative Council. Sixteen are elected under a strictly limited franchise and eight are appointed by the Governor General.

Group Purely Advisory

The Council's function is purely advisory.

Nevertheless, the Council gives an opportunity for an expression of views that hitherto had not been possible. It also is a training ground for legislative experience.

There are other limits on the Council's activities. Its sessions are restricted to two each year of thirty days each. The meetings are public except when the Governor General, who also is President of the Council, decides otherwise. The Council may be disbanded by the Overseas Minister for strong reasons of national interest.

An important aspect of the creation of the Council is that two members are appointed specifically to represent the interests of the country's 5,700,000 Negroes. Neither of the representatives is a native, as the Negroes here are called, but one is part African.

Portuguese officials say it is not inconceivable that a qualified native may one day take a seat in the Council.

Political representation is by no means the most difficult problem in Mozambique. The most difficult—a common problem in sub-Saharan Africa—is the backwardness of the Negro population.

In the 300,000 square miles of this Portuguese East African territory there are nearly 6,000,000 inhabitants. About 100,000 are whites, Asians, Indians, persons of mixed blood or so-called civilized or assimilated Negroes.

The Mozambique Negro leads a strictly regulated life. However, unlike most of his African brothers, he may, by meeting certain requirements, become assimilated into the civilized community and live on equal terms with the white man.

The absence of official color bars in Mozambique and Angola also eliminates an irritation that is building up the dangerous stream of resentment in other African areas.

Mozambique's safety valve is known as the assimilado system. To qualify for its privileges of full Portuguese citizenship, a Negro must be older than 18, speak Portuguese correctly, be of good conduct and have an occupation that provides sufficient income for him and his dependents to live on the same scale as the average white men of the community.

4,555 Assimilated

There are 4,555 Assimilados in Mozambique. Since 1950 the number has increased by only 206. Basically this is caused by the Negro's difficulty in obtaining the necessary education and income.

Most of Mozambique's Africans are treated as wards of the state. They do not have freedom of movement. Those who live in the cities are subject to a 9 P. M. curfew.

About 2,000,000 Africans (Negroes) here have emerged from primitive life to take up employment. This includes about 1,500,000 in the production of cotton, Mozambique's chief crop and export. Nearly 4,000,000 others eke out subsistence in the bush.

Mozambique is chiefly an agricultural country and the annual national income is small. Nevertheless, a number of steps are being taken to improve things.

There is a six-year economic development program that started three years ago. Major emphasis is being given to transportation.

Modern agricultural methods are being taught to the Negro farmers and they are being assisted by the Government in forming cooperatives. Irrigation is being developed.

The more progressive officials of the Provincial Administration are eager to provide extensive education facilities; they complain they are limited by a shortage of funds.

March 2, 1956

RACIAL ATTITUDES HELP MOLD CITIES

Lourenco Marques Differs From Johannesburg as Much Physically as in Policy

By LEONARD INGALLS

Special to The New York Times.

LOURENCO MARQUES, Mozambique, March 2—The principal cities of Mozambique and the Union of South Africa, Lourenço Marques and Johannesburg, are close to each other on the map of Africa but they have little in common.

As an Indian Ocean port this capital city of Mozambique owes much of its economic strength to the annual parade of ships carrying goods to and from South Africa. As a resort it bears the same relation to Johannesburg as Atlantic City does to New York.

In size there is no comparison. Johannesburg has just reached 1,000,000 in population. Lourenço Marques has barely more than 100,000 inhabitants. Life here is conditioned by a hot tropical climate and is gentle and easy going. Johannesburg's elevation of nearly 6,000 feet contributes to the city's brisk atmosphere.

Broad Tree-Lined Streets

In a municipal beauty contest Lourenço Marques would win easily. Its streets are broad and lined with trees. Its buildings and homes are clean and well kept. A great white cathedral dominates the central area from its hillside site on a broad public square.

By contrast, Johannesburg's central area is a maze of narrow crowded streets clustered with trolley cars, badly designed buildings and too much traffic—all reflecting poor city planning. The South African metropolis has few natural attractions.

The major part of the population of both cities is Negro and it is in the treatment of their Negroes that difference between the two cities is most apparent. Johannesburg's racial practices have given it an air of bitterness, fear and tension. Because Lourenço Marques' Negroes are treated more like human beings there is a friendlier more relaxed atmosphere.

The New York Times March 4, 1956

A TALE OF TWO CITIES: There is little in common between Lourenço Marques and near-by Johannesburg (cross). The former is easy-going and the latter brisk.

While Johannesburg is busy keeping its Africans beyond the city limits—most of them in squalid slums—Lourenço Marques is developing a plan of Negro communities that will be spotted around the center of the city and well within its limits.

There are no separate entrances and counters for whites and Negroes in banks and post offices here such as there are in Johannesburg. The churches have mixed congregations and the schools have mixed classes, practices that are frowned upon in Johannesburg.

Public transportation is open to all races on a first-come first-served basis. So are the motion picture theatres, although there is censorship of films that results in many being ruled out for Africans.

There are still many restrictions on Negroes in Mozambique and some meanness toward them by individual whites that none of the authorities here will deny. South African visitors often wag their heads in disapproval of Portuguese policy, which is generally favorable, but the Portuguese note that the sky has not fallen because of it. They also are proud of the fact that the crime rate here is minute compared with the Johannesburg record of robberies, burglaries, assaults and murders involving Negroes.

March 4, 1956

MOZAMBIQUE BARS AFRICAN FERMENT

Stern Rule by Portuguese Keeps Nationalistic Wave From Reaching Area

By LEONARD INGALLS

Special to The New York Times.

LOURENCO MARQUES, Mozambique, July 9—The most striking aspect of Mozambique, the Portuguese possession on the east coast of Africa, is the absence of African nationalism.

While nearly all of sub-Sahara Africa bubbles with the ferment of African political aspiration, there are no discernible signs of it here. Instead, the visitor returning after an absence of four years finds there has been no change. The Government of Portugal, under Premier Antonio de Oliveira Salazar, still rules with a stern and unyielding hand.

In Mozambique, about 70,000 Europeans dwell at the upper level of the social and economic scale while 6,000,000 Africans are at the lowest level.

In between are an assortment of 18,000 Asians, 30,000 persons of mixed blood, known here as mulattoes, and about 5,000 so-called civilized Africans, known as assimilados. The assimilados have met certain social literacy and vocational requirements. They have been assimilated into the Western type of society and live on terms of relative equality with the Europeans.

The Portuguese rulers of Mozambique are shocked at events around them in Africa.

In discussions of violent nationalism in the Congo, which gained its independence from Belgium June 30, Nyasaland and South Africa, they declare: "We will have no trouble with our natives. They know what would happen to them if they made trouble."

To understand what is happening in Mozambique, the outsider must keep in mind that he is visiting a dictatorship with all the trappings of absolutism and a strong and watchful police force. African nationalism simply does not get a chance to raise its head. For that matter, neither does any other type of nationalism except the one that is loyal to the Government in Lisbon.

The New York Times July 10, 1960

A COLONY IN REPOSE: The people of Mozambique (cross-hatching) are evincing no African nationalism.

An example of what happens to those who attempt to criticize the Government was given last year. Two Portuguese residents of Mozambique published a political pamphlet that was critical of Dr. Salazar and called for demonstrations against the Governor General. They were expelled from Mozambique and sent back to Portugal. The printer lost his business license and was banished to a remote town in the north for six months.

The Government said the pamphlet jeopardized internal order in Mozambique.

Agitators Cross Border

Occasionally political agitators slip across the long border from neighboring Nyasaland. The Africans in the area belong to the same tribe even though they live in different countries.

It does not take the Portuguese police long to find out about the agitators and send them back to Nyasaland. If the Portuguese feel that a Mozambique African has been influenced by the agitators, it is soon made harshly clear to him that African nationalism is not acceptable here.

To the vistor it appears that Mozambique Africans have accepted their position, at least for the present.

Part of the explanation is that they are not subject to some of the daily restrictions on movement that apply to Africans in South Africa. Moreover, they are not constantly hounded by the police as Africans are in South Africa.

July 10, 1960

AUTONOMY URGED FOR MOZAMBIQUE

Strong Groups of Whites Are Opposed to Portugal's Rule

By LEONARD INGALLS

Special to The New York Times.

LOURENCO MARQUES, Mozambique, June 20—Strong groups of Mozambique's white population opposed to Portugal's Government are demanding autonomy for this East African territory.

The administration of Premier Antonio de Oliveira Salazar governs Mozambique from Lisbon as a province of Portugal.

Among Mozambique's white population of 100,000, there are elements that foresee ultimate independence for the territory, which is seven times the size of Portugal and has a population of 6,000,000 Africans. The anti-Government whites also envisage a Mozambique government with more Africans than whites.

Anti-Government political expression is discouraged in Mozambique and the dissidents must be careful to avoid arrest. A tough new Governor, Rear Admiral Manuel Maria Sarmento Rodrigues, a former Portuguese Minister of Overseas Provinces, arrived from Lisbon this month. Unlike his predecessor, Admiral Rodrigues holds both civil and military authority.

It is understood this concentration of power was decided upon to enable the admiral to deal with any unrest. The tightening of administration here was influenced by the uprising in Angola, Portugal's West Coast territory, and by certain indications of discontent here.

Some observers believe that if Portugal fails to quell the Angola rebellion, trouble will develop swiftly in Mozambique.

One demonstration of discontent, which resulted in the arrest of seven business men in April, was the circulation of an anti-Government petition in Beira, Mozambique's second largest city and a major port. More than 600 signed the petition, and troops were called to disperse the crowd that gathered to protest the arrests.

A list of fifty suggested economic changes and a statement that whites here are willing to share equal rights of citizenship with non-whites has been circulated in Lourenco Marques. Business men are becoming more anti-Government because of restrictions of their import licenses.

One of the most forceful anti-Government political groups was the Association of Natives of Mozambique, a former social and cultural organization of whites born here. Membership was opened to Africans and swelled to 10,000 including about 2,000 Africans.

An election of officers in December was prohibited and the association was placed under a Government administrator to curb its political activities.

Nevertheless, talk of radical changes in Mozambique goes on. "We want to educate all non-whites politically as well as otherwise, because we know that the only solution is self-determination for these people," one Salazar opponent said.

June 22, 1961

ANGOLA'S NEGROES RISE BY SELF-HELP

Portuguese Colony in Africa Makes Work Obligatory, but Shuns the Color Bar

By MICHAEL CLARK

Special to The New York Times.

LUANDA, Angola, April 16—The Portuguese are confident that the example of Angola will prove that assimilation is the best answer to the race problem in Africa.

The Belgians, next door, say they practice segregation out of respect for African custom. In the Belgian Congo the emphasis is on economic and social rather than political development, although town councils with African representation are soon to come.

The South African Government goes a step further. Its leaders have made segregation the basis of an elaborate doctrine of separate development and racial purity.

The British, up the coast, are in effect segregating whole areas by making them, in appearance at least, self-governing African states. In Nigeria and the Gold Coast, a handful of educated Africans, avid for power, wish to become big frogs in small, backwater pools. Personal ambition cloaked in African nationalism is the winner, not real equality.

Many Avenues Open

The French, who stand for equality and association, have pushed integration and interlocking institutions in the hope that mutual interests will promote a form of assimilation.

Many avenues of advancement also are open to the African in Portuguese territory, even though the authorities are committed to a policy of large-scale white settlement designed to help relieve the population pressure in Portugal.

There is nothing "bush" about Luanda. Besides being the capital of a prosperous and rapidly developing country, this city is one of the few in colonial Africa where the visitor finds all the amenities of Europe.

The Portuguese know that their hopes for Angola depend on a successful native policy, but, unlike Europeans in some other parts of Africa, they appear to have not apprehensions about the future.

The New York Times May 2, 1954

JOBLESSNESS ILLEGAL: All persons are required to work in Angola (diagonal shading).

With four centuries of African experience behind them, the Portuguese do not doubt that their system is proof against unrest and the rise of African nationalism. Certainly the present atmosphere of the place is one of exceeding peace.

In the Portuguese view, the native must be taught and protected as if he were a child, but accepted as an equal once he comes up to European standards. There is no sympathy here for the South African approach, held to be "suicidal" on the ground that it tends to build up a hostile community of great numerical superiority.

Assimilation is not a vain word in Angola, officially a province of Portugal and the birthplace of many Portuguese of mixed blood.

The color bar has all but vanished, but a sharp distinction is made between "civilized" and "non-civilized" Africans. The former enjoy European status while the latter suffer all the disabilities inherent in an intensely paternalistic system. By 1950 the number of "civilized" Africans had reached 30,112.

Accession to European status is an administrative procedure involving the grant of a revocable certificate of assimilation. The candidate for European status must be sponsored by a Portuguese administrator or two Europeans of good repute. A searching inquiry is made into his education and way of life. Polygamy and animism are equally forbidden. In practice the candidate must be a Christian.

May 2, 1954

PORTUGAL FACING BIG JOB IN ANGOLA

Poverty and Illiteracy Slow Pace of Development for West African Territory

By LEONARD INGALLS

Special to The New York Times.

LUANDA, Angola, Aug. 3—The task of converting this backward bit of Africa into a relatively civilized place is proceding more slowly than in most places south of the Sahara. Poverty and illiteracy are the main reasons.

Four million Negroes and 100,000 white persons who dwell in this Portuguese possession on Africa's West Coast draw their livelihood mostly from agriculture. But the output even of the vast coffee, sisal, maize and cotton plantations is limited by mountainous and desert terrain. Transportation is another great problem.

Angola is in the tropics. When the rains come, roads through the thick green countryside and forests turn to mud, frequently miring the tracks for months.

Nevertheless the Portuguese administration has been pressing forward with a development program that includes highway building and improvement of the railroad lines to the Belgian Congo and Northern Rhodesia. Modernization of the harbors at Luanda, Lobito Bay and Mossamedes, and hydroelectric power and irrigation projects are also in progress. However the scale is moderate because of limited funds.

Luanda Not Backward

Visitors to Luanda often come expecting to find some kind of ramshackle tropical town inhabited by dissolute whites and shiftless Africans. Such notions are soon dispelled.

Angola, like its sister Portuguese territory Mozambique on Africa's East Coast, is administered as a province of Portugal. Luanda, the capital, could easily be a place in the mother country.

Luanda, more than 300 years old, is a tidy town. Buildings of pink, white and yellow stucco with red tile roofs line the waterfront boulevards and the wide streets that climb the bluffs overlooking the sea. Sidewalk cafes are numerous and well patronized. The airport, fifteen minutes from the city, is one of the most modern in Africa.

There is an absence of urgency in the atmosphere, although the Luandans seem to drive their automobiles in a constant frenzy.

Away from Luanda, however, the picture changes drastically. Most Negroes live in mud or grass huts. Disease and undernourishment are widespread. Education is meager or nonexistent. Modest efforts to improve the situation are being made, but inadequate funds here too are a big obstacle.

Oil Provides Bright Spot

A bright spot in the country's economy developed last year with the discovery of oil in commercial quantities north of Luanda. Plans are under way for construction of a refinery here. There is also talk of expanding the present small-scale copper and manganese mining.

Meanwhile, the United States, chief customer for Angola's exports, has provided funds through the International Cooperation Administration for studies of possible hydoelectric and irrigation projects and of means of utilizing Angola's mineral resources.

In recent years a shortage of manual labor has handicapped the development of Angola's expanding economy. The Government still retains a policy of forced labor, and in many cases able-bodied African men, with no choice of employment, are compelled to work for long hours and at low pay on plantations. However, the administration has recently indicated that it intends to discontinue this policy.

Portugal's basic aim is to make both Angola and Mozambique integral parts of the mother country.

One of the ways of accomplishing this is the settlement of Portuguese peasants on farms in Angola. It is expected that by the end of this year more than 400 families will be established here in twelve villages.

Example to Africans Sought

Although the transplanted farmers are not permitted to employ Negro labor, even as domestic servants, it is hoped that by their use of comparatively advanced agricultural methods and Portuguese customs they will set an example to be followed by the backward Africans.

Angola's Negroes are regarded as citizens of Portugal but they do not enjoy full rights until they can pass certain tests and win official recognition as being of civilized status.

Preference in the resettlement of white Portuguese is given to tough stocky peasants with large families. This plan also is expected to help solve the problem of Portugal's expanding population at home.

A key resettlement project is at Cela, 4,000 feet up on a plateau southeast of Luanda. The land is irrigated by water from nearby mountains that rise to 7,000 feet.

Each family lives in a white stucco cottage and has fifteen irrigated acres for growing crops and several hundred acres for grazing stock. Each farmer also receives six head of cattle, either cows or oxen, three pigs, some poultry and some sheep.

Everything is provided by the Angola Government, which is spending nearly $3,000,000 on the plan.

August 5, 1956

PORTUGUESE BACK REIN OVER AFRICA

See Congo Crisis Justifying Strong Rule for Angola and Mozambique

By LEONARD INGALLS

Special to The New York Times.

LOURENCO MARQUES, Mozambique, July 18—The events in the Congo, the Portuguese in Mozambique say, have convinced them of two things.

One is that their policy of stern paternalism is the correct one for the 11,000,000 Africans under their control in Mozambique and Angola.

The other is that the Soviet Union is responsible for much of the trouble that has occurred in Africa in the last two years.

The main concern of the Portuguese is that the violence that has disturbed many neighboring areas, such as South Africa, Nyasaland, Northern Rhodesia and now the Congo, shall not happen in the Portuguese-controlled territories.

Additional troops from Portugal have been stationed in both Mozambique and Angola—just in case.

However, the Portuguese are basing their hopes principally on continuing to be a strict parent to what many of them describe as their African "children." They say that their aim is to bring about a gradual improvement in the lives of all the Africans and, not to concentrate on creating an African élite.

Some Portuguese believe the Belgians were guilty of incredible folly in granting independence to the Congo without first preparing the Africans there for the responsibility. Others speculate on whether the Belgians acted cynically, knowing that trouble would follow and expecting that they would have to resume control of the Congo.

Independence Not Planned

There is no question of preparing the Africans for eventual independence in Mozambique and Angola, since both territories are regarded as provinces of metropolitan Portugal and the Portuguese intend that this status shall continue.

Meanwhile, the Portuguese say that they are doing what they can with the limited means of their relatively poor country to provide Africans with education, health services, better housing and opportunities to advance.

They admit that most Africans benefit little from these efforts and say that Portugal could use financial assistance in her African areas from such wealthy countries as the United States.

The Portuguese say there has been no evidence of Communist activity in their areas, but because both Mozambique in the east and Angola in the west have long coastlines they fear that Communist agents could be landed to make trouble in each place.

Although they are unable to support their beliefs with any detailed evidence, the Portuguese strongly suspect that Soviet agents have been active in the Congo, South Africa and Nyasaland.

Portuguese Defend Policies

One official said: "Africa is vulnerable, and giving unprepared primitive Africans independence is giving the Russians a chance to step in. We hope the United States will recognize that what we are trying to do here is not unwise."

At the same time, the Portuguese are quietly critical of neighboring South Africa. There is no official color bar in Mozambique or Angola as there is in South Africa. Nor do the Portuguese sympathize with the South African policy of separate racial development. They feel that it can only lead to trouble.

"We are a multiracial country and we look forward to the day when all our Africans will be full Portuguese citizens," one Portuguese official said in explaining the aims of his Government.

July 19, 1960

Portuguese Africa Dreams of a Middle Way

Criticism grows over Lisbon's rule of 11,000,000 Africans, but Portugal hopes for a harmonious solution.

By BENJAMIN WELLES

LUANDA, Angola.

PORTUGUESE Africa has long withstood the winds of change but the winds now are rising to gale force throughout Africa. The veteran dictator-premier Dr. Antonio de Oliveira Salazar has repeatedly proclaimed to his nation and the world: "Stand firm! That is all that is needed for the storm to pass."

But the storm is not passing. Portugal's allies are reminding her with polite insistence that the slowest ship in the cold-war convoy is endangering the rest, and the Portuguese are beginning to understand and weigh the criticism showering in on them from Afro-Asian critics in the United Nations, from liberal opinion throughout the Western world and from such rebellious former officials of Salazar's regime as Maj. Gen. Humberto Delgado and former Colonial Inspector Henrique Galvão. These are the two men who directed the seizure of the liner Santa Maria a few weeks ago—with resultant outcries against Salazar and riots in Angola.

The leaders in Lisbon do not like criticism from outside, being sensitive Latins well aware of their shortcomings and disinclined to have others point them out. But their problem is to reconcile two seeming irreconcilables.

On the one hand they must modernize—but keep—their "overseas provinces" or former colonies, for without them Portugal would revert to a farming-fishing enclave in a Spanish-dominated Iberian peninsula. Yet they equally know that by continuing to rule (or as they say "civilize") 11,000,000 Africans in an anti-colonialist age they are open to rising criticisms in the rest of the world.

Until the last few months the Salazar regime maintained a "red tape" curtain around its overseas possessions, especially in Africa. It did not actually refuse foreign visitors, journalists and writers permission to visit the colonies; it achieved the same effect much more subtly by merely making it so complex and tenuous a process that most inevitably lost interest.

OF late, however, a new though somewhat hesitant sense of public relations has begun to affect high Portuguese circles. Salazar remains personally as shy and aloof as ever but some of his high aides have begun to repair Portugal's sorry international image. They have urged several journalists to visit Portuguese Africa, promising complete freedom to travel, investigate and interrogate.

"You will be perfectly free to write whatever you feel is bad about our provinces," they said. "We only ask in fairness that if you think there is anything good, too, you say so."

Over the coming years, as Afro-Asian pressures mount, there will be great and perhaps insurmountable pressure on Portugal to quit and turn Angola over to some form of "independence." That this will provoke a violent Algeria-type reaction from the 250,000 Angolans in the ruling class (including, it must be remembered, Negroes and mulattoes, too) is very likely. They do not want to be dispossessed. Yet it may not have to come to this: an intelligent middle way may still be found.

The Portuguese say that there is virtually no unrest in Angola. Their political enemies, such as Liberia, claim that conditions in Angola are "terrible." The truth lies in between, but from firsthand impressions gained in two weeks' travel about Angola if there is indeed discontent or if conditions are indeed "terrible" it is not easily apparent.

The chances of revolt in the foreseeable future seem remote—unless there is professionally organized and persistent outside agitation. This is obviously very likely in Africa today, but the tight Portuguese administrative rule over the country, the traditional easy interbreeding between whites, mulattoes and blacks plus the chronic apathy of the vast majority of illiterate Angolans would make renewed violence improbable—yet.

FOR THE FEW—A landscaped swimming pool is provided for European employes of Angola's railroad, at the inland city of Nova Lisboa.

PORTUGUESE AFRICA consists of three provinces: Angola (the biggest and richest), Mozambique and little Portuguese Guinea. Angola covers 481,000 square miles, has a 1,000-mile coast line and a population of 4,500,000 tribal Africans governed in varying degree by 250,000 Portuguese whites, mulattoes and blacks. It is the chief ornament of Portugal's imperial diadem.

With its sister province Mozambique, Angola absorbs about 23 per cent of Portugal's exports—captive markets that might not easily be replaced. Between them their exports of coffee, diamonds, sisal, mica and other minerals have long provided Portugal with the dollars she appropriates and distributes as she sees fit—seldom to the colonies' satisfaction.

Both these territories also provide native labor for surrounding white-ruled areas such as the Union of South Africa, the Rhodesias and until recently the Belgian Congo. But Angola is growing and needs native labor increasingly, so wages and conditions here are being improved as time goes by.

Angola, particularly, gives Portugal the status of an international power. It has good deep-water ports at Lobito and Luanda. Its Benguela railway is a vital link with the only transcontinental railroad in Africa; it emerges on the east coast at Portuguese Beira. For the landlocked Rhodesias, as for the once-flourishing Belgian Congo, Angola and Mozambique provide outlets.

BUT also psychologically these provinces give 9,000,000 homeland Portuguese a continuation of their historic Christianizing *mystique* which marked their finest hour. Without provinces, Portugal would see her better sons emigrate while the rest would sink back into sloth beside the rivers of time.

Up in Cabinda, a long-neglected Portuguese enclave now cradled in the embrace of two new African republics—the former French Congo and the former Belgian Congo—there is a dingy little town which has the curiously appropriate name of Dinge, pronounced "dinzh." It lies on a plain by the palm-fringed Atlantic and in its half-paved streets pigs and ducks and babies and motorcycles compete noisily for space.

In a local bar, where a tired refrigerator wheezes asthmatically through the heat, four men can generally be seen each afternoon throwing dice at a corner table There is nothing particularly striking about them. They are dressed in work-worn open shirts and pants. One wears a beret. Another clutches the dice in his fingertips and raps them sharply on the table before allowing them to drop.

They sip beer and murmur fitfully in Portuguese and the only reason that they are significant is that two of them are whites, one is a mulatto and the fourth is a Negro. Here in microcosm is a cross-section of Portuguese Angolan society. All four of these men are socially equal: equally "civilized under the law"; equally members of Angola's ruling class.

IT is a curious phenomenon about Portuguese Angola. If, as an African, you prefer tribal life, the Portuguese will make no effort to force you out of it. You will be officially protected by Portuguese law from exploitation and you will be controlled from cradle to grave by as highly organized a system of native administration as has possibly ever been devised. This will seek to insulate you against the two unpardonables here: political nonconformity and idleness.

On reaching eighteen you will acquire at a slight cost a *caderneta* in plastic with your photograph, fingerprints, work record and record of payment of head-tax (which is compulsory and comes to $7 per year). For not paying your head-tax you will be invited to contribute a month's work on roads or on some equally character-building enterprise.

The luxury of idleness under Portuguese law is permitted only to those already rich. So all others—the 250,000 "civilized" and 4,500,000 "noncivilized"—fall under the shadow of "vagrancy" unless proved to be usefully occupied. As an *indigena* or noncivilized native, you will be excused from further effort after six months' labor per year for a "civilized" employer who will be required by law to provide you with food, housing, clothes, medical care and the equivalent of $7 in cash for each month's work.

OF course, if you can prove that you are cultivating the land or otherwise assisting the economy that will be accepted. But if you should grow weary of toting that bale for the Belgian-controlled cotton monopoly and be so unwise as to strike (as happened recently at Malange, inland from Luanda) the hand of the law is merciless.

VIEWS OF PORTUGAL'S AFRICA—In Angola, Portuguese west coast province, a European directs farm workers.

Corporal punishment, the traditional flogging with a hippo-hide whip or beating of hands with the perforated wooden *palmatoria* have been banned by law now and the law is frequently observed, with prison the regulation punishment. But since the Portuguese have come to know in four centuries that the native finds prison a haven of security in an otherwise insecure world, prison terms can be and often are commuted into "light work." You find yourself back on the roads again.

Now for the other side of the coin. If you, as an African, wish to emerge from the "noncivilized" masses of the ruled into the civilized ranks of the rulers, the Portuguese will not only do nothing to prevent you; they will actually encourage you. All you will need to do is learn to speak, read and write Portuguese; to swear fealty to Portugal and to adopt a "Western" way of life.

YOU will now exchange your *caderneta* for a *Bilete de Identidade* which serves precisely the same function but has more prestige. You will put away all except one wife and if you are caught continuing the old atavistic concupiscence of tribal life it will henceforth be severely punished by Portuguese law. Your costs will suddenly go up, for now you will be paying your own health, legal, documentation and other fees. But in recompense you will be permitted to enter cinemas, restaurants and public conveniences barred to you before when you were "noncivilized." All this is yours provided you mind your manners, of course.

There is, needless to say, only one unspoken condition in this so-called process of "assimilation." That is that in joining the Portuguese ruling class the African helps perpetuate the system. Reluctance to do so—along with the fact that there are few schools for Africans and that the costs of becoming *assimilados* are high—may contribute to the fact that there are only 70,000 *assimilados* (half of them Negro, half mulatto) so far out of 4,500,000 Africans.

The Portuguese have always clung to the African coasts, only settling inland at the end of the last century. Itinerant traders, however, have moved about in the interior since the seventeenth century and they provide the authorities with an excellent information system. They settle down in jungle or bush towns, build one-or-two-story storehouses, equip them with shelves, counters, a variety of tinned foods, mirrors, candles, bolts of cloth, toilet goods, screws, nails and flour and trade them for native coconuts, bananas or palm oil.

Up country you can see Portuguese traders who have been there thirty or more years; some with mulatto or African lady friends, some married in the odor of sanctity. Generally keener than the slow-witted native, these traders prosper but they are a raffish breed—unkempt, uncouth, illiterate and harsh.

The Africans, generally, live in the bush or in the jungle, depending on the region in this huge land. Their houses are of plastered lath or bamboo with dirt floors and occasional appurtenances of civilization, such as an odd chair in front, where the patriarch can take his evening ease. Sanitation is rudimentary. Here and there a local African becomes a builder and quotes you about $1,000 for a three-room house of wood, stone and plaster.

IN outlying areas, especially among the handsome, bellicose *Cuanhamas* of the extreme south, men and women tend to disdain any clothing more than loin coverings. This goes down very well with visiting journalists but it slightly distresses American, Canadian and English Protestant missionaries who have been doing yeoman work in Angola for eighty years in fields of education, sanitation and deportment.

In the northern regions, African men universally wear shorts or pants, go sandaled or barefoot and while they may work in nothing from the waist up during the daytime heat, they are beginning to step out in style in the evenings, according to traders who are now stocking shirts worth three days' work and shoes worth a month's salary.

Let the spotlight shift now to a smart garden party in Luanda, the capital, with its skyscrapers, air-conditioned bars and handsome oceanside villas. Well-groomed women and white-uniformed officials are merry as deft Negro servants pass drinks. Suddenly there is a slight commotion and all eyes turn.

OUTSIDE the gate a Negro soldier is hustling away a slightly tipsy *indigena* who has come to peer at the guests. There is a brief scuffle and suddenly—in full view of the guests—a high-ranking Portuguese strides angrily over and violently slaps the tipsy native around the head and face. The Negro is hauled away and the official calmly resumes chatting. The Portuguese are not in the least perturbed and only the foreign guests are shocked or uneasy.

a monument salutes the "rebirth" of the land from its primitive state.

"We are not brutal," contended a young traveled and humane Portuguese. "We are only as strict with our blacks as we are with our children Africans are like big children and when they misbehave they must be punished. Don't you slap a puppy if he soils the carpet? Isn't he the better for it?"

Here in a breeze-swept palace with its ocean view, gardens, monkey-puzzle trees and Negro sentries, Governor General Alvaro Rodrigues da Silva Tavares seems quietly confident that Portuguese Angola will resist the changes now sweeping throughout Africa.

One gets the impression that, for Portugal, the débâcle in the adjoining former Belgian Congo has in some ways been a blessing in disguise. The Portuguese believe that Western "anti-colonialists" — the United States primarily—have now seen that precipitate freedom for unready Africans can be more dangerous than colonialism, however slowly it may be shedding its old cocoon.

TAVARES is a "new look" Portuguese administrator, a jurist in his late forties, perceptive and firm but not harsh. He comes from the multiracial Cape Verde Islands, and is himself of mixed ancestry. He has been here only one year and has gathered around him a small band of liberals of his own stamp.

It is these younger administrators who may save Portuguese Africa and stave off the subversion, racial hatreds and tribal wars that have been scarring the face of the adjoining former Belgian Congo. For nearly two years refugees—whites, mulattoes and blacks—have fled from the Congo to haven in Angola and the sight has borne in on the Portuguese here the need for a combination of iron nerves and progress.

Tavares and his aides know, however, that they are few: that down the centuries successive "liberal" governors in Portuguese Africa have been defeated by the ruthless, skilled opposition of local vested interests. Some are shadowy commercial interests who will brook no cut in their profits. Others are bureaucrats who mean to run their empire as they want to.

Yet a start on the right road seems to have been made. More investment capital is now flowing out here from Lisbon than is returning home in the form of profits and dividends for the first time in memory. Salazar's Second Six-Year Development Plan (1959-1964) has budgeted a $165,000,000 investment here for roads, railways, ports and airports, telecommunications, education, health and local improvements.

To the question of where is Portugal leading Angola, the Portuguese reply: "We are an empire without imperialism. This is unique in the world. Our goal is civilizing all races under our flag to live in harmony. If you want an example —look at Brazil."

Brazil, Portugal's onetime colony, is always evoked as the final solution for and justification of Portugal's colonial policies. The Portuguese are confident that there is no real hostility to them here among their African protégés. They feel sure that by a combination of police troops and social-economic development they can combat any subversion directed against them by their Afro-Asian enemies abetted by renegade Portuguese operating from Brazil, Venezuela, Guinea or from the Congo.

They are less certain, however, about the future influence of growing numbers of poor homeland Portuguese peasants who are being encouraged to settle in Angola and whose numbers have grown by more than 200,000 in the last ten years. They are tough, resourceful colonists, but they have an intense proprietary feeling toward the land and the same disdain for the "backward" native as is held by Algerian Europeans vis-a-vis the Arabs. This new influence in Angola may endanger interracial amity.

When asked how a total of about 350,000 "civilized" Portuguese in Africa can go on much longer administering about 11,000,000 "noncivilized" Africans, the Portuguese answer seems slightly Utopian.

Someday, somehow, they murmur, Angola, Mozambique and even little Portuguese Guinea will evolve into African replicas of Brazil, where men and women of every hue and race cherish the Portuguese language and culture and live in sun-drenched harmony.

March 19, 1961

ANGOLA CRUSHES ARMED UPRISING

3 Bands of Africans Attack Prisons in Move Linked to Santa Maria Seizure

By The Associated Press

LUANDA, Angola, Feb. 4 – The Government announced today the crushing of an armed uprising supposedly timed with the seizure of the liner Santa Maria. The uprising was the strongest evidence of African nationalism in this Portuguese West African territory so far.

[In Recife, Brazil, the Santa Maria was returned to her owners. Henrique M. Galvão, leader of the band that seized the liner, promised that his rebellion against the Portuguese regime would continue.]

A communiqué from the Governor General of Angola, Alvaro Silva Tavares, said three bands of armed Africans had attacked Luanda's police headquarters and the civil and military prisons during the night in an attempt to free prisoners.

"In this they failed," the communiqué said. "Those responsible are already under arrest and for the most part order is re-established."

Losses Not Explained

The Governor General said that both sides had suffered losses and that the attacking force was small. The attackers were reported armed with "native weapons and firearms."

Senhor Silva Tavares said that in the last few days he had received information from abroad that changes were threatened in Angola's public order and "this information insisted there was a plan for agitation from within to coincide with the attack on the liner Santa Maria."

If the attack had been planned to coincide with the Santa Maria's seizure, it was ill-timed. It came only hours after the surrender of the liner to Brazilian authorities.

Several days ago opponents of the Portuguese Premier, Antonio de Oliveira Salazar, said they had abandoned their plans for even a "bloodless revolution" here because they were shocked by the way the Santa Maria had been seized.

Most of these opponents—who operate underground and have no leader or program—are white. Thus the impetus for the African uprising could have come from across the border in the Congo.

White men do all but the most menial jobs here. Africans can achieve "assimilado" status and have all the privileges of whites, but only if they can find some way to get an education and learn white ways. Less then 1 per cent of the African population has managed to surmount the hurdle.

The rest live on farms in a tribal existence. Many must do months of road work in payment of taxes.

February 5, 1961

PORTUGAL DELAYS ANGOLA REFORMS

Officials Reacting Against U. S. Criticism—Drive to End Revolt Is Planned

By BENJAMIN WELLES

Special to The New York Times.

LISBON, Portugal, April 15 —The Portuguese Government has decided to postpone urgent political, social and educational reforms in Angola because of international criticism of its policies there, particularly by high United States officials.

Steps to liberalize Portuguese rule in Angola now, officials here believe, might be widely interpreted as yielding to the foreign pressures. In view of the angry mood of this nation, they say, this could jeopardize the life of the Government.

Dr. Antonio de Oliveira Salazar, the Premier-director, has just forestalled a move by a powerful bloc in the armed forces to force him into retirement and to replace him with a military junta more likely to suppress the uprising in Angola with vigor.

Dr. Salazar has abruptly dismissed Defense Minister Julio Botelho Moniz and several generals loyal to him. He is now reported planning to make the suppression of the fast-spreading rebellion in Angola a matter of national priority, and he is recasting his Cabinet with younger men of unquestioned loyalty to him.

Under his direction the Cabinet recently completed plans for a long set of reforms, the most important of which would end the much criticized "dual status" of the Angolan population and grant full political equality under Portuguese law to whites, mulattos and Negroes. The 4,800,000 population of Angola is divided into the preponderantly white "civilized" citizens, numbering about 250,000, and the African "tribal natives" who make up the remainder.

Other reforms now drafted but whose implementation will be postponed include an expanded program of primary and secondary schools for Africans, more school teachers, more transportation to take native children to and from school, and more university scholarships in Portugal for intelligent natives.

Sweeping social reforms have also been planned to enable trained Africans to rise to higher positions in Angola and to benefit from the political equality that awaits them when the former dual-status system ends.

High sources here say Dr. Salazar has decided to postpone these reforms until next October, after the election of 120 members of the National Assembly, or parliament, for four-year terms.

"These reforms admittedly should be introduced as quickly as possible," a liberal official here conceded yesterday, "but we are a sensitive people passing through a very difficult time. Outside criticism, particularly from our American friends, has had the reverse effect of making us rally even more strongly around Salazar in refusing to be pushed."

Portuguese officials are still angry over the decision of the Kennedy Administration to vote with the Soviet Union in the Security Council on March 15 for an inquiry on Angola.

"You can push the Portuguese only so far at any one time," said a foreign diplomat yesterday. "The new Administration has pushed them too far and too fast. Now they're beginning to back up."

The Portuguese Government has been advised by its friends in Washington that President Kennedy now has conceded in private conversations that he had no concept of the far-reaching results of the American vote.

Pro-U. S. Mood Fades

To an observer who has just come from Angola the situation here is sobering. Pro-American sentiment, which used to be taken virtually for granted, has disappeared overnight. Yet, with the generous Latin distinction between official disapproval of Government policy and personal friendliness toward officials called to carry out that policy, individual Portuguese have been inviting United States Ambassador and Mrs. Burke Elbrick and their staff to luncheons and dinners here as never before.

Nine killings were reported in tonight's edition of the Lisbon newspaper Diario Popular.

The Archbishop of Luanda, Angola's capital, and four bishops issued the appeal for improved social conditions in a pastoral letter.

April 16, 1961

The Bell Tolls in Angola

Behind a screen of censorship, Africans and whites in Portugal's 'overseas province' are waging a struggle bloodier than all that has happened in Kenya and the Congo.

By HAMILTON FISH ARMSTRONG

PORTUGAL'S "overseas province" of Angola, a land nearly twice the size of Texas, presents a problem at least as complex as the one the Belgians and, afterward, the United Nations have faced in the Congo, and the manifestations of it have already been more bloody than all that happened in the Congo and in Kenya during Mau-Mau days put together.

Angola has year by year been giving the anemic Portuguese economy indispensable infusions of tropical strength. Along with Portugal's other African territories, Mozambique and Portuguese Guinea, it also has given the Portuguese people, uneasy after thirty years of dictatorship, a sense of continuing mission in the world, a relic of the departed grandeur of nearly five centuries. Today Portugal's hold on Angola is slipping. Indeed, by any long-term measurement, her position there seems quite desperate.

Since March 15, a large triangular slice of Angola—its base along the Congo frontier and its apex reaching 200 miles south, uncomfortably close to the capital city of Luanda—has come almost completely into the hands of African revolutionaries. Portuguese plantation owners, farmers and village traders have been massacred or evacuated to Luanda by the planeload. Bands of terrorists, glassy-eyed from marijuana, confident that witch-doctor potions make them immune to the white man's bullets, come silently into villages and farms, swinging their long bush knives, the curved *catanas*.

In return, Army planes are strafing African villages, and civilians have been armed not only for defense but for revenge. Together they have disposed of at least five Africans for every Portuguese victim.

The civilians act in vigilante groups with little official restraint. On the edges of the rebel-held area, and in the *muceques*, the native district where three-quarters of Luanda's 200,000 inhabitants live, reprisals are savage. Suspicion is law, and where specific grounds for suspicion are lacking hatred and chance take their place.

Arrests are also beginning in parts of the country far removed from the rebellious Bakongo and Kimbundu tribes. They are considered a necessary precaution; but perhaps they are a psychological error, since they spread fear and unrest among tribes that for many years have been causing little trouble.

THUS two forces are in reckless collision—one entrenched, immensely stubborn, courageous, prepared to be cruel to whatever point is necessary to protect its heritage, living blindly on from the nineteenth century into the twentieth; the other swarming out of the bush, lying in wait to kill, savagely reckless of lives whether white or black, intoxicated by its first successes, sure of its tomorrow.

The scattered news items allowed to trickle out of Angola have given little warning of the ferocity, scope and probable consequences of this conflict. Even so, the world will very soon find it placed high on its agenda of the most difficult international problems.

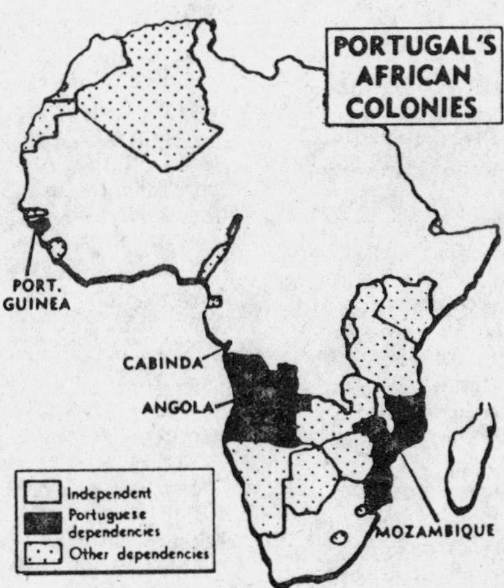

The immediate question is whether the hastily reinforced troops in Angola—they now number about 15,000, perhaps half of them African contingents that would not be used in forward operations—can recover the rebel-held area and pacify it. If so, how soon? And at what cost?

Even more important in the long run is the question of what the effect of the effort will be on the stated policy of ultimate assimilation that has been the basis of Portugal's hopes for the future, and the moral and political justification for the position she has taken before anti-colonialist world opinion. It is the probable answer to this last question that forces the visitor to Angola to view Portugal's future there so pessimistically.

Anything that happens in Angola outside the range of one's own eyesight is hard to verify. The number of Portuguese so far murdered has not been confirmed, but officials do not deny that it is more than 600. The refugees being cared for by the Red Cross in makeshift shelters in Luanda number four or five thousand, including some Africans. The bags and bundles of women and children being sent at least temporarily to Portugal line the counters in the airport; the men are kept behind.

In the absence of coherent and credible official information, and with the newspapers censored, every story in Angola has at least two versions. There was no dispute, for instance, that a band of refugees from a Red Cross camp marched to the *muceques*, set fire to the thatched mud huts and started shooting the occupants as they tumbled out.

By one account, given me by a Red Cross official who sincerely believed it, the police were alerted in time to prevent a massacre, arrest the attackers and put them in jail; by another account—this from three neutral Europeans who happened to be near the scene—the police tarried until after several dozen Africans of both sexes and all ages had been shot down.

UCUA is a small town on the main road out of Luanda leading east and north; travelers used often to stop there for a meal. At noon, one recent day, when the Portuguese shopkeepers had gone home for lunch and a siesta, a band of about 200 Africans surrounded the town and went from house to house, killing white families with their knives. The first reports were that only a dozen of the forty Portuguese in Ucua escaped; the Governor-General told me that he thought only a dozen had been killed. In any event, the town remained in the hands of the rebels. It still is, though it is only about fifty miles from the capital.

WHAT makes the long-term outlook for Portugal in Angola seem so desperate is that no solution can be imagined at present, or indeed is contemplated, except one obtained by force. No one knows of any responsible leaders with the rebel bands—not even a group of semi-educated Africans such as existed in Leopoldville and other towns of the Belgian Congo before independence. With whom, then, negotiate?

At least two revolutionary organizations exist outside Angola. One, the *União das Populações de Angola*, or U. P. A., headed by Angolan-born Holden Roberto, has its headquarters in exile in Leopoldville. It is considered the more moderate. Its leaders probably recognize that immediate independence would produce chaos worse than that in the Congo, and so might consider some sort of intermediate international regime advisable. But they are more and more being outbid in claims and promises by the group called FRAIN, which is based in Conakry, the capital of Guinea. This is a radical front dominated by Communist elements.

PORTUGUESE authorities accuse both groups of smuggling in agents to mastermind the rebellion. As evidence, they cite their capture of Ghanaian nationals fighting with the rebel bands. They claim that as the outside organizations grow in size they contain a smaller and smaller number of native Angolans, and become more and more an instrument of the international Communist revolution. They say they will never have any dealings with them whatsoever.

So far, Portuguese troops have been largely inactive. Until the rains stop—probably about the end of this month—roads are impassable and large-scale operations out of the question. Officials express confidence that with dry weather the troops can move in, exterminate the terrorist bands and pacify the population rapidly.

To an outsider, this seems optimistic. There are stretches

WORK—Angolan women pour salt into barges for transport. The Portuguese system of forced labor has been a principal cause of unrest.

of rain forest that are almost impenetrable away from the main roads; other areas are mountainous, or covered with grass higher than a man's head; the rest is bush, much of it trackless. Plantations and villages are scattered, without any means of rapid communication (though radio equipment is being imported by the authorities). It is a country made for effective guerrilla defense.

FAR more than a military scouring of the bush is involved. The Dembos area, part of the territory in rebel hands, produces 10 per cent of the coffee output of Angola—and coffee is the land's chief crop. With *bandoleiros* roaming about, killing at random, the coffee crop obviously cannot be gathered. The harvest begins in June and lasts until early August. Time, therefore, is anxiously short.

Nor is the prospective loss limited to districts where the rebels are in effective control. The German owner of an outside plantation told me that his workers, frightened by rumors from the north and excited by the drums in the night, had simply melted away into the bush. Of the hundred hands needed to work the plantation only a dozen remained, so he had come down to the coast to wait and see what happens.

Unless what happens is that the Portuguese troops contain the rebel bands within their present limits, and subdue them there within a few weeks, there will be little or no coffee harvested on much more than 10 per cent of the plantations. Coffee exports bring in about 40 per cent of Angola's foreign exchange. It is said that 50,000 tons of coffee from previous harvests remain in storage. Even so, the loss of a considerable portion of a crop that is worth twice as much as the next Angolan product, diamonds, and as much as all the other exports put together, would be a crippling blow.

NOR would it hit the Angolan economy alone. Angola is Portugal's milch cow. The effects of Angolan bankruptcy on the tightly controlled economy of the Portuguese corporate state might be enough to tumble down Dr. Salazar's dictatorship. The fall of one Iberian dictator could hardly fail to affect the position of the other, next door in Spain.

Even if what happens is the best that the Portuguese authorities dare hope—a clean-up of the rebels within the next few weeks—what will be the psychological results? What will be left of the pretense of interracial amity and the dream of many benevolent Portuguese that Angola might become another Brazil, a genuine amalgam of black and white?

It is true that, after almost 500 years of rule, the Portuguese have produced only about 50,000 mulattoes and have brought only some 30,000 full-blooded Africans to a degree of education and social progress that in Portuguese eyes justifies their being considered "civilized" and given Portuguese citizenship—this in a population of about 4,500,000.

Nevertheless, it is indisputable that both in theory and practice the Portuguese (particularly the older settlers) have shown themselves singularly free from color prejudice. The mulattoes in Angola carry no social stigma of any sort and, provided the white or partially white parent has taken the trouble to legitimize them (as usually happens), they have all the rights of citizenship—which for everyone, in Angola as in Portugal, are strictly limited.

BUT however the Portuguese have felt in the past about their black brothers, one wonders whether they can ever again regain enough confidence to live among them with the old sense of security. Two servants who had been in the household of a Portuguese planter since childhood—one for fifteen years, the other for twenty—were captured after they had cut him to pieces.

"Wasn't he a good master?" they were asked.

"Yes, he was a good master."

"Then why did you kill him?"

"It had to be."

On the other side, what will be the feelings of the tribes? After being bombed, hunted, slaughtered more or less indiscriminately and in the end defeated (supposing that is the result), will they resume their peaceful pursuits, submit as in the past to being recruited for compulsory labor and, having "learned their lesson"—a favorite Portuguese phrase—wait patiently for later generations to attain slowly, slowly, the education and economic and political advantages which will blend them all—not just a tiny fraction, but all—into a racially homogeneous society?

Tribes have revolted in different parts of Angola several times in the past fifty years. The fact that these risings were successfully suppressed may give the Portuguese false confidence today, for the conditions now are entirely different.

The system of forced labor, with its abuses and hardships, was this time as always a principal cause of tribal unrest; but the present revolt is taking place in a new context. Behind it rises the full surge of the African independence movement, sweeping the continent, overwhelming one colony after another. The Congo next door no longer is controlled tightly by Belgian authorities; it is wallowing in misery and chaos—but what does that matter in African eyes? It is

ON GUARD—Portugal's tanks and armored cars rumble through Luanda, capital of embattled Angola.

free. Communist agents operating out of Conakry and Accra provide encouragement, money and supporting propaganda. The dictatorial regime in Portugal is on the defensive after two recent attempted coups against it.

ABOVE all, the world now has its eyes on the revolutionaries, watching their struggle, considering the conditions out of which it arises, discussing it in the United Nations.

In these circumstances, the Portuguese tend naturally enough, though quite incorrectly, to attribute their troubles in Angola mainly to outside interference. They are particularly indignant with the United States because of Ambassador Stevenson's vote in the Security Council on March 15 in favor of an inquiry into the racial conflict there. A mob promptly threw Consul William Gibson's car into the Luanda harbor, and the next day broke the windows of the Evangelical Mission church.

Several African pastors and catechists trained by American Protestant missionaries have been killed, many have been imprisoned, others have seen their schools closed and their chapels burned.

The Portuguese complain bitterly that if the United States was going to take what they consider an unfriendly stand against a NATO ally it should have thrashed out all aspects of the problem with them well in advance, heard their counter-arguments and tried to work out some plan that might have minimized the dangers ahead.

THEY cannot claim that the widespread raids staged by the terrorists in northern Angola at dawn on March 15 were the result of the American vote later the same day in the United Nations; but they point out that the operation had clearly been designed to coincide with that week's discussion of Angola in New York. They also emphasize that the February riots in Luanda were planned in connection with Capt. Henrique Malta Galvão's seizure of the Santa Maria and were intended to spark a general rising in his favor; if that was the case, however, the affair was stage-set and managed both at home and abroad by Portuguese, with no foreign instigation required.

If anything, the American vote in the United Nations hardened Dr. Salazar's determination to suppress the rebellion in Angola by force unmixed with conciliatory gestures or reforms. As a high official said to me in Luanda (and his sentiments were echoed by others both there and in Nova Lisboa):

"Dr. Salazar has stated that everything about Angola can be discussed except the fact that it is, and always will be, part of Portugal. But at this juncture concessions would seem a sign of weakness. The first duty is to restore order. No outside pressure, certainly not the alliance [*sic*] of the United States and the Soviet Union, will stop us. Afterward, we can take up the various administrative changes that we have been thinking of for some time."

This confident statement hardly reflects the prevalent state of mind among the Portuguese in Angola. They fluctuate between anger and fear, hatred and remorse, determination and something like despair. They see a fierce struggle ahead and are resolved to wage it stubbornly. As one official said: "We have not the slightest intention of quitting as the Belgians did in the Congo."

Yet they cannot help asking themselves (and sometimes, very obliquely, even a visitor) what they will gain by striking at the formless, elusive and endlessly proliferating hostile mass that lurks out there in the tall grass and the jungle. They do not know precisely what malevolent forces nourish it; and they misinterpret, as being specifically hostile to them, what is simply a world-wide realization that—come what may in Angola or any other African territory—the colonial era is done for.

Many of the Portuguese in Angola were born there; some families have been Angolan for generations, a few, it is said, for four or five. Their position is desperate, for like the Afrikaaners in South Africa they have "nowhere to go." Portugal would not encourage them to return en masse. It is a cramped and crowded country, only a tiny fraction the size of Angola, affording a meagre enough living for most of its present population.

The Lisbon Government refuses to admit that the United Nations has a right to concern itself with race relations in Angola. Its thesis is that Angola is not a colony, subject to an accounting in accordance with the principles concerning dependent peoples enunciated in the U. N. Charter, but an integral part of Portugal.

THIS is, of course, a subterfuge, and one fact is enough to prove it. If a resident of Angola wants to change Angolan escudos for Portuguese escudos, he is permitted to do so only up to a limit of 1,000 escudos ($35) per month. If he needs to change more than that, he must (with certain exceptions) go to the black market, where he will lose up to 25 per cent on the transaction.

A considerable number of Angolan Portuguese have come to think that the only chance of securing fairer economic treatment and an efficient administration responsive to local needs is to win provincial autonomy or outright independence. Many local officials are men of character and ability, but they are in tight leash to Lisbon. They reportedly have urged that an elected council be set up to advise the Governor-General; if so, Dr. Salazar said no.

Frustration has been endemic in Luanda for so long that it has produced not only revolutionaries but fanatics. Some of those talking about independence go so far as to assert that the first necessary step is to kill all educated Africans (a pitifully small number) and, of course, expel the missionaries who have so mischievously taught them to read, write and think. As one industrialist said to me in justification: "After all, this is white man's country"—something of an exaggeration in view of the fact that whites and mulattoes together make up about 4 per cent of the population.

Another current of thought favors the formation of a confederation with neighboring territories where the white population feels itself in similar jeopardy. The idea of "a white bulwark against the black tide," built up of Angola, Mozambique, the Rhodesias, the Union of South Africa (including, of course, South West Africa) and, perhaps, Katanga, represents a strange turnabout for a people which has preached and, to some extent, practiced racial integration. That anyone even daydreams of joining with the land of apartheid shows how deeply the fears engendered by the present rebellion have eaten into the old Portuguese racial concepts.

Such schemes are whimsical, and in any case they come too late. Too late, too, is Dr. Salazar's rumored project of giving Angola and Portugal's other African territories some sort of commonwealth status and then asking Portuguese-speaking Brazil to join them in a "Lusitanian confederation."

Too late because, whether Angola is "forever Portugal," or autonomous, or independent or part of some larger grouping, whatever government attempts to rule it will have to deal with the Africans.

If this were a rational world and there were rational antagonists in Angola, the United Nations would now come forward with a plan for "holding the ring" while Portugal worked to get the Angolan Africans ready for self-government, and in the process endeavored to restore a basis for future racial cooperation.

The technical, economic, financial and educational aid which this or some other Portuguese Government would need in order to carry out an agreed international program over a period of, say, ten years would be very great. But it would cost a fraction of what the world will pay not just in money and effort, but in tension and risk of war if the U. N. must intervene later to rescue Angola from a chaos worse than was found in the Congo.

But even if the U. N. could agree to make constructive proposals, the Portuguese are not in any mood to listen to them; and even if they did, the African rebels would not be willing to wait while a plan for their benefit could mature. Both are under a compulsion at present to kill and be killed.

In the unlikely event that a stalemate comes and the antagonists weaken, the United States should be ready with proposals for international action, regardless of the inevitable Soviet opposition, and with offers to help largely in underwriting it. This course would be infinitely cheaper and less risky than to undertake a salvage operation in the ruins left by a savage racial war.

May 21, 1961

PORTUGAL DRAFTS AFRICAN REFORMS

Acts to Give Legal Equality to All in 3 Territories

By BENJAMIN WELLES
Special to The New York Times.

LISBON, July 26—The Portuguese Government is preparing to grant constitutional equality with whites to 10,000,000 Africans in the three Portuguese African provinces of Angola, Mozambique and Portuguese Guinea.

Final touches are being put on a new law to take effect in the coming three or four months, perhaps sooner, if Portuguese military forces succeed in quelling the Angolan revolt before then.

This measure, plus other reforms now being introduced, will give rebellion-torn Angola and the other Portuguese territories more self-determination than they have ever had in the five centuries of Portuguese rule, officials here said.

The reforms are being introduced cautiously despite the four-month-old rebellion against Portuguese rule in northern Angola and new trouble in Portuguese Guinea.

Two nights ago, a band of 200 armed Africans tried to invade Portuguese Guinea from Senegal. According to Portuguese sources, they were easily driven off.

A similar attack from Senegal occurred last Friday, in which six of the invaders were reported killed and four Portuguese wounded, one of them seriously. Senegal has broken off diplomatic relations with Portugal and the Portuguese are preparing against further efforts to foment "rebellion."

The constitutional reform being prepared throughout Portuguese Africa will consist of eliminating the "indigenato" system, which was introduced in the Nineteen Twenties to protect the Africans from exploitation. This system placed the overwhelming majority of Africans under strict state paternalism, but it also denied them nearly all civil rights.

When the reform takes effect, there will be no further legal distinction in Angola between the ruling minority of 250,000 "civilized" whites, mulattoes and Africans and the 4,500,000 "noncivilized" tribal Africans. The same will apply in the two other Portuguese African provinces.

In Angola, which has been wracked since March 15 by an African rebellion that has cost an estimated total of 1,500 casualties among Portuguese whites and loyal Africans, all inhabitants will henceforth enjoy the same constitutional rights to vote or hold public office.

These will be conferred on the basis of educational standards, as is the case now in metropolitan Portugal and in various other overseas territories. No longer will 95 per cent of the Angolan Africans be automatically disfranchized because they are legally "noncivilized."

14 Reforms Introduced

Africans who learn to read and write Portuguese and who can pay 200 escudos ($7) a year in taxes will be "voting citizens." The same education qualifications will be required for those who apply for administrative positions as for whites or mulattoes.

The Portuguese Government of Premier Antonio de Oliveira Salazar has introduced fourteen administrative reforms into the overseas territories in the last eighteen months, officials here reported.

The most important reform to date, they said, has been the granting of far wider local home rule by permitting communities of 500 or more inhabitants to form municipal councils and elect theirofficials. The officials, formerly were appointed by the government.

The impending enfranchisement of the Africans, the increased local self-rule and the educational reforms are part of a broad colonial reform program.

"Carry these reforms to their logical conclusion and you arrive at self-determination both in Angola and in our other African possessions," a ranking Portuguese authority commented.

"Self-determination is an unpopular word in Portugal at the moment but that's precisely what it is," he added. "Remember, we are doing this of our own accord and not under pressure either from our friends or our enemies."

The reforms introduced into Angola by the Portuguese Government in the last eighteen months cover the following: collective bargaining on wages and work conditions, insurance and industrial hygiene, labor inspection, the prohibition of forced cultivation by Africans and the abolition of penalties for violation by Africans of labor contracts.

Others cited by Portuguese officials include the legal recognition of a weekly rest day, the prohibition of discrimination in employment because of race or color, minimum working age legislation, greater local self-government, the formation of technical assistance cooperatives, improved health and social welfare services and an accelerated two-year industrial capital investment program.

July 27, 1961

Portuguese Army Is Digging In For Long War on Angola Rebels

Lisbon Spending $1,700,000 a Week to Press Drive on Ragged Insurgents

By HENRY TANNER
Special to The New York Times.

LUANDA, Angola, Aug. 15—About a mile from the small town of N'gage, there are a new mile-long runway of red earth in desolate African country, a barbed-wire enclosure protected by sandbags and wooden watchtowers that guard six small planes.

The site is one of the Portuguese Army's principal bases in its war against the insurrection of the Bakongo tribe. The rebellion swept the northern part of Angola last spring.

From N'gage Portuguese planes fly up to the border of the former Belgian Congo in pursuit of elusive rebel bands and in support of army columns that launched a general offensive against the rebels two weeks ago.

The army is settling down for a long campaign. The base commander will soon move from a shack of corrugated iron that now serves as his headquarters to a permanent terminal building with a regular control tower.

Large hangars and living quarters are under construction. Huge yellow bulldozers trailed by clouds of red sand are changing the African landscape in preparation for concrete runways and for roads.

The military campaign against the Angola rebels is costing the Portuguese the equivalent of about $1,700,000 a week. Over a period of a year this is twice the amount of dollars that Angola's coffee crop brought in annually before rebels burned most of the plantations. Coffee is the largest Angola crop and Portugal's biggest dollar earner.

The commander of Portuguese ground forces in the northern part of Angola has made his headquarters at N'gage. His command area spreads over 50,000 square kilometers (19,300 square miles) of partly virgin African territory.

The colonel is optimistic. He

and his troops came to Angola about three months after the insurgents first attacked on March 15 and burned plantations and killed hundreds of Europeans.

"Until two weeks ago we were on the defensive," he said. "Now we are attacking everywhere."

Rebels formerly attacked in groups up to 1,000 or 2,000 strong. Now they are split up into small bands. They rarely attack and are limiting their actions to sporadic ambushes.

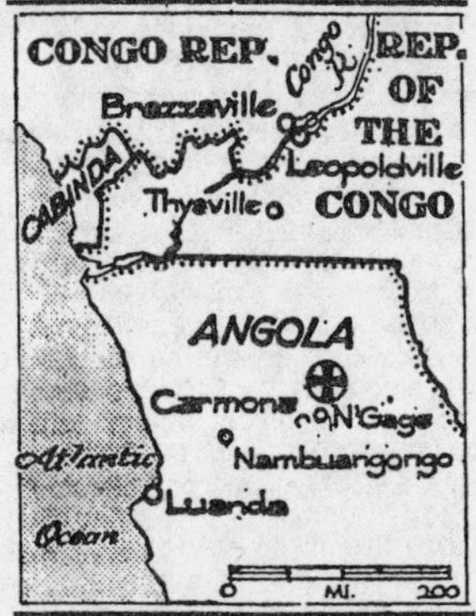

The New York Times Aug. 17, 1961

The Portuguese forces in Angola operate from a base a mile from N'Gage (cross).

Whenever the army is able to flush them out, the rebels suffer heavy losses, the colonel said. Yesterday alone the rebels lost more than 100 men in various actions. The Portuguese losses were two killed and fourteen wounded.

Town Is Recaptured

Last week the Portuguese Army recaptured the town of Nambuangogo, west of here, in the largest military operation to date. The rebels had hoped to proclaim Nambuangongo their capital. Its loss is a severe military and psychological blow for them.

The colonel is pleased with his operations and confident of the overwhelming power of a modern army facing a ragged, primitive enemy.

This is the dry season. In six weeks or so the rains will start. From sometime in December until about April, most of the roads in this part of the country will become impassable.

The army is getting ready for difficult months. It is building airstrips near towns that have never seen a plane. Elsewhere, existing airfields that are too remote and too exposed have been abandoned and are being rebuilt on the edge of towns.

The high command obviously expects a period when its garrison and the remaining islands of the Portuguese population will have to be supplied by air.

August 17, 1961

Angola Revolt Poses Questions As to Who Is Rebelling and Why

Portuguese Still Puzzled About Origins of Uprising, Its Size and Goals—Discipline of Insurgents Noted

By HENRY TANNER

Special to The New York Times.

LUANDA, Angola, Aug. 27—One of the most striking features of the anti-Portuguese insurrection in northern Angola is that its origins and character are still largely a mystery.

Angola may become another Algeria or another Congo, but neither Portuguese officials nor foreign observers have been able to form any precise notions about the size and composition of the rebel force, its goals, or the men who lead it.

The rebellion started at 2 A. M. March 15. The first shots were fired at a police car in the small town of São Salvador, about forty miles south of the border of the former Belgian Congo. São Salvador is the birthplace of Holden Roberto, acknowledged leader of the rebellion, who makes his headquarters in Leopoldville.

Between 5 and 6 o'clock that same morning, the rebels struck simultaneously at about forty points all over the coffee country of northern Angola, almost as far south as Luanda, the capital, which is about 400 miles from the border.

During that first night the rebels killed 250 to 300 Portuguese, including many women and children, according to Portuguese reports. Many Africans living on plantations that were attacked also were killed.

Foreign observers believe that the rebels hoped to frighten the Portuguese into a mass exodus similar to that of the Belgians in the Congo last year. When the Portuguese struck back after the first night of terror, the rebels changed their tactics and started large-scale destruction as a form of economic warfare, observers believe.

Portuguese at a Loss

Simultaneous attacks all over the vast territory obviously required effective coordination and advance planning. Yet Portuguese officers are still at a loss to say how the coordination was achieved. No means of effective communications other than drums and brush fires have been found, although the officers suspect that the rebels had "a few radios" that they had stolen from local administrators.

Portuguese pilots during the early days of the rebellion sighted rebel units operating in military formations, some wearing red or blue uniform-type clothing.

Yet no military experts and especially no foreign officers have been captured, according to the Portuguese. Captured weapons are homemade muzzle-loaders, heavy wooden clubs and machetes.

The greatest mystery is the size of the rebel force. After five months of contact with the enemy, the Portuguese Army still has only the vaguest estimates. There might be "about 20,000" rebel fighters, a high-ranking officer says. But then he adds that he might as easily have said 8,000 or 50,000.

The Portuguese call the rebellion "Communist-inspired." They accuse Ghana and Guinea and cite inflammatory broadcasts in Portuguese by the Moscow, Prague and Peiping radios.

But the army command concedes that no tangible proof of foreign intervention has been found so far beyond the fact that a number of captured rebels had checks made out on a bank in Leopoldville.

Portuguese and neutral observers agree that the organizers of the uprising came to Angola from the Congo and that the Bakongo tribe, which straddles the border, is playing a dominant role in the rebellion.

The testimony of the few prisoners that have been taken appears to establish Mr. Roberto as the single most powerful figure behind the rebellion. Mr. Roberto belongs to the Bakongo tribe and is head of a movement called the Union of Angolan Populations.

The name of Patrice Lumumba, the slain former Premier of the Congo, also has cropped up in prisoners' testimony and pamphlets. Some prisoners believed Lumumba was alive and asserted that they were fighting for an African movement of which he was the leader, Portuguese officers say.

The emergence of a "Lumumba cult" among the rebels; the popularity enjoyed in northern Angola by the Congolese President, Joseph Kasavubu, "King of the Bakongo," and the fact that the rebellion was directed from Congolese soil all point to "African nationalism" as a major source of the rebellion. The rise to independence of the neighboring Congo undoubtedly had key importance.

But persons who have lived among them say that the Angolan Africans have little or no awareness of political concepts such as "nationalism" and "independence." Very few of them have sufficient education to understand these terms.

Instead, these observers believe that economic and psychological factors were prime causes of the rebellion—resentment over bad working conditions on coffee plantations, low wages, lack of education, ill treatment by despotic local administrators and especially abuses in the system of "contract labor" to which African workers on coffee plantations are subject.

The system of "contract labor" is part of the "indigina law," which divides the population of Angola into two categories: "civilized" and "non-civilized."

Whites, mulattoes and about 30,000 "assimilated" Africans who have fulfilled strict requirements as to education, income and so forth are "civilized." All others, virtually all of the territory's 4,500,000 Africans, are "noncivilized," or "indigina."

Under the law each indigina has to work a minimum of six months a year. He may satisfy the requirement on land that was given to him for personal use and cultivation and on which he has to produce a minimum crop specified by the state.

If he meets the requirement, he is entitled to a certificate from a local administrator stating that he has done the required work on his own land. If he is not eligible for the certificate, he has to work for someone else—for a coffee or cotton planter, or any other employer hiring Africans on contract.

Theoretically an African can refuse a contract. But practically he seldom has that freedom. There is usually only one bidder for a contract. The employer makes his bid through a local administrator, an all powerful "chief of post," who then provides the number of laborers required.

On the basis of this law Portugal has been accused in the United Nations and elsewhere of practicing "forced labor," a charge that the Portuguese indignantly reject.

August 29, 1961

ANGOLANS ASSAIL LISBON'S POLICIES

Business Men Protest Curbs on Territory's Progress

By HENRY TANNER

Special to The New York Times.

LUANDA, Angola, Aug. 28—Portuguese business men and others in Angola are bitterly critical of what they call the Lisbon Government's past "policy of neglect" toward this African territory.

They charge that economic interests dominated by a few families in Portugal are seeking to exploit Angola to the limit and have deliberately obstructed the territory's economic and educational development.

They say that living standards have been kept low by a refusal to permit the establishment of local industries. All this, critics contend, has contributed directly to the African rebellion in the north. The outbreak of terrorism and raiding, which began last winter, has taken the lives of many white settlers and Africans.

The overwhelming majority of Africans in Angola live on a subsistence level. Only a few work in industry or business, usually as unskilled laborers.

The critics also note that only thirteen Africans were graduated from high schools last year. But they add that the Government's record was not much better with respect to the Portuguese settlers; the number of white high school graduates was 190.

They complain that Angola still has no university, though visiting professors are being brought in for special courses.

Some charge that high school teachers have been instructed to fail students in final examinations so that the number of white and Afrlican Angolans who would have a right to go to Portugal on university fellowships would be kept at a minimum.

Feelings of this kind are so strong here that highly respected, prominent citizens predict a "rebellion" by the white population of Angola unless Portugal makes sweeping reforms in the near future.

They believe there is growing awareness of this danger among Government officials in Lisbon. They hope that the shock of the African rebellion and the subsequent need to send 20,000 soldiers to Angola have jolted the Portuguese leaders and awakened them to the needs of Angola.

Election Poses Test

In a campaign spearheaded editorially by the influential newspaper Provincia de Angola, local citizens have been insisting that in the coming election for the National Assembly in Lisbon, seats representing Angola should be given to men who live here and know local problems. The election is scheduled for October. Angola has had three seats in the Assembly. It will have seven in the future.

In the past the practice has been to name retired generals and high-ranking officials living in Portugal to the seats for Angola. Under Portugal's authoritarian system a candidate of the ruling party is certain of election.

One of the principal complaints of local business men is that development of new industry in Angola requires concessions from Lisbon. Business sources here say such applications frequently have been rejected.

Thus Angola has no textile industry, even though cotton is one of the major crops. The cotton goes to Portugal and is returned in the form of finished goods. The textile industry has been given high priority in the development plans of many African countries because it can easily absorb relatively large amounts of untrained labor.

A series of reforms announced by Lisbon earlier this week appears to have general approval here, provided the reforms are followed by a large-scale effort to develop the local economy.

The main feature of the announced reforms is that the 4,500,000 Angolan Africans will be given, at least in theory, constitutional equality with the white Portuguese settlers.

The Portuguese Overseas Minister, Dr. Adriano Moreira, also promised increased economic autonomy for Angola. He announced that the coffee and cotton boards that regulate production and exports of these crops would move their headquarters from Lisbon to Luanda.

Except for fisheries, Angola has no food-processing industries and there is no dairy industry.

Two breweries, some cement plants and a cigarette industry have been introduced in recent years. This is a welcome but inadequate beginning in the Angolans' opinion.

Angolan business men are also critical of the fact that the currency is not interchangeable with that of mainland Portugal. It can be bought at a discount in Lisbon, despite the fact Angola, with its $45,000,000 annual coffee crop, has been a major hard-currency earner and covers a large part of Portugal's dollar deficit.

An importer must apply to the Exchange Council for a license and foreign currency. His application must be accompanied by a deposit, in local currency, of an amount equal to the price of the proposed import. The deposit remains tied up while the application is under study, which may be for a period of several months.

Following complaints the required deposit was reduced recently to 50 per cent of the price of the import.

September 3, 1961

Algerians Training Angolan Guerrillas

By LLOYD GARRISON

Special to The New York Times.

UNITED NATIONS, N. Y., Dec. 17 — A contingent of African rebels from Portuguese Angola is being trained in guerrilla warfare by Algerian nationalists at camps in Tunisia.

The Algerian National Liberation Front began training forty Angolans three months ago. Twenty-five of the Angolans are reported on their way back to Angola, accompanied by six Algerian advisers.

According to an Algerian source at the United Nations, the six advisers will help the rebels to organize militarily and politically. The source said the advisers would particularly stress the importance of political indoctrination along the lines of the Algerian rebels' slogan, "The leaflet precedes the bullet." More advisers may follow, the source said.

The disclosure of the Algerian rebels' role is the first evidence that the Angolans are getting organized outside support in their resistance to Portuguese rule. It is also an indication that the Angolan rebellion, which erupted last March, has not been quelled despite recent statements by the Portuguese.

All the Angolans being trained by the Algerians are members of the Union of Angolan Peoples, led by Holden Roberto, with headquarters in Leopoldville, the Congo.

The Angolan leader is in New York to attend the forthcoming debate on Angola in the United Nations.

The Angolans' training is said to have included experience with Algerian rebel forces battling the French in Algeria.

These and other developments are expected to be discussed by Mr. Roberto at a news conference tomorrow morning.

The Algerians are expected to train sixty other Angolans soon, with a goal of producing a core of 100 men qualified to give leadership and instruction to rebel cadrés within the Portuguese territory.

Aid Offered by Tunis

The Algerians have offered to supply arms to the Angolans. Similar offers of assistance have been made by Tunisia, and several undisclosed African states.

According to reliable sources, a small but undetermined amount or arms has already reached Angolan rebels in the northernmost part of the territory bordering the Congo.

What has been described as a "sizable" shipment of modern weapons is expected to reach the rebels shortly. The origin and number of the weapons have not been revealed.

Mr. Roberto, who traveled here on a Tunisian passport, is on his fifth visit to the United States.

During a news conference several weeks ago, he conceded the rebels had been "hurt" by a Portuguese counter-offensive

ANGOLAN REBELS TRAIN IN TUNISIA: A group of Angolans with instructors. Training in guerrilla tactics is being conducted by Algerian nationalists in Tunisia.

during the dry season, which ended early this fall.

Since then, he said, the onset of seasonal rains has restricted Portuguese mobility and the rebels have regrouped.

The Portuguese have said the rebellion was fermented by "terrorists" from outside Angola.

Mr. Roberto conferred at some length in 1959 with John F. Kennedy, then a member of the Senate Foreign Relations Committee.

According to informed Government sources, President Kennedy personally ordered a State Department representative to Europe last summer to offer assistance to Angolan students who had fled Portugal.

As a result of the President's initiative, seven Angolan exiles are enrolled at Lincoln University, near Philadelphia. As many as a dozen more are expected to arrive within the next few weeks.

Many are enrolled in Switzerland, and others are scattered about in France and West Germany. Some have accepted scholarships behind the Iron Curtain. Forty are in Ghana, and several dozen are expected to go to Brazil, a Portuguese-speaking country.

A few are reported to be among those being trained by the Algerians in Tunisia.

December 18, 1961

Angola Rebels Form Government in Exile

By LLOYD GARRISON

Special to The New York Times.

LEOPOLDVILLE, the Congo, April 5—Rebels from Angola announced today the formation of an African government in exile for the Portuguese-ruled territory adjacent to the Congo.

The announcement was made at a news conference by Holden Roberto, president of the newly formed National Front for the Liberation of Angola.

He said the move had the approval of the central Congolese Government of Premier Cyrille Adoula.

Mr. Roberto said he was "in contact" with other African governments and hoped for recognition from some of them.

"We are not seeking recognition at the moment from any countries outside Africa," he added. "We will avoid any commitments with either East or West."

Mr. Roberto declared that a contingent of Angolans trained by the Algerian Liberation Front in Tunisia would arrive in the Congo, "probably within a week."

Rebel forces have been fighting the Portuguese for more than a year in the northern part of Angola on the Congo frontier.

While leaders of Mr. Roberto's group claim the loyalty of those rebels actually fighting in northern Angola, the new organization met with bitter opposition from one important party of exiles here, the Popular Movement for the Liberation of Angola.

At a separate news conference, a member of the movement's executive committee denounced the formation of the organization as a "propaganda maneuver."

Party to Go Own Way

He described Mr. Roberto as a "traitor to the cause of true unity," and said his party would continue to press for a united front of its own.

Mr. Roberto was listed as Premier of the exile government. He was formerly the founder and president of the Union of Angolan People, which started the rebellion in Angola March 15, 1961.

His new organization was formed a week ago when the Union of Angola People merged with the Angolan Democratic party, a largely tribal group with strength in northwest Angola.

The Union of Angolan People and the Popular Movement for the Liberation of Angola have been bitter rivals for several years.

Members of the exile government are from a wide variety of Angola's tribal, regional, and religious groups.

Four of the ten cabinet posts are held by the Angolan Democratic party.

A list of the cabinet members was given as follows:

Premier—Holden Roberto
Vice Premier—Emanuel Kounzika
Second Vice Premier—Manuel Das Neves
Foreign Affairs—Jonas Savimbi
Information—Rosario Neto
Interior—Dr. Jose Liahuca
Finance—Emanuel Ziki
Social Affairs—Ferdinand Dombele
Defense—P. John Eduardo.

April 6, 1962

Angolan Revolutionary

Holden Roberto

HOLDEN ROBERTO, a leader of the Angolan rebel movement who announced the formation yesterday of a National Front for the Liberation of Angola, is scholarly and dignified in appearance. He does not fit the popular image of a firebrand revolutionary.

Man in the News

But there is no question in his mind that he is a revolutionary.

"I am a revolutionary because a Christian who remains silent before a crime becomes a participant in that crime," he has explained.

The crime against which he protests, Mr. Roberto avers, is Portugal's control over Angola, a West African territory fourteen times larger than Portugal.

Mr. Roberto is a third-generation Christian, but he does not identify himself with any denomination. The eight-page monthly newspaper he has published for some time in Leopoldville is heavily laden with Biblical quotations, mostly on the theme of universal brotherhood.

He was born Jan. 12, 1925 in São Salvador, a small town in northern Angola, about forty miles south of the border of the Congo.

His convert grandfather helped to translate the Bible into the Bakongo dialect and the Christian influence was strong throughout his childhood. When the family moved to Leopoldville, where Mr. Roberto grew up, he began study of Portuguese, French and English. He is fluent in the first two of the languages and speaks passable English.

Fight Began in 1954

He is a graduate of a French Protestant secondary school in Leopoldville. Upon finishing, he went to work in the Government finance office in Leopoldville and then joined a Portuguese company.

Mr. Roberto plunged into politics in 1954. After several visits to Angola he was convinced that he must "fight for its independence."

Despite what he termed colonization "by the whip" on the part of the Portuguese, Mr. Roberto declared himself unalterably opposed to violence. But he became equally convinced that Portugal would never respond to nonviolence, as the British did in India.

"Portugal will not respect nonviolence," he declared.

He began his travels abroad in 1959 when he made his way to Accra, Ghana. While in Accra he attended his first All-Africa Peoples Conference. His relations with Ghanaians were warm.

He sees the dilemma of Angolan nationalism as having to avoid being viewed as a "tool" of the United States or any other non-African power. He is personally considered an active anti-Communist.

In 1959, when he visited the United States he came in secret to avoid "reprisals" against members of his family remaining in Angola.

While he decries terrorism, he has wryly observed, in response to criticism of Angolan terrorist actions:

"Perhaps if the rebels had military uniforms and were provided with modern arms and equipment and could slaughter more efficiently, therefore, they would no longer be referred to as 'terrorists.'"

The New York Times

"Portugal will not respect nonviolence."

Mr. Roberto is the father of five children. His devotion to Angolan independence virtually precludes any other interests.

April 6, 1962

Congo Gives Base To Angolan Rebels For Troop Training

By LLOYD GARRISON
Special to The New York Times.

LEOPOLDVILLE, the Congo, Aug. 20—The National Front for the Liberation of Angola announced today that it had established a military training camp for Angolan rebels on Congolese territory.

The announcement said the camp had been "generously donated" by the Central Government of Premier Cyrille Adoula.

Alexander Taty, Minister of Defense in the National Front's government-in-exile, said the camp was situated near Thysville, about 100 miles from the border of Portuguese Angola. He said the camp, which is now training several hundred recruits, would be able to accommodate 700 within a few weeks.

The announcement was viewed by diplomatic observers here as one of the most significant developments since the seventeen-month-old rebellion began.

First Strong Evidence

It was the first concrete evidence of Congolese Government backing for the Angolan exiles. Although the Government has frequently declared its sympathy with the Angolan nationalists, on numerous occasions Congolese gendarmes have interfered with the shipment of arms and men heading for border crossing points.

Within the last few weeks, however, gendarmes in the Lower Congo region have been following strict orders to cooperate with the rebels.

Portuguese air and ground forces are reported to have restricted the rebellion to the northernmost region of Angola bordering the Lower Congo.

The Portuguese are said to have between 20,000 and 40,000 troops based in the territory, which the Portuguese consider an integral province of Portugal.

The training camp in the Congo will be supervised by twenty-four Angolans who recently returned from Tunisia after more than six months of training by the Algerian nationalist army.

All of the Algerian-trained Angolans received instruction in demolition techniques. Mr. Taty said one of their most important tasks would be to train recruits in the use of plastic and other explosives that the rebels have acquired recently.

The establishment of the base also has important political consequences. It is viewed as adding to the prestige of Holden Roberto's exile government, whose validity has been challenged by the rival Popular Movement for the Liberation of Angola, headed by Dr. Agostinho Neto.

Dr. Neto escaped from imprisonment in Portugal three months ago and has been trying, thus far unsuccessfully, to form a united front with Mr. Roberto's group.

August 21, 1962

ANGOLAN REBELS FURTHER DIVIDED

Pressure for Unity Brings a New Split Instead

By J. ANTHONY LUKAS
Special to The New York Times

LEOPOLDVILLE, the Congo, July 8 — Quarreling Angolan rebel groups were splintered even further today following a weekend of denunciations and violence.

Two factions, each claiming to be the Popular Movement for the Liberation of Angola, held out in different sections of Leopoldville.

The Popular Movement, one of the two major Angolan rebel organizations, split Saturday when a dissident faction led by Viriato da Cruz and Matias Migueis repudiated the movement's leadership.

The present leaders promptly expelled the dissidents.

Yesterday Mr. Da Cruz, Mr. Migueis and some of their supporters attempted to enter a meeting in the Movement's headquarters. A melee ensued, and Mr. Migueis and a supporter were wounded by knives.

Ironically, the split appears to stem at least partly from pressure for unity among the Angolan rebels.

Agostinho Neto and Mario de Andrade, leaders of the Popular Movement for the Liberation of Angola, have long refused to join the Angolan National Liberation Front, headed by Holden Roberto.

However, Mr. Da Cruz and Mr. Miguies said today that their faction was now willing to join the Front, under certain conditions.

Some observers here believe that the division in the Popular Movement was a consequence of the recent strengthening of Mr. Roberto's Front and the Government-in-exile it supports.

The Congo last week recognized Mr. Roberto's exile regime as the legitimate Government of Angola, and pledged it all possible assistance in its fight against Portuguese rule.

Observers believe the dissidents in the Popular Movement are now convinced that the movement has lost out in the struggle with Mr. Roberto. They are believed to be acting on the political axiom: "If you can't beat 'em, join 'em."

However, Dr. Neto and Mr. De Andrade are not likely to give up. They have strong support from Ghana, Guinea and Mali. They have also been accused of accepting support from Communists.

Mr. Roberto's group is generally regarded as more moderate. It draws mot of its support from Western - oriented African countries.

July 9, 1963

U.N. COUNCIL BIDS WORLD EMBARGO ARMS TO LISBON

Resolution Urges Immediate Moves by Portugal to Give Up Territories

3 NATO POWERS ABSTAIN

U.S., Britain and France Say They Approve Principle of Action—Vote Is 8 to 0

By THOMAS J. HAMILTON
Special to The New York Times

UNITED NATIONS, N. Y., July 31—The Security Council voted 8 to 0 today to ask all nations to impose an embargo on arms shipments to Portugal for use in maintaining her rule over her African territories. The United States, Britain and France abstained.

The Council also requested Portugal to recognize the right of the inhabitants of the three territories to "self-determination and independence," and to take immediate steps for granting them independence.

Explaining their abstention, the delegates of the three major Western powers said they favored the principle of self-determination for the affected territories — Angola, Mozambique and Portuguese Guinea—but that they could not accept the language used in some paragraphs of the resolution.

Nogueira Protests

After the vote Dr. Alberto Franco Nogueira, Portuguese Foreign Minister, told the Council the resolution was "revolting." According to reliable sources, he rejected a suggestion by the Secretary General, U Thant, that they discuss compliance with the resolution before Dr. Franco Nogueira returns to Lisbon.

The Foreign Minister was understood to have told a representative of the Secretary General that he could not discuss the resolution now because any decision would have to be taken at the cabinet level. A number of delegates expressed the belief that Portugal would not comply, and that the Africans would return to the Council demanding stronger action.

Earlier Alex Quaison-Sackey of Ghana said that the 32 African members who brought the complaint against Portugal would revive the issue in the Council if Portugal "has not accepted the principle of self-determination" by Oct. 31.

Explosion Forecast

African countries also began a concerted attack in the Council on South Africa's racial policies. They were branded "undiluted racism," and called "a time bomb" that would cause an explosion in Africa.

Mr. Quaison-Sackey, speaking for Ghana, Morocco and the Philippines, authors of the proposal, thanked the other members of the Council who voted for it—Norway, Brazil, Venezuela, Nationalist China and the Soviet Union.

In addition, Mr. Quaison-Sackey thanked Sivert A. Nielsen, the Norwegian representative, for his attempt to help negotiate amendments that would have made the resolution acceptable to the United States, and Dr. Tulio Alvarado of Venezuela, whose amendments were accepted by the sponsors and incorporated in the proposal.

Stevenson Role Ignored

The Ghanaian representative did not mention Adlai E. Stevenson, the United States representative, who joined Mr. Nielsen in reaching a tentative agreement with the African representatives on the amendments that Norway was to introduce.

The agreement was subject to confirmation by the respective governments, and the State Department withheld its consent. The State Department also refused to approve the Venezuelan amendments, which did not go as far to meet Portuguese objections as those proposed by Norway.

According to reliable sources, both Britain and Portugal had been bringing pressure to bear on the United States not to vote for the resolution unless further changes were made.

Order Becomes a Request

The principal effect of the Venezuelan amendments, which incorporated most of those that Norway had intended to introduce, was to issue a request, not an order, for the partial embargo on arms for Portugal.

August 1, 1963

Salazar Vows to Risk War To Keep Africa Territories

Special to The New York Times

LISBON, Aug. 12—Portugal will defend her rights to her overseas territories at all costs, even if it means war with some independent African states, Premier Antonio de Oliveira Salazar said tonight.

The Premier pledged his Government to "go to the limit of our human and natural resources" to retain the territories.

The 74-year-old Premier, who has ruled Portugal for more than three decades, accused the United States and the Soviet Union of "liberating" African colonies to establish American and Soviet influence in Africa.

In a major policy speech, Dr. Salazar reaffirmed Lisbon's determination to pursue administrative reform and decentralization in Portugal's African "provinces" of Angola, Mozambique and Portuguese Guinea.

Response Is Defiant

The Premier's declaration was a defiant response to the United Nations Security Council, which recently requested Portugal to take steps to grant independence to her African territories.

Dr. Salazar declared that the "massive entry" into the United Nations of Asians and Africans, backed by Communists and some Western states, "has come to constitute a menace to peace and the orderly life of nations."

The Premier spoke for an hour and a half. It was his first major speech since January, 1962, after India's occupation of the Portuguese enclave of Goa.

Dr. Salazar said Portugal sought friendly cooperation or at least correct relations with independent African states. However, he warned: "If they see fit to turn threats into acts of war and bring it into our territory, Portugal will defend her territories to the end."

He Speaks From Home

Dr. Salazar was originally scheduled to make his policy statement in the library of the National Assembly before newsmen and legislators. In a last minute change the invitations were cancelled and the Premier spoke at home in his study.

On television screens the Premier appeared vigorous. His sharp, sometimes high-pitched voice was generally forceful. He occasionally punctuated his remarks with a movement of the hand.

Portugal's present difficulties are "very grave," Dr. Salazar said, adding that the "total resistance of the nation" might be required.

In response to African demands for independence for Angola, Dr. Salazar declared:

"Angola is a Portuguese creation and does not exist without Portugal. The only national conscience rooted in the province is not Angolan; it is Portuguese, just as there are no Angolans but only Portuguese of Angola."

He asserted that if Portugal pulled out of Angola, the territory would break up into multiple tribal districts. Mozambique, he said, would share the same fate or be swallowed up by its "territorially ambitious" neighbors, Tanganyika and Nyasaland.

In a long attack on both the United States and the Soviet Union for alleged support to nationalists in Portugal's African territories, Dr. Salazar asserted that Washington and Moscow were seeking to "capture and control markets" in Africa.

He asserted that competition between the leaders of the Eastern and Western blocs could lead to the establishment of new zones of influence in Africa.

As an alternative to United States or Soviet influence in Africa, Dr. Salazar declared, "We should implore Providence to grant African countries, recently led by France, Belgium, Britain or Italy, the possibility of finding a formula of close cooperation with those nations to solve the problems of independence."

Dr. Salazar said that a recent campaign initiated by African nations at a conference in Addis Ababa would have no substantial effect on Portugal. He termed severing of diplomatic and trade relations with Portugal by Africans little more than a gesture of demagogy.

Colonialism Defended

In defending colonialism's "civilizing mission," the Premier said:

"Is the language that we teach those people superior to their dialects? Does the religion preached by the missionaries surpass fetishism or not? Is not belonging to a nation of civilized expression and world projection better than to be shut up in narrow regionalism without incentives for development, means for defense or progress?"

He declared that his Government would pursue a policy of "maximum decentralization" with increased powers for territorial governments and larger territorial representation in national institutions.

Dr. Salazar's declaration, which was disclosed to very few persons before delivery, came as a surprise to some foreign observers here, who had expected the Premier to make certain minor concessions to African demands freedom.

The Premier's speech came after months of rebel activity in Portuguese territories. Recently the United Nations Security Council voted for a limited arms embargo on Portugal, calling for a ban on shipments of weapons that might be employed against nationalists.

August 13, 1963

ANGOLAN POLITICS LINKED TO COFFEE

Portuguese Depend Heavily on Exports of Province

By JOSEPH LELYVELD

Recent reports from the Congo told of the infiltration of more than 2,200 trained rebel troops into Portuguese Angola.

They crossed into the northern part of the territory—the region of the great Angolan coffee plantations, which weigh heavily on the credit side in Portugal's balance of trade.

And this balance of trade—in addition to elements of history and a fervently-held colonial mystique—helps explain why the Portuguese insist that Angola is an integral part of Portugal.

Angola is the leading coffee exporter in Africa and the third largest in the world. It grows an estimated 5.7 per cent of the world's coffee crop.

U.S. the Big Customer

Last year, according to the United States Department of Agriculture, Angola exported 156,887 metric tons of coffee. Of this, 89,199 tons came to the United States, which imports more from the territory than any other country, including Portugal.

The International Coffee Agreement places a ceiling on Angolan coffee exports, and while the rebellion of March, 1961, damaged the crop, it did not result in lower export earnings.

Coffee accounted last year for 43.7 per cent of Angola's exports. At the same time, Portugal—minus her African territories—had a trade deficit of $200,106,600. The $37,264,000 earned on Angolan coffee in the United States alone helped to strike the balance.

While Angola's major exports earn dollars and pounds, her leading imports come from Portugal and are paid for in escudos. In all, Portugal's African territories take an estimated 25 per cent of her merchandise exports.

Importance of Railroad

The one railroad that crosses central Africa starts in the Angolan port of Lobito, cuts across the mineral-rich Congolese province of Katanga, then turns down through the Northern Rhodesian copper belt and, finally, comes out at Beira in the other large Portuguese African territory, Mozambique.

This railroad, plus the lines that run up from South Africa to Mozambique, establishes the importance of the Portuguese territories in the economic life of the continent. Though their own mineral wealth is relatively untapped, their long coastlines make them the natural corridors for exports from the African heartland.

A 194-mile pipeline is now being laid between Beira and Umtali in Southern Rhodesia. It is on such installations—and the export of labor for the Rhodesian and South African mines—that Mozambique's economy depends.

About two-thirds of the development funds that Portugal puts into the territories goes for the development of ports, rail lines and highways. African nationalists are quick to point out the military significance of these investments.

Investors Are Wary

The rebellion in Angola diverted the small stream of foreign investment that was beginning to flow into the Portuguese territories. An officer of a major New York bank who deals with African affairs remarked recently that he "almost never" receives inquiries from his customers about Angola and Mozambique.

Angola started to attract cautious investment in the nineteen-fifties as Lisbon—some say for political reasons—decided to break down the barriers it had erected.

Earlier, the same British and Belgian interests that are behind Union Minière du Haut Katanga had invested in Angola's Benguela Railroad and diamond mines. Diamonds rank behind coffee as Angola's second biggest export. They all go to Britain.

Petrofina, the Belgian petroleum company, has oil fields and refineries in Angola under a joint venture with the Provincial Government.

Oil Production Climbs

Crude oil production soared from 104,000 metric tons in 1961 to 471,000 last year. The exports went to Portugal.

The Portuguese have established a development bank to assist the territories that they describe as their overseas provinces. But this assistance is limited by the comparative poverty of Portugal herself and the huge military outlays she has been making to maintain control over Angola, Mozambique and Portuguese Guiana.

The status of the three territories is anomalous to say the least. Portugal says they are an integral part of Portugal. But, for instance, when it comes to Portugal's membership in the European Free Trade Association, the African territories are simply ignored.

The trade bloc is establishing an economic development committee. Portugal, but not Portuguese Africa, will be within its purview.

Portugal levies tariffs on the products of her overseas provinces. She also maintains a separate currency. The tariffs are due to be eliminated next year with the creation of a customs union called "the Escudo Area."

The cities of Mozambique and Angola are described as handsome, cosmopolitan and full of hope. "Needless to say," one observer wrote, "these are white men's hopes, just as these are white men's cities."

November 11, 1963

Angolan Revolt Gains Recruits and Arms

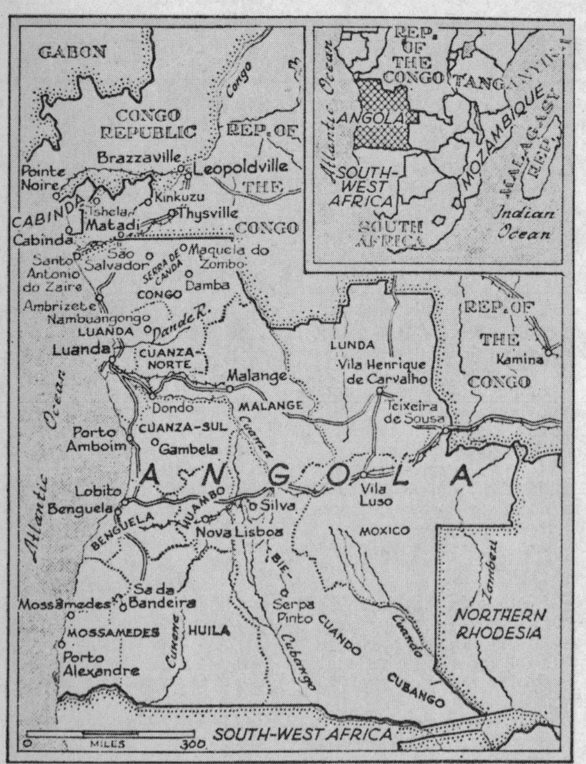

VOLUNTEERS, not yet uniformed, train at Camp Kinkuzu

The New York Times (by Lloyd Garrison)

HIDING FROM PORTUGUESE, many Angolans live in secret villages

The New York Times (by Lloyd Garrison)

Soldiers of the Angolan Liberation Army moving through high grass in northern Angola

SUPPLY DETAIL: Soldiers cross a stream in mountains

MOUNTAIN POST: Angolan rebels keep watch for Portuguese bombers

December 16, 1963

Now Angola: Study of a Rebel

As the African revolution advances onto a new battlefield, here is a report on how one man found himself in the front of the fight.

By LLOYD GARRISON

LEOPOLDVILLE.

MARCH 15, 1961, began like almost any other day in the north of Angola. Africans throughout the region arose, as usual, with the first light of dawn, lit their breakfast fires and warmed themselves against the chill of the early morning mist. Many who worked the nearby Portuguese coffee plantations began sharpening their machetes. Others cleaned old flintlock rifles which the Portuguese permitted them for shooting birds and game.

But few Africans showed up for work that day and few went hunting for game. Instead, thousands met, by plan, on the edge of Portuguese towns in the valleys. And then, by plan, they attacked.

Local Portuguese *chefs de postos* (district officers), plantation foremen, clerks and merchants were shot or hacked to death. Survivors said there seemed no limit to the Angolans' ferocity: by nightfall, hundreds of Portuguese had been slain, their bodies mutilated in the African's customary show of contempt for the enemy. Many were women and children.

Thus began Angola's revolt for independence. For many, it bore a chilling resemblance to the Mau Mau in Kenya. In the first few weeks the insurgents overran huge portions of the north, burning and looting. Then, with the arrival of Portuguese reinforcements from Lisbon, the rebels were slowly pushed back into the mountain rain forests; for a time, it seemed as if the uprising had been stilled — but only for a time.

THE revolt goes on, although its character has changed. From a base in the Congo, over the border to the north, the Angolans have developed an amazing "bush" organization with an elaborate chain of command, communications, logistics. Gone are the ragged bands of 1961; the new National Liberation Army is waging a calculated guerrilla war with machine guns and bazookas, mortars and land mines. And the army now has a hard core of 7,500 well-trained and disciplined soldiers; hundreds more are being trained and equipped every day.

Who are these "new" rebels? And what do they have in store for a country of 4,500,000 Africans, and 200,000 whites?

As with any army, there is no "typical" soldier, no single reason why men serve. Rebel recruits come from many backgrounds. A very few have had higher education. Many are barely literate. The majority were once farmers or day laborers, and most are Kikongos, the dominant tribe of the north. The story of one of them, Antonio Muandazi, reflects a great deal about who the rebels are and where they are heading.

At the headquarters of the Angolan Revolutionary Government in Exile (G.R.A.E.) in Leopoldville, the Congo, Muandazi's file card is brief:

Born in Canca, a remote village in the Canda mountains of Northern Angola. Age: 32. Formal education: none. Religion: nominal Catholic. At 12 was sent to the Congo by his parents to live with his married brother. Worked first as a house boy, then as a waiter in Thysville and Matadi. Speaks Kikongo, has picked up French and a little Portuguese. In 1948 was arrested in Thysville on charges unspecified on the card, tried in a Belgian court and acquitted.

TODAY, Muandazi appears little different from other Angolan soldiers, although at 5 feet 8 inches he is shorter than most. Everyone wears the same khaki uniform and there are no insignia to distinguish officers, sergeants and enlisted men. In the Angolan army, nobody considers it unusual that Antonio Muandazi, onetime waiter, has risen to command more than 1,000 men. (He has no formal rank, but in other armies such a unit would call for a lieutenant colonel.)

"I was lucky," he says, looking back on a life that was anything but lucky — a life that, until a few years ago, seemed one of unending pointlessness.

Muandazi operates from one of several carefully camouflaged field headquarters in the Canda mountain region, about 70 miles south of the Congo. This was the back yard of his childhood. As a boy he roamed these rain forests, climbed the steep ravines, hunted in the open rolling savanna on the high plateaus. Today, he can remember every trail and animal track. "Elephant tracks are the best for marching; after you've gone the elephants come along and stamp out your footprints."

He grew up barely seeing a Portuguese, except when the local *chef de posto* made his rounds of the district. The boy didn't like him much. His father always tipped his hat and bowed when he spoke to the *chef*. All the grownups did.

THE senior Muandazi was a carpenter and made furniture for Portuguese living in the valley towns. His mother, like most Kikongo women, tended the family plots of manioc and corn. Young Antonio and his brother and three sisters were expected to draw water, chop wood and help in the fields. In his spare time he hunted grouse with slingshots and trapped small game. There was no school near Canca and none of the villagers could read or write.

When he was 12 he was sent to join his older brother in the Congo, because, he was told, the Belgians paid Africans better wages than the Portuguese. This was true, but years later his parents said the real reason was because they did not want him pressed into work gangs on the roads — in those days a common routine for women and children.

There was no job for a 12-year-old at the Belgian cement factory where his brother worked, so Antonio moved to the nearby city of Thysville. There he got a job as a "small boy" in the home of a Belgian doctor, washing dishes, scrubbing floors, making beds.

The "No. 1 boy" was also Angolan. He had been to school in the Congo and could read and write French. At night, he tried to teach Antonio.

WHEN the doctor returned to Belgium in 1946, he got Antonio a job as a waiter in the Hotel Cosmopolite. One of his duties there was to make pre-dawn breakfast for a resident, the Belgian police chief. He was late one morning and the chief began beating him with his baton. "I finally hit him back, and the next thing I knew I was in jail."

After three days he was brought before a Belgian judge.

The police chief never appeared to testify: the judge finally heard Antonio's story, said he had broken no law and should go back to work.

Muandazi says he asked the judge: "Why don't you punish the police chief?" And the judge replied: "I suggest you forget everything and learn how to behave yourself."

The incident impressed Muandazi in two ways. It was his first realization that the white man could do pretty much as he liked and get away with it. At the same time he felt fortunate that what happened took place in the Congo. "In Angola," he said, "I never would have had a trial."

As soon as he left court Muandazi hitched a ride on a truck to the port city of Matadi on the mouth of the Congo River. For a while he did laundry for seamen off the ships.

"I saw all those foreign ships coming and going and I said to myself, the European can come here to the Congo; why can't I go to Europe? I asked if I could be a worker at sea — washing, cooking, anything at all. They always said, 'No, you are a *noir* [black],' or 'We don't hire *macacos* [monkeys].' "

So he went back to waiting on table, this time at Matadi's Hotel Metropole. These were glum years for Muandazi. His job paid well enough but there was no hope for advancement. He could still barely read and write and now, in his late 20's, it was too late to go to school.

THEN, just before the Congo became independent in 1960, Muandazi quit his job and enlisted in the Congolese *Force Publique*. It was a move taken entirely on impulse; he had been told a private could work his way up to sergeant, and this meant more pay and responsibility. He laughs about it now. There was no basic training. He was given a week of drill, shown how to handle a rifle and then put on guard duty.

Some of the Belgian officers were "haughty" and he was not surprised when the ranks mutinied just after independence. "But then every sergeant wanted to be an officer. It was madness." Three months later it was discovered that Muandazi was an Angolan and he was discharged.

At this point he met Eduardo Pinoch, now Interior Minister for the Angolan Government in Exile. Pinoch had come to Matadi to recruit Angolans for the Union of Angolan Peoples (U.P.A.), the independence movement headed by Holden Roberto, now the exile Government's Premier. Would Muandazi like to join? Better yet, would he be willing to come to Leopoldville for indoctrination, then go back to his district in Angola as a U.P.A. agent? Pinoch stressed that there would be no pay and that once in Angola Muandazi would be on his own; if he were caught by the Portuguese, death was almost a certainty.

Muandazi accepted without hesitation. He had never really thought about Angolan independence before. But now he was among Angolans who believed they could direct their own destiny and were seriously doing something about it. In Leopoldville he learned of "nationalism," of party discipline, of the need for the unity of all Angolans, whatever their tribe or region. And he learned, for the first time, of the movement's network of party cells inside Angola.

After two months in Leopoldville, he slipped across the frontier and made his way to Canca. There he found only three dues-paying U.P.A. members. Immediately, Muandazi organized secret membership meetings at night in the forest. Hundreds joined. His superiors in Leopoldville were pleased and soon he was assigned to organize other villages.

EXILES — Holden Roberto, Premier of the Angolan Government-in-Exile in the Congo, visits a wounded rebel in a Leopoldville hospital.

IN 1960 the mood of Angola's Africans was one of deeply repressed bitterness. The elders had been pressed into forced labor; the younger men who had acquired skills as carpenters or mechanics knew that Portuguese performing the same jobs were paid twice, sometimes three times, as much as an African. In many areas women and children were still being conscripted to do road maintenance.

On the surface, all was tranquil. Africans continued to bow and smile to the *chefs de postos;* the Portuguese continued clinging to their belief that they "knew" their Africans and their Africans didn't want to be "independent," they wanted to be "Portuguese." This illusion was so strong that not even the secret police had any inkling that Angolans were preparing to strike. Portuguese officials assured themselves and the few foreign correspondents permitted to enter the territory that all was well, that "gradual assimilation" was Lisbon's unique alternative to "the winds of change." (And just to make sure no other thought seeped in, any African caught listening to Radio Leopoldville was packed off to jail.)

ON March 8 word was passed to U.P.A. agents that the time had come—in seven days all Angolans in the north should rise up against Portuguese towns, plantations and army posts. On the night of the 14th Muandazi assembled the villagers of Canca and explained his plan. Their first target would be Tamfu, a newly built Portuguese administrative post near Canca. There were 20 Portuguese there: nine men, five women and six children. Three of the men were Portuguese officials.

The next day, the men hid in the forest near Tamfu until noon, when the Portuguese began their siesta. Then, armed with their machetes and flintlocks, they attacked. The three officials managed to escape in a jeep. Everyone else was slain after a bitter hand-to-hand struggle in which five Angolans were killed and 19 wounded.

Muandazi's feelings about that day are mixed. He insists he had no hand in killing the women and children. His people, he said, were "blinded" and beyond restraint. "Nothing was spared. They set fire to everything — even the money in the houses. Nobody could stop them."

Neither he nor his fellow insurgents have renounced what happened that day. But now, nearly three years later, they have come to accept the exile Government's view that killing civilians is "wrong."

Many, though not Muandazi, felt that after that first blow was struck, the Portuguese would flee, and independence would quickly follow. It was not so. Many Portuguese did flee Angola in panic. But the majority stayed put.

If March 15 was a nightmare, it soon begot another. Portuguese vigilante squads armed themselves and roamed the bush seeking vengeance. Scores of African villages were burned and thousands of African civilians were killed in random retaliation. In many villages the settlers decapitated African bodies and placed the heads on rows of pikes as a demonstration of Portuguese authority.

When Portuguese army reinforcements finally arrived the settlers were brought under control and the battle became mostly one of soldier against soldier, although the rebel "soldiers" had no uniforms, few weapons, no overall command and little formal discipline.

IN the Serra de Canda, Muandazi stood out as a natural leader whose bravery compelled other men to follow. In November, 1961, he and 22 other veterans were picked to go to Tunisia for special training with the Algerian liberation army.

"With the Algerians," said Muandazi, "we learned what an army is really like." Training consumed 18 hours a day, seven days a week, for seven straight months. In lectures, the Angolans were taught the classic theories of guerrilla warfare; in actual combat with Algerian units against the French, they learned how to apply theory to reality.

Upon their return, 18 of the 22 were made officers. Muandazi was one of them. Their task: to set up a program for retraining the entire rebel army.

The Congolese donated the site — an abandoned bivouac area near Kinkusu, a barren hilly region 70 miles from the Angolan border. The eighteen Angolans started from scratch; within 60 days they had erected thatch-roofed barracks, written a basic training syllabus, and were ready for the first group of 600 men pulled back from Angola.

TODAY Camp Kinkusu is turning out 2,200 men every eight weeks. In addition to weapons training and endless hours of practice in night fighting, recruits are lectured on everything from how to dig a latrine to the role of free trade unions in Angola after independence.

Their uniforms come from the Tunisians and the Congolese. Algeria has shipped several hundred tons of modern weapons left over from the war with France. Recently Holden Roberto announced he would accept arms from Communist China, but no one who knows him and the leaders of his exile government thinks this portends a swing to the left. Indeed, one of the most striking things about the Angolans is how little they seem concerned with the cold war on a continent where other Africans are becoming increasingly involved in it.

Locally, however, the National Liberation Army is rapidly becoming a political force within Angola. Almost 5,000 men who have passed through Camp Kinkusu have joined the General League of Angolan Workers (L.T.G.A.), the rebels' trade-union movement. Many are also members of Roberto's U.P.A. Meetings in the interior are informal but soldiers take their affiliations seriously. At one meeting Muandazi told fellow L.T.G.A. members of support from labor unions abroad: from the A.F.L.-C.I.O., typewriters and mimeograph machines; from Israel and West Germany, scholarships for Angolan trainees; from Tunisia and the International Confederation of Free Trade Unions in Geneva, money and technical assistance.

"This shows we are not alone," said Muandazi. "We have more friends than Salazar. They believe in us. We can't let them down."

Muandazi himself has led nine major attacks in the last six months and has shot his way out of five Portuguese ambushes. He admits to fear—"It's a constant feeling, no matter how long you've been fighting" — but he knows that the end is nowhere near and that there will be no clearcut military victory, not while the Portuguese have planes and armor and superior firepower. Victory, he feels, will depend on wearing down the Portuguese until they are willing to negotiate, as the French finally did with the Algerians. But it took the Algerians seven years.

WHAT then? One thing the rebels are agreed on is that post-independence Angola must not become another Congo. "The Congolese just stamped their feet a few times and they got independence," says Carlos Almeida, an enlisted man "But now what have they got? Officials taking big bribes and driving big cars." A sergeant added: "This war has taught us to respect three things — hard work, discipline, sacrifice. Our leaders know if they don't live up to these things, they won't last long."

"What happened in the Congo was crazy," Muandazi says. "You know, the Belgians used to make matches in the Congo, but when the Belgians were all scared away the Congolese had to bring matches all the way from Sweden at twice the price. That's crazy."

The Congolese example has led to the most significant change to come over the Angola rebels — the feeling that their rebellion is no longer against everything "Portuguese" but against the "system," and that there will still be a place for white men in free Angola. Thus a recent order from the exile Government: the rebel army should refrain from attacking civilians unless they are armed, and it should start taking prisoners, treat them well and send them under escort to Leopoldville.

"This is a good policy," says Muandazi. "What we did in March, 1961, is done with."

MUANDAZI'S own progression from servant boy to terrorist to soldier has suggested one answer to the personal question of what he will do when the war is won. Lately his thoughts have been turning on the belief that, after Angola is free, the revolution will spread to South West Africa and eventually into South Africa itself. There will be new "freedom fighters," using Angola as their base with their own Camp Kinkusus.

"Who knows?" he said. "If they want someone like me with practical experience, I might just join them . . . I don't like making war. But what else can I do better?"

•

As this article was going to press, the following cable arrived:

WORD HAS JUST BEEN RECEIVED THAT ANTONIO MUANDAZI IS REPORTED MISSING IN ACTION IN THE SERRA DE CANDA—GARRISON.

February 16, 1964

AFRICANS REPORT ANTI-LISBON DRIVE

Say Offensive Has Started to Free Mozambique

Special to The New York Times

DAR ES SALAAM, Tanganyika, Oct. 18—Details have been disclosed here of an offensive to free the East African territory of Mozambique from Portuguese rule.

The details were reported this weekend by Oscar Kambona, Foreign Minister of the Republic of Tanganyika and Zanzibar, speaking as chairman of the African Liberation Committee.

The committee, which has its headquarters here, was set up by the Organization of African Unity to assist nationalist movements on the continent.

A high official of the Mozambique liberation movement said the offensive began Sept. 24. Freedom fighters had infiltrated into Mozambique singly and in small groups, he said, and had linked up into assault groups at arranged points. They were said to have attacked Portuguese military emplacements along a 700-mile front.

These bases have been built by the Portuguese along Mozambique's northern frontier to bar entry of nationalists from Tanganyika.

The freedom fighters were trained mainly in Algeria, and some were trained in the United Arab Republic and elsewhere in Africa, the official said. He refused to confirm or deny that the nationalists were using arms of Soviet origin.

The official said the nationalists had been traveling in and out of Mozambique for about six months, reporting on the military build-up by the Portuguese on their northern frontier.

He said that one of the bases of the guerrillas had struck was Mueda, about 30 miles from the Ruvuma River, which is the border between Mozambique and Tanganyika.

About 7,000 people are said to have fled from Mozambique to Tanganyika in the last two weeks. Most came from the Mueda area.

Portuguese Panic Charged

Mr. Kambona described the beginning of the offensive as "a forceful assertion of the right to self-determination." The Portugese Government, the Tanganyikan minister said, had reacted with "panic, inhumanity and oppression characteristic of colonial regimes."

He declared that the Portuguese, charging external aggression and Communist subversion, had started a ruthless campaign of pillage, terrorism, torture and expropriation of Africans in the northern part of Mozambique.

This organized oppression, Mr. Kambona added, has given rise to a wave of "helpless refugees fleeing across the border into the southern region of our republic."

Mr. Kambona urged the Refugee Committee of the Organization for African Unity to study the refugee's problems and lend its aid.

"The resistance in Mozambique has started," he said, "and no amount of intimidation from Lisbon and the NATO powers will stop it."

October 19, 1964

Angola Rebellion, Now Waning, Spurring Portuguese to Reforms

Aid in Industry and Education Increases—Other Nations' Aid Called a Threat

By DREW MIDDLETON
Special to The New York Times

LUANDA, Angola, May 4—If some Portuguese businessmen had their way, there would be a statue here to the unknown rebel who fired the first shot of the insurrection five years ago.

For they say it was that insurrection, now reduced to sporadic attacks by scattered bands, that jerked the Portuguese Government in Lisbon out of its 18th-century attitude toward Angola and prompted the present program of economic and social development.

The insurrection, as one official put it, had an effect the reverse of that intended. The Portuguese not only became more determined than ever to retain Angola but also increased their investment in the country and began, belatedly, to improve the lot of Angola's estimated five million Africans.

During the second five-year development plan, Portugal, neither a large nor a rich nation, spent $140-million in Government funds in Angola. Half of that was in loans to Angola. There was also extensive borrowing in Angola for the revival of local enterprises that had come close to collapse at the start of the insurrection.

One result is that Angola is no longer largely dependent on coffee exports. Krupp of Germany is financing the development of a new iron ore field in the south and production from an older field has been expanded. German and Japanese ships are putting in at Angolese ports to pick up ore.

Agricultural products—coffee, fish, corn, nuts and sisal—still make up the bulk of the country's exports. But minerals, diamonds and manganese, as well as iron ore, are assuming greater importance.

The autumn of 1961, when Portuguese troops were moving into the north to break the insurrection, also brought a number of reforms. Africans were given full citizenship. The requirement that Africans work for a specified period each year was eliminated. The expansion of school, health and public welfare activities was begun.

Opinions differ on the amount of progress. One experienced diplomat said he believed that one in two African children now received primary education. Others say that the total of Africans in elementary schools is only about 180,000.

Vocational Training Stressed

The emphasis is on vocational education. The Portuguese believe Africa needs bookkeepers, mechanics and farmers far more than she needs lawyers or doctors. The five faculties of the new university here are medicine, engineering, agronomy, veterinary science and teacher training.

The attitude toward race here is outspoken even for the Portuguese, who draw no color bar. One senior official spent 10 minutes trying to convince a visitor that since the 16th century there has been a large admixture of Negro blood in metropolitan Portugal and that few if any Portuguese could claim to be true Caucasians.

Another said bluntly, and probably realistically, that the presence in Angola of 50,000 troops from metropolitan Portugal would increase the birth rate of mulatto children. "And it is the mulattos who will have the future of Angola in their hands," he said.

One hard-bitten general officer said he hoped that each Portuguese soldier would leave at least six mulatto children behind when he returned home.

The object, all Portuguese agree, is a multiracial, pluralistic society. They believe they have a much better chance of attaining it than the white South Africans have of achieving separate development—if they are left alone.

The Portuguese believe that the rebellion can be ended—it is very near defeat now, according to foreign diplomats—and that Angola can move forward economically and socially if only the rest of the world will keep its hands off.

By the rest of the world they mean Black Africa acting through the United Nations with, at times, the support of the United States.

The Portuguese maintain that the situation in Angola is a domestic matter because the overseas territories are considered under Portuguese law an integral part of the nation.

Foreign diplomats agree with the Portuguese that the insurrection is no longer a military danger.

The two independence movements are the Popular Movement for the Liberation of Angola and the Republican Government of Angola in Exile.

Communist Aid a Factor

The first of these movements apparently gets the lion's share of support from the Soviet Union and Communist China. The second, led by Holden Roberto, has degenerated into small bands living off the country. Recently the Portuguese have noticed that these bands change allegiance from movement to movement according to the supplies available.

The Portuguese concede that the present economic and social development owes much to the concern aroused by the rebellion. They say they have made more progress in the last five years than in the preceding five hundred.

What they ask is that the United States recognize the contribution in money and manpower by Portugal to Angola and that it understand that Portugals cannot overnight produce all the doctors, engineers and technical assistants needed.

The Portuguese are Angola's only white community. The backwoods trading posts that in Mozambique would be in Indian hands are Portuguese. The coffee farms are run by both Portuguese and Africans. Again unlike their fellow nationals in Mozambique, the Portuguese in Angola — there are about 300,000 of them—have penetrated the interior.

Most are third-generation and fourth-generation Angolas, although there has been some more recent settlement from metropolitan Portugal. They are convinced it is a good country, that it belongs to its people including the Africans, and that left alone they can make it one of the most prosperous in Africa.

May 5, 1966

Oil Is Transforming Economic Outlook in Angola

By LAWRENCE FELLOWS
Special to The New York Times

LUANDA, Angola—Favored by nature and harassed not intolerably at the moment by a seven-year insurrection, this huge Portuguese territory on the west coast of Africa is enjoying a boom. Angola, once known for mahogany forests and gorillas and not much else, presents a transformed picture.

Of the glowing new hues in the economic picture of this overseas province of Portugal, the brightest is in Cabinda, a wedge of dense, tropical forest separated from the northern tip of the territory by the Congo River.

Oil has been discovered there in enormous quantities, the extent still not fully known. In three or four months, however, oil will be coursing through a pipeline three feet in diameter to tankers waiting 10 miles out in the shallow sea.

Promise of New Wealth

Even now there is enough oil to promise new wealth to the long-suffering Portuguese. There is more than enough to give a new measure of security to the white-dominated governments of southern Africa, where an oil shortage has been the cause of gnawing anxieties.

Oil may also have altered the political balance in Africa. Cabinda must look immensely more interesting to black Africa; it is only slightly larger than Delaware, sandwiched between the two Congos—both bent on driving Portuguese and all the other vestiges of white or alien rule from Africa.

For the whites in power in southern Africa Cabina will proneedvite them with the oil, the need of which they have always felt keenly in a largely hostile world.

Apart from oil, and far down the Atlantic coast from Cabinda, on the edge of the great southern desert, high-grade iron ore from easily-worked deposits at Cassinga is spilling off the end of a conveyor belt at Mossâmedes at the rate of three thousand tons an hour, into ore carriers bound for Japan.

Americans Raising Cattle

North of the desert, on the immense, empty highlands, an American group is preparing to raise half a million head of cattle.

In the northeast, a vast, bush-covered area close to the Congo border, a million carats of diamonds and gem stones is being mined yearly.

Westware, where the ground rises steeply to forested hills around Carmona, and to the south, on the slopes and by the spectacular waterfalls around Gabela, the coffee is still growing. It is still Angola's most important single export, and makes it the third largest coffee producer in the world.

It was in these northern hills that Bakongo tribesmen started their revolt against Portuguese rule in 1961. Living astride the Angola-Congo border, spurred by independence in the Congo, the Bakongo went on a killing spree against the whites and against the Bailundo tribesmen who worked on the coffee plantations.

This brought on an even greater wave of killing, much of it indiscriminate, by the enraged white population. Tens of thousands of Bakongo were killed or sent fleeing across the border to the Congo before the Portuguese Army could restore its authority and settle down to the long war it has fought since against the hard core of the insurrections.

Angola's slow awakening cannot be marked by circling a date on the calendar, but the revolt of the Bakongo had something to do with it.

The Portuguese let the territory slumber for four centuries. They had come first in 1482 as seafaring people, interested mainly in finding ports and building forts along the African coast, to protect their route to India.

A few changes were vaguely considered before the revolt:. In 1953 the Portuguese were already spending some money on improving medical services and pest control in Angola. They were trying to encourage the migration of people from Lisbon and Oporto to step up the pace of what they call their "civilizing mission" in Africa. They were planning to do something about the appalling roads.

Settlers Not Content

But most of these things were meant to soothe the discontented Portuguese settlers, to make them less resentful of the rigid control from Lisbon, and of the drag on progress caused by Lisbon's tight grip on its own purse strings and by its objections to foreign investment.

In 1961, the changes came fast. Soldiers who had fought in Angola stayed, or went home only to fetch their families. The settler population has nearly doubled since 1961, with 400,000 whites and 100,000 mulattos now in a population of 5,500,000.

The imbalance of blacks and whites is not necessarily as frightening to whites as it might be in Rhodesia or South Africa. The Portuguese are better mixers than most. They eat in the same restaurants as the black population, sleep in the same hotels, and intermarry without bringing upon themselves any social stigma. Money is still a great barrier but not color. The civil service in Angola is about half black.

That the Africans here, although Portuguese citizens, have no really significant political rights puts them in the same boat with everyone else in Portugal whatever his color—and her other overseas territories.

Cotton Issue Resolved

The worst grievances of the Africans were taken care of when the Portuguese awakened to their problems in Angola. The black Africans were no longer forced to grow cotton in Angola and to sell it at prices below what the rest of the world was paying. The system of "contract" labor was abolished so that Africans were no longer compelled by law to work six months out of the year and to do whatever jobs their tribal chiefs agreed they should be assigned to.

A minimum wage was established, and after five hours of work a man must rest for two before he can work overtime for a higher rate of pay. At Cabinda, among the drilling rigs, hammocks hang like cocoons in a mulberry tree, and are filled with slumbering workers who have put in their five hours.

The fact that Cabinda Gulf Oil Company, a subsidiary of American Gulf, holds the concession points to the growing willingness of Portugal to let the outsiders in with their expertise and money. The company has so far invested $125-million in the venture.

Wells that have already been brought in will produce 150,000 barrels of oil a day, more than enough to cover all import needs of southern Africa for a long time to come.

In agreement with Cabinda Gulf, Portugal has retained the right to take all crude oil that is produced or the equivalent in refined products should her military or political needs dictate it.

"Well, let's just say it will never come to that," said Robert Ward, a Texan who is general manager of Cabinda Gulf.

Prosperity has already made ghe place look like invasion beach. It is littered with barges, miles of unassembled pipe, warehouses, earth-moving equipment, drilling rigs and great steel skeletons of production platforms and oil-collecting stations that still have to be floated out to sea and set on bottom among wells that have been sunk offshore.

At the end of the dock, built straight into the sea, ships bob like corks in enormous swells, unloading everything from machinery to food for drilling crews.

The first tanker is due in October when Cabinda Gulf will be well ahead of its commitment to be producing 30,000 barrels of crude a day by the end of this year.

With Portuguese and foreign money and expertise flowing into Angola, the economy is becoming less colonial and more self-sufficient. The people are making textiles, assembling cars, manufacturing agricultural equipment, building materials, wires and cables, paints, glass, tires, transistor radios, milling their own cotton, refining enough oil from the small fields south of Luanda for their own needs. With the help of two Scots, they are even distilling their own whisky.

July 7, 1968

Portuguese Curb Guerrillas in Mozambique

Tighter Defense Set Up in 2-Year-Old Struggle in North

By LAWRENCE FELLOWS
Special to The New York Times

MOCIMBOA DA PRAIA, Mozambique — In the bitter, half-forgotten war in this overseas province of Portugal, the Portuguese appear to be containing the guerrilla army operating against them.

On one side of a wide band of scorched earth the battle is toughest, and the Portuguese have built a defense system against the guerrillas, who are regarded by many not as rebels but as invaders from the north.

The guerrilla war, waged for two years by the Mozambique Liberation Front, is built largely around the Makonde, a fierce and relatively primitive tribe that lives on both sides of the Mozambique-Tanzania border.

There are perhaps 80,000 Makonde in Mozambique and 120,000 in Tanzania. Their faces are slashed in decorative scars and their teeth are filed to points, vivid reminders of their cannibalistic past.

"This has been a help and a hindrance to us," Col. Basilio Seguro, Governor of the Cabo Delgado District, explained in his office in Porto Amélia. "The Makonde are feared by some tribes and by some they are held to be superior, because of their fighting ability. I must say we have always held them in a certain respect ourselves.

"But they are also detested and this has helped us, as long as we have been able to show strength, to gain the support of the rest of the population," he added. "The side that wins the population will win the war. There is no question about that."

There are two battle zones, one along the high tablelands near Lake Malawi in the Niassa district in the northwest, and one in Cabo Delgado, around the Makonde plateau in the northeast. Both zones extend northward to the Ruvuma River, which marks the border with Tanzania and which in the hot, dry months before the rains begin, provides many shallow crossings for the guerrillas from Tanzania.

According to the Portuguese, the important guerrilla camps in Tanzania are at Mbamba Bay, Songea, Nachingwea, Newala, Tunduru, Masasi, Kitangari, Mingoyo and Mtwara.

At the first four places, the Portuguese say, they have evidence of the presence of Chinese Communist instructors. At the others the Tanzanian army and police units are helping the guerrillas, the Portuguese say. At Nachingwea, they report, the guerrillas have their toughest commando troops, and at Rutamba they draw recruits from refugees from the fighting and gives them elementary training with wooden rifles.

The Portuguese estimate the guerrillas' total strength at 3,500, but Dr. Eduardo Mondlane, the Liberation Front's leader, says he has 7,000.

About their own military strength in Mozambique, the Portuguese say nothing, but foreign estimates put the number of troops at 40,000 or higher. Under a rotation system all troops serve in Cabo Delgado or Niassa.

The guerrillas say they have killed 3,000 Portuguese and wounded 4,000 and shot down 20 planes.

The Portuguese say their own military losses, including not only those killed in combat but also those who died of sickness or in accidents, are under 300. None of their planes have been shot down, the Portuguese say.

Native of the South

Dr. Mondlane, a native of the south of Mozambique who is dedicated to the overthrow of Portuguese rule, directs the guerrilla war from Dar es Salaam, Tanzania, and declares he can get all the weapons he needs from Communist countries.

The Portuguese still regard Dr. Mondlane as non-Communist and pro-West, but they regard his second in command, the Rev. Uriah Simango, as pro-Chinese. They believe his third-ranking aide, Marcelinos dos Santos, who studied in Lisbon, is in league with Portuguese Communists.

Dr. Mondlane says he receives adequate funds from the Organization of African Unity, which is pledged to remove the last vestiges of white rule in Africa, and from private organizations in Britain, the United States, Sweden and the Netherlands. He prefers not to disclose their identity. He says he will fight a guerrilla war for 20 years, if he has to, to force Portugal out.

Dr. Mondlane, who is about 46 years old, is a Northwestern University graduate who once lectured in anthropology at Syracuse University, where he married a white woman who was a Syracuse graduate. He also worked as a minor official in trusteeship affairs at the United Nations.

Dr. Mondlane has gathered some support among educated black men in Mozambique, but many of them have been put in jail. He has also attracted some following in Niassa.

But there are no demonstrations on a national scale and no slogans are shouted in the streets. The movement has not grown substantially outside the Makonde tribe, and there has been no fighting in the south.

Dr. Mondlane describes Mozambique's economy as a straightforward colonial system. However, in the last few years Portugal has been trying to alter this situation radically —paying the going world prices

The New York Times (by Lawrence Fellows)
A Portuguese patrol prepares to leave Mocimboa da Praia for night foray against rebels

for Mozambique's agricultural commodities, putting money into industrial development and promoting new settlement.

Education Is Pressed

The Portuguese also are spending vast amounts on education and development to raise the social and economic level of the black inhabitants to make them good Portuguese as quickly as possible.

The disengagement of the other colonial powers after World War II had little immediate relevance for Portugal, for without her empire she would have to retire to an inconspicuous, inglorious slice of Iberia, and that is unthinkable.

Mozambique has been an important factor in Portugal's economy since 1520. Most of the province's wealth now comes from farming. Cashew nuts and cotton are the main export crops, with sugar, sisal and copra also figuring importantly. The territory's 2,000-mile coastline is dotted with good ports.

But the disengagement nevertheless had its impact on Portugal.

As the tide of independence rushed down the African continent, to the borders of Portugal's provinces, Portugal reacted swiftly and with determination to maintain her position in Africa. Her resistance helped to stiffen the will of neighboring South Africa and Rhodesia, whose white regimes have proclaimed they will not be moved or deprived of what they have.

Portugal is no democracy, so there is little internal pressure on the government to grant independence to the territories and Lisbon does not pay even lip service to the ideas of colonial freedom or self-determination.

In the last five years Portugal has been confronted with three insurrections in Africa. The first broke out in Angola in 1961, the second in Portuguese Guinea in 1963.

In August, 1964, in Mozambique, the third rebellion began with the murder of a Dutch Roman Catholic priest by a group of rebels that has since faded from existence.

Rebels Have Troubles

The Liberation Front began a month later, but in an attempt to assert its leadership over all the rebel movements it claimed the credit for the earlier beginning.

The rebels have had difficulty winning over the population, largely because of the economic and social reforms the Portuguese instituted after the 1961 uprising in Angola.

These efforts have been helped by the relative lack of color consciousness among the Portuguese, and this has kept the war from becoming a racial conflict.

The Government, determined to do nothing that might foster racialism, makes no racial breakdown in its population estimates, so it is difficult to judge how many whites are in Mozambique. A fair guess on the conservative side might be 150,000, out of a total population estimated at 6.9 million.

At a sidewalk table outside the Hotel Portugal in Nampula, a white professional soldier, a lieutenant, sipped coffee and spoke of the easy relations between black men and white men in the Portuguese Army.

"The Portuguese are like a milk shake," he said. "Yes, we are like a chocolate milk shake, sometimes a little more chocolate or a little more vanilla. Who can say for sure? Who cares!"

Doesn't Worry Him

And a white farmer, Francisco Maria de Sousa, declares:

"I do not worry about the blacks here. I have 15 of them working for me. The countryside is full of them. They are not violent people."

He laughed quietly over the suggestion that the Liberation Front might dislodge the Portuguese from this vast land of 297,000 square miles — almost as big as California, Oregon and Washington combined.

"I'm sure they would like to have my farm," said Mr. de Sousa, who got the uninhabited land free after he and his wife emigrated from Torres Novas, near Lisbon, 19 year ago.

But he continued:

It's crazy to think the blacks could have this. They're not ready. It would go right back to bush.

"Besides, I'm not going anywhere. This is my country. My children were born here. If someone wants to give this farm to the blacks, he can go ahead. But he should remember one thing: I'll be here."

Afonso Bomane is black, but again and again he makes the point that he thinks of himself as Portuguese and that he identifies his interests with Portugal's. Even his clothes make the point: highly polished shoes, tight-fitting trousers, white shirt with the front half-buttoned — typical Portuguese attire.

Sure of Oil Find

Sitting under a palm at the water's edge in the hot, steamy port of Quelimane, he watches admiringly as an oil-drilling rig is towed out of the harbor. He has come from the Limpopo Valley in the south, and, like almost everyone else in Quelimane, he is quite sure that oil has been discovered not far away, in spite of official denials.

In Niassa the war is quiet now. The Makonde warriors conduct military activities but leave political activities to rebels from the Nianja and Ajaua tribes, who make up lists of prospective cabinets pending the departure of the Portuguese and go through villages in search of support. At night the war ranges 40 miles inland along Mozambique's lake shore.

Gunboats Patrol Lake

Gunboats equipped with radar and 20-mm. Oerlikon guns patrol Lake Malawi in search of guerrillas paddling down from Tanzania in dugout canoes in the darkness or under cover of vegetation that hangs over the water.

But for the most part the war in the district is waged on the Portuguese side by small army patrols that go out from isolated garrisons at Villa Cabral, Metangula, Maniamba, Cobue and Olivenca.

They rarely find the enemy, for the guerrillas usually operate in small units and avoid contact with Portuguese patrols. They rely more on mines, which they plant in dirt roads in large quantities and sometimes by imaginative means.

In Cabo Delgado the sandy tracks are almost as heavily mined, but another sort of war rages on the slopes and in the valleys around the Makonde Plateau.

The Portuguese stepped up their effort there to gain the most ground and advantage possible before the summer rains started. The roads are turning quickly into deep, impassable traps of wet sand or mud or are washing away completely. For the next four months the patrols will have to slog through the bush without vehicles.

Here the Portuguese have hemmed in their enemy by a wide band of scorched earth. Except for some easily protected settlements on the coast, not a native village has been left intact in the strip between the Montepuez and Messalu Rivers, which run roughly parallel courses, 50 miles apart, to the sea.

The area of devastation between these rivers extends a hundred miles into the interior, into forbidding bush country made almost uninhabitable by the tsetse fly.

At least 250,000 villagers were moved out of this strip, some willingly, especially those who had been raided by the guerrillas. The unwilling ones were given no choice. What they could not harvest of their crops was burned, as were their huts. Nothing was left that could have been used by the guerrillas.

150 Fortified Villages

Outside this blackened, empty perimeter, the Portuguese have laid out 150 fortified villages for the displaced people and for refugees who continue to stream in from the fighting areas.

The villagers live in the mud-and-straw huts that look like the huts in any African village. But the customary jumble of huts typical of other villages is missing in these: They have been laid out in straight lines as a defensive measure against the Makonde. The villagers are given corn, flour, canned milk and other food until they begin to harvest their own crops on their new land.

Trenches and barbed wire surround each village, and in each the inhabitants are formed into the protection militia, which is strictly defensive, or the intervention militia, whose task is to go deep into the bush to root out guerrillas.

Leader of Mozambique Liberation Movement Killed by Assassin's Bomb at Cottage in Dar es Salaam

Special to The New York Times

DAR ES SALAAM, Tanzania, Feb. 3—Dr. Eduardo Chivambo Mondlane, president of the anti-Portuguese Mozambique Liberation Front, was assassinated in Dar es Salaam today in the explosion of a time bomb at a beach house where he was working.

Once described as Portugal's most wanted man, Dr. Mondlane returned to Africa from the United States in 1963 to found the front, known as Frelimo, a merger of several nationalist groups. Armed struggle to end Portuguese rule in Mozambique began a year later.

Dr. Mondlane worked regularly at the beach house, which is owned by an American, Miss Betty King, a director of a local gemstone exporting company. Miss King is a longtime friend of Dr. Mondlane and his American wife, the former Janet Johnson of Downer's Grove, Ill. She helped found the Mozambique Institute, the liberation party's educational center. [The Associated Press reported that Mrs. Mondlane was believed to be out of Tanzania. One report said she was in Stockholm.]

The police said they believed that Dr. Mondlane arrived at Miss King's house at 11 A.M., three hours after she left for work, and that in that period the killer planted a bomb in the chair where he normally worked. The explosion apparently killed him instantly. The beach house is only a quarter of a mile from the official residence of the President of Tanzania, Julius V. Nyerere.

Tanzania's top policeman, Inspector General Elangwa Shaidi, said tonight that a number of people were undergoing interrogation. The main theories on the assassination were that it was the work either of the Portuguese or of dissident Mozambicans.

February 4, 1969

LISBON TO WIDEN AFRICA HOME RULE

Premier Says Mozambique and Angola Would Become 'Autonomous Regions'

By Reuters

LISBON, Dec. 2 — Premier Marcello Caetano told Parliament today that the Government planned to give more local autonomy to Portugal's African territories, particularly Angola and Mozambique.

He said that under proposed constitutional reforms the territories would become "autonomous regions within the Portuguese unitary state."

He rejected any possibility, however, that Portugal would give up these territories, where Portuguese forces have been fighting African liberation movements for 10 years.

Dr. Caetano made his statements in outlining to the National Assembly changes that the Government proposes to make in the Portuguese Constitution, which was drawn up in 1933. The proposals are to be discussed by the Assembly.

The proposed constitutional reforms would make no drastic changes in the country's political structure. They would retain the present system of a head of state above the direct Government of the country, and a Premier who is the head of Government. However, the National Assembly would be enlarged and given greater legislative powers.

The most important proposed changes concern the African territories.

Dr. Caetano made it clear there was no change in Portugal's basic policy of retaining the huge African territories. But he said that it was natural that they should have greater local administrative autonomy.

"I know many people are shocked by the idea of autonomy for the overseas provinces," he said, "but there is no reason for shock." The territories have local geographical and social conditions that require greater administrative freedom from Lisbon, he said.

Although Portugal's African territories are recognized by the present Constitution as having autonomy, they are virtually governed by Lisbon. Mozambique is administered by a Lisbon-appointed governor general, advised by councils partly elected under limited suffrage. Angola is also administered by a Lisbon-appointed governor general and a Legislative Council, and Guinea is governed by an appointee of the central Government.

Under the changes proposed by Dr. Caetano today, a "governor delegate" would represent Lisbon in the territories. The Premier said that the territories must have their own political and administrative organization, with laws voted by their own legislative bodies.

Dr. Caetano stressed that the Government would make certain there was complete equality in these territories. "If there are any local tendencies towards segregation," he said "they will be rooted out by the central power" in Lisbon.

He asserted that Portugal's policy was and remained "racial brotherhood" and that the Government intended to continue to work toward a multiracial society.

The Premier said the constitutional changes would extend to Brazilians living in Portugal the same rights as Portuguese to reciprocate for similar rights for Portuguese included in the Brazilian Constitution.

December 3, 1970

PORTUGAL FACING GUINEA DILEMMA

African Region Is Reported Almost in Rebel Control

By TAD SZULC

Special to The New York Times

WASHINGTON, July 4 — United States Government reports indicated today that Portuguese Guinea had been virtually overrun by revolutionaries.

Although the Portuguese Government has committed close to 10,000 troops, supported by napalm-throwing jet fighters, to Portuguese Guinea, some United States experts on the situation feel that Portugal is "up against a wall" in the tiny territory on Africa's northwest coast.

Moreover, the Portuguese are suffering heavy economic losses in trying to defend a territory that is almost worthless economically. It has 2,700 white settlers in a population of 560,000.

The information available here is that the Portuguese troops are hemmed in at Bissau, the capital, and a few other townships, while being virtually unable to move elsewhere in the jungles, the rice paddies and the network of rivers and creeks.

Guerrilla attacks and terrorist incidents are reported to be occurring with increasing frequency in the vicinity of Bissau.

Military Forces Doubled

Portugal has doubled her military forces in Portuguese Guinea since 1962, at which time the rebels are said to have held only 15 per cent of the territory of about 14,000 square miles.

In the face of almost impossible odds, it was said here, the Lisbon Government will soon have to make a decision whether to go on suffering an economic drain in Portuguese Guinea almost comparable to that it has to face in defending the rich and developed territory of Angola, in southwest Africa.

The fighting in Angola is quiescent, the analysts said, and the 40,000 to 50,000 Portuguese troops there are better than holding their own against the four-year-old rebellion.

High coffee prices and the temporary inability of the rebels to interfere with the coffee-growing zones have somewhat stabilizd the situation, but the danger remains that the rebellion will pick up again later this year, probably with greater support from African states.

In such an event, the experts said, Portugal may find herself unable to maintain her over-extended military and economic position along Africa's west coast. Furthermore, if an incipient rebel movement in Mozambique, the large Portuguese territory on the southeastern coast, also gains momentum, she may have to commit additional military resources there.

A decision to cut the losses in Portuguese Guinea and pull out is immensely difficult and embarrassing for the Government of Premier Antonio de Oliveira Salazar. Such a move might encourage the rebels in Angola and Mozambique as well as create internal problems for Dr. Salazar, particularly with military groups.

The New York Times July 5, 1964

Portuguese Guinea (shown by diagonal shading) has been reported as almost overrun by rebel forces.

Issue Sensitive in Lisbon

In December, 1961, Portugal lost her enclaves of Goa, Damão and Diu in India, and the whole matter of overseas territories, or "provinces," as the Portuguese call them, is extremely sensitive in Lisbon.

The rebellion in Portuguese Guinea is spearheaded principally by the African Party for the Independence of Portuguese Guinea and the Cape Verde Islands. The party, made up of blacks of Guinean stock and Cape Verde mulattoes, is headed by Amilcar Cabral, a 39-year-old island mulateto, who is a graduate in agronomy from Lisbon University.

It is believed here that Mr. Cabral and most of his associates are primarily nationalists with relatively moderate political views. Although some are believed to have been trained in Communist China and Czechoslovakia, and some of the automatic weapons used by the movement are of Chinese and Czech origin, no serious Communist infiltration is believed to exist.

The party has received direct support from Guinea, the independent republic south of Portuguese Guinea. Two smaller rebel movements are backed by Senegal, which lies to the north of the triangular territory.

The anti-Portuguese movement is supported by the Organization of African Unity, but it has been unable thus far to decide whether to give its full blessing to Mr. Cabral's party or to the Senegal-based movements, which are known as the Front for the Fight for National Independence of Guinea and the Union of Inhabitants of Portuguese Guinea.

July 5, 1964

In Portuguese Guinea, Time Is Rebels' Ally

By WILLIAM BORDERS
Special to The New York Times

CAMPEANE, Portuguese Guinea — This swampy little corner of West Africa is being torn apart by one of the world's last colonial wars. Here, in an area twice the size of New Jersey, Portugal is trying to defend a land that her explorers discovered 500 years ago against a growing force of black guerrillas.

The rebels, led by Amilcar Cabral, a tough, Lisbon-educated agronomist, now control at least half the country, and in it they have set up hospitals, courts, stores and schools.

"In those areas, we are no longer fighting for sovereignty," asserted Mr. Cabral. "We've achieved sovereignty. Now we are just trying to get the Portuguese to leave us the rest."

Rebel Force Is Smaller

But the Portuguese show no signs of leaving. They have recently increased their European troop strength here to 25,000 and their African armed force to 10,000.

The rebel army is much smaller—perhaps 5,000 regular troops and a militia of 5,000 men and women.

Because the rebels have no planes, the Portuguese control the air, dropping bombs and napalm on guerrilla targets, including villages. Sometimes the Portuguese land a helicopter-borne patrol in a rebel stronghold like this one. But most of their ground forces are concentrated in the few urban areas, or in fortified outposts from which they venture only cautiously.

The rebels roam more freely through the rain-soaked countryside, ambushing and laying mines, sometimes striking a Portuguese-held fort with heavy artillery, and just waiting, secure in the conviction that they can wait longer than the colonialists for victory.

"We are fighting for our home, so we are prepared to keep on fighting," explained Fernando Mendonça, a 28-year-old African soldier who has spent the last two years at a rebel army camp near here—a circle of thatched huts hidden by tall trees.

"Those Portuguese, they have a home, too. But it's not here: It's Portugal. So they just sit over there and think about going home," he said, gesturing in the direction of Cacine, a well-fortified Portuguese outpost two miles away.

According to the rebels, the 100 or so Portuguese soldiers stationed at Cacine rarely leave their encampment, which is supplied by helicopter from Bissau, the capital, 60 miles to the northwest.

But Mr. Mendonça and his guerilla company, with familiarity developed over a lifetime, can easily work their way through the dense, damp forest to within sight of the Portuguese camp. Sometimes they attack it with grenades, or turn their Soviet-made rifles on a patrol that has strayed too far.

The Portuguese fire cannon from Cacine occasionally, but they do not seem to know where to aim, because of the difficulty of air reconnaissance. Most of the rebel villages and camps in the area are well hidden by trees, and when there is fear that a camp has been spotted, it is quickly moved, stick by stick.

Casualties Are Light

Neither side has many casualties any more in this southern tier of the country, much of which the rebels seized soon after they began to fight in 1962 as a ragtag group of poorly armed young men staging hit-and-run attacks.

In other areas, especially in the east, where the fighting centers now, reports of casualties conflict.

Mr. Cabral said in an interview that the rebels had killed 500 Portuguese soldiers in the whole country this year, most of them by mines and ambushes. He said the rebels had lost "a much, much smaller number." The Portuguese say they have been losing 100 men a year, while killing 1,000 rebels.

There is also wide variance as to how much of the country each holds.

The guerrillas say that they control more than two-thirds of the territory with more than two-thirds of the population. The Portuguese claim control over 85 per cent of the population and assert that population shifts caused by the war have left nearly half the country uninhabited.

A rough estimate that emerges from observations and discussions with impartial observers is that the guerrillas control more than half the country with somewhat less than half the population.

This year, no important territory has changed hands, but the rebels hailed as "a turning point" their successful artillery attacks in June on Bissau and Bafatá, an inland commercial center.

The struggle for this impoverished land began in 1956, well before most of Africa was independent, when Mr. Cabral, then 32 years old, got together with some friends who shared his dissatisfaction with Portuguese rule and formed the African Party for the Independence of Guinea and Cape Verde. The party, known here by its Portuguese initials, P.A.I.G.C., is also seeking independence for the Cape Verde Islands, 300 miles offshore. But there has been no fighting there yet.

"No power in the world will be able to prevent the total elimination of Portuguese colonialism," Mr. Cabral said at the time. And the party set about proving it, lining up support village by village before the rebellion moved into its military phase.

In the years since, European governments have granted independence to 33 African states, changing the map of the continent. But Portugal, the only substantial overseas power left, has made it clear that she has no intention of relinquishing this land or her two other major territories, Angola and Mozambique.

Late last year, Premier Marcello Caetano of Portugal announced a plan to offer them more local autonomy, but reports from Lisbon said he was not even considering full independence.

Portugal regards the areas as overseas provinces, or, as President Américo Thomaz called them during a visit to Bissau, "sacred portions of national territory."

Guerrilla forces are fighting for independence in Angola and Mozambique, too, but they are meeting with less success there, and informed observers consider the fight in Guinea the only one of Portugal's three territorial wars that she is in real danger of losing, either militarily or through a forced political settlement.

Fighting on these three fronts, the Caetano Government has a total of more than 125,000 white soldiers stationed in Africa. In proportion to her population, this is a military presence five times as great as the largest that the United States has had in Vietnam.

Lisbon calls the rebels terrorists, and points out that most of their backing comes from Communist countries. In response, the rebels say that they will take their aid as it comes.

For years, in fact, the African Party for the Independence of Guinea and Cape Verde has received substantial help from China and the Soviet bloc. Those countries still provide most of the party's support, offering more than 100 scholarships a year to young members, and shipping into the forests around here a range of gifts from heavy artillery to mosquito nets.

Now Sweden has joined the cause, providing $500,000 worth of medicine in the last two years. Private groups have begun sending in donations from Rome, Paris and New York.

"Success is very attractive," said a well-informed observer in a neighboring African country. "People are rushing to jump on the rebels' bandwagon so that when independence comes they will have been on the right side."

The rebels say that the United Nations Children's Fund and the United Nations Educational, Scientific and Cultural Organization have promised this year to start sending medicine and schoolbooks here, and African neighbors have also become friendlier as the rebels have gained ground.

The military equipment, an impressive supply that includes heavy machine guns, bazookas and mortar, all comes from the Communist countries. In some white-governed African countries, Moscow and Peking support rival guerrilla groups, but not in Portuguese Guinea, because Mr. Cabral no longer has any significant rivals.

Cubans Staff Hospital

The rebels also use the territory of their very friendly neighbor for party headquarters and for a high school and a hospital usually staffed with a few Cuban doctors who are, they say, the only foreigners actively helping in the region.

"We stress that those Cubans usually stay outside our borders," said José Araujo, the official responsible for party affairs in this southern section of the country. "The Portuguese say we're being commanded here by all manner of foreign Communists, but there is almost no one anywhere in the liberated area who is not Guinean."

Discussing help from abroad, Mr. Cabral said:

"We will take aid from anyone. In fact, we would be most grateful if those who are not aiding us — the United States, for example — would simply stop aiding the other side."

"Portugal is a poor country, unable to make her own bombs and planes," the guerrilla leader continued in an interview. "All we ask is that the world stop arming Portugal, and then we can finish up our struggle."

Mr. Cabral charges that the United States, Britain, West Germany and France have all provided aircraft or armaments that Portugal is using in Africa. Some of the military aid that reaches here, he alleged, is provided through the North Atlantic Treaty Organization, to which all five nations belong.

Americans Denies Charge

American spokesmen vehemently deny the charge, pointing out that a 1961 embargo as well as NATO regulations forbid Portugal to use such arms in her African territories.

Moreover, they stress that United States policy favors self-determination here, and that its military aid to Portugal, a small program centered on antisubmarine warfare and air defense, would have little application to this conflict.

Photographs for The New York Times by WILLIAM BORDERS

Jungle provides protection in raids against their enemy

When the subject of independence arises in Lisbon, several reasons are advanced for keeping Mozambique and Angola: they are both rich countries by African standards, they provide a market for one-fourth of Portugal's exports, and Angola has 400,000 white settlers.

But Portuguese Guinea is small and poor, with no mineral or agricultural wealth, and almost all of the several thousand European settlers who used to live here have departed because of the war. The African population is about 600,000.

The Portuguese also offer a version of the domino theory—success for the rebels here would encourage the rebels in Angola and Mozambique, and set a precedent for their independence.

Some Portuguese cite Communist influence in what might be regarded as a strategic part of the Atlantic coastline. But rebel leaders insist that they envision an independent nation beholden to no foreign power.

Premier Caetano points out that self-government in many African countries has proved no guarantee of human rights. He says he wants "to spare our Africa the calamities of phony independence." Others in Lisbon see the Portuguese role here as a continuation of the colonial civilizing mission, insuring the benefits of the Portuguese culture.

But Mr. Cabral, waving his hands in the air for emphasis, answers: "I am Portuguese-trained, and Portuguese is my language. I would be imbued with their culture and traditions even if I did not want to be. Let this country have independence, and then we and the Portuguese will naturally be friends again."

Key Anti-Portuguese Leader In West Africa Is Assassinated

By The Associated Press

DAKAR, Senegal, Jan. 21—Amilcar Cabral, one of the most prominent leaders of the African struggle against white supremacy, was assassinated last night in front of his home in Conakry, the capital of Guinea.

President Sékou Touré of Guinea announced Mr. Cabral's death in an emotional speech today over the Conakry radio.

Mr. Touré said that Mr. Cabral "was assassinated in a cowardly and horrible manner last night, Saturday, at 10:30 P.M. in front of his own house, by the poisoned hands of imperialism and Portuguese colonialism."

The "principal killers" were arrested in Conakry soon after the assassination, President Touré said.

The President did not indicate how the black nationalist leader had been killed. Mr. Cabral lived with his wife in a villa in Conakry put at his disposal by Guinean authorities.

Mr. Cabral, whose forces claimed control of more than half the territory of Portuguese Guinea in West Africa, achieved new prominence last October when he was allowed to give an address at the United Nations in New York as a spokesman for all the black African independence movements.

He was the founder and president of the nationalist group known as the African party for the Independence of Guinea and Cape Verde.

No Comment From Lisbon

LISBON, Jan. 21 (AP)—Portuguese Government spokesmen refused comment tonight on Mr. Cabral's death or on Mr. Touré's charge that Portugal had been involved in the assassination.

Headed Revolutionary Army

By ERIC PACE

As the leader of the most successful revolt against Portuguese rule in Africa, the 48-year-old Mr. Cabral was enormously respected in black and Arab Africa. But fellow African insurgents said that he lived in constant danger of being killed by agents of the Portuguese.

Mr. Cabral himself mentioned the possibility in an interview when he visited New York last year, accompanied by a bodyguard or two. In his soft, melodious English, he said the danger could not be avoided by a man in his position. Then he changed the subject and began to speak of his hopes for what he called his nation.

Amilcar Cabral's position was at the head of a ragtag force of perhaps 10,000 black men and women. They were trying to wrest their swampy corner of West Africa from the grip of the Portuguese, who first trod its steamy shores five centuries ago.

When he appeared at the United Nations last October, Mr. Cabral reported that his forces controlled three-quarters of Portuguese Guinea, which is a coastal enclave twice the size of New Jersey. It lies between Guinea and Senegal.

Independence Predicted

A short man with eyeglasses and a scholarly manner, Mr. Cabral reported to the Committee on Trust and Non-Self-Governing Territories that the insurgents had "set up regional governments and our first national assembly with 120 representatives," based on "universal and secret suffrage in all liberated areas." And he said in the interview that his "nation" would declare its independence within a few months.

Thus by Mr. Cabral's account—and in the view of independent observers—his movement was far closer to success than the other best-known anti-Portuguese insurgency in Africa, the Mozambique Liberation Front. That movement, known as Frelimo, was shaken by the assassination of its leader, Dr. Eduardo C. Mondlane, in Tanzania four years ago. African nationalists blamed the Portuguese for that killing, too, although the killer or killers were never found.

Last year the Mozambique Liberation Front's representative, Marcelino Dos Santos, told the United Nations committee that his group controlled one-quarter of Mozambique which, like Portuguese Guinea, is administered as an overseas province of Portugal. But Portuguese spokesmen disputed the claims of both Mr. Cabral and Mr. Dos Santos.

It was in metropolitan Portugal that Mr. Cabral obtained his higher education, in agronomy; something of the courtly air of his Lisbon professors stayed with him through his life.

He looked as much at ease in a diplomat's starchy white shirt as in a guerrilla's combat fatigues.

Mr. Cabral seemed always to keep a clear sense of identity as an African—although in fact he was born not on the African Continent but in the offshore Cape Verde Islands, a Portuguese possession, and was of mixed European and African ancestry.

After finishing his studies, Mr. Cabral became director of an experimental agricultural center in Bissau, the capital of Portuguese Guinea.

Then, during the nineteen-fifties, he founded the African party for the Independence of Guinea and Cape Verde, which received the backing of President Touré and of the Organization of African Unity, which has headquarters in Addis Ababa, Ethiopia.

Like other guerrilla movements, the party has been very much a one-man show, dominated from the beginning by the strong personality of Mr. Cabral. The party has no obvious successor.

His admirers said that Mr. Cabral was a skillful organizer and that one of his slogans was: "Hide nothing from the masses of the people. Tell no lies, mask no failures, claim no easy victories."

Ideologically, Mr. Cabral was a moderate compared with more leftist insurgent leaders elsewhere in the world. But some Portuguese critics called him a Communist, and he berated Western powers for providing Portugal with arms.

In 1970, Mr. Cabral was received by Pope Paul VI, an unusual honor for an insurgent chief.

And in New York last year he said he wanted his new "nation" to be like Brazil, a former Portuguese colony that has close ties with Lisbon.

Mr. Cabral traveled widely in search of foreign support, and a measure of his diplomatic skill was the fact that he was friendly with the Governments of both Senegal and Guinea, although relations between those two nations have frequently been strained.

The Guinean Government aided Mr. Cabral's movement, and provided him with a house in Conakry, the capital, where he and his wife spent much of their time and where, according to President Touré, he was killed.

January 22, 1973

CHAPTER 4

Political and Economic Development

Children play around the fallen statue of Kwame Nkrumah in Ghana after the president was overthrown by a coup.

Courtesy Compix.

AFRICAN FAVORS ONE-PARTY RULE

Guinea Minister Upholds It at Parley on Governing Newly Freed Lands

By THOMAS F. BRADY

Special to The New York Times.

IBADAN, Nigeria, March 17—A representative of newly independent Guinea declared today that the one-party system of his country was the only efficient method of government in new African nations.

Abdoulaye Diallo, Guinea's Minister to Ghana, said at a conference of African intellectuals and political leaders that his country's method was democratic because the ruling party had its roots in the people and reflected their will through constant consultation.

But, the Minister continued, there is no "opposition for opposition's sake" and no struggle by individuals to take over power from other individuals in Guinea. Such struggles are a waste of time and energy and therefore inefficient in new countries, he said, where social programs are the first consideration.

M. Diallo's position in Ghana is a dual one because of the union that has been proclaimed between the former French territory of Guinea and Ghana, formerly the British Gold Coast. He not only serves as his country's envoy but also sits in the Ghanaian Cabinet as Minister of Guinea. Ghana has a similar minister in Guinea.

The conference, a seminar on representative government and national progress in Africa, is sponsored by University College here and by the Congress for Cultural Freedom. Those attending are chiefly from British and French areas.

Self-Government Gains

It started yesterday, twenty-four hours after the British authorities had turned over local government to the Northern Region of the Nigeria Federation. Ibadan is the capital of the Western Region, which like the Eastern Region has had local self-government since 1956. The three-region federation will become independent next year.

The transfer of powers in the Northern Region will not be celebrated publicly until May, because its people are Moslems and are now observing the month-long fast of Ramadan, which virtually precludes daylight activity.

M. Diallo's proclamation of a one-party philosophy, which appears to be that of Prime Minister Kwame Nkrumah of Ghana, as well as Premier Sekou Touré of Guinea, followed a discourse on the role of political opposition in new countries by S. N. Eisenstadt, professor of sociology at Hebrew University, Jerusalem.

David Apter, a Professor of Political Science at the University of Chicago, replied to M. Diallo, stressing the value of an opposition as the representative of minority interests, as a critic of government and as a source of information for the people.

Ignatio Pinto, Minister of Justice of neighboring Dahomey, an autonomous republic of the new French African Community, spoke in support of M. Diallo's position. He said opposition in the new countries was unfortunately motivated in almost every case not by interest in the public weal but by the desire of the outs to enjoy the fruits of power.

Last night at dinner, however, M. Pinto had said in conversation that he expected to go into opposition against his own Prime Minister, S. M. Apithy, because the latter is opposing Dahomey's membership in the new Mali Confederation of West African republics, which M. Pinto favors.

Several Nigerians, members of the university faculty, spoke in favor of the Western democratic system of parliamentary majority and opposition. The Western Region of Nigeria, of which the university is the intellectual center, is probably the most advanced non-white territory in Africa, with the largest indigenous middle class and therefore with the fullest understanding and acceptance of Western political philosophy.

March 18, 1959

African Democracy

The visit of Prime Minister Kwame Nkrumah of Ghana to Britain has revived discussion there and elsewhere of the political drift of Ghana and the other newly independent countries of Black Africa. The general feeling is one of disappointment, and yet one may well ask if the criticisms are reasonable.

Certainly Ghana has drifted steadily into a one-man, one-party authoritarian state under Kwame Nkrumah. Will it stay that way? Is anything else possible today? Is the Western form of parliamentary democracy suitable for nations like Ghana?

What all of us are asking is whether newly formed states, or states in revolutionary transition, or even states recovering from the tremendous shock of a modern war, can rely exclusively on parliamentary democracy. Ask this question in Ghana, Guinea, the Sudan and elsewhere in independent Black Africa; ask it in Egypt, Iraq or Cuba; ask it in France or West Germany, not to mention Spain and Portugal, and one gets a variety of dubious answers. Every one of these countries, as The London Times pointed out a few days ago, has turned to a person, a leader, even while retaining a parliamentary structure and even—in cases like France and West Germany—while remaining democracies.

Ghana is relatively wealthy, with her cocoa crop, but generally speaking these new African countries have a narrow, rural economic base with high illiteracy and low political consciousness. There are few trained civil servants, and little grass-roots democracy, due to the tribal way of life.

Perhaps it was asking too much to expect countries like Ghana, Guinea and the Sudan suddenly to become democracies in our sense of the word. But perhaps also, with patience, we will see them evolve some form of democracy suitable to their tribal society.

August 12, 1959

Africa Needs Time—

A leader of the upwelling independence movement on that continent says the goals are clear but that Africans must be allowed to find their own ways to democracy.

By JULIUS K. NYERERE

WITHIN ten years, Africa will have won its fight against foreign domination. Then the continent will be free to concentrate on its battle for the consolidation of its freedom, the achievement of economic, political and moral equality before the whole world.

The slogan "Africa must be free" must not be confined to the idea of freedom from foreign rule. It must, if it means anything at all, mean freedom for the individual man and woman —freedom from every form of oppression, indignity, intimidation or exploitation. It must include the right of the individual citizen to re-elect or to replace the Government of his own country. It must also, of course, include the freedom of the Government to govern, without fear of any attempt to replace it by means other than that of the ballot box.

THE African claims that his fight is for democratic rights. There are many, both in Africa and elsewhere, who believe in the sincerity of that claim. There are others who question whether, in fact, the African can really understand or practice democracy. It would be naïve to think that African nationalists do not themselves sometimes question whether, once having established democratic institutions in their own countries, it will in fact be possible to use those institutions to maintain full democratic rights. But I have often wondered whether the people who question either the sincerity of the African's belief in democracy, or his ability to establish and safeguard democratic rights, are clear in their own minds as to what the essentials of democracy really are.

Too often the doubters of an African democracy have confined their idea of it to certain democratic institutions or forms which have been developed in particular countries and as the result of local circumstances and national characteristics peculiar to those countries.

JULIUS K. NYERERE is president of Tanganyika's most powerful political party, the Tanganyika African National Union, and seems assured of becoming Prime Minister when his country achieves self-government next fall. This article was adapted from a speech he gave at a symposium on Africa at Wellesley College.

For instance, the British critic when he speaks of "democracy" has a picture in his own mind of the Parliament buildings, a party in power within those Parliament buildings, and another party within the same imposing buildings, not actually in power but with hopes of getting into power if and when its turn comes to win a general election, and in the meantime enjoying the title of Her Majesty's Opposition.

So, to the Briton, democracy is an institution consisting of a debating house where one group is "for" and another "against" the motion, and each group is quite distinct from the other. Similarly, the American critic has his own picture of democracy. Each is confusing the machinery, or structure, with the essence. Each is, in fact, saying: "Can you imagine an African country where you have one party governing and another party in opposition?" To these critics an organized and officially recognized Opposition has become almost the essence of democracy.

I MAY be oversimplifying the basis of the criticism and doubts, but that is certainly the way in which most people argue when they question Africa's ability to maintain a democratic form of government. They assume that if a country is governed by one party alone, the Government cannot be a "democratic" one. In doing so, I suggest, they ignore three important facts.

The first is this: that a country's struggle for freedom from foreign domination is a patriotic struggle; it leaves no room for difference. The issue, at that stage, is a simple one, and one which unites all elements in the country. As a result you find, in Africa and in other parts of the world that face a similar challenge, the growth not of a "political party" but of a nationalist movement. It is this nationalist movement which fights for, and achieves, independence; and it, therefore, inevitably forms the first Government of the independent state.

IT would surely be ridiculous to expect a country—for the sake of conforming to a particular expression of democracy, which happens to be seen in terms of a Government party and an Opposition party, and midstream in a struggle that calls for the complete unity of all its people—voluntarily to divide itself in order to produce a ready-made Opposition at the moment of independence. Democracy has been described as a government of the people, by the people, for the people. Surely, if a Government is freely elected by the people, there can be nothing undemocratic about it just because nearly all the people, rather than only some of them, happen to have voted it into power?

Indeed, it appears to be natural that young nations which emerge as the result of a nationalist movement that has united their people shall be governed at first by a nationalist government as distinct from a party government; and no one should therefore jump to the conclusion that this means such a country is not democratic, or does not intend to remain democratic.

ANOTHER factor generally forgotten by these critics is that the presence of an organized Opposition as a visible symbol of "democracy" is not, in fact, universal. It is rather the Anglo-Saxon's symbolic demonstration of his own democracy. In particular, the two-party system one finds in countries with an Anglo-Saxon tradition implies something which Americans may not like, but which to my mind is nevertheless true —it implies the existence of a class struggle.

The third factor that is conveniently forgotten by some critics of African democracy is the history of Africa. In traditional African society the African never was — nor thought himself to be—a cog in a machine. He was a free individual in his own society. But his conception of "government" was personal, not institutional. When government was mentioned, the African thought of the chief; unlike the Briton, he did not picture a grand building in which a debate was taking place.

The colonizers of Africa did little to change this. In colo-

VOICE — Tanganyika's Julius K. Nyerere, author of this article.

nial Africa you mention the word "government," and the average person immediately thinks of the district commissioner, the provincial commissioner or the governor. When, later, the mad African like myself reads Abraham Lincoln and John Stuart Mill, and demands that government should become institutional, what happens? The district commissioner, the provincial commissioner and the governor—the very ones who have come to symbolize government in their persons—resist this demand. We have to keep on insisting and "agitating" until, at the eleventh hour, our demands are granted, elections take place, and then government becomes, almost overnight, an institution. But this happens only shortly before the country achieves independence.

In these circumstances, it would be surprising if the pattern of democratic government in Africa were to take on, immediately, the shape familiar to the United Kingdom or to the United States. But it would be unfair to assume, therefore, that it was any less dedicated to the preservation of the rights of the individual. Indeed, it is an injustice to African democrats when their fellow democrats in other parts of the world accept without thought the facile, and in fact illogical, criticisms of the very people who have delayed the establishment of democratic institutions in Africa.

It is important to emphasize the difference between democracy itself and the various forms it can take. To my mind, there are two essentials of democracy. The first of these is the freedom and well-being of the individual; the second is that the method by which the Government of a country is chosen must insure that the Government is freely chosen by the people.

When I say that Africa, today, seems to be in the best position to champion personal freedom and the democracy to preserve that freedom, I am not basing my claim solely on the moral strength which is hers because of her history. There is another, though less lofty, factor. In the world today there is a conflict between the advocates of the freedom of the individual and those who champion the primacy of the state. When one examines the differences between the ideologies of the Eastern and Western powers, one can reduce them generally to this very conflict.

The West seems to have exaggerated its idea of freedom beyond the point where freedom becomes license; to have accepted a society in which, provided a man does not too obviously steal or murder, he can defend any form of self-indulgence by calling it "freedom of the individual." The Communist world—largely, I think, as a reaction against this exaggeration—has swung like a pendulum to the other extreme; the individual in a Communist society is secondary to something called the state.

Here, then, I think is the problem: where does society, or the state, draw the boundary of its rights and obligations; and where does the individual? It is a problem that has not yet been solved by either side in a way that can be accepted by the other.

In primitive African society this question of the limits of responsibility as between the individual and the society in which he lived was not very clearly defined. The traditional African community was a small one, and the African could not think of himself apart from his community. He was an individual; he had his wife, or wives, and children—so he belonged to a family. But the family merged into a larger "blood" family which, itself, merged into the tribe.

Thus he saw himself all the time as a member of a community; but he saw no struggle between his own interests and those of his community, for his community was to him an extension of his family. He might have seen a conflict between himself and another individual member of the same community, but with the community itself—never. He never felt himself to be a cog in a machine. There could not be this all-embracing, all-powerful modern concept of society which could "use" him as a cog.

That traditional "community" is still visible in Africa today; in a sense it is one of our problems. Having come into contact with a civilization which has overemphasized the freedom of the individual, we are in fact faced with one of the big problems of Africa in the modern world. Our problem is just this: how to get the benefits of European society—benefits that have been brought about by an organization based upon the individual—and yet retain Africa's own structure of society in which the individual is a member of a kind of fellowship.

Let me put this another way. One of the complaints of the European employer in Africa is that the African is paid a wage to which he has agreed, and then complains that it is not enough after all—usually because he does not use this wage merely upon himself and his family; there are others who lay claim upon his wage.

This is a fact; but one must not think that the African is therefore a natural "Communist." He is not. To him, the wage is his wage, the property is his property; but his brother's need is his brother's need and he cannot ignore that need. He has not learned to ask, "Am I my brother's keeper?" The African is not "communistic" in his thinking; he is—if I may coin the expression—"communitary." He is not a member of a commune—some artificial unit of human beings; he is a member of a genuine community, or family.

Today, when there is this conflict between East and West—and I have said that I think this conflict is basically one between the rights of the individual and the rights of the state—Western Europe, which has had a much longer experience of its own pattern of society, is becoming self-critical. Africa is, in this sense, fortunate in that there is still to be found on our continent a form of organization of society which solves the fundamental conflict between the individual and society. It should be possible, therefore, for Africa to use both its own basic structure and the self-criticism of Western Europe to evolve a form of society that can satisfy both sides.

We are not so naïve that we do not realize the problems new countries must face, and the anxious times through which such countries must

MAN AT WORK—An African on a construction project in Togo.

pass. Nor are we unaware of the efforts, and even sacrifices, which people in new countries may be called upon to make in the national interest and in the process of consolidating their newly won freedom through economic reconstruction.

But, even when all this is granted, there should be no conflict between our commitment to freedom for the individual and our need for national effort. In fact, these can work together harmoniously as long as the emphasis is on the "national" interest, as implying the interest of the individuals who comprise the nation. What would need to be generated is a positive response on the part of the individuals and groups within the country.

The Africa we must create, the Africa we must bequeath to posterity, the Africa of our dreams, cannot be an Africa that is simply free from foreign domination. It must be an Africa that the outside world will look at and say: "Here is a continent that has truly free human beings." The outside world must be able to say: "If you really want to see how a free people conduct their affairs—if you want to see a people who live up to their ideals of human society—go to Africa! That is the Continent of Hope for the human race."

I feel that Africa's own tradition, her moral strength, her lack of ties with one power bloc or another, and that sentiment of oneness which the centuries of suffering have built among all her peoples, can together fit her for the role I have suggested—the role of champion of personal freedom in the world today.

NEW LANDS FULL OF HOPE AND PERIL

George Kimble's Broad Survey Tells Us What Tropical Africa Is and Might Be

TROPICAL AFRICA. Vol. I, Land and Livelihood. Vol. II, Society and Polity. By George H. T. Kimble. Illustrated. 603 pp. and 506 pp. New York: The Twentieth Century Fund. $15 the set.

By GWENDOLEN M. CARTER

WITH the news columns full of reports on Africa, with the United Nations welcoming Nigeria, the most populous country on the continent, as its ninety-ninth member and its twenty-sixth African state, it is hard to realize that only seven years ago when George H. T. Kimble started work, for the Twentieth Century Fund, on this important survey, tropical Africa was largely unfamiliar to the American public. Only three years ago, when Ghana became the first country of the area to graduate from colonial control to independence, there was still a paucity of first-rate reporting and also of first-rate books on Africa written by Americans.

Even today, events on that continent have far outstripped our resources for understanding them. But at least there are many works now available from which to gain understanding of the factors affecting this fastest changing section of the international community. Among these works, Mr. Kimble's is the most comprehensive.

The area with which it is concerned, more than twice the size of the United States, is bordered by the Sahara and South Africa, by the Atlantic and the Indian Oceans. It is an area whose common elements often seem overbalanced by its contrasts. It includes deserts, tropical rain forests, high plateaus and snow-capped mountains. It is comprised of forty-one political territories. Some of them are wholly African and some are multi-racial. Others are independent and some, notably Angola and Mozambique, are still tightly controlled by a European country. The area has a population of about 170 million, among whom there are about 600 recognizably distinct groups, most of them with their own language.

NO general reader should be discouraged by the fact that "Tropical Africa" comprises two volumes and over a thousand pages. This is a work which generally reads easily and wears its learning lightly. Particularly in those chapters where he describes the land and livelihood of the people, Mr. Kimble has avoided technicalities and provided the kind of setting which makes sense

Photograph by Omar Marcus from "Tropical Africa."
Africans bicycle to town on newly surfaced roads near Salisbury, Southern Rhodesia.

to the non-specialist. Of the woods, he writes: "A forest means different things to different people. To one it means raw material; to another food; to a third adventure; to a fourth fertility, and to a fifth firewood." Even the more detailed material on different types of trees that follows this introduction carries a picture of their relation to the economy.

Sprinkled throughout the book are nuggets of information interesting in themselves and significant because they illustrate broader issues:

The distribution of population throughout tropical Africa is the result less of features of physical geography than of cultural, military and other historical factors. There were migrations, the objects of which were subsistence, or work, or (as in the movement of 100,000 people from Mozambique to Nyasaland between 1900 and 1920) escape from colonial excesses.

Only 10 per cent of the people of Africa live in towns of 5,000 people or more. Two-thirds of all the area's 455 towns are in West Africa, one-quarter of them in Nigeria.

There is a lower percentage of males to females among Africans 95.6 per 100 than in any other continent except Europe.

Forty-three per cent of Africans are under 15 years of age, as compared to 27 per cent in the United States.

Contemporary trends suggest that the population will double in the next fifty years.

The power potential of the Congo basin is one-quarter that of the whole world.

Lake Victoria is three times the size of Massachusetts. Because the White Nile flows out of that lake, Uganda has a potential control over both the Sudan and Egypt.

Without the rain forest (which is less widely present in tropical Africa than the popular stereotype suggests) there would be no year-round navigation on African rivers. It is these rivers which are least subject to extensive flooding.

Some African cultivators have developed an indigenous agricultural expertness. The Kara on Lake Victoria have found out how to support 600 people to a square mile.

ON the whole, however, the soil of tropical Africa is poor, and the luxuriance of its plant life depends on what Mr. Kimble calls the "current account" of rainfall and plant decomposition. Speaking of the great danger of erosion, especially where the forest has been cleared, he points out that "hooves are often as quick as hoes to set soil in motion." This is one of the many illustrations that arise from his first-hand experience in many parts of the continent.

It is natural to compare a work of this scope with the monumental and classic volume by Lord Hailey, "An African Survey," which first appeared in 1938 and was revised in 1956. The interests of the two authors clearly differentiate both their scope and their emphasis. Mr. Kimble, a geographer based at Indiana University, is at his best in describing the physical framework within which life must be carried on in tropical Africa, the patterns of settlement and the forms of economic activity. All of these are treated in his first, and longer volume.

Society and politics are considered in his second volume. This begins with an account of social change under different conditions of life and of the influences of education and of efforts to curb the sicknesses which have long debilitated the peoples of tropical Africa. Where Lord Hailey devoted most of his attention to colonial policies and the administration of African affairs, Mr. Kimble treats these subjects with relative brevity. It is in these chapters, also, that the sense of perspective so evident in the first volume becomes somewhat blurred, that detail sometimes replaces distinctions and that the march of events has clearly outstripped the printing press.

WHAT makes tropical Africa so significant today is the fact that its recently independent states constitute a new factor in international affairs. Already we have seen the chief figures of the West and of the Soviet bloc appealing for their support in the United Nations. At the same time, we have seen the response of these newly independent states to the appeal for troops for the Congo and their support of U. N. Secretary General Dag Hammarskjold. If they are neutralists, as they maintain they wish to be, it is a positive neutralism, which sees international organization as their chief support and aid.

Can independent Africa, in spite of its Balkanization, be a stable force in the international community? The disorders in the former Belgian Congo should not be allowed to cloud the fact that fifteen other African states have achieved independence without violence or division in 1960 alone. The credit for this achievement must be divided between (1) the African leaders and their organizations that have established a national unity bridging, often with difficulty, the tribal divisions which naturally separate their people; and (2) the British and French administrations which did so much to prepare the way for stable regimes.

That problems and difficulties lie ahead goes without saying. It is also likely that many African states will fail to follow the patterns of parliamentary institutions and of administration that Europe has left to them. What is chiefly important is (1) that with outside aid they can handle their own problems of development; (2) that their governments retain popular support; and (3) that opportunities are permitted for the expression of criticism, not necessarily through a formal parliamentary opposition but possibly within open-ended, one-party regimes, or through youth or women's groups, or trade unions, or even the army, which in some new countries has a number of progressive, educated leaders.

The chief political danger spots in tropical Africa are those where tribal rivalries threaten to impede national unity, as in Uganda, or where, as in Southern Rhodesia, the balance of power between long established white residents and African majorities is still unsettled. Tropical Africa understandably still believes the slogan popularized by President Kwame Nkrumah of Ghana, "Seek ye the political kingdom and all else shall be added unto it." As independence is won, new problems appear. In the near future the African and multi-racial states alike will face their toughest strains.

So careful a survey as Mr. Kimble's makes it obvious that tropical Africa's potentialities for economic growth need careful nurturing. The leaders of every new country feel compelled to provide more for their people than did the colonial regime that they succeed. Such countries necessarily lack skilled manpower and often their people do not have a compulsion toward achievement.

Hurray for those who have
never invented anything,
Hurray for those who have
never explored anything,
Hurray for those who have
never conquered anything,
But who, in awe, give themselves up to the essence of things,

writes one of the chief exponents of a distinctive "African personality."

NO one would denigrate this concern for spiritual rather than material achievement. Yet in the light of the African leaders' ambitions for their countries, this concern may well work against achievement of the goals they have set.

It is the great merit of Mr. Kimble's work that it provides a clear, sound account of the potentialities and liabilities of tropical Africa, of what has been accomplished and what is necessary in order to achieve more.

AFRICAN NATIONS FACE A VAST TASK OF DEVELOPMENT

One-Commodity Economies and Shortages of Capital Are Among Problems

By LEONARD INGALLS

Economic progress in Africa is slow. Some improvement occurred in 1962 and more is indicated this year, but the task confronting the continent is vast and long-range.

Although great forward steps have been made in the last 15 years, many formidable obstacles remain. These include political instability, illiteracy, poor communications, malnutrition, overpopulation, single-commodity economies and shortages of development capital.

All over the continent efforts were being made to reduce the impact of these and other impediments. New oil refineries were under way in North Africa, greater inducements to foreign investment were being offered in West Africa, new roads were being cut through the jungles of East Africa, new factories were springing up in Central Africa and South Africa was on the verge of a boom.

However, the scale of all these new activities remained small in relation to the size of the problem.

Export Prices Decline

Meanwhile, economic trends in Africa in 1962 followed the pattern of the last few years. The dominant factor was the depressed level of prices on the world market for many African exports while prices of capital goods that had to be imported for development were going up.

In terms of foreign trade, exports were in the neighborhood of $6,600,000,000, imports were about $8,000,000,000.

African prospects for this and future years depend in large measure on efforts to obtain greater markets for exports in industrialized countries, and on plans to compensate those nations whose commodities are based on a single product for the fluctuations in world market prices.

Eighteen countries that formerly made up French Africa will have the aid this year of a fund provided by the European Common Market countries. This help is intended to enable them to become more efficient producers of cotton, coffee and cocoa, which France had been buying from them at inflated prices. In East Africa, moves are being made by Kenya, Uganda and Tanganyika to continue what is, in effect, a common market of the three countries. A mission representing the three traveled to Brussels early this year for preliminary talks on the possibilities of establishing a trade relationship with the European Common Market.

The possibility of regional economic associations is one of the most lively topics being discussed by the leaders of newly independent African countries.

Emperor Haile Selassie of Ethiopia has invited the heads of other African states to a conference in Addis Ababa in May to discuss continental trade, an African common market, closer economic ties and better communications.

But one of the most promising regional groupings, particularly from an economic standpoint, appears to be on the threshhold of breaking apart.

Seek to Break Away

This is the 10-year-old federation in Central Africa of Rhodesia and Nyasaland. Both Northern Rhodesia and Nyasaland have indicated they want to break their ties with Southern Rhodesia because the federation is dominated by that white-controlled British colony.

In addition to what Africans are doing themselves to improve their economic situation, they are also receiving increasing amounts of aid from the rest of the world. In 1962 the International Bank for Reconstruction and Development and its affiliates provided $89,500,000 in loans to African countries for development.

In another of Africa's most serious trouble spots, the former Belgian Congo, inflation is still a great problem. This was caused by the high level of Government expenditures and low revenues. The 1962 budget called for spending $300,000,000 and foresaw revenues of about $100,000,000, a gap that was filled chiefly by printing money.

Another country, Ghana, in which political problems have discouraged outside investment, has moved to correct the situation. President Kwame Nkrumah has introduced legislation to remove restraints on the transfer of profits, grant generous tax and tariff exemptions, and give guarantees against nationalization except in unusual circumstances and then with fair compensation.

In East Africa a flight of capital that began three years ago as the area approached independence has abated. The economies of Kenya, Uganada and Tanganyika area are basically agricultural and are considered sound.

For all Africa the problem of raising its economic standards remains enormous. The United Nation's Economic Commission for Africa has estimated that to raise the continent's consumption standards to the level prevailing in Western industrialized countries in 1960, a 25-fold increase in industrial production and doubling of agricultural output would be required.

Such an increase, the commission estimated, would take 40 to 50 years at an annual rate of 7 to 8 per cent in industry and 1 to 2 per cent in agriculture.

April 19, 1963

British Still Take Economic Responsibility in Africa Seriously

By LAWRENCE FELLOWS
Special to The New York Times

LONDON—For all practical purposes, Kenya's independence and the dissolution of the Federation of Rhodesia and Nyasaland last year marked the end of the British Empire in Africa.

Yet Britain would be the last to contend that these events marked the end of her responsibilities on that continent.

Africa, bigger than the United States, China and India put together, is throbbing with the promise of political, economic and social upheaval.

Few of its independent states are economically viable. Its imperial frontiers, drawn at conference tables in Europe, cut straight through the continent without economic or ethnic meaning.

The imperial frontiers remain, but the economic federations created by the imperial powers have broken apart.

The African politicians have inherited a system that cries out for change. Chou En-lai's tour of the continent serves as a reminder that China, as well as the Soviet Union, is standing by in the hope of picking up some of the pieces.

Britain's trade with Africa is based mainly on the primary products that come from those countries — foods, minerals, hides, timber and such. As trade continues to grow there is no expectation that it will depart radically from the old channels.

Nor is there any expectation that it will be seriously disrupted by the Common Market, the forthcoming negotiations under the General Agreement on Tariffs and Trade, or political developments elsewhere.

Britain's economic aid to Africa is still mainly committed through bilateral agreements to national development programs. It is largely designed to maintain the political stability of those new members of the Commonwealth that have old trade patterns to protect.

More and more Britain is investing and providing technical assistance on a regional basis in Africa, as it becomes increasingly obvious that only through regional development will Africa ever achieve self-sustaining economic growth and social and political stability.

Parliament last year gave the Commonwealth Development Corporation enormous new scope by enabling it to start projects in countries before they get their independence and carry the projects to completion afterward.

It has invested $42 million in the Kariba hydroelectric system in the Rhodesias. In Swaziland it has started an integrated afforestation and woodpulp program on a large scale, in partnership with private enterprise.

It is engaged in several territories in activities that range from household mortgage finance to industrial development, and is reaching out now into regional transport and telephone systems.

Britons Put to Work

Britain is also turning her own surplus industrial capacity to use in her assistance programs wherever she can. Last year she concluded a loan agreement with East African Railways to buy diesel locomotives and railroad ferries from Britain.

Algeria, Senegal and the Cameroon Republic, outside the Commonwealth, got loans tied to British products.

The British Government has been working with other donor countries, especially the United States, to achieve more by pooling resources and to avoid the kind of misplaced overabundance that could distort an economy.

In Ghana, Britain is participating with the International Bank for Reconstruction and Development and the United States Government in the Volta hydroelectric project.

In the field of technical assistance, the most notable new development of this kind of cooperation is the Anglo-American "teachers for East Africa" program, now in its third year.

The aim is to provide graduate trained teachers for secondary schools and teacher training institutes in Kenya, Tanganyika and Uganda, where political federation is still a good possibility. Britain and the United States have each undertaken to provide 134 teachers for the program this year.

In East Africa, Britain is also meeting half the cost of the regional research organizations maintained by the Governments of Kenya, Tanganyika Uganda and Zanzibar.

She is providing regional agricultural and medical assistance, and surveying and mapping the Kafue Basin development project in Northern Rhodesia, the Lower Tana Valley in Kenya, and 50,000 square miles of Tanganyika, in connection with water control projects.

In 1960 the Commonwealth prime ministers set up the Special Commonwealth African Assistance Plan to muster capital aid and technical assistance for African members.

Apart from her contributions through the United Nations and other international bodies, Britain's disbursements in capital aid in Africa last year came to a little more than $180 million.

Although the figure was $58 million down from the year before, commitments were on the rise. This year the disbursements will be higher than before.

The flow of private British capital to Africa has been leveling off and even declining in recent years. The Government is working on a number of ways of correcting this.

Britain is supporting the Organization for Economic Cooperation and Development in its attempt to draw up a convention for the protection of foreign investors.

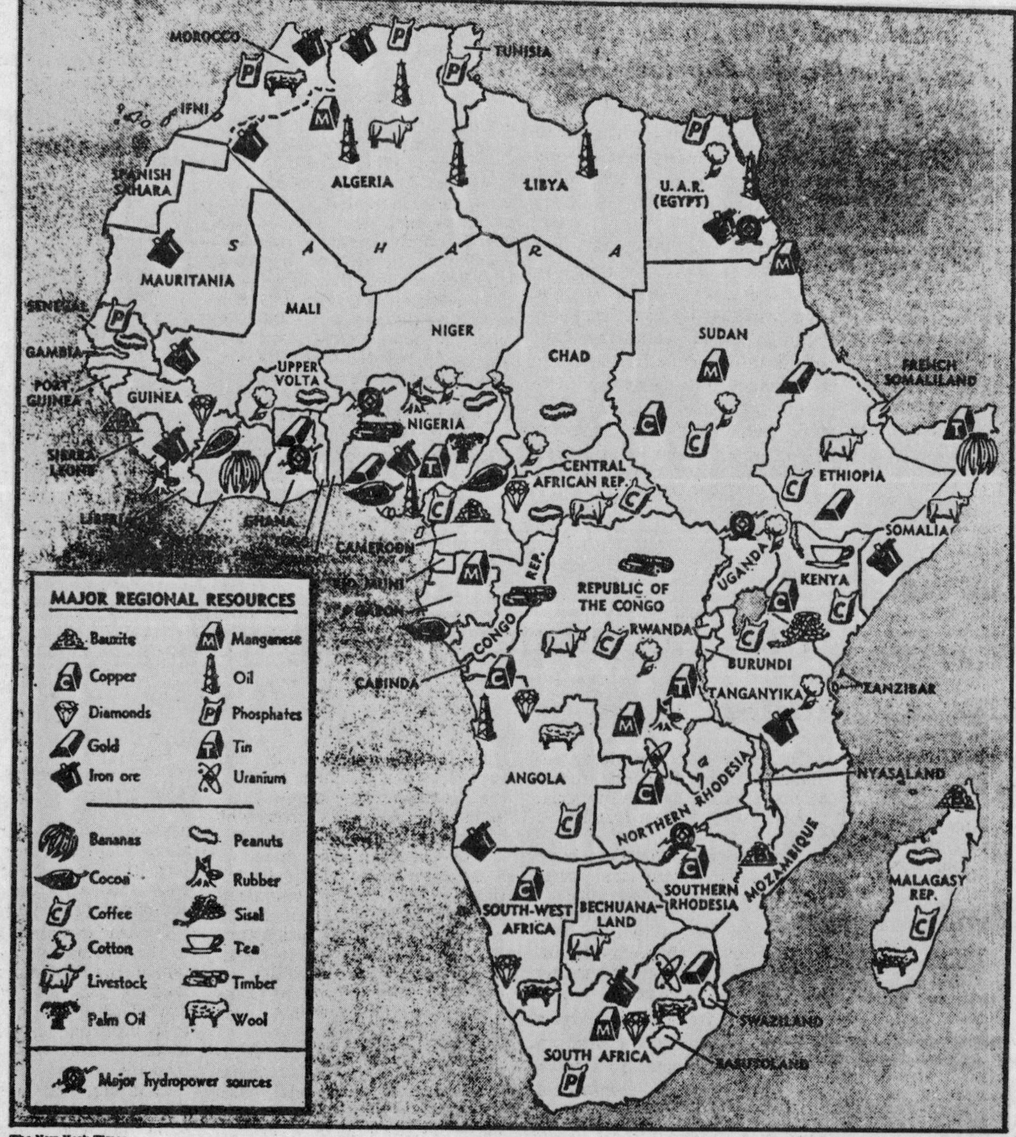

RESOURCES: The emergence of Africa, with 250 million people in some 50 areas, is keyed to its natural wealth

An African Chief Explains Tribalism

Non-Africans, he says, have a distorted idea of what it means, thinking it signifies only the primitive; in fact, 'tribe' is another way of saying 'ethnic group.'

By S. O. ADEBO

FROM the way some people write or talk about it, you would think that tribalism was just a peculiarity of the African, with no counterpart anywhere else in the world. Whereas citizens of a European country are referred to as "nationals" of that country, the citizens of an African country are generally described as "natives." And in the same way, the inhabitants of an African country are not divided, as their counterparts in Europe are, into racial or ethnic groups—they are just "tribes." This kind of terminological confusion leads inevitably to confused thinking about the effect of the perfectly natural divisions of mankind everywhere—and particularly of those in Africa.

One of the tribal groups in Nigeria numbers as many as eight million people—more than the entire population of Austria or Chile or Sweden, not to mention Denmark, Ireland, Israel, Ecuador and New Zealand. Any wish on their part, however, to retain their identity within the larger grouping of the Nigerian Federation, would be called tribalistic. The continued reluctance of the Scots, on the other hand, to lose their identity in the British personality—or the movement in Quebec for greater recognition of the five million or so French-speaking Canadians—is called, not tribalistic, but *nationalistic*.

This is not to deny that these divisions could be an impediment to national unity, but my point is that they have the same effect, damaging or otherwise, whether they occur in Nigeria, Great Britain or Canada. Tribalism is tribalism anywhere.

We must keep a sense of proportion about it. Some people seem to think tribalism is an unmitigated evil, but it is not. Every ethnic group has its own cultural features and may, therefore, have something of value to contribute to the way of life of the country or region of which it forms a part. The American of British stock, the Irish-American, the American Jew, the American Negro, and all the other tribes that compose the American nation, have contributed in different ways to make the American culture what it is today.

THE same has happened, and is happening, in Africa. There you will find that each tribe is well known for one distinctive quality. It may be industriousness, or brains, or a flair for commerce, or political sagacity, or a gift for diplomacy, or a sense of humor, or even a love of gaiety. Whatever it is, it serves to enrich the national cultural pattern.

Another point that needs to be made is the impossibility of doing away with tribal consciousness. The Welsh, for example, are as British as any other Briton. They have produced eminent political figures like the late Lloyd George (before Sir Winston Churchill, the greatest wartime leader Britain ever produced), and the late Aneurin Bevan, one of the greatest Socialist leaders of all time. They have made contributions of similar quality in other fields of British life. But they remain as conscious of their Welsh identity as ever, and as anxious to preserve that identity, particularly in its cultural aspects. As with the Welsh, so with the Walloons in Belgium, and so with African ethnic groupings—or "tribes"—in Africa.

While writing of Africa in general, I shall take my illustrations from my own country of Nigeria. In the first place, it is the African country with which I am, naturally, most familiar, and secondly, Nigeria is like the continent itself in microcosm—containing something like one-sixth of its total population and over 200 of its tribal divisions.

What makes these tribal groupings a greater source of trouble in Africa today than in other continents is the fact that the division of Africa was carried out by the old metropolitan powers with little regard to ethnic considerations. Territorial boundaries cut across ethnic boundaries in many places, not only in the division of the continent into countries but also in the division of some countries into local government areas.

Where an international boundary splits a tribe in two, placing one part in one country, and the remainder in another, it is only natural that the two halves should regret the split and wish it remedied. This could lead to a straining of relations between the countries concerned, as happened between Ghana and Togo a few years ago, and as is happening right now between Somalia and Ethiopia.

In other places, however, the wish for reunion is quiescent, so quiescent, in fact, as to be hardly discernible. A sizable proportion of the nationals of Dahomey, for instance, belong to the Yoruba tribe, the bulk of whom are citizens of Nigeria. There is no doubt that Yorubas on both sides of the border wish they all belonged to one country (I know because I am a Yoruba myself), but there is no agitation for such a reunion. Indeed, the presence of Yorubas in both Dahomey and Nigeria, far from constituting a source of friction, contributes to the promotion of the friendliest relations between the two countries.

THIS happy situation may be, at least in part, the consequence of the Nigerian Government's policy on international boundaries. Recognizing that some African frontiers need revision, it holds that this should be done only by consultation and agreement between the countries concerned. No revision should be promoted by violent means or sought or achieved unilaterally.

This policy was, in effect, adopted by the Organization of African Unity when the founding fathers, at Addis Ababa in May, 1963, wrote into the charter of the organization a clause providing that all members shall respect the territorial integrity of other member countries. They also provided for the establishment of a commission to deal with boundary disputes. While the flame of tribalism continues to burn, therefore—and to burn rather furiously in some breasts—Africans have the policy, and the instrumentality, for keeping it within reasonable bounds.

In the national context, tribalism can be a mixed blessing. On the credit side, anxiety to enhance the reputation of his tribe can inspire a man to great deeds. A number of the leading professional men in Nigeria today come from a tribe which, some 30 years ago, had only one or two members of such distinction. By no means more affluent than other tribes in the country, its members went to great personal sacrifice to raise money for a tribal scholarship scheme because they had a great urge to make themselves "a force to be reckoned with" in Nigeria's intellectual class.

Other tribes followed their example, not only by providing scholarships for promising youths, but also by organizing collections to aid development of their respective home towns. This type of intertribal competition is, of course, healthy, unexceptionable and, indeed, commendable.

The divisive effects of tribalism are felt only when this kind of competition is carried to extremes. Healthy rivalry is one thing, but to push one's claims to leadership solely on tribal grounds is tribalism of the deplorable kind. It manifests itself in several ways—in attempts to organize political parties on a tribal basis; in demands that political, cabinet or other posts should be distributed purely on a tribal basis, and, worse still, in demands for tribal quotas in the distribution of civil-service jobs and in the showing of favoritism toward their fellow-tribesmen by senior public officials.

THESE abuses harm the cause of national unity. They are roundly condemned and firmly resisted by leading African statesmen. Not a week passes in Nigeria, for instance, without the newspapers calling for vigilance against the canker of tribalism. There has been hardly an address made to the nation since independence by our President or Prime Minister that has not contained a warning to the effect that an overly tribal-conscious Nigeria would very soon cease to be one country, and that the diversity of gifts possessed by our diverse peoples should be devoted to the task of building a great and unified nation.

Where, as in Nigeria, political leaders—irrespective of their different tribal origins—are anxious that the country should remain united, the battle against the excesses of tribalism has a good chance of success. But anxiety alone to preserve a united country is not enough. Its leaders must work sincerely and realistically for the cause—sincerely, because if they do not themselves practice what they preach, the people will not follow; and realistically, because trying to ignore the existence of ethnic divisions is to invite defeat.

TO disregard ethnic considerations altogether in composing a government in a country of many different groups would be folly. No country in the world does it that way. In Great Britain, the Prime Minister is more often than not a Scot—but even he has to pay some respect to ethnic considerations by offering a few top posts to Englishmen! And the Welsh may not be overlooked with impunity either.

THE AUTHOR—Chief S. O. Adebo of Nigeria. His tribe, the Yoruba, is one of more than 200 different tribes in his country.

The United States, being a less homogeneous nation than Britain, makes concessions to tribalism even more openly. Party tickets have to contain the right proportion of Northerners and Southerners, and a sprinkling at least of representatives from minority tribal groups like the Irish. Cabinet posts are filled in the same manner. Nigeria must do—and does—likewise. So must every country in similar circumstances. To do so is not so much

tribalism as plain common sense.

As a rule, ethnic or tribal affiliations should play no part in filling civil-service posts in any country. The only workable basis of selection is individual merit. But this ideal can only be achieved, I submit, under two conditions: The appointing authority must enjoy the confidence of minority groups as to its impartiality of judgment, and the terms of competition must be fair. In Nigeria, the first point has been met by a Public Service Commission of eminent citizens selected with due regard to fair regional representation. As to the second condition, because the advance of education has, for historical reasons, been less rapid in one region than in the others, it has been necessary to adopt two different solutions to the problem — one for the short term and the other for the more distant future.

THE long-term solution, obviously, is to speed up the rate of educational advance in the region that is now behind, and this is being done. But until candidates for jobs at all levels can compete on an equal basis throughout the country, the Public Service Commission has relaxed the prescribed academic qualifications for applicants from the region in question. It is accepting, as a partial substitute, practical experience of a kind suited for the post for which the candidate is applying. Care is, of course, necessary to see that the process is not carried unreasonably far, or continued for too long.

Other measures, private and governmental, have also been

adopted in Nigeria to discourage tribalism and foster national consciousness. The most notable private effort is perhaps being staged by the Nigeria Society, which was started 15 years ago by young Nigerian undergraduates in the United Kingdom, many of whom are now holding very responsible positions.

The National Union of Nigerian Students, a voluntary association of students attending Nigerian universities, also plays a useful part. Every one of these universities admits applicants from anywhere in the country regardless of tribal or regional affiliations, thus giving the students the opportunity of studying and living together as Nigerians and getting to understand one another. Membership of the union offers an additional forum for deliberating on and discussing, with nontribal objectivity, matters affecting the students as well as matters affecting the country as a whole.

One positive step has been taken in the same direction by the Federal Government in recent years. The one school in Nigeria which, perhaps more than any other educational institution, has contributed to the creation of a Nigeria-wide outlook among today's Nigerian leadership is King's College in the Federal capital, Lagos—a secondary institution run by the Government as a sort of model for other high schools.

IT deliberately goes out for a student body with the widest possible tribal and regional spread and many of our national leaders showing the greatest degree of "tribe-blindness" graduated from King's. The Federal Government in consultation with the governments of the regions, has decided to finance the establishment of a similar institution in each of the regions, with a view to promoting on a larger scale the benefits the country has gained from King's College in the field of intertribal relations.

What does the future hold for Africa in tribalism? The struggle to contain its divisive effects may be longer and more difficult in some countries than in others, but I have no doubt that contained they will be. Other countries in other continents have had to face the same problem; indeed, which country is not still facing it?

March 1, 1964

Forecast for Africa: More Plots, More Coups

By **RONALD MATTHEWS**

IT was a decade ago that the French and British colonies and protectorates in Africa began to win — one after another—their freedom from foreign rule. Morocco and Tunisia were first on the list, in 1956; Ghana followed in 1957, Guinea in 1958. The big year was 1960, which saw independence come to the remaining French possessions south of the Sahara and to the Federation of Nigeria. Then, less than two and a half years later, a long series of conspiracies and insurrections began: in December, 1962, a group of civilians and army officers were arrested for a plot against the life of President Bourguiba in Tunisia; the same month witnessed the arrest of Mamadou Dia, Premier of Senegal, for an alleged plot against President Senghor; in January, 1963, President Sylvanus Olympio of Togo was killed in the course of a military demonstration against him.

Since then, it has been rare for a quarter-year to go by without some similar incident being reported. Today more than two-thirds of the newly independent states of Africa, and some whose independence dates further back, have been victims of such attempts against their internal order. The process appeared to have reached its climax at the turn of 1965-66, when no fewer than half a dozen coups took place in less than four months.

What is it all about? And why is it that a force which, as Western democratic opinion sees it, should be at almost any cost excluded from politics—the army—has been playing an ever-increasing part in these acts of violence?

Several possible reasons for this chronic political instability will be advanced merely to be dismissed. There are those who might suggest that it is due to the fact that not a few of the new African states are in that economic stage—between penury and solvency—which historical experience has shown to be the most propitious for the outbreak of revolutions. It is not, this thesis goes, the starvelings who arise from their slumbers, as the Communist anthem, the Internationale, summons them to; it is the prisoners of want who have perceived that the doors of their prison are opening before them.

Unfortunately for this explanation, coups and plots have by no means been confined to countries like Ghana and Gabon, whose $200-per-head annual national income puts them on the verge of unassisted economic take-off; they have also occurred in the Congo (Brazzaville), Chad and Dahomey, all with a national income more in the neighborhood of $40 per head. What is more, most of the African overturns, like those that have afflicted Latin America for a century and a half, have not been revolutions at all—in that they have been almost entirely lacking in social content.

Another conceivable ground for revolt in Africa is the conspicuous waste — of which most of its authorities are guilty. There are costly presidential palaces rising all over the continent; hundreds of privileged guests consuming luxury dishes and drinks at the annual liberation day parties while the inhabitants of the nearby shantytowns have barely enough to live on; and parliamentary deputies drawing annual salaries and allowances far higher than a local doctor, let alone a peasant, could ever hope to obtain—and this for the hardly exhausting task of regularly saying "yes" to Government measures. There has as yet, however, been no record of angry proletarian crowds breaking into lavish official receptions to satisfy their hunger, or of armed troops invading a parliament building and calling on the deputies to account for the inordinate remuneration they enjoy.

A final factor to which the discontent behind the conspiracies might be ascribed is the chronic overspending on unimportant objects by a new privileged class which all over Africa has been taking the place of the vanishing European administrators. To make things worse, the education which African countries desperately need is geared, not to the agriculture from which the greater part of their inhabitants will be forced to live, but to the requirements of this minority. But again, the birth of this new upper crust has so far provoked no particularly dangerous reactions, except the occasional peasant tax strike, though it needs very little encouragement to draw from peasants up and down the continent the disillusioned comment that national independence wasn't meant for them: the only people who have got anything out of it have been the townies.

But that is no more than resignation, and resignation is at the opposite pole from revolt.

THERE is, however, at least one other common element to be found in almost all the newly independent African states: the single-party system. As the sixties advanced, the political monopoly of the single party was being written into the constitutions of more and more African countries. Though these constitutions, patterned as they were on a European model, specifically guaranteed freedom of expression, of the press and of meeting, these can in fact hardly exist under a single-party regime.

How did the African single parties come into existence? In some countries they were the nationalist organizations which had participated in a long struggle for independence, usually under a single leader who had become a national hero, and which quite naturally assumed power when their aim was achieved. Tunisia, Ghana and the Ivory Coast are examples of this class.

"Many African army officers, trained at Sandhurst and St. Cyr, have been shocked by the economic chaos and official high living in the newly independent states."

In other lands, mostly south of the Sahara, where the former colonial power had granted independence on a platter to its erstwhile subjects, single-party systems had been established by the local political leader who had taken over the Government, largely as a means for putting an end to internal ethnic quarrels. The danger of these will be appreciated when it is recalled that six languages are spoken in Dahomey (population: 2 million) and 40 languages or dialects in Gabon, with its half-million inhabitants; while in the Congo (Brazzaville) as late as 1959 intertribal rioting in the capital had resulted in 99 fatalities and 177 persons injured.

The head of a single-party system, however it evolved, would also, naturally, when independence came, be head of state. He could count on the benevolent neutrality of the ex-colonial power, since the internal stability which his organization was expected to insure furnished the best guarantee for the security of investments from overseas.

A number of apparently plausible reasons are advanced in defense of the single party's privileged role. Its champions claim, with what looks like reason south of the Sahara, that it alone is capable of creating a sense of nationality in the newly emergent political entities, whose artificial boundaries in more than one case cut important tribal units in two, and where such a sense of nationality is almost nonexistent outside the capitals.

The single party, it is maintained, is an ideal instrument for mobilizing the population for the necessary tasks of economic construction. It is the best obstacle, it is argued, to the demagogic opposition so easily aroused in underdeveloped countries by the sometimes unpopular measures dictated by the process of development. The single party, its supporters say, forms a solid and irreplaceable transmission belt between the Government and the people, passing down instructions from above and passing up complaints from below. Finally, history is called to witness that the party reflects the will of the people, which, indeed, it did in many countries—at the moment of liberation.

THERE are specific answers to all these arguments, and to similar ones, but the most cogent general reply is that the disposition to criticize the decisions of the authorities is a part of human nature—and that criticism, like opposition, is a thing the single party cannot tolerate for long once it has taken over the apparatus of a state. So almost as soon as it is established in power, almost everywhere, a system of repressive measures is introduced, ranging from a press censorship to preventive detention laws.

Sometimes the process is gradual, sometimes it is almost instantaneous. In Ghana, the first Preventive Detention Act was adopted 16 months after independence and first made use of four months later. Across the continent, in Malawi, a similar measure was enacted a bare three months after the country had attained sovereignty, and a decree providing fines and imprisonment for anyone publishing anything likely to undermine confidence in the Government was issued about the same time.

Laws like these are by no means the only restraints on freedom in Africa's single-party states. Elections in them are consistently rigged, with the single lists of candidates represented as having been elected with 90-plus per cent majorities, when, indeed, they are not declared to have been unopposed. Every sort of organization in the single-party state is sooner or later brought under the control of the Government party, from women's and youth organizations to labor unions.

The last-named are likely to be slapped down firmly if they indulge in what most people would regard as the normal syndical activity of pressing for wage increases or fighting wage standstills when the cost of living rises, as the Ghana workers were in 1961 and those of Upper Volta just before the recent coup there. In Tunisia the head of the labor unions in 1965 opposed official policy on labor issues. He was prosecuted on what many people regarded as a trumped-up charge, deprived of his parliamentary immunity, removed from office and replaced by a man who had a month before been a high Government official.

ONE of the best brief explanations of why the single-party system makes for coups was given in 1963 by Albert Teveodjre, former Information Minister in Dahomey, who in 1964 was appointed to the International Affairs Center at Harvard. In the nineteen-fifties, Teveodjre wrote, we saw that when a people is prevented from expressing its opinion by means of a ballot, it tends to express itself by means of a gun. That was the justification for the revolts against colonialism. The single-party African state, he suggested, is leading in exactly the same direction — bombs appeared in Ghana at the very moment when the Parliament was offering Kwame Nkrumah the life Presidency.

For the single-party system doesn't put an end to political differences. It merely makes them take a new form. In a country subject to such a regime there is apparently no means by which the ordinary citizen, even if he is a party member speaking within a party cell, can express himself with any real freedom if he comes up against the viewpoint of the party chiefs. If, therefore, he wants to secure redress for his grievances from the authorities, the only means open to him is by conspiring against them.

IN few African single-party countries is it safe to discuss in public matters remotely related to politics. Plainclothes police will be listening for such conversations in the principal cafes of the capitals, and they have been known to remove for questioning people who had been talking indiscreetly. Plainclothes men have also been found in the press galleries of Parliaments. Even at home it is wiser not to express oneself too freely, for house servants are quite likely to be under orders from the police to report regularly on the talk exchanged between their master and his guests. An acquaintance who three years ago called on Dr. Albert Schweitzer at his leper colony in Gabon was astonished to find the doctor conducting all his conversations with his European staff in German, though quite a number of them would have found it far easier to understand him if he had expressed himself in French.

Dr. Schweitzer had a ready explanation: his African employes didn't understand German; when he had spoken in French, his boys, and some of his patients, had made wildly inaccurate reports to the local police on the subjects of his conversations. The police had passed on even more fanciful reports to the higher authorities, and it had been necessary for him to waste precious time and energy to iron the matter out.

Nyerere of Tanzania after re-election last fall.

One reason for this sort of curb on freedom lies in the nature of the single party, which has been defined as an exceptional concentration of powers in the hands of a man assisted and influenced by a group. (The extent of the group's influence varies considerably: it is said that in Mali, President Modibo Keita pays considerable attention to the views of his collaborators; but it may be doubted whether President Bourguiba in Tunisia would easily admit contradiction.)

Even some of its African critics agree that the single party, and the personal power that goes with it, can serve an emergent country in the transitional period—during the building up of the state, the consolidation of national unity and the establishment of new economic structures, which may require a certain measure of coercion. The trouble is that by the time that period is over, the dictator and his aides have inevitably come to believe that what is good for them is good for their fellow citizens. They started off as rulers; they become a group of interests, and they don't like their privileges to be challenged. Restrictions result.

THERE is a second reason for this curb on freedom—one involving mismanagement and corruption. Once the unifying nationalist struggle had been successful, the ordinary man found that what he had expected of independence was greatly different from the reality that emerged. In a fair proportion of independent African countries, the standard of living has dropped and not risen since the single party took over. The Ivory Coast and Gabon are the only African states south of the Sahara which can boast a favorable balance of foreign trade. In some of the lands concerned, the economic difficulties were due to hasty and inefficient nationalizations; the fall in the world market value of their exports was another factor. In a country like Guinea, which tried to take over internal as well as external trade—mistakenly as President Sékou Touré later admitted—it hopelessly alienated the sympathies of the tradesmen who had been among the stoutest supporters of the single-party's struggle for freedom.

These and other errors and extravagances had to be paid for, so customs duties and taxes were increased and forced loans introduced by compulsory deductions from workers' pay: the last-named measure was sometimes accompanied by a wage freeze.

Corruption in the single-party countries goes right down the scale. At the top, there is a stock phrase, "the corruption index," for what it will cost a visiting foreign businessman to see a Minister. Trade Ministers in some sub-Saharan states ask such excessive sums for permission to establish a factory that quite a number of potential investors have been put off.

At the bottom there are hospital attendants, from porters to nurses, who exact bribes before they will let patients in to consult a doctor. In between, selling of import licenses has been so prevalent that in Ghana special companies were at one time set up exclusively to get and resell them.

For all this, defenders of the single party claim that its existence provides no grounds for conspiratorial activities. Those whose discontents tempt them to plot against it would achieve far more by joining its ranks, they argue, for there is complete freedom of speech in meetings of party members until policy on a given issue has been decided by the party as a whole. Those of us who lived in Stalin's Russia and heard the same sort of assertion made there will be a little chary about accepting it, and indeed there is evidence that young Africans who have gone into some monopoly parties on the understanding that they would be able to speak freely within them have found themselves in a trap.

Moreover, a number of the African conspiracies reported over the last few years have led to the arrest of distinguished figures who, if speech within the single party had really been free, might have been expected to voice their grievances in its cells, where they should have been able to count on a far more attentive hearing than could any run-of-the-mill member; no one but a fool plots when he can persuade. The nine Cabinet Ministers jailed over the two Ivory Coast plots of 1963 did not stand alone. The Ghana plot of August, 1962, led to the arrest, not only of two ministers, but of the executive secretary of the Government party, and these were by no means the last incidents of this kind.

THOUGH coups d'état and conspiracies in Africa do not date from yesterday, there has been one novel element about the latest series of pronunciamentos. In two of the three 1963 coups, the army stepped in to oust the local President only after there had been large-scale and continuous demonstrations against him by crowds whose core was formed by labor unionists. In all three, the military handed over control to civilians almost at once—indeed, in Togo, where President Olympio's assassination had quite certainly been a mistake, they pleaded with something like pathos for a politician to replace him. The same handover to civilian authorities followed the success of the 1964 Gabon coup, which was put down after 36 hours by French military intervention. Though Colonel Boumediene's June, 1965, *putsch* in Algeria was entirely an army affair, the colonel did not install a military government.

But that was just what the armies did establish following their successive takeovers in Dahomey and the Central African Republic, Upper Volta, Nigeria and Ghana, and only in Upper Volta was the takeover preceded by a period of civilian demonstrations, by the local labor unions. What is more, there seems little sign at the moment of the army putschists being on the point of handing over control to civilian successors in these states, though they have indeed got in technicians, some of whom they have given ministerial rank, to help them with the work of administration.

THE discontents in the single-party states were and are, on the whole, civilian ones. Why then should it have been the armies, whose officers and men their governments took good care to pay and to feed well, which took action against the regimes? There are a number of likely reasons.

First, in countries where the labor unions had already been called to heel, the armies represented the only independent organized force there was. Second, in a state like Ghana, where the party apparatus and its spies were omnipresent, civilians who had tried to plot against the authorities ran an almost certain risk of being denounced before they had time to get along. That would not be so among the army officers, who, incidentally, had shown not the slightest sign of enthusiasm for Mr. Nkrumah's anti-Western attitudes.

Third, in the nascent armies of the new African states, no closed military caste has yet had time to come into being. The officers were therefore in close touch with the resentments felt by the civilian population—by officials and lawyers, technicians and tradesmen, and students alike. Fourth, the position of the African armed forces recalls the remark made by a Latin American about their opposite numbers on the other side of the Atlantic: "The soldiers have got to have *something* to do. Since no one is threatening from the outside, they've become one more political party."

Another factor is that the officers of African armies, with the traditions of uprightness many of them had brought down from Sandhurst and St. Cyr, have been profoundly shocked by the economic disorder and the official high living they saw in the single-party states. It is not incidental that Ghana's economy was on the verge of bankruptcy before the military coup in February—or that before the take-over in the Central African Republic, President David Dacko had shown himself incapable of interfering with Cabinet Ministers who squandered state funds. In Upper Volta, President Yameogo before his overthrow had prescribed austerity for labor unions at the same time that he had brought back a costly trousseau from Paris for his new bride and held a no-expense-spared wedding reception.

THE general lines on which the new military governments intend to conduct affairs are already fairly clear. All of them have come out for economy in public expenditure, and are preparing prosecutions of ministers and officials found guilty of corruption. They have had the good sense to take on civilian experts for departments which plainly require expert knowledge, such as that of foreign affairs. There are indications that they are likely to improve conditions for foreign investors and go back on hasty nationalizations. They may extend greater freedom to the press.

In a number of the states where the army has taken over, there was an immediate switch away from an attitude sympathetic to the Communist powers in the international field: Communist China has been a big loser in the coups. It seems likely that the new African rulers will follow a policy of neutrality in foreign affairs—though it is odds-on that it will be a neutrality like President Bourguiba's, angled toward understanding with the West.

When or whether the army leaders who have taken power in the latest series of coups will be prepared to hand over control to civilian successors—and whether, supposing they do so, they will insist on a political set-up allowing for the existence of an opposition—must still be largely a matter for speculation. One possible pointer to their future course is that Dr. Kofi Busia, who as late as 1956 took over the leadership of one of the two parties then in opposition to Nkrumah, was lately allowed back into Ghana, though it is true he was given no official reception at the airport.

If the army leaders do decide to reinstate something resembling democracy, it would appear highly likely that they will discourage the formation of more than one opposition group, since in Africa, as in Europe, the multiparty system has revealed its inefficiency. What's more, in Africa there is a grave danger that a multiplicity of parties may represent not delicately shaded differences of opinion but merely the egoistic rival interests of the manifold ethnic groups into which almost every sub-Saharan African country is divided. And that is the last thing anyone concerned with national unity, as the army putschists purport to be, would wish to see.

One thing that may discourage the soldiers from restoring civilian rule, at least for a while, is that in the past the politicians haven't shown themselves to be as capable as they should have been in doing their jobs. Thus in Ghana in 1958, the opposition's boycott of the elections to the regional assemblies—which were set up to meet their fears of dictatorship by a single-chamber central Parliament—had results that could easily have been foreseen. The Government party (the Convention People's party) gained control of the regional assemblies, which then approved a measure doing away with the very power to restrict constitutional changes with which they had been endowed.

Experience shows, however, that the longer a man or a body of men exercise dictatorial powers, the less reason they see why they should cease to wield them. If, therefore, the army officers who replaced Nkrumah don't give place to a democratic government fairly soon, and turn out to be a set of little Nkrumahs themselves, we shall probably see the same sort of split in their ranks as had been threatening within Nkrumah's own party. And there, and in other countries under army rule, we may see a new series of coups, this time by dissident soldiers.

What is as certain as anything can be is that the coups which saw the old year out and the new year in will not be the last that Africa will witness. One of the most likely scenes of a new rising would appear to be Guinea, where the economic situation is almost as perilous as it is in Ghana, whose deposed President it is now harboring. Another is Chad, where three ministers and the Vice President of the National Assembly were arrested toward the end of last year on charges of plotting against the life of President François Tombalaye. A third is Niger, where President Hamani Diori has to face up to an opposition whose armed activities against him have been directed from outside his country's frontiers.

April 10, 1966

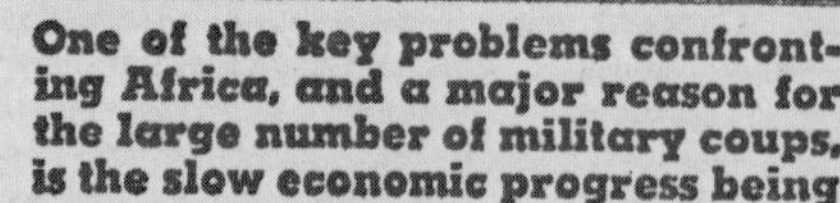

March 6, 1966

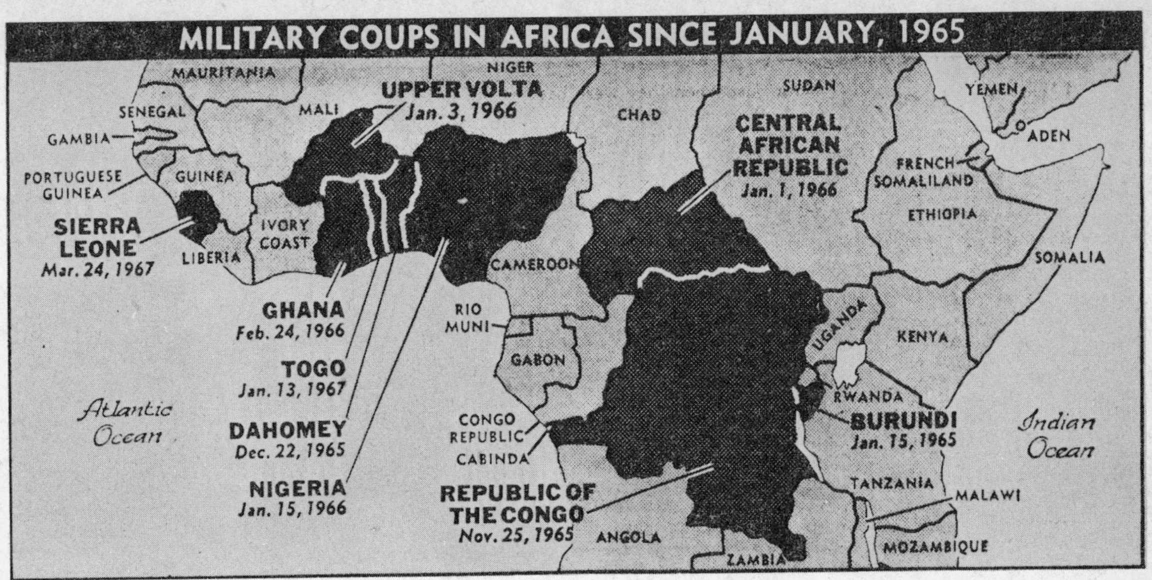

April 2, 1967

The Irony of 'Africanization': A Vital Ingredient Is Help From the Outside

By DREW MIDDLETON

Special to The New York Times

LONDON, May 5—The dramatic difference between the soaring aspirations of Africa's independent states and the appalling economic and social conditions that begin where the pavement ends is a basic continuing problem.

While this difference exists, "neocolonialism" and "neoimperialism" will vex African politics because the new states cannot exist, much less develop, without investment and technical help from abroad and with foreign markets for their products.

Until education has provided the trained Africans to take over jobs now held by whites in government, industry and commerce, the demand for jobs for Africans—"Africanization"—will plague the heads of African governments. Few of them have the confidence of the Ivory Coast's President Felix Houphouet-Boigny, who rejects what he calls "cut-rate Africanization"—that is, placement of partly trained personnel into jobs beyond them simply because they are black.

Lack of Skills Resented

This situation aggravates the sense of inferiority among educated Africans that complicates relations between white and black.

"Do you realize there's nothing on thiis airfield that we Africans have invented or made?" a young customs official asked one morning at Douala, in Cameroon. "Everything from the planes to the luggage tags is made by the white man. Yet we are told this is our continent."

Kwame Nkrumah's was the extreme African response to this situation. In an effort to increase pride in the African past he emphasized the somewhat tenuous connection of past Africans with landmarks in scientific and political development.

Less imaginative leaders today demand more study, more work and greater concentration on essentials as the slow but sure route to African independence. To them pan-Africanism, the Organization of African Unity and other prestige elements of African independence are less important than education and development of individual countries.

Schools Are 'What Counts'

"Whenever the O.A.U. gets lost in some cloudland," a Foreign Minister said at Addis Ababa, "I comfort myself by the thought that all over Africa schools are being built. That's what counts."

Though this may be true, the harsh fact is that it will be many years before education and development enable Africa to stand on its own feet. In this turbulent period of transition the new states are in many ways more dependent than independent, despite their formal political status.

Independent states such as Chad or the Central African Republic are almost as dependent upon French investment and technical aid as the Portuguese territories of Mozambique and Angola are upon the homeland's bounty. The difference is that in theory at least Chad and the Central African Republic could accept massive help from other governments.

Foreigners Stay On

The great British and French banks, industrial organizations, trading corporations and construction companies overshadow the economies of most Black African states. The shortage of trained Africans keeps French and British engineers, German and Norwegian teachers, Yugoslav and Italian doctors profitably employed.

American private industry and investment, although more modest than the British or French stake, is growing in Black Africa, but not, it appears, as rapidly as in racist South Africa.

The Agency for International Development is the principal channel for American aid. In Nigeria, for example, the agency's technical assistance program spends about $17-million yearly. The agency's contribution to the country's six-year growth plan may exceed $200-million.

Nigeria is one of Africa's economic success stories with a growth rate of more than 5 per cent of the gross national product last year. Some of its light industry is owned by Africans, a situation unusual in Black Africa.

Africans Trained to Manage

The agency's objective is to provide the technical training that will enable Africans to run the country's light industry and increase its farm production. Once trained, the visitor is told, the African is the equal of the European worker.

In less fortunate countries American aid is directed at public works, water systems for example, which will help build a viable economy in the future.

But in these states the list of necessities is discouragingly long, the political and social barriers to progress formidable.

A second important aspect of African dependence is the reliance of a majority of African states on foreign markets for their agricultural and mineral products. The development of a new synthetic in Germany, a change in American taste, a fluctuation on a London commodity market may seriously damage the economy of any one of a dozen countries.

Africa has its "rich" nations such as the Ivory Coast, Senegal, Nigeria, Ghana, and Zambia and its "poor ones like Tanania, Chad, the Central African Republic. There should be a natural development toward economic regionalism with the stronger economies attracting the weaker, complementary ones.

Nigeria Could Be Center

Nigeria with her expanding urban population should be the center of a region in which, for example, Chad's beef would feed Nigeria in exchange for Nigerian-manufactured goods and oil.

But Nigeria was British and Chad was French. France wants to keep Chad firmly anchored in her economic orbit. French support for regionalism does not venture beyond regions composed of "Francophone" states. This is logical enough from the financial point of view but illogical because the states of the "region" that was former French Equatorial Africa do not have complementary economies.

The rapid expansion of education is the key to ending African dependence. This includes education for education. For, in many parts of Africa, it is almost as important to convince the warrior tribesman that there is nothing demeaning about manual labor as it is to herd his children to school.

All of education's problems elsewhere are magnified in Africa. The labor demands of a still largely subsistence economy increases the number of dropouts. A class of children from four or five tribes has to learn a common tongue before schooling can begin. Schoolhouses, books, equipment, teacher training and salaries often lay a strain on impoverished governments.

Vocational Training Rises

There are two positive factors.

Africa generally is moving away from classical education toward the wider vocational training that an empty, undeveloped continent demands. The British, once strong on classical education, have sent more than 15,000 Africans to Britain for vocational training. The United States, with the help of American universities, has established programs in which the development of mechanical and agricultural skills is given priority.

The second factor is the emphasis placed on education by parents as well as governments.

The parents realize, as the children may not, that the future belongs to the educated and they prod their young to classes. They, themselves, often will finish a hard day's work and then attend night school for three or four hours. The enthusiasm among educators is greater than in any other field of government work.

At Kibanha secondary school outside Dar es Salaam in Tanzania, a grave 13-year-old African told a visitor he hoped "to serve my people as a teacher." His manly manner did not stand up against homesickness. Someone asked where he was from.

"Bukoba in the north," he said, his eyes filling. "This is my first month here. Bukoba is nicer, it's home."

Women More Enterprising

Education will also in time broaden the contribution of the women to African society. In those tribes where matriarchy is the rule, the woman is important. But woman's place is lesser where polygamy is practiced, as among animist tribes and the Moslems.

In many instances, the market Mammies of Accra, Ghana, and Lagos, Nigeria, for example, the women seem more enterprising than the men. The visitor repeatedly is struck by the large number of men idly chatting in the shade while women work.

Social progress in Africa will depend, too, on strong judiciaries and independent police forces. Primitive emotions are very close to the surface in Africa and require restraint and prompt punishment. Corruption, so powerful a factor in Black Africa's life, already has affected the courts and the police in many countries.

Educated Have Sense of Duty

The most encouraging factor is the manner in which a high percentage of the educated are coming to terms with 20th-century ideas and concepts outside their previous experience. Men who have fought for education and influence now apply these for their country's good.

For all the squalor and venality, there remains a singularly high concept of duty among many educated Africans. These are the people who will guide their countries when the leaders of the struggle for independence have gone and the British and French have departed.

If there is time enough to train even more of them, this difficult period of transition may end in true African independence.

May 11, 1966

Regional Links Are Solution for Many

By LAWRENCE FELLOWS
Special to The New York Times

NAIROBI, Kenya—Africa, bedraggled continent of two score countries on the verge of splitting into more, is turning earnestly to the task of pulling herself together a bit to look more attractive to potential investors.

The fragmentation of states and fireworks display of political crises and border wars are probably not over. But through smoke and billowing dust of crisis, the smell of economic realism grows stronger.

All around the continent there is growing acceptance that the land and people are perhaps the greatest untapped resources and that unless more is made of them and of the meager markets offered potential investors, there may soon be no real development at all in black Africa.

In Gambia, where the United Nations has provided a special staff to speed the country's integration into the West African economy, the splintered heritage and colonial roots of it are best illustrated. It is a sliver of a country, two banks of river as far upstream as British gunboats could penetrate in otherwise French territory.

Infrastructure is all wrong for independent development. It was inherited from colonial powers and designed mainly to facilitate trade between colony and mother country.

Roads, railways, posts and telecommunications were all designed not to tie the continent together but to tie the separate bits to different places in Europe, and this, if Africa is going to continue to attract new development money, will have to be undone.

Another of the regional groupings the Economic Commission of Africa is promoting would tie together states of the Berber north.

Another grouping, from Ethiopia southward to Zambia and Malawi, would put in a single regional organization on the eastern side of the continent, where some regionalism used to exist and where there is some promise that it will flourish again.

Kenya, Uganda and Tanzania came to independence with the Common Market and the system of common services they had inherited from the British.

In a flush of economic nationalism, brought on by ideological differences and feeling in Tanzania that Kenya was getting the lion's share of new investment, Tanzania embarked on a policy of "self-reliance," introducing her own currency, raising tariff barriers, eventually nationalizing banks and imposing exchange control against her former partners in the market.

But like Guineans, Tanzanians are part of a larger market whether they like it or not. The daily stampede across the border at Himo is not a crowd headed for a football game or a riot; it is Tanzanian women going to Kenya to do their shopping.

Zambia wants into a region, too, to help herself out of her old dependence on the white-controlled Rhodesia.

Africans are worried about the prospect of lean years ahead for foreign aid. Many are beginning to see that they need shipping lines and automobile assembly plants less desperately than roads to get their tea or peanuts or pyrethrum to market, botanists and anthropologists less desperately than technicians who can show the people how to use their land.

The trend toward economic realism is there.

This is the argument that has been thrown at them for years by the United Nations, the United States, Britain, France and other big givers.

Even private investors have been saying that no matter how sympathetic they may be to traditions and aspirations of individual countries, they are not interested in putting their money into pursuit of minimum markets.

The trouble is that even put together, Africa is not all that great as a market. It covers a fifth of the earth's land surface. According to the United Nations Economic Commission for Africa, the gross domestic product of the whole continent, apart from Portuguese territories and South Africa, is less than that of Belgium and the Netherlands put together.

This suggests that many of those 300 million people padding around Africa have not much money jingling in their pockets. In fact, a huge pro-

United Nations

Sisal being dried in Tanzania, an African country that came to inherit common services from the British. Impelled by economic nationalism, Tanzanians set a course of "self-reliance," introducing a national currency. But regional market problems still remain.

portion of them are not part of a market at all; they have no money to spend and do nothing constructive apart from trying to feed themselves. And not in every country in Africa can they do even that.

The Congo, which was a big exporter of farm products before independence and which is destined to be one of the richest countries on the continent, still depends heavily on the United States Food for Peace program for supplies.

Eventually, if plans laid out by the Economic Commission for Africa over the past two years come to something, the market will be widened to include the former Belgian Congo, Gabon, Cameroon, Central African Republic and Chad.

Another market is envisaged for the West African countries as far north as Mauretania, Mali and Niger, and preliminary talks West African countries have had so far have been promising.

Guinea is refusing to go along with others in discussing regional development. She still pursues a policy of economic nationalism and wants to look for her aid and development money directly.

But Guinea is part of a region whether she likes it or not. A farmer knows it best of all. He sells his leanest cows to the government at controlled prices. He drives others across the border.

June 10, 1967

Ebb of African 'Revolution'

President Sekou Touré of Guinea must often ask himself whether survival is possible for an African leader bent on radical revolution. The army's ouster of Modibo Keita in nearby Mali leaves Mr. Touré the only remaining revolutionary head of state in West and Central Africa.

African radicals invariably blame "neo-colonialists" or "imperialists" for the downfall of a Keita, Nkrumah or Lumumba. What is true is that a host of factors—primarily economic and military—usually make it extremely difficult for a struggling young African government to sustain a course markedly independent of its former colonial ruler.

Mr. Keita was an intelligent politician who cut a large figure in the new Africa; yet he followed a familiar African path to his downfall. He had finally confronted economic reality last year, turning back to his French colonial tutors for help in launching an austerity program and an effort to restore a convertible Malian currency. However, he was unable to prevent sabotage of his plans by Cabinet extremists. Finally, he made the mistake that had helped bring down Ghana's Nkrumah and the Congo Republic's Massamba-Debat. He created a popular "militia" with enough arms and authority to provoke the regular army and precipitate West Africa's twelfth military coup in three years.

The young officers who overthrew Mr. Keita have wisely called in able, experienced civilians to help run the government, but they must confront familiar problems of a bankrupt "revolutionary" African state: clumsy economic machinery, including two dozen state enterprises, which braked Mali's economy and eroded even its traditional trade ties. And they must urgently seek foreign aid and capital.

Mr. Touré, meanwhile, still paying rhetorical service to revolution, is forging new economic links with the World Bank, the United States and the West. He may yet be able to avert the fate of his revolutionary neighbors.

December 7, 1968

Vital Foreign Aid Drying Up in Black Africa

By R. W. APPLE Jr.

When they talk about black Africa, diplomats and scholars sometimes divide it into "countries" and "noncountries."

They define as "countries" the places where size, location, economic resources and leadership seem to offer some hope of economic self-efficiency and development—nations such as Nigeria, the Ivory Coast, the former Belgian Congo, Kenya, perhaps Ghana, perhaps Cameroon.

The noncountries, harsh though the verdict may seem, appear to have no such hopes.

They are places such as Chad, which is so isolated that it takes a gallon of gasoline to deliver another gallon to Fort-Lamy, the capital; such as Rwanda and Burundi, where as many as 500 people may live on a single, hilly, treeless square mile; such as Botswana, which has not a single mile of paved highway.

Both groups of nations need foreign aid: the "countries" to develop, to industrialize, to grow; the "noncountries" merely to keep going. Neither group is getting what it needs, and neither is likely to get it.

The Necessities Are Absent

The need is great. Africa—so big that the United States, Europe, the British Isles and India could fit into it with room to spare—lacks all the necessities of modern life. The need can be seen in the clamorous, stinking slums of Lagos, in the advancing desert of Niger, in the crowds of dirty, big-eyed urchins outside a luxurious hotel in Dahomey.

Not enough housing. Not enough water. Not enough schools.

But black Africa, having suffered through the eras of slave-trading and colonialism, has had the singular misfortune to arrive at this stage of development at a time when foreign economic aid is drying up.

French Aid Due to Ebb

The situation was concisely stated last month in a report to the World Bank—formally the International Bank for Reconstruction and Development—by a commission of eight men from eight countries. The commission said the climate surrounding foreign-aid programs is heavy with disillusion and distrust.

Britain, buffeted by economic troubles at home, is trying to retrench in Africa, where more than a dozen of her former colonies have attained an independence tempered by economic reliance on the erstwhile mother country. In Malawi, for example, the British hope to abandon budget subsidies within five years.

With the end of the de Gaulle era, France's aid to Africa is also expected to dwindle.

Gen. Charles de Gaulle never forgot that the first feeble voices raised in support of Free France during World War II came from the sultry little Congo River port of Brazzaville, and he tailored his aid program accordingly. His successor, President Pompidou, is far less responsive to the emotionalism of colonial history.

Neither Communist China nor the Soviet Union, despite intensive efforts in a few countries such as Tanzania and Mali, is prepared to invest in the continent as a whole. Western diplomats expect Communist efforts to fall off too in coming years.

As for the United States, Africa is clearly the lowest priority in an era of increasing Congressional opposition to foreign-aid appropriations.

A report drafted in 1966 by Edward M. Korry, former Ambassador to Ethiopia, represented an attempt to put the reduced available funds to better use.

With its adoption, the United States began concentrating on a few major countries — Nigeria, Liberia, the Congo, Kenya—and closing aid offices in a dozen or more African capitals, trying to persuade smaller countries to take part in regional development efforts and searching for multilateral approaches.

Most American diplomats would agree that the report has succeeded in giving greater impact to the $155-million that Washington spent on African economic assistance last year. But for the less fortunate countries the cutoff has hurt.

For the moment regionalism seems out of reach in Africa, partly because of suspicions engendered by the new nationalism, partly because the former colonial powers discourage the breaking of apron strings. For example, French-speaking Niger gets most of her imports from Dahomey, not through Nigeria, because Dahomey, though less accessible, is in the franc zone and Nigeria is not.

Tariff Barrier Raised

Similarly, Senegal has a cement plant that operates well below capacity, but tariff barriers make it cheaper for Gambia, which is almost surrounded by Senegal, to import cement from Britain.

American attempts to promote multinational aid programs have been hindered by the complex restrictions ordained by Congress. A United States Ambassador said recently that he felt humiliated every time he was forced to explain the regulations to fellow diplomats.

Many Congressmen, of course, believe that without such regulations foreign aid funds would be misdirected or wasted.

The single truly hopeful sign for African economies in recent months has been the attitude of Robert S. McNamara during his first two years as president of the World Bank. Promising to avoid "the general paralysis" of other aid officials, he plans to triple loans to African nations by 1973.

At the same time that foreign aid is declining, Africa's hopes of earning enough foreign exchange to finance development are dimming.

With some exceptions—copper for one—the commodities that tropical Africa sells bring in less money and the manufactured goods it needs cost more. A sack of peanuts will pay for only about half as much steel as it would a few years ago. What is worse, many African crops are obsolescent; for example, the use of Tanzania's sisal in rope products is threatened by synthetics.

A further problem—one that lies behind the periodic cries of neo-colonialism — is European domination of large-scale commerce and industry.

White men own and manage the rubber plantations in Liberia, the flour mills in the Ivory Coast, the aluminum smelter in Ghana, the oil fields in Nigeria, the tourist companies in Kenya, the banana groves in Somalia. They have a virtual monopoly on capital and skills.

Pressure for 'Africanization'

But pressures for "Africanization" of ownership and personnel are building up across Africa, even in the Ivory Coast, President Félix Houphouët-Boigny's citadel of laissez-faire.

Both Zambia and Tanzania have partially nationalized most of their industries. The Congo has just concluded an agreement to take over the huge Belgian mining company Union Minière du Haut-Katanga. Mixed state-private enterprises seem likely to emerge in Uganda soon.

Even in most of these, however, the key personnel remain European; the European populations of cities like Dakar and Abidjan and Nairobi, which seem about as African as Miami, have increased since independence.

Only a few companies are rapidly Africanizing their staffs, and thus giving Africans the experience they will need to start companies on their own someday. One of the notable pioneers in this area is Ethiopian Airlines, which is managed under contract by Trans World Airlines.

One great advantage over other parts of the underdeveloped world partly offsets some of black Africa's problems: with a few exceptions, such as Ethiopia, there are no indigenous economic oligarchies to be dismantled.

The road ahead—like most of Africa's highways—is potholed and perilous, but it is not blocked.

November 24, 1969

REFUGEE PROBLEM GROWS IN AFRICA

U.N. Agency Tends Some of the Million Homeless

JOHANNESBURG, South Africa, April 25 (AP)—More than a million people have been uprooted from a dozen African countries, creating a refugee problem that does not appear to have any immediate solution.

Some of the homeless at last count totaled 933,000, are tended by the United Nations High Commission for Refugees, which operates from headquarters in Geneva and 29 branch offices throughout the world. The commission, which was established in 1950, seeks to help resettle or repatriate the refugees and to safeguard their rights and interests and to improve their status.

Not included in the United Nations refugee count of 933,000 are thousands displaced by terrorism or civil war. Nor does the count cover the millions who still lead nomadic lives or hundreds of thousands who must leave impoverished homelands to find work elsewhere.

Also outside the latest official head count are tens of thousands of aliens expelled from Ghana in recent months. As many as 200,000 of Ghana's two million foreigners could be affected. They include Africans from Nigeria, Togo, Niger, Upper Volta and Dahomey. Many lived and worked in Ghana for decades.

More than 75,000 Nigerians trekked home, many of them sick, penniless and demoralized.

Many Walked

Many walked all the way. Truckers and operators of creaky, wood-bodied "mammy wagons" increased their fares as much as 40 per cent when the exodus began, to haul deportees from Ghana across Togo and Dahomey to Nigeria. One truck overturned in Dahomey, killing 21 and injuring 60.

The expulsions were heavy in Ghana where unemployment is high. The Government defended its action by saying that 90 per cent of the country's prison inmates were aliens.

Prince Saruddin Aga Khan, the United Nations High Commissioner for Refugees, hurried to Lagos to study the problem.

Although the high commissioner's office was set up mainly to help refugees from Eastern Europe, when the liquidation of old colonial empires began, it shifted its emphasis to Africans forced from their homes by tribal wars or fighting between local blacks and the remaining colonial rulers.

3-Phase Program

The United Nations High Commission has adopted a three-phase program that has shown some signs of success in aiding refugees in Africa, most of whom are subsistence farmers.

The first step involves emergency resettlement on the land with food, clothing, shelter, seeds and simple agricultural tools provided by the Red Cross and other international organizations.

The second phase includes the building of roads, bridges and a few permanent buildings and the development of water supplies on the new land in an effort to integrate the refugees into their adopted land.

The third phase to help the refugees attain the same economic standards as the original local population.

The commission faced its first major challenge in Afirca in the Congo not long after the former Belgian colony gained independence in 1960. About 70,000 Congolese fled. On the other hand, the Congo provided haven for some 475,000 refugees, mostly from Rwanda, Portuguest Angola, Zambia and the Sudan.

Refugee traffic often moves in opposite directions. The Sudan got some 30,000 from Ethiopia, many Eritreans, when the former Italian colony of Eritrea on the Red Sea became part of Ethiopia in 1952. Ethiopia has received about 20,000 of the 184,000 refugees estimated to have fled the Sudan in the civil war there.

Problems in Uganda

Other Sudanese refugees went to Uganda, the Central African Republic and the Congo.

Uganda faced thorny economic and social problems created by an influx in the nineteen sixties of some 175,000 refugees from Rwanda, the Congo and the Sudan. Politically, the difficulty was to keep refugees from plotting against those who ousted them and to prevent their persecutors from crossing into Uganda and killing them. Friction along the Sudanese border threatened to become a shooting war in 1968.

Uganda is one of the few countries where the refugee situation has slightly improved. Resettled on fertile land, many refugees no longer need help. They are harvesting good crops, sending their children to school and paying taxes.

More than 120,000 are scattered among Uganda's native population. Others stay in 11 rural settlements.

Because the refugees are mainly farmers, most find rural poverty in their new country much like rural poverty in their homeland. But some of the younger ones drift into cities in their country of haven, adding to the list of urban jobless.

April 26, 1970

U.N. LISTS 19 STATES AS LEAST DEVELOPED

UNITED NATIONS, N. Y., May 9 (UPI)—The United Nations has listed 19 nations, 16 of them African, as the least developed nations of the world.

The list, contained in a report for next week's meeting of the United Nations Economic and Social Council, was determined on the basis of literacy, gross national product and manufacturing production.

In addition to the 16 African countries, two Asian countries and Yemen were listed.

The African nations were Botswana, Burundi, Chad, Dahomey, Ethiopia, Gambia, Guinea, Lesotho, Malawi, Niger, Rwanda, Somalia, the Sudan, Tanzania, Uganda and Upper Volta. The Asian nations were Afghanistan and Laos.

In each of the 19 nations, the report said, less than 20 per cent of the adult population is literate. Per capita gross national product is less than $100, and manufacturing accounts for less than 10 per cent of total production.

May 10, 1970

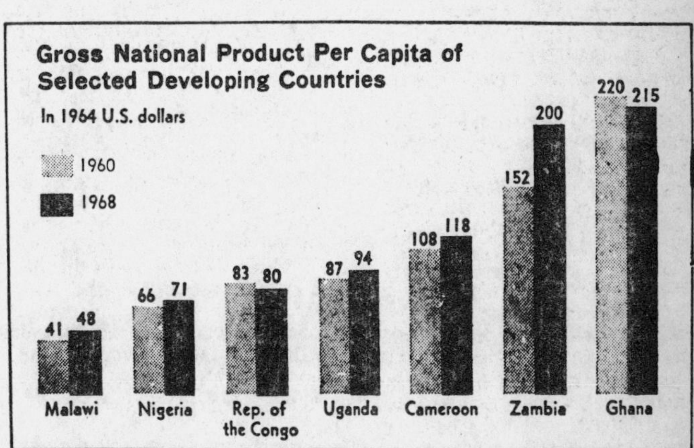

January 29, 1971

Black Africa's Cities Teem With Youths Seeking Jobs but Finding Poverty

By WILLIAM BORDERS
Special to The New York Times

LAGOS, Nigeria, April 26 — Ignatius Chukwuka has left his rural village and come to Lagos to look for a job, but his prospects are dim and growing dimmer.

"Every day I hold it strong in my mind that this will be the day I find something, but it never is," the slender 24-year-old dropout from grade school explained early the other morning as he joined the growing line outside a crowded employment office.

Like millions of other young, semieducated black Africans who have crowded into the cities seeking a brighter life, Mr. Chukwuka has found only increasing hopelessness and a poverty far worse than what he left behind on the farm.

From Kinshasa to Kampala, from Dakar to Dar es Salaam, the young unemployed populate vast shanty slums spreading around urban centers, where their presence has become one of modern Africa's gravest social problems.

"There is really no solution because these developing economies simply do not have the jobs to offer," a sociologist from the University of Lagos explained. "I cannot see any way out of Africa's urban unemployment problem."

Opportunities Are Scant

Historians point out that in the United States the migration to the cities coincided with industrial development; a young man of even meager skills could find work when he left the farm and moved to Cleveland or Chicago 50 or 100 years ago.

In Africa, with few factories and an economy that is still overwhelmingly agricultural, there is scant industrial opportunity for the man whose education has taught him to be dissatisfied with the primitive village life.

A recent study in Zambia found that the entire economy had 350,000 paying jobs. But each year 50,000 seventh-graders leave school and begin looking for work, many of them gravitating toward the cities.

Like Ignatius Chukwuka, who left school in the eighth grade, they have read about modern urban life in their European textbooks and they want to share it.

"In my village, Oba, people do not even have electricity, and there is nothing to do at night," he explained.

"In Lagos there are lively entertainments and girls and cinemas."

The urban migration depends heavily on Africa's extended family system, in which the door is never closed to kin, no matter how distant the relationship. When Mr. Chukwuka made the 250-mile trip to Lagos last October, he knew he could count on living with a cousin.

A Few Yards of Floor Space

The cousin, who already had six children and half a dozen other relatives living with him in a four-room flat 10 miles from the center of town, was able to offer only a few square yards of floor space. He could not have turned him away without insuring the ostracism of all their relatives back home.

"It's not bad, and I can get a place of my own after I get a job, if I do," Mr. Chukwuka said as he walked down the dirt road leading to the bus stop where his 80-minute ride into town begins.

Like other barely literate young men hanging around on street corners all over Africa, he describes himself as "an applicant." Just what job he settles for depends on what is offered.

At the employment office the other day he was waiting in the line for drivers, because it was the shortest, but he said it made little difference "because you almost never get a job here anyway."

A good driver in Lagos earns $55 a month, and finding a job like that would be a dream come true for Mr. Chukwuka. In the meantime he works two or three days a week in the European section at the construction site of a house that will rent for $700 a month. For a 10-hour day of carrying sand and cement there he is paid $1.30, and he regards the job as only a stopgap.

Most days, after whiling away the morning lounging in the shade of the fruit trees outside the employment office, Mr. Chukwuka moves at noon to a fetid back street where his brother runs a tiny shop that sells used nuts and bolts.

"I get some rice or soup across the road, and we sit here on the step and talk," he explained, idly fingering one of the rusty bolts that his brother sells for a penny or two each.

The shop sometimes clears a couple of dollars a day. Other small merchants are less fortunate.

One morning recently a teenage boy squatted on the sidewalk outside a branch of a European bank and stacked four boxes of imported Vicks cough drops neatly in front of him. The cough drops, presumably stolen, were for sale, but he cheerfully conceded that business was anything but brisk.

In cities all over black Africa youths can be seen standing in rows outside shops and restaurants with strange bits of merchandise for sale. One holds a single leather belt, waving it at passers-by: another has three bottle openers and a couple of watchbands. Many earn nothing in the course of a day.

"Who knows how long someone like that waits before deciding that there's easier money to be made holding up a shop?" asked a Government official in Kampala, Uganda, where unemployment is high and street crime is growing.

In Nigeria armed robbery is so prevalent that the Government has begun executing thieves publicly as a deterrent, but the crime rate, many experts say, is still climbing in direct proportion to the unemployment.

Like most statistics in underdeveloped Africa, the unemployment figures are sketchy approximations. A recent survey indicated that a third of the men in Kinshasa, the Congo, had no jobs. In Lagos no more than half the men are earning enough to support themselves without help.

Yet both of the cities—the two largest in black Africa, with populations over 1.25 million each—are growing because of migration at a rate of more than 10 per cent a year as their vast slum suburbs eat up more and more of the countryside.

Before World War II tropical Africa had five cities of more than 100,000 people. It now has 60, and most of them have meager social services, poor water supplies and grossly inadequate sanitation systems. Nonetheless the migration shows no signs of abating, and the cities still exert the pull described by Cyprian Ekwensi, the Nigerian writer, in his novel "People of the City":

"It was a way of life she liked. The glamorous surroundings, the taxis, the quick drinks. This was one reason why she had come to the city from her home 60 miles away. To eat in fashionable hotels, to have men who wore white collars to their jobs as lovers, men who could spend."

Hiring of 10% Ordered

Increasingly, Governments are becoming aware of the problem and are trying either to reverse the migration or to give the people in the cities something to do.

In Nairobi, where jobless youths by the hundreds crowd the sidewalks of an otherwise prosperous-looking downtown area, the Kenyan Government ordered employers last year to hire 10 per cent more workers whether they were needed or not. At the same time it is trying to persuade youg men to go back to the tea plantations in the west, where there is a shortage of workers.

The Zambian authorities have coordinated youth programs with their rural-development plans and opened trade-training centers to give practical knowledge to dropouts who can find no market in an underdeveloped land for the knowledge they learned from books.

The Ivory Coast, which is wealthier than most of her neighbors, is using educational television to keep young men back on the farm and out of Abidjan, the flashy capital. Programs beamed to the rural areas are portraying farming with more respect to erase the impression that it is beneath the dignity of anyone who can read. But the old attitudes die hard.

"I might like to go back to my village some day, but not to make a living from the soil," Mr. Chukwuka remarked. "It would be nice to visit, especially if I could arrive there in a car, and of course I'd have to take money to give to my mother."

Since he came to Lagos six months ago, Mr. Chukwuka said he has been able to send her $2.50, and his present assets total less than $3—"But still I am glad to be in the city,

The New York Times/William Borders

Ignatius Chukwuka, a 24-year-old unemployed Nigerian, resting on a street in Lagos with jobless countrymen

and things could be worse. I have friends and I am well."

Most of his friends are Ibo tribesmen, like himself, although the pressures of city life have eroded some of the strictures of tribalism, and now he sometimes shares a joke or a drink with Yorubas, which never would have happened at home.

"You're on the whole long bus trip with them every day, it is difficult not to speak to them," he explained

It is usually to fellow migrants from his village in the east that Mr. Chukwuka turns for companionship as evening comes to the block of rude stone houses that they now call home, bringing slight relief from the oppressive heat.

He and his friends sit outside, chatting over a bottle of palm wine or, if someone has had a particularly good day, over a couples of bottles of beer.

Like Mr. Chukwuka most of them are bachelors, but they talk of making a trip back to the village to find a wife as soon as they have saved enough to pay the bride price.

They also talk about their temporary work, about cadging a shilling here and a shilling there, and sometimes about stealing. So far, they concede, no one has found the job they are all looking for. Maybe tomorrow.

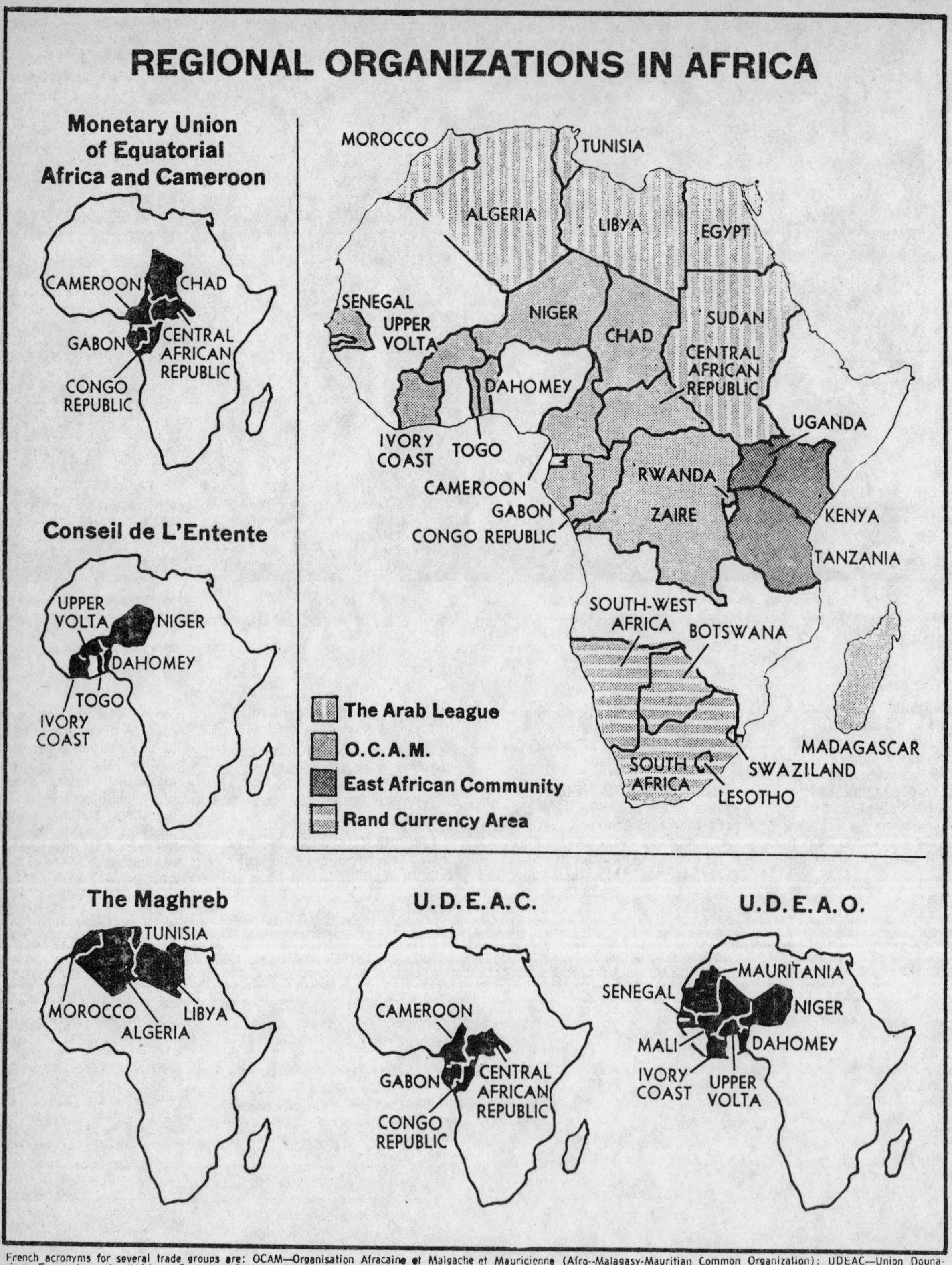

French acronyms for several trade groups are: OCAM—Organisation Afracaine et Malgache et Mauricienne (Afro-Malagasy-Mauritian Common Organization); UDEAC—Union Douaniere Economique de l'Afrique Centrale (Central African Customs-Economic Union); UDEAO—Union Douaniere des Etats de l'afrique et l'Ouest (Customs Union of West African States).

REGIME IN GHANA WARNS OPPOSITION

Reprisal Talk Is Held Device to Avert Chaos—But Foes See Dictatorship Trend

By RICHARD P. HUNT
Special to The New York Times.

ACCRA, Ghana, Oct. 5 — Seven months after independence, Prime Minister Kwame Nkrumah's Government feels it must threaten its political foes with reprisals to avoid bloodshed and authoritarianism in Ghana.

This is the explanation being given today in circles close to the Government for the recent spate of warnings that any outburst of violence could lead to suspension of the Constitution and wholesale imprisonment of leaders of the opposition.

The Prime Minister is portrayed as being eager to keep Ghana on the path of parliamentary democracy. To do so, it is said, he sanctions threats as a means of heading off a situation that, he feels, would require the sternest measures.

The nature of these measures is indicated in the preface to his autobiography, published this year, in which he said: "Even a system based on social justice and a democratic Constitution may need backing up, during the period following independence, by emergency measures of a totalitarian kind."

Interior Minister Krobo Edusei was even more specific this week. He said at a rally of the governing Convention People's party that any attempt to assassinate the Prime Minister, a Cabinet minister or a party leader, would be "the beginning of a dictatorship in this country."

Government Held Vague

Amid all this the Govern ment is being vague about what it fears. Assassination and violence are alluded to, but no specific charges have been leveled and there has been no attempt to amplify the Government's version of the situation.

In the camp of the opposition, however, it is said that "there would have been a bloody revolution" a year ago except for the intervention of Mr. Nkrumah's parliamentary foes. These sources blame the Government for having revived bad feeling recently in the deportation of two leaders of the Moslem community at Kumasi, the upcountry center of the opposition.

Kumasi is the capital of the Ashanti people, the cocoa-farming sons of some of the fiercest warriors in Africa. Around their beloved king, or asanthahene, they form the core of loyalty to a traditional tribal political organization.

With those under the influence of other great upcountry chiefs there is perhaps a body of 1,000,000, or roughly a quarter of Ghana's population, that has not yet been won over to the kind of Western political organization exemplified here by Mr. Nkrumah's party.

In a strange alliance with this group are a number of intellectuals, who contend that Mr. Nkrumah is only trying to find an excuse to establish the dictatorship that has always been his objective.

One of these is Joseph Appiah, a member of the Ghana Parliament, who for six years was Mr. Nkrumah's personal representative in London during the struggle for independence from British rule. Mr. Appiah, who is a son-in-law of the late Sir Stafford Cripps, once British Laborite Chancellor of the Exchequer, broke away from the conventional People's party about three years ago.

To Fight Authoritarianism

Speaking with that special vehemence of an old comrade in arms who has gone over to the other side, Mr. Appiah told this correspondent that Mr. Nkrumah for years had been "always thinking in terms of the police, the army and taking the salute."

Mr. Appiah declared that his group would fight with all the constitutional means at its disposal to prevent authoritarianism. To this end six opposition parties and two independent M. P.'s will join forces at Kumasi tomorrow in a new unified opposition, probably to be called the National Progressive party. It will have thirty-three M. P.'s against the Government's seventy-one.

Another party leader said it was hoped that this new organization could crystalize opinion throughout the country and force the Government to continue the observance of democratic principles. It was denied, however, that the opposition would do anything to precipitate an emergency.

October 6, 1957

GHANA VOTES BIAS BILL

Deputies Act to Bar Parties Based on Race or Religion

ACCRA, Ghana, Dec. 11 (Reuters)—Parliament adopted today on the second reading a bill that would prohibit the formation of political parties based on race, tribe or religion. It rejected by a 40-to-7 vote an Opposition amendment to throw out the measure—the avoidance of discrimination bill.

Owusu Ansah of the opposition United party, said there was no need for the bill now that all Opposition parties had united. He added that the measure sought to supress political activity.

Interior Minister Krobo Edusei said he hoped to introduce a preventive detention bill empowering the Government "to imprison without trial any person suspected of activities prejudicial to the state's security." He told newsmen the bill would cover "local deportations" of Ghana citizens and said it was not intended that such persons should be brought before the courts.

December 12, 1957

Ghana Curbs Opposition Party

ACCRA, Oct. 4 (AP)—The Government has banned public meetings by the Opposition United party in campaigning for regional elections. The Foreign Ministry said the party "might provoke ill-disposed persons to indulge in breacnes of the peace."

October 5, 1958

JAILINGS IN GHANA AROUSE PROTESTS

By JOHN B. OAKES
Special to The New York Times.

ACCRA, GHANA.

This country's tough Preventive Detention Act, passed last fall, has resulted in the imprisonment for up to five years of about forty-five persons, without hearings, trials, or appeals.

The Act is one of several security measures that have aroused bitter criticism from such opposition as still exists.

It is not easy to be active in the Opposition United party. For all practical purposes, this is a one-party state. In fact, it is virtually a one-man state. The man is Prime Minister Kwame Nkrumah, under whose statue in front of the Parliament building here is the phrase: "Founder of the Nation."

Dr. Nkrumah rules Ghana's politics, economics and almost every other phase of Ghanaian life through the People's Convention party, without fear of contradiction. He controls eighty-six of the 104 seats in Parliament. His opponents, a number of whom are in jail, are disorganized and leaderless, but not entirely without hope.

There is at least one outspoken Opposition newspaper, The Pioneer. There is also universal suffrage and genuine secrecy of the ballot box. At least there was in a municipal election here.

The voters filed past election officials, including watchers for both political parties, and proceeded into a screened booth, which contained two boxes, each marked with a party symbol. It was impossible for the officials to see the box in which the voter placed his ballot. The Opposition won two of the four offices contested.

Ghanaian leaders assert with some heat that this two-year-old state's Government is in constant danger of forcible overthrow by a discontented minority. Quick to point to the recent assassination of the Prime Minister of Ceylon, S. W. R. D. Bandaranaike, as justification for their own severe security laws, they recall that only a few months ago a plot was exposed against the life of Dr. Nkrumah.

November 1, 1959

Ghana Changes to a Republic, Retaining Commonwealth Ties

West African State Makes Transition—Nkrumah President Today

Special to The New York Times.

ACCRA Ghana, Friday, July 1—Ghana made a complete break today with the Constitution bequeathed her by Britain in 1957. Her Parliament was prorogued and a few minutes after last midnight she became a republic within the British Commonwealth.

The prorogation was the last state function by the Earl of Listowel, the Governor General and Queen Elizabeth II's representative as head of state. In ceremonial regalia Lord Listowel told the hushed National Assembly:

"I come to prorogue this Parliament and bid you farewell. By midnight the monarchy of Ghana will cease and the new republic will be born."

The New York Times
Kwame Nkrumah

He read a message of good wishes from Elizabeth, in which she said: "From midnight I shall cease to be your Queen."

Message and Reply

"I am proud I am head of a Commonwealth in which every nation may choose for itself the form of government which best suits it," her message added. "Now that Ghana has chosen for itself a republican form of constitution it will not affect the interest which I have always taken and shall continue to take in the welfare of its people."

Ghana's reply in effect was made by Kwame Nkrumah, former Prime Minister and now President-elect, at a farewell state dinner last night for Lord Listowel.

The Ghanaians had not adopted a republican Constitution "through any lack of affection for Her Majesty nor because of any dissatisfaction with the way in which the office of Governor General has been discharged," Mr. Nkrumah said.

"We have enacted for ourselves a new Constitution because it is our conviction that we need a form of government that will more truly interpret the aspirations and hopes of the people of Ghana and give full expression to our African personality," he added.

At the state dinner, the toast was for the Queen as head of state and in Parliament last evening the Speaker and clerks wore the traditional wig and gown.

But this forenoon, when Mr. Nkrumah is inaugurated as President—head of state as well as head of the Government—it will be in a wholly Ghanaian setting. The traditional drums and horns will sound his praise. The Parliament chamber will already have been fitted with furniture of a Ghanaian character by carpenters working through the night.

After his inauguration, Mr. Nkrumah will appoint his new Cabinet. Parliament will meet Monday as the legislature of the republic.

The change was taking place in an atmosphere of goodwill. Accra, Ghana's capital, was thronged and the streets gay with bunting and special lighting. Five days of merrymaking and official functions mark the transition.

Until March 6, 1957, when she became an independent state, Ghana was the Gold Coast Colony administered as such by Britain since 1874.

July 1, 1960

Nkrumah Brands All of Ghana With the Stamp of His Authority

President's Image and Name Mark Nation Struggling for Economic Gains

By A. M. ROSENTHAL

Special to The New York Times.

ACCRA, Ghana, Oct. 16—There is a fine new fountain in Accra at a traffic roundabout where a neon sign flashes "Kwame Nkrumah Circle" through the night.

Kwame Nkrumah Avenue leads into the circle and Kwame Nkrumah Road is near by. The fountain was dedicated by Kwame Nkrumah.

A couple of miles away, in front of a red-tiled Parliament building that looks like a Howard Johnson roadside restaurant, Kwame Nkrumah—by official title "Victorious Leader, the President of the Republic of Ghana"—stands in bronze.

His words are chiseled into the pedestal: "Seek ye first the political kingdom and everything else shall be added unto you."

Everywhere in this gay and jostling tropical capital on the Gulf of Guinea there is the presence of Kwame Nkrumah. He peers down from billboards, he is engraved on stamps and coins, and he stares out from the masthead of a newspaper. Praise of him blares from radios and is chanted at political rallies almost every day.

After three years of independence this former British colony of the Gold Coast is the personal political kingdom of the nationalist who once walked Harlem's streets in hunger.

The dream that inspired him from youth—the dream of African unity—remains far from a reality. But Mr. Nkrumah has as his base a country he shaped himself and that greets him with love and laughter almost everywhere he goes.

The state of Ghana is authoritarian and the authority is Mr. Nkrumah. He has followed the classic modern pattern — the creation of a personally controlled party that reaches into every village and directs every aspect of social and political life.

Control Is Centralized

In the once revolutionary Convention Peoples party Mr. Nkruham has centralized control over unions, farmers, business men, the press, youth organizations, women's organizations and social welfare. In Ghana if a man wants a job or a push forward economically or politically, the starting point is a C. P. P. card.

All effective opposition was eliminated. It did not take much—a Preventive Detention Act, under which just about anybody the Government dislikes or fears can be clapped into jail without trial, and a news censorship bill that was passed by Parliament in fifteen minutes.

About 100 of Mr. Nkrumah's opponents are now in jail. The so-called opposition paper prints through a censor's muzzle and the Government newspaper is filled with angled news and great headlines of praise for "Osagyefo"—"Victorious Leader."

Officials of the nominal opposition group, the United party, are either bullied out of holding meetings or are too frightened to call them. Enemies of the Government generally are not jailed, but they find it harder and harder to make a living.

Still, this is not a grim land of silence ruled by a feared man with a whip. In Ghana, Mr. Nkrumah is beloved, perhaps not by so many people as he says he is, but by a majority, even according to his opponents.

His enemies can talk against him, but not in public. His opponents do fear him, but the city is busy trading and building and there is music in the streets and a great deal of laughter.

Ghanaians smile a great deal and the outdoor dance halls are filled with people shuffling to the quick beat of the "High Life" dance; these things may not be politically significant but they do affect the tone of life in the city.

Nobody denies Mr. Nkrumah's one-man rule. "But you have to understand conditions and not judge by Western standards," say the Ghanaians and foreigners who are embarrassed by the worship with which Mr. Nkrumah is surrounded and the power with which he has armored himself.

The argument is that when Mr. Nkrumah took power he found not a united country but four chunks of territory divided by custom, tribe and language. It was a geographic entity only by grace of British colonial decision. It was his job as he saw it to weld these bits into a whole and to do it he had to break the feudal power of the Ashanti tribal chiefs in the North.

The chiefs were broken and Mr. Nkrumah increased his power.

His followers offer this explanation: Unity was too new to stand on its own and anyway Mr. Nkrumah's next job was to push the country forward economically. Parliamentary tradition was weak, they say, and authority was what was needed.

There is another argument put forward for Mr. Nkrumah and it runs this way:

"You come from the West and you may be startled by what looks like a tough dictatorship. But the people in this country are involved in a moral and political battle against colonialism and Nkrumah is their leader."

His toughness does not mean much to them when they think of prison camps in South Africa or police shootings in Rhodesia."

"He has brought benefits; you can't take that away from him," is a statement heard often in Accra.

Foreign economists here say readily that Mr. Nkrumah has supplied a push that has indeed brought benefits. The number of children in schools has been tripled and with new roads and airlines the Ghanaians are for the first time moving easily about their own country.

The individual income in Ghana of about $170 a year was the highest in Africa when he took over and it has risen slowly but steadily at a rate of 1 per cent a year. The cost of living has gone up at about the same rate, but part of the reason is that consumption has increased and broadened. A worker who once was content with yams may now buy tinned fish.

The British may have created the base for this advance, but Ghanaians and many foreigners believe that it would not have taken place so rapidly without independence and Mr. Nkrumah.

The benefits of independence do not change the fact that among many of the educated here there is a bitterness toward Mr. Nkrumah for having wiped out real political freedom. His opponents concede he is popular, but they do not think popularity excuses oppression.

"That party of his is an octopus but it is also a fraternal society," one of them said. "It knows how to make people feel good. He gives people a feeling of being lifted up.

"If you are a party member in a village and you die, why, a big man comes from Accra and makes a speech and brings flowers and everybody says Nkrumah loves even the lowliest."

Another political opponent of Mr. Nkrumah said:

"Even now if he meets me he puts his arm around me. Yes he is a charmer. But he had me sacked from my job.

"That man, he makes people feel like somebody, but if you are against him, watch out, you become nobody."

October 17, 1960

NKRUMAH SEVERS AIDES' TRADE TIES

Special to The New York Times.

ACCRA, Ghana, April 8—President Kwame Nkrumah announced tough measures today to curb the activities of some members of his party that he said were weakening the regime and dissipating confidence in Ghana abroad.

The measures, announced in an early-morning broadcast, include the cutting of all business connections by members of Parliament and ministers belonging to his party. The President made clear that he meant foreign as well as Ghanaian businesses. Anyone not prepared to end his business ties must resign his parliamentary seat or public office, he decreed.

In addition, the President declared that in the future he alone would make statements for the Government. Any member of the party or the Government, including ministers, who want to make a statement dealing with official policy must have it approved by the Cabinet, he instructed.

'Ruling Class' Barred

The President said his "business or politics" move was directed against a group of party members who "by virtue of their functions and position [as senior and junior ministers and members of Parliament] are tending to form a separate new ruling class of self-seekers and careerists in contradiction to the party's socialist aims."

At the same time the President announced a program to tighten the party organization. Four organizations that are often referred to as party wings —the workers', farmers', women's and cooperators' organizations—are being brought under rigid party control and their independent activities considerably curbed.

Their organization flags and membership cards are to be abolished and only party flags and cards allowed. Outlying branches of the organizations will be grouped in the same premises as the party organizations. Control of their finances is to be given to Ghana's Auditor General.

The President announced that he was shelving a proposal to set up a state agency to take over cocoa buying. This project had aroused discontent among farmers, who have their own purchasing organization. The Labor and Cooperatives Ministry is to be abolished.

Mr. Nkrumah also said he was cutting down expenditure by ministers, directors of state corporations, foreign service and other officials when traveling abroad. Ambassadors, diplomats and other officials serving abroad will no longer be allowed take their children along unless they are under 5 years of age.

Mr. Nkrumah said he was taking action to tighten party discipline because of "petty misunderstandings and squabbles" between various wings of the party while he was in Britain attending the Commonwealth Prime Ministers' conference. The quarrel was between party men in big business and Parliament and others leading workers' cooperatives and farmers' organizations.

Of the party members in business, the President said many used their positions to collect money and to set up agencies to collect money for themselves. This, he said, was a "degrading, shameful, highly criminal tendency which must be crushed in the most ruthless manner."

Trade Unionists Rebuked

Of the workers' leaders he said: "Some trade union officials now and again indulge in loose talk and reprehensible statements which do no good to either the party or the Government. This is not the time for unbridled militant trade unionism in our country."

Mr. Nkrumah also revealed plans to extend and intensify Ghana's influence on African affairs.

He said a Ministry of African Affairs would be set up, separate from the Ministry of Foreign Affairs. The new ministry will be responsible for all African matters and will take over the Bureau of African Affairs and the African Affairs Center.

The announcement came at a time when other African states had been challenging Ghana for African leadership. Liberia, Nigeria, Ivory Coast, Cameroon, Guinea, Mali and other states are organizing a conference of African states to be held in Monrovia, Liberia, May 8 to 13.

April 9, 1961

GHANA DEFEATS CRITICS

Beats Down Move to Ease Bill on Foes of Nkrumah

Special to The New York Times.

ACCRA, Oct. 17—The Government used its majority in Parliament today to defeat an opposition attempt to insure that legislation to make disrespect of the person of President Kwame Nkrumah a criminal offense would not result in the denial of a citizen's right to criticize the activities of the Ghana Government.

Before the House was a bill providing for £350, or $980, fine or three years in prison or both as punishment on summary conviction for an act calculated to bring the person of Presisdent Nkrumah into ridicule, contempt, or hatred.

An attempt to get the Parliament to reject a Government plan to make the bill retroactive was also defeated. Government spokesmen denied that the bill would result in the denial of the right to criticize the Government.

October 18, 1961

Nkrumah Steps Up Nkrumahism

To achieve his 'pan-African' goals, Ghana's President is building an ever stricter regime, and moving ever closer to the Eastern bloc.

By HENRY TANNER

ACCRA, Ghana.

PRESIDENT KWAME NKRUMAH passionately believes that "the independence of Ghana is meaningless unless it is linked up with the total liberation of the African continent." This passion, bordering on obsession, has shaped his personality, his life and his foreign and domestic policies down to the most trivial detail.

A suspicious man, Nkrumah also is deeply convinced that the colonial powers which gave political independence to their possessions have recently launched a vast, ignoble campaign to "take back with one hand what they gave with the other." For "total liberation" to Nkrumah means "African unity" and who stands in the way of unity if not the "colonialists" who hope to play African leaders off against each other? Liberation means "total economic independence"—and who is seeking to perpetuate commercial privileges and industrial monopolies in Africa if not the "capitalists" who came to the continent under the colonial administrations?

Total liberation also means new, specifically African institutions "neither Westminster nor the Kremlin." It means "socialism," but the "African brand" of socialism. It means assertion of the "African personality." In one word, it means "Nkrumahism."

This newest of "isms" has never been defined either by the "Osagyefo" (Redeemer), as Nkrumah is officially called, or by his disciples. But it makes huge banner headlines and fills pages in Accra's two Government-controlled newspapers.

"Nkrumahism is the new philosophy and code of life evolved by Osagyefo for the nation. It is our 'Mein Kampf' [spelled 'Mien Kamph'']," declared The Evening News recently, probably without realizing all the implications of the phrase. "Leaders like Gandhi, Jinnah and Nehru were a new orientation to their people. Osagyefo means more * * * he means the birth of a new era of work, peace and happiness; the dawn of a new hope, brilliant in its unique mission of obedience, sacrifice and service. It is divine in its wisdom and love."

ALTHOUGH he has never spelled out Nkrumahism, the Osagyefo pursues it with a terrible impatience. So impatient has he become in recent months that in order to achieve his goal of African unity and total economic independence more quickly he is imposing an ever more authoritative regime on his country, and abroad is moving for the first time into ever closer relationship with the Eastern bloc.

As a result, many of his own people have turned their backs on him for the first time since independence in a sullen, if ineffectual, gesture. The only organized opposition to his Convention Peoples party is the Unity party, which has been opposed to Nkrumah since the days before independence, but which is now weak, with most of its leaders in jail or exile. More important is the widespread disaffection among the people because of the mass arrests, the austerity budget, new taxes, rising prices, reduced incomes and the Eastward drift in foreign affairs.

For years, one of his advisers told me, Nkrumah avoided contact with the Soviets because he was afraid of being drawn into their orbit, but he is now confident that he would be able to "ride the tiger" if necessary. As is evident in his passion for "total independence," he will not consciously become a Soviet satellite; but he feels he is secure enough to accept aid from all sides, including the East.

The key factor in the estrangement between Nkrumah and much of the Western world is the Congo. What happened there has been the most telling, saddest personal defeat the Ghanaian President has suffered in his life. His bitterness is great and, according to all those who have dealt with him during this period, he blames the West, and most particularly Britain, for his disappointment.

In July of 1960 Nkrumah thought he was within reach of fulfillment of his dream. Africa, or at least a major part of it, was about to unite under his leadership. A new nationalist, Patrice Lumumba, had come to power in the largest, richest country of Africa. And Lumumba had promised to join Nkrumah's Ghana-Guinea union, making the Osagyefo the most powerful man on the African continent.

Then Lumumba was deposed and finally killed. With white mercenaries to aid "traitor" Tshombe, Britain, France and Belgium "conspired" to keep the Katanga secession alive and to kill Nkrumah's dream. He has not forgotten and will never forget, his associates say.

THESE recent tendencies of Nkrumah caused the United States to delay and reconsider its promise of one of the largest loans ever made under the foreign-aid program—for the Volta Dam hydroelectric project. When the Administration finally decided to go ahead with the loan, it was because American diplomats, like other Western observers here, hope that the trend in Ghana is still reversible and that Nkrumah, who in all probability will continue to govern his country for a long time, is still recoverable.

Whatever the outcome of Nkrumah's headlong drive for the total liberation of Africa, his moves will have repercussions throughout the continent. "Whether we like it or not," a foreign diplomat here said recently "his passions reflect the passions of all of Africa."

WHAT kind of man is Nkrumah? The answer of the men who have been close to him usually is a puzzled look and a helpless shrug. Many know him but no one claims to know him well.

The image that emerges is that of an unusually complex, even tortured figure, living in friendless, unhappy isolation, reluctant to reveal himself to any man or woman, cut off from the reality of his country, alone with the tremendous conviction that he is the man of destiny of Africa whose acts are wise and just at all times and who cannot be opposed by any honest person. "He is the most complex man I have ever known," says an international civil servant with long years of experience in a dozen countries.

One of the elements of complexity apparently is religion. Nkrumah was brought up a Catholic; he has left the Church but "cannot disbelieve," in the words of one former associate. "He would be much more happy if he could be an agnostic or a frank atheist but he can't. So he is caught between his religious faith and his ambition to be a 'Marxist - Socialist' nation-builder and emancipator, bringing industrialization and great material progress to his people."

Although he is a Christian, Nkrumah has not freed himself of ancient African superstitions. He hardly ever separates himself from the cane he carries not to lean on but as a protection from evil. A visitor to his office may at times see an array of little leather bags attached to the arm rest of his chair. They are jujus to chase evil spirits. They have been placed there with complicated ministrations, pouring of libations and perhaps the sacrifice of a sheep by one or an other of the Capital's jujumen.

There have been reports, never substantiated, that jujumen had influenced the nature or at least the timing of decisions of state: that because it feared the spirits dwelling in the dark water, the Government of this modern emancipator waited four years before dredging a malaria-breeding lagoon near the Capital.

There is complexity also in Nkrumah's being "African" and at the same time "Western." The President is swayed alternately by his Western education and his African background, almost all his acquaintances say. In recent years, one of them adds, the African part of his personality has come to the fore and the Western traits have receded with the fading of memory of his years in America and England.

IN the middle of a convertion, one frequent visitor says, he may suddenly become unfathomable, shrinking from contact with the Westerner and refusing to reveal the thoughts and emotions that went into the argument he just made. He is a man who can change abruptly from charm to utter rudeness. "He'd pour you champagne one moment and drop a brick on your toes the next," one associate says.

Another element of complexity is Nkrumah's vanity. The personality cult that has been built up around him is more extravagant than anything ever tried by Stalin.

"Nkrumah is Ghana!" an Accra newspaper proclaimed the other day, adding: "When our history is recorded the man Kwame Nkrumah will be written as the Liberator, the Messiah, the Christ of our day, whose great love for mankind wrought changes in Ghana, in Africa and in the world at large. He is our Messiah and he is immortal."

Among the titles given him, in addition to Osagyefo, are His High Dedication, The Aweful, The Achiever, The Ruthless, The Valorous, The Quencher of Fires, The Fount of Honor, The Father of the Nation, The Brave Warrior, The Renewer of All Things.

His name and his image are everywhere—in all the Government offices and most private commercial establishments, on the penny stamp, on all coins from half-penny to two shillings and on the masthead of the party newspaper which he founded and which bears the slogan "The Party Is Supreme."

IN the capital alone he has a larger-than-life bronze statue, a Kwame Nkrumah Circle, Kwame Nkrumah Avenue, Kwame Nkrumah Road, Kwame Nkrumah Railway Station, Kwame Nkrumah Leadership Training School (for party youth) and Kwame Nkrumah Cooperative. One of Accra's soccer teams of course is called Osagyefo's Eleven.

Does Nkrumah himself believe he is the Messiah? There is no certain answer. Most of the men who know him seem to think that the Messiah cult is little more than a convenient political device. In a superstitious country where tribalism is still strong, it gives him the aura of a super-chief with mysterious divine powers. It makes governing easier for him.

Nkrumah did not initiate the personality cult, but neither did he lift a finger to stop it, these men say. And they add that the President is a man of great vanity who likes to be flattered and to bathe in the nation's adulation.

One of the most revealing comments came from one of his greatest admirers: "Certainly he does not think he is a Messiah. How could he? He is a deeply religious man who prays to his God and it is not to himself that he prays." Then the admirer paused and added: "He does not think he is a Messiah but he thinks he is the Saviour of Africa."

Nkrumah, the single-minded nation-builder, has no private life. He spends up to eighteen hours a day at his desk. He does not drink. He does not smoke. And when a visitor asked him what he did for recreation, he answered, "I talk."

Even in his marriage he seems to have deferred to political strategy and to the idea of African unity. Like a medieval king entering into union with a foreign dynasty, he had decided that his bride should be a Moslem from Egypt. In 1957 he married Fathia Ritz, a pleasant-looking light-skinned woman who was discovered by his emissaries in Cairo after a systematic search and whom, the story goes, he had never seen before.

FOR all his self-denial in the interest of his mission, Nkrumah is not a selfless man according to his intimates. On the contrary, they say, he has a towering ambition and a great lust for personal power. "I'm the leader of Ghana," he is said to have told a group of politicians, "and since Ghana was the first independent African state, I am the leader of Africa." The theme is recurrent in many of his public statements.

It has never occurred to him, one of his collaborators says, that his own drive for personal power might clash with the ambitions of other African leaders. This is one of the several flaws in the leadership he is attempting to give to the African continent. It is easy to find evidence that Nkrumah is not liked but sometimes held in ridicule by powerful Africans who are supposed to be his allies.

More and more, Nkrumah is a lonely figure cut off from the realities of the world, according to the men who have watched him over the years. His great tragedy, these men say, is that he no longer has any disinterested, rational advisers capable of leading him back onto solid ground whenever his dreams and ambitions have carried him away.

HIS great friend and mentor for many years was George Padmore, a brilliant figure from the West Indies who was a member of the Soviet Politburo in the early days, turned to the extreme Right for a while before World War II and finally with a famous book, "Pan-Africanism or Communism?", became the father of pan-Africanism.

Nkrumah and Padmore met in London. All through the pre-independence struggle and the post-independence trials, Padmore was Nkrumah's closest and most influential adviser. Then in the fall of 1959 he died suddenly. He has never been replaced.

Up until that time it was possible for those who were close to Nkrumah, and for quite a few comparative strangers, to see him casually and discuss matters freely with him. That is no longer possible.

This summer, after there had been an unsuccessful rebellion against him within his Cabinet, he dismissed the only two ministers who had dared to stand up to him. Ever since, he has been surrounded mainly by party hacks who, while scraping before him and pushing his personality cult to ridiculous extremes, have managed to create a void around him.

THERE is evidence that Nkrumah himself no longer respects any of the men surrounding him. Visitors say they have heard him shout them down like schoolboys. So complete is the isolation in which he now lives that most of those who still see him doubt that he is aware of the mood of the country—of the disaffection that has set in among his countrymen.

Nkrumah is a sensitive man who wants to be admired and respected. His sensitivity is a key factor in the anti-Western stance he has recently adopted. Like so many African leaders, he has been disappointed and hurt by what he considers the "duplicity of the white man," especially in the Congo. The fury of his drive for total emancipation has doubled as a result.

January 14, 1962

Nkrumah Charges 'External Enemies' Backed Plot

By LLOYD GARRISON
Special to The New York Times.

ACCRA, Ghana, Oct. 2—President Kwame Nkrumah declared today that a recent attempt to assassinate him was linked to enemies of Ghana.

Speaking at the opening of Parliament, he described the assassination plot as a "desperate attempt to arrest our progress and halt the fight against imperialism and its handmaidens, colonialism and neocolonialism."

He added that "external enemies" were behind the strikes a year ago against the Government's austerity program.

Shortly after the assassination incident nine weeks ago, Parliament voted to make Mr. Nkrumah President for life.

Today he declined the offer and said it was "essential" that the people exercise their will through national elections every five years.

The 53-year-old President arrived at Parliament escorted by 48 motorcycle guards and a mounted troop of lancers.

Mr. Nkrumah spoke for 90 minutes and appeared fit and in a confident, jovial mood. He frequently paused in his address to exchange quips and banter with the lawmakers, who interrupted him more than fifty times with shouts of "Hear! Hear!" and "That's right!"

The vast majority of the Deputies are members of Mr. Nkrumah's ruling Convention People's party. The President congratulated them for having "echoed the will of the people in calling for a one-party state."

United States officials here were generally pleased with what they felt was Mr. Nkrumah's moderate tone in speaking of Ghana's foreign policy.

Several weeks ago party newspapers accused the United States and other Western nations of being behind the recent waves of terrorist bombings that have taken 15 lives and wounded more than 250 persons. President Nkrumah later dissociated the Government from these allegations.

In today's speech he stressed that "when we in Ghana speak of imperialism, colonialism and neocolonialism, we do not necessarily refer to, or aim our attack at any government or country. Our stand is against the system."

In his only reference to foreign aid, he thanked the United States for assistance in setting up Ghana's National Investment Bank.

He went on to ask Parliament to pass an act to "define the nature of concessions that the Government proposes to make to foreign investors."

Mr. Nkrumah emphasized that Ghana welcomed foreign capital. "We have absolutely no intention to take over any private enterprises," he said. "We never have and we never will."

October 3, 1962

GHANA ENACTS LAW TO DETAIN PRISONERS

ACCRA, Ghana, Nov. 4 (Reuters)—An amendment allowing the Government to detain a prisoner for five years after he has served a five-year sentence was passed by Parliament today.

Enacted under a certificate of urgency, the amendment would permit such detentions if they were considered in the interests of defense and security.

It was understood that a group of persons being detained were nearing the end of the five-year terms.

The Defense Minister and Leader of the House, Kofi Baako, said the Government did not want the preventive detention act, but that it was a "distasteful necessity." Some Members had compared the act to measures adopted in South Africa.

November 5, 1963

NKRUMAH ESCAPES ASSASSIN 5TH TIME

Security Guard Fatally Shot —Assailant Is Arrested

By Reuters

ACCRA, Ghana, Jan. 2—President Kwame Nkrumah escaped another attempt on his life today when five shots were fired at him from close range, the Government reported.

An official statement said the shooting had occurred while Mr. Nkrumah was walking toward his car outside his office. The assailant was arrested immediately.

The President was unhurt, but a security guard was seriously wounded and died soon afterward at the military hospital.

There have been four previous attempts to kill the 54-year-old President, who led the Gold Coast, a British colony, to independence in 1957.

Two men were sentenced to death after a previous attempt on his life.

The first hint of a new assassination attempt came in midafternoon, when policemen suddenly massed around the Presidential residence, Flagstaff House. Mr. Nkrumah actually lives in a 300-year-old castle about two miles away.

Armored cars from a nearby army camp formed a cordon around Flagstaff House. Top police and military officials called at the President's office, which is part of a group of Government buildings.

The Ghana Association of Journalists and Writers celebrated Mr. Nkrumah's escape with a vigil of thanksgiving at the press club, the first of a series expected throughout the nation.

Apart from police activity around Flagstaff House, business went on normally in Accra.

The first attempt on Mr. Nkrumah's life was made early in 1956, before Ghana became independent. A bomb exploded in his house in Accra while he was meeting with several government ministers. No one was injured.

Last August Mr. Nkrumah was injured when a grenade was thrown at him on Ghana's northern frontier near Upper Volta. Several persons in the crowd near him were killed.

Seven persons were condemned to death by the Special Criminal Division of the Ghana Court on charges arising out of the assassination attempt.

Last Jan. 9 a bomb exploded amid a crowd cheering the President as he drove from a political rally in Accra.

More than 60 persons were wounded by a blast near the President's residence Sept. 9, 1962.

President Nkrumah is officially styled Osagyefo, or the Redeemer, and is hailed as immortal by the pro-Government press.

On New Year's Eve he announced plans to create a one-party state and to take power to dismiss judges of the Supreme Court and High Court at any time.

He recently dismissed the Chief Justice, Sir Arku Korsah, and discarded the verdict in a treason trial that had acquitted three persons, two of them former Cabinet ministers.

In announcing his plan for a single-party nation, Mr. Nkrumah said that a referendum would be held Jan. 24 to 31 and that if Ghana approved, his ruling Convention People's party would be the only national party.

In effect Ghana has been a one-party state for some years, with the opposition United party all but defunct. A few legislators have represented the Opposition in Parliament, where they are officially known as the minority.

January 3, 1964

GHANA IS VIEWED AS GOING MARXIST

Regime Proclaiming 'Total War' on Capitalism

By LLOYD GARRISON
Special to The New York Times

LAGOS, Nigeria, Jan. 8—Diplomats in Accra, the capital of Ghana, have concluded, almost unanimously, that that country is rapidly becoming an undisguised Marxist state.

They hold that the Government of President Kwame Nkrumah is seeking complete ideological control over the judiciary, education, the civil service, the army and the police.

These views are confirmed almost daily by the Government-owned press and radio, which have proclaimed "total war" on capitalism and are demanding a nationwide purge of all "anti-progressive" elements.

[The Government reported the arrest of Dr. Joseph B. Danquah, one of the country's leading lawyers, under the Preventive Detention Act, Reuters said. The Police Commissioner and nine other senior police officials were dismissed and two were jailed.]

The most radical change in the Government's policy is sudden emphasis on the "class struggle." Until recently, President Nkrumah maintained that Ghana was seeking to develop "African Socialism" and that, because of the "communal" nature of African society, class frictions were nonexistent.

Reports from abroad and all domestic news are tailored to fit the prevailing line of the ruling Convention People's party. Outgoing dispatches are subject to tight censorship.

Among them was the detention of Sir Arku Korsah, Ghana's Chief Justice, who was dismissed by Mr. Nkrumah last month after he had acquitted three ranking officials of treason charges.

Sir Arku was picked up by the police Saturday, questioned throughout the night and returned to his home Sunday morning.

The Government press continued its stepped-up attacks against the United States and what it called other "imperialists" countries of the West. Typical was a commentary in The Ghanaian Times that demanded the expulsion of all Peace Corps volunteers. They were described as "spies and meddlers."

Trend Believed Irreversible

Diplomats in Accra see the trend toward a Marxist state as irreversible. They expect that Ghana will increasingly identify herself with Communist policies.

However, they found out that President Nkrumah apparently has no intention of formally aligning Ghana with the Communist bloc.

The morale of militant members of the ruling party has never been higher. Last month they were cheered by Mr. Nkrumah's decision to dismiss Sir Arku and declare his decision in the treason case "null and void."

Party members were further heartened by an announcement by the President on New Year's Eve. He said that a constitutional amendment making the Convention People's party Ghana's sole political party would be put to a referendum Jan. 24.

Soviet Parallel Noted

The proposed amendment is taken almost word for word from Article 126 of the 1936 Soviet Constitution.

The abortive attempt on Mr. Nkrumah's life last Thursday has served to intensify the drive against "reactionaries" and "counter-revolutionaries." The President was not hurt in the attack, but a bodyguard was killed.

The tone of the Government's campaign was set by Kofi Baako, the Defense Minister. Hailing the President's escape in the attack, he declared: "Kwame is to Africa today what Lenin was to the Soviet Union in 1917."

But for hundreds of silent civil servants, lawyers, teachers and students these developments have inspired disillusionment and fear.

Many Ghanaians who once maintained friendship with Westerners are now avoiding contact for fear of being tarred with the "imperialist" brush.

One foreign embassy has reported that a number of Ghanaians have come to it to ask what the embassy would do if they sought asylum.

Capital Outwardly Calm

Outwardly Accra is calm. But as one civil servant remarked: "Things are so quiet all you can hear are the whispers."

Many responsible observers question the Government's version of what happened last Thursday when a police constable fired at Mr. Nkrumah as he was leaving Flagstaff House, his official residence.

The Government's account was as follows: At 2:15 P.M., as the President was walking to his car, the constable fired five shots with an Enfield bolt-action rifle. One of the shots killed a bodyguard. The President, displaying great courage, disarmed the constable and threw him to the ground with a jujitsu grip.

In support of this account the Government distributed a picture taken by the official photographer of Flagstaff House. It showed the President pinning the constable to the ground.

A cropped version appeared in the press in Ghana and in many newspapers overseas.

Indoor Photo Indicated

An examination of the original print indicates that it was taken indoors. Mr. Nkrumah appears relaxed and composed, his arms on the constable's shoulders. On his right are two policemen, one standing, one kneeling.

A nurse in a white uniform can be seen behind the President with her left hand resting lightly on his shoulder. The constable's wristwatch reads 2:15, the time the Government said the attack took place.

However, diplomats in Accra are convinced that the shooting actually took place between 1:15 and 1:30 P.M.

Diplomats from Western and African embassies pieced together the following version from information they consider reliable:

When Mr. Nkrumah walked out of Flagstaff House the constable fired one shot, which was wild. The President and his bodyguard ducked behind the car. All other security officers fled.

2d Bullet Hit Constable

When the bodyguard raised his head he was hit with the second shot and collapsed. The constable then fired three more shots, all wild.

Policemen at Flagstaff House carry only one five-round clip of ammunition and after the fifth shot Mr. Nkrumah ran into the kitchen of Flagstaff House with the cons'able in close pursuit.

At this point the diplomats' version ends and rumor begins. Some reports say Mr. Nkrumah pushed the kitchen's swinging door, knocking the constable down.

Others say that when guards finally reappeared they found the President and the constable standing in the kitchen, arguing heatedly.

Some Ghanaians who distrust the Government press believe the incident was stage-managed to evoke support for Mr. Nkrumah. This view is also widely held here in Nigeria.

One Lagos newspaper, The Daily Express, commented that on examination of the official photograph the whole assassination story seemed to be a "ruse" to get Ghanaians to "rubber-stamp the new one-party Constitution."

There are also persistent rumors in Accra that the constable was not out to kill Mr. Nkrumah, but was aiming only at the bodyguard, against whom he was said to have had a grudge.

These rumors have been carefully weighed and discarded by most diplomatic observers.

They all agree that the photograph was carefully posed after the actual shooting and that the Government version does not match several known facts.

But after consideration of all these things, the view remains that the constable intended to assassinate the President and that only bad aim kept him from succeeding.

January 9, 1964

GHANA BALLOTING MARKED BY FRAUD

Intimidation Widespread in Vote for One-Party State

By LLOYD GARRISON
Special to The New York Times

ACCRA, Ghana, Feb. 2 — Ghana has become an official one-party Socialist state following a nationwide referendum marked by widespread fraud and intimidation.

The Government contends that in the week-long voting that ended Friday, 99.9 per cent of those who cast ballots voted "yes" for proposals giving President Kwame Nkrumah dictatorial power.

In many areas thousands of voters had no choice. In all but a few wards in the Northern Region, voters found that the "no" boxes had been removed by Government-appointed polling officials.

In many other areas in the central and coastal districts, the slits of the "no" boxes were sealed.

Ghanaians were repeatedly warned by the Government-controlled press and radio that anyone who failed to vote or dared to vote "no" would be punished as a "counterrevolutionary."

To back up this threat, the Government proclaimed that it had the "machinery" to detect the "no" voters. There was no attempt to disguise this detection process: every voter's ballot was marked with his serial number, which appears in the listing of registered voters.

Many African states have established one-party governments and foreign observers were not surprised when Ghana did so.

But what sets Ghana apart, the observers note, is that the ruling Convention People's party now has unrestricted power to control all phases of Ghanaian life. This includes the army, the police, civil service, the schools and universities, sectors that have always been considered above politics.

The key to the Government's extraordinary new powers is a clause in the referendum establishing the Convention People's party as the "leading core of all organizations and the vanguard of the people in their struggle to build a Scialist society."

Close to Soviet Clause

This clause is taken almost verbatim from Article 126 of the 1936 Soviet Constitution, tution, which makes the Communist party "the leading core" of private as well as Government institutions.

Another clause in the referendum eliminates the last existing check in Ghana against dictatorial rule—that of a free judiciary. President Nkrumah may now dismiss any judge of the Supreme Court or High Court "at his discretion."

In practical terms, according to the party-operated Evening News, the referendum means that the party "has a mandate to transform all expressions of the state—economic, social and cultural—into organizations for the interest of the revolutionary classes."

The paper added: "It follows automatically that it is illegal for nonparty elements to conduct propaganda or any form of agitation against the People's party."

New Purges Hinted

The party press has strongly hinted that the judiciary and the universities will be the first to be purged of "counter-revolutionary" and "bourgeois" elements.

President Nkrumah dismissed Sir Arku Korsah as Chief Justice after the justice acquitted three high officials accused of treason last December.

Armed with the referendum's new powers, the President is expected to move against other judges regarded as unreliable.

A purge of faculty and students at the University of Ghana is also expected. Last week the Government indicated it wanted a shake-up of the Law School, whose dean is an American from the University of Michigan.

Police Are Disarmed

Three weeks ago the police underwent a top-level purge after an unsuccessful attempt by a policeman to assassinate President Nkrumah.

The entire 9,000-man police force has now been disarmed by the army, which has been given sole responsibility for guarding the President.

Since the assassination attempt, Mr. Nkrumah has remained secluded in Christianbourg Castle, the 17th-century slave fortress perched on a cliff overlooking Accra harbor.

Soviet armed Ghanaian troops backed by armored cars and antiaircraft guns have ringed the walls of the fort and blocked all approaches for several hundred yards around.

The Government's latest figures on the referendum put the "yes" votes at 2,523,385 and the "no" votes at 2,452.

Polling officials and presiding officers who counted the ballots were, with rare exceptions, members of the ruling party. All vote totals were forwarded to the Ministry of Justice before they were announced.

In several wards the number of those who actually voted and the number announced by the ministry differed by more than 100 per cent.

There was no campaigning against the referendum. In Accra several cars were seen with homemade "Vote No" signs on their bumpers. The drivers were arrested.

February 3, 1964

Nkrumah Is Reported Out After Ghana Army Coup

A Broadcast From Accra Announces Takeover—President in Asia

By Reuters

LONDON, Thursday, Feb. 24—The Army has taken over in Ghana and dismissed President Kwame Nkrumah who is at present on a trip to Peking and Hanoi, according to an Accra radio broadcast heard here this morning.

Reports reaching London said there was sporadic firing in the center of Accra.

The broadcast, by an unnamed colonel commanding a brigade, said the police had joined the Ghanaian Army in the coup. It added that parliament had been dissolved, the President and his ministers dismissed, and the ruling Convention People's party—the only one in the single-party state—dissolved.

The Army acted three days after Mr. Nkrumah had left Accra by air on his way to the Far East. He is at present in Rangoon, and was due to leave there today on his way to Peking and Hanoi. Mr. Nkrumah has been reported planning a move aimed at ending the Vietnam war.

Reliable reports reaching London said that the army had sealed off Accra airfield early today. The army also took over radio communications.

President Nkrumah had several times in recent years faced threats to his life. Since an evident attempt to assassinate him in the summer of 1964, he had kept an extra guard at his mansion in Accra.

The state of Ghana came into being on March 6, 1957, when the former British colony of the Gold Coast and the trusteeship territory of Togoland achieved dominion status.

The name of the country recalls a powerful monarchy that ruled the Middle Niger region in the fourth to the 13th centuries A.D.

The country is divided into nine regions with Accra the capital, population around 337,-000. Each region has been administered by a commissioner with the rank of minister. The regional assemblies were dissolved in 1959.

The 56-year-old Dr. Nkrumah was Prime Minister of Ghana when it became the first British black-ruled colony in Africa to attain independence. He was elected the country's first President when it became a republic in 1960.

President Nkrumah introduced the one-party state in January, 1964, in which only his Convention People's party was permitted to operate. A referendum approved the measure by a 99.99 per cent majority.

Washington Hears of Appeal

WASHINGTON, Thursday, Feb. 24 (AP)—The State Department said American officials in Ghana reported that the military officer who announced the government seizure had appealed to the people of the country to be calm and cooperative.

He said also that all persons held in detention by the Government would be released in due course. Officials at Ghana's Embassy in Washington withheld comment on the situation in Accra.

February 24, 1966

OUSTERS BY GHANA END KEY FOOTHOLD OF REDS IN AFRICA

East Germans Join Soviet and Chinese Exodus—Nkrumah in Guinea

By LLOYD GARRISON
Special to The New York Times

ACCRA, Ghana, March 2 — Ghana's new military government today dealt the Communist world a major setback in Africa by ordering the expulsion of all Soviet, Chinese Communist and East German teachers and technicians.

The expulsions have brought to an abrupt end one of Communism's footholds in Africa. The Communists' presence here was cultivated by President Kwame Nkrumah, who was flying to Peking on a Vietnam peace mission when the army and police overthrew his avowedly Marxist regime last Thursday.

[Former President Nkrumah arrived Wednesday in Conakry, Guinea, from Moscow and vowed again to make a comeback in Ghana. His Foreign Minister, Alex Quaison-Sackey, returned to Accra and pledged allegiance to the new leaders, but was placed in protective custody. Page 3.]

Two planeloads of Russians left yesterday. Others followed by commercial flights today. All of the 1,000 Russians working in schools and on aid projects here are expected to be out of the country in 10 days.

Chinese Already Leaving

A few Chinese took off on an Air Mali Ilyushin-18 this morning. The 150 who remain will be evacuated by tomorrow aboard chartered French jets that will fly them as far as Karachi, Pakistan.

The break with the East Germans was complete. Their trade mission, which served their interests in the absence of an embassy, has been told to close.

Lieut. Gen. Joseph A. Ankrah, head of the new ruling National Liberation Council, has made it plain that Ghana has no intention of breaking diplomatic relations with any country, at least for the time being.

But the council has ordered the Soviet Embassy staff reduced from 67 to 18. These would consist of 10 diplomatic officials and 8 on the clerical staff.

One high Ghanaian official said that most, if not all, of the other East European embassies and aid programs here would be permitted to function.

"We don't care about the small fry," he said.

It was known at the outset of the coup that the rebels were basically conservative in their thinking, but few expected them to sever almost completely Ghana's trade and aid relations with Communist countries.

The reasons are partly political, partly practical, with a large share of emotion thrown in.

Politically, the Army has always resisted Mr. Nkrumah's efforts to make officer training dependent on Soviet aid. The military particularly resented the former President's personal guard, trained and equipped by the Soviet Union.

From a practical viewwpoint many Communist aid programs were inefficient, costly and often unnecessary to the Ghanaian economy.

For example, Ghana put three times more money into the six Soviet-sponsored state farms than the value of the farms' produce.

The new economic and financial advisers of the military regime are civil servants or academic people who knew of the shortcomings of the Communist aid programs, but whose advice was disregarded by Mr. Nkrumah.

But sheer dissatisfaction throughout the country was perhaps the most important motive behind the rebellion. For years Mr. Nkrumah's press and radio had identified Ghana with Moscow and Peking, and the United States as the main enemy.

When Mr. Nkrumah put opponents in jail, or built a useless superhighway and neglected the price of bread, or held a rigged referendum to give his Convention People's party sole power, these acts tended to be seen also as Soviet and Chinese acts.

Since last Thursday's coup there have been demonstrations demanding that the Communists "go home."

Non-Communist diplomats could scarcely contain their delight with the turn of events. For years they had endured a barrage of Communist-inspired propaganda designed to vilify the West.

But some expressed second thoughts over the economic impact of the severance of Communist aid. The Soviet Union and China combined have earmarked more than $132-million in aid. The halting of several projects under way will put hundreds of Ghanaians out of work.

Hardest hit will be the school system. About 100 Soviet teachers have filled mathematics and science positions in secondary schools. There are also 24 Soviet physicians at Ghana's new medical school, and other Soviet advisers in technical training colleges and universities.

March 3, 1966

Major Reforms Guide Ghana Out of Nkrumah Era

Nation's U.N. Mission Says New Rulers Junk Grandiose Plans and Cut Ministries

By DREW MIDDLETON

Special to The New York Times

UNITED NATIONS, N. Y., June 15 — Ghanaian ministries have been abolished, diplomatic missions cut and grandiose economic plans junked as the National Liberation Council has guided the country out of the Nkrumah era.

According to data made available through the Ghanaian mission to the United Nations, the council's administrative, economic and legal reforms have swept away the apparatus of the authoritarian state that President Kwame Nkrumah was building until he was ousted Feb. 24.

Private investment once scorned is now courted. Communist-dominated pseudopolitical organizations such as the Ghana Young Pioneers have been scrapped.

Foreign policy seeks what Lieut. Gen. Joseph A. Ankrah, chairman of the council, calls "a balanced neutralty."

The balance he seeks may be disturbed, however, in the long run by Ghana's reliance on aid and investment from the United States and Western Europe.

Mr. Nkrumah's failure to get all civil servants to do what he wanted resulted in the establishment of aides in parallel ministries that would do his bidding.

At his downfall, there were 32 ministries and 168 administrative districts in a country with a population of 6,726,000. There now are 18 ministries and 47 administrative districts.

Many of the experienced civil servants who, under the old system of parallel and supraministerial secretariats, had been eliminated from policy-making have been restored to their former positions.

The work, Ghanaian officials note, is just beginning. They say that, if the country is to recover from the paralyzing effect of the Nkrumah regime, the whole apparatus of administration will have to be overhauled. A Commission on the Public Services has been appointed to do so.

The National Liberation Council's program of action for economic recovery envisages three phases.

The first, or "emergency," phase is to end with the introduction of a new budget next month.

The second, or "review," period is to extend until the end of June, 1968, when it is expected that a new development plan will have been formulated and the third phase will begin.

4 Soviet Planes Returned

Ghana's economic reforms stress the elimination of the unnecessary expenditures contracted by the former regime as one means of restoring foreign confidence in the country's eventual economic stability.

Ghana Airways, a major spender of foreign exchange, has eliminated uneconomic routes.

Four Soviet-built Ilyushin aircraft have been sent back to Moscow. The Government has decided not to take delivery of a third British VC-10.

Orders for two ships of the Black Star Line, the national shipping line, have been canceled, with a saving of $8.4-million.

Under the former President, Ghana's diplomatic representation abroad was on a lavish scale. The number of embassies has been reduced by 40 per cent, saving the country about $3-million in foreign exchange.

After a prolonged review, the council has decided to transfer nine state enterprises to private ownership. These include the Timber Products Corporation.

Private investment is being sought in six other state enterprises, including the Cocoa Products Corporation, the Diamond Mining Corporation, the national steel works, shipping line and airline.

Public works also have been cut back. The Accra-Tema motorway's construction will not proceed beyond the first phase, with a saving of nearly $11-million.

The third phase of the dredging of Tema harbor has been discontinued. Work on the construction of the $16-million Tamale airport has been halted.

The effect of these economies will be reflected in the budget. When Mr. Nkrumah fell, Ghana's external obligations amounted to $58.6-million, and the reserves stood at about $112-million, almost all of them pledged against borrowings.

Consequently, Ghanaian officials here say, it will not be possible to balance the budget for 1966-1967, but every effort will be made to reduce the deficit to a level that can be financed through production and revenue.

June 16, 1966

Religious Fervor Rising in Wake of Nkrumah Fall

All Churches in Ghana Report Big Increase in Members Since President's Ouster

By LLOYD GARRISON

Special to The New York Times

ACCRA, Ghana, Feb. 27 — One year after the downfall of President Kwame Nkrumah, who warred on organized religion, there is striking evidence here of a revival of religious fervor.

The evidence was on display yesterday afternoon, when thousands of Ghanaian Protestants attended a service in Accra Stadium marking the first anniversary of last year's Feb. 24 coup.

The sermon was delivered by the Right Rev. Richard Roseveare, the Anglican Bishop of Accra, who was expelled by President Nkrumah in 1962 and, for more than three months, denied re-entry into Ghana.

In an allusion to Mr. Nkrumah's nine-year-long campaign first to isolate, then to control church leaderships, Bishop Roseveare declared:

"History teaches us over and over again that you can force a man to fear but you cannot force a man to love. You can force a man to conform but you cannot force him to believe."

A year ago, under Mr. Nkrumah, such an open-air service in a Government-owned stadium would have been unthinkable.

Seven Are Christians

Yesterday, the Government not only made the stadium available, but also provided the Ghanaian Army band to lead the hymns and permitted the service program to be printed on Government stationery.

Seven of the eight members of the ruling National Liberation Council are Christians and all seven attended the ceremony. The eighth member is a Moslem.

Religion permeates many of the Government's recent actions. The Ghanaian national anthem has been rewritten to include numerous references to God. At Friday's anniversary parade in Black Star Square, Roman Catholic, Protestant and Moslem church leaders were present and pronounced special prayers before the unveiling of a plaque honoring the seven soldiers who lost their lives in the coup.

The religious leaders were also invited to bless the army's colors before the march began.

All religious denominations report that church attendance has increased markedly since the coup.

But Bishop Roseveare cautioned against overemphasizing the significance of what he called the "numbers game."

"It is not the quantity but the quality of the faith that counts," he said in his rectory office before the stadium service yesterday.

The Bishop, who is 64 years old, is a pipe-smoking Briton who has been in Ghana 11 years and at one time knew Mr. Nkrumah well.

He attributed the rise in religious observance since the coup to "natural reaction against the public neglect of God for so many years."

He recalled Mr. Nkrumah's success in isolating the churches and noted that after his own expulsion the Government-controlled press and radio did not run any of the protests raised by the United Church Council or the Roman Catholic diocese. His eventual return was also unreported.

The expulsion followed an attack by the Bishop on a youth group whose oath attempted to deify Mr. Nkrumah.

Throughout his presidency, Mr. Nkrumah was repeatedly hailed in the press as the "Redeemer" and "his Messianic Majesty".

An avowed Marxist, Nkrumah ordered red party agents to infiltrate the churches in 1963 in a bid to take over their direction. But resistance forced Nkrumah to call a temporary retreat.

"There is considerable evidence that he was prepared to mount a final confrontation with the churches in 1966, just before the coup", said the Bishop.

February 28, 1967

Ghana Struggles Under Burden of Nkrumah's Debt

By R. W. APPLE Jr.
Special to The New York Times

ACCRA, Ghana, May 3—No matter who comes to power when the military-police regime relinquishes control in Ghana this fall, he will face all-but-insoluble economic problems.

Ghana is a 98-pound weakling trying to be a weightlifter. For an underdeveloped agricultural country, the burden of debt left by former President Kwame Nkrumah, who was overthrown Feb. 24, 1966, is unmanageable.

The total debt amounts to about $800-million, of which $547-million is accounted for by short-term obligations to foreign companies. Even after two renegotiations, the country must look forward to 13 years of outlays ranging from $22-million to $58-million a year.

People talk of repudiation, but the ruling National Liberation Council rejected that course in 1966. It still insists that it will meet its obligations, if it does nothing else.

Little Left to Invest

The payment must be made out of Ghana's meager stock of foreign exchange. The country's trade surplus in 1968– the first in years—amounted to only $68-million, and almost half went to the creditors.

That leaves very little for investment in national development, which is what every young African state needs most.

If exports could be stepped up sharply, things would look better. But Ghana's prime crop is cocoa, and although she remains the world's largest producer by a wide margin, she is gradually losing her share of the market to other countries. In the early sixties Ghana accounted for more than half of world output, but this year the figure will probably be less than 40 per cent.

The usual explanation for the decline is bad weather, but some experts argue that the cocoa farmers have become demoralized. With the price at eight cents for 60 pounds—the amount a bearer can carry on his head—the farmers have no money for replanting, insecticides or improved technology.

A further drain on the economy is the vast network of state enterprises set up by Mr. Nkrumah, many of which still lose money and most of which operate with minimum efficiency.

The state fishing corporation, for one example, has invested $40,000 an employe in boats and other equipment, compared with an investment of about $12,000 an employe at a typical United States fishing port.

It also owns 10 Soviet-built trawlers that have never been used. A United States consultant recently reported that they were hopelessly dilapidated. He suggested towing them out to sea, filling them with concrete and leaving them there as breakwaters.

The Liberation Council has tried to persuade foreign companies to take over the unprofitable state enterprises, with some initial success. The Firestone Tire and Rubber Company, for instance, operates a tire factory and rubber plantations.

But Abbott Laboratories backed out of a deal after public criticism of the contract price, and the Government stalled for more than a year before rejecting bids from four or five countries for the operation of the French-built state textile factory.

Early this year the Government embarked on an Africanization program, which, though primarily directed against Lebanese and Indian small-business men, has had a damaging psychological effect on foreign investment. A reduction in the amount of money expatriate workers can send home has not helped, either.

"There's a sign out at the airport: 'Ghana welcomes foreign investment,'" an English businessman commented the other day. "Don't believe it."

Finance Minister John H. Mensah, an economist who once worked for the United Nations, conceded in a speech this week that less private capital was flowing into Ghana now than under the Nkrumah regime. He said that the national debt was alarming.

"I can only see one way out for Ghana in the long run," he said, "and that is to pursue a policy of self-reliance. What foreign money comes into the country must be on such terms that we are sure we will be able to pay it off and to pay off all its attendant obligations."

May 6, 1969

Progressives Winners in Ghana In First Free Elections Since '56

ACCRA, Ghana, Aug. 30—The Progress party of Dr. Kofi A. Busia was assured today of a majority in Ghana's 140-member Parliament in the first free general elections since 1956.

As a result of yesterday's election, the six-man National Liberation Council of army and police officers, which has been ruling the country since deposing President Kwame Nkrumah in February, 1966, will hand over power to a civilian administration on Oct. 1.

However, under the new Constitution promulgated a week ago a Presidential Commission of three of the members of the National Liberation Commission will exercise the powers of president for the next three years unless the National Assembly decides otherwise.

Though the results of the election are not complete, the Progress party of Dr. Busia, who led the opposition United party during the rule of Dr. Nkrumah, was assured at least 82 seats in the National Assembly. The opposition will apparently be led by Komla A. Gbedemah, who served as Finance Minister under Dr. Nkrumah before going into self-imposed exile.

The election was a far cry from the last one held under Dr. Nkrumah, in which all 198 candidates of his Convention People's party were returned unopposed to Parliament. Yesterday 480 candidates, including 20 independents, offered themselves to the nation's 2.3 million voters.

The Progress party and Mr. Gbedemah's National Alliance of Liberals presented 138 candidates each. The United Nationalist party of Joe Appiah, a former aide of Dr. Busia, which campaigned vigorously in the Accra metropolitan area, put up 87 candidates.

Candidates were also offered by two minor parties—the All People's Republican party of Dr. Edward de Graft-Johnson and the Imoru Ayarna, a northern businessman's party.

With returns incomplete, the Progress party had won 82 seats, the National Alliance of Liberals 29, the United Nationalist party two and the Imoru Ayarna, or People's Action party, 2. Two independents also won seats.

Dr. Busia's overwhelming victory indicates that Ghanaians rejected the overtures of Mr. Gbedemah, who returned from exile in June, 1966. Mr. Gbedemah based his campaign on his experience in politics and his role in securing a loan from the United States to finance the large Akosombo hydroelectric dam.

Dr. Busia based his campaign on a platform of progress, honesty and integrity in the management of the country's affairs and finances.

The administration of Dr. Busia will face its first crisis, if Mr. Gbedemah insists, as he promised to during the campaign, on challenging the President Commission, composed of Brig. A. A. Afrifa, head of the National Liberation Council; John W. K. Harlley, vice chairman of the council and Maj. Gen. A. K. Ocran, Chief of Defense Staff.

Mr. Gbedemah faces possible expulsion from the National Assembly if his election is challenged under Article 71 of the new Constitution, which bars persons against whom adverse findings have been made by any inquiry commission.

August 31, 1969

Ghana Demands Urban Austerity to Improve Rural Life

By CHARLES MOHR
Special to The New York Times

ACCRA, Ghana—The Government is attempting one of the most difficult feats in politics: to sell austerity.

One of many posters plastered on walls in this West African capital shows two rural women standing deep in mud. Bold letters read: "Sacrifice for Development. Remember Us." Another poster proclaims "No Discipline, No Progress. National Discipline Campaign."

The citizens of Accra have even been asked to "discipline your throats" by cheerfully paying a new tax for poor workers—it amounts to roughly the price of a small bottle of beer each month—to help support rural development.

Public discontent might make little difference if Ghana were one of Africa's many openly dictatorial one-party states. For the past two years, however, the country has had one of the few functioning multiparty democracies on the continent. In this situation, the Progress party Government led by Prime Minister Kofi Busia seems increasingly apprehensive and sensitive — and sometimes heavy-handed—in the face of criticism.

Heritage From Nkrumah

Part of the Government's troubles are a heritage from former President Kwame Nkrumah, who led the country into independence from Britain in 1957, gradually repressed all political opposition, ran up huge debts and was deposed in a military coup d'état in 1966. He is now in exile in Guinea; independent observers believe there is little sentiment favoring his return to power, for his despotic ways are still well remembered.

A foreign observer said that "the Government's problem is that it is trying to bring back democracy after it has been asleep for many years."

Another troublesome factor is that the Government has deliberately aimed its policy toward rural development on the ground that it is only just beginning to reduce the imbalances in amenities and property between rural and urban areas.

The policy makes sense in many ways. Production of cocoa, the main export, which was 557,000 tons in 1964-65, is not much more than 400,000 tons now, and large amounts of foreign exchange must be spent to import food that could be grown domestically.

Politically, the Progress party gets most of its votes from rural people in this nation of nine million, so it is probably strengthening its main base of support.

Distressing Urban Reaction

Party spokesmen seem distressed by the urban reaction and have recently argued that urban interests have not been neglected, though the posters and propaganda stress the theme that others should sacrifice for the rural people.

The idea may be difficult for the unemployed to swallow, especially those who had jobs under Mr. Nkrumah and who may not understand, or believe, that his spending spree led to the prevailing austerity.

Mr. Nkrumah left a crushing burden of international debt. At independence Ghana was rich, with foreign-exchange reserves of about $400-million. By the time of the coup debts totaled almost $600-million, a staggering turnaround in nine years. (A new effort to reschedule about $330-million of the debt is expected soon.)

The economy was saddled with unsound and unprofitable socialist enterprises, declining exports, rising imports and a serious deterioration of the cocoa industry.

The Busia Government was elected in 1969 by a large majority after the military junta that had toppled Mr. Nkrumah voluntarily stepped aside in favor of civilian control.

"Austerity was necessary," one observer said, "and the need for austerity meant unpopular measures."

In this year's budget the

The New York Times
Prime Minister Kofi Busia heads democratic regime.

Government imposed a "national development levy," a tax of 1 to 5 per cent on the earnings of workers who make about $30 a month or more. The allowances of civil servants were deeply slashed and more import surcharges were imposed, raising living costs further. The administration also resisted labor's demands that the minimum wage be raised from about 75 cents a day to about $1.50.

Unemployment, aggravated by the earlier dismissals of workers from overstaffed Nkrumah enterprises, has not been dealt with, and one estimate is that about 25 per cent of the work force is unemployed or underemployed.

Instead of bending to the wind of criticism, the Government has tended to get tough.

This past summer a new party, the People's Popular party, began selling photographs of Mr. Nkrumah at rallies. In August the Government adopted a law making it a crime to display Mr. Nkrumah's picture or to shout slogans of his defunct Convention People's party or attempt to revive it.

In September the Government abolished the powerful Trades Union Congress, after having raided its headquarters and frozen its assets. Its Secretary General, Benjamin A. Bentum, had toured the country denouncing the development tax and the refusal to raise minimum wages.

Under new legislation the 17 member unions of the congress must be reregistered, and will lose the right of automatic deduction of members' dues on employers' payrolls.

Tight Rein on the Press

The Government has rejected proposals that the major newspapers it acquired in Mr. Nkrumah's day be placed under an independent trust. Keeping a firm grip on the papers, it dismissed the editor of one after he had criticized Dr. Busia's suggestion of a diplomatic dialogue with South Africa.

The Government has also harassed The Spokesman, a biweekly newspaper with bitingly critical views. Its editor, Kofi Badu, has a knack of turning up embarrassing nuggets about the money politicians spend on themselves in spite of austerity. The company that printed The Spokesman stopped doing so when faced with the loss of Government business, so the paper is being printed on an old press designed for producing labels for tin cans.

Some observers believe that the Government's entire attitude amounts to oversensitivity that will only make things worse.

"Cracking down on the Trades Union Congress won't end the agitation," said a Ghanaian intellectual. "The Government has been in office two years and Nkrumah has been gone for five and a half years. They can't go on blaming everything on Kwame forever."

"The threat is not from Nkrumah but from Nkrumahism," an informed source commented. "An effective socialist policy would have attractiveness."

November 23, 1971

Leaders of Coup Tighten Their Control on Ghana

By WILLIAM BORDERS
Special to The New York Times

ACCRA, Ghana, Jan. 14—The army officers who took over this West African nation in a coup d'état yesterday morning moved today to consolidate their controal amid signs that the quick, clean take-over had been widely successful.

Accra, the bustling seaside capital, returned to normal with startling speed. Its communications with the rest of the world were re-established and only a few soldiers patrolled the streets.

In the countryside north of here, there were no reports of any opposition, from soldiers or civilians, to the new Government, which is headed by Colonel I. K. Acheampong, a solidly-built brigade commander.

Explaining why the army had decided to overthrow the democratically elected Government of Prime Minister Kofi A. Busia, the 40-year-old colonel cited a long list of grievances that he summarized as "general mismanagement."

But Dr. Busia's stringent austerity program, and particularly his 44 per cent devaluation of the Ghanaian currency last month, were paramount in many conversations about the coup here today.

'No One's Sorry'

"Everybody's pocket was hurting bad, so no one's sorry to see Busia go," said one of the thousands of petty traders who line the streets of this sultry city, selling razor blades, plastic mirrors, pencils or tiny rolls of string.

Like the drivers of the colorful mammy wagons that crowd Accra's streets, and the market women who squat, selling vegetables with their babies tied on their backs, the traders said that their business had scarcely skipped a beat with the smooth change of government.

An army spokesman, indicating that the military government shares the common view that economics is the prime concern, disclosed that Colonel Acheampong and his aides had spent quite a bit of time today meeting with local bankers and financial experts of the old civil service.

He announced that tomorrow, the new Government would name special committees to consider what should be done about the marketing of cocoa, the country's major export, which is in a severe price slump, and about the devaluation of the Ghanaian cedi, which has led to a sharp increase in prices all over the country.

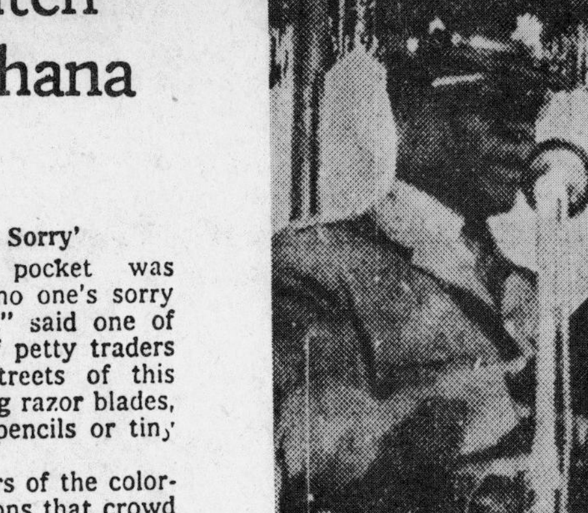

Associated Press

LEADER OF COUP: Col. I. K. Acheampong heads army group that took control in Ghana Thursday.

Economy Was Ailing

Prime Minister Busia's drastic move in devaluating the cedi was part of an attempt to cure the economy, which is still reeling from the extravagances of President Kwame Nkrumah, who was himself overthrown in an army coup six years ago.

"For the second time, the armed forces have had to come in to take over the reins of government to save the country from the maladministration and corruption of politicians, and to save the nation from total economic collapse," proclaimed an editorial today in the Government-owned Ghanaian Times.

But even some of his critics considered the comparison of Dr. Busia to Mr. Nkrumah a strained one.

"Nkrumah was a dynamic politician who was ultimately corrupted; Busia was a rather colorless sociology professor who tried but failed," said a local businessman who, like many people here, had been predicting the coup weeks ago.

Colonel Acheampong plans to govern through a National Redemption Council whose membership he announced today.

Besides himself, the nine-man body includes five other army officers, the head of the navy, the head of the air force and the inspector general of the police.

Among the officers on the council are two who have just been appointed to the positions of chief of defense staff, the highest military post, and army commander. The two men who held those jobs until the coup are now believed to be in jail. So are most of Dr. Busia's Cabinet ministers, and some other members of Parliament.

Dr. Busia, who entertained Mrs. Richard Nixon here last week, was in London for medical treatment at the time of the coup.

January 15, 1972

Nkrumah, 62, Dead; Ghana's Ex-Leader

By ALDEN WHITMAN

Kwame Nkrumah, the deposed President of Ghana and the first man to lead an African colony to independence after World War II, died yesterday in exile in Conakry, Guinea, at the age of 62.

His death, of cancer, was announced by President Sékou Touré of Guinea, one of the militant nationalist's closest friends. Mr. Nkrumah had been living in Guinea since his overthrow in a military coup in 1966. Recently he had been in Eastern Europe for medical treatment. According to some reports, his death came in Bucharest.

In Accra in the early nineteen-fifties, the sight of this husky man with melancholy eyes, finely chiseled lips and a nimbus of frizzy hair could send throngs of British Gold Coast tribesmen into paroxysms of adulation. But by 1966 the shouting had stopped, the halo had evaporated and with it the impregnability of Mr. Nkrumah, by then the supreme ruler of the independent state of Ghana. His fall was the dross of drama: A tiny group of army dissidents took over, virtually effortlessly, while "His High Dedication Osagyefo" (the Redeemer) was on a trip to Peking.

$600-Million Debt

After having led Ghana into independence in 1957 with $400-million in foreign reserves, Mr. Nkrumah ran his country into a debt of $600-million by 1966, a fearsome figure for a nation whose chief export was cocoa. Nepotism and corruption abounded among the Nkrumah ministers, a condition, of course, not peculiar to Ghana, although its flagrance was markedly open.

Outweighing even these factors, however, was Mr. Nkrumah's galloping megalomania. He caused his likeness to be on postage stamps; he put his name in lights all over Accra; he rigged an election so as to win 98.5 per cent of the votes; he dismissed the Supreme Court, making himself the final arbiter of appeal; he jailed dissenters; he elaborated an ideology called "conscientism"; he embarked on a grandiose Seven-Year Plan; and, as time went on, he burrowed himself in Flagstaff House, his official residence, which he converted into a fortress with a private zoo.

Ghanians were solemnly informed that, after one of his speeches, "the earth trembled and the trees shook [and] there was rain in Accra, which had not seen a drop of water for a long time." This (and other hyperbole) was understandable in the context of impressing the peoples of an emerging nation. But what was less comprehensible was that Mr. Nkrumah came to believe that he really did shake the earth.

There was no doubt that he had enemies, for he was the object of at least three assassination attempts. Nor was it in question that his anticolonial policy upended many of the traditional economic and social and religious relationships in Ghana, and that his pan-Africanism—he thought seriously of siring a future emperor—clashed with the nationalist aspirations of other leaders.

April 28, 1972

Touré's Country—'Africa Incarnate'

Guinea embodies the emphatic nationalism and revolutionary hopes of ex-colonial Africa, but its energetic President confronts handicaps that are also typically African.

By DAVID HALBERSTAM

CONAKRY, Guinea.

It is the day and time of the free African. In the major capitals of the world berobed African leaders arrive for state visits. In the United Nations there is an upsurge of African power and ambition (so that the South Africans, the odd men out in this time, call it "The United Natives"). Throughout the continent Africans discover other Africans, proudly pledge African unity and they eye each other suspiciously. What follows is the story of one of the newest and proudest nations on the continent.

SOMEHOW one expects an exciting city, a place where the winds of change have come, where the world is moving before your eyes, where something new and striking and yet African reaches up to the sky to symbolize all that has happened here in four years. But inevitably the reality of the new years of African independence is not so exciting as the idea; inevitably the cities are disappointing. And somehow this city seems particularly disappointing because the idea of what is happening in Guinea is so much more exciting than most African ideas. This is a city where they talk of revolution, but where the pace is slow—worse yet, listless. Are their speeches so much better than their actions? Is this the land where the awakening giant slept? Does the giant still sleep?

"Dakar is a black Paris and Conakry—well, Conakry is a black Conakry," says one Frenchman here. The particularly brutal climate, an all-enveloping mugginess, makes work here more difficult, achievement more limited, than elsewhere in Africa; the rainy season is so harsh that for two months air conditioners must run night and day to keep bedding and clothes from damp ruin. No wonder there is only one real skyscraper, and that already weather-tarnished; no wonder the roads are badly rutted; no wonder the pace is particularly relaxed; no wonder it is hard to get people to work.

And so this city doesn't bustle. Its pace, as well as its facade, is particularly relaxed and African. Along the main street are many goats, and in the center of town little boys knock mangoes out of trees, and there is always time for a beer, although now the beer is likely to be Czech or East German rather than Guinean. Yet this country is considered by many people, pan-African and colonialist alike, to be, with all its imperfections and contradictions, the purest expression of the true African will. This is the country, many white men believe, where Africans probably come closer to saying what they really believe; it is a country often regarded enviously by other young Africans.

PERHAPS this is so, that it is the purest expression of the African will, but then similarly it must be the truest expression of the African reality and the African frustration, the country where Africans themselves staff the bureaucracy, where the money is African and not backed by Western currency and therefore is not of any great value to the Africans, and where consequently the economy is in considerable trouble.

IT is not these things by chance. If this is the age of African independence, then also it is the time of the spectacular African—and perhaps the most spectacular of all is 40-year-old President of Guinea, Sékou Touré, born one of seven children of illiterate Malinké tribe peasant farmers. It is Touré, with his looks, his ideas, his will, who has projected both himself and his country so quickly and so forcefully onto both the African and international scene that they have become African independence and nationalism incarnate.

He is a powerfully built man of immense personal force and energy, so much so that he gives the impression of being taller than his five foot ten. He has the broad shoulders of a professional boxer and strong facial lines that would move a sculptor. Finally, he projects a sense of both pride and hurt befitting the leader of a young and angry country.

Just as he has put his stamp on everything inside Guinea, it is Touré who has given the idea of Guinea to the world: the world knows and cares about Ghana because it was first; the Congo, because it was fabled and violent; Nigeria, because it is a giant; but Guinea because of Touré, because in September, 1958, when all the other French West African leaders said yes to de Gaulle he gave a defiant no, because he said in public what many Africans thought in private—that the Guineans would rather be poor but free than rich and still French.

"An African statesman is not a naked boy begging from rich capitalists," he told Western statesmen with typical African pride, and curiously at that time these were the words the West expected to hear, almost seemed to want to hear.

In effect, he declared himself the African leader to be reckoned with, not just in Guinea but throughout the continent; and curiously it came to pass that he was. He made Guinea a stage: East vies with West for Guinea. The East wants to see it as yet another step in the decline of the West. Washington vows that it shall not, as the saying goes, go down the drain.

SO in this city, which has been called an overgrown African bush village, Russians light American cigarettes with Chinese matches, Poles wonder just what the Outer Mongolians are really doing, West Germans and Israelis share notes on what the Arabs and East Germans are doing. Guinea may not be big and it may not be rich, nor indeed does it hold the strategic key to Africa, but these people are all here. They all sweat and compete for the affection of Africans who seem almost indifferent to their ardor; who keep them waiting hour after hour for appointments; who ban their books and propaganda; who look on their technical offerings with cool disdain; who go to Washington and publicly complain about the quality of Russian goods (heaven only knows what they say about Americans in Moscow).

Who is this man who created — or invented — Guinea, this proud African who has proclaimed his Marxism, yet within the same calendar year received the Lenin Peace Prize and ousted a Russian Ambassador; who within a period of a month accused the Eastern embassies of plotting against him, threw out a French Archbishop, and closed the Koranic schools in Conakry?

SOME said he was a black Castro; now they have changed their minds—perhaps he is a black Nasser, or a black Tito. Certainly he is Africa's version of the angry young man, constantly talking of the African personality, rejecting the European version of it, making it constantly and abundantly clear to any visitor that he is very much in a black man's land.

The passion of his life is anti-colonialism. He claims to be descended from a famed Guinean leader, Samory Touré, who led an African war against the French until captured, in 1898. To this day an interview with Touré remains pleasant but unproductive, full of automatic responses and slogans, until the subject of colonialism comes up. Only then does Touré become excited, and seem to speak with feeling: "My first experience with colonialism was when I was in primary school, and was obliged to read from a history book in which the French insulted my grandfather. I refused. But then the High Commissioner for the area came to our class and he recited this part and I stuck him with a penknife and wounded him. I was put in jail for this. I was 10 years old at the time that happened."

He goes on about colonialism, almost unable to stop: "It was brutally forced on us and always with humiliation. Our grandfathers became a part of colonialism, but they never accepted it. For us liberation was always just a matter of time. * * * You Europeans talk about the difference between French colonialism and British colonialism but it is all the same to us. There is no good kind, no better kind. For us there is no difference. It is all evil, as if one were cutting off a leg, the other an arm."

WHERE once in Conakry there was a monument to French war dead, now there is a monument to the martyrs of colonialism. It is the same monument, and only the lettering has been changed. Perhaps, say some of his critics, it is not the only thing the colonialists have done for him.

"Without colonialism," says one Frenchman in Guinea, "I wonder whether Sékou would have ever been able to go and address the United Nations. I wonder what he would be President of — perhaps some little tribe."

It was the colonial system, plus his own fierce ambition and energy, which made Touré different from the other Malinkés deep in the forest. He attended first a Koranic school, then a French technical school in Conakry from which he was expelled at the age of 15 for leading a protest about the school food.

He soon became a voracious reader, took a correspondence course and passed the exam qualifying him for service in the French postal service.

Again both his immense energy and his highly developed sense of protest stamped Touré as different. He soon organized his fellow workers into a union, and became simultaneously a leader in African unions and thus an African political leader. It was in the unions that Africans received most of their basic political training and made their first political contacts.

In 1945 Touré was named the secretary general of the postal and telecommunications workers of Guinea and at the same time with Félix Houphouët-Boigny (now President of the Ivory Coast) became one of the founders of Houphouët's African Democratic Rally. During this period both men were considerably under the influence of Communists in the French unions. Later, when Houphouët became more conservative, the two broke.

Yet these years were a major influence on Touré. The young Africans had gone from one extreme of contact with Frenchmen in the colonial service to another extreme, the French Communists who were trying to cultivate them. In Paris it was primarily the Communists who took an interest in the young Africans; in particular they took an interest in Touré, a formidable leader and orator, and a deputy to the French National Assembly in 1956.

IT was this ideological background that made Guinea's turn to the East easier in the days following independence. Those who know Touré still believe he was stunned and shocked by the violence of the French withdrawal in 1958. The French stripped the country of technicians and equipment, ripping telephones out of the walls, smashing light fixtures, rerouting a rice ship, even, the story goes, destroying all the prison records so the Guineans had to go around asking each prisoner what offense he was in for, and how long a sentence he was serving.

The Guineans, caught in the wave of French anger, needed help desperately. Touré turned first to the United States. But Washington, after checking with Paris and being advised that the French were not interested in what happened to Guinea, turned Touré down. The next step was natural enough. The Guineans were looking for support; the Eastern bloc, just in the process of discovering Africa and wanting an entry on its west coast, was delighted by this young nation which had insulted the West.

By the end of 1959 Guinea was swarming with Russians, Communist Chinese, Bulgarians, Poles, North Vietnamese, East Germans. On the streets the ivory hawkers and cigarette peddlers approached white men. *"Camarade,"* they said. The French nodded wisely and said, "We told you so, they are all Communists; what can you expect?" The Americans gaped: Would all Africa, as Touré implied, follow his pattern? The first of the black satellites? Had the West given away another country, or—more likely—a whole continent?

Then a remarkable thing happened. The Russians turned out to be very human indeed, neither ten feet tall, nor any gentler, nor more understanding than other white men. It was their first experience in black Africa, and it is an incontrovertible fact about this part of the world that nowhere else is there such a great difference between theory and practice, nowhere else is the process of learning so painful and difficult.

RUSSIAN equipment, not top-grade anyway, and designed for Moscow weather, failed badly under the cruel test of the tropics. Disabled trucks lined Conakry's streets. No mechanics or spare parts were available. Russian school teachers arrived, were unable to speak French and needed Russian interpreters, to the delight of the Guinean students. The Russians, ill-prepared for the relaxed tempo of the tropics, found the Guineans badly lacking as worker-comrades, Marxist or not. Russians clad in wool suits and nylon shirts complained bitterly and openly of the climate.

Target dates for completion of projects, computed for Moscow conditions, came and went, leaving behind disenchanted Guineans. Russian equipment, shipped all the way here, turned out to be more expensive than the superior French goods. "It was a magnificent job of bungling," says one diplomat here. "Even you Americans couldn't have matched it."

But the problem in the Guinean-Eastern bloc relationship was even more serious than that. The Russians, unwittingly but ironically, were in Guinean eyes taking the place of the French (without even being able to speak the language). From top to bottom it suddenly seemed the Russians were telling the Guineans what to do and how to do it.

NOT only were the Russians taking all the fun out of independence; worse still, they began to represent a threat to the Guinean idea of independence. The Russians, not satisfied with Touré's ideological discipline, started to work closely with some of the younger intellectuals. When Touré saw in this the beginnings of an opposition he reacted violently to strike it down, and in the process threw out the Soviet Ambassador for plotting and then made his successor wait six weeks before being allowed to present his papers.

The Russian experience proved now zealously the Guineans intend to guard their new freedom and that they have no intention of being anyone's satellite.

In addition, the Russians had miscalculated the anti-Western feeling and had not understood the curious love-hate relationship of the French and Guineans which still exists. To this day French is the national language, and even when Touré speaks in the native dialect he must use French words to say "independence," "freedom," "liberty"; to this day it is easier for a French reporter to see Touré than a man from any other country.

Now, with the Algerian war over, Touré has moved toward a rapprochement with France; according to friends, he wants nothing so badly as a state trip to Paris. "The French shaped their thinking, their way of looking at the world. They have the French in their blood," says one diplomat. "They like the French more than they will ever admit."

TO see Touré as a Marxist, or any kind of ideologist, is something of a mistake. If he has any kind of ideology, it is perhaps a new kind, Africanism. For Touré the test appears to be whether something is good for Africa or bad for Africa. The politics he cares about are the politics of Africa, not of Laos, or even of Cuba. The cold war is judged—albeit unfairly—on its meaning to Africa. The United Nations Charter, say the Guineans, is historically in error, since it does not make anti-colonialism the U. N.'s major work. "Sékou is emphasizing the teaching of the English language, but it is not so that his young people may go to London and Washington," says an African diplomat, "it is so they can go to Accra and Lagos."

Touré's great dream, friends say, is of Conakry as the political and cultural center of a new Africa. To this end, while his country neared economic ruin he channeled most of his Soviet aid into big showy buildings which would help this dream; a powerful 100-kilowatt radio transmitter that would project his and Guinea's voice up and down the continent; a high-speed new printing plant which can print 40,000 papers an hour; a new outdoor theatre; a new and at present unneeded hotel to house visiting African delegations. His dreams, these friends say, are all African dreams.

TOURE has described his own ideas on Marxism this way: "Without being Communists we believe that the analytical qualities of Marxism and the organization of the people are methods especially well suited for our people." For a young country in a hurry to harness its resources, the economic example of the Soviet bloc is impressive. Touré apparently intended to nationalize nearly all of the Guinean economy, but eventually found that his state economy was badly lagging, while the one private corporation in Guinea was setting new records.

He has recently taken a new conservative turn on economics and is encouraging private capital. Ironically, the last business he nationalized was the local book store—this solely in order to confiscate the piles of Russian, Chinese and North Vietnamese propaganda tracts being sold there.

Yet there are many parallels between Touré's Guinea and an Eastern-bloc country: the one-party system through which Touré rules the country, from the Politburo at the top to the party organization in every village—including a press attaché—at the bottom; the integration of the trade unions into the party; the theoretical economic planning of Guinea's three-year plan (goals unachieved); the suspicion with which the Government regards all foreigners, and the restrictions on association between Guineans and foreigners; and the violent way in which Touré cut down any opposition.

Yet Touré's Guinea is not a police state. There are few policemen around. The Army is refreshingly out of view. There is no system of informers or checking in hotel rooms, as in Ghana. This, according to observers, is testimony less to the Government's relaxed view of the future than to the low-pressure attitude of the Guineans.

FOR the tempo of Guinea is slower than that of other African countries. These may be exciting years politically, but Touré's basic and most difficult job remains getting his people to go to work. The Guineans, setting up a red-tape bureaucracy, now find themselves unable to man it, and are so badly ensnarled at times they are unable to accept technical aid because of their own administrative difficulties. Because Touré, at the urging of the Eastern bloc, took Guinea out of the franc zone—his biggest mistake, say friends; he could have had the best of both worlds—his currency is weak; smuggling is widespread, as Guinean farmers refuse to sell their produce for soft money, and instead smuggle their goods over the borders for hard, European-backed currency.

ONLY when the food shortage became a political problem did it become a reality in Guinea. This has been one of the major criticisms of Touré and his Government—that the political instinct and response is first and foremost, that he and his Ministers are among the most politically sophisticated Africans on the continent, but that they are not nearly so interested in economics and finance.

"This is another legacy from the French," says one Frenchman here. "From the French they learned about trade unions and politics, but nothing about finance. We did nothing here in the colonial period to develop a black commercial class, no Guinean merchants or bankers. We developed their political instincts, that is all."

This is part of a more general criticism of Touré himself: that he was fine as the young and dynamic revolutionary leader protesting against colonialism and exploitation, but that he has been reluctant to settle down to the hard, dull, day-to-day tasks of leadership. "He would rather make a speech than work on a budget," says a Pole here.

But Touré goes his way. He is not a satellite, and yet if he receives American aid and if he wants French friendship he remains quiet about it, as if careful not to tarnish the image of the angry and independent young African. "We are not asking for aid, but what can you give us?" is in essence what he said to G. Mennen Williams recently.

IF he is more pragmatist than Marxist, then similarly he is more anti-colonialist than anti-Soviet. The Eastern bloc is here, it has a big stake here and it will remain here, although the honeymoon is over. "He is a very good positive neutralist now," says one diplomat. "He will permit both sides to help him."

Inevitably, the words of his representatives in other countries and at the U. N. will sound harsh. Yet there is more optimism among Westerners here than in recent years. Much of this Guinean anger, they say, is the sign of a young and insecure country with a chip on its shoulder; some day, and perhaps it is not so far off, Guinea will get over its anger and its hurt; it will become preoccupied with reality. And that day will not be so bad for the West. For the West only wants these people to be independent. In the long run, the East wants much more.

Guinea, Bastion of Socialism, Struggles to Make System Work

By ALFRED FRIENDLY Jr.
Special to The New York Times

CONAKRY, Guinea — The last bastion of the revolutionary "socialist option" in West Africa, Guinea lies 10 degrees north of the Equator, suspended between conflicting hopes and creeping decay.

Weeds are growing in some of Conakry's narrow, empty side streets. Nearby, on one of the capital's main arteries, a signboard above the crumbling sidewalk proclaims "The worker who has everything to gain in a revolutionary regime must be unconditionally engaged in revolutionary action."

A few blocks from the slogan, shoppers in the state-owned Printania or Nafay general stores idle between counters whose display spaces are two-thirds empty. Around the corner from the revolutionary exhortation, however, a hole-in-the-corner black market offers the goods — imported cloth, transistor radios, bicycle tires, canned foods—that long ago disappeared from the big shops. Black-market prices are three to four times higher than the cost of such merchandise in neighboring Sierra Leone, Liberia and the Ivory Coast.

Teacher Feels Pinch

"By Guinean standards I get a good salary [$80 dollars a month at official exchange rates], but I can barely make ends meet," complained an outspoken young high school science teacher who asked to be called Diallo because it was not his real name. "Things have gone on like this for years, getting worse.

"The people are tired. They want change and they are just waiting for the army to do here what it did in Mali. Ten years ago I could buy a pair of trousers for 1,500 francs [six dollars]. Now if I can find them, they cost 15,000 francs. The situation is impossible, and it cannot last.

When Diallo's remarks were repeated to him, Mahmadou Barry, an eloquent advocate of the Guinean "option," said "we did not take out independence just for trousers." Mr. Barry is director of international broadcasting for the official radio, called Voice of the Revolution.

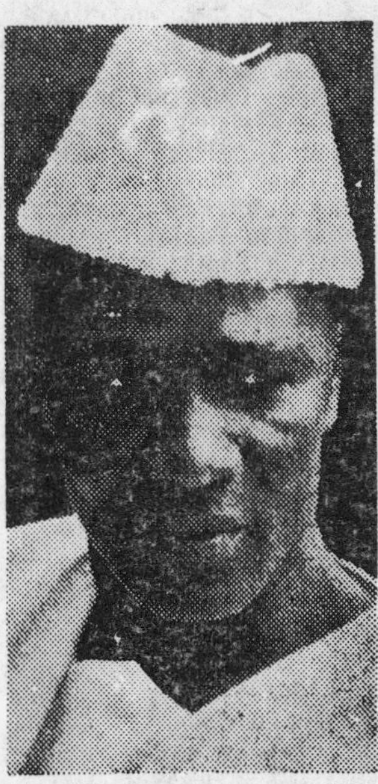

Paris Match

President Sékou Touré

The sacrifices made by Guinea's 3.6 million people in the 10 years since the nation became France's first African colony to become independent have paved the way, according to Mr. Barry, for sound rapid future development.

600,000 Leave County

Other evidence points to a different verdict. According to a knowledgeable Cabinet minister, 600,000 of Guinea's people have voted with their feet —left the country—since independence, renouncing the Atlantic coastal regions, the cool, dramatic interior highlands and the steam forests for more prosperous neighboring countries. Less official estimates put the population outflow at nearly a million.

Relatively few came to Conakry, the shabby apotheosis of the political structure, whose rhetoric is distributed to most Guineans by the efficient communication network of the nation's only party, the Democratic party of Guinea. Rarely does an important political proclamation come before the 200,000 residents of the capital without its being transmitted along party lines to the remotest village.

The flow of information and opinion from bottom to top is less orderly but still impressive. Officials, striving to get an honest reading of public opinion, have been holding "open mouth" conferences all over the nation with the aim of hearing the complaints and suggestions of ordinary citizens.

Cabinet Ministers and the President have a record of travel inside their own country that no other West African leaders can equal. To many observers it seems that they stump the interior more to be seen and heard than to look and listen.

Despite the dissenting opinions of such Guineans as Diallo and despite rationing of such products as rice, soap, sugar and cooking oil, most Government officials and many Western observers discount the obvious parallels between Guinea and neighboring Mali, where a group of young officers swiftly and bloodlessly overthrew President Modibo Keita Nov. 19.

The Lesson of Mali

Guineans say that the fall of their onetime stanch ally was mostly caused by his own political mistakes, errors they say that Guinea's President, Sékou Touré has not made and will not permit.

"When the cow in the field next to yours is struck by lightning, naturally you worry a bit for your cow," commented the Economic Development Minister, Ismael Touré, the President's half-brother. "But our enemies should not make the mistake of thinking our cow is next."

President Touré, who will be 46 years old in January, was at least distressed enough by the fall of his Socialist neighbor to take up his familiar position behind a podium 10 days after the Mali coup. For eight hours over two days, he lectured his party and Government supporters on the meaning of it all.

His immediate reaction, however, was more cautious, a far cry from the now-regretted speed with which he proclaimed the deposed Ghanaian leader, Kwame Nkrumah, co-president of Guinea after the military seized power in Ghana in February, 1966.

This time Guinea simply called for quick consultation among the four members of the Organization of Senegal River States—Guinea, Senegal, Mauritania and Mali. When the new Malian regime declined the invitation to a heads-of-state meeting in Conakry, pleading a press of business, President Touré scolded them with uncharacteristic mildness.

Mr. Touré has outgrown his "tub-thumping stage," maintains a French businessman, whose experience in Guinea goes back to the years before 1958, when President de Gaulle washed his hands of one of France's most promising territories. "The man has held on to power here for 10 years because he is a political genius. He is not going to let it slip away now for the sake of ideology."

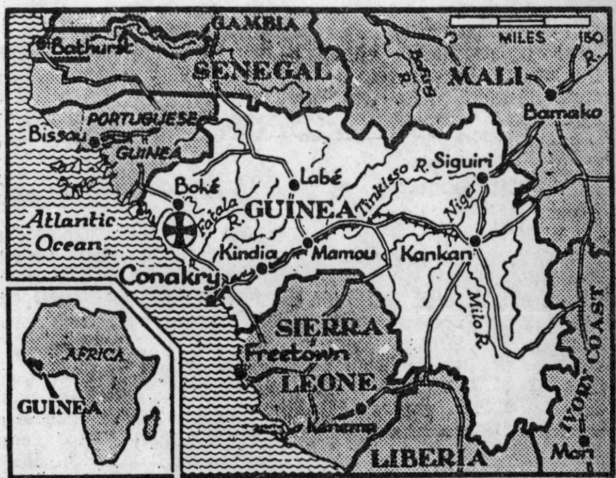

The New York Times Dec. 16, 1968

Guinea's bauxite deposits around Boké (cross) are major factor in nation's hopes for prosperity in the 1970's.

As further proof, American diplomats cite a recent agreement that will bring two major American aluminum companies and five West European partners, with an initial invest ment of $100-million., into the development of rich bauxite reserves around Boké. The World Bank has lent $64.5-million and the United States Government $21-million in counterpart Guinean francs for Guinea's share of the project's cost.

With close to half the world's known bauxite reserves and an annual production of 1.5 million tons now, Guinea is looking forward — too optimistically, some experts believe — to an era of real prosperity.

Guinea's present import bill is a $30-million a year. Her earnings are only $11-million and, even after debt payments on the Boké project are brought to manageable size, Guinea's annual hard currency deficit at present rates seems likely to run indefinitely between $5-million and $9-million.

With improved agricultural techniques Guinea might be able to redress this imbalance. Only in one field—pineapple exports—has her production risen since independence, from zero to about 6,5000 tons.

Officially, 1968 is "Agriculture Year," but it is also the year in which the Centers of Rural Education became Centers of Revolutionary Education.

A Guinean student said, "my friends do nothing but talk all the time about revolution, but they are afraid to take action themselves. They say the army has to save them and they act as if it were going to happen any day."

Ismael Touré, among others, sees no likelihood of the 4,500-man army moving to overthrow a government that pays it well and treats it respectfully. Surrounded by young tech-decisions made and carried out, their ability to get pragmatic decisions made and came out, he argues that Guinea's order of priorities does not include making Conakry a model city before the interior of the country can catch up. Proud of the Boké agreement and of other private investments, he says of Guinea's socialism: "We are not doctrinaire."

Less involved observers believe that Guinea is simply becoming less doctrinaire. Fodé Bereté edits Horaya, the official Government newspaper, and on most subjects he is a resolute party-liner. At the end of a recent talk, however, even he relaxed a little.

"Guineans put a lot of importance on development," he remarked. "Guineans want to be as realistic as possible. Se don't want to live on slogans."

December 16, 1968

U.N. Council Votes To Condemn Lisbon For Guinea Invasion

By HENRY TANNER

Special to The New York Times

UNITED NATIONS, N. Y., Dec. 8—The Security Council voted overwhelmingly today to condemn Portugal for "its invasion of the Republic of Guinea."

It demanded that the Portuguese Government "pay full compensation" to Guinea for the loss of life and property caused by the reported attack and urged all nations to refrain from giving Portugal "any military assistance and material assistance enabling it to continue its repressive actions" in Africa.

The resolution, which had been submitted by five African and Asian members, was adopted by a vote of 11 to 0, with 4 abstentions.

The United States, Britain and France, each of whom could have vetoed the resolution, abstained, as did Spain.

Portugal did not participate in the Council debate. Her delegate, António Patrício, explained to reporters at the outset of the debate last Friday that the Council had long been unfair to Portugal. The Portuguese Government has denied all involvement in the events in Guinea, and declared in advance that it would reject any resolution that "may seek to establish the culpability of Portuguese entities or individuals."

The resolution specifically endorsed the findings of the five-member United Nations mission that reported last Friday after a three-day visit to Guinea, that it had found conclusive evidence that the West African country was invaded on the night of Nov. 21-22 by an armed force consisting mainly of members of the Portuguese armed force under the command of white Portuguese officers. The mission's report said that the invasion had originated in neighboring Portuguese Guinea.

The delegates of the United States and Britain made it clear that they did not care to defend Portugal against the charges made against her.

Sir Colin Crowe, the British delegate, specifically endorsed the report.

Charles W. Yost, the American delegate, declared that the United States had "no reason to question the mission's considered opinion and judgment." Mr. Yost noted that according to the mission "elements of the Portuguese armed forces participated" in the attack on Guinea and added that this was "an action which my Government must condemn."

The French delegate, Jacques Kosciusko-Morizet, said that although some of the circumstances remained unclear, there could be no doubt that Guinea had been the victim of an armed attack involving elements of the Portuguese armed forces coming from Portuguese Guinea.

December 9, 1970

Toure Steers Strict Course for Guinea

By WILLIAM BORDERS

Special to The New York Times

CONAKRY, Guinea, Oct. 14—The socialist Government of Guinea once sponsored a basketball team to compete with neighboring West African countries. While the other teams devoted most of their time to practicing, the Guinean players spent long afternoons in a party school, studying social theory instead of dribbling and shooting.

"Naturally, when the competition came, the Guineans lost," said a man who had participated in the program.

"But I doubt if Sékou Touré cared much," he added, "because for him ideological correctness is always the prime consideration."

The story illustrates the basic manner in which President Sékou Touré has guided his country during the 13 years since he shepherded it into independence from France. It may also help to explain the baffling political convulsions that Guinea is suffering now.

"Touré is unwilling to tolerate any kind of compromise with what he sees as strict morality, and strict loyalty to pure Marxist principles," said a man who admires the President, with some reservations.

Spurned Aid From French

This trait is a reason not only for the current purge, in which 250 Government officials, businessmen and civil servants have been arrested for disloyalty, but also for the austerity of a regime that has steadfastly refused to let foreign powers lure it into a position of dependence.

After independence, President Touré declined continued financial affiliation with the French, disdainfully explaining that "an African statesman is not a naked boy begging from rich capitalists."

His attitude immediately made him one of the authentic heroes of the new Africa, exemplifying proud independence from European colonialism.

His position was reinforced last November, when Conakry was invaded by a naval force that even many neutral observers now believe came from Portuguese Guinea, a colony 150 miles north of here.

"It was a brazen attempt by the dying forces of colonialism

who are determined that we shall not succeed, and we stood up to it and defeated it—that's what our African neighbors admired," an official explained, echoing the theories that President Touré has expressed in his revolutionary poetry and in his nearly two dozen volumes of political philosophy.

But now, after 58 death sentences, the public executions of at least three former cabinet secretaries and the increasingly hysterical tone of the move against what the Government describes as an "S S Nazi spy network," some doubts are being raised.

Touré Stays in Guinea

"I am afraid Touré is straying from the mainstream of current African thinking," said one sympathetic African politician.

In an era when many African leaders seem constantly to be flying to conferences and state visits with one another, President Touré has spent at least the last two years without setting foot outside of Guinea. His life here is extremely insulated and dominated by the fervor of domestic politics.

Only a few years ago, the handsome 49-year-old President used to stroll out of the palace in the evenings and chat with passersby here, explaining to a friend: "I will never put guards between me and my people."

Now he is more afraid of assassination; he appears only in a car preceded and followed by men with machine guns.

But even detractors of Mr. Touré, who is a former trade union leader, usually stop short of questioning the purity of his intentions. They insist that, as an African in a neighboring country put it: "If Sékou is wrong this time, at least he's honestly wrong."

President Touré, a Moslem so religious that one acquaintance considers him "almost a guru," is said to feel a mystical reverence for "the people."

According to this view, the people have been betrayed and they must be uncompromising in punishment of traitors. That is why the purge is called a people's trial, and why the prisoners' lengthy confessions are being broadcast in several tribal languages as well as in French.

Suggestions of verdicts will work their way from the 8,000 local party committees all the way up to the National Assembly, which will pass the final sentences, probably in a few weeks.

"And when it does," said a resident who expects another round of executions, "The President will say and devoutly believe that his people's will has been done and that Guinea will be a better and stronger land for it."

October 25, 1971

Nigeria Republic in Commonwealth

Dispatch of The Times, London

LAGOS, Nigeria, Oct. 1—A 21-gun salute and a blast from ships' sirens ushered in Nigeria today as a republic within the British Commonwealth. The new republic of 50 million people is the most populous country of Africa.

Its birth was marked by the calling off of a national strike, the shadow of which had hung over the celebrations.

Few Nigerians have had pay rises since Nigeria won her independence from Britain three years ago. Nigeria had been a British protectorate since 1900.

Dr. Nnamdi Azikiwe, Governor General since November, 1960, stressed the importance of loyalty to one's fatherland in his inaugural address as Nigeria's first President.

October 2, 1963

NIGERIA UPHOLDS DEMOCRATIC WAY

Authoritarian Trend Loses in Defeat of Detention Act

By LLOYD GARRISON

Special to The New York Times

LAGOS, Nigeria, July 27—The defeat of a proposed preventive detention act here this week would appear to confirm Nigeria as one of Africa's democratic countries.

Nigeria has long been conspicuous for not having succumbed to the trend toward authoritarianism so prevalent elsewhere on this continent.

The reason for the defeat of preventive-detention powers is not simply that Nigerians respect democracy more than other Africans do. In fact, many responsible persons in and out of government believe Nigeria can progress only with a tough-minded central government with executive powers.

Many who hold this view are attracted by the views of President Kwame Nkrumah of Ghana and his one-party, one-leader philosophy.

Without such an approach, these persons say, no Nigerian government will ever be able to cut across tribal boundaries and reflect a truly national outlook.

It was this very tribalism that finally prevented acceptance of preventive detention.

A real fear emerged that one of Nigeria's three main tribes might use preventive detention to gain the upper hand over the others.

This fear prevailed, and for the time being at least Nigeria will continue to exist as a delicate balance of three antagonistic tribal groupings of the Eastern, Western and Northern Regions.

Why were the detention powers considered in the first place? The answer lies in the Government's concern about security after having discovered what it called a plot. Leaders of the Action Group party were arrested and their trial on treason charges is now nearing its end.

Government witnesses declared that Ghana served as a haven for the accused and also provided training facilities for Action Group recruits.

Since independence was won in 1960 the Federal Government has been composed of a coalition of the two parties of the Northern and Eastern Regions.

The Northern is by far the most populous. It is dominated by Hausa-speaking Moslems and it is a stronghold of conservatism.

The coalition with the Eastern Region was a political convenience. There is a long tradition of suspicion of the north on the part of southerners of both the Eastern and Western Regions.

July 28, 1963

REPUBLIC IN PERIL: Elections held in Nigeria last week were boycotted in almost all areas of the Eastern, Midwestern and Western regions, threatening to split the country in two. The dominant party in these three southern regions contended that many of its candidates had been denied the right to contest seats in the Northern region, which covers almost two-thirds of the land and is the most populous. Also, the major tribes in the southern part of the country—animist for the most part—have long had a fear of being overwhelmed by the larger Moslem Hausas in the North.

January 3, 1965

NIGERIANS SETTLE ELECTION DISPUTE

President Says Balewa Will Form a Unity Regime

By LLOYD GARRISON
Special to The New York Times

LAGOS, Nigeria, Jan. 4—President Nnamdi Azikiwe said tonight that he would appoint a new government headed by Prime Minister Sir Abubakar Tafawa Balewa under a compromise solution of the election crisis, which has threatened to break up Nigeria's federation.

In a dramatic broadcast, first the President and then the Prime Minister went on the air and reaffirmed their confidence in each other and their faith in Nigerian unity.

The President, a Southern Christian who had sided with the Opposition and the Prime Minister, a Moslem Northerner whose Nigerian National Alliance won the elections after a massive Southern boycott, together pledged a "broadly based national government" representing all shades of opinion.

The break in the deadlock between the North and the South ended Nigeria's greatest crisis since she won independence from Britain in 1960.

American diplomats and many African and Western representatives made no secret of their pleasure at the agreement. The most populous nation on the continent and one of the last democracies in black Africa, Nigeria has been regarded as a symbol of freedom where the trend elsewhere has been more and more toward one-party dictatorship.

During th efive-day crisis, which developed after last Wednesday's elections, the Eastern Region threatened to break away from the federation and set up an independent state.

This threat evaporated tonight with the President's promise of new elections in districts where the Southern boycott was heaviest.

The East, a stronghold of the opposition United Progressive Grand Alliance, conceded a key point: it agreed to drop its demand for new nationwide elections. Opposition candidates had complained of widespread intimidation in their attempts to run in the North and in some pro-Government areas of the West.

The Northern Region's election results will stand. Mr. Azikiwe urged that where "irregularities" had occurred candidates "should seek redress in the law courts."

The holding of new elections in the South will reduce but not eliminate the Northern alliance's majority in Parliament.

It is widely assumed that Sir Abubakar's new Cabinet will not differ much from the old Government coalition of Northerners and Easterners.

President Azikiwe said that in the West, where the boycott cut sharply into the voting in most areas, "the results, in the interests of democracy, should be re-examined."

Many pro-Government candidates won in the West by only a few hundred votes out of a possible 100,000. The main issue of the campaign in the West was the release of the action-group oppositeion leader in Parliament, Chief Obafemi Awolowo, who was imprisoned last year for plotting the Government's overthrow.

January 5, 1965

Nigeria Army Chief Heads A Provisional Government

By Reuters

LAGOS, Nigeria, Jan. 16 — Maj. Gen. Johnson Aguiyi-Ironsi, commander of the Nigerian Army, announced tonight that he had accepted an invitation by the Council of Ministers to head a provisional federal military Government to maintain law and order. He acted in the wake of yesterday's attempted coup d'état.

The general said that the military Government had suspended Parliament and the offices of President and Prime Minister, as well as regional Governors and Premiers and the regional legislatures.

He appointed a military governor for each region, with the former governors as advisers to the new military governors.

Broadcasting just before General Aguiyi-Ironsi, the acting President, Nwafor Orizu, told the nation that the Council of Ministers had called on the army unanimously and voluntarily to form a military government.

The general said in his broadcast that the Chief Justice and all members of the judiciary, the civil service and police would continue their normal duties.

He said that the army was determined to suppress the current disorders in Western and Northern Nigeria.

Speaking on external affairs, the general said the military Government would respect international financial obligations, honor all international agreements and maintain Nigeria's present diplomatic relations with foreign states.

He appealed for the cooperation of all Nigerians in restoring law and order.

It was reported earlier that rebel troops appeared to be consolidating their position in the Northern Region's capital of Kaduna while troops loyal to the Lagos Government assumed control of most of the rest of the country.

General Agufyi-Ironsi also said in his broadcast the army would guarantee the safety of all members of the Council of Ministers, an executive body appointed by the President.

He pledged that the army would maintain law and order in the federation until a Constitution could be drawn up in accordance with the wishes of the people.

January 17, 1966

ARMY AIDE TAKES POWER IN NIGERIA

Chief of Staff Announces He Heads Regime—Fate of Ironsi Still Uncertain

Special to The New York Times

LAGOS, Nigeria, Aug. 1—The Chief of Staff of Nigeria's Army announced today that he had taken over the Government after an army mutiny and the kidnapping of the chief of state.

The new leader is Lieut. Col. Yakubu Gowon, 32 years old. He is a Hausa tribesman from Nigeria's Moslem North, as are the soldiers who started the mutiny. He was third in command of the junta that took over power after the coup d'état Jan. 15.

Colonel Gowon told Nigeria's 55 million people in a broadcast that the head of state, Maj. Gen. Johnson T. U. Aguiyi-Ironsi, had been kidnapped by mutineers during a visit to the town of Ibadan. He said his whereabouts and fate were not known.

The broadcast signaled success for the mutineers' aim—the end of the policy pursued by General Ironsi to convert Nigeria into a unified country under a strong central government.

Policy Aroused Suspicions

His policy aroused the suspicions of the Hausas in the North and of the Yoruba tribes from the West, who feared domination by the more advanced Ibo people.

At least 600 people were reported killed in fighting in the North earlier after General Ironsi, an Ibo, announced the abolition of the federal system, in which the country was divided into regions, each with a powerful government.

In last week's mutiny the Governor of the Western province, Lieut. Col. Adekunle Fajuyi, also was kidnapped. His whereabouts, too, is unknown, according to the broadcast.

It made no mention of the second in command to General Ironsi in the deposed junta, Brig. Babafemi A. O. Ogundipe, chief of staff of the army supreme headquarters, but he is believed to be alive.

Colonel Gowon said he was assuming control of the military Government with the support of a majority of the Supreme Military Council.

"All is now quiet," he said. He promised a decree soon that would lay a foundation for national unity.

He praised General Ironsi for his efforts to reconstruct the country after what he called the "sad and unfortunate" January revolt, but said that recent disturbances in Northern Nigeria showed that the basis of trust and confidence necessary for a unitary system of government did not exist in Nigeria.

For this he blamed those military men who in conjunction with certain civilians overthrew the legal government in January and killed many army officers. Most of the officers, he said, came from one section of the country.

The new head of the Government assured all foreigners of their safety. He said his Government would respect all treaties, financial agreements and obligations entered into by the previous Government.

Colonel Gowon joined the army in 1954 after having attended Zaria Government College. He was sent to an officers' training school at Teshie in Ghana and received further military training in Britain.

He served in the Southern Cameroons when it was still part of Nigeria and later with the United Nations force in the Congo. He was promoted to adjutant general of the Nigerian Army in 1963 and in 1965 returned to Britain for a course at the staff college.

When the army took over the Government in January, he was appointed Chief of Army Staff.

August 2, 1966

Poiltical Break-up Looms in Nigeria as Ibos Challenge Regime

By LLOYD GARRISON
Special to The New York Times

LAGOS, Nigeria, Aug. 2—Nigeria appeared to be moving toward political dissolution today with the Ibos of the Eastern Region openly challenging the new Northern-dominated Government in Lagos.

In a broadcast over the Eastern Region radio last night, the region's military Governor protested that only the army rebels and their Northern supporters had been consulted on the formation of the new Government of Lieut. Col. Yakubu Gowon, a Northerner who took over after a mutiny ousted Maj. Gen. Johnson T. U. Aguiyi-Ironsi last Friday.

Lieut. Col. Odumegwu Ojukwu, the East's Governor and an Ibo, said the terms of an Army cease-fire were imposed by Northerners and accepted by Southerners in the army's ranks solely to avert bloodshed.

Scores Basis of Settlement

He said the terms called for splitting Nigeria into component states and for sending all Southerners living in the North and all Northerners in the South back to their home regions.

"In spite of the fact that the only representations made at these cease-fire negotiations were those of the rebels and their Northern followers, it was agreed to accept these terms to stop further killing," Colonel Ojukwu said.

"I now consider that the next step will be to open negotiations at the appropriate level to allow further sections of the Nigerian people to express their views."

The government issued a denial tonight that it planned to partition the country into separate tribal components and that Northerners and Southerners were to be sent back to their own parts of the country.

The cease-fire negotiations to which Colonel Ojukwu referred came over the weekend after the dissident Northerners in the army mutinied and kidnapped General Ironsi and other leaders, whose whereabouts remain unknown.

As a result of the negotiations, Colonel Gowon, 32 years old, the Chief of Staff of the army, was able to announce yesterday that he had taken over the Government.

The Northern mutiny came as a surprise to most veteran observers. Northerners are outnumbered by Southerners in the army and most of the top-ranking Northerners were slain in last January's coup by Southern "young Turks," thus depriving the North of its most capable officers.

Now that the army has undergone two bloodlettings in less than seven months, its ability to recover as a cohesive and disciplined force is seriously in doubt.

Role in Plot Unclear

It is not yet clear whether Colonel Gowon was in on the Northern plot to seize power. He went out of his way yesterday in his speech announcing his assumption of power to praise General Ironsi.

But it is plain that Colonel Gowon reflects the North's fears of Southern domination and tha he is determined to turn the political clock back to where it stood before the original coup d'état in January overthrew the Prime Minister, Sir Abubaka Tafawa Balewa. Mr. Balewa and the premiers of the western and northern regions were killed.

The new take-over seems to mean that General Ironsi's "unification" campaign, an attempt to combine the disparite tribal and geographic elements in a cohesive nation, will be scrapped in favor of a reimposition of regional autonomy.

Colonel Gowon also hinted broadly that his regime would seek an alliance of Northern Hausas and conservative Western Yorubas—the same alliance Prime Minister Balewa forged, which plunged the western region into a bitter fratricidal conflict last year between pro-Northern and anti-Northern Yorubas.

The consequences of any return to the old Balewa power base cannot yet be accurately measured because the loyalty of Southern Yoruba and Ibo troops is still in question.

But just as the Northerners feared that the January coup signaled an end to the North's grip over the Federal Government, now progressive Southerners can only interpert Colonel Gowon's takeover as meaning a decline in Southern and particularly Eastern Ibo influence. The Ibos and their anti-Northern Yoruba allies are not likely to take any such development lying down.

Colonel Gowon's most critical challenge is to placate Southern fears of domination by the Moslem Hausas of the North. General Ironsi, faced with the opposite problem, obviously failed to reassure the North during his brief tenure.

If Colonel Gowon fails to effect a new spirit of national reconciliation, there is a very real prospect that the Ibos will secede and declare themselves an independent nation.

Secession might well lead to the break-up of Africa's most populous and potentially most prosperous nation, with the very real possibility of an outbreak of civil war.

The Government announced that it would release six prominent political prisoners, confirming a promise made by Colonel Gowon.

The most prominent among the six, all of whom were accused of plotting to overthrow the Nigerian Government, is Chief Obafemi Awolowo, a former premier of the Western Region and the leader of the opposition Action Group, now banned. He was sentenced to 10 years imprisonment in 1963 and is believed to be in Calabar jail in Eastern Nigeria.

His deputy, Chief Anthony Enaharo, was also released. He had been extradited from Britain to face trial after a bitter battle in the High Court and in Parliament. He was sentenced to 15 years, but last year the Nigerian Appeal Court reduced the sentence to 7 years.

The four other prisoners were also leading members of the Action Group.

In a political change, Colonel Gowon appointed Lieut. Col. R. A. Adebayo military governor of the Western Region. He takes over from Lieut. Col. F. Adekunle Fajuyi, who was one of those kidnapped by mutineers in Ibadan Friday.

Gowon Not a Hausa

LAGOS, Aug. 2 (Reuters)—Colonel Gowon is not a member of the Hausa tribe, as was first reported yesterday after he had announced his assumption of power. He is from one of the smaller tribes who dwell among the Hausa of the North and had a Christian, not a Moslem, education.

August 3, 1966

REVOLTS CRIPPLE ARMY IN NIGERIA

Tribal Warfare Decimates and Divides the Military

By LLOYD GARRISON
Special to The New York Times

LAGOS, Nigeria, Aug. 8—Two bloody coups d'état within less than seven months have left the Nigerian Army all but destroyed as a unifying national force.

In the first coup, which occurred last January, the main victims were high-ranking Northern officers. They were killed by young Southern officers, who also assassinated Prime Minister Abubakar Tafawa Balewa and the Northern region's Premier, the Sarduana of Sokoto.

The mutineers were almost all Ibo tribesmen from the South. Northern Hausas in the army were suspicious of an "Ibo plot" to dominate the North. Why else, they asked, had so many Northern leaders been killed and so many Southerners spared?

These suspicions grew when the leaders of the coup were detained, but not court-martialed, by Maj. Gen. Johnson T. U. Aguiyi-Ironsi, an Ibo who had emerged as the head of Nigeria's military Government.

Ibos Lynched in North

Northern hostility boiled over in May, when Hausa demonstrations against the Ironsi regime led to widespread lynchings of Ibo civilians living in the North.

The army's second upheaval, on July 29, may not have been conceived as a Northern countercoup, but that was its result.

General Ironsi was kidnapped and presumably killed, scores of Ibo officers and enlisted men were slain by Hausas, and a Northern officer, 31-year-old Lieut. Col. Yakubu Gowon, took over as Nigeria's supreme commander.

The killing began in the barracks at Abeokuta, 40 miles north of here.

One report says the Hausas struck to prevent a second coup by Ibo officers seeking to free the detained leaders of the January coup.

The mutiny spread rapidly. "It was an orgy of revenge that just had to come," remarked one Hausa officer who had tried in vain to restrain his troops.

More than 30 Ibo officers have been confirmed dead.

One reliable army source reported that nearly all Ibos in Abeokuta, perhaps as many as 40, were killed and that 37 were killed in Abadan, 40 in Ikeja and 7 in Kano.

The army, which once numbered 8,500 men, has been reduced to a decimated and divisive force.

Ibos once made up more than a third of the officers and numbered nearly 2,000 in the enlisted ranks. Because the Ibos had more education than the Hausas of the less developed North, they occupied key positions in ordnance, administration, logistics and communication.

The consensus among most diplomats here is that, even if Colonel Gowon succeeds in his avowed determination to hold the country together, reintegration of the army is out of the question.

What most diplomats forecast is a loose federation of Nigeria's four regions, each raising its own army to maintain internal security.

Tribal Passions Surface

To many long-time observers, the sudden resurgence of latent tribal passions is the most significant and tragic consequence of the two coups.

"Just look what's happening," a high-ranking Ibo civil servant said recently with contempt. "The goats are taking over."

This was his way of alluding to the Hausas. Until the Northern coup, the civil servant had been a passionate and articulate exponent of national unity. Only a few weeks ago, he had spoken warmly of the Hausas.

But now his tribal pride and prejudice had gained the upper hand.

"I am not sorry about the Ibos," remarked a Hausa guard at the airport today, "They killed us first."

A Yoruba policeman from the West agreed.

"The Ibos aren't happy with their own homeland," he said. "They want to live everywhere, take the best jobs, be the masters. Let them secede. Good riddance."

Later, speaking in a whisper, an Ibo airlines clerk confided:

"We're sending our wives and children back home. We have our plans. We will cool it for a month. The Hausas will relax. Then we will strike back. When it comes, stay in your house. It will be another Congo."

Return to Tribalism

The alarming fact is that such talk has become common among the very Nigerians who once appeared to be tribally emancipated—the doctors, civil servants, lawyers.

To many seasoned Western diplomats, Nigeria gained independence from Britain in 1960 as the most promising of African states. It was 55 million strong, it was a democracy, and it had a thriving free-enterprise economy.

Now secession and recrimination are the dominant themes; to most outside observers, tribalism has emerged as Nigeria's tragic flaw.

The voices of unity may yet be heard. But for now, these voices are stilled.

August 9, 1966

300 IBO TRIBESMEN KILLED BY TROOPS AND NIGERIAN MOB

Refugees Trying to Board Plane in North Are Shot—Week's Toll Near 1,000

By LLOYD GARRISON
Special to The New York Times

LAGOS, Nigeria, Oct. 2—Troops in the Northern Region city of Kano mutinied last night and joined civilian mobs in attacking members of the Eastern Region's Ibo tribe. More than 300 Ibos were reported killed, and this was said to be a conservative estimate. Hundreds were injured.

The latest killings are likely to bring the toll in the North to well over 1,000 slain since widespread attacks on Ibos began last week.

The mutiny at the airport began last night when troops apparently defied orders and opened fire on Ibo refugees waiting to board a Lagos-bound Nigerian Airways VC-10 from London.

Army officers at the airport fled after the shooting and the mutineers drove into town, where, aided by Northern civilians, they assaulted Ibos congregated at the railroad station and in the "dangerous quarter" outside the old city walls.

Some Control Restored

Lieut. Col. Mohammed Shuwa, who once commanded the Kano battalion, was sent to Kano early today from Kaduna, the regional capital, to get the troops under control. He said shortly before noon that he had succeeded in getting most of the rebellious troops back to their barracks. But rioting and looting continued in three sections of the city.

The seeds of the current anti-Ibo rioting go back to the army coup in January, when young Southern army officers, most of them Ibos, killed four Northern superior officers and assassinated the Northern Prime Minister, Sir Abubakar Tafawa Balewa.

The North first reacted in May in riots against Ibos in which more than 600 lost their lives. Two months later army officers mutinied and assumed control of the military government.

The Ibos had filled many of the more highly skilled jobs in the vast but underdeveloped North. Since May they have been fleeing the North in a steady exodus, crippling many essential services.

Communications Are Cut

Railroad communication from the North to the sea has been cut, and electricity, telephones, mail and telegraph services have been suspended in half the region. As of 1:45 P.M. today all telephone contact was suspended from Lagos to Kaduna and Kano.

Earlier telephoned reports from Kano said the bodies of Ibos lay in the streets. Many had been mutilated and their limbs severed by machetes.

An American passenger on the VC-10 said 24 Ibos had boarded the plane in Kano but had been ordered off by the troops. The Ibos were marched back to the departure gate, where scores of other refugees were clamoring for space.

Passengers on the plane watched in horror as the refugees panicked and the troops opened fire with automatic weapons.

The American plane passenger related that one Ibo who

had been shot in the leg and the back climbed the ramp just before it was pulled away. The refugee, according to the passenger, was carried aboard, the steward closed the door and the plane took off.

Other Towns Report Toll

Earlier reports from remoter areas of the North said that more than 60 Easterners had been killed in Maiduguri, 40 in Bukuru and more than 90 in Jos. The reports were two days old and were considered preliminary estimates.

Before last night's outburst, Kano had escaped the violence that swept many other Northern cities last week. Attempts by a civilian mob to storm the Kano airport last Tuesday were blocked by troops and policemen.

A round-the-clock airlift of Ibo personnel working for foreign companies in the North continued today, but Kano airport was reported closed to all traffic.

Fears were expressed that the Ibos might retaliate against Northern residents in the Eastern Region. Although swollen with more than 100,000 embittered refugees, the East has emained quiet.

The continuing wave of anti-Ibo incidents has given a severe setback to hopes that Nigeria may yet unite. At the root of the unrest that has brought the country's four regions — Eastern, Northern, Western and Mid-Western — to the brink of disunity is the Northerners' traditional fear of domination by the Ibos, who are better educated and more highly skilled.

The Moslem Hausas are dominant in the North, and the Government's problem is the fear of each tribe that a regime headed by another tribe will crush it.

For weeks a conference of regional leaders has been held in Lagos to determine whether there is still a foundation for national unity. The delegates now have returned to their own regions for further consultations.

October 3, 1966

HOPES OF NIGERIA EBB IN THE STRIFE

Fears Seem to Be Tearing Nation Into Tribal States

By LLOYD GARRISON
Special to The New York Times

LAGOS, Nigeria, Oct. 5—A massive population shift borne of insecurity and fear appears to be dividing Nigeria's four regions into separate tribal states.

In spite of official appeals for calm, this once-unified nation is witnessing a spontaneous drama of total disengagement, with each tribe retreating into the sanctuary of its traditional boundaries.

Aggrieved Ibo tribesmen are being trucked and airlifted by the thousands out of the North to their Eastern Region homeland.

The more than 10,000 Hausas who lived in the East are being repatriated to save them from becoming targets of retaliation for the slaying of more than 2,000 Ibos in the North over the last two weeks.

Now, Yorubas, fearful of being caught in the Hausa-Ibo conflict are fleeing home to the Western Region from both the North and the East. So, too, are minority tribesmen of the Mid-West Region.

Refugee Train From Kano

Yesterday a 13-car refugee train pulled out of the Northern mud-walled city of Kano packed with more than 800 Ibos and 200 Yorubas. An additional 1,000 have been flown out.

Reliable sources in Kano said the weekend death toll was more than 600, twice the number originally reported.

The violence is not confined to the North. In Lagos last week, troops acting on their own killed the Ibo personnel manager of Nigerian Airways and seriously wounded the Ibo principal of the Lagos City College.

The East still insists that it has no intention of seceding. But it has functioned as a virtually autonomous state with its own all-Ibo army since July when Northerners mutinied, executed scores of Ibo officers and men and took control of the federal military Government.

Authority Questioned

Lieut. Col. Odumegwu Ojukwu, the East's Ibo military governor has refused to recognize Lieut. Col. Yakubu Gowon, the Northerner who is supreme commander here in Lagos.

Easterners say that Colonel Gowon has no sanction to rule because he has not yet publicly conceded the death of his superior, Maj. Gen. T. U. Aguiyi-Ironsi, who was executed in the July mutiny.

On Colonel Gowon's shoulders has now fallen the burden of trying to restore discipline among Northerners in the army who have joined in the attacks against the Ibos.

The restoration of security and mutual trust will take weeks if not months of extraordinary statesmanship—if the nation holds together that long.

Many Nigerians applauded the editorial in the Government newspaper, The Morning Post, calling on Colonel Gowon to turn over security to the police.

But observers wonder how ill-armed policemen can disarm troops who have looted and killed, and who refuse to turn in their guns.

A Turning Inward

As each day passes without a solution, each tribe within each region seems to be turning more and more inward, if only for self-preservation.

Nigeria is in a state of shock. No one group, no one figure, seems to be able to stem this tribal reversion.

As The Daily Sketch in the Western Region put it today:

"Will no one save Nigeria?

"Is there no one whose love for Nigeria transcends love of tribe or personal safety, who is willing to come forward and seek others like himself to nurse this sick nation?

"If there be a man, let him come forward. Today, for God's sake!"

October 6, 1966

Eastern Region Quits Nigeria; Lagos Vows to Fight Secession

LAGOS, Nigeria, May 30 — Nigeria's Eastern Region seceded early today, declaring itself an independent republic, Biafra. The Federal Government immediately ordered a mobilization and said it would use force to thwart the secession.

The break, after five and a half years of Nigerian independence, culminated a violent struggle between Northerners, predominantly Moslems of the Hausa tribe, and Easteners, Ibo tribesmen of Christian and animist religions.

The secession announcement was made in a somber hour-long broadcast by the region's 33-year old military Governor, Lieut. Col. Odumegwu Ojukwu.

The Oxford-educated colonel concluded his declaration with these words: "Long live the Republic of Biafra, and may God protect all who live in her!"

The reaction of Lieut. Col. Yakubu Gowon, head of the Federal Government, was swift. He declared the secession treasonous, said it would be met with force, imposed economic sanctions and ordered army veterans recalled to service.

At least two Federal battalions and an armored reconnaissance squadron are already positioned on the Eastern Region's northern frontier.

Late in the day the Federal Government announced a freeze on currency transactions with the East and forbade all imports or exports of the Nigerian pound, to protect it. All exchanges of foreign money will have to be cleared in advance by the national bank.

Foreign Ships Cautioned

Colonel Gowon also alerted the Nigerian Navy to stand by, and said that any foreign ships putting into the Eastern Region would do so "at their own peril."

With more than 55 million inhabitants, Nigeria is the most populous nation of Africa — a variegated people ranging from the highly sophisticated in the capital to small pagan tribes dressed in leaves.

Nigeria attained independence from Britain on Oct. 1, 1960, and three years later changed from a dominion to a republic within the Commonwealth. Until her regional rivalries became overpowering, Nigeria was acclaimed in the West as Africa's most promising democracy.

The East's secession has all but buried hopes that Nigeria's three remaining regions — the North, the West and the Mid-West — can hold together.

The leader of the Yoruba tribesmen of the Western Region, Chief Obafemi Awolowo, warned two weeks ago that if the East broke away the West would immediately follow.

Chief Awolowo was silent after the East's announcement. Colonel Gowon has decreed a ban on the publication of political statements.

The Eastern Region's break-away rises problems for Africa and the world powers, which must decide whether to recognize the new leadership. Britain and the United States have the most at stake economically, with heavy investments in oil explorations in the region's Niger delta.

To date, the oil companies have been paying royalties and taxes to the federal authorities. They will now come under heavy pressure to pay these revenues into the East's treasury, risking federal retaliation.

The secessionist state takes its name from the Bight of Biafra, the body of water that washes its shores.

14 Million Inhabitants

With 45,700 square miles and nearly 14 million inhabitants—the majority Ibo tribesmen—the Eastern Region is larger than Pennsylvania in both size and population. As a state in Africa, it would outrank such nations as Algeria, Morocco, Kenya and Ghana.

In addition to its petroleum deposits, the area exports rubber and timber and has growing industries.

The Ibo tribesman is Eastern Nigeria's most important and controversial resource.

Outside his region, the Ibo may be hated or mildly resented or publicly respected, but he is seldom loved. Like the Biblical Israelites, with whom the Ibos share some cultural parallels, the East's predominant tribe is individualistic, clannish, enterprising, with an unbending will that some describe as arrogance. Others equate it with the character of modern-day Israelis, a people the Ibos admire.

The secession had its roots in the coup d'état of January, 1966, in which Eastern officers, most of them Ibos, assassinated the Northern Region Governor, several top-ranking army officers from the North, and the Prime Minister, Sir Abubakar Tafawa Balewa, also a Northerner.

Many Nigerians welcomed the end of the corrupt and discredited civilian Government, but in the North the suspicion grew that the coup had been part of an Ibo plot to dominate the country.

In July, Northern ranks in the army struck back, slaying 200 Ibo officers and men and elevating Colonel Gowon to power.

Two months later the North erupted in the mass killing of thousands of Ibo civilians, setting off an exodus of more than a million refugees seeking the sanctuary of their Eastern homeland.

After the massacre, Colonel Ojukwu and Colonel Gowon fought an increasingly bitter war of words over the future make-up of the federation. Colonel Ojukwu demanded a loose association of nearly autonomous regions. Colonel Gowon sought to preserve the federation with a strong central government based on the establishment of 12 new states.

The East's secession came as no surprise. Over the weekend, Colonel Ojukwu was voted a mandate by the region's 300-man Consultative Assembly.

The final decision was obviously weighed carefully in advance.

After midnight, ranking judges, civil servants and foreign consular officials in Enugu, the East's capital, were awakened by telephone calls and told to appear at the Premier's Lodge, Colonel Ojukwu's residence.

There they found Colonel Ojukwu sitting before a battery of microphones and motion-picture cameras. Behind him hung the new flag of Biafra: horizontal stripes of red, black and green with a rising sun in the middle.

Colonel Ojukwu began his address at 3 A.M. with a lengthy summary of the East's grievances, with special emphasis on the massacre last September.

The proclamation ended with a police band playing the new national anthem: a hymnlike song reminiscent of the stirring theme from "Finlandia" by Sibelius.

Prolonged applause greeted the end of the ceremony, but diplomats present said there had been no jubilation. "The atmosphere," one said, "was somber, touched with sadness that this had to happen."

Champagne was poured for the guests, who stood talking quietly with Colonel Ojukwu for 5 or 10 minutes and then drifted home and back to bed.

May 31, 1967

The Ibos Go It Alone

By LLOYD GARRISON

LAGOS, Nigeria.

THREE years ago, Chief S. O. Adebo, Nigeria's respected delegate to the United Nations, wrote an article for this Magazine in which he rightly protested that too many Westerners think of "tribal" as the same as "primitive," when in fact "tribe" really means "ethnic group." African tribes, he pointed out, are as different from one another as Swedes are from Spaniards or Welshmen from Walloons.

Nigeria encompasses more than 50 tribes, each with its own distinctive culture, language, religion. The three largest of these ethnic units are the tribes known as the Yoruba (Chief Adebo's) in the west, the Hausa (who are Moslems) in the north, and the Ibo (most of whom are Christians, but some of whom are animists) in the east. It is precisely the mutual suspicions, jealousies—indeed, hatreds—among these three that prompted the Eastern Region—the homeland of the Ibos—to break away 12 days ago and declare itself the independent Republic of Biafra. It takes its name from the Bight of Biafra, the body of water that washes its shores.

Unless the East's secession is swiftly crushed, hopes are dim that Nigeria's three remaining regions—the Northern, Western and Mid-Western Regions—can hold together. The shock waves already extend far beyond Biafra's borders. For Washington and London, Nigeria's crisis means an end to the self-delusion that this former British colony, whose 55 million people make it Africa's most populous nation, would develop into a showcase of what parliamentary government, Western aid and creative private enterprise in Africa could do. For leaders of many other African countries, presiding over nations composed of equally fractious tribal elements, the fear has arisen that if the secession virus spreads it could become a disease from which few governments could claim immunity.

THE tribal antagonisms that brought about the Ibos' secession began to harden in 1960, when Nigeria attained independence. Three years later, it changed status from that of a dominion to that of a republic within the Commonwealth. From the start, the Hausas, dominating the vast Northern Region, where roughly 60 per cent of all Nigerians reside, controlled the vote, the Federal Government, the patronage and the purse strings.

Nigeria's first Prime Minister was Sir Abubakar Tefawa Balewa, a Northerner. His Government was overthrown—and he was assassinated—in a *coup d'etat* staged in January, 1966, by a group of non-Northern army officers, mostly Ibos. The Government had been corrupt, but Balewa was killed because he was a Northerner. To the army's Young Turks, he personified the Moslem North's "regressive" domination over the political life of the rest of the federation.

The conspirators, in fact, hoped to install, not an Ibo, but a Yoruba, the jailed opposition leader, Chief Obafemi Awolowo, as Prime Minister.

But to many Hausa tribesmen, the coup seemed clearly a plot to establish an Ibo stranglehold on the nation. The result was a countercoup in July, in which Northern ranks in the army killed some 200 Ibo officers and men and installed their man, Maj. Gen. Yakubu Gowon, as Prime Minister. Then, in September, the Hausas staged a mass slaughter of Ibo civilians living in their territory—including women and children. A million or more survivors fled home to the Eastern Region. Now the upshot has come with the region's secession, and Lieut. Col. Chukuemeka Odumegwu Ojukwu's assumption of the role of chief of state of Biafra.

WITH nearly 14 million people—the majority are Ibos—Biafra is no ministate. It is bigger than Bulgaria, more populous than Sweden. Within Africa itself, it embraces more people than Algeria, Morocco, Ghana or the Congo.

Left alone, free of blockade and civil war, Biafra could become a viable nation. It has untapped quantities of sulphur-free oil, now in high demand in the pollution-stricken cities of Europe and North America; Biafra also exports palm oil and timber, and has a growing number of fledgling industries.

But any nation's greatest asset is the quality of its people, and Biafra's Ibos are its most important—and controversial—resource.

Outside his region, the Ibo is variously hated, mildly resented, grudgingly respected—seldom loved. Like the Biblical Israelites—with whom the Ibos share striking cultural parallels—Biafra's predominant tribe is individualistic, clannish and enterprising, with an unbending will that some describe as arrogance, and that others equate with the modern-day, do-it-yourself Israelis — a people whom the Ibos greatly admire.

In little more than two generations, Iboland has produced skilled statesmen, doctors, writers, scholars and millionaire entrepreneurs at a pace and with a determination that can only be described as breath-taking. And they have achieved these advances not from any fallout from British paternalism, but by pulling themselves up by their own bootstraps.

BY contrast, the Hausas of the Northern Region have a centuries-old heritage rooted in the Arab world. Their ruling families are drawn from the Fulani, who can trace their lineage back to the Prophet Mohammed.

Long before the first Portuguese mariners tacked into Lagos Harbor and officially "discovered" Nigeria, Hausa men could read and write in Arabic script; they had their own political kingdoms, their own courts and Koranic schools; Hausa traders, setting forth from Kano, their principal city, plied across the Sahara all the way to Tripoli and Khartoum. Through trade, Northern Nigeria had been in contact with the Middle East and the Mediterranean for more than 10 centuries.

When Britain's Lord Lugard subdued the Northern Region at the turn of the century, he was so impressed with the orderliness of the Hausa-Fulani political structure that he decided to leave it alone, letting the local emirs continue to run things through a system of "indirect rule." Lugard also agreed to the Hausa demands that Christian missionaries—with their textbooks as well as their Bibles—should be kept out of Moslem territory.

The Islamic North was protected from alien religious ideas. But it was also left to stagnate while mission education in the rest of Nigeria produced the country's future lawyers, doctors, technicians and civil servants.

In many ways, the Yoruba tribesmen of the Western Region were the first to capitalize on the European presence. They entered the colonial period with a highly developed political and cultural past of their own. (Much was exported to the New World; the best of the African strains in Latin-American music and art stem from Yoruba culture.) The British were quick to recognize their talents, and by 1900 nearly all the Nigerians in the lower ranks of the civil service were Yorubas. So, too, were most of the new lawyers, doctors and businessmen.

MEANWHILE, the Ibos were coming up fast. They took to Christianity with an ease and ardor that amazed the first missionaries who managed to penetrate the swamps of the Niger delta only around the turn of this century. Time after time, the religious pioneer discovered that he was welcome—as long as he promised to build a mission school as well as a church.

No one knows where the Ibos originated. Their society has become a source of endless fascination to anthropologists, especially the former British missionary G. T. Basden. He suspects they may have migrated from the Nile Valley centuries ago. As evidence, he cites the fact that there are not only Ibos who are jet black, but others with light-colored and reddish-tinted skin as well. Furthermore, the faces on their masks and carvings are not Negroid, but Eastern.

Basden has also noted similarities between Hebrew and Ibo speech patterns. And he feels he has found corresponding practices related to capital punishment, land tenure, childbirth, circumcision, stealing, witchery, trial by ordeal and the remission of sin.

In contrast to some African tribes, such as the Yorubas, the precolonial Ibos seem to have had no political cohesion. Theirs was a region of small clans, bound to no hierarchy beyond the legal authority of village elders. Status and power were not inherited, but acquired by deeds. Significantly, the village elder was always elected. Upon his death, his son had no better chance to succeed him than the boy next door.

AS soon as roads and rail lines were built, linking the Eastern Region with the rest of the colony, the inquisitive Ibo left his homeland in search of new opportunity. His own land was vastly overpopulated; there were fewer and fewer job opportunities.

Ibos also went abroad. By 1945, more Ibos were studying in American universities than all other Nigerian tribesmen put together, and the number of Ibos in British institutions was at least equal to the number of Yorubas.

Within the space of only one generation, the Ibo had emerged as an economic as well as a political threat outside his homeland. Yorubas, for example, could no longer command the best jobs in Lagos or in the rapidly expanding civil service.

At the same time, as independence approached, Hausa tribal leaders in the Northern Region suddenly realized the price they had paid for living in an educational vacuum. Clearly, the North had to catch up if it was to compete on the job front in the new federation.

Even before independence, thousands of Southern Nigerians—mostly the mobile and enterprising Ibos—had moved north to fill the jobs in the 20th-century side of the region's economy. Ibos were middlemen in the markets, clerks in the post offices, engine drivers and station masters on the railway. Ibos served in the hotels, ran trucking lines, worked as bank tellers, telegraph operators, garage mechanics, salesmen and accountants for the big European trading firms.

As far as Europeans were concerned, the Ibo influx was all to the good.

"Mind you, I don't necessarily love the Ibo," is the way one English insurance executive in Kano puts it. "But who else is as honest with money, as willing to work

WORSHIP—Hausa tribesmen, who are Moslems, gather for prayer before the mosque in Kano.

long hours? Who else appreciates what it means to plan ahead, and isn't afraid to burn the candle all night studying to advance himself on the job?"

This is a commentary you hear over and over, and it is not exclusively a white man's judgment. Take the view of the South African writer, Ezekiel Mphahlele. In his autobiography, he recalls his days as a grammar-school teacher in predominantly Yoruba Lagos. He writes:

"The complacency of most of the boys struck me forcibly and I became progressively annoyed by it. . . .

"But the small number of Ibo boys in the school were a source of inspiration: critical, self-confident, challenging, generally pushful; they have the guts to challenge authority (even if sometimes obstructionist). They seldom beg for favors, and I admire a man who does not beg for favors."

WHEREVER they went, the Ibos maintained an abiding loyalty to their family, their village, their district, to the Ibo "nation" as a whole. In Lagos, in Kano, in Ibadan, the capital of the West, Ibos banded together in tribal "Progressive Unions." These unions were, in effect, close-knit social cooperatives.

If one Ibo member was found to have stolen from another, for example, he was not reported to the police, but taken before the elected union elders, tried and, if found guilty, punished in private.

Every member paid dues. Special subscriptions — taxes, really — were levied to provide scholarships for the most promising Ibo youngsters. Ibo communalism extended even to buying and selling in the market place. If there were two bars in town, one run by an Ibo and one by a Yoruba, the Ibos would patronize the Ibo bar, even if it were smaller and served less appetizing fare.

As if in some hidden alliance with the Puritan ethic, young Ibo writers, with almost Babbittlike zeal, churned out a whole new literature on how to get ahead by trying. Shrewd Ibo publishers in the bustling market town of Onitsha sold their booklets, for as little as a nickel a copy, at a rate of 100,000 copies a title per year. Some sample titles: "How to Avoid Poverty," "Master of Money," "Determination Is the Key to Success."

Ibo consciousness was carefully cultivated by tribal leaders, especially Nnamdi Azikiwe, who is perhaps West Africa's most prominent nationalist and who, in 1949, declared: "It would appear that the God of Africa has specially created the Ibo nation to lead the children of Africa from the bondage of the ages. . . . The martial prowess of the Ibo nation at all stages of human history has enabled them not only to conquer others but also to adapt themselves to the role of the preserver. The Ibo nation cannot shirk its responsibility. . . ."

Such statements, however pleasing to Ibo ears, were badly designed to encourage intertribal fellowship. Not surprisingly, the Ibos came to be widely regarded as too "combative," too "clannish," too "pushy" for their own good.

THE feeling grew particularly acute in the Northern Region. Long before the current crisis, it flared into violence in the Kano riots of

CONTACT—A Yoruba tribeswoman and a Hausa mother and son walk together to a UNICEF-sponsored class in a North Nigerian town. Such intertribal association is rare.

1953. Months later, British authorities produced a White Paper analyzing the reasons for the riots, and what could be done to avoid their repetition.

The White Paper included scores of letters and transcripts of interviews with the Hausa man-in-the-street, all of them complaining of crude discrimination by Ibos in offices, at ticket counters, even in hospitals. Ibos, they testified, had no respect. Ibos laughed at the Prophet. Ibos considered every Hausa not only stupid but inferior if he could not speak English.

The depth of Hausa resentment was enshrined in this letter to the editor of a local Arabic-language weekly: "We were conquered by the white man, but he did not enslave us, and now those who did not conquer us will enslave us. Editor, lead us. God, show us the way."

The authors of that 1953 White Paper concluded: "Given statesmanship, there can be a future for this country. Given an acceleration of the present trends, there can be none."

Acceleration, of the worst sort, happened. One might have hoped that there would have been a third force among the tribal groups. What is particularly discouraging to the foreign observer here is the failure, for the most part, of even the educated and socially established Yoruba élite to speak up and transcend tribal isolationism.

A few have: Wole Soyinka, the Yoruba writer who is Nigeria's foremost playwright, wrote with compassion about the traumatic effects of the September slaughter on the Ibos in the North, and argued that only a massive outpouring of national remorse could rescue the country from moral and political bankruptcy. But for the most part, Yorubas reacted to the Ibo bloodletting with ostrichlike withdrawal.

Last November, only a few weeks after the pogrom, I had lunch with a Yoruba diplomat, just returned from abroad. He was breezily optimistic.

"We Nigerians have a history of going to the brink and then compromising," he assured me. "What's needed," he went on, picking at his shrimp cocktail, "is for everyone to let bygones be bygones."

If he had been to Kano or Jos or Kaduna the week of the pogrom, his attitude might have been different. But one doubted it. He listened impassively to my unsolicited description of the aftermath: the bullet holes in the bedspreads, in children's cribs. The bayoneted Bible on the floor of the Baptist church. The smashed typewriters and blood-stained newspapers on the floor of the O.K. Jazz Stationery Store.

Kano's *Sabon Gari*, the "strangers' quarter" where the Ibos had lived, was like a ghost town, I recalled. When the shutters of empty houses banged shut in a sudden gust of wind, even stray dogs crouched trembling in fear. The sound was like rifle shots, and the vultures took flight.

But my diplomat seemed as unconcerned as the waiter—a member of the small Ijaw tribe of the Mid-Western Region—who summed up the slaughter of the Ibos: "It was too bad, what happened, but then—well—they really had it coming to them."

WHOEVER is to blame for Nigeria's break-up, it could be said that, from the very start, Nigeria never really had a chance to make it. Perhaps Nigeria always should have been recognized for what it was when the British first arrived: at least three countries, and perhaps four, five or six more, instead of one.

Clearly, what has happened in Nigeria is not necessarily the last time that Africans will seek to realign themselves along more truly ethnic lines. The number of other states burdened with tribal imbalances, or encompassing tribes split by European-drawn frontiers, suggests the magnitude of the problem. The list includes Ethiopia, Somalia, Kenya and the Sudan, Ruanda and Burundi, Cameroun and Dahomey, Uganda, Zambia, Mauretania and Togoland.

The West may recoil from the prospect, but Africa may be in for an extended period of more violence and uncertainty as its new nations sort themselves out. Yet to ignore the problem and wish it would go away, and to expect Africans to conform to nation-making decisions they were never consulted on, is to deny postcolonial Africa its right to risk failure as well as success in reshaping its own destiny. ■

Nigerians Report Invasion of the East,

By ALFRED FRIENDLY Jr.
Special to The New York Times

LAGOS, Nigeria, July 7 — Troops of Nigeria's federal military Government have begun their long-anticipated attack on the secessionist regime of the Eastern Region, the Nigerian radio announced here tonight.

According to the broadcast, the clash began early yesterday morning when Government positions were fired on along the northern border between Nigeria and the Eastern Region, which has declared its independence as the Republic of Biafra.

Federal troops were said to have returned the fire and to have received orders from Maj. Gen. Yakubu Gowon "to penetrate into the east central state and capture Ojukwu and his rebel gang."

The Nigerian radio announced tonight that federal troops had taken two towns in the Eastern Region. Obolo, which is 10 miles from Nsukka on the main road to the regional capital at Enugu, 45 miles away, and Obudu, at the opposite, eastern end of the northern border in Ogoja state.

The official announcement said that federal troops "had inflicted heavy casualties on the rebel forces."

Lieut. Col. Odumegwu Ojukwu, who was dismissed last week from the federal army, was military governor of the Eastern Region when he declared it independent on May 30.

Before taking military action against the secessionists, the Government had imposed an extensive economic blockade on the East, extending it earlier this week to prohibit the export of oil from the region.

The Nigerian broadcast came some four hours after the Biafra radio said that Eastern forces had repulsed a four-pronged federal attack that it said began yesterday. The rebel broadcast said that Eastern troops had pushed back federal forces near Nsukka and had crossed into federal territory north of the border.

While federal spokesmen had long been saying that the military action was inevitable, it had appeared to many observers here that the Government was hoping that its tightening blockade on the East would produce enough internal unrest in the area to topple the secessionists.

The blockade, which was imposed by the Nigerian Navy even before the formal announcement of secession, was reported to have been extremely effective in cutting off the importation of industrial materials and consumer goods by the East.

Until July 4, the federal Government had been allowing oil tankers to enter the Bonny terminal at Port Harcourt to load oil, which is produced in the region at the rate of more than half a million barrels a day.

The Government prohibited this activity after the combined Royal Dutch-Shell and British Petroleum Company, which produces 85 per cent of Nigeria's oil exports, offered to make a token deposit of a quarter of a million pounds to the Ojukwu regime on its quarterly royalty payments.

Colonel Ojukwu had demanded that the full royalty payment, estimated at close to £7-million, be made to him by July 1 instead of to the federal Government. He threatened to seize oil installations in the East, including the refinery at Port Harcourt, if the payment was not made.

The secession of the Eastern Region with 12 million of Nigeria's estimated population of 55 million came after a long period of tension between the Ibo population centered in the East and the dominant ethnic groups in the West and North, Yorubas and Hausas respectively.

Some 20,000 Ibos living in the North were killed there last October in bloody clashes at Kano and along the railroad line that the Ibos used to flee South and East.

Efforts to negotiate a settlement that would satisfy the Easterner's demands for security through autonomy and yet retain Nigeria's federal structure broke down in May. On May 27, General Gowon announced the formation of 12 states in the country out of what had been four regions, creating three states in the East.

The boundaries of the two southern states, Rivers and Southeast, were drawn to give local minority groups their own protection against domination by the heavily Ibo East Central state.

At the time of the announcement, the Eastern Region Consultative Assembly had already given Colonel Ojukwu power to declare the East independent at any time. He did so on May 30.

Both sides have accused the other of employing white mercenaries and the Biafra radio broadcast said that the federal offensive had been led by them.

July 8, 1967

NIGERIAN REGION SEIZED BY REBELS

By ALFRED FRIENDLY Jr.
Special to The New York Times

LAGOS, Nigeria, Aug. 10 — The federal Government suffered a major reverse when mutinous Nigerian Army troops, and soldiers from the secessionist Eastern Region seized control of the Midwestern Region yesterday.

Confirming the loss of major towns throughout the 15,000-square-mile region, an official announcement said today that rebel troops had "engaged in confiscating food and other commodities" for transport back to the east.

Spokesmen also implied at a midday briefing that the secessionist forces, which made a lightning dash across the Midwest yesterday and captured its capital, Benin, were more likely to be a raiding party than a permanent occupation force.

Two Czechoslovak-made jet trainer aircraft equipped to carry rockets and bombs arrived in Nigeria yesterday.

Federal spokesmen declined to comment on the report from a reliable witness who saw both planes at the Kaduna airfield or to comment on informed speculation that two to four more such aircraft were scheduled for delivery to the Nigerian Air Force soon.

The official announcement about the rebel take-over in the Midwest said it had been made possible by the deception of officers of Ibo origin in the garrisons there. These officers, it was said, told others that the federal military Government was planning to use them in an attack on the east, the home of most of Nigeria's Ibos, who number about six million.

Of the 2.5 million inhabitants estimated in the Midwest, 500,000 to 750,000 speak the Ibo language, and all the colonels and lieutenant colonels in the federal garrison there are Ibos.

The federal regime's statement about the Midwestern troops said that "under this guise they deployed troops to their advantage and later proceeded to disarm those loyal to the federal Government." A spokesman added that except in Benin, federal garrisons throughout the Midwest usually consisted of only a dozen soldiers or fewer.

He said the number of federal soldiers in the area at the time of the take-over was fewer than 1,000. In Benin, he said, reports indicated that loyal troops resisted the take-over until about 4 P.M. yesterday.

Restoration Sought

The official statement concluded by expressing the Government's determination "to restore the situation in the Midwest to normal within the shortest possible time consistent with minimum damage to life and property in the area."

Spokesmen said they had no reports yet that troop columns sent yesterday from the Western Region and from Lagos, 130 miles west of Benin, had made contact with the rebels or mutineers.

Spokesmen said Lagos had been cut off from all communications to the Midwest since 10 A.M. yesterday, but that early reports of the action there indicated Eastern forces had crossed into the region "in small numbers."

If many troops have moved into the Midwest, they added, resistance to federal forces along the East's northern border will be weakened and "the push to Enugu will be much easier now."

Enugu is the capital of the secessionist East, which declared independence as the Republic of Biafra on May 30.

The hostility between the regions centers on the federalism-regionalism issue, but Ibo anger over slaughter of many of their tribe by Northerners last year added to the bitterness that led to the secession.

No Shift Indicated

The East's gains in the Midwest brought no signs that the federal troops would be diverted from battle sectors in the Nsukka area of the East, or from the Bonny area, which the federal forces captured July 26, according to well-informed sources in Lagos.

While conceding a major psychological defeat, federal officials appear to regard the loss of the Midwest as a minor military irritant that will not deflect them from their main drive to cut off the East's access to the sea and, eventually, to capture Enugu.

There was no repetition of the rebel bombing raid on Lagos yesterday. The attack resulted in the slight wounding of four persons, the police said, and in setting one house afire. It caused no damage to oil storage or harbor installations, which were the apparent targets of the crude explosives.

The first of about 500 foreign nationals being evacuated from the Midwest by ship arrived in Lagos today. Three other ships with refugees are to arrive tomorrow.

August 11, 1967

poster circulated in Biafra showing three Ibos—the dominant tribe in the East—at left, and an enemy Hausa from the North, at right. The poster reflects the intense tribal rivalry felt by both sides.

October 27, 1967

Hunger as a Political Weapon in Nigeria

LONDON—The starving Ibo tribesmen of Biafra are the pawns in a political and military chess game being played between the leaders of the Federal Republic of Nigeria and the secessionist state of Biafra.

The federal aim is to eliminate Biafra; the Biafrans' is independence or some form of far-reaching autonomy.

The federals' method is basically military. They have nearly won the war militarily, in the opinion of most outside observers. But they are finding it difficult to make the final kill in the deep Ibo heartland, whose population is 13 million. They are superior by far in numbers and material but the terrain now is difficult and favors defense. Guerrillas lurk in the undergrowth and along the banks of a thousand streams that criss-cross the jungle.

Isolated

The federal forces have surrounded a densely populated area in Ibo territory which normally depends on meat from the north. War and the fear of war have greatly reduced the production of local farms. Transportation from the north is cut off.

As a result, the Ibo people are suffering from a rapidly progressive form of malnutrition, caused by protein deficiency, combined in many cases with absolute starvation.

In the camps into which hundreds of thousands of Ibo refugees from other parts of Nigeria are crowded, missionaries and others from outside the country see to the maintenance of a certain level of sanitation and distribute such relief supplies as are available. In the villages where the local population looks after itself conditions are usually worse.

This, then is the federal Government's weapon in its attempt to break the last Biafran resistance. The issue is also a weapon for Biafran leaders who hope to save what can be saved of their position by political means. Their calculation is that the horror of mass starvation—13,000 dying daily now, according to the International Red Cross, perhaps two million dead within two months—will force the world to force the Nigerian federal Government to agree to a cease-fire and a settlement.

To save the greatest possible number from death by starvation and acute malnutrition, the immediate need is for an airlift from Fernando Po Island off the African coast, where Oxfam, a nongovernmental, nonsectarian British relief organization, has already accumulated the necessary supplies, with more on the way. The organization took an option last week on the charter of a Hercules aircraft which, Oxfam officials calculate, could fly in 100 tons of food a day to an airstrip that the Biafrans have set aside for the purpose. The plane would be supervised by the International Red Cross and would be painted with I.R.C. insignia.

In the long run, Oxfam officials emphasize, an overland relief program is essential. But it will take months to organize even if the Biafrans agree to it.

This question of airlift versus overland relief is the technical question about which Biafrans and the federal Government are arguing this weekend through the intermediary of British officials and the head of the Commonwealth Secretariat, Arnold Smith. The federals are offering to open a land corridor with a local cease-fire for movement of supplies. The Biafrans are objecting that this is not only too slow but is unacceptable because Biafrans fear food coming through federal lines would be poisoned.

Proudly the Biafrans are maintaining that they would rather die than touch food from Lagos. They have also declared they would not accept any part of the £250,000 which the British Government has allocated for relief in Nigeria. Their position is that it would be dishonorable to accept relief from a government that is at the same time arming their enemies.

The British are deeply embarrassed by the suggestion of their responsibility for this frightful human tragedy. It has been British policy to deliver arms to the legitimate Government in Lagos except for aircraft and bombs—a distinction that the Commonwealth Office hopes would exculpate Britain from some of the blame for the suffering caused.

Life and Death Role

The Federal Government's offer to let relief cargoes pass through its territory by land would put it in the position of controlling life-and-death supplies for the rebel territory. This undoubtedly accounts for the Biafrans' initial refusal to accept overland relief through federal territory more than the Biafran claim that the food might be poisoned. The latter fear may seem irrational at a distance, but it is understandable in the poisoned atmosphere of the civil war in Nigeria.

The effort to get political advantage out of the food crisis was made even more obvious last Friday, when Lagos said it would shoot down any planes flying to rebel areas, whether they were carrying relief packages or not. It is thus clear that the relief of starvation has become another aspect of the Biafran struggle to obtain independent recognition through contact with the outside world and the federal Government's determination to prevent the same.

—DANA ADAMS SCHMIDT

July 7, 1968

Anger in Africa Over West's Help to Biafra Rises

By LAWRENCE FELLOWS
Special to The New York Times

LAGOS, Nigeria, Sept. 29 — "We don't want your custard and your wheat," a young Nigerian officer told a Swiss relief worker the other day. "The people here need fish and garri. We can give them that, so why don't you find some starving White people to feed?"

Accusations like this are heard more and more frequently in Nigeria now that Biafra's attempt to secede from the Nigerian federation, after nearly 15 months of fighting, appears on the edge of collapse.

In fact, relief teams have been distributing fish and garri too. Some of it has even been confiscated by army commanders making their own distributions of food.

Feeling Similar Elsewhere

But the accusations reflect deep resentment that is gathering not only in Nigeria but elsewhere in Africa against white people of Europe and the United States who have rallied to the support of Biafra, even though most of the support has been sent for humanitarian grounds.

In the last few days in Nairobi, Addis Ababa, Khartoum and Lagos, political leaders seem to express similar feelings when the discussion turns to the war in Nigeria — that outsiders are meddling again in Africa's affairs.

There is evidence that the outpouring of sympathy in the West did not do Biafra any good, especially in Africa, in its quest for support for the cause of independence.

Algiers Parley Backed Lagos

At the summit meeting of the organization of African Unity in Algiers this month, the Nigerian Government won a resounding vote of confidence and Biafra was left almost without friends or hope of meaningful support in Africa.

Odumegwo Ojukwu, Biafra's leader, is usually given credit abroad for one ringing diplomatic victory after another and for a masterful exercise in propaganda that evoked the deep sympathy of people around half the world for Biafrans—trapped and encircled by the advancing Nigerian Army and starving by the thousands.

But in much of Africa it is not viewed that way at all, as relief workers who have been pouring into Biafra and the rest of Nigeria have had to learn to their astonishment and dismay.

Starvation and the other forms of human distress do not evoke quite the same emotions here as they do in richer, happier places. Around the continent there are people living on the margin of starvation from the time they are born until they die. And death usually comes to an African sooner than it does to people in most places.

In many parts of the continent a family considers itself fortunate if half the children survive hunger and disease. In many places it is the smallest children who are allowed to slip away to starvation first when food is short.

Africans love their children as much as any others do, but death is commonplace, and if someone in the family has to go without eating, the smallest children represent the smallest investment in food and clothes already paid.

True in Congo and Sudan

This is true in the Congo and in the southern Sudan, where human devastation has been wider and longer-lasting than in Biafra.

It happened that way last year in southeastern Tanzania, when floods and then drought left people without food. It happened in the Machakos district in Kenya about two years ago, when corn withered on the ground.

Three years ago in Rhodesia, when drought struck a remote region, a worker for Save the Children was astonished to discover that he could not give away food designated exclusively for the children.

"If you want a tree to grow, you do not water the leaves, you water the roots," he was told.

Red Cross teams working among starving people emerging from the bush behind advancing Nigerian troops are accustomed now to seeing people eating on one side of the road and starving on the other side. Usually some obscure tribtribal animosity keeps the healthy ones from giving away their surplus food.

Within the shrinking perimeter of Biafra, where starvation may be causing thousands of deaths a day, Red Cross workers have been buying food in abundantly supplied markets and giving it to the desperately hungry.

In fact, the Red Cross has spent only about $15,000 buying food in Biafra and has spent much more—about $650,000—buying food in other parts of Nigeria to feed dislocated and hungry people now outside the fighting area.

Arguments Increasing

Relief workers are on all sides of the fighting area now, and they are getting deeper and deeper into arguments with Nigerians over matters of access and transport. There is resentment over the unspoken assumption that white people must still do for blacks what they are unable or unwilling to do for themselves.

All evidence so far suggests Mr. Ojukwu's campaign, though it has won Biafra sympathy in the Western world, has lost Biafra's cause a great deal of sympathy among African politicians. While Mr. Ojukwu was appealing to the humanitarian instincts of Americans and Europeans, Nigeria's ambassadors in Africa were quietly warning of the dangers that could befall the whole continent if one seccession were seen to work, and if political pressures from abroad helped ease Biafra out of the Nigerian fold.

BIAFRANS CAPITULATE TO NIGERIA, ENDING 30-MONTH-LONG CIVIL WAR; U.S. INCREASES GRANT FOR RELIEF

ARMISTICE SOUGHT

Gowon Accepts Offer —Toll of Dead May Be Two Million

By LAWRENCE FELLOWS

Special to The New York Times

LAGOS, Nigeria, Tuesday, Jan. 13—Biafra, with its last defenses crumbling and its supplies of food and ammunition exhausted, capitulated yesterday to the Nigerian Government.

Brig. Philip Effiong, the Biafran Chief of Staff, who took over the leadership Saturday night when Gen. Odumegwu Ojukwu fled the besieged remnant of the secessionist region, announced on the Biafran radio this afternoon that the attempt at secession had failed.

[Unconfirmed reports from Lusaka, Zambia, said Monday night that General Ojukwu was expected to arrive within the next day. It was understood that Zambia had offered him asylum. Page 15.]

Brigadier Effiong ordered Biafran forces to disengage from battle in an orderly fashion and said that he was sending representatives to Nigerian field commanders to negotiate an armistice.

Gowon Accepts Offer

Immediately after the broadcast Gen. Yakubu Gowon, head of the Nigerian Government, issued directives to troops in the field to provide full protection of surrendering Biafran forces and to shoot only if they encountered resistance.

He ordered that particular care be taken to insure the safety of civilians in the liberated areas. To relieve some of the fears of soldiers and civilians in the vanquished republic, he ordered civilian policemen to accompany troops.

At midnight, more than seven hours after the offer of surrender, General Gowon made a broadcast to the nation stating that he accepted in "good faith" the surrender offer.

"We have arrived at one of the greatest moments in the history of our nation," he said, "a great moment of victory for unity and national reconciliation.

"Our objective was to crush the rebellion, to maintain the territorial integrity of our nation, to assert the ability of the black man to build a strong, progressive and prosperous modern nation." he said.

News Spread Slowly

The news of the capitulation had taken a while to spread into the streets of Lagos. There was little obvious excitement. Not everyone has a radio good enough to receive the frail Biafran transmitter, but by last night the news was moving rapidly through Lagos.

A crowd gathered in Independence Square, just passing the news to all who came by. The Daily Times published an extra edition with the huge headline "Rebels Surrender."

The brutal, bewildering civil war in Nigeria had lasted just over 30 months. There may never be an accurate reckoning, but it probably cost Nigeria more than a billion dollars and something like two million lives.

It has been estimated that at most there are four million people left in what remains of Biafra. It had a population of 14 million when General Ojukwu, then a lieutenant colonel, raised the flag of independence on May 30, 1967. On July 7 that year it was plunged into this wasting war. Most of the two million dead were lost to starvation. At the very least, 1.5 million will need quick relief now from some measure of starvation.

"I thank the civil population for their steadfastness and courage in the face of overwhelming odds and privation," Brigadier Effiong said in his broadcast. He spoke solemnly, but without faltering, in English. His six-minute message was then rebroadcast by the Biafran radio in four other languages of the country.

Disillusionment Cited

"I am convinced now that a stop must be put to the bloodshed which is going on as a result of the war," he continued. "I am also convinced that the suffering of our people must be brought to an immediate end. Our people are now disillusioned."

He continued: "Those elements of the old government regime who have made negotiation and reconciliation impossible have voluntarily removed themselves from our midst."

The reference was to General Ojukwu and some of the other leaders of the secession movement. It was still not known in Lagos where General Ojukwu, his closest followers and his family had gone.

The Nigerian Government said yesterday that it had certain knowledge that General Ojukwu and 19 others, including him immediate family, three tons of luggage and a Mercedes Benz were flown out of Biafra Saturday night in a Super Constellation—"an aircraft supplied by a certain foreign government supposedly for relief flights."

Whether the government's statement was true was an unimportant matter before the day was out. It was made long before 4:40 P.M., when Brigadier Effiong spoke.

For two days the Biafran radio had broadcast nothing but music. Some indication had been awaited from the Biafrans of the effect on them of the recapture of Owerri by Nigerian troops and of the destruction by artillery fire of the airstrip at Uli, the only significant means they had of receiving shipments of food and ammunition.

Last night the Government announced that its forces had captured Uli airstrip and the town of Orlu, the home of General Ojukwu in Ibo the heartland.

Just before Brigadier Effiong spoke, the radio played Beethoven's Fifth Symphony, a symbol of the resistance to Hitler in the dark, early days of World War II. It caused more than one heart to sink among the Nigerians who had listened to the Biafran radio faithfully all day.

"I urge on General Gowon in the name of humanity to order his troops to pause while an armistice is negotiated," the Brigadier said.

"We have always believed that our differences with Nigeria could be settled by peaceful negotiations," he said. "A delegation of our people is therefore ready to meet representatives of the Nigerian federal Government anywhere to negotiate a peace settlement on the basis of O.A.U. resolutions."

By accepting the resolutions of the Organization of African Unity, the Biafran leader showed the completeness of his surrender. The organization has never accepted Biafra's secession, and was against any settlement of the civil war that would violate the integrity of the Nigerian nation.

Resistance Ruled Out

Brigadier Effiong also said there was no thought of a Biafran government-in-exile, and came out strongly against further resistance either passively or in some form of guerrilla warfare.

"Any question of a government in exile is repudiated by our people," he said.

"The whole population are hereby advised to remain calm

and to cooperate with the armed forces and police in the maintenance of law and order," he said. We should remain in our homes and stop the mass movements which have increased suffering and loss of life."

How swift would be the effect of the orders General Gowon has sent to his troops in the field could not be ascertained immediately. Discipline is not always ideal in Nigeria's army, which grew from a force of 8,000 men at the time of Biafra's secession to 150,000 men now. Communications are not always easy in a country four times the size of Britain, more populous than any in Africa and more turbulent than most, even in peacetime.

The Nigerians were already moving relief supplies of food staples to the edge of the battlefronts yesterday. A shipment of 500 tons of rice, beans and fish—staples in this part of the world—was sent to the Southeastern State for distribution to refugees slipping through the lines, most without knowledge of the capitulation.

Another shipment of 18 tons of food went to the Rivers State, which Biafra claimed but which was lost early in the war.

Relief Shipments Ready

More shipments of food were being organized by the Nigerian Government to be placed at depots close to the shrunken borders of Biafra for quick distribution.

The Americans, British and others are standing by with enormous means of transport and food aid for the moment the Nigerian Government gives the word.

No one really knows the dimensions of the problem. Not even the population of Biafra is known, nor can it be known, for the borders are uncertain and shifting always in the vagaries of warfare in these damp West African forests.

In his broadcast Brigadier Effiong said:

"On behalf of our people I thank those foreign governments and friends who have steadfastly given us support in our cause. We shall continue to count on their continued help and counsel.

"I also thank His Holiness the Pope, Joint Church Aid and other relief organizations for the help they have given for the relief of suffering and starvation."

He concluded his broadcast by saying, "I appeal to all governments to give urgent help for relief and to prevail on the Federal Government to order their troops to stop all military operations."

January 13, 1970

Biafrans Returning Home to Uncertainties

By WILLIAM BORDERS
Special to The New York Times

OWERRI, Nigeria, Jan. 19—The hard-pressed people of Biafra finally have peace—but little else.

Still starving by the thousands in their overrun territory, they are returning to their homes and beginning to be fed again.

But the future is unclear.

"The only thing anyone got from this war was hunger," said a tired old man in a dusty white robe as he gestured at the aimlessly milling crowds that filled Owerri's square this morning.

[A dispatch from Lagos, the Nigerian capital, said Wednesday that 80 foreign journalists, including Mr. Borders, were being detained by Nigerian military authorities in Port Harcourt after having visited Owerri.]

Biafra's last capital, the town whose fall a week ago signaled the ultimate end of the 30-month-old rebellion, Owerri is crowded now with refugees, most of them hungry, some dying.

Naked children with bellies swollen from starvation sit at the side of the road and stare, restless, as their mothers tear up pumpkin leaves to put into soup.

A few merchants are selling Italian tomato juice, Spanish sardines, or beer. But they now accept only Nigerian money, and people have nothing but worthless Biafran currency. Red Cross food is beginning to reach the towns of what was Biafra, but slowly.

In the damp, dense forests outside the towns, the suffering is thought to be much worse, although no one knows.

So far as can be ascertained from a tour of the area seized by Nigerian troops in their final advance, there has been no pattern of purposeful starvation by the conquerors in the week since the end of the war, although bureaucratic snags in their emergency relief effort enrage many of the doctors and nurses involved.

Nor were there any signs of massacre or genocide as Gen. Odumegwu Okukwu, the Biafran leader, had said there would be, although the proud occupying troops can be seen subjecting civilians to routine bullying brutalities.

Swaggering in their camouflage uniforms the soldiers push the people around and swing their Russian-made rifles carelessly. Reports of rape and looting are not uncommon.

"I had a wrist watch when the war ended; it was all I had," said a man who was walking barefoot down a road near Orlu, bound for the port city of Calabar 150 miles away. He added: "They took it, for now I have nothing."

The man lived in Calabar when the war began in July, 1967, and then fled farther and farther inland as the Biafran enclave shrank. Now, like hundreds of thousands of others, he was going home.

Some carried baskets and suitcases, or even chairs and tables on their heads as they made their way up and down the narrow roads. Since the army has taken most of the vehicles in the area, walking is the only way to get around.

In its final days of secession, the Republic of Biafra had shrunk to an area half the size of Connecticut, with a population of perhaps three million or four million. As the Nigerian troops took the last few towns in the heart of the traditional Ibo land, many of the people fled in panic to the countryside into the big brush that Africans call "the bush." Only now are they coming back.

Most of the Biafrans, though certainly not all, were of the Ibo tribe, a proud people that still feels itself discriminated against and even hated in much of the rest of Nigeria.

They declared complete political independence. Toward the end they were talking of negotiating for just a measure of autonomy. Now, having been heavily defeated, they are to get nothing from the fight in which it is estimated that as many as two million lives were lost.

"It was bad, but it will happen again," said a well-educated 30-year-old man named Joseph who had introduced himself last night as "a Biafran." "The Ibo men will not tolerate being in one Nigeria with the others."

Joseph was captured near Aba in the final weeks of the baffling civil war. He became not a prisoner but a house guest of the officer who captured him because they had gone to school together, a tie apparently stronger than the antipathy for which the war was fought.

"Him, I liked," Joseph said of his host. "But most of them the Ibos cannot live with. They are jealous of us and they treat us as second-class. This will not work, and there will be another war. You will see."

But other Ibos, questioned as they waited for food to come to the crowded, dirty refugee camps that have suddenly dotted their land, said, "Never again, never again."

Despite what are generally considered to be the sincere good intentions of the Nigerian Government, food was just beginning to reach any of these people, even along the main roads, a full week after the war ended.

In the opinion of a number of relief workers, both foreign and Nigerian, the delay arises at least in part from the Government's insistence that all relief be channeled through the Nigerian Red Cross and from its ban on relief workers and organizations that were in the area when it was Biafra.

"I am trying to do all I can," said a European nurse who was feeding a meal to starving children near Owerri. "But I only got here three days ago. I certainly don't know anything about these people.

Associated Press

BIAFRAN CHILDREN: Ibo youngsters, refugees from the former secessionist state, at a maternity home in Port Harcourt, Nigeria, yesterday. They were suffering from dysentery, with their stomachs swollen from malnutrition.

Meanwhile, more than two dozen Irish priests who have worked in Biafra and who knew its people and its problems intimately, were being held in Port Harcourt, 70 miles away, pending deportation.

To the occupying Nigerians, it is logical that foreigners who have helped the enemy should not be allowed to continue their work after the end of the war. Furthermore, stung by criticism from abroad, the Nigerians are eager to show the world that they can do the job themselves.

But an exasperated European nurse said, "Another factor in the whole thing is just that they don't care very much if an Ibo dies."

Insisting on anonymity, some doctors here complain that the insistence on Nigerian direction of the relief effort is badly snarling it because it tends to bog down in Government bureaucracy.

At a hospital at Port Harcourt, where 550 Ibo children were taken last week to be nursed back from the brink of death, a British doctor exploded in indignation:

"On Saturday, we couldn't get drugs, not because they weren't there, but because the pharmacy had closed at 2 o'clock on Saturday! On Sunday it was closed all day, just because that's the way it always is!

"We have forms to fill out and officials to check with and then just at the last minute we find the man with the key to what you want has gone home to lunch. I tell you, it's the bloody end!"

Sitting lethargically around the young doctor, whose regular job is with an oil company in Port Harcourt, were dozens of his patients, small children with nearly no flesh on their bony bodies and sagging skin that gives them an oddly aged appearance.

This hospital, like most of the others, finally has food, though; most of the children who were beyond saving have already died. The others, the doctor said, will live and ultimately, he hopes, be sent back to their own villages.

At the Uli air strip, which served as Biafra's lifeline with the world, a man sat in the shade this afternoon, sipping palm wine as he talked of the war.

"We Ibo men are proud," he said. "Maybe that was wrong."

"We thought we were right and I still think we were," he continued, squinting into the hazy sunlight, stroking a beard caked with red clay dust. "But I don't know; if we did not gain anything by the war, why then, I wonder what its purpose was."

OWERRI, Jan. 21 (Reuters)—At the Uli airstrip, at which 280 tons of relief food arrived each day before Biafra's surrender, there is little but desolation. A wrecked DC-6 that overshot the runway almost blocks the approach road.

Aside from two small craters, the wide, 1½-mile runway appears in perfect condition, and C-130 aircraft could land here with ease. But the landing lights have been pulled out and destroyed.

Scores of women with babies on their backs and children at their side, stood waiting outside the barbed wire fence of the Red Cross compound here today while sacks of cornmeal were unloaded from a truck.

Four little girls carrying clay bowls waited under the truck's tailgate, frantically gathering the grains of cornmeal that filtered through.

Suddenly, a sack burst and dozens of people clambered or fell over the barbed-wire fence. Babies went flying as about 40 women and children fought and rolled on the ground, scrambling for the cornmeal.

The observer team from four nations—Sweden, Canada, Poland and Britain—invited by Nigeria during the war to report on charges of atrocities, was visiting Orlu, the last secessionist town to fall.

Asked about widespread charges of rape and looting by Nigerian soldiers, Brig. Gen. John Drewry of Canada said he did not consider it serious.

He said 10 cases of rape at the same time and at the same spot might be worth investigating. But, aside from that, he said, rape was something that sometimes happened in war.

Several soldiers tried to abduct a young wife in view of several foreign correspondents in Owerri today.

Col. Ipola Akinrinade, the commandant of Owerri, said, "I don't think it is true there has been general looting and raping. In every war, you will find odd soldiers who behave this way."

January 22, 1970

In a Former Biafran Town, Palm Wine Flows Again

By WILLIAM BORDERS

Special to The New York Times

IFAKALA, Nigeria, Aug.12—The shabby infirmary that houses the sickest people in this Ibo bush town has fewer patients now than it has had in years, and most of Ifakala's young army veterans have left their hiding places to come back home.

The palm wine is flowing again. And as the town elders pull their grass mats together into a circle, the talk is not only of their bitter past, but also, increasingly, of a brighter future.

Like hundreds of other towns and villages in the land that used to call itself Biafra, Ifakala is resuming the routine and appearance of the days before it was engulfed by Nigeria's bloody civil war. But it is still far from what its residents consider normal.

"Surely it will be years—perhaps after I am dead—before Ifakala knows again the days it used to know," said a bare-chested old man who was digging a water hole in the hard red earth outside his hut.

'None Too Good'

But the degree of recovery that places like Ifakala have seen in the seven months since Government troops overran the rebel territory surprises some Nigerians.

In most parts of the region, the Government is tapering off its emergency food distributions because the emergency is over, even though hard times continue.

A doctor who is close to the relief operation predicted that by the end of next year the area would be back to normal. But then he added, "Of course, normal for the bush country of West Africa is none too good."

Ifakala, which is in the very heart of Iboland, has a population of perhaps 20,000. But a Westerner strolling along its mud paths would never guess it because the rude houses blend so completely into the bush.

During the 30 months of war, the town sent 1000 men off to the Biafran Army. About 200 of them died, and most of the rest are back now, lounging about restlessly because there are no jobs.

Some of the older men and women of the village murmur darkly that unemployed young veterans, trained in the use of weapons, are responsible for the banditry that has made some of the former Biafran territory's highways hazardous at night.

Girls Face Cloudy Future

Among the others who have come back to Ifakala are the several dozen girls who were taken away last January by conquering federal soldiers. Some of them are pregnant, and all of them face a cloudy future.

"It would be a man of rare courage who would take one of those women for his wife," said Cyril Ahaneku, the son of the village chief. "Most will stay here without marrying."

Mr. Ahaneku has resumed his studies at the University of Nigeria in Nsukka, which is open again. Some of his younger brothers and cousins are back in the bombed-out classrooms of the local schools. But many children here still stay home because their parents have no money to pay the tuition of a few dollars a term.

In a town like this one, wealth is measured in yams, the staple of the Nigerian diet. The men of Ifakala cultivate yams and the women sell them in the towns, such as Owerri, which is seven miles to the south.

This harvest season there are few yams because months ago, when they should have been planted, hungry townspeople ate the seed yams instead.

But some cassava, a potato-like crop, has been harvested, and every day now women pad out of Ifakala carrying loads of it on their heads. They sell it on the nearest paved road, which is two miles away and return with bits of dried fish or a few highly prized shillings.

"None of us had any money six months ago, except for the worthless Biafran currency," said a young man sitting under a palm tree reading a Bible. "Now a few of us have a little, so I guess that is an improvement."

"My two children—we almost lost them in February—have now come back from the hospital," he said. "Have a look at the son." He gestured toward a naked but healthy-looking boy about 5 years of age who sat splashing happily in a puddle left by a violent tropical storm.

A neighbor suddenly appeared out of the thick rain forest that separates Ifakala's earthen compounds from one another, and the two men began talking about the bombs that had fallen here during the war and then about the desperate days that followed the surrender.

"Every person expects the future will be better than the past," one of them concluded, as the other nodded thoughtfully. "We are just barely getting on, but at least now we know we will survive."

August 15, 1970

Oil Fuels the Nigerian Economy

By WILLIAM BORDERS

LAGOS, Nigeria—The oil industry in this West African land is burgeoning, and is becoming a key factor in Nigerian economic growth.

General Yakubu Gowon, the head of state, said a few months ago in reviewing the 11 years since Nigeria became independent from Britain:

"Our country is blessed with all the resources necessary to enable us to remove poverty from our midst in this century, and to join the ranks of developed countries."

Some of the investors and businessmen who swell the population of this sultry capital thought the deadline he set was too hopeful, but many regarded the goal, at least, as realistic. As one of them explained simply: "The reason is oil."

In the two years since her bloody civil war ended, Nigeria has become one of the top 10 oil producers in the world, and this industry is expected to yield the Government revenue of close to $1-billion in 1972.

Every day, 1,700,000 barrels of oil are pumped out of the rich green wetlands of eastern Nigeria, and new fields are being discovered regularly. Among the major companies taking part in the exploration are Shell, British Petroleum, Gulf and Mobil.

One oil economist, riffling through a stack of charts and projections, said: "You just run out of adjectives to describe how good the future looks."

Low in Sulphur

He was optimistic not only because Nigeria, on Africa's west coast, is close to world markets, but also because the oil here, being particularly low in sulphur, meets the requirements of American buyers increasingly conscious of pollution.

Largely because of the oil, Nigeria's foreign exchange reserves have increased to more than $300-million, and the Government has recently made sharp reductions in the backlog of exchange releases to overseas suppliers.

The Government has also balanced its budget for the first time in years, even though it expects to be spending several hundred million dollars extra this year in the first stage of a four-year development plan.

The four-year plan, a broad shopping list of postwar improvements in agriculture, roads, education and health facilities, is just getting under way, one year after it was introduced. The delay was apparently caused more by the relaxed pace of the tropics than by any lack of money.

A varied land twice the size of California, Nigeria has problems to match her sudden new wealth. The population of more than 55 million—the largest in Africa—yields political strength and provides a ready consumer market.

But it also stands as a measure of the educational needs, in a country where no more than one man in four can read, and of the health needs, in a country where even the most rudimentary medical care is rare.

One direct way the Government is trying to spread the wealth is by its increasing insistence on "Nigerianization," the replacement of foreign workers by Nigerians, although most large companies are still run by white foreigners.

In the last year, the Government also set new requirements for at least partial Nigerian ownership of many small businesses, although some foreign investors are expressing doubt about the local availability of private investment capital.

Draws Businessmen

But businessmen continue to flock to Nigeria, despite such discouragements. A visiting European manufacturer of small hardware, perspiring through an exhausting amount of red tape at the Lagos airport, explained why:

"I wasn't going to do anything in this country, because there's so much corruption, and it's all such a hassle Then I did some figuring. It will take just seven months for us to gross $1-million. I'll be back."

January 31, 1972

Nigeria Moves Boldly to Gain Control of Her Economy

By THOMAS A. JOHNSON

Special to The New York Times

LAGOS, Nigeria, Aug. 31—Nigeria is making bold moves toward controlling her own economy—for the first time.

Such words as "indigenization" and "Nigerianization" are most often used here to describe these attempts.

While their meanings are not always clearly expressed, many Nigerians are certain that both spell out a future when the greatest share of this nation's potential wealth will go to Nigerians.

They insist that both terms really mean reversing of conditions disclosed by the Federal "Industrial Survey of Nigeria 1968" that showed non-Nigerians controlled 70 per cent of the nation's 625 largest manufacturing establishments.

In addition, the Central Bank of Nigeria's "Economic and Financial Review" for 1967-68 showed that British concerns controlled 56 per cent of Nigeria's fixed foreign assets and that American companies controlled 20 per cent. Nigerians controlled less than 6 per cent.

Nigerian Managers Required

The Nigerian Enterprises Promotion Decree, 1972, issued last February, has been the most public of the "indigenization" moves. It stated that as of March 31, 1974, some 55 categories of business enterprises, services and trades would be operated solely by Nigerians or Africans.

Bank loans are to be provided, the decree stated, to Nigerian businessmen who seek to buy out foreigners now engaged in such enterprises.

Major expatriate-owned concerns not affected by the decree, must "Nigerianize" a percentage of their management positions. In addition, these concerns — many are international, multimillion dollar operations—are required to allow Nigerians to purchase at least a 40 per cent ownership.

"The big difference today is that we are on much happier grounds for bargaining, and it is getting better and better for us," said Dr. J. E. Adetoro, Nigeria's Commissioner of Industries, during a recent interview.

The happier grounds, he added, are directly above great pools of crude oil.

"We have recently struck new oil fields," Mr. Adetoro said, "and it appears we are sitting on a huge lake of oil."

And it is oil—a two-million-barrel-a-day production was predicted by the Standard Bank Review last February—that has lessened this generally underdeveloped nation's need for foreign investments.

At the same time the oil revenues have permitted Nigeria's 62 million citizens to greatly increase their role as consumers.

Writing for the Nigerian Bulletin of Foreign Affairs, a British economics writer, Andrew C. E. Hiton, contended that foreign investors would not quit Nigeria because they "cannot afford to be excluded from a market which, it has been estimated (by Nigeria's Ministry of Development and Reconstruction), will grow at over 10 per cent per annum."

Mr. Adetoro said there had been no lessening of foreign companies' wanting to come into Nigeria, and he reported an expansion of Nigerian trade talks with several nations, including, the United States, Scotland, Italy, Britain, the Soviet Union and China. He said Nigeria did not intend to chase expatriate businessmen out of the country.

Auto Plants Planned

Both Volkswagen, A. G., of West Germany and Peugeot of France have recently contracted to set up assembly plants here, and Nigeria will soon contract with another foreign automobile maker to do the same, Mr. Adetoro said.

The Peugeot contract, made with a nation that supported Biafra during the Civil War that ended just 30 months ago, calls for Nigerians to own 60 per cent of the local company.

Talks have been going on for some weeks now between major expatriate-controlled oil concerns and the Government-backed, Nigerian National Oil Corporation. The corporation's chairman, Philip Asiodu, has emphasized that Nigeria will need a "majority participation" in the oil industry to create an atmosphere of confidence between the Government and the concerns.

There have been rumors that expatriate companies, now operating in the areas that will be reserved for Nigerians, have been inflating the value of their concerns for the best possible price when they sell out to Nigerians. But there are also reports that a number of major corporations are cooperating fully with the Nigerian aims. A number of businessmen say they are waiting to seen how the Nigerian Federal military Government will move.

Thomas Schropshire, however, the managing director of Philip Morris Nigeria, Ltd., which is said to produce 18 per cent of the cigarettes bought in Nigeria, since January has reduced the expatriate management staff among his 863 employes at the corporation's factory in Ilorin from 28 to 11.

Mr. Schropshire, who is a black American, said, "There had been some resistance, some reports that 'we can't find qualified Nigerians.' I couldn't accept this—it was the same thing we heard so often about blacks in the United States."

Shares to Be Offered

He said Nigerians were in training to take over other expatriate positions, and that, "We will be offering shares to the public for a percentage of ownership."

Stephen Abodunion, a 24-year-old Yoruba who earned a bachelor's degree in mechanical engineering two years ago at the Ahmandu Bello University in Zaria, recently took over the job of manager of the tobacco-redrying plant from a Briton, Frank Rigby, at the Philip Morris factory.

He said that while he favored Nigerian control, he would not want to see a totally Nigerian operation. This was echoed by other factory workers.

"We need experience and new ideas, if we are to prosper," Mr. Abodunion said. "We need input from all people and all countries."

One of hte biggest helps for the "indiginization" and "Nigerianization" processes came when Chief Simeon Adebo, the Nigerian Under Secretary-General to the United Nations, announced earlier this summer that he would resign and become a consultant on research and training to the multimillion dollar, multinational United Africa Company Amalgamation.

During a recent talk in Lagos, Mr. Adebo, who had been the executive director of the U.N.'s Institute for Training and Research, said he left the United Nations, because "I am anxious to join the struggle for the salvation of this country, whether in or out of Government."

He continued, "The United Africa Company does intend to indiginize. I have no higher interest than to apply myself in this way to the betterment of this country."

September 2, 1972

LIBERIA IS MAKING ECONOMIC STRIDES

U. S. Technical and Monetary Aid Has Played Large Part in Developing Resources

By MICHAEL CLARK
Special to THE NEW YORK TIMES.

MONROVIA, Liberia, Dec. 10—Liberia, though extremely backward, has come a long way in the past few years. Her economy still is gathering momentum, thanks largely to United States technical and financial assistance.

Now in its 107th year of independence, this republic, founded by freed American slaves, is just beginning to reveal its possibilities.

When William V. S. Tubman was elected President in 1943, the country was still almost wholly undeveloped. There were virtually no roads outside the two Firestone rubber plantations. Liberia was without a port worthy of the name and had nothing that could be called a railway.

In Monrovia, the capital city, there were a few dilapidated mansions vaguely reminiscent of the old South of the United States, many houses of corrugated iron and any number of tar-paper hovels amid the tropical vegetation. There was no telephone system, no piped water supply or sewage disposal.

Nation Was Isolated

The outgoing President, Edwin James Barclay, had been more concerned with the problem of safeguarding the country's ingrity and of keeping foreign interests out. He apparently felt that Liberia could be true to herself only by remaining a purely Negro creation.

The door that President Barclay had held so firmly shut was thrown wide open by President Tubman, whose strong personality now dominates the scene.

The war gave Liberia her first impetus. Roberts Field, the country's only good airport, was built by the United States under the 1942 Defense Areas Agreement. The $5,000,000 field is now operated by Pan American World Airways.

The free port of Monrovia, ordered by President Roosevelt in 1943 after his visit to Liberia, was constructed under naval supervision at a cost of $20,000,000 in lend-lease funds. The property to revert to Liberia once the original cost has been refunded from port revenues. However only $150,000 has been repaid since the port was opened to shipping in 1948.

The Monrovia Port Management Company, a United States concern, is custodian of the property. The port remains at the disposal of the United States in the event of war.

The most dramatic success in Liberian economic history has been that of the Bomi Hills mining venture, promoted by Lansdell K. Christie of New York. Republic Steel bought a controlling interest in Mr. Christie's Liberia Mining Company in 1949. Since then production has soared to well over 1,000,000 tons of high-grade iron ore a year, bringing Liberia about $2,000,000 a year in royalties.

Liberia is collecting about $2,500,000 a year from the Firestone plantations in the form of income tax. Her total revenues this year are expected to reach $10,000,000. The total in 1934 was $467,000.

Two Export-Import Bank loans totaling $6,350,000, authorized in 1952, have enabled Liberia to begin road construction and to give Monrovia a water and sewerage system. A dial telephone exchange also has been put in.

Liberia signed a Point IV agreement in 1950 and embarked in 1951 on a five-year economic and social development plan to cost $32,000,000. The United States public health and economic missions sent to Liberia in 1944 were merged into the United States Operations Mission. A joint Liberian-United States commission is responsible for planning and coordination.

The Liberian Government, having agreed to allocate 20 per cent of its annual revenue to the plan, is putting up $2,000,000 this year. The United States is contributing $1,283,000.

President Tubman now is working on an expanded, nine-year development plan for which he is seeking a $50,000,000 loan from the United States that might be amortized from the royalties of the Liberia Mining Company.

An increasing number of foreign groups, both United States and European, are negotiating concessions for mineral and other rights in Liberia. All this means additional revenue and employment. The country still is very poor, but the outlook is brighter than ever.

December 26, 1953

INNER WEAKNESS HAMPERS LIBERIA

Differences With Hinterland on Outlook Forced Policy of Indirect Rule

By MICHAEL CLARK
Special to THE NEW YORK TIMES.

MONROVIA, Liberia, Dec. 10—The Liberian Republic, now in its 107th year of independence, aspires to be the showpiece of African democracy. However, progress in this respect has been impeded by inner contradictions and weaknesses.

The handful of freed American slaves who settled on the African coast many years ago under the auspices of the American Colonization Society were unwelcome guests in a hostile land. The little republic that was proclaimed in Monrovia in 1847 managed to survive, however, and with time its Americo-Liberian oligarchy was able to win a secure position along the coast and in parts of the interior.

But the Americo-Liberians and their natives subjects remained worlds apart. The United States heritage of the rulers made them complete strangers to the natives, who were, and are, among the most primitive peoples in Africa.

Today Liberia is in the paradoxical position of being a Negro republic obliged to have a native policy just as if it were a colonial power.

Tribal Law Prevailed

The Government has had to pursue a policy of indirect rule in the hinterland, where native chiefs continue to function according to tribal law and custom. But lately the process of fusion, encouraged by the present administration, has begun to make headway.

In 1946 the natives in the bush, called to the polls for the first time, sent three chiefs to the House of Representatives in Monrovia. Since then the number of native Representatives has reached eight. The House has thirty-one members. There is no native representation in the Senate.

Meanwhile, educated Liberians of native descent are entering public service in increasing numbers. One of them, a member of the Grebo tribe, is Chief Justice of the Supreme Court. Another, a Kru, is director general of the National Public Health Service.

An upsurge of Afro-Liberians may well be a feature of the years ahead, but the task of assimilation and integration, not to say emancipation, is just beginning.

Stand Against Bias

Liberian officials have consistently taken a firm stand against colonialism and racial discrimination. Their position would, perhaps, be stronger if Liberia herself could be cited as a model of liberalism and successful nationalism.

In Liberia, however, the racial bond is a primary concern. The country is conceived as a Negro commonwealth; by some as a land of redemption, as a Negro Jerusalem. That is why the blessings of Liberian citizenship are limited to Negroes.

Liberians have not always been of one mind as to how best to serve their race. Many have believed in going it alone so that, good or bad, Liberia would remain a purely Negro creation.

This attitude prevailed until William V. S. Tubman became President in 1944. He began to build up his country. Loans, grants and technical assistance came from the United States. Ports, bridges, roads, railways, telephones and waterworks appeared where there were none before, and with them came whites. Liberia is no longer, and will probably never again be, a purely Negro creation.

The French and British West African territories are far ahead of Liberia, even in political training. Liberia has had to concede mineral and agricultural rights to foreign interests. Foreign companies operate the port, the power plant and the airport. A United States Operations Mission is the mainstay of the development program, and the United States has strategic rights in the country. And things are getting done.

December 27, 1953

LIBERIAN UPHOLDS COLONIAL BENEFIT

U.N. Envoy Explains Factors for the Prosperity of Ghana Compared With Own Land

By WAYNE PHILLIPS
Special to The New York Times.

UNITED NATIONS, N. Y., March 23—The Liberian representative here declared this week that his country lagged materially behind the new nation of Ghana because it had always been independent and had never reaped the advantages of colonialism.

Charles T. O. King, Ambassador here for the last two years, made the statement in an interview that was prompted, he said, by the recent tour of Vice President Richard M. Nixon in Africa.

Reporters acompanying Mr. Nixon had noted, he said, that Liberia, which has been independent for more than a century, was still largely primitive, while Ghana, which has just obtained independence after long colonial rule, was relatively well developed.

"It is the difference between the home of a man who has had to accomplish everything by his own sweat and toil," Mr. King said, "and that of a man who has enjoyed a large inheritance."

Injustices Conceded

By seeking to explain the benefits colonial rule had brought to Ghana, the former Gold Coast, he said he was by no means trying to justify its injustices. His own family, he said, had fled from British oppression in Nigeria for the free political air in Liberia.

Nor, he said, is he in any sense trying to stir political controversy between his country and Ghana. "We are not jealous," he said, "we are proud and glad of the progress they have made and the independence they have obtained."

The material differences, however, are clear to see, he said. Ghana had better roads, better schools, better harbor facilities, a more highly developed industry, agriculture, and public revenue.

Liberia was founded in 1847 by freed United States slaves, who returned to the continent from which their forebears had come and staked out a territory on a primitive coast where the European colonizers were yet to come.

"The United States did not care about a colony on the coast of Africa," he said, "and we were left alone and struggling, to vegetate in the midst of developing European colonies."

Firestone Interest Noted

Until twenty years ago, when the Firestone Rubber Company began to take an interest in rubber plantations in Liberia, the United State was uninterested in the tiny republic for anything beyond sentimental reasons.

By contrast, he said, the liberal colonial policy of Britain was to extend great efforts to develop her colonial holdings and build them up materially.

"The students from the Gold Coast went to the best schools in England, to Oxford and Cambridge," he said. "They were not denied admission to those schools because of their race, as we were in the United States."

The European colonial powers wanted the raw materials of their colonies to feed their industry, he said, while the United States was more isolationist in its economic policy and had little interest in the raw materials of Liberia.

March 24, 1957

Liberia Is Changing After the Tubman Era

By CHARLES MOHR
Special to The New York Times

MONROVIA, Liberia, Oct. 17 —There is a new atmosphere of pride, relief and expectation in the small West African nation of Liberia.

The people are proud because power passed constitutionally and peacefully to Vice President William R. Tolbert Jr., with no murmur of coups or conspiracies, when their strongman President, William V. S. Tubman, died last July after 27 years in office.

Mr. Tubman had made big strides in turning his country from a stagnant backwater into a more modern nation. However, there is a tastefully restrained but real sense of relief that the formidable old autocrat is finally gone.

E. Reginald Townsend, Minister of Information and the author of much lavish praise of the late President, said mildly that "after 27 years a change is always welcome."

Expectations have been raised by Mr. Tolbert's first three months in office. Emerging from the deep obscurity of 19 years in Mr. Tubman's shadow, the new President has made a promising start toward reform and faster change and has displayed both political skill and idealistic rhetoric.

Something Very Refreshing

There is a consensus that, as a foreign diplomat phrased it, "something very refreshing is happening in Liberia."

All of this is particularly satisfying to many here because the nation, for most of its history, was the victim of diplomatic humiliation and faint ridicule.

Liberia was founded by freed American slaves, sponsored by the white-run American Colonization Society. The 150th anniversary of the landing of settlers will be marked on Jan. 7 amid considerable ceremony. The colony became an independent republic in 1847.

Despite the long history—in fact, because of it—Liberia, the size of Ohio but with only 1.5 million people, still lags behind most of her neighbors.

A major motive of the Colonization Society was to try to solve the problem of "unowned Negroes" in slave-owning America by depositing them back on the western bulge of Africa. Only a few thousand blacks and mulattoes ever came. Almost all of those who did had been in America for several generations and were imbued with Christian and middle-class values of Southern Americans.

The handful of "Americo-Liberians" were vastly outnumbered by what they called the aborigines, or tribal Africans already here, but the settlers were dominant politically and culturally. So it is that Liberia, a unique amalgam of cultures, settlers and tribes, still gives the superficial impression of a small community in the Old South.

English is the official language and the United States dollar is the currency. When politicians try to explain the workings of the governing True Whig party, they sometimes say that the best comparison is the old one-party Democratic primary in the American South.

Monrovia, named for President James Monroe, who encouraged the Liberia experiment, was once one of the shabbiest capitals in the world.

Today, with about 100,000 people, it is a curious mixture of peeling old pillared houses reminiscent of the United States South, some modern office buildings, a $6-million seven-story presidential mansion that looks like a Miami Beach resort hotel, tin shacks and comfortable new houses for the upper class.

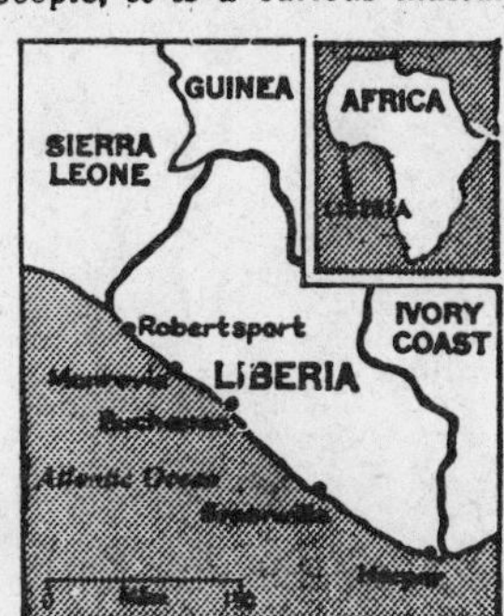

The New York Times/Nov. 1, 1971

On Sundays the streets are filled with the strong, pure voices of church congregations. But even on that day Lebanese, Syrian and Turkish bar girls and prostitutes stand in the doorways of saloons to lure sailors inside for a drink. The bar area is on a road with the phonetically appropriate name of Gurley Street.

Liberia was for most of her life the target of slurs from a white-dominated international community. Her people's love of formal dress and dignity gave birth to bad jokes about top hats and tom-toms.

More important, because the country had almost no revenue and could get neither economic aid nor adequate international credit, it suffered from economic and social stagnation until after World War II. Because it was never a colony, it had not received the economic benefits of colonialism—roads, harbors, commerce, markets, education and health.

As late as 1953 the author John Gunther, noting that the Liberians had only 10 miles of paved road, said that they "might almost be called a kind of perverse advertisement for imperialism" because they were much more backward than neighboring British and French colonies.

If there was little compassion in such a judgment, there was considerable accuracy. The national seal bears the motto "The love of liberty brought us here." Sensitive but not stuffy, Liberians at one time joked: "The lack of money kept us here."

"The fact that we survived at all is a miracle," a Liberian intellectual remarked.

So, while Liberia has made rapid progress in the last 20 years, no one denies that she still has a task ahead. As Africa's newest President, in its oldest Republic, Mr. Tolbert said in a recent speech that "the swell of pride contains the salt of much humility."

Wealthy Rubber Grower

A heavy-set, baldish man of 58, Mr. Tolbert, whose father came here as a boy from Charleston, S. C., has become wealthy as a rubber planter. He is a part of what Liberians like to call the Establishment or the Old Guard—the network of closely intertwined leading families (the late President's son, Senator Shad Tubman, is married to Mr. Tolbert's daughter).

But since taking office Mr. Tolbert, moving with unexpected vigor to break with the past in both style and substance, has promised greater social and economic justice.

In his first few weeks in office, he has dismissed a Cabinet Under Secretary for corruption, suspended two much-hated officers of the secret police forces, replaced the director of the civil service and two of the powerful superintendents, or governors, of counties (the equivalent of states).

He also dismissed the Secretary of Commerce because that official had approved Mr. Tubman's orders for a private monopoly in the imports of rice, the staple food.

Mr. Tolbert then abolished the monopoly, of which his son-in-law was an owner. The price of rice has dropped from more than $13 a hundredweight to $9.80.

Under Mr. Tubman every civil servant was forced to contribute a month's salary each to the True Whig party, which has controlled Liberia since the eighteen-seventies. His successor abolished this year's assessment and is thought likely to eliminate the practice. Payments have been sharply reduced for a group of down-at-the-heels Tubman loyalists and informers who received monthly stipends from the treasury.

"The whole style is different, even the style of dress," an observer said.

Liberia used to be fantastically conscious of protocol and fashion. Morning coat and white tie were worn for official and ceremonial functions and dinner jackets were the rule in the evenings.

Although the new President often wears business suits, he has taken to appearing at official functions and on street tours in an open-necked bush jacket and slacks—a break in precedent that caused Liberians to gasp.

The change seems popular, particularly with young people who resented the idea that their country resembled a running convention of a Negro fraternal organization. A letter to a newspaper recently said, "It is a known fact that a tedious preoccupation with dress entails waste of time."

No More Presidential Yacht

Mr. Tolbert has also decided to sell the presidential yacht, which was costing $250,000 a year in maintenance.

Liberia has never been like Haiti, and Mr. Tubman, who was known as "Uncle Shad," was not a vicious dictator, but he did inspire awe approaching fear, a foreign resident said.

His successor's style, manner and statements have encouraged greater freedom of speech and a new attitude of relaxation. A newspaper recently printed a letter from a reader who offered "profound thanks" that "the iron box of freedom of speech once sealed up for years" had been opened.

According to Liberians, Mr. Tubman continued to insist on making most decisions when he was too ill and feeble to bear the load. He also placed loyalty above competence, they said, and tolerated both inefficiency and corruption.

On the subject of corruption, he used to point to his wrist and then to his shoulder and say, "Up to here, O.K., up to there, no."

A Liberian commented: "There was also a feeling that the country was in the hands of an oligarchy, a club. Tolbert has been appealing to young people and to the people out in the tall bush, saying the whole country should begin to participate and share. It's a different attitude."

One of Mr. Tubman's Cabinet members said: "Everyone is looking forward to getting something done in the country."

BRITISH PUT DOWN AFRICAN MUTINIES IN THREE NATIONS

London Sends Troops After Calls From Tanganyika, Kenya and Uganda

3 DIE AT DAR ES SALAAM

Action Lasts 40 Minutes— Warships in Indian Ocean Fire Blank Ammunition

By ROBERT CONLEY
Special to The New York Times

NAIROBI, Kenya, Jan. 25—British forces went into action in three newly independent East African countries early today to put down mutinies by African troops.

Striking at the request of the three governments, the British troops disarmed mutinous soldiers in Tanganyika, seized a camp of mutineers in Uganda and broke a sitdown strike by soldiers in Kenya.

The action in Tanganyika began at dawn in answer to an urgent appeal from President Julius K. Nyerere. Sixty commandos, transferred by helicopter from the aircraft carrier Centaur, subdued 800 mutineers in a 40-minute assault. They used one bazooka antitank rocket launcher and a lot of sharp fireworks.

Blank Charges Fired

Blank powder charges were used in a naval "barrage" from the aircraft carrier and her escort destroyer, the Cambrian, off the Indian Ocean coast. The din was thunderous, but no shells were fired.

Three Tanganyikan mutineers were killed and an undisclosed number wounded in this first British military operation in Africa since the 1956 invasion of the Suez Canal area. No commando casualties were reported.

In Uganda, troops from the Staffordshire Regiment moved in before dawn at the request of Prime Minister Milton Obote to seize a rebel camp at Jinja on northern Lake Victoria, near the headwaters of the Nile.

Kenyatta Asked Aid

In Kenya, elements of the Royal Horse Artillery were called out in response to a request by Prime Minister Jomo Kenyatta.

Arriving in armored cars, the troops broke up the strike at the army post near Nakuru, in the Rift Valley, the great cleft that runs up the spine of Africa.

The British military action came at the end of a week in which successive mutinies broke out in East Africa. The uprisings in the three countries were over demands for more pay and for the dismissal of British officers still commanding the African units.

Late in the day President Nyerere announced that he would disband Tanganyika's 1,350-man army, known as the Tanganyika Rifles, and set up a new one.

In a radio broadcast, Mr. Nyerere called on all members of the Youth Wing of his Tanganyika African National Union to register as recruits.

"No popular government can tolerate an army that disobeys its instructions," Dr. Nyerere said in Swahili. "An army that does not obey laws and orders of the people's Government is not an army of that country. It is a danger to the whole nation."

The President condemned the mutineers as men "intoxicated with the poison of disloyalty and disobedience." He called their rebellion the "most disgraceful" event in Tanganyika's history and promised that they would be punished severely.

In Kenya, Mr. Kenyatta made a similar broadcast. He termed his soldiers' insurrection a "grave betrayal" of Kenya's African leaders and her people. The mutineers will be "dealt with firmly," he added.

Seven hundred additional Royal Marine commandos arrived after dark from Britain. Four-engine Royal Air Force turbojet troop carriers arrived at Nairobi's International Airport in two-hour intervals through last night.

By midmorning 600 commandos with trucks and equipment had been airlifted to follow up the initial assault at Colito, 10 miles north of Dar es Salaam, the Tanganyikan capital.

By noon, 450 commandos had moved into the capital to protect strategic points. One detachment sealed off the State House, the President's official residence, which overlooks the Indian Ocean. Other units stood guard at the radio station, the telephone exchange, the overseas cable office, the airport and the homes of Government officials.

British paratroopers dropped on two centers of mutiny inland from the palm-fringed coast. One unit overpowered mutineers at Tabora, 450 miles west of Dar es Salaam. Another disarmed mutineers at Nachingwea, 260 miles to the south, near the border of Mozambique.

In Kenya, British artillerymen used six Ferret armored cars to end a sitdown strike of the Lanet barracks, headquarters of the 11th Battalion of Kenya Rifles, near Nakuru. More than 150 rebellious troops armed with weapons taken from the arsenal, occupied the parade grounds. A sniper fired on the armored cars from a roof.

One of the cars moved up closer, brought its turret to bear on a hut with a tiled roof and, with a sustained burst from its .50-caliber machine gun, raked the empty hut. All its windows were smashed, and the sitdown strike collapsed.

Wives and children of the British officers and troops attached to the unit were given refuge at the Rift Valley Club and at the Stag's Head Hotel in Nakuru, six miles away. In Nairobi a Scots Guardsman manned a machine gun on the roof of the Kenya Broadcasting Corporation station. Others guarded the Prime Minister's office, the police headquarters and the post office.

Troop carriers flew in and out of Nairobi all day.

At Jinja in Uganda, 30 men from the Scots Guards and the Staffordshire Regiment, armed with burp guns, captured about 300 mutineers of the Uganda Rifles.

The Britons burst through the camp's main gate, secured the guardroom and seized the armory before the mutineers awoke, and 450 British troops surrounded the camp.

British women and children were removed from the camp immediately after the raid. They included 34 wives of the unit's British officers and men, 52 children and 2 grandmothers.

The dependents were taken 70 miles down the lake's west shore to the Lake Victoria Hotel at Entebbe to await an airlift to Nairobi.

The barrage on the coast of Tanganyika started about 6 A.M. (10 P.M. Friday, New York time). In Dar es Salaam, Arab and Indian merchants were unlatching the wooden shutters of their whitewashed shops to begin the day.

At 6:20 the first wave was airlifted to shore from the flight deck of the Centaur. The assault troops were from the 45th Royal Marine Commandos, rushed in from the British protectorate of Aden at the tip of the Arabian Peninsula.

Brig. Patrick Sholto Douglas led the attack. He was deposed Monday as commanding officer of the Tanganyika Rifles when insurgent African soldiers seized the capital and set off a day of rioting, looting and killing. Twenty persons died then, and at least 100 others were injured.

January 26, 1964

Tanganyika's Guardian

Julius Kambarage Nyerere

ON the White House lawn one day last summer, President Julius K. Nyerere of Tanganyika heard President Kennedy liken his work in office to that of Thomas Jefferson and George Washington. He also heard him remark that leading Tanganyika to independence was only part of the struggle, that it was more difficult "to build a cohesive society once independence has been founded."

Man in the News

That day, President Nyerere told a questioner at the National Press Club that he still regarded it as a "dangerous game" for African states to seek outside military assistance.

Yet last week the 42-year-old teacher - turned - politician found himself seeking just such help. He called back British troops to disarm his own forces, the Tanganyika Rifles, who had turned against their British officers.

The turmoil had spread to his capital, Dar es Salaam, from another newly independent state, the nearby island of Zanzibar. Mr. Nyerere withheld public criticism of the mutineers until the British had disarmed them. Those who know him are inclined to regard this delay as a sign not of weakness but of prudence in dealing with the crisis.

Camera Press-Pix

Country is his classroom

Issued a Warning

The mutiny must have come as a shock, but not necessarily as a surprise. A year ago he warned the third Afro-Asian Peoples Solidarity Conference in Tanganyika that Communist countries had the same purpose as the European colonialists of the nineteenth century, "to get control of our countries."

Julius Kambarage Nyerere (pronounced NY-a-REH-ray) probably learned his first lessons in politics as one of 26 children of a polygamous tribal chief. Twenty years ago as a student at Makarere College in neighboring Uganda, he organized the Tanganyika Students Association.

Mr. Nyerere interspersed teaching at Roman Catholic mission schools with study in Scotland that brought him a master of arts degree from the University of Edinburgh in 1952. He adopted Catholicism at the age of 20.

He turned to politics in 1954, when he founded what is still the country's only party, the Tanganyika African National Union. It was dedicated to preparing for independence. Previously Tanganyika was a German colony, then a mandated territory of the League of Nations and a United Nations trusteeship territory with British supervision.

Mr. Nyerere was determined to build a party that would be strong in the black country try rather than a city-based coterie of office-holders. It was with this in mind that, when independence was achieved in December, 1961, be strong in the back counhe held office as Prime Minister for only six weeks. He yielded his post to a colleague and returned to party building until his election to the Presidency of the republic. He was inaugurated on Nov. 9, 1962.

The Tanganyikan President works long hours at his job. Off the job he will relax over a martini, gin and tonic or Scotch. He also likes to relax by playing table tennis with his wife, the former Maria Magige, or with their children. The Nyereres have five sons and two daughters.

Tanganyika has been spared some of the tragedies of transition. It has had a comparatively small number of white settlers. Tribal loyalties are less of a threat to the central Government than they are in some other new African states.

The mild, moderate, hard-working figure of Mr. Nyerere is symbolic of enlightenment on both sides. As a result, the transition has been almost too easy.

President Kennedy's prediction has already been confirmed. Mr. Nyerere, an admirer of the literature of American independence, is now faced by an African variant of "the times that try men's souls."

He still thinks of himself as a teacher and is sometimes addressed by that title in Swahili—"Mwalimu." His classroom authority over a new nation is being tested.

January 27, 1964

African Revolt Overturns Arab Regime in Zanzibar

All Strategic Buildings Seized After Fight—Sultan Flees Capital

By ROBERT CONLEY
Special to The New York Times

DAR ES SALAAM, Tanganyika, Jan. 12 — African rebels overthrew the predominantly Arab Government of Zanzibar today. Striking before dawn, the armed rebels swept the Prime Minister, Sheik Mohammed Shamte Hamadi, and his Cabinet from power in a revolution apparently inspired by racial antagonism.

Late reports from Zanzibar, an island in the Indian Ocean off the east coast of Africa, indicated that there had been fighting and that casualties were heavy.

"Many lives have been lost," one rebel radio broadcast said.

[A Reuters report from Zanzibar said three persons had been killed and 24 wounded.]

Zanzibar, a former British protectorate, became independent Dec. 10, but remained in the Commonwealth. The island has a population of 340,000.

Within six hours after they struck the rebels had captured all strategic buildings in the town of Zanzibar, the island's capital. They seized the cable office, airstrip and radio station.

Repeated bursts from automatic rifles echoed through the narrow, winding streets of the capital, once the center of the Arab slave trade in East Africa. The sultan, Seyyid Jamshid Bin Abdullah, the island's traditional monarch, was reported to have fled to a yacht anchored in the harbor, just out of range of the rebel guns.

The Prime Minister and the remnants of his Government were believed to be on the yacht with the Sultan.

The rebel radio proclaimed Zanzibar a republic and announced the formation of a revolutionary government.

Abeid Karume, a former trade union leader, took over as President. Kassim Hanga, another

The New York Times Jan. 13, 1964

Cross denotes Zanzibar

labor leader, became Prime Minister. Sheik Abdul Raman

Mohammed, the firebrand of Zanzibar politics, became Minister of External Affairs and Defense.

Rebels Lean to Left

All three revolutionary leaders have a pronounced leftist outlook. The Sheik, known as "Babu" or "father," was in close touch throughout the day with the Chinese Communist and Cuban Embassies here in Dar es Salaam, the capital of Tanganyika, 45 miles southwest of Zanzibar.

The Sheik arrived here yesterday from the island. He was reported to have returned tonight by special boat.

Zanzibar was sealed off to all other ships and planes. The revolutionary government imposed a dusk-to- dawn curfew and warned that anyone found in the streets after dusk would be shot.

The United States destroyer Manley was recalled at the last minute as it raced to Zanzibar to remove 61 Americans caught in the revolution. The Americans fled to the English Club on the waterfront of Zanzibar town.

The Americans included the 16-man staff of the United States space-tracking stations on the island. The fate of the tracking station, operated by the National Aeronautics and Space Administration, was uncertain.

The destroyer had been on a goodwill visit to Kenya's port of Mombasa, north of Zanzibar. She was ordered to turn back after an unidentified rebel, who

Involved in Zanzibar Power Change

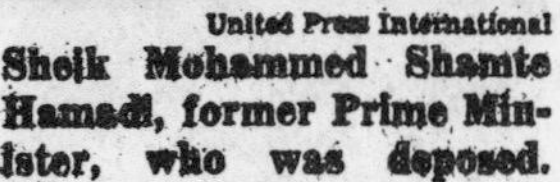

United Press International

Sheik Mohammed Shamte Hamadi, former Prime Minister, who was deposed.

Associated Press

Abeid Karume, former trade union leader. He took over as President of the island.

called himself "field marshal," broadcast a warning that the revolutionary government would brook no interference from foreign powers.

British authorities, meanwhile, were prepared to rescue 300 British subjects on Zanzibar if necessary.

The revolution gave every impression of being the culmination of years of racial bitbitterness between Zanzibar's 230,000 Africans and 50,000 Arabs.

Zanzibar's Police Commissioner, J. M. Sullivan, reached by telephone from here, said there were about 600 insurgents.

Revolt Laid to Party

The revolution was the work of Mr. Karume's Afro-Shirazi party—Zanzibar's black nationalist movement—and the militant leftist Umma party, led by Sheik Abdullah Raman Mohammed.

"The Afro-Shirazis provided the manpower and the Umma provided the brain power," a diplomat reached by telephone in Zanzibar said.

The word Shirazi derives form Zanzibar's original Moslem settlers, who came from the town of Shiraz in southeast Persia in the seventh centruy. They are now almost indistinguishable from the mainland Africans. Umma means "forward."

The rebels struck at 3 A.M. (8 P.M. Saturday, Eastern standard time.) They broke into the police arsenal and into the Government armory, stealing hundreds of automatic rifles and submachine guns.

All telegraph contact with the outside world was shut down when the rebels seized the cable office in the middle of Zanzibar town.

By 2:18 P.M., they had seized the airstrip about eight miles south of town. The airstrip's control-tower operator was allowed to remain.

"It is getting serious," the tower operator, Edward Cheek, sai dover his radio. "A truck with 30 men has just arrived. We are shutting down."

"Are you signing off?" interrupted the regional air control officer in Dar Es Salaam. "Yes," said Mr. Cheek. "there is a large armed party here. We are going down to meet them."

January 13, 1964

Zanzibar Long Divided by Arab-African Rivalry

Tensions of 25 Centuries Brought to a Critical Point in New Independence

Since the movement toward African independence gained momentum in the early nineteen-fifties, Zanzibar has been a place where the African and Arab brands of nationalism intersect.

The conflict between the Arabs, who make up about 15 per cent of the 307,000 population, and the indigenous Africans broke out into the open in the election disorders of June, 1961, when a coalition of Arab-dominated parties won control of the Legislative Council.

The common desire of the African and Arab parties for independence from Britain helped keep some differences below the surface until independence was granted Dec. 10. Since then the split has widened. It culminated in the banning of the Umma party, a left-wing African group, by the Arab-dominated Government last week.

Arabs There 2,500 Years

The Arab-African conflict has its roots in more than 2,500 years of Arab influence. Since about 600 B.C. the Arab dhows have come south from Arabia and Persia on the northeast monsoon and returned on the southwest monsoon with ivory, spices and slaves.

In 1832 Seyyid (Lord) Said bin Sultan, ruler of Oman, established his capital at Zanzibar. His great-great-grandson, Seyyid Jamshid bin Abdulla, was removed from power by the coup yesterday.

Seyyid Said held extensive territories on the East African coast in addition to the islands of Zanzibar and Pemba. In the late 19th century these fell to Britain, Germany, Italy and Portugal. The last mainland part of the sultanate, a coastal strip including the deep-water port of Mombasa, was signed over to Kenya last October.

In 1890 the islands were placed under British protection. Under the protectorate, the Sultan and the British resident ruled jointly.

Under the British, Arab influence continued. It was said that, in general, the Arabs owned the land, the Indians controlled the trade and the Africans did the work.

In 1955 the British offered a measure of self-government through representative elections. The Arabs, comprising the wealthiest and best-educated portion of the population, demanded property and literacy qualifications for voting. A compromise was reached.

In the first elections of 1957, for six seats in the Legislative Council, the Afro-Shirazi party won five and the party of the Indian minority won one. The Zanzibar Nationalist party of the Arabs had no successful candidate.

Elections Ended in Tie

The next general elections, in January, 1961, ended in a tie. The Afro-Shirazi party and the Zanzibar Nationalist party each won 11 seats. To prevent another tie an additional seat was established and a second election was held in June.

In the June voting the Zanzibar Nationalist and Afro-Shirazi party each won 10 seats. The new Zanzibar and Pemba People's party, which had a pre-election alliance with the Zanzibar Nationalists, gained three seats.) Thus the first fully elected Legislative Council was Arab-dominated, and Mohammed Shamte Hamadi, leader of the People's party, became Prime Minister.

After the elections, riots broke out and 68 people, 64 of them Arabs, were killed. British troops were moved in to quell the disturbances. An official inquiry later found that the cause of the disorders had been racial animosity between the African and Arab groups.

It was feared that the pre-independence elections last July would also be disorderly, but there was peace at the polling places. The Arab coalition won 18 seats and the Afro-Shirazi party 13, although the latter capured 54 per cent of the popular vote. A third party emerged when Sheik Abdul Rahman Mohammed Babu resigned from the Arab coalition to form the Umma party, which is now aligned with the African group.

Zanzibar, a constitutional monarchy before the coup, is made up of the islands of Zanzibar, having an area of 640 square miles,

January 13, 1964

CUBA BEGAN ROLE IN ZANZIBAR IN '61

Havana's Part in Revolution Outlined in Washington—Guerrilla Course Cited

By TAD SZULC

Special to The New York Times

WASHINGTON, Jan. 22 — Preparations for last week's pro-Communist revolution in Zanzibar began quietly in Cuba late in 1961, when a Zanzibari political office was established in Havana. They reached their peak with the arrival six weeks ago of a Cuban chargé d'affaires in Dar es Salaam, Tanganyika.

The detailed story of Cuba's involvement in the Zanzibar revolt and Cuban activities in connection with the training of East African and South African guerrillas and other African groups has been pieced together from reliable reports that became available today.

In addition to tracing the Cuban strategy in preparing for the revolution in Zanzibar, which lies off Tanganyika, the information, which comes from many quarters, discloses that several hundred African "students" are being trained in Cuba. The training is said to include guerrilla warfare tactics.

The students are divided into four main groups. Special emphasis is being placed on the first group, trainees from South Africa, and on the second group, trainees from the East African countries of Kenya, Tanganyika and Zanzibar.

This is believed to indicate that Cuba, working with the Soviet Union and possibly Communist China, is centering her attention and activities on South Africa and the east coast of Africa, where the successful revolt in Zanzibar took place Jan. 12 and an army uprising broke out in Tanganyika on Monday.

Students from Ghana, Mali, the Congo and Nigeria are said to form the third group. The fourth group is made up of students from Spanish Guinea, on Africa's northwestern coast, where there have been pro-independence movements.

Facts that once seemed insignificant, such as the establishment in 1961 of the Havana office of the Zanzibar National party, were being pulled out of files and studied.

For example, the man who ran the Zanzibari political office in Havana has emerged as a top aide of John Okello, the self-styled field marshal of the Zanzibari revolution. His name was not available here tonight, but dispatches from Zanzibar last Wednesday quoted an aide of Mr. Okello as having said that he had been trained in Cuba along with other Zanzibaris.

How much power Mr. Okello has at this point is not known here, but the available information suggests that Cuban "graduates" still play an important role in the Zanzibari situation.

Link to South Africa Seen

Informed sources here also saw a relationship between Cuban operations and the activites of a nine-man South African Liberation Committee based in Tanganyika.

It was suspected that Dar es salaam might have become a center for revolutionary activities for East and South Africa and that the Cuban Embassy there, which began functioning suddenly last month, might be one of the key elements in this effort.

Also under study here was a report that the Algerian vessel Khaladoun arrived in Dar es Salaam on Jan. 2 with a cargo of arms, supplies and uniforms.

Some specialists here were checking the possibility that these may have been some of the arms sent by Cuba to Algeria last October during Algeria's brief border conflict with Morocco. The Cubans sent two shiploads of weapons, including tanks, to Algeria and, according to intelligence sources, they have not been returned to Cuba.

Cuban military personnel accompanied the arms and they, too, are believed to have remained in Algeria. There was interest here whether the Cuban military men might have traveled with the shipment that arrived in Tanganyika 10 days before the Zanzibar revolution.

January 23, 1964

Tanganyika and Zanzibar Sign Agreement to Unite

Parliaments Must Ratify Surprise Decision by Two Presidents

Dispatch of The Times, London

DAR ES SALAAM, Tanganyika, April 23 — President Julius K. Nyerere of Tanganyika and President Abeid Amani Karume of Zanzibar have signed articles of union under which their countries will become one sovereign state, it was officially announced here today.

President Nyerere unexpectedly visited Zanzibar yesterday. The announcement, which coincided with a Moslem feast day, came as a surprise. It was generally welcomed.

[Dr. Nyerere would be President and Mr. Karume and Vice President R. M. Kawawa of Zanzibar the Vice Presidents of the new state, said a Reuters report.]

Details of the proposed union are expected to be announced at a special session of the National Assembly here tomorrow. The union is subject to ratification by both Parliaments.

Reports here said the announcement had been greeted with great relief in Zanzibar, where President Karume's position is generally regarded as precarious in the face of strong Communist influences. The feeling now is that union will create greater economic and political stability in the island, and prevent Communist infiltration.

The New York Times April 24, 1964

Tanganyika (1) and Zanzibar (2) have agreed to unite.

Signing of the agreement is the culmination of frequent exchanges between the two governments during the absence on a Far Eastern tour of Zanzibar's Foreign Minister, Abdul Rahman Mohammed, known as Babu, who is considered to have strong pro-Chinese sympathies.

Tanganyikan and Zanzibari cabinet ministers had made numerous flights between their countries' capitals before Dr. Nyerere himself flew to Zanzibar.

It is generally believed that Dr. Nyerere will head the new state. It is considered possible that the two islands, Zanzibar and Pemba, will become regions of the new state, each with its own members in the National Assembly.

One immediate effect of the union will be to ease the financial strain on Zanzibar, whose economy has steadily deteriorated since the revolution in January.

Tanganyika became independent on Dec. 9, 1961, and Zanzibar on Dec. 10, 1963. The predominantly Arab government of Zanzibar was overthrown by a revolt in mid-January.

Mr. Karume heads the Afro-Shirazi party, which is closely allied with the ruling Tanganyika African National Union, led by Dr. Nyerere. In recent weeks the pro-Communist leanings of the regime in Zanzibar have been causing concern on the mainland.

April 24, 1964

TANGANYIKA ONCE UNDER ARAB RULE

Zanzibar Was Base of Raids on Mainland for Slaves

The decision of Tanganyika and Zanibar to form a single state will restore to the region the common government it had during much of the 18th and 19th centuries—with one vital difference.

After the Arabs of Oman drove the Portuguese traders from Zanzibar at the end of the 17th century, the coastal plain, as far as the mountains that ring Lake Tanganyika, was systematically raided for slaves by the Arabs based on Zanzibar.

Mungo Park, Richard Burton and David Livingstone all visited the Arab overlords of the region and found the mainland tribes the helpless prey of the islanders.

Presumably in the new nation Tanganyika, with its 9.2 million inhabitants, will dominate the union with Zanzibar's 300,000.

Disparity of the Lands

Geographically, the disparity between Tanganyika and Zanzibar is even greater than that of population. The mainland area is about 363,000 square miles; the islands of Zanzibar and Pemba no more than 1,100 square miles together.

Dar es Salaam, with a population of 128,742 in 1957, is Tanganyika's capital and chief port. Other cities include Tanga, a port with 38,000 population; Tabora, on the central plateau. Kigoma, on Lake Tanganyika, and Moshi, on the Tanga railway in the farm country.

Zanzibar island is separated from the mainland by a channel 22½ miles across at its narrowest part. It lies due north of Dar es Salaam. The island is 50 miles long and 24 miles wide with an area of 640 square miles. It had 165,253 persons at the 1958 census.

Most of the 300,000 people of Zanzibar and Pemba are Africans of the Watumbatu, Wahadimu, Wapemba and 50 other mainland tribes.

First Explored by Portuguese

The Tanganyika coast was explored by the Portuguese about 1500 and held by them until the 17th century. At the end of the 17th century the inhabitants of Zanzibar drove out the Portuguese with the assistance of the Arabs of Oman. The interior remained in the hands of a local ruler, known as the Mwinyi Mkuu.

During the 18th century Zanzibar and the Tanganyika coast were ruled by the Sultanate of Oman through an Arab governor sent from Oman on the Persian Gulf.

Seyyid Said, Sultan of Oman established his capital at Zanzibar in 1832 and thereafter Zanzibar, Pemba and a large strip of the East African mainland coast came under his rule. He died in 1856. Five years later the British declared his former African possessions independent of Oman, and they were divided between Britain and Germany.

In 1884, under treaties signed by local rulers, Germany took over the area that is now Tanganyika, and fought Arab and African dissidents for 15 years. Britain made Zanzibar and Pemba a protectorate in 1890.

After World War I Britain got the area, under a League of Nations mandate, and it was first called Tanganyika. The country became a fully self-governing member of the British Commonwealth in 1961, with Dr. Julius K. Nyerere as President. A mutiny in January of this year was put down with British help.

Britain granted Zanzibar independence last December. The island was to remain a member of the Commonwealth, under an Arab-dominated Government On Jan. 12 Abeid Amani Karume, leader of the Afro-Shirazi party, and Abdul Rahman Mohammed, known as Babu, leader of the People's party, joined in a successful revolt.

Mr. Karume became President, Abdullah Kassim Hanga Premier and Babu Foreign Minister. Many Arabs were killed. Others were deported to Oman in dhows, and about 1,000 were placed in detention camps.

The island's new rulers proclaimed Zanzibar a people's republic, the designation by which many Communist governments are known. Correspondents said that the rebel troops who overthrew the Arab regime were Cuban-trained guerrillas.

April 24, 1964

Union Renamed Tanzania

Special to The New York Times

DAR ES SALAAM, Tanganyika, Oct. 29 — President Julius K. Nyerere announced today that the Union of Tanganyika and Zanzibar would be renamed Tanzania. The name was chosen in a contest.

October 30, 1964

Troubled Tanzanians Have a Long Row to Hoe

A Start Has Been Made, but Land Cries Out for Help

By DREW MIDDLETON
Special to The New York Times

BAGAMOYO, Tanzania, March 17—This is the old Africa. A listless town under the pitiless sun, a decaying state house where once German officers sweated into their high collars and longed for the pines of Prussia, old men dozing in the sun, children running naked in the dusty streets, a coconut plantation.

Besides the Indian Ocean lie the remains of an Arab fort and the stockade in which Africans were kept before being shipped across the ocean to slavery. Some boys unload poles from a beached dhow—the only activity in sight.

Half an hour's drive away are the outposts of a new Africa—a British-built cement plant on a hilltop, a university aided by American money outside Dar es Salaam, the Kibaha secondary school where 300 boys from all over Tanzania study under Swedes, Finns, Norwegians and Danes sent there by the Nordic Center.

$7-Million for Schooling

The four Nordic governments have invested $7-million in the center being built on the rolling hills 24 miles west of Dar es Salaam. The center maintains an agricultural school for farmers at which more than 1,200 adults have studied. In these schools and in light industrial plants lies hope for the new Africa.

The problems, contradictions and pressures that confront all East Africa appear to weigh heaviest on Tanzania.

The Tanzanian Republic is not yet five years old. In that short lifetime problems at home and abroad have accumulated that would tax a great power.

Tanzania's area is 363,000 square miles, about the size of Texas, Louisiana and Arkansas combined. The population is estimated at 10 million, give or take a million. Accurate statistics do not exist. The life expectancy is between 35 and 40 years and one objective of the present five-year plan is to raise it to 50. The annual per capita income is less than $55.

Little Land Cultivated

The main crops are sisal, cotton and corn, but only about 10 per cent of the country is cultivated. Of the cultivated land, 90 per cent is devoted to grain and other food crops for local consumption on a subsistence basis.

The poverty in the roadside villages is bad enough. But off the roads the visitor moves into the stone age, to little clusters of huts in which there are no manufactured articles, where women still carry water for two or three miles, where life is short, brutal and hopeless.

The land cries out for help and development. Britain, the United States and West Germany have helped. But circumstances make it impossible for Tanzania to tend to her domestic affairs.

Geography and the high principles of President Julius K. Nyerere, "the teacher" as he likes to be called, have involved Tanzania deeply in the affairs of Africa.

The Portuguese territory of Mozambique lies to the south and Tanzania supports training camps for Freedom Fighters on her territory and assists a guerrilla government. So do the Chinese Communists.

The Congo, potentially the richest of African states, lies to the west and arms for the Congolese rebels went from China through Tanzania.

Break With Britain

To show his dissatisfaction with what he considered British weakness on the Rhodesian independence issue, Mr. Nyerere broke relations with Britain, a country that provided most of the economic guidance and assistance to Tanzania as she emerged into nationhood and maintained civil servants, doctors and teachers.

The high cost of principle and of agitated involvement in African affairs contrasts sharply with the example of neighboring Kenya. There President Jomo Kenyatta's Government, operating on a sounder economic base, has turned inward, intent on building the country's economy.

Mr. Nyerere, knowing his country's difficulties and aware of his ministers' problems, places his faith in education. Even there, he concedes he is in difficulties. There are just too many who want to go to school and not enough classrooms or teachers. But he has the faith his people need—just as they need about everything else.

March 21, 1966

TANZANIA IS BESET BY DECLINE IN JOBS

Strikes and Unrest Hamper What Little Output There Is

By LAWRENCE FELLOWS
Special to The New York Times

DAR ES SALAAM, Tanzania, May 31—In the sticky, oppressive heat of the decaying courtroom, 10 forlorn-looking black Africans stood in the dock, shifting uneasily as the charges were read to them.

They were accused of having taken part in a strike of bus drivers here last Friday in an effort to force the dismissal of the company's British manager and open his job to a black.

The accused were led away to jail to await trial and the Government said that more arrests would follow. Strikes are illegal in Tanzania.

The number of people in paid employment has gone down steadily in the six years since the British gave the territory independence. There were 412,000 people working when the British left, but now there are not many more than 200,000 at work in a population of 10 million.

An initial setback in employment was unavoidable. Independence came at the end of a year that showed no increase in national income. The production of sisal fiber for rope slumped. A drop in world prices had hit the farmers, starting layoffs on sisal and coffee estates that have continued year after year.

The Government has persuaded some peasant farmers to plant cotton, but not all of them have found the prices attractive enough to make it worthwhile to pick it.

The confusion, disappointment and resentment that began to build up around the country found an outlet in bursts of racialism. White men's farms were confiscated. Indian traders and artisans were berated by politicians and last year hundreds were deported. That cost black Africans some jobs.

Last February, when labor troubles began and some of the more radical members of the Cabinet applied pressure, President Julius K. Nyerere nationalized the banks and several foreign-owned industries.

Meat Packing Reduced

They have not proved easy to run. By taking over the banks, Mr. Nyerere largely shut himself out of the London money market, where bankers here had always gotten what they needed to finance crops. The country is so short of banking talent that it has still not been able to restore even ordinary commerce. Among the first victims have been the nationalized industries and the Tanzanians who work for them.

At the Metal Box Company, one of those the President said was being taken over, there was a decline in orders soon after his announcement. The company, which was still managing its affairs, laid off some workers. The rest retaliated with a go-slow strike, which is not illegal and which cut production by 90 per cent.

The immediate effect was to reduce production at Tanganyika Packers, the major food-processing plant. Without cans they had to cut back on slaughtering. There were some layoffs and a strike is in prospect.

The Bata Shoe Company has refused to accept nationalization on Mr. Nyerere's terms. The company has told the Government that it can have 30 per cent if it pays for it and leaves management alone; otherwise, it said, the Government can have the whole factory for nothing and run it if it can.

The workers called the British and Canadian managers "bloodsuckers" and "saboteurs" and started a go-slow that almost halted production and triggered a mass of new layoffs.

The company has said that it will have to let two-thirds of the staff go anyway as a result of a drop in orders, presumably because of the dwindling number of Tanzanians with money to buy shoes.

June 1, 1967

Tanzania Begins a Cultural Revolution, Kenya an Economic One

By LAWRENCE FELLOWS
Special to The New York Times

NAIROBI, Kenya, Jan. 1—Two neighboring countries in East Africa opened separate limited revolutions today—one "cultural" and one economic.

In Tanzania, Operation Vijana got under way at midnight when patrols of "green guards" started out to clear the country of miniskirts, wigs, skin bleaches, hair straighteners and trousers that hug hips or are very tight or have bell bottoms or are fitted with wide belts.

"Tanzanian youths must do away with these obscene foreign influences," insisted Joseph Nyerere, secretary general of Tanzania's Youth League.

His brother, President Julius Nyerere, calls the league "green guards," who will lead the country's cultural revolution.

Swahili Word Is Used

Vijana is the Swahili word for youths.

"Youths in Europe are frustrated," Joseph Nyerere said two days ago at a rally in the national stadium at Dar es Salaam. "Now we seem to want to imitate the way they behave, even the way they smile. We will eradicate such illusions. Our youths will not be strangers in their own country."

The guards seem to have taken the campaign seriously, for 500 who roamed through Dar es Salaam today reported no incidents. From Tanga it was reported that 11 young women who frequent bars in that port on the Indian Ocean burned their miniskirts before a big crowd this morning and vowed to oppose all alien cultural trends.

The Green Guards had been given two months of intensive

police training. There was still no word today about whether any allowances would be made for tourists who violate the new rules.

Here in Kenya, a law came into force today that is expected to put about 3,000 Indian traders out of business and that may start another mass exodus of Indians to Britain. The new law is aimed at "Duka Wallahs," shopkeepers, of Indian origin whose families have lived in East Africa for generations but who did not obtain Kenya citizenship when the country became independent five years ago.

Mwai Kibaki, Kenya's Minister for Commerce and Industry, said today that in the next six months trading licenses would not be granted to noncitizens except in a few areas in Nairobi, Mombasa, Nakuru, Kisumu, Eldoret and Thika.

The exceptions were being made, he said, because there were not yet citizens in these places ready to take over. "Within the next six months the Government estimates that about 3,000 noncitizen traders will have been refused licenses, he said. "This is a conservative estimate. There could be more."

As many at 20,000 Indians may head for Britain, an exodus on the scale of the one in February when many Indians left to beat immigration barriers Britain was setting up.

Dr. G. S. Sandhu, president of the Association of British Citizens in Kenya, said yesterday he assumed that holders of British passports, if they are unemployed and homeless, even if they are of Indian origin, would not be turned away by Britain.

An official of the British High Commission said here tonight that the law enacted in Britain last year empowers the Home Secretary to restrict immigration of passport holders who have never had close family ties to Britain. The law sets no limit in numbers, but the House of Commons has been told the number would be about 1,500 a year.

The High Commission here has had no word from London on the number to be allowed to enter Britain.

"I did not think the Kenya Government would enforce this act so severely," Dr. Sandhu said. "But they have and most of these poor people will have nowhere else to go except Britain."

In Nakuru, the secretary of the Indian Association, M. R. Thakar, was asked if he expected an exodus of Indians from his area.

"Very much so," he said. "It will take a few months, but it will happen."

Of the 10 million people in Kenya, about 160,000 are Indians and they control about 80 per cent of the commerce in the country. It is estimated that as many as 120,000 might be eligible to seek entry into Britain.

The exodus, if it comes, may be more spread out than it was last year. The trading licenses will be withdrawn over a period of six months, Mr. Kibaki said. He also said traders would be given varying times of between one and six months to wind up their affairs.

January 2, 1969

Tanzanian Self-Help Villages Crowded

By MARVINE HOWE
Special to The New York Times

KEREGE, Tanzania — "We have too many people here," a leader of Kerege Ujamaa Village said. "Everybody wants to join the ujamaas."

That is the main trouble with Tanzania's self-help village plan, known as ujamaa, or familyhood; it is too popular.

Ujamaa villages are voluntary, socialistic communes, an African version of the Israeli kibbutzim.

Kerege, 25 miles north of Dar es Salaam on a busy dirt road, looks like a progressive oasis in the bush. On one side of the road is a neatly painted school, a small clinic and the office of the only political party, the Tanganyika African National Union, known as TANU. Across the way is a large water tower, a carpentry shop, a dairy and barn with several tractors and harvesters, and a modest cashew-nut "factory" opened a month ago.

"Ujamaa villages are coming up like mushrooms," according to Ntimbamjayo Melinga, party secretary for the program. "We are being overtaken by events and haven't got enough good leadership."

There are over a thousand villages all over this country of 13 million people, some with as few as 30 families and others with more than 2,000.

President Pushes Plan

Ever since independence in December, 1961, President Julius K. Nyerere has tried to bridge the economic and social gap between the urban minority and the vast rural majority. His views on rural development were published in April, 1962, in an essay, "Ujamaa—the Basis of African Socialism."

His Government made various attempts to begin to regroup the rural population into villages to facilitate the introduction of technical progress and modern necessities such as potable water, electricity, schools and dispensaries.

The main impetus for the program came in 1967, when the governing party adopted a policy of socialism based on hard work, self-reliance and the development of agriculture.

There are said to be some 1.5 million small private farmers on scattered holdings who in most cases continue to work along traditional lines.

The Government and the party have waged an aggressive campaign to spread the ujamaa spirit. "Prosperity through a cooperative life" is the slogan at public meetings.

Numerous incentives have been put at the disposal of ujamaa villages: land-bank credit, veterinary services, free seeds and fertilizer. The movement seems to have caught on, and every day some group announces that it has created a village.

"The Government handles the technical side of things and we deal with ideology," Mr. Melinga said. It is up to the party to set up a kind of government in the village, which eventually adopts its own charter.

Earlier Plans Failed

René Dumont, director of research at the Paris National Agronomy Institute, was invited by President Nyerere to visit Tanzania shortly after the ujamaa program got under way and to advise the Government on agricultural development plans. In a report he said: "The 'villagization' of the Tanzanian countryside, which was the aim in 1962, certainly appears desirable, on condition that it does not cost too much."

Earlier Tanzanian settlement plans failed because the change was too rapid and there were too many subsidies and too much mechanization.

Kerege actually started out as a settlement but, like many others, was converted to an ujamaa village when the authorities saw that settlements were too expensive.

Now, however, Kerege is a model ujamaa village that is attracting new workers every day.

Another example is Kumuhasha Ujamaa Village in the Kigoma region, near Lake Tanganyika. A group of seven jobless men got together in 1968 and, aided by a missionary and the party district officer, set up a farming community on a 17-acre site. Encouraged by the results and with their group enlarged to 32, they decided to form an ujamaa village in 1969.

The group has doubled its acreage and raises peanuts as a cash crop and corn, millet and beans for its own use.

The first ujamaa village will soon be opened on the slopes of Mount Kilimanjaro, with 129 families taking over a 177-acre farm formerly operated by two cooperative societies.

Notwithstanding the ujamaa rush, many people are skeptical about the program, which they consider too utopian.

On the other hand, the United Nations Economic Commission for Africa has cited the ujamaa villages as the only African attempt to restructure the socio-economic system of the peasantry.

October 5, 1970

Tanzania, in Mood of Leftist Urgency, Seizes Property and Attempts to Rally People

By CHARLES MOHR
Special to The New York Times

DAR ES SALAAM, Tanzania, May 9—After a long period of relative political somnolence, left-wing forces seem to be increasingly in command of this East African nation of 13 million.

The abrupt shift to the left is accompanied by volleys of revolutionary rhetoric and seizure of private property. The Government has published a new list of buildings nationalized under a law to end what was termed exploitation by landlords. It brought the total of buildings seized to 1,341 since the law was passed April 23.

The new atmosphere of urgency and militancy began after the army of Uganda seized control of that neighboring country Jan. 25 from President Milton A. Obote, who had taken tentative steps to initiate socialism there.

President Julius K. Nyerere was "unquestionably shaken by the Uganda coup," said one foreign observer. Mr. Nyerere probably viewed the coup d'état—the first in the immediate area—as dangerous precedent.

Amin Is Criticized

In addition, Tanzanians were summoned to mass rallies to be told that Uganda's leader, Gen. Idi Amin, was a tool of Western nations that hoped to stop the development of African socialism.

Emergency meetings of the only party, the Tanzanian African National Union, led to the announcement that a people's militia would be formed. Presumably such a militia would discourage any possible coup by Tanzania's regular army, estimated to total about 7,000 men.

Campaigns were begun to politically "educate" the masses and there were attacks by the press on civil servants and other "bourgeois foot draggers" who were said to be holding back socialization.

Then late last month the bill authorizing the seizure of buildings worth more than 100,000 shillings, or about $14,300, was quickly passed.

President Nyerere referred to the bill as a "mopping up," measure. Since 1967 he has nationalized banks and insurance companies, taken shares ranging from 51 to 100 per cent in industries and has placed the export and import trade in national hands.

Many well-informed sources, however, believe that President Nyerere is not through and will soon nationalize such remnants of private enterprise as trucking and bus companies, garages and automobile sales agencies. Some of his party's leftists would like to see the take-over of retail trade but this may be postponed indefinitely, according to some observers.

The buildings take-over, which exempts owner-occupied houses and very cheap houses, will affect most urban office buildings, shops, apartments and middle-class houses. Compensation will be paid only for buildings less than 10 years old, on a sliding scale.

Owners Mostly Asians

The list of owners names published so far confirm the belief that most such buildings are owned by the Asian Community, people of Indian or Pakistani extraction.

The loss of income from rents, coming on top of exclusion from wholesaling and import trade, has hit the economic interests of the Asian community, which numbers about 90,000, with considerable severity. Asians are still permitted to deal in retail trade, however.

Since there is considerable animosity toward the Asians, whose shrewd and tireless enterprise have made them masters of small business, the takeovers have apparently been a popular step so far. On the other hand, the take-overs will do nothing to end a current housing shortage here and will, in fact, throw the burden of building onto the state, which has already been forced to reduce funds for development because of shrinking currency reserves.

Tenants have been ordered to pay their next rent to the Government through the national bank. It is unclear how maintenance will be handled, how tenants will rent space in the future and how much pressure the measure will bring on an already burdened bureaucracy.

10,000 Chinese There

What triggered the move to the left is a matter of speculation and doubt. Apparently, however, it was not a result of the growing presence of Communist China. About 10,000 Chinese are here working on the Tanzania—Zambia Railway and hundreds of others are giving military training.

However, diplomats say there is still no evidence that the Chinese have become involved in local politics or have worked to guide the activities of young radicals.

"There would be little point anyway" said one observer. "On every major foreign policy question important to China, Tanzania is already acceptable to China and the country is certainly trying to develop in a socialist way."

All Communist Asian nations are represented here and even the exiled Cambodian faction of Prince Norodom Sihanouk is to open an embassy.

A combination of alarms and frustrations, both foreign and domestic, are discussed as factors behind the shift.

Tanzania was stirred more than many African nations last fall by the incursion into Guinea by forces hostile to President Sékou Touré and sent funds to Guinea for defense. President Nyerere may also have become convinced, sources said, that Guinea's "people's militia" saved the day.

Stirring the People

"Nyerere has clearly felt ever since the Uganda coup," one observer said, "that he must arouse mass consciousness and stir the people up or they may just sit idly by if the Tanzanian revolution is threatened."

President Nyerere also has cause to feel frustration about foreign policy goals. An increasing number of conservative African states have shown interest in a dialogue with South Africa.

Domestically, there is beginning to be serious talk that First Vice President Abeid Karume might like to succeed Mr. Nyerere as President.

In a recent speech Mr. Karume, who is head of the Revolutionary Council of Zanzibar Island, criticized a policy that forbids office holders to own remunerative property. He said that private citizens, including Asians, had been permitted to do so. This was generally interpreted as a veiled hint that Mr. Nyerere was not radical enough.

For Blacks Only

Mr. Karume has also taken such steps as donating free housing projects to workers in Dar es Salaam. He argues that citizenship should be restricted to blacks and says that all foreigners shouuld leave by 1972.

Although President Nyerere has developed a more egalitarian society than in many African nations, this has not speeded economic growth or changed living conditions much. Rural people have been slow to respond to calls to join cooperative villages and only a small fraction of the rural population belongs.

"Nyerere is under increasing pressure from the left and the moderates are more and more afraid to expose themselves."

An example of recent criticism is the remark of a left-wing minister that the present examination system in education should be scrapped because "if we accept that one student has failed and one has passed we are admitting that some people are better than others."

May 16, 1971

4 Gunmen Murder Zanzibar Chief and Wound 2 Aides

DAR ES SALAAM, Tanzania, April 8 (AP) — Sheik Abeid Amani Karume, the onetime sailor who ruled Zanzibar under a stern socialist regime and brought in Peking technicians to help develop the island, was shot to death there last night by four men.

The Tanzanian Government, with which Zanzibar is united, reported today that Sheik Karume had been killed and two members of the Revolutionary Council, of which he was chairman, had been wounded in the shooting at a political headquarters. Sources said Sheik Karume was playing cards with friends when the assassins struck.

Thabit Kombo, secretary-general of the Afro-Shirazi party, Zanzibar's only political group, was reported seriously wounded. Another council member, Ibrahim Sadala, also was shot, reports from the island added.

One assassin was killed and the island's army and police fanned out in a search for the other three, the reports said.

The Revolutionary Council announced over the Zanzibar radio that it would continue Sheik Karume's leftist policies. The council of about 30 persons remained in control. Tanzanian sources said the assassination had not been followed by an attempt to overthrow the government. There was no word, however, on who might have been behind the killing.

The council lifted a curfew for three hours this afternoon to allow Zanzibaris to shop, then reimposed the curfew until further notice. Armed troops and civilians were in the streets. Public buildings were guarded.

President Julius K. Nyerere of Tanzania announced that he and his Cabinet would attend a state funeral for Sheik Karume on Zanzibar Monday. The island, less than 20 miles off East Africa, is part of Tanzania, but the Karume regime had broad local autonomy.

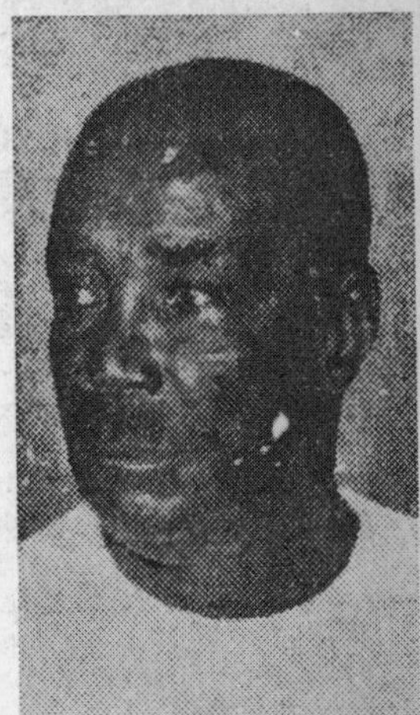

Associated Press

Sheik Abeid Amani Karume

April 9, 1972

One-Party State Planned in Uganda

KAMPALA, Uganda, Jan. 7 (Reuters) — Uganda will restrict the growth of political parties and develop as a one-party Socianst State, Prime Minister Milton A. Obote said today.

In a statement issued in Lango, Mr. Obote said there was an urgent need to cultivate national consciousness and to promote national parties, "as opposed to the present situation that allows for factional and tribal groupings."

Opposition leaders in Uganda have still to win the respect of the public, the Prime Minister declared, and opposition leaders outside Parliament have been "irresponsible, opportunist and subversive."

"We are firmly convinced that a one-party state does not inevitably and necessarily remove the opportunity of giving voice to the expression of individual opinion and the giving of constructive criticism," he said.

January 8, 1964

Making of a President, Uganda Style

By EDWARD R. F. SHEEHAN

UGANDA is an enchanted country, at once equatorial and salubrious, situated some several thousand feet above the level of the sea, a land of grassy hills, glinting lakes and crested cranes, of the sources of the Nile and the Mountains of the Moon. It is, like the other nations of East Africa, a British invention, and one of which the British have some reason to be proud, for they ruled it rather well from the day they imposed their protectorate in 1894 until they made the country independent four years ago.

Lord Lugard, soldier and adventurer, created Uganda partly out of the Bantu kingdoms of Buganda, Bunyoro, Ankole and Toro—all but one of which have, in their anomalous African way, kept their tribal monarchies intact, even though the modern Uganda which comprises them is officially a unitary state. In this epoch of galloping egalitarianism such kingships should have the right to be retained for the resonance of their nomenclature if for nothing else. How many hierarchies elsewhere can rival a Sir Charles Godfrey Gasyonga II, Rubambansi the Mugabe of Ankole? Or a Sir George David Kamurasi Rukidi III, Rukirabasaija the Mukama of Toro? Or a Sir Tito Gafabusa Winyi IV, the Mukama of Bunyoro? One might even mention His Highness Sir Edward Frederick Mutesa II, K.B.E., the Kabaka of Buganda—"King Freddie" to his friends—were it not for his recent and very involuntary retirement.

In fact, if we intend to talk about Uganda, we can hardly avoid mentioning either the Kabaka of Buganda or the exceedingly unceremonious circumstances of his deposition. A gregarious, easy-going gentleman, the Kabaka sat on a lion-headed throne in robes of almost papal splendor, an object of intense reverence among his people, who are Uganda's richest and most advanced, though they embody but a seventh of the country's total population of about seven million. In view of his kingdom's resources, it was understandably disturbing to the Central Government when, last May, the Kabaka's legislature ordered the Central Government out of Bugandan territory forthwith. Indeed, since the national capital, Kampala, is situated in the very heart of Buganda, it is not surprising that President A. Milton Obote considered the eviction notice an act of rebellion. Thus did a prolonged war of nerves between Uganda's two most prominent personalities—the Kabaka and Obote—escalate into a final confrontation.

On May 23, much of Buganda rose up in revolt against the Central Government. Police stations were put to the torch, a policeman in one was burned alive, some civilians were killed, roadblocks were erected, communications were cut. Mobs of Baganda (as the tribesmen of Buganda are called) began to rampage about; some wielded *pangas*, others had firearms. A few of those arrested with firearms confessed they had obtained them from the Kabaka's great-walled, silver-domed palace atop Mengo Hill outside Kampala. President Obote declared a state of emergency, and, so it is said, was moved to quote a maxim popular among African revolutionaries: "When an old society is pregnant with a new one, the only midwife is force." He ordered the Uganda Army to surround the Kabaka's palace.

At dawn of May 24, the army (possibly exceeding Obote's instructions) launched a heavy assault on the palace, where hundreds of Baganda had gathered to defend their ruler against just such a danger. After 12 hours of savage combat, interrupted at one point by a heavy rainstorm but costing in the end perhaps 200 or 300 lives, the Government troops overran the palace and seized a large quantity of illegal arms and ammunition.

In the meanwhile, the Kabaka himself had managed an escape which has already become part of the mythology of his people. In his own version of the events, recounted later in London, he jumped from the high wall of the palace—and hailed a taxi which happened to be passing by. ("My brother, Prince Henry, was less fortunate," the Kabaka has written. "Prince Henry found no taxi and had to queue for a bus.") The Kabaka then related a heart-rending tale of his own trek for several weeks and many hundreds of miles through the bush, forests and savanna of Uganda, living on wild berries and sweet potatoes, sleeping in thorn thickets. Eventually, he says, he reached the Congo and then hitchhiked to Burundi, whence he flew to his present exile in London.

The Kabaka placed full blame for his downfall on the misdeeds of Dr. Obote. "He considered me a rival, a fact which might surprise those who think of me as a playboy monarch, gay King Freddie, late of Cambridge University and the Brigade of Guards. Uganda is fast becoming a totalitarian, one-party police state. Milton Obote is an intelligent man, and an able one, but in power and seeking power he has learned all the wrong lessons. He has become a schemer; his mind dwells always on plots and plotting, and he suspects everyone else is the same. It was not always so. He once had a strain of humanity which now seems to have become lost. . . ."

THE collision of the Kabaka and President Obote dramatizes the clash between tribal tradition and the new nationalism that is raging throughout all of Africa. History is the mother of irony, and it is interesting that the Kabaka of Buganda, whose ancestors were noted for the savage speed with which they dispatched all suspected rivals, should now himself become the victim of precautionary violence. Indeed, unless we understand something of the history of Buganda, the country's most recent convulsions make little sense.

In contrast to the highly civilized contemporary Kabaka, his namesake and ancestor, Mutesa I, who ruled Buganda at the time of its first penetration by the British a century ago, was (in Alan Moorehead's phrase) "a savage and bloodthirsty monster." On becoming king he instantly burned alive some 60 of his brothers (which was regarded as a normal precaution against rebellion), and on one particularly horrendous day he had 2,000 victims tortured and burned at the stake as an offering to the spirit of his father, Suna.

Nevertheless, Mutesa was a gifted ruler. In fact, for centuries before the coming of the British, the Baganda had belied the myth that, left to themselves, untouched by Western civilization, Africans could not rise above the most primitive forms of human society. Before having any contact with the outside world, they had achieved a culture well in advance of any other south of the Sahara; though they were illiterate and their religion was a barbarous witchcraft, they were accomplished in weaving, music and architecture.

Following the imposition of the protectorate, the British used the Baganda to wage wars of pacification against many of the 25 or 30 other tribes in Uganda. As a reward, Buganda was granted a privileged status together with portions of other tribal kingdoms. Its system of tribal administration was extended by the British over the whole protectorate. After World War II, Britain's hesitant efforts to develop Uganda into a democratic, integrated nation constantly stumbled over the special rights previously granted to Buganda. The intensely tribalistic Baganda wanted nothing to do with a united Uganda, and in our own time they have, under the most recent Kabaka, ceaselessly intrigued for their independence as a separate nation. Before Britain granted Uganda independence in 1962, Buganda made several attempts to secede from the rest of the country. It took a most delicately balanced federal Constitution to delay the day of judgment that finally came this year with the uprising of the Baganda and then the Central Government's reprisal against the royal palace. With that reprisal, nationalism seemed to triumph over tribalism; President Obote seemed to have vanquished his great antagonist. But the Baganda will not soon forget the dishonoring of their king—nor can anyone insure that, despite their present mood of impotence, they will not one day rise up again to inflict on President Obote the traditional vengeance of the Mutesas.

WHAT sort of man is this who toppled King Freddie from his throne? Apollo Milton Obote was born in a mud hut, sometime in 1924—he knows neither the month nor the day—in the small village of Akakoro on Lake Kwania, Lango District, in northern Uganda. He is the third of nine children born to Stanley Opeto, a minor chieftain, and his wife Pulisikira. (Opeto was polygamous and had three other wives.)

Obote is a Lango, one of the northern Nilotic tribes, tribal origins always being significant in the career of any African politician. Even today a visit to his birthplace reveals much of the man: The crooked thatch-roofed huts of his childhood are gone, but nearby, amidst tall green grass and flat-topped acacia trees, identical dwellings have replaced them. His elderly father inhabits a neat, painted mud hut to this day, and has journeyed to the capital, Kampala, only once in his lifetime.

"It is not true that I began life as a poor boy, as so many say," Dr. Obote remarked in a conversation I had with him recently in Kampala. "I was born of a ruling family. My grandfather, great-grandfather and great-great-grandfather were all rulers. But the story of my having been a shepherd, and a goatherd, is true. My father wanted to keep me near him. All my brothers and sisters went to school, but I remained at home with my father. Odd as it might appear, I took this as a sign of my father's love for me. I used to spend hours a day tending to my sheep, cattle and goats—all alone. I started school when I was 12 years old."

Obote's academic history is not a glittering one; he joins Sir Winston Churchill on the list of drop-outs of distinction. He was discharged from more than one secondary school for failing to meet required standards, and at Makerere University College in Kampala he withdrew (but was not expelled) after two years.

"I left Makerere because I decided I wanted to practice either law or politics," Obote says. "I was offered a chance to study law by an American university, but the Uganda Government (that is, the British) turned me down because they said that American law was no good for this country. Then they refused me a place at Gordon Memorial College at Khartoum because they said I could not make up my mind where or what I wanted to study. So I gave up and took some correspondence courses instead." Obote's attitude toward the British today seems to reflect the classical compound of envy, reverence and resentment so common among his generation of African intelligentsia.

His relatively scant formal education—his failure either to achieve distinction as a scholar at home or to attend a university in England or America—has unquestionably marked Obote psychologically and has given him what one of his critics claims is "a painful inferiority complex which he seeks to conceal in various pretentious ways." These considerations may help to explain some of the interesting, and by no means obnoxious, poses which Obote strikes as President today—the conscious and somewhat strained elegance of his conversational English (despite a very difficult accent), his obvious disdain of native costumes, the impeccability and deliberate good taste of his British-cut wardrobe, the title of "Doctor" that he brandishes before his name. His "doctorate" is purely an encomium, an honorary LL.D. awarded to him by Long Island University during a visit to America, and most probably arranged by the State Department.

AT 26, not long after leaving Makerere, Obote took a job in Kenya as a common laborer at a sugar works, for about $3 a month. "I had become interested in the trade-union movement, and I decided that the best way to learn about trade unionism was at the bottom," he says. He drifted in Kenya from one humble job to another—laborer, clerk, salesman—engaging (despite British displeasure) in union organizing, and learning something of African street politics as a founder-member of the Kenya African Union.

In 1957, having returned home, Obote was named by the Lango District Council as a representative in the national Legislative Council in Kampala, the precursor of the present Parliament. From that moment, his rise to prominence and power was phenomenally swift, and he soon became a skillful craftsman in the black Byzantium of Ugandan tribal politics.

Though he entered Parliament as a member of the Uganda National Congress (and soon became its head), he broke away from the U.N.C. following a factional dispute and founded the Uganda People's Congress (U.P.C.) in 1960, with himself as president. A boycott by Buganda removed many more experienced leaders from Parliament, and in 1961 Obote emerged as leader of the Opposition. In the following year, he led his party to victory in the national elections which preceded Uganda's full independence.

As Prime Minister, Obote played a major role in framing the Ugandan Constitution at a conference in London on the eve of independence. In his bargaining, he was forced to make full allowances for Bugandan particularism; the ultimate independence Constitution granted Buganda a large measure of self-rule and seemed to perpetuate the kingdom's special position as first among equals.

In fact, Obote's party, though the largest, lacked a majority in Parliament. The second-largest faction was the predominantly Roman Catholic Democratic party; the balance of power was held by the radical Bagandan Kabaka Yekka (Kabaka Only) party. To govern, Obote was obliged to forge an unnatural and exceedingly uneasy coalition with the Kabaka Yekka — a coalition that attempted to accommodate two totally contradictory visions of Uganda's future. Even then, it was no secret that Obote aspired to a unified country which would eventually adopt a unitary Constitution within a one-party state.

AS a means of integrating Buganda with the rest of the nation, Obote — with great difficulty — persuaded his party to accept the Kabaka as President of the whole country. It did not take Obote and the Kabaka terribly long to have a falling out. But by offers of Government patronage and other means, Obote began to lure M.P.'s of the other two parties into his own U.P.C. When he had a clear majority, he broke off the coalition. By mid-1965, the country seemed on the verge of becoming a one-party state.

Then the U.P.C. ran into trouble. The Cabinet began to split up along tribal lines. One clique was identified with Obote and labeled "the Northerners"; the other, labeled "the Bantu faction," was composed mostly of Southerners. By the beginning of 1966, tribal, religious, ideological, factional and personal disputes within the U.P.C. became so serious that the party appeared on the point of disintegration. From without, Buganda's hostility to the Central Government was renewed with growing force.

A major crisis was inevitable, and it exploded at the beginning of last February. Obote left Kampala for a fortnight's tour of his home area in the north. Hardly was he out of the capital when the Cabinet joined Parliament in accusing him and three associates of corruption and of plotting to overthrow the Constitution.

Kampala reeked with rumors of coup and countercoup; whispers whirled of mysterious troop movements; ministers vanished from their ministries. But though his Government seemed about to topple with an ignominious thud, the Prime Minister did not panic. He calmly continued his tour of the north, dedicating schools and addressing throngs of his own people, carefully considering his next moves and—given his character—probably plotting 50 steps ahead of his enemies.

Then he returned to Kampala and immediately seized the initiative. He publicly denied the charges against him, and, surprisingly, prevailed upon the Cabinet to create an impartial and irreproachable commission of inquiry composed of three distinguished judges from Kenya and Tanzania. The testimony at the hearings was tortuous and contradictory. One key witness disappeared, and many questions—such as the fate of some smuggled Congolese gold—remained unanswered. But the hearings produced no conclusive evidence against Obote or his supporters.

MEANWHILE, Obote was maneuvering to regroup his forces and consolidate his power. At a Cabinet meeting in late February, police burst in, and — despite some understandable kicks and screams—dragged the five dissident "Bantu" ministers (whom Obote accused of having plotted with the Kabaka) off to imprisonment in the North. Obote then announced that, to avert an anti-Government army coup, he was temporarily assuming all powers, suspending the Constitution and dismissing the Kabaka from his office as President. The rest of the Cabinet rallied to the Prime Minister and he entrusted effective control of the army to a friend and fellow Northerner, Idi Amin.

On April 15, Obote suddenly convened Parliament and informed the members that they were sitting as a constituent assembly to pass on a new Constitution. The document proclaimed Uganda henceforth a unitary state—depriving the Kingdom of Buganda of both its federal status and many of its entrenched privileges. The roar of Uganda Air Force jets could be heard overhead, armed troops gazed down from the galleries; the Speaker forthwith called for the vote. Not surprisingly, Parliament chose to ratify. Prime Minister Obote was promptly sworn in as Uganda's new President—an office which he had taken care to provide with very strong powers—and the Chief Justice took an oath of allegiance to the new Constitution, thereby intimating that its legality would be upheld in the courts. Despite its highly unorthodox manner of presentation, Obote's Constitution retained many provisions of the old one, nor did it deal a deathblow to the system of checks and balances.

There followed the disastrous decision by the Buganda Legislature to order the Central Government out of Buganda, and Obote's angry rejoinder in dispatching Government troops to the palace of the Kabaka.

PRESIDENT OBOTE appears obsessed with his private vision of becoming a nation builder, the acknowledged founding father of a united and integrated Uganda, and the architect of a major and lasting transformation of its feudal society. As yet, he enjoys neither the prestige nor the personal fame of East Africa's other two Presidents—Jomo Kenyatta of Kenya and Dr. Julius Nyerere of Tanzania—but he probably surpasses both of them as a tactician and as a pure political animal who possesses an almost mystical understanding of the mechanics and sources of power. He does not inspire the awe or reverence that Kenyatta's charismatic history commands in Kenya. Nor, despite his intelligence and omnivorous reading habits, can he claim to possess the intellectual brilliance of Nyerere, but then, neither is he burdened with the excessive introspection, diffidence and indecisiveness which so often seem to have immobilized the President of Tanzania.

In the misty forest of Ugandan tribal politics, however, Obote has proved himself to be a maneuverer whose foresight and cunning have invariably overturned the most ingenious stratagems of his enemies. When his political fortunes were at their lowest ebb, and just as he appeared to be losing his grip, not only did he surprise his opponents by creating the commission of inquiry, but he took the brilliant gamble of assuring that its composition was beyond his political control, free to scrutinize his personal probity as it pleased. Then he turned the attention of the country from the debate over his honesty to the controversy over his new Constitution.

In their repeated confrontations, Obote has consistently outwitted the Kabaka, who never really had the stomach for the power game in the first place. The Kabaka was under pressure from his own people to prove that he was running Buganda, and pushed by foolish advisers to take untenable positions from which there was no retreat.

DESPITE some lingering suspicions of his probity, even Obote's severe critics concede that avarice is not one of his primary motivations. He has not enriched his family, nor does he live luxuriously himself. He has yet to move to the Presidential mansion from the more modest Prime Minister's residence, where he lives with his third wife, Miria—a Baganda tribeswoman—and some of his children. He is a notoriously frugal eater with a bad stomach, and at public gatherings he does little more than pick at his food.

Like other leaders of his type, Obote has surrounded himself with a Cabinet now composed for the most part of nonentities. Well aware of the limitations of his own lieutenants, and apparently convinced that he is the one man in Uganda who can do things properly, he finds it difficult to delegate authority and reserves virtually all major decisions to himself, determining even such matters as agricultural or mineral policy over the heads of the ministers concerned. He is of course careful not to permit any rivals to his power, and each time he leaves the country he deputizes a different minister. He watches the army very closely, as well he should; he has been purging Bantu officers, replacing them with Northerners, and giving the new leadership pretty much what it wants. But what will happen if one day the army decides that Obote is not giving enough?

Obote is extremely moody. He oscillates between congeniality and belligerency. At times he rages at his ministers as if they were schoolboys. People who have argued with him say that he has an irrational hatred of being challenged. His eyes flame; at times he becomes violent and, some believe, unbalanced; when he is caught in this temper there is no reasoning with him. In the past, moreover, he has displayed not only a certain tendency toward deceit but a highly developed talent for rabble-rousing. He is, one acquaintance says, "congenitally suspicious—ready to believe anything."

His suspicions used to turn rather often against the United States, but his relations with Washington have improved remarkably in recent months, due in no small measure to the arrival of Henry Stebbins as American Ambassador.

The Soviet influence in Kampala is much stronger than the Chinese. As for his own ideology, Obote says: "I have none, except pragmatism." Nor is he necessarily as dazzled by the doctrines of the one-party state as he once appeared to be. Now that there are few more than a handful of Opposition members left in Parliament, he is said to believe that "any majority of more than 50 is dangerous." He is apparently disillusioned because the lop-sided predominance of his own party has invited division and decay, not to mention subversion, nepotism, inefficiency, apathy and the arrogance that accompanies too much power.

UNITARY STATE— Three of Uganda's ancient Bantu kingdoms, Bunyoro, Ankole and Toro, have kept their tribal monarchies intact, but the Kabaka of Buganda was deposed when he crossed President Obote.

OBOTE is now said to recognize the need for a free and effective Opposition as he casts his eye across Africa and discerns the general failure to devise workable alternatives to the stimulus of rival parties.

Despite all the high-flown theories propounded for Africa by Western liberals, the single-party state does not necessarily represent all of the people or even a substantial part of them; neither does it guarantee a stable government nor a liberation from tribalism. Even in Tanzania, Dr. Nyerere felt obliged to put up rival candidates within his single-party system to provide his people with a genuine choice during their most recent national elections.

Does this mean that President Obote will allow early, free elections to submit his new Constitution and his own popularity to the judgment of his people? He has been vague about that.

Benedicto Kiwanuka, the president of the Democratic party (the once-upon-a-time Opposition), who was Chief Minister of Uganda before independence, is much more definite. "I don't know what's in Obote's mind," he told me, "but we mean to have free elections by April, 1967, or earlier.

"Obote has become a dictator. If the Kabaka should test his deposition in the courts and win, Obote might decide to imitate Nkrumah and depose the judges.

"I don't hold any brief for the Kabaka—I had my own battles with him when I was Chief Minister—but we mean to have free elections and we mean to put an end to Obote's dictatorship, and I invite you to believe me."

My encounter with Dr. Obote himself came in his modest office in the modernistic Parliament building in Kampala. He was faultlessly tailored in a dark business suit; black, small-buckled shoes; a tie emblazoned with a tiny, crested-crane, the symbolic bird of Uganda. He smoked incessantly; on occasion he would reach out from his chair to finger his quilted walking stick. Leisurely, and sometimes eloquently, he gave voice to his convictions.

The violent events of last May? "I'm ruined and heartbroken by what happened. I feel that Uganda, our precious pearl, has been soiled."

African corruption: "It stems simply from the failure of the corrupted politicians to appreciate their role in society."

The C.I.A.: "I'm not supposed to know that they're around. I'm afraid of them. Probably they spy on their own Ambassadors."

Red China: "I told Chou En-lai that if I found his men working against our Government, I would close their Embassy. I have a lot of problems here, and I would like to solve them in my own way. I have no need, thank you, for Chinese solutions."

Personal ambition? "I've thought of nothing except to serve the people. When my party won the general election just before independence, I was in my constituency at Lira, 130 miles from the capital. The first thing I did was to jump into a tribal dance. I had no idea at all that at that time I should be thinking about forming a Government. Then a police car came, and we thought it was to stop the dancing. An officer got out . . ."

"A Ugandan?"

"No, he was British. He saluted me and his words were: 'Sir, there is a message for you from the Governor . . .'"

DUSK began to invade the President's parliamentary office. His voice grew low, almost drowsy, but it did not seem that he wished just yet to terminate his reminiscence. We were in the middle of modern Kampala, but even in that marble building we could hear the croakings of the African twilight and the distant calling of exotic birds. The President's skin glowed like a black boot; at the nape of his neck he pulled absently—dreamily—at his long, coarse hair; he surrendered himself to a great nostalgia.

I faintly suspected that I was being treated to some sort of performance—and yet I was moved. I wondered: Is he an Ataturk, a Machiavelli or just a good actor, this goatherd in the Savile Row suit? Or perhaps all of that at once? Would he survive to consummate the building of his nation, or would he be intercepted by the ancient justice of the Kabakas?

"This ambition, this 'will to power' that you speak of, never bothered me at all," he said. "When I was a herdboy watching my flocks I thought about my brothers and sisters at school, and at times during the holidays they were very nasty. At times they even called me a great fool because I did not know how to read or write, and because I was not at school. At the same time, my uncle, the elder brother of my father, was a big chief, and my father was a subcounty chief. I knew that neither my father nor my uncle had gone to school, yet their work was to look after the affairs of men. I therefore turned my cattle, sheep and goats into human beings, and I tried—so to speak—to govern them."

MAN TO MAN—Prime Minister Harold Wilson greets Obote at a London meeting of Commonwealth leaders.

"Was it then that you began to glimpse what you are today?" I asked.

"At times I tried to talk to them, and to pretend that I was myself a chief governing men," he said. "But, since they were animals, I had to care for them. In the afternoons, when I used to drive them home, I had a big problem of doing things in such a manner that some would not run too fast and leave me behind with the others. Perhaps you can see what my position was? They were animals. I needed their cooperation. . . ." ■

January 22, 1967

OBOTE IS OUSTED BY UGANDAN ARMY

Coup Comes as President, Leader Since '62, Is Out of Country for Parley

By Reuters

KAMPALA, Uganda, Tuesday, Jan. 26—Uganda's Army ousted President Milton Obote yesterday and set up a military government.

Thousands of cheering Ugandans thronged the streets of this East African capital celebrating the army take-over, while the President himself was still heading home after attending the conference of Commonwealth leaders in Singapore.

[During a brief stopover at the Bombay airport, the 46-year-old President refused to comment on the developments in Uganda, Reuters reported. He later arrived in Nairobi, Kenya, where he went to a hotel.]

Army Enforces Curfew

Kampala was placed under a strict curfew, enforced by army patrols, from 7 P.M. to 6:30 A.M. Essential workers were escorted to their jobs.

Sporadic gunfire was heard in Kampala at night, after the curfew was in effect.

Residents said that the shots appeared to be bursts fired into the air to deter people breaking the curfew. [Agence France-Presse reported rumors of efforts for a countercoup.]

The new leader in Uganda is Maj. Gen. Idi Amin, who rose from private to become commander of the army and air force and who will now head the military government. One broadcast on the national radio—believed to have been by the general himself—said that General Amin had accepted the task on the understanding that there would be an early return to civilian rule.

"Free and fair general elections will soon be held in the country, given a stable security situation," the broadcast said. Mr. Obote has been leader of Uganda, as Prime Minister and then President, since she became independent of Britain in 1962. Murchison Falls and the legendary "Mountains of the Moon" are in Uganda, the Commonwealth's largest producer of coffee.

The first act of the new Ugandan leaders was to order the release of all political prisoners detained by the Obote Government—believed to number 92, including five former Cabinet ministers—and to authorize the return of political exiles.

The announcement of the army take-over came after hours of confusion in the capital, during which shooting spread across the city and was interpreted as a sign of clashes between rival army factions. Some fighting was also reported around the Entebbe airport, about 20 miles from here. Fighting was also reported in scattered parts of the country, which with 91,000 square miles of territory is dwarfed by four of her five neighbors—the Sudan, Kenya, Tanzania, Rwanda and the Congo.

No Resistance Reported

Announcements over Ugandan radio gave no indication of any major resistance to the army take-over, which is evidently backed by the police force.

International reference books give the strength of the Ugandan Army as 5,700 men and of the Air Force as 260 men and about 60 planes, most of them trainers.

The police force is numbered at 5,500 men in a population of over seven and a half million.

The coup started at 2 A.M. yesterday when small arms, mortar and tank fire were heard in Kampala.

Soldiers chased civilians from the streets as sporadic shooting echoed across the city and troops ringed the parliament buildings, seized the radio station, the post office, the railway station and banks and other strategic positions.

The Entebbe airport was closed after a tank drove up and put a shell through the front entrance. One report said several people had been killed by the shell.

A soldier said to a British reporter outside the parliament buildings that seven people had been killed in the area, adding: "I don't mind making you the eighth."

When the news of the take-over was announced on the radio, people flocked into the streets to celebrate. Cars decorated with green branches—a traditional sign of rejoicing—drove down the streets and trucks were loaded with drummers and dancers.

The announcement of the coup d'etat came in the form of a denunciation of President Obote by an unidentified speaker who said he had the backing of army officers. He said the army had taken control of the country because it believed the President's policies would lead to bloodshed. The Government's economic policies were benefiting "the rich, big men" while other Ugandans were becoming poorer, he said.

The speaker also accused Mr. Obote of having developed his own home region in the north at the expense of other parts of the country.

Uganda was a British protectorate until independence on Oct. 9, 1962. She was later declared a republic, but remains a member of the Commonwealth.

Mr. Obote became President early in 1966, when as Prime Minister, he ousted the President, Sir Edward Mutesa, who had earlier been a regional king.

Mr. Obote was popularly elected to the Presidency under the 1967 Constitution, which made the country a republic.

In 1969, President Obote was wounded by an assassin's bullet as he left a Kampala conference. A nationwide state of emergency was declared and all major opposition parties banned as a result.

In a pamphlet circulated to Uganda's ruling People's Congress party last August, the President denied that he alone ruled the country or that the Ugandan Government was being directed by the army or the police.

January 26, 1971

Uganda's New Military Ruler

Idi Amin

Man in the News

Maj. Gen. Idi Amin, Uganda's new head of state, was the Ugandan army's heavyweight boxing champion for nearly 10 years.

He retired undefeated. And he has promised to try to do the same thing in the presidency: Retire unbeaten and hand over control to an elected government. General Amin—a large, bluff informal man known to almost everyone as "Idi"—led the military coup that deposed Milton Obote Monday.

He made it clear, however, that in doing so he was not changing his role: "I'm a professional soldier," he said on the Uganda radio 14 hours after starting the coup, "and I've always emphasized that a country's military should support a country's government while that government has the support of the people. I have not changed my views about this."

Idi Amin (the name is pronounced EE-dee ah-MEEN) was born about 1925 in the village of Koboko in the northern section of Uganda, then a British protectorate. He is a member of the Kakwa tribe, and as a boy he worked in the lush fields of the West Nile area and tended the family's goats. He did manage to acquire a primary-school education, although his school attendance was sporadic, varying with his father's ability to pay the fees.

In 1944, he enlisted in the Fourth (Uganda) Kings African Rifles. He saw service as a rifleman before the end of World War II in Burma, and when interviewed by British journalists in Kampala Tuesday, he was wearing the Burma campaign ribbon.

Fought the Mau Mau

He was promoted to corporal in 1949, and took part in punitive expeditions against tribal marauders in Northern Uganda. In 1953, he saw action in the forests of Kenya against Mau Mau terrorists. General Amin, who is an enthusiastic rugby player, is reported to have described hunting Mau Mau as "the finest physical training a footballer could have."

Before the Ugandan battalion returned home in 1957,

he had been promoted to sergeant. Then, in 1959, as efforts were being made to prepare Africans for self-government, the East African command of the British Army decreed the establishment of a new rank—"effendi"—for African noncommissioned officers who were potential officers.

General Amin was one of the first Ugandans to acquire this Kiplingesque title, and two years later he was commissioned. By the end of 1963, he was a major and by 1964 a colonel and deputy commander of Uganda's Army and Air Force.

Set Up Camps

In that same year, he carried out a special mission in the Congo on President Obote's orders, setting up training camps for Christophe Gbenye, the political heir of Patrice Lumumba and an opponent of General Joseph B. Mobutu. He was also in charge of collecting gold and ivory to buy arms for the "Simba" rebellion against General Mobutu, commander of the Congolese army. His handling of that affair led to a commission of inquiry in 1966 that showed both his and Mr. Obote's integrity.

Associated Press

"Just a soldier" concerned about country and people

Gen. Amin, right, holding news session in Kampala yesterday

General Amin and Mr. Obote were close friends; General Amin's fourth wife—as a Moslem he can and does have four wives, who have borne him seven children—is a member of Mr. Obote's Langi tribe. But General Amin has never tried to conceal his distaste for politics. He is, for example, entirely unknown to the members of Uganda's United Nations mission.

As a Moslem, too, General Amin would tend toward the conservative side of the political spectrum in Uganda, putting him increasingly at odds with Mr. Obote's announced "move to the left." When Mr. Obote acted to nationalize foreign-owned business, for example, there were rumblings of discontent in Moslem quarters.

General Amin's growing disaffection with Mr. Obote's policies became increasingly public, and Mr. Obote worked in a variety of ways to weaken General Amin's position.

But General Amin, heavier now than in his championship days but still displaying the boxer's springy walk, stayed very much the former sergeant, and maintained his popularity with the ranks. "I am not an ambitious man," he was quoted as saying earlier this week, "I am just a soldier with a concern for my country and its people."

January 28, 1971

Uganda President to Curb Nationalization Plans

Amin Says Free Enterprise Has Vital Role in Nation's Economic Development

By CHARLES MOHR
Special to The New York Times

KAMPALA, Uganda, May 1—Uganda's President, Gen. Idi Amin, announced today that his Government would substantially curtail the programs of the deposed former President, Milton A. Obote, aimed at nationalizing industry and commerce.

In a May Day speech at Kabale in southwestern Uganda, General Amin said that private enterprise "has an important and vital part to play in the economic development of Uganda."

His speech came a year to the day after Dr. Obote had announced that Uganda would assume 60 per cent ownership of the nation's largest industries, banks and commercial establishments.

Because of prolonged and difficult negotiations, the Obote Government had signed takeover agreements with only seven concerns by Jan. 25, when General Amin seized power in a military coup d'état.

The President said today that he would honor those agreements "unless the companies concerned ask for a review."

He went on to say that his Government had decided to take a 49 per cent interest in 11 other companies. Although he did not specifically mention the 62 other companies, his remarks seemed to indicate that they would be left in private hands.

The new policy was thus a severe curtailment of Dr. Obote's "move to the Left" but not a total reversal of it.

Dr. Obote's policies had shattered confidence among private investors, brought new investment to a virtual standstill, caused a rapid outflow of capital and saddled Uganda with a huge compensation bill. Heavy spending had also brought a large budget deficit.

Many observers believed that the most important task facing General Amin was the restoration of economic confidence and this he tried to do in his speech.

He said it was absolutely necessary that the Government "give a clear indication of those areas in which it wishes to participate" and that "uncertainty and confusion" had made the private sector unwilling to take risks.

President Amin called Dr. Obote's policies "ill conceived" and said that a mere change of ownership of existing enterprises would not bring this nation of 10 million people the required economic expansion.

Saying that a balance between public and private enterprise was desirable, the general remarked, "I am one of those who believe that pure capitalism like pure communism or socialism is neither desirable

The seven concerns that signed agreements with Dr. Obote included three oil companies that distribute petroleum products here—Shell-British Petroleum, Agip and Total.

May 2, 1971

Abrupt Shifts Mark Amin Rule of Uganda

By BERNARD WEINRAUB
Special to The New York Times

KAMPALA, Uganda, Aug. 23—The 19 puzzling months of President Idi Amin's reign have been marked by the disappearances of about a dozen prominent officials, the murder of two Americans, perilous economic problems, an erratic foreign policy and tribal strife within the Uganda Army that has left thousands of soldiers dead.

Members of the small Western comunity here of British, Americans, Germans and French, as well as antigovernment Ugandans, are plainly frightened. They describe the current political climate with such phrases as "unstable," "unpredictable," "bizarre," "out of control" and "dangerous."

With General Amin's planned expulsion of at least 55,000 Indian and Pakistani businessmen, doctors and lawyers in store, the future is viewed with some alarm by Ugandans and Westerners here. "There's always a need for a scapegoat," a senior Western official said. "Earlier in the year it was the Israelis. Now it's the Asians. After they leave, who's next?"

Tension and Furtiveness

Tourists—and 65 per cent of Uganda's 80,000 yearly visitors are Americans — are warned now not to leave the capital. Journalists are told to keep their notes hidden and to send critical articles from Nairobi, an hour's flight. Letters mailed to the United States are sometimes opened and diplomats say privately that their phones are tapped.

The radio news, in English and Swahili, is limited solely to General Amin's activities: Condemning the Asian "saboteurs" at a meeting of farmers, denouncing "imperialism, Zionism, colonialism and neocolonialism" to students, meeting church leaders, undergoing a 20-minute operation for warts, cheerfully attending the farewell ceremonies for a British high school headmistress who has been here for 30 years.

"It is very much a one-man show with advisers who are too frightened to say and do anything," a knowledgeable Uganda source said. "The President feels that there is an ever-present threat from the outside world—and he's always felt that way."

British Welcomed Coup

General Amin's take-over in a military coup on Jan. 25, 1971, was welcomed by the British, who looked upon President Milton Obote as a brilliant but devious and troublesome politician.

General Amin, a bluff paratrooper with a fourth-grade education, dominates a nation of 9.5 million where all political activity is banned, the Opposition is silent and figures on expenditures are secret. Government policies veer abruptly—almost by the week—with the 46-year-old President seeming, at times, like a new driver who has lost control of his car.

Financially, Uganda is virtually bankrupt because of heavy spending on armaments. The nation's reserves are believed to have slipped below $15-million, or less than would be needed to pay for two weeks of the current rate of imports In the past year, President Amin has spent millions of dollars—perhaps as much as $20-million—building his 10,000-man army, constructing military runways and buying arms.

A 'Mythical Threat'

"General Amin feels that his neighbors, Tanzania and Rwanda, are somehow threatening him," said an official. "He also sees Israel, Britain and the United States as threats. He's built up the army against a totally mythical threat."

The Israeli presence, which began during Dr. Obote's reign, grew in strength and influence in the early months of the Amin administration. In fact, his closest allies were Britain and Israel. General Amin still wears parachute wings earned while training in Israel. He paid several personal visits to Premier Golda Meir and the Defense Minister, Gen. Moshe Dayan, and he openly welcomed Israeli technicians and advisers to Uganda.

By last year, a total of 700 Israelis were working in Uganda and building a major foothold in east Africa. They served as advisers to the air force—some Israelis complained, privately, that the pilots were undisciplined and often showed up drunk—and helped construct two buildings in downtown Kampala and roads north and west of the city.

Turnabout and Expulsion

Last March. quite suddenly, President Amin turned in a rage upon the Israelis, expelled them and now denounces "Zionism" in virtually every public utterance. One reason for the swift reversal of policy toward Israel is believed to be financial—that the Ugandans owed Israel about $24-million. Political pressures from the Sudan and Libya also contributed to the move.

But there is some feeling, too, that President Amin feared that the Israelis, who had access to Government intelligence, might depose him. (Ugandans and Western diplomats are convinced that the Israelis played a role in deposing Dr. Obote in favor of President Amin.)

General Amin's relations with Britain were also unpredictable. Initially he praised Prime Minister Heath, supported Britain's policy of selling arms to South Africa and even offered to speak to the racist Government there. There are rumors that President Amin turned on Great Britain when Mr. Heath refused to sell him Harrier aircraft; there is also some belief that President Amin asked the Israelis to help him seize Tanga from nearby Tanzania to provide landlocked Uganda with a port.

President Amin now says that he can crush Israel in a week and South Africa in two weeks. (Officials here say that he is counting on Libya as well as Soviet support in case of a break in relations with Britain, which provides assistance totaling more than $10-million a year.)

Britain, which has 7,000 residents here, and Israel were known to be especially disturbed about the undisciplined Uganda army, riven by tribal feuds that have led to widescale killings. Estimates on the number of deaths within the army range from 3,000 to 10,000. Most of the soldiers from two northern tribes, the Acholi and Lango, were slaughtered by other soldiers in barracks and towns between July and October.

Although President Amin sought to win the support of the tribes, indications are that he failed and was forced to rely on low-ranking soldiers from his own northern area of the West Nile. These tribes and others are alleged to have rounded up and slaughtered thousands of northerners.

In the garrison town of Mbarara, 250 miles northwest of Kampala, two Americans, investigating the tribal massacres, were murdered in an army barracks. The victims, Nicholas Stroh, a freelance journalist, and Robert Siedle, a lecturer at Makerere University here, were believed killed to prevent news of the massacre from leaking out.

A Dozen Have Vanished

Within the last year there have also been at least a dozen disappearances of prominent Ugandans, including Anil Clerk, an Indian lawyer, Martin Okello, a former Member of Parliament, and former police and army officials.

Temperamentally, General Amin has acquired a reputation for mercurial moods and bizarre public comments.

Yesterday, he sent a 2,000-word telegram to President Julius K. Nyerere of Tanzania, who had attacked him for racism in the move against the Asians.

President Amin said that Mr. Nyerere would have expelled Tanzania's Asians if he had the necessary courage. The Uganda president said, nevertheless, that he "loves" Mr. Nyerere and if he were a woman, would have married him, "despite your grey hairs."

President Amin, a Moslem with four wives, added, "but as you are a man the possibility does not arise."

August 26, 1972

Uganda's Crisis Seems to Be Abating, But the Underlying Problems Persist

By CHARLES MOHR
Special to The New York Times

NAIROBI, Kenya, Oct. 9—As Uganda celebrated the 10th anniversary of her independence today, observers in East Africa and concerned residents were convinced that the country's real problems were those of leadership.

The current crisis—the expulsion of Uganda's resident Asians and border hostilities with Tanzania—seemed to be abating, but the East African nation's fundamental difficulties seemed far from solved.

Most of Uganda's alien Asian residents will probably be deported by the deadline, a month from now. As they disappear, so will much of the racial and emotional issue that the Uganda President, Maj. Gen. Idi Amin, has exploited since August.

Also, Uganda and Tanzania have arrived at a "peace agreement" which, if honored, should end their small-scale but recurrent border hostilities.

President Amin's own remarks indicate that a handful of exile guerrillas opposed to his Government are still at large in southern Uganda, but the exile force that invaded from Tanzania on Sept. 17 has been militarily crushed and dispersed.

More Basic Problems

If the Asians and the exile security threat were Uganda's main problems, these developments might lead to a period of relative tranquility. But Uganda's main problem is more basic—can the Government effectively run the country? And from this has sprung other problems of economic decline, ethnic hatred and public fear and insecurity.

Guessing the future in Uganda is hazardous, but the following factors raise serious questions:

¶President Amin has a tendency to seek, or create, external and internal enemies to distract not only the public but also himself from difficult domestic problems. Many observers in East Africa fear that he might turn his ire next on a small neighbor, Rwanda, which he has repeatedly accused of plotting against him. These fears were increased last week when he agreed to confer with Rwanda's President, Gregoire Kayibanda, then suddenly canceled the plan, saying he had to direct national defense against an invasion plot that included Rwanda.

¶The "peace" agreement with Tanzania might break down, as did a previous accord quietly negotiated by Kenya's President, Jomo Kenyatta.

¶The possibility of further trouble with Tanzania grew more ominous when responsible diplomatic sources let it become gradually known that last year President Amin asked Israel for help in planning the military annexation of a broad strip of northern Tanzania to give landlocked Uganda an outlet to the sea at Tanga. It is not known how serious President Amin was, and his small army is unequal to the task, but he is one of the few African leaders to complain of unfair boundaries.

¶Tribal uncertainties and frictions in Uganda are serious and may increase. The country's largest and most advanced tribe, the Baganda seems increasingly disenchanted with President Amin, although it welcomed his coup d'état in January of 1971. President Amin himself recently accused people of other tribes in Ankole and Kigezi Provinces of sympathy with the former President, Milton Obote, and the refugee guerrilla army. The main basis of President Amin's strength is among troops from the northwest, but one major tribe there, the Lugbara, seems to have stirred suspicion and hostility among the others.

¶The Asian exodus is expected to accelerate a process of economic decline in Uganda and eventually to hurt such neighbors as Kenya.

The Bank of Uganda said last week that as of July Uganda's liquid foreign exchange reserves (not counting certain credits such as with the International Monetary Fund) were $20.5-million, which is low but not disastrous.

Transactions Halted

In August, however, Uganda virtually stopped international transactions by requiring importers to revalidate all permissions to remit money abroad. Shipping and import companies in the Kenya port of Mombasa said goods for Uganda were simply piling up there and traders were trying to sell them elsewhere.

President Amin had denounced the Uganda Asians as parasites and "economic saboteurs" who dominated commerce and kept black traders out of the business world. The grievance against Asian dominance was justified in some ways, but the sudden departure of the Asians could be damaging.

"The whole distribution and credit system of the country is disappearing overnight," said one neutral foreign economist. "The cash situation is only one problem."

In a flood of other comment the words got little attention, but last week President Amin told the visiting President of Zaïre, Mobutu Sese Seko, that Asians were "refusing" to sell such vital items as drugs and gasoline. Asians, naturally, were not reordering as inventories dwindled and the deadline for their own expulsion neared.

Credit a Problem

Because so many shops are owned by Asians, a majority will probably close, at least temporarily. Precise figures are not available but a witness said that about half of the stores on side streets already seem to have gone out of business and somewhat fewer on the main shopping boulevard, Kampala Road.

This in turn, departing Asians said, has already resulted in unemployment for thousands of blacks who worked for the Asians.

The Uganda plan is for Africans to take over commerce and for a new state trading corporation to assume much of the Asians' role in importing and exporting.

Although managerial experience could be a problem, a greater one is likely to be the obtaining of credit to get the African traders started and of foreign exchange to permit them to buy abroad.

In 1971 Kenya, which by African standards is a booming economic success, sent about 20 per cent of her exports to Uganda, and this market is gravely endangered by Uganda's growing inability to pay.

Uganda is linked with Kenya and Tanzania in the East African Community, which operates many joint services, including a railway, an airline and a postal service. The community also provides a relatively accessible joint market of more than 36 million east Africans.

Because Tanzania's President, Julius K. Nyerere, has steadfastly refused to recognize President Amin, the three East African Presidents, who constitute the governing authority of the community, have not met since General Amin took power.

The real threat to the community is now less political than economic, observers feel.

Assessments are necessary, for instance, to operate and make viable the railroad and airline. If Uganda cannot pay her share, which is an increasing possibility, continued joint operation will be severely compromised.

Still another problem involves Rwanda, a poor nation of about 3.6 million people in the heart of Africa. She has traditionally imported and exported most of her goods through Uganda. Even if President Amin does not precipitate hostilities, the truck route from the Kampala railhead to Rwanda is now insecure and unsatisfactory.

Estimates Inaccurate

In the meantime, it seems that the original estimate of the number of Asians living in Uganda was inflated. The British High Commission says that only 25,000 Asians have been processed as British citizens, instead of the original estimate that there were 50,000 to 55,000 holders of British passports in Uganda.

A total of 3,500 Asians are expected to go to India or Pakistan. As many as 10,000 Asians may be confirmed as Uganda citizens. An informed estimate is that Uganda will offer deportation "exemptions" to about 5,200 Asians and permit—or even compel—them to stay. Some 12,000 to 16,000 people may become stateless because Uganda officials have torn up or otherwise rejected their Uganda citizenship papers as technically inadequate.

Having already created an international uproar over the expulsion of foreigners, President Amin may create another by refusing to allow some to leave.

The loss of professional men, teachers and other technicians poses so many problems for Uganda that there have already been reports that officials have refused to allow some citizen Asians to go.

October 10, 1972

COMMON MARKET FOUND IN AFRICA

Kenya, Uganda, Tanganyika Near Economic Integration

By KATHLEEN McLAUGHLIN
Special to The New York Times.

UNITED NATIONS, N. Y., Feb. 12—In East Africa the oldest existing common market has grown up gradually in Kenya, Uganda and Tanganyika over the last fifty years. The three countries are just short of full economic integration, the Economic Commission for Africa reports in its latest bulletin, which raises the question of the market's future extension to adjacent nations.

At present, the bulletin notes, the trio of member states form a Customs and Currency Union with almost complete internal freedom of trade. They have, in addition, a common income-tax system, as well as common excise rates. There are no restrictions on the movement of capital from one country to another.

For many years the largest proportion of goods mutually traded comprised locally produced foods in a raw or partially processed condition. More recently there has been a marked increase in the scope of manufactured goods, and of those packaged and processed. The trend is sure to continue and to increase, the commission feels.

Concurrently, it is pointed out, the growth of internal trade has provided an important element of stability in the economies, "which are so sensitive to external influences." But while the evolution of inter-territorial trade has brought benefits, they have not been shared equally. Uganda and Tanganyika remain much more dependent on world commodity markets than does Kenya, whose income is less dependent on earnings from exports.

Continued Gains Seen

The introduction of manufacturing industry into East Africa—a comparatively recent change—is unlikely to bring replacement of foreign imports for some time, in the opinion of the commission. There are, on the contrary, "strong expansionist forces" in inter-territorial trade that would be sufficient to maintain its rate of growth even if developments are slow in other sectors under the influence of falling global prices.

Three items alone — foods, beverages and cigarettes — account for more than half of all territorial exports. These traditional items are diminishing in importance in relation to the total value of trade, for "there has been a very considerable increase in the quantity of local manufactured goods." Out of Kenya's $34,440,000 of total sales to Tanganyika and Uganda, $11,940,000 now consists of manufactured articles.

The three East African territories occupy a strategic position in the eastern part of the continent, the bulletin comments. They are well integrated economically, have access to the sea and to the markets of the world and have economies that have grown prodigiously in the last fifteen years even against unfavorable terms of trade in the last five years. They are already geared to provide at least some goods and services to their neighbors.

Although arguments have been raised that only minor advantages are to be gained by enlarging their commercial contacts with such neighboring countries as the Sudan or Ethiopia, because "they have nothing that we want to buy," the commission expresses a divergent view.

Even if the situation remains static and trade a one-way channel for some time, the comment runs, increased regional cooperation through negotiated agreements with certain countries would form the basis of a long-term program to encourage the growth of inter-African trade.

February 13, 1962

Factory Hand: $62 a Month—and Hope

Special to The New York Times

NAIROBI, Kenya — Marco Libwana retreads tires during the day and studies English at night. He earns $62 a month and on the side owns a shop for which he meets a $27 monthly payroll.

At the age of 27, Marco Libwana is attaining membership in East Africa's middle-class élite.

Mr. Libwana, a Tiriki tribesman, has a wife and three children younger than 5. When he was 16 he left his father's house about 200 miles north of Nairobi to seek his fortune in the capital, and talked his way into a job as kitchen boy in a restaurant.

He worked there for 10 years, and by 1962 he was assistant chef, earning $58 a month, double the Nairobi average for Africans.

A Wife for $100

Mr. Libwana saved nearly every penny he earned. First he chose a wife, for whom he paid a bride price high by African standards.

"She's a good wife, but she cost me 700 shillings [$100], nine cows and six goats," Mr. Libwana recalled recently. After the marriage he saved for a piece of land his wife could work; he finally bought three acres near his father's home for $430 and planted it with maize.

Soon the small holding — shamba, as it is known in Swahili — was supporting his wife and his family and showing a net cash profit of $85 a year. Mr. Libwana continued saving, and recently he bought a shop in his home village. There he sells clothes, sugar, salt, tea, soap, baking powder, flour and cigarettes.

The shop was soon employing two other Africans — a shopkeeper, whom he pays $17 a month, and an assistant, whom he pays $10—and it now returns a net profit of $30 a month.

Because East Africa has little industry and very large labor queues, the few Africans in skilled factory jobs are rising rapidly.

Generally they are brighter and harder-working than the laborers, sweepers and office boys, and many, like Mr. Libwana, have more than one iron in the fire.

In the middle of 1962 Mr. Libwana took a look at the industries beginning to mushroom in Nairobi. He decided that factory work was more a man's job and applied for a trainee job in a new Goodyear factory.

His starting salary was $58 a month, but he was soon adept at handling tire machinery. Now he gets $62. He also bought a second-hand sewing machine; until recently he made clothes for sale in his village shop after his daily stint in the factory.

Now Mr. Libwana retreads tires during the day and studies English in a correspondence course from 6 P.M. until 10 and all through his weekends.

"I want to be the foreman of this factory," he explains, "and you can't get anywhere nowadays if you don't speak English."

Like thousands of other urbanized Africans, Mr. Libwana **lives in Nairobi's overcrowded "locations." He pays $14.80 a month to rent the house, and he rents the smaller of the two rooms to another African for $5.80.**

The day begins at 6 A.M. Mr. Libwana cooks his breakfast, which usually consists of two eggs and bread, and he takes a bus to the factory, where he starts work at 8.

Lunch hour is 1:15 P.M. to 2:30. Mr. Libwana has a bottle of soda water and a slice of bread, which he has taken to work.

At 5:30 P.M. the factory closes, and Mr. Libwana rides home to study.

Boxing is popular in East Africa, and Mr. Libwana used to be a well-known welterweight, but has given up sports to have more study time. His only recreation nowadays is a Sunday visit to the movies.

About 8 P.M. Mr. Libwana cooks his evening meal on a charcoal stove. The main meal of the day, it consists of a basic pudding made from boiled maize meal, flour and water, occasionally flavored with meat. It is washed down with hot, sweet tea. Mr. Libwana goes to bed regularly at 10.

The thirst for learning is by no means unusual here. Private schools and correspondence schools of all kinds have for several years been Kenya's most thriving businesses.

Mr. Libwana says he has seen the higher standards of living of educated Europeans and aspires to them.

January 20, 1964

Kenyatta Opens a 'Socialist' School

By ROBERT CONLEY
Special to The New York Times

KAMITI, Kenya, Dec. 12—A Soviet-sponsored political training center for Kenyans—and ultimately other Africans—was opened on an isolated hill here today in memory of Patrice Lumumba, the first Premier of the Congo, who was murdered early in 1961. The institute also intends to help African nationalist organizations in other countries to train what are termed militant "cadres." An atmosphere of mystery surrounded the ceremonies as Jomo Kenyatta opened the school in his first official act as President of the new Republic of Kenya. He had been sworn in only a few hours before, when Kenya abandoned the status of a dominion in the British Commonwealth.

Moscow's share of the costs was understood to amount to $84,000. The rest of the money was said to have come from "friends and organizations in African-Asian and the Socialist countries."

The Soviet Union was said to be prepared to provide two professors for the institute which is surrounded by a barbed-wire fence seven feet high.

As far as can be determined, the institute will act as the political training center for selected leaders from the country's ruling Kenya African National Union party. The institute already has $140,000 deposited in a Nairobi bank to support its work. The origin of the funds, held as the Lumumba Trust, has not been revealed.

The institute in broad terms, intends to indoctrinate young politicians and labor leaders in Kenya with "Socialism." Its charter lists the detailed objectives as:

¶ To define teach and popularize African Socialism "in the context of universally accepted principles and practices of Socialism."

¶ To organize courses for party cadres, trade unionists cooperative workers, civil servants and journalists for the "realization of Socialism."

¶ To instill "patriotism," conduct research in problems of African progress and cooperate with other organizations having similar objectives in other parts of Africa.

All of this came to light after Mr. Kenyatta had unveiled a bust of Lumumba at the institute's entrance.

The man chosen as the school's principal is Matthew M. Mutiso, a 30-year-old Kenyan with a political science degree from the University of Delhi. He was of the charter, a "patriot with selected for being, in the words a proved knowledge of Socialism."

December 13, 1964

LEADER DEFINES KENYA SOCIALISM

Kenyetta Pledges to Permit Many Kinds of Ownership

By LAWRENCE FELLOWS
Special to The New York Times

NAIROBI, Kenya, April 27—President Jomo Kenyatta presented to Parliament today his long-awaited definition of what "African Socialism" is intended to mean in Kenya.

It will differ both from capitalism and Communism, the President said. It will combine political democracy with social responsibility and will draw on the best of African traditions, he declared.

Mr. Kenyatta's definition, contained in a 56-page document prepared under the direction of Tom Mboya, Minister for Economic Planning and Development, is the first real attempt to give meaning to the term that has become a favorite of politicians throughout East Africa.

Since Kenya became independent in December, 1963, the words "African Socialism" have been bandied about by both far left and far right as though the term were their own.

Definition Will Be 'Bible'

Mr. Kenyatta said the definition offered today would be the "bible" of Kenya, guiding the lines of the country's policy. It carries with it the promise that various forms of ownership will still be encouraged, he said.

"African Socialism differs politically from Communism because it insures every mature citizen equal political rights, and from capitalism because it prevents the exercise of disproportionate political influence by economic power groups," the document states.

The President's definiton recognizes the difficulties of preventing individuals or small groups from accumulating so much wealth as to exercise undue influence on the country.

But it proposes to try by means of heavy death duties and progressively steepened taxes on income, inheritance and capital gains.

At the same time, Mr. Kenyatta's brand of African Socialism would not contenance taxes on high that they would inhibit accumulation of savings or discourage flow of capital into the country.

State ownership, joint state private ventures, cooperatives, corporations and partnerships are all to be encouraged.

Nationalization a Tool

"Nationalization is a useful tool that has already been used in Kenya and will be used again when circumstances require," the document states.

But it also makes clear that the Government remains committed by the Constitution and by the manifesto of the Kenya African National Union, the country's only party, to" prompt payment of full compensation whenever nationalization is used."

The tax structure, according to Mr. Kenyatta's document, would eventually remove any burden from the lowest income groups.

April 28, 1965

Tea Crop Changes Life for Kenya Smallholder

He Earns Cash for First Time Under a New Program

By LAWRENCE FELLOWS
Special to The New York Times

KERICHO, Kenya, Aug. 21—Beyond the Mau Forest, in the cool, rolling highlands near Kericho, a young African farmer has planted two acres of tea.

With these two acres, Kibet arap Chepkwony is not going to change things much in his country. But his own life has been changed in the most fundamental way: instead of planting his 12 acres with just enough maize, millet and potatoes to keep himself and his family alive, he is growing something that, for the first time in his life, has brought him money and shifted him into the country's cash economy.

Because there are 22,000 smallholders like Kibet arap Chepkwony who, with help and encouragement from the Kenya Tea Development Authority, have planted a total of 12,000 acres in tea, things are happening to the country.

Big Factor in Economy

Perhaps 20 per cent of the tea plants are four years old and already in full production. But even without the African smallholders, tea has become one of Kenya's most valuable plantation crops. The area around Kericho looks like one sprawling, green - checkered carpet of glistening leaves.

With almost 50,000 acres in production, these big tea estates provide employment for more than 36,000 Kenyans, nearly one-tenth of the country's workers. They account for exports of more than 32 million pounds of tea yearly, and earnings of close to $13 million.

Since the world markets for both coffee and cotton have grown increasingly sluggish, and with a need to pull more Kenyans out of their old patterns of subsistence farming, the Government, through the Special Crops Development Authority and its successor, the Kenya Tea Development Authority, has spent the last five years encouraging smallholders to plant tea.

Things went slowly at first. But the gleaming geometric patterns of tea extend far beyond Kericho now, to the Kisii Highlands to the west and the Nandi Hills to the north. In Bugoma, tea has been planted on the slopes of Mount Elgon, as it has on Cherangani Mountain, and on the slopes of Mount Kenya, and straight through the Aberdare Range.

Tea Authority Helps

The tea authority has been selling young plants to the farmers, showing them how to prune and care for the bushes, how to pluck just the top two leaves and a bud to get the best tea.

The authority has also built collecting stations and processing factories, and has been selling the tea for the farmers at the auctions that are held twice a month in Nairobi.

Because tea must be processed quickly after it is plucked, a program to build or improve 900 miles of road has been set up. To help, a credit of $3 million has been approved by the International Bank for Reconstruction and Development.

If all goes well, Kenya's smallholders will have planted 25,000 acres by 1970. A survey shows that there are still more than a million acres in Kenya that would be ideal for tea growing.

August 29, 1965

3 AFRICAN LANDS UNABLE TO AGREE

Kenya, Uganda, Tanzania Still Split on Economic Tie

By LAWRENCE FELLOWS
Special to The New York Times

NAIROBI, Kenya, May 10—President Jomo Kenyatta disclosed today that Kenya, Uganda and Tanzania had been unable to agree on means of preserving the economic cooperation the three countries began before any of them were independent.

Addressing the Central Legislative Assembly, the parliamentary body that governs what remains of the common market and shared services of the three countries, Kenya's President said he had not given up hope that an agreement could still be reached.

"Our people can benefit greatly from a form of cooperating between the countries of East Africa that is founded on reality and trust," he said.

The President's speech was by way of explanation of the failure to get a report from the mixed commission he and Presidents Milton Obote of Uganda and Julius K. Nyerere of Tanzania set up last August to see whether they could not halt the erosion of their old cooperation.

Report Was Due on May 1

Under the independent chairmanship of Prof. Kjeld Hisip of Denmark, an economic expert provided by the United Nations, the commission was due to report May 1.

"But it has been found in practice impossible to complete a report," Mr. Kenyatta told the Assembly. He said the deadline had been extended, but did not say for how long.

Nor did Mr. Kenyatta say what the main causes of prolonged disagreement were. The well-known ones begin with Tanzania's decision to break up the common currency of East Africa and issue currency and set up a central bank of her own.

The new Tanzanian currency is to be issued next month, and Uganda, which shares some of Tanzania's complaints that Kenya has always had the most to gain from the common market, has advanced plans for her own currency and central bank as well.

The common institutions — currency, railways and harbors, postal services, customs, rail lines and many others—were inherited by Kenya, Uganda and Tanzania from the days when all three were governed by the British.

Nairobi was always the commercial center of East Africa, and after independence Kenya came under increasing pressure from the two others to allocate industries and accept quotas in trade to reduce the adverse balances Uganda and Tanzania were running.

May 11, 1966

Odinga of Kenya Quits Post as Vice President

NAIROBI, Kenya, April 14 (AP) — Oginga Odinga resigned today as Kenya's Vice President and strongly hinted he would launch a new party to oppose President Jomo Kenyatta's Government.

His announcement threatens a bitter fight that could divide Kenya along ideological and tribal lines. The 54-year-old former teacher is the acknowledged leader of Kenya's leftists and commands formidable support among his own Luo tribe, second only to Mr. Kenyatta's Kikuyu in numbers.

Mr. Odinga charged Kenya was being ruled by an "invisible government" representing foreign ideological and commercial interests.

He said at a news conference that he had become an "unwanted person" among his Cabinet colleagues and that there was "pressure and desire" that he leave the Government.

April 15, 1966

The Duka-Wallas Are Outcasts in Africa

By LAWRENCE FELLOWS

NAIROBI.

IN Nairobi's big municipal market, fruits and flowers and African curios are spread among the moving crowd in a profusion of colors and aromas: lilies and delphiniums, shields and spears and zebra skins, oranges, mangoes, avocado pears. At one of the stalls a portly, alert-looking Hindu presses a couple of pineapples on a friend, and is asked how his business is going. He smiles wanly and shrugs his shoulders.

This is Surajnarain Maya Ram. He is doing all right, but he does not regard the future as very bright, not for him and not for the vast majority of people like him—Punjabis, Gujeratis, Rajasthanis and all the others who came, or whose forebears came, to Africa to escape the distressing poverty of the Indian subcontinent. They have become the victims of a peculiar form of prejudice, in part self-induced.

In the three newly independent countries of East Africa—Kenya, Uganda and Tanzania (which is made up of the old Tanganyika on the mainland and the island of Zanzibar)—all such people are known simply as "Asians." They began to come as traders, centuries ago, borne on the monsoon winds across the Indian Ocean. By far the greatest influx, however, came toward the end of the last century, when the British imported more than 30,000 of them to build the railway, and the whole complex around it, from Mombasa to Lake Victoria. They were tradesmen, craftamen, clerks and coolies.

The immigrants followed the railway as it was laid into the interior, spreading a line of communication and a civilization of sorts that was as deep and penetrating as anything the missionaries or conquerors had been able to do. For a while the Indian rupee was the official coinage. Indian laws for marriage, divorce, succession and a host of other religious and personal matters were extended to the area.

And the immigrants prospered. There are fewer than 400,000 Asians living and trading among the 27 million Africans of Kenya, Uganda and Tanzania, yet they control probably four-fifths of the commerce, from the biggest trading houses to the smallest *dukas* where pennies are squeezed out of hard bargains with Africans.

In the remotest parts of the interior one finds the *duka-wallas*, the Asian shopkeepers. At a place called Kajiado, where there is nothing to see but a great empty plain stretching away from Kenya toward distant, purple-furrowed hills in Tanzania, a *duka-walla* makes a living out of selling spears from Birmingham to the Masai warriors. At Bundibugyo, on the far side of the Mountains of the Moon, the Uganda police do not venture far out of their barracks for fear of the poisoned arrows and the hooked long knives of the tiny, wizened rebels of the Bakongo and Bwamba tribes. But a *duka-walla* is there, buying their monkey skins and bhang, selling them salt and kerosene and whatever trinkets they fancy.

THE Asians' religious, traditional and social divisions make them as different from one another as can be imagined—Goan Christians, Ismaili Moslems, Sikhs with their beards tucked up into their puggrees. A few of the women have taken to modern dress, but most stick to their banian ways, or to fashionable new versions of their traditional dress: the form-hugging *khamis* and *salwar* of the Moslem women, the bright saris wrapped in misty folds around the gliding, dusky figures of the Hindu women.

To Africans, however, these people all seem pretty much alike—remote, rather mysterious. In the evenings and on Sundays, whole families stream out of their blocks of shops and flats to promenade, walking in groups a little apart. When they ride, the whole family gets into the car until the springs are compressed and the oil pan drags on the ground. Then they drive at the same unchanging, slow pace, whether pulling out of a driveway into oncoming traffic, or cruising down the center of a wide and lonely road, never hurrying, never dallying, almost always a calm, unhurried picture of politeness and grace. With their obvious wealth and strange ways, and their ties to communities far away, the Asians are a world apart from the Africans, and are becoming more and more the objects of outbursts of envy and smoldering resentment.

"BLOODSUCKERS," shouted Joseph Nyerere, who is secretary general of the Youth League of the Tanganyika African National Union (TANU), Tanzania's mainland political party. He is also the brother of Tanzania's President, Julius Nyerere, and was speaking then in his former role as regional commissioner in Mwanza, on the shore of Lake Victoria. He was telling a big crowd at a rally there that an Asian mill owner had bought diamonds and taken them out to India. Mr. Nyerere asked the crowd what ought to be done to the man.

"Kill him!" the crowd demanded. Such men deserved hanging, the commissioner agreed, but this one had already been deported. Only the mill was still in Tanzania.

"Confiscate it!" the crowd yelled. This, too, had already been done; the mill was turned over to the TANU Youth League.

Anti-Asian outbursts like this are common in East Africa. They betray frustration and a deep sense of grievance. The Africans have won political power in their countries, but economic power eludes them. Programs of Africanization, of reserving jobs for Africans, have got them into the civil service, but not into commerce. Programs of Government help to aspiring African businessmen have not very often proved a good substitute for hard work and the good business sense that is acquired through experience.

The Africans rarely blame themselves; more often they speak of their plight as a legacy of their colonial past. Comparatively few yearn to have the big productive farms, the industries or the high administrative positions the white men still hold. But many think the Asians in small shops are doing work that is within reach. Only a few years ago the African politicians were promising that independence would be followed by a better life. To the Africans who believed it and who still hunger for it, the Asians stand first in the way.

"I am in the retail trade, so I am resented," complained a baldish, soft-spoken Ismaili with a cluttered general store on the edge of Jinja, in Uganda. "I run this place with my brothers. My cousin is a wholesaler. They say we conspire together to keep the Africans out of the retail trade. They say we cut prices on them, or keep them from getting credit. I'll tell you how I conspire."

He unwound a woeful story about how he had taken an African into his business, and loaded up a small truck with £150 worth of soaps, cosmetics and other small items for him to sell on a long round of tribal villages.

"He came back three months later," the Ismaili continued. "That's all right. He gave me £50. I said: 'Everything's gone. Where's the rest of the money?' He said: 'I sold everything, so I spent the money.' What could I do? I let him go and now he calls me an exploiter. He doesn't know how I exploit myself. The African is not ready for business."

In the Nairobi market Maya Ram chose not to talk about Africans and their chances of doing well in business. He didn't want to push his luck. Just before Christmas last year the Nairobi City Council declared that Asians holding stalls in the market would soon be displaced—whether they were citizens of Kenya or not—to make room for African traders and so "redress the imbalance of race in trade."

"You know they did this already in Mombasa," Maya Ram recalled, wrinkling his nose to suggest his poor opinion of the move, yet not daring to voice it. There was no point in his arguing the unconstitutionality of the Nairobi order on grounds of its racial discrimination. Some of Kenya's Cabinet members have hinted that criticism of the order might be regarded as racial in itself. For a moment Maya Ram studied the line of pitiful stalls just outside the entrance to the market. African peasant farmers or their wives sat there silently behind wilted flowers and wrinkled apples. Finally he said: "I haven't heard anything official. I'm a Kenya citizen. I'm not leaving yet."

He was born in Kenya in 1918, and has been working at the stall in the market for as long as he can remember; his father had opened it 10 years before Maya Ram's birth. Yet Maya Ram is not really alarmed about the prospect of leaving, if one day he must. He has property in Delhi. His wife is there, as are his five daughters, all married or waiting to finish school so that their marriages can be arranged. Two of his sons work in the Nairobi market stall with him, but the other three are in school in Delhi.

To the Africans, ties like these outside the country smack too much of the quality they consciously dislike most in Asians: the divided loyalty, the foot in the door between two worlds to have the best of both and the obligations of neither. The Africans suspect them of being mere birds of passage who are beginning to sense now that they are at the end of their season in East Africa.

But many know no other homes even though, in all the uncertainty and confusion about citizenship the Asians have endured in East Africa since independence, some have clung to alien passports. Not all the passports are Indian or Pakistani. Some are British, issued in the colonial days, although their holders may be utterly foreign to Britain and may never have lived there. When Kenya, Tanzania and Uganda were British there was no such thing as local citizenship. Most people in these territories were British or British-protected subjects, and on that basis legally where they were.

After independence, most Asians could have applied for citizenship in the countries where they worked and lived, but many did not, partly out of worry about the implications of citizenship and doubts about the protection it offered them. The Asians were as uncertain as the whites of their future under African rule, perhaps more so.

Quite naturally, the more the Asians hesitated, the more did the Africans come to regard the taking of citizenship as a necessary act of faith. Few of those who chose not to apply could be regarded as disloyal, or even as mutely hostile. Many of them have obligations to friends or relatives who are citizens with a stake in Africa and who are definitely hoping to stay. Some see no long-term future for themselves or for their children in Africa, but are prepared to stay as long as they are needed, or as long as they are making money. In some ways, these may be less a problem eventually than the Asian who is a citizen and wants to stay. Sooner or later, those without passports will get up and go. The trickle of voluntary leavers has already started. With each isolated bit of new trouble, the trickle grows.

When Kenya expelled six Asians last year for misdeeds that were never specified, not only had two of them first to be stripped of their newly acquired Kenya citizenship but the incident brought down on the whole Asian community a deluge of official wrath. The Voice of Kenya, the Government radio station, started it off with a bitter attack against the Asians for not showing unstinted support of President Kenyatta and for failing to relax their communal inclinations. A group of prominent Asians replied that by being condemned for the misdeeds of a few, the whole Asian community was being made the victim of racialism. Not only had the Asians supported President Kenyatta, they said, but they had also demonstrated their goodwill by their donations to national charities.

The radio station came back with an even stronger attack against the community. The Opposition party, the Kenya People's Union, complicated the issue by taking the side of the Asians and accusing the Voice of Kenya of stirring up racial hatred, much against the spirit and letter of the Constitution. In hope of keeping the Asians from becoming a major political issue, Mr. Kenyatta's party, the Kenya African National Union (KANU), issued what was meant to be a quieting and conclusive statement:

"We have no wish to prevent any man worshiping with his co-religionists. We do not want to see people prevented from choosing their own husbands and wives.

"Yet it is a fact that while the other tribes and races of this country are coming closer in so many matters, the majority of Asians live out their lives in a communal cocoon, having only the most superficial contact with their fellow inhabitants.

"If that is the kind of isolated and insular life they want, they will always come into conflict with the spirit and even the Constitution of Kenya."

The tone of the statement was echoed by President Kenyatta when he spoke afterward at a KANU luncheon in Mombasa. He appealed to Africans and Asians to live in harmony, but threw in a remark to show his dislike of the Asians' trumpeting about their generosity.

"People of immigrant communities have a duty and obligation to intensify their efforts in the process of building a nation free of bigotry and color consciousness," the President said. "There is no room in Kenya for patronage built on wealth, and those who dislike our way of life must pack up and go."

This sort of sensitivity is fairly general, as was discovered by an Asian in Dar es Salaam when he wrote to The Nationalist, a newspaper owned by the Tanzanian Government, to protest against dropping a Hindustani program on Radio Tanzania. He made the mistake of referring to the "colossal" amounts of money the Asians had given to help develop the nation.

"By contributing to this or that fund, these people actually do nothing but merely reimburse the country the wealth they have exploited out of its labor and natural resources," The Nationalist retorted in a stinging editorial. "These are the same people who are prepared to exploit the real owners of the country remorselessly under the guise of brotherhood. These are the people who are prepared to call themselves Tanzanians only as long as they remain a privileged group."

Incidents like this suggest the importance of the Asians' aloofness as an element in the prejudice they are now encountering. In the old days they took easily and happily to the colonial system. By separating the races the British gave them a niche and a certain security, protected areas of employment and housing. The system suited the Asians' temperament and allowed them to make up from their own resources the things the system did not adequately furnish—the mosques and temples, schools, clubs, hospitals and places of entertainment. Each of the Asian communities was left to its own way of life, its own introverted world.

As for the conduct of national affairs, there was never a very high level of political consciousness among the Asians. There was communal representation in politics, a fact that made communalism and racial self-interest inevitable as political issues, and helped to solidify the separatism in the system. What little sensitivity there was among Asians on matters of human rights was a new phenomenon, with all their history of caste differences, and did not get any real sympathy out of the Asian communities. Now the Africans are in control of government, and the Asians are willing to accept a new political allegiance. Beyond that they would prefer not to change.

They do not show up at political rallies, for example; to do so faithfully would be very time-consuming. Instead, they watch from the rooftops or send the children, and this irks the African politicians. Tanzania's regional commissioner in Moshi accused those who missed one of his recent rallies of "undermining the Government." The regional commissioner in another town simply shut all the local Asian shops for a day, to teach them not to take his rallies so lightly.

This sort of inconvenience and the occasional bit of drum-beating do not bother the Asians so much as the threat of mass deportations like the one carried out in Tanzania at the beginning of the year. Officially, the purge was supposed to be restricted to Asians who had no legal right to be in Tanzania, and whose departures would open up jobs and hasten the process of Africanization. The Asians remain unconvinced that this was all the Government wanted. Some were illegal residents only in the most technical sense. Some had been trying for years to get African officials to put their permits and papers in order. Some of the purged Asians had papers that were in order.

"Barbers, shoemakers, dry cleaners," Home Affairs Minister Lawi Sijaona proclaimed when the deportation drive began. "I call on all people in these categories to start packing." Hundreds of families in these and other categories were served with deportation notices. A barber in Dar es Salaam complained that his entry permit, which had another two months to run, was canceled on the spot. Five Asians who claimed to be the only important potmakers in the country were given notice. Four were British subjects and one was an Indian citizen, but all their children were Tanzanians. In the town of Arusha, both the Asian barbers were deported, but no African could fill the gap. An Asian with a Tanzanian passport had to come over nights from Moshi, 45 miles away, and the price of a haircut jumped from three shillings to five shillings. Two new Asians from out of town have since set up barber shops in Arusha, and the price of a haircut is back to normal again.

In a crowded little clothing store on Kilindini Road in Mombasa an unwealthy man with a gentle manner and slick gray hair waits stoically to see what will happen to him and his family. He watches a few Africans staring into his store from the sidewalk, and decides in an instant what they want. They are not waiting for work, nor thinking of buying clothes, nor preparing to serve a deportation notice; they just like to stare.

The storekeeper is a Hindu, but from a part of India that is now Pakistan. He left with his parents in 1921 because of religious fighting that threatened their lives. He has a British passport, but has never been to Britain. He never got a reply to his application for Kenya citizenship. Both his small sons, who are sorting through boxes of cut-rate clothes in the back of the store, are Kenya citizens, having been born in the country.

"I would like to do something, but I cannot put an African in my shop," the store owner says. "What could he sell? Maybe 300 shillings in a month? Can they take away my business and make me leave for that? Maybe they can; it is their country. I left my own country because of trouble. Do I have a right to stay in this one? I have an uncle and a brother in Bombay. Maybe I'll go there, but I am a stranger in India. It is very nice in Africa." ■

June 25, 1967

Kenya, Uganda and Tanzania Forcing Indians Out

By LAWRENCE FELLOWS
Special to The New York Times

NAIROBI, Kenya, Feb. 5 — "Can a mouse roar like a lion?" asked Meghji Shah, a Hindu who has lived all his life in Nairobi and worked all his adult years as an accountant here.

He was particularly bitter because he had just been to the airport to see his brother off to London on a charter flight.

Under pressure by the Governments of Kenya, Uganda and Tanzania, the Indians in East Africa appear to have started their largest exodus from these countries.

The airports at Nairobi, Entebbe and Dar es Salaam are packed with Indians now. In Nairobi, more than 100 are leaving every day, mostly men thrown out of their jobs by governmental regulations designed to break the Indians' grip on commerce and crafts and to move Africans into the resulting vacancies.

A Question of Skill

When Mr. Shah referred to the mouse, he was not thinking of the harassed Indian, once again on the run; he was thinking of the unskilled African who got his brother's clerical job in the post office or perhaps the African who would eventually, however meager his qualifications, squeeze him out of his accountant's job with a private company in town.

"These are the mice," Mr. Shah said. "Can they manage my job?" he asked. "Can they run a shop like my friend they pushed out of the municipal market?"

"They are unskilled or idle," he said. "What country can afford to pay an unskilled worker enough to support his family in idleness? The United States? A few Western European countries? I am skilled and my wife still has to work."

"The Africans cannot do this; they do not know what work is involved," Mr. Shah said. "And they have the nerve to roar like lions. I know my brother will find work for all of us and we will see who suffers."

Most of the Indian men are going to Britain on British passports that were acquired in the days when East African countries were part of Britain's colonial empire. The women and children who see them off at the airports hope to follow, presumably when the men find work and places to live. No one in authority here seems willing to venture a guess as to how many of the 400,000 Indians in East Africa will join the exodus.

Training Problem Encountered

The problem would seem to be a minuscule one as there are 30 million Africans in the three East African countries. But it has been so difficult to train sufficient numbers of Africans to fill vacancies that the Kenya Government had to re-admit some Indian masons, electricians and plumbers to keep the boom in office and hotel construction from collapsing in that country. Still, there has been some success in training Africans for jobs now held by Indians and the exodus continues.

One senior immigration official in Nairobi suggested that close to 100,000 Indians might leave Kenya alone. But he also said records of population and citizenship were so muddled that probably no one could really tell

Some of the Indians in East Africa are descended from traders who had crossed the Indian Ocean for centuries. Most, however, are descended from artisans and laborers whom the British brought over toward the end of the last century to build a railroad from Mombasa to the interior.

In some families, one member holds a British passport, another an Indian passport and still another a passport from some East African country. In that way they seek some protection against all eventualities.

The police and immigration officials in Tanzania grew so frustrated a year ago, when there was a purge of smaller dimensions, that they canceled many valid work permits on the spot just to get the Indians moving out of the country.

Several rackets have sprung into existence as a consequence of the exodus. Poor Indians are getting their fares paid by rich ones on condition that they take some money out of the country for them.

In Kenya, many Indians have lost their jobs because their employers have balked at a new requirement that every noncitizen employe and every member of his family be bonded to the extent that all their plane fares can be paid if the man should be deported.

February 6, 1968

Kenya Is Halting the Purge of Indian Shopkeepers

By LAWRENCE FELLOWS
Special to The New York Times

NAIROBI, Kenya, March 15 —A purge of Indian traders has ended in Kenya, at least for the rest of this year, it was learned today.

Perhaps a thousand shopkeepers and small traders around the country have been given notice to wind up their affairs, this is less than third of the number that were expected to be put out of business when Mwai Kibaki, Minister of Commerce and Industry, announced the start of the purge at the beginning of the year. At that time he said: "Within the next six months the Government estimates that about 3,000 noncitizen traders will have been refused licenses. This is a conservative estimate. There could be more."

No public announcement has been made yet that the Government has abruptly brought a halt to its policy of canceling trading licenses for aliens and, in some cases, for citizens if they are of Indian origin.

Joseph Kibe, Permanent Secretary of the Ministry of Commerce, confirmed, however, that it had.

No Reason Is Given

He would give no reason for the move, but it is known that the Government wanted to avoid a panic exodus of the sort that took place a year ago when 20,000 Indians with British passports who expected to lose shops or jobs left for Britain to get in before immigration was restricted. Many Indians also left Uganda and Tanzania under similar circumstances.

This exodus did have a certain short-term political usefulness in Kenya, where the presence of large Indian communities has always fed a strong undercurrent of racial and political tension, as it has elsewhere in Africa.

But the shopkeepers among them—the duka wallah—have dominated small trade almost from the time the British brought 30,000 Indians here as tradesmen, craftsmen and clerks and as labor to build the railroad into the interior toward end of the last century.

In the five years since Kenya became independent, the Government has ousted most of the Indians from lower paid clerical jobs in Government offices and replaced them with Africans.

Difficult for Africans

But for most Africans in this country, the ways of small trade have been difficult to understand.

Although the panic departure of Indians last year was caused more by the approach of Britain's restrictive immigration laws than by the action of the Kenya Government, there was a disruption of business that made investors hesitate.

As a result, the Government tried to balance what seemed politically necessary with what seemed economically advisable.

Even so, retail and wholesale trades in Nairobi were in a state of chaos for two weeks after the Government started canceling trading licenses early this year. Banks stopped even considering loans, the stock market slipped precipitously. As rumors spread, creditors were clamoring for quick payment of debts and debtors were making themselves hard to find.

Even Indians who had not received notices closed and shuttered their shops and many made plans to leave. The Government quickly stopped canceling licenses in Nairobi and slowed the process in Mombasa, Nakuru, Kisumu, Eldoret, Thika, and other sizable towns.

The drive against Indian shopkeepers in smaller places continued, however, and now some measure of economic dislocation can be felt almost anywhere in the country.

Because of this, the Government has apparently decided that the time has come to let up, at least for a while.

Among the many people in Kenya who are heaving sighs of relief are consumers who had grown accustomed to buying things they needed in well run, well stocked shops and also British diplomatic representatives. The British High Commission, the equivalent of an embassy, estimates that as many as 120,000 Indians here either hold British passports or are dependents of those who hold them.

March 16, 1969

Gunman Kills Tom Mboya, Kenyan Leader, in Nairobi

Special to The New York Times

NAIROBI, Kenya, July 5 — Tom Mboya, Kenya's Minister of Economic Affairs, was shot and killed by an unidentified assassin today as he emerged from a drugstore on a busy downtown street.

As Mr. Mboya appeared in the doorway, an auto reported to be carrying three men pulled up in the street and one of them jumped out and fired three shots, two of which are believed to have struck the Kenyan leader.

The gunman then sped away in the car, according to reports. Mr.Mboya was taken to Nairobi Hospital, where he was pronounced dead.

Mr. Mboya, who was 38 years old, was also Secretary General of the governing Kenya African National Union (KANU), and was regarded as the third most powerful man in the Government behind President Jomo Kenyatta and Vice President Daniel Arap Moi.

When the shots were fired, there were hundreds of shoppers in the area, many of whom fled. Mr. Mboya's bodyguard, who had preceded him through the doorway, crouched over his body weeping.

The police quickly put a cordon around the area and began questioning passersby. A widespread search for the three men was launched.

There were fears among Kenya's political leaders that the assassination might be regarded as the work of Mr. Mboya's political enemies and that the murder might spark reprisals.

The death of Tom, as he was known to thousands of his supporters, was greeted with sorrow throughout the nation, where he was regarded by many as Kenya's greatest hope for the future.

He had been active recently in organizing his party's campaign for general elections scheduled to be held in the next few months.

Mr. Mboya returned yesterday from Addis Ababa, Ethiopia, where he had attended a meeting of the Economic Commission for Africa, a group sponsored by the United Nations.

His assassination was the first in Kenya since 1966, when Pio Gama Pinto, a supporter of Oginga Odinga, the opposition leader, was shot down at his home in Nairobi.

July 6, 1969

Tribal Tension in Kenya

Arrest of Opposition Leader Is Sign Of Disintegration of Political Stability

By R. W. APPLE Jr.

Special to The New York Times

LONDON, Oct. 27—Last Saturday, in the lakeside town of Kisumu, President Jomo Kenyatta of Kenya seized a microphone and shouted at Oginga Odinga, the leader of the opposition Kenya People's Union:

"If you hadn't been a friend of mine from long ago, you know what would have happened to you by now." That outburst, so uncharacteristic of the 79-year-old President, was dramatic evidence of the rapid disintegration of political stability in what had until recently been regarded as the healthiest and most prosperous young country in all of East Africa.

News Analysis

Today threat became fact, as Mr. Odinga and his deputy, J. M. Nthula, were placed under house arrest along with the six other members of the parliamentary opposition.

President Kenyatta's position has worsened rapidly in the four months since the assassination of Tom Mboya, the Minister for Economic Development.

A Break With Tradition

The process has been evident to most observers in Nairobi, as this correspondent learned during a nine-month trip through Africa that has just been completed.

Jealous of its reputation for stability, eager to attract foreign investors and American tourists, Kenya has tried to avoid doing anything that would suggest chaos or crisis. The arrests and detentions, a clear break with the country's tradition of relatively free democracy, thus appear to constitute an extreme measure.

The death of Mr. Mboya, who was a Luo but was perhaps the most detribalized of Africa's younger politicians, was like the opening of a spigot, out of which poured pent-up tribal and regional animosities and fears.

Members of the Luo tribe, the country's second largest, after the Kikuyu tribe of President Kenyatta, rallied around Mr. Odinga. Members of the Kikuyu tribe were subjected to secret oath-taking rituals, countenanced by Mr. Kenyatta, which committed them to fight to the death if necessary to keep the Kikuyus in power. Members of the other tribes, which together form a majority, began thinking and acting not as Kenyans but as clan members.

The oaths, reminiscent of rituals used during the Mau-Mau rebellion against Britain, terrified non-Kikuyus but apparently failed to cement Kikuyu unity. Kikuyu Christians and their clergymen have resisted oath-taking ceremonies, one has been killed and several have been beaten up.

Finally, on Saturday evening, things got out of control.

The President drove to Kisumu, a port on Lake Victoria where Mr. Odinga's party holds sway. More than 5,000 Luos, still bitter over the shooting of Mr. Mboya by a Kikuyu, began stoning the cars in Mr. Kenyatta's motorcade. The police moved in, clubs swinging.

The crowds heckled the President with People's Union slogans. Swiftly the meeting dissolved in shouts and catcalls, fistfights, gunfire from the police, and a stampede. The police put the casualties at 11 dead and about 70 injured.

This morning came the arrests, plus a Cabinet meeting blaming Luo oppositionists for the events on Saturday. The Government-owned Voice of Kenya said in a special broadcast that the Cabinet had decided to deal firmly "with subversive elements who had been working with some foreign and unfriendly elements to destroy the peaceful running of the country."

The last phrase was presumably an allusion to Mr. Odinga's past Communist leanings.

It seems inevitable that the crackdown will make the Luos feel even more shut out of a role in governing Kenya and that that in turn will lead to further violence. Luo disaffection does not yet appear to have become as severe as that among the Ibos in Nigeria, who felt so aggrieved that they seceded and set up the state of Biafra. But Luo disaffection is not likely to recede quickly.

In these circumstances, the smaller tribes can be expected to become more and more insular, which can only make the country more difficult to govern.

It is therefore difficult to see how a successful parliamentary election can be held late this year or early next year, as is now planned. It, too, would be subject to disruption and to charges of Kikuyu intimidation.

October 28, 1969

SWAHILI DECLARED KENYA'S LANGUAGE

Switch From English Meets With Little Enthusiasm

Special to The New York Times

NAIROBI, Kenya, May 9—The Government has issued orders establishing Swahili as the national language in Kenya, as it is in neighboring Tanzania.

Under the program, which has met with little enthusiasm among the 10 million people of this former British territory, English is to be displaced except in institutions of higher learning by the end of next year.

Swahili, which is also widely used in Uganda, is basically a Bantu tongue that originated among the peoples of the East African coastal areas and absorbed many words from Arabic, Portuguese and English as well as from Urdu, a Persianized form of Hindustani.

During the colonial period in Kenya, the British administrators and private employers required that their people know Swahili, and it has long been the lingua franca of the country.

Use of English Spread

Since Kenya gained independence in December, 1963 ,English has become much more widely used. In Nairobi it became almost an insult for a foreigner to address a Kenyan in Swahili because a knowledge of English had become regarded as the hallmark of education.

But toward the end of last year, the governing council of the Kenya African National Union, the ruling party, decided that the widespread use of English language smacked of neo-colonialism, or at least was un-African. The alternative was Swahili.

Last month Robert Matano, secretary general of the party and Assistant Minister of State in President Jomo Kenyatta's Government issued a directive — in English — stating that Swahili would become Kenya's national language.

"All Kenyans," it said, "shall speak in Swahili at all times either to fellow Kenyans or to non-Kenyans, whether officially or unofficially, politically or socially."

It requires Kenyans to speak to their children in Swahili "instead of English as the case is today" and to speak to foreigners only in Swahili "to make them learn it."

The use of English in addition to Swahili, the directive said, will be tolerated until 31, December, 1971. At that time "Swahili shall then be spoken by all people at all times whether officially or unofficially, politically or socially" and National Assembly and local council business will be conducted in Swahili, it said.

"All civil servants will have to pass both oral and written Swahili tests at elementary and advanced levels," the order said. "Promotion, demotion or even forced retirement will depend on the outcome of these tests."

A concession to the dozen or so principal vernacular languages was made in the directive by permitting their use among people of the same tribe, although they are to be encouraged to attend an Academy of Swahili that is to be established.

The directive acknowledged the usefulness of English as a world language and exempted institutions of higher learning from the order against its use "officially or unofficially, politically or socially."

May 10, 1970

Ethiopians Get New Constitution And Right to Vote for First Time

Haile Selassie Also Announces Nation's Laws Are Codified—Electoral Statute Said to Call for Vote in Two Years

By KENNETT LOVE
Special to The New York Times.

ADDIS ABABA, Ethiopia, Nov. 4—Emperor Haile Selassie promulgated today a new Constitution for Ethiopia. It grants the people the right to vote for the first time in their 3,000 years as a nation.

The Constitution provides that a lower house of Parliament will be elected by universal franchise. It incorporates a liberal bill of rights. It also provides for an independent judiciary, regulates the imperial succession and defines the reserved powers and prerogatives of the Emperor.

In line with Haile Selassie's gradualist policy of liberalizing one of the world's few remaining absolute monarchies, the Constitution reserves the imperial veto over legislation and does not permit the legislature to override it. The Emperor will appoint judges and Cabinet ministers.

One of history's most revolutionary limitations voluntarily imposed by an absolute monarch on his own powers is contained in the ninety-second of the new Constitution's 131 articles. It provides for the Emperor to legislate by decree when Parliament is not in session. but it gives Parliament the right to abrogate such degrees by disapproval.

Theoretically it would appear that enmity between Parliament and the Emperor could paralyze the legislative process. but the Emperor retains the right to dissolve Parliament.

Although the bill of rights insures full religious freedom, the Constitution states that the Ethiopian Orthodox Church, founded in the fourth century on the doctrines of St. Mark, is the established church of the state.

The new Constitution was announced in a speech from the throne. The Emperor addressed a joint session of Parliament in the presence of foreign representatives assembled for the twenty-fifth anniversary of the Emperor's coronation, celebrated yesterday.

A few minutes before the speech the monarch signed the proclamation of the new Constitution and the Constitution itself in a simple ceremony in the throne room. The splendor of the room, containing the thrones of Haile Selassie and Empress Menen, and the glittering uniforms of foreign and Ethiopian dignitaries contrasted with the simplicity of the historic event.

Haile Selassie then proceeded to the imperial box above the rostrum in the Hall of Parliament and announced his action, which had ben a closely guarded secret.

The Emperor said the Constitution, replacing Ethiopia's first Constitution, which he promulgated in 1931, had been six years in preparation and "is therefore no superficial achievement." He said Parliament had approved it before it received his final authorization.

The speech included the announcement that "the most enlightened jurists of the continent of Europe" had aided in codifying the civil, penal, commercial and maritime laws of Ethiopia. This was described by international authorities gathered here as of scarcely less importance than the new Constitution. The legal code is being printed.

The Monarch also disclosed he had prepared a national electoral law for submission to Parliament.

Women will have the same right to vote as men. Ethiopian women of the Christian majority are free of the traditional restrictions on women in Moslem countries.

Describing the bill of rights, the Emperor said:

"No less than twenty-nine articles have been inserted in the Constitution to provide for the protection of the essential liberties and rights of the people. Thus we have provided that 'no one shall be denied equal protection of the laws' * * *; that 'freedom of speech and of press is guaranteed throughout the Empire in accordance with the law'; 'correspondence shall be subject to no censorship except in time of declared national emergency.'"

November 5, 1955

COUP IN ETHIOPIA OUSTS SELASSIE; SON CLAIMS RULE

KING FLYING HOME

Cuts Visit to Brazil—Palace Guard Acts With Prince's Aid

By DANA ADAMS SCHMIDT

Special to The New York Times.

WASHINGTON, Dec. 14—Emperor Haile Selassie I of Ethiopia was overthrown today by Crown Prince Asfa-Wossen, his son.

The State Department confirmed that a coup d'état had been carried out by the Imperial Household Guard.

Haile Selassie, whose titles include King of Kings and the Lion of Judah, was in Saõ Paulo, Brazil, on a state visit.

The Emperor's first reported reaction to the coup came in an announcement by a spokesman that he was "perfectly calm" and would "keep his schedule while awaiting information from official sources in Addis Ababa on this revolution."

[Late Wednesday night, Haile Selassie left Sao Paulo, Brazil, by plane for Ethiopia. Soon afterward, The Associated Press reported, the new regime in Addis Ababa barred the flight of any aircraft into the country, apparently to prevent the Emperor's return.]

Coded reports received from Western embassies suggested that the 44-year-old Crown Prince, a retiring, shy man who was known as a dutiful son, was the respectable front for other political forces. But the names of those leading these forces were not available.

In the absence of more detailed information, the State Department declined to interpret the meaning of the overturn. Officials said there had been no advance indications and that the coup took them by surprise.

Emperor Haile Selassie

A Foreign Ministry spokesman with the Emperor in São Paulo said it was "impossible" that the Emperor's son could "of his own free will" be involved in a palace coup.

The spokesman also doubted that the Imperial Guard, "the most pampered force in Ethiopia," could be involved.

The Imperial Household Guard consists of 6,000 specially trained troops. The Ethiopian Army, trained by British and United States officers, numbers about 25,000, of whom 2,500 are in the Congo with the United Nations force.

United Press International

Crown Prince Asfa-Wossen

The first radio announcements by the new regime had a socialistic, nationalistic touch akin to that of the revolutionary regimes of the neighboring United Arab Republic and Sudan.

The announcements protested against privileges given by the 68-year-old Emperor to the few at the expense of the "common people" and proclaimed the need for "concrete action" to improve the standard of living.

Ambassador Arthur L. Richards reported to the State Department that there had been no reports of civil disorder and nothing to indicate any danger to Americans in Ethiopia.

The State Department estimated there were 2,500 Americans in Ethiopia, including 1,200 to 1,500 military men and their families at a military relay base at Asmara, about 1,000 missionaries and about 200 State Department and other Government employes and their families.

The United States has spent about $115,000,000, mostly for technical assistance, in Ethiopia in the last decade. This has included setting up an agricultural school for which the University of Oklahoma provided the staff, a nursing school and other forms of vocational training.

The United States also has drilled wells and carried out a geodetic survey of the Blue Nile. A small group of American military advisers has participated in training the army.

The Soviet Union extended a $100,000,000 credit to Ethiopia after the Emperor visited Moscow in July, 1959, but little if any of it has been used yet. A few Soviet technicians have arrived at Addis Ababa to begin surveys for possible projects.

Parliament Reported Dissolved

The Addis Ababa radio announced today that Parliament had been dissolved.

In a statement to the people of Ethiopia, the Crown Prince said he had taken power and that "any decision by this Government—including changes in appointments—will be strictly adhered to."

He said he would serve his people "in accordance with the Constitution," on a fixed salary, like any other Ethiopian."

The broadcast attacked the rule of the Crown Prince's father without mentioning him by name. "The laws and regulations of the country have been abused to deprive the common people of their rights and privileges in order to boost up the riches of the favored few," it said.

"The people of Ethiopia have waited for a long time with patience in the hope that they would be free some day of oppression, poverty and ignorance.

December 15, 1960

SELASSIE RETURNS TO ETHIOPIAN RULE

19 of His Officials Feared Slain in Brief Revolt—Fate of Rebels Unclear

Special to The New York Times.

LONDON, Dec. 17—Emperor Haile Selassie I of Ethiopia returned today to his capital, Addis Ababa, and resumed control of a Government shaken four days ago by an attempted revolt.

The Ethiopian Embassy here reported that the Emperor was greeted at the airport by his son, Crown Prince Asfa-Wossen, who had been identified earlier as the leader of the rebellion.

A report from Djibouti, in French Somaliland, said that nineteen leaders of the Emperor's Government were believed to have been executed by the rebels.

Some of the rebel leaders also were dead. General Mulugeta Bullie, who had been named rebel army chief, was reported slain. There were conflicting reports as to how the rebels died, but some mentioned suicide.

The arrival of the Emperor in the city from which he has ruled Ethiopia since 1928 marked the end of thirty-six hours of desperate battling between loyal troops and the Imperial Guard rebels who attempted to overthrow him last Wednesday.

The 68-year-old Emperor was on a state visit to Brazil when the rebels struck. He flew to Asmara, about 450 miles from Addis Ababa yesterday and then made his entrance into the capital today.

It was said that he went immediately to his palace and "took control of the situation at once."

With the serious rebel resistance apparently over, Addis Ababa was said to be returning swiftly to its peaceful routine.

Although amateur radio rereports said that some skirmishing continued, 124 persons were returning or preparing to return to their homes from the British Embassy compound, where they had taken refuge.

Three Ministers Slain

But the bodies of at least three Cabinet ministers testified to the bitter, last-ditch stand of the rebels. Reports credited as reliable said that the Ministers of Defense and Commerce and the Acting Minister of Foreign Affairs had been slain when their rebel guards retreated to the palace and saw the hopelessness of their position.

The Minister of the Interior was reported to have been wounded, and the Ministers of Public Works and Finance were said to be in hiding.

As of late this afternoon, little was known of the fate of the other rebel leaders. Ras (Duke) Imru, a distant member of the royal family, who had been proclaimed rebel Premier, was said to be dead. Reports about him were conflicting.

A message reaching Aden from Djibouti, sporadically in telephonic communication with Addis Ababa, said that Germane Wondafrash, chief of the Ethiopian Imperial Guard, had been killed by the loyalist forces.

Units of the Imperial Guard have been accused of spearheading the rebellion. They were apparently overpowered by the army and air force.

Behind the uprising were Gen. Mangistou Neway, chief of the Imperial Guard, some of his officers and a small group of civilians.

Among the crucial victories of the loyalists was the recapture of air force planes that had been seized by some of the Imperial Guard. The planes were then used in a combined land and air attack against the rebels.

December 18, 1960

The Future of Ethiopia

Younger Educated Class Unhappy With Selassie's Moderate Pace of Reforms

By DREW MIDDLETON
Special to The New York Times

ADDIS ABABA, Ethiopia, March 7—This ancient empire has so far survived the storms that have swept Africa, toppling rulers and deposing governments.

But Ethiopia cannot escape change in a changing Africa. The central issue is whether mild social reforms, gradual economic growth and slow methodical progress toward political responsibility will suffice to meet the demands of a growing class of educated and restive young people.

News Analysis

Haile Selassie, Regent from 1916 to 1928, King from 1928 to 1930, and Emperor since 1930, to a great extent is the victim of his own progressive program. Half a century ago this gentle-mannered autocrat set his 3,000-year-old empire on the road to modernity.

"Ten years, even five years ago, the Emperor was ahead and leading us," a young Ethiopian explained. "Now it is we, the educated élite, educated by his order, who are leading, and the Emperor who lags behind."

His Imperial Majesty Haile Selassie I, Conquering Lion of the Tribe of Judah, Elect of God, Emperor of Ethiopia, remains the center of power and the fountain of honors. Under his guidance, the beginnings of democratic rule are discernible in the two-chamber Parliament.

Parties Do Not Exist

There are no political parties. Members of the Chamber of Deputies, or lower house, elected by direct universal suffrage, represent localities.

Recently groups of members have found themselves in agreement on some issues. The questioning of ministers in Parliament has been introduced. These first steps toward the evolution of parties bear a resemblance to the emergency of Tories and Whigs in Britain and of the Federalists and Democrats in the United States. Shared political ideas are bringing men together.

The Emperor is 74 years old. Asfa-Wossen, his eldest son, is the Crown Prince. But the Emperor has not designated him his successor. The question of the succession is of the utmost importance to Ethiopia's future stability.

The death of the Emperor, regarded as the father of his country, may shake Ethiopia. If he can pass on some of his prestige and influence to his heir, the transfer of power may go smoothly. The Crown Prince would have the support of the army, the church and a large segment of the young élite.

For Haile Selassie's position is far greater than that attainable by any transient politician. Few of his countrymen can remember any other rule. An Amhara himself, he is above tribal rivalries, the focus of loyalty and patriotism among the unlettered peasants.

Wishes of Young

"We want an end to absolute rule," one young man educated abroad said, "but we cannot do away with the monarchy. Wise men must guide the new Emperor while a constitutional monarchy is developed. A President? Look at the rest of Africa. We have our own way of doing things."

Others assure the visitor that "blood will flow" and remind questioners that the Ethiopians, unlike other Africans, have arms and know how to use them.

The privilege and corruption that surround the emperor, the favors shown the Orthodox church, the powers of great landowners must be swept away they say. They add that the system of rule in which favorite is balanced against favorite, while bright young men are shunted aside, must go.

The less pessimistic say that an old civilization like Ethiopia's has the flexibility to withstand the death of the Emperor because it will understand the crown is necessary as a unifying factor.

Nation Set Apart

And the visitor is told continually, "Ethiopia is not Africa."

Ethiopia is in Africa, but not of it. For centuries its people have held themselves remote and proud. Even with the headquarters of Organization of African Unity and the United Nations for Africa in Addis Ababa, Ethiopians maintain a remarkable objectivity toward the tumult and the shouting elsewhere.

But the Emperor has plunged Ethiopia into that Africa. The two organizations are in the capital because of his diplomacy and help. His voice has been raised on all the great issues confronting Africans—and always on the side of moderation.

This idea of moderation has guided Haile Selassie in the development of Ethiopia. Much remains to be done, he concedes, but it must be done deliberately.

This nation, whose 395,000 square miles vary from towering mountains to wide deserts, is potentially very rich. It has changed rapidly, especially in the last five years, yet much remains to be done.

The central plateau is fertile. Yet only about 15 per cent of the cultivatable land is farmed. The beginnings of land reform may induce peasants to farm more extensively.

Coffee is the main crop, with almost three-quarters of the production eventually reaching the United States. Foreign-owned companies have successfully grown sugar and cotton.

Mussolini Had Plans

Yet around the capital lie vast stretches of fertile untilled land. Of the country's 22 million cattle only a fraction reach market. Mussolini, who conquered Ethiopia, in 1936 but was driven out by Allied forces in 1941, said that properly developed, Ethiopia could feed half of Europe or all of the Middle East.

Industry, despite efforts to stimulate it, still accounts for less than 10 per cent of the gross national product. Foreign investment is courted; Americans are building a potash plant, the Russians have built an oil refinery.

Ethiopia escaped the colonial system except for a brief unhappy period of Italian rule. But the nation has had to build the roads, dams, schools, hospitals that the colonial powers built elsewhere in Africa. Moreover, Ethiopia has had to train the administrators, civil servants, teachers and doctors. Elsewhere the colonialists often trained and bequeathed them to subject peoples on their departure.

Education has been the key to the Emperor's modernization. But of 4 to 5 million children of school age only about 300,000 are in school, according to the United States Peace Corps. There is too little vocational training, young Ethiopians insist, although they concede this is natural among a people traditionally disdainful of manual labor.

Ethiopia needs, a young official said, "foreign investment, a skilled labor force and better communications."

The United States is the most important outside power in Ethiopia. Nearly $70-million has been spent here since 1953 in technical assistance in education, public health and geographical surveys. Airport and highway construction has been assisted by loans and advice. The Peace Corps and the military assistance group have been successes.

Ethiopia is ready to take off. The question is whether the last step can be accomplished without disturbance and bloodshed.

March 8, 1966

In Selassie's Ethiopia, Muted Voices Urge Change

By MARVINE HOWE

Special to The New York Times

ADDIS ABABA, Ethiopia, Aug. 18—"Awake, oh people, awake!" the dark-robed chorus cries. But everyone sleeps on, and only a nervous figure, symbolizing time, continues to move.

This is the conclusion of a new play, "Face of the Earth," a kind of Ethiopian "Hair," which attacks familiar institutions — weddings, funerals, witchcraft, prostitution, the courts, the press and radio.

The most important Ethiopian institution, the 2,000-year-old monarchy does not come under fire. But then—except in private conversation—it almost never does in this closely controlled society, in which the secret police reportedly have penetrated every milieu, including that of university and high school students. The press is Government-owned, and books and other publications are censored.

In the face of this, an increasing number of voices are calling for change. There is subtle pressure from intellectuals. Some manage to record some criticism, as did the author of "Face of the Earth."

Ethiopian authors have various ways of circumventing censorship. Some strike up friendly relations with the censors to get controversial works published. Others write novels or plays about repression and corruption in some other country or age, although the implications are clear.

"Censorship has had a devastating effect in Ethiopia," one author said. "What happens to a culture in a country where the works of some of the best writers are lying in desk drawers and where you're afraid to tell the story of 'Aida' because it mentions an Ethiopian king who is killed?"

Some potential force for change comes from within the regime. Nearly half the high Government officials are 40 years of age or younger and are exerting increasing influence for reform, although they are apparently still outweighed by the strong conservative forces.

A new liberal press bill is scheduled to be presented to the Council of Ministers in the fall. But conservative elements strongly oppose the measure because it does not provide for press censorship, leaving sanctions to the courts.

A liberalizing land reform bill has been in the mill for about six years and is also scheduled to be brought before Parliament in the fall. But important land-owning interests are expected to delay it again.

The students, who are considered among the most radical in Africa, constitute the principal opposition force in this feudal land, and the loudest and most vigorous pressure for change has come from them.

But 78-year-old Emperor Haile Selassie, who has been absolute ruler for 40 years, is still the principal instrument of reform, because no other figure or institution has the power to introduce change. However, he believes, Government sources say, that change must come slowly and that the country is not ready for mass education.

Aside from the student movement, there is no organized political opposition in Ethiopia. Political parties are illegal, and the labor unions are in an embryonic apolitical stage.

The students have put land reform at the top of their list of demands, which include expansion of education, freedom of speech and of demonstration, abolition of the detention act and more social welfare measures. Their conflicts with the authorities have often resulted in bloodshed and widespread detentions.

The feudal pattern of land tenure, against which the students inveigh, has been unchanged for centuries. One third of the land is owned by the state and the royal family, one third by the Ethopian Orthodox Church and the rest by large and small landowners and communal groups.

Ethiopia, whose heartland is a high plateau, is generally described as one of the world's least developed countries. More than 95 per cent of her 25 million people are dependent on agriculture for their livelihood, and most of the land is still tilled by tenant farmers. The principal crop is coffee.

"The students are right," Abebe Retta, the Minister of Agriculture, said in an interview, "but the method they propose is wrong.

"The students think the landlords should give their land to the peasants, but this isn't necessary now because the Government owns a great deal of land that is not inhabited, which can be distributed."

The new bill would provide that the tenant would have to pay no more than 30 per cent of what he produces to his landlord. In the past the figure has been as high as 50 per cent.

Modern World Touches Capital

A modern superstructure of educational, economic and political institutions has been built in Ethiopia in recent years, mainly in this capital city. Addis Ababa, generally called Addis, is a city of vast imperial palaces and other stately structures and handsome embassy compounds, but it is also a city of shantytowns and of crowded hovels in the old quarter.

The capital has no real center, and its half a million people live in a municipal area that sprawls over several hills.

Haile Selassie University, chartered in 1961, has 12 faculties, or schools, and an enrollment of 4,000 day students, 3,000 night students and 1,500 in summer school, impressive numbers in Africa.

As everywhere, the students' main grievance is against the "system," which they hold responsible for corruption, poverty and delayed progress. They do not as a rule attack the Emperor directly, except in clandestine pamphlets, but they appear ready to support any move that aims to weaken his regime.

Backed Attempted Coup

The student movement openly backed an unsuccessful attempt by the Imperial Bodyguard to overthrow the regime in 1960, when the Emperor was in Brazil on a state visit. The movement has also shown sympathy for the Eritrean Liberation Front, which seeks to unite Ethiopia's northernmost province, or at least its Moslem lowlands, with the Sudan and the rest of the Moslem world.

Many students are strongly anti-American because they feel that the United States is the major support of the imperial regime.

"The United States should pull out its professors and aid program and leave us alone," a spokesman for a group of six students from various schools said in an interview.

"If it hadn't been for American aid, the whole system would have crumbled long ago," an economics major said.

Ethiopia's main foreign support comes from the United States, which has provided $250-million in grants or loans and surplus commodities since 1952. The current aid program —adapted to the priorities of Ethiopia's third five-year plan, which ends this year—emphasizes agriculture and industries related to farming and puts education projects ahead of health and other social measures.

The United States is currently also Ethiopia's chief foreign supplier of military equipment, about $13-million worth a year. But troubled border situations are impelling the Ethiopians to look for more arms.

Besides the activities of the insurgents in Eritrea, there is a problem with the Moslem country of Somalia, which claims a large part of southwestern Ethiopia on the ground that one million Somalis live there.

'Just Like Israel'

"We are an island, encircled by hostile Arab states, just like Israel," is a comment heard often in ruling circles here.

The Soviet Union has made recent offers of military equipment, according to high officials, who add that the Emperor has rebuffed these overtures.

"The Emperor is a very sentimental person and believes the Americans will send us more help if we're in trouble, but there are many other people who don't have so much faith," a Government source said.

Technical assistance has been given Ethiopia by Eastern Europe but it has been relatively low-key. The Soviet Union has built the oil refinery at Assab on the Red Sea. Yugoslavs operate a joint construction company in Addis Ababa and have built several hospitals. Poland has built a plant for making hand tools. Czechoslovakia has put in a joint fishing venture.

Assistance from the West includes a cotton plantation operated by the British and a Dutch sugar plantation east of the capital. Swedes have launched an important agricultural project south of Addis Ababa.

The New York Times (by Marvine Howe)

Students in the John F. Kennedy Memorial Library of Haile Selassie I University, Addis Ababa. Students are the principal opposition in Ethiopia and press the hardest for change.

Despite varying pressures for change, Ethiopia seems likely to continue on her slow road to modernization as long as Haile Selassie remains in power. In recent years, the Emperor has delegated some of his administrative duties to his Premier, Aklilu Habite Wold, but he continues to direct foreign policy and to make all important internal policy decisions.

According to his intimates, the Emperor is not an arbitrary ruler but governs more by consensus, balancing interest groups around him. However, he remains the sole arbiter among competing factions.

Younger leaders are looking forward to the day when Crown Prince Merid Azmatch Asfa Wosen will become the "inheritor of the bed," as the successor to the throne is described in the Amharic language. These leaders believe that the Prince will not inherit his father's absolute authority and will increasingly share his powers with the Government and Parliament, thereby propelling Ethiopia toward democratic rule.

The Unknown War In the Sudan

By LAWRENCE FELLOWS

KHARTOUM, the Sudan.

A SUDANESE Army captain lay sprawling out of a wicker chair on the covered deck of the steamer El Mirrech. He was half-asleep and rolled uncomfortably as the steamer and its half a dozen barges made their way down the upper reaches of the White Nile, bumping from one bank of matted vegetation to the other in a fetid, mauve-green sea of reeds. The captain's long, white robe clung to his skin where the perspiration had soaked through. He had been reading, but the oppressive heat and the heavy progress of the steamer were overpowering and his book lay open on its crumpled pages on the deck by his chair.

When the barges started to heave up onto the bank at one sharp bend in the river, the sun crept up to his eyes and he half-consciously sheltered them against the hard light. The cables groaned and snapped like great, cracking whips and the waves pushed out by the sidling barges rushed hissing into the reeds. We knew we would hit the bank hard. Yet the captain seemed startled by the bump when it came. He sat bolt upright and, still not really awake, tried to concentrate on a plume of smoke rising from a distant point on the horizon. It might have been nothing more than a camp of Dinka tribesmen burning off the coarse grass so that fresh grass for their cattle could come up later. It might also have been a village burning after an army raid, or perhaps after a raid by the Anya'nya rebels. A frown deepened on the captain's face, and he looked away.

"Oh," he said, "I had already forgotten about the war."

IT is easy enough to forget about the savage, awful war that has raged through the three southern provinces of the Sudan for the last six years. It is a war that involves neither foreign ideologies nor foreign powers, fought over distant and isolated territory of no special economic value, and by Africans with feeble political and military power. And yet it will not go away; it has rent the physically biggest state in Africa disastrously, perhaps irreparably; it has spilled over the borders into five neighboring countries, creating recurrent diplomatic, military and refugee problems; and it has taken already perhaps half a million lives, making it a far more costly war than Vietnam, and the rebels vow that they will continue to fight for 20 years more if need be.

In simplest terms, the war is a rebellion run by a ragged organization of guerrillas hoping to lead the 3 or 4 million black, Christian or pagan, Africa-oriented people of the southern third of the Sudan away from the 9 million Moslem and Arab-oriented people of the north. The rebels are fighting the Arab-dominated Government in Khartoum and its well-equipped, growing army of 22,000 men with a raggle-taggle organization known as the Anya'nya, whose name is taken from the deadly powder made by drying and grinding the whole head of the cobra, a slow but invariably fatal poison. Their political arm is the Southern Sudan Provisional Government, headed by ex-civil servant Aggrey Jaden, and the military is a force of perhaps 5,000 men splintered into small uncoordinated bands, nominally commanded by Col. Tafeng Lodongi.

FLYING low over the south, you can get an idea of the chaotic effect of this hidden war. Nearly every village in the south has been burned to the ground by troops trying to stamp out support for the rebellion, or by rebels punishing villagers who accepted the army's authority. The survivors in the bush live a hunted, half-starved existence. They can be seen in scattered camps, away from the river, away from the roads, where neither the army nor the Anya'nya can get at them.

Even there, whole camps are easily wiped out by diseases that sweep over them—malaria, dysentery, black fever. They are hungry and have little resistance. They have no doctors, no medicines. They do not even have salt. African priests and merchants who still move around a bit in the south reckon there can hardly be a family left that has not lost someone.

"Half a million dead," reflected Hamid Ali Shash, the soft-spoken, intense looking Commissioner of Equatoria Province, flush against Uganda and the center of the rebellion. He was shaking his head.

"Half a million," he said. "That's one in six, or one in eight. No, it cannot be. It must be less."

"How many?" I asked.

"I don't know," he said. "How can anyone know?"

Certain knowledge about anything in the Sudan is hard to come by. It is extremely difficult to gauge the progress of the rebellion, both because the Khartoum Government does not normally allow outsiders, including journalists, free access to and around the south, and because this war — like Vietnam's, without definable fronts—is largely a matter of ambush, political murder, occupation and pacification, where the allegiance of the countryside is always uncertain. But indications are that the Government in recent months has managed to make considerable progress in isolating the Anya'nya bands, opening thin corridors of authority along the major roads and, through soldiers and police, keeping the peace in many newly established villages.

HOW long the rebellion can stay under control is anybody's guess, and the Government is hoping fervently for a continuance of the disunity and tribal antagonisms that have plagued both the political and military sides of the Anya'nya. But it is clear that the guerrilla force has won overt allegiance from many southerners and tacit support from many more because it expresses their very real and long-standing religious, racial, tribal, economic and historical grievances against the northerners. As long as these grievances remain unsatisfied, the brutal business of guerrilla war will continue for years to come.

In the barges, northerner and southerner did not talk to each other, but neither did they argue. When they ate, Arab and African leaned together over the sides, stripping sugar cane with their teeth, spitting the chewed-out pulp into the water. Sometimes the soldiers would watch the southern women nursing their children, listen to their plaintive songs, study the carefully patterned scars that decorated their backs and chests. When a woman stood and loosened her robes to rub ghee over her body, the Arab soldiers turned discreetly away, looking out into the river.

Only the Nile and a long, unhappy history tie together north and south. As a British colony, the Sudan had value only as a buffer for the strategic Nile, and hence Egypt itself; in fact, the British made the south a part of their colony only to keep the French away from the headwaters of the Nile.

British rule extended only slowly over the south, but the British decided the area had to be closed off to Arab influence from the north. Christian missions were made responsible for education. Northern merchants were excluded from the south, Greek and Syrian traders encouraged. Northern clerks and officials were transferred back to the north. Arabic patois and Arabic names were discouraged. One zealous district commissioner even forbade the sale of Arabic clothing.

After World War II, in the rush to independence, this policy gave way. The southerners were suspicious of the northerners, and hesitant about throwing in their lot with them, but in the end they had no choice. The British began to withdraw. Northern merchants and civil servants flocked into the south. Few southerners got jobs; probably few were eligible, but the south grew morose and a demand welled up for some form of federation to protect southern rights.

At Nazara, on July 26, 1955, half a year before independence, a mob of southerners demonstrated against some mass dismissals from a cotton-growing and processing scheme. The soldiers sent to quell them lost their nerve and fired into the mob; northern merchants stood beside the soldiers, firing with them.

Three weeks later more trouble came. In the garrison of the Equatoria Corps an Arab officer drew his revolver and shot an unruly African soldier. The African soldiers went on a rampage and swept through the province killing every northerner they could find. Men, women and children were butchered or whipped and skinned and hung from trees. Northern troops were flown to the south to restore order, but not until hundreds had been killed. The whole south was locked under emergency regulations which are still in effect.

The rebellion failed. The mutiny had been unorganized and leaderless and not even the southern politicians in Khartoum had supported it. But it left hundreds of African soldiers armed, vengeful and scattered in the bush.

THE military regime that took over power from the inept politicians in Khartoum in 1958 tried to bear down on the south, but only made things worse. Talk about federation was banned, and the southerners began thinking of secession. Fighting finally broke out again in 1962, villagers dug ditches in the roads or felled trees across them to immobilize the army. The next year, the Anya'nya was formed and the rebellion enveloped the whole of the south.

In 1964 the army regime fell. The caretaker government that took over was more acceptable to the southerners, but there seemed to be no turning back. A cease-fire was proclaimed, but it did not work. When Mohammed Ahmed Mahgoub took over as Prime Minister in 1965, he pursued a hard line with the rebels. There were fierce massacres of civilians in Wau and Juba. Refugees were pursued in the bush, and sometimes across the borders. Every village school in the south was destroyed, and there were more than 500 of them. The mission stations were shot up and sometimes bombed.

This spring southerner Ottiafano Amauro returned home to his village of Liria, to his father and his family. After six weary years with the Anya'nya he had had enough. Not that he liked the Arabs of the north any better than any other southerner. He knew from his childhood all the old stories about the 19th-century Arab raids for slaves and ivory. He had been cheated by Arab merchants and had suffered the brutal excesses of Arab soldiers and policemen. He had no wish to become a Moslem or wear the loose-wrapped turban and long, white robe that might help ease him into the fringes of the establishment. He just wanted to be let alone.

Ottiafano had been a corporal in the Sudanese Army at the time of the army mutiny in 1955 which had first set north against south. He and all the 140 other southerners in his company stole 12 army trucks, headed for the Uganda border and walked across as refugees. He wandered back to the Sudan in 1959, heading for Liria, and was thrown into a Sudanese jail. After a month he was let out, then stayed at home until the Anya'nya rebellion started.

In 1963 he was captured by the Anya'nya in a field outside his village. Of the 75 men in the gang that captured him, two had rifles. The rest were armed with spears, clubs, bows and arrows. Because of Ottiafano's military training, they pressed him into service as a lieutenant, and gave him one of the rifles—a Chinese .375 that was built to hold five cartridges, but jammed if more than four were put into it.

Eventually his group was reduced to seven men—five lieutenants and two privates. All had rifles. They roamed usually through the dense forest around Yei, near the Uganda border, living on the game they could shoot, possibly on the food they were given by villagers or stole from them. Ottiafano refuses to talk about that, or about the battles he had with the soldiers. But when he finally gave himself up this year, he would not surrender to a soldier. He waited in the forest at the edge of Liria until a policeman walked by. Then he surrendered.

The Anya'nya followed him to the village a few months ago, and shot his father and 10 other villagers in revenge before the army chased them away.

MOST of the southerners are Nilotic, with scars drawn on their deep-black faces to distinguish them by tribes—the Dinka, the Nuer, the Shilluk, the Annuak. They live in the marshes with their beloved, long-horned cattle, and care for little else. Some live by nothing more than hunting crocodiles, or burning the marsh grass to catch and eat the rats when they come skittering out.

Usually they wear nothing, and smear their bodies with mud when they are in the marshes, to discourage the mosquitoes that choke the hot, evening air. But when the Dinkas clamber into the barges on the river, they wear their best: half-shaven heads daubed with earthy hues of orange or red, ears powdered white, necklaces of blue-dyed beads, perhaps a shawl to cover the shoulders. One Dinka wore a wrist watch and nothing else.

Along the southern borders are the smaller tribes, Sudanic, Nilo-Hamitic or Nilotic: the Bari, the Moru, the Azande, the Madi, the Acholi, the Latuka and dozens of others. Some of the tribes have cattle, but most of them in the forest areas are cultivators of the most primitive sort—planting cassava or durra, occasionally raising chickens. Many were never reached by the missionaries. Some never saw a white man before, and when one came they touched his skin and looked under his shirt to see if he was white all over. Almost all of these tribes are represented in the Anya'nya.

THE President of the Southern Sudan Provisional Government, Aggrey Jaden, is a mission-educated Bari tribesman. His Vice President, Camillo Dhol Kwach, who once served as a member of the Sudan's Parliament, is a Dinka. The Minister of Finance, Tadeo Bidai, is a Zande. The Minister of Education, Othwonh Dak, is the son of the Shilluk king.

All the tribes are represented, too, in the military side of the Anya'nya, but it doesn't take much imagination to picture the generally primitive state of their weapons and organization. The guerrillas began by raiding police posts and army garrisons for their guns and then in 1964 bought and bartered from the Congo rebels the very same weapons the Sudanese had shipped through in a vain effort to support that rebellion before it collapsed. Today, however, the army has tightened its control, the Congo is quiet and the rebels do not come by weapons so easily; ammunition is especially scarce.

There are always weapons floating around Africa as items of barter, but they usually have to be paid for. The Anya'nya collect taxes in most places in the south, even where the Sudanese Army feels it has really good control, but the rebels lose when they exchange the Sudanese money; in Nairobi, for example, they get 10 shillings for a pound. Some church groups collect money for them abroad, but very often it arrives in the form of food and medicine, and these things are useless to an army that needs sometimes five or six months to get things from one remote point to another.

Other troubles are plaguing the rebels' organization these days. Though the Anya'nya claim now to have an army of 5,000 men, to think of it in terms of an organized force of that size would be wildly wrong. The Sudanese Army probably with more than 12,000 troops in the south, has broken the Anya'nya into isolated bands, somtimes of only three or four men. Without effective central command, the guerrillas live like brigands, sniping at army convoys when they have the chance, raiding villages that refuse to give them food or recruits to go with their rebel army as soldiers or bearers or wives. There are incidents almost every day; any place in the south can be unsafe if a rebel or two happen to be in the area. But only rarely now can the Anya'nya muster the resources to take a sustained attack on a police post or an army garrison, or lay a really deadly ambush for northern troops or for southerners they feel have gone over to the other side.

Col. Tafeng Lodongi, the commander of the rebel army, is a Latuka tribesman, a former corporal in the Sudanese Army who never went to school, a very bitter man. Not long ago two nieces of his, Veronica and Angelica, were taking part in a funeral dance, after an army raid on their village. A second army patrol drove into the village during the dance, and asked the village headman if there were any of Colonel Tafeng's relatives there. When the headman presented the two girls, the officer in charge of the patrol drew his pistol and shot them dead.

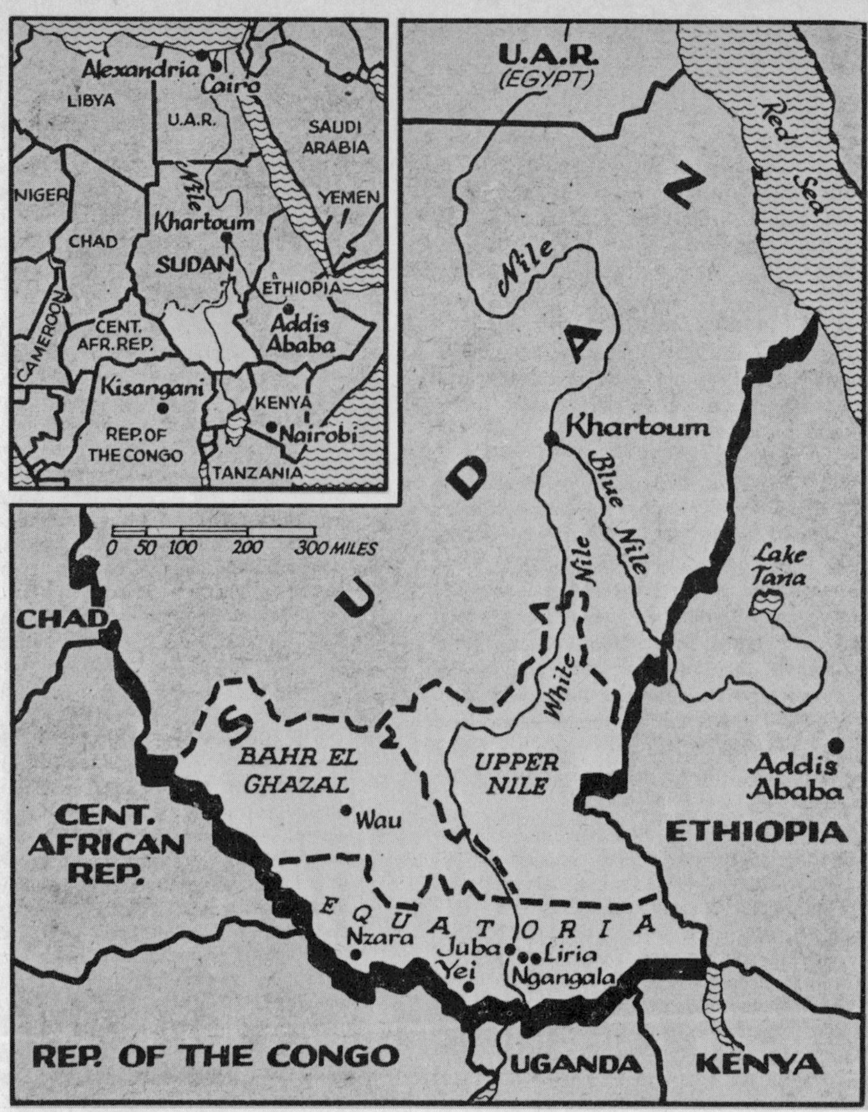

BATTLEGROUND—The Sudan's war-torn southern provinces—Bahr el Ghazal, Upper Nile and Equatoria—where the strife has spilled over the borders into five neighboring countries, "creating diplomatic, military and refugee problems."

THE northerners live in a world apart. They look to Cairo, not Juba; their interests lie more in the Arab world than in black Africa. It is as if the vast swampy region between them and the south were a stone wall.

They are Nubians and Jaalin, who live on the watered banks of the

Nile where it courses through the northern desert to Egypt. They are Hadendoa and Amarar from the rugged hills on the Red Sea coast, who trace their ancestry through lines of fierce warriors to the Fuzzy-Wuzzies who fought the British and to the Blannyes who fought the Romans. They are the Baggara, who hunt on horseback for lions and elephants on the western plains; and the Kabbabish, who wander into the southern reaches of the Libyan desert, living for months on nothing but the milk and meat of their camels.

Some are very dark, for over the centuries the Arabs have moved, in conquering armies or as hunters of ivory and men, into all but the most remote and inaccessible regions of the south. They have taken their wives from around them, and the differences in color and facial characteristics now are very often blurred. Because of this, the racial issues are too obscured to be an explanation of the savagery of the war.

Yet the northerner lives in an Islamic culture and is proud of his Arab connections. He can scorn the southerner today as his ancestors did only a few generations ago, his ancestors who captured pagan tribesmen and shipped them in chains to the slave blocks of the Middle East, leaving a bitter residue that survives today.

"We are not slave traders," said Hamid Ali Shash, the Commissioner of Equatoria. "Perhaps our grandfathers were. But they were not the only ones. It doesn't matter. We want to impress on the people that they have nothing more to fear. How else can we get them into the villages? How else can we begin the task of reconstruction?"

He sounded worried. He was an intense man who worried about the task as he worried about a lot of things, the unending rain, the time it took the coffee to arrive for the guest in his office.

In Juba, I met a nervous, well-dressed man, a Kresh tribesman far from home, headed for Khartoum; he hated the Arab's world, but he was venturing into it to seek his fortune. Together we watched women running to a dance starting in an open field, looking gay in their printed cotton dresses and bare feet. We could hear the drums beating and the sad, shrill voice of a woman. These people were not of his tribe, and their songs must have been different. Yet he was reminded of one, and sang along quietly in halting English:

I don't like you,
But you keep calling me.
What for?

A love song, he said. Rather, sometimes it was a love song; that is what they always told the Arabs who asked. Really, it was a song about the slave trade. He knew nothing more about the slave trade than what his grandmother had told him by the cooking fires at night. Now it was wrapped up in the traditions of bitterness in his tribe, in the secretive instincts, the lingering suspicions. There were other words, he started to say, but he was listening again to the music, and started singing again:

The man is still calling me
And I do not like him.
My mother, I am the only dead one
Here in this town.

SOME signs of normality are now evident in the troubled south. Southerners can be seen walking along the roads these days, at least near the villages in the army's narrow corridors of newly established, still tenuous authority. At the Juba ferry, southerners cross to the west bank of the Nile with bundles of thatch, reed mats and baskets of grain to sell in the Juba market. On the east bank a squat old woman ladles *marisa* out of five-gallon cans and sells the thick, vinegary brew to the people crossing back from the market with their hard-won piasters. Not so long ago there would have been nobody in sight.

The northerners in the Government in Khartoum seem to be making an effort to return to normal, too. White missionaries are still kept out of the south, but two Tanzanian priests—Father Barnabas Temu and Father Mark Riwa—have just been permitted to take up teaching posts in the Theological College at Malakal and help minister to the untended flocks of Roman Catholics in Upper Nile Province.

In Equatoria Province, schools have been reopened in Juba and half a dozen big villages. Schools are an indication of the Government's good intentions. They also indicate, more accurately than the army reports, the areas that can be considered fairly secure.

In Bahr el Ghazal the thin lines of apparent security stretch outward from the provincial capital of Wau for several hundred miles eastward, some 50 or 60 miles north and west. In Upper Nile, the quietest of the three provinces, the rebels appear to be blocked into a narrow margin of territory behind the swamps close to the Ethiopian border.

I traveled 50 miles eastward from Juba to the village of Liria, where the authorities are hoping to open another school. I could travel only in a military convoy. At one time, this stretch of road was broken in a dozen places by deep trenches and vehicle traps, but the army engineers have it open now. We stopped when we saw a trail of vines and branches scattered across the road, but it was nothing. Perhaps a rhinoceros had crashed across the road toward some real or imagined enemy. Farther along, a tree lay across the road, but there was no ambush; probably the work of an elephant.

THE Anya'nya were on this road last November, at the end of the rainy season, burning off the elephant grass by the road before the grass was completely dry. By burning early they made it impossible for the army to set the grass afire when it was completely dry and thus clear the whole roadside of hiding places. Little clumps of grass were still standing, possible cover for the Anya'nya, which the army had not got around to clearing out. But no one fired at the convoy that day.

At Ngangala, on the way, a new village was being built under the watchful eye of the army. It was the only village on a stretch that used to be full of them.

At Liria itself, there were 6,000 people in a village that looked like almost any other. There were no fortifications, no barbed-wire barriers thrown around. There were 10 policemen and 25 soldiers living in their own camp on one side of town. Eventually, the soldiers were to be withdrawn and the police force enlarged. It would have to be quiet around Liria for a long time before the police, too, could be withdrawn.

There had been a stampede to get aboard the El Mirrech steamer at Juba; there had been at every landing. Old women and children were thrown from the narrow gangplank in the clamor; everywhere people seemed to be grasping at outstretched hands, grabbing eggs or chickens or canes of sugar, arguing about money. Some merely wanted to get aboard as passengers, and they tumbled against the side of the barge or fell into the river. Police whacked them with sticks, canes and lengths of knotted rope in a hopeless effort to maintain order.

"We treat them like animals," the army captain on the deck said, long after the steamer had moved out of the vast expanse of melancholy swamp, and the sea of reeds had turned to desert. Only a few palms and acacias grew by the river, where

the water soaks into the banks. The clouds had disappeared from the sky and it was steel blue, but it ought to have been another color—orange or red—for it burned mercilessly on the barren landscape. The fine sand was driven by the wind into a wild, tireless whirlwind that skidded erratically over the hot surface.

"The devil is dancing," the captain said, watching the desert. "He will make me forget." ■

September 22, 1968

Sudan Appears at Peace After Long, Fierce War

By RAYMOND H. ANDERSON

Special to The New York Times

WAU, the Sudan, March 14—The sounds of drums and chanting drifted over this provincial capital in the Southern Sudan from grass-hut encampments on the outskirts. Black warriors, painted and armed for battle, brandished spears and stirred up clouds of red dust as they stomped with bare feet.

The warriors were celebrating peace, not preparing for war.

The silence of cease-fire has fallen over the bush, grasslands and forests of the Southern Sudan after nearly 17 years of fierce intermittent fighting by pagan and Christian tribesmen against the Arab Moslems of the North.

The dreaded Anya-Nya guerrillas are laying down their rifles, spears and bows as word of an accord granting regional autonomy to the four million Southerners spreads by radio, runner and drum through the provinces of Upper Nile, Equatoria and Bahr el Ghazal, which are larger in area than France.

The Sudanese Army has suspended forays against the guerrillas and released Southerners imprisoned during the long struggle for self-rule.

Since the announcement of the peace agreement in Addis Ababa, Ethiopia, late last month, the guerrillas have been emerging from their well-concealed camps, some to surrender and others to dig up antivehicle mines buried in the dirt roads of the southern provinces.

"This is the most encouraging sign so far that the Anya-Nya are serious about the Addis Ababa peace agreement," Maj. Gen. Fadlella Hamad, Sudanese commander in the South, commented after he had accompanied President Gaafar al-Nimeiry on a 10-day tour. "But it will take four or five months before we can expect all of the Anya-Nya to learn of the cease-fire. And there will be some, of course, who will never agree to stop fighting."

A Southerner from Equatoria Province echoed the caution:

"Some of the younger Anya-Nya have known nothing but war. They are bitter and they are extremists. They want independence for the South, not just self-rule in union with the North.

March 24, 1972

STRAIN BESET MALI FROM THE OUTSET

Sudan and Senegal Appear Too Diverse in Population and Wealth to Keep Tie

Special to The New York Times.

PARIS, Aug. 20 Senegal and Sudan, former French territories, united in January, 1959, to revive in modern form the old Mali empire that flourished six centuries ago.

Although the two countries complemented each other to a certain extent, from the beginning of the union there were strains that resulted from differing political conceptions, personal rivalries and national jealousies. The strains proved too much in the end.

Senegal is the smaller but richer of the two states. This has contributed to the strain. Of some 523,900 square miles constituted by Mali, only 75,750 are occupied by Senegal, with a population of 2,300,000. Sudan, which is to be distinguished from the country of the same name in east-central Africa, occupies 443,200 square miles with a population of 3,700,000.

Senegal has one of the most developed ports in Africa, Dakar. A modern city of tall buildings, with a population of 180,000, it formerly was the capital of French West Africa and has become the capital of Mali, the chief business and administrative center of Senegal and an object of envy for landlocked Sudan. The Sudanese capital of Bamako is a sleepy provincial town of about 100,000.

Senegal's major source of wealth is peanuts and their byproducts, such as cooking oil and glycerine, which are extracted in plants near Dakar.

Sudan, in her northern area, is largely desert. In the south agriculture is carried on in a wide variety of products, but in general the economy is less developed than that of Senegal.

The sharing of political power between a Sudan predominate in numbers and a Senegal predominate in wealth was worked out with difficulty.

Always wary of their bigger partners, the Senegalese from the beginning favored a loose federation that would leave each state with a maximum of control over its affairs. The Sudanese favored a tight federation, with wide powers concentrated in the hands of the Federal Premier.

The Federal Premier in this case was a Sudanese, Mobido Keita, Premier of Sudan and Mayor of Bamako. He is a 45-year-old former schoolteacher, who has long been a fervent partisan of African unity. He is a Moslem, as are most Sudanese. He and the circle around him have a reputation for aggressiveness and authoritarianism tinged with Marxism.

The Deputy Premier was Mamadou Dia, Premier of Senegal. He is 50 years old, a specialist in economic questions and a fervent Moslem. He is considered a moderate, with a matter-of-fact turn of mind.

The head of the Federal Assembly was also a Senegalese, Leopold Senghor, philosopher, grammarian, poet ond orator, who speaks better French than many Frenchmen. It had been more or less agreed that the President of Mali would be a Senegalese. Mr. Senghor was slated for the job, but Mr. Keita has long been opposed to him.

Having been one of the oldest of French possessions, Senegal is considered more moderate in political thinking. She has a tendency to be more French-oriented than Sudan. She tolerates political opposition, while Mr. Keita and the Sudanese Union party have complete control over the country in the manner of President Sékou Touré in Guinea.

The Sudanese population and many of its leaders have long been attracted to Mr. Touré, who refused to enter the French Community in September, 1958. The Sudanese are also described as attracted to Communist states by the authoritarian methods employed in economic development.

August 21, 1960

MINERALS BOOST GABON'S ECONOMY

Benefits of Mining Projects Widespread in Nation

By KATHLEEN McLAUGHLIN

Special to The New York Times.

UNITED NATIONS, N. Y., Nov. 10—The Gabon Republic, a West African country hitherto associated primarily with the hospital founded by Dr. Albert Schweitzer, or with the Babingas, a tribe or pygmies, is facing rapid transition.

By mid-1962, exports of processed manganese ore are scheduled to start from a point deep in the interior. The mine is only one square kilometer (.386 square mile) in area, and is estimated to contain 9,000,000 tons of the mineral. Initially, the rate of shipment is expected to be 500,000 tons a year.

By the time the first cargo of ore steams away from Pointe Noire in the Republic of the Congo (Brazzaville), three years will have been spent in fairly monumental construction projects to make it possible. The International Bank for Reconstruction and Development (World Bank) has lent $35,000,000 to the Compagnie Miniere de L'Ogooue (Comilog), incorporated in Gabon in 1953. The United States Steel Corporation owns a 49 per cent share, with French and Gabonese interests holding the rest.

Various aspects of the operation characterize it as unusual.

Obstacles Are Many

The location of the deposits on a jungle-girt plateau deep in the interior near Franceville—with so rich a potential that they may hold a maximum of 200,000,000 tons of ore with a metal content of 48 per cent—prevented access by rail or by vehicle. Gabon has 3,200 miles of roads, but no railway. The mined ore will therefore begin its journey to the seaport via the world's longest single-line cableway—forty-five miles in length—to M'Binda, near the border with the neighboring Congo Republic.

The cableway has been a feat of engineering. Crossing both wide marshes and thickly forested hills, it was made possible by the use of a helicopter, which airlifted workers, tools, bags of cement, concrete-mixing machinery, and the ponderous trestles for 858 steel pylons that carry the overhead trolley-line, with its 3,000 buckets.

At the railhead at M'Binda the ore will be dumped automatically onto a conveyor belt to a stockpile. From there the mineral will traverse a 300-foot tunnel of reinforced concrete and be loaded automatically onto a slow-moving train. The weight of ore in each load will be restricted to 3 per cent of the weight of the freight car in which it is carried.

For its trip south across Congo territory to connect with the existing Congo-ocean railway, stretching from Brazzaville to the coast, a new 180-mile railroad is now in its final stage of construction.

Mechanization Widespread

The junction point of the old line and the new one—presently being pushed doggedly through dense forest—will be at Mont Belo, northeast of Dolisie. From there 124 more miles must be covered to Pointe Noire and the special wharf in prospect for the ship-loading operations—to be handled at minimum cost through mechanized apparatus.

Throughout the years of construction thousands of Gabonese have been acquiring many new skills, as well as enjoying a steady wage. About 3,000 are employed in building the railroad; 250 at a quarry at Mont Belo, which produces crushed stone for the ballast required for rail track; 200 in the prefabrication shop at the same point, where they have become welders, operators of electric-powered gantry cranes and bolt-tightening machines, and 2,500 on the cableway installation.

Since the start of the Comilog program, several communities have sprung up where previously there was nothing but jungle or isolated plateau. At Moanda, for instance—the site of the first mining operations—a six-mile road from the town has been completed, together with two modern guest houses, 100 homes for African employes, and twenty-seven of the fifty houses slated for permanent staff members. Water pipelines, sewerage and electrical installations have been finished and a hospital and sizable restaurant are being built.

Two towns that have arisen in the jungle are Bakumba, the main cableway camp, and Makamba, about 50 miles from Mont Belo. The former has maintenance workshops, supplies and houses for personnel, and the administrative office of the railway. The latter is headquarters for all rail personnel and for maintenance.

Yet the importance of Gabon as a supplier of minerals lies well in the future. An already thriving economy built essentially on forestry—with a turnover of $32,000,000 a year and added export-duty income of about $2,000,000—is expected to profit handsomely when exploitation begins at the iron ore field at Mekambo, in the north. Known deposits are estimated at 250,000,000 tons of 60-63 per cent iron content, and reserves may on later investigation prove to be more than three times as large.

To bring it to the coast, however, another Comilog must be formed that will undertake to provide the 450-mile railway needed for its transportation.

November 11, 1961

Ivory Coast's Economy Remains Under French at Leader's Wish

Houphouet-Boigny Calls People Unready to Take Over Booming African Country —Nationalists Do Not Oppose Him

Special to The New York Times.

ABIDJAN, the Ivory Coast, March 14 — President Felix Houphouet-Boigny, whose rule over the Ivory Coast is patterned on the example of his friend and hero, General de Gaulle, is embarked on an experiment that violates the doctrines of most African nationalists.

With a haughtiness worthy of the French President, he dismisses his fellow African leaders' talk of "African socialism" and the "African personality." He ridicules the warnings of Kwame Nkrumah of Ghana that political independence is meaningless without total economic independence and that imperialists are trying to impose a new economic yoke on their former colonies.

On the contrary, having won political independence from France under "the best of circumstances," as he puts it, Mr. Houphouet-Boigny puts off the day of economic independence. He has asked the French to continue to run the country economically and technically until his own people are able to, in a few years.

He Invites Help

"Our internal means are insufficient for the rapid and harmonious construction of our young state," he told the National Assembly a few weeks ago, laying down his political and economic program. "We invite the help . . . of all those who wish to assist us without intervening in our internal affairs."

He added: "The first country toward which we have turned is France, the former colonizer, whom we regard as our best friend."

Thus, while his Government ministers and almost all the political administrators in the interior are Africans, he relies on French technicians and advisers whose salaries are paid by France under an almost all-inclusive technical-aid agreement.

France last year gave the Ivory Coast $50,000,000 in aid in the form of technical assistance, coffee subsidies and outright financial support. This is equal to one-third of the annual exports of the Ivory Coast, and without it the country's economy would collapse.

France still has a near-monopoly on trade. Seventy-four per cent of the country's imports last year came from the franc zone, almost entirely from France but some from Morocco. Exports to the franc zone were 63 per cent of the country's total.

Investors Flock to Capital

French investors are coming to Abidjan, the capital, in droves. French companies are building factories. Renault has an assembly plant for cars and trucks almost ready for production. There are plans for a flour mill, an oil refinery and for ambitious expansion of the already impressive harbor, which was built only eight years ago.

The most striking anachronism to radical African nationalists is that Mr. Houphouet-Boigny has practically abdicated sovereignty in the military field. The Ivory Coast has only a small force for internal security. And even this force has French officers.

The French Army assures the external defense of the country. It has been asked to do so, Mr. Houphouet-Boigny says, because "we wish to devote our modest means to the economic and social development."

With French money and personnel, a great effort goes forward in public welfare. Cheap but attractive housing developments have been built for Africans and are being expanded.

Surge in Education

There has been a great surge in education. About 45 per cent of the children are now in school compared with a little above 5 per cent a few years ago.

This year for the first time the Ivory Coast is trying to raise a development fund of its own to add to the money received from France.

A "national contribution" of 10 per cent has been imposed on the highest salaries, but not on those of workers. There will be a levy on a company's profits amounting to a forced loan but it can be recovered if the company shows it has reinvested a substantial part of its profits.

Mr. Houphouet-Boigny has given strong assurances against nationalization. He envisions a system under which foreign companies, if they desired, would sell some of their shares to the Government to assure a degree of "Africanization."

As a whole, the Houphouet-Boigny policy is a gamble. It assumes that the two leopards that have been clawing at each other in Africa—colonialism and nationalism—are both capable of changing their spots.

Wait of 5 Years Seen

It assumes that African nationalists here are willing to wait five years or more before insisting on running the country themselves. It assumes also that the former colonizers—the French Government and French citizens here—will be content to make a great effort only to work themselves out of their jobs.

Neutral observers believe the French Government is seriously pushing "Africanization."

"On almost every visit to an administrative service one finds an African sitting at a desk that was occupied by a Frenchman the last time," a foreign diplomat says.

The same apparently is true in most of the big French companies that are training Africans here and in France.

But foreign observers have great doubts that the transition will be as smooth for the rest of the French community — the small-business men, shopkeepers, craftsmen, clerks and the women who sell vegetables in the market.

Jealous of Newcomers

There are about 12,000 French citizens in Abidjan. Many of them speak with the accent of Algeria. Others have been driven out of Indochina. They are making a comfortable living here, under the hot sun and in the easy-going atmosphere they understand. They are quick to express their jealousy of all newcomers, especially Americans. "This is not Indochina and not Algiers," they say. "Make no mistake about it: we are here to stay."

All the timber, all the bananas and most of the coffee in the Ivory Coast are planted by Europeans. Practically all the commerce is in their hands.

However, many observers believe the experiment can succeed if the President "lives long enough to see it through himself."

The President, who added Boigny, which means "irresistible force" in the native language, to his original name, is running the country single-handed. But at 56 years of age he is in precarious health. His periods of rest, on doctor's orders, get more frequent and longer. Even the smallest decisions wait for his return, for instance, from a visit to neighboring Mali (last month), to the United States (in May) or from a cure in Switzerland (where he is now).

Leader for 20 years

His prestige stems from the fact that for nearly twenty years, as a local politician, as Mayor of Abidjan, as a Deputy in the French Parliament and a minister in several French Governments, he led the struggle for African emancipation.

He was the principal founder of the Rassemblement Démocratique Africain (RDA), a regional party. Sékou Touré of Guinea and Modibo Keita of Mali as very young men were co-founders. Today, as presidents of their countries, they are on the opposite wing of African nationalism. But they have not lost their respect for Mr. Houphouet-Boigny.

Like President de Gaulle, the Ivory Coast President appears to believe he is the incarnation of the nation and its interests. There is only one party in the country, his own, and outside of it there is no political life. Would-be dissenters are brought into the Government and given responsibilities and honors and are generally kept too busy to think of working against the chief.

He Brings Aide Back

Jean-Baptiste Mockey, once a vice premier, resigned in 1959 in opposition to the President. But two years later the President brought him back, first in a marginal position. Now Mr. Mockey is generally assumed to be in line for a key ministry and may be the President's choice as heir.

Two left-wing labor leaders who lived in exile in Guinea got amnesty early this year and returned to Abidjan. One of them, Camille Adam, is believed to have adjusted without difficulty. The other, Ngu Blaise, was found to have tried to indoctrinate soldiers aboard ship and was met by the police when he docked here. No one appears to know where he is. He may be in jail, although the President recently said that the Ivory Coast was one of the few countries in the world where no one was in jail for political reasons.

Neutral observers say it does not seem possible that a continent in the throes of nationalist passion can contain an island of complete complacency. But they agree there is no evidence of ferment.

One of the President's closest advisers, an African, says the Government complains of an extension of this apparent calm.

"The majority of Ivoriens still are shy about making use of their new-found equality with the whites," he said. "They stay in their own parts of town, at Treichville across the lagoon and in Adjame. They hardly ever come to the Plateau [the predominantly European center of the city] except to shop or find jobs."

Observers explain the reticence by saying progress of any kind came later in the Ivory Coast than in almost any other territory on the African west coast.

Eight years ago, Abidjan was little more than a village, a

The New York Times March 25, 1962

TRAINING PROGRAM: The Ivory Coast (diagonal shading) wants the French to run the economy of the country until her people can take over themselves.

railhead with a port that consisted of a ramshackle building. Lighters battled the surf to bring passengers and goods from an occasional steamer anchored far out in the sea.

Then in 1954 the French built a channel that opened the lagoon on which the town is built to oceangoing vessels. The new port, one of the best in West Africa, started the current boom.

March 25, 1962

FRANCE AFFIRMS A ROLE IN AFRICA

Ready to Put Down Coups in Areas She Once Held

By HENRY GINIGER

Special to The New York Times

PARIS, Feb. 26 — France served notice today that she was prepared to intervene with military forces at any time to maintain political stability in French-influenced areas of Africa.

Alain Peyrefitte, Minister of Information, made the statement after a Cabinet meeting that discussed France's recent intervention in Gabon to put down a revolt.

He said France would meet the obligation she had contracted in signing accords of cooperation with her former territories, most of which, he said, are in "a state of gestation."

Mr. Peyrefitte said "it is not possible that a few men carrying machine guns be left free to seize a presidential palace at any time."

He declared: "It is precisely because such a threat was foreseeable and foreseen that the new born states signed accords with France to guard against such risks."

Mutual Defense Pacts

The minister referred to mutual defense agreements signed with most of the former French territories under which the new governments may request French help against internal and external threats.

An accord to that effect was invoked to justify the French military action last week that restored President Léon Mba of Gabon shortly after he had been arrested by a military junta.

Mr. Peyrefitte said France did not seek to become involved in a country's internal politics or to decide who should govern.

The Gabon action provoked criticism here by opponents of President de Gaulle's Government who felt that France did indeed decide in favor of Mr. Mba. The latter's authoritarian methods are widely considered a major factor in creating tensions in Gabon.

The Information Minister reported that France had intervened on at least 10 occasions in various parts of what was formerly French Equatorial Africa. All these actions, he said, were in accordance with defense agreements.

In 1960 and 1961 French troops helped restore order in Cameroon, it was recalled. In the Congo Republic (Brazzaville) French forces helped end tribal massacres in 1960 and in September, 1960, the French ended attacks by Gabonese and Congolese on each other.

The French, the Minister said, intervened "several times" in Chad. Last December they made a show of force in Niger to save the Government of President Hamani Diori.

Three cases of intervention in 1961 were cited in Mauritania. Mr. Peyrefitte recalled that similar trouble had recently broken out in Tanganyika, Kenya and Uganda, former British territories and had brought about the intervention of British troops.

February 27, 1964

CAMEROON WOES MIRROR AFRICA'S

Tribalism and Dual Culture Temper Hope for Unity

By LLOYD GARRISON

Special to The New York Times

YAOUNDE, Cameroon, Aug. 16—Africa's hopes for continental unity, and all the stumbling blocks that surround these hopes, can be seen in many ways in Cameroon.

The country is extraordinary among African states, for in its legacy of European language and culture it reflects the division of the continent: It is part English, part French.

Like most West African states, Cameroon has proud, conservative Moslems in the north and equally proud, better-educated Christians along the coast. Added to this mixture are 129 tribal and linguistic groups, many bitter enemies of one another.

As if this were not enough, Cameroon has been torn since infancy by a little-publicized civil war that has claimed more than 70,000 victims, a fact all but eclipsed by the spotlight on the Congo.

A small but determined army, trained by the French, has almost eliminated the rebellion, which was once openly backed by the Soviet and Chinese Communists. But the blood-letting has left deep scars that will take years to bind.

Such are the immense problems facing Ahmadou Ahidjo, the country's young, self-educated President. He is a soft-spoken former Teletype operator with a penchant for history books and Georges Simenon novels about Inspector Maigret.

A Moslem northerner of common birth, he has sought to whittle away the power of the feudal Moslem kings without destroying his political base.

To southerners and English-speaking Africans in West Cameroon, Mr. Ahidjo has sought to be as progressive as a northerner can be without adopting the slogans of the London- and Paris-educated young radicals.

"Ahidjo is a political pro," an admiring American diplomat said. "Put him down in Chicago's South Side and within a year he'd have a ward all his own."

Yet for all his political skills, Mr. Ahidjo faces an uphill, seemingly endless task in his campaign to mold a national consciousness.

The New York Times Aug. 24, 1964

AFRICA IN PROFILE: Cameroon (diagonal lines) typifies hopes and perils facing the new nations. Heavy line shows border of former British trust area.

In this fourth year of Cameroonian independence, it is still possible to drive past public buildings in Yaoundé, the serene hilltop capital, and see the flag—green, red and yellow vertical stripes, with two gold stars in the upper part of the green stripe—flying upside down.

Bowing to political realities, Mr. Ahidjo has had to choose most officials on the basis of their tribes, not their merits. This has perpetuated an uneasiness common throughout Africa: Africans appointed because of their tribes tend to put those tribes first and the Government second. So, if the national flag flies upside down, who cares?

Not long ago the European manager of an airline office here reluctantly discharged his booking clerk, an African Negro. "I had no choice," he said.

The manager had employed two Negroes: a counter clerk to take reservations and a booking clerk to send messages confirming the reservations. When they were hired, the manager had no idea that they were from hostile tribes.

"The booking clerk sent the cables all right," the manager said, "but they were all for the wrong flights. It was a deliberate attempt to sabotage his tribal rival."

According to the manager, both men were efficient and well educated—"emancipated Africans." "If tribalism comes before professionalism with people like this," he asked, "what is this country's future?"

The same question weighs heavily on Mr. Ahidjo. "I think," he remarked to a visitor the other day, "that for the next five years we will be watching Africa in the balance. Certainly we need aid, but I think political maturity is needed far more than economic development."

In stressing his hope for political maturity, Mr. Ahidjo voiced concern not only over tribalism but over the "negative" attitude of many Africans toward government itself.

For a long time, "the Government" meant the French or, in West Cameroon, the English. For Cameroonians who worked for the Government, performance didn't matter: The Government was not theirs.

With a few variations, this view lingers. The Government has become the country's biggest single employer. Many see it as a huge, impersonal corporation that gives the civil servant a fine house and a big car and at the end of 20 years a fat pension—just what the Europeans used to have.

Mr. Ahidao knows this, and he has tried to stamp it out. Last week, for example, he issued warrants for the arrest of 125 officials accused of embezzling Government funds intended for new cocoa cooperatives.

Perhaps the most subtle and successful transition taking place in Cameron is the blending of French and English culture.

It was in 1961 that West Cameroon voted to team up with French-speaking East Cameroon. It could instead have joined English-speaking Nigeria, Africa's most populous country.

The vote indicated that most West Cameroonians were afraid of becoming "poor cousins" under Nigerian rule. Now some of them complain that they do not have enough representation in the Federal Government here. Others charge that West Cameroon is neglected when Yaoundé distributes economic aid. But few regret the merger, and most credit Mr. Ahidjo with strict impartiality.

French and English are compulsory languages in schools throughout the country, and the new university here is bilingual. French cuisine and couture are fashionable in the English-speaking West. In the French-speaking East, some Cameroonians are taking to afternoon tea.

But there remain many striking differences between the regions, which are still largely autonomous. Westerners are extremely sensitive about their civil liberties and about due process of law. Newspapers are free to criticize the Government. Labor unions may strike, and they often do.

In the East the unions, the press and the radio are arms of the Government. Mr. Ahidjo's Cameroonian Union amounts in effect to a one-party system; opposition parties are permitted only in the provinces.

"It will take years for us to mold one nation," said the student who had lamented corruption. His language, as it happened, was French, and he could speak only halting English. But he was trying.

August 24, 1964

French Consolidate Forces in Africa

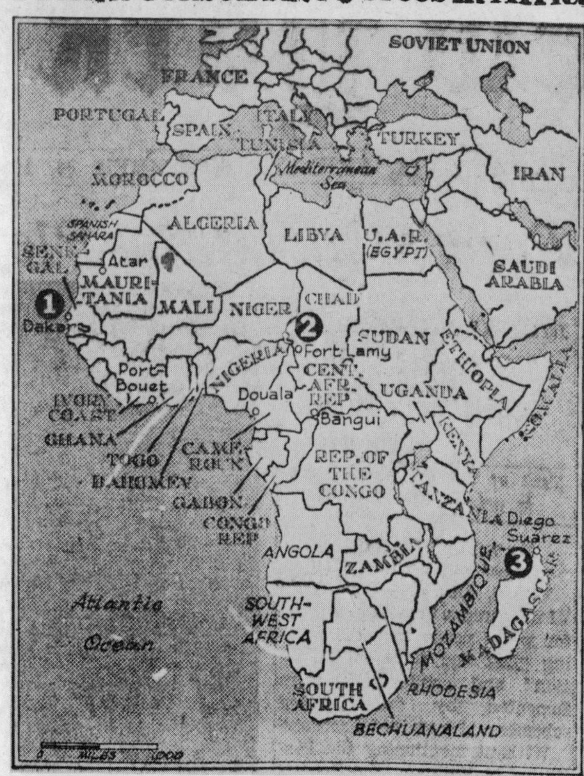

The New York Times Dec. 24, 1965

The principal French bases in black Africa will be at Dakar (1), Fort Lamy (2) and Diégo Suarez (3).

Special to The New York Times

PARIS, Dec. 23—The Defense Ministry announced today that France's reduced 6,600-man force in black Africa would be concentrated next year in three main bases: Dakar, Senegal; Fort Lamy, Chad, and Diégo Suarez in Madagascar.

Under various defense pacts with her former colonies France will also continue to hold air base rights at Port-Bouet, Ivory Coast; Douala, Cameroon; Bangui, Central African Republic, and Atar, Mauritania. Small units will remain in Gabon and Niger.

In 1964, France had 27,800 troops in Africa, south of the Sahara. The bases still being retained are primarily for emergency use by the airborne "intervention force," the two parachute brigades of the 11th Division, stationed in southwest France.

The French also have bases in Algeria, which are gradually being phased out.

December 24, 1965

Old Way of Life Lingers in Chad, A Chapter in Storybook Africa

By DREW MIDDLETON

Special to The New York Times

FORT LAMY, Chad., April 16 — With the rains still a month away, the Chari River, which flows through modern Africa into the past, is very low. The fishermen of the Bananas tribe stand shoulder deep in the river holding a chain of nets along the bottom from bank to bank. The outboard motorboat thumps against the sandbars in midstream.

Fort Lamy, with its airport, its presidential palace, its hotels, its shops, drops astern. The life of the old storybook Africa emerges in the blistering heat along the banks.

From their nesting holes in the clay, fly hundreds of birds, their bodies bright orange in the sun. Marabou storks, as solemn as civil servants watching cricket, survey the river life. Crested cranes and fish eagles fly overhead.

Tribes Come for Fish

Out in the river four enormous heads surface to watch the boat. The tiny pig eyes of the hippopotamuses follow the craft. Then the great beasts submerge again. When night falls, they will climb the banks leaving a trail like a small tank, to feed on some villager's garden patch.

These are fishing villages. The Bananas and other tribes come to the Chari each year from farther south to net the great capitain and the other fish that are among the republic's few natural resources.

Some of the catch, dried or smoked, is exported to Nigeria, the Sudan and other nearby countries. The capitain, some of them man-sized, are flown to Paris where as "the prince of the Chari" they bring enough in the best restaurants to keep a fisherman's family for a week.

But mostly the fish are eaten here. For Chad's is still largely a subsistence economy.

Chad, in fact, poses one of Africa's most difficult questions: How can a country be developed if there is next to nothing in it to develop?

Half of this landlocked country, which is three times the size of California, is desert, sparsely populated by black Arab Moslems who not so long ago raided the south for slaves. But the peoples of the south, the Seras, the Massa and the Mouneangs, more amenable to education and training by the French, are the masters now.

More than 90 per cent of Chad's economy is agriculture at subsistence level. The main industrial crop is cotton, with a production of about 100,000 tons yearly. Cotton makes up 80 per cent of Chad's exports.

Livestock is the second most most important commodity. There are over 4 million head of cattle and 4.5 million sheep and goats. The developing countries of the west coast need meat. Chad sells some to Nigeria and more to her neighbors in the south.

Beyond beef, cotton and fish, Chad has very little. Natron, a low quality salt, is found in the north and around Lake Chad. There are processing plants for raw cotton, cottonseed oil and peanut oil. The peanut-oil mill in Fort Lamy, which produces the region's cooking oil, is powered by two elderly and misanthropic camels working in shifts.

Despite its poverty, the country and its 3 million people have their charm for the visitors.

As the sun sinks in Fort Lamy, people come out to gossip, for it is cooler now—probably under 100 degrees.

Beside the river, four boys dance slowly and gravely. Beyond them across the river a drum begins to beat. Paris is five hours away by air.

April 17, 1966

14 AFRICAN NATIONS APPROVE UNITY PACT

TANANARIVE, Madagascar, June 25 (Reuters)—Fourteen French-speaking African nations approved a charter here today for political and economic cooperation.

The charter brings together 12 former French African territories and two former Belgian ones in the African-Malagasy Common Organization.

President Hamani Diori of Niger was named president of the organization. The post was previously held in an acting capacity by President Philibert Tsiranana of Madagascar.

All but Rwanda and the Congo, the former Belgian territory, sent heads of state to the meeting.

The conference decided to press efforts to solve the problem of exporting primary products. The president of the organization is to take up the problem with European countries, particularly France and the European Economic Community.

June 26, 1966

FRENCH IN AFRICA PREFER OLD WAYS

By DREW MIDDLETON

Special to The New York Times

DOUALA, Cameroon, April 19—"They are happy, are they not?" a French official asked as he watched village dancers. "So why should we teach them to want things they will never get?"

The question expressed one aspect of the French attitude in the independent African countries once under French rule.

A nostalgia for the imperial past coupled with a determination to hold French-speaking countries—"the Francophones"—under France's economic and political influence seems to dominate thinking among the administrators, soldiers, technicians and teachers who remain to guide and counsel in the young African states.

Instinct must have told the British, even in such strongholds as Kenya, that they would have to surrender power one day, so they began—in in some cases reluctantly, in others gladly—to prepare Africans for that day.

A Difference of Outlook

When the British taught an African to drive a tractor, they were pleased and thought about the next step. When the French did it, they worried about accidents and repairs for the tractor.

There are many Frenchmen who have been in western and equatorial Africa for 20 or 30 years and who love and understand the land and its people. But they, no less than the newly arrived teachers who work in Africa for two or three years to make money and return to France, freely express their doubts about the Africans' ability to compete in the modern world.

French officers called their African soldiers "My children" in the old days. Much of that approach remains in the general attitude.

Both the British and the French were slow in providing the technical and vocational training emergent Africa needs. The British have recognized the mistake and are shifting Africans to studies that will fit them for commerce, agriculture and industry. The French still emphasize classical education, although there is a start in vocational teaching. Furthermore, the French are slow to embrace United States help.

Burden on the Budget

The French emphasis on classical education has had and continues to have political and social repercussions. The newly educated consider themselves fitted for government jobs. In Chad, for example, the Government has created such jobs at the rate of about a thousand a year.

This is a burden on the budget. In Chad and elsewhere it produces political malcontents temperamentally unprepared for agriculture, commerce or industry. In former French Africa even more than in former British Africa they are an explosive element clamoring for "Africanization," meaning jobs and power.

The French emphasize the Africans' share in French culture. This may have been the tie that bound when the Africans had nowhere else to go, but only a depressingly few of them share the delights of Molière or Racine with the remaining Frenchmen. To the masses, French culture means a limited French vocabulary.

The educated elite, always small, has become aware of its own African culture and of other cultures. Its members are as likely to find intellectual stimulus in Hemingway or Denis Brogan as in Raymond Aron or Camus.

Africans in the francophone states are most irritated by the reluctance of the French to take their hands from the wheel and let the Africans drive.

April 22, 1966

Foreign Affairs: Black Orpheus

By C. L. SULZBERGER

DAKAR, Senegal—Leopold Senghor, the poet of *Negritude* and President of Senegal, embodies the best in France's colonial legacy. Dutch imperialism stressed commerce and British imperialism stressed leaving behind efficient civil services wherever it withdrew. The French placed emphasis on culture.

They produced an élite of black Frenchmen in Africa before abandoning it, and Senghor—who served in the French Army (and was a war prisoner in Germany), in the French National Assembly and in the Cabinet of Premier Edgar Faure—is a remarkable representative of this élite. He speaks elegant French and is married to a Norman woman one of whose ancestors invaded England with William the Conqueror.

And Withal a Poet

He is also a first-rate poet whose works have been published in many countries. Senghor believes the only other poet-Presidents are Mao Tse-tung and Ho Chi Minh, although he protests softly with a smile that he doesn't share all their other interests. He considers Mao a better writer than Ho, less political.

Senghor is delightfully free of complexes. A small, frail man, very well-tailored, he has a photograph of de Gaulle on his office wall. But he writes: "We will take from our conquerors their arms as we have always done." Proudly, unabashedly, he preaches *Negritude*. Let me cite from his poetry:

"Listen to our dark blood beat, listen to the deep pulse of Africa beating in the mist of forgotten villages." Or: "I have chosen my toiling black people, my peasant people, the peasant race through all the world." Or: "I grew up deep in Africa, at the crossroads of cases of races and routes." He writes of "The love of my black-skinned people" and: "How black he is. . . . How splendid he is."

In this age of confused intolerance and bigotry it is a pleasure to talk with President Senghor and to acknowledge in him the civilizing genius of France which, despite the persistence even in Senegal of narrow-minded white *colons*, has lit a special flame in Francophone Africa.

Like the rest of the Senegalese élite, Senghor admires France. Twelve of his seventeen ministers retain French passports and dual citizenship. He takes annual vacations in Normandy. He talks easily about the steady injections of French economic aid and the presence here of a French military establishment capable of swift intervention anywhere in Francophone Africa.

French Heritage

Furthermore, he extols the French language as "a classic tongue, a useful intellectual instrument, logical and clear." But he has also made English compulsory in schools, and concludes: "We inherited from France both qualities and defects." Among the defects he considers Francophone Africa far less efficient than Anglophone Africa. Yet he sees as more than making up for this a French testament of tolerance.

"The French have gone beyond prejudice," he says. "Take my own case. I am a Catholic in a country that is 90 per cent Moslem. My wife is French. However, none of this counts here. In Anglophone Africa tribalism became far more developed." He is sponsoring a scientific conference to which South Africans and Portuguese will be invited—despite acrid policy differences with their governments.

He wishes to unite the various sectors of contemporary Africa and to combat the present tendency toward Balkanization. He hopes for West African confederation, including both its French- and English-speaking components. With this in mind he will confer Nov. 6 with the chiefs of state of Mauretania, Guinea and Mali and is summoning a subsequent meeting of ministers from eight Francophone and four Anglophone lands.

An 'Atlantic' Nation

Nevertheless, while striving to encourage regional ties, he wants to avoid linking Senegal to the kind of restrictive Afro-Asian bloc that has occupied the attentions of many neutralist leaders. "After all," he protests, "we are an Atlantic nation. Senegal is closer to Latin America than the Far East."

Senghor has limited influence because Senegal is tiny, but his maturity, his tranquillity and his tolerance in a world riven by fanaticism are as refreshing as his literary talent.

He is proud of his French culture, but insists on national independence. He is pleased to have a black skin, but is not aggressive about it. And he is deeply humanitarian. All this makes Leopold Senghor, the black Orpheus, an unusual man.

October 27, 1967

Niger Begins to Succumb to Progress

By ALFRED FRIENDLY Jr.
Special to The New York Times

NIAMEY, Niger, Jan. 27 — Niger is beginning to succumb to progress despite the penchant for apathy and fatalism of many of her 3.5 million people.

This capital city was recently graced by a number of improvements on the occasion of a meeting here of leaders of 14 French-speaking African countries.

Stop signs went up on previously uncluttered corners and the number of traffic lights rose from one to four. While the conference lasted, a jet of water played in the green oasis of a traffic circle from which three paved and two sand roads radiated out into the dry heat. Niger, north of Nigeria and south of Algeria and Libya, includes part of the Sahara, and the climate is excessively hot.

Back to Everyday

After the conference delegates departed, there was only the original traffic light winking and blinking with the symptoms of overwork. The 2,600 camels who had passed in gaudy review before the heads of state went back to their ordinary lives carrying firewood and fodder. A small herd of goats reappeared beside the Grand Hotel's swimming pool.

Nevertheless, President Hamani Diori was able to report on some progress toward modernity.

"For us," President Diori said at a news conference in a high-ceilinged, white-walled room of his offices, "a processing mill that turns millet into flour is just as revolutionary in one of our towns as the steam engine was in its time and place." Less essential revolutions will have to wait, he added.

The first of what is hoped to be a chain, the mill cost $241,000 and now processes only 1 per cent of the annual consumption of millet. The rest of this diet staple — a grain particularly difficult to store— is still pounded by women with heavy wooden pestles.

TV Education Used

A two-year-old educational television program is an even prouder accomplishment, although the scale is tiny. In 20 bush villages outside Niamey, 800 primary school students sit on sand floors and watch televised instruction that uses marionettes and cartoons to teach elementary mathematics and reading.

Niger each year graduates only 27 persons with the equivalent of a junior college diploma; she would need 15,000 qualified teachers to handle the 600,000 school-age children in the country.

With television, minimally trained "monitors" can take the place of teachers, enabling the President to boast of having 12 per cent of the children in school, half in the television classes. Television may hold great promise eventually; Niger is vast, 449,400 square miles in area, which is larger than Texas and California together.

In five years, Niger may be reaping the fruits of a substantial uranium deposit. The deposit, on the edge of the Sahara, will be developed by a company in which Niger holds only a 15 per cent interest. Taxes and royalties, however, are supposed to bring the country's share to 50 per cent. The $5-million anticipated in annual revenues will be a welcome addition to a budget that now runs $39-million a year, some of it supplied indirectly by French aid and loans, estimated at $15-million a year.

Not all the development prospects are as promising as uranium, and the worst — aside from the problematical future on the world market of peanuts, Niger's main cash crop — is a projected $2.8-million American-financed bridge across the Niger River at Niamey. The cornerstore was laid last month. The bridge, to be called the Kennedy Bridge, would replace a leisurely ferry service, but would add another obstacle to navigation on the 2,600-mile waterway, once called the Nile of the Negroes, that winds through Mali, Niger and Nigeria.

The river is now only sporadically navigable in stretches, but the new international Niger River Commission is studying possibilities for shipping, irrigation, power and fishing. An official of the Commission believes that the bridge would be a disaster. Officials of Niger, including the President, appear to believe that because there is already one bridge under which barges cannot pass, a second will make little difference.

President Diori is slow but patient, a man who finds time for weekly English conversation lessons with Peace Corps volunteers, but can indulge his passion for golf only on a driving range. To some of his people, he is too patient, particularly with the continuing and expanding French presence here. Niger gained autonomy from France in 1958 and declared herself independent in 1960.

Yet, French advisers are in every ministry. Behind the counter of the Banque Internationale de l'Afrique Occidentale, there are more white faces bent over ledgers than black.

Niger, however, has rejected extremism in the pursuit of any of her goals, even such a touchy one as Africanization.

February 4, 1968

Mood of Cameroon Is Optimistic in 10th Year of President Ahidjo's Rule

By ALFRED FRIENDLY Jr.
Special to The New York Times

YAOUNDE, Cameroon, March 1—The mood of this breezy upland capital is so upbeat these days that it is almost smug. The outlook brightened by the flowering of scarlet flame trees, purple Jacarandas and yellow trumpet vines, politicians and ordinary citizens alike are counting their blessings and finding them considerable.

The occasion for this public stocktaking was the 10th anniversary on Feb. 18 of the coming to power of President Ahmadou Ahidjo. A taciturn, slightly dumpy Moslem, he is widely credited here with combining politician's instincts with an autocrat's decisiveness to carry his West African republic to a degree of unity, stability and prosperity that few prophesied for it when French rule ended on Jan. 1, 1960.

As "the father of the nation," the 43-year-old President, a former telegraphic operator, has been making triumphal appearances throughout the country, which, with an area of 183,000 square miles, is larger than California. Preaching no ideology but success, he has been delivering a low-key rendering of "You never had it so good" to the five million Cameroonians.

'Good Thing for Cameroon'

To correspondents attending his third news conference in 10 years, Mr. Ahidjo blandly remarked, "I see quite simply that I've been here 10 years and that it has been a good thing for Cameroon." Mr. Ahidjo was Premier of Cameroon before its independence, after which he became President.

In an anniversary speech after opening Yaoundés handsome air terminal, he said: "Our strongest, most tenaciously held passion is called Cameroon."

At the inauguration of the aluminum rolling mill at Edea, in the south, he noted that investments in the nation's economy had more than doubled since independence.

Simultaneously, however, he called on Cameroonians to realize that the acceleration of industrial growth—manufacturing accounted for 6 per cent of the gross national product in 1960 and 10 per cent six years later—had brought the country to a period of "considerable fiscal sacrifices."

Liberal tax holidays for new investors and a drop in revenues from duties on imported goods that are being replaced by local manufacture caused a budgetary squeeze. Anticipated though it was, the temporary revenue shortage almost certainly means delays in meeting several of the goals in the ambitious second five-year plan, which ends in 1971.

Also a matter of real concern to Yaoundé's financial planners is the phasing out of American assistance programs that have brought $13-million in loans to road and rail construction and $7.5-million in technical-assistance grants from 1961 to 1967. Cameroon can now expect to benefit only from aid to regional-development projects.

"We understand the policy," remarked Daniel Masuke, the Minister of Development, "but we are not required to like it."

One cheerful sign reflecting Cameroon's solid international credit rating and her determination to diversify the agricultural base that permits five crops (coffee, cocoa, cotton, bananas and peanuts) to make up over 60 per cent of exports was the approval last summer of an $18-million World Bank loan. With another loan of $6.4-million from the European Common Market, economic planners are embarking on a program to raise palm oil production by one third to nearly 70,000 tons a year by 1971.

Despite such outside support, Cameroonians occasionally complain that their undramatic steady progress—an over-all annual growth rate since independence of 7.3 per cent in current prices—is forcing them to accept virtue as its own reward.

"We are paying the price of success," said one second-echelon official, only half in jest. "Since we are not in serious trouble, no one seems to worry or even talk about us very much."

In recent weeks, speakers have recalled the terrorism of bygone years, when political quarrels seemed certain to pitch the more than 200 tribes in Cameroon into bloody fratricide. With considerable satisfaction, the Cameroonians have noted the inaccurate prophesies of outsiders who forecast failure for the reunification of British and French Cameroon, accomplished after a plebiscite supervised by the United Nations seven years ago.

Except for minor banditry in some areas and an occasional border raid by political terrorists based in the former French Congo, Cameroon is now remarkably quiet. It is kept that way by an army and a constabulary that are constantly watched by each other and by the President's special security police.

March 10, 1968

AUSTERITY IS RULE IN UPPER VOLTA

A Balanced Budget Does Not End Economic Woes

By R. W. APPLE Jr.
Special to The New York Times

OUAGADOUGOU, Upper Volta, April 15—In Upper Volta, they talk about the "Garangose" the way Americans talk about the income tax.

Named for Capt. Témoko Marc Garango, the Minister of Finance, the Garangose is the military Government's austerity program. It was put into effect shortly after Gen. Sangoulé Lamizana assumed power in this landlocked West African state Jan. 3, 1966.

General Lamizana, who is 53 years old, took over from Upper Volta's first President, Maurice Yaméogo, at the hight of demonstrations by unemployed workers and disaffected students. The national treasury was short about $8-million—a quarter of the annual budget—but Mr. Yaméogo had blithely taken a lavish honeymoon in South America with his second wife.

General Lamizana, a modest man, tried to set a different example. Instead of moving into the Presidential palace that Mr. Yaméogo had built, he remains in his small military bungalow, where his wife does the housework.

Taxes Increased

The new regime forbade the purchase of more governmental air-conditioners — no small step in a country where noontime temperatures of 115 degrees are common—and said it would replace champagne with Coca-Cola at official receptions.

Many taxes were sharply increased, including import duties and head taxes. A Voltan visa now costs $12, one of the highest figures in the world. At the same time, Government salaries were cut by as much as 50 per cent.

For most of the five million people of this wretchedly poor country, the changes made little difference. No more than 25,000 Voltans, according to most estimates, work for money. The rest live on what they can grow themselves. Four million people in Upper Volta consider themselves lucky if they have as much as $4 in their pockets during the course of a year.

But for the city dwellers, the Garangose has constituted a near-disaster. A primary-school teacher now earns less than $20 a week and the Minister of Planning less than $70 a week. The prices in Ouagadougou are no lower than those in Lagos or Dakar.

To make matters even harder, employment is growing more slowly than the population.

Upper Volta is an intensely

moral country, where the bribe, which is endemic to much of West Africa, has been almost unknown. But the economic stress created by the austerity program is so great that burglary has become a serious problem.

Several men have been murdered for money in the last year, including a guard who was killed and robbed of tax receipts—the first such crime anyone in Ouagadougou can recall.

The goal of the Garangose, balancing the budget, has been achieved, with a surplus of almost a million dollars this year. Much of the country's indebtedness to private business has been paid off, and the minuscule exports of peanuts, sesame and other commodities have begun to increase slightly.

But even the balanced budget has failed to attract the new foreign investment that General Lamizana has hoped for. "We must learn to live within our means," the general is fond of saying.

It seems doubtful, however, that Upper Volta—which was so unpromising economically that during the colonial period France once broke it up and parceled out its land among surrounding territories — will ever have enough means of her own to live by.

General Lamizana is nonetheless determined that Upper Volta hew to her present course and not revert to free spending on travel and prestige projects. He has promised a return to civil rule by next year, but the politicians will believe that when they see it.

April 20, 1969

French Still Maintain 7,000-Man Force in Africa

By R. W. APPLE Jr.

Special to The New York Times

ABIDJAN, Ivory Coast, April 28—Port-Bouet, a few miles southeast of Abidjan, has one of West Africa's busiest airports, with daily flights to Paris and other capitals.

But it also has something else—one of a string of French military bases, manned by French troops in French uniforms, that stretch across sub-Saharan Africa. The unit at Port Bouet, commanded by a colonel, resembles an American reconnaissance battalion, with about 500 men, a large number of armored vehicles and a complement of advanced communications equipment.

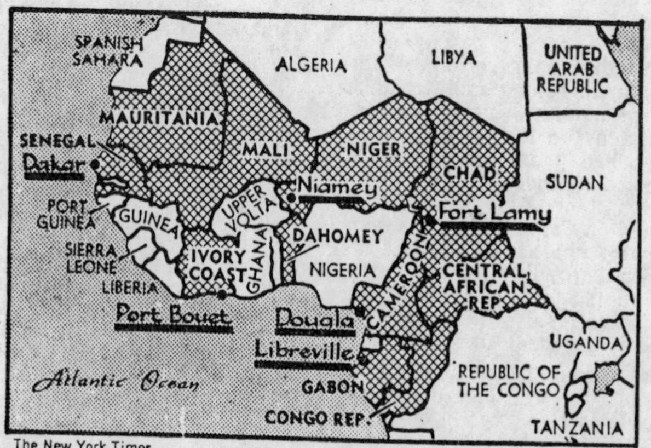

The New York Times May 4, 1969

Eleven African countries (crosshatching) have military intervention pacts with France, which maintains string of military bases (underlines) across sub-Saharan area.

Other French officers serve as advisers in the Ivory Coast's small army, wearing Ivorian shoulder patches on their uniforms. But the Port-Bouet force—like other units based at Niamey, Niger; Dakar, Senegal; Diego-Suarez, Madagascar; Fort Lamy, Chad; Douala, Cameroon, and Libreville, Gabon—is designed for combat, not for training.

Force Now 7,000 Men

For that reason, the 7,000 men who make up this force are unique in black Africa. Spain and Portugal, of course, maintain troops in colonies they still control, but neither of the other one-time colonial powers, Britain and Belgium, has armed forces stationed in Africa.

Moreover, the French maintain a special unit—the Force d'Intervention, also known as the 11th Mixed Arms Division, numbering about 16,500 men—at Pau, near Toulouse, in southwestern France.

It can be airlifted anywhere in Africa in a matter of hours, with the small permanent forces at various airfields to allow for the landing and refueling of troop transports.

In September, 1967, the French gave a vivid demonstration of their ability to deploy these forces in large-scale maneuvers called Operation Alligator III. Paratroops, fighter-bombers, warships and helicopters carried out a mock assault against a hypothetical aggressor in the western part of the Ivory Coast.

France's military presence did not cease with the granting of independence to her African colonies. Instead, in 1960 and 1961, the Government of Premier Michel Debré made a series of secret agreements, permitting intervention in stated circumstances, with the governments of 11 newly independent countries.

They were: Cameroon, the Central African Republic, the Congo Republic, the Ivory Coast, Dahomey, Gabon, Mauritania, Mali, Niger, Senegal and Chad.

Ostensibly, the troops are here to protect against external aggression — for example, the Ivory Coast has from time to time feared invasion from Guinea. But a larger, though unspoken purpose has been to guarantee the security of French nationals and to help keep in power regimes amenable to the French viewpoint.

In 1964, in Gabon, French paratroops helped reinstate President Léon Mba by recapturing his capital, Libreville, from a group of young Gabonese Army officers who were trying to overthrow him. Later, after the death of Mr. Mba, the French helped to insure a smooth transition to his chosen successor, Albert-Bernard Bongo.

"There has been almost no external aggression in Africa since independence," said a western military attaché recently, "and I don't think Ghana is about to invade Niger. The French troops have been put here to help General de Gaulle's friends."

Without the troops, a French businessman with wide interests in West Africa said, French companies would be less willing than they now are to invest here and individual Frenchmen would be less willing to come to work.

The French troops evoke little protest from either the Governments or people of the countries where they are based, and many heads of state, including President Félix Houphouët-Boigny of the Ivory Coast, have been unhappy at the progressive reduction in French strength in Africa: from 68,000 in 1962 to 28,000 in 1964 to 7,000 now.

What course President De Gaulle's successor will follow is not known, but up until the eve of his resignation the general continued to undertake military actions in Africa.

Only two weeks ago, 100 Foreign Legionnaires and 160 marines were flown to Chad, where French units last August went into combat against rebellious Toubou tribesmen in the north.

Paris is not believed to be prepared, particularly in the post-de Gaulle era, to respond militarily whenever it is asked to do so. But where French interests are considerable, as in Gabon, with its iron, manganese and urnaium, or where the governments are particularly friendly, at in the Ivory Coast and Chad, future uprisings might well be met by French intervention.

May 4, 1969

AIR OF UNREALITY ENVELOPS BANGUI

But Central African Republic Is Ruled With Firm Hand

By R. W. APPLE Jr.
Special to The New York Times

BANGUI, Central African Republic, June 13 — Gen. Jean Bedel Bokassa, President of this landlocked state in the heart of Africa, decided recently to close a bank whose manager he suspected of unsavory methods.

He told the police to seize the man's bank. They did—but unknown to them or to President Bokassa, the man had changed jobs, so they acted against the wrong bank.

Unhappily, the institution they closed turned out to be the Government - owned central bank, which supplies currency to everyone else. Until things were sorted out a few days later, business in Bangui was in a snarl.

Life in this sleepy capital along the Ubangui River is like that. The place has a remote, slightly bizarre atmosphere, a Graustarkian unreality.

General Bokassa, a short, bullnecked veteran of the French Army with a distinguished combat record, often

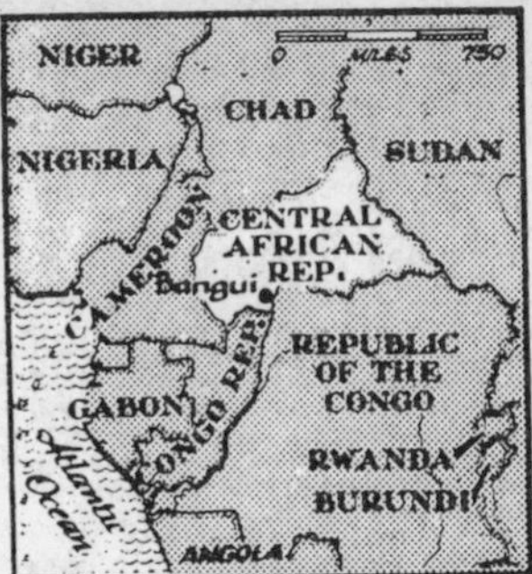

The New York Times June 16, 1969

does things that strike foreigners as disproportionate for a poor, sparsely populated country whose 1.5-million people are scattered across an area slightly smaller than Texas.

Last year, for the 10th anniversary of the country's independence, the President staged a celebration worthy of a nation of 50 million people—a seven-hour parade, a dinner party on the presidential palace grounds for 3,500 guests, a gift of 13 polished diamonds for the wives of each of the visiting ambassadors.

He Rules Firmly

It is easy to mock 48-year-old General Bokassa—as do many of Bangui's French residents, when they are sure no one is listening -for his habit of wearing so many medals that his uniform looks like a suit of chainmail. But the general, who took office after a coup d'état on Jan. 1, 1966, is deadly serious about his country and about maintaining his power.

Although he often praised President de Gaulle in extravagant terms, he has dealt sternly with what he considers foreign threats to national sovereignty.

Diplomats are forbidden to invite cabinet ministers to their homes, unless they invite the President and the Cabinet as a whole. They must receive permission before traveling in the countryside. A dozen French businessmen have been jailed in recent months on charges of subversion.

All direct contacts between Government officials and foreign diplomats, said a decree issued last month, "should be considered matters to be brought to the attention of the security police."

General Bokassa's xenophobia is in part a product of the history of this area.

Arab and European slave traders roamed across the central African plateaus for decades, depopulating whole villages. When slavery ended, it was replaced by a system of forced labor imposed by French corporations. So many Africans were tortured and killed while he was here in 1926 that André Gide wrote a book denouncing "the shameless exploitation" of the "frightful" colonial regime.

But the suspicions of General Bokassa also grow out of what he describes as an assassination plot by Lieut. Col. Alexandre Banza, who had once been his closest associate and Minister of Finance. Last April 12, after a secret predawn trial, Colonel Banza was executed.

Control Is Firm

General Bokassa's swift action appears to have left him more firmly in control than ever. He has pressed ahead with his economic development program, which has achieved some success.

The 1968 cotton crop reached a record level of 49,000 tons, up 25 per cent from 1967. An agreement to develop uranium resources was signed with the French. Small factories have been built near here.

More important, diamond production has increased steadily, amounting to more than $18-million last year. Several times each week, American, Israeli and other merchants here put wooden cases, about the size of cigar boxes, aboard Air Afrique flights to Paris. Each box contains $100,000 or more in gems.

But the long-term economic prospects are disheartening. The Central African Republic is too far from the sea, too poor in mineral resources and too short of trained manpower to sustain itself economically. It is hard to see how it will ever be able to overcome the cruel handicaps imposed by geography and history.

June 16, 1969

Unnoticed Chad Revolt Spreads

Blacks Battling Arab Rebels in Central African Nation

By R. W. APPLE Jr.
Special to The New York Times

FORT-LAMY, Chad, June 22 — Almost unnoticed by the outside world, a rebellion is slowly spreading across this parched Central African nation, pitting Arabs against black men.

In three years of episodic fighting, several thousand people have been killed. No one knows the exact figure; in a country with no all-weather roads, few airplanes and a primitive communications system, reliable statistics do not exist.

The war in Chad, which has an area of 485,750 square miles — as big as Texas, California and Oklahoma combined — is part of a struggle that extends across Africa, from the Red Sea to the Atlantic Ocean.

Black and Arab Africa meet in the belt between the Sahara and the grasslands that extend across the continent — a belt that has been torn by conflict for hundreds of years. The struggle in the Sudan, Chad's eastern neighbor, is one example; the hostility between Moslems and Christians in Ethiopia is another.

Rebels in Two Areas

Opposition to the regime of François Tombalbaye, Chad's only President since independence from France in 1960, is centered in the eastern and northern parts of the country.

Through the scrub - covered plains in those regions wander dozens, perhaps hundreds of bands of Arab guerrillas. In a group of 50 men there may be no more than five rusty rifles. The rest of the rebels—called "bandits" by the Government — are armed only with homemade sagai, or spears.

But they have almost completely isolated Fort-Lamy, the capital, from large areas of the country. The roads from here to Mongo and Abéché have been unsafe for more than a year, and only armed convoys are permitted.

Murdering and torturing uncooperative chiefs, kidnapping others, burning villages, ambushing motor columns and destroying tax records, the guerrillas move almost at will, except in the towns where government prefects or subprefects are stationed.

A year ago a French doctor and nurse were killed on the road to Abéché. Last month a village only 15 miles from Mongo was destroyed, and the rebels stole everything of value, including a cache of arms. At about the same time a convoy carrying 1,114 bales of cotton, Chad's main export, was ambushed on the road from Am-Timan to Fort-Archambault. As a result, the big cotton gin at Am-Timan has been closed by its French owners.

Rebel Leader Killed

Since their principal leader, Ibrahim Abatcha, was killed in battle in February, 1968, the guerrillas have been disorganized.

And last April the President asked the French to send more troops here and to help him reform the local governments. The move evoked wide criticism among younger Chadians and must have hurt the President's own pride.

The French, who have maintained an 800-man garrison at the strategic Fort-Lamy air base for several years, responded by building their strength up to 1,600, including 450 Foreign Legionnaires dispatched from Corsica and a helicopter squadron. With the new troops came Brig. Gen. Michel Arnaud, an officer who had served twice in Chad during the colonial era.

Deployed in the Mongo area, the Legionnaires seem to have considerably calmed things there. They have fought only one major battle, an ambush in which they piled out of their vehicles and killed seven rebels while suffering only one man wounded.

For generations before the arrival of the French in Chad at the turn of the century, the black people in the south were the slaves of the northern Arabs. But when independence came, the former masters suddenly found themselves dominated by the blacks, particularly by the Sara tribe, of which President Tombalbaye is a member.

Chad's population of 3.3 million is divided about evenly between the Arabs of the north and east — who are mostly of Sudanese origin, with some lighter-skinned Libyan stock mixed in — and the southern Bantu tribes. In the south, the people tend to be sedentary farmers who grow cotton and food crops; in the arid north, many of the Moslems are nomadic herdsmen. Chad has far more cattle than people.

Banditry had long been prevalent in eastern Chad, even under the French, and as the Arabs found themselves increasingly excluded from power, banditry evolved into guerrilla warfare.

In the opinion of most impartial observers here, there is no question that the Arabs have been exploited. They have been victimized, for example, by rapacious tax collectors who triple the rates decreed by Fort-Lamy, then pocket the difference.

Nearly all prefects in Arab areas are black Christians or pagans from the south. Only two Arabs have become officers in the Chadian Army — both lieutenants. The Minister of Defense, an Arab, is often excluded from key military conferences.

Chad's own military and paramilitary forces of 4,000 to 5,000 men have been unable to cope with the rebel challenge. On occasion, they have made things worse by going into villages suspected of sympathizing with the guerrillas and "shooting everything that moves," as one foreigner here puts it, "even the chickens."

President Tombalbaye, who is 51 years old, demonstrated last fall in coping with a short-lived revolt by the Toubou tribesmen in the far north that he was capable of the political flexibility needed to solve complex issues. The Toubous, enraged by heavy-handed treatment by the local prefect, went on a rampage, ambushing convoys and killing Government troops. The President quieted things down by cordoning off the area, calling in the Toubou chiefs, and meeting most of their demands.

Sensitive to Criticism

Although he continues to be hypersensitive to criticism — he arrested Dr. Outel Bono, the Director of Public Health, and several other intellectuals on subversion charges last month — Mr. Tombalbaye has recently begun to show a new determination to bring the war to an end.

But French officers in Chad operate under no illusion about their chances of success.

"Unless something is done in political terms, we will not be able to help very much," said one officer. Marking off an inch on a ruler with his fingers, he added, "Only this much of the problem is military."

Another French veteran of the colonial period, Pierre Lami, a former governor of the Ivory Coast and Senegal, arrived at the same time as General Arnaud. His job is to decide what reforms are needed to draw the country together — and his success or lack thereof will go far toward determining whether the war in Chad will end quickly or drag on for years.

Gamma—Pix

François Tombalbaye

June 26, 1969

Revolt in Chad Drags On Despite Help by French

By WILLIAM BORDERS

Special to The New York Times

FORT-LAMY, Chad, May 10—In parched desert lands near the center of Africa, French soldiers are fighting Moslem nomads in a battle that some describe as neocolonialist and others call legitimate foreign aid.

The guerrilla insurgency has dragged on for years, and the lack of French progress has contributed to demands in Paris for a quick withdrawal.

"But what the critics there do not understand is that if we left, Chad would simply fall apart," a French officer here said the other day.

Opponents of the French involvement are fond of describing Chad as "France's Vietnam," and there are some parallels.

One point of similarity is the presence of several hundred French advisers, who are really in command of Chadian troops. Another is that defenders of the intervention use the domino theory to support their stand.

According to that view, this arid land, formerly a French colony, which is three times the size of California, has a strategic location at the crossroads of Africa. If bands of rebels are permitted to make chaos of it, French and other interests all over the continent will be endangered.

France has now built up her force in Chad to 3,500 men, including the advisers. But since more than half of them represent a permanent garrison that was already in Fort-Lamy before the Chad Government requested reinforcements in April, 1969. Paris usually uses the figure of 1,500 to describe the size of its involvement.

When the French troops began to join in the fighting, draftees were pulled out of Chad, presumably to make the intervention less controversial in France. This is now a post only for men who have enlisted, including, at present, 400 members of the Foreign Legion.

Most of the French troops are in Fort-Lamy, the sleepy capital, where the Chadians see them speeding along on motor bikes and crowding the bars to dance with local girls who have taken to wearing miniskirts since the escalation.

"I would prefer to spend a year in hell," said a 19-year-old French marine, dismissing with a gesture of disgust the miles of red powdery dust, baking in 110-degree heat, that surrounds the military base here.

In the year since the build-up, 12 Frenchmen have been killed by the guerrilla bands that roam the deserts in the north and east of the country, armed with spears and daggers as well as German and Italian rifles left over from the North African campaigns of World War II.

Casualties among the Chadian Army, which fights beside the French, have been heavier, and the rebels are thought to have lost several hundred men, at least.

According to military men here, the rebels have reacted to the foreign intervention by breaking down into groups of only a dozen or two, which hit and run and then disappear. As a result, there have been few large armed clashes in recent months.

Nevertheless, by raiding government outposts and ambushing both military and civilian travelers, they have made whole sections of the country even more a hazard than such no man's lands of Africa are anyway, discouraging the trickle of tourists who used to come to Chad to hunt elephants and giraffes.

It is the policy of President François Tombalbaye's Government to dismiss the rebels as "bandits," and even observers who consider that an oversimplification concede that there is little political unity among them, short of a common opposition to the central government.

The opposition grows out of a widespread feeling that the Government, which is run by Christians and animists, has not fairly treated the eastern and northern regions, which are largely Moslem.

In common with states all across central Africa, Chad has traditionally been split between Moslems in the north and non-Moslems in the south.

The non-Moslem rulers decided to tax wives, for example, hitting the polygamous Moslems, and to put a heavy tax on the underfed longhorn cattle that are the only thing most of the northern nomads possess.

Tax collectors sent out from Fort-Lamy often doubled or tripled the tax rate, pocketing the difference. Since most of the wandering cattlemen live in tents that they move with their herds, they found themselves taxed at one water hole, then forced to pay the same tax again the following month at another drinking spot miles away.

With a faltering administration running an impoverished government, such meetings with the tax collector have often been the only contact that many of the nomadic Moslems had with the state, which gave them no hospitals, no schools and no roads.

In a move toward reform this year, President Tombalbaye, a Christian member of the dominant Sara tribe, brought more Moslems into his government, and promised a greater effort to keep tax returns in the regions from which they were collected.

But with a national budget of only $48-million, half of it supplied by France, there is little he can provide to make life any better for most of Chad's 3.5 million people.

Leading the fight against him are thought to be at least two resistance organizations, neither with any definite ideology, and each claiming considerably wider support and control than it has.

The Front de Libération Nationale, called Frolinat, says it speaks for parts of the north. In the east, some sloganeering has been done in the name of the Front de Liberation Tchadienne.

Frolinat is based on the other side of Chad's 650-mile border with Libya, which passes through the Sahara, scarcely defined and poorly patrolled.

The border crossings, and the feeling in Tripoli that Chad is fighting Arabs, have contributed to some strain in relations between the two neighbors, and the French are thought to be anxious lest this unsettle their own relations with Libya.

May 17, 1970

Glittering Facade of Dakar, the Capital, Masks Economic Malaise That Grips Senegal

By WILLIAM BORDERS

Special to The New York Times

DAKAR, Senegal, Oct. 30 — This glittering metropolis, with its rows and rows of tall white buildings, seems busy and brisk, giving an impression of great prosperity. The impression is false.

Other African capitals, like Lagos and Kinshasa, are struggling to catch up with economic booms. But Dakar, a city almost surrounded by the shimmering sea on the westernmost point in Africa, is going in almost the opposite direction.

The New York Times Nov. 8, 1970

As the capital of a small and backward country that depends heavily on its uncertain peanut crop, Dakar is in many ways less important than it was before independence 10 years ago, when it was the administrative capital of all of French West Africa.

"True, true," conceded one of the 500,000 residents, sipping espresso at one of the many sidewalk cafes, "it may have declined in relation to the rest of Africa, but, certainly, it is still Dakar."

With its broad, tree-shaded boulevards and its mood of graceful chic, Dakar has long been called "the Paris of Africa" and is regarded as one of the continent's most European cities.

$4 a Pound for Beef

Its handsome main square is surrounded by elegant restaurants, smart boutiques and grocery stores in which French housewives pay $4 a pound for beef tenderloin flown from Paris.

In the opinion of many here, however, Senegal's future can be read more accurately a few miles away from the growing European quarter — in the much more rapidly growing black slum.

The Government of President Léopold S. Senghor is building houses to replace the acres of tin shacks and schools to raise the literacy rate, now 5 per cent. Restricted by its poverty, it is barely keeping up.

Two years ago discontent spilled briefly into the downtown streets, where unemployed youths rioted and looted the shops, almost all of which are run by Frenchmen.

Peanut Crop Reduced

The urban disorder has not been repeated, but out in the countryside east of Dakar there is a new kind of revolt—"the peasants' malaise," as concerned Government officials describe it.

Dissatisfied by a declining return, the peasants have sharply cut back their peanut crop. A traveler across the rolling inland plains still sees women on their way to market carrying peanut plants on their heads like elaborate green crowns, but there are not so many of them. The farmers are turning their land to cereal crops to feed their families.

The informal strike, coupled with less than ideal weather, has reduced the current crop to perhaps 600,000 tons, half what it was a few years ago.

Since 80 per cent of Senegal's export earnings come from peanuts, the revolt puts additional strain on a budget already heavily subsidized by the French, and builds political pressure on the Government.

In response, the 64-year-old President, the country's leader since before independence, has recently moved to make his Government more popular among the 3.8 million Senegalese.

He has established the post of Premier, to achieve what he called "a less concentrated presidential system," and has even hinted that he could tolerate an opposition party.

On an otherwise bleak horizon, economic surveys of Senegal usually find one hopeful note: tourism. Dakar is one of the few cities in West Africa that is a genuine attraction, equipped to international standards.

Its pleasant climate and its position as a logical first stop in Africa have created something of a boom, with 50 per cent increases in the number of visitors in each of the last two years.

Some of the tourists are Americans, including, increasingly, Negroes for whom Africa has acquired new significance.

Such a tourist was Shorty—the name was the only one he cared to divulge—a young college graduate from the Bedford-Stuyvesant section of Brooklyn who spent several hours here the other day searching the past on Gorée Island.

Gorée, less than two miles offshore, was discovered by the Portuguese years before Columbus landed in America and it was one of the first European settlements on the coast of black Africa.

It was the rocky little island's later history that had impelled Shorty to take the ferry across the clear, calm Dakar harbor. During the 18th and 19th centuries Gorée was a major transshipment point for slaves from all over West Africa en route to the New World.

As American blacks had done before him, Shorty, striding past the postcard vendors and the stand that sells carvings, headed for the pastel stucco House of Slaves, where thousands and thousands were crammed into tiny rooms, awaiting shipment to America or death.

November 8, 1970

French Influence Pervades Marxist Congo

By MARVINE HOWE

Special to The New York Times

BRAZZAVILLE, Congo — The monuments to General Charles de Gaulle and the French colonial explorer Count Savorgnan de Brazza coexist steadfastly here with an array of Marxist-Leninist slogans, photos of Mao Tse-tung and red flags with golden star, hammer and hoe.

The Congo, Africa's only people's republic, receives considerable aid and attention from the Soviet bloc but remains closely linked to her former French rulers.

Capital and communications center of what was once French Equatorial Africa, the Congo has a population of one million that is one of the most urbanized and politicized in Africa.

The country is firmly committted to revolutionary socialism, but until now the revolution has been largely verbal. The sedate capital is adorned with red slogans for the governing Labor party and the revolutionary youth and women's organizations.

The press is full of Marxist sayings and attacks on imperialism, colonialism and neocolonialism. A banner at the central post office exhorts "proletarians to assault the bureaucratic bourgeoisie."

Nevertheless, the Protestant and Catholic churches are full every Sunday, and there is a rash of new African religions. The French still run secondary and higher education and control much of the economy.

The French community here generally shrugs off the hostile slogans as part of the trappings of independence. There are French complaints but no evidence of general departure. The population of 8,000 French—including 700 technical assistants—has remained stable over the last five years.

Most Industry French

Private enterprise, mostly French, is flourishing. Shops charge high prices and make good profits. A pair of shoes selling for $25 in France is priced at $50 here.

But the Congolese still like their luxuries, and when they can afford to do so, they drink Evian mineral water and Bordeaux wine, eat Camembert cheese and wear Pierre Cardin clothes.

The French also control most of the industry, including the promising new offshore oil concession, which is scheduled to produce 1.5 million tons next year and 10 million tons in 10 years.

The Congolese Government has nationalized only those industries that were on the verge of closing down, such as sugar and cement, neither of which are doing well. The state sector is said to be in debt for over $4-million, almost 5 per cent of the national budget.

In fact, the French have tried to get the Congolese to nationalize the Congolese Potassium Company but they refused. The French admit they made "a bad calculation" on the potassium and would like to get rid of it. The company is producing only half a million tons this year, or 50 per cent of the target. Expensive port installations at Point Noire were built for an overly ambitious 8 million tons.

France is also engaged in a program for renewing this country's vital transport system with the help of the World Bank and the European Fund for Development.

France's pervasive presence here, 12 years after independence, has been a factor for stability but at the same time is one of the basic causes of the country's continuing political malaise.

Many Coup Attempts

The Congo has been afflicted with coups and coup attempts since the early days of independence. The first President, Fulbert Youlou, a pro-French defrocked priest, was overthrown in 1964 by a coalition of militant anti-French students and labor unionists.

The succeeding left-wing Governments of Alphonse Massemba-Debat and currently Maj. Marien Ngouabi tried, unsuccessfully, to appease the extremists with revolutionary rhetoric, anti-Americanism and closer contacts with Communist countries.

"American imperialists will never be allowed back as long as they persist in policing the world," President Ngouabi asserted recently.

American visitors here are looked upon with awe. An occasional American tourist has been allowed a 48-hour transit visa but most requests are turned down or ignored. The stately white house overlooking the Congo River that was once the American Embassy has been deserted since August 1965. The United States pulled out after being accused of sending agents from Leopoldville—capital of what was then the Congo Republic, now called Zaïre—to overthrow the Massemba-Debat Government

On the other hand, a parade of missions from Communist countries has come here to sign every kind of cultural, economic and technical accord. The latest were the Hungarians and Rumanians.

Peking has provided the most valuable aid, according to Congolese sources, who reproach the Chinese only for remaining aloof and not mixing with the population. The Chinese have built a textile factory and shipyard and are now working on a hydroelectric dam. They have also planted rice farms and given considerable medical and military aid.

The Soviet Union has provided teachers, doctors and military aid. The Congolese complain, however, that four Antonov planes supplied by the Soviet Union were costly and must be repaired frequently—in Moscow. The new Russian-built Hotel Cosmos is austere and already shabby and would be better suited to a Siberian landscape.

The East Germans have been generous with short scholarships and propaganda but have not yet come up with capital aid.

"The Communists seem more interested in public relations than economic development," a Western observer remarked.

On the whole, Communist aid has not provided a valid alternative to French participation.

There is nevertheless a growing sector of the élite that believes that nationalization of French enterprises is the prerequisite for effective revolutionary socialism. They are supported by students and workers who cannot find satisfactory jobs under the present "neocolonial system."

The trouble is that 90 per cent of the Congo's youth goes to school—the highest rate in formerly French Africa—and the country does not know what to do with them. Last year, the secondary school graduates were asked to do an extra year because there were no jobs for them.

"Once the young people learn to read and write they don't want to go back to the farm," a French teacher said. "They spend all their time at rallies, talking politics in cafes or plotting—because they have nothing else to do."

The last nearly successful coup took place on Feb. 22 and was led by Ange Diawara, a pro-Peking member of the governing party's Political Bureau. Mr. Diawara, who was supported by student and union radicals, is said to be still hiding somewhere in the country and presents a permanent threat to the Government.

Major Ngouabi still controls the army, but his political apparatus has been seriously eroded by political purges and trials. The party's Political Bureau, which had nine members a year ago, has three now. The Central Committee has been reduced from 18 to 5. Party membership has dropped from 500 to 160.

President Ngouabi has called for a national conference in a few weeks to patch up the Labor party and review policy. He is expected to face strong pressure from the radicals to nationalize French interests.

July 17, 1972

Congo Revolt: An Intricate Mercenary Adventure

By HENRY TANNER
Special to The New York Times

KINSHASA, the Congo, July 18—The Congo, after seven years of independence, is still a country where simple things are intricate and where the obvious is implausible. The story of the brief revolt of white mercenaries is no exception.

Striking before dawn July 5, they shot up the Congolese Army camp at Bukavu, the Congo's eastermost city, and simultaneously, [illegible]00 miles to the northwest, [illegible] to capture Kisangani, a town [illegible]dged between the Congo River and the African forest.

A week later the mercenaries disappeared into the forest with their commandeered brewery trucks and radio transmitters to wait for planes to evacuate them to Rhodesia and Portuguese Angola.

The Congolese Army, which fought well against the mercenaries and showed discipline, reverted to former ways. As soon as the fighting stopped, it went on a looting spree until there was no beer left in Kisangani.

The death toll in the revolt is several hundred Congolese soldiers, women and children and at least 12 European civilians, including a Belgian couple who had lost three of their four children during the violence in Kisangani two years ago. The toll of the mercenaries is not known here.

Many of the reports that gained currency at the beginning of the revolt have been proved wrong. There is no evidence, for instance, that the mercenaries held hundreds of hostages.

Thirteen visiting newspapermen, most of them Belgians, who arrived in Kisangani on the first day of the fighting were confined to a downtown hotel.

Captured Congolese officers were held there. European residents sought refuge and food at the hotel.

The mood of the mercenaries was closer to despair than to cockiness, according to witnesses.

In Kisangani they cleaned out the Banque du Congo, but, to the delight of the Congolese, did not touch the Congolese National Bank. The Banque du Congo belongs to Société Générale of Brussels, which controls Union Minière du Haut-Katanga and had close though not always easy relations with Moise Tshombe when he ran Katanga Province and, later, was national Premier.

Why did the mercenaries strike just five days after the kidnapping of Mr. Tshombe, who is being held in Algeria? Were they part of an international plot to seize power in his name? Was there an "invasion" from abroad, as the Congo alleged?

Most foreigners here were convinced that the invasion claim was wrong when it was made. But as the story unfolded it became clear that the mercenaries had received men and planes from abroad.

There is strong evidence that John Puren, a South African who once was a ranking member of the mercenary corps, returned illegally and took part in the revolt.

The newsmen and other witnesses noticed that several of the mercenaries exercising command functions were speaking English among themselves with Rhodesian and South African accents.

The obvious conclusion was that members of an English-speaking mercenary force that was disbanded in May had returned. Since May the only mercenaries operating with the approval of the Government of President Joseph D. Mobutu were in a French-speaking force headed by Col. Bob Denard.

The New York Times July 19, 1967

Abortive Congo revolt began with attacks on Bukavu (1), and Kisangani (2).

There are indications also that a plot existed before the mercenaries struck.

The Kisangani uprising was preceded by sabotage directed at the Congo's two vital links with the outside world — the Benguela railroad, over which at least half of Katangese copper is exported through Angola, and the railroad linking the capital with Matadi, the only seaport.

On July 12 a major bridge between Kolwezi and the border of Angola was destroyed. At almost the same time saboteurs blew up pylons of the powerline feeding industries in the Lubumbashi area.

A little earlier the Kinshasa-Matadi line was interrupted several times by wrecks and landslides.

A Frenchman named Savant who is suspected by the Congolese of having masterminded the sabotage in Katanga showed up at the mercena[illegible] headquarters in Kisangani [illegible] according to reports.

A dissident Congolese officer from Katanga, a Captain Mungo, who was one of the most active men in the mercenary camp, told visiting newsmen that it was he who blew up the Kolwezi bridge. He said that the man of the same name who had been arrested was a Government plant.

Finally, Colonel Denard is known to have been in radio contact with journalist friends in Paris and to have invited them to fly to Kisangani.

Many diplomats here are convinced that there was some scheme to seize control of the eastern provinces, bring Mr. Tshombe back and proclaim a Free Congo in the hope that the Government's control over the rest of the country would disintegrate sooner or later.

Observers close to the situation believe that the kidnapping of Mr. Tshombe, who faces a death sentence on treason charges, upset the plan when it was still in its early stage and that the mercenaries struck sooner and with less preparation than they had intended.

They must have felt events closing in on them. On the day before the uprising several of them had a stormy session with President Mobutu in the capital. The President, it is reported, charged that Colonel Denard had visited Mr. Tshombe in Madrid.

When the group reached Kisangani in the evening, it had a run-in with Congolese soldiers at the airport. The next morning the mercenaries struck.

July 19, 1967

Mobutu Seeking Stronger Federal Control in Congo

By HENRY TANNER
Special to The New York Times

KINSHASA, the Congo, July 31—General Joseph D. Mobutu has gained a little weight and a great deal of self-confidence since that September evening in 1960 when he climbed on a cafe table on the terrace of the Regina Hotel here and proclaimed to all within earshot that his army had taken over the country.

He was the power behind the power of President Joseph Kasavubu and three successive Premiers until he assumed full power and the Presidency in November, 1965.

Men who are close to him assert that, more than any of his predecessors, the general is concerned with the need for national administrative and political structures that would permit the central government to reach into the provinces and begin to govern the whole huge country rather than just the cities and towns.

He has recently founded his own political party, the Popular Revolutionary Movement, which he hopes will become a nationwide organization.

His admirers say that he is doing early in his regime what preceding leaders, notably two former premiers, Cyrille Adoula and Moise Tshombe, attempted too late—only a few months before their ouster.

Detractors Fear Police State

His detractors say that the Movement is the beginning of a one-party police state.

The 36-year-old general's desire to bring order into the habitual chaos of the Congo came out in an interview the other day. He listed as his greatest achievements since 1960 his action to reform the army and give the Congolese a feeling of "national pride."

"Congolization is no longer a

bad word," he said proudly. An intimate later explained that "it tears him apart" to see foreign newspaper reports of Nigeria or any other African country in crisis as "another Congo."

He suspended Parliament, it is believed, partly because he felt that the actions of the senators, who turned their debates into tribal palavers, were giving the country a bad name in the rest of Africa.

General Mobutu's greatest ambition since taking over the presidency has been to gain recognition for himself and his country among Africans. He wants to be the first Congolese to become a leading African nationalist.

In the interview he said: "Before I came to power, all Africa turned its back on us. I put the Congo into the heart of Africa as soon as I took over."

He has no hesitation in using the first person singular in describing what the Congo is doing, and there are those who detect the beginnings of a mild cult of personality in the newspapers and on the radio.

Before General Mobutu came to power the Egyptians and Algerians, as well as all of the Congo's immediate African neighbors, were giving military support to the left-wing nationalist rebels in the Eastern province.

Now this aid has stopped almost entirely; that from Burundi is the only exception.

In 1964, Mr. Tshombe was put under house arrest by the Egyptians when he arrived in Cairo to attend an African summit meeting. Two years later, the summit leaders made General Mobutu's Foreign Minister, Justin Bomboko, their president. This year's summit, scheduled for next month, is to be held here.

This meeting, the first major African conference to be held in the Congolese capital since 1960, is looked upon as the consummation of General Mobutu's bid for African recognition.

Associated Press

General Joseph D. Mobutu, President of the Congo, at a news conference early last month during the rebellion.

The general is building a conference site behind the Presidential Palace at a cost of about $10-million. This is relatively modest as African summit arrangements go.

There are 41 bungalows, one for each head of state, and a central main building plus a swimming pool, tennis courts and a miniature golf course.

Twenty Cadillacs, 20 Lincolns and a Chrysler have been ordered, and tall modern street lamps are going up on the airport road and on streets that the visitors are likely to travel.

The only cloud that is hanging over the project is the Tshombe affair.

Congolese ambassadors in West Africa are hard at work trying to persuade moderate African leaders to agree to come to Kinshasa next month even if Mr. Tshombe is extradited and executed.

Mr. Tshombe, who had been living in exile in Spain after his ouster as Premier, was kidnapped when his plane was hijacked over the Mediterranean early this month. He was flown to Algeria, where he is awaiting extradition to the Congo. Mr. Tshombe had been tried in absentia for treason, convicted and sentenced to death.

It is believed that it would be a tremendous loss of face for General Mobutu if the summit conference was canceled or poorly attended.

Another crucial test facing the Mobutu regime is internal.

With the backing and advice of the International Monetary Fund and the United States, the Congolese have just carried out a major monetary reform. The Congolese franc has been devalued from 150 to the dollar to 500 to the dollar, the new valuation being just about equal to the black-market rate before reform.

The new monetary unit is called the zaïre (pronounced za-eer), and the question asked by the local punsters inevitably is "Ca ira ou ça n'ira pas?" ("Will it work or won't it?").

Would Stimulate Exports

The main purpose of the reform is to arrest the steady deterioration of the currency and to stimulate exports of such plantation products as palm oil, rubber and coffee. But since the Congo is an importer of food and almost all the other consumer goods, the wage earners and Government employes in the cities will suffer if, as is expected, many prices double within the next few months.

The purchasing power of these two groups of Congolese is already down to 60 per cent of what it was in 1960, at the time of independence. Specialists predict that it will go down to 40 per cent in spite of the limited wage increases that are contemplated.

One of the big questions is whether this will produce social unrest in the urban centers.

August 2, 1967

Belgians Returning to a Stabler Congo

By R. W. APPLE Jr.
Special to The New York Times

KINSHASA, the Congo, Oct. 18—"The Congo," said a Belgian businessman, "is a honeypot. The bees may fly away for a while, but they always come back."

With a population of 16 million, huge deposits of copper, cobalt, diamonds and perhaps oil, hydroelectric resources, soils and climates that can grow almost any agricultural product, a strategic geographical position and a vast system of navigable rivers, the former Belgian Congo seems to economists to have the best chance of any black African country of reaching economic self-sufficiency.

The relative political stability achieved by the Government of Gen. Joseph D. Mobutu in the last four years and the radical economic reforms of June, 1967, in which a new currency, the zaïre, was introduced, have begun to pay substantial dividends.

Talk of Achievements

Analysts in Kinshasa talk less these days about potential and more about performance. These are some of the items they talk about:

¶Reserves of gold and foreign exchange, which vanished during the bedlam of revolt and corruption that marked the Congo's first years after independence in 1960, reached $203-million last year.

¶Agricultural production, which collapsed during the bad old days, has rebounded, though declining commodity prices have put a crimp in profits. Exports of palm products, rubber, and coffee increased last year, and for the first time since independence, some cotton was exported.

¶Copper production, which is in the hands of a state company called Gecomin, is expected to set a record of about 356,000 tons this year. With the help of a new Japanese-Congolese consortium, Sodimico, the Congo should double its output in 10 years.

¶The black market rate in currency, which once stood at two and a half times the official rate, has contracted. The premium is now only 20 per cent.

And the bees have returned. Tens of thousands of Belgians have come back to the Congo to earn bonus salaries as pilots, managers, advisers, engineers and architects—reversing the flow of the post-independence era, when Europeans flew out of Ndjili Airoprt, often unloading their property at fractions of its true value to men who stood with bags of dollars in the departure lounge.

The wives of the people whom the Congolese call "les techniciens" can be seen with huge wads of zaires in their hands, shopping in Kinshasa stores full of modern imported goods.

Overseas investment, essential if the Congo is to realize her potential, is also beginning to return, encouraged by a new, liberal investment code. A settlement this month with the Belgian mining corporation, Union Minière du Haut-Katanga, whose assets have been taken over by Gecomin, the state company, has prompted the World Bank to begin looking for projects here.

General Mobutu is trying to bridge the technology gap in the Congo by turning over the operation of certain agencies to private companies. He has already signed agreements, or hopes to do so soon, with Bell Telephone to oversee telecommunications services, Pan American World Airways to oversee Air Congo, Caterpillar Tractor Company to oversee river transport and the Radio Corporation of America to oversee Congolese television.

He keeps copies of Jean-Jacques Servan-Schreiber's book, "The American Challenge," in his office, to hand to members of his Cabinet as he extols the virtues of American managerial skills.

Kinshasa is in the midst of an extraordinary construction boom, with new villas going up quickly in the suburbs. A 260-room hotel, a project of Pan American, is under construction, and two others are planned.

The streets are thronged with new vehicles. Standing for two minutes at a corner, a visitor sees three glistening green German buses, a yellow Corvette, three Mercedes sports cars and a stream of Cadillac limousines.

Stagnancy in the Interior

But Kinshasa is only a part of the picture. Even here, the working man has suffered a short-term reduction in his buying power while gaining a long-term prospect of real increases in income. In parts of the seemingly limitless interior, the economy still lies stagnant.

Only one riverboat a week heads downstream from Kisangani, formerly Stanleyville, which was devastated first by the Simba revolt of 1964, then by an uprising of Katangese gendarmes in 1966, then by the rebellion of white mercenaries under Jean Schramme in 1967.

"The port," says a European who knows Kisangani, "is a stage waiting for its players."

Agriculture in Orientale Province, of which Kisangani is the capital, is coming back, both on plantations and on small farms. But the network of roads has been allowed to fall into such disrepair — the main feeder route from Kisangani toward Uganda is closed—that a great deal of the produce never reaches the marketplace.

Transportation, in fact, has proved to be the Congo's main weakness. The Government has shown itself incapable of maintaining even the marginal system left behind by the Belgians, partly because it seems unable to provide even rudimentary maintenance for heavy equipment.

More than 100 year-old Fiat dump trucks sit in a yard near Kinshasa, all of them broken down and many totally unrepairable.

The other seemingly insoluble economic problem is corruption, which has always flourished here with a fine tropical luxuriance. To do business in Kinshasa, one must indulge in the "matabus"—the bribe. Despite presidential pronouncements on probity and public service, a recent arrival was asked four times for bribes before he left the airport terminal.

October 28, 1969

Congo Changes Name To the Zaire Republic

KINSHASA, Zaire, Oct. 27 (Reuters)—The Congo, a former Belgian colony, changed its name to the Zaire Republic today. The new name was taken from the original name of the Congo River, which in Zaire will be called the Zaire River.

This country became independent in 1960. Its capital, Kinshasa, was formerly known as Léopoldville.

Across the river to the west is the Congo Republic, a former French colony once known as the Middle Congo, which gained independence in 1960. Its capital is Brazzaville.

October 28, 1971

The Rise and Fall Of the Watusi

By ELSPETH HUXLEY

FROM the miniature Republic of Rwanda in central Africa comes word of the daily slaughter of a thousand people, the possible extermination of a quarter of a million men, women and children, in what has been called the bloodiest tragedy since Hitler turned on the Jews. The victims are those tall, proud and graceful warrior-aristocrats, the Tutsi, sometimes known as the Watusi.* They are being killed by their former vassals, the Hutu (or Bahutu).

Who are the Tutsi and why is such a ghastly fate overtaking them? Is it simply African tribalism run riot, or are outside influences at work? Can nothing be done?

The king-in-exile of Rwanda, Mwami (Monarch) Kigeri V, who has fled to the Congo, is the 41st in line of succession. Every Tutsi can recite the names of his 40 predecessors but the Tutsi cannot say how many centuries ago their ancestors settled in these tumbled hills, deep valleys and volcanic mountains separating the great drainage systems of the Nile and Congo basins.

Nor is it known just where they came from—Ethiopia perhaps; before that, possibly Asia. They are cattle folk, allied in race to such nomadic peoples as the Somali, Galla, Fulani and Masai. Driving their cattle before them, they found this remote pocket of central Africa, 1,000 miles from the Indian Ocean. It was occupied by a race

*According to the orthography of the Bantu language, "Tutsi" is the singular and "Watutsi" the plural form of the word. For the sake of simplicity, I prefer to follow the style used in United Nations reports and use "Tutsi" for both singular and plural.

of Negro cultivators called the Hutu, who had themselves displaced the aboriginal pygmy hunters, the Twa (or Batwa). First the Tutsi conquered and then ruled the Hutu, much as a ·r-man ruling class conquered and settled down in Anglo-Saxon England. Like the Normans, they established their own laws and customs but adopted the language of their subjects.

In the latest census, the Tutsi constitute about 15 per cent of Rwanda's population of between 2.5 and 3 million. Apart from a handful of Twa, the rest are Hutu. (The same figures are true of the tiny neighboring kingdom of Burundi.)

For at least four centuries the Tutsi have kept intact their racial type by inbreeding. Once seen, these elongated men are never forgotten. Their small, narrow heads perched on top of slim and spindly bodies remind one of some of Henry Moore's sculptures. Their average height, though well above the general norm, is no more than 5 feet 9 inches, but individuals reach more than 7 feet. The former king, Charles III Rudahagwa, was 6 feet 9 inches, and a famous dancer and high jumper—so famous his portrait was printed on the banknotes—measured 7 feet 5 inches.

THIS height, prized as a badge of racial purity, the Tutsi accentuated by training upward tufts of fuzzy hair shaped like crescent moons. Their leaps, bounds and whirling dances delighted tourists, as their courtesy and polished manners impressed them.

Through the centuries, Tutsi feudalism survived with only minor changes. At its center was the Mwami, believed to be descended from the god of lightning, whose three children fell from heaven onto a hilltop and begat the two royal clans from which the Mwami and his queen were always chosen. Not only had the Mwami rights of life and death over his subjects but, in theory, he owned all the cattle, too — magnificent, long-horned cattle far superior to the weedy native African bovines. Once a year, these were ceremonially presented to the Mwami in all their glory — horns sand-polished, coats rubbed with butter, foreheads hung with beads, each beast attended by a youth in bark-cloth robes who spoke to it softly and caught its dung on a woven straw mat.

"Rwanda has three pillars," ran a Tutsi saying: "God, cows and soldiers." The cows the Mwami distributed among his subchiefs, and they down the line to lesser fry, leaving no adult Tutsi male without cows.

Indeed, the Tutsi cannot live without cattle, for milk and salted butter are their staple food. (Milk is consumed in curds; the butter, hot and perfumed by the bark of a certain tree.) To eat foods grown in soil, though often done, is thought vaguely shameful, something to be carried out in private.

THE kingdom was divided into districts and each had not one governor, but two: a land chief *(umunyabutaka)* and a cattle chief *(umunyamukenke)*. The jealousy that nearly always held these two potentates apart prompted them to spy on each other to the Mwami, who was thus able to keep his barons from threatening his own authority.

Below these governors spread a network of hill chiefs, and under them again the heads of families. Tribute — milk and butter from the lordly Tutsi, and grain, bananas, beer and goats from their Hutu vassals—escalated upward to the royal court, each subchief, chief and governor taking his cut on the way.

Just as, in medieval Europe, every nobleman sent his son to the king's court to learn the arts of war, love and civility, so in Rwanda and Burundi did every Tutsi father send his sons to the Mwami's court for instruction in the use of weapons, in lore and tradition, in dancing and poetry and the art of conversation, in manly sports and in the practice of the most prized Tutsi virtue —self-control. Ill-temper and the least display of emotion are thought shameful and vulgar. The ideal Tutsi male is at all times polite, dignified, amiable, sparing of idle words and a trifle supercilious.

THESE youths, gathered in the royal compound, were formed into companies which, in turn, formed the army. Each youth owed to his company commander an allegiance which continued all his life. In turn, the commander took the youth, and subsequently the man, under his protection. Every Tutsi could appeal from his hill chief to his army commander, who was bound to support him in lawsuits or other troubles. (During battle, no commander could step backward, lest his army retreat; at no time could the king bend his knees, lest his kingdom shrink.)

The Hutu were both bound and protected by a system known as *buhake*, a form of vassalage. A Hutu wanting to enter into this relationship would present a jug of beer to a Tutsi and say: "I ask you for milk. Make me rich. Be my father, and I will be your child." If the Tutsi agreed, he gave the applicant a cow, or several cows. This sealed the bargain.

TROUBLED LANDS—In Rwanda, Hutu tribesmen have been killing Tutsi; in Burundi, a Tutsi-Hutu government maintains an uneasy peace.

The Hutu then looked to his lord for protection and for such help as contributions toward the bride-price he must proffer for a wife. In return, the Hutu helped from time to time in the work of his protector's household, brought occasional jugs of beer and held himself available for service as the Tutsi's man—not slave, certainly, but retainer.

The densely populated kingdoms of the Tutsi lay squarely in the path of Arab slavers who for centuries pillaged throughout the central African highlands, dispatching by the hundreds of thousands yoked and helpless human beings to the slave markets of Zanzibar and the Persian Gulf. Here the explorer Livingstone wrote despairingly in his diaries of coffles (caravans) of tormented captives, of burnt villages, slaughtered children, raped women and ruined crops. But these little kingdoms, each about the size of Maryland, escaped. The disciplined, courageous Tutsi spearmen kept the Arabs out, and the Hutu safe. Feudalism worked both ways.

Some Hutu grew rich, and even married their patrons' daughters. Sexual morality was strict. A girl who became pregnant before marriage was either killed outright or abandoned on an island in the middle of Lake Kivu to perish, unless rescued by a man of a despised and primitive Congo tribe, to be kept as a beast of burden with no rights.

SINCE the Tutsi never tilled the soil, their demands for labor were light. Hutu duties included attendance on the lord during his travels; carrying messages; helping to repair the master's compound; guarding his cows. The relationship could be ended at any time by either party. A patron had no right to hold an unwilling "client" in his service.

It has been said that serfdom in Europe was destroyed by the invention of the horse collar. In Africa, slate and pencil played the same role. Literacy and Western education, brought to Rwanda by Christian missionaries, awoke the subject peoples to an awareness of their subordinate condition.

UNTIL the First World War the kingdoms were part of German East Africa. Then Belgium took them over, under the name of Ruanda-Urundi, as a trust territory, first for the League of Nations, then under the U. N. Although the Belgian educational system, based on Roman Catholic missions, was conservative in outlook, and Belgian administrators made no calculated attempt to undo Tutsi feudalism, Western ideas inevitably crept in. So did Western economic notions through the introduction of coffee cultivation, which opened to the Hutu a road to independence, bypassing the Tutsi cattle-based economy. And Belgian authority over Tutsi notables, even over the sacred Mwami himself, inevitably damaged their prestige. The Belgians even deposed one obstructive Mwami.

About ten years ago, the Belgians tried to persuade the Tutsi to let some of the Hutu into their complex structure of government. In Burundi, the Tutsi ruling caste realized its danger just in time and agreed to share some of its powers with the Hutu majority. But in Rwanda, until the day the system toppled, no Hutu was appointed by the Tutsi overlords to a chief's position. A tight, rigid, exclusive Tutsi aristocracy continued to rule the land.

The Hutu grew increasingly restive and resentful. Their young men, emerging from Western-run schools, were unwilling to accept Tutsi overlordship. When they realized that the Belgians, hustled on by the United Nations, really intended a complete withdrawal, they recognized their moment of destiny. Hastily throwing together skeleton political parties, they gathered forces for a showdown with their hereditary masters.

It came in the form of an uprising on Nov. 1, 1959, triggered largely by a pastoral letter sent out by the Archbishop of Rwanda calling the inequality between Hutu and Tutsi incompatible with Christian morality. In the bloody fortnight that followed, many Tutsi were slaughtered, and at least 100,000 fled before vengeful Hutu mobs armed with arrows, pangas and swords. With them went an untried Mwami, Kigeri V, whose elder brother's death a few months earlier had weakened the Tutsi grip.

WHEN order was restored, there were reckoned to be 21,000 Tutsi refugees in Burundi, 14,000 in Tanganyika, 40,000 in Uganda and 60,000 in the Kivu province of the Congo. The Red Cross did its best to cope in camps improvised by local governments.

Back in Rwanda, municipal elections were held for the first time—and swept the Hutu into power. The Parmehutu—*Parti d'Emancipation des Hutus*—founded only in October 1959, emerged on top, formed a coalition government, and after some delays proclaimed a republic, to which the Belgians, unwilling to face a colonial war, gave recognition in terms of internal self-government.

In 1962, the U.N. proclaimed Belgium's trusteeship at an end, and, that same year, a general election held under U.N. supervision confirmed the Hutu triumph. With full independence, a new chapter began — the Hutu chapter.

Rwanda and Burundi split. Burundi has the only large city, Usumbura (population: 50,000), as its capital. With a mixed Tutsi-Hutu government, it maintains an uneasy peace. It remains a kingdom, with a Tutsi monarch. Everyone knows and likes the jovial Mwami, Mwambutsa IV, whose height is normal, whose rule has lasted since 1915 and who sometimes plays the drums in Usumbura's nightclubs.

As its President, Rwanda chose Grégoire Kayibanda, a 39-year-old Roman Catholic seminarist who, on the verge of ordination, chose politics instead. Locally educated by the Dominicans, he is a protégé of the Archbishop of Rwanda whose letter helped spark the first Hutu uprising. Faithful to his priestly training, he shuns the fleshpots, drives a Volkswagen instead of the Rolls or Mercedes generally favored by an African head of state and, suspicious of the lure of wicked cities, lives on a hilltop outside the town of Kigali, said to be the smallest capital city in the world, with some 7,000 inhabitants, a single paved street, no hotels, no telephone and a more or less permanent curfew.

Mr. Kayibanda's Christian and political duties, as he sees them, have fused into an implacable resolve to destroy forever the last shreds of Tutsi power—if necessary by obliterating the entire Tutsi race. Last fall, Rwanda still held between 200,000 and 250,000 Tutsi, reinforced by refugees drifting back from the camps, full of bitterness and humiliation. In December, they were joined by bands of Tutsi spearmen from Burundi, who with the courage of despair, and outnumbered 10 to 1, attacked the Hutu. Many believe they were egged on by Mwami Kigeri V, who since 1959 had been fanning Tutsi racial pride and calling for revenge.

THE result of the attacks was to revive all the cumulative hatred of the Tutsi for past injustices. The winds of anti-colonialism sweeping Africa do not distinguish between white and black colonialists. The Hutu launched a ruthless war of extermination that is still going on. Tutsi villages are stormed and their inhabitants clubbed or hacked to death, burned alive or herded into crocodile-infested rivers.

What will become of the Tutsi? One urgent need is outside help for the Urundi Government in resettling the masses of refugees who have fled to its territory. Urundi's mixed political set-up is reasonably democratic, if not always peaceful (witness the assassination of the Crown Prince by a political opponent in 1961), and the Tutsi should be able to avoid obliteration there. They must become politically subordinate, however, and intermarriage with the Hutu seems likely to increase. In Rwanda, there is no future for the Tutsi.

In a sense the Tutsi have brought their tragic fate on themselves. They are paying now the bitter price of ostrichism, a stubborn refusal to move with the times. The Bourbons of Africa, they are meeting the Bourbon destiny—to be obliterated by the people they have ruled and patronized.

The old relationship could survive no longer in a world, as E. M. Forster has described it, of "telegrams and anger;" a world of bogus democracy turning into one-party states, of overheated U.N. assemblies, of press reports and demagogues, a world where (as in the neighboring Congo) a former Minister of Education leads bands of tribesmen armed with arrows to mutilate women missionaries.

THE elegant and long-legged Tutsi with their dances and their epic poetry, their lyre-horned cattle and superb basketwork and code of seemly behavior, had dwindled into tourist fodder. The fate of all species, institutions or individuals who will not, or cannot, adapt caught up with them. Those who will not bend must break.

For the essence of the situation in an Africa increasingly convulsed by violence is that the liquidation of colonialism is taking place in the context of a mighty social revolution, affecting profoundly the lives of perhaps 100 million people and turning upside down beliefs and practices that have endured for many centuries. The age-old social system, universal throughout Africa, vested political and social power in the hands of mature men with grown sons, the elders in whom resided all wisdom and authority, and who could often rely for guidance on the world of spirits in whose reality no tribal Africans disbelieved.

NOW, not just the white men have gone, or are going; far more importantly, the elders and their authority, the whole chain of command from ancestral spirits, through the chief and his council to the obedient youth are being swept away. This hierarchy is being replaced by the "young men," the untried, unsettled, uncertain, angry and confused generation who, with a thin veneer of ill-digested Western education, for the first time in Africa's long history have taken over power from their fathers.

It is a major revolution indeed, whose first results are only just beginning to show up and whose outcome cannot be seen. There is only one safe prediction: that it will be violent, unpredictable, bloody and cruel, as it is proving for the doomed Tutsi of Rwanda.

Slaughter in Burundi: How Ethnic Conflict Erupted

By MARVINE HOWE

Special to The New York Times

BUJUMBURA, Burundi, June 9—This nation is just beginning to realize the extent of the slaughter that has taken place here over the last six weeks in struggles between the country's two major ethnic groups.

The complete story of an attempted coup at the end of April, and the counteroffensive that followed, cannot be told since only official sources can be quoted and they are clearly biased. Other sources, as well as foreigners, are still generally terrorized and reluctant to jeopardize lives of friends or risk expulsion. However, a six-day visit to Burundi has produced a plausible account of the catastrophe out of a web of rumors, lies and contradictions.

Clear statistics on the extent of the massacres are hard to come by. Information is limited because movement has been severely curtailed by official barricades and curfews. Foreigners must have travel permits and these are very difficult to obtain. Above all, most people are terrorized and reluctant to talk. Nevertheless, authoritative sources on the scene estimate that about 2,000 people were killed in the initial rebellion, mostly members of the ruling Tutsi tribe, a numerical minority. The reprisals are said to have cost the lives of 2,000 more Tutsis and about 100,000 members of the Hutu, the majority tribe, mainly in Bururi Province and in the area of Bujumbura, the capital.

The New York Times/Marvine Howe

Hutus in Kiganda listen as a Government official announces that rebellion has ended

The President of Burundi, Lieut. Col. Michel Micombero, acknowledges that 50,000 to 100,000 people have been killed in the last six weeks, while many foreign residents estimate the number of victims at closer to 150,000.

The basic struggle involves an attempt by the Hutu majority to overthrow the ruling Tutsi aristocracy, as the Hutus in neighboring Rwanda did in 1959. Here the attempted coup has failed, at a terrible price, particularly among the Hutus.

"We have won a reprieve but the final showdown is irreversible," a member of the Tutsi minority said. The dominant Tutsi account for only 15 per cent of the 3.5 million inhabitants of this country, which is about 10,750 square miles in area, roughly equivalent to the state of Maryland.

Colonel Micombero still speaks of his "program of national unity," but most people believe that the progress that had been made toward integration has now largely been erased by the violence.

Province Is Devastated

Bururi Province in the south, where the main part of the Hutu rebellion took place, is now a scene of devastation. The population has almost disappeared from a once densely inhabited area in a 40-mile stretch along Lake Tanganyika.

Some people, estimated to number 10,000 have fled to neighboring Tanzania, and 15,000 have escaped across the lake to Zaire, the former Republic of the Congo, leaving 175,000 unaccounted for. Many of these people are known to have taken refuge in the bush and marshes but many more are believed to be dead.

Only recently a small trickle of human life has begun to return to Rumonge, the lakeside fishing center, to Bururi, the inland farming center, and to some of the hill towns. In the Bururi region alone, 2,000 grassroof huts have been burned. Some 5,000 women and children have taken refuge in the Bururi missions.

The reprisals, on the other hand, have taken a heavy toll not only in the south but in Bujumbura and towns throughout the country. The Hutu élite has been decimated in the government administration, in the commercial world, in the church and in schools down to the secondary school level.

Local Officials Criticized

There have been excesses and atrocities during both the rebellion and the subsequent repression, according to foreign testimony. The burden of private criticism, however, has been directed against the local authorities for neglecting to curb reprisals.

"It is natural to demand greater moral restraint from the established authority than from drugged rebels," a churchman declared.

Foreign diplomats and other residents have generally followed the events in impotent silence, fearing that any intervention would bring grave repercussions for the foreign community of Burundi. The 6,000 or so missionaries, technicians, school teachers and businessmen and their families are considered hostages.

Until now, foreigners have not been the target of either the rebels or the repressers The only foreigner to be killed was a Belgian technician who lost his life by accident when he sought to observe the first assault at Bujumbura.

The explosion of ethnic antagonism is regarded by many missionaries as evidence of a failure of the Western church, both Roman Catholic and Protestant.

"The church has been humiliated and must start again from zero," a priest said. "Both those who provoked the rebellion and those who carried out the repression were Christians," he noted.

Representatives of seven missionary institutions broke their silence on May 20, with a strong letter to their superiors, aimed also at the Burundi Government, condemning persons responsible for the rebellion as well as the "systematic repression" of the Hutus.

The letter also protested against arbitrary arrests and the ban on priests' visits to the prisons. The only response to the letter seems to have been increased difficulties for missionaries who seek to obtain travel permits.

At the end of last month, a group of diplomats, led by the papal nuncio, applauded the President for starting what was called his "pacification" program and pledged support for "all victims" of the violence. Even this action brought no direct response.

Protest by Priests

Troubled by the continued repression and the official silence around it, three Italian priests and one Spanish priest in the north spoke severely about arbitrary punishment. They were promptly called to Bujumbura for interrogation by the police. Accused of political activity, the four young priests have been put under surveillance.

These protests, however timid and belated, coupled with strong criticism in the international press, seem to have spurred the authorities to move to halt the repression. "Or maybe it's merely that there are no more Hutus who can lift their heads," a churchman observed.

The Burundi Government has publicly blamed "foreign influences for the ethnic war," but has not specifically attacked any country. Diplomatic speculation about this accusation runs from China and North Korea to the Vatican and the United States Central Intelligence Agency.

President Micombero cleared Belgium, which until 1962 exercised a colonial mandate here, of the charges. However, the colonel did accuse Belgian Christian trade unions and former trusteeship administrators "of sowing division among us."

Burundi's ethnic troubles are considered to have been inevitable by scholars who have followed the evolution of this area of Central Africa. The problem can be attributed above all to a rapid breaking up of the old feudal structures.

Royal Line Established

More than three centuries ago, the tall handsome Tutsis came with their flocks from the high plateaus in East Africa to settle on the gentle hills of what are now Rwanda and Burundi. The local kings accepted them as colonizers and married the Tutsi women, establishing a royal line of mixed Tutsi and Hutu blood. A feudal hierarchy was established with the Tutsis as lords and the Hutus their serfs.

This feudal harmony was disturbed by the arrival of European colonizers and by the teachings of the Catholic Church. The area became part of German East Africa in 1899 and after World War I was ruled by the Belgians for 40 years under a League of Nations mandate, followed by United Nations trusteeship. The outside forces brought basic education and new ideas to the Hutus, such as the injustice of slavery.

In neighboring Rwanda, the Hutus carried out their revolution in the presence of the Belgian administration — and probably with some Belgian complicity. The king there was overthrown in 1959 and the Hutus later won control of the Government through elections held under sponsorship of the United Nations.

Some 20,000 Tutsis were killed in this revolt and 300,000 were forced into exile — about 100,000 of them to Burundi.

The Belgians, who granted both territories independence in 1962, generally felt that the transition could be smoother in Burundi, where there were many Hutu-Tutsi marriages and a Hutu middle class was gradually emerging.

Hutu Discontent Evidenced

Two Hutu risings, in 1965 and 1969, however, were evidence of a growing dissatisfaction within the majority.

The attempted coup of April 29 this year, to all appearances, follows in the same line of rebellions but was organized on a much broader and more violent scale. It was also complicated by the involvement of some monarchist Tutsis as well as opposition elements in Zaire. But independent sources generally agree that essentially this was another attempt by the Hutus to assume what they consider their rightful place as the majority in Burundi.

The fullest account of the initial attack was given this week by President Micombero in an informal interview by a small group of newsmen. The 31-year-old leader, who ousted young King Ntare V in 1965 to proclaim a republic, discussed for the first time the role of the former King in the recent events.

Ntare was duped by the Hutu plotters, according to President Micombero, who said the former King's name had been used to get as wide backing as possible for the uprising. Ntare returned to Burundi after "they convinced him that my regime was very unpopular and that it was now or never to make a comeback," Colonel Micombero said.

The New York Times

Lieut. Col. Michel Micombero giving official version of the events.

Assurances Given to King

The President acknowledged that he had given assurances that the former King would be protected on his return. But he stressed that since Ntare was "trying to trap me," he could not be allowed to move about freely and had been put under house arrest.

After the former King's return, preparations for the plot were intensified, the President said. The army was put on alert two weeks before the rising occurred.

Colonel Micombero declined to link the dissolution of his Government on the morning of April 29 with the attack that came that evening. The timing, he said, was a matter of "providence."

Monarchists and rebels acted together on the night of the rebellion, the President said. He disclosed for the first time that the former King was immediately tried and executed on the night of the attack. Earlier, official reports said that Ntare had been killed in the fighting when his supporters tried to free him.

The initial rising, according to the first official account broadcast over the Burundi radio on May 29, took place on the night of April 29 between 7 and 8:30 P.M. Some 10,000 Hutus and a number of "Mulelists," followers of the late Congolese revolutionary leader Pierre Mulele, carried out nearly simultaneous attacks in four areas of the country.

The rebels were said to have come mainly from a training base in the woods of northern Tanzania. They were reportedly armed with poisoned machetes, clubs, a few automatic weapons and gasoline bombs.

At Bujumbura, fewer than 100 persons took part in the attack, which was aimed principally at the radio station, near a military camp.

An argument at a service station over payment for the fuel for the gasoline bombs is said to have alerted the army camp. Two officers who came out to investigate the incident were killed before the rebels were dispersed. Another group of rebels clashed with troops in front of the cathedral and a third band attacked private vehicles at an intersection near the military camp, burning a dozen cars and killing about a dozen persons.

Main Attack in South

The main attack took place in the south in an area along the main highway between Rumonge and Nyanza-Lac. It was said that 4,600 rebels took part in a systematic slaughter of Tutsis in the region. Local Hutus were ordered to join in the hunt and shared the Tutsis' fate if they refused.

Another group of 3,000 rebels attacked in the Bururi region, the homeland of the President and most of the present Tutsi rulers. Nearly every army officer is said to have lost some member of his family in the attack. President Micombero said his brother-in-law had been slain.

Forty of the chief administrators were also killed, including the district commissioner, the attorney general and his assistants, doctors and accountants, as well as many of their wives and children.

At the same time, about 100 attackers from Tanzania assaulted the military post of Cankuzo in the east, where a large number of Tutsi refugees from Rwanda had settled. However, this band was rapidly "cut into pieces" by the defending forces, the Bujumbura radio said.

A fourth attack was said to have taken place at Kitega, where the former King was being held. However, although the town was beseiged by rebels, according to the official report, residents of Kitega said they had heard no fighting.

Eyewitnesses at Bururi confirmed official reports that the assailants were mainly Hutus, using Mulelist tactics. They were said to have smoked hashish, to have worn white saucepans stained with blood as helmets, and to have had their bodies tattooed with magic signs as immunity against attack.

The rebels, fired with drugs, were said to have killed all the

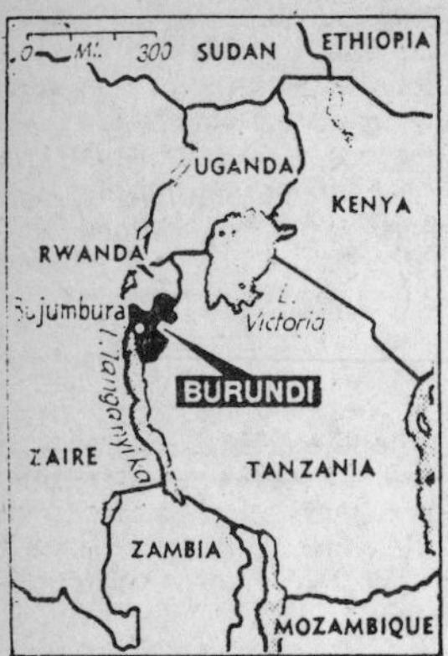

The New York Times/June 11, 1972

Tutsis they could find, generally cutting them to pieces with their machetes.

Normally Burundi people are not drug users, but witchdoctors played an important role in this attack, according to Colonel Micombero. He said that the Mulelist trainers would shoot blank bullets at a man to show his immunity and then shoot a dog or cat with real bullets to show that the animal had died because it did not cry out the words that conferred protection.

"We have tangible proof that Mulelists from Zaire participated in the rising," President Micombero said. He charged that the Zairian oppositionists wanted to use Burundi as a base to attack the regime of President Mobutu Sese Seko. He asserted that Martin Kasongo, a well-known Mulelist, had taken part in the Burundi rising, had stolen four million francs at Nyanza-Lac and had disappeared.

"I want his head," said Colonel Micombero.

Asked how long the repression would last, the President snapped: "They're still tracking down the persons responsible for the genocide of Jews in World War II and that's more than 20 years ago. You can easily understand that we are still taking action against criminals six weeks after the genocide here."

The initial slaughter took place in a period of 24 hours, but isolated attacks lasted for two weeks. At Martyazo, in the Bururi region, the rebels set up a "people's republic" and remained entrenched for nearly two weeks before they were routed out, the President said.

The army, gendarmes and youth brigades rapidly put the rebellion down in most areas of the south, according to available information. However, some 100 rebels are believed to be still hiding in the bush, coming out at night to steal food.

The repression that followed the attack has been extreme, according to all independent sources. The authorities announced that they had uncovered a secret "organization for genocide and coup d'état" and said they had proof that the aggressors not only wanted "to overthrow the republican institutions but also had a highly detailed organized plan for the systematic extermination of the whole Tutsi race."

The President said that "thousands" of Hutu names were on the lists of persons paying dues to the rebel organization.

Large-scale arrests started with the four Hutu members of the Government. Pascal Bubiriza, Minister of Telecommunications, was said to have confessed that the massacre had been aimed at the Tutsis.

On May 7, it was announced that "a good number" of Hutus had been found guilty of taking part in the plot and had been executed.

The Revolutionary Youth brigades took the lead in what are widely described as arbitrary arrests and killings. These were aggravated by personal acts of revenge, with people being denounced as plotters because of disputes over land or a cow.

"It was barbaric, unbelievably inhuman," said a foreign resident who had seen a man clubbed to death in front of the Bujumbura post office by a gang of Revolutionary Youth.

"They picked up almost all the Hutu intellectuals above secondary school level," a Tutsi professor said.

Many Students Vanished

The universiy here was severely affected. Students were seen assaulting Hutus in the university grounds, beating them to death with rocks and clubs. In the beginning, soldiers came into the lecture halls, threw them into trucks and took them away.

In the first week of repression at Bujumbura, witnesses said, Hutus were piled up in trucks and taken off for burial at a mass grave at the airport. "I used to see the trucks almost every evening at around 9, after the curfew, going down Avenue Lumumba in front of the cathedral and sometimes I could hear people screaming inside," one resident said.

The churches have been particularly hard hit. Twelve Hutu priests are said to have been killed and thousands of Protestant pastors, school directors and teachers. In the Bujumbura hospitals, six doctors and eight nurses were arrested and are believed to be dead.

In its "truth broadcasts," the Burundi radio has said almost nothing about the repression that has followed the rebellion. The rebels were given "the punishment they deserved" and "only the guilty Hutus" were arrested, it has said. "One cannot even speak of repression but legitimate defense because our country is at war," the state radio emphasized.

Evidence Viewed as Flimsey

Most independent observers are inclined to accept the official position that there was a Hutu plot. However the origin of the name lists, the evidence of guilt and the severity of the punishment are widely questioned.

It is also increasingly asked why the authorities did not act to prevent the initial outbreak, since there had been reports of unusual movements in the south six weeks before the rising. Some church sources wonder whether the staging of the attack was permitted so as to provide justification for broad repression.

The slaughter has been a serious blow to the economy. In the south, the missions are trying to get refugees out of the bush to harvest the cotton, bananas and coffee, but it seems that much of the crops will be lost.

Foreign observers generally question whether reconciliation can ever be possible after so much killing. In the city area here where Hutus and Tutsis live side by side, the two tribes are terrified of each other, and word has spread that all Tutsi families should get rid of Hutu houseboys for fear of poison or some other form of retaliation.

June 11, 1972

Zambia Cutting Trade Dependence on Rhodesia

By ANTHONY LEWIS
Special to The New York Times

LUSAKA, Zambia, Aug. 16—The great mines and smelters of the Zambian Copperbelt turn out 60,000 tons of refined copper a month. Until this year all of it reached the outside world by way of the Rhodesian railways.

This month 24,000 tons of Zambian copper will have gone out by rail, road and air without crossing Rhodesia. By about next March routes outside Rhodesia should be ready to handle Zambia's entire copper output.

Copper is just one example of a remarkable economic story—the effort to reorient the whole Zambian economy as a result of Rhodesia's declaration of independence from Britain last November.

Outside experts here are convinced now that, no matter what happens in Rhodesia, Zambia will push on to cut free of Rhodesia economically. They regard the progress so far as dramatic in the light of the difficulties Zambia has faced.

Economy Looked South

For 40 years under British rule and then in the Federation of Rhodesia and Nyasaland, Zambia's economy was arranged to look south. The main artery was the rail line crossing the Zambezi River to Rhodesia at Livingstone. The principal surfaced road out of this landlocked country went south.

Rhodesia's declaration of independence brought overwhelming political motivation for a change in that pattern. Zambia wants to cut ties to do what damage she can to white-ruled Rhodesia and to end her own dependence on the Rhodesians.

Gasoline is a good example of the difficulties and the accomplishments. At the end of last year Zambia was using about 15,000 tons a month, all of it brought in by Rhodesian rail. Most observers were skeptical that alternative routes were feasible.

Rhodesia offered to let the gasoline go through by rail to Zambia although Rhodesia herself faced oil sanctions. Zambia said no.

At first Zambia's needs were met — barely — by an emergency airlift operated by Britain, Canada and the United

States. But the cost was extremely high, and the desire was for a more economical surface route.

The only immediate possibility was the Great North Road running 1,200 miles northeast from Lusaka to the railhead near Dar es Salaam in Tarzania. But it was this road that aroused skepticism. Almost all of it is unsurfaced and many miles are extremely dangerous.

Road Operates Successfully

Over that road now trucks are bringing in more than the previous requirement of 15,000 tons a month. How much more the Government will not say. The need is up and stockpiling is going on.

Apart from driving conditions, the Great North Road presented economic obstacles as a practical gasoline route. When tank trucks were used they had to go back empty. If steel drums were carried on ordinary trucks, the trucks could return carrying copper, but then the drums piled up at the Zambian end.

American ingenuity helped to solve the problem. The United States Rubber Company, Inc., developed a rubber gasoline container that looks like a giant inflatable camp pillow.

Two pillow tanks with a capacity of about 3,000 gallons are carried on a special truck designed by Fiat, an Italian company. When emptied the rubber tanks roll up to take only a few inches of space and the trucks can go back full of copper.

Eight hundred pillow tanks have been ordered for $1.4-million, as well as 450 trucks. One hundred twelve trucks and many tanks have already arrived.

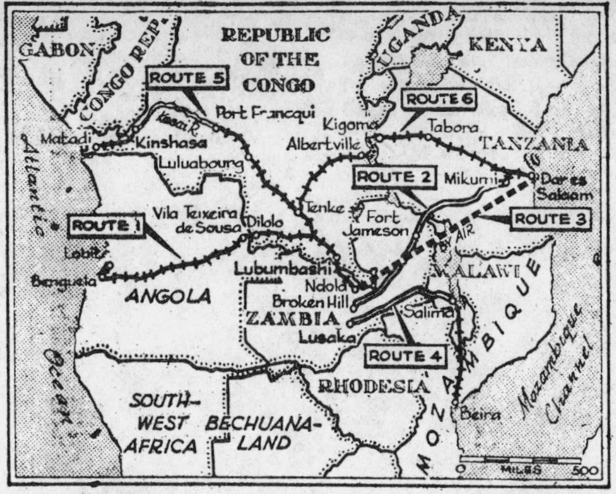

The New York Times — Aug. 17, 1966

Map shows six routes now in use or envisaged to move Zambia's copper ingots to the sea for the export market.

Operators of Trucking

The trucks are operated by Zamtan Road Services, Ltd., in which Zambia and Tanzania own a 35 per cent share each and Fiat 30 per cent. Fiat manages it.

Gasoline rationed to ordinary users at 12 gallons a month, sells for 56 cents an imperial gallon (1.2 United States gallons). It costs the Zambian Government a good deal more—how much is not made public.

Government sources say the subsidy ran as high as 50 cents a gallon but is down to 25 cents as road shipments replace the airlifts. The only airlift still going on is a British one, bringing aviation fuel at considerable expense from Dar es Salaam.

There are two giant copper companies, Anglo-American and the Roan Selection Trust. Their natural economic inclination is to keep established links southward. But they now recognize that they cannot and are fully committed to altering their trading pattern.

Plans for handling copper ingot exports reflect ingenuity, to say the least. Six different routes are in use or envisaged.

The first route is by rail up into the Congo and west through Portuguese Angola to Lobito. This is now carrying more than 15,000 tons a month, and extra cars and improvements to the line are expected to double the capacity.

The second route is the Great North Road, over which more than 5,000 tons a month move now. Traffic is scheduled to build up to 25,000 tons after the rainy season, which runs from November to March.

The third route is the airlift in two C-130 jets bought by the Roan Selection Trust. They carry more than 2,000 tons a month now to Dar es Salaam, usually bringing in gasoline on the return trip. Next month two more of the planes, ordered by the Government, will arrive, doubling the capacity.

A Route to Mozambique

The fourth route is by the mostly unsurfaced road east to Salima, in Malawi, there transferring to the rail line running south to Beira, in Portugese Mozambique. This month's figure for that route is 2,000 tons. Next month it is expected to be above 6,000 tons and the eventual goal is double that.

The fifth route, projected to carry more than 5,000 tons a month beginning perhaps six months from now, starts on the Congolese railroad and goes north to the Kasai River. Then barges are to take the loads to Kinshasa (formerly Leopoldville) and from there a railroad line leads to the mouth of the Congo at Matadi.

Finally, there is another complicated route by rail north and east through the Congo to Albertville, across Lake Tanganyika by barge to Kigoma and from there by rail to Dar es Salaam. That is projected to carry 4,000 tons a month starting next winter.

August 17, 1966

Development Programs Pushed In Zambia to Recast Economy

By ANTHONY LEWIS
Special to The New York Times

LUSAKA, Zambia—Within the next few weeks final approval is expected to be given for a 1,000-mile oil pipeline to supply this landlocked country in the heart of Africa.

The pipeline will run from Dar es Salaam, Tanzania, to Ndola in the Zambian copper belt. It will cost about $50-million and take two years to build.

Before the end of this year a West German contractor will start surfacing the Great North Road that connects Lusaka with Dar es Salaam. This project, including major reconstruction of the road in Tanzania, is also scheduled for completion in two years.

To improve the harbor at Dar es Salaam, new lighter vessels have been ordered, and a 100,000-square-foot goods shed is under construction. Contracts for three new deep-water berths are to go out in the fall.

These projects are examples of one of the most ambitious development programs in Africa. Zambia is trying to do no less than to recast her economic structure.

The motive here is more urgent than the general desire to become more prosperous. White-dominated Rhodesia's unilateral declaration of independence has made Zambia desperate to end her economic reliance on Rhodesia.

Last year more than 97 per cent of Zambia's exports and imports went through or came from Rhodesia. Food and coal and electric power came from the white-led land south of the Zambesi, and Zambian copper moved out over Rhodesian railways.

The development plan for the next five years is fundamentally designed to disengage Zambia from Rhodesia. In addition to the items mentioned above, it includes these projects:

¶The long-discussed proposal for a rail link between Lusaka and Dar es Salaam. Anglo-Canadian consultants are understood to have filed a favorable report on the line, which would cost more than $300-million.

¶Major improvements to the main alternative rail line, which goes up into the Congo, then west and out through Portuguese Angola to the port of Lobito on the Atlantic. Officials of this railroad have asked Zambia for a 10-year commitment to rebuild parts of the line and buy new rolling stock.

¶A huge new hydroelectric power dam at Kafue, costing $150-million. The aim of this project will be to end Zambia's dependence on power from the generators on the Rhodesian side of the Kariba Dam.

A Different Situation

The formidable list of investment plans is not so fanciful as some Western observers, grown skeptical about Africa because of past disappointments, might believe.

Zambia is different because she is so rich in copper. This basic wealth makes possible loans from the International Bank for Reconstruction and is expected to be built as a strictly business proposition by a private company. More than one are believed to have expressed interest.

The lucky winner of the building authorization is the Lonhro Corporation. Its main asset, a pipeline from Beira in Portuguese Mozambique to Umtali in Rhodesia, has been shut off by the oil sanctions against Rhodesia. But Rhodesia is compensating Lonhro for that loss.

The plan is to pump finished oil products through the pipe at first. When demand grows large enough, a refinery would be built in Zambia and crude oil brought through the pipeline.

Economic planners in Zambia, most of whom are white advisers to the Government, are convinced that Rhodesia's declaration of independence will actually help Zambia economically in the long run. Their argument is that it has forced this country to begin a desirable kind of development.

August 27, 1966

Zambia Is Attempting to Steer a Neutral Course

By BENJAMIN WELLES
Special to The New York Times

NDOLA, Zambia, May 19—One of the world's richest copper lodes, discovered here 40 years ago, has helped to make this landlocked nation one of the richest of the new African states.

However, the vast copper wealth, which brings Zambia more than $500-million in yearly export earnings appears to have increased rather than diminished her domestic and foreign problems—especially the complex racial issue.

Independent from Britain since 1964, ruled firmly but paternalistically by Dr. Kenneth Kaunda — "K.K." to his friends —Zambia is surrounded by seven African neighbors, at least four of which are ruled by white minorities: South-West Africa, Portuguese Angola, Mozambique and Rhodesia. This has stirred deep passions in this sensitive new nation, formerly Northern Rhodesia.

Rhodesia's unilateral declaration of independence from British rule on Nov. 17, 1965, has not only put Zambia economically at the mercy of her neighbor to the south, but has made Zambians question the loyalty of the 60,000 white "Europeans" who live in Zambia alongside the 3.5 million Africans. The great majority are believed to accept Zambian independence loyally, but periodic "plots" are widely reported in the Government-controlled news media and the nerves of many Zambians are tense.

Copper Goes Through Rhodesia

About half of the 700,000 tons of top-grade copper mined here every year passes 1,500 miles to the sea over Rhodesian railways through Rhodesia and out through Portuguese Mozambique to the port of Beira. A fourth travels twice as far, through the Congo and out through Portuguese Angola to Lobito. The final quarter is shipped by truck on Lockheed C-130 transports that fly 20-ton loads 840 miles twice daily from here to Dar es Salaam — at $140 a ton compared with about $50 a ton on the railroads.

Shipping its major export through white-ruled areas is economically vital to Zambia, but politically it is humiliating. Nonetheless, President Kaunda is grappling against odds to preserve a multiracial society in Zambia where Africans and Europeans can live in harmony.

"So long as white minority rule continues in Rhodesia, Portuguese Africa and South Africa," he is understood to have told Under Secretary of State Nicholas de B. Katzenbach yesterday, "African relations with the West will remain distorted and we Africans will challenge those concepts of majority rule, democracy and Christianity that the West has taught us to believe."

Students Question Katzenbach

Mr. Katzenbach, who is making an orientation tour of a dozen African nations, met President Kaunda yesterday for a private talk in Lusaka, the capital. The two men conferred at the stately brick colonial mansion that was the residence of British Governors.

As President Kaunda and Mr. Katzenbach posed on the terrace with their wives and advisers for photographers, Mr. Kaunda, clad in a well-tailored gray bush jacket and trousers, drew his guests' attention to the surrounding park. Zambian security men could be seen discreetly pacing behind the trees.

President Kaunda's emphasis on racial complaints is shared by the nation's intellectuals. Mr. Katzenbach was challenged by a dozen students at the University of Zambia in Lusaka about racial inequities in the United States, about North Vietnam and about the United States so-called intervention in the affairs of small nations such as Vietnam and the Dominican Republic.

"Why does the United States continue to supply arms to Portugal for use against African freedom-lovers?" asked one African student.

Mr. Katzenbach recalled the United States' treaty obligations with the North Atlantic Treaty Organization, of which Portugal is a charter member, and of Portugal's agreement not to use American arms in connection with any African problem.

While he succeeded in presenting the United States viewpoint, it was evident that these issues deeply impair the United States impression among young African intellectuals.

Mr. Kaunda is fully conscious of this concern among his people. He is trying to steer a neutralist course and not be committed to either of what many Africans call the two world blocs: United States-West or Communist China.

A speech given unexpectedly in Lusaka a fortnight ago by Justus Paletskis, chairman of the Soviet assembly who was leading a goodwill mission at the inauguration of the new Zambian House of Parliament, created a diplomatic storm here and exacerbated fears of involvement in cold war politics.

Communists Are Assailed

"Just who do these Russians and Chinese think they are to bring their venomous ideological battles to Zambia?" protested the Zambia News editorially after the Chinese Communist Ambassador had in turn assailed the Russian visitor.

As a result, according to Western residents, President Kaunda has tightened orders restricting contacts between foreign embassies—of West or East—and the Government and people of Zambia. All Embassies are limited to 12 officers, except Commonwealth missions, which may have 15. Diplomats are forbidden to go more than 25 miles from Lusaka without permission.

Not only is Mr. Kaunda now isolating himself from visiting journalists, but as the President's example spreads down the bureaucratic grapevine, Zambian officials who formerly dealt with Americans are now apologetically disassociating themselves. In theory, all foreign contacts with Zambians must in the future be arranged by the Foreign Ministry.

But, as one diplomat said, "If we obeyed Kaunda's orders literally his Foreign Ministry would be so swamped with paperwork that it would grind to a halt within 24 hours." In a variety of ways Mr. Kaunda is determined to steer a meticulously neutral foreign policy line, although he has accepted some $9-million in United States aid in the three years since independence. Half of this has gone to underwriting the copper airlift.

"You can't really blame Zambians for feeling jumpy," said one long-time resident.

"They're training Zambian technicians as fast as they can for mines, for education, for agriculture and for other things," he added, "but they'll still be dependent on Europeans for 10 or 15 years at least. In time, this edginess will pass. At the moment, there's a strong undercurrent of suspicion between blacks and whites here."

May 21, 1967

Zambians Feel Threat on 3 Sides

Kaunda Warns 'Mad' People of Action

By ALFRED FRIENDLY Jr.
Special to The New York Times

LUSAKA, Zambia—Zambia's black leaders see themselves menaced by the white-ruled regimes to the south, east and west.

In a recent speech President Kenneth D. Kaunda said that Zambia's independence was meaningless as long as colonalists were plotting against her.

"They are mad people," he said. "They need treatment, and the treatment we can give them is action." His country is offering hospitality and moral support to black nationalist organizations from all three of the neighboring lands—the Portuguese territories of Angola to the west and Mozambique to the east, and Rhodesia to the south—and from South Africa and South-West Africa as well.

Despite the bravado of the 43-year-old President, he has had difficulty in the 41 months since independence from Britain in matching his means to his goals.

Before November, 1965, when Rhodesia declared herself independent, 98 per cent of Zambia's imports came either from or through that country. Rhodesia, formerly known as Southern Rhodesia, and Zambia, formerly Northern Rhodesia, had once been partners in the Federation of Rhodesia and Nyasaland.

Black Africans Bitter

Black Africa, including Zambia, responded with bitterness to the Rhodesian independence move, which sought to assure continued white rule despite the black majority.

But Zambia has been unable to make a complete break either with Rhodesia or with her other white-ruled enemies. She has had to content herself with strong words and compromise. Cynics refer to the combination by the acronym ZANY, which stands for Zambia Almost Never Yields.

Since April, 1966, Zambia's main supplier has been Rhodesia's leading backer, South Africa. Of all the essential imports that used to cross Rhodesia, only oil has been completely shut off.

Coal for Zambia's copper smelters still comes from the Wankie colliery south of the Zambezi River and about 40 per cent of the 666,000 tons of copper that Zambia exports each year continues to travel by Rhodesian railroads.

In May, 1966, bitter-enders in Lusaka forced through a decision to stop exporting copper from this landlocked country through Rhodesia. Two months later the exports were resumed because the backlog of the mineral had grown so large. Copper accounts for 93 per cent of Zambia's exports and 55 per cent of governmental revenues.

The present modus vivendi is an uneasy one. Rhodesia can cut off Zambia's electric power from the Rhodesian side of the Kariba Dam with one flick of a switch. This has not been done, but Zambia, believing that it might be, is anxiously seeking outside financing for her own $103.6-million hydroelectric project in the gorge of the Kafue River.

Pipeline Is Speeded

Italian engineers are speeding construction of an oil pipeline from Dar es Salaam, Tanzania, to Zambia's copperbelt. With promised United States aid, Zambia is hoping to see the worst stretch of the 1,200-mile road link to Dar es Salaam resurfaced. She is also slowly negotiating an agreement that would have Communist China construct the parallel Tanzam railroad.

These efforts are costing Zambia dearly in deferred development.

The slim, dapper Finance Minister, Elijah Mudenda, estimates that because of the violent readjustment of planning that followed Rhodesia's independence move, nearly half of Zambia's capital outlays are going into basic economic development that yields few immediate returns.

This year he presented the first budget to include outside loans and grants as a major source of Zambia's capital expenditures. This amount is $120-million.

"It is like a left arm trying to transplant itself from one body to another, one businessman said in describing Zambia's what is called a prudent disengagement from traditional suppliers and transporters. But however painful the operation, Zambians insist that it be carried through.

President Kaunda accompanies these economic moves with an advocacy of nonviolence, a political philosophy that he calls humanism and easily aroused suspicions of white antagonism.

During a pre-independence campaign against discrimination by butchers who sold meat to blacks that was often rotten, Mr. Kaunda, already a teetotaler, became a vegetarian as well. And when whites who stayed in Zambia showed themselves sympathetic to the Rhodesian regime, the President felt himself compelled to emasculate his own police force by dismissing 15 whites in the Special Security Branch.

There are still about 3,000 whites in government service here, but many of them are young technocrats without the strong ties in Zambia of earlier settlers.

Even they are nevertheless suspect in a country where Rhodesian warplanes and South African soldiers occasionally make peaceable incursions. "To the Government's mind," declared one of the 10 whites in Parliament, "every white face in this country is a potential saboteur."

Recently, when a crowd marched through Lusaka's wide streets on the anniversary of the slaughter of demonstrating South African blacks at Sharpeville in 1960, President Kaunda declared to the throng: "If I had to choose between nonviolence and slavery and violence and freedom I would choose violence and freedom."

But while Zambia makes black nationalist organizations from neighboring white-ruled countries welcome, she is showing signs of being embarrassed by their presence and their relative lack of success.

"If you are not cowards, stand up!," Mr. Kaunda told youthful demonstrators against South Africa recently. "We will organize you and give you the tools to finish the job."

The exiles have heard the message before, but still seem unable to respond with coordinated attacks on the white regimes below the Zambezi. "One cannot blame them very much if they get disappointed and start drinking,'" said Mr. Mudenda.

Observers are asking whether Zambia can keep up her militant pan-Africanism in the face of strong tribal divisions, which are beginning to show through the political fabric. A hard-fought party election last August brought victory to the faction led by Vice President Simon Kapwepwe. Mr. Kapwepwe, a long-time colleague of the President, has brought members of his Cibemba language group—a third of all Zambians—to positions of leadership in both the party and the Government.

In February, however, resentment against his maneuvering broke out at another party meeting. Mr. Kaunda threatened to resign, and forced Mr. Kapwepwe, in tears, to beg him to stay on.

"The President is our indispensable man," said a Cabinet Minister. "We were really on the brink of a complete breakdown."

The President is also deeply concerned over the possibility of race war in southern Africa. He warned Britain, France, the United States and the Soviet Union, all of which he said were supporting South Africa with capital, that if they did not "arrest the madness of white people, the black people of Africa will act on their own."

"It's going to be white against black," he said.

A race war is a complete contradiction of Mr. Kaunda's devoutly held principles.

In Lusaka, where handsome new buildings can hardly go up fast enough to meet the housing needs, the prospect of such violence seems distant and unreal.

Nontheless, "the conflict is almost in the situation itself," George Silundika, a black Rhodesian nationalist leader said, "whether Zambia likes it or not."

April 3, 1968

Tanzanian Pipeline to Zambia Opened

By LAWRENCE FELLOWS

Special to The New York Times

NDOLA, Zambia, Sept. 2—With the formal opening today of the oil pipeline from the Tanzanian port of Dar es Salaam to this town in Zambia's copperbelt, the long and difficult oil famine in Zambia has at last been brought to an end.

The ceremony marked a new step ahead for Zambia in her struggle to extricate herself from her historic, but unwanted, economic partnership with Rhodesia, the white-dominated state on her southern border.

The pipeline represented more than just a new economic link with Tanzania, the black-governed state to the north. It was a line thrown into the East African community, the whole network of trade and tariff agreements and essential services shared by Tanzania, Kenya and Uganda.

The ceremony today also marked the end of one of the most perilous, uncertain and wildly uneconomic routes of fuel supply. The hazardous 1,250-mile route of truck drivers led through swamps and along treacherous escarpments, through dust and mud and families of snarling baboons. It was known as "Hell Run."

Oil Run Built Up in 1965

It cost the lives of a hundred truck drivers from the time the oil run built up gradually after supplies from Rhodesia were cut in 1965, when it proclaimed independence from Britain and Zambia started looking for new sources of oil.

Both President Kenneth D. Kaunda of Zambia and President Julius K. Nyerere of Tanzania paid tribute to these men today at the ceremony at the oil terminal in Ndola.

Both spoke of the hardships Zambia had endured in tearing loose all her old economic ties with the south and fixing them anew with black-governed countries to the north. Both spoke realistically of the difficulties that lay ahead of Zambia before she could be cooperating fully with the three East African countries.

"Our application to become a member of the community is an expression of faith," President Kaunda said.

Zambia's ties to Rhodesia had been built up in four decades of British rule, and then tightened in the short-lived partnership with Rhodesia in political federation.

The two countries shared an airline with Malawi and its assets have finally been divided up.

The two countries shared a railway system, and the outlet it provided for Zambia's copper was southward through Rhodesia and Portuguese Mozambique to the sea.

Zambia still uses the line, but reluctantly. The copper companies are instructed to try all other means before using Rhodesian railways. But, on the average, a quarter of the copper still goes out that way.

Zambia always got the coal she needed for the copper smelters from Rhodesian fields at Wankie. The Zambians have opened their own coal fields, but the quality of the coal is poor and there is not nearly enough of it yet to free Zambia from her need for Rhodesian coal.

The Rhodesians still supply Zambia with hydro-electric power from their jointly owned dam on the Zambezi, at Kariba. The power plant is on the Rhodesian side.

Zambia has always relied heavily on Rhodesia's secondary manufacturing industries. She has cut that trade back to about half of its old level by permitting only essential goods to come in. South Africa has jumped in to fill most of the breach, but eventually Zambia will have enough lines open to the north so she can cut back on the South African trade, too.

Virtually all of Zambia's oil supplies came from Rhodesia's refinery at Feruka. That was shut down when the British blockaded Beira, and stopped the flow of crude oil to the refinery. Rhodesia offered to refine crude for Zambia, without taking any for itself, but Zambia refused and the oil run down from the north was on.

An oil airlift was organized by Britain, Canada and the United States, but it was an expensive measure meant only for temporary relief.

Trucks and oil drums were gathered from half the world, but the rough course over "Hell Run" rubbed holes in the drums, and very often half the gasoline was lost. Sometimes dishonest drivers took it, and blamed the road. Huge rubber sausage-like containers were tried, but these also failed to take the strain. A road tanker fleet was finally built up, but these trucks were of no use in taking copper out on the return run to Dar es Salaam.

September 3, 1968

Kaunda Assumes Control Of Zambian Industries

Special to The New York Times

LUSAKA, Zambia, Jan. 29—President Kenneth Kaunda took virtual control of Zambia's mining, industry and commerce today.

He named himself chairman of a new Mining and Industrial Development Corporation, which will succeed the present Industrial Development Corporation on April 1.

The new group will have two subsidiaries, Indeco, to handle industrial investments, and Mindeco, to control mineral developments.

The mining subsidiary will hold the 51 per cent share, taken over by the Zambian Government Jan. 1, of the two copper producers—Roan Selection Trust, Ltd., partly owned by United States interests, and Anglo American Corporation of South Africa, Ltd., partly South African and British.

To Control New Ventures

The subsidiary will also administer the Government's control of any new ventures.

In setting up the new organization, the President said, he is trying to keep mining and industry in touch with the political feeling of the country, while leaving a large part of management in the care of experts.

The board of directors named to the new corporation by Mr. Kaunda includes Cabinet ministers, civil servants, trade unionists and other representatives of Zambian society.

The President said that the industrial subsidiary would become increasingly self-financing, with dividends invested in places of fastest expansion. He said he expected to see Indeco borrow more from nongovernment sources both inside and outside Zambia.

Andrew Sardanis, permanent secretary in the Ministry of State Participation and chairman of the existing Industrial Development Corporation, will become managing director of the subsidiaries.

Copper is a billion-dollar industry in Zambia, which is the world's third largest producer of the metal, with an output in 1968 of 655,000 short tons. Zambia also has deposits of talc, tin, mica, amethyst, coal, manganese and lime, which are being developed.

Under the terms of the takeover, to which the companies acceded, Zambia will pay compensation for the shares with negotiable dollar bonds issued over a 12-year period at the rate of about $20-million a year. The Government put the value of the mines last November at about $575-million.

The new arrangement also provides that the companies pay 51 per cent of their profits to the Government corporation. The companies have contracts with it as management consultants under which they will retain day-to-day supervision of production.

January 30, 1970

ZAMBIA TO PURCHASE CORN FROM RHODESIA

Special to The New York Times

LUSAKA, Zambia, July 11—Zambia, faced with a heavy drain on her foreign exchange and the problem of keeping four million landlocked people from going hungry, is to modify her policy against trading with Rhodesia and buy corn from that country.

The Zambian Government announced last night that it was ordering 1.5 million bags of corn—a direct breach of United Nations sanctions against Rhodesia. Zambia has been one of the most outspoken critics of white domination of African masses in southern Africa.

She has accused the Portuguese of blockading Zambian food imports at the Mozambique seaports of Beira and Nacala.

The Zambian Government had achieved a large measure of success, after heavy sacrifices, in reducing economic links with Rhodesia. Imports from Rhodesia decreased from $76.8-million in 1965 to less than $24-million last year, and much of this was in electric power from a joint undertaking. Zambia had halted almost all food imports from Rhodesia and has withdrawn from common rail services.

July 12, 1971

OPPOSITION PARTY BANNED IN ZAMBIA

Ex-Vice President Is Among 134 Leaders Arrested

Special to The New York Times

LUSAKA, Zambia, Feb. 4—President Kenneth D. Kaunda banned one of Zambia's two Opposition parties today, arrested its leader, former Vice President Simon M. Kapwepwe, and ordered the arrest of 133 other leaders of Mr. Kapwepwe's United Progressive party.

The ban leaves only one Opposition party, the African National Congress. Mr. Kaunda has said he favors a single-party system instead of the multiparty parliamentary system inherited from British colonial days. He is now expected to appoint a committee to recommend the constitutional changes.

In an early-morning broadcast the President said that he

Camera Press
Simon M. Kapwepwe

had acted after "most careful and exhaustive investigations" and alleged that the party was "bent on violence and destruction" and had "shown no respect for life and property."

The United Progressive party was founded by Mr. Kapwepwe, a boyhood friend of Mr. Kaunda's, after he and others broke away from the governing United National Independence party.

Mr. Kapwepwe's wife said by telephone that her husband was taken away by two policemen at 5 A.M.

Mr. Kaunda charged that Mr. Kapwepwe's party had carried out "outrageous actions aimed at the destruction of life and property."

There have been numerous acts of violence in this landlocked Central African nation in the last month, and Mr. Kaunda said that their incidence was increasing. He charged that attempts had been made to blow up Freedom House, his party's national headquarters here.

Mr. Kaunda said that the police and army had been put on an alert, but the country appeared calm.

The arrests, under security regulations that enable suspects to be held indefinitely without trial, followed a similar wave of detentions four months ago, when more than 100 of Mr. Kapwepwe's supporters were detained. Some had been released, but the exact number still held has not been made public.

February 5, 1972

NEGRO CONGRESS TO MEET HERE

Fourth Pan-African Meeting Will Have Delegates From Several Countries—Problems of The Dark Continent to Be Discussed

TO the fourth Pan-African Congress meeting in New York Aug. 21 to 24, will come representatives of the negro populations of the Gold Coast, British West Africa, Nigeria, Sierra Leone, French Africa, Belgian Congo, Guadaloupe and the United States. This conference is not to mark a recrudescence of the now defunct "Back to Africa Movement," originated by Marcus Garvey, the self-styled Provisional President of All the Africas. Instead, it aims to develop an international sentiment on the negro's problems by exposing them fully to view. It will meet unostentatiously in the negro churches of Harlem, with hardly more than one hundred delegates.

The congress represents the Pan-African movement, which is intended to reinforce the efforts of negroes to improve their conditions in their present homes. Its effort is to draw the negro's problems and interests in all parts of the world into a common cause so that they may be faced with a united front. One of the announcements issued by the Committee on Foreign Policy of the Fourth Pan-African Congress reads:

"The question of the status of the negro in modern society is no longer a domestic problem of the United States, or a parochial problem of Jamaica, or a colonial policy problem. It is rather a great world-wide problem to be viewed and considered as a whole, and the congress particularly desires that the relations of the black and white races in various countries be considered to the end that greater harmony may ensue."

How the Race Is Faring.

The program arranged, while dealing mostly with Africa, begins with descriptions by the delegates of conditions existing at present in various countries. Opportunity will be provided to question the speakers and debate the points raised. The other topics included are: African missions, education in Africa, art and literature in Africa, the political partition of Africa, the history of Africa, the slave trade and the dispersed children of Africa, the economic development of Africa and its importance in the world and the future of Africa.

The congress centres in the personality of Dr. W. E. B. Du Bois, editor of Crisis and the leading protagonist of liberal opinion among negroes. The idea of the congress came into being in 1900, at the time of the Paris Expositon, when a Pan-African conference was held in London. Coleridge Taylor, the negro musical composer, of London; Dr. Du Bois, the Colenso family, Alexander Walters and T. J. Colloway were among the participants. But it took almost a score of years for the idea germinated at this conference to come to fruition.

Just after the World War, when the political atmosphere was charged with the doctrines of self-government, the negro manifested unrest. His demands for a greater degree of participation in economic and political life were let loose in the midst of acclamation of President Wilson's Fourteen Points. Out of this general political confusion and racial unrest issued the first Pan-African Congress, which met in Paris in February, 1919.

Since then there have been the second and third Pan-African congresses. The second, that of 1921, met in London, Brussels and Paris; the third met in Lisbon in 1923.

A Voice in Their Government.

The first congress laid down its fundamental objective when it resolved that, "Wherever persons of African descent are civilized and able to meet the tests of surrounding culture they shall be accorded the same rights as their fellow citizens; they shall not be denied on account of race or color a voice in their own government, justice before the courts and economic and social equality according to ability and desert." For the natives of Africa it advocated participation in their "government as fast as their development permits, in conformity with the principle that Government exists for the natives, and not the natives for the Government."

The methods sanctioned by the congress for the realization of its ideals were solely moral suasion and the arousing of international public opinion. Its recommendation to the Peace Conference read:

"Whenever it is proved that African natives are not receiving just treatment at the hands of any State or that any State deliberately excludes its civilized citizens or subjects of negro descent from its body politic and cultural, it shall be the duty of the League of Nations to bring the matter to the attention of the civilized world."

The Negro's Eight Points.

The second Pan-African Congress petitioned the League of Nations to set aside a section in the International Bureau of Labor to deal with the conditions and needs of native labor, especially in Africa. The labor problems of the world, it asserted, could never be solved so long as colored labor "is enslaved and neglected," and it urged a thorough investigation.

The third Pan-African Congress took up the needs of the race as a whole. It urged the League to "appoint direct diplomatic representatives in the mandated territories with duties to investigate and report conditions," and to appoint representatives of the negro race on the Mandates Commission and in the International Labor Bureau. The Executive Committee, as well, formulated at that time the following needs of its people:

1. A voice in their own government.
2. The right of access to the land and its resources.
3. Trial by juries of their peers under established forms of law.
4. Free elementary education for all; broad training in modern industrial technique, and higher training of selected talent.
5. The development of Africa for the benefit of Africans, and not merely for the profit of Europeans.
6. The abolition of the slave trade and of the liquor traffic.
7. World disarmament and the abolition of war; but failing this, and as long as white folk bear arms against black folk, the right of blacks to bear arms in their own defense.
8. The organization of commerce and industry so as to make the main objects of capital and labor the welfare of the many, rather than the enriching of the few.

These were proclaimed as the eight "irreducible needs of our people."

Its Policy Peaceful.

The Congress has never sought to expropriate whites now in Africa, nor to engender feeling prejudicial to what has been conceded as the white man's portion in Africa. This absence of inflammatory racialism has earned for it much approbation.

Some of the leading delegates to the congress are expected to be Chief Amoah III of the Gold Coast, British West Africa; L. C. Delmonte, Deputy from Martinique; Lamin Senghor President of the Committee for the Defense of the Negro Race, Paris; Dantes Bellegarde, Port au Prince, Haiti, and Georges Sylvain, a young Haitian physician.

August 14, 1927

SEES BRITAIN 'IN DUTCH'

Dr. Du Bois Scores Labor Party's Policy Toward Colonies

The British Labor party is already "in Dutch" with the British colonies, with a policy "sometimes worse than the Tories, and at no time better," Dr. W. E. B. DuBois declared yesterday on his return from London and Manchester, England. Dr. DuBois presided at sessions of the fifth Pan-African Congress, made up of representatives of sixty countries and colonies and attended by representatives of African and West Indian labor groups as well as representatives of the various professions.

"The tempo of the colored peoples has changed," Dr. DuBois said. "Either the British Government will extend self-government in West Africa and the West Indies or face open revolt."

The Pan-African Congress has established permanent offices in London. Since its beginning in London in 1900 sessions have been held in London, 1919; Paris, 1921; London, Paris and Brussels, 1923; London and Lisbon, 1927, and New York, 1927 and 1929.

After thirteen years as Professor of Sociology at Atlanta University, Dr. DuBois has returned to the National Association for the Advancement of Colored People as director of special research.

November 18, 1945

WORLD ROLE GOAL OF WEST AFRICANS

Negro Leaders in Gold Coast and Nigeria Also Hope for Federation, but Are Wary

Special to The New York Times.

ACCRA, Gold Coast, April 1 —Now that independence from Britain is virtually assured in the Gold Coast and eventually will be in Nigeria, nationalists of both countries are able to focus their efforts on broader objectives.

The Negro African politicians have set themselves a double goal. Their first aim, according to observers in Accra and Nigeria, is to establish a powerful commonwealth of Negro-governed African states. The other goal is an early and active role on the international scene in association with the African-Asian bloc of states, which hitherto has been almost entirely a combination of North African, Middle Eastern and Asian countries.

Full independence from Britain will enable the Gold Coast to be the first major Negro African state to qualify for such a role. It is embarking upon its first adventure on the international scene this month by sending a powerful delegation to the African-Asian conference in Indonesia. The conference marks the first successful attempt to bring African Negro and Asian representatives together.

The West African goal of participation in international events holds the greatest immediate significance. The ideal of West African union and a commonwealth of interest has ardent supporters in all the territories but is bedeviled by politics. Nigerian leaders, who were among the first to sponsor the movement, have expressed fear that any move toward federation, would be dominated by Prime Minister Kwame Nkrumah's Convention People's party, the most powerful political machine in West Africa. They point to the fact that Mr. Nkrumah already has established a Pan-African Conference office in Accra.

West Africans find themselves politically on more solid ground in their support of involvements beyond this general area. There also is the prospect of winning for the African Negro his first real voice in international councils.

This desire to look abr[illegible] has drawn the approval of members of the African-Asian bloc, particularly India and Egypt. Both those countries have done much to foster relations with West Africa.

There is a turmoil of thought in West Africa at the moment. The region's traditional associations, commercially and politically, are almost wholly with the West. Nigerian and Gold Coast nationalists, almost to a man, are products of local and American or British-guided mission schools and, in their higher educati[illegible] of British universities. But the rapid growth of local universities and a steady influx of litera[illegible]ure and ideas from the African-Asian countries are [illegible]iving new political guidance.

West Africa, with its rich natural resources and strategic geographic situation, commanding as it does some of the most vital reaches of the Atlantic, has always been taken for granted as a friendly bastion.

While there is nothing at this stage to indicate that final removal of British control will radically alter this situation, development of new ideas and alignments by the Gold Coast's Negro administrators, as well as in Nigeria, may create a different political climate in the future.

Following the general election victory of his party last June, Prime Minister Nkrumah declared that an independent Gold Coast would stand, like India, between East and West. Asked recently whether he considered India as the leader in the free world of the nonwhite peoples, he replied: "Certainly not. But we admire India tremendously and could learn a lot from her. We will develop a course of our own."

April 17, 1955

LEVEL OF PARLEY IS BLOW TO GHANA

Few Government Chiefs Will Be Present at African Meeting in Accra

By KENNETT LOVE
Special to The New York Times.

ACCRA, Ghana, April 13—A conference of independent African states scheduled to open here Tuesday has all but completed an unplanned descent from the summit to the foreign ministers level.

A proposal for an African summit meeting to include the chiefs of state or government of the independent Arab and Negro nations was first made public a year ago by Prime Minister Kwame Nkrumah of Ghana during celebrations attending the transition of Britain's Gold Coast colony into the independent Commonwealth nation of Ghana.

The purpose of the conference was to strengthen the collective voice of independent Africa in world affairs and enhance the international prestige of Ghana.

Nasser Going to Moscow

As the date of the conference approached, the Government chiefs began to drop out. First President Gamal Abdel Nasser of the United Arab Republic decided he would go to Moscow instead. President Habib Bourguiba of Tunisia declined next, it was announced here yesterday, because of the urgency of the French-Tunisian crisis.

The Libyan delegation, first to arrive, was greeted at the airport this morning by Mr. Nkrumah and a smartly turned out guard of honor. But it was headed by Foreign Minister Wahl al Buri instead of Premier Abdel Majid Kubar.

Other than Mr. Nkrumah, the only Chief of State still scheduled to participate in the conference is President William V. S. Tubman of Liberia.

Ghana's leaders are acutely disappointed and more than a little hurt at the way distant events have whittled down the caliber of the conference. But they are determined to make it an effective beginning to search for an African policy.

The agenda is expected to include the Algerian revolt against French rule, the future of the still dependent African territories, economic cooperation, an exchange of technical and scientific information and experts, coordination of foreign policy and United Nations policy, and cultural relations.

Nigerians Annoyed

In addition to the disappearance of the names of government chiefs from the program, the organizers of the conference have had other difficulties. Nigeria, which is almost but not quite independent, was annoyed at not being given some kind of a place at the table. The annoyance was increased when Mr. Nkrumah had to turn down a visit to Nigeria last week because of the pressure of preparations for the meeting.

South Africa was invited as a last-minute afterthought, but the invitation came to nothing when that country proposed that all nations having African colonial interests should be invited too.

All these burdens and embarrassments sat lightly on the average Ghanaian, who is characteristically cheerful. They were more than offset by the thrilling victory over a Togoland eleven in an international soccer match here. Ghana won 5 to 2, scoring twice in the last three minutes.

April 14, 1958

NKRUMAH WARNS AFRICAN 'RULERS'

Ghana Chief Sets Liberation of Colonial Lands as Aim of 8-Nation Parley

By KENNETT LOVE
Special to The New York Times.

ACCRA, Ghana, April 15—Liberation of colonial Africa was the keynote of the first conference of independent African states, which opened here today.

Prime Minister Kwame Nkrumah of Ghana, who organized the conference, set the tone of the meeting. After asserting that a major purpose of the conference was "to find workable arrangements for helping our brothers still languishing under colonial rule," he closed the speech by saying:

"Today we are one. If in the past the Sahara divided us, now it unites us. And an injury to one is an injury to all of us. From this conference must go out a new message: 'Hands off Africa!' Africa must be free."

Five Arab and three Negro nations are officially represented at the conference. The United Arab Republic of Egypt and Syria, the Sudan, Libya, Tunisia and Morocco are the Arab states represented. Ghana, Liberia and Ethiopia are the Negro nations in attendance.

In addition, three representatives of the Algerian rebels, headed by Mohammed Yazid, New York representative of the National Liberation Front, are here as advisers to the Tunisian and Egyptian delegations. Among unofficial observers are an exiled nationalist leader from the French Cameroons and a Somali from the Italian-administered trust territory.

The liberation theme heads a seven-point agenda prepared during the last two months by meetings at the ambassadorial level in London and Cairo. The first item reads:

"Exchange of views on foreign policy, especially in relations to the African continent, the future of the dependent territories of Africa, the Algerian problem, the racial problem and the steps to be taken to safeguard the independence and sovereignty of the independent African states."

The second item concerns economic cooperation, with special regard to industrial and agricultural development and exchange of technical, scientific and educational information. Item three deals with cultural exchanges.

Item four concerns the problem of international peace, to be considered on the basis of the United Nations Charter and the Bandung conference of Asians and Africans.

The fifth item is headed "foreign subversive activities in Africa." The sixth deals with African maritime nations. The seventh provides for setting up permanent machinery to continue the work of the conference.

Throughout his thirty-minute speech Dr. Nkrumah warned again and again against the dangers of colonialism and imperialism.

"Colonialism is not dead," he said. "It is alive today as ever before with new forms and methods."

The Prime Minister of this one-year-old British Commonwealth nation urged a policy of "positive nonalignment." He said:

"It is only by avoiding entanglement in the quarrels of the great powers that we shall be able to assert our African personality on the side of peace."

Support for the Algerian rebels was voiced by all other delegates except President William V. S. Tubman of Liberia. Dr. Sadok Mokkadem, Tunisian Foreign Minister, said:

"Despite the stubbornness of the French Government, despite border violations and extensions of the conflict, my Government will not give way to any pressure or any threat and it will continue to make every effort for the restoration of peace in Africa and realization of the legitimate aspirations of the Algerian people."

April 16, 1958

CAIRO NAMES UNIT TO GHANA PARLEY

Action Is Held Recognition by Nasser of Nkrumah's Prestige in Africa

By FOSTER HAILEY
Special to The New York Times.

CAIRO, Nov. 29—A strong delegation of intellectual leaders and publicists has been named to represent the United Arab Republic at the All-African Peoples' Conference at Accra Ghana, beginning Friday.

The naming of the delegation is recognition by Cairo of the growing importance of Dr. Kwame Nkrumah, Prime Minister of Ghana, as spokesman for the burgeoning independence movements throughout Africa.

When the invitation came to attend the second Nkrumah-led conference in nine months there had been some question here whether to send anyone at all. Despite disclaimers of any rivalry, the latest by President Gamal Abdel Nasser himself in a fiery anti-Western speech Thursday night, Dr. Nkrumah's new prominence is not relished in Cairo.

There are several reasons for this. President Nasser is much too busy with affairs more immediate and closer to Cairo at the moment than are the struggling African colonies and protectorates. But he likes to think of himself as an African leader as well as an Arab one.

When Dr. Nkrumah and his Egyptian wife visited Cairo last summer after the first Accra conference, he was accorded honors not often extended to state guests. His picture, twinned with that of President Nasser, was pasted up all over town.

The famed Nasser charm apparently did not convert Dr. Nkrumah. He still is frankly pro-Western. This was made quite evident for the whole world to read in an article he wrote for the American quarterly Foreign Affairs in its October issue.

In that article Dr. Nkrumah did not mention President Nasser but he did speak of cooperation between Ghana and Tunisia, with whose President Habib Bourguiba, President Nasser now has a fued in full swing.

Ghana also has close commercial relations with Israel, even a joint shipping line. And that is a cardinal sin in Arab lands.

There were several reasons, therefore, that could have been used to precipitate a break. Instead, a decision was taken to cooperate. There was some question whether Dr. Nkrumah could be beaten. The better plan seemed to be to join him and to send a delegation that might overshadow others, and even Ghana's own.

Mohammed Fuad Galal, president of the Arab Graduates Association, will lead the United Arab Republic delegation.

The Arab Graduates are a strong group that has influence throughout the Middle East and North Africa.

Two other members of the delegation are the editors of the Cairo morning newspaper Al Shaab and of the influential weekly Rose el Youssef. The remainder are university professors of high standing. Two members of the delegation of ten are from Syria.

Their task at Ghana obviously is to see that the conference does not show too strong a Western feeling and to keep prominently before the delegations the name of Nasser and his role as freedom leader of Africa and the Middle East.

November 30, 1958

Africa Is Warned Of New Colonialism

By KENNETT LOVE
Special to The New York Times.

ACCRA, Ghana, Dec. 8—Prime Minister Kwame Nkrumah of Ghana warned African nationalists today to beware of new forms of colonialism and imperialism carried out by non-European powers.

Addressing the opening session of the first All-African People's Conference, Dr. Nkrumah also endorsed nonviolence in the struggle for African independence. This was in blunt opposition to the policy championed in preliminary sessions by the United Arab Republic and the Algerian National Liberation Front.

"Do not let us also forget that colonialism and imperialism may come to us yet in a different guise, not necessarily from Europe," Dr. Nkrumah declared. "We must alert ourselves to be able to recognize this when it rears its head and prepare ourselves to fight against it."

Many Africans said later they presumed the warning was against communism, since the Soviet Union is an Asian as well as a European power. Others believed Dr. Nkrumah also referred to Egyptian expansionism. Some insisted that "economic imperialism" by the United States could not be ruled out.

Tom Mboya, anti-Communist head of the Kenya Federation of Labor, who was elected conference chairman, declared East African approval of Dr. Nkrumah's sentiments.

"There is nothing that any of us can add to what Kwame Nkrumah has said," Mr. Mboya remarked.

The Ghanaian leader pointedly omitted any reference to the Bandung, Indonesia, conferences of Africans and Asians, which for more than three years have been as important a rallying symbol as the United Nations Charter. Dr. Nkrumah told intimates late last week that he would ignore Bandung because he felt that President Gamal Abdel Nasser of the United Arab Republic had corrupted its principles of noninterference and intruded Asian and Communist influences into African affairs.

The purpose of the current conference of delegations from political parties and trade unions from all of Africa, Dr. Nkrumah declared, is "planning for a final assault upon imperialism and colonialism."

On the stage behind the speaker were the heads of delegations. Ahmed Boumandjii of the Algerian rebel group wore an open-neck shirt and blue jacket and looked more like a hearty Brooklyn delicatessen owner than an outlaw in exile. Beside him was Taieb Slim, Tunisian Ambassador to Britain, representing his country's Neo-Destour party. Near by was Arthur Ochwada of the Kenya Federation of Labor, wearing a Western suit and a Luo tribal headdress of black plumes on a tall stalk.

Fred McEwen of Eastern Nigeria, a conference secretary, told the assembly that 200 delegates representing fifty organizations from twenty-five African countries, colonies and other territories had arrived.

There appeared to be a claque centered on delegations from Cairo, including a number of exiled nationalists from Negro Africa and the Afro-Asian Solidarity Council, which has a Soviet Uzbek and a Chinese Communist among its members.

No greetings were read from Mr. Nasser or from United States Government leaders.

Dr. Nkrumah, who led his country to freedom within the British Commonwealth, wore a toga of brilliant cloth woven by Ashantis instead of the Western dress he wore at the governmental conference of eight independent African states here in April.

Other themes he spoke on were: pan-Africanism, or the desire for regional or continental unity through federation; "the African personality" and the evolution of African communalism into a modern Socialist pattern of society, and tribalism, which is regarded officially here as a feudal and traditional barrier to democratic progress.

Neutralism, or nonalignment, which was endorsed at the April conference, was another notable omission from Dr. Nkrumah's speech. It was endorsed briefly by Mr. Mboya in a wildly applauded off-the-cuff speech at the end of the day.

Mr. Mboya, wearing a beaded tribal hat and lionskin pouch and a dark double-breasted suit, threw away his prepared text and made a speech during which one could have heard a pin drop in the pauses between bursts of cheering and clapping.

"Some have said Africans are not yet ready to be free," he remarked. "Others have said we are not civilized enough. To this we give a simple answer:

"Civilized or not civilized, ignorant or illiterate, rich or poor, we, the African states, deserve a government of our own choice. Let us make our own mistakes, but let us take comfort in the knowledge that they are our own mistakes."

"We will not tolerate any attempt by any country—and that means any—to undermine the independence that we are fighting for," he said. "We shall never sell our freedom for capital or technical assistance."

Then he made a point of singling out for welcome fraternal delegations from the United States, especially the American Committee on Africa.

December 9, 1958

Tubman's Views Prevail

By HENRY TANNER
Special to The New York Times.

SANOQUELLI, July 18—The leaders of Liberia, Guinea and Ghana apparently have decided to delay practical steps toward unification until three more territories of this region gain independence next year.

According to conference sources, President Tubman's go-slow approach has carried the day over the "union now" concept of Dr. Nkrumah. The final declaration was expected to stress the close ties between the three countries and contain a strong but general pledge for continued efforts toward African unity.

The conference outcome appears to represent a bitter disappointment for the Ghanaian Prime Minister, who had hoped to weld the three countries immediately into a close union in which each would surrender a significan part of its sovereignty.

Dr. Nkrumah envisaged this "union" as the nucleus for a future "United States of Africa." Other African territories were to join upon achieving independence later on, according to his plan.

This would have established Dr. Nkrumah, and to a lesser extent President Tubman and President Touré, as a dominant force in West Africa before the balance of power in the region undergoes drastic changes with the emergence of independent Nigeria.

Nigeria, a British colony, is larger and economically stronger than Ghana, Guinea and Liberia together. It is scheduled to gain independence next year along with the neighboring French Cameroons and Togoland.

President Tubman, opposing Dr. Nkrumah's plan, wants to wait until Nigeria is independent and can assume a founding role in the projected organization. Mr. Tubman also favors a much looser "Association of African States," modeled after the Organization of American States and involving no sacrifice of national sovereignty by its members.

The conference has shown that President Touré of Guinea is closer to Mr. Tubman than to Dr. Nkrumah, informed sources said.

Guinea and Ghana proclaimed a bilateral union last year, but took no effective steps to implement it. Instead, they widened their consultations to bring in Liberia.

There is no common border between Guinea and Ghana. Guinea and Liberia, on the other hand, are contiguous for hundreds of miles and share potentially close economic interests. President Tubman managed to demonstrate convincingly during this conference what Guinea might gain from association with Liberia.

Sanoquelli, the conference site, is a small village of regional administration buildings and mud huts with thatched roofs, not far from the Guinea border.

On a mountain immediately above is the budding mining camp of Nimba, where the Liberian - Swedish - American industrial and financial group known as Lamcoe has started work on a $200,000,000 mining project that will make Liberia one of the world's largest iron ore producers by 1963.

Lamco is building a large harbor on the Liberian coast and will run a railroad and highway 175 miles to Nimba Mountain to move out the iron ore.

It has already proved the existence of 250,000,000 tons of iron ore of the highest quality and expects to find 250,000,000 tons more.

Large but unexplored iron ore deposits are believed to exist also on the Guinean side of the border. Unless the Guineans use the railroad and road facilities now being built on the Liberian side, they would have to transport their ore over 500 miles of roadless and undeveloped country to the port of Conakry.

Observers suggest that President Tubman may have chosen Sanoquelli instead of Monrovia, the capital, for the conference to impress his visitors.

The discussions here also dealt with the question of Algeria, the prospect of French nuclear tests in the Sahara, French policy in the Cameroons and racial discrimination in South Africa.

July 20, 1959

AFRICANS AT ODDS ON PLAN FOR UNITY

12-Nation Parley to Debate Issue of Alliance in Addis Ababa Session Today

By JAY WALZ
Special to The New York Times.

ADDIS ABABA, Ethiopia, June 19 — The delegates of twelve independent African nations will turn tomorrow to the task of building a working union with their newly won freedom.

In their conference here that began last Tuesday, the delegates have expressed divergent views on the practical form that should be taken to achieve African unity. They will debate the issue in closed sessions starting tomorrow and hope to resolve it by the time the conference adjourns next week-end.

The delegation sent by Kwame Nkrumah, Prime Minister of Ghana, has strongly supported the establishment of a United States of Africa, presumably with Mr. Nkrumah as its leader.

However, the delegate from the young African state of Nigeria—Malam Maitama Sule, Minister of Mines and Power—has issued an oblique attack on that idea. Africans do not want a "messiah or a Hitler type" leader, he has declared.

Besides Ghana and Nigeria, the African states represented at the parley here are Morocco, the United Arab Republic, Tunisia, Libya, Liberia, Guinea, Togo, Ethiopia, the Cameroons and the Sudan.

Emperor Haile Selassie of Ethiopia has stated repeatedly that his nation should have a key role in the movement toward a union since Ethiopia has been "independent" for thousands of years.

Despite their differences on the pace and shape of an eventual African union, the delegates here were nearly unanimous on two other African issues after their public sessions last week. These are Algeria and the Union of South Africa's racial segregation policies. Algeria should be free from French authority and South African apartheid must be ended, the delegates have declared.

Hardly any speakers in the last five days failed to denounce France for holding Algeria under an "imperialist yoke" and for setting off nuclear blasts in the Sahara Desert. When the leader of the Algerian delegation, M'hammed Yazid, accused American bankers yesterday of financing French operations against the Algerian rebels, some delegates cried, "Shame on America!"

It is no secret that Cairo wants the new African countries to look not to Premier David Ben-Gurion of Israel for a "big brother" but to President Gamal Abdel Nasser.

June 20, 1960

AFRICANS DRAFT ECONOMIC UNITY

Addis Ababa Parley Lays Plans for Self-Sufficiency and Foreign-Fund Curb

By JAY WALZ
Special to The New York Times.

ADDIS ABABA, Ethiopia, June 25—Ambitious plans for building African economic unity among newly independent states were advanced here in the last fortnight.

A program approved by the twelve-nation conference of independent African states that adjourned last night envisages continental self-sufficiency and a sharp curtailment of foreign loans and investments. Nationalist leaders eye foreign capital with suspicion of "imperialist" motives.

The programs approved by the conference require not only long-range planning but also much capital, whose sources must still be found.

One resolution, approved unanimously, recommended the establishment of a joint African development bank and a joint African commercial bank. These banks would set up funds to be made available for economic and social-welfare projects in the twenty African states and territories that are free or approaching independence.

The conference also recommended the establishment of a council for African economic cooperation to "organize, coordinate, implement and maintain African economic unity."

Among the responsibilities of the council are expected to be the drafting of measures for organizing the banks, the setting of capital quotas and the study of payment difficulties the member states might encounter.

Transport Study Set

The conference also assigned to the proposed economic council the task of mapping improvement in cross-Africa transportation, communications and trade exchanges. It urged closer cooperation among African airlines and standardization of inspection procedures for civil aviation.

The delegates recommended that the council study tariffs to simplify them and to accord member states preferential treatment.

The conference recognized the "important role" already played in such matters by the United Nations Economic Commission for Africa, but said that there was a "further need" for the promotion of African economic cooperation.

The conference report did not specify the role it envisioned for such agencies as the International Development Agency and the special program for technical assistance supported by Britain, France, Belgium and other colonial powers. However, it authorized the proposed council to seek assistance from "appropriate international bodies."

Observers sensed a theme of "go it alone" running through the conference's statement of policy.

For example, a resolution calling for the eradication of colonial rule from Africa noted that "new forms" of colonialism could be introduced into territories under the guise of economic, financial and technical assistance. It called on colonial powers to "refrain from any action which might compromise the sovereignty and independence of emerging states."

June 26, 1960

5 Neutrals to Form 'NATO' for Africa; Proclaim a Charter

By HENRY TANNER
Special to The New York Times.

CASABLANCA, Morocco, Jan. 7—The heads of five neutralist African states announced today their intention to establish a NATO-like African organization to coordinate their policies and insure common defense.

They proclaimed what they called the African Charter of Casablanca. In it they vowed their "determination to liberate the African territories still under foreign domination" and to "liquidate colonialism and neo-colonialism in all their forms."

King Mohamed V of Morocco and Presidents Gamal Abdel Nasser of the United Arab Republic, Kwame Nkrumah of Ghana, Sékou Touré of Guinea and Modibo Keita of Mali announced their decisions in a unanimously adopted statement closing a four-day conference here.

Other States Invited

They launched an "appeal to all independent African states" to associate themselves with this action for the "consolidation of liberty in Africa."

The organization patterned on the North Atlantic Treaty Organization, which will be set up as soon as conditions permit, according to the statement, includes an African Consultative Assembly having a permanent seat and holding periodic sessions.

A Joint African High Command comprising the Chiefs of Staff of the independent African states also is planned, the statement said.

There will be a committee each for political, economic and cultural affairs. The one on political affairs is to be made up of heads of state.

A far-reaching statement issued at the close of the conference concerned Israel, which had not originally figured on the agenda but was added later at Mr. Nasser's request. It branded Israel as an "instrument of imperialism and neo-colonialism not only in the Middle East but also in Africa."

In an implied reference to the important program of economic and technical assistance Israel has been carrying out in several West African countries, the conference appealed to all African states to oppose this "new" way by which imperialism was trying to "create bases for itself."

The Casablanca Charter formalizes African neutralism by pledging its signers to a "policy of nonalignment." In addition to calling for independence for remaining colonial territories, it asks members to rid the continent of "economic interventions and pressures" and opposes the maintenance of foreign troops and the establishment of bases.

Ferhat Abbas, Premier of the Provisional Algerian Government; Abdelkader el-Allam, Foreign Minister of Libya, and Alwin B. Perera, Ambassador of Ceylon in Cairo, also participated in the conference. The text of the final statement made it clear, however, that they had not participated in the charter and the call for the continent-wide defense organization.

In a separate communiqué, the conference participants declared their intention to withdraw their troops from the United Nations command in the Congo unless the United Nations adopted a policy favorable to Patrice Lumumba, deposed premier. The communiqué listed conditions the United Nations would have to meet if troops of Morocco, Ghana, Guinea and the United Arab Republic were to remain.

No Time Limit Is Set

The conditions were the disarming and disbanding of "lawless bands" of troops, that is, those loyal to Col. Joseph D. Mobutu, head of the military regime; the release of all members of Parliament and of the "legitimate Government"; reopening of Parliament; the release of all airports and radio stations, and action to prevent Belgians from using their trust territory of Ruanda-Urundi as a base for "aggression against the Congo."

The communiqué did not set a time limit. It appeared to leave it up to each government to decide at what point it wished to implement the withdrawal decision.

Mr. Nasser and Mr. Touré, who went on to Belgrade yesterday, pressed for a definite deadline, but Mr. Nkrumah is understood to have held out against it. Throughout the conference the Ghanaian leader appeared in the role of a moderate while Messrs. Nasser, Touré and Keita were consistently reported to take the most radical stand. Morocco, according to conference sources, kept to a middle position.

The Moroccans' views prevailed on the Congo, on the charter and on the African defense organization, which was proposed by King Mohamed at the opening of the conference.

Observers interpreted the resolution on Israel as a slap at Mr. Nkrumah and, to a lesser degree, at Mr. Keita.

January 8, 1961

3 AFRICAN LANDS TAKE UNITY STEP

Ghana, Guinea and Mali Sign Charter for New Grouping

Special to The New York Times.

ACCRA, Ghana, April 29—The heads of three states on the West Coast of Africa advanced today toward their ultimate goal of union of their countries.

President Kwame Nkrumah of Ghana, President Sékou Touré of Guinea and President Modibo Kieta of Mali announced that their agreement in principle last December to form a union had now become "a firm decision. They signed a charter, which will be submitted to their parliaments for ratification.

The charter provides for the establishment of the Union of African States. It provides that other African states or federations may later join the union.

The Presideent's joint communiqué came at the end of three days of secrecy talks. The idea for a union of African States was originated in November, 1958, when the heads of Ghana and Guinea proclaimed the Ghana-Guinea Union as a nucleus of a broader union. When the former French Sudan became the Madi Republic, she announced that she was joining the union.

At a meeting last December in Conakry, capital of Guinea, the three heads of state formally agreed in principle to enlarge the union to include Mali. A committee was appointed to study practical ways of effecting the union, particularly in regard to a merger of the military commands, currencies, foreign affairs and cultural policies of the three countries.

The three heads of state took into their conference their ministers of defense and foreign affairs, senior officials of their national banks and other key government officials.

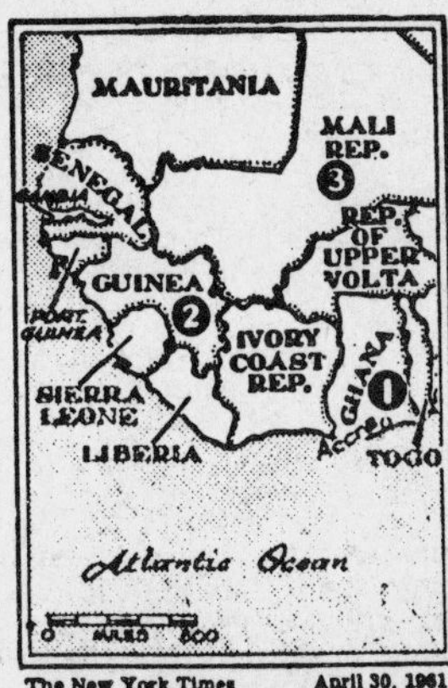

The New York Times April 30, 1961

The Presidents of Ghana (1), Guinea (2) and Mali (3) signed agreement for a union of their countries.

A unified Parliament and single flag for the three countries may not be around the corner, one observer said, but this week's conference proves the will of the three Presidents to work toward the closest possible cooperation and coordination of policies.

A significant indication was the unanimous decision of the three Presidents to demand a postponement of the conference of African states scheduled to take place in Monrovia, Liberia, May 8 to 13. The seven states sponsoring the Monrovia conference are Guinea, Mali, Nigeria, Liberia, Ivory Coast, Cameroon and Togo.

The Monrovia conference was conceived as an attempt to bridge the gap between various factions among the African states. All independent African states except the Union of South Africa were invited.

April 30, 1961

19 AFRICAN LEADERS OPPOSE GHANA AIMS

MONROVIA, Liberia, May 10 (AP)—Leaders of African nations meeting here today adopted a statement of principles aimed at recognizing the sovereignty of all.

A communiqué said the leaders, all heads of government of pro-Western or noncommitted nations, "regarded as totally unrealistic any conception of unity which entails the surrender of the sovereignty of any African state to another."

This was obviously aimed at Ghana, which is not among the nineteen nations at the Monrovia talks. Ghana's leaders have talked of acquiring territory in Togo and Ivory Coast.

Delegates also asked the conference chairman, William V. S. Tubman, president of Liberia, to try to mediate between Somalia and Ethiopia on a border dispute.

NKRUMAH STAYS FIRM

Backs African Unity Despite Parley's Rejection of Aim

Special to The New York Times.

ACCRA, Ghana, May 15—President Kwame Nkrumah criticized tonight the twenty African states at the recent conference in Monrovia, Liberia, for having rejected his ideas on Pan-Africanism and a United States of Africa.

Mr. Nkrumah addressed 500 guests at a state dinner in honor of President Sukarno of Indonesia.

"In the new Africa," he said, "we must be prepared to scrap outright the frontiers that were drawn to suit the convenience of colonial powers without regard whatsoever to ethnic and social groupings or the economic needs of the people."

Ghana, a sponsor, withdrew from the Monrovia meeting before it opened.

May 16, 1961

5 IN AFRICAN BLOC TO BOYCOTT TALKS

Rift Between Groups Widens on Eve of Lagos Parley

By HENRY TANNER

Special to The New York Times.

LAGOS, Nigeria, Jan. 21—The rift between two rival blocs of African nations was substantially widened today when members of the so-called Casablanca group announced their refusal to attend a foreign ministers' conference called here for tomorrow.

The foreign ministers of Ghana, Guinea, Mali, Morocco and the United Arab Republic, the five principal members of the Casablanca bloc, announced their decision in Accra, Ghana.

Their announcement came as a surprise and a disappointment to the delegates who have been gathering here since yesterday.

The conference here is sponsored by the nineteen members of the Monrovia group of independent African nations that first met in the Liberian capital last May. The Monrovia powers, which are regarded as moderate, include most of the former French territories and seven other countries.

The Casablanca group, which first met in the Moroccan city a year ago, has taken a more aggressively nationalistic and neutralist position.

The conference plans call for a three-day preliminary meeting of foreign ministers, to be followed Thursday by a meeting of African heads of state.

The sponsors had expected several heads of state of the Casablanca powers to stay away from the conference. But they had assumed that the foreign ministers would attend the preliminary meeting.

Blow to Unity Seen

The Casablanca powers' decision to boycott the preliminary meeting is regarded by delegates here as a deliberate affront and a severe blow to the cause of African unity.

The immediate reason for the boycott was the failure of the sponsors of the conference to invite the Algerian Provisional Government to take part. The Algerian rebels participated in the Casablanca conference a year ago.

A communiqué issued in Accra charged that this failure "may undermine the struggle of the Algerian people for their survival and independence at a critical state." It said the Algerians' absence from the conference would cause "grave harm to all members" of the group.

Nigeria, the conference host, has asserted that an invitation to the Algerians may yet be forthcoming. Nigeria intends to put the issue before the conference tomorrow as the first item of debate.

The Nigerians say that, since some of the former French territories objected to inviting the Algerians, they had to wait for the conference itself to decide.

Nigeria is known to favor inviting the Algerians. Liberia has given diplomatic recognition to the Algerian Provisional Government and is on record as favoring its representation here.

Tunisia, another influential member of the Monrovia group, declared last week that it would come to Lagos only if the Algerians were present.

The members of the Casablanca group favor achieving African unity by erasing political boundaries. The Monrovia powers believe in building unity through practical cooperation in such fields as commerce, industry, transport, commmunications, health and education.

The Lagos conference was expected to advance the views of the moderate group. Members of the Casablanca bloc, therefore, have been reluctant to accept the invitation. They have been promoting a meeting of African heads of state to be held in Tunis in April.

January 22, 1962

SENEGAL'S LEADER HAILS LAGOS UNITY

Senghor Says Talks Created an African Confederation

By HENRY TANNER

Special to The New York Times.

LAGOS, Nigeria, Jan. 31—In the view of President Leopold S. Senghor of Senegal, the Lagos conference of African countries set up "a confederation of independent African states that will follow a concerted policy in the most varied fields."

The six-day conference, attended by twenty heads of state or government, adjourned last night after having adopted in principle a charter of an organization of African and Malagasy states.

After further study by the member governments during a period of not more than three months, the charter will be submitted in revised form to the next conference.

Among other things, the charter provides for a permanent secretariat with a provisional seat in Lagos, a council of ministers that will meet at least once a year and for a council of heads of state that will meet at least once in three years.

Isolation Not Implied

Mr. Senghor, summing up the results of the conference, declared that the new organization did not imply that Africa intended to "isolate itself."

Sixteen resolutions adopted by the conference were made public today. The resolutions amounted to an ambitious blueprint for cooperation in almost all fields.

One of the most important decisions was financial. Twenty governments decided their cooperation in this field would include the following:

The stabilization of prices of basic products by means of national funds; the creation of regional funds for specific purposes and a common fund.

The creation of an organization for regulating exchanges between states employing different currencies.

The creation by stages of regional customs unions.

The drafting of a complete table of trade statistics between member states for the purpose of an inventory of African production.

A standing committee was formed to work out the means to implement these decisions.

The conference decided to create an Organization for Health, Labor and Social Affairs to coordinate the campaign against major diseases in all member states. The organization is to provide for the joint training of a medical staff and for the pooling of certain health and rehabilitation facilities.

Also set up was an Educational and Cultural Council of African and Malagasy States. This organization will have the task of coordinating educational systems between member states and of breaking down language barriers represented by the French and English inherited from colonial times.

Crop Protection Favored

The conference decided in favor of coordinating programs for the eradication of major animal diseases. It endorsed the creation of joint veterinary schools and the integration of efforts to protect crops through pest control.

One of the political resolutions adopted by the conference called on all colonial powers to declare publicly their acceptance of the principle of the right of all colonies to become independent. It urged the colonial powers to take steps immediately to insure that all colonies attained independence "at the earliest possible date."

The conference called for "concrete and immediate measures" to arrange an economic and diplomatic boycott of the colonial powers that refused to accept these principles.

The countries represented at the conference were Cameroon, the Central African Republic, Chad, the former French Congo, the former Belgian Congo, Dahomey, Ethiopia, Gabon, the Ivory Coast, Liberia, the Malagasy Republic, Mauretania, Niger, Nigeria, Senegal, Sierra Leone, Somalia, Tanganyika, Togo and Upper Volta.

February 1, 1962

30 AFRICA STATES FORM LOOSE UNION WITH BROAD AIMS

Political and Economic Ties Set in Charter—Action on Colonies Pledged

By JAY WALZ
Special to The New York Times

ADDIS ABABA, Ethiopia, May 25—The leaders of 30 independent African states formed today an Organization of African Unity. They adopted an all-Africa charter calling not only for unity in a loose federation but for far-reaching cooperation in politics, economics, education and defense.

Before adjourning their four-day conference, the heads of state or government also pledged to join in an effort to eradicate colonialism from the continent. They agreed to set up a fund to help freedom fighters in territories remaining under foreign control.

The charter was drafted by the foreign ministers of Ethiopia, Nigeria, Cameroon, Senegal, Ghana and the United Arab Republic. The heads of state and government had overruled an earlier decision of the foreign ministers to put off drafting the charter to a future date.

The signing took place at a public ceremony tonight.

Leaders to Meet Annually

The charter provides for an annual assembly of heads of state and government, who could pass resolutions by a two-thirds majority. A Council of Ministers is to meet every six months and will also approve resolutions by a two-thirds vote.

A Commission on Mediation and Conciliation was established to settle disputes.

The African leaders adopted a series of resolutions. One expressed the "deep concern" of the African people over racial discrimination throughout the world, saying they were particularly distressed about the situation in the United States.

The resolution voiced "appreciation for the efforts of the Federal Government of the Unit- States to put an end to these intolerable malpractices." It was plain that the Africans had in mind the incidents in Birmingham, Ala., though these were not specifically mentioned.

Conference Adjourns

One resolution called on the great powers to cease support of colonialist governments, "particularly the Portuguese Government, which is conducting a real war of genocide in Africa." This was directed primarily against Portuguese rule in Angola and Mozambique.

The conference afterward adjourned. The leaders and delegations plan to leave tomorrow.

Addis Ababa was chosen as the site of temporary headquarters of the Organization of African Unity. The secretariat will be established in Africa Hall, where the conference was held.

The new charter is the first instrument bringing together free African states on a continental basis. The countries of the new organization occupy most of Africa from the Mediterranean to the boundaries of the still colonized territories in the south of the continent. South Africa, although independent, is excluded from the organization because of its racial segregation policy.

The countries that took part in the conference are Algeria, Burundi, Cameroon, the Central African Republic, Chad, the Congo Republic (Brazzaville), the Congo (Leopoldville), Dahomey, Ethiopia, Gabon, Ghana, Guinea, Ivory Coast, Liberia, Libya, Madagascar, Mali, Mauritania, Niger, Nigeria, Rwanda, Senegal, Sierra Leone, Somalia, Sudan, Tanganyika, Tunisia, Uganda, Upper Volta and the United Arab Republic. Morocco sent an observer.

Looser Association Urged

The heads of state and government worked in closed session this morning on a final draft of the charter prepared by their foreign ministers. The session followed two and a half days of speeches in which the leaders all favored unity but differed sharply on how to approach that goal.

President Kwame Nkrumah of Ghana was the sole advocate of a union of African states that would unify the nations under a strong central government.

Other states followed the lead of Emperor Haile Selassie of Ethiopia. President Sékou Touré of Guinea; Sir Abubakar Tafawa Balewa, Prime Minister of Nigeria; President Julius Nyerere of Tanganyika, and President William V. S. Tubman of Liberia. Those leaders favored a loose association in which the various states would preserve their sovereignty while agreeing to cooperate in economics, culture, education, transport and communication.

President Gamal Abdel Nasser of the United Arab Republic and Premier Ahmed Ben Bella of Algeria supported this view.

Mr. Nyerere, who made a moving appeal for unity in the last speech yesterday, appeared to have been the peacemaker. Mr. Nkrumah, who believes that Africa must "unite or perish," appeared to be ready to join the majority.

Mention of Israel Omitted

The new charter follows in most respects the unity proposals adopted by the foreign ministers of the Monrovia group of 20 states last December in Lagos. The document also is in agreement with much of the charter adopted in 1961 by the six states of the Casablanca group, Ghana, Guinea, Mali, Morocco, Algeria and the United Arab Republic. However, the Casablanca states, in subscribing to the new, all-Africa charter, modified their determined neutralist stand.

The new charter omits any expression of concern about economic and cultural "infiltration" of the continent by Israel.

President Nasser said in a speech on Thursday that in interests of African unity the United Arab Republic would forego submitting for consideration "this serious problem for us."

The charter says all free African states shall be "dedicated" to liberation of all African territories still under foreign rule. There are 14 major territories so ruled, including Portuguese Angola and Mozambique and the British colony of Kenya, which is now in the process of achieving independence.

Unity is to be promoted through understanding and collaboration, and the states affirm their adherence to the United Nations.

In form and machinery, the African organization follows the pattern of the Organization of American States. The charter provides for a permanent headquarters, at a place yet to be chosen, and for a permanent Secretariat.

Assembly to Govern Group

The organization will be governed by the assembly of heads of state and government. The Council of Ministers will direct the Secretariat. Other agencies will include an economic and social committee, an education and cultural committee, a defense board and a scientific training and research institute.

The ceremonies of the conference culminated last night in a state banquet given for 2,000 guests by Emperor Haile Selassie in the brilliantly illuminated great hall of King Menelik II, Ethiopia's monarch half a century ago. A fireworks display was held outside, and the orchestra of the imperial guard played. Myriam Makeda, the South African singer, also performed.

Emperor Haile Selassie, in black tie and dinner jacket, and President Nasser, in a gray business suit, entered the hall arm in arm, leading the procession of dignitaries.

May 26, 1963

32 AFRICAN LANDS URGE SLOW UNION

Dakar Group Defeats Move to End Moderate Body

By J. ANTHONY LUKAS
Special to The New York Times

DAKAR, Senegal, Aug. 11—Advocates of a gradual approach to African unity won out today as the African foreign ministers closed their conference here.

The 32 ministers expressed a "wish" to see African regional groupings "melt gradually" in the new Organization of African Unity.

This formula appeared to resolve, at least temporarily, a struggle that threatened to tear the new continental organization apart.

The fight centered on the African and Malagasy Union, a moderate league of 14 former French and Belgian territories. The union, dealing with social, projects, has been a force for close relations with Western Europe. Several countries, led by Guinea, have been calling for the immediate dissolution of the union, the only African regional grouping still active. The opponents contend that the unions continued existence would impede the march toward African unity.

Most of the union's members have vigorously resisted these attacks. They say they are ready to "harmonize" its activities with the new organization's and even to fuse gradually with it. But they refuse to disband until the new organization proves itself.

When the ministers gathered at Senegal's Foreign Ministry last night for their final plenary session, they had two resolutions before them.

One, proposed by Mali, Guinea and Ghana, called for the "immediate dissolution" of regional groupings. The other, by Dahomey, the Malagasy Republic and the former French Congo, called for "gradual realignment."

After a bitter debate, the ministers scrapped both and restricted themselves to the wish for "gradual melting."

In the early morning, the ministers also completed action on the other issues that they had been considering for 10 days.

They called on all African states to recognize the Angolan government in exile headed by Holden Roberto. So far, only the Congo and Tunisia have recognized it.

The resolution was decisive victory for Mr. Roberto in his campaign to lead the splintered movement seeking to free Angola from Portuguese rule.

The ministers decided to make no recommendation, however, on a group to lead the liberation movement in Portuguese Guinea. They referred it for further study to the nine-nation Coordinating Committee for the Liberation of Africa.

In other resolutions approved this morning, the ministers took these actions:

¶Urged African heads of state to attend the 18th General Assembly of the United Nations which starts next month in New York.

¶Expressed approval of the treaty for a limited ban on nuclear tests and called for further efforts on disarmament.

¶Set rules and procedures for the Organization of African Unity.

¶Recommended Addis Ababa, Ethiopia, as the permanent headquarters of the organization.

In a surprising last-minute move, the delegates decided to make no recommendation for secretary general of the organization. After a bitter fight, they refused to accept a commission's nomination of Diallo Telli, Guinean representative at the United Nations. The vote was 15 to 15, with two abstentions.

The choice will now be left to the African heads of state, who are scheduled to meet in Tunis next May. The heads of state must also approve the selection of Addis Ababa.

The minister set their next meeting for February in Lagos, Nigeria. Mongi Slim, Tunisia's Foreign Minister, and John Karefa-Smart, Foreign Minister of Sierra Leone, reported on recent African initiatives in the United Nations.

At the closing public session, which began at 11 A. M., more than a dozen ministers took the floor to express their view that the conference had been an important step toward unity.

August 12, 1963

East Africa Misses Its Chance for Unity

By ROBERT CONLEY
Special to The New York Times

NAIROBI, Kenya—The most important step toward unity yet contemplated by African nationalism on this continent—creation of an East African Federation—failed last year because of uncertainty, jealousy and mistrust.

Kenya, Uganda, Tanganyika and the spice island of Zanzibar attempted to transform their loose economic union into a full political federation. But they failed because none of them could ease the others' doubts of "what is in it for me?"

Tanganyika's president, Julius K. Nyerere, said that the lack of agreement was Africa's "greatest disappointment" of 1963.

"One of the hard facts we have to face on our way to African unity," he said, "is that this unity means, on the part of the countries, surrender of sovereignty, and on the part of the individual leaders, surrender of high positions. We must face squarely the fact that so far there has been no such surrender in the name of African unity."

Federation would have drawn four East African countries in a single political unit larger than all of Western Europe. It would have had 25.2 million persons and one head of state.

Moreover, federation had been expected to become the means of changing the entire economic orientation of the Eastern half of the continent.

Ethopia, Somalia, Ruanda, Burundi, Nyasaland and Northern Rhodesia were interested in allying themselves with the federation to form a common market of Greater Eastern Africa that would reach from the shores of the Red Sea on the North to the edge of the Zambezi River on the south.

Whether any part of those aspirations can be realized now is open to question. More and more East Africans are convinced that political federation may not be possible here for a few more years at least and perhaps not in this decade.

Federation was to have been created in December as the last vestiges of British colonial rule disappeared from East Africa with the independence of Kenya and Zanzibar. That had been the announced intention of Kenya's Prime Minister, Jomo Kenyatta; Uganda's Prime Minister, Milton A. Obote, and Mr. Nyerere.

Few parts of this emerging continent seemed better prepared for political unification than East Africa. Its long history of economic intergration had brought Kenya, Uganda and Tanganyika into a common market, with Zanzibar as an associate member.

Many Things in Common

East Africans use the same money in the four territories, buy the same postage stamps and speak the same languages, English or Swahili. A single system of railroads, airlines and ships links the area.

On the mainland, borders are hardly marked. Immigration stations are rarely encountered.

The mechanism for carrying all this out is an interterritorial body called the East African Common Services Organization.

With its headquarters in Nairobi, Kenya's capital, the Common Services Organization collects East Africa's income and corporate taxes and its customs and excise duties.

It operates more than 3,600 miles of railroads from the Indian Ocean to the Nile; runs steamers on four lakes, Victoria, Tanganyika, Albert and Kioga; and manages the three main East African seaports of Mombasa, Dar es Salaam and Tanga.

Through a central currency board the organization regulates the common money of the four territories—with the East African shilling being equal to 14 United States cents. The organization also operates East Africa's postal and telecommunications, supervises her civil aviation and provides her weather reports and forecasts.

"Our mistake," said one influential East African, "was to believe that political integration would follow naturally from economic union."

Trouble arose in the efforts to reach agreement on essentially political matters such as establishing a central bank, unifying defense forces, merging diplomatic corps and locating the Federal capital. At one point it was suggested that the issue of the capital might be settled by putting it on an island in the middle of Lake Victoria, which is bounded by Kenya, Uganda and Tanganyika, but is inside none of them.

Equally unsolvable were the problems of finding a basis for federation, wide economic planning, deciding how to spread industrial development as evenly as possible and determining what benefits each country would be willing to give up for the larger advantage of political union.

Trouble Arose on Bank

East Africans tend to believe that they can keep their common services intact without having to create a federation.

Yet every indication points to the possibility that the present services may wither without political authority at the top to enforce decisions and equalize mutual costs and benefits. Fragmentation already is apparent.

In one case Uganda withdrew financial support from a desert locust control program because the foraging insect was not a threat to her own crops. In another, Tanganyika questioned the costs of increased weather services required by international jetliners. Most of the jets land at Nairobi, and bring tourists and money to Kenya.

Uganda also withdrew from the East Africa Tourist Travel Association, another common service, on the ground that she paid a quarter of the association's costs and received less than 9.5 per cent of the area's tourist revenue.

Publicly, East Africa's leaders still are committed to political federation although no more negotiations on it have been scheduled. Privately they say that none will be—not right now, anyway.

January 20, 1964

Africans Widen Rebel Aid; Form a Border Group

By LLOYD GARRISON
Special to The New York Times

LAGOS, Nigeria, March 2—Western diplomats here are carefully weighing two steps taken by the Foreign Ministers of countries in the Organization of African Unity. One was on the coordination of aid to African "freedom fighters." The other was the setting up of a permanent commission to arbitrate border disputes.

Both these developments tended to be obscured by more spectacular resolutions adopted yesterday, recommending a boycott of planes and ships trading with South Africa.

The Ministers ended their six-day meeting here yesterday with the adoption of more than 20 resolutions for consideration next summer at a meeting of African heads of state.

The arbitration commission, however, will not have to wait for approval by the heads of state. It is expected to be set up at the next meeting of the unity organization's secretariat in May. Thus it could have an important bearing on the frontier conflicts between Ethiopia and Somalia and between Somalia and Kenya.

Some conference delegates, particularly those from Ghana, had been hopeful that the organization would agree at this meeting to a far more dramatic move — the formation of a continental African army. They argued that only such an army could have properly intervened in the recent rash of African border disputes, coups d'état and mutinies.

Tanganyika, Uganda and Kenya recently asked British help in ending army mutinies. France intervened in Gabon last month to restore President Léon Mba after he had been deposed.

The Angolans have been the chief beneficiaries. Six months ago they received $95,000. They were reported to have left this meeting with a second donation of at least $16,000 and the promise of much more soon.

Liberation movements from Mozambique, Portuguese Guinea, South-West Africa and South Africa lobbied for part of the fund. Informed sources said a tentative formula was reached determining each movement's share.

Three months ago Holden Roberto, leader of the Angolan rebels, announced his acceptance of Chinese Communist aid. However, Mr. Savimbis said that no arms had actually arrived from Peking and that the aid was accepted only "in principle."

The proposal for an African force bogged down over the questions of who would pay for it, what country would command it and under what circumstances it would act.

But in the absence of a standing army the arbitration commission is viewed as an important buffer between feuding African states.

In many respects the work of the Committee of Nine, dealing with decolonization, could have the most important long-range effects.

For the first time since the organization was born last year in Addis Ababa, Ethiopia, all 34 member states have now contributed at least a token sum to the "Freedom Fighters Fund." The exact amount of the fund is a secret, but it is reliably reported to be close to $500,000.

March 3, 1964

NYERERE, AT CAIRO, ASSAILS NKRUMAH

Tangangikan Says Ghanaian Only Preaches Unity

By JAY WALZ
Special to The New York Times

CAIRO, July 20 —President Julius K. Nyerere of the United Republic of Tanganyika and Zanzibar made a bitter attack on President Kwame Nkrumah of Ghana before the conference of the Organization of African Unity here today.

He accused Mr. Nkrumah of preaching rather than practicing unity and of advocating African union with reasons that were "absurdities." He said Mr. Nkrumah was "extremely petty" in refusing support of the organization's liberation committee.

"This union government business has become a cover for doing some of the most unbrotherly things in Africa," the 43-year-old Tanganyika leader declared.

It was the first personal assault on a fellow African leader the conference had heard. Mr. Nkrumah remained in his seat throughout Mr. Nyerer's speech, his face impassive, his hands folded.

Mr. Nkrumah had repeated his call for a strong federal union of all independent African sates yesterday. He argued that this was the only way Africans could maintain their freedom in the face of outside imperialism.

Mr. Nyerere espoused the more popular step-by-step approach, on the ground that full final union now was impossible. The Tanganyikan received an ovation at the close of his speech, which he said he had not wanted to make.

Formal addresses were suspended at noon and the African leaders joined committees assigned to the specific problems of promoting unity, driving out the remaining "colonialists," handling boundary disputes and developing trade and better standards of living for Africa's 250 million inhabitants. They hope to prepare and adopt resolutions so the conference can end tomorrow night.

Mr. Nyerere was plainly angered by various remarks made by Mr. Nkrumah yesterday, including one accusing the organization's liberation committee of inaction throughout the last year. Mr. Nyerere said this was a "curious accusation" to come from the leader of the "only country that has not paid a single penny to the committee since its establishment."

The committee was established to organize and aid freedom fighters' movements in territories under foreign control, notably Mozambique, Angola and Portuguese Guinea.

Yesterday Mr. Nkrumah referred to the army mutiny in Tanganyika last winter and spoke of the "humiliation" of an African state's having, as Mr. Nyerere did, to call troops of the "former colonial power"—Britain—to restore order and save the government.

Mr. Nyerere charged today that Ghana's Ambassador in Tanganyika at the time "rejoiced" in this humiliation, and "I was forced to request that he be removed."

The heads of state, before adjourning the conference, are expected to strengthen the Organization of African Unity by choosing a permanent headquarters and selecting a permanent secretary general.

July 21, 1964

Congo Issue Dividing African Group

By LAWRENCE FELLOWS
Special to The New York Times

NAIROBI, Kenya, March 7 —The Organization of African Unity, less than two years after it was founded amid widespread enthusiasm, was described today as a forum full of "hollow verbalism and outdated phrases."

Foreign Minister Doudou Thiam of Senegal, addressing the organization's Council of Ministers, said that after listening to more than 10 days of speeches he had come to the conclusion that the words colonialism, neo-colonialism and imperialism were being bandied about by some delegates who did not know what the words meant.

"There is a kind of internal imperialism in Africa," he said. "Some of the states here seem even to want to impose their own regimes on all of Africa."

At the root of Mr. Thiam's complaint and at the center of a controversy that has brought the organization to a state approaching paralysis is the Congo, with her recurring strife and underlying racial bitterness.

Nearly all of the 36 member states of the organization have became involved in arguments over the Congo. Some of them have reached the point of open intervention, in spite of pledges to respect one another's sovereignty and territorial integrity.

The governments of Algeria and the United Arab Republic have never tried to conceal the help they have been giving to Congolese rebels. They have covered their efforts with fierce denunciations of the support Premier Moise Tshombe is getting from the United States and Belgium.

Mr. Tshombe, apart from his accusation against these two Arab states, condemned the Sudan, Uganda and the former French Congo yesterday for the shelter and support he said they had given the rebels.

A Congolese rebel leader, Capt. Rachel A. Kissonga, said in Dar es Salaam recently that Nigerian troops had been fighting for Mr. Tshombe in the Congo. This charge was denied before the organization's Council of Ministers Friday by A. I. Osakwe, the Nigerian Ambassador to the Congo.

Rigid Camps Formed

Members of the organization have settled into fairly rigid camps. One side is not strong enough to unseat Mr. Tshombe and the other is not strong enough to force his antagonists to disengage.

Behind Algeria and the United Arab Republic are ranged the former French Congo, where Chinese Communists are making their first firm foothold in West Africa, and Burundi, where the Chinese are trying to regain influence after the suspension of diplomatic relations by that country.

Ghana, Guinea, Malawi, the Sudan and Somalia belong to the anti-Tshombe camp, as do Kenya, Uganda, Tanzania and Zambia.

Not all those delegates who are backing Mr. Tshombe at the conference can be numbered among his friends. But these states support him for the sake of legitimacy in government and to promote orderly political development in Africa.

The states whose support Mr. Tshombe can almost surely count on are Nigeria, Liberia, Cameroon, Senegal, Togo and Malagasy.

The rest are likely to abstain in voting on the Congo issue. Since a majority of all those at the conference must be obtained, a stalement seems a certainty in any decisive vote affecting Mr. Tshombe.

Even the abstainers, when they are shaken out of groups by events or pressures put on them by their neighbors, are believed likely to fall into the camp behind the Congolese leader when the chips are down.

March 8, 1965

MEETING IN ACCRA WINDS UP QUIETLY

African Unity Group Unable to Solve Finances Problem

By LLOYD GARRISON
Special to The New York Times

ACCRA, Ghana, Oct. 26—The Organization of African Unity wound up its third annual conference of heads of state early today as somberly as it had begun it.

The organization took no startling steps. It did little to strengthen its own secretariat, which is inadequately staffed and is already in arrears by nearly $2.5 million.

And much to the dismay of exiled insurgents lobbying in the corridors, the heads of state declined to give more year-round initiative to the liberation committee, which gives funds to African rebel forces. The committee must still report directly to the heads of state—who meet only once a year.

The delegates appeared to bury for good the repeated appeal of Ghana's President, Kwame Nkrumah, for a continentwide union government.

President William V. S. Tubman of Liberia summed up the views of many when he spoke the day after the meeting opened. Describing union government as "Kwame's hobby," President Tubman declared:

"I have no objection to it in principle. But with the kind of confusion we have seen among ourselves right here—can we have one government functioning for us all?"

Tubman Leaves Early

Mr. Tubman concluded by saying he felt compelled to leave the conference early "because I have just received a cable of the death of an old friend." He then flew to Monrovia on a flight for which he made reservations three days before.

The attendance perhaps represented the organization's most conspicuous failure.

Only 18 of the organization's 36 heads of state attended Five went home early. Eight French-speaking countries boycotted the meeting to protest Ghana's aid to African exiles who are attempting to subvert their home governments.

If the meeting lacked drama it did pass a number of practical resolutions.

It warned Britain of the consequences of alienating much of Africa if she permits Rhodesia's white minority Government to declare independence.

The heads of state also condemned subversion and called for curbs on political refugees who agitate against their own governments.

October 27, 1965

AFRICAN UNITY TALK ENDS IN ADDIS ABABA

ADDIS ABABA, Ethiopia, March 6 (Reuters) — The Organization of African Unity formally closed a six-day meeting here early today, shaken by the walkout of eight members nations.

Some of the eight left the 36-member organization's Council of Ministers in protest against the representation of the new Ghanaian leadership that deposed President Kwame Nkrumah 10 days ago. Others felt a resolution against Rhodesian independence was too weak.

March 7, 1966

BLACK AFRICANS REJECT 'DIALOGUE'

Leaders at Talks Bar Any Approach to South Africa

By CHARLES MOHR
Special to The New York Times

ADDIS ABABA, Ethiopia, June 23—The Organization of African Unity reaffirmed today—but by a split vote—its opposition to any moves by black states to open an independent diplomatic dialogue with the white Government of South Africa.

A declaration critical of such dialogue was adopted by 28 votes to 6 at the closing session here of the organization's eighth annual conference of heads of governments. Five states abstained. Two members, Uganda and the Central African Republic, boycotted the meeting, but both might have voted no.

The charter of the organization requires that two-thirds of the members endorse resolutions at the leaders' level and, therefore, the declaration barely squeaked through.

President Félix Houphouët-Boigny of the Ivory Coast, in a last-minute attempt to advance his own previous suggestion that the time was ripe for a dialogue with South Africa, issued a statement proposing that a special meeting of heads of government be convened to discuss the issue further.

'Weapon of the Strong'

No action was taken on his proposal, which, since he was not present, was read to the conference.

In his statement President Houphouët-Boigny said that "dialogue is the weapon of the strong and not the weak." He said that some effort to attain harmony with South Africa was necessary to keep the cold war and its tensions out of Africa.

Most members, however, made clear they felt that any move to open talks with South Africa without some prior reform in racial policy by that Government would hamper efforts to isolate it internationally.

The President of Gambia, Sir Dauda K. Jawara, said in a speech that the organization had achieved what he called "quasiunanimity."

This phrase expressed the strong desire of a majority of African leaders to maintain the appearance of almost complete unity of past years on taking a tough line toward South Africa and its policy of racial separation.

The six nations that voted against the declaration opposing any dialogue with South Africa were the Ivory Coast, Gabon, Lesotho, Malawi, Mauritius and Madagascar.

The five that abstained were Dahomey, Niger, Togo, Upper Volta and Swaziland. The first four are relatively conservative French-speaking states on Africa's west coast that are closely associated with the Ivory Coast. Swaziland, like Lesotho, is a small black nation bordering on South Africa.

'No Basis' for Dialogue

The declaration, first adopted last week by a preparatory meeting of foreign ministers, said that "there exists so basis for a meaningful dialogue" with South Africa. It said that no African state should make an approach to the South Africa Government without the organization's approval and unless South Africa had first begun discussions with her own black population.

Only one black state, Malawi, has diplomatic relations with South Africa. Whether the declaration will deter others such as the Ivory Coast and the Central African Republic from beginning discussions was unclear.

At a news conference this evening the chairman of the organization, President Moktar Ould Daddah of Mauritania, said he felt that "these decisions are binding to member states." He added that he believed the organization would take a "very stern" attitude to any member that defied the declaration.

The conference, which adjourned today, was orginally scheduled to be held in Kampala, Uganda. But after the army overthrew the Government of Uganda last January, some members worked successfully to move the session to Ethiopia. This and other actions by leaders of the organization angered some members and probably contributed to the fact that few heads of government attended.

Only 10 heads of government attended the conference, the smallest number since the organization was formed in 1963. Two vice presidents attended and 27 governments were represented by cabinet ministers or even lower officials.

June 24, 1971

WITCHING HOUR FOR REDS

British Say Communists Woo African Native Doctors

LONDON, July 29 (UP).—Russian Communist agents are filtering into the ranks of the witch doctors in West Africa in an attempt to break down the tribal system, British intelligence reports said today.

The Communists are encouraging a revival of the secret native Jujy ritual, the reports said.

Activity by the Communist agents was reported in British and French West Africa and in the Negro republic of Liberia.

The Communists are seeking to get controlling influence in African trade unions, centering their activities in the seaports, and trying to get a political following, according to the reports.

In the interior the Communists are seeking to gain a following in tribal secret societies and among prominent witch doctors, especially those known to be anti-European, the reports said.

July 30, 1949

Positive Policy in Africa Held Vital If West Is to Keep Position There

By WILLIAM S. WHITE
Special to THE NEW YORK TIMES.

ACCRA, Gold Coast, May 17—The Western World's position in Africa south of the Sahara is in urgent need of strengthening. If war should be forced by the Soviet Union, this vast continental area, with all its indispensable minerals from uranium on down, might well be lost to the free side through passive resistance among the 200,000,000 Negroes or even through rebellions.

Conditions in many African areas are ideal for Communist agitation and penetrations already are going on to a degree that, one feels, should cause the West grave anxiety.

To one who has been on the scene for two months Western policy, speaking generally, seems weak and confused. This is particularly true in the Union of South Africa, the most critical point at the moment. There Prime Minister Daniel F. Malan's Nationalist Government is marching along a road that in the past has led to Right Wing dictatorship. It is taking a course of repression toward the natives that, quite apart from any moral consideration, is believed by many foreign observers to be fatally reckless in the hatreds it is building.

The West is not doing much to stop Dr. Malan or to alter his course and this is especially true of the United States, which potentially has by far the most powerful influence in Capetown of all foreign powers.

Here on the Gold Coast, at the other political extreme, the British have granted to the natives a degree of self-government for which they demonstrably are not yet prepared. Here, London, oversensitive to long attacks on its colonial policies that have led to a slow liquidation of the British Empire, may have gone too far and too fast away from colonialism.

Gold Coast Trial May Fail

While the British concept here of native self rule is no doubt noble in principle, there is great danger the experiment may fail and lead to chaos and to a loss of such uneasy stability as now exists in British West Africa.

In British Central Africa, efforts to federate Southern Rhodesia, Northern Rhodesia and Nyasaland as a barrier to "Malanism" and as a possible new area of British strength, are meeting with difficulties. If the British do not succeed, economic and perhaps ideological absorption of Southern Rhodesia by the Union of South Africa within a few years may be reasonably predicted.

All these are conclusions of two months of travel in South, Central and West Africa.

It seems clear that, in bureaucratic terminology, Africa is being given "low priority" diplomatically and especially by the United States. American diplomatic missions through these areas are on the whole well manned by capable and objective personnel, but this personnel is handicapped in many cases by a lack of clear instructions from the State Department.

In the Union of South Africa the United States Embassy takes what looks to an outsider to be a position of unnecessary timidity in its anxiety to have no interruption in the movement home of manganese and the like.

Three Steps Indicated

Some disinterested persons in Africa south of the Sahara believe that the following are essential steps to save the Western position:

1. A strong, clear and firm United States policy against the Malan regime, which understands and respects firmness, and in support of the constitutional tradition that Dr. Malan is thus far attacking with such success. It is not believed that the Malan Government would try, in resentment, to cut off its exports of minerals to the United States; after all those exports and particularly gold are the basis of South Africa's whole economy. If it was not sold to the United States who would be the buyer?
2. A United States policy of open encouragement of a Central African Federation as a strategic necessity of the first importance.
3. A continued sympathetic view by Washington toward British efforts here in the Gold Coast—in spite of the fact that these efforts look extreme—as a means of promoting what seems absolutely necessary in Africa—some sort of a concession to the political demands of the natives of this Continent.

Explosion Is Feared

It is felt by many that unless there is at least some degree of a general white retreat the rising pressure of this black world will lead to a terrible explosion.

While the Gold Coast experiment plainly is a doubtful one, the British nevertheless are irrevocably committed to it now and however unwise may have been that commitment it is clearly in the Western interest that the plan be given every chance to work. This is considered now a must. Either it works or much of West Africa will become a political jungle in which no one but the Communists can win anything.

It appears that there is wisdom in the proposals being made by Belgian Congo administrators that the United States encourage the calling of a Central Africa conference to try to find some sort of agreement of view among the white man's varying policies in Africa.

It is felt by many that while success for such a conference would be highly unlikely it nevertheless would be worth the try. As matters stand now there is absolutely no coherence between one area and another in meeting the questions posed by the demands of the native populations.

May 18, 1952

Moscow Spurs Africa Drive With Diplomacy and Trade

Communists Also Use Cultural Methods In Seeking Predominance in Continent —Action by West Is Held Urgent

By KENNETT LOVE
Special to The New York Times.

LONDON, May 25—The Soviet Union, using the international machinery of communism, is concentrating its attention on Africa, according to evidence accumulated here by authoritative analysts.

United States and British officials have conferred about Communist penetration of Africa. However, responsible sources here believe that more than conferring is needed. They say it is high time for large-scale coordinated counter-action by the West.

Soviet, Chinese Communist and satellite penetration is being carried out by varied means. Arms are offered and sold to independent Middle Eastern and African countries.

Diplomatic and trade missions are multiplied. Engineers, entertainers and botanists, motion pictures, publications and radio programs are flowing from the Communist world through the Middle East to Africa in a growing stream. African and Middle Eastern leaders, students and technicians are invited to visit Communist capitals.

Communist experts are studying hard, on a widely organized basis, to learn African languages, attitudes, customs and political patterns. On the Dark Continent itself, the Russians are diligent in cultivating African friendships.

According to a highly authoritative statement, "the recent moves are part of a concerted plan to follow up the Soviet thrust in the Middle East and to penetrate south, using Egypt as a bridge to establish contact with Communist networks in French North Africa as a preliminary to the main objective."

The "main objective" is described as achieving political and commercial predominance in Africa by non-military means. Africa contains one-fifth of the world's land surface, a population of 200,000,000 and a rich repository of strategic and other natural resources.

On the diplomatic level, the Kremlin recently opened missions in Libya, Liberia and the Sudan. It previously had embassies in Cairo and Addis Ababa, Ethiopia. Both Poland and Hungary have diplomatic missions in Egypt and the Sudan, and Poland plans to open one in Ethiopia. Bulgaria and Rumania are represented in Cairo.

Czechoslovakia has missions in Egypt and Ethiopia and a consulate in the Belgian Congo. East Germany has permanent trade missions in Egypt and the Sudan. Communist China has an embassy in Egypt, whose recent recognition of the Peiping regime is expected to influence other Middle Eastern and African countries to do the same.

Studies Intensified

Meanwhile, the Kremlin has ordered the Institute for the Study of Contemporary Capitalism at Moscow's Academy of Sciences to intensify its studies of Central and South African languages, literature and economics. The recently established Moscow Institute for the Study of Contemporary Imperialism is concentrating on colonial affairs.

The Academy of Sciences has announced the formation of a group in its Africa section to compile dictionaries of African languages.

At present the Moscow radio broadcasts to Africa only in Arabic and English. However, Moscow has been getting a free ride on radio waves emanating from Cairo, which broadcasts several African languages in addition to Arabic.

Broadcasts Analyzed

A British Broadcasting Corporation analysis of monitored broadcasts from Cairo this month states:

"In concentrating more on the general effects of Western, or NATO, policy than on British or French actions in the Middle East [and North Africa], the Cairo radio has set the West as a whole, as compared with Soviet Russia or Communist China, in a light unfavorable to the interests of the Arabs."

Recent Cairo broadcasts have portrayed the Communist bloc as helping in "liberation from the West's restrictions."

Soviet-bloc trade missions are concentrating their sales efforts on whole factories and other technical items that require a substantial number of technicians to go with them.

British colonial officials in Africa have been alerted to watch Communist activities in their areas. British information offices and broadcasters are doing what they can to slow the tide of Communist influence. But informed circles here admit that counter-action has not been effective so far.

May 26, 1956

U. S. IS BECOMING AFRICA-CONSCIOUS

Will Open 4 New Consulates —Congress to Be Asked for Funds for More

By RUSSELL BAKER
Special to The New York Times.

WASHINGTON, March 23—The Administration has suddenly become Africa-conscious.

As a result, four new United States consular offices will be opened on the once "Dark Continent" during the next few weeks, and Congress is being asked for funds to set up several more during the year ahead.

African affairs, the most neglected realm of State Department activity, are soon to be brought out of bureaucratic limbo at the department and invested with new dignity.

As has been disclosed, this will involve the creation of a new Bureau of African Affairs under its own Assistant Secretary of State. Legislation to carry out this reorganization is now before Congress, and the new bureau is expected to start operating about Sept. 1.

Planned Before Nixon Trip

These moves all were planned before Vice President Richard M. Nixon's successful African tour and cannot be described as one of its results. Rather, the Vice President's trip was, like the reorganization and expansion plans, a symbol of Washington's awakening to Africa.

All these developments, one State Department official said today, reflect a sudden awareness that history is beginning to move at a swift pace on the African continent.

Persons in the department who are not given to overstatement are talking in terms of "dramatic" and "breath-taking" developments there within the next few years.

Officials here are sensitive to the new nationalism as the explosive force in Africa. Behind the Administration's sudden concern there also is the disturbing memory of events in Asia dating from World War II.

Parallel With Asia Drawn

There is a tendency here among persons who think about foreign-policy planning to draw a parallel between under-developed Asia in the immediate post-war era and under-developed Africa today.

Africa, the theory goes, is just now beginning to tremble under the nationalist pressures that hit Asia a dozen years ago and shaped the present political constellation of the Pacific and Indian Ocean areas.

Few are content with the outcome of events in Asia. The preponderance of neutralism, the weakness of pro-Western sympathy and the communization of China have created what many policy planners regard as an unpleasant model of what happens when the new nationalism shakes under-developed or colonial lands.

In the Republican party, moreover, there is the hint of an uneasy awareness that Republican success in making political capital out of events in Asia during Democratic Administrations might conceivably boomerang if the Asian pattern is repeated in

Africa under Republican policy in the State Department.

Hence, what is happening now in Washington is the first act in a play aimed at preventing a repetition of the Asian pattern on the African continent. Ideally, it is recognized, United States policy not only should stop communism from rooting in the under-developed nations that will be emerging to independence in the years ahead but also achieve positive results.

It should guarantee the West a large fund of goodwill and intimate relations as among equals with the new nations. It also should insure that Africa's gigantic and largely untapped reservoir of natural resources should not be closed to Western markets.

There is general agreement on the goals. But there is still no comprehensive policy to attain them.

The State Department suffers from a dearth of African experts, and Vice President Nixon's remarks about the quality of United States diplomatic representation in Africa testify to the hardship psychology that permeates the department's present view of African duty.

On the credit side of the ledger, there is heavy commercial pressure on Congress to protect the future of increasing United States investment in Africa.

This pressure seems to insure that Congress, in the face of demands for slashing economies, will approve the money needed for expanding diplomatic work in Africa and creating the new State Department bureau.

There is some speculation already that the new Assistant Secretary might be Representative Frances P. Bolton, a Cleveland Republican and a leading Congressional exponent of African development.

The new consular posts to be opened this spring are at Yaounde, in the French Cameroons; Abidjan, in the Ivory Coast, French West Africa, Mogadishu, in Somalia, which is due to become independent in 1960, and Kampala, the commercial center of Uganda. At present there are no United States missions in these territories.

The organization of an African Bureau will bring all but three nations of Africa under a single department officer. The exceptions will be Algeria, a French territory, which will continue to be dealt with as a West European responsibility, and Egypt and the Sudan, which will remain the responsibility of the Bureau of Middle Eastern Affairs.

March 24, 1957

REDS SEEK TRADE OF WEST AFRICA

Soviet Stays in Background, Satellites Do Spadework in Economic Warfare

Special to The New York Times.

MONROVIA, Liberia Jan. 3—Soviet-bloc traveling salesmen are energetically bringing economic warfare aginst Western countries to West Africa south of the Sahara. The long-cherished Russian dream of obtaining a foothold in Negro Africa appears to be becoming a reality.

But the Soviet Union is remaining discreetly in the background for the time being, preferring to let its satellites do the spadework.

The first results have been highly promising. East Germany already has signed a trade and cultural agreement with the newly independent West African republic of Guinea on the basis of "lasting and fruitful cooperation." Under the agreement, East Germany will supply industrial plants, textiles, chemical products and consumer goods.

In return Guinea will deliver, presumably under a partial barter arrangement, coffee, oleaginous goods, bananas and other agricultural products.

Other Tempting Vacuums

There are other tempting vacuums in Guinea that are not escaping the attention of the Eastern bloc. Three thousand French technicians and other skilled personnel have departed. The Soviet Union and its satellites are willing and eager to supply experts.

It is no secret that Guinea, which voted for independence from France, is facing financial difficulties. A loan offer from the East cannot be ruled out.

Besides, Guinea has been left with some uncompleted industrial projects, the chief of which would appear to be the large Fria hydroelectric project on the Souapiti River at Konkoure. Its estimated cost is $140,000,000.

Guinea is rich in mineral resources such as bauxite, diamonds and iron ore. The capital city of Conakry alone is reported to rest on a great deposit of iron ore. Still richer deposits exist in the interior.

Quick penetration into Guinea by the Eastern bloc was made comparatively easy by a combination of factor's including the wait and see policy of Western countries.

Attitude of President

Primarily, the penetration has been made smooth by the attitude of Guinea's President, Sekou Touré. He visited behind the Iron Curtain before his country became independent. He is known to have been deeply impressed and is reported to have deep sympathies for Eastern bloc countries and their form of government and economy.

Also, like Ghana's Prime Minister, Kwame Nkrumah, Mr. Touré is said to be convinced that some form of socialist economy will be best suited for his country and people.

Hard on the heels of the East Germans, a five-man Czechoslovak trade mission flew into Conakry with ample sample cases.

Farther down the West African coast, Polish representatives were busy negotiating for a shipping line between Szczecin (Stettin) and Ghana for transporting East European wares and carrying back West African products.

January 7, 1959

WEST IS GAINING FAVOR IN GUINEA

Makes Up for Early Soviet Bloc Lead by Economic and Diplomatic Moves

By HENRY TANNER

Special to The New York Times.

CONAKRY, Guinea, July 9—One morning last week two freighters, tied up side by side in the port of Conakry, were discharging gifts for this small new republic.

One had come across the Atlantic with 1,500 tons of United States surplus rice, the first installment of a gift that will eventually include 5,000 tons of rice and 3,000 tons of wheat flour.

The other ship, coming from Communist China, was carrying gifts of 5,000 tons of Chinese rice.

The Guinean Government acknowledged receipt of the American rice in a gracious ceremony and a cordial communiqué broadcast over the state radio.

At the request of Chinese authorities, nothing was done to welcome the Chinese gift.

The reaction of the Government was indicative of the problems and contradictions of this country's relations with East and West. The East has been winning a race here, but the West is catching up.

Half a dozen governments rushed in to bring unsolicited aid to the nation when it was born last September.

The Communists were first. Today there are well over a hundred Communist bloc technicians and diplomatic officials, according to most conservative estimates. Some place the figure closer to 200.

The technicians work as advisers in agriculture and public works. They have collected an enormous amount of goodwill.

They came at a time of need, when France was trying to isolate and even blockade Guinea and when other Western powers, including the United States, withheld recognition.

The United States recognized Guinea last December. But most Soviet bloc countries had concluded trade agreements by November.

Under these agreements, which are on a barter basis, the greater part of Guinea's principal crops, such as bananas, are going to Eastern Europe in exchange for industrial equipment and textiles.

Brighter Side Seen

Western diplomats do not deny that the Communists have made the most of their early chance and have established a potentially dangerous bridgehead in the economy of Guinea.

But there is also a brighter side, they say. Guinean contacts with the West have multiplied in the last two months.

United States assistance is beginning to arrive. An International Cooperation Administration mission is here. A United Nations mission is laying the groundwork for a technical aid program under which $800,000 will be spent in the next twelve months.

The most important event in the apparent normalization of Guinea's relations with the West, according to neutral observers here, was a United States invitation to President Sekou Touré for a state visit to Washington next October. The President welcomed this invitation.

At the same time he refused similar invitations from Moscow and other Eastern European and Middle Eastern capitals.

July 10, 1959

ISRAEL PRESSES ASIA-AFRICA TIES

Uganda Minister of Social Development Is Latest Guest to Seek Advice

By SETH S. KING

Special to The New York Times.

JERUSALEM (Israeli Sector), Oct. 3—Y. K. Lule, Minister of Social Development in the British protectorate of Uganda, visited Israel this week as a guest of the Government.

During his ten-day stay, Mr. Lule has been shown what a tiny state has been able to do with its educational, health and welfare services in the last eleven years.

Mr. Lule is only one of the scores of government officials from Asian and African areas who have already come to Israel or will do so during the rest of this year.

But he has the distinction of being the first Cabinet Minister from a "dependent" state in East Africa, and his arrival signified another Israeli foot in the door of Asia and Africa.

Israel has always been in need of friends, anywhere, and the new countries of Africa and Asia, born at the same time or soon after Israel, have been excellent prospects.

In addition, isolated as she is by the Arab states, Israel has been even more in need of trade outlets and political understanding in a section of the world where the United Arab Republic has been trying so hard to establish its influence.

Since the opening of the Gulf of Aqaba in late 1956, Israel has been quietly pushing outward in these directions with two commodities — trade and the offer of technical assistance from a young nation not formally aligned with either of the great-power blocs.

This week Mr. Lule is having his opportunity to study Israel's techniques.

Next week the Premier and three Cabinet Ministers from Chad, one of the new West African republics within the French Community, are scheduled to begin a two-week "exploration tour" of Israel.

For the last eleven months thirty-three officers and enlisted men of the Burmese Army, some with their families, have been living in agricultural settlements to learn how Israel has developed her farms and defended those that lie along the Arab borders.

In November six Indian specialists in community development will arrive in Israel for a six-week study. This is the second Indian delegation to come here for this purpose. The man in charge of the first one is now head of all community development in India.

Israel's ties are ever firmer with Ghana, wether among the newly independent states of West Africa. There are now 280 Israelis living in that country as advisers or officials in joint Ghanaian-Israeli companies.

At the moment Israel is providing instructors at Ghana's flying school and her nautical college. Ghana's Black Star shipping line includes Israeli maritime experts among its officials. Solel Boneh, the construction company of the Histadrut, Israel's federation of labor, is now operating in Ghana.

In East and West Nigeria, Israel now has representatives in joint Nigerian-Israeli water development companies. She also has them in a joint construction company in West Nigeria.

The first Israeli adviser, this one on agricultural development. has gone to the new Republic of Sudan in the French Community.

In addition to all these, Israeli technicians and advisers (the Foreign Ministry dislikes the term "expert") are now functioning in the Philippines, Thailand, Burma, Ethiopia and Liberia. All of these states have either sent people here or are planning to do so.

El Al, the Israeli airline, last week quietly began a regularly scheduled weekly flight to Teheran, detouring around the Arab states and through Turkey to reach Iran.

Israel's exports to Asian and African nations modestly grew from $10,100,000 in 1957 to $11,850,000 in 1958, and a further increase is expected this year.

October 4, 1959

NKRUMAH ASSAILS NON-AFRICA PACTS

He Calls Defense Alliances Threat to Independence —Again Urges Union

Special to The New York Times.

ACCRA, Ghana, March 14—Prime Minister Kwame Nkrumah warned African independent states today against defense pacts with powers outside Africa. Such pacts, he said, would compromise and undermine the independence and sovereignty of African states.

Mr. Nkrumah issued his warning in a speech to Parliament during a debate on the Government's draft constitution for a republic. Africa, he said, must be free of defense and political commitments "not entirely African in complexion."

"Entanglement in military politics with foreign powers is a danger to African unity," he said. "It will bring the cold war to Africa."

One of the clauses in the proposed constitution enjoins the Government to work for a union of African states.

Observers here believe Mr. Nkrumah's remarks were aimed at Ghana's neighbor, Togoland, due to become independent next month.

Togoland was reported recently to be contemplating a defense pact with France after independence as a precaution against Ghana's expansionist policies and a threat by Mr. Nkrumah to integrate Togoland as a province of Ghana.

Mr. Nkrumah said integration, which he termed as the removal of barriers between two countries, would be pursued "by all legitimate means available to us, including negotiation."

Mr. Nkrumah restated his plans to save Africa from imperialism and from the holding of nuclear tests on African soil.

"The African peoples will never forgive France for any repetition of atomic tests in the Sahara." he said.

He told the cheering members of Parliament to plan a conference for positive action "to mobilize world opinion against the horrors of French tests in Africa."

"Ghana," he said, "has a duty to speak for Africa."

March 15, 1960

West Fears Ghana Drifts Further Left

By HENRY TANNER
Special to The New York Times.

ACCRA, Ghana, Nov. 24—Ghana is going through a phase that is considered ominous from the Western point of view.

Internally, observers say, the trend is toward totalitarianism. Externally, they add, the country has been moving gradually toward adoption of a pro-Soviet brand of neutralism.

This is the conclusion reached by almost everyone talking politics in Accra.

When President Kwame Nkrumah went to the conference of nonaligned nations in Belgrade, Yugoslavia, he supported Moscow's foreign policy on a wide range of issues from Berlin to nuclear disarmament.

When he returned, he dismissed his British chief of staff, Gen. Henry T. Alexander, and all British officers from army command posts. He then said that Ghana would buy Soviet military equipment to supplement its British arms.

His Minister for Light and Heavy Industries has concluded an as yet unpublished agreement for loans and technical assistance with almost every member of the Soviet bloc.

Hundreds of members of most of the political organizations in the country—the ruling Convention People's party, trade unions, women's organizations and the youth movement—accompanied the President on various parts of his nine-week trip through Eastern Europe, the Soviet Union and China.

A trickle of Soviet technicians is gaining volume as aircraft engineers are being joined by agronomists making surveys for collective farms, by Czech labor leaders and by others.

Cadets Train in Moscow

About seventy Ghanaian cadets have been flown to Moscow for military training. Hundreds more will follow.

Accra's two Government-controlled newspapers imitate Soviet terminology down to attacks against "colonialists" and "neocolonialists" and occasionally, with or without attribution, run dispatches from the Soviet and Chinese press agencies.

November 25, 1961

AFRICA AND ASIA WARNED ON REDS

Tanganyikan Voices Fear of Colonizing 'Scramble'

By ROBERT CONLEY
Special to The New York Times.

MOSHI, Tanganyika, Feb. 4 — One of Africa's prominent but uncommitted leaders attacked the Communist countries today, implying that they were intent on colonizing Africa and Asia.

The accusation was made by Tanganyika's President, Julius K. Nyerere, who warned his neutralist colleagues of an impending "second scramble" for the two continents.

Mr. Nyerere said this new colonialism would be different from the ninteenth century "scramble" for Africa and Asia by the European countries.

"But its purpose will be the same—to get control of our countries," he said.

Mr. Nyerere questioned Communist motives both politically and economically in the opening address at the third Afro-Asian Peoples Solidarity Conference here on the slopes of Kilimanjaro in northern Tanganyika.

His address was understood to be an attempt to redefine the role of a nonaligned state, or one that refuses to be politically committed to either the East or West in a world that many neutrals feel has been unalterably changed by Communist China's invasion of India.

From the economic viewpoint, he charged Communist countries with the "same crime that was committed by the capitalists before." He said they were now beginning to use wealth for the capitalistic purpose of acquiring "power and prestige."

Mr. Nyerere did not cite the Communist world directly as political colonialists, but there appeared little doubt that he had them in mind.

Moreover, it was widely felt he was referring to the Soviet Union and Communist China in particular.

At one point in his half-hour address he told the Africans and Asians among the delegations from about 60 countries in the conference hall that they should not allow themselves to "think of this new imperialism solely in terms of the old colonial powers."

"Imperialism is a byproduct of wealth and power," he added. "We have to be on guard against incursions by anyone."

At another point he confided, "I wish I could say that I believe that the second scramble for Africa or Asia is going to be a scramble only between the capitalistic powers."

Although the Chinese Communist and Soviet delegates fell silent at his words, the Africans cheered.

One delegate tonight called the speech "the strongest attack ever made on the Communist bloc by a non-aligned leader at such a conference."

Had Mr. Nyerere's remarks about Communist colonialism been made elsewhere, his speech might have been regarded as ambiguous with its use of the term "Socialist countries" to mean the uncommitted states in one breath and the Communist governments in another.

Many Reds Present

But in the context of the solidarity conference, the speech was looked upon as remarkably frank. Two-thirds of the more than 400 delegates and observers are either from Communist countries or leaders of Communist movements in other countries.

Mr. Nyerere's speech also came at a time when the lexicon of invective against the colonialists employed by most other non-aligned leaders is restricted to Britain, France and the United States.

It is an open secret here that Mr. Nyerere was none too pleased with the political cast of the week-long conference and had tried to find some other official engagement in the hope of being able to avoid attending.

Addressing himself to the Communistsh, he said no state had enough wealth to "satisfy the desire of a single individual for power and prestige." Once wealth was divorced from its essential purpose of banishing poverty — as he charged was beginning to happen in the Communist countries—it became a means of domination and of humiliating other people

If his view of the new role of a nonaligned country could be defined simply it could be found in his warning to the African and Asian delegates: "Be on your guard."

February 5, 1963

U.S. IMAGE CALLED MARRED IN AFRICA

Nigerian Says Racial Strife Results in Loss of Goodwill

By ARNOLD H. LUBASCH
Special to The New York Times

CORNING, N. Y., May 19—"If the Government only knew how much damage was being done they would not continue this costly indulgence."

The remark referred to racial discrimination in the United States. The speaker was an African Cabinet Minister who is attending an international conference here.

"For every penny of aid poured into Africa," he added, "America continues to lose tons of goodwill because of the racial discrimination in this country. Something drastic must be done, fast, before it is too late."

The speaker, Chief Joseph Modupe Johnson, Nigerian Minister of Labor, was conversing with colleagues at a week-long conference on African leadership.

The main address at the session on "The American Negro and Africa" was delivered by the Rev. James H. Robinson, director of Operation Crossroads Africa.

The conference, attended by leaders from 25 African nations and private representatives from the United States and Europe, is designed to help develop young African leadership.

Mr. Robinson reported that some African countries had made it known that they would not accept Negro ambassadors from the United States.

"Shame! shame!" shouted several African leaders in the audience.

"The indictment is not upon the Africans," Mr. Robinson said. He explained that some Africans feared that Negro ambassadors would not be listened to in Washington "because they are second-class citizens."

May 20, 1964

REDS' AFRICA GAIN BELIEVED LIMITED

U.S. Analysts Cite Wariness on Continent and Chinese Quarrel With Russians

By TAD SZULC
Special to The New York Times

WASHINGTON, July 5—The Communists have had only limited and spotty success in winning meaningful influence in Africa in recent years despite some spectacular instances of infiltration in the view of United States Government specialists.

This was the assessment made last week by highly qualified analysts against the background of events of the last several months in such places as Zanzibar, the Congo, Burundi, Algeria, Angola and Somalia.

The analysts here have not contended in their evaluation that the Communist political offensive in Africa has altogether failed. They also do not deny that either the Soviet Union or Communist China may eventually gain some victories in Africa.

In fact they believe that, for example, the situation in Zanzibar is still touch-and-go and that the problems in the Congo may well lead to an increase in Communist influence.

The specialists also foresee situations in which Communism may benefit from the emerging and spreading movements of young radicals impatient with the relatively moderate leadership in many of their countries in the first phase of independence.

The assessment is designed principally to measure the African situation as it stands in mid-1964, following visits to the continent by Premier Chou En-lai of Communist China and Premier Khrushchev and other occurrences in the region in the last few years.

The chief finding is that, with the possible exception of Zanzibar, the Communists have not won a firm foothold anywhere in Africa, even though they exert varying degrees of influence in many African countries and independence movements.

Specifically, the experts have found that the impact of the Chinese-Soviet split has seriously affected the effectiveness of the Communist effort in Africa. The Russians and the Chinese are viewed as directly confronting each other in Mali, Guinea and Somalia and to be working at cross-purposes in Zanzibar and Tanganyika.

The second point that appears to emerge is that the leaders in most African countries are extremely wary of unquestioning acceptance of Communist aid or influence.

Guinea and Algeria Cited

This is notably true in Guinea, which three years ago seemed to be sliding fast into the Communist orbit, and in Algeria. In the latter, despite sizable Soviet aid and the regime's official socialism, President Ahmed Ben Bella has been as suspicious of domestic Communists as President Gamal Abdel Nasser is in the United Arab Republic.

The impact of Communist economic aid to Africa has likewise been limited, according to the United States analysts. Its size is dwarfed by contributions from the United States, France and other Western powers.

In many instances, the experts said, the Russians find it difficult to deliver capital goods or other supplies to African countries or to maintain their flow.

United States specialists have discovered that both Russians and Chinese frequently run into racial problems in Africa. Soviet technicians are said to have failed to develop popular acceptance among Africans, even to the degree of acceptance enjoyed by Americans or Western Europeans.

There is some concern over Kenya, where leftist pressures are rising at a time when Prime Minister Jomo Kenyatta's power is lessening.

Congo Sway Discounted

In Somalia, which has a border problem with Kenya and an on-and-off war with Ethiopia, the Russians and Chinese are openly vying for influence.

Last autumn the Soviet Union signed a $30 million military agreement with Somalia, but the arms have been arriving slowly and mainly in the form of small items. It is believed Moscow wishes to avoid antagonizing Ethiopia, which Mr. Chou visited earlier this year.

In the Congo, the present judgment is that extreme leftist influences have been exaggerated. United States specialists feel that tribal and local problems are chiefly at the root of the present provincial rebellions, although growing attention is given to the "jeunesse," or youth, movement in the eastern Congo, which is becoming increasingly radical in its clamor for social reforms and economic betterment.

Officials here tend to think that the support given to the rebels in Kivu Province by Chinese Communists operating from Burundi, where they have an embassy, has been much exaggerated. They said there was no evidence of any Chinese arms traffic reaching the Bafulero-tribe rebels.

July 6, 1964

Peking's Frustration

China Finds Efforts to Widen Influence With Africans and Latins Often Balked

By RICHARD EDER
Special to The New York Times

WASHINGTON, Aug. 15—For six years Communist China has been seeking to spread its influence through Africa and, to a lesser degree, Latin America.

News Analysis

It has trained guerrillas, given away softly colored picture magazines, built canneries, sent acrobats to tumble in the dust of African villages, bribed officials and sometimes killed them, and steadily preached the example of the great revolution made by some of the world's poorest people.

The results have been inconclusive. If they suggest anything, it is that the Chinese are learning, as the United States and the Soviet Union already have, that to be a great international power is to be subject to great international frustrations.

Much Tangible Bafflement

The Chinese effort in Africa is fully developed and moving rapidly. In Latin America it can barely be called incipient. In both areas, however, the Chinese can find some intangible promise and a great deal of tangible bafflement.

Dealing with new, nationalist governments has not been notably easier for the Chinese than for the Russians and the Americans. Politically, China seems better able to project a sense of inspiration to revolutionary leaders than does the Soviet Union, let alone the United States.

But even in the event of successful new revolutions in Africa or Latin America, inspiration and influence are not necessarily the same. In sending its revolutionary example abroad, China is apt to find as it already has in Cuba—that revolutions rarely have sons; at most, they have sons-in-law, and even these tend to be intractable.

China Widens Ties in Africa

In Africa, China has diplomatic relations with 16 nations. Four years ago it had relations with six.

At the end of 1964 it had cultural agreements with nine countries. Two years before it had four such agreements. In 1964 alone, China extended grants and credits valued at $94 million; in all of the 10 preceding years these had totaled only $138 million.

Chinese-dominated groups control the Government of the Congo Republic at Brazzaville, their power threatened only by the problematical disposition of the army. In Tanzania, Chinese influence in Zanzibar and in some political circles in Tanganyika has limited, though by no means eliminated, the margin for independent action by President Julius K. Nyerere.

On the other hand, Burundi broke relations with China and threw out its mission for interfering in Burundi's internal affairs. In Kenya, President Jomo Kenyatta has reacted sharply against elements in his party showing signs of Chinese influence. Malawi's Prime Minister, Dr. H. Kamuzu Banda, has denounced what he said was a Chinese bribe in the form of a promise to extend $18 million in aid in exchange for recognition.

Mali, which has especially warm relations with China, has made a point this year of showing signs of friendship for a number of Western countries, including the United States. In Somalia, where both China and the Soviet Union are contending, the Russians appear to have the upper hand.

Even in Tanzania, where the Chinese are reported to have made their largest aid offer so far—the building of a railroad to Zambia that would cost about $145 million—a recent trip by Premier Chou En-lai was considerably dampened when his aggressive cold war language offended his hosts.

The collapse of this year's African-Asian conference, scheduled to take place in Algiers, could furnish a script for what could only be called "the ugly Chinese." China's quick recognition of those who overthrew President Ahmed Ben Bella offended many African leaders who had close links with the deposed Algerian chief.

Analysts here attempting to define Chinese objectives in Africa break them down into short-range and longer-range categories. In the first category are the establishment of relations, the setting up of trade and aid links, and an effort to win the governments to as anti-Western a brand of neutralism as possible.

In the second category are the efforts to train groups of revolutionaries whose mission will be to transform the African nationalist political temper into a Communist one. The two categories are not completely compatible. When Premier Chou spoke recently of Africa being ripe for revolution he infuriated many old revolutionaries—Mr. Kenyatta, among others.

Chinese Poorly Trained

In the first category of efforts—those aimed at forging national links—the Chinese, as indicated by the figures cited above, have been quite successful. They have two principal handicaps, however.

One is the fact that they are materially unprepared to furnish aid on anything like the scale of the Soviet Union, let alone that of the United States. This disadvantage extends not only to the quantity but to the manner of assistance. Russian diplomats and advisers are schooled in the customs and the language—sometimes even the dialects—of the country. The Chinese are much more poorly trained.

The second handicap is the fact that China's position toward the Soviet Union obliges Peking to be militant and aggressive about cold war matters. On the other hand, the Russians can talk about neutralism, independence and peaceful coexistence—something much more to the taste of the Africans, who generally want to stay out of both the cold war and the Chinese-Soviet feud.

At the very least, however, the Chinese have established a firm presence in Africa from which they may be able to advance some longer-range goals.

August 16, 1965

Extensive Efforts in Africa Yield Little Results for Communists

By DREW MIDDLETON
Special to The New York Times

LONDON, May 5—International Communism, despite an extensive and expensive campaign, has failed thus far to win to its cause any significant number of black African states, peoples or political parties.

African versions of representative government have held their own against the Communist political challenge. Communist economic assistance and technical aid have reduced only slightly the West's position as the principal source of help in developing Africa.

Yet the political, economic and ideological contest will continue. There is no prospect of a final defeat of Communism on a continent whose peoples desperately seek national identity during a period of rapid, drastic and explosive change.

In his "Prologue to African Conscience" the Ethiopian poet Tsegaye Gabre Medhen saw this African dilemma:

Tamed to bend.
Into the model chairs.
Carpentered for it.
By the friendly pharos of its time.
The black conscience flutters
Yet is taken in.
It looks right
It looks left.
It forgets to look into its own self.

African leaders see the Communist presence in ways as varied as their continent.

Chinese Feared by Some

One view is shared by Presidents Félix Houphouët-Boigny of the Ivory Coast, François Tombalbaye of Chad, and Lieut. Gen. Joseph A. Ankrah, head of Ghana's National Liberation Council, which has ruled the country since the ouster of President Kwame Nkrumah. To them, the long-term threat is that Chinese Communism might spread into underpopulated Africa, using subversion, sabotage, bribery and economic infiltration to win control of individuals, organizations and Governments.

But President Julius K. Nyerere of Tanzania sees Communism merely as one of two competing political forces. And he considers it harmless enough to be asked for help if his country cannot get what it wants, politically or economically, from the rival Western force.

To President Kenneth Kaunda of Zambia, Communism is part of a world struggle from which his nation should stay aloof, taking help not from the Soviet Union or the United States, the great antagonists, but from nations less committed to the cold war.

Kenya's President, Jomo Kenyatta, advocates what he calls democratic African Socialism. He finds that Marx's description of Victorian industrial society has little similarity to Kenya today, and has become an enemy of Communism as promoted in Africa by outsiders.

Communism in South Africa is widely and often wildly interpreted to mean anything from subversion to a few kind words for Abraham Lincoln. The Portuguese assert that the arms and ammunition of the rebels in northern Mozambique and Angola come from Communist sources and that Portugal's forces are fighting Communism there just as much as the Americans are in Vietnam.

Communism in Africa met and failed to defeat conditions it had not encountered in Europe and Asia. The chief of these was tribalism, often a curse to developing Africa.

Communism's state ownership ran afoul of the African belief that land belongs to the tribe or the clan and its individual members. And the antireligious stand offended Moslems.

Another obstacle was the persistence, despite all the harsh things said and done in various struggles for independence, of Western political concepts and training. Leaders of these struggles who had done more than flirt with Communism returned, once in power, to governmental systems modeled after those they knew best and to the advice and help of the Americans, British and French.

Picture Changes in Ghana

For some years Ghana was the most conspicuous Communist success. President Nkrumah's overthrow and the complete elimination of Communism was the movement's worst reverse. Today most Ghanaians beleve that the Russians, who were the stronger Communist influence, overplayed their hand and underestimated the latent anti-Communism in the army and the civil service, both trained in the British traditon.

"Even those who adopted the Soviet line could see that the Russian assistance was intended to serve the Soviet Union, not Ghana," a civil servant said. "And the Russians were such fools about it, they thought we were completely ignorant. Imagine, they established state farms so that they could teach us about agriculture. As though we didn't know about the failures on their own farms."

Teacher from Soviet Union instructs high school mathematics class in Conakry, Guinea

Tanzania is a prime objective of Chinese and Soviet Communists, with the Chinese more numerous and influential than the Russians. But Tanzania's rulers, desperate for help from any quarter, complain that Chinese performance does not square with Chinese promises. The country, President Nyerere acknowledged, remains under Western economic influence because the Chinese have not made good on their offers of help.

President Kenyatta, who as a revolutionary was familiar with Communism, has been one of its bitterest foes as a national leader. Kenya's security service has thrown out Chinese and East European agents and provided the President with evidence of corruptions of his rivals by the Communist powers.

The evidence produced by the counterintelligence service led to the ouster of Oginga Odinga from the Vice-Presidency. It convinced Mr. Kenyatta that "Double O" was in Peking's pay.

Guinea remains under Communist influence, and Africans report food shortages and commercial stagnation there.

There is considerable agreement among Africans and Western advisers on basic Communist strategy in Africa. The Communists apparently want to cut Africa in half, moving westward from a base in Tanzania on the east coast through the two Congo republics to the Atlantic coast.

Such a movement would take many years. It would end with Communism controlling the Congo area, potentially the richest in Central Africa, and within striking distance of the politically explosive black populations of Rhodesia, Mozambique, Angola and South Africa.

The Potential Is There

For as long as white supremacy flourishes in South Africa and Rhodesia, and colonialism rather than self-determination rules the Portuguese territories, Communism has a fertile field for growth.

Africans know that the Government forces of Rhodesia and South Africa will be superior for some time to any forces black Africa might mobilize against them. Meanwhile the depth of feeling against the two white regimes cannot be doubted. To Africans the existence of these Governments insults the whole idea of African maturity and independence and perpetuates the concept of the African as a lower order of being in a white man's world.

Although most black Africans detest the South Africans and Rhodesians, they abhor the idea of a real war in Africa now. But it is obvious that if independent Africa fails to get Western help in overthrowing racism in the southern third of the continent it will look for help in the East.

More Openings Likely

The future will present other opportunities for Communism.

Education, social reforms, industrialization and the movement into cities, which is very marked in Nigeria, the Ivory Coast and Ghana, are bound to weaken tribalism as a bulwark against Communism.

The growth of slums and labor troubles following the expansion of industry will create conditions more favorable to Communist agitation than those in a semiprimitive society.

Most African countries are primary producers depending on Western markets. A small change in the price of one commodity can ruin an African country's economy for a year. When this occurs the Communists make the most of it, advocating closer commercial links between themselves and the Africans.

The Ultimate Ingredient

Finally, Communism thrives on chaos. There probably will be 5 to 10 years more of political turbulence in Africa, promising opportunities for Communist agents who already have found African politicians susceptible to bribes and blackmail.

There remains one human element in the equation that the Communists must overcome.

"You know the Russians don't really like Africa," a Ghanaian said. "I'll go further. They hate it.

"The British, the French, the Americans find it exciting. They want to learn more, to taste every experience. The Rusians just want to go home. And the Chinese, well, they're so conceited, so arrogant, that they just cannot make contact with Africans, even those who favor Communism."

May 10, 1966

Chinese Communist Presence in East African Nations Grows

By **LAWRENCE FELLOWS**
Special to The New York Times

DAR ES SALAAM, Tanzania, May 24—Although the Chinese are rarely seen on the streets here, Chinese communist projects seem everywhere.

The technical help and the loans and gifts the Chinese have bestowed on the Tanzanians exceed by far what the Tanzanians are getting from anyone else.

The Chinese have helped set up a joint shipping line with Tanzania, employing two 10,000-ton freighters. Tanzania paid her share with an interest-free loan from Communist China that the Tanzanians must start repaying only in 10 years and then from the profits they make on the line.

The Chinese have just finished building a textile mill at Ubungo, near Dar es Salaam, which Tanzanians are to pay for with another interest-free Chinese loan.

They also provided the Tanzanians with a 50-kilowatt radio transmitter at Mabibo, also near Dar es Salaam, with the same financing arrangement. A police-training camp at Moshi is staffed by the Chinese. They are also running a $15-million farming project at Ruvu. And they are providing loans and grants that the Tanzanians need to resume agricultural and road-building projects suspended when diplomatic relations were broken off with Britain and that source of money dried up.

Last Engineers Arrive

About 150 engineers and technicians from Communist China arrived in Dar es Salaam yesterday. They are the last of a team surveying for a 1,000-mile railway that the Chinese have undertaken to build from here to the Copper Belt in neighboring Zambia.

There were no Government announcements or fanfare about their arrival, but a crowd of Africans stood on the thin white shore that lines the harbor and watched the glistening blue-and-white liner Yao Hua slip into harbor and drop anchor.

It was a curious spectacle: the Chinese stepping into launches one after another, without smiling or speaking, to be carried ashore and driven away in crowded minibuses. The Africans giggled, but seemed not to talk much to one another about this evidence of China's growing presence in black Africa.

For the other foreigners in Dar es Salaam, swilling beers and exchanging alarming tales under paddling overhead fans in crowded bars these sticky nights, there is no more favorite topic of discussion than the Chinese. What do they hope to achieve in Africa? Why have they done so well in Tanzania when they have failed so miserably in so many other places in Africa?

Relations Turn Sour

After a promising start, China's relations with Ghana and the Central African Republic turned sour. From Burundi the Chinese supported the rebellion in the Congo and eventually got themselves thrown out. Their relations were strained in Kenya and Uganda when they were caught providing funds for the opposition, Dr. H. Kamuzu Banda, President of Malawi, called their hand for having tried to bribe some of his ministers into joining the opposition. In the Congo and Mali the Chinese were well received, but they failed to make any headway in the rest of the continent.

China's big initial success in Africa was in helping to stage a revolution in Zanzibar in 1964. It has never relinquished its hold on the island and has never made a political misjudgment serious enough to jeopardize its influence there.

With the unon of Zanzibar and the mainland state of Tanganyika to become the state of Tanzania, even those who thought the islanders had been swallowed up wondered if they would ever be digested. Tanzania's politics have moved erratically but unmistakably to the left ever since.

This enormous, primitive country of more than 360,000 square miles—as big as France and Germany together—has 12 million people, most of whom care little about politics, scratching out no more than a peasant's existence on land that is abundant and that could be as productive as any in Africa. There is remote, scattered mineral wealth in the southern highlands that no one has bothered to exploit.

It is difficult to accept the idea that the Chinese are very interested in anything Tanzania has to offer now, or that the Chinese very badly need Tanzania's reassurance that China is leading a revolutionary force

The New York Times May 25, 1968

Projected railroad: From Dar es Salaam (1) to the Copper Belt in Zambia (2).

in the world. But Tanzanian Government leaders are easily excited about the continued presence of white governments in southern Africa.

The Tanzanians are receptive to the flow of Chinese weapons, for they can get them nowhere else as easily. A grip in Tanzania, whose vast area touches eight other countries, would give the Chinese a wide periphery in Africa and a base on the western littoral of the Indian Ocean. A project like the railway will give them valid reason to put thousands of people into the mineral-rich heart of the African Copper Belt that runs from Zambia into Katanga Province of the Congo.

Of enormous potential importance is the military equipment and training that the Chinese provide for the dozen "liberation" movements based in Tanzania.

But not all of the weapons have gone to rebels operating against the white-dominated southern region. The rebellion in the Congo was kept alive by weapons sent by rail from Dar es Salaam to Kigoma. And a convoy of weapons bound for Uganda was stopped by the police in Kenya.

Dr. Banda has accused President Julius K. Nyerere of Tanzania of allowing plots against him to be hatched in Tanzania. Even the Watusis, in their long-bogged down invasion of Rwanda, got their Chinese weapons through Tanzania.

But the railway that the Chinese have undertaken to build is a far more spectacular idea, and they have wasted no time getting the project under way.

The job could be done in 15 months and the construction could begin then The Chinese have already promised to finance the construction to extend of $280-million in an terms for repayment.

The Chinese have also offered to talk about providing diesel locomotives and rolling stock for the railway.

Both President Nyerere and President Kenneth D. Kaunda of Zambia were anxious to get the railway. Mr. Nyerere sees it as a way to open up his southern region to development and to enhance the value of the port of Dar es Salaam. Mr. Kaunda wants the railway so that he need not ship copper out through white-governed Rhodesia and Portuguese Mozambique.

Mr. Kaunda was at first reluctant to accept the Chinese offer to build the railway, but he changed his mind when he failed to arouse any interest in the project in Britain, France, West Germany or the United States.

All of the nations seemed worried by the big initial investment and the time it would take for the railroad to start turning a profit. The United States offered to pay for a comprehensive transportation survey that would establish the economic facts of the matter, but the Africans were not interested.

President Nyerere was less worried than was President Kaunda about the political implications of bringing in the Chinese. He has always argued that big slices of Communist aid would help offset the old preponderant influence of the West in Africa.

Mr. Nyerere approached Soviet leaders and was turned down. The world bank was also approached, but it advised the Africans to ask instead for help to improve the crude road that is now being used to some extent to truck copper to Dar es Salaam.

Eventually Presidents Nyerere and Kaunda accepted the offer the Chinese had made to Mr. Nyerere when he visited China in 1956.

Several diplomats in this city are frankly puzzled about the intentions of the Chinese. The railway could take seven or eight years to build, they say, terming it an unusually long period for any country to commit herself to a project so sensitive and unsettled a part of Africa.

They feel that the Chinese will inevitably run into frictions that have been met by Britain, the United States, West Germany, Israel, Nigeria and every other country that has made any major contributions in Tanzania.

The Chinese are obviously aiming at the rich heart of Africa, but it is considered a long shot.

May 25, 1968

U.S. Officials Say China Widens African Aid to Extend Influence

By TAD SZULC

Special to The New York Times

WASHINGTON, Sept. 3—China has negotiated or renewed aid and trade agreements with 24 African countries in the last two years, closely following the resumption of active diplomacy after the isolation of the Cultural Revolution in the late nineteen-sixties.

According to information compiled by United States specialists, Peking is concentrating on expanding economic relations with Algeria, Egypt, the Sudan. Ethiopia, Tanzania and Zambia, demonstrating considerable flexibility in all cases.

The Chinese have also established trade and aid links with smaller African nations, such as Burundi, Rwanda, Equatorial Guinea, Mauritania, Mauritius and Sierra Leone.

In addition, China signed in May and July two civil air agreements with Ethiopia—presumably as the first step in extending to Africa planned worldwide aviation routes. She is also negotiating airline services with Zambia.

In the judgment of United States specialists, this effort is designed in large part to increase China's influence where there has been an erosion of Soviet and Western positions.

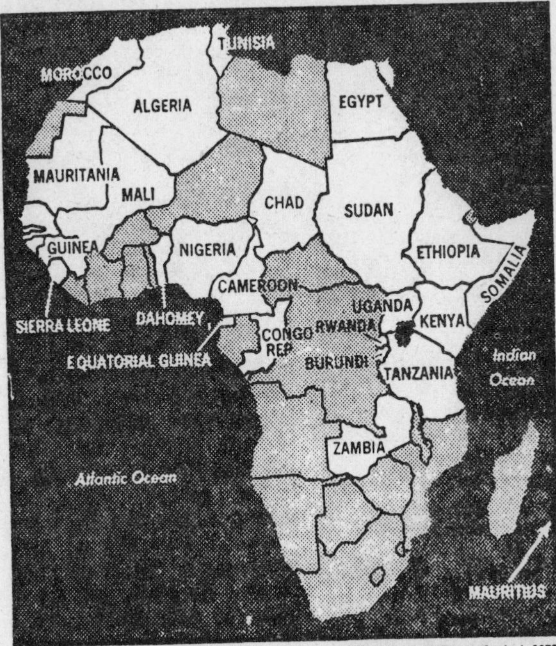

The New York Times/Sept. 4, 1972

The Chinese have negotiated or renewed agreements for aid or trade with countries designated in white.

Egypt, which has mounting problems with Moscow, is a case in point. Chinese-Egyptian trade, which had totaled $12.5-million a year, is to be increased to $85-million in an agreement signed last March.

In the Sudan, China supplied Khartoum with $80-million in loans, after an attempted take-over of the Government, reportedly backed by Moscow, failed. A trade agreement signed in May provided for $70-million in annual trade exchanges.

Ethiopia received $87.5-million in loans from China last October and a Peking commitment to purchase a large volume of coffee.

Burundi and Rwanda each received $20-million in interest-free loans earlier this year with provisions for repayment in commodities over 15 years.

Railway Is the Big Project

China's principal economic project in Africa remains the Tanzam Railway linking Tanzania and Zambia. About 15,000 Chinese technicians and workers are building it and construction costs are financed from the sale of Chinese goods imported on credit.

Since mid-1971, China has been buying 1,000 tons of copper monthly from Zambia. In July, Tanzania announced that China had replaced Britain as her principal source of imports. Soap traditionally imported by Tanzania from Kenya was replaced early this year by Chinese soap.

During 1971, China bought $3.5-million in cotton from Kenya, nearly three times what she had originally contracted to import.

Along with the emphasis on trade, American experts said the expansion of air routes was closely related to China's new economic programs in African nations and in other developing countries, with the new agreements in Africa looming as the principal example.

September 4, 1972

CHAPTER 5

Africa and the Modern World

he future of the New Africa.

urtesy Compix.

TRIBAL RULE EBBS IN THE GOLD COAST

Local Chieftains Giving Way to More Modern Methods of Government in Africa

By THOMAS F. BRADY

Special to The New York Times.

KETA, Gold Coast, Aug. 6—Tribal organization and the institution of the chieftaincy, which British colonial administration once encouraged as a means of indirect rule, still exist everywhere in the Gold Coast. But in many parts of the country they have become more vestigial than the British peerage.

Chief Ocloo, the seigneur of this town of 10,000 souls, died last week. His family and friends and fellow citizens have combined the funeral solemnities with the British bank holiday, and today, Monday, is the end of the week-end festivities.

The notable fact at the funeral was the absence of gloom or any atmosphere of mourning. Two men in open-throated white European shirts presided over three deep drums that looked like barrels tapered to a point at one end and covered with hide at the other, tipped at forty-five-degree angles on wooden supports.

The chief drummer smiled broadly at white visitors and began to beat out a rhythm with L-shaped drumsticks made from small tree branches. He said in English: "That meant you are welcome."

Opposite him on benches were other cheerful folk who shook hands and said: "How are you?" A few wore European dress, more were in wonderfully printed calicos made in Europe exclusively for the African trade, with twisting geometric designs that seem to move with their wearers. The men use their swatches of calico as togas, the women as bodices and generous wrap-around skirts.

In an inner enclosure were two distinguished members of the Ocloo family, Daniel Chapman, secretary to the Gold C ast Cabinet, and his brother, C. H. Chapman, member of the Legislative Assembly (Parliament). They belong to a branch of the Ocloo family, and their name in Ewe, the language of this region, is Oclootse, which means Little Ocloo, "tse" being a diminutive suffix.

Their father went to school in Cape Coast, west of here, where he lived with an English family named Chapman, whose name he adopted. Now that the Gold Coast is approaching sovereign independence as the first Negro nation in the British Commonwealth, the sons are thinking of going back to the Ewe name.

The funeral seemed to illustrate the gamut of transition from tribalism to modern nationalism and independent government. Daniel Chapman, who is said to be the author of the most lucid and polished speeches of cabinet members, had to get back to Accra, the capital. C. H. Chapman, who is deputy speaker of the assembly, said he could not leave the funeral, but suggested a visit to another brother, Shaw Chapman, president of the Keta municipal council.

Keta (pronounced k'tah) is a completely African town in the middle of a long sand spit between the Gulf of Guinea and a lagoon. This correspondent and his companion, a Gold Coast information officer from Accra, saw no other white men in town. Shaw Chapman lived down the street in a two-story building above his cold storage and refrigeration plant, which he is just getting under way.

The problem now, he said, is to find a new chief. Nobody wants the job. Chiefs are not very well paid and modern methods of government are reducing them more and more to the status of semi-religious figureheads, forced by tradition and fetish always to wear sandals and cloth togas, and walk about in the shade of an umbrella borne by an attendant.

Mr. Chapman went on to talk of more serious things. He had been defeated overwhelmingly in a neighboring consistituency in the recent general election because, he said, he had voted three years ago as a regional councilor for local taxes the people did not like.

He discussed the prospect of local land reclamation with possible United States aid after independence; the problems of the fishing, farming and salt-making economy of Keta; and the hoped-for unification of the Ewe people, who live partly in the Gold Coast and partly in the French and British trust territories of Togoland.

August 19, 1956

AFRICAN RALLIES MARKED BY SONG

Hymns and Chants Provide Rhythm and Morale for Nationalist Meetings

By MILTON BRACKER

Special to The New York Times.

JOHANNESBURG, South Africa, April 17—Songs, hymns and chants give both rhythm and morale to African nationalist meetings throughout east, central and south Africa.

In a country like South Africa, the music is a characteristic and particularly important part of the meetings. That is because they are held under restricted conditions and police scrutiny, and often in dilapidated premises.

Massed voices joining in Zulu, Xosa or Sotho parodies of familiar melodies are sure to play a big part in the gathering at Alexandria Township which will wind up Africa Week Sunday.

As slow processions of Negroes from small meetings converge on a large one, they invariably move to the swelling beat of a vernacular chant.

A tour of native meetings in three areas Wednesday night, when Africa Week officially started, was a revealing experience.

Basement Used as Hall

The first site was a baseball hall in downtown Johannesburg, where several hundred men and women met under the scrutiny of a half dozen white members of the security branch of the South African police.

A white speaker of the multi-racial Liberal party spoke in English; an African translated into Sotho. It was a rather painful process. On the rear wall a picture of Lana Turner lent an incongruous touch, while the cluster of security men near the doorway provided an unmistakable damper.

Yet somehow the entire mood of the meeting lifted when the group stood and began singing to the tune of "Clementine." Instead of "Oh, My Darling," the four-syllable begining was "Mayibuye."

'Come Back' Is Theme

This is the Zulu equivalent of "Come Back."

The song went:

Mayibuye, Mayibuye,
Mayibuye Afrika
Makaphele Amapasi
Mayibuye Afrika.

Thus the crowd was singing, in effect, "come back Africa, come back to your original heritage and let the pass laws [for identity cards carried by Africans] come to an end."

It was not necessary to understand a single word to feel the impact of the voices. Throughout, the security men looked on in alert silence.

Out in Sophiatown five miles from the city, there was no overt scrutiny, although in African locations African agents are often used. Sophiatown was one of the few places where Negroes could own homes. It was an easy-going good-natured community that outside natives called "Soft Town." It had a more-or-less famous illicit bar, or "shebeen," called "The Thirty-nine Steps."

In 1955 demolition of Sophiatown began. The area had been assigned to whites, and of 58,000 Negroes only 15,000 remain. The others have been moved to places called Meadowlands and Diep Kloof. Sophiatown is now two-thirds rubble.

The Wednesday meeting in Sophiatown was held on Gold Street, in a place called Diggers Hall. The place was lighted by two bulbs. Every time a person moved, hulking shadows crept across the dark green walls.

In the rear, one whole corner of the wall was a raw concrete patch. The windows were studded with missing panes.

Robert Resha, a leader of the African National Congress and a defendant in the protracted treason trial that is to resume in Pretoria Monday, spoke articulately in English. At his side a youth translated the address into Sotho.

Several hundred persons were present. The men and women sat apart on plain benches divided by a center aisle. Most of the women wore bandannas and many carried infants.

Another speaker, an old, bearded Zulu, made a strong attack on the past laws as applied to women. Then the crowd started for a larger meeting in a near-by African Township.

Their close shuffling gait was to a chant in which the name of the South African Prime Minister, Dr. Hendrik F. Verwoerd, was readily identifiable:

Doctor Verwoerd, open the jails;
The volunteers are coming ***.

On the way across dusty roads to the township, they also sang: "The Pass is the Enemy of the People" and "God Save Africa."

Arrivals Join in Song

The township hall was of solid brick with better lighting. As the last residents of Sophiatown filed in, their voices joined in "Somlandela." This is a parody of an old nondenominational hymn, with the theme line: "I will follow Jesus."

But as the Negroes sang it:

Somlandela somlandela Luthuli
Somlandela somlandela izikhathi zonke.

Roughly it is "We will follow Luthuli forever." Albert Luthuli is president of the African National Congress.

A speaker said:

"In places like Ghana the flags are flying high. In places like Egypt the flags are flying high."

He paused, breathed deeply and resumed:

"In places like South Africa, where people are oppressed, the flags are rising . . ."

April 18, 1959

NUDITY FORBIDDEN BY GUINEA REGIME

Dresses of Young Women Now Cover Torso, as Do Those of Ghanaians

By THOMAS F. BRADY
Special to The New York Times.

CONAKRY, Guinea, May 2—Nationalism here has been as severe as puritanism in New York in making the girls of Guinea cover their torsos.

While Paris chuckled at Manhattan moralists who forced brassieres on the young women of the African ballet, directed by Fodeba Keita, Guinea's Minister of the Interior, President Sekou Touré of Guinea was doing the same thing at home.

Mr. Touré said in a speech that "No longer will we see young women, torso nude, carrying a tray with two bananas."

Women still carry bananas on their heads, as they do almost everything else from ink bottles to a bedsteads. But after seven months of independence, the torsos of the tall, handsome women for whom Guinea is famous have been covered with the same brilliant calicos they use for skirts.

A Difference in Welcomes

This new formalism was one of the noticeable differences between the welcome accorded to Prime Minister Kwame Nrumah of Ghana ten days ago and the welcome given to Gen. Charles De Gaulle last August, a few weeks before Guinea became independent of France.

Glineans and Ghanaians alike have adopted European disapproval of nudity.

Thus Mr. Nkrumah presumably was more comfortable last week than he would have been in pre-independence Guinea. Back in Ghana he had left the women of the advanced coastal region waging a campaign to persuade their sisters of primitive Northern Ghana to adopt clothing.

Habits of dress apart, Conakry remains one of the pleasantest cities of West Africa to look at: wide streets lined with enormous shade trees, mango, kapok and palm; white colonial houses set in big gardens, and an occasional modern building of concrete and glass jutting out of the hot, sleepy sun and shade below.

But the "African quarters" are pitifully different: dusty, treeless masses of ramshackle huts.

And Marxist though the Government's philosophy may be, Conakry, where the inflated French colonial franc is still the medium of exchange, remains a relatively expensive place to live. At the only modern hotel in town, the Hotel de France, a room and meals cost $17.50 to $20 a day.

Although Guinea has concluded barter trade agreements with the Communist world, French goods still predominate in the stores.

Of the 6,000 French who lived in Guinea before independence, 4,000 remain, most of them in the capital.

The Government and the public services, except for the port and the airfield, are run by Africans and work surprisingly well, in view of the precipitate departure of French civil servants and technicians last fall. But at the lowest echelons of government the notion seems to exist that courtesy to foreigners is a form of colonial servility to be dispensed with in an independent state.

In this respect, Conakry differs markedly from Accra, the capital of Ghana, where African cordiality and gentle good manners have survived independence.

While in Conakry, Mr. Touré, a man of dynamic charm and forthright manner, is extremely difficult to see nowadays because of the load of work he has assumed personally.

The change since last October is marked. Then, the day after independence, this correspondent interviewed Mr. Touré in his office.

In front of the hotel he had a sudden thought because we had talked of African food. "Are you free for lunch?" he asked.

At his large and comfortable house nearby Mrs. Touré, a noted beauty and a gracious hostess, showed no surprise at an unexpected visitor. We ate fonio, a paste made of pounded millet, and stewed chicken.

May 18, 1959

2 AFRICANS FREED IN CONTEMPT CASE

Traditional Legal System Is Upset by Decision on Two Rhodesian Catholics

Special to The New York Times.

NDOLA, Northern Rhodesia, Sept., 22—The foundations of African customary law were swept away here this week when the Northern Rhodesia High Court acquittted two Bemba tribesmen charged with contempt of their chief.

The defendants, both Roman Catholics, admitted they had prevented fellow Catholics from contributing grain for the worship of ancestor spirits in a traditional ceremony.

Bemba tribal courts and government lower courts had found the two men guilty. They were judged to be in contempt of customary law by their "refusal to worship the land," and in contempt of traditional ways of worshiping the dead.

Tribal Courts Curbed

Although the High Court's acquittal of these charges was made because of substantive technicalities, Government administrators here agreed the practical effect of the decision would be that tribal courts no longer could convict African Christians of opposing traditional customs if they were acting in accordance with their religious teachings.

The case, first heard in Chief Mwamba's Bemba court in September, 1958, was appealed to the High Court by the seven Catholic Bishops of Northern Rhodesia.

Joseph Mubanga and Fitaliano Sakeni, the men acquitted, were acting on their Bishop's instructions when the original charge was made. They persuaded fellow tribesmen to withhold finger millet requested by Chief Mwamba for a rainmaking ceremony.

Lower courts convicted the two Africans on interpretations of Bemba law that make a man guilty of the act of persuasion and prevention, even if the action itself is not illegal. Lower courts agreed that failure to contribute millet was no longer an offense by itself.

October 11, 1959

Drums of Change Beat For Africa's Tribes

Old customs are dying, but tribal enmities smolder against the day white rulers depart.

By ELSPETH HUXLEY

TROUBLE in Africa generally suggests a revolt of Africans against their colonial overlords—black versus white. This alignment is rapidly becoming out of date. The recent riots in Ruanda, which caused the Belgian Government to declare a state of emergency, were not directed against whites; they were the outcome of an age-old enmity between two tribes: the Watusi, a race of aristocrats who grow seven feet tall, and the Bahutu, 4,000,000 Africans who were once their slaves.

Like all other colonial powers, the Belgians have promised the Africans under their tutelage self-government within the next few years. This led to rumors among the Bahutu majority that the Watusi, whose powers have been curbed by the Belgians, would resume their onetime rule, when the white men go.

The Ruanda riots bring into sharp relief what is probably Africa's greatest danger today—a revival of tribalism once white rule is withdrawn.

Colonialism has fallen into such disrepute that few people recall the state of Africa in precolonial days. The normal condition was one of intertribal war. African tribes are as different from one another as Danes from Italians or Irish from Germans and, like the Europeans, they have been fighting throughout their history. The Europeans, because of their superiority in weapons and organization, were able to put a stop to tribal wars. But many of the deep-seated fears and enmities between the various tribes have rumbled under the surface all along.

It was fear of civil war that toppled the democratic system left by the British in the Sudan and created a military dictatorship within three years of their departure. If intertribal warfare like that in Ruanda should break out all over Africa, other newly established African Governments may find themselves obliged to impose dictatorships, too. Democracy, in fact, may be the first casualty of African nationalism.

ELSPETH HUXLEY, an English woman, grew up in Kenya and has written several books about Africa. Her latest is "The Flame Trees of Thika: Memories of an African Childhood."

MASAI—This herdsman belongs to one of the proudest of the tribes.

NO one knows exactly how many tribes there are in Africa, but nearly 1,000 languages are spoken and each language must denote a separate group. The linguist and administrator Sir Harry Johnston listed 276 Bantu languages alone, and the New Testament has been translated into eighty-two major tongues. Even in Ghana, with less than 5,000,000 inhabitants, over twenty vernaculars are spoken and Radio Ghana broadcasts in six African languages.

A young Masai girl.

Many of Africa's tribes are quite large. The Somalis, who will have their own independent state, Somalia, next year, probably number about 3,000,000. The Ibo of Nigeria number around 6,000,000, the Yoruba at least 5,000,000, the Baluba of the Congo 3,500,000, and there are about 9,000,000 Hausa-speaking peoples on the fringes of the Sahara. Smaller groups include the Galla of Ethiopia (a minority ruled by the dominant Amhara), the Ruanda of Ruanda-Urundi, the Zulu, Bechuana and Basuto of South Africa, the Barotse and Bemba of Rhodesia, the Suku and Chaga of Tanganyika, the Kikuyu and Jur of Kenya, the Baganda and Ankole of Uganda, the Wolof, Mandingo, Mossi, Nupe, Tiv and many others.

TODAY the very word "tribe," because of its association with the primitive and savage, is shunned by the new African leaders. So sensitive are they that a Nigerian writer has suggested it should be applied only to small, backward groups "running at most into a few thousands"—which would exclude most African peoples. Nothing insults an educated African more than to refer to tribal customs, and to ask what tribe such a man belongs to is to drop a very heavy brick indeed.

I talked not long ago with a peasant in a remote region, who explained how he was working his small farm. He was proud of his improved bull, his home-made cattle shed and the corrugated iron with which he had roofed his new hut. "White men used to come and photograph us as if we were gorillas," he said. "Now I hope they will see that we are human beings like everyone else."

This is the mainspring of the educated African's revolt against tribalism—the deep, desperate wish to be the same as everybody else, to join the twentieth century as full members.

If you wear beads, wrap your limbs in copper wire, plug your nose or lips, stretch your ear lobes, cut cicatricial patterns on your flesh, you belong to a past your children intend to bury. The young man of today pictures himself in a collar and tie and pin-stripe suit at the desk of a company or Government office—or, better yet, as a lawyer or politician who can talk back to white men on equal terms or even give them orders as their superior.

THUS, tribal customs are dying, but not so fast as those who have outgrown them would like to believe. This summer I encountered, in a little store way out in the bush, a skin-clad young woman in a wide ruff of beads, her legs and arms encased in coils of wire, escorted by her husband who wore feathers in his mud-packed hair and a metal cylinder stuck through his upper lip. She stared at me so much that I asked, through

PYGMIES—These tiny inhabitants of the deep forest (here shown making arrows) are allies of the powerful Watusi tribe in Ruanda, Central Africa, mandated to Belgium.

OUOLOF—A woman of the Louga region of French West Africa.

an interpreter, if anything was wrong. "No," he replied, "there is nothing wrong, it is only that she has never seen a European before." Yet we were within a day's drive of Nairobi with its hothouse politics and traffic jams, its drive-in cinemas and parades for freedom based on "one-man-one-vote."

Though skins and beads have all but given way to dresses and trousers, many traditional customs remain. Bride-price, for example—the custom by which a man pays his future father-in-law a sum to compensate for the loss of a daughter—is still practiced. Payments used to be made mainly in cattle, or in beer and hoes. Now cash often replaces cows.

A British Governor in South Africa, many years ago, made illegal what he called "the sin of buying wives." Africans do not look at it like that. The payment is a guarantee of the young man's good faith, on the one hand, and of the girl's stability, on the other—if she misbehaves her father must refund it. They disapprove of the white people's easy divorces.

THIS summer, too, I met an African girl who was especially attractive. She was about 23, spoke English well, was nicely dressed, had trained as a nurse and had charming manners. She lived in a small town, in a way still extremely uncommon anywhere in Africa—as a bachelor girl, earning her living as a clerk. A white woman friend of hers told me that she was a keen Christian and that her moral code was strict.

Her life seemed to me desperately lonely. Her girlfriends were all married, with their own families. She never went out with boys. Outside the few big cities, young men don't take out girls unless they are prostitutes. The bubbling spirit of all African girls I've ever met seemed crushed

HOLDOVER—A Matabele woman—her neck and limbs banded in copper wire—and her children illustrate the many survivals in dress and other folkways that are still typical of Africa.

and stilled in her. Why, I asked hadn't she married?

"It's a tragedy," said her white woman friend. "Because she's a Christian, she refused to be circumcized, and now none of the young men will have her. Even teachers and clerks, the educated ones." Girls of her tribe are still circumcized (clitorodectomy) at 12 or 13, even those at boarding school who must come home to face this ordeal during the holidays. They are glad to undergo it, for they know that if they don't their own people will look on them as outcasts for the rest of their lives.

Once, in West Africa, I met an oldish man being pushed along a forest path in a so-called "bush chair." He was on the way to visit a famous witch doctor. What about the modern hospital near his home? Oh, yes, he'd tried that; London-trained doctors there had cured his fever but he still had stomach trouble, so he was going to give the native doctors a chance.

In Lagos, fast-growing capital of Nigeria, there are glass-fronted stores that sell anything from Cadillacs to Paris hats; just a few paces away, in the market, you may buy a withered monkey's skull, dried bats' wings and nameless claws to make you a potion as eerie as anything cooked up by Macbeth's witches.

AND there is a darker side to African magic that doesn't often emerge into the open. A recent outbreak of ritual murders in Basutoland, conducted with appalling cruelty, resulted in the uncovering of scores of other such crimes. They had been committed to obtain parts of living bodies for "medicines" used, among other things, to bring success in college examinations. Nearly seventy people have been executed for their part in these murders, one of which was largely performed by a fully trained hospital doctor.

Although journalists and other visitors have stressed these more sensational rituals, not all tribal customs are bad, by any means. In addition, they vary so considerably from place to place that no single pattern will fit all tribes.

One, for example, may have a chief so sacred that his feet must never touch the ground lest some of his supernatural powers escape. Another may have no chief at all but a council of elders who meet under a tree to settle public business and extend the law.

THE NEW WAY—Western-style education, here exemplified in a school in the Belgian Congo, is a principal weapon of the new African nations against the divisive force of tribalism.

BUT one thing that almost all tribes have in common is a sense of closeness. Almost everyone is a relation, however distant, of everyone else, and no self-respecting African would let a fellow tribesman go hungry. For centuries Africans have got along very well without any state provision for old age, sickness, widowhood, orphans or mental

WATUSI—A typically tall tribal chief, whose people are being attacked by the more numerous Bahutus, asks refuge in Ruanda.

illness, because the family looked after its needy or afflicted members.

The tribe has always formed a compact, self-sustaining unit. Its members gave absolute loyalty to their chief, and whatever he said was obeyed without argument. But as a rule the chief himself was not dictatorial. He embodied the will of the tribe; he did not impose his own will upon it—or if he did he was generally thrown out. Among the Yoruba, for example, if a chief found a parrot's egg in his doorway he knew that he had gone too far and his only course was to disappear into the bush and commit suicide.

Each tribe had its own territory, rites, history, legends and beliefs. No tribesman ever felt alone or unwanted and no woman ever lacked a husband and the protection of her husband's clan. To anyone who deviated from the norm or challenged its authority, the tribe could be ruthless. As a result, there were few rebels in tribal society.

All this was shaken by the European decision to establish democracy. Many tribes are in themselves democratic in certain ways; but their methods of government by elders and chiefs could not be adapted to a system of universal suffrage wherein young men have an equal say with elders, women with men, the chief has no function, and people are elected to political office instead of holding it by virtue of age or similar criterion.

So tribalism has been busted wide open by the democratic system which the Europeans set up and which they propose to hand over when they relinquish authority. But there has been very little time to solidify the democratic system and to train the people in its use. Major reforms have been made in Africa only in the past fifteen years. The consequence is that, although tribalism, as such, is declining and being replaced by elected councils, parliaments and national assemblies, you do not have to dig very deep to find many of the tribal loyalties that have existed for centuries, waiting for a chance to emerge.

THE situation is further complicated by the fact that very few of the new African states correspond with any ethnic or cultural units. Most often their boundaries were drawn on maps for reasons of power politics quite unconnected with tribal distribution or historical fact.

The boundary between Kenya and Tanganyika is a straight line originally drawn in London and Berlin to divide British from German "spheres of influence." At one point it wiggles around Mt. Kilimanjaro—because Kaiser Wilhelm II was interested in the mountain's fauna and flora and asked his aunt, Queen Victoria, to pop it into his sphere. Apparently it bothered no one that the line ran smack through the middle of Masai grazing grounds.

Some of these bisected peoples now represent the danger spots of Africa. The Somalis—a proud, united, tough, warlike people—are so divided: the Ethiopians, their hated foes, hold part of the territory they graze with great herds of camels. The more outspoken of their leaders in Mogadishu, Somalia's capital, told me that sooner or later the "Greater Somalia" movement, aimed at uniting Somalis now living under five administrations, will clash with Emperor Haile Selassie's determination to hold on to his empire.

The sooner they get matters back into their own hands, they indicated—and the last vestiges of Italian trusteeship end next year—the sooner they will be able to settle accounts with Ethiopia.

In short, two contrary forces are at work on Africans today. One is the tribal spirit which urges divided people to reunite under their own leaders and develop their own particular cultures. The other is the anti-tribal force of African nationalism—a force fed by the nationalist leaders, who are making a deliberate, full-scale effort to smash the tribal system to smithereens.

So long as freedom is the goal, this force fuses tribal groups together in a common aim. But once freedom is achieved, the nationalists' real troubles begin. Tribal groups start to assert themselves again and ancient jealousies and hatreds are revived.

By whipping up national pride and loyalty, the nationalist leaders may create a spirit of aggression that they will later be unable to control. Or the leaders may find power a heady draught and drink so much of it that they will turn into dictators. Or, finally, they may fail in their attempts to suppress tribalism, and in this case freedom could lead straight to civil war.

THESE are dangers: but, of course, no one expects a great continent of 225,000,000 people, which for the first time has joined its history to the rest of the world's, to undergo a revolution without trouble. Tribalism, the ancient way of life in Africa, is in transition. No one can say whether it will vanish into a national melting pot or endure as the focus of new cultures—only that it is changing fast, and that, either way, it cannot ever again be just what it was.

Despite survival in backwaters, primitive customs are disappearing from the continent almost as fast as its wild animals. The spear, the ostrich feather, the juju mask, the thumping dance with naked breasts and swinging monkey-tails—all these soon will be as extinct as the redskin stockade and the pony express. And not until this is so will modern nationalist leaders be satisfied.

From Veld to City: The Bantu Drama

Behind South Africa's crisis is a people's march from Stone Age to twentieth century.

By **ANTHONY SAMPSON**

CUTTING through the middle of the lives of the black people of South Africa is one of the swiftest and sharpest breaks in the history of any race. It is the crossing from the placid, Stone-Age existence of the tribal reserves to the bustling, twentieth-century cities of modern South Africa—Johannesburg, Durban or Capetown. It is a contrast that lies inside the minds, to a greater or lesser extent, of all black South Africans. This contrast is at the very core of the current South African crisis, for as firmly as the Government of Dr. Verwoerd believes that the native people should remain in their primitive tribal state, so do the natives themselves desire passionately and unchangeably to become part of the modern cities.

To white observers, indeed, the metamorphosis of the Africans from country to town is the most fascinating aspect of South Africa. The image of the blanketed tribesman, with bare, feet, tribal scars and plugs in his ears, arriving bewildered and innocent in the middle of industrial Johannesburg is one which runs through the white literature of South Africa with a repetition that irritates the Africans themselves.

William Plomer's "Ula Masondo," Alan Paton's "Cry, the Beloved Country," Mopeli-Paulus' "Blanket Boy's Moon" all have the same basic theme. More recently, Lionel Rogosin's film called "Come Back, Africa," shot in Johannesburg last year, has the same tribal hero.

THE theme is, undoubtedly, an evocative one, but it is perhaps less simple than it appears. Educated Africans, who resent the white men's dramatizations of their tribal antecedents, suspect that the writers' interest is based on the old myth of Rousseau's "noble savage"—the quest for some imaginary innocence which sophisticated man has lost. They argue that their own transition has been no more abrupt than that of the English of Shakespeare's time—the "country gulls" who swagger into Elizabethan plays. Above all, they suspect that nearly all white men prefer their Africans to be primitive and untouched, and like to think that black men cannot be assimilated into white cities. In fact, the African intellectuals say, most white men believe in *apartheid* in their hearts.

Certainly, few white visitors could fail to be attracted by the outward appearance of life in the tribal reserves. Only a hundred miles from the industrial cities of Port Elizabeth or Durban, you can see the clusters of plain mud huts, with nothing but grass mats for furniture, and old women pounding maize with tree stumps outside. A Xhosa girl, her hair wound into a headdress of red clay, and her brown arms jangling with rings, walks by the side of the main road, balancing a pitcher on her head, staying erect and unworried as the Chevrolets and Jaguars swish past her.

TO the nerve-racked white business men living their complex urban lives, it is hardly surprising that the tribal Africans stand for all the peace they miss in their own existence.

Their tribal life appears magnificently unchanged. The community is dominated by two ancient leaders: the chief and the witch doctor. The chief, it is true, has not the gaudy splendor of the West Africans, with their umbrellas, embroidered gowns and rich jeweled headdresses. A South African chief is likely to wear white man's mufti, or a vague, cast-off uniform, with only a ceremonial blanket, a leopard skin or a shield to signify his status. But the chiefs retain a splendid dignity and apparent authority: they rule through a gathering of elders, and when important issues arise they hold a special meeting of the tribe, or *kgotla*, which constitutes a kind of *ad hoc* democratic process. On festive occasions, they hold a beer-drink, sitting around the floor of a mud hut, and passing a calabash of home-brewed beer from man to man.

There are many aspects of this tribal life that are endearing. There is the responsibility of it—the sense of duty to the family, the chief and the tribe. There is the courtesy, the consideration and the dignity of individuals, particularly old men and women. There is the laughter, the peasant wisdom, and the straightforward human values. Even the witch doctor, hung with bones, hides and bangles, is far from a figure of fun. He is, as a missionary doctor will tell you, a home-grown psychoanalyst who can, in a society riddled with fears and superstitions, cure a psychosomatic illness when Western medicine has failed.

BUT in this attractive-looking community, there is one indication of a fatal flaw: there are no young men, and even among the older generation there is a vast disparity between men and women. The reason is obvious: the dry, cracked land cannot support the men. They go, as soon as they reach manhood, to earn their livings in the gold mines of Johannesburg or the kitchens of Durban, and to send back money to their families.

The lack of men has corrupted the character of tribal life. The pivot of the community is no longer the chief's court, but the little hut, which exists in every small community, called Wenela — from W. N. L. A., the initials of

ANTHONY SAMPSON is a London newspaper man (The Observer), who once edited a paper for Africans in Johannesburg called Drum. He has periodically revisited South Africa.

MAIN STREET—A cow forages in the street of an African township. Most shops are run by Indians.

Witwatersrand Native Labor Association, the organization of mine-owners which brings 400,000 Africans every year to the gold mines.

They are taken in train loads for six- or nine-month contracts, and come back with new suits, hats and phonographs. They leave for second contracts, and then, perhaps, they take permanent city jobs, and never come back again.

THEY leave behind them a community demoralized by their absence. The land, eroded and poor as it is, is not properly cared for. The women, without their husbands, become undisciplined, promiscuous or prey to mysterious mental diseases and imagined pregnancies. Families are disorganized, and the children are often brought up by an aged grandfather or a drunken uncle. Above all, the country remains desperately poor. The 13 per cent of South African land on which the 3,000,000 tribal Africans live was never enough to sustain them; but the system of migratory African labor, while it provides the reserves with pocket money from remittances, insures that the country areas can never be developed properly.

Doctors, however, more than economists, are the ones who can perceive the true misery of the tribal reserves. To the mission doctors who deal with underfed children, fear-ridden mothers and miners sent back with TB, there is nothing romantic about tribal life; it is nasty, brutish and short.

THE main cause of African migration is necessity. Ever since Cecil Rhodes devised a poll tax for rural Africans, to insure a labor supply for his diamond mines in Kimberley in the Eighteen Seventies, Africans have been forced by taxes and poverty to go to work in the cities.

But even without compulsion, many of them would go; it is more than poverty that brings Africans to Johannesburg from as far away as Nyasaland or Mozambique. All the lure and the glory of Johannesburg—*Geoli*, the Golden City—is summed up for Africans in two letters—"TJ," standing for "Transvaal Johannesburg"—on the number-plates of Johannesburg cars. As the big cars screech past the dry mud huts, the little pot-bellied Zulu or Xhosa children dance up and down with delight, and shout, "Tee Jay! Tee Jay!"

"TJ" stands for everything that is exciting: not only cars, but skyscrapers, trains, elevators, cinemas and radios. "TJ" stands for everything that the young tribal recruit sees ; he gazes out at the street from the Johannesburg station. But "TJ" does not mean only the half-million whites of Johannesburg and the white men's wonders: indeed, it is noticeable that the raw Africans are never quite as astonished by the "houses on wheels" or the "huts on top of each other" as the white men expect them to be. No, "TJ" means more than anything else the black metropolis—the city with 700,000 Africans, the biggest black city in the continent.

MODERN TEMPO—Near Johannesburg, a citified Zulu girl dances to a phonograph.

IT is a very different place from white Johannesburg, and to the Europeans it seems far less attractive than the reserves. The "locations," or "townships," where the Africans live are mostly clusters of boxlike brick houses, beginning ten miles southwest of the city center in the area known as the "Orlando Complex," and spreading over the brown hillsides in bleak, unvarying rows, like huge chicken farms.

The locations, although they have become more hygienic and less slummy in the past few years, are uniformly dismal. The houses are all single-story, built at minimum cost. Although there is a large power station near by, the rooms in the African townships have no electric light. The roads are unpaved, full of ditches and boulders. The largest building in most locations is the police station, with the administrative offices of the location superintendent next door.

THE skyline of bungalows is unbroken, except for billboards advertising beauty cream, corn flakes, or flashlights ("Be safe at night — carry a torch!"). One house is distinguished from another only by its number: a typical African address is 3586B, Orlando West Extension, Johannesburg. The country Africans call a boy born in the city "the son of a number."

But to the Africans who live in Orlando so named, before the war, after a paternalistic city councilor who laid out the "model township" — there is nothing impersonal about their city. In spite of the police raids, the mass removals and the pass laws designed to circumscribe and control their daily lives, they love the city, and out of it they have built a new and vibrant society.

THE streets which seem so impersonal and bleak to the white visitor have, to the Africans, all the nuances and variations of Manhattan or Mayfair. The extensions and postal districts, or the townships named by the municipality after tribal heroes, are quickly renamed by the Africans after snob white districts or American Negro heroes, like "Killarney," or "Satchmo." Many of the bleak numbers turn out to be "shebeens," or illicit African drinking places, with names like "Falling Leaves," "Back o' the Moon" or "Thirty-Nine Steps."

The shebeen might be taken as the cornerstone of this new metropolis, for it is here that the new society is most vocal and expressive. The contrast with the chief's beer-drink in the reserves is a bizarre one. Instead of the chief and elders, sitting on the mud floor, passing a calabash around, the superior shebeens have a mixture of teachers, bus drivers, nurses and gangsters, sitting around a polished mahogany table, drinking European brandy under a kerosene lamp.

THERE is little connection with the old society: a teacher might turn out to be a chief's nephew, but descendants of the old Zulu royal family are quite likely to end up as messenger boys or domestic servants. The conversation in a shebeen will not be about tribal customs or chiefly intrigue, but about Hollywood films, football, jazz or Shakespeare. If some newly arrived innocent, perhaps, raised the subject of tribal ritual, he might well be met with a shout of, "Jeez, man, go back to the kraal! We don't want blanket-boys here."

There are, of course, many tribal relics embedded in this new society, particularly among the newly arrived groups. Some, like the Basutos or the Vendas, still in their multicolored blankets, stride through the crowds as if they were among their native mountains.

Tribal myths and superstitions still play their part in urban life. Five years ago a story suddenly became current that a *tokoloshe*—a kind of Zulu imp—had been discovered in Johannesburg, and for two weeks copies of the local African newspaper, The Bantu World, were sold out with stories of the *tokoloshe*—which turned out to be an otter.

SOMETIMES the tribal relics are of a grimmer kind, as when a homemade liquor brew is discovered with bits of flesh mixed in it, supposed to strengthen the courage of its drinkers. Witch doctors still do business in Johannesburg, in musty little shops hung with skins, bones and medicines;

and when a paramount chief such as King Cyprian of the Zulus or King Sobhuza of the Swazis comes up to Johannesburg, he is besieged by humble tribesmen and guarded in his small location house by bus drivers or municipal clerks.

These tribal memories are often said by whites to be a sign that Africans will never be assimilated into city life, and the Government of Dr. Verwoerd has done everything possible to encourage the continuance of tribal feeling, with special "ethnic grouping" in the layout of the townships, and special entries in the passbooks for each person's chief and tribe.

BUT to hundreds of thousands of urban Africans these subdivisions mean nothing: some of them have lived for three generations in the towns, have intermarried among tribes, and speak English and Afrikaans at home. For them, it would be as unthinkable to return to the reserves as for the Afrikaners to return to Holland.

The black cities of South Africa are kept separate from the white cities by all the elaborate devices of apartheid. By day the Africans work in the same offices, factories or shops as the white men, and jostle in the same streets; but every night they are separated, and travel in their segregated trains to their segregated townships.

To the whites, the lives of their black office boys or chauffeurs seem unimaginably separate and isolated from their own. Although African jazz has lately become fashionable among white liberals, very few white South Africans have ever made their way into a shebeen, and even to be found drinking with an African constitutes an offense. But to the urban Africans, the "Europeans" are the ones who seem isolated, in their remote and hidden mansions in the superior suburbs. The Africans no longer feel themselves reliant on white patrons or promoters for their education and cultural development; they see themselves as the heirs of Western civilization, and the "Europeans" as the impostors.

IN much of the black metropolis, there is a fearful rootlessness—the other side of the imbalance which shows itself in the reserves. There are too few girls, no land, no freehold rights, broken families; often husbands who work as domestic servants are not allowed, because of the Group Areas Act, to sleep with their wives. And all the time, the townships are subject to the perpetual insecurity which comes from the police state—the threat of being waked at midnight for not having a pass, of being exiled to the farms, of being jailed indefinitely for suspected political views.

All these factors have produced ugly elements in the African townships—violence, gangsters, promiscuity and wild drunkenness. They show themselves at their worst each Christmastime when, maddened with liquor and frustration, the wilder Zulus and Basutos engage in atavistic faction fights, and a score or so are murdered.

But against these grimmer sides, there is much that is infinitely exciting and hopeful about this African "Harlem." "The truest optimism in South Africa," wrote the greatest of South Africa's historians, Dr. De Kiewiet, "is in the crowded, disease-ridden and crime-infested urban locations." Anyone who spends some time in the shebeens or social gatherings of Orlando, Meadowlands or Sophiatown can understand what he means. The Africans have not, as a race, been demoralized by the white men's cities; they have taken to them with all the enthusiasm of a London Cockney, and in them have built their own society, hierarchies and prides.

HUNDREDS of thousands of the new Africans are no longer men of two worlds, but of one—the world of the city, *their* city. Out of their varied backgrounds—motorcars, blankets, cinemas, witch doctors, physicians, chiefs, lawyers—they have forged something new, confident and civilized.

Signs of this new amalgam take many forms: the new African jazz blending old monotonous tribal chants with sharp new rhythms from America; the all-African musical "King Kong," which appeared last year in Johannesburg and will come to New York next year; the young African writers and journalists who have produced a jazzy, expressive English of their own; even the curious Johannesburg wedding ceremonies, with their mixture of tribal courtesy, Western formality and all-African prolixity.

But the new character can be seen most simply in the urban Africans themselves. Though the whites may view them as clowns, dandies, imitative monkeys, the Africans are fundamentally confident—of themselves, and of their right to Western civilization. The more one sees of them, the more one feels that Dr. Verwoerd, who is determined that they shall have no place in the white men's cities, has bitten off more than he can chew.

A New African 'Personality' Emerges

One tie that binds all Africans together is suffering. That theme, perhaps more than any other, will determine the nature of the New African.

By ANTHONY SAMPSON

"I SAY that once Africa is free and independent," said Kwame Nkrumah, President of Ghana, in December, 1958, "we shall see a flowering of the human spirit second to none * * * Some of us, I think, need reminding that Africa is a continent on its own. It is not an extension of Europe or any other continent. We want, therefore, to develop our own community and an African personality. Others may feel that they have evolved the very best way of life, but we are not bound, like slavish imitators, to accept it as our mold."

Since Dr. Nkrumah spoke these words, the phrase "the African personality" has become a catchword throughout the continent. Parallel with the arrival of political independence in the new black states of Africa, there has been a passionate, though often hazy, desire for cultural independence—an insistence that Africa should assert herself not only in diplomacy and power politics but in art, writing and philosophy.

But what exactly constitutes the African personality? In the months to come, the nature of this "personality" will become increasingly important to the rest of the world. Will it, indeed, be "a flowering of the human spirit second to none"? Will Africa achieve a common sense of identity and purpose, comparable to that of Western Europe or of America? Will it disintegrate into ancient often inimical tribal patterns? Will it become culturally parochial and secondhand, defying the influence of the West, yet remaining subservient to it?

IT is necessary to ask these questions, because Africa does not have an obvious, unifying cultural heritage as have other assertive parts of the world—India, for example, or China or the Arab states. In spite of recent archeological discoveries, which have revealed much stronger ancient African cultures in West, East and Central Africa than had previously been imagined, Africa remains a continent without a history—or at least without a sense of history.

Western Nigeria, for instance, has magnificent wood-carvings and bronzes from the Yoruba kingdoms of the sixteenth century, but few modern Nigerians are aware of or proud of them and you will never see them in Nigerian homes. Africans, except in a few feudal pockets, such as Buganda, Basutoland or Northern Nigeria, have little of the confidence in their own past such as that which exists among modern Indians. Most of the educated élite of Africa have been detribalized and uprooted by the European invasion; their first desire is to become part of the world of the white teachers, conquerors or administrators under whose spell they grew up.

"I cannot rest/Satisfied with half a loaf or less/When I know you can give the whole bread * * *", wrote the Nigerian poet Dennis Osadebay, complaining that the white man had withheld the full fruits of his culture. This attitude, which shows itself in many parts of the continent, is very different from that of other new nations. For the past three centuries, Africans have been conditioned by slavery, conquest and the impact of Western civilization to regard themselves as inferior, negative people.

There is an old joke in South Africa about a "non-European," as Africans there are commonly described by the white authorities. "Where do you come from?" a white policeman asked a non-European. "I come from non-Europe," he replied. The black South Africans, of course, have a far greater sense of inadequacy than the liberated Africans in the north; but the feeling of belonging to "non-Europe" pervades the whole of Africa. It was this feeling that Dr. Nkrumah was attacking when he insisted that "Africa is a continent on its own."

But now, as the independent states spread over the map of Africa, the sense of inadequacy is rapidly disappearing, and is giving way to a conscious, urgent cultivation of things African. In the past, it was the foreigners who searched for the African soul—most notably the small group of American Negro intellectuals, from Garvey to Du Bois, who looked for their roots in Africa.

WHILE the Europeans and Americans were exploring Africa, studying her anthropology and tribal structures, the Africans were far more interested in acquiring the Europeans' skills. Now, their interests are turning back to themselves. "In the last century," said Dr. Nkrumah in April, 1958, "the Europeans discovered Africa: in the next century the Africans will discover Africa."

Paradoxically but understandably, it is among the Africans who have been most assimilated into Europe—the educated, French-speaking Africans—that the search for the "African personality" is most insistent; it was, indeed, the French Africans, rather than Dr. Nkrumah, who first invented the phrase "*négritude.*"

THE French-speaking African élite, whether from the new republics of what was French West Africa or from the Congo, have become much more absorbed into European culture than have the English-speaking Africans. You have only to compare a Nigerian student in London with a Senegalese student in Paris to perceive the difference: the man from Senegal will be smooth, confident, moving with ease among French intellectuals; the Nigerian is likely to be surrounded by his fellow-students, talking in nationalistic terms and on guard among English friends. But the effect of the warm embrace of Parisian life has been to turn many of the African intellectuals back in search of their roots—because they had the feeling that they were being "Frenchified" out of existence.

The first and greatest exponent of *négritude* was the Negro poet from the West Indies, Aimé Césaire, who idealized Africa in vague, romantic terms: "Hurray for those who never invented anything." In his famous poem, "To New York," he attacked the hollowness of white men's materialism and glorified the flamboyance of Harlem:

New York! I say to you New York!
let black blood flow into your blood
*That it may rub the rust from your steel joints, like an oil of life * * **

Since Césaire's first revolt against European and American culture, which began as early as 1939, a school of French African writers has grown up around him, dedicated to the "African personality." They have established in Paris their own periodical, Présence Africaine, which publishes much of the best African writing and criticism in the continent, and they have organized special cultural congresses in Paris and Rome to stimulate discussion among intellectuals from all parts of Africa.

HERE and elsewhere they have tried to map out the bases of the African personality. "The more African writers are inspired by African culture," wrote Léopold-Sedar Senghor, the African politician-poet from Senegal, "the more they will raise themselves to international rank: the more they turn their back on Africa, the more they will degenerate and weaken."

But these grand discussions about the nature of the African character have not really spread beyond the frontiers of French-speaking Africa — or even much outside its small group of sophis-

STRAINS OF THE NEW AFRICA

ticated writers. In recent years these writers have become less idealistic and more down-to-earth in their attitudes; but the French intellectuals still have something of the nostalgic, idealized attitude toward their continent which American Negro poets like Countee Cullen or Langston Hughes have shown in the past.

To the English-speaking African writers, the French preoccupation with *négritude* seems merely boring. When Dr. Nkrumah spoke of the "African personality" he meant something more practical and political than mere philosophizing; and when, at the Pan-African conference in December, 1958, a group of French Africans tried to pass a motion about the importance of *négritude*, the English-speaking delegates, who formed the majority, showed little interest.

It is here that the generalizations about the "African personality" begin to dissolve. For while the idea of "Mother Africa" or the "African soul" is being invoked all over the continent, it is clear that the "soul" means something quite different in one territory from what it means in another. The soul of the French African writers, for example, which has been partially molded by the *lycées* of Paris and the Sorbonne, often bears striking resemblances to the personality of the French themselves; similarly, though to a lesser extent, British Africans become "British."

In spite of the fervent nationalism of Ghana or Nigeria, a great deal of the energy of young educated Africans goes into the frank emulation of British habits and correctness; adjectives like "been-to" (meaning that an African has visited Britain), or "jagua" (describing a girl with all the glamour of a Jaguar car) remain part of the vocabulary of excellence. Immaculate British dress is still a mark of status.

The Nigerian poet Wole Soyinka, in his satirical poem "And the Other Immigrant," described the studied Britishness of the young Nigerian thus:

My dignity is sown
Into the lining of a three-piece suit.
Stiff, and with whiteness which
Out-Europes Europe,
My crisp Van Heusen Collar
Cradles an All-Wool Tootal tie . . .

Outside West Africa, the "African personality" appears even more nebulous. The Kikuyu of East Africa and the Zulus of South Africa have very few characteristics in common, apart from their distant common racial origin.

In the past, communications in the continent have been so slender that one territory has been virtually unaware of its next-door neighbor. Before the arrival of the European explorers in the last century, the only link between many parts of East Africa, ironically

WATUSI SENEGALESE ZULU BUSHMAN

enough, was the slave trade. Even today, most visitors to Africa are astonished by the parochialism of African territories.

IN Nigeria, it is hard enough to find news of Ghana let alone of East Africa, while residents of the Kingdom of Buganda often seem entirely unaware that there are Africans outside their frontiers. African visitors between one territory and another are rare. When a black South African comes to Ghana, he complains of being treated as if he were "as foreign as a white man."

Even when Africans have migrated in large numbers to a strange country, as the Nyasas have to South Africa or the Nigerians to Ghana, they usually retain their own closeness and are preoccupied with the affairs of their home countries.

None of this is surprising, when one examines the diverse histories and backgrounds of African territories. They are as different as the countries of Europe, with far fewer communications and cross-currents: no Holy Roman Empire has ever bound Africa together. And on top of the original differences of tribes have been superimposed the new differences of the several European invaders.

The British and French on the West Coast, the Arabs and Indians on the East Coast, or the Afrikaners in the south, however much they have been hated by their African subjects, have each left their mark on the African character, as indelibly as the Romans left theirs on Europe itself.

WHAT, then, can an "African personality" amount to? Even a "Congo personality" or a "Nigerian personality" is hard enough to define. To many skeptics it seems that the African personality can offer no more than a distorted mirror-image of Western ideas, debased and corrupted by the voyage to Africa, and mixed up with lingering elements of tribal mumbo-jumbo: a kind of parody of Europe, which the more satirical writers have already observed in Ghana or Liberia.

But much the same, no doubt, could have been predicted of Europe after the Roman Empire, and equally wrongly. For if there is one common characteristic that can be detected in all the muddle and variety of Africa, it is that the whole continent south of the Sahara—excluding, that is, the Arab states to the north—has grasped the Western idea of progress with immense enthusiasm, and do not mean to let it go. It may be true that it was not until the Europeans arrived that Africans were stirred from their long apathy and isolation. But now stirred, they show no signs of relapsing; the catalyst has set off the chemical change and is no longer needed.

It is the boast, indeed, of many African leaders that they are more Western than the West; not only in the whiteness of their collars, but in the vigor and purity of their ideas—in their humanism, their nonracial Christianity, their passionate desire for education.

In South or Central Africa, where they see white civilization being corrupted by oligarchy and fear, the Africans view themselves as the inheritors of the Western mission and the whites as the betrayers of it. Nigerian or Kenyan intellectuals visiting Oxford or Cambridge are often ap-

BANTU

SUK

palled by the lack of enthusiasm and excitement in the ancient seats of learning. It is they, as they see it, who are the true Renaissance men; the European civilizers have passed on the elixir and lost it.

It is, indeed, the *newness* of Africa that is its most important characteristic. The very lack of cultural luggage, or of the ancient prides which hold back older nations, supplies a perpetual stimulus. Like Australia or post-war West Germany, the new states of Africa have little desire to dwell on their pasts. Once liberated from their tribal loyalties—and that liberation will still take time—they are determined to become part of the "Great World," to catch up with the other continents, learning from all their mistakes and teaching them their own proud message.

In many respects, no doubt, the newness of Africa will make it an easy prey for the spread of materialistic values—large cars, flamboyant mansions and grand outward symbols which already, as a matter of fact, play a large part in West African cities, particularly in Nigeria. There are plenty of depressing facets to the African personality that are showing themselves in the newly independent states.

BUT under this surface, there are signs of a more promising Africa: the gay and reckless use of language of West African writers, the thoughtful, brittle verse of the French African poets, the half Western, half-tribal work of Nigerian sculptors, the passionate melancholy of South African jazz.

And behind all these varied manifestations, up and down the length of Africa, there is one theme that is constantly reappearing—the theme of suffering. For there is one common experience which *does* bind together Africa, and that is slavery and the destruction of the society which came from it. The idea of suffering, and the nobility that comes from it, run all through African writings.

My wives crushed their painted mouths
On the hard thin lips of the steel-eyed conquerors,
And my children abandoned their peaceful nudity
*For the uniform of iron and blood * * **

The theme of "uniform of iron and blood," here expressed by the French African poet David Diop, is a recurring one. From this common experience of slavery and its aftermath has evolved all the African emphasis among its leaders on humanity, compassion, passivity—the idea that Africa, which was subjugated by guns, can now teach the world the true meaning of peace.

HOW far that ideal will be reflected in reality still remains to be seen: the interaction of African states is only now developing. Newspapers, airplanes and television are just beginning to open up one part of the continent to another. Africa is still preoccupied with the fight against poverty and disease and the sheer physical problems of government, including inter-tribal hostilities.

The "flowering of the human spirit" which Dr. Nkrumah speaks of is still no more than a bud. But one thing is certain: Africa has come alive through the mysterious touch of the West, and it will remain so. No one visiting the noisy market places of Ghana, or the political beer halls of Nyasaland, or the townships of South Africa can doubt that. Out of it all, some kind of African personality—laughing, suffering, new and boundlessly optimistic—is emerging.

THE NAMES OF AFRICA

Today's headlines are crowded with names from Africa —names whose derivations reflect the color and variety of African history. Some of them come from local words for geographical features or from tribal legends; others were coined by European discoverers. These are some of the names and their derivations:

DAHOMEY (republic)—from the native "Da home" meaning "city on the belly of Da." Da was a sixteenth century chief who was killed by a rival. The rival split open his stomach, buried him, and founded a city on his grave.

GHANA (republic)—from a medieval African empire.

CONGO (republic)—from the Congo River, which is derived from the native "kong" meaning mountains.

GUINEA (republic)—from the native "ginnie" meaning town. The British made gold pieces, also known as guineas, in the ginnies.

KENYA (British crown colony and protectorate)—from Mount Kenya, which takes its name from the native word for mist. The summit of the mountain is often hidden in clouds.

LIBERIA (republic)—from the liberty of the freed American slaves who colonized the country in 1822.

ETHIOPIA (empire)—from a Greek word meaning "the burnt faces."

TANGANYIKA—"Nyika" means water in a native dialect, and "tanganya" means to collect. The lake was thus a gathering place of waters.

IVORY COAST (republic)—from the tusks gathered in the region.

CHAD (republic)—from the native word for lake.

SIERRA LEONE (British colony and protectorate)— from Portugese for lions' range—although there are no lions along the rocky coast. Portugese explorers mistook the sound of the surf for the roar of lions.

August 14, 1960

Two Tribes Tell Africa's Story

By ELSPETH HUXLEY

AS the tide of colonialism ebbs throughout Africa, rocks are surfacing which threaten to wreck the great experiment of African self-rule before it even gets out to sea. The rocks are those of tribal strife. Most African countries are little more than names on a map. In them dwell not united peoples but collections of tribes who have often fought each other for centuries and don't see why they should stop now.

The extent to which tribalism is a serious problem varies from country to country. At one extreme lies Ghana, where President Nkrumah has effectively sealed over the tribal cracks with a strong central government and what some observers believe to be virtually a personal dictatorship. At the other extreme lies the Congo, where rampant tribalism, uncontrolled by any strong central authority, has made a shambles of the country. Somewhere between these two ends of the spectrum lie most other African countries either newly independent or well on the way to becoming so.

What does it seem like to be born into an African tribe? In what respects does the tribal outlook differ from that of a more advanced society? The answers depend largely on what tribe you consider. No tribe is untouched by the "wind of change," but while some expose themselves to it with enthusiasm, others have sought shelter from its revolutionary blast. The tribal outlook is illustrated by two peoples who represent tribalism, one at its best-preserved, the other at an advanced stage of decomposition.

The Masai of the East African steppes of Kenya and Tanganyika are in the first group. They have resisted change deliberately, almost fanatically, and live as close to the age-old primitive tribal system as any important group today. In this they contrast sharply with their neighbors, the Kikuyu. The largest tribe in Kenya, the Kikuyu have embraced Westernism with both hands, from Christianity to white bread and trade unions, and already play a major part in the stormy progress of their country toward independence.

* * *

WHILE most African peoples have been pressing hard for more and more Western education quickly, the Masai have spent the last fifty years trying to keep it out. Only a few individuals have defied this tribal ban on Western education and sent their sons to school outside Masai territory.

A Masai I knew who graduated from a university and became a headmaster told me that during vacations he would strip off his Western clothes, put on again the short calico cape and buffalo-hide sandals of the warrior, grease his limbs with sheep's fat and red ochre, take a spear and herd his father's cattle as his own father had herded them.

"Cattle are in our hearts," he said. "Their smell is sweet even to those of us who are educated." There are stories told of safari parties reaching remote Masai camps and asking the way of a semi-naked herdsman—to be answered in English with an Oxford accent.

Masai custom was based on two allied things: war and cattle. Like Scots in the Middle Ages, they were the great cattle-raiders, the scourge of peaceful cultivators. God gave all cattle, according to their legend, to their ancestors, so in raiding other peoples' cattle they were merely getting back stolen property.

WHAT does life look like to a young Masai? He is born into a *manyatta* consisting of from a half dozen to twenty or thirty long, low huts made of branches and cow dung, so low that an adult must stoop almost to all fours to enter. These windowless huts are dark and thick with smoke from an open fire with no chimney. A thorn-branch fence encloses them. Inside the enclosure, the ground is pulverized into thick red dust by the cattle, sheep and goats which share the *manyatta* with their owners. Clouds of flies settle so thickly on the children's eyes that nearly all suffer from ophthalmia.

The baby rides everywhere in a sling on his mother's back and, after weaning, eats the staple Masai food—milk mixed with blood taken from a bullock's jugular vein and curdled into cheese with a little cow's urine. The Masai are nomads and pastoralists, and do not cultivate. When the head of the *manyatta* gives the word, calabashes, pots and hides are bundled on to the backs of donkeys and of women, the huts abandoned to crumble away, and the Masai move on to seek fresh grazing grounds.

To build a new *manyatta* is women's work, not men's. Women wear up to thirty pounds of copper wire coiled around their limbs from shoulder to wrist and thigh to ankle, and wound around their necks into a sort of ruff, so they look as if their heads rested on platters.

A Masai boyhood is all preparation for the moment of circumcision and entry into the tribe with the status of a warrior. Every three or four years, circumcision ceremonies are held in sacred places when the whole clan gathers—the Masai are divided into about a dozen clans—and witch doctors make magic to insure fertility and success in war.

WHEN the boys' hair grows long enough to plait into pigtails, they take their new weapons and live apart from their families in young men's dormitories. They hunt, feast, practice their military skills, adorn their handsome bodies and make love to the unmarried girls, who live with them in a sort of free-love colony. Anything goes except getting a girl pregnant, which is considered a disgrace to both parties.

In the past, these warriors were in training for one thing: cattle raids. The time and place of raids were decided by witch doctors who read omens in the entrails of goats and the behavior of birds, just like the Roman augurs. On the warpath, each warrior wore a tall headdress of ostrich plumes, a short cape of black vultures' feathers and anklets of monkey fur, and carried a heavy oval shield painted with his clan insignia, a long spear, a sword and a club.

Now the purpose of these proud, savage warriors' existence has withered. The young men prepare for something that no longer takes place. Now and again raids do still occur, but the young men slink off in darkness and, after the raid, instead of dances, booty and glory, there are inquiries and fines.

Despite this, young Masai still plait their pigtails, grease their bodies, hurl their spears at lions or hyenas, make love, walk about in their finery and play for hours on end a game with beans and rows of shallow holes in the ground. Most of them still refuse all forms of manual labor.

When the time for marriage comes, the warrior picks out a young girl, and long bargaining sessions follow between the two fathers. Bride price is a custom that persists over most of tropical Africa. When the amount is settled—three heifers, say, and two bulls—a feast clinches the bargain.

LATER on, when the couple's children are themselves approaching circumcision, another ceremony, the *e-unoto*, marks the father's entry into the next age group. All Masai life is stratified into these levels, each of which has a name and which determine a man's status, his duties and even his costume. As the climax of the feasting and ceremony, our Masai's pigtail is shaved; he lays aside his weapons and takes on the duties of a magistrate.

With the *e-unoto* the rule of the tribe passes from the senior generation to the next below it. The old men now become respected elders but, as it were, pensioners, no longer in charge. If they are rich they will have a number of wives to look after them.

When the British first came about seventy years ago, they found that the real tribal rulers were the witch doctors. These men were seers and priests, who alone could speak to God on His high mountain. The British dealt with the senior witch doctor Lenana, who advised his people not to fight the "iron snake"—the railway—but to make terms. So they put their mark to a treaty which preserved for their exclusive use a large tract of country.

Now the Masai are frightened not of the British but of African politicians who are taking over the government. These men belong to once-despised, now land-hungry tribes. Will they observe the treaty, as the British have done since 1911? The chances look slender. If they try to move into Masailand, warriors in warpaint and ostrich plumes will rally once again—for the last time. They would stand no chance against the well-armed, British-trained troops who would be ordered to enforce the policy of an African government.

UNDER strong pressure from British officials, the Masai reluctantly sanctioned a couple of boarding schools for boys only. When the first school started, five thousand acres were set aside because the fathers agreed to send their sons only if a herd of cattle and a female relative went with each boy. At first, the boys lived in typical *manyattas* among smoke and flies and cattle. Now, the fathers have agreed to let their boys sleep in clean, airy dormitories; and several others schools have opened. On a recent visit to one of these, I saw boys in regulation shorts and shirts mulling over sums and essays like any other schoolboys—though brighter than most.

This is a big break-through in Masai education. Is it too late? At the eleventh hour the Masai realized that only if they produce enough lawyers, journalists, politicians, teachers and business men will they be able to hold their own. Men they despised as savages are now the bosses—and the Masai have fifty years of lost time to make up.

So they send their boys to school. But their hearts are still with their great herds of small, humped, wiry cattle grazing the vast semi-arid plains.

* * *

THE Kikuyu are a tribe the Masai formerly harried and despised. Their homeland stretches from the outskirts of Nairobi, Kenya's up-to-date capital, northward to the silent forests of Mount Kenya where elephant and buffalo dwell and Mau Mau gangs used to hide.

In Nairobi, prosperous Kikuyu business men, lawyers, doctors and politicians drive their own cars and act like middle-class Europeans. But go out a couple of miles and you will see shaven-headed, bare-footed women, in beads and copper wire, bent double under heavy loads of produce, or beneath a hundredweight of wood to feed the fire that always burns between three cooking stones in the middle of the family hut.

Most of the older women speak no tongue but Kikuyu, and guard tenaciously tribal traditions and ways. But the young are poised uneasily between old and new.

Kamau wa Mathenge—a young Kikuyu I know—is an example. Until he was 9 or 10, his world was bounded by his mother's hut and *shamba*—the patch of land she cultivated—and, mentally, by the Kikuyu lore, tradition and custom he imbibed with her milk. She taught him how to address each type of adult according to age group and degree of relationship, how to eat politely with his fingers from a calabash—the father always first, men and women separately—and the religion and folklore of his people.

HE learned that God lived on the snow-capped peak of Mount Kenya and created the first man and his wife, and that their nine daughters founded the nine Kikuyu clans; that women had once ruled the tribe until one day the men, hatching a plot to get them all pregnant simultaneously, had seized power; that the cause of all misfortune was the anger of dead men's spirits, who must at all times be appeased; that witch doctors alone can intervene between the living and the dead to put matters right; and that wicked men, the sorcerers, know the secrets of deadly curses taken on the sacred stone of the Kikuyu, whose seven apertures represent the seven apertures of the body.

When he was 8 or 9, Kamau's father sent him to school to learn the new magic of writing, which would open the door to the white man's world of wealth and prestige. So Kamau went to a little primary school run by one of the Christian missions. Here he learned to read and write in his own tongue, and a smattering of English.

He learned also of a world of astonishing size and complexity beyond the green ridges of his own land. He learned that the Kikuyu God was of no importance, but that the true God meant everyone to be equal, black and white, rich and poor. He saw that this had not happened; so that either the Christian God was a failure, or the white men who were supposed to worship him were hypocrites. And he learned that most of what his mother had taught him was false.

At fourteen he was circumcised. This was not just a painful operation, at which he mustn't even wince, carried out by an elder with a knife; it was a course of instruction about his tribal traditions and beliefs, his rights and duties as a man, the technique of sex and many other matters.

When Kamau fell sick he was taken to a witch doctor, medicines were rubbed into his body and he drank and vomited a concoction made from herbs and the contents of a goat's stomach. But he got no better, so his father took him to a dispensary, where a white doctor sent him to a hospital. He came back cured, and converted to a total belief in European medicine; he never went again to a witch doctor except to get charms to wear on a journey.

ONCE a distant relative visited Kamau's father. He came in a shining motorcar, dressed in the smartest imaginable suit and carrying a briefcase. He was a business man in Nairobi who had turned politician, and had been to Britain to a conference, and hoped to become a Cabinet minister.

Yet he was only a Kikuyu like Kamau, who called him "uncle," and he gave Kamau's father five pounds to help with Kamau's schooling. Kamau resolved that one day he, too, would become as rich and powerful. He began to despise the customs of his fathers and the young men who dressed in beads and feathers and oiled their bodies, to go to dances when the moon was full.

At 16, Kamau went away to boarding school for two years. By now his hopes were centered on a college education. He went to dances and made love to the girls—in particular to one girl, who in time told him that she was pregnant. Her father claimed the bride price in goats, beer, blankets and tobacco to the value of about $150.

KAMAU'S father paid, and Kamau found himself a married man while still a schoolboy. Gone were his dreams of a lawyer's briefcase and a motorcar; on the other hand, he had too much education to go back to his father's land and cultivate the *shamba* he had been offered, even though his young wife, following tribal custom, would do all the field-work. So he found a job as an assistant schoolteacher at a primary school maintained by a group of white farmers for their employes' children.

All went well until the roving eye of the foreman's 15-year-old daughter proved too magnetic. An informal council of elders, the *Kiama*, which settled all domestic cases on the farms, fined him $150 for "spoiling" her by pregnancy. To find the money, Kamau resorted to theft, and this led to a further fine.

One night he decamped and vanished into the shifting underworld of Nairobi, where he lived from hand to mouth, kept company with dubious characters and pinned such faith as remained to him on the political party that promised a golden age for everyone when the great day of independence dawned.

Here we must leave Kamau. His story can end in one of several ways, in tragedy or in rehabilitation. Whatever the outcome, he must continue to inhabit a world halfway between tribalism and the Western economy.

In the city, life is wholly Western in pattern; but his wife, cultivating the *shamba*, her baby on her back in a leather sling just as he was carried, still lives a mainly tribal life. His son, like himself, will be brought up with a foot in both worlds.

How does Kamau think of himself? As a Kikuyu, as an African, as a citizen of his country, as a member of the British Commonwealth or even of the world community?

FIRST and foremost, as a Kikuyu: that is his race and nation, as people are Russians or Japanese, English or Frenchmen. Nothing will ever supplant Kamau's feeling of belonging to the Kikuyu; it is a spiritual matter. His body may travel across the seas, may even die there, but his spirit will return to his own country under the peak of Mount Kenya.

Kamau also knows that the Kikuyu are only one of many tribes, and that the deep divisions which have hitherto separated them must be bridged if political freedom is not to fizzle out in bickering and perhaps civil war. So he knows that he must not quarrel with the Masai or other tribes but must even vote for their members if he thinks they will make better leaders than his own brothers.

But as to marrying one of their women—that's a different matter. He wants his sons to be brought up as true Kikuyu, and in their time circumcised. He believes this to be the spirits' wish. It is the same with land; to sell any part of his family's *shamba* to a non-Kikuyu would be unthinkable. Outside the townships and mission centers, not a single non-Kikuyu lives within the borders of Kikuyuland.

Peaceful coexistence is Kamau's aim, not a tribal merger. He doesn't see why tribes can't agree at the level of government, so long as each keeps its identity and minds its own business at home.

And while some outside, colonialist control remains, this peaceful coexistence is quite possible. Will it continue when all outside control has gone? That is the great question all over the continent.

Two forces pull in opposite directions on the emerging African. Education, the growth of industries and cities, easy communications, the urge to prove that Africans can govern themselves—all these work to destroy tribalism. But when African nationalists like President Nkrumah of Ghana talk of expressing the "African personality," they imply a revival, to some extent, of African customs, languages, dress and political methods. These could strengthen the tribal spirit.

JOMO KENYATTA, the Mau Mau leader and the man Kenya nationalists want as their first Prime Minister, wrote a book glorifying Kikuyu customs and urging that some of those condemned by Europeans, like the circumcision of girls, should be retained in the new society.

Tribes are bound to change but that does not mean they will disappear. They offer the bemused individual a form of spiritual security, and the need for this today is greater, not less, than formerly. It will be a long time before Kamau and thousands like him, even if they become Westernized, cease to regard themselves first and foremost as Kikuyu, and to want their sons brought up to know Kikuyu ways.

Advertising: Pepsi Courts African Market

By ROBERT ALDEN

As the drums of political change boom across tropical Africa, other changes are in the making on the continent.

Not the least of these is the matter of marketing. Africa has a population of 230,000,000, perhaps not large as some of the continents go, but certainly one of substantial importance.

Africa is a difficult marketing area because complications arise that ordinarily are not encountered by marketing men accustomed to selling their wares along the familiar streets of North America or Europe.

It is hard to advertise in Africa. The continent lacks the media through which to advertise. A West Nigerian salesman who crosses over into East Nigeria not only will not sell his product but also is apt to be stoned in the bargain.

Add to local pride the strong tides of nationalism that tug at the African, and the problems of the man trying to sell a truckful of made-in-the-United States kazoos to the Africans become apparent.

One American who has just had a brush with the African market is Harvey Russell, director of special markets for the Pepsi-Cola Company. Pepsi, because of the nature of its product, is especially interested in Africa. Africa is a hot continent, where all men and animals get thirsty and (save for the camels) get thirsty often.

For this reason the company recently sent Louis Armstrong on a jazz safari to Africa. For this reason also, Pepsi has opened bottling plants in romantic sounding places like Mombasa, Kano, Ibadan, Onitsha, Moshi, Fernando Po and Dar es Salaam.

Mr. Russell, a modest man, denies that he is any particular authority on the African market. But he has just spent seven weeks there in a sweep across Nigeria, Ghana, Sierra Leone, Liberia and Senegal—all in Pepsi's Western African marketing area.

Research Need Seen

In an interview, Mr. Russell said that he felt that the most significant thing about the African market was that so little was known about it. His feeling was that the first order of business was some "good, sound market research."

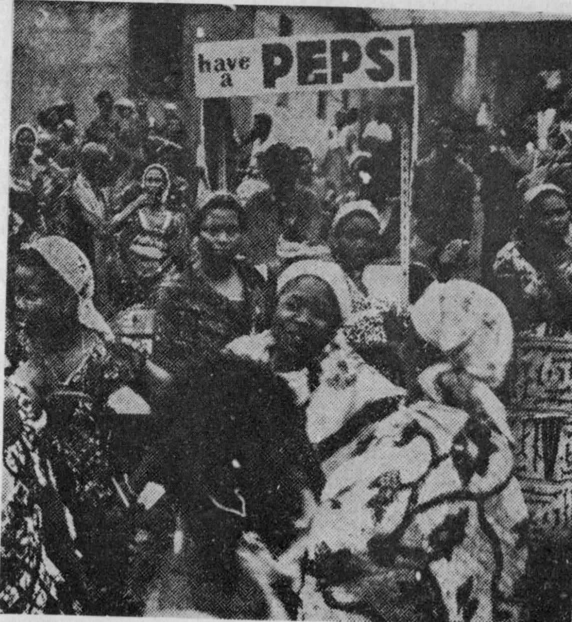

Residents of North Accra, Ghana, surround a dispensing unit set up by local bottler during a tribal festival.

Until now, there has been little mass marketing in Africa. Most of the products available to the Africans, Mr. Russell said, were products of monopolies and lack of competition made mass marketing unnecessary.

In addition, there is hardly any middle class. The small upper class generally dictates what is bought and sold. The poor are so poor that they have no money to buy anything. As a result, barter is a common method of trade.

It is not unusual, for example, Mr. Russell said, for a tribesman to come to a trading post with goods from his village and leave with a case of Pepsi-Cola. It is up to the local Pepsi vendor to convert the native goods into cash. (Catch the man in the local candy store in the Bronx who is willing to do that.)

The bulk of advertising in Africa is of the plaster-it-on-the-wall variety. Only there are not many walls. There is, however, public transportation—hundreds of little lorries roaming all over the bush country. These trucks are usually covered with advertising messages. No worries about triple-spotting there.

Newspapers would be all right for advertising but most people do not buy newspapers and could not read them if they did. Radio is fine and there are several radio stations. But not many of the Africans own radios. Radios often are community property—one to a village square. The people cluster around them the way people used to cluster around the radios in taxicabs in the United States during the World Series twenty or more years ago.

There is a television station in Lagos, Nigeria. But there again, no matter how radiant the star, what does it mean when few people in Africa own television sets?

That is why Mr. Russell believes that the most effective way of selling products in Africa is through promotion. Louis Armstrong's tour is a case in point, although many of the Africans did not understand the jazz music, which is, after all, native to America.

Lack of Salesmen

Another marketing problem is posed because educated Africans usually want to enter the civil service. They do not want to be salesmen (actually driver-salesmen) as Pepsi-Cola would have wished.

Mr. Russell found no strong antagonism toward Americans or American products as such. The people are happy to have skilled workers among them, regardless of their race.

But the fact remains that resentment of the treatment the Africans received at the hands of their recent colonial masters and the bitterness over the treatment of Negroes in South Africa overflows occasionally into business relationships.

"Sending a Negro over is an extra plus for Americans who want to open markets in West Africa," Mr. Russell said.

Summing up the situation, Mr. Russell said: "As far as marketing in Africa is concerned, I would guess that they are about where we were fifty years ago. They do things that we did when I was a kid—like painting ads on the sides of buildings.

"But I think they are going to catch up in a lot less than fifty years. They will start with modern communications. Radio, television, newspapers, education, income will grow by leaps and bounds and marketing methods will grow with them. The people are vital and inquisitive.

"There is room for American business in West Africa now, as long as it does not enter on a basis of exploitation. These new countries, fresh from colonialism, are leery of anything that smacks of exploitation and they will remain so for a long time to come."

May 25, 1961

NEGROES' TIES DEBATED

Views Differ on Link Between Americans and Africans

The identity between American Negroes and Africans was discussed yesterday at the fourth annual meeting of the American Society for African Culture, held in the Biltmore Hotel.

William Conton, a writer from Sierra Leone, told the 200 educators, writers, artists and students attending that the African man of culture had more in common with the European man of culture than with uncultured men of his own race. He and other speakers advocated a view of Africans as human individuals first and as Africans second.

Others, however, saw deep ties between the Negro of Africa and of America—ties of cultural traits and of a shared experience of subordination, whatever their position.

June 25, 1961

Change Comes To Africa's Villages

As new ways impinge on the old in these communities, a paradox of progress results.

By BARBARA WARD

THAT the politics of tropical Africa today is marked by a continuous turbulence is not really surprising. Every problem of transition confronts the continent in its most violent form—authoritarian colonial rule has to give way overnight to largely unfamiliar democratic processes; racial attitudes born of superiority and dependence have to be painfully readjusted; tribes must form nations; their leaders must adapt themselves, whether they like it or not, to the pressures of the cold war. It would require super-human wisdom to ride out this upheaval without shipwreck here and there.

Yet, of all the problems of transition, the deepest, the most enduring and probably the most difficult does not lie on the surface of politics. It is to be found at the very foundation of the new states in the effort to take the African village—where 70 or 80 per cent of the peoples of Africa still live—out of its millennial communal and tribal past into the modern world of general education and dynamic farming.

Just how far the village has to go can best be judged not in abstractions but in a concrete image of the village itself. First of all, in spite of tribal differences, in spite of the spectrum of climate and vegetation running from the arid rim of deserts through park-like savannah country to the dense, green, matted walls of the rain forest, the villages have a family resemblance. Mud huts stand in small compounds, roofs and wall tops thatched with straw or sorghum stalks or the big leaves of plantains—with an increasing incursion of stained and rusty corrugated-iron roofing in townships nearer the cities and the ports.

MUD walls, mud compounds, mud underfoot, all baked in the sun or slimy with tropical rain, make the village a splash of chrome or gray in the green ring of shade trees or the all-encompassing green of the forest. At the doors of the huts, women pound millet or Guinea corn or cassava for the family meal while the men sit under the trees and talk and smoke and talk again. Somewhere in the center, hidden behind a thick hedge or a laterite wall, is the place of the fetish. In Moslem villages, a tiny baked-mud mosque takes its place. The house of the headman or the chief stands out by reason of the extra carving above the lintel of his door or the dignity of a large Victorian armchair in his living room. And in and out of the compounds and the alleyways run little black goats while scraggy, squawking hens peck millet from the dust.

One would say: "This has not changed in half a millennium." But everywhere the signs of change are there. In many of the villages a plain, square, concrete community hall stands upright among the sagging huts. It has been built by the villagers themselves. The market economy is reaching out to them. They have their village stores where women traders conduct transactions which vary from a hundredweight of firewood down to the transfer of a single cigarette.

IMPORTED canned goods are displayed on trestle tables besides wood stoves roasting local plantains—the African equivalent of the hamburger. The "mammy wagons," open trucks using extravagant titles as trademarks "God Deliver Us," "Never Say Die," "Don't Trust a Lovely Woman") roar up the village street, depositing visitors and taking on a load of passengers and yams for the near-by market. Even if the forest is a around and trees block the view beyond the first turn of the road, the wider world is pouring through and eroding the old isolation.

The economic basis of the village is beginning to change, as well. The starting point is still traditional farming in which the land is held by the village group and no one outside the clan may claim a share (although some tribes are more lenient than others in allowing strangers to rent a temporary strip). Within the group, families have the use of individual holdings and this use, but not any form of ownership, is heritable.

Whether the surrounding area is forest, savannah, or semi-arid land, the farming family's usual practice has been to clear no more that the three or four acres needed for food crops, grow yams and Guinea corn and cassava for four years and then, as the soil's fertility petered out, move on to another four-acre plot, leaving the vegetation to flow back over the old site. In fifteen years or so, the soil is restored.

THE system seems confusing to the outside observer. So much land appears not to be in use at all. Forest and farm overlap in ways repugnant to tidy Western concepts. And some aspects are confusing even to the Africans themselves. There are few complete and adequate surveys; endless litigation arises over the delimitation of clan lands. Family plots, fixed by tradition, become unbelievably complex as the family grows and subdivisions occur. A village can become a patchwork of interlocking farm and fallow where no farmer can change methods or rotation without the agreement and cooperation of everyone else.

But the system has had signal virtues. Above all, it has kept a vegetable cover over Africa's friable soils and neither tropical rains nor tropical heat has washed or baked the earth into sterility.

The system is also incredibly durable. In fact, it is the special order which man has lived for by far the longest part of his history; civilization is a newcomer compared with a hundred thousand years of tribal life.

Yet change is on the way. Nature may have isolated the African farmer. But it certainly did not deprive him of the power to seize opportunities once he could see them. Wherever new openings entailed only small amounts of capital (no village community can produce massive saving) the farming communities have taken them up with purpose and vigor. Truck gardening is increasing near the cities. Where the growing of cash crops does not demand elaborate organization or plantation lines, the peasant farmers provide the bulk of the crop.

COCOA in Ghana and Western Nigeria is grown on small farms in the forest. Ninety per cent of Nigeria's palm kernels are picked from wild palms. And there can be little doubt that many more villagers would have entered the timber trade if the initial cost of equipment had not been so high, and if the European middleman had been more ready to help. It is not dour conservatism but lack of capital that keeps the more enterprising farmers from changing the scale of their operations.

But the chief key to change in Africa today lies in the schoolhouse. In more and more of the villages, the passer-by will see a green clearing with a couple of insecure football posts stuck up in the middle and, around it, a square of low mud buildings, white-washed, roofed with thatch or corrugated iron, veranda posts painted black, cannas growing scarlet and yellow in the corners. Here the children in khaki shorts and shirts or tidy mission dresses of butcher blue chatter and race and cheer the passing cars with extravagant gaiety, or sit in the shade frowning over their reading books.

IN the dark little classrooms they are quiet, attentive scholars. They try to learn their letters and figures with an almost alarming concentration. So much turns on the outcome, so many family ambitions, so many personal hopes. And they feel the cold breath of failure when their teacher says: "If you don't learn better than that, you'll have to stay on the farm"

And here begins the reasons why, although there is change in the villages of Africa, there must be more. Some of the compulsions are shared by all developing lands. More food must be grown if towns and industries are to expand. Farmers must earn more income if they are to buy the goods from an expanding industries sector. And, with or without industrial growth, traditional farming cannot indefinitely support a steadily growing population. As land runs short, the subdivisions increase, fallowing is cut, a fatal depletion of the soil sets in.

This pressure is not yet tropical Africa's main problem. But the shape of things to come is already visible in some areas. Around Owerri, in Eastern Nigeria, the fallowing time is already too short to allow the soil to recover. Trees and bushes are stunted, streams run down raw, red gulleys where the bones of the land stand out like the limbs of a starving man; eroded sheets of the clayey laterite earth appear in the clearings and on them nothing grows at all. No sight is more grim than this slow murder of the soil—our planet's "flowery earth-rind" upon which the continuance of life itself depends.

BUT in Africa the overwhelming need for rapid change starts not so much in eroded fields as in the tidy white buildings and noisy compound of the village school. All through the continent, education is seen—rightly—as the door to the future. "Universal primary education" is a symbol of statehood. Politicians must promise it to parents. The timetable is under constant pressure for revision —to enlarge it, to speed it up, to provide the schooling without fees. But the boy who leaves school no longer wants to work in the village where perhaps 80 per cent of the opportunities for a livelihood are still to be found.

The isolation, the oppression of forest life, the endless struggle with hoe and machete against recalcitrant vegetation, the closed-clan system, the authority of the elders—all these make up an environment stifling to the young mind that has learned something of the world beyond. The boy is up and away to the city.

In colonial times, when education covered perhaps 5 per cent of the population, his school - leaving certificate would secure him an apprenticeship in the town, or open the way to the lower rungs of the bureaucracy.

TODAY, such doors are closing fast. The number of school-leavers multiplies with the end of each school year. The opportunities for absorbing them in the towns do not. Already in Eastern Nigeria there may be as many as 300,000 school-leavers looking for work. Four years from now the figure may have grown to 700,000—or 40 per cent of the employable men. Estimates for Western Nigeria are not much different. There is talk of 900,000 unemployed school-leavers by 1967. No one can doubt that a social and political explosion on an incalculable scale may be in the making.

What can be done about this vast exodus from the villages? The answers are, of course, as wide as the whole strategy of development. At one end of the scale is large-scale industrialization. But modern industry does not in the short run match its heavy capital cost with any heavy increase in employment. For example, an oil refinery that may be built at Port Harcourt in Eastern Nigeria should cost about $30 million. But it will provide only 350 jobs. This is an extreme example, but even medium-sized industries may require as much as $2,800 in capital for each worker taken on.

Another series of answers lies in stimulating small-scale and workshop production, replacing imports with local goods and introducing more efficient methods into traditional trades. Firms like Sears Roebuck in Latin America have shown what marketing organizations can do to stimulate the production of local consumer goods. The big European importers in Africa — Britain's United Africa Company, the Swiss Union Trading Company, the various French firms, S. C. O. A. and C. F. A. O.—have a big part to play here.

EVEN so, on the analogy of other lands, industrialization, large and small, would not do much more than absorb the future increase in rural population. The present numbers, including the present flood of school - leavers, cannot be wholly absorbed in the cities. Means have to be found to keep them, productively, on the land. And so development policy has to double back on its tracks and return to the problem of the village.

One of the possible methods of change is found not only in Africa but all through the developing world. It is to persuade the villagers to consolidate their holdings in economic plots and to provide them with the credit, the fertilizer, the improved seeds, the pattern of crop rotation, the insecticides, the storage and the marketing facilities which make intensive farming safe for the land and profitable for the farmer.

This pattern has proved possible in Kenya and in Southern Rhodesia. There, native holdings have begun to be as productive as highly capitalized European farms. But the basic reason for the improvement is the same—the very large input of capital which made the consolidation of holdings and the provision of services possible. Moreover, the crucial change in Kenyan and Rhodesian land tenure was imposed by authoritarian European governments. Change by persuasion will cost no less and it will take much longer.

For this reason, African governments are looking for other models. One is to tempt the educated sons of farmers into new farm settlements as soon as they leave school. In Nigeria, new lands have been cleared in the bush by Government bulldozers. Here, on each new settlement, about 200 school-leavers, with a year's training in a farm institute, work together to get the land ready for farming.

Each boy can look forward to owning freehold about a 20-acre plot on which he will farm according to modern methods, with a proper rotation, fertilizers, imported seed and some farm animals to make mixed farming possible. Each plot will have its cash crops, too, and the settlement provides good housing, water, light, roads and community services.

CONDITIONS and earnings should begin to compare with those of urban life. The boys are, in fact, pioneers of the belief that better living is possible on the land and even though the capital cost for each farmer may be as high as $8,400, a town family will pay as much today to make a son into a lawyer or a doctor. Equal expenditures may give a professional stamp to farming and also create a lasting asset in the shape of better land.

This is the argument and the boys seem cheerful enough as they drive the tractors—symbols of emancipation—out to the fields of Guinea corn or feed their N'dama cattle on the husks. Moreover, last year perhaps 40 per cent of the school-leavers in Western Nigeria applied for openings in the farm settlements—the first sign of the tide of young opinion turning back to the farm.

Some of these farm settlements will be dedicated almost wholly to cash crops and, while each boy will own his own plot, the settlement itself is to be run on the lines of a plantation. A general strategy of planting and development will be adopted and individual farmers will thus gain the advantages of modern methods of cultivation and of larger-scale operations.

THE archetype of such experiments is the successful growing of cotton by peasant proprietors on individual plots in the vast irrigated estate of the Gezira in the Sudan. Such a combination of private ownership of land with a collective strategy of planting and marketing seems to combine the most productive features of both types of farming and many Africans wonder whether the idea of the cooperative plantation may not prove a master idea in tropical agriculture. The Chagga tribe in Tanganyika has shown that its communal tribal system of landholding could be adapted for the extensive production of coffee as a cash crop. May there not be here an alternative method of modifying village agriculture—one which, by persuading the community as a unit to become producers of cash crops, gives the farmers all the gains of large-scale cooperative enterprise?

But whatever the approach — community development, new farm settlements, cooperative plantations—one thing is clear. All methods, without exception, demand massive investment of fresh capital. To give only one example, Eastern Nigeria would need to spend perhaps $20 million a year to coax even a quarter of its school-leavers into new settlements. Yet the region's whole annual development budget is not much above $60 million and the agricultural estimates have to cover all the other interrelated needs of village life—water, power, extension services, roads—while $10 million and more has to be found for the recurrent costs of education alone.

This is the final universal dilemma of village development. Villages produce barely any surplus capital because they are not developed. But they cannot develop until they find the capital. The consequences are to be seen all around the world—in thrusting cities, growing ports and brisk industrial enclaves surrounded, engulfed, held back, weighed down, even stopped in their tracks by the drag of a vast, unchanging, stagnant countryside.

YET there could be a really effective speeding up of rural change if, in the next decade of sustained economic development, the Western donor nations were prepared to put a wholly new emphasis upon capital assistance to the farms and villages in developing lands. In the past, the countryside has, of course, gained from outside aid. Road building, the construction of dams and extensions of electric power all help, directly or indirectly, to raise rural standards and a good deal of technical assistance has been made available to agricultural extension services and community development.

But what has been lacking has been any large-scale, multiple - sided, consistently thought-through program for accelerating rural development in *all* its facets. In the Indian subcontinent, governments are feeling their way toward such a concept—in India's "special project districts," in Pakistan's plans for agricultural corporations charged with the task of planning over-all development for specific areas. That such an approach would be applicable in Africa has been shown by the success of the Swynnerton Plan in Kenya in which heavy doses of capital and competently integrated planning were used to resettle Kikuyu farmers on economic holdings and to give them the stock, the credit and the extension services needed to make a success of the new methods.

IF, now, a similar systematic concentration of forethought, capital and technical skill were applied to farming in other African regions, there could be a corresponding adoption of more dynamic techniques and the creation in the countryside of a new kind of life for the farmers.

The opportunity is more than economic. Political and social instability is the price paid for stagnant agriculture and the uncontrolled drift of semiliterates to towns where no work—and the political agitator—await them. In the end, we return to the point at which we began. There can be no halt to the turbulence of African politics without some restoration of social cohesion at new levels of skill and choice. The village still holds the key to this cohesion. Restore it there, and Africa regains a foundation upon which to build up securely and productively its new, adventurous, post-colonial, post-tribal patterns of life.

November 19, 1961

Words to the Wise —From Africa

By GEORGE H. T. KIMBLE

IN the recent Peace Corps postcard incident, the indiscretion of a young American teacher, which looked for a while as if it might cause international complications was cut down to size by a Nigerian newspaper editor with the proverb "Every black fold has its own white sheep." Some of us might be inclined to reverse the color scheme of this saying, but the point of it is as clear as black or white, and we can be grateful to the editor for making it. It won the day for reason.

In Africa, proverbs provide, in the words of my former colleague, George Herzog, "almost the exclusive, certainly the most important, verbal instrument for minimizing friction and effecting adjustment—legal, social or intellectual. Far from being the dead clichés which proverbs are to us, they form a vital and potent element of the culture they interpret." They also give spice and punch to everyday talk. Without them, as one African saying has it, "Talking is like spearing an animal with a sharpened 'palm rib": it simply does not "go home."

Almost every African society that has been studied by the folklore specialist has been found rich in proverbs relevant to its point of emphasis and the needs, individual and corporate, of its members.

In some societies the number of proverbs that have come to light as the result of such studies is very large. Mr. Herzog lists 416 in his study of the Jabo people of Liberia. C. M. Doke's work on the folklore of the Lamba people of Northern Rhodesia lists 1,695 proverbs, and J. G. Christaller's collection of Ghanaian proverbs runs to 3,600.

BECAUSE many of the points of emphasis in African societies are identical with those of our society, the meaning of many African proverbs is immediately self-evident. Some of them look as though they were "lifted" from European and American folklore, or vice versa. Be this as it may, they speak to the condition of all men in language that any man can understand. For example:

"Ashes fly back in the face of him who throws them."

"No man is clever enough to lick his own back."

"People look for strayed black goats in the day."

"A greatly worried person will even answer to the braying of an ass."

"Borrowing is a wedding: paying back is mourning."

"Pipe a tune in Zanzibar, and the drums of the Great Lakes will echo the refrain."

"The crab never gives birth to a bird."

"No incense is strong enough to hide a bad smell."

"When two bulls fight, it is the grass that suffers."

"God makes the rain to fall even on the wizard's garden."

"One tree alone does not make a forest."

"However long a stream may be, the canoe eventually lands."

Some African proverbs, however, do not yield their accepted meaning to the outsider—for two reasons. First, because they are fashioned from raw material—physical and cultural, economic and psychological—of everyday experience, and this is frequently quite different from the raw material of Western experience.

TAKE the following proverb, for instance. "A beast that is passing finishes no grass." This is the Zulu's way of saying that strangers are to be treated with consideration. It is based on his pastoral economy, which involves the seasonal movement of cattle from one pasture to another. As every herder, sooner or later, needs the right of passage over another man's land, it is to his own gain to think more of the "beast" than of th; "grass."

Another proverb of the same type asserts, "If God dishes your rice in a basket, you should not wish to eat soup." This is the Mende (Sierra Leone) way of saying that if you are a poor man, you should not aspire to be rich. It is based on the dietary standards of the people; only the more well-to-do can regularly afford the palm oil, meat and other ingredients that go into the local "chop," or soup.

The second reason many African proverbs do not strike a responsive note in Western ears is that not all of the African's points of emphasis are shared by us, nor are all his thoughts our thoughts. Thus, the Banyankole people of Uganda have the saying, "An old hare suckles at the breasts of its offspring." Odd and unseemly as this practice may appear to us, it reflects the deeply felt obligation of the Banyankole and of almost all African peoples, to provide material support in old age for those who bore and raised them.

Then, the Swahili-speaking people of East Africa have the saying, "The log cannot be moved save with the help of rollers." This is a comment on the widespread "dash" system in which every favor has its price. Again, in parts of West Africa it is commonly said (contrary to the accepted Western view that honesty is the best policy), "A lie in court saves the case." Among the Jabo and others, a crime against the tribe is not considered to be proved, nor the culprit convicted, unless a confession has been made.

Because African proverbs form "a vital and potent element" of culture, some may like to argue that they do more than "interpret" the culture; that, perhaps, they adumbrate the future of it or, at any rate, provide us with some signposts to it.

WHAT can be surmised about the future from such sayings as "He who blazes the trail determines its straightness," "If you cannot build a house, be content to live in a hut," "A roaring lion kills no game," "He who is waiting for a huge helping * * * isn't going to stand and wait for a handful," and "When you see your neighbor's beard catching fire, bring water for your own."?

Much depends on one's point of view. Some, no doubt, will find grounds for concern in these sayings; others, for comfort. But at least there is not likely to be more than one point of view about the East African saying, "When minds are the same, that which is far off will come."

With so much wisdom embedded in the proverbial lore of Africa, is it too much to hope that "the far off will come" someday, and that it will have been worth waiting for?

January 28, 1962

ETHIOPIANS ENDING CONFUSION ON NAMES

Special to The New York Times.

ADDIS ABABA, Ethiopia, April 20 — Ethiopia is trying to end the chaos created by the country's archaic custom on names.

As matters now stand, it is impossible to tell by names who is related, who are brothers and sisters, or who are husbands and wives.

For example, the son of a man named Abebe Tadessa automatically is named Tadessa Abebe. He in turn must name his son Abebe Tadessa.

Further confusion has been caused by marriage customs. A girl does not take her husband's family name, but retains her father's last name. But the children of such a marriage would assume their own father's last name, with the sons reversing first and last names, as described above.

To clean up this confusion, Ethiopia's new civil code requires that henceforth every family must adopt one surname and keep it, giving all the children only a new first name.

April 29, 1962

AFRICANS WORRIED BY CROWDED CITIES

Special to The New York Times.

ADDIS ABABA, Ethiopia, May 7—Massive migration of Africans into urban centers has become so serious that a special conference discussed the problems for ten days in Africa House here.

Twenty-four African countries participated in the conference, which was sponsored by the United Nations Economic Commission for Africa, the World Health Organization, the United Nations Educational, Scientific and Cultural Organization and the International Labor Organization.

The conference found the problems created by the influx into cities so complex that no easy solution could be found.

Among the many proposals offered to stem the flow to the cities were two calling for administrative control of urban migration and large-scale industrialization programs to provide jobs for the migrants.

Too much centralization of social amenities and public services—schools, hospitals, cinemas, electricity, running water, etc.—in urban centers was given as one of the main causes of the flow of people into cities.

May 13, 1962

New Nations Sing Out

The creation of national anthems for ex-colonials raises language problems.

By EMIL LENGYEL

United in harmony and fraternity,
Arise, Gabon, as the dawn breaks;
Thrill to thy vibrant and sustained ardor,
The fountainhead of our felicity.

THE national anthems of Africa's newly independent countries are composed of basically the same ingredients as are the old patriotic hymns we know. They celebrate a nation's traditions and aspirations and—of special concern to Africans—love of a unified mother country as opposed to attachments to the tribe.

One of the great problems the new nations faced in the creation of their hymns was language. What language was to be used, for instance, in Nigeria, whose people speak with about 270 tongues? Or in the Republic of Ghana, with some 70 languages and major dialects? Or in the Republic of Senegal, where half a dozen languages are spoken in the capital of Dakar alone?

The problem was solved in a somewhat paradoxical way. Even though most of the new nations gained their independence by freeing themselves from British or French rule, when it came time for them to express their patriotic feelings in anthems, they turned to the languages they had learned in colonial times. Thus the anthem of Gabon, the first lines of which are quoted above, was written in French.

THE title of Gabon's anthem, "La Concorde," is expressive of a preoccupation of the new African countries to harmonize discordant interests. Exhortation to national unity is also, for example, the keynote of the hymn of the Congo Republic. Its title, "La Congolaise," is reminiscent of France's "Marseillaise" and its text displays some similarities:

Arise, Congolais,
Marching proudly,
Let's proclaim our national unity,
Forgetting the divisive forces.
Let's be united more than ever,
Living for the watchword: work, progress, unity.

The virtues of one's ancestors and the glories of precolonial days are evoked in several of the new African hymns. Representative of this type are the national anthems of the Central African Republic and of the Republic of Upper Volta.

The first, titled "Centrafricaine," goes:

O, Central Africa, the Bantus' cradle
Resume the right to the respect of life
Long suppressed and restrained by all.
Henceforth destroy tyranny:
Work, order, dignity.

Upper Volta's "The Hymn of the Republic" contains the lines:

Proud Volta of my ancestors,
Thy glowing and glorious sun
Invests thee with radiance and gold.

THE fact that no fewer than four authors are credited with composition of the "New Dawn," the national anthem of the Republic of Dahomey, suggests that the anthem had to be written in great haste in order to have it ready for the celebration of independence. It begins:

Without faltering, our ancestors
Responded to the call,
With courage, ardor, and light heart,
Fighting brilliant battles with heavy loss of blood.

The Republic of Senegal was fortunate in having a statesman-poet ready at hand to write the text of its national anthem. President Leopold Senghor is the best-known French-writing indigenous poet of sub-Saharan Africa. He is the author of the impressionistic hymn:

Grasp your karas [harps], sound the balafons [cymbals],
The red lion has roared,
The tamer has bounded out of the bush,
The darkness is dissipated.

The anthem continues, apparently influenced by the "Marseillaise":

But if the foe sets fire to our land
We shall stand ready to seize arms,
United in faith and defying reverses,
The young and old, men as well as women,
Death! Yes, we say death, but shame, never!

The Malagasy Republic, formerly Madagascar, has a national anthem written in both French and the Indonesian tongue used on the island. The French version is "O Notre Patrie Chérie" and the Malagasy version, "Ry Tanindrazanay Malata O"—in each case, "O Our Dear Native Land." The Gold Coast, now Ghana, was the first British colony in Africa to win independence after World War II. Its national anthem, in English, follows the American pattern, glorifying the flag:

Lift high the flag of Ghana,
The gay star shining in the sky,
Bright with the souls of our fathers,
Beneath whose shade we'll live and die,
We'll live and die.
Red for the blood of heroes in the fight,
Green for the fruitful farms of our birthright,
And linked with these the shining golden band
That marks the richness of our fatherland.

MOVING north, we encounter Arabic as a dominant language. Thus the anthem of the Sudan is titled "Jundi al-Allah" ("Soldiers of God"). It goes like this:

Soldiers of Allah and of our land,
We are standing our ground,
Challenged to offer our blood,
Facing hardships, suffering and death . . .
May our land of Sudan endure for ever, we pray,
Guiding our nation the right way.

In Morocco, while the official language is classical Arabic, a large segment of the people speak Moorish Arabic or any of three major Berber dialects. It may be for this reason that the Moroccan anthem is a song *without* words. Anthems without words are, in fact, found in several Moslem countries—Afghanistan and Saudi Arabia, for example—a circumstance that also may be ascribed to religious reasons. Glory is due to Allah and to Him alone, and not to secular concepts, such as the nation.

TUNISIA'S national anthem does, however, have words and is distinguished by the fact that it glorifies not only the country but also President Habib Bourguiba. It is written in march time:

For our beloved fatherland
We have shed undying, precious blood.
All hardships we gladly stand
So as to free our verdant land.
Sweet is the fight when victory is sure
When shedding the yoke we had to endure.
Fire we face staunchly and with heart light,
Cherishing the spirit of our Habib, the great guide.

The United Kingdom of Libya has a national anthem, also a march, that invokes Allah's aid to crush the foe:

May God cast off the hand that seeks to harm,
May thou live forever, as eternally we are thy warriors,
We care nought who perishes amongst us,
As long as thou survivest.

And so the process goes on. As new countries in Africa have emerged, announcements in the local press such as the following have become routine: "The Constituent Assembly is engaged in the task of creating the Constitution, the flag, and the national hymn."

SACRED KENYA TREE MAY BACK PROPHECY

Dispatch of The Times, London

NAIROBI, Kenya, Oct. 30—A sacred fig tree of Kenya's Kikuyu Tribe is rapidly crumbling and many Africans believe that it will fall on the country's independence day as forecast by the most famous of the tribe's prophets, Mugo Kibiru, about 70 years ago. Independence Day is set for Dec. 12.

Kibiru is said to have foretold the coming of the white man and colonialism to Kenya and to have told the tribe that the sacred tree at Thika, 26 miles north of Nairobi, would wither and die when the white men left the country.

The tree, which was recently struck by lightning, is rotting more every day.

Jomo Kenyatta, Prime Minister of Kenya, recalled the prophecy some years ago at a meeting held under the tree.

At the height of racial friction here settlers in Thika built a 3-foot-high concrete wall encased in iron around the tree to avert an "accident" to it. They feared that the Africans would take such an accident as a "sign" that Kibiru's prophecy was coming true.

November 3, 1963

Africans Face $400 Question: A Wife or Status-Filled TV Set

Special to The New York Times

NAIROBI, Kenya — Thousands of Africans face a decision these days—should they save for a television set or a wife?

Wives cost up to $400 when paid for in cattle, sheep, goats and money. Television sets cost about the same—and among the African people the possession of a sinema kidogo (Swahili for tiny cinema) is a peak of distinction today.

Many parts of the continent now boast electricity and television transmission. There are stations in Sierra Leone, Northern and Southern Rhodesia, Ghana, the Ivory Coast, Kenya, Uganda and the United Arab Republic. Stations are being built in Aden and Mauritius and they are contemplated in Zanzibar and Tanganyika.

Throughout the continent the pattern is approximately the same. Governments install community sets in tea gardens, community centers and public halls, and each set draws hundreds of viewers nightly.

English is the main language medium in East and Central Africa, French in parts of West Africa and Arabic in the north. Cairo boasts Africa's most powerful station, reaching into Jordan and Israel and providing the United Arab Republic with strong pipeline for propaganda—the object of most of its programs.

Local Material Educational

Elsewhere in Africa, transmissions average three to four hours nightly, of which about 90 minutes consists of local material. The remainder is received from major United States, British and French networks. Local transmissions have a high percentage of educational broadcasts, health lessons and promotions of local social projects.

Such surveys as have been carried out indicate that Africans prefer cowboy films, newscasts and music programs. In Kenya, Hickleberry Hound and Top Cat also have high popularity ratings.

All African stations are subsidized in one form or another by governments and all the governments involved regard television costs as a necessary investment. Many point out that there is no better medium for civilizing and developing a nation. Although no leader will acknowledge it, a claim to have given the people television is a big vote-catcher in contemporary Africa.

Roy Thomson, the British newspaper magnate, has extensive television interests in Africa. Thomson Television Ltd. has been making funds available for developing countries to buy television equipment and amortize it over a number of years. The organization is providing more than $1.5 million yearly for these services and for educational television programs.

The company's latest venture is the installation of portable television apparatus, based in Nairobi, for use to cover major events throughout the continent.

pay its way with commercial

The start of television broadcasting in African countries is a momentous occasion. At least two countries, Sierre Leone and Uganda, inaugurated telecasting services in 1963 on their national independence days.

Sierre Leone, which boasts that its new studio in Freetown is the largest in West Africa, began four to five hours of daily telecasts on April 27, the second anniversary of her independence. Education rather than entertainment was proclaimed as the main purpose of programs.

Uganda began regular television broadcasts from a Kampala station on Oct. 9, the country's first anniversary of independence. Program fare has been a free-wheeling mixture of sports, news, cultural and children's shows, jazz and other music.

January 20, 1964

800 Languages

Not the least of the problems of the Pan-Africanist is how to get on speaking terms with those he wishes to win over to his cause, for Africa is a Babel of more than 800 tongues. Most of them cannot be written down and have only local currency. Some are spoken by less than a thousand people, while fewer than fifty are spoken by as many as a million.

Of the "African" languages, only Arabic and Swahili are understood widely enough for each to serve as a lingua franca, but even so, there are large areas where neither would help a motorist find his way, and even larger areas where any attempt to impose either as the official language would run into grave difficulty.

By the look of things, one or the other, or both, of the two most widely used European languages must continue to serve the cause of African unity. "Speak English . . . Parlez Francais" were the cries that went up at the recent meeting of the foreign ministers of the Organization of African Unity when the Egyptian delegate rose to address his colleagues in Arabic.

No doubt there is irony in the fact that the search for unity—and identity—has to be pursued in an alien tongue, but maybe there is also wisdom in it. After all, most educated Africans (including the Egyptian delegate) are as fluent in English or French as they are in their mother tongues. And most uneducated Africans would like to be.

March 29, 1964

Clerics Hear Islam Is Spreading Swiftly in Africa

By LLOYD GARRISON
Special to The New York Times

ENUGU, Nigeria, Jan. 13 — African delegates to the meeting here of the World Council of Churches have reported a sharp rise in the spread of Islam throughout black Africa.

Many African church leaders credit the Moslems' success not only to an increase in the small Islamic missionary work but also to a failure of Christianity in adapting to African customs —including polygamy.

According to the Rev. Jean Kotto of Cameroon, Islam is "growing rapidly" in all the former French territories in West Africa.

"The percentage of Moslems is at least equal to if not greater than that of Christians," he told the World Council's policy-making central committee.

Delegates from English-speaking African states reported similar Moslem inroads. Nigerian churchmen said that while Islam was winning thousands of converts, the rate of Christian growth was barely keeping pace with the rise in population.

There are no reliable figures on the Moslem advance. "Islam doesn't stop to count pagans like we do they just convert them," said the Rev. E. A. Adegbola, Nigeria's leading Methodist theologian.

The challenge of Islam has brought many African clerics into direct theological conflict with their European counterparts assembled here in the palatial Hotel Presidential overlooking Enugu, the capital of Nigeria's Eastern Region.

Many European theologians feel that their churches in Africa should adhere rigidly to traditional moral principles. The Archbishop of Canterbury, the Most Rev. Arthur M. Ramsey, reflected this view when interviewed shortly after his arrival in Nigeria for the conference.

When a Nigerian reporter asked the archbishop whether he thought the church could bring itself to accept an African with more than one wife, he replied: "Certainly not."

But a number of prominent African churchmen, including Mr. Adegbola, disagreed.

"It is not just because Islam is gaining but because the church must adapt to African reality," he said.

His opinion was echoed by Samuel H. Amissah, a Methodist layman from Ghana who is general secretary of the All-Africa Conference of Churches.

"We don't have to accept all African customs wholesale," he said. "But if Christianity is going to be really meaningful to us, it must take into account our indigenous culture. And this can be done only by Africans who have the culture in their blood."

Tolerance of polygamy is considered here one of the main reasons for Islam's attraction in Africa, where polygamy is a deeply ingrained custom.

"Islam also is tolerant of its followers worshiping tribal gods and taking part in traditional dances and ceremonies that European missionaries have long considered sacrilegious," said Mr. Adegbola.

The Moslems "also make conversion easy by demanding only that a man profess his belief in one god, Allah, and his prophet, Mohammed" he added.

"Further instruction can come later, and much of it is oral, which appeals to the mass of Africans who can neither read nor write.

January 14, 1965

Art Under Apartheid

JOHANNESBURG.

There is a curious paradox about race-haunted South Africa. Under the ironclad *apartheid* laws the ring of racial separation is complete—except for one link. This link is art: there is no bar whatever to the free mixing of blacks and whites at art exhibitions. Africans can attend opening-night shows patronized by the top levels of society in Johannesburg, Capetown and Pretoria, the three leading art centers. And they do. The artists among them are free to exhibit their paintings and sculptures on exactly the same terms as the whites. And they do.

In fact, in a country where the black man is held down and the white man is determined to keep him there, the best-known, most admired and most sought-after figurative sculptor is a Negro—Sydney Kumalo, currently exhibiting his work in an international show in London's West End.

But he is only one member of a new and developing school of

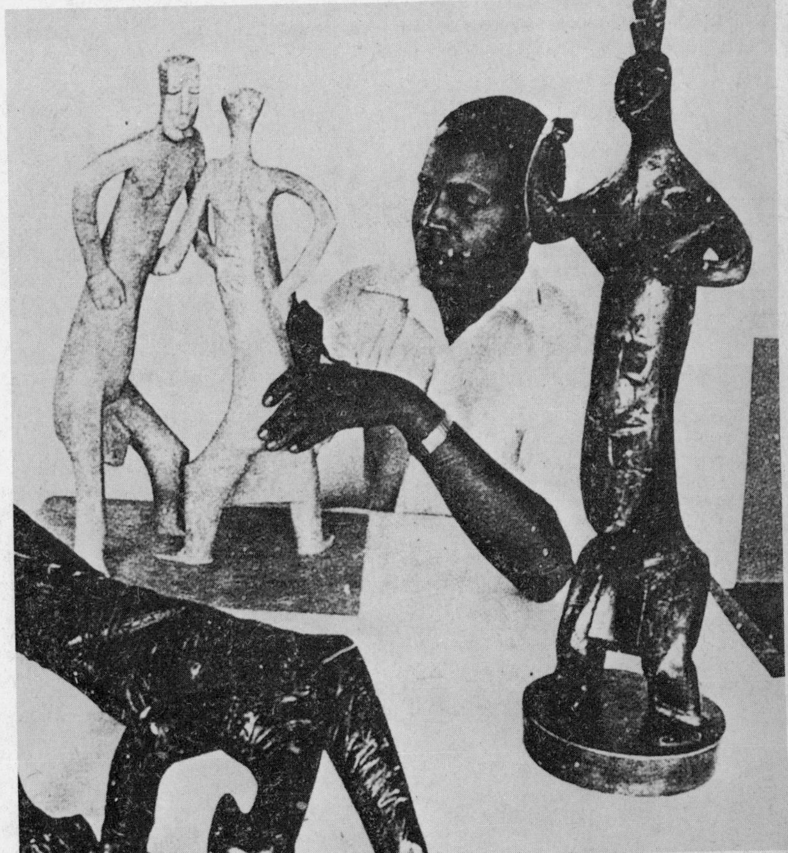

Sydney Kumalo, 30, has more commissions for cathedrals, churches, homes and offices than he can handle. Born in Johannesburg, he was trained there in South Africa's first all-African art school, the Polly Street Center. He has had no less a patron than the Government itself.

urban African art flourishing in the republic. Other prominent African artists are currently exhibiting in one of Johannesburg's most fashionable galleries, including Andrew Motjouadi, Lucas Sithole and Louis Maqhubela. Examples of their work are shown here.

The painting, "Washday," above, is by Louis Maqhubela, 26, whose work is much in demand among collectors of African art. Maqhubela is a teecher at the Polly Street Center.

The painting at right, "Township," is by Andrew Motjouadi, who grew up under tribal chiefs in the hot, dry bush country of the Northern Transvaal and became an artist after moving to Johannesburg.

Lucas Sithole (above with one of his works, "Guitar Player") is 34, and represents the new school of African artists who work and exhibit in South Africa despite apartheid. At right is his "Mother and Child."

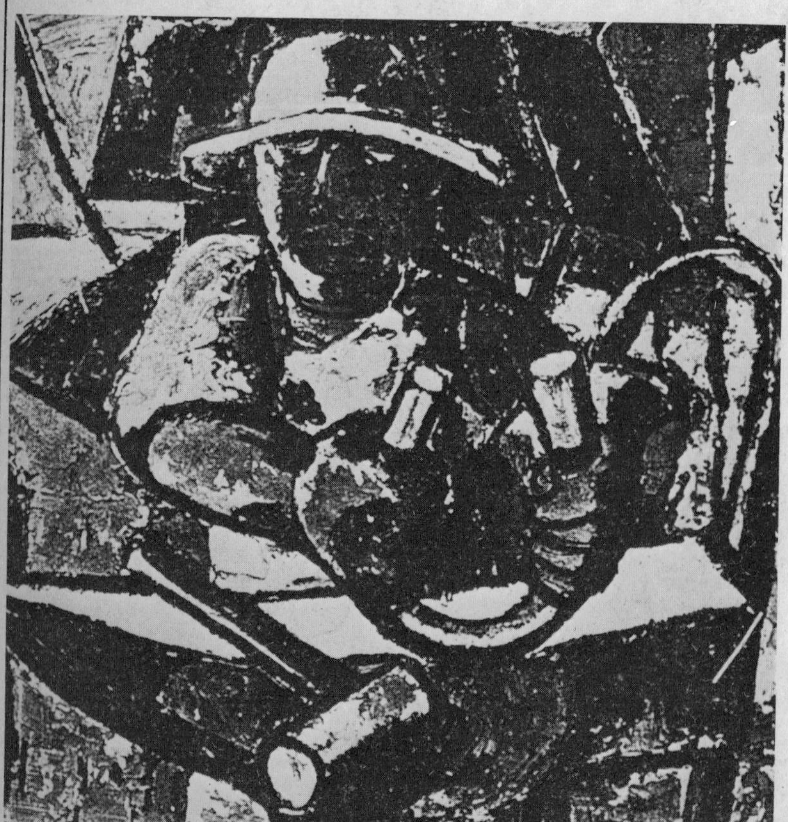

"The Blacksmith" is another work by Louis Maqhubela. Artistically his future—like that of his associates—looks good, but there is a cloud on the horizon. While the Government permits racially mixed art shows now, the question is whether under its tightening policy of *apartheid* they will continue.

March 28, 1965

AFRICAN SAVAGES AT END OF TRAIL

Uganda Nomads Plagued by Disease and Civilization

By LAWRENCE FELLOWS
Special to The New York Times

NAMALU, Uganda, July 24—The proud savages of Karamoja, caught between an advancing tide of disease on one side and of civilization on the other, stand uneasily at the end of the lonely nomadic trail they have followed for ages.

The vast majority of these tall, naked Karamojong, perhaps 140,000 in all, live as their fathers lived. They follow their huge herds of cattle from pasture to pasture, according to the seasons, over the bush that seems to roll interminably from Mount Elgon along the border of Kenya to the Sudan in the north.

Like the Masai in Kenya and other Nilo-Hamitic tribes who are presumed to have wandered up the Nile from Egypt in some long-forgotton era, the Karamojong lived on the milk and blood of their cattle and cared nothing for maize or millet or any of the other seed that other people and ants had been seen to eat.

The Karamojong bowed to no overlords. Their warriors drove the Bantus and any others who would encroach on their plain down toward Mount Elgon. Now the slopes of this ancient volcano, brushed by a misty lilac cloud, are covered with a deep green canopy of banana fronds and coffee and oozing with prosperity.

And now the Karamojong are hungry, yet not for failure of their pastures. For this is the rainy season and everything is green. A haze hangs heavily over the plain at dusk and thunderstorms mutter and crackle on the horizon.

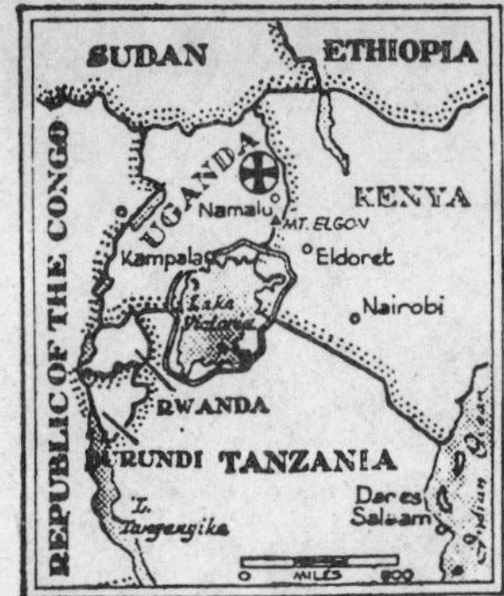

The New York Times July 25, 1965

A TROUBLED REGION: Nomadic tribesmen in the Namalu area (cross) are hurt by disease that has swept their cattle herds.

But rinderpest, pleuro-pneumonia and the encroaching tsetse fly have taken a heavy toll of cattle.

Raids against the Turkana in Kenya and against the Sebeti to the south have brought some new cattle into the herds of the Karamojong, but the raids have also been costly in lives. The raids got so bad in the last few weeks that Uganda's army moved in and relieved the Karamojong of their spears.

Still hungry and thirsting more than ever for battle, the Karamojong warriors have taken to doing something they could never have done before: raiding a handful of their own number here at Namalu to steal not their cattle but the maize they planted in desperation two years ago.

Farmer States His Case

Last night a sort of peace council was summoned at this crossroads by clan heads and chiefs of the Karamojong. At dusk, with the women and children gathered and with a platoon of armed soldiers standing by, 60 warriors in three neat files of 20 came chanting and loping in perfect step over a distant rise toward the meeting ground.

The Karamojong warriors, their hair plaited with mud and dung and dangling with brilliantly colored feathers and their bodies covered only with shoulder cloths and painted with zigzags of ochre, were each carrying a long willowy reed instead of the spear the authorities had forbidden.

Ahead of them crested hoopoe birds fluttered and lurched from bush to bush and winged ants rose in dun-colored clouds from their red earthen towers.

The meeting, like most African meetings, was not a short one, but when the point of complaint was reached, that someone had been stealing maize, the warriors went into a frenzied, fearful-looking dance, leaping over and over again into the air and chanting as they do before they go into battle.

One of the farmers, whose contact with civilization was already obvious from the torn pink undershirt and khaki shorts he was wearing, took a reed in his hand, ran screaming around the whole group twice and then dropped to one knee in front of the group with the reed poised as if he were ready to blood it in his worst enemy.

The farmers are few but they are not afraid to fight, he shouted. Anyone who is hungry enough to eat maize can plant it for himself, he added.

That his argument was effective was evident from the moaning that set in among the warriors. The meeting was over and as the warriors loped off into the darkness, a Karamojong on a tractor swerved casually around them and out of the way.

July 25, 1965

A King at Work

In Nigeria, Africa's most populous nation (57 million), social progress is making strides without upsetting all traditions. A leader in this work is the Deji of Akure, 40, a modern oba (king) who for eight years has ruled 230,000 subjects in Akure Province. A British-trained lawyer, he has made it clear that while traditions will be upheld, "superstitions will have to go." A day with the king can be a mixture of old and new concepts. At left he emerges from his palace (its corrugated roof is in background) to a fanfare.

Royal dress contrasts sharply with wig and robe, right, symbolic of the Deji's legal practice in England and Lagos, the Nigerian capital, before he ascended the throne.

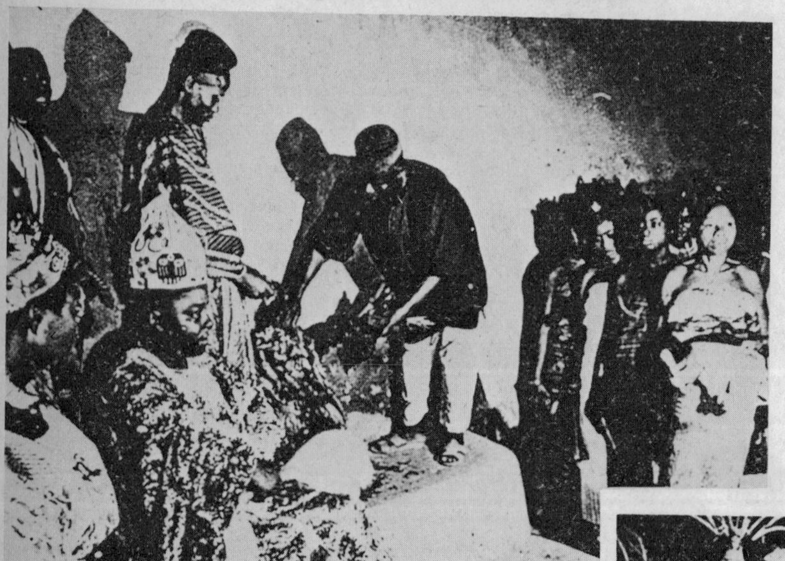

Among the local traditions is the worship of ancestors. Above, the Deji of Akure, wearing his royal robes and attended by some of his many wives, presides at the sacrifice of a chicken at an ancestral shrine. In another ceremony, below, he wears a special beaded crown and a latticed veil, while some of his young wives kneel before him.

At right he employs his legal knowledge to settle disputes before the palace court.

April 25, 1965

Swazi King's Ritual Dancing Stresses Tradition as Political Change Nears

By JOSEPH LELYVELD

Special to The New York Times

LOBAMBA, Swaziland, Jan. 11 — King Sobhuza II, the Ngwenyama, or lion, of Swaziland, joined thousands of his people today in a ceremonial singing of dirges and lullabies as he dismissed the old year and its evils and welcomed the new.

It was the high point of the six-day incwala, the central ritual in the life of the Swaziland, symbolic of the renewal of the people, land and King.

The Ngwenyama, who wears three-piece suits when he addresses Parliament or dedicates factories, was dressed like his warriors. That is, he wore a headdress of fancy plummage, a leopard-skin girdle and a mantle of ox tails. He danced barefoot on the earth of the royal cattle corral, where the ceremony took place.

Some of the more sophisticated young Swazis added woolen knee socks to the traditional garb, but the remarkable thing was that they were there at all.

"I used to shy away from these ceremonies," one university graduate said. "But there has been a remarkable change of late. We all realize now that this is our national dance. It's something we've got to support and be proud of."

The blending of old and new in Swaziland carries over into politics. Most of the bright young men have joined the Imbokodvo National Movement, which is for all practical purposes the King's party.

In the new year that he was summoning, King Sobhuza will almost certainly become the constitutional monarch of his small but potentially rich land, which has a population of only 290,000. The next year, probably the beginning of 1968, Swaziland will be independent, ending its status as a British protectorate, which dates from 1903.

Site of ceremony (cross)

Independence will necessitate a certain change in the ritual of the incwala. The British commissioners have been here so long that their entrance and departure from the royal corral has been built into the ceremony. The commissioner wears plumage every bit as fancy as the Ngwenyama's.

Sobruza's emergence as a political force in the modern context occurred only in the last few years. The King was apparently motivated by a determination to make certain that independence does not undo Swazi traditions.

He has celebrated more than

40 incwalas in Lobamba, a large village of beehive-shaped huts that is presided over by the Queen Mother, who is called the Indlovukati, or She Elephant.

A dozen of the King's wives and a score of his daughters took a central part in the ceremony. Their dress included red headfeathers and beaded belts. Apparently there is no one in Swaziland, including the King, who is entirely sure of the size of his harem or the number of his progeny.

According to some interpretations, an important part of the ritual is the renewal of the monarch's virility. At one stage of the ceremony, from which foreigners are barred, he is said to sit naked on the back of a bull while he is annointed with sea water, brought especially from the Indian Ocean, and other substances.

This prepares him to take the leading role in the renewal of people and land, which he does by biting into a gourd, the symbolic first fruit of the new harvest.

The dance Sobruza does with his warriors is little more than a shuffling and swaying in place, accompanied by slow, deliberate gestures of the hands, which hold spears and oxhide shields. The British officials, decked out in ceremonial white sunsuits, cough politely and exclaim at regular intervals, "Very interesting. Very interesting, indeed."

Other onlookers, under the mistaken impression that something dramatic is about to happen, keep asking, "When does it begin?"

January 13, 1966

Ivory Coast Acting to Eliminate Polygamy and Bride Purchase

By DREW MIDDLETON
Special to The New York Times

ABIDJAN, Ivory Coast, April 10—Matriarchy, polygamy and the purchase of brides are the targets of a sweeping program of social and political change that is planned to accompany the present rapid expansion of the Ivory Coast's economy.

President Felix Houphouet-Boigny's Government, pioneering beyond the purely agricultural and industrial development sought by other African states, is trying to fashion a traditional society into a contemporary one quickly and relatively painlessly.

Changes that the Government and foreign diplomats here consider revolutionary are being advanced. One is the introduction of a modern civil code that abolishes matriarchy, polygamy and the "bride price," the sale of brides to prospective husbands by the father of the bride, a practice followed in many African states.

Another step is to award appointive positions on merit rather than tribal affiliation, clan or religion.

In addition, a new property law encourages the extension of private holdings and the productive use of agricultural land.

The three measures are aimed at encouraging individual enterprise and speeding the transition from a subsistence to a money economy.

The new civil code, approved by the National Assembly in 1964, is gradually being implemented. Modeled on the French code, it includes laws on birth registration, marriage, divorce, adoption and inheritance. A special section abolishes the bride price.

The most significant result will be the suppression of polygamy and the matriarchial system as the code takes effect.

Under polygamy the woman is more of an economic factor—an extra pair of hands—than a person. She also is often a status symbol her husband cannot afford. Under the new code the wife can marry whom she likes and she is encouraged to seek education and to play a constructive role in Ivorian society.

The younger, educated elements in the country have attacked the matriarchial system, especially inheritance through the mother, for some years. They saw it as deterring economic incentive and disrupting home life in the center, south and southeast of the country, where it is most prevalent.

The abolition of the bride price also has economic importance. The ardent suitor forced to pay $50 for a bride out of a yearly income of about three times as much was hard hit. Only the bride's father, who got the cash or cows given for his daughter, profited.

Officials conceded that the new code would not work until monogamy and patrilineal succession were accepted as normal. Consequently enforcement has been gradual, with care being taken for the feelings of the Moslem community, which numbers about a fourth of the population.

Agricultural diversification, expanding education and new rural housing are being counted on to help the new code win acceptance. When villagers turn to the Government for loans for housing or fertilizer or to enroll their children in school, their papers will have to be in order.

District government executives called prefects and subprefects, in accordance with the French tradition, also are doing their best to end some of the old tribal customs. This includes the liberalization of traditional initiation rites and the encouragement of salaries for young initiates. In some villages young men no longer are required to work exclusively for their elders during the seven years following initiation.

Tribalism Still Vigorous

Tribalism's continued vigor is deplored by forward-looking officials throughout Africa. Here the Government is trying to do something.

The rural housing program has involved relocation of many villages, even the destruction of sacred forests. This has reduced the influence of traditional religion and customs and promoted new ideas.

The slow breakdown of the tribal system — there are 60 tribes in the country — also is being accomplished by not replacing provincial and tribal chiefs when they die. Village chiefs still are replaced.

Meanwhile, the power of the prefects and subprefects continues to grow. These officials come from outside their districts, usually are not members of the dominant tribe and speak French rather than local dialects in public dealings. They represent the "meritocracy" that the Government is encouraging.

Deputies to the National Assembly and officials generally now are chosen solely on the basis of merit. The young educated élite doctors, engineers and teachers taking their places in Government symbolize the second of the Government's measures of social reform.

April 11, 1966

A famous Benin bronze, exhibited at the Dakar festival, an example of how "Africa has created style out of emotion itself."

Malraux Looks At African Culture

Behind the Mask Of Africa

How can modern Africa develop its arts? How can it make use of its rich cultural and artistic heritage? And how can it relate this heritage meaningfully to the present world of machines and modernity? These are the questions that lay behind the recent First World Festival of the Negro Arts in Dakar, Senegal, which attracted some 2,000 Negro artists from all over the world. And they are the questions to which André Malraux—novelist, French Minister of Cultural Affairs and author of the noted study of art, "Voices of Silence"—addressed himself in a speech to that gathering. The following article is an adaptation of the speech.

By ANDRE MALRAUX

A CULTURE is primarily a people's intrinsic response to the universe. But in Africa today the word has two different—though complementary—meanings. On the one hand, it means the artistic heritage of Africa; on the other, it means its creative life. So, on the one hand we are speaking of a past, and on the other of a future.

The artistic heritage (I repeat *artistic*) of Africa does not include all the arts—not, for example, architecture. It does include dancing, music, literature, sculpture.

Africa has transformed dancing throughout the world—this is its first contribution to the art of dancing. But there is also a field of dancing uniquely her own, her secular and sacred dancing. This is dying out and it is the responsibility of African governments to save it. But this second aspect is quite different from the first. Sacred dancing is one of the noblest expressions of Africa, as it is of all cultures at their peaks. The fact that no American, Englishman or Frenchman now dances as his grandmother did is quite another thing.

We see the same thing in music. Africa has two musics. One is the music born of despair long ago in the United States; it is the great lamentation, the eternal voice of affliction which, with its searing originality, has passed into European music as the blues. I remember asking Yehudi Menuhin, "What does music most constantly convey to you?," to which he replied, "And to you?" I was moved to reply: "Nostalgia." The great music of Europe is the song of Paradise Lost. Now observe this: the first great music of Africa does not sing of a lost or even an unknown paradise, but of a very simple, very ordinary human happiness wrested forever from the unfortunate men who improvised songs on the banks of the Mississippi. But nevertheless this music is like our own, only physically more exciting.

And then there is jazz. It is a species apart by virtue of its rhythm; it is an invented music. It is also a species apart by virtue of its musical content, which we can relate not to the classical or traditional music of the West, but to modern music—sometimes to Stravinsky or Boulez. But jazz came first. Here Africa has invented in a highly complex field of art — musical content — something which today reaches the entire world as powerfully as her contribution to dancing has reached dancers.

In sum, jazz started with certain European or American melodic elements through which Africa has rediscovered her soul, or, more exactly, has discovered a soul which she did not possess before. For although her soul of despair is expressed in the blues, her ancient soul is not expressed in jazz, for jazz is a modern invention.

And perhaps in much the same way Africa, starting out from a poetry akin to Western poetry, has charged it with an emotional fury which has disrupted its models and sources.

FINALLY, the greatest of African arts: sculpture. It is through her sculpture that Africa again takes her place in the culture of man. It has often been said that this sculpture is a sculpture of signs—signs, let us add, charged with emotion and creating emotion. But it is also a sculpture of symbols, in the sense in which Romanesque art is an art of symbols.

These works were born as magic works, as we all know. But they are experienced by us today as esthetic works. It is said: Only by you Westerners. I don't believe this. I do not believe that there is one of my African friends—writers, poets, sculptors—who responds to the art of masks, or any other works of the past, in the same way as the sculptor who created these figures. I do not believe that any one of us Europeans responds to the figures on the main door of Chartres as the sculptor who created them.

The truth is that a magic or sacred art is created in a universe of which the artist is not the master. When the sacred element disappears, all that remains in the artist's creation is an obscure communion or sympathy, a sympathy which, in its root sense, runs very deep in all of Africa. But for the sculptor of Chartres, the statues on the main door *were to be prayed to but not admired;* and for the sculptors of Africa, their masks were to refer to a religious truth and not to an esthetic quality.

To believe that we—even Africans—can recover the world of magic is vain and dangerous for two reasons: First, it is false, and second, it prevents us from receiving from this august art all that it can bring to us, to all of us.

Metamorphosis has played a primary role here. Certainly African sculpture seems very closely related to modern sculpture. But the fact remains that when we look at a sculpture by Lipchitz or Laurens we know that we are not looking at a mask because, though we do not have a magical relationship with a mask, we know that magic is *in* the mask. African sculpture had a sphere of reference which is not that of modern art: it referred to the supernatural, whereas modern art refers simply to art.

THIS brings us to a fundamental issue. When African sculpture appeared before the world—that is to say, when certain artists began to be aware that they were in the presence of a great art—the field of reference for sculpture of all kinds was that of Greco-Roman art. Sculpture referred to what was then called nature, either by imitation or by idealization.

It is well known that African sculpture is not concerned with imitation and still less with idealization. What is less well known is that, in the slow but decisive process of establishing itself throughout the world, African sculpture has destroyed that earlier field of artistic reference. It has not imposed its own field of reference; the sculptor who created masks has not imposed magic on the modern world. But African art has destroyed the system of reference which once denied its existence and it has powerfully contributed to establishing a great period of art in place of Greco-Roman antiquity. On the day that Africa reawakened art to the vast realm of the supernatural (which had once included our Romanesque sculpture), on that day Africa made her triumphal entry into the artistic life of humanity.

This has not happened because one particular mask happens to be better than another particular Greek sculpture. It is because, from the moment Picasso began his Negro period, that spirit which had reigned in the world for thousands of years, and had disappeared for a brief period (from the 17th to the 19th centuries in Europe), recovered its lost rights. Of course we do not today approach art as we

MASK AND MASTER—African sculpture like this Congolese mask inspired Picasso's famous "Negro period" (below, an example) and "reawakened art to the vast realm of the supernatural."

did in the 12th century, but we have resuscitated the immense field of art which in the 12th century covered all the regions of the earth.

This is where African art finds its supreme justification. This is what commands our recognition. When Africa is in her own realm of spirit and form, we are no longer concerned with just one more art, or even with what was once called "naiveté" or primitivism. We are concerned, when confronted by the genius of Africa, with nothing less than the nature of world art. And inevitably world art acclaims the genius of Africa as part of its own.

Of course, the specific elements remain: Africa is not India. Africa represents a very particular power of communion with the universe. Its vehemence and pathos place it in direct opposition to the solemn ballet of Asia, make it very different from the European world which we all know. Here is the difference between Africa and the rest of the world: her rhythmic urge and pathetic power.

We have to remember that what we call a great epoch of art is nearly everywhere the negation of the pathetic principle, in other words, of emotion. Egypt and Asia have created style by implying emotion. On the contrary Africa has created style out of emotion itself, a style more discretionary and perhaps more powerful than that of any other civilization. This perhaps will prove to be her decisive contribution to the cultural heritage of mankind.

WHAT is the problem of culture? It is partly the problem of our past heritage, but it is more than that. It is also a problem of our changing world.

Since the beginning of this century the world has undergone a greater transformation than in the previous 10,000 years. Both Einstein and Oppenheimer have pointed out that there are more research workers in science alive today than the sum total of past researchers since the world began.

One cause of this transformation is that humanity has decided that the purpose of thought is to discover the laws of the universe and no longer to answer the question of why man is on earth. The search for the laws of the universe has, in some measure, taken the place of religious questionings.

The other cause is obviously the influence of machinery. Note how our machine civilization has multiplied the dream life of humanity in a way hitherto unknown; just as there are machines to transport us physically, there are machines to make us dream. Dream factories never existed before today, but now we have radio, television and cinema. A hundred years ago 3,000 Parisians a night went to some form of entertainment. Today there are several million television sets in the Paris area.

Thus the problem of culture is not to establish a realm of the mind *in opposition to* a realm of the machine (which in any case is impervious to the mind), for the machine is the most powerful means of diffusing the world of the imaginary that we have ever known. The principal problem is to discover what the mind can now bring to bear against the kind of diffusion of the imaginary which the machine has so far brought about.

The cinema was not born to serve humanity—it was born to make money. It relies therefore on those very emotions (with the exception of the comic) that are most suspect. The task, then, must be to combat its power as a dream factory which generates money by setting up dream factories which generate spiritual values—in other words, to combat images of sex and death by projecting immortal images.

Culture is that endeavor. Culture is that mysterious power of things so much older and deeper than we ourselves, things which, in the modern world, are our strongest allies against the power of the dream factories. That is why each country of Africa needs its own cultural heritage, needs the heritage of the African continent and needs, too, to create its own world heritage.

IT has been said that we should try to re-create this heritage out of the past, should try to recover the African soul which conceived the masks—this is how to reach the African people. I don't believe a word of it. What once inspired the masks, no less than what once inspired the cathedrals, is forever lost. But an African country such as Senegal is the heir to its masks and can say: "I have an affinity with my masks that nobody else has. And when I look at them and ask them to tell me their message of the past, I know that they speak to me, and that it is to me that they speak."

Africans must take into their hands all that was Africa. But they must take it knowing that they are in the throes of a metamorphosis. When the Egyptians believe themselves to be the descendants of the Pharaohs, that is unimportant; what is important is when they relate themselves to the Pharaohs and say to themselves: How can we be worthy of them?

Make no mistake about the ancient spirits. They are truly the spirits of Africa. They have greatly changed, yet they are there to be questioned. But Africans will make no communion by studying the ceremonies of the bush. It is right for Africa to claim her past; but it is still more important for her to be free enough to conceive a new past in the terms of the present world which belongs to her. Men believe themselves less strong and less free than they really are. It is not necessary for Africa to *know* how she will make her "imaginary museum." Did she know how she would create her dance? Did she know what jazz would be? Did she know that, one day, those trifling fetishes which used to be sold like firewood would cover the world with their glory and be bought by our greatest artists? There you have the supreme mystery of metamorphosis.

Africa is strong enough to create her own cultural domain, present and past, provided only that she dares to try. Nothing more is needed.

May 15, 1966

Kenya Report: Market in Brides

By LAWRENCE FELLOWS

NAIROBI.

"WOMEN are different now," said Chief Njiri Karanja, leaning forward on his stool to pull one stiff, sinewy leg over the other. "Women are getting clever. They are wearing expensive dresses instead of skins. They are painting their faces with cosmetics instead of mud. They are wearing high wigs that look like beehives. All these things cost money, and women didn't know about money before. Now there are school fees, too; it is very expensive to educate many children.

"Let me tell you: I had 52 wives, and finally they were like 52 pots of poison. If I had to start over now, I think one at a time would be plenty."

This ancient Kikuyu chief is more than just a quaint relic of Kenya's ancient past. He symbolizes not only the old values and customs—of marriage, of family and of social stability—but the new problems brought about by money, industrialization, urbanization and the other 20th-century attributes which Africa has become heir to. In his time he has seen the old ways in frontal attack from the new, has watched them bend and blend, and has known some of them to buckle entirely.

In the old days, under the old customs, Chief Njiri was a man of power. He was rich, as the Kikuyu reckoned wealth, and could afford many wives. Because of the competition to marry his daughters, he could demand as many as 15 cattle in bride-price instead of the usual five or six, some of which he added to his herds and some he set aside to acquire more wives.

As long as land was plentiful each wife got her own *shamba*, her patch of ground on which to grow the corn and beans she needed to support herself and the children she brought into the world. To Chief Njiri each wife, apart from being a fresh and lively new soul-mate, was another pair of hands. Finally, he had his women hoeing acres of corn up and down most of the hillsides around Kinona, north of Nairobi. His big herds of cattle wandered over the uncultivated slopes and his sons were spread as far as Kijabe, in the Rift Valley.

In the old days Chief Njiri had to guard against being plundered by the Masai or some other neighboring tribe looking for cattle, women and other valuable items of booty. The bigger his family and the bigger and stronger the tribe, the less likely was that sort of disaster. In addition, infant mortality and famine made family-building a matter of survival.

Each new bride brought interlocking and unending responsibilities to new clans within the tribe, and this helped give cohesion to the tribe. Polygamy and the practice of marrying the girls off as soon as they were nubile insured that the most was got out of a woman's fecundity, and helped secure the future for the tribe.

IN such a system, the place of the woman was special, but quite low. The virtues she was supposed to bother about were discipline, childbearing and the unity of the family and clan. It worked out well for the family and the clan, and also for the man. But not so much for the woman, who was pretty much of a chattel.

Even today the women retain much of this old position. Few have broken through the old barriers to an education and a career. Any day on the paths around Nairobi the evidence is there to see: a man, if he can bring himself to carry anything, will be swinging a little stick, while his wife staggers on behind, bent almost horizontal under a heavy load of firewood held from her forehead by a leather strap that wrinkles her shaven head and heightens her earnest and unhappy look. At home she wields the hoe; he sits in the shade and drinks *pombe*, the thick brew she made from the corn she grew and harvested.

In Uganda the more prominent Bahima men are still in a position to insist that their brides be fattened on milk, and the Bahima women are some of the most statuesque and beautifully built women on the continent. They have to be forcibly fed, and are beaten and stuffed so full that sometimes they cannot stand up alone and have to creep through the wedding ceremony on all fours, or be pushed through it by a gang of old women in attendance.

In the kingdom of Ankole in Uganda the keepers of the morals no longer lightly throw wayward girls into the Kagera River. Yet when a well-behaved girl is married, she is expected to provide sexual entertainment for all her husband's brothers as well. The same goes for the Masai in Kenya, although the service is extended to any visitor from the tribe, provided he is in the right age group. If the Masai visitor puts the woman in a family way, her husband is flattered; to him it is a matter of building his social security.

Yet, under the traditional system, no woman in Africa should ever find herself destitute. None should be turned into a nervous wreck, none should feel her life is unfulfilled. Even if she should somehow feel discontented, under the comfortably old shelter of custom, there was no expectation that she would be left unmarried.

Moreover, in some corners of Tanzania there is still polyandry, where the women take on as many husbands as they can afford, or think they have time for. (The Kikuyu tradition is that their tribe was polyandrous until the men in their resentment of the system finally overthrew it by a brilliantly executed plot in which they managed to immobilize the women by making them all pregnant at the same time.) And among the Langi in Uganda a woman may divorce her husband for impotence, nonmaintenance, cruelty, practicing witchcraft, quarrelsomeness, incompatibility, assault, laziness or foolishness. While some may wonder that there are any Langi women at all who stand by their husbands, it is true in most African societies, even where a woman cannot divorce her husband, she can leave him if he is too cruel to her or if he refuses to eat the food she puts before him.

BRIDE-PRICE, whether by the Zulu name of *lobola* or the Kikuyu label of *ruracio*, was another of the old steady customs with which the social fabric was knit. The idea of placing a monetary value on a woman is deeply imbedded in many societies around the world, but bride-price in Africa was more than just that. It had some of the flavor of playing cards for money: the game was still the prime consideration, but playing even for pennies tended to spice the hand and make it a less trivial undertaking.

CHIEF NJIRI, with his 52d wife and their son. Twenty wives survive; he has never counted his children, he says, for fear of bad luck.

It was, first, the way the suitor paid compensation to his bride's parents for all they had spent on her from the time she was born. Before cash crept into it, the price might have been in cattle, sheep, goats, copper ingots, gold, beads, spears or anything valuable, and would have covered even the calabashes she broke and the honey she spilled as a child. It was an earnest of the suitor's good faith, for not only was it expensive but it meant he would have his bride's clan around his neck for the rest of his life. And it was a way of stabilizing the marriage, because if the bride ran home on her wedding night the father would have to hand back the whole lot. (Or more likely, he would give his daughter a good thrashing and send her back to her new husband.)

BUT the old days of close tribal cohesion and huge, interlocked families are going. Disease is being controlled, famine is being relieved, tribal wars are being discouraged, the arguments for polygamy are therefore weaker—and the women are beginning to feel the time has come for a change. Peace among wives in some of the larger households is becoming more and more difficult to maintain. The letters columns in newspapers from one side of the continent to the other are loaded with complaints that demonstrate how fiercely the women resent both polygamy and the unmistakable air of purchase that seems to be settling around bride-price.

In some places the women are gradually getting their way.

In Ruanda, the Ivory Coast and elsewhere in Africa where the pressures from the Catholic Church and from organized groups of women have been too strong to resist, polygamy has been abolished by law; yet these governments know it will be years before their people will pay full attention to the new laws.

In Ethiopia, where polygamy is forbidden by law to all but Moslems, the Ethiopians have a traditional form of marriage called *Be Damoz*, a fairly casual arrangement fixed usually on a monthly basis with a salary for the woman. The children from these marriages are considered legitimate, but the woman has no real claim on her husband's estate apart from whatever salary there might be in arrears. The courts are beginning to treat these women more generously, especially those who entered into marriage as virgins.

URBANIZATION and the evolution of a money economy are having a much faster effect on the old customs than the whole chorus of angry female voices. The need for money has been made inevitable by the desire for education and by the growing demand for bicycles, radios, suits, motor scooters and all the other accoutrements of "civilization."

Even a skilled and relatively well-paid worker in Nairobi, earning as much as $150 a month, will have to weigh his resources carefully before he thinks seriously about taking on a second wife, especially if her family is going to find out how much he is earning. The new importance of money is shaking the ground under polygamy, bride-price and the whole lot of customs around marriage and the family.

MORE often than not, however, bride-price is accepted by educated Africans as a worthwhile institution. A lot of young people would like to see bride-price retained, but brought back down to reasonable proportions, so that the traditions of family solidarity can be preserved without sending newlyweds deep into debt. It need not be regarded as any more commercial than the presentation of an engagement ring.

The Africans who argue for the retention of bride-price like to talk about the awful examples of inexpensive marriage and easy divorce in the United States. They liken taking a wife there to checking a book out of the public library: you can have it if you are attracted by the cover, and return it if you tire of it after the first couple of chapters. The Africans pay for their books and brides, and think carefully before they decide which ones they want to keep. It is just that the prices, at least of brides, are increasing so rapidly.

With bride-prices rising, payment on the installment plan has become almost universally accepted in Africa. It was always that way among the Karamojong in Uganda. The difference there was that the marriage was not considered binding until the whole bride-price had been paid. As this could take up to 15 years, it was sometimes hard on the woman who happened to marry a slow-moving husband.

Generally, however, there are said to be few defaulters on wife-buying installment plans. Men who fall behind in their payments are hauled before tribal elders who examine their means and lay out schedules for future payment. The elders have no legal standing in most places in Africa, but to disobey them means to cut loose permanently from the clan.

And the ties to the clan, even in the new Africa, are still strong—but, in the new Africa, they create their own special problems. For obligations of hospitality apply to clan members wherever they go, and when they move off the land into the cities this can make their lives very complicated indeed.

A family with a house in town is almost never without house guests, some of whom can be expected never to leave. Any African home is a reception center for all clan members. In the village a visiting relative might bring a chicken and, if it is a woman, help with the work and the children. But in the city the visitors more often sit and mope and, if they are waiting for paying jobs, sit and mope for a long, long time. Among the Bantu tribes, the parents are the worst hazard; they can come when they are hard up and take whatever they want out of the house.

One young family man in Salisbury, where overcrowding in African homes is strictly against the law, simply slips out of his home when it gets too crowded and calls the police. He acts as surprised and unhappy as all the others when the premises are cleared by the long arm of the law, but he is laughing inside; he will not be blamed and he knows it will be at least a week before the relatives begin piling up in his home again.

Yet the same man takes advantage of the system when he heads on vacation trips to visit his second wife in a village deep in the bush. He takes a bus for about half the distance. It costs him only half as much that way, and from where he gets off the bus he can make his way from clan member to clan member, by a slightly circuitous route, to his second home at no additional cost.

This man's approach to the clan responsibilities he acquired with each of his wives may be a twisted one, but he is keeping his own two immediate families together on a single salary, and sending his two batches of sons to school. If he were to treat his two sets of in-laws as custom requires, he would soon have nothing. He has long since cast out any thought of acquiring a third wife and a third network of expense and responsibility. Like Chief Njiri in Kinona, he appreciates that the custom has been overtaken by the times. ■

February 19, 1967

VILLAGERS SHARE IN KENYAN JUSTICE

Manhunt Shows Adjustment of Africa's Rule by Law

By LAWRENCE FELLOWS
Special to The New York Times

EMBU, Kenya, Nov. 3—In a deep valley south of here, where thorn-covered hills begin to rise toward Mount Kenya, a man wanted by the police as the "maddened bow and arrow killer" was captured last night after a week-long search by a posse of a thousand villagers.

In the process, the growing concept of civilian involvement in East Africa's law enforcement was made a little firmer.

That the wanted man, Njenga Fundi, was still alive today and in the hands of the police came as a surprise, especially since he still had a sheaf of six poisoned arrows when he was caught.

The size of the posse was also a surprise; it would have put to shame most of those drawn up in American West in even its wildest days and was certainly bigger than anything seen in these parts for years.

Crowds Beat Thieves

Civilian interest in order and in law of sorts is not new in East Africa. Market thieves, purse-snatchers and even people involved in automobile accidents are often trampled and beaten to death if they are caught by an excited crowd before the police get to the scene.

The crime that Fundi is charged with was much worse. As the police tell it, he went berserk a week ago last night when he found his wife in Marinani, the village where her mother lives. She went there after an argument. Her husband, according to the police, shot his mother-in-law with one poisoned arrow and his wife with another, then his brother-in-law, then his two sons and another boy they were playing with, then that boy's father.

Another man and his wife and another child were also shot with poisoned arrows, but these three survived and are being treated at a hospital in Embu.

The police permitted villagers to bring their spears, staves and bows and arrows and join the search for Fundi. Perhaps the police could not have prevented the villagers' participation. But the whole incident is indicative of the adjustments that are being made between African villagers' concept of justice and the old rule of law that the British practiced in the East African countries before they won independence in this decade.

In Uganda, where the Government is trying to make established rules of law prevail, the question has grown into a heated national debate since a mob intercepted policemen and a tribal chief escorting seven suspected thieves to police headquarters at Gombola in September.

Four of the men, handcuffed together, were beaten to death on the spot. Another was caught on the run and killed. Even the chief and the policemen were beaten severely.

Two weeks ago, Sir Udo Udoma, Uganda's Chief Justice, declared:

"The rule of law means that no man shall be punishable or can be lawfully made to suffer in body or goods except for a distinct breach of law established in the ordinary legal manner before the ordinary courts of law."

Tanzania Shifts Powers

But debate continues in Uganda. And in Tanzania, where debate seems further advanced, some powers of trial and punishment have already been handed over to villagers.

Under directives issued last month by President Julius K. Nyerere on "nation-building," village development committees may impose fines and other "customary punishments" still to be specified on "lazy people who shirk their role" in well-digging, road improvement and other communal projects found by the committees to be worthy.

The Tanzanian Government has also bypassed the courts in a round-up, now in progress, of "suspected criminals." They are being imprisoned now but are soon to be put to work clearing bush and growing crops under prison supervision.

On the island of Zanzibar, which is part of Tanzania, a unification of law and authority with the mainland is still in progress. Courts on Zanzibar have been deprived of much of their own power. Since July, only those charged with murder and armed robbery have been tried in the courts. All other defendants are automatically sentenced to five years' imprisonment and are trained in a trade in that time.

November 4, 1968

'Negritude' Outmoded

By ERIC PACE

Special to The New York Times

ALGIERS, July 27—The concept of "négritude," long a watchword of African cultural nationalism, has come under sharp attack at the Pan-African Cultural Festival being held here.

The word in French means simply "blackness," but French-educated black writers in the nineteen-thirties and nineteen-forties used it to label a vague and sentimental doctrine affirming the value of black culture.

At this gathering of Africans from more than two dozen countries, négritude, variously defined, has been denounced as outmoded and even colonialistic.

"'Negritude' is really a good, mystifying anesthetic for those who have been whipped too long and too hard," the head of the Guinean delegation, Keita Mamadi, said in the domed Palais des Nations outside Algiers.

Mr. Mamadi and other Marxist-influenced dignitaries at the 12-day gathering have said Africans should reject the romanticism of négritude and consider their culture, as Mr. Mamadi put it, an "arm of economic and social liberation." Speakers have also urged Africans to consider their common cultural heritage as defined by the borders of their continent and not by color.

These views are welcome to the extreme leftist Government of Algeria, which wants to enhance its influence and prestige among Black African countries. In staging the gathering, now in its sixth day, they are working to promote their revolutionary philosophy and to assuage the centuries-old rancor between the continent's Arabs and blacks.

The view was also welcome to American black militants among the 4,000 people at the festival, which is being held under the aegis of the 41-member Organization of African Unity.

"It's what you do with your culture that counts," observed one militant at the busy information center of the Black Panther party, seconding Mr. Mamadi's view.

Among the delegations that have not rejected négritude is that of Senegal. That West African nation's President, Léopold S. Senghor, was one of the many formulators of the concept in his days as a student in Paris.

President Senghor, who is reported to be vacationing in France, avoided the term in a statement published by the Algerian Government newspaper, El Moudjahid. He said: "I think we cannot open ourselves to modernity if we are not first ourselves."

President Senghor has not been named in the criticism of négritude, however, or even in the qualified defense of it that was put forward yesterday by Hunga Kabonga, a respected scholar from Kinshasa, the Congo.

He said that Africans had managed to "bring to the world the rhythm of our dances, the rhythm of our songs, the rhythm of our suffering.

The idea of négritude, he said, played an early and important role, "returning to us our identity and, quite simply, our humanity" at the end of the colonial era.

But now, he said, it is outmoded and Africans should try to work out more constructive ways to come to grips with their identity.

Similar views were expressed by Henri Lopez, Education Minister of the former French Congo. He contended in an address that Africans should define themselves by geography now—that is, in a way that would include the nonblack countries of North Africa—and not by race.

Publicly, speakers have not dwelled on the past friction between African blacks and Arabs, some of whom were engaged in black slaving.

Privately, however, many participants have acknowledged the depth of the differences. And some Arab private citizens in Algiers have told foreign visitors that they were not greatly impressed by the degree of sophistication shown in the black African performances at the festival.

But working-class Algerians appeared delighted with the black singers and dancers, who have drawn vast crowds and left-wing intellectuals, Arab and black, have said they hope their revolutionary ideology can help to unify the continent in a way that négritude, however widely espoused. could not.

July 28, 1969

A Search for the Black Eldorado

By ANTHONY LEWIS

TIGONI, Kenya—"I've been here four months, and I have to say there is no Kikuyu culture. You know, nothing you could call a real culture."

The young man was an American Negro, call him Roy, born in Newark, a graduate of Rutgers, now working for his master's degree at the Harvard School of Education. He was spending a year teaching history and English to high school students in a Kikuyu village 25 miles from Nairobi, living in a typical small village house without electricity or running water. He wore blue jeans and sandals, his hair Afro style; the voice was educated New York.

He was talking to a Kikuyu girl, Ruth, a bright student at University College, Nairobi, who works in her spare time for American anthropologists, gathering data for them and learning their techniques. In her soft African diction she replied:

"You are completely wrong. You overstate, Roy; you do not know enough."

Roy: "They think only of American culture. They want to be like us. They want things."

Ruth: "Oh no, not American culture. We don't want that, we are not going to have it. We shall have our own."

Roy: "Well, Western values. They ask why I don't wear shoes in school, why I wear jeans. You know, they think any man with position or money has to wear shoes, and that doesn't mean sandals. It's a material thing. They want money and possessions, and that means Western ideas."

Ruth: "Yes, we do want some Western things. We are poor, we want a better life. But we don't have to be like Americans. I have seen American children, and certainly we are not going to bring up our children like that — ordering their parents around, greeting the guests as if they ran the house. No, I am going to beat my children if I have to, to make them behave . . . like children."

Roy: "In the sense of the future, the culture of the future, they are going to have Western desires and ideas about status."

Ruth: "No, you don't understand, you haven't seen, you don't know what culture means. For example, men and women will always be a different thing here. Men will run things. I used to think I would be different, but now I know that I shall be happy only by letting my husband decide."

Roy: "When women move into an apartment in Nairobi, and they have a refrigerator and a stove, and a servant to take care of the children—and they do not have all their grandparents and aunts with them—that will change. The women will think differently. It is inevitable."

Ruth: "You're too sure again. Maybe those Western material things will have an effect for a while, but people will come back to the African way—respect for the man, bringing up children to be respectful. The wife can have power in the home, she can have ideas, but the credit must go to the man; he has to make the decisions. When he asks her to explain, she must explain; but he goes where he wants and does what he wants and does not explain."

Roy: "I come here, and all I find is people wanting to be like bourgeois American Negroes."

Ruth: "I think you came here with romantic expectations, Roy. You wanted something completely distinctive from American values, from white values—a different civilization, a different ideology. Now you are disappointed because people are not so different."

Roy: "No. I came without any expectations, so I'm not surprised or disappointed. I just say I have not found a culture."

Ruth: "But you do not know. You have not felt the ties of a family, the welcome to relations, the security. You live alone in your house and you don't see anyone except the boys from the university when they are there between terms. Perhaps you miss city life and conveniences."

Roy: "I don't want company, I'm a loner everywhere. I'm enjoying this okay, I just say the Kikuyu are going for the same things as in American society. It doesn't matter to me; I'm going to go back and teach at a university, to students who understand.

January 12, 1970

The Struggle to Liberate Women

By ANGIE BROOKS

IN 1947, the United Nations Trusteeship Council received a petition which vividly described what used to happen to some young girls of the Bikum tribe in the Bamenda Province of what was then the British-administered Cameroons.

A girl was grinding corn in the small space in front of her father's hut. She was about 13 years old, a fine child clad in her home-spun dress. Two or three men walked down the road, looking from side to side; they stopped, looked hard at the girl who, quite unconscious of their looks, continued her back-breaking task.

Then the leader, or "Chinda" as he was called, stepped forward, dragged the child to her feet, marked her forehead with a piece of red camwood and stripped off her clothes. The girl howled like a wounded animal — she was doomed. Her father came out and knew the mark meant she was branded.

Off the "Chinda" and his men went; their day's work for the King had been done. (The King was the 80-year-old Fon of Bikum.)

Next day, Papa, arrayed in his tribal splendor, set off for the King's Compound. The girl, with nothing but a string of large seeds around her neck, came sobbing behind. They came to the King's Compound; guards stood in costume with erect spears. The King sat on the throne, a leopard under his feet. About 100 of his 600 wives stood around him in a semi-circle — naked — as was the privilege and custom of the "Kings Own."

The father stepped forward, bent his knees so that, although bent forward, he was still on his feet, clapped his hands three times, then standing upright dragged his daughter forward, threw her on the ground in front of the King, who stepped forward and put his right foot on top of the girl's body, which meant, "I accept this piece of cargo."

This unforgettable picture of the custom prevalent in the Cameroons under British administration led the Trusteeship Council to request its visiting mission to investigate the complaint.

The mission drove across the mountainous roads of the Bamenda Province, climbed some 3,000 feet, partly on foot and partly on horseback, to the lofty heights of the Fon's village accompanied by hundreds of the Fon's subjects.

The Fon, who claimed himself to be more than 100 years old, took a lenient view of this "interference" in what he regarded as his private affairs. That the outside world should think otherwise or take exception to an age-old custom of chiefs — having many wives — looked rather odd to him.

He remained calm and polite throughout the discussion, which, by his standards, appeared to him as an unwarranted interference, but there was little doubt that he and his councillors were clearly annoyed about the inquiry.

That was understandable from his point of view, since it was the tradition and custom among the chiefs of this region to have many wives who worked for him. It was an economic arrangement under which young girls became wives, servants of the Fon; and widows of close male relatives became an inherited chattel of the nearest male kin, who, in exchange, protected them and looked out for their subsistence.

The mission which investigated this custom was given a memorandum by the Fon's wives, who expressed the opinion that they were "living with the Fon according to the natural law and custom." The mission was told that any wife had the liberty to leave the compound if she wished to do so, and, in point of fact, a number of them have done so.

•

MAYBE this was an isolated case in the whole of Africa, but it was not an isolated case in the British Cameroons.

In any case, the United Nations found this custom unacceptable and accordingly certain ancient laws and customs relating to marriage and the family have been termed by resolutions of the General Assembly and the Commission on the Status of Women (which specifically deals with the status of women all over the world), as impediments to the attainment of women's basic rights as contemplated in the Charter and in the Declaration of Human Rights.

The United Nations Commission on the Status of Women has studied the question of marriage, especially from the point of view of requiring the free consent of both parties to establish a minimum age to marry. In 1962, it prepared texts for a draft convention, and a draft recommendation on these subjects that were subsequently adopted by the General Assembly and were opened for signatures. The convention provides that no marriage shall be entered into without the full and free consent of both parties and prescribes the minimum age. The convention has been ratified by 18 states.

The birth of the new states in Africa was generally interpreted as liberation. The temptation to approach everything from a political angle was inevitable. The accession to an international life was felt as a sort of promotion, and in particular people were convinced that this kind of life was incompatible with maintaining an internal legal system whose character was customary and oral.

Old customs in the name of development and of the freedom of the rising generations were condemned. Clearly, individualist and feminist movements have developed which were supported by most of the governments of the newly independent states in Africa. Modern laws were enacted, which, opposed to customary law, became the instrument for development and unity. Immediately after some states in Africa became independent, they announced that they were drawing up codes of civil law which would better the condition of women in their states.

At present women in most of the newly independent African countries have now, from the constitutional point of view, full rights of vote at the age of 16 or 18.

Most of these changes took place between 1946 and 1965. This is particularly due to the efforts of the United Nations in building up the status of women in general as well as to the contribution which women in Africa have

ANGIE Elizabeth Brooks, who became President of the 24th General Assembly of the United Nations last September, brought with her to that high post the vivaciousness and dynamism that had always marked her career. She warned her colleagues, some of whom are not known to share Miss Brooks's drive to get things done, that they must deal with the issues that they had "either sidetracked or ignored," thus contributing to "the gradual decline of the United Nations in the eyes of public opinion." Miss Brooks, born 41 years ago in Liberia, showed her own unwillingness to accept the status quo early: She became the first woman lawyer in her country after working her way through Shaw University, a Negro college in South Carolina, and the University of Wisconsin Law School. She is the second woman to head the General Assembly; the first was Mrs. Vijaya Lakshmi Pandit of India in 1953-54. High posts are not unknown to the General Assembly's President. She served as Liberia's assistant secretary of state in 1958 and served as the nation's chief executive for 10 days when the President and Secretary of State were out of the country. "Not bad for a woman," she remarked.

made to the nationalist movement, the struggle for independence and to the vital role they have always played in raising the standards of living in these countries.

Further, United Nations assistance for the advancement of women through its various organs and technical agencies has contributed to the rapid development of the status of women in Africa.

•

SINCE independence, women in Africa have generally exerted their will and have gained political recognition, but that is not the case as far as African women under the minority regime of the Republic of South Africa are concerned. There, Africans have irreversibly become absorbed into the Western exchange economy. Women, who under archaic tribal law were always subject to a man's guardianship, have in many cases become wage-earners and often contribute to the support of their families or maintain themselves and their children by their own efforts.

But even there traditional tribal attitudes to women are changing.

There is a widespread awareness in Africa today of the enormous problems of education and economic disabilities as well as social, religious and legal obstacles with which women in Africa are still faced. There is also a widespread awareness of the need of the majority of women to receive adequate training in the right and duties of citizenship to enable them to participate fully in public life or to exercise freely and effectively their constitutional rights.

It is therefore all the more remarkable that in the newly independent states of Africa, many women have taken advantage of the opportunities open to them, for qualifying themselves, and are now exercising political responsibilities equal to those of women in the developed nations of the world.

January 30, 1970

African Literature—From the Breath of Gods

By JAN CAREW

The titles reviewed in the following article are from the Doubleday Africana series. Chivuzo Ude, an Igbo from Nigeria, became editor of the project in 1969 and, since then, 14 titles have been published. According to Ude, "the series is intended to provide a better understanding of the African heritage and to enable American readers to appreciate the value, dignity and relevance of other cultures. Works of fiction, poetry, drama, history, anthropology and politics are included in the series, and many of the authors are among Africa's leading writers."

One of the central facts of contemporary African writing is that it has evolved quite recently from an oral into a written form, and that much of the vitality, the immediacy and the rhythmic cadences of the one have been carried over into the other. And when one talks of Africa as a cohesive cultural entity, one is dealing with a continent which, for all its vastness and diversity, is most accessible from within. It forms a continuous shelf broken here and there by deserts and jungles. Because of its size, it required minimal population pressures for major migrations to take place. It is not surprising, therefore, that throughout its history there has been continuous movement of population from one area to another.

So when an Ethiopian recites the deeds of his ancestors in heroic verse, although cultural particulars might differ, he is nevertheless working in a tradition and with a creative form that closely resembles that of the Zulu, the Sotho or the Ashanti. In the same way, the Ancient Egyptian and the Akan have startlingly similar forms in their songs of the dead.

What are the origins then of the enduring oral forms in African literature? In order to answer this question, one has to turn to the Hereros of South West Africa, a pastoral people with an ancient tradition of oral literature. They claimed that their song-poems to the living and the dead, their mytho-poetic dreams, which were danced, acted and sung, were born out of the breath of the gods. In their cosmology all creative life begins with the rhythmic breath of the gods, which in turn regulates the flow of seminal life-juices in men. These life-juices then bind men to plants, living creatures and, in fact, to all objects.

It is partly because this cosmology of breath, rhythm and substance is eternally linked together that a strong vein of realism threads its way through most African myths; these myths are in essence fables about beings that incarnate, under a symbolic form, forces of Nature and aspects of the human genius or destiny. What the Hereros were implying

Ayi Kwei Armah, top left, Isidore Okpewho, below, Ama Ata Aidoo, center, Kofi Awoonor, top right, Peter Abrahams.

by their claim was that there is a concrete and organic relationship between man, land, myth, magic, time and space.

Léopold Sédar Senghor, the Senegal poet-President, explains the evolution from the oral to the written form in African literature when he describes the word as encompassing a reality which, "linked the African man with the invisible power through the mediation of visible concrete things." He then explains further the link between the written word and the myth. "The myth had to be lived before being acted and acted before being sung, recited and, at last, explained. It is at the stage of poems and fables that the verbal symbol, which is but a thread in the web, appears."

As a former student and admirer of the German ethnologist and philosopher, Leo Frobenius, Senghor had little difficulty in becoming an eloquent advocate of the idea of Negritude. By asserting this idea of Negritude—and the word was coined by Aimé Césaire, the black poet from Martinique—African and the black writers in the New World were creating a new image of themselves and their people and shattering forever the servile one created by slavery and colonialism. It was Frobenius who defined Africa for Europe at a time when colonialism was already losing its certainties. He traveled from Europe to Africa and with brilliant and facile insights at once crystallized and added new dimensions to the myth of the noble savage.

"The most typical fact of Africa," he wrote, "is the inclination and the faculty to form precise and opposing styles." The opposing forces as he defined them had their origins in the character of the Negro-African whom the Greeks called "Ethiopians," and the Arab-Berbers, who were called "Hamites." The Ethiopian civilization was mystic while the Hamitic one revolved on an axis of magic. For the Ethiopian time and space were centrifugal while for the Hamite it was centripetal. The Ethiopian civilization was conditioned by plants while the Hamitic one was conditioned by animals. The Hamite was a nomad living under a tent made of animal skins whereas the Ethiopian made his hut out of earth and herbs and leaves.

But Senghor was moving away from the Frobenius thesis and closer to the Negritude idea when he wrote that the African personality preceded the Arab conquest and the "unity of African civilization is so strong that cleavages within it do not follow the boundaries of races but, more ofter than not, those of geography: of the environment. A great many Southern Saharans who are marginal Negroes are classified as Hamites: Somalis, Massai, Peuls and Nubians. Some of them are even unquestionably Negroes such as the Soninkes and Sarakoles who founded the Empire of Ghana."

Negritude gave some fresh impetus to literary creations for a while and then it passed away. It barely survived into the initial period of freedom from colonial rule. Contemporary African writers are now concerned with neo-colonialism and liberation; Senghor, one of the original prophets of Negritude, is now being denounced as a "black imperialist." In literature and politics alike fashions change like seasons.

Four of the novels reviewed here deal with African societies and Africans abroad in the throes of neo-colonialism, while the fifth, "Wild Conquest" by Peter Abrahams, is a reprint of a novel published 20 years ago. But after this span of time —and two decades send most novels into oblivion—the Abrahams novel still retains a pristine strength. Set in the 1830's, it captures very vividly that initial moment of impact when the Boers, armed with rifles and a simple and unshakable faith in their divine right to seize and settle upon African lands, met and destroyed the heretofore invincible Zulus.

There was an inevitability about the destruction of the Zulus under Mzilikazi, their king. He was tormented by the anguish of his own indecision. He no longer believed the simple Zulu war ethic. He carried within him premonitions of doom and these are fed by the truths that Mkomozi, his medicine man, reveals. When the king learns about the white man's arrogance and his awesome weapons, Mkomozi tells him: "Only people go on, their power comes and their powers go, but they go on." For Gubuza, the king's general, the choices are simple, liberty or death, and he fights to the finish. Before the final battle he said, "Time has an end for us too, my brothers."

"Wild Conquest" is a novel created with extraordinary skill, but it is its profound and compassionate understanding of the Boer and of the African that gives it its enduring quality and there are times when one feels that Abrahams is not only a writer but also a literary magician.

"This Earth, My Brother" and "Why Are We So Blest?" are books of the same genre. They deal with the private anguish of young Africans who take that fateful journey from the family, the clan, the tribe into the 20th century. It is a journey not only across distances, but also across several hundred years. Kofi Awoonor's "This Earth, My Brother" is an expressionistic work taking us swiftly from continent to continent, from country to country. But one never loses track of the author. He is a persuasive and ubiquitous narrator who shows and illuminates even the most trivial experience through his own eyes.

"Why Are We So Blest?" by Ayi Kwei Armah, is more of an inspired travelogue than a novel. The real journey that the author deals with, however, is an uneasy one taken by Modin, a young African intellectual, in and out of the peripheries of revolutionary involvement. Modin is a young man inspired not by hope but by a death wish. One of the revolutionary bureaucrats declares in his Algiers office after Modin's first visit with his white American mistress: "He is one of those intellectuals who wants to die. He should have the courage to do it himself." There is an obsessive preoccupation with black-white sexual relations throughout the book and the author offers far too many unnecessary and repetitive clinical details, which in the end produce yawns instead of fresh insights. This novel, unlike the other two by Armah, is one bereft of genuine emotions. Somehow in dissecting characters, situations, settings, there is an absence of tension. It demonstrates the sterility of a purely intellectual involvement in revolution, sex or life itself.

"This Earth, My Brother" has more of a gut quality. Awoonor, like Armah, is a Ghanaian but his African roots are stronger. He, too, is a prophet-writer in a wilderness of neocolonialism, but there is a living pulse inside his disillusionment and an insatiable appetite for living. He describes his book as "an allegorical tale of Africa"; Senghor's definition of allegory ("a metaphor that starts from the subject and is transferred to the object") fits perfectly. The author seems intoxicated not only with life but with language. His words assault the senses and the intellect simultaneously. Images leap from the pages — butterflies, a dunghill, the womb, the sea, a kind of drowning amniotic fluid out of which swims the lady he loves—and yet the book is serious and its message of new and positive forces emerging from the African chaos, unmistakable.

"The Victims," by the Nigerian author Isidore Okpewho (with "Bound to Violence" by Yambo Ouologuem and "Prostitute" by Okello Oculi) marks the end of an epoch in which the past was romanticized and the present tethered to illusions. "The Victims" probes remorselessly into the realities of polygamy and in doing so illuminates aspects of the human condition that few writers in any age or culture are able to deal with so well. The story is simple. Obanua Ozoma, a born loser and someone afflicted with the curious optimism of the weak, is driven to deal with one set of troubles by rushing foolishly into others. Obanua, unable to cope with his job as a truck driver or with his wife and son, takes on a second wife who is young, promiscuous and the mother of twin daughters who all move in to make his already difficult life, desperate.

The tragedy in the end is inevitable, but as the main characters move slowly towards it the author reveals both their outer and inner lives. Obanua, always drunk and dreaming his life away, touches the reader's heart with the sheer banality of his dreams and the certainty that he can never change and therefore they can never be fulfilled. The writing is disciplined to the point of austerity, and yet there is poetry in the inner tensions of the most ordinary situations: a fight between Obanua and Nwabunor, his first wife; her passionate addiction to standards that he can never meet; his blind resistance to her anguish as an aging and neglected woman; the real and imagined fears afflicting him every time he thinks of going home after a day's work or a session at the toddy shop. In the course of all this, one sees the reality of polygamy, and that indisputable truth that one cannot free oneself by restricting the liberty of others.

This is a superior work of fiction that places Okpewho in the vanguard of contemporary African writing. The author succeeds in making a social unit as small as a village as meaningful as an entire society.

"No Sweetness Here" is a collection of short stories by Ama Ata Aidoo, and they give the reader gentle, polished but profound and ironic insights into the manner, morals and esthetic sensibilities of contemporary West African society. The first of the stories is about wigs — the whole business of wearing wigs is abandoned by a young African woman who studies abroad, but she returns home to find the young women there frantically adopting them. And apart from the wigs there are her relatives asking her, "What car are you bringing home, Sissie? And oh, we hope you brought a refrigerator." In another story, "For Whom Things Did Not Change," there is a dedicated young doctor trying vainly to break down class barriers between himself and his cook and caretaker.

All of these stories are low-keyed; the irony is so muted that at times it almost escapes the reader. But they are worth reading and there is in all of them a quality which makes the reader feel he is being nudged quietly toward a more profound understanding of modern Africa.

Still, African literature has developed beyond the point where any general definition might adequately characterize it, and the five books considered here only partially reflect its variety and resonance. Authors such as Chinua Achebe, Wole Soyinka, Ezekial Mphahlele, Camara Laye, and many others would have to be considered before even approaching an understanding of the literature of the African continent. Yet these books, while each is distinct, provide tangible evidence of the vitality and effective fusion of oral and written forms that are dominant features of the emerging African literary tradition. ■

Muffling the Drums of Africa

By ANATOLE BROYARD

WARRIORS AND STRANGERS. By Gerald Hanley. 320 pages. Harper & Row. $7.95.

What is happening in Africa now is like the shattering of an enormous diamond in order to make working parts for thousands of industrial machines. Of course, a diamond is useless, in a sense. Its only virtue is its rarity and beauty, but it is precisely these two qualities that our homogenized world can least afford to lose. Watching Africa change is like seeing our children grow up, allowing their pure egoism and astonishing creativity to be curbed and cramped into practical patterns. The very idea of Africa had always been a sort of psychological escape-valve: its "darkness" had helped absorb the harsh light of reason. Halfway between hell and the Garden of Eden, it affected many whites like a fever-produced delirium, a germ that never gets out of your blood. Men who have lived in Africa always talk of it with extremes of emotion: love, hatred, or both.

And it is a land of extremes. Usually, there is too much water, or too little. There is the threat of structureless space in the dry country and the claustrophobia of the deep bush. Almost always, there is pressure: heat, humidity, insects and loneliness for one's own kind. Desperation was the white man's answer, and he was hypnotized by the imperturbability of the African. Only a semicrazed commitment could keep the white man going, while the Africans—like our own Muhammad Ali, who resembles a fattened-up Somali or Masai—could "float like a butterfly, sting like a bee."

Worlds of Machismo

White men used to be drawn to Africa as people were once drawn to Harlem—by a vitality they admired even as they tried to destroy or explain it away. They generally sentimentalized the black man in both places, making him both more and less than he was. Above all, both places were worlds of machismo: the challenge of self, sex and violence, to the rhythm of drums. As a musician once said: every man at some time in his life wants to play the drums.

Gerald Hanley had seen Africa just before it began to change; he had been there during World War II, and in "Warriors and Strangers," he went back to see it a third time, to compare the three periods, to try to separate good and bad, to guess what was going to happen. He found, as William Empson said, that "earth has shrunk in the wash." The Africa of boundless spaces, countless animals and cultures stranger than any disturbing dream has almost disappeared.

The sound of drums has been replaced by the droning of schoolrooms. The stories around the campfires have given way to the rhetoric of politics. "The bulldozers are massing on the horizon," and civilization looms like a locust plague over the land. It was inevitable: progress, in the beginning, is rarely pretty. Order is largely a matter of reduction. No longer could Mr. Hanley find in Africa that "true solitude . . . when the most restless part of a human being, his longing to forget where he is, born on earth in order to die, comes to rest and listens in a kind of agreed peace."

Plight of the Masai

The Masai, whom he had called "the true nihilists . . . who seemed to have no past and no future, only a silent sun-glowing now . . . who had lived in a sort of in-between time, a dreaming halt between their old pre-white-man tribal world and that of the cement mixer," were now to be governed by their former "slaves," the Kikuvu, who, as one of the old chiefs put it, "would *eat* a book if you gave it to them." "The village," said another old chief, "is finished. Everything is money now."

The whites may be finished, too, for, as Mr. Hanley says, "There is no one so puzzled as the pioneer who has lost his frontier, who has dissolved what challenged him, the wilderness." Christianity, as well, may be delivering a hopeless sermon: Islam, which has never had a color bar, is more to the new African's taste. "The destructive myths," the author says, "are melting away in a flood of lifegiving despair."

The black man in Africa can no more be expected to stand still, to remain "picturesque," than the black man in Harlem. And yet, one thinks, and yet . . . wasn't he more than that? Isn't he making a poor Faustian bargain with civilization, trading his soul for a transistor radio? Africa had laws protecting its now rare animals, but has anyone dared to suggest a law or a plan to protect its peoples' enviable "animal" qualities—that vitality that all our vitamins, diets, doctors and amenities can never begin to compensate them for?

CHAPTER 6
Update

The African who kicked out the Asians, who said Hitler was right, who has made his country a state sinister

If Idi Amin of Uganda is a madman, he's a ruthless and cunning one

By Christopher Munnion

The dreams of Gen. Idi Amin, heavyweight boxer, flyweight philosopher and the seemingly punch-drunk President of the Second Republic of Uganda, have transformed life in his lush, landlocked East African state into a nightmare of terror for inhabitants of all hues. In one dream last August, according to the burly ex-sergeant, God appeared in person and instructed him to exorcise Uganda of its 50,000 Asian residents, most of them third-generation Ugandans who collectively form the country's economic middle class. The Asians, Amin charged, had been sabotaging Uganda's economy, deliberately retarding economic progress, fostering widespread corruption and treacherously refraining from integrating in the Ugandan way of life. He gave them 90 days to quit the country, "or they will find themselves sitting on the fire."

This decision, its cause and effect, has created a dark whirlpool of uncertainty in the heart of Africa. It has brought Uganda to the brink of Congo-style turmoil, outraged world opinion, enraged and embarrassed moderate African leaders and exposed the continent's susceptibility to raw and ruthless military despots.

Idi Amin Dada (the latter is his family name and has no relevance to his media tag of "big daddy") has broken every rule of statesmanship, even the emergent-Africa brand, and boggled diplomatic minds everywhere with his verbal buckshot, exhortations, pronouncements and threats. He has established a state sinister that would startle fiction writers. Dissidents, real or potential, are dragged screaming from bar or cafe by gun-toting young men in dark glasses; bodies of well-known former citizens are washed up on the shores of otherwise picturesque lakes; swaggering glazed-eyed soldiery waylay and molest tourists and travelers in the bush. Entire army units have been massacred in their barracks; policemen suspected of less than wholehearted loyalty have had their heads smashed with sledgehammers; more fortunate citizens of other countries have been deported almost daily; and the jails are witnesses to unmitigated brutality.

In the midst of all this, Idi Amin has called on his army to be prepared to liberate South Africa,

Christopher Munnion, a correspondent for Britain's Daily Telegraph who reported from Uganda until his jailing and expulsion in September, is now based in Salisbury, Rhodesia.

"Idi the Terrible," above, with pistol on his hip and Israeli paratrooper's wings on chest, delivers one of his notorious impromptu speeches. Left, the former heavyweight boxer takes a dip.

offered to help Britain solve the Ulster crisis, disclosed that the United States has been seeking his help to end the Vietnam war and appointed himself a one-man peace emissary to the Middle East. He has also found time to entertain his first state visitor, Gen. Jean Bédel Bokassa, Life President of the Central African Republic, whose last public appearance was at the head of an army unit which toured the country's jails beating, in some cases to death, prisoners accused or convicted of petty theft.

A bemused world has pondered aloud on Amin's sanity. Britain's Opposition leader, Harold Wilson, told a television audience recently that he considered Amin "mentally unbalanced." President Kenneth Kaunda of Zambia described him as "a madman . . . a buffoon." London's tabloid Sunday Mirror screeched in heavy front-page type: "He's nuts!"

But having watched the man and his ways at close quarters during the last three months, I doubt if any doctor would find Amin certifiable. Capricious, impulsive, violent and aggressive he certainly is, but to dismiss him as just plain crazy is to underestimate his shrewdness, his ruthless cunning and his capacity to consolidate his power with calculated terror.

Last month, Uganda's 10 million people were marking a decade of independence from British colonial rule. They have not been happy years, despite the economic promise of the bountiful coffee and cotton crops which flourish in the rich soils on the northern shores of the equatorial inland sea of Lake Victoria. Political trouble beset the country from the time of independence in 1962. The problems have been predominantly tribal, emanating in no small degree from the arbitrary boundaries traced by colonial administrators who paid scant attention to ethnic and tribal factors.

British rule in the protectorate of Uganda was conducted through the five ancient kingdoms in the south, in particular the sophisticated people of Buganda, whose comparatively civilized way of life had impressed the earliest 19th-century explorers. But the Bugandans' power, prosperity and arrogance made them unpopular with the 40 other tribes in Uganda, most of them impoverished Nilotic peoples in the northern regions. This intertribal disaffection prevails today. Open animosity is never far below the surface.

Britain's hope, at the time of independence, rested in a federal relationship between the kingdoms and a central government. The first president was the Kabaka — the royal ruler—of Buganda, Sir Edward Mutesa, familiarly known as King Freddie. The Prime Minister and executive head of Government was a young trade unionist from the northern Lango tribe — Milton Obote. Obote, ambitious son of a goatherd, also led the Uganda Peoples' Congress, a left-leaning party broadly representing all tribes outside the kingdoms.

Obote saw himself as an intellectual African messiah in the Nkrumah-of-Ghana mold. To that end he purchased for himself a doctorate of philosophy and, in 1966, made a successful bid for absolute power. He suspended the Independence Constitution, abolished the tribal kingdoms and declared the country a republic and himself President.

In his palace atop one of the seven hills of Kampala, the Uganda capital, King Freddie's guard attempted a futile resistance which was rapidly crushed by Obote's army. The Kabaka fled to exile in London, where he died a few years later. The attack on his palace was led by the army commander and the man most Ugandans regarded as Obote's close friend — Maj. Gen. Idi Amin.

It was, as it turned out, merely a friendship of convenience. The devious Obote, surviving no fewer than five assassination attempts, came to rely increasingly on his army for his security and power. He leaned heavily on the mercurial Amin, who had worked diligently at making himself the force's favorite.

In January last year, with Obote overconfidently attending a Commonwealth conference in Singapore, Amin and the army seized power. More delighted with the overthrow of the corrupt and oppressive Obote than with the prospect of military rule, joyful Ugandans danced in the streets. The genial general announced an amnesty for political prisoners, disbanded Obote's notorious secret service, appeased the Bugandans by permitting King Freddie's body to be returned from London for a royal funeral, and blandly assured the people that he would be handing over the reins to civilian rule as soon as the situation permitted.

Amin insisted that he had staged the *coup d'état* merely to foil an Obote plot to kill him. But there has emerged much evidence to suggest that on that bright, hot Kampala morning, the Uganda heavyweight had grabbed the title he had been coveting for many years—President of the Second Republic.

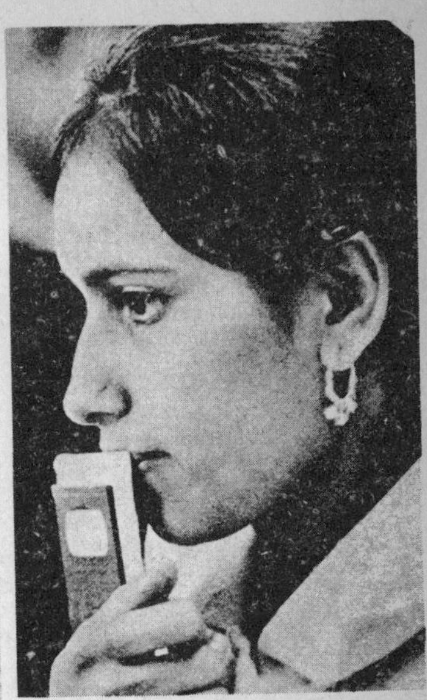

At a former R.A.F. camp in Suffolk, Asian refugees—some of the 50,000 who were ordered evicted from Uganda by President Idi Amin last August — wait despondently (left), apply at the employment bureau (above), and queue up patiently for meals (below).

Idi Amin (pronounced EE-dee ah-MEEN) revels in peasant oratory and barrack-room philosophy. His tribal background and military career gave him a thorough training in both. Essentially, he is a product of African village politics and colonial parade-ground pugnacity. A Moslem Kakwa tribesman, Amin was born in the remote village of Arua in Uganda's West Nile district, close to the confluence of the Congo and Sudan borders. His parents scratched a subsistence living from the land and young Idi, like other sons of this impoverished soil, enjoyed only a sparse education.

But his brawn and energy gave him the advantage he needed. The King's African Rifles, one of Britain's crack colonial regiments, deprived Arua of the village bully when the 18-year-old Amin, already 6 feet 3 inches tall and weighing 230 pounds, enlisted.

The beefy teen-ager took readily to army life. He served with the regiment in Burma and later, brawling and bawling his way to the rank of sergeant major, he fought with the British against the Mau Mau insurgents in Kenya. By all accounts, he relished the fight against fellow Africans.

He excelled, not unnaturally, at robust sports. He played a ferocious but fair game of Rugby, swam energetically every day and, in 1951, won Uganda's heavyweight boxing championship. The army taught him to read and write English, somewhat uncertainly, and he picked up the basic, colorful Swahili which was the regiment's lingua franca.

His sporting prowess, coupled with his tough but genial nature and a popularity with ordinary troops which he constantly sought and won, stamped him with some affection on the memories of the white officers. Col. Hugh Rogers, once Amin's company commander and more recently the leader of a 17-man British military training mission to Uganda which was peremptorily expelled by the President last September, said of him, "He was a splendid and reliable soldier and a cheerful and energetic man."

In fact, Amin's ambivalent attitude toward Britain in the present crisis stems largely from his nostalgia for the King's African Rifles. When he asked for a British military mission shortly after seizing power, he specifically asked for a pipe major to be included, recalling with affection the skirl of the regimental bagpipes. And, having accused the British officers in the team of preparing to lead an invasion force against him, he radioed a message to their departing aircraft thanking them for their work in Uganda. "My argument is not with the British officers. It is with the British politicians," he said.

Another of his former colonial officers, who has been his presidential guest in Kampala on several occasions, summed up Amin the soldier. "He was one of nature's sergeant majors." That, in the view of many of his former friends, is where he should have ended his career — and, anywhere else but in Africa, he probably would have.

Amin's big break, and most likely the point at which his eyes were opened to the heady prospects of power, came in the immediate pre-independence period. Britain's colonial administration, with some haste, was preparing to hand over political and institutional responsibility to the Africans. An army selection board, dispatched to Uganda to find officer material, interviewed two possible candidates—Idi Amin and his long-standing army rival, Shaban Opoloto, who were then both "effendis," the highest non-commissioned rank.

Much to Amin's chagrin, they chose Opoloto. But a few weeks later, on instructions from London's War Office, they returned to find another Ugandan officer. There was little to choose from. Idi Amin became a second lieutenant and managed to hold the rank despite a threatened court martial for insubordination a few weeks before independence.

Self-government found the two Uganda officers leap-frogging each other in a rapid promotion race. Opoloto made it to army commander, but so great was the friction between them that Obote promoted Opoloto to the post of defense minister, leaving Amin in charge of the army.

That was the end of Opoloto. Within months he was accused of plotting against the state and Idi Amin was in total control of the armed forces, by then the country's crucial power base. Sitting at the side of the crafty Milton Obote, Amin sensed the proximity of absolute power. It was no more than a couple of tank shells away.

It is only since the coup that the full measure of Amin's ruthlessness and cunning has emerged. Despite his benevolent protestations and apparent lack of political ambition at the time of the military takeover, every action he has taken has been designed to consolidate his position as an unassailable dictator. Even as he released Obote's political prisoners, his soldiers were rounding up the members of the ex-President's secret police, and potential dissident tribal elements in the army. Some 700 detainees were herded into a remote military prison. In small groups each day, they were taken from their cells for execution.

Some of the prisoners, mostly Langi and Acholi people from Obote's tribes, managed to escape and flee to join the former President in exile in neighboring Tanzania. They told horrifying stories of the executions by Amin's hatchet men. The most fortunate had been shot; some had been crammed into a tiny cell which had then been dynamited; others had been carved with knives or had been suffocated with their own dismembered genitals.

The rumors of this tribal purge spread, unnerving other Langi and Acholi units in the army. In June last year, fighting broke out in barracks throughout the country. At the end of it, more than 800 soldiers from the two tribes had been massacred and another 1,000 had fled to Tanzania.

Thus assured that the main threat of dissidence had been purged from his army, Amin began to build his military base with tribal elements whose loyalty was more certain. In six months, he doubled the size of the armed forces to 16,000 men, mostly from his own Kakwa people and other West Nile groups. Regardless of cost, new barracks and quarters were built, expensive military equipment purchased and perquisites lavished on officers and men. Corporals and sergeants, particularly those who shared Amin's Moslem faith, found themselves promoted overnight to brigadiers and colonels, while the few trained officers who survived the Purge were eased into political posts well away from the barracks.

This program effectively bankrupted Uganda. Without reference to his treasury Amin had spent an estimated $50-million on defense and armaments and had sliced the country's already meager foreign-exchange reserves to less than $5-million, enough to pay for just two weeks of imports.

The Uganda economy, based almost entirely on its high-quality coffee and cotton crops, had been the envy of neighboring states. Although the annual per-capita income was about $70, just over half the average for Africa, the Ugandan crop-exports sustained a healthy balance of payments. But Amin's régime inherited an economy enfeebled by a slump in world cotton and coffee prices, by wild overspending on such prestige projects as lavish conference halls and by a drastic loss of overseas investment confidence as a result of Obote's nationalization program. Immediately after seizing power, Amin made some encouraging noises about thrift and denationalization but, in fact, he indulged himself and his army in reckless military spending, doubling Uganda's trade deficit to more than $30-million in one year.

His hapless Minister of Finance, like most other post-coup Ugandan ministers a former civil servant portfolioed overnight, attempted to report the parlous economic position to the President. Amin rewarded him by slapping him hard across the face in front of other Ministers and Government officials. The Minister broke down in tears.

The general is deeply suspicious of intellect, higher education and white collars. His ministers are merely the Administration staff, there to carry out orders unquestioningly. Incidents like the one with the Finance Minister rendered them and the civil service into quaking and sycophantic impotence.

Amin has only slightly more regard for his officer corps. In his frequent, almost compulsive, upcountry tours, he delights in gathering the troops around him and telling them, with a jerk of his thumb at their officers: "If you think they are wrong you come and tell me. . . . If they give you any trouble you must arrest them." And more often than not he will relate the latest coarse barrack-room joke as the soldiers sit around drinking beer.

He is a man of immense energy and no little physical courage. Despite his accumulation of enemies, he scorns personal security, preferring to drive his conspicuous self around the streets in an open Jeep. He puts in an average 14-hour day and travels several thousand miles each week to talk to the people. Popularity with the ordinary people means much to Amin. He has the peasant's contempt for the pretentiousness of other social orders. On formal occasions, he insists on stumbling through prepared speeches in his faltering English, clearly not understanding many of the words he mispronounces.

But his stiffness and discomfort disappear miraculously when, as he invariably does, he throws the prepared speech aside and stands to harangue his audiences in crude, spontaneous Swahili. Recently, he addressed students from Kampala's Makerere University. His prepared speech was an explanation of his policy to "liberate the economy" by expelling Asians. It was dry stuff, and Amin detected some restlessness. He broke from the text and announced he had "a rocket" for them. "I am told that venereal disease is very high with you. . . . You had better go to the hospital to make yourselves very clean or you will infect the whole population. I don't want you spoiled by gonorrhea." The students were suddenly attentive.

Again, stumbling through an opening address to an agricultural conference, he suddenly switched the topic to a lecture on the evils of Kondo-ism —a rife brand of armed robbery. Some evil people were informing the authorities that innocent people were Kondos, he said. "Sometimes a girl has rejected them so they say the girl is keeping Kondos in her house. . . . This is not good. I only want factual reports. If the girl refuses you, go to another girl."

It is of such spontaneous thoughts that much Ugandan policy is created these days. On average, Idi Amin makes 20 speeches a week, many of them off-the-cuff. And, as in the case of the Asian expulsion decree, the decisions appear to form in his own mind as he speaks. Certainly, they are usually as big a surprise to his ministers and civil servants as they are to the world.

Many theories have been advanced on the real reason for the anti-Asian move. Ignoring for a moment the method by which Amin declared they should leave, the expulsion of Asians is undoubtedly popular with the *wananchi* — the masses — not only in Uganda but throughout East Africa.

The Asian communities, descendants of Indian traders who moved into Africa last century, are insular and self-contained. Contemptuous of the Africans in general, they dominate the trading sectors throughout East Africa. Intermarriage is rare, and African-Asian cooperation rarer. Since independence, the writing has been on the wall for the Asians in Africa. It could be that Amin ordered them out in an unrealistic and callous fashion merely to win some instant popularity.

Another theory, more strange but in the unlikely land of Uganda today not easily dismissed, is that Amin decided to scourge the Asians because he was rebuffed by the widow of one of the wealthiest Asian families in Uganda. This story has wide currency in Kampala but its credence is impossible to check. Amin, a nonsmoker and nondrinker, has a large sexual appetite. His former army colleagues have testified to this and it is further evidenced by his concubines. In addition to the four wives permitted him by the Koran, he has three others who comfort him in various up-country staging posts. Apart from any concupiscence on his part, a selection of wives from different tribes helps traditionally to cement factional relationships. In these terms, he once unnerved expatriate maidens by announcing that in the interests of harmony among all the peoples living in Uganda he would like to take an Asian and a European wife. There is no record of him making any approach to a white woman, but the story runs that he did propose to the aforementioned Asian widow. He was rejected with a shuddering refusal and the widow's family immediately arranged for her to leave the country. Hell hath no fury like a military dictator scorned, the Asians say.

The third, and most likely, theory is that the Asians of Uganda were yet another readily available alien enemy, the specter of whose subversion Amin could conjure up to divert attention from the very real social and economic problems his country faces. The technique is not new but Amin has given it dimensions dreamed of by few other dictators. Like the barrack-room brawler he is, he finds it spectacularly easy to raise his fists, box with substance or shadow and make fearsome threatening noises. It keeps his troops on their toes, their concentration on the threat, real or imaginary, internal or external, and keeps their minds off the prospects of receiving no pay or equipment when the exchequer runs dry.

Tanzania, whose peaceable philosopher-President, Julius Nyerere, gave succor and sanctuary to the deposed Obote, was the first and most obvious target for Amin. Although, with Kenya, the countries constitute the East African Community, one of the most hopeful economic groupings in Africa, Amin's opportunist belligerence has brought them to the brink of war on three occasions.

When Nyerere expostulated on Amin's behavior, the general fired off a 3,000-word cable to the Tanzanian leader, pleading, cajoling, threatening and finally professing a desire for peace and love. "I want to assure you that I love you very much and if you had been a woman I would have considered marrying you although your head is full of gray. . . . As you are a man that possibility does not arise."

While Western diplomats reeled in disbelief at this weird extreme in African diplomacy, the point was not lost on Julius Nyerere. In grass-root African terms, the proposal amounted to a cutting double-edged insult. This was Amin the peasant speaking.

Eventually, with exasperated ineptitude, Tanzania played into the Ugandan leader's hands, equipping and permitting a small force of Obote loyalists to mount an ill-fated September invasion into Uganda. The imagined threat had become real, and Amin gleefully crushed the infiltrators with a crescendo of saber-rattling.

Earlier this year, when some of the consequences of his economic recklessness struck home, Amin rounded on the Israelis who, for some years, had regarded Uganda as a secure and convenient foothold in sub-Saharan Africa. Israelis were building roads, houses, office blocks, schools and airports. Their 150-strong military mission was training Ugandan armed forces and flying its aircraft. Amin himself had been treated to a paratroopers' course in Israel and had survived to win a pair of bright blue wings, which he still wears.

Suddenly, Idi Amin ordered them out with a verbal barrage of anti-Semitic, anti-Zionist abuse. The 1,000 Israelis downed tools and convoyed themselves into neighboring Kenya, leaving an estimated $20-million worth of construction work unpaid for. No doubt, the Israelis' impatience for some kind of payment influenced Amin's decision but the Moslem President, returning from a visit to the Middle East, had found himself a new soul mate—none other than the equally unpredictable, but infinitely wealthier, Col. Mo'ammar Mohammed Qadhafi of Libya.

Amin's expulsion of the Israelis, whose presence below the southern border of the Sudan had been viewed uneasily by the Arab world, was an easy and effective coup for Qadhafi, who immediately promised Uganda $30-million worth of aid and military assistance. (The latter was forthcoming during the recent invasion scare, but there is no sign of the former.)

Whatever Qadhafi told the Ugandan leader, it obviously made a deep impression. Long after the Israeli departure, Amin would foam at the mouth whenever Jews were mentioned. In an interview with me last month, he disclosed an Israeli plot to "poison the waters of the Nile." A little later, he fired off a telegram to the United Nations with the astounding assertion that, "Germany was the right place where, when Hitler was the Prime Minister [*sic*], he burned over six million Jews."

But with the Israelis gone from Uganda and the economic position worsening, Amin had to find another scapegoat. Just as suddenly, and with an abusiveness that branded him indelibly as a black racist, he turned on the Asian community. His advisers have managed to keep the official record of the expulsion order to "noncitizen" Asians, meaning those who have failed to become Ugandans, but the general fails to make that distinction when he speaks off the record.

The Asians took the decision with an amazing calm. Grief, despair and fear were—and still are—prevailing among them but there were no stirrings of revolt or aggression. The British Government, having bestowed citizenship on most East African Asians as a retreating colonial power, reluctantly accepted responsibility for absorbing the exodus. The general, often on record as wanting to teach "British imperialism a lesson," has sat back cheerfully to watch his bombshell of colored immigration explode on the British domestic political scene.

"The British are very worried," Amin declared, accurately. "I have taught them a lesson and that is why I am the best politician in the world." All Britain could do, in fact, was to suspend a $25-million loan to Uganda and "review" the annual $10-million aid program.

The highly suspicious Amin obviously could not believe he would get away with things so easily. Seizing on a personal letter, written by an emotional expatriate, that had been confiscated by his security men, he announced the discovery of a British plot to invade Uganda and assassinate him. The 7,000 Britons in the country would have to be "watched and marked," he said.

He reinforced the point by unleashing his four different but equally sinister security branches on the expatriate community. In one day they arrested 40 European men, women and children and jammed them into the cells of Kampala's central police station. Eight British newspaper correspondents, including myself, were also arrested at gunpoint, accused of spying and incarcerated in the infamous Makindye military barracks.

For four days, before being deported, we learned from our fellow black prisoners what it takes to keep Amin in power. Four senior police officers, arrested two weeks before during an Amin purge, were led from our cell and murdered by what turned out to be the favorite Makindye method—a "tap" on the skull with a 20-pound sledgehammer.

As we were leaving, a further 30 police officers were being marched into the barracks. There was no reason to suppose their fate would be any less horrifying. An Asian youth, caked in blood from a split jaw, was thrown headlong into our cell late one night, having been seized by soldiers at a military roadblock. What had he done? A shrug. Nothing more, it seemed, than encountering a military roadblock—and being an Asian.

Among our African cellmates was a university lecturer who had been debating, too loudly, the iniquities of military government; a businessman whose large American car had been coveted by an army officer; and a Kenyan who had been caught negotiating to buy some saucepans from a departing Asian. We were, in effect, the luckier victims of a pampered, ill-disciplined army which ex-Sergeant Major Amin allows unlimited license, perhaps because he could not bring them into line if he tried.

Can Amin survive? Impossible, say the fleeing, impoverished Asians; unlikely, say the terrorized intellectuals; hopefully not, think the British and Uganda's African neighbors. But Idi Amin's considerable energy and resourcefulness have been applied to eliminating any viable alternative leadership. The alternatives at present to Idi the Terrible are few and fearsome—either an even more sinister military junta or total and bloody anarchy. ■

November 12, 1972

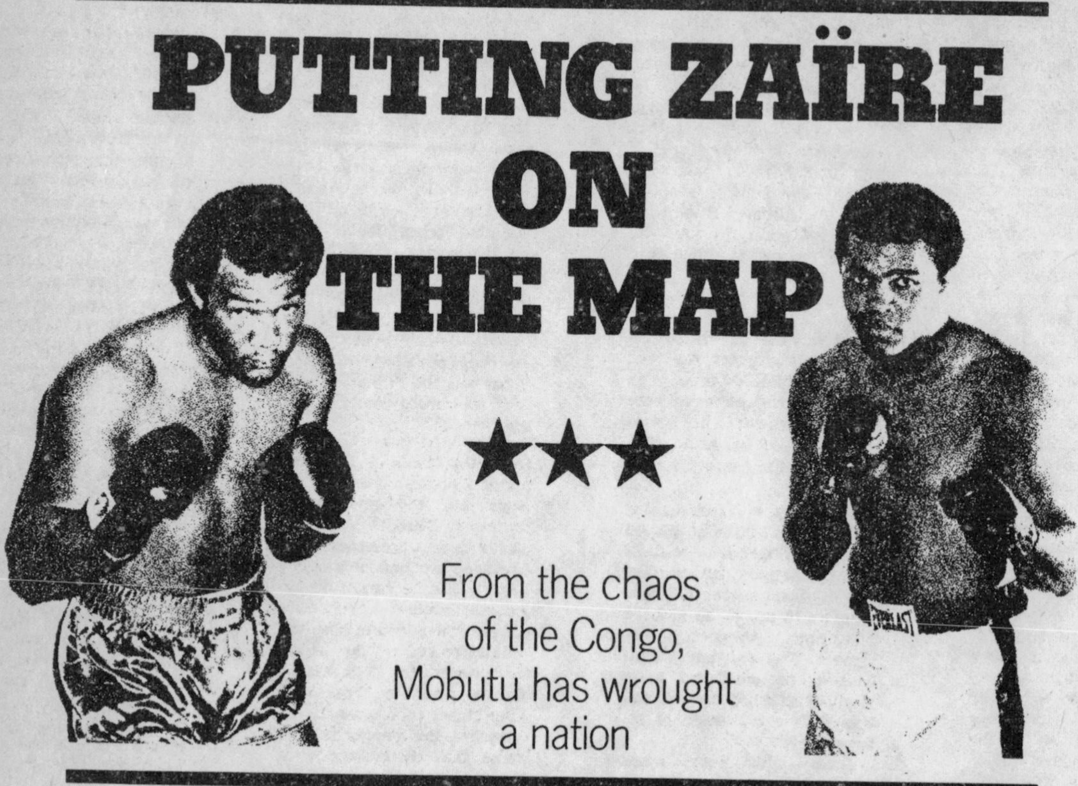

PUTTING ZAÏRE ON THE MAP

★★★

From the chaos of the Congo, Mobutu has wrought a nation

By J. J. Grimond

Why Zaïre? It seems bizarre that Muhammad Ali should make his challenge against George Foreman for the world heavyweight boxing title on Sept. 25 in a Central African country whose name means little even to the few people who can correctly pronounce it (it's not Zaïre to rhyme with Claire, but Zye-eer to rhyme with Die-ear). To those who do know Zaïre, the event is not quite so incongruous. "In Africa, think big," was the advice of Cecil Rhodes, and no one has taken it more seriously than Zaïre's President Mobutu Sese Seko. For him, nothing could be more natural than to hold the biggest fight in history—it will cost nearly $12-million to stage—in Zaïre's capital, Kinshasa.

President Mobutu landed a smaller catch a few years ago when he persuaded the organizers of a beauty contest for the title of Miss Europe to hold it in Zaïre. This year's international event is a much bigger fish: Boxing fans the world over will now know that Zaïre is a country to conjure with. That is the point. Both the fight and the beauty contest should be seen as part of the President's scheme to put Zaïre on the map as a stable and important country.

Not that it is exactly off the map; on the contrary, it takes up a very large part of a very large continent. It is equivalent in size to Austria, Belgium, Britain, Denmark, France, East Germany, West Germany, Ireland, Italy, Portugal, Spain and Switzerland together; in the United States, it would be the equivalent of Alaska, Texas and Colorado. Yet it is little known. This is in part because the world has some difficulty in keeping up with a country that in the past 15 years has changed its name from the Belgian Congo to Congo (Leopoldville) to Congo (Kinshasa) to Zaïre. But it is also in part because Zaïre has some difficulty in keeping up with the world.

Zaïre's size promises now to make it one of the two most important countries of black Africa (the other being Nigeria). But in the past its immensity was its undoing. When the Belgians pulled out in 1960, they had grappled with the country for more than half a century but had done almost nothing to prepare it for independence. Primary education was widespread, but there was only a handful of university graduates; copper and diamonds helped to make the country rich by African standards, but most of the wealth went out to Belgium; the civil service relied heavily on Belgians, most of whom fled the country after less than a fortnight of black rule.

Above all, no sense of national unity existed. The Congo's boundaries, like those of many African countries, owed more to drainage than to population, for, at the end of the 19th century, King Leopold II of the Belgians had simply annexed as much of the basin of the Congo River as he could, caring little for the people he happened to catch in his net. As a result, a heterogeneous collection of tribes and kingdoms, many of them divided by the arbitrary frontiers created by European powers in their scramble for Africa, came to be administered by the Belgians.

Their descendants, the 23 million people of modern Zaïre, are still a very diverse lot. About four-fifths of them live in the countryside where some—such as the Pygmies of the Ituri forest, who live mainly by hunting and gathering fruit—lead an existence hardly touched by modern civilization. Others may be fishermen on Lake Kivu or Lake Tanganyika; but most Zaïrans, be they Alur or Azande, Bemba or Baluba, are peasants who survive mainly by subsistence farming and by earning a little cash on the side. Their counterparts, in the cities are more sophisticated, but few Zaïrans are far removed from their rural origins and all Zaïran women are alike in their taste for elaborate hair-dos and clothes of brightly colored material. The town dwellers have, however, married their traditional music with urban influences to produce a kind of music now found throughout much of Africa, but still heard at its best in the nightclubs of Kinshasa's *Cité*.

The vastness of the country and the absence of any system of communications except a network of rivers meant that until recently the tribes of any one part of the country had little or nothing in common with those of any other part. All but two of the embryonic political parties that were allowed to operate before independence were ethnically based and made a specifically regional appeal. Little wonder, then, that 11 days after Patrice Lumumba became the Congo's first black Prime Minister in June, 1960, Moise Tshombe declared the independence of the copper-rich province of Katanga (now Shaba), and that before long a similar attempt at secession was made in Kasai.

Breakaway groups, some of them encouraged by outside powers, threw the country into turmoil for seven years, despite the presence of a United Nations force that stayed until June, 1964. Fear of a return to the early nineteen-sixties, to the days when the Congo *(Continued)*

J.J. Grimond is the correspondent in Africa for The Economist.

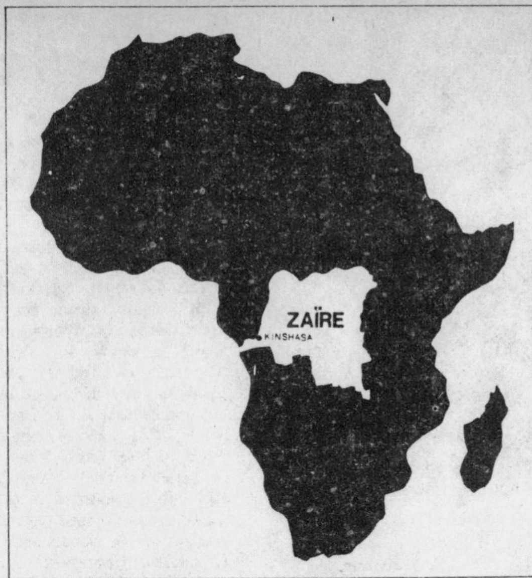

was a byword for chaos, has colored most of the actions of Joseph-Désiré Mobutu, the lieutenant general who stepped in to seize power briefly in 1960 and then did the same in November, 1965—on that occasion to hold on to it.

Mobutu's second coup was both effortless and bloodless. Backed by the 25,000-strong army, he faced no opposition worth speaking of. He had personally built up the army since the return to constitutional government in 1961 and had shown his qualities of courage and leadership on a number of occasions. On one of these, in 1963, he strode alone into a mutinous police compound and ordered the mutineers to put down their weapons. This they did. The police were then stripped to their underpants by Mobutu's troops and exhibited to an appreciative crowd that had gathered.

The army remains Mobutu's power base to this day; he is solicitous in keeping the soldiers sweet with little favors but at the same time maintains a policy of divide-and-rule by imposing a complex pattern of command under which different officers report directly through different channels. This strategy of maintaining separate links with different subordinates is followed throughout the entire administration. Provincial and district governors are never posted to their own areas lest they be tempted to rebel or to secede. Incipient political alliances are quickly broken by the frequent changes of office that take place—often to the detriment of efficiency.

The President is careful to maintain a tribal balance in government and to play ambitious individuals off against each other. Potential rivals are often dispatched from the country to take up ambassadorial posts abroad and, until recently, those that could not be trusted on their own at home were taken by Mobutu to accompany him on his foreign travels.

It is a sign of his new self-confidence that this no longer happens. But it is a self-confidence born of supreme strength rather than nationwide popularity. For Mobutu remains, in spite of the widespread support that he unquestionably enjoys, an unloved man without, for instance, the infectious warmth of Tanzania's Julius Nyerere, the uninhibited humor of Uganda's Idi Amin or the disarming honesty of Nigeria's Yakubu Gowon.

Mobutu rules the country from Kinshasa, a city of more than one million people that lies on the southern bank of the great Zaïre River opposite Brazzaville, the capital of the former French Congo. One can stand on the bank of the river in Kinshasa and watch the ferry fight its way to the other side, buffeted by the flotsam brought down from deepest Africa on its 2,900-mile journey to the sea. The width of the river at this point makes it difficult to see much on the opposite bank, yet the force of the current carries down gigantic trees like matchwood on a torrent. To see the river at Kinshasa gives some idea of what lies upstream—the vast area that Conrad called the Heart of Darkness, and that Swift must have had in mind when he wrote:

So geographers, in Afric-maps
With savage-pictures fill their gaps
And o'er unhabitable downs
Place elephants for want of towns.

There *are* towns in Zaïre but they are remote. It is a four-hour flight by Air Zaïre from Kinshasa to Lubumbashi, the capital of Shaba, and the journey by road takes between three and four weeks in a Land-Rover (ordinary cars cannot make it). Kisangani, in the northeast, is scarcely more accessible and most traffic somnolently reaches it by river. The poverty of the transport system poses formidable problems for the country's development. The copper from Shaba—which provides 65 per cent of the nation's foreign earnings—makes its way to the sea by four tortuous routes. About half of the total production (some 460,000 tons last year) goes north by rail to Ilebo where it is transferred to a boat that takes it down the Kasai and Zaïre rivers to Kinshasa; there it takes to the rails again to make the final journey to the Atlantic port of Matadi. Other shipments go by rail to Kalemi, there to be transshipped by boat across Lake Tanganyika to join the East African railway system which carries them to the Indian Ocean port of Dar-es-Salaam. Between 60,000 and 100,000 tons of copper go west by rail through war-torn Angola to Lobito. And the remainder finds its way south through Zambia, Rhodesia and Mozambique to the sea at Beira and Lourenço Marques.

At least the copper gets out. No such good fortune for the agricultural produce of much of eastern Zaïre. In colonial days, agriculture was the country's mainstay, and its principal export was palm oil, even though the Congo was always a large exporter of copper and industrial diamonds. Nowadays it is a different story, as Zaïrans from the President down will tell you. The inadequacy of the marketing system and the lack of investment in irrigation, fertilizers and farm machinery have led to a dismal drop in production in many areas. In others—like Kivu in the east — fruit and vegetables have rotted for want of transport to take them to the towns.

The Government's response to the situation is unorthodox. The slogan *salongo*—self-help—has been bandied about for several years and for a period after President Mobutu's visit to Peking in January, 1973, was mouthed even more vigorously than before. But for all that, the kind of Socialist and cooperative rural development programs favored by such African countries as Tanzania have little appeal for Mobutu or his chief economic adviser, Bisengimana Rwema. They have opted instead for a back-to-the-land policy based on rural capitalism. The plan is that the educated élite in commerce, industry and the civil service should be encouraged to invest in farming as a secondary activity. Cooperatives and such have been rejected because it is thought they take too long to develop.

So, although Chinese advisers will help to establish "green zones" and, although the World Bank will assist with cattle raising, Zaïre is pinning its main hopes for progress in farming to the efforts of private entrepreneurs. To encourage them, the President announced last November that more than 1,920 foreign-owned plantations would be taken over and put into the hands of Zaïrans, and ministers would thenceforth spend three or four days each month in the rural areas, where they would be expected to tend their private farms. The President added, however, that "the replacement of foreigners by our nationals is not aimed at favoring a minority of Zaïran citizens or creating a national *bourgeoisie.*" Yet that will surely be its effect.

The Government's plans for industrial development are less at odds with its objectives. As long as the price of copper remains high, copper will be worth developing, so the vast, open-cast mines of Lubumbashi and Kolwezi owned by the state company, Gécamines, will be expanded to produce 472,000 tons this year and 600,000 tons by 1977.

Cobalt production may also be expanded. Zaïre is already the world's largest producer of cobalt (used in strengthening steel), which is the second biggest mineral export after copper. And the huge workings at Mbuji-Mayi, where Gargantuan machines claw through thousands of tons of earth daily, are responsible for nearly half the world's diamond production, although very few of these are gemstones. Zaïre, with only 23 miles of coastline, can also count itself lucky to have discovered enough offshore oil to satisfy its own domestic requirements.

But none of these minerals, or the manganese, zinc, tin or gold that are also found, are likely to eclipse copper as the country's foremost resource. So new copper mines are to be developed at Tenke

Fungurume, where a consortium led by British interests hopes to produce 100,000 tons by 1978, and at Musoshi, where a Japanese company, Sodimiza, is already exploiting the deeper deposits there. This Japanese project has given rise to a new spectacle in Africa—that of a Japanese settlement deep in the African bush, where signs are written in Japanese as well as French and Swahili, and where small Japanese children can be seen in schools reminiscent of those built for the sons and daughters of European colonizers.

These efforts to draw in foreign companies to help mine Zaïre's resources are part of a deliberate plan to free the country from its dependence on the skills and capital of its former colonial masters. Mobutu has called Zaïre "the world's most exploited country" and always points his finger first at Belgium, which, he says, still receives $300-million to $375-million a year in transfers from Zaïre — and that excludes salaries, administration expenses, dividends and commissions. Now the President is continuing the trend he started in 1966 when he moved to take over Union Minière, the Belgian mining concern that became the first large company to be nationalized in black Africa. In deference to the need to attract foreign investment through the late nineteen-sixties and early seventies, he then soft-pedaled on nationalization.

Today there are still rich pickings for foreign investors if they participate with Zaïran interests, but Mobutu reckons the country is now strong enough to take over most of the operations of the Greek, Portuguese and Asian traders in addition to a number of other foreign enterprises such as palm-oil plantations. The state has also taken a 50 per cent share in all mining companies and has said all its copper production will be refined in Zaïre by 1980.

To help it in this last aim, Zaïre is fortunate to have a fair contender for the eighth wonder of the world. At Inga, the Zaïre River drops by 330 feet in a distance of nine miles where the water rushes past at an average rate of 11 million gallons per second. If fully exploited, it is reckoned the river at Inga could yield 40 million kilowatts of electricity—more than four times the maximum that the Grand Coulee could give. That possibility is still far off, but the first stage of the dam, which involves no barrage but only a childishly simple diversion scheme, already yields 300,000 kilowatts; and the second stage, due for completion in 1976, will add one million kilowatts. Thus the power needed to refine Zaïre's copper —and fuel its other development plans—will be readily available by 1980.

President Mobutu with Queen Elizabeth in London last year.

But will it be in the right place? The copper is in Shaba, more than 1,000 miles from Inga. A power line is therefore being constructed to link the two, a project that involves the clearing of thousands of square miles of scrub and jungle and an investment of $326-million, some of which will be provided as a loan from America. However, at the end of it all, the mines of Shaba will have their power. And, just as important for President Mobutu, the richest part of the country will be firmly attached to the center by an umbilical cord that should be decisive in discouraging any future attempt at secession.

This is a political consideration that is still important in President Mobutu's thinking. The disorders and revolts of the nineteen-sixties may be history now, but their memory lingers on—prompted occasionally by events. A number of Bakongo secessionists were arrested in Bas-Zaïre province a year ago for handing out leaflets, and seven former supporters of the late Lumumbist rebel leader Pierre Mulele were jailed in April for plotting to overthrow the President. The Government admits to reservations about developing tourism in the eastern part of the country lest it should become "economically detached" from Zaïre by being linked to the East African tourist circuit.

The past is usually referred to only obliquely in President Mobutu's speeches — unless he is castigating the Belgians —yet it is hard to overemphasize its importance in molding his thinking. The chaos of the early years was a humiliation, not just for Mobutu but for nearly all Congolese politicians. There were particular incidents, the most famous of which was the Belgians' decision to land their paratroops in the Congo a mere eight days after it had theoretically become independent. Carried out in order to protect Belgian citizens still in the country, this action was seen throughout black Africa as an example of supreme European arrogance.

There were many other such occasions on which those who were nominally in charge of the country were frustrated by individual Belgians acting with impunity above the law. For example, the plane carrying both the Prime Minister, Patrice Lumumba, and the then President, Joseph Kasavubu, was forbidden to land at Elisabethville (now Lubumbashi) on the instructions of the Belgian in charge of the airport. And apart from these individual instances, there was the crowing of the rightwing colonists that the chaos showed that blacks were not fit to govern themselves. For most Congolese, what ought to have been the thrill of liberation — *dipanda* in Lingala, *kimpwanza* in Kikongo and *uhuru* in Swahili — turned into a nightmare.

Mobutu clearly shared this nightmare. His feelings toward the Belgians had been ambivalent ever since he was expelled from school for throwing ink at a Belgian schoolmaster in 1948 and was conscripted into the army. But he has never really rejected Belgium or what it stands for. It is true that he claims to have done so, and that many of his actions—from the nationalization of Union Minière to the recent cancellation of the two countries' friendship and cooperation treaties because of the publication in Belgium of a hostile biography—have been directed against Belgium. But he still keeps a house in Brussels (as well as in Paris, Lausanne and the Ivory Coast) and sends his children to school in Belguim.

This love-hate relationship with Belgium seems to rest upon Mobutu's fundamental wish to show his former colonizers that he is just as good as they are, that anything they can do he can do better. This perhaps explains some of the astonishing excesses of his regime. The foreign villas (justified thus by the Government news agency: "He purchases houses instead of staying in hotels where he could through overconfidence expose himself to the madness of an irresponsible") and Mercedes cars are probably among his cheaper extravagances.

His taste in aircraft is particularly expensive for the budget of an underdeveloped country. As well as 15 Mirage jet fighters, Zaïre also ordered or bought last year a DC-10 to accompany the Boeing 747 that it leased from Pan Am, a DC-8, a Boeing 737 and 30 Puma helicopters; Air Zaïre's fleet already included Fokkers and Caravelles, making it one of the most diversified in Africa. And though President Mobutu has warned against "bourgeois revolutionaries who become rich at the expense of the masses," the members of his own family are strikingly successful entrepreneurs. His cousin, Mboti Litho, for instance, who has many business interests, recently opened in Kinshasa the largest supermarket to be found anywhere in Africa or Europe. Patronized largely by foreigners and rich Zaïrans, it boasts 50 cash desks, three floors of underground parking and a surface area large enough to accommodate six football fields. All of which seems rather out of place in a country whose national income per head is little more than $90 a year.

It is even more out of place when one remembers that the prevailing catchword in Zaïre these days is "authenticity." It was in the name of authenticity that the Congo became Zaïre in 1971, a change that curiously replaced one corruption of an African name with another. At the same time, the President decreed that all Christian names were to be dropped and replaced by African ones. He himself discarded Joseph Désiré and took instead Sese Seko Kuku

Belgian King Baudoin, with Premier Patrice Lumumba, left, and President Joseph Kasavubu on Independence Day, 1960.

Ngbendu Wa Za Banga, which, loosely translated, means "the all-powerful warrior who, because of his endurance and inflexible will to win, will go from conquest to conquest, leaving fire in his wake." It has also been suggested that, more literally, it means "the cock that leaves no chicken intact."

Apart from this round of name-changing, authenticity has led to the outlawing of the collar and tie: Zaïran men are now obliged to wear an open-necked outfit referred to as the "abacos" (*à bas la costume*). All titles, including "excellency" and "honorable," have also been abolished; everyone, including the President, is now known as "citizen."

But the President is known by many names. *Le Guide* (The Guide), *Le Chef* (The Chief), *Le Timonier* (The Helmsman), *Le Redempteur* (The Redeemer), *Le Père de la Révolution, defenseur perpetuel des biens et des personnes* (The Father of the Revolution, Perpetual Defender of Property and People) are just some of his sobriquets. Everywhere he goes, he is greeted as a savior by squads of gyrating dancers swinging and stamping, waving and winnowing, and all the time singing the President's praises. As cults of personality go, Mobutu's is very much jollier than Mao's or Kim Il Sung's, let alone Stalin's. Zaïrans dance like no other nationality on earth; the women are beautiful; the music is the best in Africa.

Yet orchestrated adulation, however presented, becomes tedious after a time and there are signs that even Mobutu is conscious of some of its dangers. For the first time ever, the President spoke of an excess of flattery among the *militants* in a major speech to the National Assembly last November. And he drew attention to the risks involved if he were told only what it was thought he wanted to hear.

Isolation from reality is a real problem for Mobutu, for he is undeniably remote from the people. This is in part by design: He has held onto his power by insuring that no one else becomes strong enough to usurp it. And he is intelligent and tough. But Mobutu is by nature an introverted and distant character: He is said to have been unusually pleased with a biography entitled *"L'Homme Seul"* ("The Man Alone"). And he has made few friendships in his political life, even among his former associates in the Binza group, an informal circle of politicians of whom Mobutu was one.

Understandably, he has made enemies. For his part in the decision to send the captive Lumumba to Katanga, where he was murdered in 1961, Mobutu is credited with complicity in his death. Certainly, Mobutu was not directly implicated in the assassination, but he must have known what would happen to Lumumba if he was sent to Katanga. Mobutu has also been attacked by those who believe that he was promoted in his first coup by the American Central Intelligence Agency; certainly, the United States has had a closer relationship with Zaïre than with any other African country except, perhaps, Liberia. He has dealt ruthlessly with such political enemies as Pierre Mulele, who was executed in 1968 after he had returned to Zaïre on the understanding that he had been granted amnesty.

But there are no obvious challengers to Mobutu's power in sight at the moment. Through Zaïre's only legal party, the Popular Revolutionary Movement, he has channels of information to all sectors of the population in all parts of the country. His only trouble in recent years has come from students and churchmen. The students have been dealt with uncompromisingly—more than 20 were shot during a demonstration in 1969 and the whole student body at Kinshasa University was conscripted into the army, albeit briefly, two years later.

The church is now quiescent. It has, however, been more of a problem to Mobutu than anything else in the past few years, chiefly because Catholics resisted the abolition of Christian names and the subsequent take-over by the Popular Revolutionary Movement of the Catholic seminaries. Since more than two-thirds of the country's primary students and nearly half its secondary students were educated in Catholic schools, the church has always been an important influence in Zaïre. And as the only nongovernmental institution organized on a nationwide basis, it was the only possible source of national opposition to the regime. The conflict, however, now seems to be in abeyance.

President Mobutu, indeed, seems to be on the crest of the wave. Still only 43, he is becoming a major third-world statesman. His growing association with the radical Presidents of Tanzania and Zambia, Julius Nyerere and Kenneth Kaunda, is a measure of the respect accorded to him in black Africa. His friendship with the Arabs is likewise strong. At the same time, his traditionally close relationship with America is unimpaired. And a state visit to Britain last December opened new doors for him in Europe.

But perhaps his trip to Peking in January, 1973, has pleased him more than anything else recently. There he was told by Chairman Mao of all the money that China had spent backing Mobutu's subversive opponents in the nineteen-sixties; the cordiality of the exchange was a reflection of the respect Peking now has for Zaïre.

Zaïre is certainly a country to reckon with. It is still desperately poor, desperately "underequipped," as Mobutu often points out. It is a country of great disparities of income, both between regions and between classes, and if nothing is done to spread the country's wealth more evenly, there will undoubtedly be trouble. Further, it seems improbable that the concentration of power in one man's hands can lead to long-term continuity and a constitutional hand-over.

But Mobutu's achievement is a formidable one: He has wrought a nation out of chaos and brought it stability. Whether George Foreman or Muhammad Ali goes home to the United States as the world heavyweight champion, there will be no doubt that, in Zaïre, Mobutu Sese Seko Kuku Ngbendu Wa Za Banga will still be the greatest. ■

The main event

The Ali-Foreman fight will begin at 3 A.M. on Sept. 25 in Kinshasa, Zaïre, in order to reach closed-circuit television receivers in the United States at 10 P.M. Eastern Daylight Time on Tuesday, Sept. 24—prime time. A New York company called Video Techniques is handling the closed-circuit television coverage and has arranged viewing sites in the United States in most major cities. The potential gross in the United States is estimated at $50-million; another $3.5-million may be collected in other countries. The two fighters will each get $5-million, regardless of who wins.

Those who can afford the trip to Zaïre—package deals including air fare, hotel and the fight have been offered for well over $2,000—will watch the fight in Kinshasa's 20th of May Stadium, where ticket prices range from $250 at ringside to $10 in the bleachers. Some have predicted that 12,000 foreigners and 16,000 Zaïrans will descend upon the city for the fight, and they may have trouble finding places to stay. Although promoters have been advertising "de luxe accommodations," only about 500 beds are available in first-class hotels in the city; other accommodations include publicly owned one-family houses that might be packed with visitors for the week of the fight, and dormitory rooms at the University of Kinshasa.

Those who do make the trip, however, will have access to a complementary event—a music festival that is expected to fill the stadium for the three days preceding the fight, featuring a roster of African performers and big-name U.S. acts reported to include Aretha Franklin, James Brown, Stevie Wonder and B. B. King.

South Africa: The end is inevitable but not predictable

The relentless arithmetic of the future:
Already four blacks for every white.
By the year 2000, five.
By 2020, seven.

By Anthony Lewis

JOHANNESBURG. Friends met me at Jan Smuts Airport. We walked through the domestic side of the terminal, past the signs for the non-European toilets and lunch counter, across the road to the parking lot. There was the first surprise: a black cashier; when I was last here, four years ago, an African would not have had that job. More of the same downtown: Asian and African salespeople in the OK Bazaars and Woolworth's, black bulldozer drivers, black bank clerks. And Africans sitting in the city parks and libraries, desegregated by vote of the local council.

There it was, what I had come to see: change in South Africa. The most frozen of states has been telling the world that it is changing, by advertising campaigns ("Could the Next Olympics Be in Pretoria, South Africa?") and by diplomacy. Last fall, R. F. (Pik) Botha, then South Africa's representative at the United Nations, soon to be Ambassador in Washington, told the United Nations: "My Government does not condone discrimination purely on the grounds of race or color. Discrimination based solely on the color of a man's skin cannot be defended. And we shall do everything in our power to move away from discrimination based on race or color."

Those black clerks and cashiers one sees in Johannesburg are barred by law, however, from living in the city or its white suburbs. They spend up to four hours a day commuting, on dangerously overcrowded buses and trains. Home is probably Soweto, an African township 10 miles from Joburg, past a belt of wasteland left to separate the races. (Some say, not altogether cynically, that the separation would make possible "surgical strikes," as the Pentagon would say, in the event of trouble.)

Soweto is one of the largest cities in southern Africa, with a population of roughly a million. Very roughly; so many are there without the legally necessary pass that there is no sure

Anthony Lewis is a columnist for The New York Times.

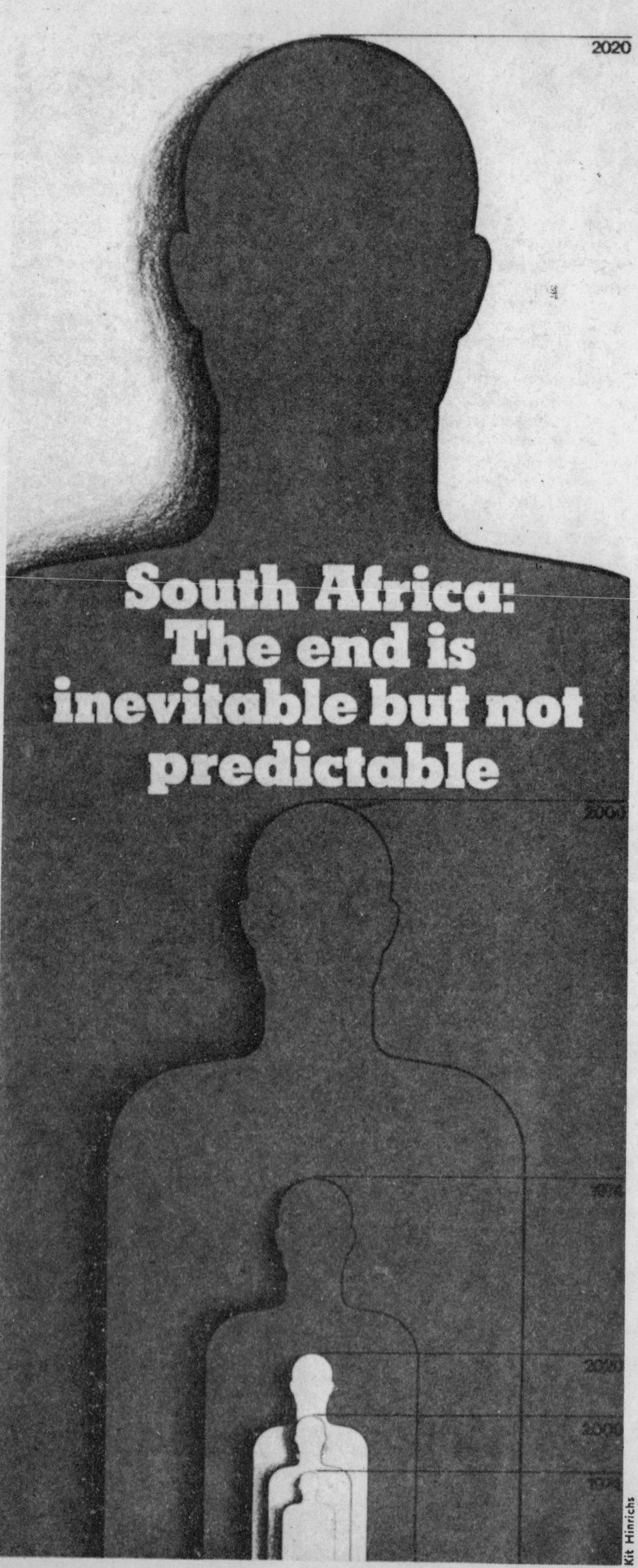

Kit Hinrichs

count. But you will not find Soweto on a road map, and I did not see the name on a road sign. You just drive along, and suddenly over a rise there is an endless vista of tiny one-story houses, marching in close rows to the dusty horizon.

It is a city in numbers but in no other sense: It has no center, no high-rise buildings, no supermarkets or department stores. (White businesses may not invest in stores there, and strict rules on African enterprise have limited commerce to small shops.) As for facilities, these are some statistics of Soweto: 20 per cent of the houses have electricity; 25 per cent, running (cold) water; 15 per cent, inside bathrooms. In the average house, 6.7 persons live in just under four, small rooms.

One night, I got the Government permit required for a visit to Soweto and went out there to see a play. It was "How Long?" by Gibson Kente, an African playwright, and its subject was life in Soweto. It dramatized the problems that are on people's minds in Soweto by showing a family (widowed father, son, grandmother) confronting them:

□ The son has not been properly registered, at some point in the past, and so does not have the pass that every African needs to be in a white area—including all cities, and Soweto as part of the Johannesburg area. You get a pass only if you have a job in a particular area, and ordinarily a child is not entitled to be with the working parent unless born there and registered. Recently, an 8-year-old was ordered removed from her mother in Soweto and sent back to her birthplace.

□ The father, in rags, sacrifices everything to get the boy through school. Africans have to pay for many things that are free to white pupils—schoolbooks, examination fees, stationery—costing up to $60 a year. The state spends about $700 a year on whites, $41 on black pupils, Education is not compulsory for blacks, and places in school are desperately short: one high school for every 1,300 white families in Johannesburg, one for every 16,000 in Soweto.

□ The family is evicted by white officials from the hovel where they live. Africans have had no security of tenure in Soweto. The law forbids them to own property in "white" areas. They could only rent a home from the authorities, month by month, until the Government last spring announced that it would allow 30-year leases.

□ The father staggers home one night covered in blood. Crime and violence are so common in Soweto that many people's greatest concern is physical safety—getting home on Friday night with the pay packet. A newspaper headline the day I saw "How Long?" said: "Blood Flows in Soweto —14 Killed at Weekend."

The boy's name in the play was Africa, and (Continued)

there were moving songs of praise and hope for Africa —choruses, almost hymns. "You shouldn't be ashamed of your color," one character said. Another, looking at a pass, said, "Even the most beautiful African looks ugly in a pass. I suppose he's in an ugly mood when he has the picture taken for it." The relentless misery of the plot came to a climax when the family bought a forged pass for Africa, the police detected the forgery and the boy went to prison.

When the lights went up at the end, Gibson Kente, the author, came on stage in extravagant African robes. "We hope you got the message," he said, and cupped his hand to his ear. The audience shouted back a single word: "Courage."

Americans would notice the approach to black power, the overtones of antiwhite feeling. Yet the yearnings that were expressed in the play were so bourgeois, so nonrevolutionary by our standards: for physical safety, equality before the law, security in a home — above all, the chance for an education. The chorus at the end appealed to God:

Hear the black child in the streets,
Let his days ahead be leaps.
Make him read and write,
Make his future bright.

I was taken to the play by Dr. Selma Browde, a cancer specialist who went into politics a few years ago as a Progressive — the small, liberal-minded opposition party—and got herself elected to both the Johannesburg and the provincial councils. Because nonwhites cannot vote, she has made a point of trying to represent their interests and even of hearing individual complaints.

As we walked out of the hall, an African woman came up to Dr. Browde. She had a pathetic look; there were five small children behind her. "Oh, hello," Dr. Browde said, "you're here." I drifted away. A few minutes later, Dr. Browde rejoined me and explained, "She was on my doorstep this morning, asking for help. She's been a nurse's aide for eight years, but somewhere along the way she didn't get the right piece of paper signed, and now they've dismissed her. No job, she'll lose her pass, and she's divorced—no money to feed the children. So she forged a nurse's name to a document, they caught her, and now she's up for forgery."

My God, I thought: You see a play about people trapped by the system, in their desperation forging a document and getting caught. You think it is melodrama, and then as you walk out the door of the theater you run into it as reality.

A visitor who gets at all beneath the surface of South Africa inevitably finds himself swirling about in deep emotions. He begins to ask himself how people live in such a state. How do they handle the strain? How does any sensitive white person cope with the constant knowledge of what the others feel?

"Existential schizophrenia is the answer in this country." That was said to me, in a voice of Oxonian irony, by a Roman Catholic bishop named Stephen Naidoo, a Capetown man of Indian descent. What did he mean? "You have to live, so you live in compartments. You stop seeing things that are too painful or too worrying. You get used to things that are, you know. No one can live at an emotional pitch all the time."

In that statement is one reason why South Africa is such a fascinating place—and why it matters, even to people as far away as America. As Francis Wilson, an economist at the University of Capetown, put it, "South Africa is us in microcosm. Each of us draws boundaries around himself and doesn't worry about those outside—the man in New Delhi does, the man in New York. That's why I stay in South Africa. It's not the good guys against the bad guys here, it's the struggle within each of us."

One last word about that evening in Soweto: When I saw "How Long?" officials had started proceedings to ban the play. A woman who lives in Soweto said, "It's like banning life."

To understand the peculiarities of South Africa—the laws and attitudes — one must begin with arithmetic, the arithmetic of population. The last official estimate, for mid-1974, put the country's total at just under 25 million. The estimate broke that down by race as follows:

Whites	**4,160,000**
Asians	**709,000**
Coloreds	**2,306,000**
Africans	**17,745,000**

The birth rate among Africans and Colored persons (as South Africa denotes those of mixed race) is nearly double that of the whites. A recent estimate puts the growth of white population at 1.54 per cent a year, Colored 2.99 per cent, African 2.87 per cent—and the African figure is expected to climb over 3 per cent in the next few years.

Prof. J. L. Sadie of Stellenbosch University did a population study, published by the Industrial Development Corporation of South Africa, that is used by the Government. The study makes these projections to the years 2000 and 2020:

	2000 (in millions)	2020 (in millions)
Whites	**6.890**	**9.204**
Asians	**1.215**	**1.617**
Coloreds	**4.890**	**7.720**
Africans	**37.293**	**62.798**
Total	**50.288**	**81.339**

Those projections assume substantial white immigration; the Government campaigns for it. Without it, the figures for whites would be much lower—5,726,000 in the year 2000, 7,039,000 in 2020. But, even including immigration, the study foresees a sharp decline in the white proportion of the population: from 16.7 per cent last year to 11.3 per cent in 2020.

The diminishing minority status of the whites helps to explain one curious and chilling phenomenon of life in South Africa. Again and again, one detects the unspoken assumption among white people that their privileged position will end—by gradual change, by explosion or whatever. People think in a time frame of perhaps 20 years, the intransigent and the liberal alike. An elderly man advises his grandson not to study law, because the young man will probably have to leave, and South Africa's Roman-Dutch law is useless elsewhere. A prominent politician, asked what he foresees for his grandchildren, says, "I can do arithmetic, you know. I've done what I can to make this country and keep it what it is. They will have to take care of themselves."

"A hundred years from now this country *will* be different," a liberal-minded white said. "The population figures tell you that. But how do we get from here to there? I cannot tell you that." Dr. Richard Rive, Colored, a literary scholar, put it more succinctly: "The end is inevitable, but not predictable."

□

The sense of being a beleaguered group runs through the history of the people who now rule South Africa—the Afrikaners. Their ancestors came to the Cape of Good Hope from Holland starting in 1652. That is not so long after the Mayflower landed at Plymouth—which gives some idea of why the Afrikaners think of South Africa as their country. The Dutch settlers were farmers, Calvinist, fiercely independent of any civil authority, wanting to live by themselves in their large family units almost in search of loneliness. When the British came, they resisted British dominion and, finally, in 1835-43, left the Cape in the Great Trek. In wagons like the American prairie schooners, they traveled hundreds of miles to the north and east.

The Great Trek "was something more than an outflanking movement to escape from the British," John Fisher writes in his book "The Afrikaners." "It was a severing of the direct lifeline to Europe; a renewed recognition of the fact that as Afrikaners their lives depended on the soil beneath their own feet, and that they no longer had any ties with any other home."

That sense of being without ties outside, of having to survive in South Africa, remains strong in the Afrikaners. They speak Afrikaans, a variant of Dutch; they are about two-thirds of the country's whites now, and they tend to think of the other, English-speaking, third as not totally committed to South Africa—as having an anchor to windward in the form of a second, British, passport or of connections in other English-speaking countries.

The Boer War (*boer* means "farmer" in Afrikaans) ended in a British military victory, but in the long run the Afrikaners were the political winners. Their superiority in numbers and will finally told in 1948, when the Afrikaner-based Nationalist party won at the polls and took a grip on political power that has become overwhelming in the all-white electorate. In the present Assembly, the Nationalists hold 123 of the 171 seats. The United party, the traditional opposition, based largely on the English-speaking electorate, has 37 seats, but seems to be in the process of dividing, with some moving toward the Nationalists and some to the Progressives and the Reform party, which have just merged and hold 11 seats.

The Nationalists—which is to say, the Afrikaners in their political guise—are nowadays divided, in popular description, into two categories: *Verligte* (enlightened) and *Verkrampte* (strict or narrow). I spoke with a Nationalist backbencher in Parliament who is known as a *Verkrampte*: Daniel Van der Merwe, young, open in manner, plainly committed in belief.

"The first Van der Merwes came here in 1660," he said—"10 generations. In my line of the family, I was the first to go to a university. We were farmers, teachers, ministers of religion, not businessmen or engineers. We were struggling to make this country habitable. We didn't have time to go to university."

Why was he called *Verkrampte?*

"The newspapers call me that. I suppose it may be because I believe in the Bible as I read it. I'm strict—Victorian, perhaps. I'm for Sunday laws, like my father and grandfather.

"But I remember my grandfather and the respect he had for black people. And I don't feel any hatred. I am not going to throw my arms around them, as some liberals would, but I haven't got a feeling of hatred and I wasn't taught that way."

Van der Merwe has a B.A. in divinity, a master's degree in anthropology. He lectured in anthropology at Pretoria University before entering politics, and he said it taught him that people must "respect their own culture." I asked what he would do with the Africans living in "white" areas, five million in the cities and 3.5 million on white farms.

"The presence of millions of black people in what I think is my country is a very tough problem to handle," he said. "When we moved into the open spaces in Africa, we brought a lot of things to these people—we brought an end to tribal wars and so on. They came to us and asked to work on our farms. We accepted them—my grandfather did—but we never had the

Soweto: Population, about a million. "But you will not find it on a road map or its name on a road sign."

idea that they would have a share in our Government, that they would be given political rights in *our* country.

"Our economy does need these people, so they are in areas that historically we think of as ours. So I think we must accept, for a decade or two or three or four, that they will stay—until industrial machinery changes.

"I just know that if we have *one* Government, then the Africans will be in a majority. I just feel that if there is a Minister of Education, I want one of my own to look after me, or a Minister of Justice."

The apparatus of law and regulation by which the Afrikaners maintain their control in South Africa is well-known to the world through literature and drama—currently, for example, in "The Island" and "Sizwe Banzi Is Dead," the electrifying plays by Athol Fugard, John Kani and Winston Ntshona. There are the pass laws, the Immorality Act forbidding sexual relations between white and nonwhite, the intricacies of racial classification, the apartheid laws excluding nonwhites from most public facilities, and, not least, the Draconian statutes against political dissent.

But the reality is still numbing when observed close up. To see blacks in long lines at *their* windows in the post office. To meet a sensitive, educated man who spent years on Robben Island, where political prisoners are held, subjected to assaults and indignities. Or to meet a matronly woman who for 10 years was "banned"—confined to her home every night, not allowed to meet more than one person at a time or to be quoted. (The law has recently been relaxed to allow quotation from banned persons after their death.)

It is easy to put South Africa down as a totalitarian country, but that is too simple. Anomalies abound. The press is guardedly free. The censors have just banned "Jaws" and "The Thoughts of Chairman Mao," but let by Nadine Gordimer's profound and subtle new novel, "The Conservationist." Mrs. Helen Suzman, the courageous Progressive who was for years a lonely voice for human rights in Parliament, has made the criticism that while 180 policemen were convicted of assault in 1974, most of them remained on the force; but in a true totalitarian state, no policeman would be convicted or even charged.

And the repressive apparatus may not be a matter of ideology, as with fascism. A critical scholar—Pierre van den Berghe, in his "South Africa: a Study in Conflict"—argues that the law has been manipulated to keep alive a pastoral vision: that of the Boer republics, with the rugged farmer living the simple life, master of all he surveyed. But it is another century now, and pastoral isolation is a myth that the most extreme means cannot maintain. The world is too much with the Afrikaners. And so they are adjusting—painfully, grudgingly, under external pressure—to new realities.

The big external change has been the coming to power, in the brief period since World War II, of the independent states of black Africa. With that, lately, have come the rise of nonwhite consciousness in the world and the formal rejection by most white societies of the old assumptions of white supremacy. Instead of saying the world be damned, as in the old days, South Africa's leaders have lately been seeking its good opinion. That meant giving an impression of change, of at least some accommodation to the world's modern ideas of racial justice. But how could that be done without losing control? As Dr. J. H. Moolman, of the Africa Institute in Pretoria, put it: "The dilemma for South Africans was that if they granted democratic political rights in the same way as in the rest of Africa, fate would have played a trick on them: There would be an African majority ruling European people."

The Nationalist answer to the dilemma was "separate development." This was a policy of letting the Africans develop institutions and political rights in their areas, leaving the whites sovereign in theirs: a formula for change without any real loss of status. For years, the Government paid little more than lip service to separate development. Lately, with the rising concern for world opinion, it has given great emphasis to the idea. Eight tribal "homelands" have been designated, each with a rudimentary form of government. The aim is to give them legal independence, so they will exist as countries within the borders of South Africa. (Colored people and Asians have no geographical homelands, so they present an embarrassment to the theory, but that is another and complicated question.)

Separate development is what enables Ambassador Botha to tell the United Nations that his Government does not condone racial discrimination. The fact that Africans cannot vote in South Africa or ride in "white" trains or meet the most ordinary expectations of most people elsewhere is explained by saying that they will be able to make the rules in their own areas.

It is something of a conjurer's trick, and easy enough to expose. First of all, there is the size of those "homelands." The whites, with less than 17 per cent of South Africa's population, have 87 per cent of its land reserved for them by law. And only one of the homelands, the Transkei, the first scheduled for independence, has reasonably contiguous territory. The other seven are scattered among "white" areas—"dots all over the map," as one black scornfully put it.

One would have to be quite an optimist to foresee the homelands as flourishing independent countries, whatever their size and shape. They are mostly areas of uninviting land—what was left by the pioneer farmers and miners—with virtually no industry. And in any event, nearly half of South Africa's Africans do not live in them. For a person in Soweto to vote for officials in a homeland he has never seen may not seem to him an overwhelming gain in human rights or practical self-government.

Nevertheless, the theory of separate development is expounded whenever one talks to Nationalist politicians. One articulate advocate is Dr. P. G. J. Koornhof, the Minister of Mines, Immigration and Sports and Recreation. I met him the day before Capetown was to see its first international Rugby match with a racially mixed South African side, and Dr. Koornhof was feeling good about having made that possible. He is a big man, with large hands and features, and he has an expansive manner.

"Separate development has a positive content," he said. "It is multinational development, like Germany and France—the separateness does not have the content the world thinks. Historically, Zululand has always been a separate bloody country, with its own language and culture, and the same with each of the black nations. How do you undo that sort of thing?"

I asked Dr. Koornhof what separate development would do for the millions of Africans in urban areas—like those in Soweto.

"It is a problem," he said. "But insoluble? Nonsense. We are making excellent progress because we are facing it squarely."

Politically, he said, the people of Soweto would gain rights as the homelands achieve independence. "Then each person in Soweto will be able to vote for his or her own parliament." As for living conditions in Soweto itself, Dr. Koornhof referred enthusiastically to what he saw on a trip to the United States.

"Look at Chicago," he said. "It was very bad once. Then that excellent Mayor—what's his name? Daley—did a job of renewal. I admire America, the way it goes for development. It is possible that Soweto can be built into one of the great cities of Africa."

Dr. Koornhof said separate development was necessary to avoid violence as South Africa industrialized. "Engels said riots were epidemic in Britain's industrial revolution," he said, "and you had yours in America. Since World War II, South Africa has had more rapid industrialization than Britain did. How come we've gone through it without riots? I maintain that in an integrated system there would have been violence. We escaped it—and historians will consider that a miracle. Your integrated system is right for you, but here the top would have blown off."

Dr. Koornhof did not mention the series of riots among black miners in the last two years; 130 of them have been shot dead by police.

In the brief period since World War II, South Africa has had, as Dr. Koornhof said, its own industrial revolution. An impressive capital base in manufacturing has been added to the traditional mining and farming. In the last decade, the country has tripled its gross domestic product. The real annual growth, discounting inflation, has averaged 5.5 per cent.

Most of the increased wealth has naturally gone to whites. The disparities in white and black income remain, to American eyes, grotesque. A white miner earns 12 times as much as a black. The *average* pay of Africans employed by the Government is below the official poverty line. While I was there, newspaper stories told of a manufacturing plant in a distant location that paid its women employes $6 a week. The millions of Africans working on white farms typically are paid $150 a year, plus a bag of corn, some old clothes and the right to cultivate a small plot of their own.

But the rapid industrial growth has had dramatic effects in the way of new jobs for blacks. An industrial economy that now includes, say, 12 million people cannot function with a skilled labor pool limited to 4 million. The reason for those African cashiers and bulldozer drivers I noticed on arrival is not any change of theory. It is economic necessity: There are no white applicants for the jobs.

The laws reserving skilled occupations to whites remain on the books, but they are ingeniously avoided. Instead of being a railroad "shunter," the black employe is called a "train assembler." White unions are politically rightwing and highly resistant to change in job reservation; there is a collective memory of the hard days of the nineteen-thirties, when Afrikaners came from farms to cities and competed with blacks for jobs. But deals are made, gradually, and all over one sees crews of workers with a token white in charge.

Along with that trend, there has been a less-noticed change among the Afrikaners. They used to be poor whites—farmers, ministers and blue-collar workers. But, in the last 10 or 15 years, many have found affluence, and enjoy it. There are Afrikaner big-business men now, and the old ideology of separateness and Afrikaner identity grows dimmer for them. Like other businessmen, they think of the figures. And so they go to Prime Minister B. J. Vorster and say, "We can't get drivers for our oil trucks. We need a trained, stable work force, no matter what color. You've got to do something to help us."

The pressure from business has had its effect, and it is not stopping. For example, one businessman told me that absenteeism is very bad among African employes—and that it is not their fault. They spend a whole day getting a pass renewed, or finding medical treatment. They have no telephone. Getting to work is a long and exhausting process. One of this man's employes has a car, and one day he drove friends to work. He was stopped by the police and told to report next day and pay a $150 fine for transporting passengers without a carrier's license. His employer spent a day fixing that up.

And so business is a force for bringing blacks into the economy on an open basis, without all the hampering restrictions that made one employer say to me, "Half the population of this country is busy giving passes to the other half." Experts think it is already too late, economically. The training of new workers has fallen so far behind need that competence is noticeably dropping and shortage of the skilled is feeding inflation.

Some politically conscious blacks fear that their people will be bought off by a little economic amelioration of their lot. One said, "I'm afraid that when you make money, you lose your compassion. You begin to think that other people deserve the way they live." But I wonder. The black cashier will see that, at the end of the day, his white colleague goes to a good home nearby and lives a relatively unfettered life, while he jams into an appalling train to make his way to a house without a bath or electricity in Soweto. Is that a recipe for contentment? American blacks taught us about the power of rising expectations.

Official spokesmen say that people live better in Soweto than they do in most of Africa. That is true, but it is not necessarily relevant. A man who becomes aware of the way whites live may not continue to accept schools with 75 children in a bare, unequipped classroom.

But what does a black South African do if he does not accept the status quo?

□

Politics in the ordinary sense does not exist for nonwhites in South Africa. Anyone who speaks out puts himself at risk. It is a capital crime to encourage hostility toward whites so as to endanger "law and order"; a black teen-ager is serving a five-year sentence for writing an antiwhite poem and showing it to one person, a girl friend.

The old African political movements are banned, their leaders out of action. Nelson Mandela is on Robben Island. Robert Sobukwe was in jail three years for inciting demonstrations against the pass laws, then was detained six years without trial—alone, in a stockade on Robben Island. Somehow, he retained his great personal magnetism and his sense of humor, but he is banned still, and restricted to the mining town of Kimberley.

But, underneath, pressure builds. There have been African strikes in the last two years, with some violence. Black student leaders, arrested and banned for making antiwhite statements, have had surprising support from middle-aged blacks. One said to me, "They suppress more and more, but the people they suppress are in fact the barometer of black opinion."

The one opportunity for significant political activity in the open is provided, curiously, by the homelands. That is curious, because the intention of separate development was to reduce the African political threat by isolating and dividing it.

At the end of the policy, in theory, every African in South Africa would be a citizen of a foreign country — a migrant worker there on sufferance, an alien without rights. And, in the meantime, the Government pursues the theory to the remorseless extent of insisting on separate schools for Soweto children of different tribal origins, even though that worsens the already desperate school problem.

But there has turned out to be a political catch in separate development. If the world is to take it seriously, as desired, then logically the leaders of the homelands cannot be altogether repressed. They must be allowed to speak, even to be heard. And that has started to happen. The eight homeland leaders do say things that would get other blacks into trouble. And Prime Minister Vorster met and listened to them in 1974 and again last January.

The homeland leader who has made most forceful use of his new political position is Gatsha Buthelezi, a hereditary Zulu chief who was chosen by the assembly of the Kwazulu homeland as chief executive councilor. At the 1975 meeting with Vorster, Chief Buthelezi warned that blacks might "resort to civil disobedience and disruption of services" if their frustrations were not eased, though he said he did "not intend leading my people in this direction at the moment." Vorster was not pleased by those words.

Chief Buthelezi is a bridge between the old tribal world and modern life—a relative of Zulu kings, a university graduate, a shrewd user of his special position. When a new Zulu king, Goodwill Zwelethini, was to be crowned, the Government saw to it that Buthelezi was not invited to the ceremony. But he appeared — wearing a leopard skin, waving a battle-ax and leading 1,000 men with spears in a charge that stopped just a few yards short of the king and his white advisers. In silence, Chief Buthelezi bowed.

Afrikaner soldiers during the Boer War. The sense of being a beleaguered people lives on.

I went to see him in his temporary capital, Nongoma, a one-horse town with no paved roads connecting it to anywhere else. That meant chartering a little plane from Durban—a take-off point that nicely represented the anomalies, the chameleon varieties of life in South Africa. Durban is a sprawling port and seaside resort on the Indian Ocean. It is achingly English, down to the rude seaside postcards, the fun fair, the Victoria Embankment, the rococo city hall copied from Belfast's. You might think yourself in a tropical Blackpool until you see the signs on the edge of the sand: European Beach, Indian Beach, Colored Beach. . . .

Flying north from Durban into the sun (an odd experience for someone from the northern hemisphere), one sees the impressive farms—stock ponds, sugar cane growing on terraces cut into the hills—sugar mills, steel plants. Then the terrain turns dusty, twisting, and there are the little clearings of African settlements, the kraals of round mud huts with thatched roofs. The plane lands in a grassy field. A small boy watches from the fence and opens the gate for us.

Chief Buthelezi conveys the sense of inner power that is called charisma in politicians. He is 47 but looks younger, with a flow of words broken by occasional deep laughter. On one wall of his modest office are pictures of Vorster and other South African officials; on another, one of Dr. Martin Luther King Jr. —symbols of his contradictory position as a figure in the official system he opposes.

"This is one country," he said when I asked whether he accepted the idea of independence for the homelands. "And the destiny of black people is one." He continues to believe in a single multiracial South Africa, with political and economic rights for all. I asked how that goal could possibly be achieved.

"We can struggle for it," he said, "as American blacks do." He has made four trips to the United States and is immensely fond of Americans.

Did he mean protests?

"What else is there to do?"

The Kwazulu offices are in a ramshackle one-story building. I remarked to Chief Buthelezi that its public toilets were segregated. He explained that this was because Nongoma is a "white" town—a new capital is being built at Ulundi, and that will be unsegregated. But he went on to say, with annoyance, that the Government would not allow Kwazulu's white civil servants to live in Ulundi; their homes will be 33 miles away. "All the rules in this country! A white person is even supposed to get a pass from the Government to enter Zulu territory —how ridiculous. It's a waste of time and money, and spiritual wear and tear."

There are more Zulus—4.8 million — than whites, and Chief Buthelezi travels around the whole country speaking to them. I asked whether it was true, as I had been told, that antiwhite feeling was growing.

"I agree that it exists," he said. "I find impatience everywhere. There are shouts from the audience that there is no alternative to violence—and that in a country where everyone is watched by the security police.

Tokenism: Gatsha Buthelezi, chief executive councilor of the Kwazulu homeland, delivers a speech, and an Afrikaner civil servant pours him a glass of water. "There is a change. A new politeness, for example," says Buthelezi. "In terms of human rights and dignity, no."

"It's unrealistic to think we can get rid of whites as in a colonial situation. It's their country, too. If it comes to confrontation, it will be a Pyrrhic victory for whoever wins, white or black. These white administrators seem to have a death wish. I don't know why they want to go on a death spree with all of us."

Was he worried that his outspokenness might get him into trouble?

"Oh, they have the power to do anything," he said. "But in terms of their own myths, how can they do anything to me?"

I asked whether he thought South Africa—that is, the ruling structure—was changing.

"In terms of human rights and dignity, no. And I am not convinced that they are sincere at all about the urban blacks. But there is change. A new politeness, for example, and they do meet us. I held a prayer breakfast in Durban last year and this year, and Mr. Vorster encouraged his own pastor to come.

"Even if people haven't moved, it's nice if they face in the same direction. But they really are not doing that yet—not as long as they think they can monopolize power in this country and keep its riches for themselves."

What could the Government do, I asked, to convince him of its good faith—not far-out wishes, but realistic possibilities?

"First," he said, "provide a free and compulsory education for our children.

"Second, give professional people, at least, equal pay. To treat doctors and lawyers alike would not bankrupt the country.

"Third, end one of the most iniquitous things in the country—the influx [migrant labor] controls that separate people from their families."

To people in most Western societies, those must seem modest demands indeed, expressing middle-class yearnings, just like the sentiments in the play "How Long?" It is a measure of where South Africa stands that at least the first and the third would represent profound changes. Compulsory schooling for Africans through six grades, even at the low standards of "Bantu education" that blacks bitterly resent, would mean enormous new costs. Allowing families to accompany blacks to work in "white areas" would mean a radical change in the old assumptions about using blacks as labor units without allowing them the rights of citizenship.

If the demands of a man like Gatsha Buthelezi cannot be met, what hope is there of avoiding the explosion he fears? He is a classic moderate, in the mold of Dr. King, who wants to live with the whites. After him will come angrier men. Already, he is regarded by some urban blacks as too soft.

Like many with whom I spoke, Chief Buthelezi said that hope must lie in two factors outside his control or any politician's. One is the economy. Almost everyone sees, now, that all South Africans' prosperity depends on the existence and nurturing of a single economy. The trend is to bring Africans into the society, not remove them. And so, in the opinion of those whose judgment most impressed me, the fantasy of South Africa as nine countries is visibly unraveling.

The other factor is pressure from outside. Some could come from the world at large, notably from the United States. South Africans worry more about American opinion than any other, and it would make a difference if the State Department and American companies were more insistent on decent standards in their own businesses in South Africa. But the more immediate pressure comes from right across South Africa's borders.

Politics does not exist for non-whites in South Africa. Anyone who speaks out puts himself at risk.

The big political word in South Africa these days is "détente." Visitors from the north quickly get used to the idea that it refers to an easing of relations not between the Communist and capitalist worlds but between South Africa and her black-governed neighbors. In pursuit of the policy, Prime Minister Vorster has flown secretly in the dead of night to meet the leaders of Liberia, the Ivory Coast and Senegal. Then, three weeks ago, he met President Kaunda of Zambia in a dramatic public effort to force whites and blacks to a settlement in Rhodesia.

The new policy is a response to reality. Until now, South Africa has never had a black state of any real significance on her borders. She has been insulated by the Portuguese colonial territories, by a white-run Rhodesia and by such weak new countries as Botswana, with black governments but totally dependent on the South African economy.

The Portuguese revolution transformed that picture. Mozambique, which has a long common border with northeastern South Africa, became independent in June, under a left-wing black Government. Rhodesia, across the Limpopo River in the north, looks increasingly shaky for the small (5 per cent) white minority that holds control. And world pressure has grown for South Africa to give independence to Southwest Africa, which she has held since 1920.

Months ago, it is understood, Vorster assured the neighboring black leaders that he would work for a peaceful transition to majority rule in Rhodesia and to independence for Southwest Africa. And he has acted. He withdrew South African police from their front-line posts in Rhodesia and put heavy pressure on the white Rhodesian Government—without early success—to make concessions. He has taken at least preliminary steps toward letting Southwest Africa go, and recently he ordered a sudden end to petty apartheid rules there: segregation in public facilities.

The leaders of the black countries have very different interests from Mr. Vorster in a new relationship. He wants to gain time for a white South Africa. They see peaceful transition in the states around her borders as a preferred way toward the inescapable goal of transforming the Afrikaner redoubt itself. What the two have in common is a fear of uncontrolled, violent change—for that, on the pattern of Angola, could sweep away established political systems, black or white.

In any event, the reality of black political power has moved hundreds of miles closer to South Africans. The implications are large. For one: When the rise of a radical new black state in Mozambique makes the loyalty of South Africa's blacks crucial, is it sensible to go on trying to create a series of homelands near that very border?

'If it comes to a confrontation, it will be a Pyrrhic victory for whoever wins, white or black.'

Every black person I asked said the single most transforming event in recent years had been the victory of the anti-Portuguese movement, Frelimo, in Mozambique. No one confuses the Afrikaners with the Portuguese, in terms of will or power, but the example is there. The big pending political prosecution is of African, Indian and Colored student leaders who organized a rally in Durban last year to hail Frelimo.

The fascinating question is what Vorster makes of all this in his heart of hearts. In seeking détente, in pushing Rhodesia and apparently Southwest Africa toward some form of adjustment to black numbers, does he mean to prepare the way for genuine change in South Africa? Does he understand, as one shrewd resident American guessed he did, that "he's got a loser of a policy in separate development?" If he does, how can he slip change past his narrow, conservative constituency? And always, in South Africa, there is the question: How much time does he have?

What is called change in South Africa — a mixed football match, a park bench, a meeting with a black President — has not so far affected the fundamentals of life for blacks. But there is a sense of movement underneath, not least in attitudes and expectations. I asked a black woman, a professional, what she thought about détente. She answered:

"If you want to talk about change, about détente, don't go to Liberia. Look at me. I'm here. I'm going to stay with you. Listen to me.

"In my language, they say, 'The child who doesn't cry dies on its mother's back.' You don't know if the child is hungry, if a needle is piercing it, if its nappy is wet. So, in this country, we are not supposed to be crying babies. We are supposed to be quiet on our mother's back." ■

SUDDENLY, ANGOLA

Left to themselves, the rival factions would have skirmished to a decision or a compromise in a 'war of decibels.' But outside powers have come in.

By Michael T. Kaufman

HUAMBO, Angola. It is a big land, twice the size of Texas, a mosaic of high plateau, broad rangeland, craggy mountains, stretches of desert, and rain forest with elephant grass standing tall along the riverbanks. For centuries, the land lay in colonial slumber, largely ignored by its absentee landlords in Lisbon, who were interested in Angola only as a source of slaves for Brazil, though a few investors talked shrewdly of the territory's untapped wealth in coffee, diamonds and oil. When the slave trade was outlawed, the land became nothing more than a penal colony for Portuguese convicts. It was not until 1912 that the Portuguese subdued the last tribal revolts. It was not until after World War II that the Salazar Government turned its energy to the development and colonization of Angola.

And now, suddenly, the Portuguese are gone and the Angolans are left to themselves—except for the superpowers. Over this square on the African checkerboard, the powers of East and West again meet in confrontation, with lesser adherents entering the fray. Soviet-made rockets soar over the jungle and chew up the countryside. Cuban soldiers operate these and other Soviet weapons and serve as infantry alongside their Angolan allies. South Africans fight alongside black Angolans on the other side of the civil war, in the name of anti-Communism and to protect their apartheid ramparts to the south. Western military analysts worry about the strategic importance of the thousand-mile Angolan coast. The American Government rebukes Soviet adventurism; the United States Senate, fearing gradual involvement, votes to cut off covert American military aid.

Here in the city of Huambo (Nova Lisboa under the Portuguese), several hundred women gathered outside the former Portuguese Governor's Palace. Less than 200 miles to the northwest, a battle was said to be raging, but in Huambo life was peaceful. In the streets, the luckier citizens were joyfully racing their liberated cars to the whir of stripped gears. Others sat on the statues of Patience, Fortitude, Justice and Temperance that had been toppled in the square before the palace on the eve of the Portuguese withdrawal. And in the palace courtyard, the women sang and danced.

Half of them were dressed in the yellow and white colors of the National Front for the Liberation of Angola. The other half wore the red, green and black of the National Union for the Total Liberation of Angola. While inside the palace officials of the two groups sought, day after day, to reach an agreement of common purpose against the third warring faction, the Popular Movement for the Liberation of Angola, the women outdid each other with hymns of praise to their respective leaders.

The dancers were euphoric. As babies slept soundly on their backs, they moved with vigorous grace, their faces beaming with rapture. Watching them from the balcony, I wondered about the nature of the emotion so lavishly expended. Was it, as the leaders declaimed, the soul of the nation exulting in the promise of a democratic future and a share in the riches of the ancestral land? Or was it a case of the Bakongo women in yellow and white cheering for the leader of the Bakongo tribe, while the Ovambundu dancers of the rival group sought to sing *their* tribal leader into pre-eminence? The printed legend on the skirts of the latter contingent did little to clarify. It said: *"Independência Pronto! Liberdade Pronto! Pole Pole Pronto!"* *"Pole pole"* is a Swahili expression meaning "slowly, slowly."

Unable to distill the national aspirations of the Angolan people from the people themselves, I turned toward their officials, all educated men. "Ideology is secondary," said an official of the National Front. "It's really just a power struggle. We have all been fighting [the Portuguese] so long, we have too much invested in blood to allow the others to win."

□

If, as many observers would agree, the Angolan civil war is a tribal and regional struggle magnified by outside intervention, then the responsibility must be shared by the colonizing power for having failed to prepare the country for orderly transition to independence, or even self-government. Partly, this may stem from the failure of the Portuguese to realize how soon their sun of empire would set. As late as 1920, there were only 20,000 Portuguese in Angola. Lisbon's postwar offer of free passage for those who wished to settle in Angola brought many poor Portuguese to the territory; even so, there were never more Portuguese in Angola than there are today working in France and West Germany. The newness of the Portuguese commitment is seen in the Mediterranean villas and pastel apartment houses *(Continued)*

Troops of the Western-backed National Front capture a road junction from the Soviet-supported Popular Movement.

Michael T. Kaufman is a New York Times correspondent in Africa.

that have been built in the cities within the past decade.

The Portuguese did seek to expand educational facilities in the urban centers in recent years, but outside of the cities few blacks went to school, and most of them, if they worked at all, picked beans at the coffee plantations or dug in the diamond mines. Also, to their credit, the Portuguese were generally regarded as the least racist of the colonial powers. There was considerable mixing between the races; intermarriage was not uncommon, and blacks and whites were often neighbors in the slums, with whites often working as chambermaids and sidewalk fruit peddlers. Under the concept of *assimilado*, an African could prove, by dint of education and economic position, that he was sufficiently civilized to merit Portuguese citizenship. But at the height of the system (dropped some five years ago), there was scarcely more than 1 percent of the blacks who qualified. There were whites who drove Lamborghinis and Lotuses, kept speed boats and lived in huge villas, but there were no blacks who did.

Rebellion broke out in the early 60's. Small units of independence fighters armed with mortars and machine guns began attacking critical road junctions; similar revolts broke out in Portuguese Guinea and Mozambique. A colonial army sent overseas to put down the revolts was gradually transformed into the radicalized force that, in 1974, overthrew the Lisbon Government and decided to grant independence to the African possessions. At Lisbon's encouragement, the three nationalist movements that had come into being in the course of the independence struggle met in Portugal, and again in Kenya, to negotiate for coalition. A transitional regime that was to accept sovereignty from Lisbon and prepare for national elections was installed in Luanda, the principal port city. The coalition broke down, was reformed, and collapsed again. Last August, troops of the Soviet-supported Popular Movement chased the other two factions out of Luanda. On Nov. 11, independence day, the last of the Portuguese withdrew, and Angola was abandoned to its fate.

I have visited the sectors now held by each of the three factions; in each sector, the political and military commanders talked in the ideological metaphors of Angolan nationalism, while the people only seemed to want some food, some land, and healthy children. All three of the top leaders are sons of Protestant lay preachers, in a predominantly Catholic country. All three were educated in mission schools. All three took part in the long struggle for independence, sometimes as allies, sometimes as enemies.

Holden Roberto, 52, has spent most of his life in Zaire —the Belgian Congo before independence 15 years ago— and has been associated politically with the "Binza group" of Western-oriented Congolese whose sole survivor is the President of Zaire, Mobutu Sese Seko. In 1954, Roberto organized a political movement in northern Angola, where he was born, to press for advantages for the Bakongo, a tribe whose lands cover parts of Angola, Zaire and the (formerly French) Republic of the Congo. His movement, based in Kinshasa, capital of Zaire, launched the first guerrilla attack on the Portuguese in 1961. Soon afterward, it was expanded into the National Front for the Liberation of Angola.

Taking President Mobutu as his mentor, Roberto has modeled his views on Mobutu's efforts to instill a sense of Zairois nationalism by extolling traditional culture and promoting a cult of his own personality. Roberto even resembles Mobutu in appearance: He always wears dark glasses, he is trim, and he looks 10 years younger than his years. He is not jovial, seldom smiles, and neither smokes nor drinks.

Roberto's African enemies often picture him as Mobutu's stooge, more Zairois than Angolan, with a constituency confined to the Bakongo, Angola's second- or third-largest tribe, depending on which set of statistics is cited. The charge makes him bristle. He has been fighting longer than any of his rivals. While his forces were ambushing Portuguese patrols and he was in Europe or the United States raising money and trying to popularize the independence war, the men who are now his critics, he gibes, met over after-dinner coffee and cakes to deplore Portuguese oppression.

Politically, he depicts himself as a moderate. During the early years of his struggle, his support came largely from church groups in the United States. Like Mobutu, he is suspicious and fearful of Russian Communism. In 1973, after Mobutu drew closer to the Chinese, Roberto went to Peking and elicited a pledge of support from Mao Tse-tung. That support has been limited to some arms supplies and 200 military advisers for his National Front guerrillas in Kinshasa; the advisers left at the end of 1975.

It is to the West that Roberto has now turned for weapons for the civil war. "I do not understand the United States," he lamented over lunch in Uige, a pleasant city in northern Angola that used to be called Carmona. "While the Russians pour in weapons, the United States debates and discusses. The situation is urgent. This is not Vietnam. This is just the opposite. We have the people with us, and the other side has the weapons and equipment."

Dr. Jonas Savimbi, 42, holds a Ph.D. in political philosophy from the University of Lausanne. He started out in the independence struggle as a protégé of Roberto. A member of the Ovambundu tribe in the south, he came to feel that Roberto was concentrating too much on the Bakongo, and, in 1966, he broke with the National Front to start his own movement, the National Union for the Total Liberation of Angola, deep in the southern bush.

Savimbi is a burly man with a bushy beard who habitually wears camouflage coveralls, a brown beret and a .45-caliber pistol. In Huambo, his present base, he swaggers bearlike into adoring hordes, who reach out to touch him or tell him of their family problems or trouble with the electricity. He listens to all of them like a ward-heeler, and gives orders to his lieutenants to remedy their small complaints. Though the poorest armed of the three movements and the one with the smallest foreign backing, Unita, as it is popularly known, has won respect by being the only guerrilla army to remain continually inside Angola during the liberation war.

In line with his image of himself, in those years, as a disciple of Che Guevara, Savimbi camped with his men in remote expanses in the southwest. He is quick to add, however, that his other hero during that period was George Grivas, the right-wing guerrilla leader of the Greek Cypriote movement. Like Roberto, with whom he has now made common cause, he describes himself today as a moderate and an opponent of Communism. He is also an admirer of President Kenneth Kaunda of Zambia, with his vision of a "humanist" nonracial nation. Savimbi adds, however, that political philosophizing is a luxury he cannot afford—not while his ill-equipped men must sustain endless rounds of 122-millimeter Soviet rockets. His aim now, he says, is to counter the Russian-supported blitz by any means necessary.

Would that include the use of South Africans? He laughs, and asks why the issue of South Africans so fascinates the West. There are, he asserts, 3,000 Cubans fighting with the other side; some have been captured and shown publicly. There are Africans from Mozambique and the Republic of the Congo on the other side, as well as 3,000 political refugees from Zaire. Why, he asks, are these mercenaries considered less offensive than the handful of South Africans who may, he concedes, be serving as advisers with some units on this side of the war?

Dr. Agostinho Neto, 54, comes from a family of *assimilados*. Sent to Lisbon to complete his medical training, he returned to Angola to set up practice as a young gynecologist near the *museques* of Luanda — the teeming multiracial slums that sprawl between the port's modern avenues. He also began writing poems for the literary journals, despairing poems of Africans under the colonial yoke. In a country attuned to the Portuguese love of language and verbal imagery, his poems earned him prestige—and the troubled attention of the Portuguese police. The following stanza, from a poem called "Farewell at the Moment of Parting," gives a sense of his poetic style:

We the naked children of
the bush
unschooled urchins who
play with balls of rags
on the noonday plains
ourselves
hired to burn out our
lives in coffee fields
ignorant black men
who must respect the
whites
and fear the rich
we are your children of
the native quarters
which electricity never
reaches
men dying drunk
abandoned to the rhythm
of death's tom toms
your children
who hunger
who thirst
who are ashamed to call
you mother
who are afraid to cross
the streets
who are afraid of men.

Poems like that were deemed seditious by the Portuguese authorities. Neto was arrested and jailed.

By the mid-1950's, having come out of prison, Neto joined a small clandestine discussion group of Angolan intellectuals and labor leaders. Some of the members had links with the Portuguese Communist Party, and the group moved from discussion to revolution, with the formation of the Popular Movement for the Liberation of Angola. In 1958, Neto was arrested again—in his own office, before his patients' eyes. The patients carried word of his arrest to the *museques*, and a protest demonstration moved on the police station. Portuguese troops fired on the marchers, killing six and wounding some.

Neto was sent to Portugal, where he was kept under house arrest. But in 1962, he escaped and returned to be named president of the Popular Movement. Under his leadership, the group sought to broaden its appeal to all classes and races. Working largely from Brazzaville in the Republic of the Congo, it participated in a limited way in the guerrilla attacks on Portuguese patrols. Neto, by now, was a friend of Alvaro Cunhal, the long-exiled Portuguese Communist leader, and under Cunhal's tutelage he made a trip to Moscow. In 1968, he visited Moscow again, and the Popular Movement began receiving military equipment from the Soviets. In addition, several hundred of its members have been trained in

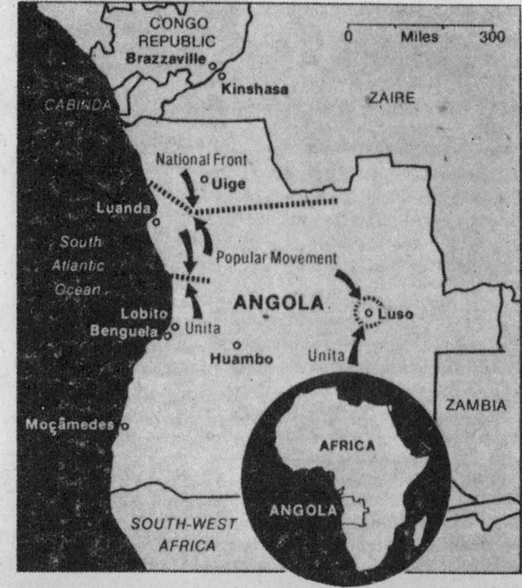

Fluid fronts (dotted lines): The fighting in Angola.

Russia, Czechoslovakia and Bulgaria.

Neto today is a modest, soft-spoken man of austere demeanor, who dresses in Western clothes, with a jacket and tie. Together with his white wife, he leads what seems to be a bourgeois existence in a pleasant house above Luanda's yacht club. In his public appearances, he seems aloof, while his deputies rally the cheering crowds. In his interviews, he makes light of the current military imbroglio and concentrates on the need for schools and technological training to transform Angola into a modern nation, capable of reaping and distributing the fruits of its natural abundance. Though certainly a Marxist, with long-standing ties to Moscow, he rejects charges that he has sold the nation out to Moscow for the arms and Cubans that have transformed his faction, once thought to be the weakest of the three, into a position of considerable advantage. Private investments will be necessary from all sectors, he says; there will be no confiscations. The Russians, he insists, are acting only out of comradely solidarity. What of the widely held belief that the Russians want a quid pro quo in the form of a naval base that would give them control of the sea lanes around the Cape of Good Hope? Neto insists that he has given them no commitments.

□

Neto's coup last August against the other two factions of the transitional regime left him in control of the *museques* of Luanda, while the Portuguese retained nominal control of the modern parts of the city and the port. But elsewhere in the country, the skirmishing that had sputtered along since early in 1975 mounted in tempo, as the rival factions counterattacked. The Popular Movement was pushed back, until it controlled only the area around Luanda; a narrow corridor running hundreds of miles east to the border of Zaire; and the oil-rich province of Cabinda, which is wedged between Zaire and the Congo, unattached to the rest of Angola. A column made up largely of Portuguese and other Europeans, fighting with one wing of

Popular Movement militia at a midnight rally in Luanda, Nov. 11, 1975, as Angola became independent.

the National Front, had moved up the coast from the south, taking back the ports of Moçâmedes, Benguela and Lobito.

It had not been, up to that point, a particularly bloody engagement. "It was in large part a war of decibels," said one Portugese who was fighting with Unita. "The side with the biggest noise usually won." Then, on Nov. 10, on the eve of the final Portuguese withdrawal from Angola, the Popular Movement seized the port of Luanda, and a new phase began.

Vessels with Japanese television sets on board were ordered out of the harbor. Yugoslav ships waiting outside the port were towed in. Their cargoes of tanks and rockets were quickly and openly transported through the city. Within two weeks, these weapons were in use at the front.

I have not witnessed the fighting, since all three movements have been reluctant to transport the independent press to the front—presumably for fear, on the Popular Movement side, that they would see Cubans or Soviet technicians, and for fear, on the other side, that they would see South Africans. Obtaining independent transport has so far proven impossible. Nonetheless, in numerous conversations with soldiers of both sides who have returned from the front, a picture of the war emerges.

There are, at this writing, three main fronts—(1) a line running inland from the coast about 90 miles north of Luanda, where the Popular Movement faces soldiers of the National Front; (2) a parallel line about 160 miles south of Luanda, where the Popular Front is opposed by Unita; and (3) an area of military action around the town of Luso, about 400 miles in the interior. The largest of the armies — the National Front's—probably has no more than 10,000 men.

The major fighting is over strategic road junctions some distance from the principal cities. The armies now seldom meet within rifle range, or even mortar range. Instead, the 122-millimeter rockets are set up in batteries of 24 on the backs of jeeps, and fired at National Front and Unita positions some nine miles away. The barrage continues for hours. Those National Front and Unita units that have artillery answer back as best they can, while their infantry digs in against the Popular Movement soldiers moving up behind the rocket barrage. In this way, the Popular Movement has captured territory in nine-mile chunks.

In the modern city of Luanda, with its broad boulevards, neon lights and tiered layers of apartment houses facing a scimitar bay, Agostinho Neto has proclaimed the People's Democratic Republic of Angola. Bolstered by Soviet arms shipments, controlling the banks and the financial institutions, and with concessions concluded for foreign exploitation of oil and diamonds, the Popular Movement feels itself the inheritor of Portuguese sovereignty. Its partisans, most of them young, urbanized and educated, and many of them mestizos, talk endlessly and with innocent conviction of building an African Socialist society that is not Marxist in the classic sense. "We are Soviet-supported," said one young militant, "but that does not mean we are pro-Soviet." He has read Frantz Fanon, and in the deserted farm village of Porto Quipiri, some 30 miles north of Luanda, where I met him, he had organized the 20 men under his command into study groups on such questions as "the divisiveness of tribalism" and "the cultural oppression of African women."

In the inland city of Huambo, seat of the precarious new coalition between Unita and the National Front, there is not even a phone line to the outside world, and the airport radar tower does not work. The troops of Holden Roberto and Jonas Savimbi are in desperate need of sophisticated weapons, their leaders feel, to counter the Soviet rockets and tanks. So far, except for light Belgian-made arms paid for covertly by France and the United States, nothing has been forthcoming, according to knowledgeable officials in Africa—and nothing that I have seen in Angola has contradicted that information.

Roberto and Savimbi would like the weapons they need to come from some respectable quarter, in African political terms. But, if they are thwarted there, there is always South Africa. South Africa has the weapons and the expertise, and it seems willing to help, since by battling the Soviet intrusion it is forcing the Western democracies to admit it as a partner. But can Roberto and Savimbi afford to accept help from Pretoria?

When Savimbi asked me rhetorically what was wrong with South African mercenaries, he, of course, knew the answer. For black Africa, South Africa is the devil. So far, the greater part of the black African states have remained neutral in the Angolan conflict, though Zaire backs the National Front, Zambia supports Unita, and a few states in the leftist camp, such as the Congo, Mozambique and Guinea, have recognized the Popular Movement. But were South African involvement in the war to grow, it would tip black African sentiment in favor of the Popular Movement. Already, Nigeria has reluctantly recognized the Neto Government, solely because it believed that the other side was getting South African help. Yet both Roberto and Savimbi seem to feel that they are rapidly running out of choices.

Where is Angola heading?

"From the beginning," said Roberto, "we and Unita understood that there would have to be a political solution." Any government of Angola, he said, would have to represent all factions; and he conceded that the Popular Movement did speak for much of the organizational talent that would be needed to run a modern bureaucracy. "We entered the transitional government in good faith, and so did Unita, but the Popular Movement even then was planning and building for a military solution. We are even now prepared to talk, but it is obvious that the other side, knowing it can't win through elections, is going for military victory."

"I was in the bush for seven years against the Portuguese," said Savimbi, "and now I am prepared to stay another seven years against the Russians."

Left to their own devices, the three Angolan movements could have skirmished and fought with their rather small armies over the tribal, vaguely ideological but mostly personal rivalries that are at the nub of the conflict. People would have been killed and maimed and taken prisoner. The wealth of the land would have temporarily gone to seed. But sooner or later, one of the movements, or perhaps one not yet formed, would win. Or else the factions would compromise and merge.

Now, the big powers have come in, with too much prestige invested to make it easy for them to withdraw. What with Soviet rockets and Cuban soldiers, the war is becoming more lethal, and South Africa is obviously looking to the United States for a signal before raising its own commitment. If that happens, it could lead to the use of air power on both sides—and if *that* happens the war could well boil over into Zaire, South Africa and other parts of the African continent. And the principal sufferers will be the Angolan people. ■

Black victory in Rhodesia: How bloody will it be?

By Richard Hall

Nationalist leader Joshua Nkomo during his abortive negotiations in Salisbury earlier this year.

I remember Joshua Nkomo in the early 60's—a burly figure, full of vitality. Laughing and joking, he used to come into the offices of the newspaper I edited in Lusaka, in the heart of the central African plateau, to look up what the British Government was saying about Rhodesia. He had been in the forefront of the independence struggle for a decade, and we all assumed he would become President of Rhodesia—or rather, Zimbabwe, as the blacks had resolved to rename it —within three or four years. The tide of nationalism was advancing down the continent at breakneck speed in those days.

We reckoned without Ian Smith, the World War II fighter pilot who combined ruthlessness at home with scorn for international opinion. He became Rhodesian Prime Minister in 1964 with an overwhelming mandate from the white electorate to stem the tide at the Zambezi River, his country's northern boundary. Smith thrust Nkomo and all the other black political leaders he could get his hands on into jail or detention, and took off into the unknown with his Unilateral Declaration of Independence from Britain (U.D.I.).

Eleven years in detention, mainly in the lonely and malarial Gonakudzingwa camp, have taken their toll of Nkomo, and when I interviewed him in his suite at London's Savoy Hotel June 4, just after his return from a week in Moscow, I found him tired and tetchy. The guerrillas, who have grown into a formidable force in Rhodesia, are winning; the next rainy season from October to March could well prove decisive. But it is not clear that they recognize him as their national leader—him or any of the other men who have arisen to contest his claim to authority. What had looked like a prospect of more or less peaceful takeover by relatively moderate African leadership has been replaced by the danger of a bloody cataclysm. The outlook beyond that is just as uncertain. When Prime Minister Smith and his diehard followers go down at last, a totally unpredictable force may emerge from the forests to take power.

□

Most of the Rhodesian whites came to the country less than 30 years ago, in a surge of emigration to escape the bleakness and rationing of postwar Britain. One thing the immigrants and the earlier settler stock have never lacked, until now, is total self-confidence. It has allowed them to shrug off the fact that, after more than 10 years, not one country in the world—not even neighboring, white-supremacist South Africa—has recognised their U.D.I. as legal. It blinds them to the brutal arithmetic of their situation—of being outnumbered 20 to 1 and surrounded, apart from their vital corridor to South Africa, by black-ruled countries where the guerrillas wait to pounce.

When you ask the whites just why they are willing to fight on despite mounting losses, they say, almost as a reflex, that they are defending civilization against Communism and barbarity. They really mean they are defending their way of life, with its swimming pools, sunshine and unlimited cheap labor. In any case, they cannot sell their homes and businesses these days because nobody wants to buy; even if they could, it would be impossible to get the proceeds out because of Draconian currency controls. But even if they were free to go tomorrow, most would not. They are fatefully in thrall to their myths.

These go back to 1890, when a column of 200 pioneers, recruited by the "empire builder" Cecil Rhodes and protected by 500 mercenaries, trekked north in ox wagons from South Africa to occupy a wilderness thought to contain vast deposits of gold. Bringing the African tribes to heel entailed a massacre of the Matabele, a warrior offshoot of the Zulus; an African rebellion in 1896 in which nearly 500 of the colony's 4,000 whites were slaughtered; and a ferocious British revenge.

In Salisbury today, you are not allowed to forget the pioneers who "made a place for the white man." Several of the capital's wide streets, flanked by tall office blocks and shaded by jacaranda trees, are named after them. The main public holidays in Rhodesia are called "Rhodes and Founders" and "Pioneer Day." They are marked by military parades and church services to honor the white national heroes. Their statues are in the streets, and their portraits hang in the Parliament building.

There is no yardstick in recent African history to measure the white resolve. In the heyday of colonialism in Kenya, there were 60,000 whites in the country, and by independence day the figure had fallen to 30,000. But Kenya offers no real parallel with Rhodesia. The Mau Mau warriors, who killed only a few score whites and were armed with nothing more sophisticated than shotguns, could never seize control of the country; the whites left not because they were driven out but because they were compelled to sell their vast farms for distribution to the African peasants. And there was a vital social difference between the Kenya settlers, who were largely middle class (in some instances, decidedly aristocratic), and the predominantly working-class white Rhodesians. It was financially much easier for the Kenyans to "up sticks" and start new lives in other parts of the Commonwealth, or simply to retire to thatched cottages in the West Country of England.

And there was Jomo Kenyatta. Emerging when memories of the Mau Mau uprising were still bitter, Kenyatta almost miraculously won the trust of Kenya's whites, overcame tribal rivalries by a combination of adroitness and blatant repression, and has kept the country safe for big business. The white population has climbed back to 40,000. In fact, the beguiling likeness between Kenyatta's background and Joshua *(Continued)*

Richard Hall, who is on the staff of the Financial Times of London, spent 13 years reporting from central Africa and has written five books on the region.

Nkomo's has contributed to hopes in the West that Nkomo might be able to "do a Kenyatta" in Rhodesia. Both men were born of humble village parents, both threw themselves into politics after struggling against huge odds to get a university education; then both were swept into temporary oblivion by white administrations. How well such hopes are founded, however, is another matter; great as were the odds against Kenyatta, the odds against Nkomo are incomparably greater.

Zambia, in some respects, provides a better comparison. The two countries, sharing a 40-mile border along the Zambezi River, have closely interwoven histories. Zambia was Northern Rhodesia until independence in 1964, and Rhodesia was Southern Rhodesia; for the first quarter of the century they were administered as one, and during the years 1953-63 they were linked in the Central African Federation. The whites of pre-independence Zambia were, like their counterparts farther south, predominantly working class, and the majority were settled in the Copperbelt; they were technicians in the mines, they ran the garages, they drove the locomotives.

Yet as independence neared, the whites were never able to resist. The odds of 4 million blacks to 50,000 whites were just too much—and London held the reins. There were threats of a "scorched-earth" policy and white farmers talked of poisoning their wells, but there was never more than token action, and when that was over and the independence timetable had been set, nearly half the whites just got up and left.

You would have to look as far north as Algeria to find a real parallel to Rhodesia—a country with settlers psychologically ready and able to fight it out to the bitter end. And even Algeria was a colony, and General de Gaulle was the *deus ex machina*, able to dictate the fate of the *colons* from Paris. The Rhodesians have brooked little interference in their domestic affairs since being granted self-government in 1923; and, of course, they have had effective independence since 1965.

Everywhere else in colonial Africa the metropolitan powers stayed in charge until the flag had to come down. When the pressures grew too great, or the will was too weak, they overrode the white communities and bestowed sovereignty on the apparent leaders of the black majority. Whatever the consequences might be after that, the ultimate decision was seen to be theirs. This is as true of Kenya or the Congo as it was more recently of the Portuguese colonies of Angola and Mozambique. It may have been a desperate scramble at the end—and in Algeria it entailed an abortive French Army revolt—but the ritual of handover was still carried through. It is this lack of a transfer mechanism, added to the whites' assertion of a right to indefinite mastery based upon occupation and conquest, that makes Rhodesia different.

Few of the Rhodesian whites will admit, as yet, that black power is on the horizon. Although white emigration has been rising markedly this year, it is still far from catastrophic for the Smith regime. Some young men are slipping away to avoid being drafted into the war against the guerrillas, but most show every sign of wanting to stay and battle it out. At a recent parade of newly enlisted men, their commanding officer, Col. Peter Rich, proudly told the assembled parents, "They just want to kill houties." "Houties" is a derogatory term, meaning "wooden-heads."

Rhodesia has some 6,000 men in its regular army, of which about half are black troops, an equal number of paramilitary police, and about 5,000 reservists in the field at any one time (to call up more would put an unbearable strain on the economy). Notwithstanding an indefinite enlistment for men between the ages of 18 and 25, the security machinery is patently overstretched. It is just not possible to kill enough houties, in a country the size of Spain, or to be sure that you are killing the right ones. It is now estimated that at least 1,000 guerrillas are active on Rhodesian soil and another 10,000 are being trained in Mozambique and Tanzania to press forward on four separate fronts.

Two years ago, the guerrillas received little help from local villagers, who were still more scared of the white "search and destroy" units. That no longer applies. It is a fair guess that the blacks see things going their way and will want to get on the nationalist side—as happened in the pre-independence phase elsewhere in Africa. Mao Tse-tung's image of the guerrillas swimming like fish in the sea of the populace becomes increasingly apropos. Even the readiness of the black troops in the settlers' army to keep killing guerrillas must grow more problematical.

But the whites are still a long way from surrender. Ian Smith, whose Scottish-born father arrived in 1898 to start a farm and open the first butcher shop in the small town of Selukwe, and whose own roots are still in the town's red soil, never tires of reminding visiting journalists of the time in 1965 when Prime Minister Harold Wilson forecast that it would take "weeks rather than months" to bring the settlers' rebellion to an end. "After 11 years," Smith says proudly, "we are still here."

The main weight of the guerrilla attacks is being taken by the farmers, who make up a fifth of the white population. Their farmhouses are surrounded by tall wire perimeters, and many of them sleep with guns beside their beds. When daylight comes and they drive out to visit their workers or buy supplies, they risk being blown up by land mines planted in the night. The tempo of death among the farmers keeps increasing, but a high proportion of them are of Afrikaans stock and they do not flinch. They are the backbone of Smith's ruling Rhodesia Front, and if, for any reason, he were to go, they would incline to a new leader farther to the right.

But how long can such obduracy and such courage prevail if the guerrilla movement catches fire in the black villages and in the black townships clustered around the cities?

The broadcasts from Mozambique, which call upon the young men to cross the border and join the guerrillas in their camps, talk of the *chimurenga*. It is a word meaning strife or rebellion, and the warriors of the Mashona tribe used it when they took up their spears and pangas in 1896. The difference is that in the *chimurenga* of 1976, the blacks are using Kalashnikov AK-47 assault rifles, grenade launchers and 60-mm. mortars. The complication is political — uncertainty over how much support any of the present claimants to nationalist leadership enjoy in the guerrilla ranks.

Joshua Nkomo, now 59, has some powerful backers outside Rhodesia, including President Kenneth Kaunda of Zambia and President Julius Nyerere of Tanzania, but he also has fierce denigrators who regard him as an "Uncle Tom." Early this year, he held his chin out to his critics by participating in "settlement talks" with Smith that were foredoomed to failure. (Smith's timetable for a shift to black majority rule was "never in a thousand years.") Within Rhodesia, Nkomo's support is limited to his own people, the Matabele tribe, who number less than a quarter of the population, and to older, middle-class Africans in the Salisbury suburbs. There was revealing asperity in his words when I asked him in London about the allegiance of the guerrillas: "They cannot go around waving guns and saying they are in charge. They are not fighting to be the bosses. It is not everybody that must shoot."

Nkomo's leading rival is Bishop Abel Muzorewa, a 51-year-old Methodist who has studied at colleges in Fayette, Mo., and Nashville, Tenn., and whose following comes essentially from the massive American Methodist Episcopal congregations within and beyond his own Manyika tribe. A small, rather bumbling figure in his clerical collar and dark suit, Muzorewa has captured the imagination of the Rhodesian black population by his aura of total sincerity since his arrival on the political scene four years ago. When I mentioned the Bishop to Nkomo, he was heavily contemptuous: "How can he be a leader? He was appointed by me to organize African opinion in 1971, because I was in detention."

Nkomo is equally dismissive about another cleric, the Rev. Ndabaningi Sithole, 56, who led a faction that broke away from Nkomo's Zimbabwe African People's Union (ZAPU) 13 years ago. Today, according to Rhodesian Government estimates, the breakaway group, known as the Zimbabwe African National Union (ZANU), is far ahead of Nkomo's party in the number of guerrillas in training and in the field. Sithole is a respected Congregationalist, and also American-educated, but after years in prison for political offenses he is in bad health.

Outside of Nkomo, Muzorewa and Sithole, it is from the ranks of the freedom fighters that a leader may emerge. A veteran radical, Robert Mugabe, has lately been claiming to speak for the guerrillas, but the claim must be reckoned unproven. The men in the guerrillas' camps have been dubbed by Julius Nyerere "the third force," but they are shadowy and silent.

One name and personality has come to the fore—Josiah Tongogara, who has been the supreme military commander of the ZANU forces. Tongogara, who is 35, was trained in China and fought with the Frelimo forces, the victors in Mozambique, before turning to leading attacks on the whites in his own homeland. Tongogara has become something of a cult figure in central Africa, and it is fashionable to name babies after him. But he is in a Zambian prison, charged with the murder of a ZANU leader in Lusaka (now the capital of Zambia) who was blown up when he started his car one March morning last year.

With the guerrillas growing in power without united political leadership and the Smith regime refusing to bend before the oncoming storm, the switchover from white rule to black is likely to come with traumatic suddenness, almost overnight. Nkomo predicted to me that the whites would collapse within a year. He admitted that a highly dangerous situation could result; the 270,000 whites would start to flee toward South Africa—"They have done so much harm they are afraid to stay"—and the 6 million blacks would rise up and take action. It is likely, in any event, to be a moment of confusion and panic, fraught with peril for both races, unless the incoming regime can assert its dominance throughout the land at lightning speed.

Unless, in other words, Nkomo or one of the other black leaders can "do a Kenyatta" and carry the guerrillas with him. The prospects for such an outcome must have been discussed at Secretary of State Henry Kissinger's recent meeting with South African Prime Minister John Vorster in West Germany. Both statesmen have implied support for Nkomo—Vorster joined Kaunda in arranging for a historic, if unsuccessful, confrontation between Ian Smith and his black political opponents at the Victoria Falls conference last August; and Kissinger when he met with Nkomo at Lusaka during his African tour last April. Kissinger now seeks legal independence for Rhodesia, with legal safeguards for the rights of the white minority under black majority rule; and all indications are that Vorster has come around to seeing this as the least dangerous solution for South Africa. But that would require a last-minute assertion of unified black Rhodesian leadership, to steer the country through peril toward compromise, and the auguries for that are far from good.

One key to the situation is the whites' fleet of 40 helicopter gunships. The guerrillas' main force is encamped in Mozambique, from where they slip across the border to harass the Rhodesian farms. The gunships patrol the 800-mile border, forcing the guerrillas to hide by day and thus limiting their striking power. Nkomo, who badly needs to buy more support from the guerrillas, is understood to have asked for SAM-7 missiles for use against the choppers when he met in Moscow with Leonid Brezhnev. A great deal depends on how the Russians respond.

There is another possibility that must be threatening to the Smith regime. The helicopters happen to be on loan from South Africa, and are flown mainly by South African Air Force pilots. Vorster, through an understanding with Kissinger, might just decide to withdraw the gunships from Rhodesia.

The helicopters are the crucial military factor in the present struggle. If they go—or are shot out of the skies by Soviet missiles—the 11th anniversary of Smith's U.D.I. on Nov. 11 could well be the last. Without them, the Rhodesian forces can scarcely survive through the rainy season. If they stay, white rule could cling on for another two years. And that, considering the explosive alternatives to a settlement, could turn out to be a good thing for all the races in Rhodesia. For the longer it takes to get the whites out of the way, the better becomes the admittedly slim hope of the blacks' finding some kind of unity, whether by consent or by coercion, and keeping the situation under control at the moment of takeover.

There is an assumption in many quarters that, at the last moment, an international peacekeeping force will be put into Rhodesia to defend the whites against a black uprising in the cities and to smooth the path for an "interim government of national unity." But there is great doubt about who could mount such a force.

Nightmarish memories still exist at the United Nations of the Congo operations of the 60's: The morass into which the international body was drawn played havoc with its finances, besmirched its reputation and caused the death of Secretary General Dag Hammarskjold in an air crash. Moreover, the racial and ideological overtones of the southern African conflict would almost certainly create near-paralysis in the Security Council and prevent such a force from being assembled quickly enough to do any good.

The Rhodesian Army on an antiguerilla operation: "They just want to kill houties."

Would the United States be forced by humanitarian considerations to give a lead? After all, in 1964, a combined American-British-Belgian task force flew to Stanleyville to rescue white hostages from a rebel Congolese regime. But that was 12 years ago, and when Ronald Reagan floated the idea of an American peacekeeping force for Rhodesia, he reaped a "never again" whirlwind of protests.

In legalistic terms, the British should certainly be the ones to step in, but most of their troops are tied down in Northern Ireland. It is scarcely likely that the canny and newly appointed Prime Minister, James Callaghan, will divert his attention from his country's economic malaise to plunge into the Dark Continent. Honor will be saved, in a fashion, if Britain can take the stage for the final ritual: The last British Governor will be brought from retirement and told to don his plumed hat, and Princess Anne may even be flown out to take a decorous turn on the floor with Joshua Nkomo—or whoever else may become President—at the Independence Ball.

The country in the best strategic position to intervene is South Africa. Its military forces are well equipped, the terrain is familiar, and one out of four Rhodesian settlers has family ties in the "white south." But Vorster will hesitate for a long time before risking such a move, for he learned a hard lesson in Angola. He backed a loser there, and the fierce reaction from the Organization of African Unity has temporarily blighted his attempts at détente with the black African leaders. Moreover, a South African relief operation could well stimulate a Soviet-backed invasion from Mozambique and an infinitely more dangerous replay of the Angolan conflict — a war along the borders of South Africa itself.

The manner of any outside intervention, and the nature of the last scenes in the Rhodesian tragedy, must depend upon two factors. First, how long will the whites fight on, and how many would rather cut and run before the end, regardless of what they have to leave behind? Second, will Joshua Nkomo, still the strongest influence for racial harmony, stay the course in the Presidential stakes?

Prime Minister Ian Smith: "Never in a thousand years."

And what of the independent Zimbabwe that, one way or another, comes into being?

In the past two decades, Africa has given a surfeit of bloody evidence that the continent's endemic tribalism induces feverish conflict at the moment of independence unless a country has certain basic strengths. These necessities for escaping anarchy are, first and foremost, a national leader who stands head and shoulders above any potential challenger, and a political party standing above the tribes and chiefs with which youthful activists can identify. It is also a distinct advantage to have a tolerably efficient civil service loyal to the new regime, as well as enough economic potential to meet in some measure the invariable "crisis of expectations."

None of these prerequisites for stability is much in evidence in Rhodesia. The nationalist movement is fragmented along tribal lines. The Matabele have remained faithful to ZAPU; the ZANU leadership is overwhelmingly Mashona-speaking, and the old precolonial hostility between the two tribes has been flaring up in bouts of vicious fighting. And there is small likelihood that many of the white bureaucrats running Rhodesia will care to stay around after independence (though Nkomo still says he hopes many of them will). The outlook for Zimbabwe is thus a desperately troubled one. If stability is somehow achieved, it can only be along authoritarian lines. One luxury no African state can afford much of is democracy: The centrifugal forces that are set loose in countries carved out by white men, without regard for ethnic diversity, are just too great.

In London, the executives of the London and Rhodesia Mining and Land Company, with their extensive investments in Rhodesia, are betting on Joshua Nkomo and eventual stability. Lord Duncan-Sandys, chairman of Lonrho, as the international conglomerate is known, has assured shareholders that their interests in Rhodesia are safe and that the company has "nothing to fear from majority rule." His lordship's public optimism remains to be borne out by events. All that is certain is that the "place for the white man" created by the pioneers of 1890 is about to pass into history. ■

'Must everything be destroyed?'

The author of 'Cry, the Beloved Country' asks whether there is any hope for South Africa.

By Alan Paton

DURBAN, South Africa—I write not to express my detestation of the policies of apartheid, not because my Government has cruelly and ruthlessly treated its more articulate opponents, including many of my friends, but because I fear for the future of Afrikanerdom. I fear it is going to be destroyed and I fear that the process of destruction has actually begun. If so, it began on June 16, 1976. The riots in Soweto, Cape Town and other cities—this burning down of shops and clinics and schools and universities—are they going to stop, or is this a chain reaction that cannot stop until everything is destroyed?

It is hatred that is at work, the hatred of a people who for generations, *but in particular for the last 28 years,* have been treated as persons of no account, with no voice in their own affairs, forbidden to buy land or houses in the towns and cities whose wealth they made and doomed to be domiciled in some remote homeland* that many of them have never seen.

Worst of all, this hatred is being manifested for the greater part by *schoolchildren,* who won't go to school, who burn down their classrooms, who terrorize their own parents, who threaten their own fathers if they go in the morning to their work in the cities, who warn them not to come back at night if they value their lives.

The immediate cause of these demonstrations was the regulation that certain high-school subjects must be taught in the Afrikaans language. Black parents and children were not demanding that black languages be used; they wanted to be taught in English. That, they believe, is the gateway to the modern world. This was, naturally, a bitter pill for our rulers. A black child named Hector Peterson was killed. Just how and why is not certain but the demonstration turned into a riot, and the riots have spread over the land.

The deep cause is not Afrikaans. It is the long, terrible burden of the cruel and discriminatory laws. It is the rising in the small hours of the morning, the congested buses and trains, the work for wages on which it is often impossible to live a human life, the congested, often dangerous journey back home on paydays, the arrival home too tired to worry about what the children have been doing, or how they are growing up.

It is that the Afrikaners [whites who speak Africaans—a modern Dutch-based language], whose leaders represent one-tenth of the population of 25 million, decide not only where I and all black Africans shall be confined but also with whom I may or may not make common political cause. In 1968, they decided that I could not make common political cause with any person who was not white. So they destroyed the Liberal Party of South Africa, of which I was the president, and which was open to any person who espoused the cause of one common society. We were lovers of our country and *all* its peoples.

Our Afrikaner rulers had already done great damage to the party by "banning" some 40 of my associates from public life, usually for five years, sometimes much longer. Under a law known as the Suppression of Communism Act, my friends were forbidden to attend any gathering—even to play a game of bridge—forbidden to say or write anything for publication, forbidden to speak to one another. Being banned is a kind of living death, and it is one of the things I cannot write about without pain and anger, though I was never banned myself. Nor do I think I take much risk in writing now, partly because I have been free from surveillance since 1968, partly because my opposition to racial separation has been expressed publicly for 25 years. And I do not vituperate.

There is another deep cause of the current, destructive demonstrations—the stirring of black consciousness and the realization of black power, which was given powerful impetus by the fall of Marcello Caetano in Portugal and the liberation of Angola and Mozambique, filling many with fear.

I have my own fears, too. If Afrikanerdom is destroyed there will be no room here for any white person anymore. It does not matter so much to me, but I believe it will matter a great deal to my children and my children's children.

Why should this country and the many lifetimes of service devoted to establishing fairness and justice for everyone, regardless of race, be brought to nothing by arrogant men who have devoted all their gifts—which are not inconsiderable—to their own preservation? If those men have managed to destroy themselves, many of the rest of us will be destroyed also. Nearly 300 people have died in the present rioting.

In 1948, when the Afrikaner Nationalist came to power, he enacted a series of racial laws the like of which the world had never seen before, and will certainly never see again. These laws had two purposes, each inseparable from the other. The first was to insure the supremacy of the white man, and especially the survival of the Afrikaner. The second was to separate the races, and by that is meant white, Asians, colored, (that is, of mixed blood) and Africans, from one another in every possible place and on every possible occasion, in trains, buses, schools, universities, hospitals, residential areas, cinemas, concerts, theaters, sports fields (both as players and spectators) and, wherever possible, in industrial occupations and places of work. In addition the Mixed

Alan Paton: "The Afrikaners are as afraid to make changes—as not to."

*The homelands are conquered territories set aside solely for black occupation. There are eight, the largest being the Transkei and Kwazulu. Together they constitute one seventh of the area of the Republic of South Africa, although black people constitute seven tenths of the total population. The South African Government aims to steer all the homelands to political independence. The Transkei will become independent next month.

Alan Paton, whose most recent book is "Knocking on the Door," an anthology, was president of South Africa's now outlawed Liberal Party.

Marriages Act and the Immorality Act forbade sexual relations between white persons and all others.

In the philosophy of apartheid there are two main strands: the first is the simple unvarnished insistence on white survival, the second is the ethical resolve that each race (and in the case of the Africans, each group—Zulus, Basotho, Xhosas, etc.) should achieve its own destiny, preserve its own culture, conduct its own education and, finally, govern itself. Hostile critics and cynics maintain that the second is only the first in disguise. There is truth in this, but not the whole truth. It was in fact the existence of the ethical strand that enabled many decent Afrikaners to support a policy that had a cruel element. But the persistence of the cruel strand and the rioting and violence of the past three months have since caused many of them to suffer agonies of mind. They understand too well what they have done.

Before moving on, I must make one thing clear. These authoritarian laws evoked strong opposition, and this opposition had to be dealt with firmly. Hence, the Suppression of Communism Act (in 1950), to be followed by acts such as the Sabotage and Terrorism Acts, and now in 1976 the Internal Security Act. This last Act virtually empowers the Minister of Justice to imprison a person forever, without recourse to any court of law, provided that *in the Minister's opinion* such a person is a danger to the security of the state. Thus, white South Africa has given to one man a power greater than that exercised by Parliament or by our highest court of law.

If you are a murderer or a rapist you will still have the protection of the rule of law; but if you are a political danger to rulers, you will have none.

□

Our rulers have always argued that the making of these laws was their *domestic concern*. At first it seemed that they might get away with it. They ignored all protest, both from within and without. In election after election they went from power to power. Starting with the barest of majorities in 1948, they now hold 123 seats in a house of 171. They have abolished all parliamentary representation of African and colored people. Mr. John Vorster is the most powerful Prime Minister that South Africa has ever had.

But inexorably the anger of the outside world mounted in intensity. It reached a high point in 1960 when South African police—initially in panic, I believe—killed 69 black people at Sharpeville. We recovered economically from that, but Sharpeville came to be commemorated year after year in many countries of the world. South Africa has now virtually been thrown out of the world of sport. We are debarred from one international congress after another. But two powerful weapons have not yet been used against us—the military and the economic. White South Africa could not withstand them. That is why I fear for the future.

Apartheid, the policy of race separation, introduced with such arrogance, is no longer a matter of domestic concern. From our perspective it seems to have become the concern of the world. It overshadows nuclear war, population explosion, the energy problem, even poverty and starvation in the deliberations of the United Nations. I don't think Dr. Kissinger really understands the problem. Perhaps his successor will. Our rulers fear that he may understand it too well. Yet, there is no evidence from their recent talks in Zurich that Dr. Kissinger has brought strong pressure on Mr. Vorster to relax his race policies.

Prime Minister John Vorster and caddie.

□

The fall of Caetano in Portugal on April 25, 1974 resounded throughout Africa, most loudly in the South. It was the first intimation to our rulers that the age of white supremacy had come to its end. But it was an intimation to our black people, too. There was a new sense of expectation, of self-confidence, of certainty in the air. Black consciousness, still in its infancy, was to become black power.

The fall of Caetano led soon to another event. In November 1974, our Ambassador to the United Nations, Mr. Pik Botha, announced that the Government of South Africa would now begin to move away from racial discrimination. A month later Mr. Vorster appealed to the world to give South Africa a chance of six months, and it would be surprised "where we will stand." And even if the chance were refused, "you will still be surprised where South Africa stands in six to 12 months' time."

These pronouncements filled me with hope. I was lecturing in Cambridge, England, and was asked time after time if I thought the promises fraudulent. I said I did not, but I did not think the Prime Minister and his Ambassador understood what they were promising. I think the same today, but I see now that the answer is even more complicated.

How does one move away from racial discrimination when one has for 28 years been constructing a new order based upon it? The Afrikaner Nationalist has a quibble that he does not *discriminate*, he only *differentiates*. No one understands this except himself. In any event, how does one cease discrimination and retain differentiation? The answer is that it is impossible.

But the Afrikaner Nationalist is not a man of reason. He is a Christian who is determined to remain a Nationalist, and he has therefore constructed a culture called Christian-Nationalism. It is a culture that judges education, literature, art, morality, religion, law-making, sexual behavior and ultimately thought itself, by the standards of its own tribalism. It has up till now judged sport by the same standards, and has all but destroyed it. Although some of our rulers have no doubt been cynical and opportunistic, others believe they have been given authority by God, who having created so many separate and different races, wishes above all things that they should stay separate and different. And if you have been entrusted with a divine mission, then surely you must at all costs carry it out. Reason enjoys no freedom in this culture. One can employ reason only if one reasons within the irrationality of the culture. Afrikanerdom has produced as clever persons as any culture, but they are clever only in the confines of their irrationality. They could no doubt produce mathematicians and physicists and engineers and doctors to compete with all the world, but their philosophers, psychologists, sociologists, and above all their political theorists, are crippled by the irrational axioms of the culture. I state at once that there are exceptions, but they are Afrikaners who have rejected the irrational axioms. There are not many such.

The supreme irrational axiom is that you can develop separately—that you can in fact *compel* people by law to develop separately—the dozen or more races with their dozen or more languages, that inhabit one and the same piece of land. It is the fundamental axiom of separate development, and its collapse is bringing down the whole superstructure of reason in ruins about those who held it.

□

Why is there this fundamental irrationality in Christian-Nationalism? It is because the belief that man's most important possession is his nationality—that nationality is the only thing that gives meaning and purpose to his life—is entirely irreconcilable with the Christian belief that man's most important possession is his humanity; in Christianity, man's dignity comes, not from his nation, but from the fact that he is made in the image of his Creator. You can't have it both ways.

The Afrikaner was a creature of the earth if ever there was one, and being faced, on the one hand, by the fierce warriors of the Xhosa, and the Zulu and, on the other, by the empire-hungry British, he found a more earthy security in being an Afrikaner, a son of Africa, than in being merely a son of God. No man was ever more fit to hold the motto: Have faith in God but keep your powder dry.

But the day of the gun has gone—for him at least. He dare not use the gun anymore. If he were to use the gun again—and here I am not talking about police action—the anger of the world, including the West—would burst its bounds, and Afrikanerdom would come to its end. More and more Afrikaners know this. Police action during this current period of rioting and burning has been relatively restrained, with the inevitable excesses that characterize antiriot measures in most countries of the world, but it must be said that the mere presence of the police is, for many, an incitement to violence.

Afrikaner Nationalism is now torn in two. One part of it believes that this rioting and unrest is the work of enemy forces—Communists, liberals, radicals, black power—and that they can be contained by stricter and harsher laws and by police action when the law is defied. That is Mr. Vorster's greatest weakness, that he thinks he can delay or control change by police methods. He is immovable in his devotion to law and order, but this is not for him a lofty moral principle. It is *his* law and order that must be maintained. When it was Gen. Jan Smuts's law and order in the years of World War II, Mr. Vorster saw things differently. He is therefore not morally qualified to demand an unconditional obedience from others. And all over South Africa many are refusing to give it, just as he once did. The other part of nationalist Afrikanerdom recognizes that the roots of the present unrest go deeper, and that the unrest is the result of resentment and frustration. But it is psychologically difficult for a devout Afrikaner to go one step further and to recognize that the resentment and frustration are caused by the laws of apartheid and separate development, which the late Dr. Hendrik F. Verwoerd, the predecessor of Mr. Vorster, exalted to the status of a gospel.

I must make it clear that the Government has already modified the Afrikaans language requirement, but not before one of its ministers, Dr. Andries Treurnicht, had said that because these schools were in "white South Africa, the Government had the right to determine the medium of instruction." What is more, Mr. M. C. Botha, the Minister who controls the schools, has, since the riots began, stated categorically that black urban dwellers are transients, and must look to the homelands for their rights. It is this that makes many of us despair. The Nationalist Party appears to have no conception of the gravity of its crisis.

The prime political aim of Afrikanerdom is to preserve its unity. Only by preserving its unity can it find security in a hostile world. To question apartheid seriously, in the mind of the Afrikaner, is to threaten Afrikaner unity. Therefore one does not question apartheid seriously. How then does the Afrikaner politician deal with the danger?

I don't know the answer. Afrikaner politicians have for the last 28 years been digging for their people—and mine—a grave so big and so deep that I don't know if they will ever get out. They know that change is imperative, but they are as afraid to make change as they are not to make it.

Thirty years ago, in "Cry, the Beloved Country," I put these words into the mouth of the black priest Msimangu—*I have one great fear in my heart, that one day when they turn to loving, they will find we are turned to hating.* Has that day come?

I wrote earlier in this article that Mr. Vorster is the most powerful Prime Minister that South Africa has ever had. And so he is, but so far he has done almost nothing in this time of crisis. Why? It is the question we are all asking ourselves.

Is he afraid that if he embarks on social change, he will lose his right wing, and therefore commit the unforgivable sin of destroying Afrikaner unity?

Or is it the right wing in his own personality that he cannot overcome? And is he also afraid of the left wing in his own personality? I might add that some of his critics say he hasn't got one.

Is it true that he has no deep political belief, and that therefore he is pulled right and he is pulled left, and has no conviction to urge him ahead?

We all know that it is dangerous to hold down the lid of the boiling pot. It is just as dangerous to take it off. One must first damp down the fires underneath. That means that internal change is imperative if we are going to avoid external intervention and internal unrest. The chief responsibility for making change lies with the Prime Minister and his Government. Is he, and are they, politically and psychologically able to discharge it? Again, I do not know.

There is a not very nice picture that comes often to my mind. A man lives in a house full of his possessions. The poor and the hungry and the dispossessed keep knocking at the door. Some members of his family urge him to open the door and others tell him that he must never open the door. Then comes the final imperious knock, and he knows at last that he must open. And when he opens it, it is Death who is waiting for him.

May it not be so. ■

September 19, 1976

The case for Africa's white tribe

The Afrikaners, says one of them, believe they are in Africa for a high purpose transcending their own survival.

By P. J. Cillié

CAPE TOWN. It may be that, politically speaking, they are the loneliest people in the world today—Africa's unique white tribe of Afrikaners, numbering only about two and a half million and currently at the center of an inordinate amount of international politics. Were they born to this fate, did they bring it down on their own heads, or was it thrust upon them?

Answers vary, even among themselves, for they are as given to self-pity, self-analysis and self-admiration as any other branch of humanity. However, they have moved to near consensus on the proposition that they are passing through the most decisive phase of their more than three centuries of history in Africa. Making allowances for quite important differences, they see themselves as a sort of Israel in Africa, with a sense of God-guided destiny that it would be as perilous to discount as in the case of the original model. The writer of this article is a member of this people, sharing some of their qualities, good and bad. If he may presume to sum up their present world view from the southern tip of the continent from which they take their name, he would do so as follows:

Deriving from many sources, there seems to be operating in the world community these days a widespread and passionate craving for a whipping boy, a scapegoat, a victim to burn at the stake or to crucify, in order to gain at least temporary relief from the collective burden of guilt, meaninglessness and complexity oppressing the nations. Thoughtful Afrikaners have a feeling, possibly exaggerated, that a growing forest of fingers is pointing their way as the most likely candidates for such an expiatory role. The Kremlin imperialists must find some grim delight in this scene, as Russian rifles are handed down to any young bully of the African bush who chooses to call himself a freedom fighter.

P. J. Cillié is editor of the Afrikaans newspaper Die Burger in Cape Town.

The Afrikaners know, from their not so distant past, what it is to go down to superior force; total national tragedy is not beyond their imagination. They do not presume to be a nation of heroes, but they have in their makeup some of the stuff that heroes are made of. They have stood up stubbornly to what they regard as false ideals and systems of human unity with arrogant pretensions to universality. By way of reaction, they have tended to overstress diversity, ethnicity and differentiation by separation and exclusion.

Their greatest need now seems to be to define the *common* aims of *all* the peoples sharing their land with them. The most obvious of these aims must surely be the defense of a common civilization that, with all its defects, has raised the average quality of life of the black peoples of South Africa far above that found in most parts of the less-developed continents. Even now, prospects are opening up of enhanced human dignity and self-realization undreamed of a decade or two ago. "There are no inferior people in South Africa," Prime Minister John Vorster has said, voicing a prospect rather than the reality—but a sincere one, with untold liberating potentialities.

He was speaking as majority leader of quite a small people in African continental and subcontinental terms. The Afrikaners amount to maybe 1 percent of the total population of Africa, and less than 10 percent of that of their own Republic of South Africa. The rest of the country's 25 million people is made up of fewer than 2 million non-Afrikaners, mostly English-speaking, whites of British and other immigrant extraction; about 2½ million people of mixed race, known as coloreds or browns—predominantly Afrikaans-speaking and sometimes daringly called "brown Afrikaners"; fewer than 1 million Asians, and about 18 million black Africans belonging to eight or nine distinct tribal groupings, peoples or emergent nations. Through the ruling Nationalist Party, the Afrikaners are very much in political control of this intricate conglomeration of peoples and cultures—as well as of a country that ranks as a major power in African terms and, at least potentially, as a medium power in a global context.

Who and what are the Afrikaners? They find it a most absorbing question. Their learned men and artists show an intense preoccupation with "identity." And there exists among Afrikaners, as among white South Africans in general, a sincere conviction that, on this score as on others, they are being woefully misunderstood and misrepresented abroad. Their conception of what they are and what they are up to is completely different from their image in the world.

A typical Afrikaner is supposed by many, including sometimes himself, to be a strict Calvinist in his theological views, an austere puritan in matters of sexual morals, an uncritical hero worshiper as regards his past, and a passionate son of the soil (even when he is a third-generation city clerk or mineworker). Up to the end of the 19th century, most Afrikaners were indeed conservative agrarians, but secularization, urbanization and social stratification have changed the picture, and intelligent generalization about the modern Afrikaner has become difficult.

He may combine a fanatical attachment to the Afrikaans language with considerable liberalism in matters of race and color; or a devotion to avant-garde art with hard-line *(Continued)* views on the perniciousness of "English" progressivism in politics. A refusal to be stereotyped expresses itself in a crop of Van der Merwe jokes in which the "typical" bucolic Afrikaner, alternately stupid and shrewd, is lampooned:

☐ Koos van der Merwe sets forth from his farm for a visit to the city, taking his black farmhand with him. On the way, he fraternizes with the black in accordance with Prime Minister Vorster's détente policy, as he understands it, and invites the man to call him by his first name. Just then the tire blows. "Now, Koos," says the farmhand, "where the hell do we find a black ———— to change the wheel?"

☐ Van der Merwe visits Cape Town from Zambia, where he has become an expatriate farmer. A friend takes him to the opening of Parliament and points out the President and the Prime Minister. "What an old-fashioned set-up you have here," comments Van der Merwe. "Where I come from, we have blacks doing these inferior jobs."

☐ Van der Merwe, on a trip to London, goes to a restaurant, and a colored man from South Africa sits down at his table. Van der Merwe expresses his displeasure in vigorous Afrikaans. Tears roll down the other man's cheeks. Says Van der Merwe: "First you have the effrontery to share this table with me, and now you are crying like a woman. What the devil is the matter with you?" "Baas," says the colored man, "you make me feel so homesick."

☐ Van der Merwe is called upon to take over the leadership of Rhodesia. Deciding on a high-powered, top-level approach, he flies to America and Britain and picks up Gerald Ford and Harold Wilson for an on-the-spot conference. On the way back, the two statesmen get into an argument, each claiming his country builds things faster than the other's. Flying over the Zambezi River, they look down on the huge expanse of the Kariba Dam and ask what it is. "I don't know," says Van der Merwe. "It wasn't here when I flew north to fetch you."

The Afrikaner's concept of what he is trying to achieve is rooted in his stirring history. The Dutch settlement at the Cape of Good Hope in 1652 was conceived as simply a halfway station for ships on the profitable route to the East. However, much against the East India Company's policy, the early settlers took root, and by the beginning of the 18th century the Cape Dutch, strengthened by a modest influx of French Huguenots and German employees of the company, were already evolving a subnationality of their own. The term "Afrikaner" (African) became current to distinguish the permanent white settlers from the colonial birds of passage. At the same time, their speech was diverging from the Dutch prevalent in the Netherlands; by the 20th century it had become a full-fledged modern language.

The early and unconscious tribe- or nation-forming process among the settlers was accelerated during the Napoleonic wars when the Cape was cut off from its European homeland by preventive British occupation. An important section of the Cape Dutch came to resent British domination. In the 1830's, they set off northward in their ox wagons in search of a promised land where they could live as they liked.

British power and cupidity—or, more charitably, imperial law and order—followed them. In the Anglo-Boer War of 1899-1902, the Transvaal and Free State Republics were beaten down in a devastating struggle. In Afrikaner thinking, it still ranks as their most tragic as well as their finest hour. The moral victory was indeed theirs, and in a sense the decline of British imperialism and Western European colonialism in general can be dated from this war. In 1910, with a postwar change of government in Britain from Conservative to Liberal, the four British colonies in South Africa were brought together in a strongly centralized and self-governing Union of South Africa—under Afrikaner political leadership and British-minded financial hegemony.

The mainstream of Afrikaner tradition has thus never been colonialist in the sense in which the term is applied in our time. The Cape Dutch were anticolonialist in their behavior toward Dutch authority; and after that British imperialism became the most feared and resented evil in their political demonology, outranking by far their sporadic and sometimes extremely bloody troubles with southward-moving African tribes. An Israeli diplomat said recently to a leading Afrikaner, "Your people, very much like mine, seem to be fated to get in the way of movements with universal pretensions."

The Boer republics got in the way of Pax Britannica and had to pay the price of subjugation. Then, when British policy changed to gradual emancipation of colonial peoples, the Afrikaners got in the way of a new, sweeping and still prevalent pretension: that what the emerging societies in colonial areas needed was an expanding franchise within a unitary parliamentary structure of the Western type. Thus would self-governing and eventually free nations be created in the Western, and especially English, image. Bundles of diverse tribes arbitrarily grouped within manageable colonial areas were now expected to become viable parliamentary democracies. It has not worked anywhere in black Africa, where political parties on the Western model inevitably become vehicles of tribal interests and power, and Western democracy ends up in authoritarian rule based on a dominant tribe or grouping of tribes.

Parliamentary democracy has lasted so long in South Africa because it has been confined largely to the whites, who, although themselves divided along lines of language and tradition, did have enough Western values and conventions, as well as interests, in common to make the system work. Even so, over the past 28 years, it has given the Afrikaners a virtual monopoly of political power.

The ruling Nationalist Party, founded in 1914-15, started off as a militant splinter group dedicated to sovereign independence, republicanism, equality for the Dutch-Afrikaans language, and the economic interests of Afrikaners impoverished by the Boer War. In coalition with the predominantly English-speaking Labor Party, the Nationalists ruled during the 1920's, winning independence for South Africa and laying the foundations of industrialization. Afrikaner unity collapsed during the world depression of the 1930's and power shifted to an Afrikaner-English-speaking combination. It wasn't until the election of 1948 that the Nationalist Party regained control. The dour mood of the period can be gauged by a remark of the Nationalist leader Daniel Malan: "Now we feel at home once again in our own country!"

It was during the 1948 election campaign that the fatal word "apartheid" was first launched—ironically as a more positive and acceptable label for ethnic separation and differentiation than the shopworn term "segregation." With a tidal wave of anticolonialism building up in the wake of the Second World War, "apartheid," and the negative aspects of the policies it stood for, created the impression of a South Africa flying in the face of the whole world. A semantic changeover to "separate development" did not fare much better.

In fact, although a great deal of Nationalist policy, with its proliferation of Jim Crow legislation, amounted to a gut reaction against laissez-faire race-mixing under the previous regime, thoughtful Afrikaners were at the same time coming to grips with the central problems of their minority role in a multiracial or multinational society. Very early in the reign of the Nationalist Party, which has now lasted uninterruptedly for almost three decades, Afrikaner intellectuals and churchmen posed the dilemma more or less in these terms:

"In our very essence as a distinct African people, we are anti-imperialist. Our forefathers rejected alien domination by the British to the point of plunging into a hopeless war against fearful odds. They lost, but won their moral point at a ghastly economic and demographic price.

"We have come to inherit what is, in effect, a white-dominated empire containing a variety of underdeveloped colonial peoples, black, brown and Asian. Having fought for national freedom—first militarily, and then constitutionally—we cannot forever deny it to others. Like everybody else, we have to liberate the nonwhite peoples under our care, leading them to self-determination and freedom.

"However, since a shared freedom in a common society inside a single state structure is bound to lead to black numerical domination, probably expressing itself through tribal tyranny, the only option seems to be territorial separation of peoples, each one growing to political maturity, autonomy and freedom in its own part of a commonwealth or confederation of South Africa."

Such areas for the attainment of separate freedoms by the black (or Bantu) peoples did indeed exist in embryo in the shape of "native" reserves, later more grandly called black homelands. However, these lands set apart for blacks had, to a large extent, stagnated into rural slums, from which the able-bodied migrated to the fast-growing industries in the "white" cities. The idealistic Afrikaner vision during the 50's and 60's was one in which these homelands, with their great economic potential, would be extended, consolidated and developed into viable self-governing states, which could, in due course, become independent. This would at once remove the specter of black domination by numbers and the prospect of internecine struggle among black peoples as distinct as the various nationalities of Europe. Above all, it would supply a lasting foundation for cordial relations between blacks and whites within the geographical area of South Africa.

As happens to most grand political concepts, the reality has been trailing the ideal. True, the Transkei Republic, homeland of the four-million strong Xhosa people, has this year attained statehood and independence (although international recognition is being withheld on the grounds that Transkei is a phoney creation, with no prospect of viability, a large percentage of its able-bodied citizens working outside its borders). Still, even among the orthodox Afrikaners, questioning of the homelands policy has become more insistent. To what extent is the master plan of the 60's valid and adequate for the 70's? The other homelands are fragmented to a degree that makes their future statehood seem less than credible. To consolidate them properly would involve political and financial risks beyond the foreseeable resources of South Africa.

Time has grown short, and the ambitions of South Africa's labor force of millions of blacks have been fired by the withdrawal of Western colonial government from other parts of southern Africa. The blacks are demanding rights and privileges in the urban centers where they work, not in a distant homeland. Also, the browns and Asians, who

At the Roosevelt High School in Johannesburg. "Afrikaners have a fanatical attachment to the Afrikaans language."

have residential areas separate from the whites but no "homelands" of their own, are asking, through their representative bodies and, recently, by violent youth demonstrations: "What about us?"

There is indeed no lack of clamor in present-day South Africa. It has withal remained a surprisingly open society, maintaining a measure of press freedom equalled or surpassed in few other countries in the world, none of them in Africa.

Afrikaners today are sorting out their reactions and responses, and the superficial impression is one of some confusion. Like all originally rural peoples, they tend to an individualism that sometimes distresses their leaders mightily. Afrikaners are to be found in all South African parties, from the underground extreme left, with its racial integration, to the vociferous extreme right, with its racial supremacy or baaskap (bossism). The common feature is passionate involvement, the rightists stressing white or Afrikaner national freedom at any price, and the leftists and liberals finding present inequities, discrimination and administrative restrictions on civil liberties unbearable.

South Africa does indeed have a formidable apparatus of security legislation. It can be used by the Government to prohibit persons from addressing or attending meetings or entering certain areas, and to place individuals under house arrest or preventive detention for indefinite periods of time. The Communist Party, the African National Congress and the Pan-African Congress are proscribed, and active membership in these bodies is a criminal offense. Arrests and detentions have mutliplied in the wake of the recent urban unrest.

The arguments over the rights and wrongs of these executive powers are interminable in South African politics. Government apologists say that however unpleasant these laws may be, they are indispensable in the present situation, which demands that people who are likely to bring dangerous situations to a boil should be taken out of harm's way in time. Some hundreds of individuals are affected, few of them nationally known. Revelations of subversion made during some recent court cases tend to augment public support for the Government's hard-line approach.

Such divisions, as well as much of Afrikaner history, suggest a persistent Protestant inclination toward schism and factionalism, which in turn evokes a deep hankering after unity, discipline and strong leadership.

The Nationalist Party's power base has broadened considerably during the last few decades. A growing percentage of non-Afrikaner whites has been attracted by Vorster's strong-man image and his uncompromising stand on law and order—tempered by a show of reluctant flexibility in the face of powerful evolutionary forces inside the country and mounting pressures from the outside.

Reacting to the latter, Vorster in 1974 launched an active policy of détente in Africa, with some initial success. The main aim is to create an area of peace and prosperity in the subcontinent; the alternative, he said, is "too ghastly to contemplate." Since he spoke those words, Russian imperial power, using Cuban soldiers as its cat's-paw, has intruded into southern Africa by way of Angola. When the American Congress stopped covert American military aid to Moscow's enemies in the Angolan civil war, South Africa had perforce to cease its own concurrent—and liberally interpreted—"hot pursuit" across the Angolan border. The way was opened for a Marxist takeover in Angola—and the propaganda boast that the "Boers" had suffered defeat at the hands of the black forces of freedom.

All the time, Vorster has been plugging away at the two immediate problems that stand in the way of more constructive relations with at least some black African states: Rhodesia and South-West Africa. In the handling of both matters, basic Afrikaner philosophy has been operative.

Since Rhodesia's white Government has never accepted the idea of separate freedoms for white and black in that country, Afrikaner logic demanded the alternative of moving with all deliberate speed toward shared freedom in a common society. Moreover, only rightist fanatics in South Africa ever entertained the idea of direct military support for Rhodesia against the guerrilla warfare being waged against it from bases in Mozambique and Zambia. It is very much against Afrikaner principle to go to war in order to maintain a form of colonialist domination left by the retreating tide of British imperialism.

A similar attitude has emerged toward South-West Africa, wrested from the Germans by South African troops during the First World War at the request of the British Government and administered by South Africa under a League of Nations mandate. This legacy of British imperialism by proxy landed in due course in the lap of Afrikaner Nationalist Governments, which reluctantly veered away from the idea of incorporating the territory to the present policy of self-determination and independence by way of a constitutional consensus. What makes this solution difficult is the wide disparity of the peoples of that country.

The immensity of Vorster's agenda will have become apparent. Both a Rhodesian and a South-West African settlement would have to be negotiated in the face of Russian and militant African pressures that threaten to—and may be designed to—wreck orderly evolution in southern Africa. Even without these pressures, the outlook would have been pretty formidable.

The Rhodesian blacks, about six million of them, next to 250,000 whites, are politically and tribally as diverse as the population of any black African state. The prospect of the whites handing over power within two years to a so-called black majority may reveal that there is no such thing. In the process, an Angolan-type civil or tribal war may break out between the Matabeles and the Shonas, leading most likely to the loss of a managerial and specialist elite consisting mainly of whites, a collapse of those economic and other standards associated with civilization, and the creation of another rural slum area in South Africa's vicinity.

In South-West Africa, also, a simple one-man-one-vote system will not work. The largest black group there is the Ovambo people, who have their home immediately south of Angola. The other peoples will not accept Ovambo domination willingly, and it could probably be imposed only by Russian power, exercised brutally through the South-West African People's Organization (SWAPO), a mainly Ovambo tribal movement conducting a terrorist war from Angola. SWAPO, by intensive lobbying, has gained exclusive recognition at the United Nations, and its political wing may have to be granted some say in the multinational constitutional consultation initiated at Windhoek. However, if SWAPO's ambitions are not trimmed, it is all set to become a Marxist agent of disruption and disaster, which may or may not be the aim of its Russian promoters.

This helps to explain why Vorster has opted to work closely with Secretary of State Henry Kissinger. Both Rhodesia and South-West Africa have become superpower concerns as a result of aggressive Russian ambition and planning in the subcontinent.

Afrikaner Nationalists have a natural affinity for the extroverted, friendly, hospitable type of ordinary American, but they also have profound misgivings about some American policies and the workings of the unfamiliar American political system. They are praying — more than really hoping, after Angola—that the United States will in due course come round to the view that what is at stake in southern Africa is not white minority government, apartheid or antiblack fanaticism but the whole structure of Western civilization, threatened by Russian-backed terrorism as vicious, if not yet as sophisticated, as anything in the Arab world or Northern Ireland. It is not to be appeased by outbidding the Marxists in anticolonialist gestures, but can perhaps be countered by understanding and encouraging, by all available means, the genuine evolutionary anticolonialism inherent in Afrikaner Nationalist thinking.

Segregation at a South African railway station. Such "petty apartheid," says the author, is gradually being eliminated.

In South Africa itself, the Vorster Government is committed to moving away from discrimination. Already, overt segregation notices are gradually coming down; post-office apartheid is being dismantled; a number of first-class hotels have been desegregated; multinational sport down to the club level has been sanctioned, and representative South African teams will in future be multiracial. The matter of open churches and theaters is being argued heatedly. South Africa has set its foot on an evolutionary course that, if followed, will eliminate these and other forms of "petty apartheid" and carry our society to a normalization of human relations unthinkable 10 years ago. The exceptions will be measures whose removal can be shown to endanger elementary law and order. This would entail changes in the traditional way of life, more or less along the lines followed in the American South during the last two decades, but with a greater potential for adventurism and backlash, on account of a very different numerical and cultural situation.

Politically, the black homelands policy will have to be pursued with all possible vigor as a means of devolving and decentralizing power among the black peoples. These comparatively backward areas will have to be developed economically much faster than in the past. In South Africa's present circumstances of financial stringency, the homeland leaders themselves are more and more looking for international aid from friendly Western sources, not without modest success and against utterly misguided liberal opposition in Western capitals. As for the constitutional position of the browns and Asians—and of the urban blacks—that will have to be handled in ways still to be properly explored.

The urban blacks, sometimes called the nub of the South African problem, have been promised political rights at municipal level, and conditions for property ownership have recently been eased considerably. Whether and to what extent full citizenship rights should be envisaged for those of them who can be regarded as permanently denationalized—in the sense of not really belonging to any homeland—is probably the most touchy question in South African politics. Nationalist intellectuals are arguing that if there is a comparatively safe way of accommodating the brown minorities in a new constitutional framework, a certain percentage of urbanized blacks may be acceptable under the same or a similar formula. So far, they have met with a firm no from the top.

These intellectuals can by no means be called integrationist in the American sense: While they favor a perspective of full citizenship for browns and some urban blacks, their approach presupposes separate freedoms in viable homelands for the vast majority of blacks. Their "liberalism" excludes any prospect of black majority domination of the white and brown minorities. They, in fact, argue that South Africa is populated by a collection of national minorities, the blacks themselves consisting of a number of distinct peoples, each of whom would resist domination by any of the others.

South Africa's whole internal program, according to present indications, will have to be carried out in the teeth of unceasing Russian and militant African subversion, United Nations propaganda pressures and Western liberal sensitivities concerning human rights and racism.

Will there be time? The recent civil-rights rioting among urban blacks and browns has shaken up South African thinking. Timetables of reform will have to be shortened. At the same time, the question is being posed whether South African society, under constant threat and potential siege, can afford a degree of openness and freedom of expression unique in Africa.

To prophesy in detail how the Afrikaners are likely to react to the problems confronting them would be foolish. But having regard to their Western European makeup, their history of radical adaptation and innovation, and a powerful national ethos based on the belief that they are in Africa for a high purpose transcending their own survival, it is safe to predict that they will give as good an account of themselves as any other people similarly placed. "If we have to go under," runs a somber saying current among Afrikaners in troubled times, "let it be our fate and not our fault." ■

NIGERIA'S DISSIDENT SUPERSTAR

By John Darnton

A flamboyant musician named Fela mixes radical politics with pidgin English in songs so explosive the Government has banned his performances.

Up until five months ago, he was only the best musician in Nigeria — a raucous, insolent, flamboyant superstar, the inventor of the new music called Afro-beat. His morals were the scandal of his countrymen. He lived behind barbed wire in a Western-style commune, smoked pot religiously, called himself "the chief priest" and was idolized by thousands of young Nigerians as a sort of African Bob Dylan. His records, churned out at the rate of six and seven albums a year, were banned on Government radio because of a dispute over copyright payments, but they boomed out of shantytown shops on every other street in the congested capital of Lagos with a subliminal, perhaps even subversive, message, and they sold coast to coast across the continent.

Then, Fela Anikulapo-Kuti became the center of a controversy that rocked the Nigerian Government. Last February, Nigerian Army soldiers attacked his house, burned it, beat him and wounded scores of others, including innocent bystanders. Altogether, some 60 civilians were hospitalized, and Fela was jailed. The case became a cause, and today Fela, though free, is forbidden to perform and is considered Nigeria's foremost dissident. His wild life style and his songs critical of the authoritarian military Government, official corruption and the breakdown of such basic necessities as electricity, telephones and transportation had rankled the ruling officers for years. But his treatment last winter in what is now known as "The Fela Affair" has raised worrisome questions among Nigerians about civil liberties and about the large, undisciplined army that now runs the country — the richest and biggest nation in black Africa — as it prepares to shed 10 years of military control for the uncertain future of civilian rule in 1979.

The affair began on the sultry afternoon of Feb. 18, when a mob of 1,000 soldiers gathered ominously around Fela's house, a two-story yellow building in the sprawling slum of Surulere called "the KalaKuta Republic" (once, while in prison, Fela stayed in a cell nicknamed KalaKuta). Ostensibly, the soldiers were there to arrest some of Fela's "boys" who, after a fight with a lance corporal over a traffic violation, had burned up an army motorcycle. But in reality the soldiers had come for deeper vengeance, goaded beyond endurance by the singer's arrogance: his increasing gibes at the military, his mocking lyrics, his harem of beautiful women and the sea of clenched-fist, black-power salutes that surrounded him wherever he went.

By the time the siege was over, the KalaKuta Republic was burned to the ground. Most of its 60 occupants were in the hospital and so were a number of innocent bystanders who ran past the flames with their arms held straight in the air, a gesture of surrender, but were clubbed anyway by drunken, red-eyed soldiers.

Fela himself, beaten unconscious, was held under armed guard in a hospital room, and as rumors about his condition swept the city, he awoke to find that he had become, overnight, Nigeria's superstar dissident. He promptly flashed a clenched fist for photographers and announced a $40-million damage suit against the army chief of staff. The military Government, shaken, announced a public tribunal to investigate the incident and "apportion blame, if any."

□

A Saturday night before Feb. 18: A block from Fela's home is his nightclub, the Shrine, one of the most notorious underground haunts in international music. It is a ramshackle structure in the courtyard of the seedy Empire Hotel, threaded by open sewage drains and roofed, like most houses in Lagos, with sheets of corrugated metal. The motif is Pan-Africanism: Painted flags of admired sister states — Nkrumah's Ghana, Sékou Touré's Guinea, Nyerere's Tanzania — are peeling off the walls. A four-foot map of Africa, outlined in red neon, hangs over the creaking wooden stage.

At the door, men in sunglasses and four-inch platform shoes make patrons stand, palms out, against the wall, where they are frisked for weapons. On four elevated scaffolds, women undulate to the music, perspiring heavily in the smoky, tropical heat.

The show begins at 1 A.M. Inside the nearby KalaKuta Republic, Fela prepares for it laboriously. From a jar he spoons up liberal doses itter, gooey substance nicknamed "Fela gold," distilled extract of marijuana. A full-length mirror is brought before him and held by two young boys. He slowly slips into skintight sequined pants and a white shirt open to the waist, arranging his strings of juju beads as if he were smoothing a necktie. Members of his Afrika '70 band, scattered about on pillows, stamp out cigar-sized joints and finger their instruments expectantly. Six bodyguards draw near. "Let's go," Fela says, and the entourage moves outside, where there is a crowd of several hundred people. Some have been waiting for hours, clinging to the barbed wire to catch a glimpse of him. He steps out onto the Agege Motor Road and strolls jauntily down the center strip, raising first one fist and then the other. The traffic stops, and drivers get out to return the salutes. As the throng moves to the Shrine a block away, a chant — "Fel-a, Fel-a, Fel-a" — rumbles out of the darkness.

At first glance, Fela seems an unlikely focus for such adulation. At 39, he is not prepossessing, certainly not handsome, slight in stature, with a narrow face, high cheekbones and widely set eyes. But when he moves on stage, in restrained, graceful motions like a coiling snake, and when he sings, hunching over the microphone and spitting out the words, the magnetism is unmistakable in any culture: superstar. He struts, turns his backside, arches an eyebrow, twirls the microphone cord like a whip. He pumps a wailing saxophone and pounds an electric organ whose high notes set the tin roof rattling. The audience, mostly men in their 30's, does not applaud at the end; they raise clenched fists and yell for more.

Westerners first hearing Fela's Afrobeat music find it an acquired taste. The numbers seem too long, often lasting 20 minutes or more, with the brief snatches of lyrics in pidgin English, the lingua franca of the lower classes. Unlike Jamaican reggae, it is difficult to understand without a grounding in fundamentals. There is a heavy, driving sound from an unusual array of instruments: Western drums, trumpets and trombones mixed in with Konga drums, klips sticks and the sekere, a percussion instrument made from a calabash.

□

Fela is the scion of a well-known Nigerian family from Abeokuta, a Yoruba town in the western part of the country.

John Darnton, a New York Times correspondent in Africa, was based in Nigeria until March, when he was expelled while covering Fela's trial.

Drinking a cup of "Fela gold," a marijuana extract, surrounded by some of his harem and members of the band, Fela prepared for a performance in his compound.

His father, the Rev. Ransome-Kuti, now deceased, was perhaps Nigeria's best-known minister and educator. The family was raised with the best of bourgeois aspirations and a respectful eye toward England, the colonial ruler. Two of his brothers became doctors. Fela's mother, Funmilayo, had a rebellious streak, and by independence she had become the country's foremost woman nationalist. Today, she is one of the few women chiefs. She followed Fela's lead in de-Anglicizing the family name: "Ransome" was dropped for "Anikulapo," a name from Yoruba mythology that means "he who carries death in a sack."

Like most aspiring Nigerian musicians in the 50's, Fela began his career playing calypso-influenced high life and imitating the sounds of local stars like Victor Olaiya and Roy Chicago. Then he went to England to study at the London School of Music, where he was exposed to American jazz and fell under the spell of Charlie Parker, John Coltrane and Miles Davis. By combining the bouncy high life and American jazz, he invented Afro-beat, a new sound. Heard live, it becomes habit-forming.

In the late 1960's, Fela left England and returned to Nigeria, but his new Afro-beat sound did not catch on. American jazz is not especially popular in Africa, and even in hybrid form it seemed too ponderous and complicated for the light-hearted dance steps of Lagos music halls.

The turning point of his career seems to have come after he visited the United States in 1969. In San Francisco he met Sandra Isidore, a young woman on the fringes of the Black Panther movement who gave him books to read and introduced him to men who were stirring crowds with radical rhetoric. There were long discussions into the dawn about white oppression, colonialism and revolution. He became politically aware.

"It was incredible how my head was turned. Everything fell into place, man," Fela says. "For the first time, I saw the essence of blackism [black nationalism]. It's crazy; in the States people think the black-power movement drew inspiration from Africa. All these Americans come over here looking for awareness. They don't realize they're the ones who've got it over there. Why, we were even ashamed to go around in national dress until we saw pictures of blacks wearing dashikis on 125th Street.

"I started thinking. I saw how everything works there, everything functions. I saw how great America is. I realized that to be a great man you have to have a great country behind you. I had no country, just a bunch of Africans running around in suits trying to be Englishmen. I decided to come back and try to make my country African."

At the same time, Fela came under the influence of an equally heady stimulant, marijuana. Until then, he recalled, shaking his head at the memory, he had warned his band that any member caught smoking would be expelled. "I used it a couple of times to relax. Then one night I went on stage stoned. Man, I used to just stand there stiff as a stick. My feet were glued to the floor. This night I started jumping, dancing, flying. The music poured out. From now on, I said, we all turn on."

When he returned to Lagos, he underwent the shock of many Nigerians who cross the "Pan Am barrier," seeing for the first time the naked, begging children and the unending sprawl of squalid shacks. It was then that Fela's songs took on their driving force: outrage and irony.

His lyrics do not sound politically radical to Western ears, but they deal with themes that touch Africans to the quick. One of his favorite targets is "colonial mentality," the psychological sense of inferiority, almost as palpable as the legacy of slavery to American blacks, that drives Nigerians to mimic British mannerisms. "African man do de bare African name, African man no de think African style, African man he no be African," Fela sings.*

In "Yellow Fever," one of his most popular songs, he rails against women who use bleaching creams to lighten their complexions. "Fool-ish," the audience chants back, in a litany that parodies the rotelearning of Nigerian schoolrooms, as he sings:

Teacher, teacher
Your precious bleaching
You buy am for shopping for 40 naira
You wan go yellow
You wan go fine now
Your skin go scatter
You go die-o
*You go die-o foolish Africa woman.**

The male counterpart is J.J.D., the Westernized Nigerian who goes to England to study and comes back all airs. "You all know J.J.D.," Fela chatters, introducing the song. "He's the senior brother of J.J.C. — Johnny Just Come. Johnny Just Come wears a necktie" — he grasps his throat and lopes about with buffoon pretension — "Johnny Just Come talk funny. Johnny Just Come always just come from someplace. He just come from Looon-don. He just come from Neew Yoork. He get lost in Jankara market. He got sense and common sense, but he no wise at all."

Increasingly, with homages to Kwame Nkrumah and other Pan-African idols, Fela's songs became overtly political. In "No Bread," the theme is exploitation of Africa. The continent is rich in gold, diamonds and oil, but the African man is no better off than the Lagos night-soil men who carry human excrement in pails upon their heads:

For Africa here him to be home
Land boku from north to south
Food boku from top to down
Gold dey underground like water
Diamond dey underground like sand sand
Oil dey flow underground like river
Everything for oversea
Na from here him dey come
Na for here man still dey
*Carry—for head.**

*Copyright © 1975 Fela Ransome-Kuti.

But the lyrics carry an apocalyptic and-the-last-shall-be-first message that could apply equally to exploitation of Africans by other Africans. Someday, he sings, "who no know go know" — the oppressed will see their oppression — and the hungry monkey's eye will come open:

Everyday everyday
I dey hungry
Everyday everyday
na house to stay
Monkey dey work
baboon dey chop
Baboon dey hold
they key of store
Monkey dey cry
baboon dey laugh
The day monkey eye
*come open now. . . .**

*Copyright © 1976 Fela Anikulapo-Kuti.

Interestingly enough, a song that is most popular among his followers is not about politics at all — directly. It is called "Upside Down," and it has a simple theme: A traveler goes around the world, and everywhere he finds an orderly, functioning system. Telephones work, the lights stay on, the buses run. He comes home to Africa, and here everything is "head for down, *yansh* for up." There are a lot of villages, no roads, a lot of land, no food, a huge area, but no houses, and, of course, education, agriculture, communications, electrical supply, all are "disorganize." These things are the daily lot of all Lagosians. They are often joked about but rarely addressed so directly because they call up a sense of frustration and even shame, and when Fela sings this song, the listeners nod their heads solemnly and look into their beers.

"Most Africans hate to hear themselves compared with the West," Fela says. "When politicians do it, they say, 'We're better than the West,' which nobody believes, or, 'The West has a bunch of racists keeping us down.' I don't say, 'The white man is bad, he's got more than you, go out and kill him.' I say, 'The white man is smart, and so you better get smart. If they're organized, get yourself organized.' "

Fela is not a sophisticated political thinker. One of his heroes, up until recently, has been President Idi Amin of Uganda, for the simple reason that Amin is a titanic figure and, viewed from afar, an African who is strong is an African who leads. Authoritarianism has an appeal for Fela, who, despite his sympathies for the underdog, is in many respects a mirror image of the militaristic society he criticizes. He ruled over the KalaKuta Republic with an iron hand, settling disputes by holding court and meting out sentences — cane lashings for men and a tin shed "jail" for women in the backyard. Members of the commune treat him subserviently, holding his cigarette between puffs and quoting his lyrics like the Gospel. His women are treated little better than slaves. He wants to run for the presidency of Nigeria in 1979 — and he is convinced he can win.

To some degree, these trappings of power account for his popularity among authority-conscious Nigerians. The 5 A.M. climax of the Saturday show at the Shrine:

The lights dim, the Konga drums thunder, and a shrouded figure of death leaps on stage. Fela strips down to the waist and dashes to the center of the room where he "worships" at the shrine itself, a collage of Africana, while his women gyrate on the floor around him, offering themselves. As he symbolically takes them, one by one, a vicarious virility surges through the breathless spectators.

Fela's bullying bodyguards and his zeal for "Nigerian natural grass" — a term that he has coined to replace "Indian hemp," which he views as an outrage upon nationalism — have gotten him into scrapes with the law. He has been arrested some half-dozen times. During a raid in November 1974, the police invaded the compound with tear gas and clubs and were held off for several hours. They got their man, but Fela extracted sweet revenge: He wrote the episode into a best-selling album, "KalaKuta Show," complete with photographs on the back cover showing his scalp wound from a policeman's baton.

In Nigeria, though, the police are not as rough as the military, and in recent months Fela's songs became openly mocking of the armed forces. One recent album, "Zombie," is about robot soldiers blindly following idiotic orders. When he sang it, he marched around the stage with his saxophone tucked against his shoulder like a rifle. The sight cracked up his audience but infuriated the men in nearby Abalti Barracks. On Sunday afternoons, when he laced his show with rambling, pot-inspired diatribes against Christianity and the rich people on Ikoyi Island — a response, no doubt, to his father's sermons — he began saying things no Nigerian newspaper would dare publish. "You think dey go go give up power," he scoffed at the military's promise to hand the Government over to the civilians in 1979. Then, lapsing into Oxford English, "Tell me, what African man in a uniform with shiny brass buttons has ever done that?"

He quit the Second World Black and African Festival of Arts and Culture after a dispute with the military men running it, and mocked the Government's program to unsnarl the Lagos traffic jam by posting military policemen on the streets with horsewhips to beat dawdling motorists. When the Government launched a program called "Operation Feed the Nation," he relabeled it "Operation Beat the Nation."

"The Government won't touch me," he said at the time. "For one thing, they think I'm crazy. If I were a respectable professor at a university saying these things, that would be something different. But to them, I'm just a musician, a crazy artist saying a lot of crazy things. And then they take a look at what I stand for — nationalism, Pan-Africanism, anti-colonialism. These are things they say they stand for. So if they come down on me, they would be coming down on themselves."

That was just a few weeks before the afternoon of Feb. 18.

After more than a decade of military rule, Nigerians have become accustomed to occasional abuses of power from "the boys" in the army. Sometimes, during the lean days just before payday, a soldier will threaten a civilian with some imagined offense to receive a bit of "dash," or bribe. Men in uniform have been known to set up roadblocks to engage in highway robbery; the Government claims they are imposters and, to stop the practice, has outlawed army-colored green cars for civilians.

These are seen as nothing more than irritations, really, accepted within the ethos of fatalism expressed by the phrase, uttered with a shrug, "This Nigeria." While heavy-handed, the military regime is not repressive or dictatorial along the lines of a Latin American banana republic. When it embarks on a program that meets public resistance, it persuades and cajoles and, if need be, backs down. If an honest poll could be taken, perhaps a majority — excluding journalists, intellectuals and bureaucrats — would want the military to stay on, since the memories of chaos and strife in the pre-1966 days of civilian government are still vivid.

Nigeria emerged from the Biafran war in 1970 with the largest standing army in black Africa, with no debts, an abiding suspicion of Western journalists and a sense of self-confidence. She became the big, bold country of black Africa, the one whose size and resources enabled her to stand up to both West and East. Foreign businesssmen who flocked there and encountered venal bureaucrats, torrid heat and the traffic jam euphemistically called the "Go Slow," put up with it all in the name of money, of which more could be made, faster, than anywhere else on the continent. Throughout West Africa a caricature sprang up-the "ugly Nigerian," who pushes to the front of the airline counter, berates the hotel clerk and tosses his money around — a stereotype Fela sings about. It was prompted by envy, of course, and was simply testimony to Nigeria's growing naira-power.

Careering along on two million barrels of sulfur-low oil pumped every day from the lush Niger Delta, Nigeria's currency is stronger than the British pound and her external holdings enough to precipitate a run on it. Her gross national product, $27 billion last year, is expected to outstrip South Africa's in a year ot two. Her population of between 70 million and 80 million — the figure is imprecise because there is no reliable census — means that one out of every four Africans is a Nigerian.

But her size is matched by her problems, and toward the end of the nine-year rule of Gen. Yakubu Gowon, who presided over a harmonious postwar reconciliation, the problems gained the upper hand. Corruption became rife, and there was government drift and scandal, epitomized by the placement of orders for 20 million tons of cement, which paralyzed Lagos harbor and made prideful Nigeria a laughing-stock among businessmen around the world. Gowon reneged on his pledge to return the country to civilian rule, and when he was ousted in a bloodless coup in July 1975, there was jubilation.

His successor, Gen. Murtala Muhammed, instilled a sense of purpose and discipline into national life with a flurry of decisions from Dodan Barracks, the military headquarters. He fired corrupt state governors, announced plans to move the capital and created seven new states, thus further eroding the power bases of the three major tribes, the Yorubas, Hausas and Ibos. He fired thousands of incompetent civil servants, appointed a constitutional drafting committee and promised civilian rule for October 1979. He began clearing up the port backlog and even made some headway against the traffic congestion.

Lincolnesque legends, shaped by the travail of everyday life in Lagos, grew up around him: In civilian clothes, he entered a post office to buy stamps with a five-naira ($8) note. Rebuffed at every window because he did not have exact change, he retraced his steps and fired every teller. In foreign policy, the Government dropped a low profile, with the vigorous backing of Agostinho Neto's faction in the Angolan civil war. In the West, this was read as a leftward tilt, but it was really a move toward honest nonalignment, although it was soon accompanied by an outpouring of anti-Americanism, jingoism and paranoia about the C.I.A.

The Supreme Military Council, the body of officers that runs the country, declared, rightfully, that it had no ideology. Into the vacuum rushed a new nationalism and symbols for it were searched out. A new national anthem was commissioned, because the old one was composed by an Englishwoman.

The withdrawal of Nigerian athletes from the Montreal Olympics was touted as a military operation comparable to the Israeli raid upon Entebbe Airport. Nigeria, where capitalism thrives in its rawest form, identified herself rhetorically with the "progressive" African nations. Newspapers began speaking of the Nigerian "revolution"; they meant that things seemed to be getting done. The "amazing 201 days" of Muhammed came to an end with his assassination, while caught in a traffic jam, during an abortive coup on Feb. 13, 1976. The plotters were largely disgruntled junior officers, reportedly communicating with Gowon, who was then in exile. Their half-baked scheme plunged Nigeria into a crisis of self-confidence it has yet to slough off. Under the new head of state, Lieut. Gen. Olusegun Obasanjo, Muhammed's policies are being followed, but the image of dynamic leadership has evaporated.

With two coups, an attempted coup and ever-present rumors of coups to come, a curious mythology has evolved to explain their success or failure. According to this thesis, the coup against Gowon triumphed because his Government had lost "the support of the people," in the same way that the coup against Muhammed floundered because his Government retained that support. In both instances, of course, the people cleared off the streets and had nothing to do with the outcome whatsoever.

The myth is perhaps dangerous, for it created the illusion of almost democratic participation where none exists, and on the day two years hence when civilian rule does come, the tensions unleashed in campaigns and elections will seem anarchic compared with the placid days of military leadership. The myth has a corollary in the notion that Nigeria's problems are so vast that only the military can handle them.

It is true that the problems seem overwhelming. The people are deserting the land and flooding into the cities, unemployment and inflation are running rampant, agricultural production is declining and the infrastructure — telephones, lights and water supply — is crumbling under the weight of the demands placed upon it. To some degree, these are problems not of underdevelopment but of an overly rapid development, fueled by the mixed blessing of oil revenues. At the root of Nigeria's malady is the simple fact that so far the development has not bettered the existence of most of its people: One-half of 1 percent of the population controls 75 percent of the wealth. Without massive redistribution, it is impossible to imagine any long-term stability.

Nigeria, like the rest of black Africa, is still trying to figure out a way to rule itself. The political modes inherited from the colonizers have clearly failed, but the political aspirations linger on, and so a search for some workable format of civilian rule continues. The constitutional drafting committee has chosen the American Presidential mode, on the principle that a strong central executive is required. But the supporting institutions — a strong judiciary, a free press and a system of national, not tribal, political parties — are not there.

The ability of a civilian regime to cope with instability is doubtful because the military has not accomplished two tasks necessary for a civilian regime to survive. It has not performed a census, so that the competing ethnic groups can agree on their respective representations in a national assembly. And it has not demobilized itself, because this would invite another coup attempt. Thus, the politicians who take office in early 1980 will be faced with a 250,000-man army that has a history of usurping power and that commands the respect, though not the affection, of a great many Nigerians.

In this context, the arrest and beating of a dissident musician was an alarming omen. As one Nigerian journalist remarked, privately, "If the commanders can't control their own troops, then who can?"

The first sign that the army raid on Fela's compound had struck a nerve was the fact that the Government-owned, mass-circulation Daily Times did not print a word about it the following morning. When it did the day after, it highlighted the Government's version: The soldiers had come to make a legitimate arrest. Because the barbed wire was electrified, they prevailed upon the electric company to turn the power off. Fela's gang then set up a portable generator to re-electrify it, the generator somehow short-circuited, and the house caught fire.

This was an explanation that not even the gullible could swallow, and it was not surprising a few days later when the Nigerian Bar Association offered its services to any civilian harassed or harmed by the military.

Fela was held on two charges — not preventing his boys from attacking a motorcycle, and being in possession of a rifle. Conviction on the latter charge could bring a prison term of up to five years. Fela claimed the rifle was planted as an afterthought by the soldiers, and he noted pointedly that it seemed to have been the only object to have survived the blaze. He was released on bail and then, walking down the courthouse steps in bandages, was promptly rearrested, this time under a special state security law not open to challenge in any court. After pleas from his lawyer, Tunji Braithwait, that a public tribunal that did not hear from him would be a mockery, the Government released him again.

The tribunal was convened in the new national theater built for the black arts festival. It had two members, a court justice and an air-force wing commander. Security was tight: Spectators were searched thoroughly at the doors. Although the proceedings were in theory open, when this correspondent attended, he was evicted by the police and the following day was arrested and expelled from the country.

The panel sat day after day, taking testimony from 183 witnesses. Among them were firemen, who said the soldiers turned them back when they came to fight the fire, and neighbors, who said they saw soldiers carrying jerrycans presumably filled with gasoline. A photograph of this was introduced. Fela's women, who had been stripped and carted naked to the police station, charged that they were raped.

The tribunal's report was most acceptable to the Lagos state government, which issued a "white paper" incorporating its findings and recommendations. It said the fire was started unintentionally by "an exasperated and unknown" soldier. It rejected the charges of sexual abuse. Some soldiers were no doubt "overzealous," but the real fault lay with the police for "the levity with which they treated allegations of crimes reported against Mr. Fela Anikulapo-Kuti." Since there was no hope that KalaKuta house and the military barracks could co-exist peacefully, it suggested moving one or the other — preferably the former. Finally, it condemned Fela for using the word "republic" to describe his domain "in defiance of the Constitution" and suggested that the Government probe his political activities.

The white paper ended: "Government wishes to point out that no single individual, no matter how powerful or popular, can set himself above the laws of the land and Government will not allow or tolerate the existence of a situation which is capable of undermining the very basis of civilized society." The warning was not directed to a military commander. It was directed to Fela. And to drive it home, perhaps, the Government decided to close down the Shrine for good.

Since February, Fela has not been allowed to perform in public, although he is appealing the court orders that prohibit it. The KalaKuta Republic was bought by the Government. Fela will not be able to return to it and he is now living in a Lagos hotel. Fela's lawyer, Tunji Braithwait, says Fela is planning to cut a new record, though his records are banned on Government radio. Still, the Government has made Fela more than a superstar; he is now a symbol, more powerful than ever before. And they can't stop little shantytown shops from booming out either the Fela Afrobeat or Fela's defiant message. ■

July 24, 1977

Suggested Reading

For those readers whose interest in the history and culture of Africa might have been excited by this volume, a select bibliography is appended. Among the best available general books on Africa are:

Cartey, Wilfred, and Martin, Kilson. *The Africa Reader* 2 vols., Colonial and Independent Africa. New York: Vintage Books, 1971.

Gibbs, James, ed. *The Peoples of Africa.* New York: Holt, Rinehart and Winston, 1965.

Hatch, John. *A History of Postwar Africa.* New York: Frederick A. Praeger, 1965.

The Horizon History of Africa. New York: American Heritage Publishing Co. Inc. 1971.

July, Robert. *A History of the African People.* New York: Charles Scribner's Sons, 1970.

McKay Vernon. *Africa in World Politics.* New York: Harper and Row, 1963.

Murphy, E. Jefferson. *History of African Civilization.* New York: Thomas Y. Crowell, 1972.

Oliver, R., and J. D. Fage. *A Short History of Africa.* Baltimore: Penguin, 1962.

Rotberg, Robert I., and Ali A. Mazrui. *Protest and Power in Black Africa.* New York: Oxford University Press, 1970.

Thompson, V. B. *Africa and Unity: The Evolution of Pan-Africanism.* New York: Humanities Press, 1969.

West Africa

Crowder, Michael. *West Africa Under Colonial Rule.* Evanston, Ill.: Northwestern University Press, 1968.

Webster, J. B., and A. A. Boahen. *A History of West Africa: The Revolutionary Years.* New York: Frederick Praeger, 1967.

Central Africa

Keatley, P. *The Politics of Partnership.* Baltimore: Penguin, 1963.

Lumumba, Patrice. *Congo My Country.* London: Pall Mall Press, 1962.

Marcum, John. *The Angolan Revolution.* Cambridge, Mass.: M.I.T. Press, 1969.

Slade, Ruth. *The Belgian Congo.* New York: Oxford University Press, 1962.

East Africa

Barnett, Donald. *Mau Mau From Within.* London: MacGibbon and Kee, 1966.

Ingham, Kenneth. *A History of East Africa.* New York: Frederick Praeger, 1965.

Ogot, B. A., and J. A. Kiernan, eds. *A Survey of East African History.* Humanities Press, 1969.

South Africa

Carter, Gwendolen M. *The Politics of Inequality: South Africa Since 1948.* New York: Frederick Praeger, 1958.

Luthuli, Albert. *Let My People Go.* New York: McGraw Hill, 1962.

Roux, Edward. *Time Longer Than Rope: A History of the Black Man's Struggle for Freedom in South Africa.* Madison: University of Wisconsin Press, 1964.

Wilson, M., and L. Thompson. *The Oxford History of South Africa.* 2 vols. New York: Oxford University Press, 1966 and 1971.

African Biographies

Ayandele, E. A. *"Holy" Johnson.* London: Frank Cass, 1970.

Bennett, Norman. *Mirambo of Tanzania.* New York: Oxford University Press, 1971.

Fyfe, Christopher. *Africanus Beale Horton, West African Scientist and Patriot.* New York: Oxford University Press, 1972.

Haliburton, Gordon. *The Prophet Harris.* New York: Oxford University Press, 1973.

Lynch, Hollis R. *Edward Wilmot Blyden, Pan-Negro Patriot.* New York: Oxford University Press, 1967.

Weinstein, Brian. *Felix Eboué.* New York: Oxford University Press, 1972.

Index

Abako, 136–40, 142
Abazi Party, 140
Abbookuta, 6
Abrahams, Peter, 500
Acheampong, Col. I.K., 353
Action Group, 87, 89
Adebo, S. O., 274, 327–29
Aderemi, Sir Adesoji, 90
Adoula, Cyrille, 139, 156, 158–59, 167, 171
Adowa, Battle of, 36, 49
Africa, partition of, 9–11, 36
African Charter of Casablanca, 442, 444
African Democratic Rally, 68, 122, 125, 128
African International Association, 2–5
African National Congress (South African): and day of prayer, 178; support of United Party, 182; opposition to resettlement, 187; and proposed boycott, 194; and Sharpeville riots, 196–98; strike call, 201; early history of, 202–03
African Solidarity Party, 140
Aguiyi-Ironsi, Maj. Gen. Johnson, 360, 362
Ahidjo, Ahmadou, 419
Ahmadu, Sardauna, 88, 90
Aidoo, Ama Ata, 500
All People's Congress Party (Sierra Leone), 94
Amin, Idi, 389, 392–94
Anglo-Portuguese Convention (1884), 4
Angola: forced labor in, 42; U.S. aid to, 281, 288; population distribution of, 289–90; rebels attack prisons in, 292; revolutionary organizations in, 294; Bakongo tribe of, 296–97, 310; Portuguese army strategy in, 296–97; business men criticize Lisbon policy, 298; rebels trained by Algerians, 298–99; rebels form government in exile, 299; rebels receive Congo base, 300; rebels factionalism in, 300–01; importance of coffee in, 303; importance of oil in, 310; General League of Angolan Workers in, 308
Ankrah, Lieut. Gen. Joseph A., 349–50
Ansah, Owusu, 341
Anya'nya (Sudanese rebels), 408–12
Apartheid, 176–231 *passim:* description of, 179; and Negro resettlement, 186–88; extension of, 192–94; word dropped, 209; and black women, 229
Appiah, Joseph, 341
Arab-African tensions: in Ghana, leading to Moslem deportations, 341; in Zanzibar, 381–83; in Tanganyika, 383; in Ethiopia, 406; in Sudan, 408–12
Arden-Clarke, Sir Charles, 79–82, 84, 87
Armah, Avi Kwei, 500
Art, 485–87, 491–93
Arusha, 7
Asfa-Wossen, Crown Prince of Ethiopia, 404–05
Ashanti, 83–84
Asian-African Solidarity Conference, 125
Asians: British denial of rights to, in Kenya Colony, 39; in South Africa, 224–25; Kenya policy toward, 385; under Ugandan threats, 394; population estimates of, in Uganda, 395; in Kenya, 398–401
Awolowo, Obafemi, 89, 92, 360–61
Awoonor, Kofi, 500
Azikiwe, Dr. Nnamdi 89, 92, 360, 362, 366

Badoglio, Marshal Pietro, 55, 57
Baganda, 98–99
Bahutu: tribal war with Watusi, 134–35; *see also* Hutu
Bakongo, 138, 142, 296–97, 310
Balewa, Sir Abubakar Tafawa, 88–90, 92–93, 252, 360–62
Ballinger, Margaret, 178, 182
Baluba, 140–42, 150, 157

Banda, Dr. H. Kamuzu, 230, 246–50, 257, 262
Bantu', 46–47, 202–04, 468–70
Bantustans', 194, 212
Barclay, Edwin James, 376
Baring, Sir Evelyn, 109–10
Basutoland, 236; *see also* Lesotho
Baudouin, King of Belgium, 137, 139–40, 145
Bayaka, 142
Bechuanaland, 69–71, 236; *see also* Botswana
Belgian Congo, 68, 71–2, 136–37, 139, 140–42; *see also* Congo (Republic of the), Congo Free State, Zaire Republic
Belgium: and claims in Congo, 3; and partition of Africa, 11; and annexation of Congo Free State, 15; mandate of German East Africa to, 33; African possessions, 59–60; report on Ruanda-Urundi in UN, 64; aid to Congo and Ruanda-Urundi, 68; and Ruanda-Urundi, 134–35; Congo policy, 136–37; and Katanga secession, 146–50; sends troops to Congo, 168–69
Bello, Sir Alhaji Ahmadu, 92–93
Benson, Sir Arthur, 249–50
Berlin International Conference, 3–5, 37
Biafra: declaration of independence of, 363; economic blockade of, 368; starvation in, 369–70, 372–74; unsupported by African nations, 370; reports rape and looting, 372–73; capitulation to Nigeria, 371–72; condition of women in, 374
Bismarck, Prince Otto von, 3, 5, 9
Black Sash, 229
Blundell, Sir Michael, 111–12, 119
Boers, 18–24
Boer War, 25–29
Bokassa, Jean Bedel, 421
Bolikango, Jean, 144, 156, 158
Bomboko, Justin, 153, 156, 158
Botha, Gen. Louis, 29–32
Botswana, 237, 239–40, 275, 337; *see also* Bechuanaland
British Cameroons, 64, 88, 90; *see also* Cameroon, French Cameroons
British East Africa (census), 67
British East Africa Company, 7–8, 10
British Somaliland, 121
British South Africa Company, 20–22, 24
British Togoland, 64, 82, 85; *see also* French Togoland, Togoland
Broederbond, 189, 204
Buganda, 98–99
Bunche, Dr. Ralph J., 146–47, 151
Burns, Sir Alan, 66, 72
Burundi, 135, 337, 430
Bushongo, 140
Busia, Dr. Kofi A., 84, 332, 351–53
Buthelezi, Gatsha, 222, 224–25

Cabral, Amilcar, 314–17
Cameron, Sir Donald, 46
Cameroon, 30–33, 415–16, 419–20; *see also* British Cameroons, French Cameroons
Cape Colony, 18–20, 24, 29
Cape Coloreds, 176, 191, 226–27
Cape-to-Cairo Railway, 35
Carnegie Corporation, 72–73
Central African Federation, *see* Federation of Rhodesia and Nyasaland
Central African Republic (Ubangi-Shari), 130, 132, 421
Chad: exports beef by airlines, 123–24; votes for federation with France, 127; as autonomous republic, 129; independence of, 132; and low GNP, 337; economic development of, 416–17; uses French troops to quell revolt, 420–23
Chamberlain, Joseph, 22–25, 28
China, 386, 456, 458–9
Chinese, 226, 386
Chou En-lai, 456
Churchill, Winston, 27, 61
Cocoa, 83–85
Colonialism (evaluation), 76–78
Coloreds, *see* Cape Coloreds
Communists: expelled from Ghana, 349; in Guinea, 355–56; role of, in Zanzibar revolt, 382
Comore Islands, 126–27, 130
CONACO (Congolese National Convention), 169–70
CONAKAT (Confederation of Associations of Katanga), 142, 164
Congo Free State, 4–5, 15–16; *see also* Belgian Congo, Congo (Republic of the), Zaire Republic
Congolese National Movement, 138–40
Congo Republic, 129, 132
Congo, Republic of the: contrasted with Nigeria, 91; independence of, 145; and Katanga secession, 146–51, 159, 165–66; economic crisis in, 148; and secessionist movement in Kasai, 150–51; coup in (1960), 152; military regime in, 153–56; tribalism in, 162; and rebellion in Kwilu, 166; use of South African and Rhodesian mercenaries, 167–69; coup in (1965), 170; and UN Rhodesia sanctions, 275; and refugee problem, 337; and high unemployment, 338; students from, in Cuba, 382; keeps French influence, 424; mercenary revolt aborted in, 425; Belgian interests in, 426–27; changes name to Zaire Republic, 427; *see also* Belgian Congo, Congo Free State, Zaire Republic
Congo River, 2–5
Convention People's Party, 79, 82, 84–85
Council of the Entente (Ivory Coast, Niger, Dahomey, and Volta), 131–32
Crowther, Bishop Samuel (Adjai), 6
Cuba: role of in Zanzibar revolt, 382

Dahomey, 8, 127, 130, 131, 337
De Gaulle, Charles, 125–27, 131–33
Devonshire Declaration, 119
Diori, Hamani, 418
Djoumessi, Mathias, 69
DuBois, Dr. W.E.B., 438
Duka-Wallas, *see* Asians
Dupont, Clifford W., 277

East Africa, 396, 398, 446–47
Economic development and planning: and foreign aid appropriations, 336; in Ghana, 83, 350; in Guinea,

356; in Nigeria, 374; in Liberia, 377–78; in Uganda, 393; in Ethiopia, 405–06; in Ivory Coast, 414; in Zambia, 432–36; linked to cultural change, 479–81
Economic unity, 334–35, 396, 398, 442
Education, 95, 333–34, 384, 411
Endeley, Dr. E. M. I., 88
Erasmus, Francois C. 197, 199, 201
Ethiopia (Abyssinia): and Italian colonial ambitions, 11–13; as independent republic, 36; Italian ambitions in, 49–51; Italian conquest of, 54–58; gets development loans from World Bank, 71; suit over South-West Africa, 232–33; and refugee problem, 337; new constitution in, 403; attempted coup in, 404–05; foreign investments in, 406–07; codes reform surnames in, 482
Ethiopianism, 2
Ewe nationalist movement, 82

Federation of Rhodesia and Nyasaland (Central African Federation): formation of, 241–43; African nationalism in, 244–45; Nationalist riots in, 246–47; African nationalism in, 248–51; collapse of, 252–53, 257–58; *see also* Northern Rhodesia, Nyasaland, Southern Rhodesia
Ffrench-Beytagh, Very Rev. Gonville A., 231
Field, Winston, 258–59
Foreign aid: British, 325–26, 383, 364; United States, 326, 346, 358; to revolutionary Guinea, 335; from former colonizing nations, 336; Chinese, 458–59
France: and claims in Congo, 2–3; and colonial activity in West Africa, 8; and partition of Africa, 10–11; and colonial claims in West Africa, 14; gains Moroccan protectorate, 17; mandate of Cameroons and Togoland to, 33; sovereignty over Sahara, Morocco, Algeria, Tunis, and Madagascar, 36; and colonial policy of assimilation, 48–49; interests in Ethiopia, 50; African possessions, 59–60; and colonial policy of assimilation, 69; policy of assimilation, 122; sends troops to Cameroons, 124; invests in Ivory Coast, 414; role of, in Chad and Gabon, 415–17; maintains African forces, 420–23; influence on socialist Congo, 424
French Cameroons, 69, 124–25, 128, 130; *see also* British Cameroons, Cameroon
French Equatorial Africa, 124–27, 130–31
French Somaliland, 126–27, 130
French Togoland, 82, 124, 127; *see also* British Togoland, Togoland
French West Africa, 68, 122–27; *see also* Mali Federation
Fulani, 92

Gabon, 129, 132, 413, 415–17, 420
Gambia, 94, 336–37
Gandhi, Mohandas K., 61, 224
Garvey, Marcus, 32, 438
German East Africa Company, 7–8
Germany: and claims in Congo, 3; and partition of East and Central Africa, 9–11; colonial concessions for recognition of French protectorate in Morocco, 17; and protest of British invasion of Transvaal, 22–23; and loss of African colonies in World War I 30–33; and trade with Ethiopia, 50
Ghana: independence of, 85–86; one-party rule in 320, 330, 343, 347–48; and neo-colonialism, 336; and refugee problem, 337; bars parochial parties, 341; becomes a republic, 342; legislates against Nkrumah foes, 344; foreign policy of, 346; becoming a Marxist state, 347; military coup in, 349–50; national debt of, 351; elections in, 351; economic policies in, 352; students from, in Cuba, 382; summit attempt fails in, 439; signs Union of African States charter, 443; *see also* Gold Coast, Kwame Nkrumah
Gizenga, Antoine, 155, 158–59, 161, 167
Gold Coast: riots against British in, 66; moves toward independence, 79–85; exports of, 80; early federation hopes in, 439; tribalism ebbs in, 462; *see also* Ghana
Gowon, Lieut. Col. Yakubu, 360–64, 371, 374
Great Britain: and partition of Africa, 3, 9–11, 14, 59–60; and colonial trade, 8, 34–37; and South Africa, 18–25, 209, 225; and the Boer War, 25–29; and East Africa, 33, 39, 40–41, 46, 96, 100–01; colonial policy of, 48–49, 64, 69–70; and Ethiopia, 50; and colonial aid, 61, 63; and trust territories, 66, 72; and West Africa, 79, 81, 87, 89; and protectorates, 236; and Federation of Rhodesia and Nyasaland, 241–43, 247, 258; and Rhodesian independence, 259, 266–67, 271, 278–80; investments and trade, 325–326; interest of, in Nigeria, 364; sends troops to Kenya, Tanganyika and Uganda, 379; role of in Zanzibar revolt, 381; investments in Tanzania, 383; relations with Uganda, 394; interests in Ethiopia, 407
Gross National Product in poor African nations, 337
Guinea: Communist bloc agents settling in, 93; chooses independence, 125–27; intention to unite with Ghana, 129; relations with Soviet Union and People's Republic of China, 133; one-party rule discussed, 320; and regional economy, 335; and low GNP, 337; Communists in, 355–56; under socialism, 357; invaded by Portugal, 358; signs Union of African States charter, 443; and aid from United States, Soviet Union and China, 452–53; bans traditional women's dress, 463; *see also* Sékou Touré

Hamadi, Mohammed Shamte, 380
Hammarskjold, Dag, 146, 149–51, 153, 160, 201
Hanga, Kassim, 380
Hausa, 92, 359, 361–63, 366–67
Hertzog, General J. M. B., 43, 177
Hottentots (Bondels), 39
Houphouet-Boigny, Felix, 68, 122, 125, 128, 449
Huggins, Sir Godfrey, 241–42
Hutu, 427–32, 464

Ibo, 92, 361–72, 374–75
Ileo, Joseph, 53, 155–56, 158
Islam, 73, 485
Israel, 394, 442–43
Italy: and frustration of colonial ambitions in Ethiopia (Abyssinia), 11–13; sovereignty over Somaliland

and Libya (Tripoli), 36; as late-comer in Africa, 48; and designs on Ethiopia, 49–51; conquest of Ethiopia, 54–58; and possessions in Africa - Libya, Eritrea, Ethiopia, Italian Somaliland (Italian East Africa), 59–60
Ivory Coast: riots in, 68; allegiance to French federal community, 125; votes for federation with France, 127; as autonomous republic, 130; independence of, 131; and neo-colonialism, 336; unemployment in, 338; economy under French, 414; laws eliminate matriarchy in, 490

Jameson, Sir Leander Starr, 22–23
Jawara, David K., 94
Jonathan, Leabua, 237

Kalonji, Albert, 140–42, 150, 157, 167
Karume, Abeid Amani, 380–84, 386–87
Kasavubu, Joseph: Abako president, 139–40; and Congo independence, 143–45; and Katanga secession, 146–47, 151; backed by Congo military regime, 152–55; names provisional government, 156; and draft constitution, 157; and election of Adoula, 158; signs bills stripping Tshombe of power, 166; names Tshombe head of transition government, 167; dismisses Tshombe government, 169; deposed in coup, 170
Kasongo, Joseph, 144
Katanga, 146–51, 157, 159, 161, 165–66
Kaunda, Kenneth: and Congo resolution backing UN, 166; head of African National Congress, 245; president of Zambia African National Congress, 248–50; campaign of civil disobedience, 255–56; plan to secede, 258; becomes President of Zambia, 263; and Rhodesia, 272; President of Zambia, 434–37
Kayibanda, Gregoire, 134–35, 429
Kennedy, John F., 166, 299, 380
Kenya: British denial of Indian rights in, 39; British educational progress in, 40–41; Mau Mau rebellion in, 100–08; multi-racial government in, 109–12; independence of, 120; and regional economy, 334; and neo-colonialism, 336; unemployment in, 338, 396; mutiny disarmed by British, 379; students in Cuba, 382; Indian business outlawed in, 385; in East Africa common market, 396; teaches socialism, 397; halts Asian purge, 401; Mboya killed in, 402; declares Swahili official language, 403; bride price in, 484, 493–95
Kenya African Democratic Union, 112–13, 117, 120
Kenya African Union: headed by Kenyatta, 101; outlawed, 105; emerges as dominant party, 112; backed by Kikuyu, 113; replaces Kikuyu Central Association, 114; majority party, 117; manifesto of, 118–19; increases majority, 120
Kenya Somalis, 116
Kenyatta, Jomo: British arrest of, 101; sentenced for alleged Mau Mau activity, 103; as leader of African Union, 105; and Kenya's future, 112–15; becomes Prime Minister, 116–17; and Kenya independence, 120; and Congo resolution backing UN, 166; requests British troops, 379; opens socialist school, 397; and Kikuyu tribalism, 402
Khama, Seretse, 69–71, 237, 239–40
Khrushchev, Nikita, 147–48
Kibanguism, 144
Kikuyu: and Mau Mau rebellion, 100–08; friction in, between Mau Mau and non, 112; and politics, 113–15; tribesman kills Mboya, 402–03; customs of, 476–77; traditions of, 494
Kikuyu Central Association, 55, 101, 105, 114
Kimba, Evariste, 169–70
Kimble, George H.T., 323–24
Kruger, Pres. Paul, 20–23, 25, 28

League of Nations: and World War I mandates, 33; and mandate responsibility, 37; and concern with Hottentot revolt over dog tax, 39; appeal to, over forced labor in Angola, 42; and Italian invasion of Ethiopia, 55; ineffectiveness in Ethiopia, 56
Leopold II, King of Belgium, 2–6, 15–17, 138
Lesotho, 237, 337; *see also* Basutoland
Liberia, 35–36, 59, 232–33, 336, 376–78
Lloyd George, David, 33
Louw, Eric H., 176, 208–09, 232
Lulua, 140–42, 150
Lumumba, Patrice: president of part of Congolese National Movement, 139–41; and Congo independence, 143–45; and Katanga secession, 146–47; and Kasai and Katanga secession, 150–51; ousted as premier, 152–53; arrested, 154–55; murdered, 156–57; and Pan-Africanism, 162; Kenya school dedicated to, 397; African Charter of Casablanca backs, 443
Luthuli, Albert, 194–95, 198–99, 203, 206–07
Lyttelton, Oliver, 81–82, 88, 95, 98, 101, 109, 241–42

Madagascar, 124–128, 420; *see also* Malagasy Republic
Macmillan, Harold, 252
Makonde, 311
Malagasy Republic (Madagascar), 131; *see also* Madagascar
Malan, Daniel F.: Belgian view of, 72; Gold Coast as contrast to Malanism, 81; becomes Prime Minister of South Africa, 176; racial plans stymied by court, 180; election victory of, 181; and militarization of Africa, 183; resigns as Prime Minister, 184; and Broederbond, 204; and British protectorates, 236
Malawi, 230, 262, 275, 337; *see also* Nyasaland
Mali, 382, 413, 443
Mali Federation, 130–31, 132; *see also* French West Africa
Mandela, Nelson R., 214
Marealle, Thomas Lenana Mlanga, 96
Margai, Albert, 93
Margai, Sir Milton, 93–94
Masai, 7, 475–76
Matabele, 11
Mauritania, 129, 132–33
Mawema, Michael, 252
Mau Mau, 100–11, 114
Mbadiwe, K. Ozuomba, 64
Mboya, Tom: at Uganda independence, 100; general secretary of Kenya Federation of Labor, 110; leader of Kenya Independence Movement, 111; leader of Kenya African National Union, 112; ends jury trials,

117; on whites in Kenya, 118–19; directs "African Socialism" project, 397; assassinated, 402; head of Kenya Federation of Labor, 441
Menelick, emperor of Ethiopia (Abyssinia), 11–13, 49–52
Micombero, Lieut. Col. Michel, 430–32
Missionaries, 6–7, 147
Mobutu, Gen. Joseph: heads Congo military regime, 152–56; releases Tshombe, 158; remains army head under Tshombe, 167; becomes President in coup, 170; and C.I.A., 171; President of Congo, 425–26
Monckton Commission report, 253
Mondlane, Dr. Eduardo, 311–13
Moslems, 58, 87, 90
Mozambique: rebellion in, 13; U.S. aid to, 281; Catholic influence on, 282, 284; land policy in, 283; Portuguese paternalism in, 284, 288, 291; forced labor in, 285; reforms planned by Portugal, 285; whites urge autonomy in, 287; population distribution in, 289–90; Portuguese strategy in, 311–12
Mulele, Pierre, 166
Munongo, Godefroid, 159, 164, 167
Mussolini, Benito, 49–50, 55, 57–59
Mutesa II, Kabaka of Buganda, 98–99, 387–89

Namibia, *see* South-West Africa
Nasser, Gamal Abdel, 440–42
Natal, 18–19, 26–29
National Council of Nigeria and Cameroons, 89
National Democratic Party (Southern Rhodesia), 252
National Front for the Liberation of Angola, 299–300
Nationalist Party (South Africa): as governing party, 176; and apartheid, 179; election victory of, 181; and packing of Supreme Court and Senate, 189; and Verwoerd's election, 192; tie with Broederbond, 204; internal divisions in, 219; loss of support, 221
Nationalized industry: in Tanzania, 336, 384, 386; in Zambia, 336, 436; Nkrumah against, 346; lags in Guinea, 356; Idi Amin curbs, 393; and Congolese socialism, 424
National Liberation Committee (Congo), 166–67
National Liberation Movement (Gold Coast), 83–84
National Progress Party (Congo), 139, 141
Negritude, 496
Netherlands, the, 3, 18
Ngouabi, Maj. Marien, 424
Nguvulu, Alphonse, 140
Niger, 126, 131, 337, 418, 420
Niger Convention, 14
Nigeria: riots in, 87; federation of, 88–89; independence of, 90–93; economic development, 333–34; and neo-colonialism, 336; tribalism in, 328, 359, 361–71; becomes British Commonwealth republic, 359; civil war in, 363–72; elections disputed in, 359–60; provisional government in, 360; Army takeover and revolts, 360–362; importance of oil in, 364, 374–75; starvation of Ibos in, 369–70, 372–74; "Nigerianization" of economy, 375; early federation hopes in, 439; unemployment in, 480
Nixon, Richard M., 85–86, 278, 377, 451
Nkomo, Joshua, 253–54, 260, 266, 268–70
Nkrumah, Kwame: demands annexation of Togoland, 73; Gold Coast independence, 79–85; and establishment of Ghana, 86–87; and Uganda nationalists, 99; warns opposition, 341; personality cult of, 342–46; escapes assassin, 347–48; ousted by army, 349; dies in exile, 353; Ghana's Prime Minister, 439–43, 445; criticized by Nyerere, 448; warns of non-African defense, 453; stresses "African personality", 471
Nkumbula, Harry, 250–51, 258
Northern People's Congress (Nigeria), 87–89
Northern Rhodesia: white resentment of British policy in, 68; African franchise rights in, 242–43; African nationalism in, 244–45, 248–50, 255; African economic progress in copper belt, 253–54; economics and race in, 261; *see also* Federation of Rhodesia and Nyasaland, Zambia
Nyasaland, 243, 246–47, 257; *see also* Federation of Rhodesia and Nyasaland, Malawi
Nyerere, Julius K.: and Tanganyika independence, 95–97; one-party rule and democracy, 322–23; receives British troops, 379; profile of, 380; nationalizes industry, 384; on Ujamaa villages, 385; President of Tanzania, 436; assails Nkrumah, 448; warns of Communist colonialism, 454; directives of on "customary punishments", 495

Obote, Milton, 100, 166, 379, 387–91
Odinga, Oginga, 398, 402
Ojukwu, Lieut. Col. Odumegwu, 361, 363–65, 368, 370–71
Okello, John, 382
Okpewho, Isidore, 500
Oliveira, Dr. José Nunes de, 281
One-party rule: in Ghana and Guinea, 320, 387; Nyerere on democracy and, 322–23; excesses and abuses in Congo, Ghana and Malawi, 330–31; economic development under, 343; in Ghana, 347; in Ivory Coast, 414; Zambia moves toward, 437
Oppenheimer, Harry, 196, 210, 224
Orange Free State, 18–19, 26–29
Organization of African Unity: role in Angola, Mozambique and Portuguese Guinea, 308, 311, 314–15; foreign trade and development, 333; supports Nigeria, 370–71; in Ethiopia, 405; formation of, 445–46; aids liberation movements, 447; divides on Congo issue, 448; opposes South Africa, 449; decries "negritude", 496
Ovambo, 235

Padmore, George, 346
Pan-African Congress, 438
Pan African Freedom Movement for East, Central and South Africa, 166
Pan-Africanist Congress, 195–98, 201, 203
Party of African Regrouping (Fr. W. Africa), 128
Paton, Alan, 182, 186–88, 224
Pemba, 121
People's Convention Party (Kenya), 111
People's National Party (Sierra Leone), 93
Peters, Carl, 8–9
Portugal: and claims in Congo, 2–3; ends Mozambique rebellion, 13; African possessions, 59–60;

refuses support to Southern Rhodesia rebellion, 261; plans provincial reforms, 285, 296, 313; pro-U.S. mood fades, 292; policy criticized by Angolan business men, 298; United Nations votes embargo on, 301; and Angolan reforms, 309; use of napalm in Portuguese Guinea, 314–15; invades Guinea, 358; role of in Zanzibar, 383
Portuguese Guinea, 314–16
Prince of Wales, 34–35
Progressive Party (South Africa), 221
Preventive Detention Act (Ghana), 341, 347

Racial antagonism: spurs Zanzibar revolt, 380–82; in Kenya, 399–401; in Chad, 422; in Zambia, 434–35; in U.S. mars African relations, 455
Reeves, Ambrose, 192, 200
Refugee problem, 337
Rhodes, Cecil, 21–24, 34–35, 47
Rhodesia: independence of, 266–67; and black nationalism, 268–70; and oil embargo, 271; and pressure from black Africa, 273; and UN sanctions, 274–75; and white immigration drive, 276; declares Republic, 277; and attempted agreement with Britain, 278–80; Zambia cuts trade to, 432
Rhodesian Front, 259, 263
Roberto, Holden, 294, 298–99, 300
Rockefeller, David, 193
Ross, Dr. Edward A., 42
Ruanda-Urundi, 64, 68, 134–35; *see also* Burundi and Rwanda
Rwanda, 135, 337, 394–95, 427–29

Salazar, Premier Antonio Oliveira, 281, 287–89, 292, 302
Selassie, Haile (Ras Taffari): as a progressive ruler, 40; and Italian invasion of Ethiopia, 50–54, 56; hopes for border adjustments with Somalia, 121; grants new constitution, 403; coup attempted against, 404–05; on African unity, 442
Senegal: only colony to send representative to legislature in Paris, 48; as autonomous republic, 129; independence of, 133; and tariff barriers, 336; splits Mali union, 413; keeps French troops, 420; economy flounders in, 423
Senghor, Léopold Sédar, 122, 417–18, 423–24, 444, 499–500
Sharpeville riots, 196–200
Sierra Leone, 93–94
Sierra Leone Peoples' Party, 93
Sithole, Rev. Ndabaningi, 266, 270
Skiet Commando, 179–80
Slave trade, 2, 7, 34–37
Smith, Ian D.: becomes Prime Minister of Rhodesia, 259–60; and South Africa's and Portugal's refusal of support, 261; election victory of, 263–64; and Rhodesian independence, 266–67; and Zambia, 272; and declaration of Republic, 276–77; and attempted agreement with Britain, 278–80
Smuts, Gen. Jan Christian, 30, 32–33, 43, 46–47, 176, 204
Sobhuza II, King of Swaziland, 238, 489–90
Sobukwe, Robert Mangaliso, 195–96, 203
Socialism: under Nkrumah in Ghana, 343; in Guinea, 357; in Tanzania, 385; defined by Kenyatta, 397
Socialist People's Party (Congo), 140
Somalia (Italian Somaliland), 121, 145, 336–37, 407
South African Communist Party, 178
South African Foundation, 196
South African Indian National Congress, 177, 182
South African Institute of Race Relations, 229–30
Southern Rhodesia: white resentment of British policy in, 68; African nationalism in, 244; crisis builds, 245–47; repressive laws passed in, 249–50; riots in, 252; land apportionment in, 254; approves new Constitution, 254; Rhodesian Front in, 257; riots in, 260; *see also* Federation of Rhodesia and Nyasaland, Rhodesia
South-West Africa (Namibia), 39, 232–35
Soweto, 213
Spain, 3, 59–60
Stanley, Henry M., 2–4, 10, 100
Stevenson, Adlai E., 210, 255
Strauss, J. G. N., 180, 182, 184
Strydom, Johannes G.: on supremacy of Parliament, 181; as possible successor to Malan, 182; becomes Prime Minister, 184; regime strengthened, 189; and cooperation with black Africa, 190; and apartheid policy, 191; death of, 192
Sudan: as autonomous republic, 129; and end of Mali Federation, 133; and low GNP, 337; relations with Uganda, 394; Moslem-Black African conflict in, 408–12; splits with Senegal, 413
Suppression of Communism Act (South Africa), 178, 191, 194
Suzman, Helen, 221, 226–27, 229, 235
Swahili, 403
Swart, Charles R., 181, 189, 194, 206
Sweden, 383, 407
Swaziland, 236, 238, 489–90

Tanganyika: British educational progress in, 40–41; submitted by Britain to UN trusteeship, 64; UN reports on, 66; independence of, 95–97; mutiny disarmed by British, 379; will unite with Zanzibar, 382–83; in East Africa common market, 396; land policy of, 480; *see also* Tanzania
Tanganyika African National Union, 95–97, 385
Tanzania: and regional economy, 334; and low GNP, 337; formed by Tanganyika and Zanzibar, 382–83; cultural and economic change in, 384–86; relations with Uganda, 394–95; and Asian deportations, 400; and Zambia build pipeline, 433–35; opens pipeline to Zambia, 436; Chinese building railroad in, 458; *see also* Tanganyika, Zanzibar
Tavares, Alvaro Rodrigues da, 291–92
Thant, U, 166
Todd, Garfield, 243, 245, 259
Togoland, 30–33; *see also* British Togoland, French Togoland
Tolbert, William R., Jr., 377–78
Tombalbaye, Francois, 421
Tomlinson Commission report, 190–91, 194
Torch Commando (South Africa), 179–80, 182

Touré, Sékou: and Albert Margai in Sierra Leone, 93; and independence of Guinea, 125–27; on African unity and independence, 129; relations with Soviet Union and People's Republic of China, 133; President of Guinea, 335, 354–56; on Marxist principles, 358–59
Transkei, 207, 212–13
Transvaal Republic, 18–19, 22, 25–29
Treaty of Uccialli, 13
Tribalism: and problem of federal union in Nigeria, 89; and nationalism in Tanganyika, 96; Portuguese use of in Mozambique, 311; S.O. Adebo compares to nationalism, 327–29; in Nigeria, 359, 361–71; and one-party rule in Uganda, 387; in Uganda, 395; in Kenya, 402; in the Sudan, 409; in Cameroon, 415–16; and Watusi, 427–29; in Burundi, 430–32; ebbs in Ghana, 460
Tshombe, Moise: president of Conakat Party, 142; and Katanga secession, 146, 149–51; arrested, 157; denounces central government, 158; and UN victory in Katanga, 159; and Hammarskjold's death, 160; and Katanga's wealth, 161; character sketch of, 162–65; and end of Katanga secession, 165–66; as Congo Premier, 167; dismissed as Premier, 169; and C.I.A., 171
Tubman, William V.S., 376–77, 440–41
Tutsi, *see* Watusi

Ubangi-Shari, *see* Central African Republic
Uganda: and British colonialism, 8; climate of, preventing European settlement, 10; British educational progress in, 40–41; independence of, 98–100; and regional economy, 334; and low GNP, 337; and high unemployment, 338; mutiny disarmed by British, 379; one-party rule in, 387, 389; farm policy in, 390; army ousts Obote, 392; economic planning in, 393; and inter-African tensions, 394–95; in East Africa Common Market, 396; Minister visits Israel, 453; Karamojong near extinction in, 487; treatment of women in, 494
Uganda Nationalist Congress Party, 98–99
Ujamaa villages, 385
Um Nyobe, Ruben, 124–25
Unemployment: in urban areas, 338–39; in Ghana, 352; in Tanzania, 384; high in Upper Volta, 419
Union Minière du Haut Katanga, 142, 150, 161
Union of Central African Republics, 132
Union of South Africa: establishment of, 29; and South-West Africa, 31–33, 232–35; segregation policy proposed in, 43–45; and Negro resettlement, 183–88, 190, 194, 212; and British protectorates, 190, 236–37; and Sharpeville riots, 196–200; becomes republic, 205–06; and black Africa, 218–19, 228; growth of economy, 219; black education in, 220; and developing black consciousness in, 222–23; refuses support to Southern Rhodesia rebellion, 261; and Mozambique compared, 285–86; opposed by Organization of African Unity, 449; nationalist meetings in, 460; Bantu lifestyle in, 468–70; art in, 485–87; *see also* Apartheid, Boers, Boer War, Cape Colony, Natal, Orange Free State, Transvaal Republic
U.S.S.R.: economic mission expelled from Ethiopia 50; and Katanga secession, 147–48, 151; ignores U N sanctions on South Africa, 209; oil interests in Ethiopia, 406; opening missions and expanding trade, 451
United Country Party (Kenya), 109
United Nations: charter provisions, 62; and trust territories, 71; reports on African agricultural techniques, 73; and problem of French and British Togoland, 82; approves merger of British Togoland with Gold Coast, 85; grants independence to French Cameroons, 130; and Ruanda-Urundi, 134–35; and Katanga secession from the Congo, 146–51; seats Kasavubu delegation, 153; charges brutality in Stanleyville, 154–55; troops in Katanga, 156–57; and Adoula election, 158; troops seize Katanga, 159; troops in Katanga, 161; final offensive in Katanga, 165–66; and economic sanctions on South Africa, 208–09; censure of Union of South Africa, 232; rescinds South Africa's mandate over South-West Africa, 234; and Southern Rhodesia, 256; imposes economic sanctions on Rhodesia, 274; votes arms embargo on Portugal, 301
United Party (South Africa): opposition party, 176; and apartheid, 179; election defeat of, 181–82; opposition to Strydom regime, 189; challenges Cape Colored separate voting act, 191; election gains of, 221
United States: and recognition of African International Association, 3–4; and mandate policy, 33; and African trade, 35; and U N trusteeships, 62; policy on Katanga secession, 165; intervention in Congo, 168–69; and C.I.A. in Congo, 170–73; opposition to UN South Africa sanctions, 209; investment in South Africa, 210, 229–30; and Rhodesian oil embargo, 271; and Rhodesian chrome, 278; aid to Angola and Mozambique, 281, 288; interests in Angola, 303, 310; denies charge of aiding Portugal, 316; technical assistance to East Africa, 326; Agency for International Development, 333–34; aid to Ghana, 346; and Ghana economy, 351; aid to Guinea, 358; interest of in Nigeria, 364, 374–75; role in Liberian economy, 376–78; role of in Zanzibar revolt, 381; interest of in Tanzania, 383; role of in Uganda, 390; relations with Uganda, 394; and Ethiopian interests, 406; opens new consulates, 451–52; racism in, mars African relations, 455; marketing in Africa, 478
United Tanganyika Party, 96–97
Upper Volta, 130–31, 337, 419–20

Verwoerd, Hendrik: bill for Negro resettlement, 183; and tribal subdivision of Negro settlements, 184; and Negro resettlement, 187–88; elected Prime Minister, 192–93; and Sharpeville riots, 197–98; attempted assassination of, 200–01; membership in Broederbond, 204; and vote for republic, 205; British support of, 210–11; assassination of, 217
Volta River project, 81, 83
Vorster, Balthazar Johannes, 211, 218–19, 221, 231

Watusi, 134–35, 427–32, 458, 464–67
Welensky, Sir Roy: leader of Northern Rhodesian Legislative Council, 242–43; Federal Prime Minister, 245–46, 250–51; rejects Monckton report, 253; and new constitution, 254; and dissolution of Federation, 258
Welles, Sumner, 63
Whitehead, Sir Edgar, 245–47, 250, 252, 257
Williams, G. Mennen, 94, 168
Wilson, Harold, 259, 266–67, 271
Women: conditions of, in South Africa, 43–45; nominated to legislature in Tanganyika, 95; and antigovernment violence in South Africa, 195; under apartheid, 229; Guinea dress laws for, 463; economic enterprise, 334; clitorodectomy of, 466; Bantu, in South Africa, 469; bride-price in Kenya, 484; under Ivory Coast anti-matriarchy laws, 490; United Nations policy on, 497–98
World Bank, 71, 325, 336, 358
World War I, Germany's loss of African colonies in, 30–32
World War II, disposition of Italy's former colonies, 61–62

Xuma, Dr. A. B., 180, 187–88

Yoruba, 6, 92

Zaire Republic, 427; *see also* Belgian Congo, Congo Free State, Congo (Republic of the)
Zambia: independence of, 263; sabotage in, 272; unemployment in, 338; cuts trade with Rhodesia, 432–34; and Tanzania build pipeline, 433–36; seeks political neutrality, 434–35; nationalizes industries, 436; purchases Rhodesian corn, 437; *see also* Northern Rhodesia
Zanzibar, 7–8, 121, 380–83, 387; *see also* Tanzania
Zimbabwe African National Union (ZANU), 259, 270
Zimbabwe African Peoples Union (ZAPU), 268–70
Zulu, 19–21, 177
Zululand, 7, 44–45

Update Index

Afrikaner Nationalists, 513-515, 523-26
Algeria, 521
Ali, Muhammad, 508, 511
Amin, Idi, 504-07, 509, 531
Angola, 527; history of, 517; civil war in, 517-19
Anikulapo-Kuti, Fela, 529-32
Anti-Semitism, in Uganda, 507
Apartheid, 514-15, 523-25, 526
Asians: expelled from Uganda, 504, 505, 506-07

Bakango, 510
Banned persons, in South Africa, 514
Belgian Congo, 508
Belgium: and Zaire, 510
Berghe, Pierre van den, 514
Boer War, 513, 526
Bokassa, Jean Bédel, 505
Botha, M.C., 525
Botha, Pik, 524
Braithwait, Tunji, 532
Brezhnev, Leonid, 522
Browde, Dr. Selma, 513
Buthelezi, Gatsha, 515-16

Caetano, Marcello, 523, 524
Callaghan, James, 522
Catholics: in Zaire, 511
Central African Federation, 521
Central African Republic (Ubangi-Shari), 505
Central Intelligence Agency (CIA): and Zaire, 511
China, 509, 511
Congo, Republic of the, *see* Zaire
Cuba: role in Angola, 518
Cunhal, Alvaro, 518

Dada, Idi Amin, *see* Amin, Idi
de Gaulle, Charles, 521
Duncan-Sandys, Lord, 522

East African Community, 507

Fisher, John, 513
Foreman, George, 508, 511
Freddie, King, *see* Mutesa II, Kabaka of Buganda
Frelimo, 516, 521
Fugard, Athol, 514

Gordimer, Nadine, 514
Gowon, Gen. Yakubu, 509, 531, 532
Great Britain: and South Africa, 513; and Rhodesian guerrillas, 522
Grivas, George, 518
Guerrillas: in Rhodesia, 520, 521, 522
Guevara, Che, 518

Immorality Act (South Africa), 514, 524
Isidore, Sandra, 530
Israel, 507

Japan: investments in Zaire, 510

Kabaka, the, *see* Mutesa II, Kabaka of Buganda
Kani, John, 514
Kasai secession movement, 508
Kasavubu, Joseph, 510
Katanga, 508
Kaunda, Kenneth, 505, 511, 518, 521
Kente, Gibson, 512-13
Kenya: Mau Mau rebellion in, 520-21
Kenyatta, Jomo, 520
Kinshasa, Zaire, 509
King, Dr. Martin Luther, Jr., 515, 516

Kissinger, Henry, 521, 522, 524, 528
Koornhof, Dr. P.G.J., 514

Liberal Party (South Africa), 523
London and Rhodesia Mining and Land Company, 522
Lumumba, Patrice, 508, 510, 511

Mao Tse-tung, 511, 521
Matabele, 520
Mau Mau, 520
Mixed Marriages Act (South Africa), 524
Mobutu, Gen. Joseph, 509, 510-511, 518
Moolman, Dr. J.H., 514
Mozambique, 518, 521, 522; and South Africa, 516
Mugabe, Robert, 521
Muhammed, Gen. Murtala, 531-32
Mulele, Pierre, 510, 511
Mutesa II, Kabaka of Buganda, 505
Muzorewa, Bishop Abel, 521

Naidoo, Stephen, 513
National Front for the Liberation of Angola, 517, 518, 519
Nationalist Party (South Africa), 513, 514, 526, 527
National Union for the Total Liberation of Angola, 517, 518, 519
Neto, Dr. Agostinho, 518-19, 532
Nigeria: recognition of Neto Government in Angola by, 519; persecution of singer in, 529-32; economy of, 531; government of, 531-32
Nkomo, Joshua, 520-22, 530
Northern Rhodesia, *see* Zambia
Ntshona, Winston, 514
Nyerere, Julius K., 507, 509, 511, 521

Obote, Milton, 515, 516, 517
Opoloto, Shaban, 506
Ovambo, 528

Political prisoners: in Uganda, 506; in Zaire, 510
Popular Movement for the Liberation of Angola, 517, 518, 519
Popular Revolutionary Movement (Zaire), 511
Population projections: for South Africa, 513
Portugal: and Angola, 517, 518; revolution in, impact on South Africa of, 516, 523; and independence of Portuguese colonies, 518
Portuguese Communist Party, 518
Portuguese Guinea, 518
Progressive Party (South Africa), 513

Qadhafi, Col. Mo'ammar Mohammed, 507

Ransome-Kuti, Rev., 530
Reagan, Ronald, 522
Reform Party (South Africa), 513
Rhodes, Cecil, 508, 520
Rhodesia: and South Africa, 516; history of, 520-22
Rhodesian Front, 521
Robben Island, South Africa, 514
Roberto, Holden, 518, 519
Rogers, Col. Hugh, 505
Rwema, Bisengimana, 509

Sabotage and Terrorism Act, 524
Sadie, J.L., 513
Savimbi, Dr. Jonas, 518, 519
Second World Black and African Festival of Arts and Culture, 531
Sharpeville riots, 524
Sithole, Rev. Ndabaningi, 521
Smith, Ian D., 520, 521-22
South Africa, 512-16; population projections for, 513; black homelands policy, 514, 526-27, 528; economy of, 514-15; and independence for South West Africa 516; and Angola, 517; and Rhodesia, 522; future of, 523-25; Afrikaners of, 525-28
South Africans: as mercenaries in Angola, 518, 519
Southern Rhodesia, *see* Rhodesia
South-West Africa (Mamibia), 516, 527-28
South-West African People's Organization, (SWAPO), 528
Soviet Union: and civil war in Angola, 518, 527
Soweto, 512-13, 514, 515, 523
Suppression of Communism Act (South Africa), 524
Supreme Military Council, Nigeria, 532
Suzman, Helen, 514
SWAPO, *see* South-West African People's Organization, 528

Tanzania, 507, 521
Tongogara, Josiah, 521
Transkei, 526
Treurnicht, Dr. Andries, 525
Tshombe, Moise, 508

Uganda: under Idi Amin, 504-07; history of, 505; economy of, 506; expulsion of Israelis from, 507
Uganda Peoples' Congress, 505
Unita, *see* National Union for the Total Liberation of Angola
United Nations: Amin's telegram to, 507; and Congo intervention, 508, 522; recognition of SWAPO by, 528
United Party (South Africa), 513
United States: relations with Zaire, 511

Van der Merwe, Daniel, 513-14
Verwoerd, Hendrik, 525
Victoria Falls Conference, 522
Vorster, Balthazar Johannes, 515, 516, 521, 522, 524, 525, 527

Wilson, Francis, 513
Wilson, Harold, 505
Women: Zairan, 508, 511
World Bank, 509

Zaire Republic: Ali-Forman fight in, 508, 511; historic background of, 508-09; economy of, 509-10; Mobutu's rule in, 509, 510-11
Zambia: compared with Rhodesia, 521
Zatabele, 522
Zimbabwe, *see* Rhodesia
Zimbabwe African National Union (ZANU), 521, 522
Zimbabwe African People's Union (ZAPU), 521, 522
Zwelethini, Goodwill, 515